D0742351

# THE BRONTË SISTERS

# Wuthering Heights
### EMILY BRONTË

# The Tenant of Wildfell Hall
### ANNE BRONTË

# Shirley
### CHARLOTTE BRONTË

# Jane Eyre
### CHARLOTTE BRONTË

octopus

*Wuthering Heights*
first published in Great Britain in 1847

*The Tenant of Wildfell Hall*
first published in Great Britain in 1848

*Shirley*
first published in Great Britain in 1849

*Jane Eyre*
first published in Great Britain in 1847

This edition first published in Great Britain in 1980 by

Octopus Books Limited,
59 Grosvenor Street,
London W.1.

ISBN 7064 1348 2

Printed by Kingsport Press, USA

# CONTENTS

# BIOGRAPHICAL NOTES

1816    Charlotte born at Thornton in Yorkshire on April 21st

1817    Branwell born on June 26th

1818    Emily born on July 30th

1820    Anne born on January 17th
        Their father, Patrick Brontë, is appointed to the Perpetual Curacy of Haworth in Yorkshire and the Brontë family move to Haworth Parsonage

1821    Mrs Brontë dies and her older sister, Elizabeth Branwell, comes to care for the family

1825    Death of Maria and Elizabeth, the two eldest Brontë girls, from tuberculosis. Charlotte and Emily return from their boarding school at Cowan Bridge, which was to appear as Lowood School in *Jane Eyre* and whose poor conditions had been a major cause of the two girls' deaths. Charlotte, Emily, Anne and Branwell create imaginary worlds and start writing about them at home

1831–44 The three sisters attend Miss Wooler's school at Roe Head, then take positions as governesses; Charlotte and Emily go to teach in Brussels

1845    Family all at home together. Branwell out of work and drinking heavily

1846    Publication of *Poems* by Currer, Ellis and Acton Bell—the pseudonyms adopted by Charlotte, Emily and Anne respectively

1847    Charlotte's novel *Jane Eyre* is published and achieves immediate popularity. Emily's *Wuthering Heights* and Anne's *Agnes Grey* are also published but do not share *Jane Eyre*'s success

1848    Publication of Anne's novel *The Tenant of Wildfell Hall*. Branwell's dissolute life finally causes his death in September and in December Emily dies of tuberculosis

1849    Anne dies in May, leaving Charlotte as the sole survivor of the six Brontë children. Her novel *Shirley* is published in October

1853    Charlotte's last novel *Villette* is published

1854    In June, Charlotte marries her father's curate, the Rev. A. B. Nicholls

1855    Her happiness is shortlived as on March 31st Charlotte also dies

1857    Posthumous publication of Charlotte's first novel, The *Professor*, written in 1846

1861    Patrick Brontë dies on June 7th

# Wuthering Heights

# Chapter 1

*1801.* – I have just returned from a visit to my landlord – the solitary neighbour that I shall be troubled with. This is certainly, a beautiful country! In all England, I do not believe that I could have fixed on a situation so completely removed from the stir of society. A perfect misanthropist's Heaven – and Mr Heathcliff and I are such a suitable pair to divide the desolation between us. A capital fellow! He little imagined how my heart warmed towards him when I beheld his black eyes withdraw so suspiciously under their brows, as I rode up, and when his fingers sheltered themselves, with a jealous resolution, still further in his waistcoat, as I announced my name.

'Mr Heathcliff?' I said.

A nod was the answer.

'Mr Lockwood, your new tenant, sir. I do myself the honour of calling as soon as possible, after my arrival, to express the hope that I have not inconvenienced you by my perseverance in soliciting the occupation of Thrushcross Grange: I heard, yesterday, you had had some thoughts –'

'Thrushcross Grange is my own, sir,' he interrupted wincing, 'I should not allow any one to inconvenience me, if I could hinder it – walk in!'

The 'walk in' was uttered with closed teeth, and expressed the sentiment, 'Go to the Deuce'; even the gate over which he leant manifested no sympathizing movement to the words; and I think that circumstances determined me to accept the invitation: I felt interested in a man who seemed more exaggeratedly reserved than myself.

When he saw my horse's breast fairly pushing the barrier, he did pull out his hand to unchain it, and then sullenly preceded me up the causeway, calling, as we entered the court:

'Joseph, take Mr Lockwood's horse; and bring up some wine.'

'Here we have the whole establishment of domestics, I suppose,' was the reflection, suggested by this compound order, 'No wonder the grass grows up between the flags, and cattle are the only hedge-cutters.'

Joseph was an elderly, nay, an old man, very old, perhaps, though hale and sinewy.

'The Lord help us!' he soliloquised in an undertone of peevish displeasure, while relieving me of my horse: looking, meantime, in my face so sourly that I charitably conjectured he must have need of divine aid to digest his dinner, and his pious ejaculation had no reference to my unexpected advent.

Wuthering Heights is the name of Mr Heathcliff's dwelling. 'Wuthering' being a significant provincial adjective, descriptive of the atmospheric tumult to which its station is exposed in stormy weather. Pure, bracing ventilation they must have up there at all times, indeed: one may guess the power of the north

# Wuthering Heights

wind, blowing over the edge, by the excessive slant of a few stunted firs at the end of the house; and by a range of gaunt thorns all stretching their limbs one way, as if craving alms of the sun. Happily, the architect had foresight to build it strong: the narrow windows are deeply set in the wall, and the corners defended with large jutting stones.

Before passing the threshold, I paused to admire a quantity of grotesque carving lavished over the front, and especially about the principal door, above which, among a wilderness of crumbling griffins, and shameless little boys, I detected the date '1500,' and the name 'Hareton Earnshaw.' I would have made a few comments, and requested a short history of the place, from the surly owner, but his attitude at the door appeared to demand my speedy entrance, or complete departure, and I had no desire to aggravate his impatience, previous to inspecting the penetralium.

One step brought us into the family sitting-room, without any introductory lobby, or passage: they call it here 'the house' pre-eminently. It includes kitchen, and parlour, generally, but I believe at Wuthering Heights the kitchen is forced to retreat altogether into another quarter, at least I distinguished a chatter of tongues, and a clatter of culinary utensils, deep within; and I observed no signs of roasting, boiling, or baking, about the huge fire-place; nor any glitter of copper saucepans and tin cullenders on the walls. One end, indeed, reflected splendidly both light and heat, from ranks of immense pewter dishes, interspersed with silver jugs and tankards, towering row after row, in a vast oak dresser, to the very roof. The latter had never been underdrawn, its entire anatomy laid bare to an enquiring eye, except where a frame of wood laden with oatcakes, and clusters of legs of beef, mutton, and ham, concealed it. Above the chimney were sundry villainous old guns, and a couple of horse-pistols, and, by way of ornament, three gaudily painted canisters disposed along its ledge. The floor was of smooth, white stone: the chairs, high-backed, primitive structures, painted green: one or two heavy black ones lurking in the shade. In an arch, under the dresser, reposed a huge, liver-coloured bitch pointer surrounded by a swarm of squealing puppies; and other dogs haunted other recesses.

The apartment and furniture would have been nothing extraordinary as belonging to a homely, northern farmer with a stubborn countenance, and stalwart limbs, set out to advantage in knee-breeches, and gaiters. Such an individual, seated in his armchair, his mug of ale frothing on the round table before him, is to be seen in any circuit of five or six miles among these hills, if you go at the right time, after dinner. But, Mr Heathcliff forms a singular contrast to his abode and style of living. He is a dark skinned gypsy, in aspect, in dress, and manners a gentleman, that is, as much a gentleman as many a country squire: rather slovenly, perhaps, yet not looking amiss with his negligence, because he has an erect and handsome figure, and rather morose; possibly, some people might suspect him of a degree of underbred pride – I have a sympathetic chord within that tells me it is nothing of the sort; I know, by instinct, his reserve springs from an aversion to showy displays of feeling – to manifestations of mutual kindness. He'll love and hate, equally under cover, and esteem it a species of impertinence, to be loved or hated again – No, I'm running on too fast – I bestow my own attributes over liberally on him. Mr Heathcliff may have entirely dissimilar reasons for keeping his hand out of the way, when he meets a would be acquaintance, to those which actuate me. Let

me hope my constitution is almost peculiar: my dear mother used to say I should never have a comfortable home, and only last summer, I proved myself perfectly unworthy of one.

While enjoying a month of fine weather at the sea-coast, I was thrown into the company of a most fascinating creature, a real goddess, in my eyes, as long as she took no notice of me. I 'never told my love' vocally; still, if looks have language, the merest idiot might have guessed I was over head and ears; she understood me, at last, and looked a return – the sweetest of all imaginable looks – and what did I do? I confess it with shame – shrunk icily into myself, like a snail, at every glance retired colder and farther; till, finally, the poor innocent was led to doubt her own senses, and, overwhelmed with confusion at her supposed mistake, persuaded her mamma to decamp.

By this curious turn of disposition I have gained the reputation of deliberate heartlessness, how undeserved, I alone can appreciate.

I took a seat at the end of the hearthstone opposite that towards which my landlord advanced, and filled up an interval of silence by attempting to caress the canine mother, who had left her nursery, and was sneaking wolfishly to the back of my leg, her lip curled up, and her white teeth watering for a snatch.

My caress provoked a long, guttural snarl.

'You'd better let the dog alone,' growled Mr Heathcliff, in unison, checking fiercer demonstrations with a punch of his foot. 'She's not accustomed to be spoiled – not kept for a pet.'

Then, striding to a side door, he shouted again.

'Joseph!'

Joseph mumbled indistinctly in the depths of the cellar, but gave no intimation of ascending; so, his master dived down to him, leaving me *vis-à-vis* the ruffianly bitch, and a pair of grim, shaggy sheep dogs, who shared with her a jealous guardianship over all my movements.

Not anxious to come in contact with their fangs, I sat still; but, imagining they would scarcely understand tacit insults, I unfortunately indulged in winking and making faces at the trio, and some turn of my physiognomy so irritated madam, that she suddenly broke into a fury and leapt on my knees. I flung her back, and hastened to interpose the table between us. This proceeding aroused the whole hive. Half-a-dozen four-footed fiends, of various sizes, and ages, issued from hidden dens to the common centre. I felt my heels and coat-laps peculiar subjects of assault; and, parrying off the larger combatants, as effectually as I could, with the poker, I was constrained to demand, aloud, assistance from some of the household, in reestablishing peace.

Mr Heathcliff and his man climbed the cellar steps with vexatious phlegm. I don't think they moved one second faster than usual, though the hearth was an absolute tempest of worrying and yelping.

Happily, an inhabitant of the kitchen made more dispatch; a lusty dame, with tucked-up gown, bare arms, and fire-flushed cheeks, rushed into the midst of us flourishing a frying-pan; and used that weapon, and her tongue, to such purpose, that the storm subsided magically, and she only remained, heaving like a sea after a high wind, when her master entered on the scene.

'What the devil is the matter?' he asked, eyeing me in a manner I could ill endure after this inhospitable treatment.

'What the devil indeed!' I muttered. 'The herd of possessed swine could have

# Wuthering Heights

had no worse spirits in them than those animals of yours, sir. You might as well leave a stranger with a brood of tigers!'

'They won't meddle with persons who touch nothing,' he remarked, putting the bottle before me, and restoring the displaced table. 'The dogs do right to be vigilant. Take a glass of wine?'

'No, thank you.'

'Not bitten, are you?'

'If I had been, I would have set my signet on the biter.'

Heathcliff's countenance relaxed into a grin.

'Come, come,' he said, 'you are flurried, Mr Lockwood. Here, take a little wine. Guests are so exceedingly rare in this house that I and my dogs, I am willing to own, hardly know how to receive them. Your health, sir.'

I bowed and returned the pledge, beginning to perceive that it would be foolish to sit sulking for the misbehaviour of a pack of curs; besides, I felt loath to yield the fellow further amusement, at my expense; since his humour took that turn.

He – probably swayed by prudential considerations of the folly of offending a good tenant – relaxed, a little, in the laconic style of chipping off his pronouns, and auxiliary verbs; and introduced what he supposed would be a subject of interest to me, a discourse on the advantages and disadvantages of my present place of retirement.

I found him very intelligent on the topics we touched; and, before I went home, I was encouraged so far as to volunteer another visit, to-morrow.

He evidently wished no repetition of my intrusion. I shall go, notwithstanding. It is astonishing how sociable I feel myself compared with him.

# Chapter 2

esterday afternoon set in misty and cold. I had half a mind to spend it by my study fire, instead of wading through heath and mud to Wuthering Heights.

On coming up from dinner, however (N.B. I dine between twelve and one o'clock; the housekeeper, a matronly lady taken as a fixture along with the house, could not, or would not comprehend my request that I might be served at five) – on mounting the stairs with this lazy intention, and stepping into the room, I saw a servant-girl on her knees, surrounded by brushes and coal-scuttles and raising an infernal dusk as she extinguished the flames with heaps of cinders. This spectacle drove me back immediately; I took my hat, and, after a four miles' walk, arrived at Heathcliff's garden gate just in time to escape the first feathery flakes of a snow shower.

On that bleak hill-top the earth was hard with a black frost, and the air made me shiver through every limb. Being unable to remove the chain, I jumped over, and, running up the flagged causeway bordered with straggling gooseberry bushes, knocked vainly for admittance, till my knuckles tingled, and the dogs howled.

'Wretched inmates!' I ejaculated, mentally, 'you deserve perpetual isolation from your species for your churlish inhospitality. At least, I would not keep my doors barred in the day time – I don't care – I will get in!'

So resolved, I grasped the latch, and shook it vehemently. Vinegar-faced Joseph projected his head from a round window of the barn.

'Whet are ye for?' he shouted. 'T' maister's dahn i' t' fowld. Goa rahnd by th' end ut' laith, if yah went tuh spake tull him.'

'Is there nobody inside to open the door?' I hallooed, responsively.

'They's nobbut t' missis; and shoo'll nut oppen 't and ye mak yer flaysome dins till neeght.'

'Why? cannot you tell her who I am, eh, Joseph?'

'Nor-ne me! Aw'll hae noa hend wi't,' muttered the head vanishing.

The snow began to drive thickly. I seized the handle to essay another trial; when a young man, without coat, and shouldering a pitchfork, appeared in the yard behind. He hailed me to follow him, and, after marching through a washhouse, and a paved area containing a coal-shed, pump, and pigeon cote, we at length arrived in the huge, warm, cheerful apartment, where I was formerly received.

It glowed delightfully in the radiance of an immense fire, compounded of coal, peat, and wood: and near the table, laid for a plentiful evening meal, I was

pleased to observe the 'missis,' an individual whose existence I had never previously suspected.

I bowed and waited, thinking she would bid me take a seat. She looked at me, leaning back in her chair, and remained motionless and mute.

'Rough weather!' I remarked. 'I'm afraid, Mrs Heathcliff, the door must bear the consequence of your servants' leisure attendance: I had hard work to make them hear me!'

She never opened her mouth. I stared – she stared also. At any rate, she kept her eyes on me, in a cool, regardless manner, exceedingly embarrassing and disagreeable.

'Sit down,' said the young man, gruffly. 'He'll be in soon.'

I obeyed; and hemmed, and called the villain Juno, who deigned, at this second interview, to move the extreme tip of her tail, in token of owning my acquaintance.

'A beautiful animal!' I commenced again. 'Do you intend parting with the little ones, madam?'

'They are not mine,' said the amiable hostess more repellingly than Heathcliff himself could have replied.

'Ah, your favourites are among these!' I continued, turning to an obscure cushion full of something like cats.

'A strange choice of favourites,' she observed scornfully.

Unluckily, it was a heap of dead rabbits – I hemmed once more, and drew closer to the hearth, repeating my comment on the wildness of the evening.

'You should not have come out,' she said, rising and reaching from the chimney-piece two of the painted canisters.

Her position before was sheltered from the light: now, I had a distinct view of her whole figure and countenance. She was slender, and apparently scarcely past girlhood: an admirable form, and the most exquisite little face that I have ever had the pleasure of beholding: small features, very fair; flaxen ringlets, or rather golden, hanging loose on her delicate neck; and eyes – had they been agreeable in expression, they would have been irresistible – fortunately for my susceptible heart, the only sentiment they evinced hovered between scorn and a kind of desperation, singularly unnatural to be detected there.

The canisters were almost out of her reach; I made a motion to aid her; she turned upon me as a miser might turn, if any one attempted to assist him in counting his gold.

'I don't want your help,' she snapped, 'I can get them for myself.'

'I beg your pardon,' I hastened to reply.

'Were you asked to tea?' she demanded, tying an apron over her neat black frock, and standing with a spoonful of the leaf poised over the pot.

'I shall be glad to have a cup,' I answered.

'Were you asked?' she repeated.

'No,' I said, half smiling. 'You are the proper person to ask me.'

She flung the tea back, spoon and all, and resumed her chair in a pet, her forehead corrugated, and her red underlip pushed out, like a child's, ready to cry.

Meanwhile, the young man had slung onto his person a decidedly shabby upper garment, and, erecting himself before the blaze, looked down on me, from the corner of his eyes, for all the world as if there were some mortal feud

unavenged between us. I began to doubt whether he were a servant or not; his dress and speech were both rude, entirely devoid of the superiority observable in Mr and Mrs Heathcliff; his thick, brown curls were rough and uncultivated, his whiskers encroached bearishly over his cheeks, and his hands were embrowned like those of the common labourer: still his bearing was free, almost haughty; and he showed none of a domestic's assiduity in attending on the lady of the house.

In the absence of clear proofs of his condition, I deemed it best to abstain from noticing his curious conduct, and, five minutes afterwards, the entrance of Heathcliff relieved me, in some measure, from my uncomfortable state.

'You see, sir, I am come according to promise!' I exclaimed, assuming the cheerful 'and I fear I shall be weatherbound for half an hour, if you can afford me shelter during that space.'

'Half an hour?' he said, shaking the white flakes from his clothes; 'I wonder you should select the thick of a snowstorm to ramble about in. Do you know that you run a risk of being lost in the marshes? People familiar with these moors often miss their road on such evenings, and, I can tell you, there is no chance of a change at present.'

'Perhaps I can get a guide among your lads, and he might stay at the Grange till morning – could you spare me one?'

'No, I could not.'

'Oh, indeed! Well, then, I must trust to my own sagacity.'

'Umph!'

'Are you going to mak' th' tea?' demanded he of the shabby coat, shifting his ferocious gaze from me to the young lady.

'Is *he* to have any?' she asked, appealing to Heathcliff.

'Get it ready, will you?' was the answer, uttered so savagely that I started. The tone in which the words were said, revealed a genuine bad nature. I no longer felt inclined to call Heathcliff a capital fellow.

When the preparations were finished, he invited me with –

'Now, sir, bring forward your chair.' And we all, including the rustic youth, drew round the table, an austere silence prevailing while we discussed our meal.

I thought, if I had caused the cloud, it was my duty to make an effort to dispel it. They could not every day sit so grim and taciturn, and it was impossible, however ill-tempered they might be, that the universal scowl they wore was their everyday countenance.

'It is strange,' I began in the interval of swallowing one cup of tea and receiving another, 'it is strange how custom can mould our tastes and ideas; many could not imagine the existence of happiness in a life of such complete exile from the world as you spend, Mr Heathcliff; yet, I'll venture to say, that, surrounded by your family, and with your amiable lady as the presiding genius over your home and heart –'

'My amiable lady!' he interrupted, with an almost diabolical sneer on his face. 'Where is she – my amiable lady?'

'Mrs Heathcliff, you wife, I mean.'

'Well, yes – Oh! you would intimate that her spirit has taken the post of ministering angel, and guards the fortunes of Wuthering Heights, even when her body is gone. Is that it?'

Perceiving myself in a blunder, I attempted to correct it. I might have seen

that there was too great a disparity between the ages of the parties to make it likely that they were man and wife. One was about forty; a period of mental vigour at which men seldom cherish the delusion of being married for love, by girls: that dream is reserved for the solace of our declining years. The other did not look seventeen.

Then it flashed upon me – 'The clown at my elbow, who is drinking his tea out of a basin, and eating his bread with unwashed hands, may be her husband. Heathcliff, junior, of course. Here is the consequence of being buried alive: she has thrown herself away upon that boor, from sheer ignorance that better individuals existed! A sad pity – I must beware how I cause her to regret her choice.'

The last reflection may seem conceited; it was not. My neighbour struck me as bordering on repulsive. I knew, through experience, that I was tolerably attractive.

'Mrs Heathcliff is my daughter-in-law,' said Heathcliff, corroborating my surmise. He turned, as he spoke, a peculiar look in her direction, a look of hatred unless he has a most perverse set of facial muscles that will not, like those of other people, interpret the language of his soul.

'Ah, certainly – I see now; you are the favoured possessor of the beneficent fairy,' I remarked, turning to my neighbour.

This was worse than before: the youth grew crimson, and clenched his fist with every appearance of a meditated assault. But he seemed to recollect himself, presently; and smothered the storm in a brutal curse, muttered on my behalf, which, however, I took care not to notice.

'Unhappy in your conjectures, sir!' observed my host; 'we neither of us have the privilege of owning your good fairy; her mate is dead. I said she was my daughter-in-law, therefore, she must have married my son.'

'And this young man is –'

'Not my son, assuredly!'

Heathcliff smiled again, as if it were rather too bold a jest to attribute the paternity of that bear to him.

'My name is Hareton Earnshaw,' growled the other; 'and I'd counsel you to respect it!'

'I've shown no disrespect,' was my reply, laughing internally at the dignity with which he announced himself.

He fixed his eye on me longer than I cared to return the stare, for fear I might be tempted either to box his ears, or render my hilarity audible. I began to feel unmistakably out of place in that pleasant family circle. The dismal spiritual atmosphere overcame, and more than neutralized the glowing physical comforts round me; and I resolved to be cautious how I ventured under those rafters a third time.

The business of eating being concluded, and no one uttering a word of sociable conversation, I approached a window to examine the weather.

A sorrowful sight I saw; dark night coming down prematurely, and sky and hills mingled in one bitter whirl of wind and suffocating snow.

'I don't think it possible for me to get home now, without a guide,' I could not help exclaiming. 'The roads will be buried already; and if they were bare, I could scarcely distinguish a foot in advance.'

# Wuthering Heights

'Hareton, drive those dozen sheep into the barn porch. They'll be covered if left in the fold all night; and put a plank before them,' said Heathcliff.

'How must I do?' I continued, with rising irritation.

There was no reply to my question; and on looking round, I saw only Joseph bringing in a pail of porridge for the dogs and Mrs Heathcliff, leaning over the fire, diverting herself with burning a bundle of matches which had fallen from the chimney-piece as she restored the tea-canister to its place.

The former, when he had deposited his burden, took a critical survey of the room; and, in cracked tones, grated out:

'Aw woonder hagh yah can faishion tuh stand thear i' idleness un war, when all on 'em's goan aght! Bud yah're a nowt, and it's noa use talking – yah'll niver mend uh yer ill ways; bud, goa raight tuh t' divil, like yer mother afore ye!'

I imagined, for a moment, that this piece of eloquence was addressed to me; and, sufficiently enraged, stepped towards the aged rascal with an intention of kicking him out of the door.

Mrs Heathcliff, however, checked me by her answer.

'You scandalous old hypocrite!' she replied. 'Are you not afraid of being carried away bodily, whenever you mention the devil's name? I warn you to refrain from provoking me, or I'll ask your abduction as a special favour. Stop, look here, Joseph,' she continued, taking a long, dark book from a shelf. 'I'll show you how far I've progressed in the Black Art – I shall soon be competent to make a clear house of it. The red cow didn't die by chance; and your rheumatism can hardly be reckoned among providential visitations!'

'Oh, wicked, wicked!' gasped the elder; 'may the Lord deliver us from evil!'

'No, reprobate! you are a castaway – be off, or I'll hurt you seriously! I'll have you all modelled in wax and clay; and the first who passes the limits I fix, shall – I'll not say what he shall be done to – but, you'll see! Go, I'm looking at you!'

The little witch put a mock malignity into her beautiful eyes, and Joseph, trembling with sincere horror, hurried out praying and ejaculating 'wicked' as he went.

I thought her conduct must be prompted by a species of dreary fun; and, now that we were alone, I endeavoured to interest her in my distress.

'Mrs Heathcliff,' I said, earnestly, 'you must excuse me for troubling you – I presume, because, with that face, I'm sure you cannot help being good-hearted. Do point out some landmarks by which I may know my way home – I have no more idea how to get there than you would have how to get to London!'

'Take the road you came,' she answered, ensconcing herself in a chair, with a candle, and the long book open before her. 'It is brief advice; but as sound as I can give.'

'Then, if you hear of me being discovered dead in a bog, or a pit full of snow, your conscience won't whisper that it is partly your fault?'

'How so? I cannot escort you. They wouldn't let me go to the end of the garden-wall.'

'You! I should be very sorry to ask you to cross the threshold, for my convenience, on such a night,' I cried. 'I want you to *tell* me my way, not to *show* it; or else to persuade Mr Heathcliff to give me a guide.'

'Who? There is himself, Earnshaw, Zillah, Joseph, and I. Which would you have?'

# Wuthering Heights

'Are there no boys at the farm?'

'No, those are all.'

'Then, it follows that I am compelled to stay.'

'That you may settle with your host. I have nothing to do with it.'

'I hope it will be a lesson to you, to make no more rash journeys on these hills,' cried Heathcliff's stern voice from the kitchen entrance. 'As to staying here, I don't keep accommodations for visitors; you must share a bed with Hareton, or Joseph, if you do.'

'I can sleep on a chair in this room,' I replied.

'No, no. A stranger is a stranger, be he rich or poor – it will not suit me to permit any one the range of the place while I am off guard!' said the unmannerly wretch.

With this insult, my patience was at an end. I uttered an expression of disgust, and pushed past him into the yard, running against Earnshaw in my haste. It was so dark that I could not see the means of exit, and, as I wandered round, I heard another specimen of their civil behaviour amongst each other.

At first, the young man appeared about to befriend me.

'I'll go with him as far as the park,' he said.

'You'll go with him to hell!' exclaimed his master, or whatever relation he bore. 'And who is to look after the horses, eh?'

'A man's life is of more consequence than one evening's neglect of the horses; somebody must go,' murmured Mrs Heathcliff, more kindly than I expected.

'Not at your command!' retorted Hareton. 'If you set store on him, you'd better be quiet.'

'Then I hope his ghost will haunt you; and I hope Mr Heathcliff will never get another tenant, till the Grange is a ruin!' she answered sharply.

'Hearken, hearken, shoo's cursing on 'em!' muttered Joseph, towards whom I had been steering.

He sat within earshot, milking the cows by the light of a lantern, which I seized unceremoniously, and, calling out that I would send it back on the morrow, rushed to the nearest postern.

'Maister, maister, he's staling t' lantern!' shouted the ancient, pursuing my retreat. 'Hey, Gnasher! Hey, dog! Hey, Wolf, holld him, holld him!'

On opening the little door, two hairy monsters flew at my throat, bearing me down and extinguishing the light, while a mingled guffaw, from Heathcliff and Hareton, put the copestone on my rage and humiliation.

Fortunately, the beasts seemed more bent on stretching their paws, and yawning, and flourishing their tails, than devouring me alive; but, they would suffer no resurrection, and I was forced to lie till their malignant masters pleased to deliver me: then hatless, and trembling with wrath, I ordered the miscreants to let me out – on their peril to keep me one minute longer – with several incoherent threats of retaliation that, in their indefinite depth of virulency, smacked of King Lear.

The vehemence of my agitation brought on a copious bleeding at the nose, and still Heathcliff laughed, and still I scolded. I don't know what would have concluded the scene had there not been one person at hand rather more rational than myself, and more benevolent than my entertainer. This was Zillah, the stout housewife; who at length issued forth to inquire into the nature of the uproar. She thought that some of them had been laying violent hands on me

and, not daring to attack her master, she turned her vocal artillery against the younger scoundrel.

'Well, Mr Earnshaw,' she cried, 'I wonder what you'll have agait next! Are we going to murder folk on our very door-stones? I see this house will never do for me – look at t' poor lad, he's fair choking! Wisht, wisht! you mun'n't go on so – come in, and I'll cure that. There now, hold ye still.'

With these words she suddenly splashed a pint of icy water down my neck, and pulled me into the kitchen. Mr Heathcliff followed, his accidental merriment expiring quickly in his habitual moroseness.

I was sick exceedingly, and dizzy and faint; and thus compelled, perforce, to accept lodgings under his roof. He told Zillah to give me a glass of brandy, and then passed on to the inner room, while she condoled with me on my sorry predicament, and having obeyed his orders, whereby I was somewhat revived, ushered me to bed.

# Chapter 3

While leading the way up-stairs, she recommended that I should hide the candle, and not make a noise, for her master had an odd notion about the chamber she would put me in; and never let anybody lodge there willingly.

I asked the reason.

She did not know, she answered; she had only lived there a year or two; and they had so many queer goings on, she could not begin to be curious.

Too stupefied to be curious myself, I fastened my door and glanced round for the bed. The whole furniture consisted of a chair, a clothes-press, and a large oak case, with squares cut out near the top, resembling coach windows.

Having approached this structure, I looked inside, and perceived it to be a singular sort of old-fashioned couch, very conveniently designed to obviate the necessity for every member of the family having a room to himself. In fact, it formed a little closet, and the ledge of a window, which it enclosed, served as a table.

I slid back the panelled sides, got in with my light, pulled them together again, and felt secure against the vigilance of Heathcliff, and every one else.

The ledge, where I placed my candle, had a few mildewed books piled up in one corner; and it was covered with writing scratched on the paint. This writing, however, was nothing but a name repeated in all kinds of characters, large and small – *Catherine Earnshaw*; here and there varied to *Catherine Heathcliff*, and then again to *Catherine Linton*.

In vapid listlessness I leant my head against the window, and continued spelling over Catherine Earnshaw – Heathcliff – Linton, till my eyes closed; but

they had not rested five minutes when a glare of white letters started from the dark, as vivid as spectres – the air swarmed with Catherines; and rousing myself to dispel the obtrusive name, I discovered my candle wick reclining on one of the antique volumes, and perfuming the place with an odour of roasted calf-skin.

I snuffed it off, and, very ill at ease, under the influence of cold and lingering nausea, sat up, and spread open the injured tome on my knee. It was a Testament, in lean type, and smelling dreadfully musty: a fly-leaf bore the inscription – 'Catherine Earnshaw, her book,' and a date some quarter of a century back.

I shut, and took up another, and another, till I had examined all. Catherine's library was select; and its state of dilapidation proved it to have been well used, though not altogether for a legitimate purpose; scarcely one chapter had escaped a pen and ink commentary – at least, the appearance of one – covering every morsel of blank that the printer had left.

Some were detached sentences; other parts took the form of a regular diary, scrawled in an unformed, childish hand. At the top of an extra page, quite a treasure probably when first lighted on, I was greatly amused to behold an excellent caricature of my friend Joseph, rudely yet powerfully sketched.

An immediate interest kindled within me for the unknown Catherine, and I began, forthwith, to decypher her faded hieroglyphics.

'An awful Sunday!' commenced the paragraph beneath. 'I wish my father were back again. Hindley is a detestable substitute – his conduct to Heathcliff is atrocious – H. and I are going to rebel – we took our initiatory step this evening.

'All day had been flooding with rain; we could not go to church, so Joseph must needs get up a congregation in the garret; and, while Hindley and his wife basked down stairs before a comfortable fire, doing anything but reading their Bibles, I'll answer for it, Heathcliff, myself, and the unhappy plough-boy were commanded to take our Prayer-books and mount – we were ranged in a row, on a sack of corn, groaning and shivering, and hoping that Joseph would shiver too, so that he might give us a short homily for his own sake. A vain idea! The service lasted precisely three hours; and yet my brother had the face to exclaim, when he saw us descending,

' "What, done already?"

'On Sunday evenings we used to be permitted to play, if we did not make much noise; now a mere titter is sufficient to send us into corners!

' "You forget you have a master here," says the tyrant. "I'll demolish the first who puts me out of temper! I insist on perfect sobriety and silence. Oh, boy! was that you? Frances, darling, pull his hair as you go by; I heard him snap his fingers."

'Frances pulled his hair heartily; and then went and seated herself on her husband's knee, and there they were, like two babies, kissing and talking nonsense by the hour – foolish palaver that we should be ashamed of.

'We made ourselves as snug as our means allowed in the arch of the dresser. I had just fastened our pinafores together, and hung them up for a curtain; when in comes Joseph, on an errand from the stables. He tears down my handywork, boxes my ears, and croaks:

' "T' maister nobbut just buried, and Sabbath nut oe'red, und t' sahnd uh't gospel still i' yer lugs, and yah darr be laiking! shame on ye! sit ye dahn, ill

childer! they's good books eneugh if ye'll read 'em; sit ye dahn, and think uh yer sowls!"

'Saying this, he compelled us to square our positions that we might receive, from the far-off fire, a dull ray to show us the text of the lumber he thrust upon us.

'I could not bear the employment. I took my dingy volume by the scroop, and hurled it into the dog-kennel, vowing I hated a good book.

'Heathcliff kicked his to the same place.

'Then there was a hubbub!

' "Maister Hindley!" shouted our chaplain. "Maister, coom hither! Miss Cathy's riven th' back off 'Th' Helmet uh Salvation,' un' Heathcliff's pawsed his fit intuh t' first part uh 'T' Broad Way to Destruction!' It's fair flaysome ut yah, let 'em goa on this gait. Ech! th' owd man ud uh laced 'em properly – bud he's goan!"

'Hindley hurried up from his paradise on the hearth, and seizing one of us by the collar, and the other by the arm, hurled both into the back-kitchen, where, Joseph asseverated, "owd Nick" would fetch us as sure as we were living; and so, comforted, we each sought a separate nook to await his advent.

'I reached this book, and a pot of ink from the shelf, and pushed the house-door ajar to give me light, and I have got the time on with writing for twenty minutes; but my companion is impatient and proposes that we should appropriate the dairy woman's cloak, and have a scamper on the moors, under its shelter. A pleasant suggestion – and then, if the surly old man come in, he may believe his prophecy verified — we cannot be damper, or colder, in the rain than we are here.'

I suppose Catherine fulfilled her project, for the next sentence took up another subject: she waxed lachrymose.

'How little did I dream that Hindley would ever make me cry so!' she wrote. 'My head aches, till I cannot keep it on the pillow; and still I can't give over. Poor Heathcliff! Hindley calls him a vagabond, and won't let him sit with us, nor eat with us any more; and, he says, he and I must not play together, and threatens to turn him out of the house if we break his orders.

'He has been blaming our father (how dared he?) for treating H. too liberally; and swears he will reduce him to his right place –'

I began to nod drowsily over the dim page; my eye wandered from manuscript to print. I saw a red ornamented title – 'Seventy Times Seven, and the First of the Seventy-First. A Pious Discourse delivered by the Reverend Jabes Branderham, in the Chapel of Gimmerden Sough.' And while I was, half consciously, worrying my brain to guess what Jabes Branderham would make of his subject, I sank back in bed, and fell asleep.

Alas, for the effects of bad tea and bad temper! what else could it be that made me pass such a terrible night? I don't remember another that I can at all compare with it since I was capable of suffering.

I began to dream, almost before I ceased to be sensible of my locality. I thought it was morning; and I had set out on my way home, with Joseph for a guide.

# Wuthering Heights

The snow lay yards deep in our road; and, as we floundered on, my companion wearied me with constant reproaches that I had not brought a pilgrim's staff: telling me that I could never get into the house without one, and boastfully flourishing a heavy-headed cudgel, which I understood to be so denominated.

For a moment I considered it absurd that I should need such a weapon to gain admittance into my own residence. Then, a new idea flashed across me. I was not going there; we were journeying to hear the famous Jabes Branderham preach from the text – 'Seventy Times Seven'; and either Joseph, the preacher, or I had committed the 'First of the Seventy-First', and were to be publicly exposed and excommunicated.

We came to the chapel – I have passed it really in my walks, twice or thrice: it lies in a hollow, between two hills – an elevated hollow – near a swamp, whose peaty moisture is said to answer all the purposes of embalming on the few corpses deposited there. The roof has been kept whole hitherto, but, as the clergyman's stipend is only twenty pounds per annum, and a house with two rooms, threatening speedily to determine into one, no clergyman will undertake the duties of pastor, especially as it is currently reported that his flock would rather let him starve than increase the living by one penny from their own pockets. However, in my dream, Jabes had a full and attentive congregation: and he preached – good God – what a sermon! divided into *four hundred and ninety* parts, each fully equal to an ordinary address from the pulpit and each discussing a separate sin! Where he searched for them, I cannot tell; he had his private manner of interpreting the phrase, and it seemed necessary the brother should sin different sins on every occasion.

They were of the most curious character – odd transgressions that I never imagined previously.

Oh, how weary I grew. How I writhed, and yawned, and nodded, and revived! How I pinched and pricked myself, and rubbed my eyes, and stood up, and sat down again, and nudged Joseph to inform me if he would *ever* have done!

I was condemned to hear all out – finally, he reached the '*First of the Seventy-First.*' At that crisis, a sudden inspiration descended on me; I was moved to rise and denounce Jabes Branderham as the sinner of the sin that no Christian need pardon.

'Sir,' I exclaimed, 'sitting here within these four walls, at one stretch, I have endured and forgiven the four hundred and ninety heads of your discourse. Seventy times seven times have I plucked up my hat and been about to depart – Seventy times seven times have you preposterously forced me to resume my seat. The four hundred and ninety first is too much. Fellow-martyrs, have at him! Drag him down, and crush him to atoms, that the place which knows him may know him no more!'

'*Thou art the Man!*' cried Jabes, after a solemn pause, leaning over his cushion. 'Seventy times seven didst thou gapingly contort thy visage – seventy times seven did I take counsel with my soul – Lo, this is human weakness; this also may be absolved! The First of the Seventy-First is come. Brethren, execute upon him the judgment written! such honour have all His saints!'

With that concluding word, the whole assembly, exalting their pilgrim's staves, rushed round me in a body, and I, having no weapon to raise in self-defence, commenced grappling with Joseph, my nearest and most ferocious

# Wuthering Heights

assailant, for his. In the confluence of the multitude, several clubs crossed; blows, aimed at me, fell on other sconces. Presently the whole chapel resounded with rappings and counter-rappings. Every man's hand was against his neighbour; and Branderham, unwilling to remain idle, poured forth his zeal in a shower of loud taps on the boards of the pulpit which responded so smartly that, at last, to my unspeakable relief, they woke me.

And what was it that had suggested the tremendous tumult, what had played Jabes' part in the row? Merely, the branch of a fir-tree that touched my lattice, as the blast wailed by, and rattled its dry cones against the panes!

I listened doubtingly an instant; detected the disturber, then turned and dozed, and dreamt again; if possible, still more disagreeably than before.

This time, I remembered I was lying in the oak closet, and I heard distinctly the gusty wind, and the driving of the snow; I heard, also, the fir-bough repeat its teasing sound, and ascribed it to the right cause; but it annoyed me so much, that I resolved to silence it, if possible; and, I thought, I rose and endeavoured to unhasp the casement. The hook was soldered into the staple, a circumstance observed by me when awake, but forgotten.

'I must stop it, nevertheless!' I muttered, knocking my knuckles through the glass, and stretching an arm out to seize the importunate branch: instead of which, my fingers closed on the fingers of a little, ice-cold hand!

The intense horror of nightmare came over me; I tried to draw back my arm, but the hand clung to it, and a most melancholy voice sobbed,

'Let me in – let me in!'

'Who are you?' I asked, struggling, meanwhile, to disengage myself.

'Catherine Linton,' it replied shiveringly (why did I think of *Linton*? I had read *Earnshaw* twenty times for Linton), 'I'm come home, I'd lost my way on the moor!'

As it spoke, I discerned, obscurely, a child's face looking through the window – terror made me cruel; and, finding it useless to attempt shaking the creature off, I pulled its wrist on to the broken pane, and rubbed it to and fro till the blood ran down and soaked the bedclothes: still it wailed, 'Let me in!' and maintained its tenacious gripe, almost maddening me with fear.

'How can I!' I said at length. 'Let *me* go, if you want me to let you in!'

The fingers relaxed, I snatched mine through the hole, hurriedly piled the books up in a pyramid against it, and stopped my ears to exclude the lamentable prayer.

I seemed to keep them closed above a quarter of an hour, yet, the instant I listened, again, there was the doleful cry moaning on!

'Begone!' I shouted, 'I'll never let you in, not if you beg for twenty years.'

'It's twenty years,' mourned the voice, 'twenty years, I've been a waif for twenty years!'

Thereat began a feeble scratching outside, and the pile of books moved as if thrust forward.

I tried to jump up, but could not stir a limb; and so yelled aloud, in a frenzy of fright.

To my confusion, I discovered the yell was not ideal. Hasty footsteps approached my chamber door: somebody pushed it open, with a vigorous hand, and a light glimmered through the squares at the top of the bed. I sat shuddering

# Wuthering Heights

yet, and wiping the perspiration from my forehead: the intruder appeared to hesitate, and muttered to himself.

At last, he said in a half-whisper, plainly not expecting an answer,

'Is any one here?'

I considered it best to confess my presence, for I knew Heathcliff's accents, and feared he might search further, if I kept quiet.

With this intention, I turned and opened the panels – I shall not soon forget the effect my action produced.

Heathcliff stood near the entrance, in his shirt and trousers, with a candle dripping over his fingers, and his face as white as the wall behind him. The first creak of the oak startled him like an electric shock: the light leaped from his hold to a distance of some feet, and his agitation was so extreme that he could hardly pick it up.

'It is only your guest, sir,' I called out, desirous to spare him the humiliation of exposing his cowardice further. 'I had the misfortune to scream in my sleep, owing to a frightful nightmare. I'm sorry I disturbed you.'

'Oh, God confound you, Mr Lockwood! I wish you were at the –' commenced my host, setting the candle on a chair, because he found it impossible to hold it steady.

'And who showed you up to this room?' he continued, crushing his nails into his palms, and grinding his teeth to subdue the maxillary convulsions. 'Who was it? I've a good mind to turn them out of the house this moment!'

'It was your servant, Zillah,' I replied, flinging myself on to the floor, and rapidly resuming my garments. 'I should not care if you did, Mr Heathcliff; she richly deserved it. I suppose that she wanted to get another proof that the place was haunted, at my expense – Well, it is – swarming with ghosts and goblins! You have reason in shutting it up, I assure you. No one will thank you for a dose in such a den!'

'What do you mean?' asked Heathcliff, 'and what are you doing? Lie down and finish out the night, since you *are* here; but, for Heaven's sake! don't repeat that horrid noise – Nothing could excuse it, unless you were having your throat cut!'

'If the little fiend had got in at the window, she probably would have strangled me!' I returned. 'I'm not going to endure the persecutions of your hospitable ancestors again. Was not the Reverend Jabes Branderham akin to you on the mother's side? And that minx, Catherine Linton, or Earnshaw, or however she was called – she must have been a changeling – wicked little soul! She told me she had been walking the earth these twenty years: a just punishment for her mortal transgressions, I've no doubt!'

Scarcely were these words uttered, when I recollected the association of Heathcliff's with Catherine's name in the book, which had completely slipped from my memory till thus awakened. I blushed at my inconsideration; but, without showing further consciousness of the offence, I hastened to add,

'The truth is, sir, I passed the first part of the night –' Here I stopped afresh – I was about to say 'perusing those old volumes,' then it would have revealed my knowledge of their written, as well as their printed contents; so, correcting myself, I went on, 'in spelling over the name scratched on that window-ledge. A monotonous occupation, calculated to set me asleep, like counting, or –'

'What *can* you mean by talking in this way to *me*?' thundered Heathcliff

with savage vehemence. 'How – how *dare* you, under my roof? – God! he's mad to speak so!' And he struck his forehead with rage.

I did not know whether to resent this language, or pursue my explanation; but he seemed so powerfully affected that I took pity and proceeded with my dreams; affirming I had never heard the appellation of 'Catherine Linton', before, but reading it often over produced an impression which personified itself when I had no longer my imagination under control.

Heathcliff gradually fell back into the shelter of the bed, as I spoke, finally, sitting down almost concealed behind it. I guessed, however, by his irregular and intercepted breathing, that he struggled to vanquish an access of violent emotion.

Not liking to show him that I heard the conflict, I continued my toilette rather noisily, looked at my watch, and soliloquized on the length of the night:

'Not three o'clock yet! I could have taken oath it had been six – time stagnates here – we must surely have retired to rest at eight!'

'Always at nine in winter, and always rise at four,' said my host, suppressing a groan; and, as I fancied, by the motion of his shadow's arm, dashing a tear from his eyes.

'Mr Lockwood,' he added, 'you may go into my room; you'll only be in the way, coming down stairs so early; and your childish outcry has sent sleep to the devil for me.'

'And for me, too,' I replied. 'I'll walk in the yard till daylight, and then I'll be off; and you need not dread a repetition of my intrusion. I am now quite cured of seeking pleasure in society, be it country or town. A sensible man ought to find sufficient company in himself.'

'Delightful company!' muttered Heathcliff. 'Take the candle, and go where you please. I shall join you directly. Keep out of the yard, though, the dogs are unchained; and the house – Juno mounts sentinel there – and – nay, you can only ramble about the steps and passages – but, away with you! I'll come in two minutes!'

I obeyed, so far as to quit the chamber; when, ignorant where the narrow lobbies led, I stood still, and was witness, involuntarily, to a piece of superstition on the part of my landlord, which belied, oddly, his apparent sense.

He got onto the bed, and wrenched open the lattice, bursting, as he pulled at it, into an uncontrollable passion of tears.

'Come in! come in!' he sobbed. 'Cathy, do come. Oh do – *once* more! Oh! my heart's darling! hear me *this* time – Catherine, at last!'

The spectre showed a spectre's ordinary caprice; it gave no sign of being; but the snow and wind whirled wildly through, even reaching my station, and blowing out the light.

There was such anguish in the gush of grief that accompanied this raving, that my compassion made me overlook its folly, and I drew off, half angry to have listened at all, and vexed at having related my ridiculous nightmare, since it produced that agony; though *why*, was beyond my comprehension.

I descended cautiously to the lower regions and landed in the back-kitchen, where a gleam of fire, raked compactly together, enabled me to rekindle my candle.

Nothing was stirring except a brindled, grey cat, which crept from the ashes, and saluted me with a querulous mew.

# Wuthering Heights

Two benches, shaped in sections of a circle, nearly enclosed the hearth; on one of these I stretched myself, and Grimalkin mounted the other. We were both of us nodding, ere anyone invaded our retreat; and then it was Joseph, shuffling down a wooden ladder that vanished in the roof, through a trap, the ascent to his garret, I suppose.

He cast a sinister look at the little flame which I had enticed to play between the ribs, swept the cat from its elevation, and bestowing himself in the vacancy, commenced the operation of stuffing a three-inch pipe with tobacco; my presence in his sanctum was evidently esteemed a piece of impudence too shameful for remark. He silently applied the tube to his lips, folded his arms, and puffed away.

I let him enjoy the luxury unannoyed; and after sucking out the last wreath, and heaving a profound sigh, he got up, and departed as solemnly as he came.

A more elastic footstep entered next, and now I opened my mouth for a 'good morning,' but closed it again, the salutation unachieved; for Hareton Earnshaw was performing his orisons, *sotto voce*, in a series of curses directed against every object he touched, while he rummaged a corner for a spade or shovel to dig through the drifts. He glanced over the back of the bench dilating his nostrils, and thought as little of exchanging civilities with me as with my companion, the cat.

I guessed by his preparations that egress was allowed, and leaving my hard couch, made a movement to follow him. He noticed this, and thrust at an inner door with the end of his spade, intimating by an inarticulate sound, that there was the place where I must go, if I changed my locality.

It opened into the house, where the females were already astir, Zillah urging flakes of flame up the chimney with a colossal bellows; and Mrs Heathcliff, kneeling on the hearth, reading a book by the aid of the blaze.

She held her hand interposed between the furnace-heat and her eyes, and seemed absorbed in her occupation: desisting from it only to chide the servant for covering her with sparks, or to push away a dog, now and then, that snoozled its nose over-forwardly into her face.

I was surprised to see Heathcliff there also. He stood by the fire, his back towards me, just finishing a stormy scene to poor Zillah, who ever and anon interrupted her labour to pluck up the corner of her apron, and heave an indignant groan.

'And you, you worthless –' he broke out as I entered, turning to his daughter-in-law, and employing an epithet as harmless as duck, or sheep, but generally represented by a dash.

'There you are at your idle tricks again! The rest of them do earn their bread – you live on my charity! Put your trash away, and find something to do. You shall pay me for the plague of having you eternally in my sight – do you hear, damnable jade?'

'I'll put my trash away, because you can make me, if I refuse,' answered the young lady, closing her book and throwing it on a chair. 'But I'll not do anything, though you should swear your tongue out, except what I please!'

Heathcliff lifted his hand, and the speaker sprang to a safer distance, obviously acquainted with its weight.

Having no desire to be entertained by a cat and dog combat, I stepped forward briskly, as if eager to partake the warmth of the hearth, and innocent of any

# Wuthering Heights

knowledge of the interrupted dispute. Each had enough decorum to suspend further hostilities; Heathcliff placed his fists, out of temptation, in his pockets: Mrs Heathcliff curled her lip, and walked to a seat far off; where she kept her word by playing the part of a statue during the remainder of my stay.

That was not long. I declined joining their breakfast, and, at the first gleam of dawn, took an opportunity of escaping into the free air, now clear, and still, and cold as impalpable ice.

My landlord hallooed for me to stop ere I reached the bottom of the garden, and offered to accompany me across the moor. It was well he did, for the whole hill-back was one billowy, white ocean; the swells and falls not indicating corresponding rises and depressions in the ground – many pits, at least, were filled to a level; and entire ranges of mounds, the refuse of the quarries, blotted out from the chart which my yesterday's walk pictured in my mind.

I had remarked on one side of the road, at intervals of six or seven yards, a line of upright stones, continued through the whole length of the barren: these were erected, and daubed with lime on purpose to serve as guides in the dark, and also, when a fall, like the present, confounded the deep swamps on either hand with the firmer path: but, excepting a dirty dot pointing up, here and there, all traces of their existence had vanished; and my companion found it necessary to warn me frequently to steer to the right, or left, when I imagined I was following, correctly, the windings of the road.

We exchanged little conversation, and he halted at the entrance of Thrushcross park, saying I could make no error there. Our adieux were limited to a hasty bow, and then I pushed forward, trusting to my own resources, for the porter's lodge is untenanted as yet.

The distance from the gate to the Grange is two miles: I believe I managed to make it four, what with losing myself among the trees, and sinking up to the neck in snow, a predicament which only those who have experienced it can appreciate. At any rate, whatever were my wanderings, the clock chimed twelve as I entered the house; and that gave exactly an hour for every mile of the usual way from Wuthering Heights.

My human fixture and her satellites rushed to welcome me; exclaiming, tumultuously, they had completely given me up; everybody conjectured that I perished last night; and they were wondering how they must set about the search for my remains.

I bid them be quiet, now that they saw me returned, and, benumbed to my very heart, I dragged upstairs, whence, after putting on dry clothes, and pacing to and fro, thirty or forty minutes, to restore the animal heat, I am adjourned to my study, feeble as a kitten, almost too much so to enjoy the cheerful fire and smoking coffee which the servant has prepared for my refreshment.

# Chapter 4

What vain weather-cocks we are! I, who had determined to hold myself independent of all social intercourse, and thanked my stars that, at length, I had lighted on a spot where it was next to impracticable, I, weak wretch, after maintaining till dusk a struggle with low spirits, and solitude, was finally compelled to strike my colours; and, under pretence of gaining information concerning the necessities of my establishment, I desired Mrs Dean, when she brought in supper, to sit down while I ate it, hoping sincerely she would prove a regular gossip, and either rouse me to animation, or lull me to sleep by her talk.

'You have lived here a considerable time,' I commenced; 'did you not say sixteen years?'

'Eighteen, sir; I came, when the mistress was married, to wait on her; after she died, the master retained me for his housekeeper.'

'Indeed.'

There ensued a pause. She was not a gossip, I feared, unless about her own affairs, and those could hardly interest me.

However, having studied for an interval, with a fist on either knee, and a cloud of meditation over her ruddy countenance, she ejaculated –

'Ah, times are greatly changed since then!'

'Yes,' I remarked, 'you've seen a good many alterations, I suppose?'

'I have: and troubles too,' she said.

'Oh, I'll turn the talk on my landlord's family!' I thought to myself. 'A good subject to start – and that pretty girl-widow, I should like to know her history; whether she be a native of the country, or, as is more probable, an exotic that the surly indigenae will not recognize for kin.'

With this intention I asked Mrs Dean why Heathcliff let Thrushcross Grange, and preferred living in a situation and residence so much inferior.

'Is he not rich enough to keep the estate in good order?' I enquired.

'Rich, sir!' she returned. 'He has, nobody knows what money, and every year it increases. Yes, yes, he's rich enough to live in a finer house than this; but he's very near – close-handed; and, if he had meant to flit to Thrushcross Grange, as soon as he heard of a good tenant he could not have borne to miss the chance of getting a few hundreds more. It is strange people should be so greedy, when they are, alone in the world!'

'He had a son, it seems?'

'Yes, he had one – he is dead.'

'And that young lady, Mrs Heathcliff, is his widow?'

'Yes.'

# Wuthering Heights

'Where did she come from originally?'

'Why, sir, she is my late master's daughter; Catherine Linton was her maiden name. I nursed her, poor thing! I did wish Mr Heathcliff would remove here, and then we might have been together again.'

'What, Catherine Linton!' I exclaimed, astonished. But a minute's reflection convinced me it was not my ghostly Catherine. 'Then,' I continued, 'my predecessor's name was Linton?'

'It was.'

'And who is that Earnshaw, Hareton Earnshaw, who lives with Mr Heathcliff? are they relations?'

'No; he is the late Mrs Linton's nephew.'

'The young lady's cousin, then?'

'Yes; and her husband was her cousin also – one on the mother's, the other on the father's side – Heathcliff married Mr Linton's sister.'

'I see the house at Wuthering Heights has "Earnshaw" carved over the front door. Are they an old family?'

'Very old, sir; and Hareton is the last of them, as our Miss Cathy is of us – I mean, of the Lintons. Have you been to Wuthering Heights? I beg pardon for asking; but I should like to hear how she is.'

'Mrs Heathcliff? she looked very well, and very handsome; yet, I think, not very happy.'

'Oh dear, I don't wonder! And how did you like the master?'

'A rough fellow, rather, Mrs Dean. Is not that his character?'

'Rough as a saw-edge, and hard as whinstone! The less you meddle with him the better.'

'He must have had some ups and downs in life to make him such a churl. Do you know anything of his history?'

'It's a cuckoo's, sir – I know all about it; except where he was born, and who were his parents, and how he got his money, at first – And Hareton has been cast out like an unfledged dunnock – The unfortunate lad is the only one, in all this parish, that does not guess how he has been cheated!'

'Well, Mrs Dean, it will be a charitable deed to tell me something of my neighbours – I feel I shall not rest, if I go to bed; so be good enough to sit and chat an hour.'

'Oh, certainly, sir! I'll just fetch a little sewing, and then I'll sit as long as you please. But you've caught cold; I saw you shivering, and you must have some gruel to drive it out.'

The worthy woman bustled off, and I crouched nearer the fire: my head felt hot, and the rest of me chill: moreover, I was excited, almost to a pitch of foolishness through my nerves and brain. This caused me to feel, not uncomfortable, but rather fearful, as I am still, of serious effects from the incidents of today and yesterday.

She returned presently, bringing a smoking basin, and a basket of work; and, having placed the former on the hob, drew in her seat, evidently pleased to find me so companionable.

Before I came to live here, she commenced, waiting no further invitation to her story; I was almost always at Wuthering Heights; because my mother had nursed Mr Hindley Earnshaw, that was Hareton's father, and I got used to

# Wuthering Heights

playing with the children – I ran errands too, and helped to make hay, and hung about the farm ready for anything that anybody would set me to.

One fine summer morning – it was the beginning of harvest, I remember – Mr Earnshaw, the old master, came down stairs, dressed for a journey; and, after he had told Joseph what was to be done during the day, he turned to Hindley and Cathy, and me – for I sat eating my porridge, with them – and he said, speaking to his son,

'Now, my bonny man, I'm going to Liverpool to-day . . . What shall I bring you? You may choose what you like; only let it be little, for I shall walk there and back; sixty miles each way, that is a long spell!'

Hindley named a fiddle, and then he asked Miss Cathy; she was hardly six years old, but she could ride any horse in the stable, and she chose a whip.

He did not forget me; for he had a kind heart, though he was rather severe, sometimes. He promised to bring me a pocketful of apples and pears, and then he kissed his children good-bye, and set off.

It seemed a long while to us all – the three days of his absence – and often did little Cathy ask when he would be home. Mrs Earnshaw expected him by supper-time, on the third evening; and she put off the meal hour after hour; there were no signs of his coming, however, and at last the children got tired of running down to the gate to look – Then it grew dark, she would have had them to bed, but they begged sadly to be allowed to stay up; and, just about eleven o'clock, the door-latch was raised, quietly and in stept the master. He threw himself into a chair, laughing and groaning, and bid them all stand off, for he was nearly killed – he would not have another such walk for the three kingdoms.

'And at the end of it, to be flighted to death!' he said, opening his great coat, which he held bundled up in his arms. 'See here, wife; I was never so beaten with anything in my life; but you must e'en take it as a gift of God; though it's as dark almost as if it came from the devil.'

We crowded round, and, over Miss Cathy's head, I had a peep at a dirty, ragged, black-haired child; big enough both to walk and talk – indeed, its face looked older than Catherine's – yet, when it was set on its feet, it only stared round, and repeated over and over again some gibberish that nobody could understand. I was frightened, and Mrs Earnshaw was ready to fling it out of doors: she did fly up – asking how he could fashion to bring that gipsy brat into the house, when they had their own bairns to feed, and fend for? What he meant to do with it, and whether he were mad?

The master tried to explain the matter; but he was really half dead with fatigue, and all that I could make out, amongst her scolding, was a tale of his seeing it starving, and houseless, and as good as dumb in the streets of Liverpool where he picked it up and inquired for its owner – Not a soul knew to whom it belonged, he said, and his money and time, being both limited, he thought it better to take it home with him, at once, than run into vain expenses there; because he was determined he would not leave it as he found it.

Well, the conclusion was that my mistress grumbled herself calm; and Mr Earnshaw told me to wash it, and give it clean things, and let it sleep with the children.

Hindley and Cathy contented themselves with looking and listening till peace was restored; then, both began searching their father's pockets for the presents he had promised them. The former was a boy of fourteen, but when he drew

out what had been a fiddle, crushed to morsels in the greatcoat, he blubbered aloud, and Cathy, when she learnt the master had lost her whip in attending on the stranger, showed her humour by grinning and spitting at the stupid little thing, earning for her pains a sound blow from her father to teach her cleaner manners.

They entirely refused to have it in bed with them, or even in their room, and I had no more sense, so, I put it on the landing of the stairs, hoping it might be gone on the morrow. By chance, or else attracted by hearing his voice, it crept to Mr Earnshaw's door, and there he found it on quitting his chamber; Inquiries were made as to how it got there; I was obliged to confess, and in recompense for my cowardice and inhumanity was sent out of the house.

This was Heathcliff's first introduction to the family; on coming back a few days afterwards, for I did not consider my banishment perpetual, I found they had christened him 'Heathcliff'; it was the name of a son who died in childhood, and it has served him ever since, both for Christian and surname.

Miss Cathy and he were now very thick; but Hindley hated him, and to say the truth I did the same; and we plagued and went on with him shamefully, for I wasn't reasonable enough to feel my injustice, and the mistress never put in a word on his behalf, when she saw him wronged.

He seemed a sullen, patient child; hardened, perhaps, to ill-treatment: he would stand Hindley's blows without winking or shedding a tear, and my pinches moved him only to draw in a breath, and open his eyes as if he had hurt himself by accident, and nobody was to blame.

This endurance made old Earnshaw furious when he discovered his son persecuting the poor, fatherless child, as he called him. He took to Heathcliff strangely, believing all he said (for that matter, he said precious little, and generally the truth), and petting him up far above Cathy, who was too mischievous and wayward for a favourite.

So, from the very beginning, he bred bad feeling in the house; and at Mrs Earnshaw's death, which happened in less than two years after, the young master had learnt to regard his father as an oppressor rather than a friend, and Heathcliff as a usurper of his parent's affections, and his privileges, and he grew bitter with brooding over these injuries.

I sympathized awhile, but, when the children fell ill of the measles and I had to tend them, and take on me the cares of a woman, at once, I changed my ideas. Heathcliff was dangerously sick, and while he lay at the worst he would have me constantly by his pillow; I suppose he felt I did a good deal for him, and he hadn't wit to guess that I was compelled to do it. However, I will say this, he was the quietest child that ever nurse watched over. The difference between him and the others forced me to be less partial: Cathy and her brother harassed me terribly: *he* was as uncomplaining as a lamb, though hardness, not gentleness, made him give little trouble.

He got through, and the doctor affirmed it was in a great measure owing to me, and praised me for my care. I was vain of his commendations, and softened towards the being by whose means I earned them, and thus Hindley lost his last ally; still I couldn't dote on Heathcliff, and I wondered often what my master saw to admire so much in the sullen boy who never, to my recollection, repaid his indulgence by any sign of gratitude. He was not insolent to his benefactor; he was simply insensible, though knowing perfectly the hold he had on his heart,

# Wuthering Heights

and conscious he had only to speak and all the house would be obliged to bend to his wishes.

As an instance, I remember Mr Earnshaw once bought a couple of colts at the parish fair, and gave the lads each one. Heathcliff took the handsomest, but it soon fell lame, and when he discovered it, he said to Hindley,

'You must exchange horses with me; I don't like mine, and if you won't I shall tell your father of the three thrashings you've given me this week, and show him my arm, which is black to the shoulder.'

Hindley put out his tongue, and cuffed him over the ears.

'You'd better do it at once,' he persisted, escaping to the porch (they were in the stable); 'you will have to, and if I speak of these blows, you'll get them again with interest.'

'Off, dog!' cried Hindley, threatening him with an iron weight, used for weighing potatoes and hay.

'Throw it,' he replied, standing still, 'and then I'll tell how you boasted that you would turn me out of doors as soon as he died, and see whether he will not turn you out directly.'

Hindley threw it, hitting him on the breast, and down he fell, but staggered up immediately, breathless and white, and had not I prevented it, he would have gone just so to the master, and got full revenge by letting his condition plead for him, intimating who had caused it.

'Take my colt, gipsy, then!' said young Earnshaw, 'And I pray that he may break your neck, take him, and be damned, you beggarly interloper! and wheedle my father out of all he has, only, afterwards, show him what you are, imp of Satan – And take that, I hope he'll kick out your brains!'

Heathcliff had gone to loose the beast, and shift it to his own stall – He was passing behind it, when Hindley finished his speech by knocking him under its feet, and without stopping to examine whether his hopes were fulfilled, ran away as fast as he could.

I was surprised to witness how coolly the child gathered himself up, and went on with his intention, exchanging saddles and all; and then sitting down on a bundle of hay to overcome the qualm which the violent blow occasioned, before he entered the house.

I persuaded him easily to let me lay the blame of his bruises on the horse; he minded little what tale was told since he had what he wanted. He complained so seldom, indeed, of such stirs as these, that I really thought him not vindictive – I was deceived, completely, as you will hear.

# Chapter 5

In the course of time, Mr Earnshaw began to fail. He had been active and healthy, yet his strength left him suddenly; and when he was confined to the chimney-corner he grew grievously irritable. A nothing vexed him, and suspected slights of his authority nearly threw him into fits.

This was especially to be remarked if anyone attempted to impose upon, or domineer over his favourite: he was painfully jealous lest a word should be spoken amiss to him, seeming to have got into his head the notion that, because he liked Heathcliff, all hated, and longed to do him an ill-turn.

It was a disadvantage to the lad, for the kinder among us did not wish to fret the master, so we humoured his partiality; and that humouring was rich nourishment to the child's pride and black tempers. Still it became in a manner necessary; twice, or thrice, Hindley's manifestations of scorn, while his father was near, roused the old man to a fury. He seized his stick to strike him, and shook with rage that he could not do it.

At last, our curate (we had a curate then who made the living answer by teaching the late Lintons and Earnshaws, and farming his bit of land himself), he advised that the young man should be sent to college, and Mr Earnshaw agreed, though with a heavy spirit, for he said –

'Hindley was naught, and would never thrive as where he wandered.'

I hoped heartily we should have peace now. It hurt me to think the master should be made uncomfortable by his own good deed. I fancied the discontent of age and disease arose from his family disagreements, as he would have it that it did; really, you know, sir, it was in his sinking frame.

We might have got on tolerably, notwithstanding, but for two people, Miss Cathy, and Joseph, the servant: you saw him, I dare say, up yonder. He was, and is yet, most likely, the wearisomest, self-righteous pharisee that ever ransacked a Bible to rake the promises to himself, and fling the curses on his neighbours. By his knack of sermonizing and pious discoursing, he contrived to make a great impression on Mr Earnshaw, and, the more feeble the master became, the more influence he gained.

He was relentless in worrying him about his soul's concerns, and about ruling his children rigidly. He encouraged him to regard Hindley as a reprobate; and, night after night, he regularly grumbled out a long string of tales against Heathcliff and Catherine; always minding to flatter Earnshaw's weakness by heaping the heaviest blame on the last.

Certainly, she had ways with her such as I never saw a child take up before; and she put all of us past our patience fifty times and oftener in a day; from the hour she came down stairs, till the hour she went to bed, we had not a moment's

# Wuthering Heights

security that she wouldn't be in mischief. Her spirits were always at high-water mark, her tongue always going – singing, laughing, and plaguing everybody who would not do the same. A wild, wick slip she was – but she had the bonniest eye, and sweetest smile, and lightest foot in the parish; and, after all, I believe she meant no harm; for when once she made you cry in good earnest, it seldom happened that she would not keep you company; and oblige you to be quiet that you might comfort her.

She was much too fond of Heathcliff. The greatest punishment we could invent for her was to keep her separate from him: yet she got chided more than any of us on his account.

In play, she liked, exceedingly, to act the little mistress; using her hands freely, and commanding her companions: she did so to me, but I would not bear slapping, and ordering; and so I let her know.

Now, Mr Earnshaw did not understand jokes from his children: he had always been strict and grave with them; and Catherine, on her part, had no idea why her father should be crosser and less patient in his ailing condition, than he was in his prime.

His peevish reproofs wakened in her a naughty delight to provoke him; she was never so happy as when we were all scolding her at once, and she defying us with her bold, saucy look, and her ready words; turning Joseph's religious curses into ridicule, baiting me, and doing just what her father hated most, showing how her pretended insolence, which he thought real, had more power over Heathcliff than his kindness. How the boy would do *her* bidding in anything, and *his* only when it suited his own inclination.

After behaving as badly as possible all day, she sometimes came fondling to make it up at night.

'Nay, Cathy,' the old man would say, 'I cannot love thee; thou'rt worse than thy brother. Go, say thy prayers, child, and ask God's pardon. I doubt thy mother and I must rue that we ever reared thee!'

That made her cry, at first; and then, being repulsed continually hardened her, and she laughed if I told her to say she was sorry for her faults, and beg to be forgiven.

But the hour came, at last, that ended Mr Earnshaw's troubles on earth. He died quietly in his chair one October evening, seated by the fire-side.

A high wind blustered round the house, and roared in the chimney: it sounded wild and stormy, yet it was not cold, and we were all together – I, a little removed from the hearth, busy at my knitting, and Joseph reading his Bible near the table, (for the servants generally sat in the house then, after their work was done). Miss Cathy had been sick, and that made her still; she leant against her father's knee, and Heathcliff was lying on the floor with his head in her lap.

I remember the master, before he fell into a doze, stroking her bonny hair – it pleased him rarely to see her gentle – and saying –

'Why canst thou not always be a good lass, Cathy?'

And she turned her face up to his, and laughed, and answered –

'Why cannot you always be a good man, father?'

But as soon as she saw him vexed again, she kissed his hand, and said she would sing him to sleep. She began singing very low, till his fingers dropped from hers, and his head sank on his breast. Then I told her to hush, and not stir, for fear she should wake him. We all kept as mute as mice a full half hour, and

should have done longer, only Joseph, having finished his chapter, got up and said that he must rouse the master for prayers and bed. He stepped forward, and called him by name, and touched his shoulder, but he would not move – so he took the candle and looked at him.

I thought there was something wrong as he set down the light; and seizing the children each by an arm, whispered them to 'frame up-stairs, and make little din – they might pray alone that evening – he had summut to do.'

'I shall bid father goodnight first,' said Catherine, putting her arms round his neck before we could hinder her.

The poor thing discovered her loss directly – she screamed out –

'Oh, he's dead, Heathcliff! he's dead!'

And they both set up a heart-breaking cry.

I joined my wail to theirs, loud and bitter; but Joseph asked what we could be thinking of to roar in that way over a saint in heaven.

He told me to put on my cloak and run to Gimmerton for the doctor and the parson. I could not guess the use that either would be of, then. However, I went, through wind and rain, and brought one, the doctor, back with me; the other said he would come in the morning.

Leaving Joseph to explain matters, I ran to the children's room; their door was ajar, I saw they had never laid down, though it was past midnight; but they were calmer, and did not need me to console them. The little souls were comforting each other with better thoughts than I could have hit on; no parson in the world ever pictured heaven so beautifully as they did, in their innocent talk; and, while I sobbed, and listened, I could not help wishing we were all there safe together.

# Chapter 6

r Hindley came home to the funeral; and – a thing that amazed us, and set the neighbours gossiping right and left – he brought a wife with him.

What she was, and where she was born, he never informed us; probably, she had neither money nor name to recommend her, or he would scarcely have kept the union from his father.

She was not one that would have disturbed the house much on her own account. Every object she saw, the moment she crossed the threshold, appeared to delight her; and every circumstance that took place about her, except the preparing for the burial, and the presence of the mourners.

I thought she was half silly from her behaviour while that went on; she ran into her chamber, and made me come with her, though I should have been dressing the children; and there she sat shivering and clasping her hands, and asking repeatedly –

'Are they gone yet?'

Then she began describing with hysterical emotion the effect it produced on her to see black; and started, and trembled, and, at last, fell a-weeping – and when I asked what was the matter? answered, she didn't know; but she felt so afraid of dying!

I imagined her as little likely to die as myself. She was rather thin, but young, and fresh complexioned, and her eyes sparkled as bright as diamonds. I did remark, to be sure, that mounting the stairs made her breathe very quick, that the least sudden noise set her all in a quiver, and that she coughed troublesomely sometimes: but, I knew nothing of what these symptoms portended, and had no impulse to sympathize with her. We don't in general take to foreigners here, Mr Lockwood, unless they take to us first.

Young Earnshaw was altered considerably in the three years of his absence. He had grown sparer, and lost his colour, and spoke and dressed quite differently: and, on the very day of his return, he told Joseph and me we must thenceforth quarter ourselves in the back-kitchen, and leave the house for him. Indeed, he would have carpeted and papered a small spare room for a parlour; but his wife expressed such pleasure at the white floor, and huge glowing fire-place, at the pewter dishes, and delf-case, and dog-kennel, and the wide space there was to move about in, where they usually sat, that he thought it unnecessary to her comfort, and so dropped the intention.

She expressed pleasure, too, at finding a sister among her new acquaintance, and she prattled to Catherine, and kissed her, and ran about with her, and gave her quantities of presents, at the beginning. Her affection tired very soon,

# Wuthering Heights

however, and when she grew peevish, Hindley became tyrannical. A few words from her, evincing a dislike to Heathcliff, were enough to rouse in him all his old hatred of the boy. He drove him from their company to the servants, deprived him of the instructions of the curate, and insisted that he should labour out of doors instead, compelling him to do so, as hard as any other lad on the farm.

He bore his degradation pretty well at first, because Cathy taught him what she learnt, and worked or played with him in the fields. They both promised fair to grow up as rude as savages, the young master being entirely negligent how they behaved, and what they did, so they kept clear of him. He would not even have seen after their going to church on Sundays, only Joseph and the curate reprimanded his carelessness when they absented themselves, and that reminded him to order Heathcliff a flogging, and Catherine a fast from dinner or supper.

But it was one of their chief amusements to run away to the moors in the morning and remain there all day, and the after punishment grew a mere thing to laugh at. The curate might set as many chapters as he pleased for Catherine to get by heart, and Joseph might thrash Heathcliff till his arm ached; they forgot everything the minute they were together again, at least the minute they had contrived some naughty plan of revenge, and many a time I've cried to myself to watch them growing more reckless daily, and I not daring to speak a syllable for fear of losing the small power I still retained over the unfriended creatures.

One Sunday evening, it chanced that they were banished from the sitting-room, for making a noise, or a light offence of the kind, and when I went to call them to supper, I could discover them nowhere.

We searched the house, above and below, and the yard, and stables; they were invisible; and, at last, Hindley in a passion told us to bolt the doors, and swore nobody should let them in that night.

The household went to bed; and I, too anxious to lie down, opened my lattice and put my head out to harken, though it rained, determined to admit them in spite of the prohibition, should they return.

In a while, I distinguished steps coming up the road, and the light of a lantern glimmering through the gate.

I threw a shawl over my head and ran to prevent them from waking Mr Earnshaw by knocking. There was Heathcliff, by himself; it gave me a start to see him alone.

'Where is Miss Catherine?' I cried hurriedly. 'No accident, I hope?'

'At Thrushcross Grange,' he answered, 'and I would have been there too, but they had not the manners to ask me to stay.'

'Well, you will catch it!' I said, 'you'll never be content till you're sent about your business. What in the world led you wandering to Thrushcross Grange?'

'Let me get off my wet clothes, and I'll tell you all about it, Nelly,' he replied.

I bid him beware of rousing the master, and while he undressed, and I waited to put out the candle, he continued –

'Cathy and I escaped from the wash-house to have a ramble at liberty, and getting a glimpse of the Grange lights, we thought we would just go and see whether the Lintons passed their Sunday evenings standing shivering in corners, while their father and mother sat eating and drinking, and singing and laughing, and burning their eyes out before the fire. Do you think they do? Or reading

# Wuthering Heights

sermons, and being catechised by their man-servant, and set to learn a column of Scripture names, if they don't answer properly?'

'Probably not,' I responded. 'They are good children, no doubt, and don't deserve the treatment you receive, for your bad conduct.'

'Don't you cant, Nelly,' he said: 'Nonsense! We ran from the top of the Heights to the park, without stopping – Catherine completely beaten in the race, because she was barefoot. You'll have to seek for her shoes in the bog tomorrow. We crept through a broken hedge, groped our way up the path, and planted ourselves on a flower-pot under the drawing-room window. The light came from thence; they had not put up the shutters, and the curtains were only half closed. Both of us were able to look in by standing on the basement, and clinging to the ledge, and we saw – ah! it was beautiful – a splendid place carpeted with crimson, and crimson-covered chairs and tables, and a pure white ceiling bordered by gold, a shower of glass-drops hanging in silver chains from the centre, and shimmering with little soft tapers. Old Mr and Mrs Linton were not there. Edgar and his sister had it entirely to themselves; shouldn't they have been happy? We should have thought ourselves in heaven! And now, guess what your good children were doing? Isabella – I believe she is eleven, a year younger than Cathy – lay screaming at the farther end of the room, shrieking as if witches were running red-hot needles into her. Edgar stood on the hearth weeping silently, and in the middle of the table sat a little dog shaking its paw and yelping, which, from their mutual accusations, we understood they had nearly pulled in two between them. The idiots! That was their pleasure! to quarrel who should hold a heap of warm hair, and each begin to cry because both, after struggling to get it, refused to take it. We laughed outright at the petted things, we did despise them! When would you catch me wishing to have what Catherine wanted? or find us by ourselves, seeking entertainment in yelling, and sobbing, and rolling on the ground, divided by the whole room? I'd not exchange, for a thousand lives, my condition here, for Edgar Linton's at Thrushcross Grange – not if I might have the privilege of flinging Joseph off the highest gable, and painting the housefront with Hindley's blood!'

'Hush, hush!' I interrupted. 'Still you have not told me, Heathcliff, how Catherine is left behind?'

'I told you we laughed,' he answered. 'The Lintons heard us, and with one accord, they shot like arrows to the door; there was silence, and then a cry, "Oh, mamma, mamma! Oh, papa! Oh, mamma, come here. Oh, papa, oh!" They really did howl out, something in that way. We made frightful noises to terrify them still more, and then we dropped off the ledge, because somebody was drawing the bars, and we felt we had better flee. I had Cathy by the hand, and was urging her on, when all at once she fell down.

' "Run, Heathcliff, run!" she whispered. 'They have let the bull-dog loose, and he holds me!'

'The devil had seized her ankle, Nelly; I heard his abominable snorting. She did not yell out – no! She would have scorned to do it, if she had been spitted on the horns of a mad cow. I did, though, I vociferated curses enough to annihilate any fiend in Christendom, and I got a stone and thrust it between his jaws, and tried with all my might to cram it down his throat. A beast of a servant came up with a lantern, at last, shouting –

' "Keep fast, Skulker, keep fast!" '

# Wuthering Heights

'He changed his note, however, when he saw Skulker's game. The dog was throttled off, his huge, purple tongue hanging half a foot out of his mouth, and his pendant lips streaming with bloody slaver.

'The man took Cathy up; she was sick; not from fear, I'm certain, but from pain. He carried her in; I followed, grumbling execrations and vengeance.

' "What prey, Robert?" hallooed Linton from the entrance.

' "Skulker has caught a little girl, sir," he replied; "and there's a lad here," he added, making a clutch at me, "who looks an out-and-outer! Very like, the robbers were for putting them through the window, to open the doors to the gang after all were asleep, that they might murder us at their ease. Hold your tongue, you foul-mouthed thief, you! you shall go to the gallows for this. Mr Linton, sir, don't lay by your gun."

' "No, no, Robert," said the old fool. "The rascals knew that yesterday was my rent-day; they thought to have me cleverly. Come in; I'll furnish them a reception. There, John, fasten the chain. Give Skulker some water, Jenny. To beard a magistrate in his stronghold, and on the Sabbath, too! where will their insolence stop? Oh, my dear Mary, look here! Don't be afraid, it is but a boy – yet, the villain scowls so plainly in his face, would it not be a kindness to the country to hang him at once, before he shows his nature in acts, as well as features?"

'He pulled me under the chandelier, and Mrs Linton placed her spectacles on her nose and raised her hands in horror. The cowardly children crept nearer also, Isabella lisping –

' "Frightful thing! Put him in the cellar, papa. He's exactly like the son of the fortune-teller, that stole my tame pheasant. Isn't he, Edgar?"

'While they examined me, Cathy came round; she heard the last speech, and laughed. Edgar Linton, after an inquisitive stare, collected sufficient wit to recognize her. They see us at church, you know, though we seldom meet them elsewhere.

' "That's Miss Earnshaw!" he whispered to his mother, "and look how Skulker has bitten her – how her foot bleeds!"

' "Miss Earnshaw? Nonsense!" cried the dame. "Miss Earnshaw scouring the country with a gipsy! And yet, my dear, the child is in mourning – surely it is – and she may be lamed for life!"

' "What culpable carelessness in her brother!" exclaimed Mr Linton, turning from me to Catherine. "I've understood from Shielders" ' (that was the curate, sir) ' "that he lets her grow up in absolute heathenism. But who is this? Where did she pick up this companion? Oho! I declare he is that strange acquisition my late neighbour made, in his journey to Liverpool – a little Lascar, or an American or Spanish castaway."

' "A wicked boy, at all events," remarked the old lady, "and quite unfit for a decent house! Did you notice his language, Linton? I'm shocked that my children should have heard it."

'I recommenced cursing – don't be angry, Nelly – and so Robert was ordered to take me off – I refused to go without Cathy – he dragged me into the garden, pushed the lantern into my hand, assured me that Mr Earnshaw should be informed of my behaviour, and bidding me march, directly, secured the door again.

'The curtains were still looped up at one corner; and I resumed my station

as spy, because, if Catherine had wished to return, I intended shattering their great glass panes to a million of fragments, unless they let her out.

'She sat on the sofa quietly. Mrs Linton took off the grey cloak of the dairy maid which we had borrowed for our excursion, shaking her head, and expostulating with her, I suppose; she was a young lady and they made a distinction between her treatment and mine. Then the woman servant brought a basin of warm water, and washed her feet; and Mr Linton mixed a tumbler of negus, and Isabella emptied a plate of cakes into her lap, and Edgar stood gaping at a distance. Afterwards, they dried and combed her beautiful hair, and gave her a pair of enormous slippers, and wheeled her to the fire, and I left her, as merry as she could be, dividing her food between the little dog and Skulker, whose nose she pinched as she ate; and kindling a spark of spirit in the vacant blue eyes of the Lintons – a dim reflection from her own enchanting face – I saw they were full of stupid admiration; she is so immeasurably superior to them – to everybody on earth; is she not, Nelly?'

'There will more come of this business than you reckon on,' I answered, covering him up and extinguishing the light, 'You are incurable Heathcliff, and Mr Hindley will have to proceed to extremities, see if he won't.'

My words came truer than I desired. The luckless adventure made Earnshaw furious – And then, Mr Linton, to mend matters, paid us a visit himself, on the morrow; and read the young master such a lecture on the road he guided his family, that he was stirred to look about him, in earnest.

Heathcliff received no flogging, but he was told that the first word he spoke to Miss Catherine should ensure a dismissal; and Mrs Earnshaw undertook to keep her sister-in-law in due restraint, when she returned home; employing art, not force – with force she would have found it impossible.

# Chapter 7

athy stayed at Thrushcross Grange five weeks, till Christmas. By that time her ankle was thoroughly cured, and her manners much improved. The mistress visited her often, in the interval, and commenced her plan of reform by trying to raise her self-respect with fine clothes and flattery, which she took readily: so that, instead of a wild, hatless little savage jumping into the house, and rushing to squeeze us all breathless, there lighted from a handsome black pony a very dignified person, with brown ringlets falling from the cover of a feathered beaver, and a long cloth habit which she was obliged to hold up with both hands that she might sail in.

Hindley lifted her from her horse, exclaiming delightedly,

'Why, Cathy, you are quite a beauty! I should scarcely have known you – you

# Wuthering Heights

look like a lady now – Isabella Linton is not to be compared with her, is she, Frances?'

'Isabella has not her natural advantages,' replied his wife, 'but she must mind and not grow wild again here. Ellen, help Miss Catherine off with her things – Stay, dear, you will disarrange your curls – let me untie your hat.'

I removed the habit, and there shone forth, beneath a grand plaid silk frock, white trousers, and burnished shoes; and, while her eyes sparkled joyfully when the dogs came bounding up to welcome her, she dare hardly touch them lest they should fawn upon her splendid garments.

She kissed me gently, I was all flour making the Christmas cake, and it would not have done to give me a hug; and, then, she looked round for Heathcliff. Mr and Mrs Earnshaw watched anxiously their meeting, thinking it would enable them to judge, in some measure, what grounds they had for hoping to succeed in separating the two friends.

Heathcliff was hard to discover, at first – If he were careless, and uncared for, before Catherine's absence, he had been ten times more so, since.

Nobody but I even did him the kindness to call him a dirty boy, and bid him wash himself, once a week; and children of his age, seldom have a natural pleasure in soap and water. Therefore, not to mention his clothes, which had seen three months' service, in mire and dust, and his thick uncombed hair, the surface of his face and hands was dismally beclouded. He might well skulk behind the settle, on beholding such a bright graceful damsel enter the house, instead of a rough-headed counterpart to himself, as he expected.

'Is Heathcliff not here?' she demanded, pulling off her gloves, and displaying fingers wonderfully whitened with doing nothing, and staying indoors.

'Heathcliff, you may come forward,' cried Mr Hindley, enjoying his discomfiture and gratified to see what a forbidding young blackguard he would be compelled to present himself. 'You may come and wish Miss Catherine welcome, like the other servants.'

Cathy, catching a glimpse of her friend in his concealment, flew to embrace him, she bestowed seven or eight kisses on his cheek within the second, and then stopped, and drawing back, burst into a laugh, exclaiming,

'Why, how very black and cross you look! and how – how funny and grim! But that's because I'm used to Edgar, and Isabella Linton. Well, Heathcliff, have you forgotten me?'

She had some reason to put the question, for shame, and pride threw double gloom over his countenance, and kept him immovable.

'Shake hands, Heathcliff,' said Mr Earnshaw, condescendingly; 'once in a way, that is permitted.'

'I shall not!' replied the boy, finding his tongue at last. 'I shall not stand to be laughed at, I shall not bear it!'

And he would have broken from the circle, but Miss Cathy seized him again.

'I did not mean to laugh at you,' she said, 'I could not hinder myself. Heathcliff, shake hands, at least! What are you sulky for? It was only that you looked odd – If you wash your face, and brush your hair it will be all right. But you are so dirty!'

She gazed concernedly at the dusky fingers she held in her own, and also at her dress, which she feared had gained no embellishment from its contact with his.

# Wuthering Heights

'You needn't have touched me!' he answered, following her eye and snatching away his hand. 'I shall be as dirty as I please, and I like to be dirty, and I will be dirty.'

With that he dashed head foremost out of the room, amid the merriment of the master and mistress; and to the serious disturbance of Catherine, who could not comprehend how her remarks should have produced such an exhibition of bad temper.

After playing lady's maid to the new comer, and putting my cakes in the oven, and making the house and kitchen cheerful with great fires befitting Christmas eve, I prepared to sit down and amuse myself by singing carols, all alone, regardless of Joseph's affirmations that he considered the merry tunes I chose as next door to songs.

He had retired to private prayer in his chamber, and Mr and Mrs Earnshaw were engaging Missy's attention by sundry gay trifles bought for her to present to the little Lintons, as an acknowledgment of their kindness.

They had invited them to spend the morrow at Wuthering Heights, and the invitation had been accepted, on one condition: Mrs Linton begged that her darlings might be kept carefully apart from that 'naughty swearing boy.'

Under these circumstances I remained solitary. I smelt the rich scent of the heating spices; and admired the shining kitchen utensils, the polished clock, decked in holly, the silver mugs ranged on a tray ready to be filled with mulled ale for supper; and, above all, the speckless purity of my particular care – the scoured and well-swept floor.

I gave due inward applause to every object, and, then, I remembered how old Earnshaw used to come in when all was tidied, and call me a cant lass, and slip a shilling into my hand, as a Christmas box: and from that I went on to think of his fondness for Heathcliff, and his dread lest he should suffer neglect after death had removed him; and that naturally led me to consider the poor lad's situation now, and from singing I changed my mind to crying. It struck me soon, however, there would be more sense in endeavouring to repair some of his wrongs than shedding tears over them – I got up and walked into the court to seek him.

He was not far; I found him smoothing the glossy coat of the new pony in the stable, and feeding the other beasts, according to custom.

'Make haste, Heathcliff!' I said, 'the kitchen is so comfortable – and Joseph is up-stairs; make haste, and let me dress you smart before Miss Cathy comes out – and then you can sit together, with the whole hearth to yourselves, and have a long chatter till bed-time.'

He proceeded with his task and never turned his head towards me.

'Come – are you coming?' I continued. 'There's a little cake for each of you, nearly enough; and you'll need half-an-hour's donning.'

I waited five minutes, but getting no answer left him. . . . Catherine supped with her brother and sister-in-law: Joseph and I joined at an unsociable meal, seasoned with reproofs on one side and sauciness on the other. His cake and cheese remained on the table all night, for the fairies. He managed to continue work till nine o'clock, and, then, marched dumb and dour to his chamber.

Cathy sat up late; having a world of things to order for the reception of her new friends: she came into the kitchen, once, to speak to her old one, but he was

gone, and she only stayed to ask what was the matter with him, and then went back.

In the morning he rose early; and, as it was a holiday, carried his ill-humour onto the moors; not re-appearing till the family were departed for church. Fasting and reflection seemed to have brought him to a better spirit. He hung about me for a while, and having screwed up his courage, exclaimed abruptly,

'Nelly, make me decent, I'm going to be good.'

'High time, Heathcliff,' I said; 'you have grieved Catherine; she's sorry she ever came home, I dare say! It looks as if you envied her, because she is more thought of than you.'

The notion of *envying* Catherine was incomprehensible to him, but the notion of grieving her he understood clearly enough.

'Did she say she was grieved?' he enquired, looking very serious.

'She cried when I told her you were off again this morning.'

'Well, *I* cried last night,' he returned, 'and I had more reason to cry than she.'

'Yes, you had the reason of going to bed with a proud heart and an empty stomach,' said I. 'Proud people breed sad sorrows for themselves – But, if you be ashamed of your touchiness, you must ask pardon, mind, when she comes in. You must go up, and offer to kiss her, and say – you know best what to say, only, do it heartily, and not as if you thought her converted into a stranger by her grand dress. And now, though I have dinner to get ready, I'll steal time to arrange you so that Edgar Linton shall look quite a doll beside you: and that he does – You are younger, and yet, I'll be bound, you are taller and twice as broad across the shoulders – you could knock him down in a twinkling; don't you feel that you could?'

Heathcliff's face brightened a moment; then it was overcast afresh, and he sighed.

'But, Nelly, if I knocked him down twenty times, that wouldn't make him less handsome, or me more so. I wish I had light hair and a fair skin, and was dressed, and behaved as well, and had a chance of being as rich as he will be!'

'And cried for mamma, at every turn' – I added, 'and trembled if a country lad heaved his fist against you, and sat at home all day for a shower of rain. – Oh, Heathcliff, you are showing a poor spirit! Come to the glass, and I'll let you see what you should wish. Do you mark those two lines between your eyes, and those thick brows, that instead of rising arched, sink in the middle, and that couple of black fiends, so deeply buried, who never open their windows boldly, but lurk glinting under them, like devil's spies? Wish and learn to smooth away the surly wrinkles, to raise your lids frankly, and change the fiends to confident, innocent angels, suspecting and doubting nothing, and always seeing friends where they are not sure of foes – Don't get the expression of a vicious cur that appears to know the kicks it gets are its desert, and yet, hates all the world, as well as the kicker, for what it suffers.'

'In other words, I must wish for Edgar Linton's great blue eyes, and even forehead,' he replied. 'I do – and that won't help me to them.'

'A good heart will help you to a bonny face, my lad,' I continued, 'if you were a regular black; and a bad one will turn the bonniest into something worse than ugly. And now that we've done washing, and combing, and sulking – tell me whether you don't think yourself rather handsome? I'll tell you, I do. You're fit for a prince in disguise. Who knows, but your father was Emperor of China,

and your mother an Indian queen, each of them able to buy up, with one week's income, Wuthering Heights and Thrushcross Grange together? And you were kidnapped by wicked sailors, and brought to England. Were I in your place, I would frame high notions of my birth; and the thoughts of what I was should give me courage and dignity to support the oppressions of a little farmer!'

So I chattered on; and Heathcliff gradually lost his frown, and began to look quite pleasant; when all at once our conversation was interrupted by a rumbling sound moving up the road and entering the court. He ran to the window, and I to the door, just in time to behold the two Lintons descend from the family carriage, smothered in cloaks and furs, and the Earnshaws dismount from their horses – they often rode to church in winter. Catherine took a hand of each of the children, and brought them into the house, and set them before the fire, which quickly put colour into their white faces.

I urged my companion to hasten now, and show his amiable humour, and he willingly obeyed: but ill-luck would have it that, as he opened the door leading from the kitchen on one side, Hindley opened it on the other; they met, and the master, irritated at seeing him clean and cheerful, or, perhaps, eager to keep his promise to Mrs Linton, shoved him back with a sudden thrust, and angrily bade Joseph 'keep the fellow out of the room – send him into the garret till dinner is over. He'll be cramming his fingers in the tarts, and stealing the fruit, if left alone with them a minute.'

'Nay, sir,' I could not avoid answering, 'he'll touch nothing, not he – and, I suppose, he must have his share of the dainties as well as we.'

'He shall have his share of my hand, if I catch him down stairs again till dark,' cried Hindley. 'Begone, you vagabond! What, you are attempting the coxcomb, are you? Wait till I get hold of those elegant locks – see if I won't pull them a bit longer!'

'They are long enough already,' observed Master Linton, peeping from the doorway; 'I wonder they don't make his head ache. It's like a colt's mane over his eyes!'

He ventured this remark without any intention to insult; but Heathcliff's violent nature was not prepared to endure the appearance of impertinence from one whom he seemed to hate, even then, as a rival. He seized a tureen of hot apple sauce, the first thing that came under his gripe, and dashed it full against the speaker's face and neck – who instantly commenced a lament that brought Isabella and Catherine hurrying to the place.

Mr Earnshaw snatched up the culprit directly and conveyed him to his chamber, where, doubtless, he administered a rough remedy to cool the fit of passion, for he re-appeared red and breathless. I got the dish-cloth, and, rather spitefully, scrubbed Edgar's nose and mouth, affirming it served him right for meddling. His sister began weeping to go home, and Cathy stood by confounded, blushing for all.

'You should not have spoken to him!' she expostulated with Master Linton. 'He was in a bad temper, and now you've spoilt your visit, and he'll be flogged – I hate him to be flogged! I can't eat my dinner. Why did you speak to him, Edgar?'

'I didn't,' sobbed the youth, escaping from my hands, and finishing the remainder of the purification with his cambric pocket-handkerchief. 'I promised mamma that I wouldn't say one word to him, and I didn't.'

# Wuthering Heights

'Well, don't cry!' replied Catherine, contemptuously. 'You're not killed – don't make more mischief – my brother is coming – be quiet! Give over, Isabella! Has anybody hurt *you*?'

'There, there, children – to your seats!' cried Hindley, bustling in. 'That brute of a lad has warmed me nicely. Next time, Master Edgar, take the law into your own fists – it will give you an appetite!'

The little party recovered its equanimity at sight of the fragrant feast. They were hungry after their ride, and easily consoled, since no real harm had befallen them.

Mr Earnshaw carved bountiful platefuls; and the mistress made them merry with lively talk. I waited behind her chair, and was pained to behold Catherine, with dry eyes and an indifferent air, commence cutting up the wing of a goose before her.

'An unfeeling child,' I thought to myself, 'how lightly she dismisses her old playmate's troubles. I could not have imagined her to be so selfish.'

She lifted a mouthful to her lips; then, set it down again: her cheeks flushed, and the tears gushed over them. She slipped her fork to the floor, and hastily dived under the cloth to conceal her emotion. I did not call her unfeeling long, for, I perceived, she was in purgatory throughout the day, and wearying to find an opportunity of getting by herself, or paying a visit to Heathcliff, who had been locked up by the master, as I discovered, on endeavouring to introduce to him a private mess of victuals.

In the evening we had a dance. Cathy begged that he might be liberated then, as Isabella Linton had no partner; her entreaties were vain, and I was appointed to supply the deficiency.

We got rid of all gloom in the excitement of the exercise, and our pleasure was increased by the arrival of the Gimmerton band, mustering fifteen strong; a trumpet, a trombone, clarionets, bassoons, French horns, and a bass viol, besides singers. They go the rounds of all the respectable houses, and receive contributions every Christmas, and we esteemed it a first-rate treat to hear them.

After the usual carols had been sung, we set them to songs and glees. Mrs Earnshaw loved the music, and, so, they gave us plenty.

Catherine loved it too; but she said it sounded sweetest at the top of the steps, and she went up in the dark; I followed. They shut the house door below, never noting our absence, it was so full of people. She made no stay at the stairs' head, but mounted farther, to the garret where Heathcliff was confined; and called him. He stubbornly declined answering for a while – she persevered, and finally persuaded him to hold communion with her through the boards.

I let the poor things converse unmolested, till I supposed the songs were going to cease, and the singers to get some refreshment: then, I clambered up the ladder to warn her.

Instead of finding her outside, I heard her voice within. The little monkey had crept by the skylight of one garret, along the roof, into the skylight of the other, and it was with the utmost difficulty I could coax her out again.

When she did come, Heathcliff came with her; and she insisted that I should take him into the kitchen, as my fellow-servant had gone to a neighbour's to be removed from the sound of our 'devil's psalmody,' as it pleased him to call it. I told them I intended, by no means, to encourage their tricks; but as the prisoner

had never broken his fast since yesterday's dinner, I would wink at his cheating Mr Hindley that once.

He went down; I set him a stool by the fire, and offered him a quantity of good things; but, he was sick and could eat little: and my attempts to entertain him were thrown away. He leant his two elbows on his knees, and his chin on his hands, and remained wrapt in dumb meditation.

On my enquiring the subject of his thoughts, he answered gravely –

'I'm trying to settle how I shall pay Hindley back. I don't care how long I wait, if I can only do it, at last. I hope he will not die before I do!'

'For shame, Heathcliff!' said I, 'It is for God to punish wicked people; we should learn to forgive.'

'No, God won't have the satisfaction that I shall,' he returned. 'I only wish I knew the best way! Let me alone, and I'll plan it out: while I'm thinking of that, I don't feel pain.'

But, Mr Lockwood, I forget these tales cannot divert you. I'm annoyed how I should dream of chattering on at such a rate; and your gruel cold, and you nodding for bed! I could have told Heathcliff's history, all that you need hear, in half a dozen words.

Thus interrupting herself, the housekeeper rose, and proceeded to lay aside her sewing; but I felt incapable of moving from the hearth, and I was very far from nodding.

'Sit still, Mrs Dean,' I cried, 'do sit still, another half hour! You've done just right to tell the story leisurely. That is the method I like; and you must finish in the same style. I am interested in every character you have mentioned, more or less.'

'The clock is on the stroke of eleven, sir.'

'No matter – I'm not accustomed to go to bed in the long hours. One or two is early enough for a person who lies till ten.'

'You shouldn't lie till ten. There's the very prime of the morning gone long before that time. A person who has not done one half his day's work by ten o'clock, runs a chance of leaving the other half undone.'

'Nevertheless, Mrs Dean, resume your chair; because to-morrow I intend lengthening the night till afternoon. I prognosticate for myself an obstinate cold, at least.'

'I hope not, sir. Well, you must allow me to leap over some three years; during that space, Mrs Earnshaw –'

'No, no, I'll allow nothing of the sort! Are you acquainted with the mood of mind in which, if you were seated alone, and the cat licking its kitten on the rug before you, you would watch the operation so intently that puss's neglect of one ear would put you seriously out of temper?'

'A terribly lazy mood, I should say.'

'On the contrary, a tiresomely active one. It is mine, at present, and, therefore, continue minutely. I perceive that people in these regions acquire over people in towns the value that a spider in a dungeon does over a spider in a cottage, to their various occupants; and yet the deepened attraction is not entirely owing to the situation of the looker-on. They *do* live more in earnest, more in themselves, and less in surface change, and frivolous external things. I could fancy a love for life here almost possible; and I was a fixed unbeliever in any love of a year's

standing – one state resembles setting a hungry man down to a single dish on which he may concentrate his entire appetite, and do it justice – the other, introducing him to a table laid out by French cooks; he can perhaps extract as much enjoyment from the whole; but each part is a mere atom in his regard and remembrance.'

'Oh! here we are the same as anywhere else, when you get to know us,' observed Mrs Dean, somewhat puzzled at my speech.

'Excuse me,' I responded; 'you, my good friend, are a striking evidence against that assertion. Excepting a few provincialisms of slight consequence, you have no marks of the manners which I am habituated to consider as peculiar to your class. I am sure you have thought a great deal more than the generality of servants think. You have been compelled to cultivate your reflective faculties, for want of occasions for frittering your life away in silly trifles.'

Mrs Dean laughed.

'I certainly esteem myself a steady, reasonable kind of body,' she said; 'not exactly from living among the hills, and seeing one set of faces, and one series of actions, from year's end to year's end: but I have undergone sharp discipline which has taught me wisdom; and then, I have read more than you would fancy, Mr Lockwood. You could not open a book in this library that I have not looked into, and got something out of also; unless it be that range of Greek and Latin, and that of French – and those I know one from another, it is as much as you can expect of a poor man's daughter.

'However, if I am to follow my story in true gossip's fashion, I had better go on; and instead of leaping three years, I will be content to pass to the next summer – the summer of 1778, that is, nearly twenty-three years ago.'

# Chapter 8

On the morning of a fine June day, my first bonny little nursling, and the last of the ancient Earnshaw stock was born.

We were busy with the hay in a far away field, when the girl that usually brought our breakfasts came running, an hour too soon, across the meadow and up the lane, calling me as she ran.

'Oh, such a grand bairn!' she panted out. 'The finest lad that ever breathed! But the doctor says missis must go; he says she's been in a consumption these many months. I heard him tell Mr Hindley – and now she has nothing to keep her, and she'll be dead before winter. You must come home directly. You're to nurse it, Nelly – to feed it with sugar and milk, and take care of it, day and night – I wish I were you, because it will be all yours when there is no missis!'

'But is she very ill?' I asked, flinging down my rake, and tying my bonnet.

'I guess she is; yet she looks bravely,' replied the girl, 'and she talks as if she

# Wuthering Heights

thought of living to see it grow a man. She's out of her head for joy, it's such a beauty! If I were her I'm certain I should not die. I should get better at the bare sight of it, in spite of Kenneth. I was fairly mad at him. Dame Archer brought the cherub down to master, in the house, and his face just began to light up, then the old croaker steps forward, and says he: – "Earnshaw, it's a blessing your wife has been spared to leave you this son. When she came, I felt convinced we shouldn't keep her long; and now, I must tell you, the winter will probably finish her. Don't take on, and fret about it too much, it can't be helped. And besides, you should have known better than to choose such a rush of a lass!"'

'And what did the master answer?' I inquired.

'I think he swore – but, I didn't mind him, I was straining to see the bairn,' and she began again to describe it rapturously. I, as zealous as herself, hurried eagerly home to admire, on my part, though I was very sad for Hindley's sake; he had room in his heart only for two idols – his wife and himself – he doted on both, and adored one, and I couldn't conceive how he would bear the loss.

When we got to Wuthering Heights, there he stood at the front door; and, as I passed in, I asked, how was the baby?

'Nearly ready to run about, Nell!' he replied, putting on a cheerful smile.

'And the mistress?' I ventured to inquire; 'the doctor says she's –'

'Damn the doctor!' he interrupted, reddening. 'Frances is quite right – she'll be perfectly well by this time next week. Are you going upstairs? will you tell her that I'll come, if she'll promise not to talk. I left her because she would not hold her tongue; and she must – tell her Mr Kenneth says she must be quiet.'

I delivered this message to Mrs Earnshaw; she seemed in flighty spirits, and replied merrily –

'I hardly spoke a word, Ellen, and there he has gone out twice, crying. Well, say I promise I won't speak; but that does not bind me not to laugh at him!'

Poor soul! Till within a week of her death that gay heart never failed her; and her husband persisted doggedly, nay, furiously, in affirming her health improved every day. When Kenneth warned him that his medicines were useless at that stage of the malady, and he needn't put him to further expense by attending her, he retorted –

'I know you need not – she's well – she does not want any more attendance from you! She never was in a consumption. It was a fever; and it is gone – her pulse is as slow as mine now, and her cheek as cool.'

He told his wife the same story, and she seemed to believe him; but one night, while leaning on his shoulder, in the act of saying she thought she should be able to get up to-morrow, a fit of coughing took her – a very slight one – he raised her in his arms; she put her two hands about his neck, her face changed, and she was dead.

As the girl had anticipated, the child, Hareton, fell wholly into my hands. Mr Earnshaw, provided he saw him healthy, and never heard him cry, was contented, as far as regarded him. For himself, he grew desperate; his sorrow was of that kind that will not lament, he neither wept nor prayed – he cursed and defied – execrated God and man, and gave himself up to reckless dissipation.

The servants could not bear his tyrannical and evil conduct long: Joseph and I were the only two that would stay. I had not the heart to leave my charge; and besides, you know, I had been his foster sister, and excused his behaviour more readily than a stranger would.

# Wuthering Heights

Joseph remained to hector over tenants and labourers; and because it was his vocation to be where he had plenty of wickedness to reprove.

The master's bad ways and bad companions formed a pretty example for Catherine and Heathcliff. His treatment of the latter was enough to make a fiend of a saint. And, truly, it appeared as if the lad *were* possessed of something diabolical at that period. He delighted to witness Hindley degrading himself past redemption; and became daily more notable for savage sullenness and ferocity.

I could not half tell what an infernal house we had. The curate dropped calling, and nobody decent came near us, at last; unless Edgar Linton's visits to Miss Cathy might be an exception. At fifteen she was the queen of the country-side; she had no peer: and she did turn out a haughty, headstrong creature! I own I did not like her, after her infancy was past; and I vexed her frequently by trying to bring down her arrogance; she never took an aversion to me, though. She had a wondrous constancy to old attachments; even Heathcliff kept his hold on her affections unalterably, and young Linton, with all his superiority, found it difficult to make an equally deep impression.

He was my late master; that is his portrait over the fireplace. It used to hang on one side, and his wife's on the other; but hers has been removed, or else you might see something of what she was. Can you make that out?

Mrs Dean raised the candle, and I discerned a soft-featured face, exceedingly resembling the young lady at the Heights, but more pensive and amiable in expression. It formed a sweet picture. The long light hair curled slightly on the temples; the eyes were large and serious; the figure almost too graceful. I did not marvel how Catherine Earnshaw could forget her first friend for such an individual. I marvelled much how he, with a mind to correspond with his person could fancy my idea of Catherine Earnshaw.

'A very agreeable portrait,' I observed to the housekeeper. 'Is it like?'

'Yes,' she answered; 'but he looked better when he was animated; that is his everyday countenance; he wanted spirit in general.'

Catherine had kept up her acquaintance with the Lintons since her five weeks' residence among them; and as she had no temptation to show her rough side in their company, and had the sense to be ashamed of being rude where she experienced such invariable courtesy, she imposed unwittingly on the old lady and gentleman, by her ingenious cordiality; gained the admiration of Isabella, and the heart and soul of her brother – acquisitions that flattered her from the first, for she was full of ambition – and led her to adopt a double character without exactly intending to deceive any one.

In the place where she had heard Heathcliff termed a 'vulgar young ruffian,' and 'worse than a brute,' she took care not to act like him; but at home she had small inclination to practise politeness that would only be laughed at, and restrain an unruly nature when it would bring her neither credit nor praise.

Mr Edgar seldom mustered courage to visit Wuthering Heights openly. He had a terror of Earnshaw's reputation, and shrunk from encountering him, and yet, he was always received with our best attempts at civility: the master himself, avoided offending him – knowing why he came, and if he could not be gracious, kept out of the way. I rather think his appearance there was distasteful to Catherine; she was not artful, never played the coquette, and had evidently an objection to her two friends meeting at all: for when Heathcliff expressed

# Wuthering Heights

contempt of Linton, in his presence, she could not half coincide, as she did in his absence; and when Linton evinced disgust and antipathy to Heathcliff, she dared not treat his sentiments with indifference, as if depreciation of her playmate were of scarcely any consequence to her.

I've had many a laugh at her perplexities and untold troubles, which she vainly strove to hide from my mockery. That sounds ill-natured – but she was so proud, it became really impossible to pity her distresses, till she should be chastened into more humility.

She did bring herself, finally, to confess, and confide in me. There was not a soul else that she might fashion into an adviser.

Mr Hindley had gone from home, one afternoon; and Heathcliff presumed to give himself a holiday, on the strength of it. He had reached the age of sixteen then, I think, and without having bad features or being deficient in intellect, he contrived to convey an impression of inward and outward repulsiveness that his present aspect retains no traces of.

In the first place, he had, by that time, lost the benefit of his early education: continual hard work, begun soon and concluded late, had extinguished any curiosity he once possessed in pursuit of knowledge, and any love for books or learning. His childhood's sense of superiority, instilled into him by the favours of old Mr Earnshaw, was faded away. He struggled long to keep up an equality with Catherine in her studies, and yielded with poignant though silent regret: but he yielded completely; and there was no prevailing on him to take a step in the way of moving upward, when he found he must, necessarily, sink beneath his former level. Then personal appearance sympathised with mental deterioration; he acquired a slouching gait, and ignoble look; his naturally reserved disposition was exaggerated into an almost idiotic excess of unsociable moroseness; and he took a grim pleasure, apparently, in exciting the aversion rather than the esteem of his few acquaintance.

Catherine and he were constant companions still, at his seasons of respite from labour; but he had ceased to express his fondness for her in words, and recoiled with angry suspicion from her girlish caresses, as if conscious there could be no gratification in lavishing such marks of affection on him. On the before-named occasion he came into the house to announce his intention of doing nothing, while I was assisting Miss Cathy to arrange her dress – she had not reckoned on his taking it into his head to be idle and imagining she would have the whole place to herself, she managed, by some means, to inform Mr Edgar of her brother's absence, and she was then preparing to receive him.

'Cathy, are you busy this afternoon?' asked Heathcliff. 'Are you going anywhere?'

'No, it is raining,' she answered.

'Why have you that silly frock on, then?' he said. 'Nobody coming here, I hope?'

'Not that I know of,' stammered Miss: 'but you should be in the field now, Heathcliff. It is an hour past dinner time; I thought you were gone.'

'Hindley does not often free us from his accursed presence,' observed the boy, 'I'll not work any more today, I'll stay with you.'

'Oh, but Joseph will tell;' she suggested, 'you'd better go!'

'Joseph is loading lime on the farther side of Pennistow Crag; it will take him till dark, and he'll never know.'

# Wuthering Heights

So saying, he lounged to the fire, and sat down. Catherine reflected an instant, with knitted brows – she found it needful to smooth the way for an intrusion.

'Isabella and Edgar Linton talked of calling this afternoon,' she said at the conclusion of a minute's silence. 'As it rains, I hardly expect them; but, they may come, and if they do, you run the risk of being scolded for no good.'

'Order Ellen to say you are engaged, Cathy,' he persisted. 'Don't turn me out for those pitiful, silly friends of yours! I'm on the point, sometimes, of complaining that they – but I'll not –'

'That they what?' cried Catherine, gazing at him with a troubled countenance. 'Oh, Nelly!' she added petulantly, jerking her head away from my hands, 'you've combed my hair quite out of curl! That's enough, let me alone. What are you on the point of complaining about, Heathcliff?'

'Nothing – only look at the almanack, on that wall.' He pointed to a framed sheet hanging near the window, and continued:

'The crosses are for the evenings you have spent with the Lintons, the dots for those spent with me. Do you see? I've marked every day.'

'Yes – very foolish; as if I took notice!' replied Catherine in a peevish tone. 'And where is the sense of that?'

'To show that I *do* take notice,' said Heathcliff.

'And should I always be sitting with you?' she demanded, growing more irritated. 'What good do I get – what do you talk about? You might be dumb or a baby for anything you say to amuse me, or for anything you do, either!'

'You never told me before that I talked too little, or that you disliked my company, Cathy!' exclaimed Heathcliff, in much agitation.

'It's no company at all, when people know nothing and say nothing,' she muttered.

Her companion rose up, but he hadn't time to express his feelings further, for a horse's feet were heard on the flags, and, having knocked gently, young Linton entered, his face brilliant with delight at the unexpected summons he had received.

Doubtless Catherine marked the difference between her friends as one came in, and the other went out. The contrast resembled what you see in exchanging a bleak, hilly, coal country for a beautiful fertile valley; and his voice and greeting were as opposite as his aspect – He had a sweet, low manner of speaking, and pronounced his words as you do, that's less gruff than we talk here and softer.

'I'm not come too soon, am I?' he said, casting a look at me. I had begun to wipe the plate, and tidy some drawers at the far end in the dresser.

'No,' answered Catherine. 'What are you doing there, Nelly?'

'My work, Miss,' I replied. (Mr Hindley had given me directions to make a third party in any private visits Linton chose to pay.)

She stepped behind me and whispered crossly, 'Take yourself and your dusters off! when company are in the house, servants don't commence scouring and cleaning in the room where they are!'

'It's a good opportunity, now that master is away,' I answered aloud. 'He hates me to be fidgeting over these things in his presence. I'm sure Mr Edgar will excuse me.'

'I hate you to be fidgeting in *my* presence,' exclaimed the young lady

imperiously, not allowing her guest time to speak – she had failed to recover her equanimity since the little dispute with Heathcliff.

'I'm sorry for it, Miss Catherine!' was my response; and I proceeded assiduously with my occupation.

She, supposing Edgar could not see her, snatched the cloth from my hand, and pinched me, with a prolonged wrench, very spitefully on the arm.

I've said I did not love her, and rather relished mortifying her vanity now and then; besides, she hurt me extremely, so I started up from my knees, and screamed out,

'Oh, Miss, that's a nasty trick! You have no right to nip me, and I'm not going to bear it!'

'I didn't touch you, you lying creature!' cried she, her fingers tingling to repeat the act, and her ears red with rage. She never had power to conceal her passion, it always set her whole complexion in a blaze.

'What's that, then?' I retorted, showing a decided purple witness to refute her.

She stamped her foot, wavered a moment, and then, irresistibly impelled by the naughty spirit within her, slapped me on the cheek a stinging blow that filled both eyes with water.

'Catherine, love! Catherine!' interposed Linton, greatly shocked at the double fault of falsehood and violence which his idol had committed.

'Leave the room, Ellen!' she repeated, trembling all over.

Little Hareton, who followed me everywhere, and was sitting near me on the floor, at seeing my tears commenced crying himself, and sobbed out complaints against 'wicked aunt Cathy,' which drew her fury on to his unlucky head: she seized his shoulders, and shook him till the poor child waxed livid, and Edgar thoughtlessly laid hold of her hands to deliver him. In an instant one was wrung free, and the astonished young man felt it applied over his own ear in a way that could not be mistaken for jest.

He drew back in consternation – I lifted Hareton in my arms, and walked off to the kitchen with him; leaving the door of communication open, for I was curious to watch how they would settle their disagreement.

The insulted visitor moved to the spot where he had laid his hat, pale and with a quivering lip.

'That's right!' I said to myself, 'Take warning and begone! It's a kindness to let you have a glimpse of her genuine disposition.'

'Where are you going?' demanded Catherine, advancing to the door.

He swerved aside and attempted to pass.

'You must not go!' she exclaimed energetically.

'I must and shall!' he replied in a subdued voice.

'No,' she persisted, grasping the handle; 'not yet, Edgar Linton – sit down, you shall not leave me in that temper. I should be miserable all night, and I won't be miserable for you!'

'Can I stay after you have struck me?' asked Linton.

Catherine was mute.

'You've made me afraid, and ashamed of you,' he continued; 'I'll not come here again!'

Her eyes began to glisten and her lids to twinkle.

'And you told a deliberate untruth!' he said.

'I didn't!' she cried, recovering her speech. 'I did nothing deliberately – Well, go, if you please – get away! And now I'll cry – I'll cry myself sick!'

She dropped down on her knees by a chair and set to weeping in serious earnest.

Edgar persevered in his resolution as far as the court; there he lingered. I resolved to encourage him.

'Miss is dreadfully wayward, sir!' I called out. 'As bad as any marred child – you'd better be riding home, or else she will be sick, only to grieve us.'

The soft thing looked askance through the window – he possessed the power to depart, as much as a cat possesses the power to leave a mouse half killed, or a bird half eaten.

Ah, I thought, there will be no saving him – He's doomed, and flies to his fate!

And so it was; he turned abruptly, hastened into the house again, shut the door behind him; and, when I went in a while after to inform them that Earnshaw had come home rabid drunk, ready to pull the old place about our ears (his ordinary frame of mind in that condition), I saw the quarrel had merely effected a closer intimacy – had broken the outworks of youthful timidity, and enabled them to forsake the disguise of friendship, and confess themselves lovers.

Intelligence of Mr Hindley's arrival drove Linton speedily to his horse, and Catherine to her chamber. I went to hide little Hareton, and to take the shot out of the master's fowling piece which he was fond of playing with in his insane excitement, to the hazard of the lives of any who provoked, or even attracted his notice too much; and I had hit upon the plan of removing it, that he might do less mischief, if he did go the length of firing the gun.

# Chapter 9

He entered, vociferating oaths dreadful to hear; and caught me in the act of stowing his son away in the kitchen cupboard. Hareton was impressed with a wholesome terror of encountering either his wild-beast's fondness, or his madman's rage – for in one he ran a chance of being squeezed and kissed to death, and in the other of being flung into the fire, or dashed against the wall – and the poor thing remained perfectly quiet wherever I chose to put him.

'There, I've found it out at last!' cried Hindley, pulling me back by the skin of my neck, like a dog. 'By heaven and hell, you've sworn between you to murder that child! I know how it is, now, that he is always out of my way. But with the help of Satan, I shall make you swallow the carving knife, Nelly! You needn't laugh; for I've just crammed Kenneth, head-downmost, in the Blackhorse marsh:

and two is the same as one – and I want to kill some of you, I shall have no rest till I do!'

'But I don't like the carving knife, Mr Hindley,' I answered, 'it has been cutting red herrings – I'd rather be shot if you please.'

'You'd rather be damned!' he said, 'and so you shall, no law in England can hinder a man from keeping his house decent, and mine's abominable! open your mouth.'

He held the knife in his hand, and pushed its point between my teeth: but, for my part, I was never much afraid of his vagaries. I spat it out, and affirmed it tasted detestably – I would not take it on any account.

'Oh!' said he, releasing me, 'I see that hideous little villain is not Hareton – I beg your pardon, Nell – if it be, he deserves flaying alive for not running to welcome me, and for screaming as if I were a goblin. Unnatural cub, come hither! I'll teach thee to impose on a good-hearted, deluded father – Now, don't you think the lad would be handsomer cropped? It makes a dog fiercer, and I love something fierce – Get me a scissors – something fierce and trim! Besides, it's infernal affectation – devilish conceit, it is, to cherish our ears – we're asses enough without them. Hush, child, hush! well, then, it is my darling! wisht, dry thy eyes – there's a joy; kiss me; what! it won't? kiss me, Hareton! Damn thee, kiss me! By God, as if I would rear such a monster! As sure as I'm living, I'll break the brat's neck.'

Poor Hareton was squalling and kicking in his father's arms with all his might, and redoubled his yells when he carried him upstairs and lifted him over the banister. I cried out that he would frighten the child into fits, and ran to rescue him.

As I reached them, Hindley leant forward on the rails to listen to a noise below; almost forgetting what he had in his hands.

'Who is that?' he asked, hearing some one approaching the stair's foot.

I leant forwards, also, for the purpose of signing to Heathcliff, whose step I recognized, not to come further; and, at the instant when my eye quitted Hareton, he gave a sudden spring, delivered himself from the careless grasp that held him, and fell.

There was scarcely time to experience a thrill of horror before we saw that the little wretch was safe. Heathcliff arrived underneath just at the critical moment; by a natural impulse he arrested his descent, and setting him on his feet, looked up to discover the author of the accident.

A miser who has parted with a lucky lottery ticket for five shillings, and finds next day he has lost in the bargain five thousand pounds, could not show a blanker countenance than he did on beholding the figure of Mr Earnshaw above – It expressed, plainer than words could do, the intensest anguish at having made himself the instrument of thwarting his own revenge. Had it been dark, I dare say, he would have tried to remedy the mistake by smashing Hareton's skull on the steps; but, we witnessed his salvation; and I was presently below with my precious charge pressed to my heart.

Hindley descended more leisurely, sobered and abashed.

'It is your fault, Ellen,' he said, 'you should have kept him out of sight; you should have taken him from me! Is he injured anywhere?'

'Injured!' I cried, angrily. 'If he's not killed, he'll be an idiot! Oh! I wonder

his mother does not rise from her grave to see how you use him. You're worse than a heathen – treating your own flesh and blood in that manner!'

He attempted to touch the child, who, on finding himself with me, sobbed off his terror directly. At the first finger his father laid on him, however, he shrieked again louder than before, and struggled as if he would go into convulsions.

'You shall not meddle with him!' I continued. 'He hates you – they all hate you – that's the truth! A happy family you have; and a pretty state you're come to!'

'I shall come to a prettier, yet, Nelly!' laughed the misguided man, recovering his hardness. 'At present, convey yourself and him away – And, hark you, Heathcliff! clear you too, quite from my reach and hearing ... I wouldn't murder you to-night, unless, perhaps, I set the house on fire; but that's as my fancy goes –'

While saying this, he took a pint bottle of brandy from the dresser, and poured some into a tumbler.

'Nay, don't!' I entreated, 'Mr Hindley, do take warning. Have mercy on this unfortunate boy, if you care nothing for yourself!'

'Any one will do better for him, than I shall,' he answered.

'Have mercy on your own soul!' I said, endeavouring to snatch the glass from his hand.

'Not I! On the contrary, I shall have great pleasure in sending it to perdition, to punish its maker,' exclaimed the blasphemer, 'Here's to its hearty damnation!'

He drank the spirits, and impatiently bade us go, terminating his command with a sequel of horrid imprecations, too bad to repeat, or remember.

'It's a pity he cannot kill himself with drink,' observed Heathcliff, muttering an echo of curses back when the door was shut. 'He's doing his very utmost; but his constitution defies him – Mr Kenneth says he would wager his mare, that he'll outlive any man on this side Gimmerton, and go to the grave a hoary sinner; unless, some happy chance out of the common course befall him.'

I went into the kitchen and sat down to lull my little lamb to sleep. Heathcliff, as I thought, walked through to the barn. It turned out, afterwards, that he only got as far as the other side the settle, when he flung himself on a bench by the wall, removed from the fire, and remained silent.

I was rocking Hareton on my knee, and humming a song that began,

'It was far in the night, and the bairnies grat,
The mither beneath the mools heard that,'

when Miss Cathy, who had listened to the hubbub from her room, put her head in, and whispered,

'Are you alone, Nelly?'

'Yes, Miss,' I replied.

She entered and approached the hearth. I, supposing she was going to say something, looked up. The expression of her face seemed disturbed and anxious. Her lips were half asunder, as if she meant to speak; and she drew a breath, but it escaped in a sigh, instead of a sentence.

I resumed my song, not having forgotten her recent behaviour.

'Where's Heathcliff?' she said, interrupting me.

'About his work in the stable,' was my answer.

# Wuthering Heights

He did not contradict me; perhaps he had fallen into a doze.

There followed another long pause, during which I perceived a drop or two trickle from Catherine's cheek to the flags.

'Is she sorry for her shameful conduct?' I asked myself. 'That will be a novelty, but she may come to the point as she will – I shan't help her!'

No, she felt small trouble regarding any subject, save her own concerns.

'Oh, dear!' she cried at last. 'I'm very unhappy!'

'A pity,' observed I, 'you're hard to please – so many friends and so few cares, and can't make yourself, content!'

'Nelly, will you keep a secret for me?' she pursued, kneeling down by me, and lifting her winsome eyes to my face with that sort of look which turns off bad temper, even when one has all the right in the world to indulge it.

'Is it worth keeping?' I inquired, less sulkily.

'Yes, and it worries me, and I must let it out! I want to know what I should do – To-day, Edgar Linton has asked me to marry him, and I've given him an answer – Now, before I tell you whether it was a consent, or denial – you tell me which it ought to have been.'

'Really, Miss Catherine, how can I know?' I replied. 'To be sure, considering the exhibition you performed in his presence, this afternoon, I might say it would be wise to refuse him – since he asked you after that, he must either be hopelessly stupid, or a venturesome fool.'

'If you talk so, I won't tell you any more,' she returned, peevishly, rising to her feet. 'I accepted him, Nelly. Be quick, and say whether I was wrong!'

'You accepted him? then, what good is it discussing the matter? You have pledged your word, and cannot retract.'

'But, say whether I should have done so – do!' she exclaimed in an irritated tone, chafing her hands together, and frowning.

'There are many things to be considered, before that question can be answered properly,' I said sententiously. 'First and foremost, do you love Mr Edgar?'

'Who can help it? Of course I do,' she answered.

Then I put her through the following catechism – for a girl of twenty-two, it was not injudicious.

'Why do you love him, Miss Cathy?'

'Nonsense, I do – that's sufficient.'

'By no means; you must say why.'

'Well, because he is handsome, and pleasant to be with.'

'Bad,' was my commentary.

'And because he is young and cheerful.'

'Bad, still.'

'And because he loves me.'

'Indifferent, coming there.'

'And he will be rich, and I shall like to be the greatest woman of the neighbourhood, and I shall be proud of having such a husband.'

'Worst of all! And, now, you say how you love him?'

'As everybody loves – You're silly, Nelly.'

'Not at all – Answer.'

'I love the ground under his feet, and the air over his head, and everything he touches, and every word he says – I love all his looks, and all his actions, and him entirely, and altogether. There now!'

# Wuthering Heights

'And why?'

'Nay – you are making a jest of it; it is exceedingly ill-natured! It's no jest to me!' said the young lady, scowling, and turning her face to the fire.

'I'm very far from jesting, Miss Catherine,' I replied. 'You love Mr Edgar because he is handsome, and young, and cheerful, and rich, and loves you. The last, however, goes for nothing – You would love him without that, probably, and with it, you wouldn't, unless he possessed the four former attractions.'

'No, to be sure not – I should only pity him – hate him, perhaps, if he were ugly, and a clown.'

'But there are several other handsome, rich young men in the world; handsomer, possibly, and richer than he is – What should hinder you from loving them?'

'If there be any, they are out of my way – I've seen none like Edgar.'

'You may see some; and he won't always be handsome, and young, and may not always be rich.'

'He is now; and I have only to do with the present – I wish you would speak rationally.'

'Well, that settles it – if you have only to do with the present, marry Mr Linton.'

'I don't want your permission for that – I *shall* marry him; and yet, you have not told me whether I'm right.'

'Perfectly right! if people be right to marry only for the present. And now, let us hear what you are unhappy about. Your brother will be pleased . . . the old lady and gentleman will not object, I think – you will escape from a disorderly, comfortless home into a wealthy, respectable one; and you love Edgar, and Edgar loves you. All seems smooth and easy – where is the obstacle?'

'*Here*! and *here*!' replied Catherine, striking one hand on her forehead, and the other on her breast. 'In whichever place the soul lives – in my soul, and in my heart, I'm convinced I'm wrong!'

'That is very strange! I cannot make it out.'

'It's my secret; but if you will not mock at me, I'll explain it; I can't do it distinctly – but I'll give you a feeling of how I feel.'

She seated herself by me again: her countenance grew sadder and graver, and her clasped hands trembled.

'Nelly, do you never dream queer dreams?' she said, suddenly, after some minutes' reflection.

'Yes, now and then,' I answered.

'And so do I. I've dreamt in my life dreams that have stayed with me ever after, and changed my ideas; they've gone through and through me, like wine through water, and altered the colour of my mind. And this is one – I'm going to tell it – but take care not to smile at any part of it.'

'Oh! don't, Miss Catherine!' I cried. 'We're dismal enough without conjuring up ghosts, and visions to perplex us. Come, come, be merry, and like yourself! Look at little Hareton – *He's* dreaming nothing dreary. How sweetly he smiles in his sleep!'

'Yes; and how sweetly his father curses in his solitude! You remember him, I dare say, when he was just such another as that chubby thing – nearly as young and innocent. However, Nelly, I shall oblige you to listen – it's not long; and I've no power to be merry to-night.'

# Wuthering Heights

'I won't hear it, I won't hear it!' I repeated, hastily.

I was superstitious about dreams then, and am still; and Catherine had an unusual gloom in her aspect, that made me dread something from which I might shape a prophecy, and foresee a fearful catastrophe.

She was vexed, but she did not proceed. Apparently taking up another subject, she recommenced in a short time.

'If I were in heaven, Nelly, I should be extremely miserable.'

'Because you are not fit to go there,' I answered. 'All sinners would be miserable in heaven.'

'But it is not for that. I dreamt, once, that I was there.'

'I tell you I won't harken to your dreams, Miss Catherine! I'll go to bed,' I interrupted again.

She laughed, and held me down, for I made a motion to leave my chair.

'This is nothing,' cried she; 'I was only going to say that heaven did not seem to be my home; and I broke my heart with weeping to come back to earth; and the angels were so angry that they flung me out, into the middle of the heath on the top of Wuthering Heights, where I woke sobbing for joy. That will do to explain my secret, as well as the other. I've no more business to marry Edgar Linton than I have to be in heaven; and if the wicked man in there had not brought Heathcliff so low, I shouldn't have thought of it. It would degrade me to marry Heathcliff, now; so he shall never know how I love him; and that, not because he's handsome, Nelly, but because he's more myself than I am. Whatever our souls are made of, his and mine are the same, and Linton's is as different as a moonbeam from lightning, or frost from fire.'

Ere this speech ended, I became sensible of Heathcliff's presence. Having noticed a slight movement, I turned my head, and saw him rise from the bench, and steal out, noiselessly. He had listened till he heard Catherine say it would degrade her to marry him, and then he stayed to hear no farther.

My companion, sitting on the ground, was prevented by the back of the settle from remarking his presence or departure; but I started, and bade her hush.

'Why?' she asked, gazing nervously round.

'Joseph is here,' I answered, catching, opportunely, the roll of his cartwheels up the road; 'and Heathcliff will come in with him. I'm not sure whether he were not at the door this moment.'

'Oh, he couldn't overhear me at the door!' said she. 'Give me Hareton, while you get the supper, and when it is ready ask me to sup with you. I want to cheat my uncomfortable conscience, and be convinced that Heathcliff has no notion of these things – he has not, has he? He does not know what being in love is?'

'I see no reason that he should not know, as well as you,' I returned; 'and if *you* are his choice, he'll be the most unfortunate creature that ever was born! As soon as you become Mrs Linton, he loses friend, and love, and all! Have you considered how you'll bear the separation, and how he'll bear to be quite deserted in the world? Because, Miss Catherine –'

'He quite deserted! we separated!' she exclaimed, with an accent of indignation. 'Who is to separate us, pray? They'll meet the fate of Milo! Not as long as I live, Ellen – for no mortal creature. Every Linton on the face of the earth might melt into nothing, before I could consent to forsake Heathcliff! Oh, that's not what I intend – that's not what I mean! I shouldn't be Mrs Linton were such a price demanded! He'll be as much to me as he has been all his lifetime. Edgar

must shake off his antipathy, and tolerate him, at least. He will when he learns my true feelings towards him. Nelly, I see now, you think me a selfish wretch, but did it never strike you that, if Heathcliff and I married, we should be beggars? whereas, if I marry Linton, I can aid Heathcliff to rise, and place him out of my brother's power?'

'With your husband's money, Miss Catherine?' I asked. 'You'll find him not so pliable as you calculate upon: and, though I'm hardly a judge, I think that's the worst motive you've given yet for being the wife of young Linton.'

'It is not,' retorted she, 'it is the best! The others were the satisfaction of my whims; and for Edgar's sake, too, to satisfy him. This is for the sake of one who comprehends in his person my feelings to Edgar and myself. I cannot express it; but surely you and everybody have a notion that there is, or should be an existence of yours beyond you. What were the use of my creation if I were entirely contained here? My great miseries in this world have been Heathcliff's miseries, and I watched and felt each from the beginning; my great thought in living is himself. If all else perished, and *he* remained, I should still continue to be; and if all else remained, and he were annihilated, the universe would turn to a mighty stranger. I should not seem a part of it. My love for Linton is like the foliage in the woods. Time will change it, I'm well aware, as winter changes the trees. My love for Heathcliff resembles the eternal rocks beneath – a source of little visible delight, but necessary. Nelly, I *am* Heathcliff – he's always, always in my mind – not as a pleasure, any more than I am always a pleasure to myself – but as my own being – so, don't talk of our separation again – it is impracticable; and –'

She paused, and hid her face in the folds of my gown; but I jerked it forcibly away. I was out of patience with her folly!

'If I can make any sense of your nonsense, Miss,' I said, 'it only goes to convince me that you are ignorant of the duties you undertake in marrying; or else, that you are a wicked, unprincipled girl. But trouble me with no more secrets. I'll not promise to keep them.'

'You'll keep that?' she asked, eagerly.

'No, I'll not promise,' I repeated.

She was about to insist, when the entrance of Joseph finished our conversation; and Catherine removed her seat to a corner, and nursed Hareton, while I made the supper.

After it was cooked, my fellow servant and I began to quarrel who should carry some to Mr Hindley; and we didn't settle it till all was nearly cold. Then we came to the agreement that we would let him ask, if he wanted any, for we feared particularly to go into his presence when he had been some time alone.

'Und hah isn't that nowt comed in frough th' field, be this time? What is he abaht? girt eedle seeght!' demanded the old man, looking round for Heathcliff.

'I'll call him,' I replied. 'He's in the barn, I've no doubt.'

I went and called, but got no answer. On returning, I whispered to Catherine that he had heard a good part of what she said, I was sure; and told how I saw him quit the kitchen just as she complained of her brother's conduct regarding him.

She jumped up in a fine fright – flung Hareton onto the settle, and ran to seek for her friend herself, not taking leisure to consider why she was so flurried, or how her talk would have affected him.

# Wuthering Heights

She was absent such a while that Joseph proposed we should wait no longer. He cunningly conjectured they were staying away in order to avoid hearing his protracted blessing. They were 'ill eneuth for ony fahl manners,' he affirmed. And, on their behalf, he added that night a special prayer to the usual quarter of an hour's supplication before meat, and would have tacked another to the end of the grace, had not his young mistress broken in upon him with a hurried command that he must run down the road, and, wherever Heathcliff had rambled, find and make him re-enter directly!

'I want to speak to him, and I *must*, before I go upstairs,' she said. 'And the gate is open, he is somewhere out of hearing; for he would not reply, though I shouted at the top of the fold as loud as I could.'

Joseph objected at first; she was too much in earnest, however, to suffer contradiction; and, at last he placed his hat on his head, and walked grumbling forth.

Meantime, Catherine paced up and down the floor, exclaiming –

'I wonder where he is – I wonder where he *can* be! What did I say, Nelly? I've forgotten. Was he vexed at my bad humour this afternoon? Dear! tell me what I've said to grieve him? I do wish he'd come. I do wish he would!'

'What a noise for nothing!' I cried, though rather uneasy myself. 'What a trifle scares you! It's surely no great cause of alarm that Heathcliff should take a moonlight saunter on the moors, or even lie too sulky to speak to us in the hayloft. I'll engage he's lurking there. See if I don't ferret him out!'

I departed to renew my search; its result was disappointment, and Joseph's quest ended in the same.

'Yon lad gets war un war!' observed he on re-entering. 'He's left th' yate ut t' full swing, and miss's pony has trodden dahn two rigs uh corn, un plottered through, raight o'er intuh t' meadow! Hahsomdiver, t' maister 'ull play t' devil to-morn, and he'll do weel. He's patience itseln wi' sich careless, offald craters – patience itseln he is! Bud he'll nut be soa allus – yah's see, all on ye! Yah mum'n't drive him aht uf his heead fur nowt!'

'Have you found Heathcliff, you ass?' interrupted Catherine. 'Have you been looking for him, as I ordered?'

'Aw sud more likker look for th' horse,' he replied. 'It 'ud be tuh more sense. Bud, aw can look for norther horse, nur man uf a neeght loike this as black as t' chimbley! und Hathecliff's noan t' chap tuh coom ut *maw* whistle – happen he'll be less hard uh hearing wi' *ye*!'

It *was* a very dark evening for summer: the clouds appeared inclined to thunder, and I said we had better all sit down; the approaching rain would be certain to bring him home without further trouble.

However, Catherine would not be persuaded into tranquillity. She kept wandering to and fro, from the gate to the door, in a state of agitation which permitted no repose: and, at length, took up a permanent position on one side of the wall, near the road; where, heedless of my expostulations, and the growling thunder, and the great drops that began to plash around her, she remained calling, at intervals, and then listening, and then crying outright. She beat Hareton, or any child, at a good passionate fit of crying.

About midnight, while we still sat up, the storm came rattling over the Heights in full fury. There was a violent wind, as well as thunder, and either one or the other split a tree off at the corner of the building; a huge bough fell across the

roof, and knocked down a portion of the east chimney-stack, sending a clatter of stones and soot into the kitchen fire.

We thought a bolt had fallen in the middle of us, and Joseph swung onto his knees, beseeching the Lord to remember the patriarchs Noah and Lot; and, as in former times, spare the righteous, though he smote the ungodly. I felt some sentiment that it must be a judgment on us also. The Jonah, in my mind, was Mr Earnshaw, and I shook the handle of his den that I might ascertain if he were yet living. He replied audibly enough, in a fashion which made my companion vociferate more clamorously than before that a wide distinction might be drawn between saints like himself, and sinners like his master. But the uproar passed away in twenty minutes, leaving us all unharmed, excepting Cathy, who got thoroughly drenched for her obstinacy in refusing to take shelter, and standing bonnetless and shawlless to catch as much water as she could with her hair and clothes.

She came in, and lay down on the settle, all soaked as she was, turning her face to the back, and putting her hands before it.

'Well, Miss!' I exclaimed, touching her shoulder. 'You are not bent on getting your death, are you? Do you know what o'clock it is? Half-past twelve. Come! come to bed; there's no use waiting longer on that foolish boy – he'll be gone to Gimmerton, and he'll stay there now. He guesses we shouldn't wake for him till this late hour; at least, he guesses that only Mr Hindley would be up; and he'd rather avoid having the door opened by the master.'

'Nay, nay, he's noan at Gimmerton!' said Joseph. 'Aw's niver wonder, bud he's at t' bottom uf a bug-hoile. This visitation worn't for nowt, und aw wod hev ye tuh look aht, Miss – yah muh be t' next. Thank Hivin for all! All warks togither for gooid tuh them as is chozzen, and piked aht froo' th' rubbidge! Yah knaw whet t' Scripture ses –'

And he began quoting several texts, referring us to the chapters and verses, where we might find them.

I, having vainly begged the wilful girl to rise and remove her wet things, left him preaching, and her shivering, and betook myself to bed with little Hareton; who slept as fast as if every one had been sleeping round him.

I heard Joseph read on a while afterwards; then, I distinguished his slow step on the ladder, and then I dropt asleep.

Coming down somewhat later than usual, I saw, by the sunbeams piercing the chinks of the shutters, Miss Catherine still seated near the fire-place. The house door was ajar, too; light entered from its enclosed windows, Hindley had come out, and stood on the kitchen hearth, haggard and drowsy.

'What ails you, Cathy?' he was saying when I entered; 'you look as dismal as a drowned whelp – Why are you so damp and pale, child?'

'I've been wet,' she answered reluctantly, 'and I'm cold, that's all.'

'Oh, she is naughty!' I cried, perceiving the master to be tolerably sober; 'She got steeped in the shower of yesterday evening, and there she has sat, the night through, and I couldn't prevail on her to stir.'

Mr Earnshaw stared at us in surprise. 'The night through,' he repeated. 'What kept her up, not fear of the thunder, surely? That was over hours since.'

Neither of us wished to mention Heathcliff's absence, as long as we could conceal it; so, I replied, I didn't know how she took it into her head to sit up; and she said nothing.

# Wuthering Heights

The morning was fresh and cool; I threw back the lattice, and presently the room filled with sweet scents from the garden: but Catherine called peevishly to me.

'Ellen, shut the window. I'm starving!' And her teeth chattered as she shrunk closer to the almost extinguished embers.

'She's ill –' said Hindley, taking her wrist; 'I suppose that's the reason she would not go to bed – Damn it! I don't want to be troubled with more sickness, here – What took you into the rain?'

'Running after t' lads, as usuald!' croaked Joseph, catching an opportunity, from our hesitation, to thrust in his evil tongue.

'If Aw wur yah, maister, Aw'd just slam t' boards i' their faces all on 'em, gentle and simple! Never a day ut yah're off, but yon cat uh Linton comes sneaking hither – and Miss Nelly, shoo's a fine lass! shoo sits watching for ye i' t' kitchen; and as yah're in at one door, he's aht at t' other – und, then, wer grand lady goes a coorting uf hor side! It's bonny behaviour, lurking amang t' fields, after twelve ut' night, wi' that fahl, flaysome divil uf a gipsy, Heathcliff! They think *Aw'm* blind; but Aw'm noan, nowt ut t' soart! Aw seed young Linton, boath coming and going, and Aw seed *yah'* (directing his discourse to me). 'Yah gooid fur nowt, slattenly witch! nip up und bolt intuh th' hahs, t' minute yah heard t' maister's horse fit clatter up t' road.'

'Silence, eavesdropper!' cried Catherine, 'None of your insolence, before me! Edgar Linton came yesterday, by chance, Hindley: and it was *I* who told him to be off: because I knew you would not like to have met him as you were.'

'You lie, Cathy, no doubt,' answered her brother, 'and you are a confounded simpleton! But never mind Linton at present – tell me, were you not with Heathcliff last night? Speak the truth, now. You need not be afraid of harming him – though I hate him as much as ever, he did me a good turn a short time since, that will make my conscience tender of breaking his neck. To prevent it, I shall send him about his business, this very morning; and after he's gone, I'd advise you to look sharp, I shall only have the more humour for you.'

'I never saw Heathcliff last night,' answered Catherine, beginning to sob bitterly: 'and if you do turn him out of doors, I'll go with him. But, perhaps, you'll never have an opportunity – perhaps, he's gone.' Here she burst into uncontrollable grief, and the remainder of her words were inarticulate.

Hindley lavished on her a torrent of scornful abuse, and bid her get to her room immediately, or she shouldn't cry for nothing! I obliged her to obey; and I shall never forget what a scene she acted, when we reached her chamber. It terrified me – I thought she was going mad, and I begged Joseph to run for the doctor.

It proved the commencement of delirium; Mr Kenneth, as soon as he saw her, pronounced her dangerously ill; she had a fever.

He bled her, and he told me to let her live on whey, and water gruel; and take care she did not throw herself down stairs, or out of the window; and then he left; for he had enough to do in the parish, where two or three miles was the ordinary distance between cottage and cottage.

Though I cannot say I made a gentle nurse, and Joseph and the master were no better; and though our patient was as wearisome and headstong as a patient could be, she weathered it through.

Old Mrs Linton paid us several visits, to be sure, and set things to rights, and

# Wuthering Heights

scolded, and ordered us all; and when Catherine was convalescent, she insisted on conveying her to Thrushcross Grange; for which deliverance we were very grateful. But the poor dame had reason to repent of her kindness; she, and her husband, both took the fever, and died within a few days of each other.

Our young lady returned to us, saucier, and more passionate, and haughtier than ever. Heathcliff had never been heard of since the evening of the thunderstorm, and, one day, I had the misfortune, when she provoked me exceedingly, to lay the blame of his disappearance on her (where indeed it belonged, as she well knew). From that period for several months, she ceased to hold any communication with me, save in the relation of a mere servant. Joseph fell under a ban also; he *would* speak his mind, and lecture her all the same as if she were a little girl; and she esteemed herself a woman, and our mistress; and thought that her recent illness gave her a claim to be treated with consideration. Then the doctor had said that she would not bear crossing much, she ought to have her own way; and it was nothing less than murder, in her eyes, for any one to presume to stand up and contradict her.

From Mr Earnshaw, and his companions, she kept aloof, and tutored by Kenneth, and serious threats of a fit that often attended her rages, her brother allowed her whatever she pleased to demand, and generally avoided aggravating her fiery temper. He was rather *too* indulgent in humouring her caprices; not from affection, but from pride; he wished earnestly to see her bring honour to the family by an alliance with the Lintons, and, as long as she let him alone she might trample us like slaves for aught he cared!

Edgar Linton, as multitudes have been before and will be after him, was infatuated; and believed himself the happiest man alive on the day he led her to Gimmerton Chapel, three years subsequent to his father's death.

Much against my inclination, I was persuaded to leave Wuthering Heights and accompany her here. Little Hareton was nearly five years old, and I had just begun to teach him his letters. We made a sad parting, but Catherine's tears were more powerful than ours – When I refused to go, and when she found her entreaties did not move me, she went lamenting to her husband and brother. The former offered me munificent wages; the latter ordered me to pack up – he wanted no women in the house, he said, now that there was no mistress; and as to Hareton, the curate should take him in hand, by and by. And so, I had but one choice left, to do as I was ordered. I told the master he got rid of all decent people only to run to ruin a little faster; I kissed Hareton goodbye; and since then, he has been a stranger, and it's very queer to think it, but I've no doubt, he has completely forgotten all about Ellen Dean and that he was ever more than all the world to her, and she to him!

At this point of the housekeeper's story, she chanced to glance towards the time-piece over the chimney; and was in amazement, on seeing the minute-hand measure half past one. She would not hear of staying a second longer – in truth, I felt rather disposed to defer the sequel of her narrative, myself: and now, that she is vanished to her rest, and I have meditated for another hour or two, I shall summon courage to go, also, in spite of aching laziness of head and limbs.

# Chapter 10

charming introduction to a hermit's life! Four weeks' torture, tossing and sickness! Oh, these bleak winds, and bitter, northern skies, and impassable roads, and dilatory country surgeons! And, oh, this dearth of the human physiognomy, and, worse than all, the terrible intimation of Kenneth that I need not expect to be out of doors till spring!

Mr Heathcliff has just honoured me with a call. About seven days ago he sent me a brace of grouse – the last of the season. Scoundrel! He is not altogether guiltless in this illness of mine; and that I had a great mind to tell him. But, alas! how could I offend a man who was charitable enough to sit at my bedside a good hour, and talk on some other subjects than pills, and draughts, blisters, and leeches?

This is quite an easy interval. I am too weak to read, yet I feel as if I could enjoy something interesting. Why not have up Mrs Dean to finish her tale? I can recollect its chief incidents, as far as she had gone. Yes, I remember her hero had run off, and never been heard of for three years: and the heroine was married: I'll ring; she'll be delighted to find me capable of talking cheerfully.

Mrs Dean came.

'It wants twenty minutes, sir, to taking the medicine,' she commenced.

'Away, away with it!' I replied; 'I desire to have –'

'The doctor says you must drop the powders.'

'With all my heart! Don't interrupt me. Come and take your seat here. Keep your fingers from that bitter phalanx of vials. Draw your knitting out of your pocket – that will do – now continue the history of Mr Heathcliff, from where you left off, to the present day. Did he finish his education on the Continent, and come back a gentleman? or did he get a sizar's place at college? or escape to America, and earn honours by drawing blood from his foster country? or make a fortune more promptly, on the English highways?'

'He may have done a little in all these vocations, Mr Lockwood; but I couldn't give my word for any. I stated before that I didn't know how he gained his money; neither am I aware of the means he took to raise his mind from the savage ignorance into which it was sunk; but, with your leave, I'll proceed in my own fashion, if you think it will amuse, and not weary you. Are you feeling better this morning?'

'Much.'

'That's good news.'

I got Miss Catherine and myself to Thrushcross Grange; and to my agreeable disappointment, she behaved infinitely better than I dared to expect. She seemed

almost over fond of Mr Linton; and even to his sister, she showed plenty of affection. They were both very attentive to her comfort, certainly. It was not the thorn bending to the honeysuckles, but the honeysuckles embracing the thorn. There were no mutual concessions; one stood erect, and the others yielded; and who *can* be ill-natured, and bad-tempered, when they encounter neither opposition nor indifference?

I observed that Mr Edgar had a deep-rooted fear of ruffling her humour. He concealed it from her; but if ever he heard me answer sharply, or saw any other servant grow cloudy at some imperious order of hers, he would show his trouble by a frown of displeasure that never darkened on his own account. He, many a time, spoke sternly to me about my pertness; and averred that the stab of a knife could not inflict a worse pang than he suffered at seeing his lady vexed.

Not to grieve a kind master, I learned to be less touchy; and, for the space of half a year, the gunpowder lay as harmless as sand, because no fire came near to explode it. Catherine had seasons of gloom and silence, now and then: they were respected with sympathizing silence by her husband, who ascribed them to an alteration in her constitution, produced by her perilous illness, as she was never subject to depression of spirits before. The return of sunshine was welcomed by answering sunshine from him. I believe I may assert that they were really in possession of deep and growing happiness.

It ended. Well, we *must* be for ourselves in the long run; the mild and generous are only more justly selfish than the domineering – and it ended when circumstances caused each to feel that the one's interest was not the chief consideration in the other's thoughts.

On a mellow evening in September, I was coming from the garden with a heavy basket of apples which I had been gathering. It had got dusk, and the moon looked over the high wall of the court, causing undefined shadows to lurk in the corners of the numerous projecting portions of the building. I set my burden on the house steps by the kitchen door, and lingered to rest, and drew in a few more breaths of the soft, sweet air; my eyes were on the moon, and my back to the entrance, when I heard a voice behind me say –

'Nelly, is that you?'

It was a deep voice, and foreign in tone; yet, there was something in the manner of pronouncing my name which made it sound familiar. I turned about to discover who spoke, fearfully, for the doors were shut, and I had seen nobody on approaching the steps.

Something stirred in the porch; and moving nearer, I distinguished a tall man dressed in dark clothes, with dark face and hair. He leant against the side, and held his fingers on the latch, as if intending to open for himself.

'Who can it be?' I thought. 'Mr Earnshaw? Oh, no! The voice has no resemblance to his.'

'I have waited here an hour,' he resumed, while I continued staring; 'and the whole of that time all round has been as still as death. I dared not enter. You do not know me? Look, I'm not a stranger!'

A ray fell on his features; the cheeks were sallow, and half covered with black whiskers; the brows lowering, the eyes deep set and singular. I remembered the eyes.

'What!' I cried, uncertain whether to regard him as a worldly visitor, and I raised my hands in amazement. 'What! you come back? Is it really you? Is it?'

# Wuthering Heights

'Yes, Heathcliff,' he replied, glancing from me up to the windows which reflected a score of glittering moons, but showed no lights from within. 'Are they at home – where is she? Nelly, you are not glad – you needn't be so disturbed. Is she here? Speak! I wait to have one word with her – your mistress. Go, and say some person from Gimmerton desires to see her.'

'How will she take it?' I exclaimed. 'What will she do? The surprise bewilders me – it will put her out of her head! And you *are* Heathcliff? But altered! Nay, there's no comprehending it. Have you been for a soldier?'

'Go, and carry my message,' he interrupted impatiently. 'I'm in hell till you do!'

He lifted the latch, and I entered; but when I got to the parlour where Mr and Mrs Linton were, I could not persuade myself to proceed.

At length, I resolved on making an excuse to ask if they would have the candles lighted, and I opened the door.

They sat together in a window whose lattice lay back against the wall, and displayed, beyond the garden trees and the wild green park, the valley of Gimmerton, with a long line of mist winding nearly to its top (for very soon after you pass the chapel, as you may have noticed, the sough that runs from the marshes joins a beck which follows the bend of the glen), Wuthering Heights rose above this silvery vapour – but our old house was invisible – it rather dips down on the other side.

Both the room, and its occupants, and the scene they gazed on, looked wondrously peaceful. I shrank reluctantly from performing my errand: and was actually going away, leaving it unsaid, after having put my question about the candles, when a sense of my folly compelled me to return, and mutter:

'A person from Gimmerton wishes to see you, ma'am.'

'What does he want?' asked Mrs Linton.

'I did not question him,' I answered.

'Well, close the curtains, Nelly,' she said; 'and bring up tea. I'll be back again directly.'

She quitted the apartment; Mr Edgar inquired, carelessly, who it was.

'Some one mistress does not expect,' I replied, 'That Heathcliff, you recollect him, sir, who used to live at Mr Earnshaw's.'

'What, the gipsy – the plough-boy?' he cried. 'Why did you not say so to Catherine?'

'Hush! you must not call him by those names, master,' I said. 'She'd be sadly grieved to hear you. She was nearly heartbroken when he ran off; I guess his return will make a jubilee to her.'

Mr Linton walked to a window on the other side of the room that overlooked the court. He unfastened it, and leant out. I suppose they were below, for he exclaimed, quickly:

'Don't stand there, love! Bring the person in, if it be any one particular.'

Ere long, I heard the click of the latch, and Catherine flew upstairs, breathless and wild, too excited to show gladness; indeed, by her face, you would rather have surmised an awful calamity.

'Oh, Edgar, Edgar!' she panted, flinging her arms round his neck. 'Oh, Edgar, darling! Heathcliff's come back – he is!' And she tightened her embrace to a squeeze.

# Wuthering Heights

'Well, well,' cried her husband, crossly, 'don't strangle me for that! He never struck me as such a marvellous treasure. There is no need to be frantic!'

'I know you didn't like him,' she answered, repressing a little the intensity of her delight. 'Yet, for my sake, you must be friends now. Shall I tell him to come up now?'

'Here?' he said, 'into the parlour?'

'Where else?' she asked.

He looked vexed, and suggested the kitchen as a more suitable place for him.

Mrs Linton eyed him with a droll expression – half angry, half laughing at his fastidiousness.

'No,' she added, after a while: 'I cannot sit in the kitchen. Set two tables here, Ellen; one for your master and Miss Isabella, being gentry; the other for Heathcliff and myself, being of the lower orders. Will that please you, dear? Or must I have a fire lighted elsewhere? If so, give directions. I'll run down and secure my guest. I'm afraid the joy is too great to be real!'

She was about to dart off again; but Edgar arrested her.

'*You* bid him step up,' he said, addressing me; 'and Catherine, try to be glad, without being absurd. The whole household need not witness the sight of your welcoming a runaway servant as a brother.'

I descended and found Heathcliff waiting under the porch, evidently anticipating an invitation to enter. He followed my guidance without waste of words, and I ushered him into the presence of the master and mistress, whose flushed cheeks betrayed signs of warm talking. But the lady's glowed with another feeling when her friend appeared at the door; she sprang forward, took both his hands, and led him to Linton; and then she seized Linton's reluctant fingers and crushed them into his.

Now fully revealed by the fire and candlelight, I was amazed, more than ever, to behold the transformation of Heathcliff. He had grown a tall, athletic, well-formed man, beside whom, my master seemed quite slender and youth-like. His upright carriage suggested the idea of his having been in the army. His countenance was much older in expression and decision of feature than Mr Linton's; it looked intelligent, and retained no marks of former degradation. A half-civilized ferocity lurked yet in the depressed brows, and eyes full of black fire, but it was subdued; and his manner was even dignified, quite divested of roughness though too stern for grace.

My master's surprise equalled or exceeded mine: he remained for a minute at a loss how to address the ploughboy, as he had called him. Heathcliff dropped his slight hand, and stood looking at him coolly till he chose to speak.

'Sit down, sir,' he said, at length. 'Mrs Linton, recalling old times, would have me give you a cordial reception, and, of course, I am gratified when anything occurs to please her.'

'And I also,' answered Heathcliff, 'especially if it be anything in which I have a part. I shall stay an hour or two willingly.'

He took a seat opposite Catherine, who kept her gaze fixed on him as if she feared he would vanish were she to remove it. He did not raise his to her, often; a quick glance now and then sufficed; but it flashed back, each time more confidently, the undisguised delight he drank from hers.

They were too much absorbed in their mutual joy to suffer embarrassment; not so Mr Edgar, he grew pale with pure annoyance, a feeling that reached its

# Wuthering Heights

climax when his lady rose – and stepping across the rug, seized Heathcliff's
hands again, and laughed like one beside herself.

'I shall think it a dream to-morrow!' she cried. 'I shall not be able to believe
that I have seen, and touched, and spoken to you once more – and yet, cruel
Heathcliff! you don't deserve this welcome. To be absent and silent for three
years, and never to think of me!'

'A little more than you have thought of me,' he murmured. 'I heard of your
marriage, Cathy, not long since; and, while waiting in the yard below, I
meditated this plan – just to have one glimpse of your face – a stare of surprise,
perhaps, and pretended pleasure; afterwards settle my score with Hindley; and
then prevent the law by doing execution on myself. Your welcome has put these
ideas out of my mind; but beware of meeting me with another aspect next time!
Nay, you'll not drive me off again – you were really sorry for me, were you?
Well, there was cause. I've fought through a bitter life since I last heard your
voice, and you must forgive me, for I struggled only for you!'

'Catherine, unless we are to have cold tea, please to come to the table,'
interrupted Linton, striving to preserve his ordinary tone, and a due measure
of politeness. 'Mr Heathcliff will have a long walk, wherever he may lodge to-
night; and I'm thirsty.'

She took her post before the urn; and Miss Isabella came, summoned by the
bell; then, having handed their chairs forward, I left the room.

The meal hardly endured ten minutes – Catherine's cup was never filled, she
could neither eat nor drink. Edgar had made a slop in his saucer, and scarcely
swallowed a mouthful.

Their guest did not protract his stay, that evening, above an hour longer. I
asked, as he departed, if he went to Gimmerton.

'No, to Wuthering Heights,' he answered, 'Mr Earnshaw invited me when
I called this morning.'

Mr Earnshaw invited *him!* and *he* called on Mr Earnshaw! I pondered this
sentence painfully after he was gone. Is he turning out a bit of a hypocrite, and
coming into the country to work mischief under a cloak? I mused – I had a
presentiment, in the bottom of my heart, that he had better have remained away.

About the middle of the night, I was awakened from my first nap by Mrs
Linton gliding into my chamber, taking a seat on my bed-side, and pulling me
by the hair to rouse me.

'I cannot rest, Ellen,' she said, by way of apology. 'And I want some living
creature to keep me company in my happiness! Edgar is sulky, because I'm glad
of a thing that does not interest him – he refuses to open his mouth, except to
utter pettish, silly speeches; and he affirmed I was cruel and selfish for wishing
to talk when he was so sick and sleepy. He always contrives to be sick at the
least cross! I gave a few sentences of commendation to Heathcliff, and he, either
for a head-ache or a pang of envy, began to cry: so I got up and left him.'

'What use is it praising Heathcliff to him?' I answered. 'As lads they had an
aversion to each other, and Heathcliff would hate just as much to hear him
praised – it's human nature. Let Mr Linton alone about him, unless you would
like an open quarrel between them.'

'But does it not show great weakness?' pursued she. 'I'm not envious – I
never feel hurt at the brightness of Isabella's yellow hair, and the whiteness of
her skin; at her dainty elegance, and the fondness all the family exhibit for her.

# Wuthering Heights

Even you, Nelly, if we have a dispute sometimes, you back Isabella at once; and I yield like a foolish mother – I call her a darling, and flatter her into a good temper. It pleases her brother to see us cordial, and that pleases me. But, they are very much alike: they are spoiled children, and fancy the world was made for their accommodation; and, though I humour both, I think a smart chastisement might improve them, all the same.'

'You're mistaken, Mrs Linton,' said I, 'They humour you – I know what there would be to do if they did not! You can well afford to indulge their passing whims, as long as their business is to anticipate all your desires – You may, however, fall out, at least, over something of equal consequence to both sides; and, then those you term weak are very capable of being as obstinate as you.'

'And then we shall fight to the death, shan't we, Nelly?' she returned, laughing, 'No, I tell you, I have such faith in Linton's love that I believe I might kill him, and he wouldn't wish to retaliate.'

I advised her to value him the more for his affection.

'I do,' she answered; 'but he needn't resort to whining for trifles. It is childish; and, instead of melting into tears, because I said that Heathcliff was now worthy of any one's regard, and it would honour the first gentleman in the country to be his friend; he ought to have said it for me, and been delighted from sympathy – He must get accustomed to him, and he may as well like him – considering how Heathcliff has reason to object to him, I'm sure he behaved excellently!'

'What do you think of his going to Wuthering Heights?' I inquired. 'He is reformed in every respect apparently – quite a Christian – offering the right hand of fellowship to his enemies all around!'

'He explained it,' she replied. 'I wondered as much as you – He said he called to gather information concerning me, from you, supposing you resided there still; and Joseph told Hindley, who came out, and fell to questioning him of what he had been doing, and how he had been living: and finally, desired him to walk in – There were some persons sitting at cards – Heathcliff joined them; my brother lost some money to him, and, finding him plentifully supplied, he requested that he would come again in the evening, to which he consented. Hindley is too reckless to select his acquaintance prudently; he doesn't trouble himself to reflect on the causes he might have for mistrusting one whom he has basely injured – But, Heathcliff affirms his principal reason for resuming a connection with his ancient persecutor is a wish to install himself in quarters at walking distance from the Grange, and an attachment to the house where we lived together, and, likewise, a hope that I shall have more opportunities of seeing him there than I could have if he settled in Gimmerton. He means to offer liberal payment for permission to lodge at the Heights; and doubtless my brother's covetousness will prompt him to accept the terms; he was always greedy, though what he grasps with one hand, he flings away with the other.'

'It's a nice place for a young man to fix his dwelling in!' said I. 'Have you no fear of the consequences, Mrs Linton?'

'None for my friend,' she replied, 'his strong head will keep him from danger – a little for Hindley; but he can't be made morally worse than he is; and I stand between him and bodily harm – The event of this evening has reconciled me to God, and humanity! I had risen in angry rebellion against Providence – Oh, I've endured very, very bitter misery, Nelly! If that creature knew how bitter, he'd be ashamed to cloud its removal with idle petulance – It was kindness for him

which induced me to bear it alone: had I expressed the agony I frequently felt, he would have been taught to long for its alleviation as ardently as I – However, it's over, and I'll take no revenge on his folly – I can afford to suffer anything, hereafter! should the meanest thing alive slap me on the cheek, I'd not only turn the other, but I'd ask pardon for provoking it – and, as a proof, I'll go make my peace with Edgar instantly – Good night – I'm an angel!'

In this self-complacent conviction she departed; and the success of her fulfilled resolution was obvious on the morrow – Mr Linton had not only abjured his peevishness (though his spirits seemed still subdued by Catherine's exuberance of vivacity), but he ventured no objection to her taking Isabella with her to Wuthering Heights, in the afternoon; and she rewarded him with such a summer of sweetness and affection, in return, as made the house a paradise for several days, both master and servants profiting from the perpetual sunshine.

Heathcliff – Mr Heathcliff, I should say in future – used the liberty of visiting Thrushcross Grange cautiously, at first: he seemed estimating how far its owner would bear his intrusion. Catherine, also, deemed it judicious to moderate her expressions of pleasure in receiving him; and he gradually established his right to be expected.

He retained a great deal of the reserve for which his boyhood was remarkable, and that served to repress all startling demonstrations of feeling. My master's uneasiness experienced a lull, and further circumstances diverted it into another channel for a space.

His new source of trouble sprang from the not anticipated misfortune of Isabella Linton evincing a sudden and irresistible attraction towards the tolerated guest – She was at that time a charming young lady of eighteen; infantile in manners, though possessed of keen wit, keen feelings, and a keen temper, too, if irritated. Her brother, who loved her tenderly, was appalled at this fantastic preference. Leaving aside the degradation of an alliance with a nameless man, and the possible fact that his property, in default of heirs male, might pass into such a one's power, he had sense to comprehend Heathcliff's disposition – to know that, though his exterior was altered, his mind was unchangeable, and unchanged. And he dreaded that mind; it revolted him; he shrank forebodingly from the idea of committing Isabella to its keeping.

He would have recoiled still more had he been aware that her attachment rose unsolicited, and was bestowed where it awakened no reciprocation of sentiment; for the minute he discovered its existence, he laid the blame on Heathcliff's deliberate designing.

We had all remarked, during some time, that Miss Linton fretted and pined over something. She grew cross and wearisome; snapping at and teasing Catherine continually, at the imminent risk of exhausting her limited patience. We excused her to a certain extent, on the plea of ill-health – she was dwindling and fading before our eyes – But one day, when she had been particularly wayward, rejecting her breakfast, complaining that the servants did not do what she told them; that the mistress would allow her to be nothing in the house, and Edgar neglected her; that she had caught a cold with the doors being left open, and we let the parlour fire go out on purpose to vex her; with a hundred yet more frivolous accusations; Mrs Linton peremptorily insisted that she should get to-bed; and, having scolded her heartily, threatened to send for the doctor.

# Wuthering Heights

Mention of Kenneth caused her to exclaim, instantly, that her health was perfect, and it was only Catherine's harshness which made her unhappy.

'How can you say I'm harsh, you naughty fondling?' cried the mistress, amazed at the unreasonable assertion. 'You are surely losing your reason. When have I been harsh, tell me?'

'Yesterday,' sobbed Isabella, 'and now!'

'Yesterday!' said her sister-in-law. 'On what occasion?'

'In our walk along the moor; you told me to ramble where I pleased, while you sauntered on with Mr Heathcliff!'

'And that's your notion of harshness?' said Catherine, laughing. 'It was no hint that your company was superfluous; we didn't care whether you kept with us or not; I merely thought Heathcliff's talk would have nothing entertaining for your ears.'

'Oh no,' wept the young lady, 'you wished me away, because you knew I liked to be there!'

'Is she sane?' asked Mrs Linton, appealing to me. 'I'll repeat our conversation, word for word, Isabella; and you point out any charm it could have had for you.'

'I don't mind the conversation,' she answered: 'I wanted to be with –'

'Well!' said Catherine, perceiving her hesitate to complete the sentence.

'With him; and I won't be always sent off!' she continued, kindling up. 'You are a dog in the manger, Cathy, and desire no one to be loved but yourself!'

'You are an impertinent little monkey!' exclaimed Mrs Linton, in surprise. 'But I'll not believe this idiocy! It is impossible that you can covet the admiration of Heathcliff – that you can consider him an agreeable person! I hope I have misunderstood you, Isabella?'

'No, you have not,' said the infatuated girl. 'I love him more than ever you loved Edgar; and he might love me, if you would let him!'

'I wouldn't be you for a kingdom then!' Catherine declared, emphatically – and she seemed to speak sincerely. 'Nelly, help me to convince her of her madness. Tell her what Heathcliff is – an unreclaimed creature, without refinement, without cultivation; an arid wilderness of furze and whinstone. I'd as soon put that little canary into the park on a winter's day as recommend you to bestow your heart on him! It is deplorable ignorance of his character, child, and nothing else, which makes that dream enter your head. Pray, don't imagine that he conceals depths of benevolence and affection beneath a stern exterior! He's not a rough diamond – a pearl-containing oyster of a rustic; he's a fierce, pitiless, wolfish man. I never say to him let this or that enemy alone, because it would be ungenerous or cruel to harm them, I say – "Let them alone, because *I* should hate them to be wronged": and he'd crush you, like a sparrow's egg, Isabella, if he found you a troublesome charge. I know he couldn't love a Linton; and yet, he'd be quite capable of marrying your fortune and expectations. Avarice is growing with him a besetting sin. There's my picture; and I'm his friend – so much so, that had he thought seriously to catch you, I should, perhaps, have held my tongue, and let you fall into his trap.'

Miss Linton regarded her sister-in-law with indignation.

'For shame! for shame!' she repeated, angrily. 'You are worse then twenty foes, you poisonous friend!'

# Wuthering Heights

'Ah, you won't believe me, then?' said Catherine. 'You think I speak from wicked selfishness?'

'I'm certain you do,' retorted Isabella; 'and I shudder at you!'

'Good!' cried the other. 'Try for yourself, if that be your spirit; I have done, and yield the argument to your saucy insolence.'

'And I must suffer for her egotism!' she sobbed, as Mrs Linton left the room. 'All, all is against me; she has blighted my single consolation. But she uttered falsehoods, didn't she? Mr Heathcliff is not a fiend; he has an honourable soul, and a true one, or how could he remember her?'

'Banish him from your thoughts, Miss,' I said. 'He's a bird of bad omen; no mate for you. Mrs Linton spoke strongly, and yet, I can't contradict her. She is better acquainted with his heart than I, or any one besides; and she never would represent him as worse than he is. Honest people don't hide their deeds. How has he been living? how has he got rich? why is he staying at Wuthering Heights, the house of a man whom he abhors? They say Mr Earnshaw is worse and worse since he came. They sit up all night together continually: and Hindley has been borrowing money on his land; and does nothing but play and drink, I heard only a week ago; it was Joseph who told me – I met him at Gimmerton:

' "Nelly," he said, "we's hae a Crahnr's 'quest enah, at ahr folks. One on 'em's a'most getten his finger cut off wi' haudin' t' other froo' sticking hisseln loike a cawlf. That's maister, yah knaw, ut's soa up uh going tuh t'grand 'sizes. He's noan feard uh t' Bench uh judges, norther Paul, nur Peter, nur John, nur Mathew, nur noan on 'em, nut he! He fair likes he langs tuh set his brazened face agean 'em! And yon bonny lad Heathcliff, yah mind, he's a rare un! He can girn a laugh, as weel's onybody at a raight divil's jest. Does he niver say nowt of his fine living amang us, when he goas tuh t' Grange? This is t' way on 't – up at sun-dahn; dice, brandy, cloised shutters, und can'le lught till next day, at nooin – then, t' fooil gangs banning un raving tuh his cham'er, makking dacent fowks dig thur fingers i' thur lugs fur varry shaume; un' th' knave, wah, he carn cahnt his brass, un' ate, un' sleep, un' off tuh his neighbour's tuh gossip wi' t' wife. I' course, he tells Dame Catherine hah hor fathur's goold runs intuh his pocket, and her fathur's son gallops dahn t' Broad road, while he flees afore tuh oppen t' pikes?" Now, Miss Linton, Joseph is an old rascal, but no liar; and, if his account of Heathcliff's conduct be true, you would never think of desiring such a husband, would you?'

'You are leagued with the rest, Ellen!' she replied. 'I'll not listen to your slanders. What malevolence you must have to wish to convince me that there is no happiness in the world!'

Whether she would have got over this fancy if left to herself, or persevered in nursing it perpetually, I cannot say; she had little time to reflect. The day after, there was a justice-meeting at the next town; my master was obliged to attend; and Mr Heathcliff, aware of his absence, called rather earlier than usual.

Catherine and Isabella were sitting in the library, on hostile terms, but silent. The latter alarmed at her recent indiscretion, and the disclosure she had made of her secret feelings in a transient fit of passion; the former, on mature consideration, really offended with her companion; and, if she laughed again at her pertness, inclined to make it no laughing matter to *her*.

She did laugh as she saw Heathcliff pass the window. I was sweeping the hearth, and I noticed a mischievous smile on her lips. Isabella, absorbed in her

meditations, or a book, remained till the door opened, and it was too late to attempt an escape, which she would gladly have done had it been practicable.

'Come in, that's right!' exclaimed the mistress, gaily, pulling a chair to the fire. 'Here are two people sadly in need of a third to thaw the ice between them; and you are the very one we should both of us choose. Heathcliff, I'm proud to show you, at last, somebody that dotes on you more than myself. I expect you to feel flattered – nay, it's not Nelly; don't look at her! My poor little sister-in-law is breaking her heart by mere contemplation of your physical and moral beauty. It lies in your own power to be Edgar's brother! No, no, Isabella, you sha'n't run off,' she continued, arresting, with feigned playfulness, the confounded girl, who had risen indignantly. 'We were quarrelling like cats about you, Heathcliff; and I was fairly beaten in protestations of devotion and admiration; and, moreover, I was informed that if I would but have the manners to stand aside, my rival, as she will have herself to be, would shoot a shaft into your soul that would fix you for ever, and send my image into eternal oblivion!'

'Catherine!' said Isabella, calling up her dignity, and disdaining to struggle from the tight grasp that held her. 'I'd thank you to adhere to the truth and not slander me, even in joke! Mr Heathcliff, be kind enough to bid this friend of yours release me – she forgets that you and I are not intimate acquaintances, and what amuses her is painful to me beyond expression.'

As the guest answered nothing, but took his seat, and looked thoroughly indifferent what sentiments she cherished concerning him, she turned, and whispered an earnest appeal for liberty to her tormentor.

'By no means!' cried Mrs Linton in answer. 'I won't be named a dog in the manger again. You *shall* stay, now then! Heathcliff, why don't you evince satisfaction at my pleasant news? Isabella swears that the love Edgar has for me is nothing to that she entertains for you. I'm sure she made some speech of the kind, did she not, Ellen? And she has fasted ever since the day before yesterday's walk, from sorrow and rage that I despatched her out of your society, under the idea of its being unacceptable.'

'I think you belie her,' said Heathcliff, twisting his chair to face them. 'She wishes to be out of my society now, at any rate!'

And he stared hard at the object of discourse, as one might do at a strange repulsive animal, a centipede from the Indies, for instance, which curiosity leads one to examine in spite of the aversion it raises.

The poor thing couldn't bear that; she grew white and red in rapid succession, and, while tears beaded her lashes, bent the strength of her small fingers to loosen the firm clutch of Catherine, and perceiving that, as fast as she raised one finger off her arm, another closed down, and she could not remove the whole together, she began to make use of her nails, and their sharpness presently ornamented the detainer's with crescents of red.

'There's a tigress!' exclaimed Mrs Linton, setting her free, and shaking her hand with pain. 'Begone, for God's sake, and hide your vixen face! How foolish to reveal those talons to *him*. Can't you fancy the conclusions he'll draw? Look, Heathcliff! they are instruments that will do execution – you must beware of your eyes.'

'I'd wrench them off her fingers, if they ever menaced me,' he answered, brutally, when the door had closed after her. 'But what did you mean by teasing

# Wuthering Heights

the creature in that manner, Cathy? You were not speaking the truth, were you?'

'I assure you I was,' she returned. 'She has been pining for your sake several weeks; and raving about you this morning, and pouring forth a deluge of abuse, because I represented your failings in a plain light for the purpose of mitigating her adoration. But don't notice it further. I wished to punish her sauciness, that's all – I like her too well, my dear Heathcliff, to let you absolutely seize and devour her up.'

'And I like her too ill to attempt it,' said he, 'except in a very ghoulish fashion. You'd hear of odd things, if I lived alone with that mawkish, waxen face; the most ordinary would be painting on its white the colours of the rainbow, and turning the blue eyes black, every day or two; they detestably resemble Linton's.'

'Delectably,' observed Catherine. 'They are dove's eyes – angel's!'

'She's her brother's heir, is she not?' he asked, after a brief silence.

'I should be sorry to think so,' returned his companion. 'Half a dozen nephews shall erase her title, please Heaven! Abstract your mind from the subject, at present – you are too prone to covet your neighbour's goods: remember, *this* neighbour's goods are mine.'

'If they were *mine*, they would be none the less that,' said Heathcliff, 'but though Isabella Linton may be silly, she is scarcely mad; and – in short, we'll dismiss the matter, as you advise.'

From their tongues, they did dismiss it; and Catherine, probably, from her thoughts. The other, I felt certain, recalled it often in the course of the evening. I saw him smile to himself – grin rather – and lapse into ominous musing whenever Mrs Linton had occasion to be absent from the apartment.

I determined to watch his movements. My heart invariably cleaved to the master's, in preference to Catherine's side; with reason, I imagined, for he was kind, and trustful, and honourable; and she – she could not be called the *opposite*, yet she seemed to allow herself such wide latitude, that I had little faith in her principles, and still less sympathy for her feelings. I wanted something to happen which might have the effect of freeing both Wuthering Heights and the Grange of Mr Heathcliff, quietly, leaving us as we had been prior to his advent. His visits were a continual nightmare to me; and, I suspected, to my master also. His abode at the Heights was an oppression past explaining. I felt that God had forsaken the stray sheep there to its own wicked wanderings, and an evil beast prowled between it and the fold, waiting his time to spring and destroy.

# Chapter 11

Sometimes, while meditating on these things in solitude, I've got up in sudden terror, and put on my bonnet to go and see how all was at the farm; I've persuaded my conscience that it was a duty to warn him how people talked regarding his ways; and then I've recollected his confirmed bad habits, and, hopeless of benefiting him, have flinched from re-entering the dismal house, doubting if I could bear to be taken at my word.

One time, I passed the old gate, going out of my way, on a journey to Gimmerton. It was about the period that my narrative has reached – a bright frosty afternoon; the ground bare, and the road hard and dry.

I came to a stone where the highway branches off on to the moor at your left hand; a rough sand-pillar, with the letters W.H. cut on its north side, on the east, G., and on the south-west T.G. It serves as guide-post to the Grange, and Heights, and village.

The sun shone yellow on its grey head, reminding me of summer; I cannot say why, but all at once, a gush of child's sensations flowed into my heart. Hindley and I held it a favourite spot twenty years before.

I gazed long at the weather-worn block; and, stooping down, perceived a hole near the bottom still full of snail-shells and pebbles, which we were very fond of storing there with more perishable things – and, as fresh as reality, it appeared that I beheld my early playmate seated on the withered turf, his dark, square head bent forward, and his little hand scooping out the earth with a piece of plate.

'Poor Hindley!' I exclaimed, involuntarily.

I started – my bodily eye was cheated into a momentary belief that the child lifted its face and stared straight into mine! It vanished in a twinkling; but, immediately, I felt an irresistible yearning to be at the Heights. Superstition urged me to comply with this impulse – 'Supposing he should be dead!' I thought – 'or should die soon! – supposing it were a sign of death!'

The nearer I got to the house the more agitated I grew, and on catching sight of it, I trembled every limb. The apparition had outstripped me; it stood looking through the gate. That was my first idea on observing an elf-locked, brown-eyed boy setting his ruddy countenance against the bars. Further reflection suggested this must be Hareton, *my* Hareton, not altered greatly since I left him, ten months since.

'God bless thee, darling!' I cried, forgetting instantaneously my foolish fears. 'Hareton, it's Nelly – Nelly, thy nurse.'

He retreated out of arm's length, and picked up a large flint.

# Wuthering Heights

'I am come to see thy father, Hareton,' I added, guessing from the action that Nelly, if she lived in his memory at all, was not recognized as one with me.

He raised his missile to hurl it; I commenced a soothing speech, but could not stay the hand. The stone struck my bonnet, and then ensued, from the stammering lips of the little fellow, a string of curses which, whether he comprehended them or not, were delivered with a practised emphasis, and distorted his baby features into a shocking expression of malignity.

You may be certain this grieved, more than angered me. Fit to cry, I took an orange from my pocket, and offered it to propitiate him.

He hesitated, and then snatched it from my hold, as if he fancied I only intended to tempt and disappoint him.

I showed another, keeping it out of his reach.

'Who has taught you those fine words, my barn?' I inquired. 'The curate?'

'Damn the curate, and thee! Gie me that,' he replied.

'Tell us where you got your lessons, and you shall have it,' said I. 'Who's your master?'

'Devil daddy,' was his answer.

'And what do you learn from Daddy?' I continued.

He jumped at the fruit; I raised it higher. 'What does he teach you?' I asked.

'Naught,' said he, 'but to keep out of his gait – Daddy cannot bide me, because I swear at him.'

'Ah! and the devil teaches you to swear at Daddy?' I observed.

'Aye – nay,' he drawled.

'Who then?'

'Heathcliff.'

I asked if he liked Mr Heathcliff.

'Aye!' he answered again.

Desiring to have his reasons for liking him, I could only gather the sentences 'I known't – he pays Dad back what he gies to me – he curses Daddy for cursing me – He says I mun do as I will.'

'And the curate does not teach you to read and write, then?' I pursued.

'No, I was told the curate should have his – teeth dashed down his – throat if he stepped over the threshold – Heathcliff had promised that!'

I put the orange in his hand; and bade him tell his father that a woman called Nelly Dean was waiting to speak with him, by the garden gate.

He went up the walk, and entered the house; but, instead of Hindley, Heathcliff appeared on the door stones; and I turned directly and ran down the road as hard as ever I could race, making no halt till I gained the guide post, and feeling as scared as if I had raised a goblin.

This is not much connected with Miss Isabella's affair; except that it urged me to resolve further on mounting vigilant guard, and doing my utmost to check the spread of such bad influence at the Grange, even though I should wake a domestic storm, by thwarting Mrs Linton's pleasure.

The next time Heathcliff came, my young lady chanced to be feeding some pigeons in the court. She had never spoken a word to her sister-in-law, for three days; but, she had likewise dropped her fretful complaining, and we found it a great comfort.

Heathcliff had not the habit of bestowing a single unnecessary civility on Miss Linton, I knew. Now, as soon as he beheld her, his first precaution was

# Wuthering Heights

to take a sweeping survey of the housefront. I was standing by the kitchen window, but I drew out of sight. He then stept across the pavement to her, and said something: she seemed embarrassed, and desirous of getting away; to prevent it, he laid his hand on her arm: she averted her face; he apparently put some question which she had no mind to answer. There was another rapid glance at the house, and supposing himself unseen, the scoundrel had the impudence to embrace her.

'Judas! Traitor!' I ejaculated. 'You are a hypocrite, too, are you? a deliberate deceiver?'

'Who is, Nelly?' said Catherine's voice at my elbow – I had been over-intent on watching the pair outside to mark her entrance.

'Your worthless friend!' I answered, warmly, 'the sneaking rascal yonder – Ah, he has caught a glimpse of us – he is coming in! I wonder will he have the art to find a plausible excuse for making love to Miss, when he told you he hated her?'

Mrs Linton saw Isabella tear herself free, and run into the garden; and a minute after, Heathcliff opened the door.

I couldn't withhold giving some loose to my indignation; but Catherine angrily insisted on silence, and threatened to order me out of the kitchen, if I dared to be so presumptuous as to put in my insolent tongue.

'To hear you, people might think *you* were the mistress!' she cried. 'You want setting down in your right place! Heathcliff, what are you about, raising this stir? I said you must let Isabella alone! – I beg you will, unless you are tired of being received here, and wish Linton to draw the bolts against you!'

'God forbid that he should try!' answered the black villain – I detested him just then. 'God keep him meek and patient! Every day I grow madder after sending him to heaven!'

'Hush!' said Catherine, shutting the inner door. 'Don't vex me. Why have you disregarded my request? Did she come across you on purpose?'

'What is it to you?' he growled. 'I have a right to kiss her, if she chooses, and you have no right to object – I'm not *your* husband, *you* needn't be jealous of me!'

'I'm not jealous of you,' replied the mistress, 'I'm jealous for you. Clear your face, you shan't scowl at me! If you like Isabella, you shall marry her. But do you like her? Tell the truth, Heathcliff! There, you won't answer. I'm certain you don't!'

'And would Mr Linton approve of his sister marrying that man?' I inquired.

'Mr Linton should approve,' returned my lady decisively.

'He might spare himself the trouble,' said Heathcliff, 'I could do as well without his approbation – And as to you, Catherine, I have a mind to speak a few words now, while we are at it – I want you to be aware that I *know* you have treated me infernally – infernally! Do you hear? And if you flatter yourself that I don't perceive it, you are a fool – and if you think I can be consoled by sweet words you are an idiot – and if you fancy I'll suffer unrevenged, I'll convince you of the contrary, in a very little while! Meantime, thank you for telling me your sister-in-law's secret – I swear I'll make the most of it, and stand you aside!'

'What new phase of his character is this?' exclaimed Mrs Linton, in amaze-

ment. 'I've treated you infernally – and you'll take revenge! How will you take it, ungrateful brute? How have I treated you infernally?'

'I seek no revenge on you,' replied Heathcliff less vehemently. 'That's not the plan – The tyrant grinds down his slaves – and they don't turn against him, they crush those beneath them. You are welcome to torture me to death for your amusement, only, allow me to amuse myself a little in the same style – And refrain from insult as much as you are able. Having levelled my palace, don't erect a hovel and complacently admire your own charity in giving me that for a home. If I imagined you really wished me to marry Isabella, I'd cut my throat!'

'Oh, the evil is that I am *not* jealous, is it?' cried Catherine. 'Well, I won't repeat my offer of a wife – It is as bad as offering Satan a lost soul – Your bliss lies, like his, in inflicting misery – You prove it – Edgar is restored from the ill-temper he gave way to at your coming; I begin to be secure and tranquil; and you, restless to know us at peace, appear resolved on exciting a quarrel – quarrel with Edgar if you please, Heathcliff, and deceive his sister; you'll hit on exactly the most efficient method of revenging yourself on me.'

The conversation ceased. Mrs Linton sat down by the fire, flushed and gloomy. The spirit which served her was growing intractable: she could neither lay nor control it. He stood on the hearth, with folded arms, brooding on his evil thoughts; and in this position I left them, to seek the master, who was wondering what kept Catherine below so long.

'Ellen,' said he, when I entered, 'have you seen your mistress?'

'Yes, she's in the kitchen, sir,' I answered. 'She's sadly put out by Mr Heathcliff's behaviour; and, indeed, I do think it's time to arrange his visits on another footing. There's harm in being too soft, and now it's come to this –' And I related the scene in the court, and, as near as I dared, the whole subsequent dispute. I fancied it could not be very prejudicial to Mrs Linton, unless she made it so, afterwards, by assuming the defensive for her guest.

Edgar Linton had difficulty in hearing me to the close. His first words revealed that he did not clear his wife of blame.

'This is insufferable!' he exclaimed. 'It is disgraceful that she should own him for a friend, and force his company on me! Call me two men out of the hall, Ellen. Catherine shall linger no longer to argue with the low ruffian – I have humoured her enough.'

He descended, and bidding the servants wait in the passage, went, followed by me, to the kitchen. Its occupants had recommenced their angry discussion; Mrs Linton, at least, was scolding with renewed vigour; Heathcliff had moved to the window, and hung his head, somewhat cowed by her violent rating apparently.

He saw the master first, and made a hasty motion that she should be silent, which she obeyed, abruptly, on discovering the reason of his intimation.

'How is this?' said Linton, addressing her; 'what notion of propriety must you have to remain here, after the language which has been held to you by that blackguard? I suppose, because it is his ordinary talk, you think nothing of it – you are habituated to his baseness, and, perhaps, imagine I can get used to it too!'

'Have you been listening at the door, Edgar?' asked the mistress, in a tone particularly calculated to provoke her husband, implying both carelessness and contempt of his irritation.

# Wuthering Heights

Heathcliff, who had raised his eyes at the former speech, gave a sneering laugh at the latter, on purpose, it seemed, to draw Mr Linton's attention to him.

He succeeded; but Edgar did not mean to entertain him with any high flights of passion.

'I have been so far forbearing with you, sir,' he said, quietly; 'not that I was ignorant of your miserable, degraded character, but I felt you were only partly responsible for that; and Catherine wishing to keep up your acquaintance, I acquiesced – foolishly. Your presence is a moral poison that would contaminate the most virtuous – for that cause, and to prevent worse consequences, I shall deny you, hereafter, admission into this house, and give notice, now, that I require your instant departure. Three minutes' delay will render it involuntary and ignominious.'

Heathcliff measured the height and breadth of the speaker with an eye full of derision.

'Cathy, this lamb of yours threatens like a bull!' he said. 'It is in danger of splitting its skull against my knuckles. By God, Mr Linton, I'm mortally sorry that you are not worth knocking down!'

My master glanced towards the passage, and signed me to fetch the men – he had no intention of hazarding a personal encounter.

I obeyed the hint; but Mrs Linton, suspecting something, followed, and when I attempted to call them, she pulled me back, slammed the door to, and locked it.

'Fair means!' she said in answer to her husband's look of angry surprise. 'If you have not the courage to attack him, make an apology, or allow yourself to be beaten. It will correct you of feigning more valour than you possess. No, I'll swallow the key before you shall get it! I'm delightfully rewarded for my kindness to each! After constant indulgence of one's weak nature, and the other's bad one, I earn, for thanks, two samples of blind ingratitude, stupid to absudity! Edgar, I was defending you and yours; and I wish Heathcliff may flog you sick, for daring to think an evil thought of me!'

It did not need the medium of a flogging to produce that effect on the master. He tried to wrest the key from Catherine's grasp; and for safety she flung it into the hottest part of the fire; whereupon Mr Edgar was taken with a nervous trembling, and his countenance grew deadly pale. For his life he could not avert that access of emotion – mingled anguish and humiliation overcame him completely. He leant on the back of a chair, and covered his face.

'Oh! Heavens! In old days this would win you knighthood!' exclaimed Mrs Linton. 'We are vanquished! we are vanquished! Heathcliff would as soon lift a finger at you as the king would march his army against a colony of mice. Cheer up, you sha'n't be hurt! Your type is not a lamb, it's a sucking leveret.'

'I wish you joy of the milk-blooded coward, Cathy!' said her friend. 'I compliment you on your taste: and that is the slavering, shivering thing you preferred to me! I would not strike him with my fist, but I'd kick him with my foot, and experience considerable satisfaction. Is he weeping, or is he going to faint for fear?'

The fellow approached and gave the chair on which Linton rested a push. He'd better have kept his distance: my master quickly sprang erect, and struck him full on the throat a blow that would have levelled a slighter man.

# Wuthering Heights

It took his breath for a minute; and, while he choked, Mr Linton walked out by the back door into the yard, and from thence, to the front entrance.

'There! you've done with coming here,' cried Catherine. 'Get away, now – he'll return with a brace of pistols, and half a dozen assistants. If he did overhear us, of course, he'd never forgive you. You've played me an ill turn, Heathcliff! But, go – make haste! I'd rather see Edgar at bay than you.'

'Do you suppose I'm going with that blow burning in my gullet?' he thundered. 'By hell, no! I'll crush his ribs in like a rotten hazel-nut, before I cross the threshold! If I don't floor him now, I shall murder him some time, so, as you value his existence, let me get at him!'

'He is not coming,' I interposed, framing a bit of a lie. 'There's the coachman, and the two gardeners; you'll surely not wait to be thrust into the road by them! Each has a bludgeon, and master will, very likely, be watching from the parlour windows to see that they fulfil his orders.'

The gardeners and coachman *were* there; but Linton was with them. They had already entered the court. Heathcliff, on second thoughts, resolved to avoid a struggle against three underlings; he seized the poker, smashed the lock from the inner door, and made his escape as they tramped in.

Mrs Linton, who was very much excited, bid me accompany her upstairs. She did not know my share in contributing to the disturbance, and I was anxious to keep her in ignorance.

'I'm nearly distracted, Nelly!' she exclaimed, throwing herself on the sofa. 'A thousand smiths' hammers are beating in my head! Tell Isabella to shun me – this uproar is owing to her; and should she or any one else aggravate my anger at present, I shall get wild. And, Nelly, say to Edgar, if you see him again to-night, that I'm in danger of being seriously ill – I wish it may prove true. He has startled and distressed me shockingly! I want to frighten him. Besides, he might come and begin a string of abuse, or complainings; I'm certain I should recriminate, and God knows where we should end! Will you do so, my good Nelly? You are aware that I am no way blameable in this matter. What possessed him to turn listener? Heathcliff's talk was outrageous, after you left us; but I could soon have diverted him from Isabella, and the rest meant nothing. Now, all is dashed wrong by the fool's-craving to hear evil of self that haunts some people like a demon! Had Edgar never gathered our conversation, he would never have been the worse for it. Really, when he opened on me in that unreasonable tone of displeasure, after I had scolded Heathcliff till I was hoarse for *him*; I did not care, hardly, what they did to each other, especially as I felt that, however the scene closed, we should all be driven asunder for nobody knows how long! Well, if I cannot keep Heathcliff for my friend – if Edgar will be mean and jealous, I'll try to break their hearts by breaking my own. That will be a prompt way of finishing all, when I am pushed to extremity! But it's a deed to be reserved for a forlorn hope – I'd not take Linton by surprise with it. To this point he has been discreet in dreading to provoke me; you must represent the peril of quitting that policy; and remind him of my passionate temper verging, when kindled, on frenzy. I wish you could dismiss that apathy out of your countenance, and look rather more anxious about me!'

The stolidity with which I received these instructions was, no doubt, rather exasperating; for they were delivered in perfect sincerity, but I believed a person who could plan the turning of her fits of passion to account, beforehand, might,

by exerting her will, manage to control herself tolerably even while under their influence; and I did not wish to 'frighten' her husband, as she said, and multiply his annoyances for the purpose of serving her selfishness.

Therefore I said nothing when I met the master coming towards the parlour; but I took the liberty of turning back to listen whether they would resume their quarrel together.

He began to speak first.

'Remain where you are, Catherine,' he said, without any anger in his voice, but with much sorrowful despondency. 'I shall not stay. I am neither come to wrangle, nor be reconciled; but I wish just to learn whether, after this evening's events, you intend to continue your intimacy with –'

'Oh, for mercy's sake,' interrupted the mistress, stamping her foot, 'for mercy's sake, let us hear no more of it now! Your cold blood cannot be worked into a fever – your veins are full of ice-water – but mine are boiling, and the sight of such chilliness makes them dance.'

'To get rid of me – answer my question,' persevered Mr Linton. 'You *must* answer it; and that violence does not alarm me. I have found that you can be as stoical as any one, when you please. Will you give up Heathcliff hereafter, or will you give up me? It is impossible for you to be *my* friend, and *his* at the same time; and I absolutely *require* to know which you choose.'

'I require to be let alone!' exclaimed Catherine, furiously. 'I demand it! Don't you see I can scarcely stand? Edgar, you – you leave me!'

She rung the bell till it broke with a twang: I entered leisurely. It was enough to try the temper of a saint, such senseless, wicked rages! There she lay dashing her head against the arm of the sofa, and grinding her teeth, so that you might fancy she would crash them to splinters!

Mr Linton stood looking at her in sudden compunction and fear. He told me to fetch some water. She had no breath for speaking.

I brought a glass full; and, as she would not drink, I sprinkled it on her face. In a few seconds she stretched herself out stiff, and turned up her eyes, while her cheeks, at once blanched and livid, assumed the aspect of death.

Linton looked terrified.

'There is nothing in the world the matter,' I whispered. I did not want him to yield, though I could not help being afraid in my heart.

'She has has blood on her lips!' he said, shuddering.

'Never mind!' I answered, tartly. And I told him how she had resolved, previous to his coming on, exhibiting a fit of frenzy.

I incautiously gave the account aloud, and she heard me, for she started up – her hair flying over her shoulders, her eyes flashing, the muscles of her neck and arms standing out preternaturally. I made up my mind for broken bones, at least; but she only glared about her, for an instant, and then rushed from the room.

The master directed me to follow; I did, to her chamber door; she hindered me from going farther by securing it against me.

As she never offered to descend to breakfast next morning, I went to ask whether she would have some carried up.

'No!' she replied peremptorily.

The same question was repeated at dinner, and tea; and again on the morrow after, and received the same answer.

Mr Linton, on his part, spent his time in the library, and did not inquire concerning his wife's occupations. Isabella and he had had an hour's interview, during which he tried to elicit from her some sentiment of proper horror for Heathcliff's advances; but he could make nothing of her evasive replies, and was obliged to close the examination, unsatisfactorily; adding, however, a solemn warning, that if she were so insane as to encourage that worthless suitor, it would dissolve all bonds of relationship between herself and him.

# Chapter 12

hile Miss Linton moped about the park and garden, always silent, and almost always in tears; and her brother shut himself up among books that he never opened; wearying, I guessed, with a continual vague expectation that Catherine, repenting her conduct, would come of her own accord to ask pardon, and seek a reconciliation; and *she* fasted pertinaciously, under the idea, probably, that at every meal, Edgar was ready to choke for her absence, and pride alone held him from running to cast himself at her feet; I went about my household duties, convinced that the Grange had but one sensible soul in its walls, and that lodged in my body.

I wasted no condolences on miss, nor any expostulations on my mistress, nor did I pay attention to the sighs of my master, who yearned to hear his lady's name, since he might not hear her voice.

I determined they should come about as they pleased for me; and though it was a tiresomely slow process, I began to rejoice at length in a faint dawn of its progress, as I thought at first.

Mrs Linton, on the third day, unbarred her door; and having finished the water in her pitcher and decanter, desired a renewed supply, and a basin of gruel, for she believed she was dying. That I set down as a speech meant for Edgar's ears; I believed no such thing, so I kept it to myself, and brought her some tea and dry toast.

She eat and drank eagerly; and sank back on her pillow again, clenching her hands and groaning.

'Oh, I will die,' she exclaimed, 'since no one cares anything about me. I wish I had not taken that.'

Then a good while after I hear her murmur,

'No, I'll not die – he'd be glad – he does not love me at all – he would never miss me!'

'Did you want anything, ma'am?' I inquired, still preserving my external composure, in spite of her ghastly countenance, and strange exaggerated manner.

'What is that pathetic being doing?' she demanded, pushing the thick entangled locks from her wasted face. 'Has he fallen into a lethargy, or is he dead?'

# Wuthering Heights

'Neither,' replied I; 'if you mean Mr Linton. He's tolerably well, I think, though his studies occupy him rather more than they ought; he is continually among his books, since he has no other society.'

I should not have spoken so, if I had known her true condition, but I could not get rid of the notion that she acted a part of her disorder.

'Among his books!' she cried confounded. 'And I dying! I on the brink of the grave! My God! does he know how I'm altered?' continued she, staring at her reflection in a mirror hanging against the opposite wall. 'Is that Catherine Linton? He imagines me in a pet – in play, perhaps. Cannot you inform him that it is frightful earnest? Nelly, if it be not too late, as soon as I learn how he feels, I'll choose between these two – either to starve at once, that would be no punishment unless he had a heart – or to recover and leave the country. Are you speaking the truth about him now? Take care. Is he actually so utterly indifferent for my life?'

'Why, ma'am,' I answered, 'the master has no idea of your being deranged; and, of course, he does not fear that you will let yourself die of hunger.'

'You think not? Cannot you tell him I will?' she returned. 'Persuade him – speak of your own mind – say you are certain I will!'

'No, you forget, Mrs Linton,' I suggested, 'that you have eaten some food with a relish this evening, and to-morrow, you will perceive its good effects.'

'If I were only sure it would kill him,' she interrupted, 'I'd kill myself directly! These three awful nights, I've never closed my lids – and oh, I've been tormented! I've been haunted, Nelly! But I begin to fancy you don't like me. How strange! I thought, though everybody hated and despised each other, they could not avoid loving me – and they have all turned to enemies in a few hours. *They* have, I'm positive, the people *here*. How dreary to meet death, surrounded by their cold faces! Isabella, terrified and repelled, afraid to enter the room, it would be so dreadful to watch Catherine go. And Edgar standing solemnly by to see it over; then offering prayers of thanks to God for restoring peace to his house, and going back to his *books!* What in the name of all that feels, has he to do with *books,* when I am dying?'

She could not bear the notion which I had put into her head of Mr Linton's philosophical resignation. Tossing about, she increased her feverish bewilderment to madness, and tore the pillow with her teeth, then raising herself up all burning, desired that I would open the window. We were in the middle of winter, the wind blew strong from the northeast, and I objected.

Both the expressions flitting over her face, and the changes of her mood, began to alarm me terribly; and brought to my recollection her former illness, and the doctor's injunction that she should not be crossed.

A minute previously she was violent; now, supported on one arm, and not noticing my refusal to obey her, she seemed to find childish diversion in pulling the feathers from the rents she had just made, and ranging them on the sheet according to their different species: her mind had strayed to other associations.

'That's a turkey's,' she murmured to herself; 'and this is a wild duck's; and this is a pigeon's. Ah, they put pigeons' feathers in the pillows – no wonder I couldn't die! Let me take care to throw it on the floor when I lie down. And here's a moor-cock's; and this – I should know it among a thousand – it's a lapwing's. Bonny bird; wheeling over our heads in the middle of the moor. It wanted to get to its nest, for the clouds touched the swells, and it felt rain coming.

# Wuthering Heights

This feather was picked up from the heath, the bird was not shot – we saw its nest in the winter, full of little skeletons. Heathcliff set a trap over it, and the old ones dare not come. I made him promise he'd never shoot a lapwing, after that, and he didn't. Yes, here are more! Did he shoot my lapwings, Nelly? Are they red, any of them? Let me look.'

'Give over with that baby-work!' I interrupted, dragging the pillow away, and turning the holes towards the mattress, for she was removing its contents by handfuls. 'Lie down and shut your eyes, you're wandering. There's a mess! The down is flying about like snow!'

I went here and there collecting it.

'I see in you, Nelly,' she continued, dreamily, 'an aged woman – you have grey hair, and bent shoulders. This bed is the fairy cave under Penistone Crag, and you are gathering elf-bolts to hurt our heifers; pretending, while I am near, that they are only locks of wool. That's what you'll come to fifty years hence: I know you are not so now. I'm not wandering, you're mistaken, or else I should believe you really *were* that withered hag, and I should think I *was* under Penistone Crag, and I'm conscious it's night, and there are two candles on the table making the black press shine like jet.'

'The black press? where is that?' I asked. 'You are talking in your sleep!'

'It's against the wall, as it always is,' she replied. 'It *does* appear odd – I see a face in it!'

'There is no press in the room, and never was,' said I, resuming my seat, and looping up the curtain that I might watch her.

'Don't *you* see that face?' she enquired, gazing earnestly at the mirror.

And say what I could, I was incapable of making her comprehend it to be her own; so I rose and covered it with a shawl.

'It's behind there still!' she pursued, anxiously. 'And it stirred. Who is it? I hope it will not come out when you are gone! Oh! Nelly, the room is haunted! I'm afraid of being alone!'

I took her hand in mine, and bid her to be composed, for a succession of shudders convulsed her frame, and she *would* keep straining her gaze towards the glass.

'There's nobody here!' I insisted. 'It was *yourself*, Mrs Linton; you knew it a while since.'

'Myself!' she gasped, 'and the clock is striking twelve! It's true, then, that's dreadful!'

Her fingers clutched the clothes, and gathered them over her eyes. I attempted to steal to the door with an intention of calling her husband; but I was summoned back by a piercing shriek. The shawl had dropped from the frame.

'Why, what *is* the matter?' cried I. 'Who is coward now? Wake up! That is the glass – the mirror, Mrs Linton; and you see yourself in it, and there am I too by your side.'

Trembling and bewildered, she held me fast, but the horror gradually passed from her countenance; its paleness gave place to a glow of shame.

'Oh, dear! I thought I was at home,' she sighed. 'I thought I was lying in my chamber at Wuthering Heights. Because I'm weak, my brain got confused, and I screamed unconsciously. Don't say anything; but stay with me. I dread sleeping, my dreams appal me.'

# Wuthering Heights

'A sound sleep would do you good, ma'am' I answered; 'and I hope this suffering will prevent your trying starving again.'

'Oh, if I were but in my own bed in the old house!' she went on bitterly, wringing her hands. 'And that wind sounding in the firs by the lattice. Do let me feel it – it comes straight down the moor – do let me have one breath!'

To pacify her, I held the casement ajar, a few seconds. A cold blast rushed through, I closed it, and returned to my post.

She lay still now, her face bathed in tears. Exhaustion of body had entirely subdued her spirit; our fiery Catherine was no better than a wailing child!

'How long is it since I shut myself in here?' she asked, suddenly reviving.

'It was Monday evening,' I replied, 'and this is Thursday night, or rather Friday morning, at present.'

'What! of the same week?' she exclaimed. 'Only that brief time?'

'Long enough to live on nothing but cold water, and ill-temper,' observed I.

'Well, it seems a weary number of hours,' she muttered doubtfully, 'it must be more – I remember being in the parlour, after they had quarrelled; and Edgar being cruelly provoking, and me running into this room desperate – As soon as ever I had barred the door, utter blackness overwhelmed me, and I fell on the floor – I couldn't explain to Edgar how certain I felt of having a fit, or going raging mad, if he persisted in teasing me! I had no command of tongue, or brain, and he did not guess my agony, perhaps; it barely left me sense to try to escape from him and his voice – Before I recovered sufficiently to see and hear, it began to be dawn; and Nelly, I'll tell you what I thought, and what has kept recurring and recurring till I feared for my reason – I thought as I lay there, with my head against that table leg, and my eyes dimly discerning the grey square of the window, that I was enclosed in the oak-panelled bed at home; and my heart ached with some great grief which, just waking, I could not recollect – I pondered, and worried myself to discover what it could be; and most strangely, the whole last seven years of my life grew a blank! I did not recall that they had been at all. I was a child; my father was just buried, and my misery arose from the separation that Hindley had ordered between me, and Heathcliff – I was laid alone, for the first time, and, rousing from a dismal doze after a night of weeping – I lifted my hand to push the panels aside, it struck the tabletop! I swept it along the carpet, and then, memory burst in – my late anguish was swallowed in a paroxysm of despair – I cannot say why I felt so wildly wretched – it must have been temporary derangement for there is scarcely cause – But, supposing at twelve years old, I had been wrenched from the Heights, and every early association and my all in all as Heathcliff was at that time, and then converted, at a stroke, into Mrs Linton, the lady of Thrushcross Grange, and the wife of a stranger; an exile, and outcast, thenceforth, from what had been my world – You may fancy a glimpse of the abyss where I grovelled! Shake your head as you will Nelly, *you* have helped to unsettle me! You should have spoken to Edgar, indeed you should, and compelled him to leave me quiet! Oh, I'm burning! I wish I were out of doors – I wish I were a girl again, half savage and hardy, and free ... and laughing at injuries, not maddening under them! Why am I so changed? why does my blood rush into a hell of tumult at a few words? I'm sure I should be myself were I once among the heather on those hills ... Open the window again wide, fasten it open! Quick, why don't you move?'

# Wuthering Heights

'Because I won't give you your death of cold,' I answered.

'You won't give me a chance of life, you mean,' she said, sullenly. 'However, I'm not helpless yet, I'll open it myself.'

And sliding from the bed before I could hinder her, she crossed the room, walking very uncertainly, threw it back, and bent out, careless of the frosty air that cut about her shoulders as keen as a knife.

I entreated, and finally attempted to force her to retire. But I soon found her delirious strength much surpassed mine; (she *was* delirious, I became convinced by her subsequent actions and ravings).

There was no moon, and everything beneath lay in misty darkness; not a light gleamed from any house, far or near; all had been extinguished long ago; and those at Wuthering Heights were never visible . . . still she asserted she caught their shining.

'Look!' she cried eagerly, 'that's my room, with the candle in it, and the trees swaying before it . . . and the other candle is in Joseph's garret . . . Joseph sits up late, doesn't he? He's waiting till I come home that he may lock the gate. Well, he'll wait a while yet. It's a rough journey, and a sad heart to travel it; and we must pass by Gimmerton Kirk, to go that journey! We've braved its ghosts often together, and dared each other to stand among the graves and ask them to come . . . But Heathcliff, if I dare you now, will you venture? If you do, I'll keep you. I'll not lie there by myself: they may bury me twelve feet deep, and throw the church down over me; but I won't rest till you are with me . . . I never will!'

She paused, and resumed with a strange smile. 'He's considering . . . he'd rather I'd come to him! Find a way, then! not through that Kirkyard . . . You are slow! Be content, you always followed me!'

Perceiving it vain to argue against her insanity, I was planning how I could reach something to wrap about her, without quitting my hold of herself, for I could not trust her alone by the gaping lattice, when, to my consternation, I heard the rattle of the door-handle, and Mr Linton entered. He had only then come from the library; and, in passing through the lobby, had noticed our talking and been attracted by curiosity, or fear, to examine what it signified, at that late hour.

'Oh, sir!' I cried, checking the exclamation risen to his lips at the sight which met him, and the bleak atmosphere of the chamber.

'My poor Mistress is ill, and she quite masters me; I cannot manage her at all; pray, come and persuade her to go to bed. Forget your anger, for she's hard to guide any way but her own.'

'Catherine ill?' he said, hastening to us. 'Shut the window, Ellen! Catherine! why . . .'

He was silent; the haggardness of Mrs Linton's appearance smote him speechless, and he could only glance from her to me in horrified astonishment.

'She's been fretting here,' I continued, 'and eating scarcely anything, and never complaining, she would admit none of us till this evening, and so we couldn't inform you of her state, as we were not aware of it ourselves, but it is nothing.'

I felt I uttered my explanations awkwardly; the master frowned. 'It is nothing, is it, Ellen Dean?' he said sternly. 'You shall account more clearly for keeping

me ignorant of this!' And he took his wife in his arms, and looked at her with anguish.

At first, she gave him no glance of recognition ... he was invisible to her abstracted gaze. The delirium was not fixed, however; having weaned her eyes from contemplating the outer darkness, by degrees, she centred her attention on him, and discovered who it was that held her.

'Ah! you are come, are you, Edgar Linton?' she said, with angry animation ... 'You are one of those things that are ever found when least wanted, and when you are wanted, never! I suppose we shall have plenty of lamentations, now. ... I see we shall ... but they can't keep me from my narrow home out yonder – My resting-place where I'm bound before Spring is over! There it is, not among the Lintons, mind, under the chapel-roof; but in the open air with a headstone, and you may please yourself, whether you go to them, or come to me!'

'Catherine, what have you done?' commenced the master. 'Am I nothing to you, any more? Do you love that wretch, Heath –'

'Hush!' cried Mrs Linton. 'Hush, this moment! You mention that name and I will end the matter instantly, by a spring from the window! What you touch at present, you may have; but my soul will be on that hill-top before you lay hands on me again. I don't want you, Edgar; I'm past wanting you ... Return to your books ... I'm glad you possess a consolation, for all you had in me is gone.'

'Her mind wanders, sir,' I interposed. 'She has been talking nonsense the whole evening; but let her have quiet and proper attendance, and she'll rally ... Hereafter, we must be cautious how we vex her.'

'I desire no further advice from you,' answered Mr Linton. 'You knew your mistress's nature, and you encouraged me to harass her. And not to give me one hint of how she has been these three days! It was heartless! months of sickness could not cause such a change!'

I began to defend myself, thinking it too bad to be blamed for another's wicked waywardness!

'I knew Mrs Linton's nature to be headstrong and domineering,' cried I; 'but I didn't know that you wished to foster her fierce temper! I didn't know that, to humour her, I should wink at Mr Heathcliff. I performed the duty of a faithful servant in telling you, and I have got a faithful servant's wages! Well, it will teach me to be careful next time. Next time you may gather intelligence for yourself!'

'The next time you bring a tale to me, you shall quit my service, Ellen Dean,' he replied.

'You'd rather hear nothing about it, I suppose, then, Mr Linton?' said I. 'Heathcliff has your permission to come a-courting to Miss, and to drop in at every opportunity your absence offers, on purpose to poison the mistress against you?'

Confused as Catherine was, her wits were alert at applying our conversation.

'Ah! Nelly has played traitor,' she exclaimed passionately. 'Nelly is my hidden enemy – you witch! So you do seek elf-bolts to hurt us! Let me go, and I'll make her rue! I'll make her howl a recantation!'

A maniac's fury kindled under her brows; she struggled desperately to disengage herself from Linton's arms. I felt no inclination to tarry the event;

and, resolving to seek medical aid on my own responsibility, I quitted the chamber.

In passing the garden to reach the road, at a place where a bridle hook is driven into the wall, I saw something white moved irregularly, evidently by another agent than the wind. Notwithstanding my hurry, I staid to examine it, lest ever after I should have the conviction impressed on my imagination that it was a creature of the other world.

My surprise and perplexity were great to discover, by touch more than vision, Miss Isabella's springer, Fanny, suspended to a handkerchief, and nearly at its last gasp.

I quickly released the animal, and lifted it into the garden. I had seen it follow its mistress upstairs, when she went to bed, and wondered much how it could have got out there, and what mischievous person had treated it so.

While untying the knot round the hook, it seemed to me that I repeatedly caught the beat of horses' feet galloping at some distance; but there were such a number of things to occupy my reflections that I hardly gave the circumstance a thought, though it was a strange sound, in that place, at two o'clock in the morning.

Mr Kenneth was fortunately just issuing from his house to see a patient in the village as I came up the street; and my account of Catherine Linton's malady induced him to accompany me back immediately.

He was a plain rough man; and he made no scruple to speak his doubts of her surviving this second attack, unless she were more submissive to his directions than she had shown herself before.

'Nelly Dean,' said he, 'I can't help fancying there's an extra cause for this. What has there been to do at the Grange? We've odd reports up here. A stout, hearty lass like Catherine does not fall ill for a trifle; and that sort of people should not either. It's hard work bringing them through fevers, and such things. How did it begin?'

'The master will inform you,' I answered; 'but you are acquainted with the Earnshaw's violent dispositions, and Mrs Linton caps them all. I may say this; it commenced in a quarrel. She was struck during a tempest of passion with a kind of fit. That's her account, at least; for she flew off in the height of it, and locked herself up. Afterwards, she refused to eat, and now she alternately raves, and remains in a half-dream, knowing those about her, but having her mind filled with all sorts of strange ideas and illusions.'

'Mr Linton will be sorry?' observed Kenneth interrogatively.

'Sorry? He'll break his heart should anything happen!' I replied. 'Don't alarm him more than necessary.'

'Well, I told him to beware,' said my companion; 'and he must bide the consequences of neglecting my warning! Hasn't he been thick with Mr Heathcliff lately?'

'Heathcliff frequently visits at the Grange,' answered I, 'though more on the strength of the mistress having known him when a boy, than because the master likes his company. At present, he's discharged from the trouble of calling; owing to some presumptuous aspirations after Miss Linton which he manifested. I hardly think he'll be taken in again.

'And does Miss Linton turn a cold shoulder on him?' was the doctor's next question.

# Wuthering Heights

'I'm not in her confidence,' returned I, reluctant to continue the subject.

'No, she's a sly one,' he remarked, shaking his head. 'She keeps her own counsel! But she's a real little fool. I have it on good authority, that, last night (and a pretty night it was!) she and Heathcliff were walking in the plantation at the back of your house, above two hours; and he pressed her not to go in again, but just mount his horse and away with him! My informant said she could only put him off by pledging her word of honour to be prepared on their first meeting after that; when it was to be, he didn't hear, but you urge Mr Linton to look sharp!'

This news filled me with fresh fears; I outstripped Kenneth, and ran most of the way back. The little dog was yelping in the garden yet. I spared a minute to open the gate for it, but instead of going to the house door, it coursed up and down snuffing the grass, and would have escaped to the road, had I not seized and conveyed it in with me.

On ascending to Isabella's room, my suspicions were confirmed; it was empty. Had I been a few hours sooner, Mrs Linton's illness might have arrested her rash step. But what could be done now? There was a bare possibility of overtaking them if pursued instantly. *I* could not pursue them, however; and I dare not rouse the family, and fill the place with confusion; still less unfold the business to my master, absorbed as he was in his present calamity, and having no heart to spare for a second grief!

I saw nothing for it but to hold my tongue, and suffer matters to take their course: and Kenneth being arrived, I went with a badly composed countenance to announce him.

Catherine lay in a troubled sleep; her husband had succeeded in soothing the access of frenzy; he now hung over her pillow, watching every shade, and every change of her painfully expressive features.

The doctor, on examining the case for himself, spoke hopefully to him of its having a favourable termination, if we could only preserve around her perfect and constant tranquillity. To me, he signified the threatening danger was, not so much death, as permanent alienation of intellect.

I did not close my eyes that night, nor did Mr Linton; indeed, we never went to bed: and the servants were all up long before the usual hour, moving through the house with stealthy tread, and exchanging whispers as they encountered each other in their vocations. Every one was active, but Miss Isabella; and they began to remark how sound she slept – her brother, too, asked if she had risen, and seemed impatient for her presence, and hurt that she showed so little anxiety for her sister-in-law.

I trembled lest he should send me to call her; but I was spared the pain of being the first proclaimant of her flight. One of the maids, a thoughtless girl, who had been on an early errand to Gimmerton, came panting upstairs, open-mouthed, and dashed into the chamber, crying,

'Oh, dear, dear! What mun we have next? Master, master, our young lady –'

'Hold your noise!' cried I hastily, enraged at her clamorous manner.

'Speak lower, Mary – What is the matter?' said Mr Linton. 'What ails your young lady?'

'She's gone, she's gone! Yon' Heathcliff's run off wi' her!' gasped the girl.

'That is not true!' exclaimed Linton, rising in agitation. 'It cannot be – how

has the idea entered your head? Ellen Dean, go and seek her – it is incredible – it cannot be.'

As he spoke he took the servant to the door, and, then, repeated his demand to know her reasons for such an assertion.

'Why, I met on the road a lad that fetches milk here,' she stammered, 'and he asked whether we weren't in trouble at the Grange. I thought he meant for missis's sickness, so I answered, yes. Then says he, "They's somebody gone after 'em, I guess?" I stared. He saw I knew naught about it, and he told how a gentleman and lady had stopped to have a horse's shoe fastened at a blacksmith's shop, two miles out of Gimmerton, not very long after midnight! and how the blacksmith's lass had got up to spy who they were: she knew them both directly. And she noticed the man – Heathcliff it was, she felt certain, nob'dy could mistake him, besides – put a sovereign in her father's hand for payment. The lady had a cloak about her face; but having desired a sup of water, while she drank, it fell back, and she saw her very plain – Heathcliff held both bridles as they rode on, and they set their faces from the village, and went as fast as the rough roads would let them. The lass said nothing to her father, but she told it all over Gimmerton this morning.'

I ran and peeped, for form's sake, into Isabella's room, confirming, when I returned, the servant's statement. Mr Linton had resumed his seat by the bed; on my re-entrance, he raised his eyes, read the meaning of my blank aspect, and dropped them without giving an order, or uttering a word.

'Are we to try any measures for overtaking and bringing her back?' I inquired. 'How should we do?'

'She went of her own accord,' answered the master. 'She had a right to go if she pleased – Trouble me no more about her – hereafter she is only my sister in name: not because I disown her, but because she has disowned me.'

And that was all he said on the subject; he did not make a single inquiry further, or mention her in any way, except directing me to send what property she had in the house to her fresh home, wherever it was, when I knew it.

# Chapter 13

For two months the fugitives remained absent; in those two months, Mrs Linton encountered and conquered the worst shock of what was denominated a brain fever. No mother could have nursed an only child more devotedly than Edgar tended her. Day and night, he was watching, and patiently enduring all the annoyances that irritable nerves and a shaken reason could inflict; and, though Kenneth remarked that what he saved from the grave would only recompense his care by forming the source of constant future anxiety, in fact, that his health and strength were being sacrificed to preserve a mere ruin

# Wuthering Heights

of humanity, he knew no limits in gratitude and joy when Catherine's life was declared out of danger; and hour after hour, he would sit beside her, tracing the gradual return to bodily health, and flattering his too sanguine hopes with the illusion that her mind would settle back to its right balance also, and she would soon be entirely her former self.

The first time she left her chamber was at the commencement of the following March. Mr Linton had put on her pillow, in the morning, a handful of golden crocuses; her eye, long stranger to any gleam of pleasure, caught them in waking, and shone delighted as she gathered them eagerly together.

'These are the earliest flowers at the Heights!' she exclaimed. 'They remind me of soft thaw winds, and warm sunshine, and nearly melted snow. Edgar, is there not a south wind, and is not the snow almost gone?'

'The snow is quite gone down here, darling,' replied her husband; 'and I only see two white spots on the whole range of moors – the sky is blue, and the larks are singing, and the becks and brooks are all brim full. Catherine; last spring at this time, I was longing to have you under this roof – now, I wish you were a mile or two up those hills; the air blows so sweetly, I feel that it would cure you.'

'I shall never be there, but once more!' said the invalid; 'and then you'll leave me, and I shall remain, for ever. Next spring you'll long again to have me under this roof, and you'll look back and think you were happy today.'

Linton lavished on her the kindest caresses, and tried to cheer her by the fondest words; but, vaguely regarding the flowers, she let the tears collect on her lashes, and stream down her cheeks unheeding.

We knew she was really better, and, therefore, decided that long confinement to a single place produced much of this despondency, and it might be partially removed by a change of scene.

The master told me to light a fire in the many-weeks deserted parlour, and to set an easy-chair in the sunshine by the window; and then he brought her down, and she was a long while enjoying the genial heat, and, as we expected, revived by the objects round her, which, though familiar, were free from the dreary associations investing her hated sick-chamber. By evening, she seemed greatly exhausted; yet no arguments could persuade her to return to that apartment, and I had to arrange the parlour sofa for her bed, till another room could be prepared.

To obviate the fatigue of mounting and descending the stairs, we fitted up this, where you lie at present, on the same floor with the parlour: and she was soon strong enough to move from one to the other, leaning on Edgar's arm.

Ah, I thought myself, she might recover, so waited on as she was. And there was double cause to desire it, for on her existence depended that of another; we cherished the hope that in a little while, Mr Linton's heart would be gladdened, and his lands secured from a stranger's gripe, by the birth of an heir.

I should mention that Isabella sent to her brother, some six weeks from her departure, a short note, announcing her marriage with Heathcliff. It appeared dry and cold; but at the bottom was dotted in with pencil an obscure apology, and an entreaty for kind remembrance, and reconciliation, if her proceeding had offended him; asserting that she could not help it then, and being done, she had now no power to repeal it.

Linton did not reply to this, I believe; and in a fortnight more, I got a long

letter which I considered odd, coming from the pen of a bride just out of the honeymoon. I'll read it, for I keep it yet. Any relic of the dead is precious, if they were valued living.

DEAR ELLEN, *it begins.*

*I came last night to Wuthering Heights, and heard, for the first time, that Catherine has been, and is yet, very ill. I must not write to her, I suppose, and my brother is either too angry or too distressed to answer what I send him. Still, I must write to somebody, and the only choice left me is you.*

*Inform Edgar that I'd give the world to see his face again – that my heart returned to Thrushcross Grange in twenty-four hours after I left it, and is there at this moment, full of warm feelings for him and Catherine!* I can't follow it through – (those words are underlined) – *they need not expect me, and they may draw what conclusions they please; taking care, however, to lay nothing at the door of my weak will, or deficient affection.*

*The remainder of the letter is for yourself alone. I want to ask you two questions: the first is,*

*How did you contrive to preserve the common sympathies of human nature when you resided here? I cannot recognize any sentiment which those around, share with me.*

*The second question, I have great interest in; it is this –*

*Is Mr Heathcliff a man? If so, is he mad? And if not, is he a devil? I shan't tell my reasons for making this inquiry; but, I beseech you to explain, if you can, what I have married – that is, when you call to see me; and you must call, Ellen, very soon. Don't write, but come, and bring me something from Edgar.*

*Now, you shall hear how I have been received in my new home, as I am led to imagine the Heights will be. It is to amuse myself that I dwell on such subjects as the lack of external comforts; they never occupy my thoughts, except at the moment when I miss them – I should laugh and dance for joy, if I found their absence was the total of my miseries, and the rest was an unnatural dream!*

*The sun set behind the Grange, as we turned on to the moors; by that, I judged it to be six o'clock; and my companion halted half-an-hour, to inspect the park, and the gardens, and, probably, the place itself, as well as he could; so it was dark when we dismounted in the paved yard of the farmhouse, and your old fellow-servant, Joseph, issued out to receive us by the light of a dip candle. He did it with a courtesy that redounded to his credit. His first act was to elevate his torch to a level with my face, squint malignantly, project his under lip, and turn away.*

*Then he took the two horses, and led them into the stables, reappearing for the purpose of locking the outer gate, as if we lived in an ancient castle.*

*Heathcliff stayed to speak to him, and I entered the kitchen – a dingy, untidy hole; I dare say you would not know it, it is so changed since it was in your charge.*

*By the fire stood a ruffianly child, strong in limb, and dirty in garb, with a look of Catherine in his eyes, and about his mouth.*

*'This is Edgar's legal nephew,' I reflected – 'mine in a manner; I must shake hands, and – yes – I must kiss him. It is right to establish a good understanding at the beginning.'*

*I approached, and, attempting to take his chubby fist, said –*

# Wuthering Heights

'How do you do, my dear?'

He replied in a jargon I did not comprehend.

'Shall you and I be friends, Hareton?' was my next essay at conversation.

An oath, and a threat to set Throttler on me if I did not 'frame off' rewarded my perseverance.

'Hey, Throttler, lad!' whispered the little wretch, rousing a half-bred bull-dog from its lair in a corner. 'Now, wilt tuh be ganging?' he asked authoritatively.

Love for my life urged compliance; I stepped over the threshold to wait till the others should enter. Mr Heathcliff was nowhere visible; and Joseph, whom I followed to the stables, and requested to accompany me in, after staring and muttering to himself, screwed up his nose and replied –

'Mim! mim! mim! Did iver Christian body hear owt like it? Minching un' munching! Hah can Aw tell whet ye say?'

'I say, I wish you to come with me into the house!' I cried, thinking him deaf, yet highly disgusted at his rudeness.

'Nor nuh me! Aw getten summut else to do,' he answered, and continuing his work, moving his lantern jaws meanwhile, and surveying my dress and countenance (the former a great deal too fine, but the latter, I'm sure, as sad as he could desire) with sovereign contempt.

I walked round the yard, and through a wicket, to another door, at which I took the liberty of knocking, in hopes some more civil servant might shew himself.

After a short suspense, it was opened by a tall, gaunt man, without neckerchief, and otherwise extremely slovenly; his features were lost in masses of shaggy hair that hung on his shoulders; and his eyes, too, were like a ghostly Catherine's with all their beauty annihilated.

'What's your business here?' he demanded, grimly. 'Who are you?'

'My name was Isabella Linton,' I replied. 'You've seen me before, sir. I'm lately married to Mr Heathcliff; and he has brought me here – I suppose by your permission.'

'Is he come back, then?' asked the hermit, glaring like a hungry wolf.

'Yes – we came just now,' I said; 'but he left me by the kitchen door; and when I would have gone in, your little boy played sentinel over the place, and frightened me off by the help of a bull-dog.'

'It's well the hellish villain has kept his word!' growled my future host, searching the darkness beyond me in expectation of discovering Heathcliff, and then he indulged in a soliloquy of execrations, and threats of what he would have done had the 'fiend' deceived him.

I repented having tried this second entrance; and was almost inclined to slip away before he finished cursing, but ere I could execute that intention, he ordered me in, and shut and refastened the door.

There was a great fire, and that was all the light in the huge apartment, whose floor had grown a uniform grey; and the once brilliant pewter dishes, which used to attract my gaze when I was a girl, partook of a similar obscurity, created by tarnish and dust.

I inquired whether I might call the maid, and be conducted to a bed-room? Mr Earnshaw vouchsafed no answer. He walked up and down, with his hands in his pockets, apparently quite forgetting my presence; and his abstraction was evidently so deep, and his whole aspect so misanthropical, that I shrank from disturbing him again.

# Wuthering Heights

*You'll not be surprised, Ellen, at my feeling particularly cheerless, seated in worse than solitude on that inhospitable hearth, and remembering that four miles distant lay my delightful home, containing the only people I loved on earth: and there might as well be the Atlantic to part us, instead of those four miles, I could not overpass them!*

*I questioned with myself – where must I turn for comfort? and – mind you don't tell Edgar, or Catherine – above every sorrow beside, this rose pre-eminent – despair at finding nobody who could or would be my ally against Heathcliff!*

*I had sought shelter at Wuthering Heights, almost gladly, because I was secured by that arrangement from living alone with him; but he knew the people we were coming amongst, and he did not fear their intermeddling.*

*I sat and thought a doleful time; the clock struck eight, and nine, and still my companion paced to and fro, his head bent on his breast, and perfectly silent, unless a groan, or a bitter ejaculation forced itself out at intervals.*

*I listened to detect a woman's voice in the house, and filled the interim with wild regrets, and dismal anticipations, which, at last, spoke audibly in irrepressible sighing and weeping.*

*I was not aware how openly I grieved, till Earnshaw halted opposite, in his measured walk, and gave me a stare of newly awakened surprise. Taking advantage of his recovered attention, I exclaimed –*

*'I'm tired with my journey, and I want to go to bed! Where is the maidservant? Direct me to her, as she won't come to me!'*

*'We have none,' he answered; 'you must wait on yourself!'*

*'Where must I sleep, then?' I sobbed – I was beyond regarding self-respect, weighed down by fatigue and wretchedness.*

*'Joseph will show you Heathcliff's chamber,' said he; 'open that door – he's in there.'*

*I was going to obey, but he suddenly arrested me, and added in the strangest tone –*

*'Be so good as to turn your lock, and draw your bolt – don't omit it!'*

*'Well!' I said. 'But why, Mr Earnshaw?' I did not relish the notion of deliberately fastening myself in with Heathcliff.*

*'Look here!' he replied, pulling from his waistcoat a curiously constructed pistol, having a double-edged spring knife attached to the barrel. 'That's a great tempter to a desperate man, is it not? I cannot resist going up with this every night, and trying his door. If once I find it open, he's done for! I do it invariably, even though the minute before I have been recalling a hundred reasons that should make me refrain – it is some devil that urges me to thwart my own schemes by killing him – you fight against that devil, for love, as long as you may; when the time comes, not all the angels in heaven shall save him!'*

*I surveyed the weapon inquisitively; – a hideous notion struck me. How powerful I should be possessing such an instrument! I took it from his hand, and touched the blade. He looked astonished at the expression my face assumed during a brief second. It was not horror, it was covetousness. He snatched the pistol back, jealously; shut the knife, and returned it to its concealment.*

*'I don't care if you tell him,' said he. 'Put him on his guard, and watch for him. You know the terms we are on, I see; his danger does not shock you.'*

*'What has Heathcliff done to you?' I asked. 'In what has he wronged you, to warrant this appalling hatred? Wouldn't it be wiser to bid him quit the house?'*

# Wuthering Heights

'No!' thundered Earnshaw, 'should he offer to leave me, he's a dead man, persuade him to attempt it, and you are a murderess! Am I to lose all, without a chance of retrieval? Is Hareton to be a beggar? Oh, damnation! I will have it back; and I'll have his gold too; and then his blood; and hell shall have his soul! It will be ten times blacker with that guest than ever it was before!'

You've acquainted me, Ellen, with your old master's habits. He is clearly on the verge of madness – he was so, last night, at least. I shuddered to be near him, and thought on the servant's ill-bred moroseness as comparatively agreeable.

He now recommenced his moody walk, and I raised the latch, and escaped into the kitchen.

Joseph was bending over the fire, peering into a large pan that swung above it; and a wooden bowl of oatmeal stood on the settle close by. The contents of the pan began to boil, and he turned to plunge his hand into the bowl; I conjectured that this preparation was probably for our supper, and, being hungry, I resolved it should be eatable – so, crying out sharply – 'I'll make the porridge!' I removed the vessel out of his reach, and proceeded to take off my hat and riding habit. 'Mr Earnshaw,' I continued, 'directs me to wait on myself – I will – I'm not going to act the lady among you, for fear I should starve.'

'Gooid Lord!' he muttered, sitting down, and stroking his ribbed stockings from the knee to the ankle. 'If they's tuh be fresh ortherings – just when Aw getten used tuh two maisters, if Aw mun hev a mistress set o'er my heead, it's loike time tuh be flitting. Aw never did think tuh say t'day ut Aw mud lave th' owld place – but Aw daht it's nigh at hend!'

This lamentation drew no notice from me; I went briskly to work; sighing to remember a period when it would have been all merry fun; but compelled speedily to drive off the remembrance. It racked me to recall past happiness, and the greater peril there was of conjuring up its apparition, the quicker the thible ran round, and the faster the handfuls of meal fell into the water.

Joseph beheld my style of cookery with growing indignation.

'Thear!' he ejaculated. 'Hareton, thah willn't sup thy porridge tuh neeght; they'll be nowt bud lumps as big as maw nave. Thear, agean! Aw'd fling in bowl un all, if Aw were yah! Thear, pale t' guilp off, un' then yah'll hae done wi't. Bang, bang. It's a marcy t' bothom isn't deaved aht!'

It was rather a rough mess, I own, when poured into the basins; four had been provided, and a gallon pitcher of new milk was brought from the dairy, which Hareton seized and commenced drinking and spilling from the expansive lip.

I expostulated, and desired that he should have his in a mug, affirming that I could not taste the liquid treated so dirtily. The old cynic chose to be vastly offended at this nicety; assuring me, repeatedly, that 'the barn was every bit as gooid' as I, 'and every bit as wollsome,' and wondering how I could fashion to be so conceited; meanwhile, the infant ruffian continued sucking; and glowered up at me defyingly, as he slavered into the jug.

'I shall have my supper in another room,' I said. 'Have you no place you call a parlour?'

'Parlour!' he echoed, sneeringly, 'parlour! Nay, we've noa parlours. If yah dunnut loike wer company, they's maister's; un' if yah dunnut loike maister, they's us.'

'Then I shall go upstairs,' I answered; 'show me a chamber.'

I put my basin on a tray, and went myself to fetch some more milk.

# Wuthering Heights

With great grumblings, the fellow rose, and preceded me in my ascent: we mounted to the garrets; he opening a door, now and then, to look into the apartments we passed.

'Here's a rahm,' he said, at last, flinging back a cranky board on hinges. 'It's weel eneugh tuh ate a few porridge in. They's a pack uh corn i' t' corner, thear, meeterly clane; if yah're feared uh muckying yer grand silk cloes, spread yer hankerchir ut t' top on 't.'

The 'rahm' was a kind of lumber-hole smelling strong of malt and grain, various sacks of which articles were piled around, leaving a wide, bare space in the middle.

'Why, man!' I exclaimed, facing him angrily, 'this is not a place to sleep in. I wish to see my bed-room.'

'Bed-rume!' he repeated, in a tone of mockery. 'Yah's see all t' bed-rumes thear is – yon's mine.'

He pointed into the second garret, only differing from the first in being more naked about the walls, and having a large, low, curtainless bed, with an indigo-coloured quilt, at one end.

'What do I want with yours?' I retorted. 'I suppose Mr Heathcliff does not lodge at the top of the house, does he?'

'Oh, it's Maister Hathecliff's yah're wenting?' cried he, as if making a new discovery. 'Couldn't ye uh said soa, at onst? un then Aw mud uh telled ye, baht all this wark, ut that's just one yah cannut sea – he allas keeps it locked, un' nob'dy iver mells on't but hisseln.'

'You've a nice house, Joseph,' I could not refrain from observing, 'and pleasant inmates; and I think the concentrated essence of all the madness in the world took up its abode in my brain the day I linked my fate with theirs! However, that is not to the present purpose – there are other rooms. For Heaven's sake, be quick, and let me settle somewhere!'

He made no reply to this adjuration, only plodding doggedly down the wooden steps, and halting before an apartment which, from that halt, and the superior quality of its furniture, I conjectured to be the best one.

There was a carpet, a good one; but the pattern was obliterated by dust; a fireplace hung with cut paper dropping to pieces; a handsome oak-bedstead with ample crimson curtains of rather expensive material, and modern make. But they had evidently experienced rough usage; the valances hung in festoons, wrenched from their rings; and the iron rod supporting them was bent in an arc, on one side, causing the drapery to trail upon the floor. The chairs were also damaged, many of them severely; and deep indentations deformed the panels of the walls.

I was endeavouring to gather resolution for entering, and taking possession, when my fool of a guide announced –

'This here is t' maister's.'

My supper by this time was cold, my appetite gone, and my patience exhausted. I insisted on being provided instantly with a place of refuge, and means of repose.

'Whear the divil,' began the religious elder. 'The Lord bless us! The Lord forgie us! Whear the hell, wold ye gang? ye marred, wearisome nowt! Yah seen all bud Hareton's bit uf a cham'er. They's nut another hoile tuh lig dahn in i' th' hahse!'

# Wuthering Heights

*I was so vexed, I flung my tray and its contents on the ground; and then seated myself at the stairs-head, hid my face in my hands, and cried.*

*'Ech! ech!' exclaimed Joseph. 'Weel done, Miss Cathy! weel done, Miss Cathy! Hahsiver, t' maister sall just tum'le o'er them brocken pots; un' then we's hear summut; we's hear hah it's tuh be. Gooid-for-nowt madling! yah desarve pining froo this tuh Churstmas, flingin' t' precious gifts uh God under fooit i' yer flaysome rages! Bud, Aw'm mista'en if yah shew yer sperrit long. Will Hathecliff bide sich bonny ways think ye? Aw nobbut wish he muh cotch ye i' that plisky. Aw nobbut wish he may.'*

*And so he went scolding to his den beneath, taking the candle with him; and I remained in the dark.*

*The period of reflection succeeding this silly action, compelled me to admit the necessity of smothering my pride, and choking my wrath, and bestirring myself to remove its effects.*

*An unexpected aid presently appeared in the shape of Throttler, whom I now recognized as a son of our Old Skulker; it had spent its whelphood at the Grange, and was given by my father to Mr Hindley. I fancy it knew me – it pushed its nose against mine by way of salute, and then hastened to devour the porridge, while I groped from step to step, collecting the shattered earthenware, and drying the splatters of milk from the banisters with my pocket-handkerchief.*

*Our labours were scarcely over when I heard Earnshaw's tread in the passage; my assistant tucked in his tail, and pressed to the wall; I stole into the nearest doorway. The dog's endeavour to avoid him was unsuccessful, as I guessed by a scutter down stairs, and a prolonged, piteous yelping. I had better luck. He passed on, entered his chamber, and shut the door.*

*Directly after Joseph came up with Hareton, to put him to bed. I had found shelter in Hareton's room, and the old man, on seeing me, said –*

*'They's rahm fur boath yah, un' yer pride, nah, Aw sud think i' th' hahse. It's empty; yah muh hev it all tuh yerseln, un Him as allas maks a third, i' sich ill company!'*

*Gladly did I take advantage of this intimation; and the minute I flung myself into a chair, by the fire, I nodded, and slept.*

*My slumber was deep, and sweet, though over far too soon. Mr Heathcliff awoke me; he had just come in, and demanded, in his loving manner, what I was doing there.*

*I told him the cause of my staying up so late – that he had the key of our room in his pocket.*

*The adjective our gave mortal offence. He swore it was not, nor ever should be mine; and he'd – but I'll not repeat his language, nor describe his habitual conduct; he is ingenious and unresting in seeking to gain my abhorrence! I sometimes wonder at him with an intensity that deadens my fear; yet, I assure you, a tiger, or a venomous serpent could not rouse terror in me equal to that which he wakens. He told me of Catherine's illness, and accused my brother of causing it, promising that I should be Edgar's proxy in suffering, till he could get a hold of him.*

*I do hate him – I am wretched – I have been a fool! Beware of uttering one breath of this to any one at the Grange. I shall expect you every day – don't disappoint me!*

ISABELLA

103

# Chapter 14

As soon as I had perused this epistle, I went to the master, and informed him that his sister had arrived at the Heights, and sent me a letter expressing her sorrow for Mrs Linton's situation, and her ardent desire to see him; with a wish that he would transmit to her, as early as possible, some token of forgiveness by me.

'Forgiveness!' said Linton. 'I have nothing to forgive her, Ellen – you may call at Wuthering Heights this afternoon, if you like, and say that I am not *angry*, but I'm *sorry* to have lost her: especially as I can never think she'll be happy. It is out of the question my going to see her, however; we are eternally divided; and should she really wish to oblige me, let her persuade the villain she has married to leave the country.'

'And you won't write her a little note, sir?' I asked imploringly.

'No,' he answered. 'It is needless. My communication with Heathcliff's family shall be as sparing as his with mine. It shall not exist!'

Mr Edgar's coldness depressed me exceedingly; and all the way from the Grange, I puzzled my brains how to put more heart into what he said, when I repeated it; and how to soften his refusal of even a few lines to console Isabella.

I dare say she had been on the watch for me since morning: I saw her looking through the lattice, as I came up the garden causeway, and I nodded to her; but she drew back, as if afraid of being observed.

I entered without knocking. There never was such a dreary, dismal scene as the formerly cheerful house presented! I must confess that, if I had been in the young lady's place, I would, at least, have swept the hearth, and wiped the tables with a duster. But she already partook of the pervading spirit of neglect which encompassed her. Her pretty face was wan and listless; her hair uncurled, some locks hanging lankly down, and some carelessly twisted round her head. Probably she had not touched her dress since yester evening.

Hindley was not there. Mr Heathcliff sat at a table, turning over some papers in his pocket-book; but he rose when I appeared, asked me how I did, quite friendly, and offered me a chair.

He was the only thing there that seemed decent, and I thought he never looked better. So much had circumstances altered their positions, that he would certainly have struck a stranger as a born and bred gentleman, and his wife as a thorough little slattern!

She came forward eagerly to greet me; and held out one hand to take the expected letter.

I shook my head. She wouldn't understand the hint, but followed me to a

sideboard, where I went to lay my bonnet, and importuned me in a whisper to give her directly what I had brought.

Heathcliff guessed the meaning of her manoeuvres, and said –

'If you have got anything for Isabella, as no doubt you have, Nelly, give it to her. You needn't make a secret of it; we have no secrets between us.'

'Oh, I have nothing,' I replied, thinking it best to speak the truth at once. 'My master bid me tell his sister that she must not expect either a letter or a visit from him at present. He sends his love, ma'am, and his wishes for your happiness, and his pardon for the grief you have occasioned; but he thinks that after this time, his household, and the household here, should drop intercommunication, as nothing good could come of keeping it up.'

Mrs Heathcliff's lip quivered slightly, and she returned to her seat in the window. Her husband took his stand on the hearthstone, near me, and began to put questions concerning Catherine.

I told him as much as I thought proper of her illness, and he extorted from me, by cross-examination, most of the facts connected with its origin.

I blamed her, as she deserved, for bringing it all on herself; and ended by hoping that he would follow Mr Linton's example, and avoid future interference with his family, for good or evil.

'Mrs Linton is now just recovering,' I said, 'she'll never be like she was, but her life is spared, and if you really have a regard for her, you'll shun crossing her way again. Nay, you'll move out of this country entirely; and that you may not regret it, I'll inform you Catherine Linton is as different now, from your old friend Catherine Earnshaw, as that young lady is different from me! Her appearance is changed greatly, her character much more so; and the person, who is compelled, of necessity, to be her companion, will only sustain his affection hereafter, by the remembrance of what she once was, by common humanity, and a sense of duty!'

'That is quite possible,' remarked Heathcliff, forcing himself to seem calm, 'quite possible that your master should have nothing but common humanity and a sense of duty to fall back upon. But do you imagine that I shall leave Catherine to his *duty* and *humanity*? and can you compare my feelings respecting Catherine, to his? Before you leave this house, I must exact a promise from you, that you'll get me an interview with her – consent, or refuse, I *will* see her! What do you say?'

'I say, Mr Heathcliff,' I replied, 'you must not – you never shall, through my means. Another encounter between you and the master would kill her altogether!'

'With your aid, that may be avoided;' he continued, 'and should there be danger of such an event – should he be the cause of adding a single trouble more to her existence – why, I think, I shall be justified in going to extremes! I wish you had sincerity enough to tell me whether Catherine would suffer greatly from his loss. The fear that she would restrains me: and there you see the distinction between our feelings – Had he been in my place, and I in his, though I hated him with a hatred that turned my life to gall, I never would have raised a hand against him. You may look incredulous, if you please! I never would have banished him from her society, as long as she desired his. The moment her regard ceased, I would have torn his heart out, and drunk his blood! But, till then – if you don't believe me, you don't know me – till then, I would have died by inches before I touched a single hair of his head!'

# Wuthering Heights

'And yet,' I interrupted, 'you have no scruples in completely ruining all hopes of her perfect restoration, by thrusting yourself into her remembrance, now, when she has nearly forgotten you, and involving her in a new tumult of discord and distress.'

'You suppose she has nearly forgotten me?' he said, 'Oh, Nelly! you know she has not! You know as well as I do, that for every thought she spends on Linton, she spends a thousand on me! At a most miserable period of my life, I had a notion of the kind, it haunted me on my return to the neighbourhood, last summer, but only her own assurance could make me admit the horrible idea again. And then, Linton would be nothing, nor Hindley, nor all the dreams that ever I dreamt. Two words would comprehend my future – *death* and *hell* – existence, after losing her, would be hell.

'Yet I was a fool to fancy for a moment that she valued Edgar Linton's attachment more than mine – If he loved with all the powers of his puny being, he couldn't love as much in eighty years, as I could in a day. And Catherine has a heart as deep as I have; the sea could be as readily contained in that horse-trough, as her whole affection be monopolized by him – Tush! He is scarcely a degree dearer to her than her dog, or her horse – It is not in him to be loved like me, how can she love in him what he has not?'

'Catherine and Edgar are as fond of each other as any two people can be!' cried Isabella with sudden vivacity. 'No one has a right to talk in that manner, and I won't hear my brother depreciated in silence!'

'Your brother is wondrous fond of you too, isn't he?' observed Heathcliff scornfully. 'He turns you adrift on the world with surprising alacrity.'

'He is not aware of what I suffer,' she replied. 'I didn't tell him that.'

'You have been telling him something, then – you have written, have you?'

'To say that I was married, I did write – you saw the note.'

'And nothing since?'

'No.'

'My young lady is looking sadly the worse for her change of condition,' I remarked. 'Somebody's love comes short in her case, obviously – whose, I may guess; but, perhaps, I shouldn't say.'

'I should guess it was her own,' said Heathcliff. 'She degenerates into a mere slut! She is tired of trying to please me, uncommonly early – You'd hardly credit it, but the very morrow of our wedding, she was weeping to go home. However, she'll suit this house so much the better for not being over nice, and I'll take care she does not disgrace me by rambling abroad.'

'Well, sir,' returned I, 'I hope you'll consider that Mrs Healthcliff is accustomed to be looked after, and waited on; and that she has been brought up like an only daughter, whom every one was ready to serve – You must let her have a maid to keep things tidy about her, and you must treat her kindly – Whatever be your notion of Mr Edgar, you cannot doubt that she has a capacity for strong attachments, or she wouldn't have abandoned the elegancies, and comforts, and friends of her former home, to fix contentedly, in such a wilderness as this, with you.'

'She abandoned them under a delusion;' he answered; 'picturing in me a hero of romance, and expecting unlimited indulgences from my chivalrous devotion. I can hardly regard her in the light of a rational creature, so obstinately has she persisted in forming a fabulous notion of my character, and acting on the false

impressions she cherished. But, at last, I think she begins to know me – I don't perceive the silly smiles and grimaces that provoked me, at first; and the senseless incapability of discerning that I was in earnest when I gave her my opinion of her infatuation, and herself – It was a marvellous effort of perspicacity to discover that I did not love her. I believed, at one time, no lessons could teach her that! and yet it is poorly learnt; for this morning she announced, as a piece of appalling intelligence, that I had actually succeeded in making her hate me! A positive labour of Hercules, I assure you! If it be achieved, I have cause to return thanks – Can I trust your assertion, Isabella? Are you sure you hate me? If I let you alone for half a day, won't you come sighing and wheedling to me again? I dare say she would rather I had seemed all tenderness before you; it wounds her vanity to have the truth exposed. But I don't care who knows that the passion was wholly on one side, and I never told her a lie about it. She cannot accuse me of showing a bit of deceitful softness. The first thing she saw me do, on coming out of the Grange, was to hang up her little dog, and when she pleaded for it, the first words I uttered were a wish that I had the hanging of every being belonging to her, except one: possibly, she took that exception for herself – But no brutality disgusted her – I suppose she has an innate admiration of it, if only her precious person were secure from injury! Now, was it not the depth of absurdity – of genuine idiocy, for that pitiful, slavish, mean-minded brach to dream that I could love her? Tell your master, Nelly, that I never, in all my life, met with such an abject thing as she is – She even disgraces the name of Linton; and I've sometimes relented, from pure lack of invention, in my experiments on what she could endure, and still creep shamefully cringing back! But tell him, also, to set his fraternal and magisterial heart at ease, that I keep strictly within the limits of the law – I have avoided, up to this period, giving her the slightest right to claim a separation; and what's more, she'd thank nobody for dividing us – if she desired to go, she might – the nuisance of her presence outweighs the gratification to be derived from tormenting her!'

'Mr Heathcliff,' said I, 'this is the talk of a madman, and your wife, most likely, is convinced you are mad; and, for that reason, she has borne with you hitherto: but now that you say she may go, she'll doubtless avail herself of the permission – You are not so bewitched, ma'am, are you, as to remain with him of your own accord?'

'Take care, Ellen!' answered Isabella, her eyes sparking irefully – there was no misdoubting by their expression, the full success of her partner's endeavours to make himself detested. 'Don't put faith in a single word he speaks. He's a lying fiend, a monster, and not a human being! I've been told I might leave him before; and I've made the attempt, but I dare not repeat it! Only, Ellen, promise you'll not mention a syllable of his infamous conversation to my brother or Catherine – whatever he may pretend, he wishes to provoke Edgar to desperation – he says he has married me on purpose to obtain power over him; and he shan't obtain it – I'll die first! I just hope, I pray that he may forget his diabolical prudence, and kill me! The single pleasure I can imagine is to die, or to see him dead!'

'There – that will do for the present!' said Heathcliff. 'If you are called upon in a court of law, you'll remember her language, Nelly! And take a good look at that countenance – she's near the point which would suit me. No, you're not fit to be your own guardian, Isabella, now; and I, being your legal protector,

# Wuthering Heights

must retain you in my custody, however distasteful the obligation may be – Go upstairs; I have something to say to Ellen Dean, in private. That's not the way – upstairs, I tell you! Why, this is the road upstairs, child!'

He seized, and thrust her from the room; and returned muttering,

'I have no pity! I have no pity! The more the worms writhe, the more I yearn to crush out their entrails! It is a moral teething, and I grind with greater energy, in proportion to the increase of pain.'

'Do you understand what the word pity means?' I said, hastening to resume my bonnet. 'Did you ever feel a touch of it in your life?'

'Put that down!' he interrupted, perceiving my intention to depart. 'You are not going yet – Come here now, Nelly – I must either persuade or compel you to aid me in fulfilling my determination to see Catherine, and that without delay – I swear that I meditate no harm; I don't desire to cause any disturbance, or to exasperate or insult Mr Linton; I only wish to hear from herself how she is, and why she has been ill; and to ask, if anything that I could do would be of use to her. Last night, I was in the Grange garden six hours, and I'll return there to-night; and every night I'll haunt the place, and every day, till I find an opportunity of entering. If Edgar Linton meets me, I shall not hesitate to knock him down, and give him enough to insure his quiescence while I stay – If his servants oppose me, I shall threaten them off with these pistols – But wouldn't it be better to prevent my coming in contact with them, or their master? And you could do it so easily! I'd warn you when I came, and then you might let me in unobserved, as soon as she was alone, and watch till I departed – your conscience quite calm, you would be hindering mischief.'

I protested against playing that treacherous part in my employer's house; and besides, I urged the cruelty and selfishness of his destroying Mrs Linton's tranquillity, for his satisfaction.

'The commonest occurrence startles her painfully,' I said. 'She's all nerves, and she couldn't bear the surprise, I'm positive. Don't persist, sir! or else, I shall be obliged to inform my master of your designs, and he'll take measures to secure his house and its inmates from any such unwarrantable intrusions!'

'In that case, I'll take measures to secure you, woman!' exclaimed Heathcliff, 'you shall not leave Wuthering Heights till tomorrow morning. It is a foolish story to assert that Catherine could not bear to see me; and as to surprising her, I don't desire it, you must prepare her – ask her if I may come. You say she never mentions my name, and that I am never mentioned to her. To whom should she mention me if I am a forbidden topic in the house? She thinks you are all spies for her husband – Oh, I've no doubt she's in hell among you! I guess, by her silence, as much as anything, what she feels. You say she is often restless, and anxious-looking – is that a proof of tranquillity? You talk of her mind being unsettled – How the devil could it be otherwise, in her frightful isolation? And that insipid, paltry creature attending her from *duty* and *humanity!* From *pity* and *charity!* He might as well plant an oak in a flower-pot, and expect it to thrive, as imagine he can restore her to vigour in the soil of his shallow cares! Let us settle it at once; will you stay here, and am I to fight my way to Catherine over Linton, and his footmen? Or will you be my friend, as you have been hitherto, and do what I request? Decide! because there is no reason for my lingering another minute, if you persist in your stubborn ill-nature!'

Well, Mr Lockwood, I argued and complained, and flatly refused him fifty times; but in the long run he forced me to an agreement – I engaged to carry a letter from him to my mistress; and, should she consent, I promised to let him have intelligence of Linton's next absence from home, when he might come, and get in as he was able – I wouldn't be there, and my fellow servants should be equally out of the way.

Was it right or wrong? I fear it was wrong, though expedient. I thought I prevented another explosion by my compliance; and I thought, too, it might create a favourable crisis in Catherine's mental illness: and then I remembered Mr Edgar's stern rebuke of my carrying tales; and I tried to smooth away all disquietude on the subject, by affirming, with frequent iteration, that that betrayal of trust, if it merited so harsh an appellation, should be the last.

Notwithstanding, my journey homeward was sadder than my journey thither; and many misgivings I had, ere I could prevail on myself to put the missive into Mrs Linton's hand.

But here is Kenneth – I'll go down, and tell him how much better you are. My history is *dree*, as we say, and will serve to wile away another morning.

Dree, and dreary! I reflected as the good woman descended to receive the doctor; and not exactly of a kind which I should have chosen to amuse me; but never mind! I'll extract wholesome medicines from Mrs Dean's bitter herbs; and firstly, let me beware of the fascination that lurks in Catherine Heathcliff's brilliant eyes. I should be in a curious taking if I surrendered my heart to that young person, and the daughter turned out a second edition of the mother!

# Chapter 15

Another week over – and I am so many days nearer health, and spring! I have now heard all my neighbour's history, at different sittings, as the housekeeper could spare time from more important occupations. I'll continue it in her own words, only a little condensed. She is, on the whole, a very fair narrator, and I don't think I could improve her style.

In the evening, she said, the evening of my visit to the Heights, I knew, as well as if I saw him, that Mr Heathcliff was about the place; and I shunned going out, because I still carried his letter in my pocket, and didn't want to be threatened, or teased any more.

I had made up my mind not to give it till my master went somewhere; as I could not guess how its receipt would affect Catherine. The consequence was, that it did not reach her before the lapse of three days. The fourth was Sunday, and I brought it into her room, after the family were gone to church.

# Wuthering Heights

There was a man servant left to keep the house with me, and we generally made a practice of locking the doors during the hours of service; but on that occasion, the weather was so warm and pleasant that I set them wide open; and to fulfil my engagement, as I knew who would be coming, I told my companion that the mistress wished very much for some oranges, and he must run over to the village and get a few, to be paid for on the morrow. He departed, and I went upstairs.

Mrs Linton sat in a loose, white dress, with a light shawl over her shoulders, in the recess of the open window, as usual. Her thick, long hair had been partly removed at the beginning of her illness; and now she wore it simply combed in its natural tresses over her temples and neck. Her appearance was altered, as I had told Heathcliff, but when she was calm, there seemed unearthly beauty in the change.

The flash of her eyes had been succeeded by a dreamy and melancholy softness: they no longer gave the impression of looking at the objects around here; they appeared always to gaze beyond, and far beyond – you would have said out of this world. Then, the paleness of her face – its haggard aspect having vanished as she recovered flesh – and the peculiar expression arising from her mental state, though painfully suggestive of their causes, added to the touching interest which she awakened; and – invariably to me, I know, and to any person who saw her, I should think – refuted more tangible proofs of convalescence and stamped her as one doomed to decay.

A book lay spread on the sill before her, and the scarcely perceptible wind fluttered its leaves at intervals. I believe Linton had laid it there, for she never endeavoured to divert herself with reading, or occupation of any kind; and he would spend many an hour in trying to entice her attention to some subject which had formerly been her amusement.

She was conscious of his aim, and in her better moods, endured his efforts placidly, only showing their uselessness by now and then suppressing a wearied sigh, and checking him at last, with the saddest of smiles and kisses. At other times, she would turn petulantly away, and hide her face in her hands, or even push him off angrily; and then he took care to let her alone, for he was certain of doing no good.

Gimmerton chapel bells were still ringing; and the full, mellow flow of the beck in the valley came soothingly on the ear. It was a sweet substitute for the yet absent murmur of the summer foliage, which drowned that music about the Grange, when the trees were in leaf. At Wuthering Heights it always sounded on quiet days, following a great thaw or a season of steady rain – and, of Wuthering Heights, Catherine was thinking as she listened; that is, if she thought, or listened, at all; but she had the vague, distant look I mentioned before, which expressed no recognition of material things either by ear or eye.

'There's a letter for you, Mrs Linton,' I said, gently inserting it in one hand that rested on her knee. 'You must read it immediately, because it wants an answer. Shall I break the seal?'

'Yes,' she answered, without altering the direction of her eyes.

I opened it – it was very short.

'Now,' I continued, 'read it.'

She drew away her hand, and let it fall. I replaced it in her lap, and stood

waiting till it should please her to glance down; but that movement was so long delayed that at last I resumed –

'Must I read it, ma'am? It is from Mr Heathcliff.'

There was a start, and a troubled gleam of recollection, and a struggle to arrange her ideas. She lifted the letter, and seemed to peruse it; and when she came to the signature she sighed; yet still I found she had not gathered its import, for upon my desiring to hear her reply, she merely pointed to the name, and gazed at me with mournful and questioning eagerness.

'Well, he wishes to see you,' said I, guessing her need of an interpreter. 'He's in the garden by this time, and impatient to know what answer I shall bring.'

As I spoke, I observed a large dog, lying on the sunny grass beneath, raise its ears, as if about to bark, and then smoothing them back, announce, by a wag of the tail that some one approached whom it did not consider a stranger.

Mrs Linton bent forward, and listened breathlessly. The minute after a step traversed the hall; the open house was too tempting for Heathcliff to resist walking in: most likely he supposed that I was inclined to shirk my promise, and so resolved to trust to his own audacity.

With straining eagerness Catherine gazed towards the entrance of her chamber. He did not hit the right room directly; she motioned me to admit him; but he found it out, ere I could reach the door, and in a stride or two was at her side, and had her grasped in his arms.

He neither spoke, nor loosed his hold for some five minutes, during which period he bestowed more kisses than ever he gave in his life before, I dare say; but then my mistress had kissed him first, and I plainly saw that he could hardly bear, for downright agony, to look into her face! The same conviction had stricken him as me, from the instant he beheld her, that there was no prospect of ultimate recovery there – she was fated, sure to die.

'O, Cathy! Oh, my life! how can I bear it?' was the first sentence he uttered, in a tone that did not seek to disguise his despair.

And now he stared at her so earnestly that I thought the very intensity of his gaze would bring tears into his eyes; but they burned with anguish, they did not melt.

'What now?' said Catherine, leaning back, and returning his look with a suddenly clouded brow – her humour was a mere vane for constantly varying caprices. 'You and Edgar have broken my heart, Heathcliff! And you both come to bewail the deed to me, as if you were the people to be pitied! I shall not pity you, not I. You have killed me – and thriven on it, I think. How strong you are! How many years do you mean to live after I am gone?'

Heathcliff had knelt on one knee to embrace her; he attempted to rise, but she seized his hair, and kept him down.

'I wish I could hold you,' she continued, bitterly, 'till we were both dead! I shouldn't care what you suffered. I care nothing for your sufferings. Why shouldn't you suffer? I do! Will you forget me – will you be happy when I am in the earth? Will you say twenty years hence. "That's the grave of Catherine Earnshaw. I loved her long ago, and was wretched to lose her; but it is past. I've loved many others since – my children are dearer to me than she was, and, at death, I shall not rejoice that I am going to her, I shall be sorry that I must leave them!" Will you say so, Heathcliff?'

# Wuthering Heights

'Don't torture me till I'm as mad as yourself,' cried he, wrenching his head free, and grinding his teeth.

The two, to a cool spectator, made a strange and fearful picture. Well might Catherine deem that heaven would be a land of exile to her, unless, with her mortal body, she cast away her mortal character also. Her present countenance had a wild vindictiveness in its white cheek, and a bloodless lip, and scintillating eye; and she retained, in her closed fingers, a portion of the locks she had been grasping. As to her companion, while raising himself with one hand, he had taken her arm with the other; and so inadequate was his stock of gentleness to the requirements of her condition, that on his letting go, I saw four distinct impressions left blue in the colourless skin.

'Are you possessed with a devil,' he pursued, savagely, 'to talk in that manner to me, when you are dying? Do you reflect that all those words will be branded in my memory, and eating deeper eternally, after you have left me? You know you lie to say I have killed you; and, Catherine, you know that I could as soon forget you, as my existence! Is it not sufficient for your infernal selfishness, that while you are at peace I shall writhe in the torments of hell?'

'I shall not be at peace,' moaned Catherine, recalled to a sense of physical weakness by the violent, unequal throbbing of her heart, which beat visibly, and audibly, under this excess of agitation.

She said nothing further till the paroxysm was over; then she continued, more kindly –

'I'm not wishing you greater torment than I have, Heathcliff. I only wish us never to be parted – and should a word of mine distress you hereafter, think I feel the same distress underground, and for my own sake, forgive me! Come here and kneel down again! You never harmed me in your life. Nay, if you nurse anger, that will be worse to remember than my harsh words! Won't you come here again? Do!'

Heathcliff went to the back of her chair, and leant over, but not so far as to let her see his face, which was livid with emotion. She bent round to look at him; he would not permit it; turning abruptly, he walked to the fire-place, where he stood, silent, with his back towards us.

Mrs Linton's glance followed him suspiciously: every movement woke a new sentiment in her. After a pause, and a prolonged gaze, she resumed, addressing me in accents of indignant disappointment.

'Oh, you see, Nelly! he would not relent a moment to keep me out of the grave! *That* is how I'm loved! Well, never mind! That is not *my* Heathcliff. I shall love mine yet; and take him with me – he's in my soul. And,' added she, musingly, 'the thing that irks me most is this shattered prison, after all. I'm tired, tired of being enclosed here. I'm wearying to escape into that glorious world, and to be always there; not seeing it dimly through tears, and yearning for it through the walls of an aching heart; but really with it, and in it. Nelly, you think you are better and more fortunate than I; in full health and strength – you are sorry for me – very soon that will be altered. I shall be sorry for *you*. I shall be incomparably beyond and above you all. I *wonder* he won't be near me!' She went on to herself. 'I thought he wished it. Heathcliff, dear! you should not be sullen now. Do come to me, Heathcliff.'

In her eagerness she rose, and supported herself on the arm of the chair. At that earnest appeal, he turned to her, looking absolutely desperate. His eyes

112

wide, and wet, at last, flashed fiercely on her; his breast heaved convulsively. An instant they held asunder; and then how they met I hardly saw, but Catherine made a spring, and he caught her, and they were locked in an embrace from which I thought my mistress would never be released alive. In fact, to my eyes, she seemed directly insensible. He flung himself into the nearest seat, and on my approaching hurriedly to ascertain if she had fainted, he gnashed at me, and foamed like a mad dog, and gathered her to him with greedy jealousy. I did not feel as if I were in the company of a creature of my own species; it appeared that he would not understand, though I spoke to him; so, I stood off, and held my tongue, in great perplexity.

A movement of Catherine's relieved me a little presently: she put up her hand to clasp his neck, and bring her cheek to his, as he held her: while he, in return, covering her with frantic caresses, said wildly –

'You teach me now how cruel you've been – cruel and false. *Why* did you despise me? *Why* did you betray your own heart, Cathy? I have not one word of comfort – you deserve this. You have killed yourself. Yes, you may kiss me, and cry; and wring out my kisses and tears. They'll blight you – they'll damn you. You loved me – then what *right* had you to leave me? What right – answer me – for the poor fancy you felt for Linton? Because misery, and degradation, and death, and nothing that God or satan could inflict would have parted us, *you*, of your own will, did it. I have not broken your heart – *you* have broken it – and in breaking it, you have broken mine. So much the worse for me, that I am strong. Do I want to live? What kind of living will it be when you – oh, God! would *you* like to live with your soul in the grave?'

'Let me alone. Let me alone,' sobbed Catherine. 'If I've done wrong, I'm dying for it. It is enough! You left me too; but I won't upbraid you! I forgive you. Forgive me!'

'It is hard to forgive, and to look at those eyes, and feel those wasted hands,' he answered. 'Kiss me again; and don't let me see your eyes! I forgive what you have done to me. I love *my* murderer – but *yours*! How can I?'

They were silent – their faces hid against each other, and washed by each other's tears. At least, I suppose the weeping was on both sides; as it seemed Heathcliff *could* weep on a great occasion like this.

I grew very uncomfortable, meanwhile; for the afternoon wore fast away, the man whom I had sent off returned from his errand, and I could distinguish, by the shine of the westering sun up the valley, a concourse thickening outside Gimmerton chapel porch.

'Service is over,' I announced. 'My master will be here in half an hour.'

Heathcliff groaned a curse, and strained Catherine closer – she never moved.

Ere long I perceived a group of the servants passing up the road towards the kitchen wing. Mr Linton was not far behind; he opened the gate himself, and sauntered slowly up, probably enjoying the lovely afternoon that breathed as soft as summer.

'Now he is here,' I exclaimed. 'For Heaven's sake, hurry down! You'll not meet any one on the front stairs. Do be quick; and stay among the trees till he is fairly in.'

'I must go, Cathy,' said Heathcliff, seeking to extricate himself from his companion's arms. 'But, if I live, I'll see you again before you are asleep. I won't stay five yards from your window.'

'You must not go!' she answered, holding him as firmly as her strength allowed. 'You shall not, I tell you.'

'For one hour,' he pleaded earnestly.

'Not for one minute,' she replied.

'I *must* – Linton will be up immediately,' persisted the alarmed intruder.

He would have risen, and unfixed her fingers by the act – she clung fast, gasping; there was mad resolution in her face.

'No!' she shrieked. 'Oh, don't, don't go. It is the last time! Edgar will not hurt us. Heathcliff, I shall die! I shall die!'

'Damn the fool! There he is,' cried Heathcliff, sinking back into his seat. 'Hush, my darling! Hush, hush, Catherine! I'll stay. If he shot me so, I'd expire with a blessing on my lips.'

And there they were fast again. I heard my master mounting the stairs – the cold sweat ran from my forehead; I was horrified.

'Are you going to listen to her ravings? I said, passionately. 'She does not know what she says. Will you ruin her, because she has not wit to help herself? Get up! You could be free instantly. That is the most diabolical deed that ever you did. We are all done for – master, mistress, and servant.'

I wrung my hands, and cried out; and Mr Linton hastened his step at the noise. In the midst of my agitation, I was sincerely glad to observe that Catherine's arms had fallen relaxed, and her head hung down.

'She's fainted or dead,' I thought; 'so much the better. Far better that she should be dead, than lingering a burden and a misery-maker to all about her.'

Edgar sprang to his unbidden guest, blanched with astonishment and rage. What he meant to do, I cannot tell; however, the other stopped all demonstrations, at once, by placing the lifeless-looking form in his arms.

'Look here!' he said. 'Unless you be a fiend, help her first – then you shall speak to me!'

He walked into the parlour, and sat down. Mr Linton summoned me, and with great difficulty, and after resorting to many means, we managed to restore her to sensation; but she was all bewildered; she sighed, and moaned, and knew nobody. Edgar, in his anxiety for her, forgot her hated friend. I did not. I went, at the earliest opportunity, and besought him to depart, affirming that Catherine was better, and he should hear from me in the morning, how she passed the night.

'I shall not refuse to go out of doors,' he answered; 'but I shall stay in the garden; and, Nelly, mind you keep your word tomorrow. I shall be under those larch trees, mind! or I pay another visit, whether Linton be in or not.'

He sent a rapid glance through the half-open door of the chamber, and, ascertaining that what I stated was apparently true, delivered the house of his luckless presence.

# Chapter 16

About twelve o'clock, that night, was born the Catherine you saw at Wuthering Heights, a puny, seven months' child; and two hours after, the mother died, having never recovered sufficient consciousness to miss Heathcliff, or know Edgar.

The latter's distraction at his bereavement is a subject too painful to be dwelt on; its after effects showed how deep the sorrow sunk.

A great addition, in my eyes, was his being left without an heir. I bemoaned that, as I gazed on the feeble orphan; and I mentally abused old Linton for, what was only natural partiality, the securing his estate to his own daughter, instead of his son's.

An unwelcomed infant it was, poor thing! It might have wailed out of life, and nobody cared a morsel, during those first hours of existence. We redeemed the neglect afterwards; but its beginning was as friendless as its end is likely to be.

Next morning – bright and cheerful out of doors – stole softened in through the blinds of the silent room, and suffused the couch and its occupant with a mellow, tender glow.

Edgar Linton had his head laid on the pillow, and his eyes shut. His young and fair features were almost as deathlike at those of the form beside him, and almost as fixed; but *his* was the hush of exhausted anguish, and *hers* of perfect peace. Her brow smooth, her lids closed, her lips wearing the expression of a smile. No angel in heaven could be more beautiful than she appeared; and I partook of the infinite calm in which she lay. My mind was never in a holier frame, than while I gazed on that untroubled image of Divine rest. I instinctively echoed the words she had uttered a few hours before. 'Incomparably beyond, and above us all! Whether still on earth or now in heaven, her spirit is at home with God!'

I don't know if it be a peculiarity in me, but I am seldom otherwise than happy while watching in the chamber of death, should no frenzied or despairing mourner share the duty with me. I see a repose that neither earth nor hell can break; and I feel an assurance of the endless and shadowless hereafter – the Eternity they have entered – where life is boundless in its duration, and love in its sympathy, and joy in its fulness. I noticed on that occasion how much selfishness there is even in a love like Mr Linton's, when he so regretted Catherine's blessed release!

To be sure, one might have doubted, after the wayward and impatient existence she had led, whether she merited a haven of peace at last. One might doubt in seasons of cold reflection, but not then, in the presence of her corpse.

# Wuthering Heights

It asserted its own tranquillity, which seemed a pledge of equal quiet to its former inhabitant.

Do you believe such people *are* happy in the other world, sir? I'd give a great deal to know.

I declined answering Mrs Dean's question, which struck me as something heterodox. She proceeded:

Retracing the course of Catherine Linton, I fear we have no right to think she is: but we'll leave her with her Maker.

The master looked asleep, and I ventured soon after sunrise to quit the room and steal out to the pure, refreshing air. The servants thought me gone to shake off the drowsiness of my protracted watch; in reality, my chief motive was seeing Mr Heathcliff. If he had remained among the larches all night he would have heard nothing of the stir at the Grange, unless, perhaps, he might catch the gallop of the messenger going to Gimmerton. If he had come nearer, he would probably be aware, from the lights flitting to and fro, and the opening and shutting of the outer doors, that all was not right within.

I wished yet feared to find him. I felt the terrible news must be told, and I longed to get it over, but *how* to do it, I did not know.

He was there – at least a few yards further in the park; leant against an old ash tree, his hat off, and his hair soaked with the dew that had gathered on the budded branches, and fell pattering round him. He had been standing a long time in that position, for I saw a pair of ousels passing and repassing, scarcely three feet from him, busy in building their nest, and regarding his proximity no more than that of a piece of timber. They flew off at my approach, and he raised his eyes and spoke:

'She's dead!' he said; 'I've not waited for you to learn that. Put your handkerchief away – don't snivel before me. Damn you all! she wants none of *your* tears!'

I was weeping as much for him as her: we do sometimes pity creatures that have none of the feeling either for themselves or others; and when I first looked into his face, I perceived that he had got intelligence of the catastrophe; and a foolish notion struck me that his heart was quelled, and he prayed, because his lips moved, and his gaze was bent on the ground.

'Yes, she's dead!' I answered, checking my sobs, and drying my cheeks. 'Gone to heaven, I hope, where we may, every one, join her, if we take due warning, and leave our evil ways to follow good!'

'Did *she* take due warning, then?' asked Heathcliff, attempting a sneer. 'Did she die like a saint? Come, give me a true history of the event. How did –'

He endeavoured to pronounce the name, but could not manage it; and compressing his mouth, he held a silent combat with his inward agony, defying, meanwhile, my sympathy with an unflinching, ferocious stare.

'How did she die?' he resumed, at last – fain, notwithstanding his hardihood, to have a support behind him, for, after the struggle, he trembled, in spite of himself, to his very finger-ends.

'Poor wretch!' I thought; 'you have a heart and nerves the same as your brother men! Why should you be anxious to conceal them? your pride cannot blind God! You tempt him to wring them, till he forces a cry of humiliation!'

'Quietly as a lamb!' I answered, aloud. 'She drew a sigh, and stretched herself,

116

# Wuthering Heights

like a child reviving, and sinking again to sleep; and five minutes after I felt one little pulse at her heart, and nothing more!'

'And – did she ever mention me?' he asked, hesitating, as if he dreaded the answer to his question would introduce details that he could not bear to hear.

'Her senses never returned – she recognized nobody from the time you left her,' I said. 'She lies with a sweet smile on her face; and her latest ideas wandered back to pleasant early days. Her life closed in a gentle dream – may she wake as kindly in the other world!'

'May she wake in torment!' he cried, with frightful vehemence, stamping his foot, and groaning in a sudden paroxysm of ungovernable passion. 'Why, she's a liar to the end! Where is she? Not *there* – not in heaven – not perished – where? Oh! you said you cared nothing for my sufferings! And I pray one prayer – I repeat it till my tongue stiffens – Catherine Earnshaw, may you not rest, as long as I am living! You said I killed you – haunt me then! The murdered *do* haunt their murderers. I believe – I know that ghosts *have* wandered on earth. Be with me always – take any form – drive me mad! only *do* not leave me in this abyss, where I cannot find you! Oh God! it is unutterable! I *cannot* live without my life! I *cannot* live without my soul!'

He dashed his head against the knotted trunk; and, lifting up his eyes, howled, not like a man, but like a savage beast getting goaded to death with knives and spears.

I observed several splashes of blood about the bark of the tree, and his hands and forehead were both stained; probably the scene I witnessed was a repetition of others acted during the night. It hardly moved my compassion – it appalled me; still I felt reluctant to quit him so. But the moment he recollected himself enough to notice me watching, he thundered a command for me to go, and I obeyed. He was beyond my skill to quiet or console!

Mrs Linton's funeral was appointed to take place on the Friday following her decease; and till then her coffin remained uncovered, and strewn with flowers and scented leaves, in the great drawing-room. Linton spent his days and nights there, a sleepless guardian; and – a circumstance concealed from all but me – Heathcliff spent his nights, at least, outside, equally a stranger to repose.

I held no communication with him; still I was conscious of his design to enter, if he could; and on the Tuesday, a little after dark, when my master, from sheer fatigue, had been compelled to retire a couple of hours, I went and opened one of the windows, moved by his perseverance to give him a chance of bestowing on the fading image of his idol one final adieu.

He did not omit to avail himself of the opportunity, cautiously and briefly; too cautiously to betray his presence by the slightest noise; indeed, I shouldn't have discovered that he had been there, except for the disarrangement of the drapery about the corpse's face, and for observing on the floor a curl of light hair, fastened with a silver thread, which, on examination, I ascertained to have been taken from a locket hung round Catherine's neck. Heathcliff had opened the trinket and cast out its contents, replacing them by a black lock of his own. I twisted the two, and enclosed them together.

Mr Earnshaw was, of course, invited to attend the remains of his sister to the grave; and he sent no excuse, but he never came; so that besides her husband, the mourners were wholly composed of tenants and servants. Isabella was not asked.

The place of Catherine's interment, to the surprise of the villagers, was neither in the chapel, under the carved monument of the Lintons, nor yet by the tombs of her own relations, outside. It was dug on a green slope, in a corner of the kirkyard, where the wall is so low that heath and bilberry plants have climbed over it from the moor; and peat mould almost buries it. Her husband lies in the same spot, now; and they have each a simple headstone above, and a plain grey block at their feet, to mark the graves.

# Chapter 17

That Friday made the last of our fine days, for a month. In the evening, the weather broke; the wind shifted from south to north-east, and brought rain first, and then sleet, and snow.

On the morrow one could hardly imagine that there had been three weeks of summer; the primroses and crocuses were hidden under wintry drifts: the larks were silent, the young leaves of the early trees smitten and blackened – and dreary, and chill, and dismal that morrow did creep over! My master kept his room – I took possession of the lonely parlour, converting it into a nursery; and there I was sitting, with the moaning doll of a child laid on my knee; rocking it to and fro, and watching, meanwhile, the still driving flakes build up the uncurtained window, when the door opened, and some person entered, out of breath, and laughing!

My anger was greater than my astonishment for a minute; I supposed it one of the maids, and I cried,

'Have done! How dare you show your giddiness, here? What would Mr Linton say if he heard you?'

'Excuse me!' answered a familiar voice; 'but I know Edgar is in bed, and I cannot stop myself.'

With that, the speaker came forward to the fire, panting and holding her hand to her side.

'I have run the whole way from Wuthering Heights!' she continued, after a pause. 'Except where I've flown – I couldn't count the number of falls I've had – Oh, I'm aching all over! Don't be alarmed – There shall be an explanation as soon as I can give it – only just have the goodness to step out and order the carriage to take me on to Gimmerton, and tell a servant to seek up a few clothes in my wardrobe.'

The intruder was Mrs Heathcliff – She certainly seemed in no laughing predicament: her hair streaming on her shoulders, dripping with snow and water; she was dressed in the girlish dress she commonly wore, befitting her age more than her position; a low frock, with short sleeves, and nothing on either head or neck. The frock was of light silk, and clung to her with wet; and her

feet were protected merely by thin slippers; add to this a deep cut under one ear, which only the cold prevented from bleeding profusely, a white face scratched and bruised, and a frame hardly able to support itself through fatigue, and you may fancy my first fright was not much allayed when I had leisure to examine her.

'My dear young lady,' I exclaimed, 'I'll stir nowhere, and hear nothing, till you have removed every article of your clothes, and put on dry things; and certainly you shall not go to Gimmerton to-night, so it is needless to order the carriage.'

'Certainly, I shall,' she said; 'walking or riding – yet I've no objection to dress myself decently; and – ah, see how it flows down my neck now! The fire does make it smart.'

She insisted on my fulfilling her directions, before she would let me touch her; and not till after the coachman had been instructed to get ready, and a maid set to pack up some necessary attire, did I obtain her consent for binding the wound, and helping to change her garments.

'Now, Ellen,' she said, when my task was finished, and she was seated in an easy chair on the hearth, with a cup of tea before her, 'you sit down opposite me, and put poor Catherine's baby away – I don't like to see it! You mustn't think I care little for Catherine, because I behaved so foolishly on entering – I've cried too, bitterly – yes, more than any one else has reason to cry – we parted unreconciled, you remember, and I shan't forgive myself. But, for all that, I was not going to sympathize with him – the brute beast! Oh, give me the poker! This is the last thing of his I have about me.' She slipped the gold ring from her third finger, and threw it on the floor. 'I'll smash it!' she continued, striking it with childish spite. 'And then I'll burn it!' and she took and dropped the misused article among the coals. 'There! he shall buy another, if he gets me back again. He'd be capable of coming to seek me, to tease Edgar – I dare not stay, lest that notion should possess his wicked head! And besides, Edgar has not been kind, has he? And I won't come suing for his assistance; nor will I bring him into more trouble – Necessity compelled me to seek shelter here; though if I had not learnt he was out of the way, I'd have halted at the kitchen, washed my face, warmed myself, got you to bring what I wanted, and departed again to anywhere out of the reach of my accursed – of that incarnate goblin! Ah, he was in such a fury – if he had caught me! It's a pity, Earnshaw is not his match in strength – I wouldn't have run, till I'd seen him all but demolished, had Hindley been able to do it!'

'Well, don't talk so fast, Miss!' I interrupted, 'you'll disorder the handkerchief I have tied round your face, and make the cut bleed again – Drink your tea, and take breath, and give over laughing – Laughter is sadly out of place under this roof, and in your condition!'

'An undeniable truth,' she replied, 'Listen to that child! It maintains a constant wail – send it out of my hearing, for an hour; I shan't stay any longer.'

I rang the bell, and committed it to a servant's care; and then I inquired what had urged her to escape from Wuthering Heights in such an unlikely plight – and where she meant to go, as she refused remaining with us.

'I ought, and I wish to remain,' answered she; 'to cheer Edgar, and take care of the baby, for two things, and because the Grange is my right home – but I tell you, he wouldn't let me! Do you think he could bear to see me grow fat, and

merry; and could bear to think that we were tranquil, and not resolve on poisoning our comfort? Now, I have the satisfaction of being sure that he detests me to the point of its annoying him seriously to have me within ear-shot, or eye-sight – I notice, when I enter his presence, the muscles of his countenance are involuntarily distorted into an expression of hatred; partly arising from his knowledge of the good causes I have to feel that sentiment for him, and partly from original aversion – It is strong enough to make me feel pretty certain that he would not chase me over England, supposing I contrived a clear escape; and therefore I must get quite away. I've recovered from my first desire to be killed by him. I'd rather he'd kill himself! He has extinguished my love effectually, and so I'm at my ease. I can recollect yet how I loved him; and can dimly imagine that I could still be loving him, if – no, no! Even if he had doted on me, the devilish nature would have revealed its existence, somehow. Catherine had an awfully perverted taste to esteem him so dearly, knowing him so well – Monster! would that he could be blotted out of creation, and out of my memory!'

'Hush, hush! He's a human being,' I said. 'Be more charitable; there are worse men than he is yet!'

'He's not a human being:' she retorted; 'and he has no claim on my charity – I gave him my heart, and he took and pinched it to death; and flung it back to me – people feel with their hearts, Ellen, and since he has destroyed mine, I have not power to feel for him, and I would not, though he groaned from this, to his dying day; and wept tears of blood for Catherine! No, indeed, indeed, I wouldn't!' And here Isabella began to cry; but, immediately dashing the water from her lashes, she recommenced.

'You asked, what has driven me to flight at last? I was compelled to attempt it, because I had succeeded in rousing his rage a pitch above his malignity. Pulling out the nerves with red hot pincers, requires more coolness than knocking on the head. He was worked up to forget the fiendish prudence he boasted of, and proceeded to murderous violence. I experienced pleasure in being able to exasperate him: the sense of pleasure woke my instinct of self-preservation; so, I fairly broke free, and if ever I come into his hands again he is welcome to a signal revenge.

'Yesterday, you know, Mr Earnshaw should have been at the funeral. He kept himself sober, for the purpose – tolerably sober; not going to bed mad, at six o'clock, and getting up drunk, at twelve. Consequently, he rose, in suicidal low spirits, as fit for the church, as for a dance; and instead, he sat down by the fire, and swallowed gin or brandy by tumblerfuls.

'Heathcliff – I shudder to name him! has been a stranger in the house from last Sunday till to-day – Whether the angels have fed him, or his kin beneath, I cannot tell; but he has not eaten a meal with us for nearly a week – He has just come home at dawn, and gone upstairs to his chamber; locking himself in – as if anybody dreamt of coveting his company! There he has continued, praying like a methodist; only the deity he implored is senseless dust and ashes; and God, when addressed, was curiously confounded with his own black father! After concluding these precious orisons – and they lasted generally till he grew hoarse, and his voice was strangled in his throat – he would be off again; always straight down to the Grange! I wonder Edgar did not send for a constable, and give him into custody! For me, grieved as I was about Catherine, it was

# Wuthering Heights

impossible to avoid regarding this season of deliverance from degrading oppression as a holiday.

'I recovered spirits sufficient to hear Joseph's eternal lectures without weeping; and to move up and down the house, less with the foot of a frightened thief, than formerly. You wouldn't think that I should cry at anything Joseph could say, but he and Hareton are detestable companions. I'd rather sit with Hindley, and hear his awful talk, than with "t' little maister," and his staunch supporter, that odious old man!

'When Heathcliff is in, I'm often obliged to seek the kitchen, and their society, or starve among the damp, uninhabited chambers; when he is not, as was the case this week, I establish a table and chair at one corner of the house fire, and never mind how Mr Earnshaw may occupy himself; and he does not interfere with my arrangements: he is quieter, now, than he used to be, if no one provokes him; more sullen and depressed, and less furious. Joseph affirms he's sure he's an altered man, that the Lord has touched his heart, and he is saved "so as by fire." I'm puzzled to detect signs of the favourable change, but it is not my business.

'Yester-evening, I sat in my nook reading some old books, till late on towards twelve. It seemed so dismal to go upstairs, with the wild snow blowing outside, and my thoughts continually reverting to the kirkyard, and the new-made grave! I dared hardly lift my eyes from the page before me, that melancholy scene so instantly usurped its place.

'Hindley sat opposite; his head leant on his hand, perhaps meditating on the same subject. He had ceased drinking at a point below irrationality, and had neither stirred nor spoken during two or three hours. There was no sound through the house, but the moaning wind which shook the windows every now and then: the faint crackling of the coals, and the click of my snuffers as I removed at intervals the long wick of the candle. Hareton and Joseph were probably fast asleep in bed. It was very, very sad, and while I read, I sighed, for it seemed as if all joy had vanished from the world, never to be restored.

'The doleful silence was broken, at length, by the sound of the kitchen latch – Heathcliff had returned from his watch earlier than usual, owing, I suppose, to the sudden storm.

'The entrance was fastened; and we heard him coming round to get in by the other. I rose with an irrepressible expression of what I felt on my lips, which induced my companion, who had been staring towards the door, to turn and look at me.

' "I'll keep him out five minutes," he exclaimed. "You won't object?"

' "No, you may keep him out the whole night for me," I answered. "Do! put the key in the lock, and draw the bolts."

'Earnshaw accomplished this ere his guest reached the front; he then came and brought his chair to the other side of my table, leaning over it, and searching in my eyes a sympathy with the burning hate that gleamed from his: as he both looked and felt like an assassin, he couldn't exactly find that; but he discovered enough to encourage him to speak.'

' "You and I," he said, "have each a great debt to settle with the man out yonder! If we were neither of us cowards, we might combine to discharge it. Are you as soft as your brother? Are you willing to endure to the last, and not once attempt a repayment?"

# Wuthering Heights

' "I'm weary of enduring now," I replied, "and I'd be glad of a retaliation that wouldn't recoil on myself; but treachery, and violence, are spears pointed at both ends – they wound those who resort to them, worse than their enemies."

' "Treachery and violence are a just return for treachery and violence!" cried Hindley. "Mrs Heathcliff, I'll ask you to do nothing, but sit still, and be dumb – Tell me now, can you? I'm sure you would have as much pleasure as I, in witnessing the conclusion of the fiend's existence; he'll be *your* death unless you overreach him – and he'll be *my* ruin – Damn the hellish villain! He knocks at the door, as if he were master here, already! Promise to hold your tongue, and before that clock strikes – it wants three minutes of one – you're a free woman!"

'He took the implements which I described to you in my letter from his breast, and would have turned down the candle – I snatched it away, however, and seized his arm.

' "I'll not hold my tongue!" I said. "You mustn't touch him . . . Let the door remain shut and be quiet!"

' "No! I've formed my resolution, and by God, I'll execute it!" cried the desperate being. "I'll do you a kindness, in spite of yourself, and Hareton justice! And you needn't trouble your head to screen me, Catherine is gone – Nobody alive would regret me, or be ashamed, though I cut my throat this minute – and it's time to make an end!"

'I might as well have struggled with a bear, or reasoned with a lunatic. The only resource left me was to run to a lattice, and warn his intended victim of the fate which awaited him.

' "You'd better seek shelter somewhere else to-night!" I exclaimed in a rather triumphant tone. "Mr Earnshaw has a mind to shoot you, if you persist in endeavouring to enter."

' "You'd better open the door, you –," he answered, addressing me by some elegant terms that I don't care to repeat.

' "I shall not meddle in the matter," I retorted again. "Come in, and get shot, if you please! I've done my duty."

'With that I shut the window, and returned to my place by the fire, having too small a stock of hypocrisy at my command to pretend any anxiety for the danger that menaced him.

'Earnshaw swore passionately at me, affirming that I loved the villain yet, and calling me all sorts of names for the base spirit I evinced. And I, in my secret heart (and conscience never reproached me), thought what a blessing it would be for *him*, should Heathcliff put him out of misery; and what a blessing for *me*, should he send Heathcliff to his right abode! As I sat nursing these reflections, the casement behind me was banged on to the floor by a blow from the latter individual; and his black countenance looked blightingly through. The stanchions stood too close to suffer his shoulders to follow; and I smiled, exulting in my fancied security. His hair and clothes were whitened with snow, and his sharp cannibal teeth, revealed by cold and wrath, gleamed through the dark.

' "Isabella, let me in, or I'll make you repent!" he "girned," as Joseph calls it.

' "I cannot commit murder," I replied. "Mr Hindley stands sentinel with a knife and loaded pistol."

' "Let me in by the kitchen door!" he said.

' "Hindley will be there before me," I answered. "And that's a poor love of

# Wuthering Heights

yours, that cannot bear a shower of snow! We were left at peace in our beds, as long as the summer moon shone, but the moment a blast of winter returns, you must run for shelter! Heathcliff, if I were you, I'd go stretch myself over her grave, and die like a faithful dog ... The world is surely not worth living in now, is it? You had distinctly impressed on me, the idea that Catherine was the whole joy of your life – I can't imagine how you think of surviving her loss."

' "He's there, is he?" exclaimed my companion rushing to the gap. "If I can get my arm out I can hit him!"

'I'm afraid, Ellen, you'll set me down as really wicked – but you don't know all, so don't judge! I wouldn't have aided or abetted an attempt on even *his* life, for anything – Wish that he were dead, I must; and therefore, I was fearfully disappointed, and unnerved by terror for the consequences of my taunting speech, when he flung himself on Earnshaw's weapon and wrenched it from his grasp.

'The charge exploded, and the knife, in springing back, closed into its owner's wrist. Heathcliff pulled it away by main force, slitting up the flesh as it passed on, and thrust it dripping into his pocket. He then took a stone, struck down the division between two windows, and sprung in. His adversary had fallen senseless with excessive pain, and the flow of blood that gushed from an artery, or a large vein.

'The ruffian kicked and trampled on him, and dashed his head repeatedly against the flags, holding me with one hand, meantime, to prevent me summoning Joseph.

'He exerted preter-human self-denial in abstaining from finishing him, completely; but getting out of breath, he finally desisted, and dragged the apparently inanimate body onto the settle.

'There he tore off the sleeve of Earnshaw's coat, and bound up the wound with brutal roughness, spitting and cursing, during the operation, as energetically as he had kicked before.

'Being at liberty, I lost no time in seeking the old servant, who, having gathered by degrees the purport of my hasty tale, hurried below, gasping, as he descended the steps two at once.

' "Whet is thur tuh do, nah? whet is thur tuh do, nah?"

' "There's this to do," thundered Heathcliff, "that your master's mad; and should he last another month, I'll have him to an asylum. And how the devil did you come to fasten me out, you toothless hound? Don't stand muttering and mumbling there. Come, I'm not going to nurse him. Wash that stuff away; and mind the sparks of your candle – it is more than half brandy!"

' "Und, soa, yah been murthering on him?" exclaimed Joseph, lifting his hands and eyes in horror. "If iver Aw seed a seeght loike this! May the Lord –"

'Heathcliff gave him a push onto his knees, in the middle of the blood, and flung a towel to him; but instead of proceeding to dry it up, he joined his hands, and began a prayer which excited my laughter from its odd phraseology. I was in the condition of mind to be shocked at nothing; in fact, I was as reckless as some malefactors show themselves at the foot of the gallows.

' "Oh, I forgot you," said the tyrant. "You shall do that. Down with you. And you conspire with him against me, do you, viper? There, that is work fit for you!"

# Wuthering Heights

'He shook me till my teeth rattled, and pitched me beside Joseph, who steadily concluded his supplications, and then rose, vowing he would set off for the Grange directly. Mr Linton was a magistrate, and though he had fifty wives dead, he should inquire into this.

'He was so obstinate in his resolution, that Heathcliff deemed it expedient to compel, from my lips, a recapitulation of what had taken place; standing over me, heaving with malevolence, as I reluctantly delivered the account in answer to his questions.

'It required a great deal of labour to satisfy the old man that he was not the aggressor; especially with my hardly wrung replies. However, Mr Earnshaw soon convinced him that he was alive still; he hastened to administer a dose of spirits, and by their succour his master presently regained motion and consciousness.

'Heathcliff, aware that he was ignorant of the treatment received while insensible, called him deliriously intoxicated; and said he should not notice his atrocious conduct further, but advised him to get to bed. To my joy, he left us after giving this judicious counsel, and Hindley stretched himself on the hearthstone. I departed to my own room, marvelling that I had escaped so easily.

'This morning, when I came down, about half-an-hour before noon, Mr Earnshaw was sitting by the fire, deadly sick; his evil genius, almost as gaunt and ghastly, leant against the chimney. Neither appeared inclined to dine; and, having waited till all was cold on the table, I commenced alone.

'Nothing hindered me from eating heartily; and I experienced a certain sense of satisfaction and superiority, as, at intervals, I cast a look towards my silent companions, and felt the comfort of a quiet conscience within me.

'After I had done, I ventured on the unusual liberty of drawing near the fire, going round Earnshaw's seat, and kneeling in the corner beside him.

'Heathcliff did not glance my way and I gazed up and contemplated his features, almost as confidently as if they had been turned to stone. His forehead, that I once thought so manly, and that I now think so diabolical, was shaded with a heavy cloud; his basilisk eyes were nearly quenched by sleeplessness – and weeping, perhaps, for the lashes were wet then; his lips devoid of their ferocious sneer, and sealed in an expression of unspeakable sadness. Had it been another, I would have covered my face, in the presence of such grief. In *his* case, I was gratified, and ignoble as it seems to insult a fallen enemy, I couldn't miss this chance of sticking in a dart; his weakness was the only time when I could taste the delight of paying wrong for wrong.'

'Fie, fie, Miss!' I interrupted. 'One might suppose you had never opened a Bible in your life. If God afflict your enemies, surely that ought to suffice you. It is both mean and presumptuous to add your torture to his!'

'In general, I'll allow that it would be, Ellen,' she continued. 'But what misery laid on Heathcliff would content me, unless I have a hand in it? I'd rather he suffered *less*, if I might cause his sufferings, and he might *know* that I was the cause. Oh, I owe him so much. On only one condition can I hope to forgive him. It is, if I may take an eye for an eye, a tooth for a tooth, for every wrench of agony, return a wrench, reduce him to my level. As he was the first to injure, making him the first to implore pardon; and then – why then, Ellen, I might show you some generosity. But it is utterly impossible I can ever be revenged,

and therefore I cannot forgive him. Hindley wanted some water, and I handed him a glass, and asked him how he was.

' "Not as ill as I wish," he replied. "But leaving out my arm, every inch of me is as sore as if I had been fighting with a legion of imps!"

' "Yes, no wonder," was my next remark. "Catherine used to boast that she stood between you and bodily harm – she meant that certain persons would not hurt you, for fear of offending her. It's well people don't *really* rise from their grave, or, last night, she might have witnessed a repulsive scene! Are not you bruised, and cut over your chest and shoulders?"

' "I can't say," he answered; "but what do you mean? Did he dare to strike me when I was down?"

' "He trampled on, and kicked you, and dashed you on the ground," I whispered. "And his mouth watered to tear you with his teeth; because, he's only half a man – not so much."

'Mr Earnshaw looked up, like me, to the countenance of our mutual foe; who, absorbed in his anguish, seemed insensible to anything around him; the longer he stood, the plainer his reflections revealed their blackness through his features.

' "Oh, if God would but give me strength to strangle him in my last agony, I'd go to hell with joy," groaned the impatient man, writhing to rise, and sinking back in despair, convinced of his inadequacy for the struggle.

' "Nay, it's enough that he has murdered one of you," I observed aloud. "At the Grange, every one knows your sister would have been living now, had it not been for Mr Heathcliff. After all, it is preferable to be hated than loved by him. When I recollect how happy we were – how happy Catherine was before he came – I'm fit to curse the day."

'Most likely, Heathcliff noticed more the truth of what was said, than the spirit of the person who said it. His attention was roused, I saw, for his eyes rained down tears among the ashes, and he drew his breath in suffocating sighs.

'I stared full at him, and laughed scornfully. The clouded windows of hell flashed a moment towards me; the fiend which usually looked out, however, was so dimmed and drowned that I did not fear to hazard another sound of derision.

' "Get up, and begone out of my sight," said the mourner.

'I guessed he uttered those words, at least, though his voice was hardly intelligible.

' "I beg your pardon," I replied. "But I loved Catherine, too; and her brother requires attendance which, for her sake, I shall supply. Now that she's dead, I see her in Hindley; Hindley has exactly her eyes, if you had not tried to gouge them out, and made them black and red, and her –"

' "Get up, wretched idiot, before I stamp you to death!" he cried, making a movement that caused me to make one also.

' "But then," I continued, holding myself ready to flee; "if poor Catherine had trusted you, and assumed the ridiculous, contemptible, degrading title of Mrs Heathcliff, she would soon have presented a similar picture! *She* wouldn't have borne your abominable behaviour quietly; her detestation and disgust must have found voice."

'The back of the settle and Earnshaw's person interposed between me and him; so instead of endeavouring to reach me he snatched a dinner knife from the table, and flung it at my head. It struck beneath my ear, and stopped the sentence

# Wuthering Heights

I was uttering; but pulling it out, I sprang to the door, and delivered another which I hope went a little deeper than his missile.

'The last glimpse I caught of him was a furious rush on his part, checked by the embrace of his host; and both fell locked together on the hearth.

'In my flight through the kitchen, I bid Joseph speed to his master; I knocked over Hareton, who was hanging a litter of puppies from a chairback in the doorway; and, blest as a soul escaped from purgatory, I bounded, leaped, and flew down the steep road: then, quitting its windings, shot direct across the moor, rolling over banks, and wading through marshes; precipitating myself, in fact, towards the beacon light of the Grange. And far rather would I be condemned to a perpetual dwelling in the infernal regions, than even for one night abide beneath the roof of Wuthering Heights again.'

Isabella ceased speaking, and took a drink of tea; then she rose, and bidding me put on her bonnet, and a great shawl I had brought, and turning a deaf ear to my entreaties for her to remain another hour, she stepped onto a chair, kissed Edgar's and Catherine's portraits, bestowed a similar salute on me, and descended to the carriage, accompanied by Fanny, who yelped wild with joy at recovering her mistress. She was driven away, never to revisit this neighbourhood; but a regular correspondence was established between her and my master when things were more settled.

I believe her new abode was in the south, near London; there she had a son born, a few months subsequent to her escape. He was christened Linton, and, from the first, she reported him to be an ailing, peevish creature.

Mr Heathcliff, meeting me one day in the village, inquired where she lived. I refused to tell. He remarked that it was not of any moment, only she must beware of coming to her brother: she should not be with him, if he had to keep her himself.

Though I would give no information, he discovered, through some of the other servants, both her place of residence and the existence of the child. Still he didn't molest her; for which forbearance she might thank his aversion, I suppose.

He often asked about the infant, when he saw me; and on hearing its name, smiled grimly, and observed:

'They wish me to hate it too, do they?'

'I don't think they wish you to know anything about it,' I answered.

'But I'll have it,' he said, 'when I want it. They may reckon on that!'

Fortunately, its mother died before the time arrived, some thirteen years after the decease of Catherine, when Linton was twelve, or a little more.

On the day succeeding Isabella's unexpected visit, I had no opportunity of speaking to my master: he shunned conversation, and was fit for discussing nothing. When I could get him to listen, I saw it pleased him that his sister had left her husband, whom he abhorred with an intensity which the mildness of his nature would scarcely seem to allow. So deep and sensitive was his aversion, that he refrained from going anywhere where he was likely to see or hear of Heathcliff. Grief, and that together, transformed him into a complete hermit: he threw up his office of magistrate, ceased even to attend church, avoided the village on all occasions, and spent a life of entire seclusion within the limits of his park and grounds: only varied by solitary rambles on the moors, and visits to the grave of his wife, mostly at evening, or early morning, before other wanderers were abroad.

# Wuthering Heights

But he was too good to be thoroughly unhappy long. *He* didn't pray for Catherine's soul to haunt him: Time brought resignation, and a melancholy sweeter than common joy. He recalled her memory with ardent, tender love, and hopeful aspiring to the better world, where, he doubted not, she was gone.

And he had earthly consolation and affections, also. For a few days, I said, he seemed regardless of the puny successor to the departed: that coldness melted as fast as snow in April, and ere the tiny thing could stammer a word or totter a step, it wielded a despot's sceptre in his heart.

It was named Catherine, but he never called it the name in full, as he had never called the first Catherine short, probably because Heathcliff had a habit of doing so. The little one was always Cathy, it formed to him a distinction from the mother, and yet, a connection with her; and his attachment sprang from its relation to her, far more than from its being his own.

I used to draw a comparison between him, and Hindley Earnshaw, and perplex myself to explain satisfactorily, why their conduct was so opposite in similar circumstances. They had both been fond husbands, and were both attached to their children; and I could not see how they shouldn't both have taken the same road, for good or evil. But, I thought in my mind, Hindley, with apparently the stronger head, has shown himself sadly the worse and the weaker man. When his ship struck, the captain abandoned his post; and the crew, instead of trying to save her, rushed into riot, and confusion, leaving no hope for their luckless vessel. Linton, on the contrary, displayed the true courage of a loyal and faithful soul: he trusted God; and God comforted him. One hoped, and the other despaired; they chose their own lots, and were righteously doomed to endure them.

But you'll not want to hear my moralizing, Mr Lockwood: you'll judge as well as I can, all these things; at least, you'll think you will, and that's the same.

The end of Earnshaw was what might have been expected: it followed fast on his sister's, there was scarcely six months between them. We, at the Grange, never got a very succinct account of his state preceding it; all that I did learn, was on occasion of going to aid in the preparations for the funeral. Mr Kenneth came to announce the event to my master.

'Well, Nelly,' said he, riding into the yard one morning, too early not to alarm me with an instant presentiment of bad news. 'It's yours and my turn to go into mourning at present. Who's given us the slip, now, do you think?'

'Who?' I asked in a flurry.

'Why, guess!' he returned, dismounting, and slinging his bridle on a hook by the door. 'And nip up the corner of your apron; I'm certain you'll need it.'

'Not Mr Heathcliff, surely?' I exclaimed.

'What! would you have tears for him?' said the doctor. 'No, Heathcliff's a tough young fellow: he looks blooming today – I've just seen him. He's rapidly regaining flesh since he lost his better half.'

'Who is it, then, Mr Kenneth?' I repeated impatiently.

'Hindley Earnshaw! Your old friend Hindley –' he replied. 'And my wicked gossip; though he's been too wild for me this long while. There! I said we should draw water – But cheer up! He died true to his character, drunk as a lord – Poor lad; I'm sorry, too. One can't help missing an old companion; though he had the worst tricks with him that ever man imagined, and has done me many

a rascally turn – He's barely twenty-seven, it seems; that's your own age; who would have thought you were born in one year?'

I confess this blow was greater to me than the shock of Mrs Linton's death: ancient associations lingered round my heart; I sat down in the porch, and wept as for a blood relation, desiring Kenneth to get another servant to introduce him to the master.

I could not hinder myself from pondering on the question – 'Had he had fair play?' Whatever I did, that idea would bother me: it was so tiresomely pertinacious that I resolved on requesting leave to go to Wuthering Heights, and assist in the last duties to the dead. Mr Linton was extremely reluctant to consent, but I pleaded eloquently for the friendless condition in which he lay; and I said my old master and foster-brother had a claim on my services as strong as his own. Besides, I reminded him that the child, Hareton, was his wife's nephew, and, in the absence of nearer kin, he ought to act as its guardian; and he ought to and must inquire how the property was left, and look over the concerns of his brother-in-law.

He was unfit for attending to such matters then, but he bid me speak to his lawyer; and, at length, permitted me to go. His lawyer had been Earnshaw's also: I called at the village, and asked him to accompany me. He shook his head, and advised that Heathcliff should be let alone, affirming, if the truth were known, Hareton would be found little else than a beggar.

'His father died in debt,' he said, 'the whole property is mortgaged, and the sole chance for the natural heir is to allow him an opportunity of creating some interest in the creditor's heart, that he may be inclined to deal leniently towards him.'

When I reached the Heights, I explained that I had come to see everything carried on decently, and Joseph, who appeared in sufficient distress, expressed satisfaction at my presence. Mr Heathcliff said he did not perceive that I was wanted, but I might stay and order the arrangements for the funeral, if I chose.

'Correctly,' he remarked, 'that fool's body should be buried at the cross-roads, without ceremony of any kind – I happened to leave him ten minutes, yesterday afternoon; and, in that interval, he fastened the two doors of the house against me, and he has spent the night in drinking himself to death deliberately! We broke in this morning, for we heard him snorting like a horse; and there he was, laid over the settle – flaying and scalping would not have wakened him – I sent for Kenneth, and he came, but not till the beast had changed into carrion – he was both dead and cold, and stark; and so you'll allow, it was useless making more stir about him!'

The old servant confirmed his statement, but muttered,

'Aw'd rayther he'd goan hisseln fur t' doctor! Aw sud uh taen tent uh t' maister better nur him – un he warn't deead when Aw left, nowt uh t' soart!'

I insisted on the funeral being respectable – Mr Heathcliff said I might have my own way there, too; only, he desired me to remember, that the money for the whole affair came out of his pocket.

He maintained a hard, careless deportment, indicative of neither joy nor sorrow; if anything, it expressed a flinty gratification at a piece of difficult work, successfully executed. I observed once, indeed, something like exultation in his aspect. It was just when the people were bearing the coffin from the house; he had the hypocrisy to represent a mourner; and previous to following with

Hareton, he lifted the unfortunate child on to the table, and muttered, with peculiar gusto.

'Now, my bonny lad, you are *mine*! And we'll see if one tree won't grow as crooked as another, with the same wind to twist it!'

The unsuspecting thing was pleased at this speech; he played with Heathcliff's whiskers, and stroked his cheek, but I divined its meaning, and observed tartly,

'That boy must go back with me to Thrushcross Grange, sir. There is nothing in the world less yours than he is!'

'Does Linton say so?' he demanded.

'Of course – he has ordered me to take him,' I replied.

'Well,' said the scoundrel, 'we'll not argue the subject now; but I have a fancy to try my hand at rearing a young one, so intimate to your master, that I must supply the place of this with my own, if he attempt to remove it. I don't engage to let Hareton go, undisputed; but I'll be pretty sure to make the other come! Remember to tell him.'

This hint was enough to bind our hands. I repeated its substance on my return, and Edgar Linton, little interested at the commencement, spoke no more of interfering. I'm not aware that he could have done it to any purpose, had he been ever so willing.

The guest was now the master of Wuthering Heights: he held firm possession, and proved it to the attorney, who, in his turn, proved it to Mr Linton, that Earnshaw had mortgaged every yard of land he owned for cash to supply his mania for gaming; and he, Heathcliff, was the mortgagee.

In that manner, Hareton, who should now be the first gentleman in the neighbourhood, was reduced to a state of complete dependence on his father's inveterate enemy; and lives in his own house as a servant deprived of the advantage of wages, and quite unable to right himself, because of his friendlessness, and his ignorance that he has been wronged.

# Chapter 18

The twelve years, continued Mrs Dean, following that dismal period, were the happiest of my life: my greatest troubles, in their passage, rose from our little lady's trifling illnesses, which she had to experience in common with all children, rich and poor.

For the rest, after the first six months, she grew like a larch; and could walk and talk, too, in her own way, before the heath bloomed a second time over Mrs Linton's dust.

She was the most winning thing that ever brought sunshine into a desolate house – a real beauty in face – with the Earnshaws' handsome dark eyes, but the Lintons' fair skin and small features, and yellow curling hair. Her spirit

# Wuthering Heights

was high, though not rough, and qualified by a heart, sensitive and lively to excess in its affections. That capacity for intense attachments remined me of her mother; still she did not resemble her; for she could be soft and mild as a dove, and she had a gentle voice, and pensive expression: her anger was never furious, her love never fierce; it was deep and tender.

However, it must be acknowledged, she had faults to foil her gifts. A propensity to be saucy was one; and a perverse will that indulged children invariably acquire, whether they be good tempered or cross. If a servant chanced to vex her, it was always: 'I shall tell papa!' And if he reproved her, even by a look, you would have thought it a heartbreaking business: I don't believe he ever did speak a harsh word to her.

He took her education entirely on himself, and made it an amusement: fortunately, curiosity and a quick intellect urged her into an apt scholar; she learnt rapidly and eagerly, and did honour to his teaching.

Till she reached the age of thirteen, she had not once been beyond the range of the park by herself. Mr Linton would take her with him, a mile or so outside, on rare occasions; but he trusted her to no one else. Gimmerton was an unsubstantial name in her ears; the chapel, the only building she had approached or entered, except her own home. Wuthering Heights and Mr Heathcliff did not exist for her; she was a perfect recluse; and, apparently perfectly contented. Sometimes, indeed, while surveying the country from her nursery window, she would observe –

'Ellen, how long will it be before I can walk to the top of those hills? I wonder what lies on the other side – is it the sea?'

'No, Miss Cathy,' I would answer, 'it is hills again just like these.'

'And what are those golden rocks like, when you stand under them?' she once asked.

The abrupt descent of Penistone Crags particularly attracted her notice, especially when the setting sun shone on it, and the topmost heights; and the whole extent of landscape besides lay in shadow.

I explained that they were bare masses of stone, with hardly enough earth in their clefts to nourish a stunted tree.

'And why are they bright so long after it is evening here?' she pursued.

'Because they are a great deal higher up than we are,' replied I; 'you could not climb them, they are too high and steep. In winter the frost is always there before it comes to us; and deep into summer, I have found snow under that black hollow on the north-east side!'

'Oh, you have been on them!' she cried gleefully. 'Then I can go, too, when I am a woman. Has papa been, Ellen?'

'Papa would tell you, Miss,' I answered, hastily, 'that they are not worth the trouble of visiting. The moors, where you ramble with him, are much nicer; and Thrushcross park is the finest place in the world.'

'But I know the park, and I don't know those,' she murmured to herself. 'And I should delight to look round me, from the brow of that tallest point – my little pony, Minny, shall take me sometime.'

One of the maids mentioning the Fairy cave, quite turned her head with a desire to fulfil this project; she teased Mr Linton about it; and he promised she should have the journey when she got older. But Miss Catherine measured her age by months, and –

# Wuthering Heights

'Now, am I old enough to go to Penistone Crags?' was the constant question in her mouth.

The road thither wound close by Wuthering Heights. Edgar had not the heart to pass it; so she received as constantly the answer,

'Not yet, love, not yet.'

I said Mrs Heathcliff lived above a dozen years after quitting her husband. Her family were of a delicate constitution: she and Edgar both lacked the ruddy health that you will generally meet in these parts. What her last illness was, I am not certain; I conjecture, they died of the same thing, a kind of fever, slow at its commencement, but incurable, and rapidly consuming life towards the close.

She wrote to inform her brother of the probable conclusion of a four months' indisposition, under which she had suffered; and entreated him to come to her, if possible, for she had much to settle, and she wished to bid him adieu, and deliver Linton safely into his hands. Her hope was, that Linton might be left with him, as he had been with her; his father, she would fain convince herself, had no desire to assume the burden of his maintenance or education.

My master hesitated not a moment in complying with her request; reluctant as he was to leave home at ordinary calls, he flew to answer this; commending Catherine to my peculiar vigilance, in his absence, with reiterated orders that she must not wander out of the park, even under my escort; he did not calculate on her going unaccompanied.

He was away three weeks: the first day or two, my charge sat in a corner of the library, too sad for either reading or playing: in that quiet state she caused me little trouble: but it was succeeded by an interval of impatient, fretful weariness; and being too busy, and too old then, to run up and down amusing her, I hit on a method by which she might entertain herself.

I used to send her on travels round the grounds – now on foot, and now on a pony; indulging her with a patient audience of all her real and imaginary adventures, when she returned.

The summer shone in full prime; and she took such a taste for this solitary rambling that she often contrived to remain out from breakfast till tea; and then the evenings were spent in recounting her fanciful tales. I did not fear her breaking bounds, because the gates were generally locked, and I thought she would scarcely venture forth alone, if they had stood wide open.

Unluckily, my confidence proved misplaced. Catherine came to me, one morning, at eight o'clock, and said she was that day an Arabian merchant, going to cross the Desert with his caravan; and I must give her plenty of provision for herself and beasts, a horse and three camels, personated by a large hound and a couple of pointers.

I got together good store of dainties, and slung them in a basket on one side of the saddle; and she sprang up as gay as a fairy, sheltered by her wide-brimmed hat and gauze veil from the July sun, and trotted off with a merry laugh, mocking my cautious counsel to avoid galloping, and come back early.

The naughty thing never made her appearance at tea. One traveller, the hound, being an old dog, and fond of its ease, returned; but neither Cathy, nor the pony, nor the two pointers were visible in any direction; and I despatched emissaries down this path, and that path, and, at last, went wandering in search of her myself.

# Wuthering Heights

There was a labourer working at a fence round a plantation, on the borders of the grounds. I enquired of him if he had seen our young lady.

'I saw her at morn,' he replied; 'she would have me cut her a hazel switch; and then she leapt her galloway over the hedge yonder, where it is lowest, and galloped out of sight.'

You may guess how I felt at hearing this news. It struck me directly she must have started for Penistone Crags.

'What will become of her?' I ejaculated, pushing through a gap which the man was repairing, and making straight to the high road.

I walked as if for a wager, mile after mile, till a turn brought me in view of the Heights, but no Catherine could I detect, far or near.

The Crags lie about a mile and a half beyond Mr Heathcliff's place, and that is four from the Grange, so I began to fear night would fall ere I could reach them.

'And what if she should have slipped in clambering among them,' I reflected, 'and been killed, or broken some of her bones?'

My suspense was truly painful; and, at first, it gave me delightful relief to observe, in hurrying by the farmhouse, Charlie, the fiercest of the pointers, lying under a window, with swelled head and bleeding ear. I opened the wicket, and ran to the door, knocking vehemently for admittance. A woman whom I knew, and who formerly lived at Gimmerton, answered – she had been servant there since the death of Mr Earnshaw.

'Ah,' said she, 'you are come a-seeking your little mistress! don't be frightened. She's here safe – but I'm glad it isn't the master.'

'He is not at home then, is he?' I panted, quite breathless with quick walking and alarm.

'No, no,' she replied: 'both he and Joseph are off, and I think they won't return this hour or more. Step in and rest you a bit.'

I entered, and beheld my stray lamb, seated on the hearth, rocking herself in a little chair that had been her mother's, when a child. Her hat was hung against the wall, and she seemed perfectly at home, laughing and chattering, in the best spirits imaginable, to Hareton, now a great, strong lad of eighteen, who stared at her with considerable curiosity and astonishment; comprehending precious little of the fluent succession of remarks and questions which her tongue never ceased pouring forth.

'Very well, Miss,' I exclaimed, concealing my joy under an angry countenance. 'This is your last ride, till papa comes back. I'll not trust you over the threshold again, you naughty, naughty girl!'

'Aha, Ellen!' she cried, gaily, jumping up, and running to my side. 'I shall have a pretty story to tell to-night – and so you've found me out. Have you ever been here in your life before?'

'Put that hat on, and home at once,' said I. 'I'm dreadfully grieved at you, Miss Cathy, you've done extremely wrong. It's no use pouting and crying; that won't repay the trouble I've had, scouring the country after you. To think how Mr Linton charged me to keep you in; and you stealing off so; it shows you are a cunning little fox, and nobody will put faith in you any more.'

'What have I done?' sobbed she, instantly checked. 'Papa charged me nothing – he'll not scold me, Ellen – he's never cross, like you!'

# Wuthering Heights

'Come, come!' I repeated. 'I'll tie the riband. Now, let us have no petulance. Oh, for shame. You thirteen years old, and such a baby!'

This exclamation was caused by her pushing the hat from her head, and retreating to the chimney out of my reach.

'Nay,' said the servant, 'don't be hard on the bonny lass, Mrs Dean. We made her stop – she'd fain have ridden forwards, afeard you should be uneasy. But Hareton offered to go with her, and I thought he should. It's a wild road over the hills.'

Hareton, during the discussion, stood with his hands in his pockets, too awkward to speak, though he looked as if he did not relish my intrusion.

'How long am I to wait?' I continued, disregarding the woman's interference. 'It will be dark in ten minutes. Where is the pony, Miss Cathy? And where is Phenix? I shall leave you, unless you be quick, so please yourself.'

'The pony is in the yard,' she replied, 'and Phenix is shut in there. He's bitten – and so is Charlie. I was going to tell you all about it; but you are in a bad temper, and don't deserve to hear.'

I picked up her hat, and approached to reinstate it; but perceiving that the people of the house took her part, she commenced capering round the room; and, on my giving chase, ran like a mouse, over and under, and behind the furniture, rendering it ridiculous for me to pursue.

Hareton and the woman laughed; and she joined them, and waxed more impertinent still; till I cried, in great irritation,

'Well, Miss Cathy, if you were aware whose house this is, you'd be glad enough to get out.'

'It's *your* father's, isn't it' said she, turning to Hareton.

'Nay,' he replied, looking down, and blushing bashfully.

He could not stand a steady gaze from her eyes, though they were just his own.

'Whose then – your master's?' she asked.

He coloured deeper, with a different feeling, muttered an oath, and turned away.

'Who is his master?' continued the tiresome girl, appealing to me. 'He talked about "our house," and "our folk." I thought he had been the owner's son. And he never said, Miss; he should have done, shouldn't he, if he's a servant?'

Hareton grew black as a thunder-cloud, at this childish speech. I silently shook my questioner, and, at last, succeeded in equipping her for departure.

'Now, get my horse,' she said, addressing her unknown kinsman as she would one of the stable-boys at the Grange. 'And you may come with me. I want to see where the goblin hunter rises in the marsh, and to hear about the *fairishes*, as you call them – but make haste! What's the matter? Get my horse, I say.'

'I'll see thee damned, before I be *thy* servant!' growled the lad.

'You'll see me *what*?' asked Catherine in surprise.

'Damned – thou saucy witch!' he replied.

'There, Miss Cathy! you see you have got into pretty company,' I interposed. 'Nice words to be used to a young lady! Pray don't begin to dispute with him – Come, let us seek for Minny ourselves, and begone.'

'But Ellen,' cried she, staring, fixed in astonishment. 'How dare he speak so to me? Mustn't he be made to do as I ask him? You wicked creature, I shall tell papa what you said – Now then!'

# Wuthering Heights

Hareton did not appear to feel this threat; so the tears sprung into her eyes with indignation. 'You bring the pony,' she exclaimed, turning to the woman, 'and let my dog free this moment!'

'Softly, Miss,' answered the addressed. 'You'll lose nothing by being civil. Though Mr Hareton, there, be not the master's son, he's your cousin; and I was never hired to serve you.'

'*He* my cousin!' cried Cathy with a scornful laugh.

'Yes, indeed,' responded her reprover.

'Oh, Ellen! don't let them say such things,' she pursued in great trouble. 'Papa is gone to fetch my cousin from London – my cousin is a gentleman's son – That my –' she stopped, and wept outright; upset at the bare notion of relationship with such a clown.

'Hush, hush!' I whispered, 'people can have many cousins and of all sorts, Miss Cathy, without being any the worse for it; only they needn't keep their company, if they be disagreeable, and bad.'

'He's not, he's not my cousin, Ellen!' she went on, gathering fresh grief from reflection, and flinging herself into my arms for refuge from the idea.

I was much vexed at her and the servant for their mutual revelations; having no doubt of Linton's approaching arrival, communicated by the former, being reported to Mr Heathcliff and feeling as confident that Catherine's first thought on her father's return, would be to seek an explanation of the latter's assertion, concerning her rude-bred kindred.

Hareton, recovering from his disgust at being taken for a servant, seemed moved by her distress; and, having fetched the pony round to the door, he took, to propitiate her, a fine crooked-legged terrier whelp from the kennel; and putting it into her hand, bid her wisht; for he meant naught.

Pausing in her lamentations, she surveyed him with a glance of awe and horror, then burst forth anew.

I could scarcely refrain from smiling at this antipathy to the poor fellow; who was a well-made, athletic youth, good looking in features, and stout and healthy, but attired in garments befitting his daily occupations of working on the farm, and lounging among the moors after rabbits and game. Still, I thought I could detect in his physiognomy a mind owning better qualities than his father ever possessed. Good things lost amid a wilderness of weeds, to be sure, whose rankness far over-topped their neglected growth; yet notwithstanding, evidence of a wealthy soil that might yield luxuriant crops, under other and favourable circumstances. Mr Heathcliff, I believe, had not treated him physically ill; thanks to his fearless nature, which offered no temptation to that course of oppression; it had none of the timid susceptibility that would have given zest to ill-treatment, in Heathcliff's judgment. He appeared to have bent his malevolence on making him a brute: he was never taught to read or write; never rebuked for any bad habit which did not annoy his keeper; never led a single step towards virtue, or guarded by a single precept against vice. And from what I heard, Joseph contributed much to his deterioration by a narrow-minded partiality which prompted him to flatter and pet him, as a boy, because he was the head of the old family. And as he had been in the habit of accusing Catherine Earnshaw, and Heathcliff, when children, of putting the master past his patience, and compelling him to seek solace in drink, by what he termed their 'offald

# Wuthering Heights

ways,' so, at present, he laid the whole burden of Hareton's faults on the shoulders of the usurper of his property.

If the lad swore he wouldn't correct him; nor however culpably he behaved. It gave Joseph satisfaction, apparently, to watch him go the worst lengths. He allowed that he was ruined; that his soul was abandoned to perdition; but then, he reflected that Heathcliff must answer for it. Hareton's blood would be required at his hands; and there lay immense consolation in that thought.

Joseph had instilled into him a pride of name, and of his lineage; he would, had he dared, have fostered hate between him and the present owner of the Heights, but his dread of that owner amounted to superstition; and he confined his feelings, regarding him, to muttered innuendoes and private comminations.

I don't pretend to be intimately acquainted with the mode of living customary in those days, at Wuthering Heights. I only speak from hearsay, for I saw little. The villagers affirmed Mr Heathcliff was *near*, and a cruel hard landlord to his tenants; but the house, inside, had regained its ancient aspect of comfort under female management; and the scenes of riot common in Hindley's time, were not now enacted within its walls. The master was too gloomy to seek companionship with any people, good or bad, and he is yet –

This, however, is not making progress with my story. Miss Cathy rejected the peace-offering of the terrier, and demanded her own dogs, Charlie and Phenix. They came limping, and hanging their heads; and we set out for home, sadly out of sorts, every one of us.

I could not wring from my little lady how she had spent the day; except that, as I supposed, the goal of her pilgrimage was Penistone Crags; and she arrived without adventure to the gate of the farmhouse, when Hareton happened to issue forth, attended by some canine followers who attacked her train.

They had a smart battle, before their owners could separate them: that formed an introduction. Catherine told Hareton who she was, and where she was going; and asked him to show her the way, finally, beguiling him to accompany her.

He opened the mysteries of the Fairy cave, and twenty other queer places; but being in disgrace, I was not favoured with a description of the interesting objects she saw.

I could gather, however, that her guide had been a favourite till she hurt his feelings by addressing him as a servant, and Heathcliff's housekeeper hurt hers, by calling him her cousin.

Then the language he had held to her rankled in her heart; she who was always 'love,' and 'darling,' and 'queen,' and 'angel,' with everybody at the Grange, to be insulted so shockingly by a stranger! She did not comprehend it; and hard work I had, to obtain a promise that she would not lay the grievance before her father.

I explained how he objected to the whole household at the Heights, and how sorry he would be to find she had been there; but I insisted most on the fact, that if she revealed my negligence of his orders, he would perhaps be so angry that I should have to leave; and Cathy couldn't bear that prospect: she pledged her word, and kept it, for my sake – after all, she was a sweet little girl.

# Chapter 19

letter, edged with black, announced the day of my master's return. Isabella was dead; and he wrote to bid me to get mourning for his daughter, and arrange a room, and other accommodations, for his youthful nephew.

Catherine ran wild with joy at the idea of welcoming her father back: and indulged most sanguine anticipations of the innumerable excellences of her 'real' cousin.

The evening of their expected arrival came. Since early morning, she had been busy, ordering her own small affairs; and now, attired in her new black frock – poor thing! her aunt's death impressed her with no definite sorrow – she obliged me, by constant worrying, to walk with her, down through the grounds, to meet them.

'Linton is just six months younger than I am,' she chattered as we strolled leisurely over the swells and hollows of mossy turf, under shadow of the trees. 'How delightful it will be to have him for a playfellow! Aunt Isabella sent papa a beautiful lock of his hair; it was lighter than mine – more flaxen, and quite as fine. I have it carefully preserved in a little glass box; and I've often thought what pleasure it would be to see its owner – Oh! I am happy – and papa, dear, dear papa! Come, Ellen, let us run! come run!'

She ran, and returned and ran again, many times before my sober footsteps reached the gate, and then she seated herself on the grassy bank beside the path, and tried to wait patiently; but that was impossible; she couldn't be still a minute.

'How long they are!' she exclaimed. 'Ah, I see some dust on the road – they are coming! No! When will they be here? May we not go a little way – half a mile, Ellen, only just half a mile? Do say yes, to that clump of birches at the turn!'

I refused staunchly: and, at length, her suspense was ended: the travelling carriage rolled in sight.

Miss Cathy shrieked, and stretched out her arms, as soon as she caught her father's face, looking from the window. He descended, nearly as eager as herself; and a considerable interval elapsed, ere they had a thought to spare for any but themselves.

While they exchanged caresses, I took a peep in to see after Linton. He was asleep, in a corner, wrapped in a warm, fur-lined cloak, as if it had been winter. A pale, delicate, effeminate boy, who might have been taken for my master's younger brother, so strong was the resemblance; but there was a sickly peevishness in his aspect, that Edgar Linton never had.

# Wuthering Heights

The latter saw me looking; and having shaken hands, advised me to close the door, and leave him undisturbed; for the journey had fatigued him.

Cathy would fain have taken one glance; but her father told her to come on, and they walked together up the park, while I hastened before, to prepare the servants.

'Now, darling,' said Mr Linton, addressing his daughter, as they halted at the bottom of the front steps. 'Your cousin is not so strong or so merry as you are, and he has lost his mother, remember, a very short time since, therefore, don't expect him to play and run about with you directly. And don't harass him much by talking – let him be quiet this evening, at least, will you?'

'Yes, yes, papa,' answered Catherine; 'but I do want to see him; and he hasn't once looked out.'

The carriage stopped; and the sleeper, being roused, was lifted to the ground by his uncle.

'This is your cousin Cathy, Linton,' he said, putting their little hands together. 'She's fond of you already; and mind you don't grieve her by crying to-night. Try to be cheerful now; the travelling is at an end, and you have nothing to do but rest and amuse yourself as you please.'

'Let me go to bed then,' answered the boy, shrinking from Catherine's salute; and he put his fingers to his eyes to remove incipient tears.

'Come, come, there's a good child,' I whispered, leading him in. 'You'll make her weep, too – see how sorry she is for you!'

I do not know whether it were sorrow for him, but his cousin put on as sad a countenance as himself, and returned to her father. All three entered, and mounted to the library, where tea was laid ready.

I proceeded to remove Linton's cap and mantle, and placed him on a chair by the table; but he was no sooner seated than he began to cry afresh. My master inquired what was the matter.

'I can't sit on a chair,' sobbed the boy.

'Go to the sofa then; and Ellen shall bring you some tea,' answered his uncle, patiently.

He had been greatly tried during the journey, I felt convinced, by his fretful, ailing charge.

Linton slowly trailed himself off, and lay down. Cathy carried a foot-stool and her cup to his side.

At first she sat silent; but that could not last; she had resolved to make a pet of her little cousin, as she would have him to be; and she commenced stroking his curls, and kissing his cheek, and offering him tea in her saucer, like a baby. This pleased him, for he was not much better; he dried his eyes, and lightened into a faint smile.

'Oh, he'll do very well,' said the master to me, after watching them a minute. 'Very well, if we can keep him, Ellen. The company of a child of his own age will instil new spirit into him soon; and by wishing for strength, he'll gain it.'

'Aye, if we can keep him!' I mused to myself; and sore misgivings came over me that there was slight hope of that. And then, I thought, however will that weakling live at Wuthering Heights, between his father and Hareton? What playmates and instructors they'll be.

Our doubts were presently decided; even earlier than I expected. I had just taken the children upstairs, after tea was finished, and had just seen Linton

asleep – he would not suffer me to leave him, till that was the case – I had come down, and was standing by the table in the hall, lighting a bed-room candle for Mr Edgar, when a maid stepped out of the kitchen, and informed me that Mr Heathcliff's servant, Joseph, was at the door, and wished to speak with the master.

'I shall ask him what he wants first,' I said, in considerable trepidation. 'A very unlikely hour to be troubling people, and the instant they have returned from a long journey. I don't think the master can see him.'

Joseph had advanced through the kitchen, as I uttered these words, and now presented himself in the hall. He was donned in his Sunday garments, with his most sanctimonious and sourest face; and holding his hat in one hand, and his stick in the other, he proceeded to clean his shoes on the mat.

'Good evening, Joseph,' I said, coldly. 'What business brings you here to-night?'

'It's Maister Linton Aw mun spake tull,' he answered, waving me disdainfully aside.

'Mr Linton is going to bed; unless you have something particular to say, I'm sure he won't hear it now,' I continued. 'You had better sit down in there, and entrust your message to me.'

'Which is his rahm?' pursued the fellow, surveying the range of closed doors.

I perceived he was bent on refusing my mediation; so very reluctantly I went up to the library, and announced the unseasonable visitor; advising that he should be dismissed till next day.

Mr Linton had no time to empower me to do so, for he mounted close at my heels, and pushing into the apartment planted himself at the far side of the table, with his two fists clapped on the head of his stick, and began in an elevated tone, as if anticipating opposition.

'Hatecliff has sent me for his lad, un Aw munn't goa back 'baht him.'

Edgar Linton was silent a minute: an expression of exceeding sorrow overcast his features; he would have pitied the child on his own account; but, recalling Isabella's hopes and fears, and anxious wishes for her son, and her commendations of him to his care, he grieved bitterly at the prospect of yielding him up, and searched in his heart how it might be avoided. No plan offered itself: the very exhibition of any desire to keep him would have rendered the claimant more peremptory: there was nothing left but to resign him. However, he was not going to rouse him from his sleep.

'Tell Mr Heathcliff,' he answered calmly, 'that his son shall come to Wuthering Heights to-morrow. He is in bed, and too tired to go any distance now. You may also tell him that the mother of Linton desired him to remain under my guardianship; and, at present, his health is very precarious.'

'Noa!' said Joseph, giving a thud with his prop on the floor, and assuming an authoritative air. 'Noa! that manes nowt – Hatecliff makes noa 'cahnt uh t' mother, nor yah norther – bud he'll hev his lad; und Aw mun tak him – soa nah yah knaw!'

'You shall not to-night!' answered Linton, decisively. 'Walk down stairs at once, and repeat to your master what I have said. Ellen, show him down. Go –'

And, aiding the indignant elder with a lift by the arm, he rid the room of him, and closed the door.

'Varrah weel!' shouted Joseph, as he slowly drew off. 'Tuh morn, he's come hisseln, un' thrust *him* aht, if yah darr!'

# Chapter 20

To obviate the danger of this threat being fulfilled, Mr Linton commissioned me to take the boy home early, on Catherine's pony, and said he –

'As we shall now have no influence over his destiny, good or bad, you must say nothing of where he is gone to my daughter; she cannot associate with him hereafter; and it is better for her to remain in ignorance of his proximity, lest she should be restless and anxious to visit the Heights – merely tell her, his father sent for him suddenly, and he has been obliged to leave us.'

Linton was very reluctant to be roused from his bed, at five o'clock, and astonished to be informed that he must prepare for further travelling: but I softened off the matter by stating that he was going to spend some time with his father, Mr Heathcliff, who wished to see him so much, he did not like to defer the pleasure till he should recover from his late journey.

'My father!' he cried, in strange perplexity. 'Mamma never told me I had a father. Where does he live? I'd rather stay with uncle.'

'He lives a little distance from the Grange,' I replied, 'just beyond those hills – not so far, but you may walk over here, when you get hearty. And you should be glad to go home, and to see him. You must try to love him, as you did your mother, and then he will love you.'

'But why have I not heard of him before?' asked Linton. 'Why didn't mamma and he live together, as other people do?'

'He had business to keep him in the north,' I answered; 'and your mother's health required her to reside in the south.'

'And why didn't mamma speak to me about him?' persevered the child. 'She often talked of uncle, and I learnt to love him long ago. How am I to love papa? I don't know him.'

'Oh, all children love their parents,' I said. 'Your mother perhaps, thought you would want to be with him, if she mentioned him often to you. Let us make haste. An early ride on such a beautiful morning is much preferable to an hour's more sleep.'

'Is *she* to go with us,' he demanded, 'the little girl I saw yesterday?'

'Not now,' replied I.

'Is uncle?' he continued.

'No, I shall be your companion there,' I said.

Linton sank back on his pillow, and fell into a brown study.

# Wuthering Heights

'I won't go without uncle,' he cried at length; 'I can't tell where you mean to take me.'

I attempted to persuade him of the naughtiness of showing reluctance to meet his father: still he obstinately resisted any progress towards dressing, and I had to call for my master's assistance, in coaxing him out of bed.

The poor thing was finally got off with several delusive assurances that his absence should be short; that Mr Edgar and Cathy would visit him; and other promises, equally ill-founded, which I invented and reiterated, at intervals, throughout the way.

The pure heather-scented air, and the bright sunshine, and the gentle canter of Minny, relieved his despondency, after a while. He began to put questions concerning his new home, and its inhabitants, with greater interest and liveliness.

'Is Wuthering Heights as pleasant a place as Thrushcross Grange?' he inquired, turning to take a last glance into the valley, whence a light mist mounted, and formed a fleecy cloud, on the skirts of the blue.

'It is not so buried in trees,' I replied, 'and it is not quite so large, but you can see the country beautifully, all round; and the air is healthier for you – fresher, and dryer. You will, perhaps, think the building old and dark, at first – though it is a respectable house, the next best in the neighbourhood. And you will have such nice rambles on the moors! Hareton Earnshaw – that is Miss Cathy's other cousin; and so yours in a manner – will show you all the sweetest spots; and you can bring a book in fine weather, and make a green hollow your study; and, now and then, your uncle may join you in a walk: he does, frequently, walk out on the hills.'

'And what is my father like?' he asked. 'Is he as young and handsome as uncle?'

'He's as young,' said I 'but he has black hair, and eyes; and looks sterner, and he is taller and bigger altogether. He'll not seem to you so gentle and kind at first, perhaps, because, it is not his way – still, mind you be frank and cordial with him; and naturally, he'll be fonder of you than any uncle, for you are his own.'

'Black hair and eyes!' mused Linton, 'I can't fancy him. Then I am not like him, am I?'

'Not much,' I answered . . . Not a morsel, I thought, surveying with regret the white complexion and slim frame of my companion, and his large languid eyes . . . his mother's eyes, save that, unless a morbid touchiness kindled them, a moment, they had not a vestige of her sparkling spirit.

'How strange that he should never come to see mamma and me!' he murmured. 'Has he ever seen me? If he have, I must have been a baby – I remember not a single thing about him!'

'Why, Master Linton,' said I, 'three hundred miles is a great distance: and ten years seem very different in length to a grown-up person, compared with what they do to you. It is probable Mr Heathcliff proposed going, from summer to summer, but never found a convenient opportunity; and now it is too late – Don't trouble him with questions on the subject: it will disturb him for no good.'

The boy was fully occupied with his own cogitations for the remainder of the ride, till we halted before the farm-house garden gate. I watched to catch his impressions in his countenance. He surveyed the carved front, and low-bowed lattices; the straggling gooseberry bushes, and crooked firs, with solemn intent-

ness, and then shook his head: his private feelings entirely disapproved of the exterior of his new abode; but he had sense to postpone complaining – there might be compensation within.

Before he dismounted, I went and opened the door. It was half-past six; the family had just finished breakfast; the servant was clearing and wiping down the table; Joseph stood by his master's chair telling some tale concerning a lame horse; and Hareton was preparing for the hay-field.

'Hallo, Nelly!' cried Mr Heathcliff when he saw me. 'I feared I should have to come down and fetch my property myself. You've brought it, have you? Let's see what we can make of it.'

He got up and strode to the door: Hareton and Joseph followed in gaping curiosity. Poor Linton ran a frightened eye over the faces of the three.

'Sure-ly,' said Joseph, after a grave inspection, 'he's swopped wi ye, maister, an' yon's his lass!'

Heathcliff, having stared his son into an ague of confusion, uttered a scornful laugh.

'God! what a beauty! what a lovely, charming thing!' he exclaimed. 'Haven't they reared it on snails, and sour milk, Nelly? Oh, damn my soul! but that's worse than I expected – and the devil knows I was not sanguine!'

I bid the trembling and bewildered child get down, and enter. He did not thoroughly comprehend the meaning of his father's speech, or whether it were intended for him: indeed, he was not yet certain that the grim, sneering stranger was his father; but he clung to me with growing trepidation; and on Mr Heathcliff's taking a seat, and bidding him 'come hither,' he hid his face on my shoulder, and wept.

'Tut, tut!' said Heathcliff, stretching out a hand and dragging him roughly between his knees, and then holding up his head by the chin. 'None of that nonsense! We're not going to hurt thee, Linton – isn't that thy name? Thou are thy mother's child, entirely! Where is *my* share in thee, puling chicken?'

He took off the boy's cap and pushed back his thick flaxen curls, felt his slender arms, and his small fingers; during which examination, Linton ceased crying, and lifted his great blue eyes to inspect the inspector.

'Do you know me?' asked Heathcliff, having satisfied himself that the limbs were all equally frail and feeble.

'No!' said Linton, with a gaze of vacant fear.

'You've heard of me, I dare say?'

'No,' he replied again.

'No? What a shame of your mother, never to waken your filial regard for me! You are my son, then, I'll tell you; and your mother was a wicked slut to leave you in ignorance of the sort of father you possessed – Now, don't wince, and colour up! Though it *is* something to see you have not white blood – Be a good lad; and I'll do for you – Nelly, if you be tired you may sit down; if not, get home again – I guess you'll report what you hear, and see, to the cipher at the Grange; and this thing won't be settled while you linger about it.'

'Well,' replied I, 'I hope you'll be kind to the boy, Mr Heathcliff, or you'll not keep him long, and he's all you have akin, in the wide world, that you will ever know – remember.'

'I'll be *very* kind to him, you needn't fear,' he said, laughing. 'Only nobody else must be kind to him – I'm jealous of monopolizing his affection – And, to

begin my kindness, Joseph! bring the lad some breakfast – Hareton, you infernal calf, begone to your work. Yes, Nell,' he added when they had departed, 'my son is prospective owner of your place, and I should not wish him to die till I was certain of being his successor. Besides, he's *mine,* and I want the triumph of seeing *my* descendant fairly lord of their estates; my child hiring their children, to till their fathers' lands for wages – That is the sole consideration which can make me endure the whelp – I despise him for himself, and hate him for the memories he revives! But that consideration is sufficient; he's as safe with me, and shall be tended as carefully, as your master tends his own – I have a room upstairs, furnished for him in handsome style – I've engaged a tutor, also, to come three times a week, from twenty miles distance, to teach him what he pleases to learn. I've ordered Hareton to obey him: and in fact, I've arranged every thing with a view to preserve the superior and the gentleman in him, above his associates – I do regret, however, that he so little deserves the trouble – if I wished any blessing in the world, it was to find him a worthy object of pride, and I'm bitterly disappointed with the whey-faced whining wretch!'

While he was speaking, Joseph returned, bearing a basin of milk-porridge, and placed it before Linton. He stirred round the homely mess with a look of aversion, and affirmed he could not eat it.

I saw the old man-servant shared largely in his master's scorn of the child, though he was compelled to retain the sentiment in his heart, because Heathcliff plainly meant his underlings to hold him in honour.

'Cannot ate it?' repeated he, peering in Linton's face, and subduing his voice to a whisper, for fear of being overheard. 'But Maister Hareton nivir ate nowt else, when he wer a little un: und what wer gooid eneugh fur him's gooid eneugh fur yar, Aw's rayther think!'

'I *shan't* eat it!' answered Linton, snappishly. 'Take it away.'

Joseph snatched up the food indignantly, and brought it to us.

'Is there owt ails th' victuals?' he asked, thrusting the tray under Heathcliff's nose.

'What should ail them?' he said.

'Wah!' answered Joseph, 'yon dainty chap says he cannut ate 'em. Bud aw guess it's raight! His mother wer just soa – we wer a'most too mucky tuh sow t' corn fur makking her breead.'

'Don't mention his mother to me,' said the master, angrily. 'Get him something that he can eat, that's all. What is his usual food, Nelly?'

I suggested boiled milk or tea; and the housekeeper received instructions to prepare some.

Come, I reflected, his father's selfishness may contribute to his comfort. He perceives his delicate constitution, and the necessity of treating him tolerably. I'll console Mr Edgar by acquainting him with the turn Heathcliff's humour has taken.

Having no excuse for lingering longer, I slipped out, while Linton was engaged in timidly rebuffing the advances of a friendly sheep-dog. But he was too much on the alert to be cheated – as I closed the door, I heard a cry, and a frantic repetition of the words –

'Don't leave me! I'll not stay here! I'll not stay here!'

Then the latch was raised and fell – they did not suffer him to come forth. I mounted Minny, and urged her to a trot; and so my brief guardianship ended.

# Chapter 21

He had sad work with little Cathy that day; she rose in high glee, eager to join her cousin; and such passionate tears and lamentations followed the news of his departure, that Edgar himself was obliged to soothe her, by affirming he should come back soon; he added, however, 'if I can get him'; and there were no hopes of that.

This promise poorly pacified her; but time was more potent; and though still, at intervals, she inquired of her father, when Linton would return, before she did see him again, his features had waxed so dim in her memory that she did not recognize him.

When I chanced to encounter the housekeeper of Wuthering Heights, in paying business-visits to Gimmerton, I used to ask how the young master got on; for he lived almost as secluded as Catherine herself, and was never to be seen. I could gather from her that he continued in weak health, and was a tiresome inmate. She said Mr Heathcliff seemed to dislike him ever longer and worse, though he took some trouble to conceal it. He had an antipathy to the sound of his voice, and could not do at all with his sitting in the same room with him many minutes together.

There seldom passed much talk between them; Linton learnt his lessons, and spent his evenings in a small apartment they called the parlour; or else lay in bed all day; for he was constantly getting coughs, and colds, and aches, and pains of some sort.

'And I never knew such a faint-hearted creature,' added the woman; 'nor one so careful of hisseln. He *will* go on, if I leave the window open, a bit late in the evening. Oh! it's killing, a breath of night air! And he must have a fire in the middle of summer; and Joseph's bacca pipe is poison; and he must always have sweets and dainties, and always milk, milk for ever – heeding naught how the rest of us are pinched in winter – and there he'll sit, wrapped in his furred cloak in his chair by the fire, and some toast and water, or other slop on the hob to sip at; and if Hareton, for pity, comes to amuse him – Hareton is not bad-natured, though he's rough – they're sure to part, one swearing, and the other crying. I believe the master would relish Earnshaw's thrashing him to a mummy, if he were not his son; and, I'm certain, he would be fit to turn him out of doors, if he knew half the nursing he gives hisseln. But then, he won't go into danger of temptation; he never enters the parlour, and should Linton show those ways in the house where he is, he sends him upstairs directly.'

I divined, from this account, that utter lack of sympathy had rendered young Heathcliff selfish and disagreeable, if he were not so originally; and my interest

in him, consequently, decayed; though still I was moved with a sense of grief at his lot, and a wish that he had been left with us.

Mr Edgar encouraged me to gain information; he thought a great deal about him, I fancy, and would have run some risk to see him; and he told me once to ask the housekeeper whether he ever came into the village?

She said he had only been twice, on horseback, accompanying his father; and both times he pretended to be quite knocked up for three or four days afterwards.

That housekeeper left, if I recollect rightly, two years after he came; and another, whom I did not know, was her successor: she lives there still.

Time wore on at the Grange in its former pleasant way, till Miss Cathy reached sixteen. On the anniversary of her birth we never manifested any signs of rejoicing, because it was, also, the anniversary of my late mistress's death. Her father invariably spent that day alone in the library; and walked, at dusk, as far as Gimmerton kirkyard, where he would frequently prolong his stay beyond midnight. Therefore Catherine was thrown on her own resources for amusement.

This twentieth of March was a beautiful spring day, and when her father had retired, my young lady came down dressed for going out, and said she had asked to have a ramble on the edge of the moors with me; and Mr Linton had given her leave, if we went only a short distance, and were back within the hour.

'So make haste, Ellen!' she cried. 'I know where I wish to go; where a colony of moor-game are settled; I want to see whether they have made their nests yet.'

'That must be a good distance up,' I answered; 'they don't breed on the edge of the moor.'

'No, it's not,' she said. 'I've gone very near with papa.'

I put on my bonnet and sallied out, thinking nothing more of the matter. She bounded before me, and returned to my side, and was off again like a young greyhound; and, at first, I found plenty of entertainment in listening to the larks singing far and near, and enjoying the sweet, warm sunshine; and watching her, my pet, and my delight, with her golden ringlets flying loose behind, and her bright cheek, as soft and pure in its bloom as a wild rose, and her eyes radiant with cloudless pleasure. She was a happy creature, and an angel, in those days. It's a pity she could not be content.

'Well,' said I, 'where are your moor-game, Miss Cathy? We should be at them – the Grange park-fence is a great way off now.'

'Oh, a little further – only a little further, Ellen,' was her answer, continually. 'Climb to that hillock, pass that bank, and by the time you reach the other side I shall have raised the birds.'

But there were so many hillocks and banks to climb and pass, that, at length, I began to be weary, and told her we must halt, and retrace our steps.

I shouted to her, as she had outstripped me, a long way; she either did not hear, or did not regard, for she still sprang on, and I was compelled to follow. Finally, she dived into a hollow; and before I came in sight of her again, she was two miles nearer Wuthering Heights than her own home; and I beheld a couple of persons arrest her, one of whom I felt convinced was Mr Heathcliff himself.

Cathy had been caught in the act of plundering, or, at least, hunting out the nests of the grouse.

The Heights were Heathcliff's land, and he was reproving the poacher.

'I've neither taken any nor found any,' she said, as I toiled to them, expanding her hands in corroboration of the statement.

'I didn't mean to take them; but papa told me there were quantities up here, and I wished to see the eggs.'

Heathcliff glanced at me with an ill-meaning smile, expressing his acquaintance with the party, and, consequently, his malevolence towards it, and demanded who 'papa' was.

'Mr Linton of Thrushcross Grange,' she replied. 'I thought you did not know me, or you wouldn't have spoken in that way.'

'You suppose papa is highly esteemed and respected, then?' he said sarcastically.

'And what are you?' inquired Catherine, gazing curiously on the speaker. 'That man I've seen before. Is he your son?'

She pointed to Hareton, the other individual, who had gained nothing but increased bulk and strength by the addition of two years to his age: he seemed as awkward and rough as ever.

'Miss Cathy,' I interrupted, 'it will be three hours instead of one that we are out, presently. We really must go back.'

'No, that man is not my son,' answered Heathcliff, pushing me aside. 'But I have one, and you have seen him before, too; and, though your nurse is in a hurry, I think both you and she would be the better for a little rest. Will you just turn this nab of heath, and walk into my house? You'll get home earlier for the ease; and you shall receive a kind welcome.'

I whispered Catherine that she mustn't, on any account, accede to the proposal; it was entirely out of the question.

'Why?' she asked, aloud. 'I'm tired of running, and the ground is dewy – I can't sit here. Let us go, Ellen! Besides, he says I have seen his son. He's mistaken, I think; but I guess where he lives – at the farm-house I visited in coming from Penistone Crags. Don't you?'

'I do. Come, Nelly, hold your tongue – it will be a treat for her to look in on us. Hareton, get forwards with the lass. You shall walk with me, Nelly.'

'No, she's not going to any such place,' I cried, struggling to release my arm, which he had seized; but she was almost at the door-stones already, scampering round the brow at full speed. Her appointed companion did not pretend to escort her; he shied off by the road-side, and vanished.

'Mr Heathcliff, it's very wrong,' I continued; 'you know you mean no good; and there she'll see Linton, and all will be told, as soon as ever we return; and I shall have the blame.'

'I want her to see Linton,' he answered; 'he's looking better these few days; it's not often he's fit to be seen. And we'll soon persuade her to keep the visit secret – where is the harm of it?'

'The harm of it is, that her father would hate me, if he found I suffered her to enter your house; and I am convinced you have a bad design in encouraging her to do so,' I replied.

'My design is as honest as possible. I'll inform you of its whole scope,' he said. 'That the two cousins may fall in love, and get married. I'm acting generously to your master; his young chit has no expectations, and should she second my wishes, she'll be provided for, at once, as joint successor with Linton.'

# Wuthering Heights

'If Linton died,' I answered, 'and his life is quite uncertain, Catherine would be the heir.'

'No, she would not,' he said. 'There is no clause in the will to secure it so; his property would go to me; but, to prevent disputes I desire their union, and am resolved to bring it about.'

'And I'm resolved she shall never approach your house with me again,' I returned, as we reached the gate, where Miss Cathy waited our coming.

Heathcliff bid me to be quiet; and preceding us up the path, hastened to open the door. My young lady gave him several looks, as if she could not exactly make up her mind what to think of him; but now he smiled when he met her eye, and softened his voice in addressing her, and I was foolish enough to imagine the memory of her mother might disarm him from desiring her injury.

Linton stood on the hearth. He had been out walking in the fields, for his cap was on, and he was calling to Joseph to bring him dry shoes.

He had grown tall of his age, still wanting some months of sixteen. His features were pretty yet, and his eyes and complexion brighter than I remembered them, though with merely temporary lustre borrowed from the salubrious air and genial sun.

'Now, who is that?' asked Mr Heathcliff, turning to Cathy. 'Can you tell?'

'Your son?' she said, having doubtfully surveyed, first one, and then the other.

'Yes, yes,' answered he; 'but is this the only time you have beheld him? Think! Ah! you have a short memory. Linton, don't you recall your cousin, that you used to tease us so with wishing to see?'

'What, Linton!' cried Cathy, kindling into joyful surprise at the name. 'Is that little Linton? He's taller than I am! Are you, Linton?'

The youth stepped forward, and acknowledged himself: she kissed him fervently, and they gazed with wonder at the change time had wrought in the appearance of each.

Catherine had reached her full height; her figure was both plump and slender, elastic as steel, and her whole aspect sparkling with health and spirits. Linton's looks and movements were very languid, and his form extremely slight; but there was a grace in his manner that mitigated these defects, and rendered him not unpleasing.

After exchanging numerous marks of fondness with him, his cousin went to Mr Heathcliff, who lingered by the door, dividing his attention between the objects inside, and those that lay without, pretending, that is, to observe the latter, and really noting the former alone.

'And you are my uncle, then!' she cried, reaching up to salute him. 'I thought I liked you, though you were cross, at first. Why don't you visit at the Grange with Linton? To live all these years such close neighbours, and never see us, is odd;—what have you done so for?'

'I visited it once or twice too often before you were born,' he answered. 'There – damn it! If you have any kisses to spare, give them to Linton – they are thrown away on me.'

'Naughty Ellen!' exclaimed Catherine, flying to attack me next with her lavish caresses. 'Wicked Ellen! to try to hinder me from entering. But I'll take this walk every morning in future – may I, uncle – and sometimes bring papa? Won't you be glad to see us?'

'Of course!' replied the uncle, with a hardly suppressed grimace, resulting

# Wuthering Heights

from his deep aversion to both the proposed visitors. 'But stay,' he continued, turning towards the young lady. 'Now I think of it, I'd better tell you. Mr Linton has a prejudice against me; we quarrelled at one time of our lives, with unchristian ferocity; and, if you mention coming here to him, he'll put a veto on your visits altogether. Therefore, you must not mention it, unless you be careless of seeing your cousin hereafter – you may come, if you will, but you must not mention it.'

'Why did you quarrel?' asked Catherine, considerably crestfallen.

'He thought me too poor to wed his sister,' answered Heathcliff, 'and was grieved that I got her – his pride was hurt, and he'll never forgive it.'

'That's wrong!' said the young lady: 'some time, I'll tell him so. But Linton and I have no share in your quarrel. I'll not come here, then, he shall come to the Grange.'

'It will be too far for me,' murmured her cousin, 'to walk four miles would kill me. No, come here, Miss Catherine, now and then, not every morning, but once or twice a week.'

The father launched towards his son a glance of bitter contempt.

'I am afraid, Nelly, I shall lose my labour,' he muttered to me. 'Miss Catherine, as the ninny calls her, will discover his value, and send him to the devil. Now, if it had been Hareton – do you know that, twenty times a day, I covet Hareton, with all his degradation? I'd have loved the lad had he been some one else. But I think he's safe from *her* love. I'll pit him against that paltry creature, unless it bestir itself briskly. We calculate it will scarcely last till it is eighteen. Oh, confound the vapid thing! He's absorbed in drying his feet, and never looks at her – Linton!'

'Yes, father,' answered the boy.

'Have you nothing to show your cousin, anywhere about; not even a rabbit, or a weasel's nest? Take her into the garden, before you change your shoes; and into the stable to see your horse.'

'Wouldn't you rather sit here?' asked Linton, addressing Cathy in a tone which expressed reluctance to move again.

'I don't know,' she replied, casting a longing look at the door, and evidently eager to be active.

He kept his seat, and shrank closer to the fire.

Heathcliff rose, and went into the kitchen, and from thence to the yard, calling out for Hareton.

Hareton responded, and presently the two re-entered. The young man had been washing himself, as was visible by the glow on his cheeks, and his wetted hair.

'Oh, I'll ask *you*, uncle,' cried Miss Cathy, recollecting the housekeeper's assertion. 'That is not my cousin, is he?'

'Yes,' he replied, 'your mother's nephew. Don't you like him?'

Catherine looked queer.

'Is he not a handsome lad?' he continued.

The uncivil little thing stood on tiptoe, and whispered a sentence in Heathcliff's ear.

He laughed; Hareton darkened; I perceived he was very sensitive to suspected slights, and had obviously a dim notion of his inferiority. But his master or guardian chased the frown by exclaiming –

# Wuthering Heights

'You'll be the favourite among us, Hareton! She says you are a – what was it? Well, something very flattering – Here! you go with her round the farm. And behave like a gentleman, mind! Don't use any bad words; and don't stare, when the young lady is not looking at you, and be ready to hide your face when she is; and, when you speak, say your words slowly, and keep your hands out of your pockets. Be off, and entertain her as nicely as you can.'

He watched the couple walking past the window. Earnshaw had his countenance completely averted from his companion. He seemed studying the family landscape with a stranger's, and an artist's interest.

Catherine took a sly look at him, expressing small admiration. She then turned her attention to seeking out objects of amusement for herself, and tripped merrily on, lilting a tune to supply the lack of conversation.

'I've tied his tongue,' observed Heathcliff. 'He'll not venture a single syllable, all the time! Nelly, you recollect me at his age – nay, some years younger – Did I ever look so stupid: so "gaumless," as Joseph calls it?'

'Worse,' I replied, 'because more sullen with it.'

'I've pleasure in him!' he continued reflecting aloud. 'He has satisfied my expectations – if he were a born fool I should not enjoy it half so much – But he's no fool; and I can sympathize with all his feelings, having felt them myself – I know what he suffers now, for instance, exactly – it is merely a beginning of what he shall suffer, though. And he'll never be able to emerge from his bathos of coarseness, and ignorance. I've got him faster than his scoundrel of a father secured me, and lower; for he takes a pride in his brutishness. I've taught him to scorn everything extra-animal as silly and weak – Don't you think Hindley would be proud of his son, if he could see him? almost as proud as I am of mine – But there's this difference, one is gold put to the use of paving-stones; and the other is tin polished to ape a service of silver – *Mine* has nothing valuable about it; yet I shall have the merit, of making it go as far as such poor stuff can go. *His* had first-rate qualities, and they are lost – rendered worse than unavailing – I have nothing to regret; he would have more than any, but I, are aware of – And the best of it is, Hareton is damnably fond of me! You'll own that I've outmatched Hindley there – If the dead villain could rise from his grave to abuse me for his offspring's wrongs, I should have the fun of seeing the said offspring fight him back again, indignant that he should dare to rail at the one friend he has in the world!'

Heathcliff chuckled a fiendish laugh at the idea; I made no reply, because I saw that he expected none.

Meantime, our young companion, who sat too removed from us to hear what was said, began to evince symptoms of uneasiness, probably repenting that he had denied himself the treat of Catherine's society, for fear of a little fatigue.

His father remarked the restless glances wandering to the window, and the hand irresolutely extended towards his cap.

'Get up, you idle boy!' he exclaimed with amused heartiness. 'Away after them! they are just at the corner, by the stand of hives.'

Linton gathered his energies, and left the hearth. The lattice was open, and, as he stepped out, I heard Cathy inquiring of her unsociable attendant, what was that inscription over the door?

Hareton stared up, and scratched his head like a true clown.

'It's some damnable writing,' he answered. 'I cannot read it.'

'Can't read it?' cried Catherine. 'I can read it ... It's English ... but I want to know, why is it there.'

Linton giggled – the first appearance of mirth he had exhibited.

'He does not know his letters,' he said to his cousin. 'Could you believe in the existence of such a colossal dunce?'

'Is he all as he should be?' asked Miss Cathy seriously, 'or is he simple ... not right? I've questioned him twice now, and each time he looked so stupid, I think he does not understand me; I can hardly understand *him*, I'm sure!'

Linton repeated his laugh, and glanced at Hareton tauntingly, who, certainly, did not seem quite clear of comprehension at that moment.

'There's nothing the matter, but laziness, is there, Earnshaw?' he said. 'My cousin fancies you are an idiot ... There you experience the consequence of scorning "book-larning," as you would say ... Have you noticed, Catherine, his frightful Yorkshire pronunciation?'

'Why, where the devil is the use on 't?' growled Hareton, more ready in answering his daily companion. He was about to enlarge further, but the two youngsters broke into a noisy fit of merriment; my giddy Miss being delighted to discover that she might turn his strange talk to matter of amusement.

'Where is the use of the devil in that sentence?' tittered Linton. 'Papa told you not to say any bad words, and you can't open your mouth without one ... Do try to behave like a gentleman, now do!'

'If thou wern't more a lass than a lad, I'd fell thee this minute, I would; pitiful lath of a crater!' retorted the angry boor, retreating, while his face burnt with mingled rage and mortification; for he was conscious of being insulted, and embarrassed how to resent it.

Mr Heathcliff having overheard the conversation, as well as I, smiled when he saw him go, but immediately afterwards, cast a look of singular aversion on the flippant pair, who remained chattering in the door-way. The boy finding animation enough while discussing Hareton's faults and deficiencies, and relating anecdotes of his goings on; and the girl relishing his pert and spiteful sayings, without considering the ill-nature they evinced; but I began to dislike, more than to compassionate, Linton, and to excuse his father, in some measure, for holding him cheap.

We stayed till afternoon: I could not tear Miss Cathy away, before; but happily my master had not quitted his apartment, and remained ignorant of our prolonged absence.

As we walked home, I would fain have enlightened my charge on the characters of the people we had quitted; but she got it into her head that I was prejudiced against them.

'Aha!' she cried, 'you take papa's side, Ellen – you are partial ... I know, or else you wouldn't have cheated me so many years, into the notion that Linton lived a long way from here. I'm really extremely angry, only, I'm so pleased, I can't show it! But you must hold your tongue about my uncle ... he's *my* uncle, remember, and I'll scold papa for quarrelling with him.'

And so she ran on, till I dropped endeavouring to convince her of her mistake.

She did not mention the visit that night, because she did not see Mr Linton. Next day it all came out, sadly to my chagrin; and still I was not altogether sorry: I thought the burden of directing and warning would be more efficiently borne by him than me, but he was too timid in giving satisfactory reasons for

his wish that she would shun connections with the household of the Heights, and Catherine liked good reasons for every restraint that harassed her petted will.

'Papa!' she exclaimed, after the morning's salutations, 'guess whom I saw yesterday, in my walk on the moors . . . Ah, papa, you started! you've not done right, have you, now? I saw – But listen, and you shall hear how I found you out, and Ellen, who is in league with you, and yet pretended to pity me so, when I kept hoping, and was always disappointed about Linton's coming back!'

She gave a faithful account of her excursion and its consequences; and my master, though he cast more than one reproachful look at me, said nothing, till she had concluded. Then he drew her to him, and asked if she knew why he had concealed Linton's near neighbourhood from her? Could she think it was to deny her a pleasure that she might harmlessly enjoy?

'It was because you disliked Mr Heathcliff,' she answered.

'Then you believe I care more for my own feelings than yours, Cathy?' he said. 'No, it was not because I disliked Mr Heathcliff; but because Mr Heathcliff dislikes me; and is a most diabolical man, delighting to wrong and ruin those he hates, if they give him the slightest opportunity. I knew that you could not keep up an acquaintance with your cousin, without being brought into contact with him; and I knew he would detest you, on my account; so, for your own good, and nothing else, I took precautions that you should not see Linton again – I meant to explain this some time as you grew older, and I'm sorry I delayed it!'

'But Mr Heathcliff was quite cordial, papa,' observed Catherine, not at all convinced; 'and *he* didn't object to our seeing each other; he said I might come to his house, when I pleased, only I must not tell you, because you had quarrelled with him, and would not forgive him for marrying Aunt Isabella. And you won't – *you* are the one to be blamed – he is willing to let *us* be friends, at least; Linton and I – and you are not.'

My master, perceiving that she would not take his word for her uncle-in-law's evil disposition, gave a hasty sketch of his conduct to Isabella, and the manner in which Wuthering Heights became his property. He could not bear to discourse long upon the topic, for though he spoke little of it, he still felt the same horror and detestation of his ancient enemy that had occupied his heart ever since Mrs Linton's death. 'She might have been living yet, if it had not been for him!' was his constant bitter reflection; and, in his eyes, Heathcliff seemed a murderer.

Miss Cathy, conversant with no bad deeds except her own slight acts of disobedience, injustice, and passion, rising from hot temper and thoughtlessness, and repented of on the day they were committed, was amazed at the blackness of spirit that could brood on, and cover revenge for years, and deliberately prosecute its plans, without a visitation of remorse. She appeared so deeply impressed and shocked at this new view of human nature – excluded from all her studies and all her ideas till now – that Mr Edgar deemed it unnecessary to pursue the subject. He merely added,

'You will know hereafter, darling, why I wish you to avoid his house and family – now, return to your old employments and amusements, and think no more about them!'

Catherine kissed her father, and sat down quietly to her lessons for a couple

of hours, according to custom; then she accompanied him into the grounds, and the whole day passed as usual: but in the evening, when she had retired to her room, and I went to help her to undress, I found her crying, on her knees by the bedside.

'Oh, fie, silly child!' I exclaimed. 'If you had any real griefs, you'd be ashamed to waste a tear on this little contrariety. You never had one shadow of substantial sorrow, Miss Catherine. Suppose, for a minute, that master and I were dead, and you were by yourself in the world – how would you feel, then? Compare the present occasion with such an affliction as that, and be thankful for the friends you have, instead of coveting more.'

'I'm not crying for myself, Ellen,' she answered, 'it's for him – He expected to see me again, to-morrow, and there, he'll be so disappointed – and he'll wait for me, and I shan't come!'

'Nonsense!' said I: 'do you imagine he has thought as much of you, as you have of him? Hasn't he Hareton for a companion? Not one in a hundred would weep at losing a relation they had just seen twice, for two afternoons – Linton will conjecture how it is, and trouble himself no further about you.'

'But may I not write a note to tell him why I cannot come?' she asked, rising to her feet. 'And just send those books, I promised to lend him – his books are not as nice as mine, and he wanted to have them extremely, when I told him how interesting they were – May I not, Ellen?'

'No, indeed, no, indeed!' replied I with decision. 'Then he would write to you, and there'd never be an end of it – No, Miss Catherine, the acquaintance must be dropped entirely – so papa expects, and I shall see that it is done.'

'But how can one little note –' she recommenced, putting on an imploring countenance.

'Silence!' I interrupted. 'We will not begin with your little notes – Get into bed.'

She threw at me a very naughty look, so naughty that I would not kiss her goodnight at first: I covered her up, and shut her door, in great displeasure – but, repenting half-way, I returned softly, and lo! there was Miss, standing at the table with a bit of blank paper before her, and a pencil in her hand, which she guiltily slipped out of sight, on my re-entrance.

'You'll get nobody to take that, Catherine,' I said, 'if you write it; and at present I shall put out your candle.'

I set the extinguisher on the flame, receiving as I did so, a slap on my hand, and a petulant 'cross thing!' I then quitted her again, and she drew the bolt in one of her worst, most peevish humours.

The letter was finished and forwarded to its destination by a milk-fetcher who came from the village but that I didn't learn till some time afterwards. Weeks passed on, and Cathy recovered her temper, though she grew wondrous fond of stealing off to corners by herself, and often, if I came near her suddenly while reading, she would start, and bend over the book, evidently desirous to hide it; and I detected edges of loose paper sticking out beyond the leaves.

She also got a trick of coming down early in the morning, and lingering about the kitchen, as if she were expecting the arrival of something; and she had a small drawer in a cabinet in the library, which she would trifle over for hours, and whose key she took special care to remove when she left it.

One day, as she inspected this drawer, I observed that the playthings and

trinkets, which recently formed its contents, were transmuted into bits of folded paper.

My curiosity and suspicions were roused; I determined to take a peep at her mysterious treasures; so, at night, as soon as she and my master were safe upstairs, I searched and readily found among my house keys, one that would fit the lock. Having opened, I emptied the whole contents into my apron, and took them with me to examine at leisure in my own chamber.

Though I could not but suspect, I was still surprised to discover that they were a mass of correspondence, daily, almost, it must have been, from Linton Heathcliff, answers to documents forwarded by her. The earlier dated were embarrassed and short; gradually, however, they expanded into copious love letters, foolish as the age of the writer rendered natural, yet with touches, here and there, which I thought, were borrowed from a more experienced source.

Some of them struck me as singularly odd compounds of ardour and flatness; commencing in strong feeling, and concluding in the affected, wordy way that a schoolboy might use to a fancied, incorporeal sweetheart.

Whether they satisfied Cathy, I don't know, but they appeared very worthless trash to me.

After turning over as many as I thought proper, I tied them in a handkerchief and set them aside, re-locking the vacant drawer.

Following her habit, my young lady descended early, and visited the kitchen: I watched her go to the door, on the arrival of a certain little boy; and, while the dairy maid filled his can, she tucked something into his jacket pocket, and plucked something out.

I went round by the garden, and laid wait for the messenger, who fought valorously to defend his trust, and we spilt the milk between us; but I succeeded in abstracting the epistle; and, threatening serious consequences if he did not look sharp home, I remained under the wall, and perused Miss Cathy's affectionate composition. It was more simple and more eloquent than her cousin's, very pretty and very silly.

I shook my head, and went meditating into the house. The day being wet, she could not divert herself with rambling about the park; so, at the conclusion of her morning studies, she resorted to the solace of the drawer. Her father sat reading at the table; and I, on purpose, had sought a bit of work in some unripped fringes of the window curtain, keeping my eye steadily fixed on her proceedings.

Never did any bird flying back to a plundered nest which it had left brim-full of chirping young ones, express more complete despair in its anguished cries and flutterings, than she by her single 'Oh!' and the change that transfigured her late happy countenance. Mr Linton looked up.

'What is the matter, love? Have you hurt yourself?' he said.

His tone and look assured her *he* had not been the discoverer of the hoard.

'No, papa –' she gasped, 'Ellen! Ellen! come upstairs – I'm sick!'

I obeyed her summons, and accompanied her out.

'Oh, Ellen! you have got them,' she commenced immediately, dropping on her knees, when we were enclosed alone. 'Oh, give them to me, and I'll never do so again! Don't tell papa – You have not told papa, Ellen, say you have not! I've been exceedingly naughty, but I won't do it any more!'

With a grave severity in my manner, I bid her stand up.

# Wuthering Heights

'So,' I exclaimed, 'Miss Catherine, you are tolerably far on, it seems – you may well be ashamed of them! A fine bundle of trash you study in your leisure hours, to be sure – Why, it's good enough to be printed! And what do you suppose the master will think, when I display it before him? I haven't shown it yet, but you needn't imagine I shall keep your ridiculous secrets – For shame! And you must have led the way in writing such absurdities, he would not have thought of beginning, I'm certain.'

'I didn't! I didn't!' sobbed Cathy, fit to break her heart. 'I didn't once think of loving him till –'

'*Loving!*' cried I, as scornfully as I could utter the word. '*Loving!* Did anybody ever hear the like! I might just as well talk of loving the miller who comes once a year to buy our corn. Pretty loving, indeed, and both times together you have seen Linton hardly four hours, in your life! Now here is the babyish trash. I'm going with it to the library; and we'll see what your father says to such *loving.*'

She sprang at her precious epistles, but I held them above my head; and then she poured out further frantic entreaties that I would burn them – do anything rather than show them. And being really fully as inclined to laugh as scold, for I esteemed it all girlish vanity, I at length relented in a measure, and asked,

'If I consent to burn them, will you promise faithfully, neither to send nor receive a letter again, nor a book, for I perceive you have sent him books, nor locks of hair, nor rings, nor playthings?'

'We don't send playthings!' cried Catherine, her pride overcoming her shame.

'Nor anything at all, then, my lady!' I said. 'Unless you will, here I go.'

'I promise, Ellen!' she cried, catching my dress. 'Oh, put them in the fire, do, do!'

But when I proceeded to open a place with the poker, the sacrifice was too painful to be borne. She earnestly supplicated that I would spare her one or two.

'One or two, Ellen, to keep for Linton's sake!'

I unknotted the handkerchief, and commenced dropping them in from an angle, and the flame curled up the chimney.

'I will have one, you cruel wretch!' she screamed, darting her hand into the fire, and drawing forth some half consumed fragments, at the expense of her fingers.

'Very well – and I will have some to exhibit to papa!' I answered, shaking back the rest into the bundle, and turning anew to the door.

She emptied her blackened pieces into the flames, and motioned me to finish the immolation. It was done; I stirred up the ashes, and interred them under a shovel full of coals; and she mutely, and with a sense of intense injury, retired to her private apartment. I descended to tell my master that the young lady's qualm of sickness was almost gone, but I judged it best for her to lie down a while.

She wouldn't dine; but she reappeared at tea, pale, and red about the eyes, and marvellously subdued in outward aspect.

Next morning, I answered the letter by a slip of paper, inscribed, 'Master Heathcliff is requested to send no more notes to Miss Linton, as she will not receive them.' And, thenceforth, the little boy came with vacant pockets.

# Chapter 22

Summer drew to an end, and early Autumn – it was past Michaelmas, but the harvest was late that year, and a few of our fields were still uncleared.

Mr Linton and his daughter would frequently walk out among the reapers; at the carrying of the last sheaves, they stayed till dusk, and the evening happening to be chill and damp, my master caught a bad cold, that settling obstinately on his lungs, confined him indoors throughout the whole of the winter, nearly without intermission.

Poor Cathy, frightened from her little romance, had been considerably sadder and duller since its abandonment: and her father insisted on her reading less, and taking more exercise. She had his companionship no longer; I esteemed it a duty to supply its lack, as much as possible, with mine; an inefficient substitute, for I could only spare two or three hours, from my numerous diurnal occupations, to follow her footsteps, and then, my society was obviously less desirable than his.

On an afternoon in October, or the beginning of November, a fresh watery afternoon, when the turf and paths were rustling with moist, withered leaves, and the cold, blue sky was half hidden by clouds, dark grey streamers, rapidly mounting from the west, and boding abundant rain; I requested my young lady to forego her ramble because I was certain of showers. She refused; and I unwillingly donned a cloak, and took my umbrella to accompany her on a stroll to the bottom of the park: a formal walk which she generally affected if low-spirited – and that she invariably was when Mr Edgar had been worse than ordinary; a thing never known from his confession, but guessed both by her and me from his increased silence, and the melancholy of his countenance.

She went sadly on; there was no running or bounding now, though the chill wind might well have tempted her to a race. And often, from the side of my eye, I could detect her raising a hand, brushing something off her cheek.

I gazed round for a means of diverting her thoughts. On one side of the road rose a high, rough bank, where hazels and stunted oaks, with their roots half exposed, held uncertain tenure: the soil was too loose for the latter, and strong winds had blown some nearly horizontal. In summer, Miss Catherine delighted to climb among these trunks, and sit in the branches, swinging twenty feet above the ground; and I, pleased with her agility and her light, childish heart, still considered it proper to scold every time I caught her at such an elevation; but so that she knew there was no necessity for descending. From dinner to tea she would lie in her breeze-rocked cradle, doing nothing except singing old songs – my nursery lore – to herself, or watching the birds, joint tenants, feed and

# Wuthering Heights

entice their young ones to fly, or nestling with closed lids, half thinking, half dreaming, happier than words can express.

'Look, Miss!' I exclaimed, pointing to a nook under the roots of one twisted tree. 'Winter is not here yet. There's a little flower, up yonder, the last bud from the multitude of blue-bells that clouded those turf steps in July with a lilac mist. Will you clamber up, and pluck it to show to papa?'

Cathy stared a long time at the lonely blossom trembling in its earthly shelter, and replied, at length –

'No, I'll not touch it – but it looks melancholy, does it not, Ellen?'

'Yes,' I observed, 'about as starved and sackless as you – your cheeks are bloodless; let us take hold of hands and run. You're so low, I dare say I shall keep up with you.'

'No,' she repeated, and continued sauntering on, pausing, at intervals, to muse over a bit of moss, or a tuft of blanched grass, or a fungus spreading its bright orange among the heaps of brown foliage; and, ever and anon, her hand was lifted to her averted face.

'Catherine, why are you crying, love?' I asked, approaching and putting my arm over her shoulder. 'You mustn't cry because papa has a cold; be thankful it is nothing worse.'

She now put no further restraint on her tears; her breath was stifled by sobs.

'Oh, it *will* be something worse,' she said. 'And what shall I do when papa and you leave me, and I am by myself? I can't forget your·words, Ellen, they are always in my ear. How life will be changed, how dreary the world will be, when papa and you are dead.'

'None can tell, whether you won't die before us,' I replied. 'It's wrong to anticipate evil – we'll hope there are years and years to come before any of us go – master is young, and I am strong, and hardly forty-five. My mother lived till eighty, a canty dame to the last. And suppose Mr Linton were spared till he saw sixty, that would be more years than you have counted Miss. And would it not be foolish to mourn a calamity above twenty years beforehand?'

'But Aunt Isabella was younger than papa,' she remarked, gazing up with timid hope to seek further consolation.

'Aunt Isabella had not you and me to nurse her,' I replied. 'She wasn't as happy as master; she hadn't as much to live for. All you need do, is to wait well on your father, and cheer him by letting him see you cheerful; and avoid giving him anxiety on any subject – mind that, Cathy! I'll not disguise, but you might kill him, if you were wild and reckless, and cherished a foolish, fanciful affection for the son of a person who would be glad to have him in his grave – and allowed him to discover that you fretted over the separation he has judged it expedient to make.'

'I fret about nothing on earth except papa's illness,' answered my companion. 'I care for nothing in comparison with papa. And I'll never – never – oh, never, while I have my senses, do an act or say a word to vex him. I love him better than myself, Ellen; and I know it by this – I pray every night that I may live after him; because I would rather be miserable than that he should be – that proves I love him better than myself.'

'Good words,' I replied. 'But deeds must prove it also; and after he is well, remember you don't forget resolutions formed in the hour of fear.'

As we talked, we neared a door that opened on the road: and my young lady,

lightening into sunshine again, climbed up, and seated herself on the top of the wall, reaching over to gather some hips that bloomed scarlet on the summit branches of the wild rose trees, shadowing the highway side; the lower fruit had disappeared, but only birds could touch the upper, except from Cathy's present station.

In stretching to pull them, her hat fell off; and as the door was locked, she proposed scrambling down to recover it. I bid her be cautious lest she got a fall, and she nimbly disappeared.

But the return was no such easy matter; the stones were smooth and neatly cemented, and the rosebushes and the blackberry stragglers could yield no assistance in re-ascending. I, like a fool, didn't recollect that till I heard her laughing, and exclaiming –

'Ellen, you'll have to fetch the key, or else I must run round to the porter's lodge. I can't scale the ramparts on this side!'

'Stay where you are,' I answered, 'I have my bundle of keys in my pocket; perhaps I may manage to open it; if not, I'll go.'

Catherine amused herself with dancing to and fro before the door, while I tried all the large keys in succession. I had applied the last, and found that none would do; so, repeating my desire that she would remain there, I was about to hurry home as fast as I could, when an approaching sound arrested me. It was the trot of a horse; Cathy's dance stopped; and in a minute the horse stopped also.

'Who is that?' I whispered.

'Ellen, I wish you could open the door,' whispered back my companion, anxiously.

'Ho, Miss Linton!' cried a deep voice (the rider's), 'I'm glad to meet you. Don't be in haste to enter, for I have an explanation to ask and obtain.'

'I shan't speak to you, Mr Heathcliff!' answered Catherine. 'Papa says you are a wicked man, and you hate both him and me; and Ellen says the same.'

'That is nothing to the purpose,' said Heathcliff. (He it was.) 'I don't hate my son, I suppose, and it is concerning him that I demand your attention. Yes! you have cause to blush. Two or three months since, were you not in the habit of writing to Linton? making love in play, eh? You deserved, both of you, flogging for that! You especially, the elder, and less sensitive, as it turns out. I've got your letters, and if you give me any pertness, I'll send them to your father. I presume you grew weary of the amusement, and dropped it, didn't you? Well, you dropped Linton with it, into a Slough of Despond. He was in earnest – in love – really. As true as I live, he's dying for you – breaking his heart at your fickleness, not figuratively, but actually. Though Hareton has made him a standing jest for six weeks, and I have used more serious measures, and attempted to frighten him out of his idiocy, he gets worse daily, and he'll be under the sod before Summer, unless you restore him!'

'How can you lie so glaringly to the poor child!' I called from the inside. 'Pray ride on! How can you deliberately get up such paltry falsehoods? Miss Cathy, I'll knock the lock off with a stone. You won't believe that vile nonsense. You can feel in yourself, it is impossible that a person should die for the love of a stranger.'

'I was not aware there were eaves-droppers,' muttered the detected villain. 'Worthy Mrs Dean, I like you, but I don't like your double dealing,' he added,

aloud. 'How could *you* lie so glaringly, as to affirm I hated the "poor child"? And invent bugbear stories to terrify her from my door-stones? Catherine Linton (the very name warms me), my bonny lass, I shall be from home all this week, go and see if I have not spoken truth; do there's a darling! Just imagine your father in my place, and Linton in yours; then think how you would value your careless lover, if he refused to stir a step to comfort you, when your father, himself, entreated him; and don't, from pure stupidity, fall into the same error. I swear, on my salvation, he's going to his grave, and none but you can save him!'

The lock gave way, and I issued out.

'I swear Linton is dying,' repeated Heathcliff, looking hard at me. 'And grief and disappointment are hastening his death. Nelly, if you won't let her go, you can walk over yourself. But I shall not return till this time next week; and I think your master himself would scarcely object to her visiting her cousin!'

'Come in,' said I, taking Cathy by the arm and half forcing her to re-enter, for she lingered, viewing, with troubled eyes, the features of the speaker, too stern to express his inward deceit.

He pushed his horse close, and, bending down, observed –

'Miss Catherine, I'll own to you that I have little patience with Linton – and Hareton and Joseph have less. I'll own that he's with a harsh set. He pines for kindness, as well as love; and a kind word from you would be his best medicine. Don't mind Mrs Dean's cruel cautions, but be generous, and contrive to see him. He dreams of you day and night, and cannot be persuaded that you don't hate him, since you neither write nor call.'

I closed the door, and rolled a stone to assist the loosened lock in holding it; and spreading my umbrella, I drew my charge underneath, for the rain began to drive through the moaning branches of the trees, and warned us to avoid delay.

Our hurry prevented any comment on the encounter with Heathcliff, as we stretched towards home; but I divined instinctively that Catherine's heart was clouded now in double darkness. Her features were so sad, they did not seem hers: she evidently regarded what she had heard as every syllable true.

The master had retired to rest before we came in. Cathy stole to his room to inquire how he was; he had fallen asleep. She returned, and asked me to sit with her in the library. We took our tea together; and afterwards she lay down on the rug, and told me not to talk for she was weary.

I got a book, and pretended to read. As soon as she supposed me absorbed in my occupation, she recommenced her silent weeping: it appeared, at present, her favourite diversion. I suffered her to enjoy it a while; then, I expostulated; deriding and ridiculing all Mr Heathcliff's assertions about his son, as if I were certain she would coincide. Alas! I hadn't skill to counteract the effect his account had produced; it was just what he intended.

'You may be right, Ellen,' she answered; 'but I shall never feel at ease till I know – and I must tell Linton it is not my fault that I don't write; and convince him that I shall not change.'

What use were anger and protestations against her silly credulity? We parted that night hostile – but next day beheld me on the road to Wuthering Heights, by the side of my wilful young mistress's pony. I couldn't bear to witness her sorrow, to see her pale, dejected countenance, and heavy eyes; and I yielded, in

the faint hope that Linton himself might prove, by his reception of us, how little of the tale was founded on fact.

# Chapter 23

he rainy night had ushered in a misty morning – half frost, half drizzle – and temporary brooks crossed our path, gurgling from the uplands. My feet were thoroughly wetted; I was cross and low, exactly the humour suited for making the most of these disagreeable things.

We entered the farm-house by the kitchen way to ascertain whether Mr Heathcliff were really absent; because I put slight faith in his own affirmation.

Joseph seemed sitting in a sort of elysium alone, beside a roaring fire; a quart of ale on the table near him, bristling with large pieces of toasted oat cake; and his black, short pipe in his mouth.

Catherine ran to the hearth to warm herself. I asked if the master were in?

My question remained so long unanswered, that I thought the old man had grown deaf, and repeated it louder.

'Na – ay!' he snarled, or rather screamed through his nose, 'Na – ay! ya muh goa back whear yah coom frough.'

'Joseph!' cried a peevish voice, simultaneously with me, from the inner room. 'How often am I to call you? There are only a few red ashes now. Joseph! come at this moment.'

Vigorous puffs, and a resolute stare into the grate, declared he had no ear for this appeal. The housekeeper and Hareton were invisible; one gone on an errand, and the other at his work, probably. We knew Linton's tones and entered.

'Oh, I hope you'll die in a garret! starved to death,' said the boy, mistaking our approach for that of his negligent attendant.

He stopped, on observing his error; his cousin flew to him.

'Is that you, Miss Linton?' he said, raising his head from the arm of the great chair, in which he reclined. 'No – don't kiss me. It takes my breath – dear me! Papa said you would call,' continued he, after recovering a little from Catherine's embrace; while she stood by looking very contrite. 'Will you shut the door, if you please? you left it open; and those – those *detestable* creatures won't bring coals to the fire. It's so cold!'

I stirred up the cinders, and fetched a scuttle full myself. The invalid complained of being covered with ashes; but he had a tiresome cough, and looked feverish and ill, so I did not rebuke his temper.

'Well, Linton,' murmured Catherine, when his corrugated brow relaxed. 'Are you glad to see me? Can I do you any good?'

'Why didn't you come before?' he said. 'You should have come, instead of writing. It tired me dreadfully, writing those long letters. I'd far rather have

talked to you. Now, I can neither bear to talk, nor anything else. I wonder where Zillah is! Will you (looking at me) step into the kitchen and see?'

I had received no thanks for my other service; and being unwilling to run to and fro at his behest, I replied –

'Nobody is out there but Joseph.'

'I want to drink,' he exclaimed, fretfully, turning away. 'Zillah is constantly gadding off to Gimmerton since papa went. It's miserable! And I'm obliged to come down here – they resolved never to hear me upstairs.'

'Is your father attentive to you, Master Heathcliff?' I asked, perceiving Catherine to be checked in her friendly advances.

'Attentive? He makes *them* a little more attentive, at least,' he cried. 'The wretches! Do you know, Miss Linton, that brute Hareton laughs at me – I hate him – indeed, I hate them all – they are odious beings.'

Cathy began searching for some water; she lighted on a pitcher on the dresser, filled a tumbler, and brought it. He bid her add a spoonful of wine from a bottle on the table; and having swallowed a small portion, appeared more tranquil, and said she was very kind.

'And are you glad to see me?' asked she, reiterating her former question, and pleased to detect the faint dawn of a smile.

'Yes, I am – It's something new to hear a voice like yours!' he replied. 'But I *have* been vexed, because you wouldn't come – And papa swore it was owing to me; he called me a pitiful, shuffling, worthless thing; and said you despised me; and if he had been in my place, he would be more the master of the Grange than your father, by this time. But you don't despise me, do you, Miss –'

'I wish you would say Catherine, or Cathy!' interrupted my young lady. 'Despise you? No! Next to papa, and Ellen, I love you better than anybody living. I don't love Mr Heathcliff, though; and I dare not come when he returns; will he stay away many days?'

'Not many,' answered Linton, 'but he goes onto the moors frequently, since the shooting season commenced, and you might spend an hour or two with me, in his absence – Do! say you will! I think I should not be peevish with you; you'd not provoke me, and you'd be always ready to help me, wouldn't you?'

'Yes,' said Catherine, stroking his long soft hair, 'if I could only get papa's consent, I'd spend half my time with you – Pretty Linton! I wish you were my brother.'

'And then you would like me as well as your father? observed he more cheerfully. 'But papa says you would love me better than him, and all the world, if you were my wife – so I'd rather you were that!'

'No! I should never love anybody better than papa,' she returned gravely. 'And people hate their wives, sometimes; but not their sisters and brothers, and if you were the latter, you would live with us, and papa would be as fond of you, as he is of me.'

Linton denied that people ever hated their wives; but Cathy affirmed they did, and in her wisdom, instanced his own father's aversion to her aunt.

I endeavoured to stop her thoughtless tongue – and I couldn't succeed, till everything she knew was out. Master Heathcliff, much irritated, asserted her relation was false.

'Papa told me; and papa does not tell falsehoods!' she answered pertly.

'*My* papa scorns yours!' cried Linton. 'He calls him a sneaking fool!'

'Yours is a wicked man,' retorted Catherine, 'and you are very naughty to dare to repeat what he says – He must be wicked, to have made Aunt Isabella leave him as she did!'

'She didn't leave him,' said the boy; 'you shan't contradict me!'

'She did!' cried my young lady.

'Well, I'll tell *you* something!' said Linton. 'Your mother hated your father, now then.'

'Oh!' exclaimed Catherine, too enraged to continue.

'And she loved mine!' added he.

'You little liar! I hate you now,' she panted, and her face grew red with passion.

'She did! she did!' sang Linton, sinking into the recess of his chair, and leaning back his head to enjoy the agitation of the other disputant, who stood behind.

'Hush, Master Heathcliff!' I said, 'that's your father's tale too, I suppose.'

'It isn't – you hold your tongue!' he answered. 'She did, she did, Catherine, she did, she did!'

Cathy, beside herself, gave the chair a violent push, and caused him to fall against one arm. He was immediately seized by a suffocating cough that soon ended his triumph.

It lasted so long, that it frightened even me. As to his cousin, she wept with all her might, aghast at the mischief she had done, though she said nothing.

I held him, till the fit exhausted itself. Then he thrust me away, and leant his head down, silently – Catherine quelled her lamentations also, took a seat opposite, and looked solemnly into the fire.

'How do you feel now, Master Heathcliff?' I inquired after waiting ten minutes.

'I wish *she* felt as I do,' he replied, 'spiteful, cruel thing! Hareton never touches me, he never struck me in his life – And I was better to-day – and there –' his voice died in a whimper.

'*I* didn't strike you!' muttered Cathy, chewing her lip to prevent another burst of emotion.

He sighed and moaned like one under great suffering; and kept it up for a quarter of an hour, on purpose to distress his cousin, apparently, for whenever he caught a stifled sob from her, he put renewed pain and pathos into the inflexions of his voice.

'I'm sorry I hurt you, Linton!' she said at length, racked beyond endurance. 'But *I* couldn't have been hurt by that little push; and I had no idea that you could, either – you're not much, are you, Linton? Don't let me go home thinking I've done you harm! answer, speak to me.'

'I can't speak to you,' he murmured, 'you've hurt me so, that I shall lie awake all night, choking with this cough! If you had it you'd know what it was – but *you'll* be comfortably asleep, while I'm in agony – and nobody near me! I wonder how you would like to pass those fearful nights!' And he began to wail aloud for very pity of himself.

'Since you are in the habit of passing dreadful nights,' I said, 'it won't be Miss who spoils your ease; you'd be the same, had she never come – However, she shall not disturb you, again – and perhaps, you'll get quieter when we leave you.'

# Wuthering Heights

'Must I go?' asked Catherine dolefully, bending over him. 'Do you want me to go, Linton?'

'You can't alter what you've done,' he replied pettishly, shrinking from her, 'unless you alter it for the worse, by teasing me into a fever.'

'Well, then I must go?' she repeated.

'Let me alone, at least,' said he; 'I can't bear your talking!'

She lingered, and resisted my persuasions to departure, a tiresome while, but as he neither looked up nor spoke, she finally made a movement to the door, and I followed.

We were recalled by a scream – Linton had slid from his seat on to the hearthstone, and lay writhing in the mere perverseness of an indulged plague of a child, determined to be as grievous and harassing as it can.

I thoroughly gauged his disposition from his behaviour, and saw at once it would be folly to attempt humouring him. Not so my companion, she ran back in terror, knelt down, and cried, and soothed, and entreated, till he grew quiet from lack of breath, by no means from compunction at distressing her.

'I shall lift him on the settle,' I said, 'and he may roll about as he pleases; we can't stop to watch him – I hope you are satisfied, Miss Cathy, that *you* are not the person to benefit him, and that his condition of health is not occasioned by attachment to you. Now then, there he is! Come away; as soon as he knows there is nobody by to care for his nonsense, he'll be glad to lie still!'

She placed a cushion under his head, and offered him some water; he rejected the latter, and tossed uneasily on the former, as if it were a stone, or a block of wood.

She tried to put it more comfortably.

'I can't do with that,' he said, 'it's not high enough!'

Catherine brought another to lay above it.

'That's *too* high!' murmured the provoking thing.

'How must I arrange it, then?' she asked despairingly.

He twined himself up to her, as she half knelt by the settle, and converted her shoulder into a support.

'No, that won't do!' I said. 'You'll be content with the cushion, Master Heathcliff! Miss has wasted too much time on you, already; we cannot remain five minutes longer.'

'Yes, yes, we can!' replied Cathy. 'He's good and patient, now – He's beginning to think I shall have far greater misery than he will, to-night, if I believe he is the worse for my visit; and then, I dare not come again – Tell the truth about it, Linton – for I mustn't come, if I have hurt you.'

'You must come, to cure me,' he answered. 'You ought to come because you have hurt me – You know you have, extremely! I was not as ill, when you entered, as I am at present – was I?'

'But you've made yourself ill by crying, and being in a passion.'

'I didn't do it all,' said his cousin. 'However, we'll be friends now. And you want me – you would wish to see me sometimes, really?'

'I told you, I did!' he replied impatiently. 'Sit on the settle and let me lean on your knee – That's as mamma used to do, whole afternoons together – Sit quite still, and don't talk, but you may sing a song if you can sing, or you may say a nice long interesting ballad – one of those you promised to teach me, or a story – I'd rather have a ballad, though: begin.'

# Wuthering Heights

Catherine repeated the longest she could remember. The employment pleased both mightily. Linton would have another, and after that another; notwithstanding my strenuous objections; and so they went on, until the clock struck twelve, and we heard Hareton in the court, returning for his dinner.

'And to-morrow, Catherine, will you be here to-morrow?' asked young Heathcliff, holding her frock, as she rose reluctantly.

'No!' I answered, 'nor the next day neither.' She, however, gave a different response, evidently, for his forehead cleared as she stopped and whispered in his ear.

'You won't go to-morrow, recollect, Miss!' I commenced, when we were out of the house. 'You are not dreaming of it, are you?'

She smiled.

'Oh, I'll take good care!' I continued. 'I'll have that lock mended, and you can escape by no way else.'

'I can get over the wall,' she said, laughing. 'The Grange is not a prison, Ellen, and you are not my jailer. And besides, I'm almost seventeen. I'm a woman – and I'm certain Linton would recover quickly if he had me to look after him – I'm older than he is, you know, and wiser, less childish, am I not? And he'll soon do as I direct him, with some slight coaxing – He's a pretty little darling when he's good. I'd make such a pet of him, if he were mine – We should never quarrel, should we, after we were used to each other? Don't you like him, Ellen?'

'Like him?' I exclaimed. 'The worst-tempered bit of a sickly slip that ever struggled into his teens! Happily, as Mr Heathcliff conjectured, he'll not win twenty! I doubt whether he'll see spring, indeed – and small loss to his family, whenever he drops off; and lucky it is for us that his father took him – The kinder he was treated, the more tedious and selfish he'd be! I'm glad you have no chance of having him for a husband, Miss Catherine!'

My companion waxed serious at hearing this speech – To speak of his death so regardlessly wounded her feelings.

'He's younger than I,' she answered, after a protracted pause of meditation, 'and he ought to live the longest, he will – he must live as long as I do. He's as strong now as when he first came into the North, I'm positive of that! It's only a cold that ails him, the same as papa has – You say papa will get better, and why shouldn't he?'

'Well, well,' I cried, 'after all, we needn't trouble ourselves; for listen, Miss, and mind, I'll keep my word – If you attempt going to Wuthering Heights again, with or without me, I shall inform Mr Linton, and, unless he allow it, the intimacy with your cousin must not be revived.'

'It has been revived?' muttered Cathy sulkily.

'Must not be continued, then!' I said.

'We'll see!' was her reply, and she set off at a gallop, leaving me to toil in the rear.

We both reached home before our dinner-time; my master supposed we had been wandering through the park, and therefore, he demanded no explanation of our absence. As soon as I entered, I hastened to change my soaked shoes and stockings; but sitting such a while at the Heights, had done the mischief. On the succeeding morning, I was laid up; and during three weeks I remained inca-

pacitated for attending to my duties – a calamity never experienced prior to that period, and never, I am thankful to say, since.

My little mistress behaved like an angel in coming to wait on me, and cheer my solitude: the confinement brought me exceedingly low – it is wearisome, to a stirring active body – but few have slighter reasons for complaint than I had. The moment Catherine left Mr Linton's room, she appeared at my bed-side. Her day was divided between us; no amusement usurped a minute: she neglected her meals, her studies, and her play; and she was the fondest nurse that ever watched: she must have had a warm heart, when she loved her father so, to give so much to me!

I said her days were divided between us; but the master retired early, and I generally needed nothing after six o'clock, thus the evening was her own.

Poor thing, I never considered what she did with herself after tea. And though frequently, when she looked in to bid me goodnight, I remarked a fresh colour in her cheeks, and a pinkness over her slender fingers; instead of fancying the hue borrowed from a cold ride across the moors, I laid it to the charge of a hot fire in the library.

# Chapter 24

At the close of three weeks, I was able to quit my chamber, and move about the house. And on the first occasion of my sitting up in the evening, I asked Catherine to read to me, because my eyes were weak. We were in the library, the master having gone to bed: she consented, rather unwillingly, I fancied; and imagining my sort of books did not suit her, I bid her please herself in the choice of what she perused.

She selected one of her own favourites, and got forward steadily about an hour; then came frequent questions.

'Ellen, are not you tired? Hadn't you better lie down now? You'll be sick, keeping up so long, Ellen.'

'No, no, dear, I'm not tired,' I returned continually.

Perceiving me immovable, she essayed another method of showing her dis-relish for her occupation. It changed to yawning, and stretching, and –

'Ellen, I'm tired.'

'Give over then and talk,' I answered.

That was worse; she fretted and sighed, and looked at her watch till eight; and finally went to her room, completely overdone with sleep; judging by her peevish, heavy look, and the constant rubbing she inflicted on her eyes.

The following night she seemed more impatient still; and on the third from recovering my company, she complained of a headache and left me.

I thought her conduct odd; and having remained alone a long while, I resolved

on going, and inquiring whether she were better, and asking her to come and lie on the sofa, instead of upstairs, in the dark.

No Catherine could I discover upstairs, and none below. The servants affirmed they had not seen her. I listened at Mr Edgar's door – all was silence. I returned to her apartment, extinguished my candle, and seated myself in the window.

The moon shone bright; a sprinkling of snow covered the ground, and I reflected that she might, possibly, have taken it into her head to walk about the garden, for refreshment. I did detect a figure creeping along the inner fence of the park; but it was not my young mistress; on its emerging into the light, I recognized one of the grooms.

He stood a considerable period, viewing the carriage-road through the grounds; then started off at a brisk pace, as if he had detected something, and reappeared presently, leading Miss's pony; and there she was, just dismounted, and walking by its side.

The man took his charge stealthily across the grass towards the stable. Cathy entered by the casement-window of the drawing-room, and glided noiselessly up to where I awaited her.

She put the door gently to, slipped off her snowy shoes, untied her hat, and was proceeding, unconscious of my espionage, to lay aside her mantle, when I suddenly rose and revealed myself. The surprise petrified her an instant: she uttered an inarticulate exclamation, and stood fixed.

'My dear Miss Catherine,' I began, too vividly impressed by her recent kindness to break into a scold, 'where have you been riding out at this hour? And why should you try to deceive me, by telling a tale? Where have you been? Speak!'

'To the bottom of the park,' she stammered. 'I didn't tell a tale.'

'And nowhere else?' I demanded.

'No,' was the muttered reply.

'Oh, Catherine,' I cried, sorrowfully. 'You know you have been doing wrong, or you wouldn't be driven to uttering an untruth to me. That does grieve me. I'd rather be three months ill, than hear you frame a deliberate lie.'

She sprang forward, and bursting into tears, threw her arms round my neck.

'Well, Ellen, I'm so afraid of you being angry,' she said. 'Promise not to be angry, and you shall know the very truth. I hate to hide it.'

We sat down in the window-seat; I assured her I would not scold, whatever her secret might be, and I guessed it, of course; so she commenced –

'I've been to Wuthering Heights, Ellen, and I've never missed going a day since you fell ill; except thrice before, and twice after you left your room. I gave Michael books and pictures to prepare Minny every evening, and to put her back in the stable; you mustn't scold *him* either, mind. I was at the Heights by half-past six, and generally stayed till half-past eight, and then galloped home. It was not to amuse myself that I went; I was often wretched all the time. Now and then, I was happy, once in a week perhaps. At first, I expected there would be sad work persuading you to let me keep my word to Linton, for I had engaged to call again next day, when we quitted him; but, as you stayed upstairs on the morrow, I escaped that trouble; and while Michael was refastening the lock of the park door in the afternoon, I got possession of the key, and told him how my cousin wished me to visit him, because he was sick, and couldn't come to the Grange: and how papa would object to my going. And then I negotiated with

him about the pony. He is fond of reading, and he thinks of leaving soon to get married, so he offered, if I would lend him books out of the library, to do what I wished; but I preferred giving him my own, and that satisfied him better.

'On my second visit, Linton seemed in lively spirits; and Zillah (that is their housekeeper) made us a clean room and a good fire, and told us that, as Joseph was out at a prayer-meeting, and Hareton Earnshaw was off with his dogs, robbing our woods of pheasants, as I heard afterwards, we might do what we liked.

'She brought me some warm wine and gingerbread, and appeared exceedingly good-natured; and Linton sat in the armchair, and I in the little rocking chair on the hearthstone, and we laughed and talked so merrily, and found so much to say; we planned where we would go, and what we would do in summer. I needn't repeat that, because you would call it silly.

'One time, however, we were near quarrelling. He said the pleasantest manner of spending a hot July day was lying from morning till evening on a bank of heath in the middle of the moors, with the bees humming dreamily about among the bloom, and the larks singing high up over head, and the blue sky and bright sun shining steadily and cloudlessly. That was his most perfect idea of heaven's happiness – mine was rocking in a rustling green tree, with a west wind blowing, and bright, white clouds flitting rapidly above; and not only larks, but throstles, and blackbirds, and linnets, and cuckoos pouring out music on every side, and the moors seen at a distance, broken into cool dusky dells; but close by great swells of long grass undulating in waves to the breeze; and woods and sounding water, and the whole world awake and wild with joy. He wanted all to lie in an ecstasy of peace; I wanted all to sparkle, and dance in a glorious jubilee.

'I said his heaven would be only half alive, and he said mine would be drunk; I said I should fall asleep in his, and he said he could not breathe in mine, and began to grow very snappish. At last, we agreed to try both as soon as the right weather came; and then we kissed each other and were friends. After sitting still an hour, I looked at the great room with its smooth, uncarpeted floor; and thought how nice it would be to play in, if we removed the table; and I asked Linton to call Zillah in to help us – and we'd have a game at blind-man's buff – she should try to catch us – you used to, you know, Ellen. He wouldn't, there was no pleasure in it, he said; and he consented to play at ball with me. We found two, in a cupboard, among a heap of old toys; tops, and hoops, and battledoors, and shuttlecocks. One was marked C., and the other H.; I wished to have the C., because that stood for Catherine, and the H. might be for Heathcliff, his name; but the bran came out of H., and Linton didn't like it.

'I beat him constantly; and he got cross again, and coughed, and returned to his chair: that night, though, he easily recovered his good humour; he was charmed with two or three pretty songs – *your* songs, Ellen; and when I was obliged to go, he begged and entreated me to come the following evening, and I promised.

'Minny and I went flying home as light as air: and I dreamt of Wuthering Heights, and my sweet, darling cousin, till morning.

'On the morrow, I was sad; partly because you were poorly, and partly that I wished my father knew, and approved of my excursion: but it was beautiful moonlight after tea; and, as I rode on, the gloom cleared.

'I shall have another happy evening, I thought to myself; and what delights me more, my pretty Linton will.

'I trotted up their garden, and was turning round to the back, when that fellow Earnshaw met me, took my bridle, and bid me go in by the front entrance. He patted Minny's neck, and said she was a bonny beast, and appeared as if he wanted me to speak to him. I only told him to leave my horse alone, or else it would kick him.

'He answered in his vulgar accent.

' "It wouldn't do mitch hurt if it did;" ' and surveyed its legs with a smile.

'I was half inclined to make it try; however, he moved off to open the door, and, as he raised the latch, he looked up to the inscription above, and said, with a stupid mixture of awkwardness and elation –

' "Miss Catherine! I read yon, nah."

' "Wonderful," I exclaimed, 'Pray let us hear you – you *are* grown clever!"

'He spelt, and drawled over by syllables, the name – "Hareton Earnshaw."

' "And the figures?" I cried, encouragingly, perceiving that he came to a dead halt.

' "I cannot tell them yet," he answered.

' "Oh, you dunce!" I said, laughing heartily at his failure.

'The fool stared, with a grin hovering about his lips, and a scowl gathering over his eyes, as if uncertain whether he might not join in my mirth; whether it were not pleasant familiarity, or what it really was, contempt.

'I settled his doubts by suddenly retrieving my gravity, and desiring him to walk away, for I came to see Linton, not him.

'He reddened – I saw that by the moonlight – dropped his hand from the latch, and skulked off, a picture of mortified vanity. He imagined himself to be as accomplished as Linton, I suppose, because he could spell his own name; and was marvellously discomfited that I didn't think the same.'

'Stop, Miss Catherine, dear!' I interrupted. 'I shall not scold, but I don't like your conduct there. If you had remembered that Hareton was your cousin, as much as Master Heathcliff, you would have felt how improper it was to behave in that way. At least, it was praiseworthy ambition for him to desire to be as accomplished as Linton; and probably he did not learn merely to show off; you had made him ashamed of his ignorance, before: I have no doubt; and he wished to remedy it and please you. To sneer at his imperfect attempt was very bad breeding – had *you* been brought up in his circumstances, would you be less rude? He was as quick and as intelligent a child as ever you were, and I'm hurt that he should be despised now, because that base Heathcliff has treated him so unjustly.'

'Well, Ellen, you won't cry about it, will you?' she exclaimed, surprised at my earnestness. 'But wait, and you shall hear if he conned his ABC to please me; and if it were worth while being civil to the brute. I entered; Linton was lying on the settle, and half got up to welcome me.

' "I'm ill to-night, Catherine love," he said, "and you must have all the talk, and let me listen. Come, and sit by me – I was sure you wouldn't break your word, and I'll make you promise again, before you go."

'I knew now that I mustn't tease him, as he was ill; and I spoke softly and put no questions, and avoided irritating him in any way. I had brought some of my nicest books for him; he asked me to read a little of one, and I was about

# Wuthering Heights

to comply, when Earnshaw burst the door open, having gathered venom with reflection. He advanced direct to us; seized Linton by the arm, and swung him off the seat.

' "Get to thy own room!" he said, in a voice almost inarticulate with passion, and his face looked swelled and furious. "Take her there if she come to see thee – thou shalln't keep me out of this. Begone, wi' ye both!"

'He swore at us, and left Linton no time to answer, nearly throwing him into the kitchen; and he clenched his fist, as I followed, seemingly longing to knock me down. I was afraid, for a moment, and I let one volume fall; he kicked it after me, and shut us out.

I heard a malignant, crackly laugh by the fire, and turning beheld that odious Joseph, standing rubbing his bony hands, and quivering.

' "Aw wer sure he'd sarve ye eht! He's a grand lad! He's getten t' raight sperrit in him! *he* knaws – Aye, he knaws, as weel as Aw do, who sud be t' maister yonder – Ech, ech, ech! He mad ye skift properly! Ech, ech, ech!"

'"Where must we go?" I said to my cousin, disregarding the old wretch's mockery.

'Linton was white and trembling. He was not pretty then, Ellen! Oh no! he looked frightful! for his thin face and large eyes were wrought into an expression of frantic, powerless fury. He grasped the handle of the door, and shook it – it was fastened inside.

' "If you don't let me in I'll kill you! If you don't let me in I'll kill you!" he rather shrieked than said, "Devil! devil! I'll kill you. I'll kill you!"

'Joseph uttered his croaking laugh again.

' "Thear, that's t' father!" he cried, "That's father! We've allas summut uh orther side in us – Niver heed Hareton, lad – dunnut be 'feared – he cannot get at thee!"

'I took hold of Linton's hands, and tried to pull him away; but he shrieked so shockingly that I dared not proceed. At last, his cries were choked by a dreadful fit of coughing; blood gushed from his mouth, and he fell on the ground.

'I ran into the yard, sick with terror; and called for Zillah, as loud as I could. She soon heard me; she was milking the cows in a shed behind the barn, and hurrying from her work, she inquired what there was to do?

'I hadn't breath to explain; dragging her in, I looked about for Linton. Earnshaw had come out to examine the mischief he had caused, and he was then conveying the poor thing upstairs. Zillah and I ascended after him; but he stopped me, at the top of the steps, and said I shouldn't go in, I must go home.

'I exclaimed that he had killed Linton, and I *would* enter.

'Joseph locked the door, and declared I should do "no sich stuff," and asked me whether I were "bahn to be as mad as him."

'I stood crying, till the housekeeper re-appeared; she affirmed that he would be better in a bit; but he couldn't do with that shrieking, and din, and she took me, and nearly carried me into the house.

'Ellen, I was ready to tear my hair off my head! I sobbed and wept so that my eyes were almost blind; and the ruffian you have such sympathy with stood opposite, presuming every now and then to bid me "wisht," and denying that it was his fault; and finally, frightened by my assertions that I would tell papa, and that he should be put in prison, and hanged, he commenced blubbering himself, and hurried out to hide his cowardly agitation.

# Wuthering Heights

'Still, I was not rid of him: when at length they compelled me to depart, and I had got some hundred yards off the premises, he suddenly issued from the shadow of the road-side, and checked Minny and took hold of me.

' "Miss Catherine, I'm ill grieved," he began, "but it's rayther too bad –"

'I gave him a cut with my whip, thinking, perhaps he would murder me – He let go, thundering one of his horrid curses, and I galloped home more than half out of my senses.

'I didn't bid you good-night, that evening; and I didn't go to Wuthering Heights, the next – I wished to, exceedingly; but I was strangely excited, and dreaded to hear that Linton was dead, sometimes; and sometimes shuddered at the thought of encountering Hareton.

'On the third day I took courage; at least, I couldn't bear longer suspense and stole off, once more. I went at five o'clock, and walked, fancying I might manage to creep into the house, and up to Linton's room, unobserved. However, the dogs gave notice of my approach: Zillah received me, and saying "the lad was mending nicely," showed me into a small, tidy, carpeted apartment, where, to my inexpressible joy, I beheld Linton laid on a little sofa, reading one of my books. But he would neither speak to me nor look at me, through a whole hour, Ellen – He has such an unhappy temper – and what quite confounded me, when he did open his mouth it was to utter the falsehood, that I had occasioned the uproar, and Hareton was not to blame!

'Unable to reply, except passionately, I got up, and walked from the room. He sent after me a faint "Catherine!" He did not reckon on being answered so – but I wouldn't turn back; and the morrow was the second day on which I stayed at home, nearly determined to visit him no more.

'But it was so miserable going to bed, and getting up, and never hearing anything about him, that my resolution melted into air, before it was properly formed. It *had* appeared wrong to take the journey once; now it seemed wrong to refrain. Michael came to ask if he must saddle Minny; I said "Yes," and considered myself doing a duty as she bore me over the hills.

'I was forced to pass the front windows to get to the court; it was no use trying to conceal my presence.

' "Young master is in the house," said Zillah, as she saw me making for the parlour.

'I went in, Earnshaw was there also, but he quitted the room directly. Linton sat in the great arm chair half asleep; walking up to the fire, I began in a serious tone, partly meaning it to be true.

' "As you don't like me, Linton, and as you think I come on purpose to hurt you, and pretend that I do so every time, this is our last meeting – let us say good-bye; and tell Mr Heathcliff that you have no wish to see me, and that he mustn't invent any more falsehoods on the subject."

' "Sit down and take your hat off, Catherine," he answered. "You are so much happier than I am, you ought to be better. Papa talks enough of my defects, and shows enough scorn of me, to make it natural I should doubt myself – I doubt whether I am not altogether as worthless as he calls me, frequently; and then I feel so cross and bitter, I hate everybody! I *am* worthless, and bad in temper, and bad in spirit, almost always – and if you choose, you may say good-bye – you'll get rid of an annoyance – Only, Catherine, do me this justice; believe that if I might be as sweet, and as kind, and as good as you are, I would

be, as willingly, and more so, than as happy and as healthy. And, believe that your kindness has made me love you deeper than if I deserved your love, and though I couldn't, and cannot help showing my nature to you, I regret it and repent it, and shall regret, and repent it, till I die!"

'I felt he spoke the truth; and I felt I must forgive him; and, though he should quarrel the next moment, I must forgive him again. We were reconciled, but we cried, both of us, the whole time I stayed. Not entirely for sorrow, yet I *was* sorry Linton had that distorted nature. He'll never let his friends be at ease, and he'll never be at ease himself!

'I have always gone to his little parlour, since that night; because his father returned the day after. About three times, I think, we have been merry, and hopeful, as we were the first evening; the rest of my visits were dreary and troubled – now, with his selfishness and spite; and now with his sufferings: but I've learnt to endure the former with nearly as little resentment as the latter.

'Mr Heathcliff purposely avoids me. I have hardly seen him at all. Last Sunday, indeed, coming earlier than usual, I heard him abusing poor Linton, cruelly, for his conduct of the night before. I can't tell how he knew of it, unless he listened. Linton had certainly behaved provokingly; however, it was the business of nobody but me; and I interrupted Mr Heathcliff's lecture, by entering, and telling him so. He burst into a laugh, and went away, saying he was glad I took that view of the matter. Since then, I've told Linton he must whisper his bitter things.

'Now, Ellen, you have heard all; and I can't be prevented from going to Wuthering Heights, except by inflicting misery on two people – whereas, if you'll only not tell papa, my going need disturb the tranquillity of none. You'll not tell, will you? It will be very heartless if you do.'

'I'll make up my mind on that point by to-morrow, Miss Catherine,' I replied. 'It requires some study; and so I'll leave you to your rest, and go think it over.'

I thought it over aloud, in my master's presence; walking straight from her room to his, and relating the whole story, with the exception of her conversations with her cousin, and any mention of Hareton.

Mr Linton was alarmed and distressed more than he would acknowledge to me. In the morning, Catherine learnt my betrayal of her confidence, and she learnt also that her secret visits were to end.

In vain she wept and writhed against the interdict; and implored her father to have pity on Linton: all she got to comfort her was a promise that he would write, and give him leave to come to the Grange when he pleased; but explaining that he must no longer expect to see Catherine at Wuthering Heights. Perhaps, had he been aware of his nephew's disposition and state of health, he would have seen fit to withhold even that slight consolation.

# Chapter 25

'These things happened last winter, sir,' said Mrs Dean; 'hardly more than a year ago. Last winter, I did not think, at another twelve months' end, I should be amusing a stranger to the family with relating them! Yet, who knows how long you'll be a stranger? You're too young to rest always contented, living by yourself; and I some way fancy, no one could see Catherine Linton, and not love her. You smile; but why do you look so lively and interested, when I talk about her? and why have you asked me to hang her picture over your fireplace? and why –'

'Stop, my good friend!' I cried, 'It may be very possible that *I* should love her; but would she love me? I doubt it too much to venture my tranquillity, by running into temptation; and then my home is not here. I'm of the busy world, and to its arms I must return. Go on. Was Catherine obedient to her father's commands?'

'She was,' continued the housekeeper. 'Her affection for him was still the chief sentiment in her heart; and he spoke without anger; he spoke in the deep tenderness of one about to leave his treasure amid perils and foes, where his remembered words would be the only aid that he could bequeath to guide her.

'He said to me, a few days afterwards,

' "I wish my nephew would write, Ellen, or call. Tell me, sincerely, what you think of him – is he changed for the better, or is there a prospect of improvement, as he grows a man?"

' "He's very delicate, sir," I replied; "and scarcely likely to reach manhood; but this I can say, he does not resemble his father; and if Miss Catherine had the misfortune to marry him, he would not be beyond her control, unless she were extremely and foolishly indulgent. However, master, you'll have plenty of time to get acquainted with him, and see whether he would suit her – it wants four years and more of his being of age." '

Edgar sighed; and, walking to the window, looked out towards Gimmerton Kirk. It was a misty afternoon, but the February sun shone dimly, and we could just distinguish the two fir trees in the yard, and the sparely scattered gravestones.

'I've prayed often,' he half soliloquized, 'for the approach of what is coming; and now I begin to shrink, and fear it. I thought the memory of the hour I came down that glen a bridegroom, would be less sweet than the anticipation that I was soon, in a few months, or, possibly, weeks, to be carried up, and laid in its lonely hollow! Ellen, I've been very happy with my little Cathy. Through winter nights and summer days she was a living hope at my side – but I've been as happy musing by myself among those stones, under that old church – lying, through the long June evenings, on the green mound of her mother's grave, and

170

# Wuthering Heights

wishing, yearning for the time when I might lie beneath it. What can I do for Cathy? How must I quit her? I'd not care one moment for Linton being Heathcliff's son; nor for his taking her from me, if he could console her for my loss. I'd not care that Heathcliff gained his ends, and triumphed in robbing me of my last blessing! But should Linton be unworthy – only a feeble tool to his father – I cannot abandon her to him! And, hard though it be to crush her buoyant spirit, I must persevere in making her sad while I live, and leaving her solitary when I die. Darling! I'd rather resign her to God, and lay her in the earth before me.'

'Resign her to God, as it is, sir,' I answered, 'and if we should lose you – which may He forbid – under His providence, I'll stand her friend and counsellor to the last. Miss Catherine is a good girl; I don't fear that she will go wilfully wrong; and people who do their duty are always finally rewarded.'

Spring advanced; yet my master gathered no real strength, though he resumed his walks in the grounds with his daughter. To her inexperienced notions, this itself was a sign of convalescence; and then his cheek was often flushed, and his eyes were bright, she felt sure of his recovering.

On her seventeenth birthday, he did not visit the churchyard; it was raining, and I observed –

'You'll surely not go out tonight, sir?'

He answered –

'No, I'll defer it, this year, a little longer.'

He wrote again to Linton, expressing his great desire to see him; and, had the invalid been presentable, I've no doubt his father would have permitted him to come. As it was, being instructed, he returned an answer, intimating that Mr Heathcliff objected to his calling at the Grange; but his uncle's kind remembrance delighted him, and he hoped to meet him, sometimes, in his rambles, and personally to petition that his cousin and he might not remain long so utterly divided.

That part of his letter was simple, and, probably, his own. Heathcliff knew he could plead eloquently enough for Catherine's company, then –

'I do not ask,' he said, 'that she may visit here; but, am I never to see her, because my father forbids me to go to her home, and you forbid her to come to mine? Do, now and then, ride with her towards the Heights; and let us exchange a few words, in your presence! We have done nothing to deserve this separation; and you are not angry with me – you have no reason to dislike me – you allow yourself. Dear uncle! send me a kind note tomorrow; and leave to join you anywhere you please, except at Thrushcross Grange. I believe an interview would convince you that my father's character is not mine; he affirms I am more your nephew than his son; and though I have faults which render me unworthy of Catherine, she has excused them, and, for her sake, you should also. You inquire after my health – it is better; but while I remain cut off from all hope, and doomed to solitude, or the society of those who never did, and never will like me, how can I be cheerful and well?'

Edgar, though he felt for the boy, could not consent to grant his request, because he could not accompany Catherine.

He said, in summer, perhaps, they might meet: meantime, he wished him to continue writing at intervals, and engaged to give him what advice and comfort he was able by letter; being well aware of his hard position in his family.

Linton complied; and had he been unrestrained, would probably have spoiled all by filling his epistles with complaints and lamentations; but his father kept a sharp watch over him; and, of course, insisted on every line that my master sent being shown; so, instead of penning his peculiar personal sufferings and distresses, the themes constantly uppermost in his thoughts, he harped on the cruel obligation of being held asunder from his friend and love; and gently intimated that Mr Linton must allow an interview soon, or he should fear he was purposely deceiving him with empty promises.

Cathy was a powerful ally at home; and, between them, they, at length, persuaded my master to acquiesce in their having a ride or a walk together, about once a week, under my guardianship, and on the moors nearest the Grange; for June found him still declining; and, though he had set aside, yearly, a portion of his income for my young lady's fortune, he had a natural desire that she might retain, or, at least, return, in a short time, to, the house of her ancestors; and he considered her only prospect of doing that was by a union with his heir: he had no idea that the latter was failing almost as fast as himself; nor had any one, I believe; no doctor visited the Heights, and no one saw Master Heathcliff to make report of his condition, among us.

I, for my part, began to fancy my forebodings were false, and that he must be actually rallying, when he mentioned riding and walking on the moors, and seemed so earnest in pursuing his object.

I could not picture a father treating a dying child as tyrannically and wickedly as I afterwards learnt Heathcliff had treated him, to compel this apparent eagerness; his efforts redoubling the more imminently his avaricious and unfeeling plans were threatened with defeat by death.

# Chapter 26

Summer was already past its prime, when Edgar reluctantly yielded his assent to their entreaties, and Catherine and I set out on our first ride to join her cousin.

It was a close, sultry day; devoid of sunshine, but with a sky too dappled and hazy to threaten rain; and our place of meeting had been fixed at the guide-stone, by the cross-roads. On arriving there, however, a little herd-boy, despatched as a messenger, told us that –

'Maister Linton wer just ut this side th' Heights: and he'd be mitch obleeged to us to gang on a bit further.'

'Then Master Linton has forgot the first injunction of his uncle,' I observed: 'he bid us keep on the Grange land, and here we are, off at once.'

'Well, we'll turn our horses' heads round, when we reach him,' answered my companion, 'our excursion shall lie towards home.'

# Wuthering Heights

But when we reached him, and that was scarcely a quarter of a mile from his own door, we found he had no horse, and we were forced to dismount, and leave ours to graze.

He lay on the heath, awaiting our approach, and did not rise till we came within a few yards. Then, he walked so feebly, and looked so pale, that I immediately exclaimed. –

'Why, Master Heathcliff, you are not fit for enjoying a ramble, this morning. How ill you do look!'

Catherine surveyed him with grief and astonishment; and changed the ejaculation of joy on her lips, to one of alarm; and the congratulation of their long postponed meeting, to an anxious inquiry, whether he were worse than usual.

'No – better – better!' he panted, trembling, and retaining her hand as if he needed its support, while his large blue eyes wandered timidly over her; the hollowness round them, transforming to haggard wildness, the languid expression they once possessed.

'But you have been worse,' persisted his cousin, 'worse than when I saw you last – you are thinner, and –'

'I'm tired,' he interrupted, hurriedly. 'It is too hot for walking, let us rest here. And, in the morning, I often feel sick – papa says I grow so fast.'

Badly satisfied, Cathy sat down, and he reclined beside her.

'This is something like your paradise,' said she, making an effort at cheerfulness. 'You recollect the two days we agreed to spend, in the place and way, each thought pleasantest? This is nearly yours, only there are clouds, but then, they are so soft and mellow, it is nicer than sunshine. Next week, if you can, we'll ride down to the Grange Park, and try mine.'

Linton did not appear to remember what she talked of; and he had evidently great difficulty in sustaining any kind of conversation. His lack of interest in the subjects she started, and his equal incapacity to contribute to her entertainment were so obvious, that she could not conceal her disappointment. An indefinite alteration had come over his whole person and manner. The pettishness that might be caressed into fondness, had yielded to a listless apathy; there was less of the peevish temper of a child which frets and teases on purpose to be soothed, and more of the self-absorbed moroseness of a confirmed invalid, repelling consolation, and ready to regard the good-humoured mirth of others, as an insult.

Catherine perceived, as well as I did, that he held it rather a punishment, than a gratification, to endure our company; and she made no scruple of proposing, presently, to depart.

That proposal, unexpectedly, roused Linton from his lethargy and threw him into a strange state of agitation. He glanced fearfully towards the Heights, begging she would remain another half-hour, at least.

'But, I think,' said Cathy, 'you'd be more comfortable at home than sitting here; and I cannot amuse you today, I see, by my tales, and songs, and chatter; you have grown wiser than I, in these six months; you have little taste for my diversions now; or else, if I could amuse you, I'd willingly stay.'

'Stay to rest yourself,' he replied. 'And, Catherine, don't think, or say that I'm *very* unwell – it is the heavy weather, and heat that make me dull; and I

walked about, before you came, a great deal, for me. Tell uncle, I'm in tolerable health, will you?'

'I'll tell him that *you* say so, Linton. I couldn't affirm that you are,' observed my young lady, wondering at his pertinacious assertion of what was evidently an untruth.

'And be here again next Thursday,' continued he, shunning her puzzled gaze. 'And give him my thanks for permitting you to come – my best thanks, Catherine. And – and, if you *did* meet my father, and he asked you about me, don't lead him to suppose that I've been extremely silent and stupid – don't look sad and downcast, as you *are* doing – he'll be angry.'

'I care nothing for his anger,' exclaimed Cathy, imagining she would be its object.

'But I do,' said her cousin, shuddering. '*Don't* provoke him against me, Catherine, for he is very hard.'

'Is he severe to you, Master Heathcliff?' I inquired. 'Has he grown weary of indulgence, and passed from passive, to active hatred?'

Linton looked at me, but did not answer; and, after keeping her seat by his side, another ten minutes, during which his head fell drowsily on his breast, and he uttered nothing except suppressed moans of exhaustion or pain, Cathy began to seek solace in looking for bilberries, and sharing the produce of her researches with me: she did not offer them to him, for she saw further notice would only weary and annoy.

'Is it half an hour now, Ellen!' she whispered in my ear, at last. 'I can't tell why we should stay. He's asleep, and papa will be wanting us back.'

'Well, we must not leave him asleep,' I answered; 'wait till he wakes and be patient. You were mighty eager to set off, but your longing to see poor Linton has soon evaporated!'

'Why did *he* wish to see me?' returned Catherine. 'In his crossest humours, formerly, I liked him better than I do in his present curious mood. It's just as if it were a task he was compelled to perform – this interview – for fear his father should scold him. But, I'm hardly going to come to give Mr Heathcliff pleasure; whatever reason he may have for ordering Linton to undergo this penance. And, though I'm glad he's better in health, I'm sorry he's so much less pleasant, and so much less affectionate to me.'

'You think *he* is better in health, then?' I said.

'Yes,' she answered; 'because he always made such a great deal of his sufferings, you know. He is not tolerably well, as he told me to tell papa, but he's better, very likely.'

'There you differ with me, Miss Cathy,' I remarked; 'I should conjecture him to be far worse.'

Linton here started from his slumber in bewildered terror, and asked if any one had called his name.

'No,' said Catherine; 'unless in dreams. I cannot conceive how you manage to doze, out of doors, in the morning.'

'I thought I heard my father,' he gasped, glancing up to the frowning nab above us. 'You are sure nobody spoke?'

'Quite sure,' replied his cousin. 'Only Ellen and I were disputing concerning your health. Are you truly stronger, Linton, than when we separated in winter?

If you be, I'm certain one thing is not stronger – your regard for me – speak, are you?'

The tears gushed from Linton's eyes as he answered –

'Yes, yes, I am!'

And, still under the spell of the imaginary voice, his gaze wandered up and down to detect its owner.

Cathy rose.

'For to-day we must part,' she said. 'And I won't conceal that I have been sadly disappointed with our meeting, though I'll mention it to nobody but you – not that I stand in awe of Mr Heathcliff!'

'Hush,' murmured Linton; 'for God's sake, hush! He's coming.' And he clung to Catherine's arm, striving to detain her; but, at that announcement, she hastily disengaged herself, and whistled to Minny, who obeyed like a dog.

'I'll be here next Thursday,' she cried, springing to the saddle. 'Good-bye. Quick, Ellen!'

And so we left him, scarcely conscious of our departure, so absorbed was he in anticipating his father's approach.

Before we reached home, Catherine's displeasure softened into a perplexed sensation of pity and regret, largely blended with vague, uneasy doubts about Linton's actual circumstances, physical and social; in which I partook, though I counselled her not to say much, for a second journey would make us better judges.

My master requested an account of our on-goings: his nephew's offering of thanks was duly delivered, Miss Cathy gently touching on the rest: I also threw little light on his inquiries, for I hardly knew what to hide, and what to reveal.

# Chapter 27

Seven days glided away, every one marking its course by the henceforth rapid alteration of Edgar Linton's state. The havoc that months had previously wrought, was now emulated by the inroads of hours.

Catherine, we would fain have deluded, yet, but her own quick spirit refused to delude her. It divined, in secret, and brooded on the dreadful probability, gradually ripening into certainty.

She had not the heart to mention her ride, when Thursday came round; I mentioned it for her, and obtained permission to order her out of doors; for the library, where her father stopped a short time daily – the brief period he could bear to sit up – and his chamber had become her whole world. She grudged each moment that did not find her bending over his pillow, or seated by his side. Her countenance grew wan with watching and sorrow, and my master gladly dismissed her to what he flattered himself would be a happy change of scene and

# Wuthering Heights

society, drawing comfort from the hope that she would not now be left entirely alone after his death.

He had a fixed idea, I guessed by several observations he let fall, that as his nephew resembled him in person, he would resemble him in mind; for Linton's letters bore few or no indications of his defective character. And I, through pardonable weakness, refrained from correcting the error; asking myself what good there would be in disturbing his last moments with information that he had neither power nor opportunity to turn to account.

We deferred our excursion till the afternoon; a golden afternoon of August – every breath from the hills so full of life, that it seemed whoever respired it, though dying, might revive.

Catherine's face was just like the landscape – shadows and sunshine flitting over it, in rapid succession; but the shadows rested longer and the sunshine was more transient, and her poor little heart reproached itself for even that passing forgetfulness of its cares.

We discerned Linton watching at the same spot he had selected before. My young mistress alighted, and told me that as she was resolved to stay a very little while, I had better hold the pony and remain on horseback; but I dissented, I wouldn't risk losing sight of the charge committed to me a minute; so we climbed the slope of heath, together.

Master Heathcliff received us with greater animation on this occasion; not the animation of high spirits though, nor yet of joy; it looked more like fear.

'It is late!' he said, speaking short, and with difficulty. 'Is not your father very ill? I thought you wouldn't come.'

'*Why* won't you be candid?' cried Catherine, swallowing her greeting. 'Why cannot you say at once, you don't want me? It is strange, Linton, that for the second time, you have brought me here on purpose, apparently, to distress us both, and for no reason besides!'

Linton shivered, and glanced at her, half supplicating, half ashamed, but his cousin's patience was not sufficient to endure this enigmatical behaviour.

'My father is very ill,' she said, 'and why am I called from his bedside – why didn't you send to absolve me from my promise, when you wished I wouldn't keep it? Come! I desire an explanation – playing and trifling are completely banished out of my mind: and I can't dance attendance on your affectations, now!'

'My affectations!' he murmured, 'what are they? For Heaven's sake, Catherine, don't look so angry! Despise me as much as you please; I am a worthless, cowardly wretch – I can't be scorned enough! but I'm too mean for your anger – hate my father, and spare me, for contempt!'

'Nonsense!' cried Catherine in a passion. 'Foolish, silly boy! And there! he trembles, as if I were really going to touch him! You needn't bespeak contempt, Linton; anybody will have it spontaneously, at your service. Get off! I shall return home – it is folly dragging you from the hearthstone, and pretending – what do we pretend? Let go my frock – if I pitied you for crying, and looking so very frightened, you should spurn such pity! Ellen, tell him how disgraceful this conduct is. Rise, and don't degrade yourself into an abject reptile – *don't*.'

With streaming face and an expression of agony, Linton had thrown his nerveless frame along the ground; he seemed convulsed with exquisite terror.

'Oh!' he sobbed, 'I cannot bear it! Catherine, Catherine, I'm a traitor, too,

and I dare not tell you! But leave me and I shall be killed! *Dear* Catherine, my life is in your hands; and you have said you loved me – and if you did, it wouldn't harm you. You'll not go, then? kind, sweet, good Catherine! And perhaps you *will* consent – and he'll let me die with you!'

My young lady, on witnessing his intense anguish, stooped to raise him. The old feeling of indulgent tenderness overcame her vexation, and she grew thoroughly moved and alarmed.

'Consent to what?' she asked. 'To stay? Tell me the meaning of this strange talk, and I will. You contradict your own words, and distract me! Be calm and frank, and confess at once, all that weighs on your heart. You wouldn't injure me, Linton, would you? You wouldn't let any enemy hurt me, if you could prevent it? I'll believe you are a coward, for yourself, but not a cowardly betrayer of your best friend.'

'But my father threatened me,' gasped the boy, clasping his attenuated fingers, 'and I dread him – I dread him! I *dare* not tell!'

'Oh well!' said Catherine, with scornful compassion, 'keep your secret, I'm no coward – save yourself, I'm not afraid!'

Her magnanimity provoked his tears; he wept wildly, kissing her supporting hands, and yet could not summon courage to speak out.

I was cogitating what the mystery might be, and determined Catherine should never suffer to benefit him or anyone else, by my good will. When hearing a rustle among the ling, I looked up, and saw Mr Heathcliff almost close upon us, descending the Heights. He didn't cast a glance towards my companions, though they were sufficiently near for Linton's sobs to be audible; but hailing me in the almost hearty tone he assumed to none besides, and the sincerity of which, I couldn't avoid doubting, he said –

'It is something to see you so near to my house, Nelly! How are you at the Grange? Let us hear! The rumour goes,' he added in a lower tone, 'that Edgar Linton is on his deathbed – perhaps they exaggerate his illness?'

'No; my master is dying,' I replied: 'it is true enough. A sad thing it will be for us all, but a blessing for him!'

'How long will he last, do you think?' he asked.

'I don't know,' I said.

'Because,' he continued, looking at the two young people, who were fixed under his eye – Linton appeared as if he could not venture to stir, or raise his head, and Catherine could not move, on his account – 'Because that lad yonder, seems determined to beat me – and I'd thank his uncle to be quick, and go before him – Hallo! Has the whelp been playing that game long? I *did* give him some lessons about snivelling. Is he pretty lively with Miss Linton generally?'

'Lively? no – he has shown the greatest distress,' I answered. 'To see him, I should say, that instead of rambling with his sweetheart on the hills, he ought to be in bed, under the hands of a doctor.'

'He shall be, in a day or two,' muttered Heathcliff. 'But first – get up, Linton! Get up!' he shouted. 'Don't grovel on the ground there – up this moment!'

Linton had sunk prostrate again in another paroxysm of helpless fear, caused by his father's glance towards him, I suppose; there was nothing else to produce such humiliation. He made several efforts to obey, but his little strength was annihilated, for the time, and he fell back again with a moan.

Mr Heathcliff advanced, and lifted him to lean against a ridge of turf.

'Now,' said he, with curbed ferocity, 'I'm getting angry – and if you don't command that paltry spirit of yours – *Damn* you! Get up, directly!'

'I will father!' he panted. 'Only, let me alone, or I shall faint! I've done as you wished – I'm sure. Catherine will tell you that I – that I – have been cheerful. Ah! keep by me, Catherine; give me your hand.'

'Take mine,' said his father, 'stand on your feet! There now – she'll lend you her arm . . . that's right, look at *her*. You would imagine I was the devil himself, Miss Linton, to excite such horror. Be so kind as to walk home with him, will you? He shudders, if I touch him.'

'Linton, dear!' whispered Catherine, 'I can't go to Wuthering Heights . . . papa has forbidden me . . . He'll not harm you, why are you so afraid?'

'I can never re-enter that house,' he answered. 'I'm *not* to re-enter it without you!'

'Stop . . .' cried his father. 'We'll respect Catherine's filial scruples. Nelly, take him in, and I'll follow your advice concerning the doctor, without delay.'

'You'll do well,' replied I, 'but I must remain with my mistress. To mind your son is not my business.'

'You are very stiff!' said Heathcliff. 'I know that – but you'll force me to pinch the baby, and make it scream, before it moves your charity. Come then, my hero. Are you willing to return, escorted by me?'

He approached once more, and made as if he would seize the fragile being; but shrinking back, Linton clung to his cousin, and implored her to accompany him, with a frantic importunity that admitted no denial.

However I disapproved, I couldn't hinder her; indeed, how could she have refused him herself? What was filling him with dread, we had no means of discerning, but there he was, powerless under its gripe, and any addition seemed capable of shocking him into idiocy.

We reached the threshold; Catherine walked in; and I stood waiting till she had conducted the invalid to a chair, expecting her out, immediately; when Mr Heathcliff, pushing me forward, exclaimed –

'My house is not stricken with the plague, Nelly; and I have a mind to be hospitable today; sit down, and allow me to shut the door.'

He shut and locked it also. I started.

'You shall have tea, before you go home,' he added. 'I am by myself. Hareton is gone with some cattle to the Lees – and Zillah and Joseph are off on a journey of pleasure. And, though I'm used to being alone, I'd rather have some interesting company, if I can get it. Miss Linton, take your seat by *him*. I give you what I have; the present is hardly worth accepting; but, I have nothing else to offer. It is Linton, I mean. How she does stare! It's odd what a savage feeling I have to anything that seems afraid of me! Had I been born where laws are less strict, and tastes less dainty, I should treat myself to a slow vivisection of those two as an evening's amusement.'

He drew in his breath, struck the table, and swore to himself.

'By hell! I hate them.'

'I'm not afraid of you!' exclaimed Catherine, who could not hear the latter part of his speech.

She stepped close up, her black eyes flashing with passion and resolution.

'Give me that key – I will have it!' she said. 'I wouldn't eat or drink here, if I were starving.'

# Wuthering Heights

Heathcliff had the key in his hand that remained on the table. He looked up, seized with a sort of surprise at her boldness, or, possibly, reminded by her voice and glance, of the person from whom she inherited it.

She snatched at the instrument, and half succeeded in getting it out of his loosened fingers; but her action recalled him to the present; he recovered it speedily.

'Now, Catherine Linton,' he said, 'stand off, or I shall knock you down; and that will make Mrs Dean mad.'

Regardless of this warning, she captured his closed hand and its contents again.

'We *will* go!' she repeated, exerting her utmost efforts to cause the iron muscles to relax; and finding that her nails made no impression, she applied her teeth pretty sharply.

Heathcliff glanced at me a glance that kept me from interfering a moment. Catherine was too intent on his fingers to notice his face. He opened them, suddenly, and resigned the object of dispute; but, ere she had well secured it, he seized her with the liberated hand, and, pulling her on his knee, administered with the other, a shower of terrific slaps on both sides of the head, each sufficient to have fulfilled his threat, had she been able to fall.

At this diabolical violence, I rushed on him furiously.

'You villain!' I began to cry, 'you villain!'

A touch on the chest silenced me; I am stout, and soon put out of breath; and, what with that and the rage, I staggered dizzily back, and felt ready to suffocate, or to burst a blood-vessel.

The scene was over in two minutes; Catherine, released, put her two hands to her temples, and looked just as if she were not sure whether her ears were off or on. She trembled like a reed, poor thing, and leant against the table perfectly bewildered.

'I know how to chastise children, you see,' said the scoundrel, grimly, as he stooped to repossess himself of the key, which had dropped to the floor. 'Go to Linton now, as I told you; and cry at your ease! I shall be your father to-morrow – all the father you'll have in a few days – and you shall have plenty of that – you can bear plenty – you're no weakling – you shall have a daily taste, if I catch such a devil of a temper in your eyes again!'

Cathy ran to me instead of Linton, and knelt down, and put her burning cheek on my lap, weeping aloud. Her cousin had shrunk into a corner of the settle, as quiet as a mouse, congratulating himself, I dare say, that the correction had lighted on another than him.

Mr Heathcliff, perceiving us all confounded, rose, and expeditiously made the tea himself. The cups and saucers were laid ready. He poured it out, and handed me a cup.

'Wash away your spleen,' he said. 'And help your own naughty pet and mine. It is not poisoned, though I prepared it. I'm going out to seek your horses.'

Our first thought, on his departure, was to force an exit somewhere. We tried the kitchen door, but that was fastened outside; we looked at the windows – they were too narrow for even Cathy's little figure.

'Master Linton,' I cried, seeing we were regularly imprisoned, 'you know what your diabolical father is after, and you shall tell us, or I'll box your ears, as he has done your cousin's.'

# Wuthering Heights

'Yes, Linton; you must tell,' said Catherine. 'It was for your sake I came; and it will be wickedly ungrateful if you refuse.'

'Give me some tea, I'm thirsty, and then I'll tell you,' he answered. 'Mrs Dean, go away. I don't like you standing over me. Now, Catherine, you are letting your tears fall into my cup! I won't drink that. Give me another.'

Catherine pushed another to him, and wiped her face. I felt disgusted at the little wretch's composure, since he was no longer in terror for himself. The anguish he had exhibited on the moor subsided as soon as ever he entered Wuthering Heights; so I guessed he had been menaced with an awful visitation of wrath, if he failed in decoying us there; and, that accomplished, he had no further immediate fears.

'Papa wants us to be married,' he continued, after sipping some of the liquid. 'And he knows your papa wouldn't let us marry now; and he's afraid of my dying, if we wait; so we are to be married in the morning, and you are to stay here all night; and, if you do as he wishes, you shall return home next day, and take me with you.'

'Take you with her, pitiful changeling?' I exclaimed. '*You* marry? Why, the man is mad! or he thinks us fools, every one. And do you imagine that beautiful young lady, that healthy, hearty girl, will tie herself to a little perishing monkey like you? Are you cherishing the notion that *anybody*, let alone Miss Catherine Linton, would have you for a husband? You want whipping for bringing us in here at all, with your dastardly, puling tricks; and – don't look so silly now! I've a very good mind to shake you severely, for your contemptible treachery, and your imbecile conceit.'

I did give him a slight shaking, but it brought on the cough, and he took to his ordinary resource of moaning and weeping, and Catherine rebuked me.

'Stay all night? No!' she said, looking slowly round. 'Ellen, I'll burn that door down, but I'll get out.'

And she would have commenced the execution of her threat directly, but Linton was up in alarm, for his dear self, again. He clasped her in his two feeble arms, sobbing –

'Won't you have me, and save me – not let me come to the Grange? Oh! darling Catherine! you mustn't go, and leave me, after all. You *must* obey my father, you *must*!'

'I must obey my own,' she replied, 'and relieve him from this cruel suspense. The whole night! What would he think? he'll be distressed already. I'll either break or burn a way out of the house. Be quiet! You're in no danger – but, if you hinder me – Linton, I love papa better than you!'

The mortal terror he felt of Mr Heathcliff's anger, restored to the boy his coward's eloquence. Catherine was near distraught – still, she persisted that she must go home, and tried entreaty, in her turn, persuading him to subdue his selfish agony.

While they were thus occupied, our jailer re-entered.

'Your beasts have trotted off'; he said, 'and – Now, Linton! snivelling again? What has she been doing to you? Come, come – have done, and get to bed. In a month or two, my lad, you'll be able to pay her back her present tyrannies, with a vigorous hand – you're pining for pure love, are you not? nothing else in the world – and she shall have you! There, to bed! Zillah won't be here to-night; you must undress yourself. Hush! hold your noise! Once in your own

180

room, I'll not come near you, you needn't fear. By chance, you've managed tolerably. I'll look to the rest.'

He spoke these words, holding the door open for his son to pass; and the latter achieved his exit exactly as a spaniel might, which suspected the person who attended on it of designing a spiteful squeeze.

The lock was re-secured. Heathcliff approached the fire, where my mistress and I stood silent. Catherine looked up, and instinctively raised her hand to her cheek – his neighbourhood revived a painful sensation. Anybody else would have been incapable of regarding the childish act with sternness, but he scowled on her, and muttered –

'Oh, you are not afraid of me? Your courage is well disguised – you *seem* damnably afraid!'

'I *am* afraid now,' she replied; 'because if I stay, papa will be miserable; and how can I endure making him miserable – when he – when he – Mr Heathcliff, *let* me go home! I promise to marry Linton – papa would like me to, and I love him – and why should you wish to force me to do what I'll willingly do of myself?'

'Let him dare to force you!' I cried. 'There's law in the land, thank God, there is! though we *be* in an out-of-the-way place. I'd inform, if he were my own son, and it's felony without benefit of clergy!'

'Silence!' said the ruffian. 'To the devil with your clamour! I don't want *you* to speak. Miss Linton, I shall enjoy myself remarkably in thinking your father will be miserable; I shall not sleep for satisfaction. You could have hit on no surer way of fixing your residence under my roof, for the next twenty-four hours, than informing me that such an event would follow. As to your promise to marry Linton, I'll take care you shall keep it, for you shall not quit this place till it is fulfilled.'

'Send Ellen then, to let papa know I'm safe!' exclaimed Catherine, weeping bitterly. 'Or marry me now. Poor papa! Ellen, he'll think we're lost. What shall we do?'

'Not he! He'll think you are tired of waiting on him, and run off, for a little amusement,' answered Heathcliff. 'You cannot deny that you entered my house of your own accord, in contempt of his injunctions to the contrary. And it is quite natural that you should desire amusement at your age; and that you should weary of nursing a sick man, and that man, *only* your father. Catherine, his happiest days were over when your days began. He cursed you, I dare say, for coming into the world (I did, at least). And it would just do if he cursed you as *he* went out of it. I'd join him. I don't love you! How should I? Weep away. As far as I can see, it will be your chief diversion hereafter, unless Linton makes amends for other losses; and your provident parent appears to fancy he may. His letters of advice and consolation entertained me vastly. In his last, he recommended my jewel to be careful of his; and kind to her when he got her. Careful and kind – that's paternal! But Linton requires his whole stock of care and kindness for himself. Linton can play the little tyrant well. He'll undertake to torture any number of cats if their teeth be drawn, and their claws pared. You'll be able to tell his uncle fine tales of his *kindness*, when you get home again, I assure you.'

'You're right there!' I said, 'explain your son's character. Show his resemblance

to yourself; and then, I hope, Miss Cathy will think twice, before she takes the cockatrice!'

'I don't much mind speaking of his amiable qualities now,' he answered, 'because she must either accept him, or remain a prisoner, and you along with her, till your master dies. I can detain you both, quite concealed, here. If you doubt, encourage her to retract her word, and you'll have an opportunity of judging!'

'I'll not retract my word,' said Catherine. 'I'll marry him, within this hour; if I may go to Thrushcross Grange afterwards. Mr Heathcliff, you're a cruel man, but you're not a fiend; and you won't, from *mere* malice, destroy, irrevocably, all my happiness. If papa thought I had left him, on purpose, and if he died before I returned, could I bear to live? I've given over crying; but I'm going to kneel here, at your knee; and I'll not get up, and I'll not take my eyes from your face, till you look back at me! No, don't turn away! *do* look! You'll see nothing to provoke you. I don't hate you. I'm not angry that you struck me. Have you never loved *anybody*, in all your life, uncle? *never*? Ah! you must look once – I'm so wretched – you can't help being sorry and pitying me.'

'Keep your eft's fingers off; and move, or I'll kick you!' cried Heathcliff, brutally repulsing her. 'I'd rather be hugged by a snake. How the devil can you dream of fawning on me? I *detest* you!'

He shrugged his shoulders – shook himself, indeed, as if his flesh crept with aversion; and thrust back his chair; while I got up, and opened my mouth, to commence a downright torrent of abuse; but I was rendered dumb in the middle of the first sentence, by a threat that I should be shown into a room by myself, the very next syllable I uttered.

It was growing dark – we heard a sound of voices at the garden gate. Our host hurried out, instantly; *he* had his wits about him; *we* had not. There was a talk of two or three minutes, and he returned alone.

'I thought it had been your cousin, Hareton,' I observed to Catherine. 'I wish he would arrive! Who knows but he might take our part?'

'It was three servants sent to seek you from the Grange,' said Heathcliff, overhearing me. 'You should have opened a lattice and called out; but I could swear that chit is glad you didn't. She's glad to be obliged to stay, I'm certain.'

At learning the chance we had missed, we both gave vent to our grief without control; and he allowed us to wail on till nine o'clock; then he bid us go upstairs, through the kitchen, to Zillah's chamber; and I whispered my companion to obey; perhaps, we might contrive to get through the window there, or into a garret, and out by its skylight.

The window, however, was narrow, like those below, and the garret trap was safe from our attempts; for we were fastened in as before.

We neither of us lay down: Catherine took her station by the lattice, and watched anxiously for morning – a deep sigh being the only answer I could obtain to my frequent entreaties that she would try to rest.

I seated myself in a chair, and rocked, to and fro, passing harsh judgment on my many derelictions of duty; from which, it struck me then, all the misfortunes of all my employers sprang. It was not the case, in reality, I am aware; but it was, in my imagination, that dismal night, and I thought Heathcliff himself less guilty than I.

At seven o'clock he came, and inquired if Miss Linton had risen.

She ran to the door immediately, and answered –
'Yes.'
'Here, then,' he said, opening it, and pulling her out.
I rose to follow, but he turned the lock again. I demanded my release.
'Be patient,' he replied; 'I'll send up your breakfast in a while.'
I thumped on the panels, and rattled the latch angrily; and Catherine asked why I was still shut up? He answered, I must try to endure it another hour, and they went away.
I endured it two or three hours; at length, I heard a footstep, not Heathcliff's.
'I've brought you something to eat,' said a voice; 'oppen t' door!'
Complying eagerly, I beheld Hareton, laden with food enough to last me all day.
'Tak' it,' he added, thrusting the tray into my hand.
'Stay one minute,' I began.
'Nay!' cried he, and retired, regardless of any prayers I could pour forth to detain him.
And there I remained enclosed, the whole day, and the whole of the next night; and another, and another. Five nights and four days I remained, altogether, seeing nobody but Hareton, once every morning, and he was a model of a jailer – surly, and dumb, and deaf to every attempt at moving his sense of justice or compassion.

# Chapter 28

On the fifth morning, or rather afternoon, a different step approached – lighter and shorter – and, this time, the person entered the room. It was Zillah, donned in her scarlet shawl, with a black silk bonnet on her head, and a willow basket swung to her arm.
'Eh, dear! Mrs Dean,' she exclaimed. 'Well! there is a talk about you at Gimmerton. I never thought, but you were sunk in the Blackhorse marsh, and Missy with you, till master told me you'd been found, and he'd lodged you here! What, and you must have got on an island, sure? And how long were you in the hole? Did master save you, Mrs Dean? But you're not so thin – you've not been so poorly, have you?'
'Your master is a true scoundrel!' I replied. 'But he shall answer for it. He needn't have raised that tale – it shall all be laid bare!'
'What do you mean?' asked Zillah. 'It's not his tale – they tell that in the village – about your being lost in the marsh; and I calls to Earnshaw, when I come in –
' "Eh, they's queer things, Mr Hareton, happened since I went off. It's a sad pity of that likely young lass, and cant Nelly Dean." '

# Wuthering Heights

'He stared. I thought he had not heard aught, so I told him the rumour.

'The master listened, and he just smiled to himself, and said –

' "If they have been in the marsh, they are out now, Zillah. Nelly Dean is lodged, at this minute, in your room. You can tell her to flit, when you go up; here is the key. The bog-water got into her head, and she would have run home, quite flighty, but I fixed her, till she came round to her senses. You can bid her go to the Grange, at once, if she be able, and carry a message from me, that her young lady will follow in time to attend the squire's funeral." '

'Mr Edgar is not dead?' I gasped. 'Oh! Zillah, Zillah!'

'No, no – sit you down, my good mistress,' she replied; 'you're right sickly yet. He's not dead: Doctor Kenneth thinks he may last another day – I met him on the road and asked.'

Instead of sitting down, I snatched my outdoor things, and hastened below, for the way was free.

On entering the house, I looked about for some one to give information of Catherine.

The place was filled with sunshine, and the door stood wide open, but nobody seemed at hand.

As I hesitated whether to go off at once, or return and seek my mistress, a slight cough drew my attention to the hearth.

Linton lay on the settle, sole tenant, sucking a stick of sugar-candy, and pursuing my movements with apathetic eyes.

'Where is Miss Catherine?' I demanded, sternly, supposing I could frighten him into giving intelligence, by catching him thus, alone.

He sucked on like an innocent.

'Is she gone?' I said.

'No,' he replied; 'she's upstairs – she's not to go; we won't let her.'

'You won't let her, little idiot!' I exclaimed. 'Direct me to her room immediately, or I'll make you sing out sharply.'

'Papa would make you sing out, if you attempted to get there,' he answered. 'He says I'm not to be soft with Catherine – she's my wife, and it's shameful that she should wish to leave me! He says, she hates me, and wants me to die, that she may have my money, but she shan't have it; and she shan't go home! She never shall! she may cry, and be sick as much as she pleases!'

He resumed his former occupation, closing his lids, as if he meant to drop asleep.

'Master Heathcliff,' I resumed, 'have you forgotten all Catherine's kindness to you, last winter, when you affirmed you loved her, and when she brought you books, and sung you songs, and came many a time through wind and snow to see you? She wept to miss one evening, because you would be disappointed; and you felt then, that she was a hundred times too good to you; and now you believe the lies your father tells, though you know he detests you both! And you join him against her. That's fine gratitude, is it not?'

The corner of Linton's mouth fell, and he took the sugar-candy from his lips.

'Did she come to Wuthering Heights, because she hated you?' I continued. 'Think for yourself! As to your money, she does not even know that you will have any. And you say she's sick; and yet, you leave her alone, up there in a strange house! *You*, who have felt what it is to be so neglected! You could pity your own sufferings, and she pitied them, too, but you won't pity hers! I shed

tears, Master Heathcliff, you see – an elderly woman, and a servant merely – and you, after pretending such affection, and having reason to worship her, almost, store every tear you have for yourself, and lie there quite at ease. Ah! you're a heartless, selfish boy!'

'I can't stay with her,' he answered crossly. 'I'll not stay, by myself. She cries so I can't bear it. And she won't give over, though I say I'll call my father – I did call him once; and he threatened to strangle her, if she was not quiet, but she began again, the instant he left the room; moaning and grieving, all night long, though I screamed for vexation that I couldn't sleep.'

'Is Mr Heathcliff out?' I inquired, perceiving that the wretched creature had no power to sympathize with his cousin's mental tortures.

'He's in the court,' he replied, 'talking to Doctor Kenneth who says uncle is dying, truly, at last – I'm glad, for I shall be master of the Grange after him – and Catherine always spoke of it as *her* house. It isn't hers! It's mine – papa says everything she has is mine, all her nice books are mine – she offered to give me them, and her pretty birds, and her pony Minny, if I would get the key of our room, and let her out: but I told her she had nothing to give, they were all, all mine. And then she cried, and took a little picture from her neck, and said I should have that – two pictures in a gold case – on one side her mother, and on the other, uncle, when they were young. That was yesterday – I said *they* were mine, too; and tried to get them from her. The spiteful thing wouldn't let me; she pushed me off, and hurt me. I shrieked out – that frightens her – she heard papa coming, and she broke the hinges, and divided the case and gave me her mother's portrait; the other she attempted to hide; but papa asked what was the matter and I explained it. He took the one I had away; and ordered her to resign hers to me; she refused, and he – he struck her down, and wrenched it off the chain, and crushed it with his foot.'

'And were you pleased to see her struck?' I asked, having my designs in encouraging his talk.

'I winked,' he answered. 'I wink to see my father strike a dog, or a horse, he does it so hard – yet I was glad at first – she deserved punishing for pushing me: but when papa was gone, she made me come to the window and showed me her cheek cut on the inside, against her teeth, and her mouth filling with blood; and then she gathered up the bits of the picture, and went and sat down with her face to the wall, and she has never spoken to me since; and I sometimes think she can't speak for pain. I don't like to think so! but she's a naughty thing for crying continually; and she looks so pale and wild, I'm afraid of her!'

'And you can get the key if you choose?' I said.

'Yes, when I am upstairs,' he answered; 'but I can't walk upstairs now.'

'In what apartment is it?' I asked.

'Oh,' he cried, 'I shan't tell *you* where it is! It is our secret. Nobody, neither Hareton, nor Zillah are to know. There! you've tired me – go away, go away!' And he turned his face onto his arm, and shut his eyes, again.

I considered it best to depart without seeing Mr Heathcliff; and bring a rescue for my young lady, from the Grange.

On reaching it, the astonishment of my fellow servants to see me, and their joy also, was intense; and when they heard that their little mistress was safe, two or three were about to hurry up, and shout the news at Mr Edgar's door: but I bespoke the announcement of it, myself.

# Wuthering Heights

How changed I found him, even in those few days! He lay an image of sadness, and resignation, waiting his death. Very young he looked: though his actual age was thirty-nine, one would have called him ten years younger, at least. He thought of Catherine for he murmured her name. I touched his hand, and spoke.

'Catherine is coming, dear master!' I whispered; 'she is alive, and well; and will be here, I hope, tonight.'

I trembled at the first effects of this intelligence: he half rose up, looked eagerly round the apartment, and then sunk back in a swoon.

As soon as he recovered, I related our compulsory visit, and detention at the Heights: I said Heathcliff forced me to go in, which was not quite true; I uttered as little as possible against Linton; nor did I describe all his father's brutal conduct – my intentions being to add no bitterness, if I could help it, to his already overflowing cup.

He divined that one of his enemy's purposes was to secure the personal property, as well as the estate, to his son, or rather himself; yet why he did not wait till his decease, was a puzzle to my master, because ignorant how nearly he and his nephew would quit the world together.

However, he felt that his will had better be altered – instead of leaving Catherine's fortune at her own disposal, he determined to put it in the hands of trustees, for her use during life; and for her children, if she had any, after her. By that means, it could not fall to Mr Heathcliff should Linton die.

Having received his orders, I despatched a man to fetch the attorney, and four more, provided with serviceable weapons, to demand my young lady of her jailer. Both parties were delayed very late. The single servant returned first.

He said Mr Green, the lawyer, was out when he arrived at his house, and he had to wait two hours for his re-entrance: and then Mr Green told him he had a little business in the village that must be done, but he would be at Thrushcross Grange before morning.

The four men came back unaccompanied, also. They brought word that Catherine was ill, too ill to quit her room, and Heathcliff would not suffer them to see her.

I scolded the stupid fellows well, for listening to that tale, which I would not carry to my master; resolving to take a whole bevy up to the Heights, at daylight, and storm it, literally, unless the prisoner were quietly surrendered to us.

Her father *shall* see her, I vowed, and vowed again, if that devil be killed on his own door-stones in trying to prevent it!

Happily, I was spared the journey, and the trouble.

I had gone downstairs at three o'clock to fetch a jug of water; and was passing through the hall, with it in my hand, when a sharp knock, at the front door, made me jump.

'Oh! it is Green' – I said, recollecting myself – 'only Green,' and I went on, intending to send somebody else to open it; but the knock was repeated, not loud, and still importunately.

I put the jug on the banister, and hastened to admit him myself.

The harvest moon shone clear outside. It was not the attorney. My own sweet little mistress sprung on my neck, sobbing –

'Ellen! Ellen! is papa alive?'

186

# Wuthering Heights

'Yes!' I cried, 'yes, my angel, he is! God be thanked, you are safe with us again!'

She wanted to run, breathless as she was, upstairs to Mr Linton's room; but I compelled her to sit down on a chair, and made her drink, and washed her pale face, chafing it into a faint colour with my apron. Then I said I must go first, and tell of her arrival; imploring her to say, she should be happy with young Heathcliff. She stared, but soon comprehending why I counselled her to utter the falsehood, she assured me she would not complain.

I couldn't abide to be present at their meeting. I stood outside the chamber-door a quarter of an hour, and hardly ventured near the bed, then.

All was composed, however; Catherine's despair was as silent as her father's joy. She supported him calmly, in appearance; and he fixed on her features his raised eyes that seemed dilating with ecstasy.

He died blissfully, Mr Lockwood; he died so. Kissing her cheek, he murmured –

'I am going to her, and you, darling child, shall come to us;' and never stirred or spoke again, but continued that rapt, radiant gaze, till his pulse imperceptibly stopped, and his soul departed. None could have noticed the exact minute of his death, it was so entirely without a struggle.

Whether Catherine had spent her tears, or whether the grief were too weighty to let them flow, she sat there dry-eyed till the sun rose – she sat till noon, and would have remained, brooding over that death-bed, but I insisted on her coming away, and taking some repose.

It was well I succeeded in removing her, for at dinner-time appeared the lawyer, having called at Wuthering Heights to get his instructions how to behave. He had sold himself to Mr Heathcliff, and that was the cause of his delay in obeying my master's summons. Fortunately, no thought of worldly affairs crossed the latter's mind, to disturb him, after his daughter's arrival.

Mr Green took upon himself to order everything and everybody about the place. He gave all the servants but me, notice to quit. He would have carried his delegated authority to the point of insisting that Edgar Linton should not be buried beside his wife, but in the chapel, with his family. There was the will, however, to hinder that, and my loud protestations against any infringement of its directions.

The funeral was hurried over; Catherine, Mrs Linton Heathcliff now, was suffered to stay at the Grange, till her father's corpse had quitted it.

She told me that her anguish had at last spurred Linton to incur the risk of liberating her. She heard the men I sent, disputing at the door, and she gathered the sense of Heathcliff's answer. It drove her desperate – Linton, who had been conveyed up to the little parlour soon after I left, was terrified into fetching the key before his father re-ascended.

He had the cunning to unlock, and re-lock the door, without shutting it; and when he should have gone to bed, he begged to sleep with Hareton, and his petition was granted, for once.

Catherine stole out before break of day. She dare not try the doors, lest the dogs should raise an alarm; she visited the empty chambers, and examined their windows; and, luckily, lighting on her mother's, she got easily out of its lattice, and onto the ground, by means of the fir tree, close by. Her accomplice suffered for his share in the escape, notwithstanding his timid contrivances.

# Chapter 29

The evening after the funeral, my young lady and I were seated in the library; now musing mournfully, one of us despairingly, on our loss; now venturing conjectures as to the gloomy future.

We had just agreed the best destiny which could await Catherine, would be a permission to continue resident at the Grange, at least, during Linton's life: he being allowed to join her there, and I to remain as housekeeper. That seemed rather too favourable an arrangement to be hoped for, and yet I did hope, and began to cheer up under the prospect of retaining my home, and my employment, and, above all, my beloved young mistress, when a servant – one of the discarded ones, not yet departed – rushed hastily in, and said, 'that devil Heathcliff' was coming through the court, should he fasten the door in his face?

If we had been mad enough to order that proceeding, we had not time. He made no ceremony of knocking, or announcing his name; he was master, and availed himself of the master's privilege to walk straight in, without saying a word.

The sound of our informant's voice directed him to the library: he entered; and motioning him out, shut the door.

It was the same room into which he had been ushered, as a guest, eighteen years before: the same moon shone through the window; and the same autumn landscape lay outside. We had not yet lighted a candle, but all the apartment was visible, even to the portraits on the wall – the splendid head of Mrs Linton and the graceful one of her husband.

Heathcliff advanced to the hearth. Time had little altered his person either. There was the same man; his dark face rather sallower, and more composed, his frame a stone or two heavier, perhaps, with no other difference.

Catherine had risen with an impulse to dash out, when she saw him.

'Stop!' he said, arresting her by the arm. 'No more runnings away! Where would you go? I'm come to fetch you home; and I hope you'll be a dutiful daughter, and not encourage my son to further disobedience. I was embarrassed how to punish him, when I discovered his part in the business – he's such a cobweb, a pinch would annihilate him – but, you'll see by his look that he has received his due! I brought him down one evening, the day before yesterday, and just set him in a chair, and never touched him afterwards. I sent Hareton out, and we had the room to ourselves. In two hours, I called Joseph to carry him up again; and, since then, my presence is as potent on his nerves, as a ghost; and I fancy he sees me often, though I am not near. Hareton says he wakes and shrieks in the night by the hour together; and calls you to protect him from me;

# Wuthering Heights

and, whether you like your precious mate or not, you must come – he's your concern now; I yield all my interest in him to you.'

'Why not let Catherine continue here?' I pleaded, 'and send Master Linton to her. As you hate them both, you'd not miss them – they *can* only be a daily plague to your unnatural heart.'

'I'm seeking a tenant for the Grange,' he answered; 'and I want my children about me, to be sure – besides, that lass owes me her services for her bread; I'm not going to nurture her in luxury and idleness after Linton is gone. Make haste and get ready now. And don't oblige me to compel you.'

'I shall,' said Catherine. 'Linton is all I have to love in the world, and, though you have done what you could to make him hateful to me, and me to him, you *cannot* make us hate each other! and I defy you to hurt him when I am by, and I defy you to frighten me!'

'You are a boastful champion!' replied Heathcliff; 'but I don't like you well enough to hurt him – you shall get the full benefit of the torment, as long as it lasts. It is not I who will make him hateful to you – it is his own sweet spirit. He's as bitter as gall at your desertion, and its consequences – don't expect thanks for this noble devotion. I heard him draw a pleasant picture to Zillah of what he would do, if he were as strong as I – the inclination is there, and his very weakness will sharpen his wits to find a substitute for strength.'

'I know he has a bad nature,' said Catherine; 'he's your son. But I'm glad I've a better, to forgive it; and I know he loves me and for that reason I love him. Mr Heathcliff, *you* have *nobody* to love you; and, however miserable you make us, we shall still have the revenge of thinking that your cruelty arises from your greater misery! You *are* miserable, are you not? Lonely, like the devil, and envious like him? *Nobody* loves you – *nobody* will cry for you, when you die! I wouldn't be you!'

Catherine spoke with a kind of dreary triumph: she seemed to have made up her mind to enter into the spirit of her future family, and draw pleasure from the griefs of her enemies.

'You shall be sorry to be yourself presently,' said her father-in-law, 'if you stand there another minute. Begone, witch, and get your things.'

She scornfully withdrew.

In her absence, I began to beg for Zillah's place at the Heights, offering to resign mine, but he would suffer it on no account. He bid me be silent, and then, for the first time, allowed himself a glance round the room, and a look at the pictures. Having studied Mrs Linton, he said –

'I shall have that home. Not because I need it, but –'

He turned abruptly to the fire, and continued, with what, for lack of a better word, I must call a smile –

'I'll tell you what I did yesterday! I got the sexton, who was digging Linton's grave, to remove the earth off her coffin lid, and I opened it. I thought, once, I would have stayed there, when I saw her face again – it is hers yet – he had hard work to stir me; but he said it would change, if the air blew on it, and so I struck one side of the coffin loose – and covered it up – not Linton's side, damn him! I wish he'd been soldered in lead – and I bribed the sexton to pull it away, when I'm laid there, and slide mine out too. I'll have it made so, and then, by the time Linton gets to us, he'll not know which is which!'

189

# Wuthering Heights

'You were very wicked, Mr Heathcliff!' I exclaimed; 'were you not ashamed to disturb the dead?'

'I disturbed nobody, Nelly,' he replied; 'and I gave some ease to myself. I shall be a great deal more comfortable now; and you'll have a better chance of keeping me underground, when I get there. Disturbed her? No! she has disturbed me, night and day, through eighteen years – incessantly – remorselessly – till yesternight – and yesternight, I was tranquil. I dreamt I was sleeping the last sleep, by that sleeper, with my heart stopped, and my cheek frozen against hers.'

'And if she had been dissolved into earth, or worse, what would you have dreamt of then?' I said.

'Of dissolving with her, and being more happy still!' he answered. 'Do you suppose I dread any change of that sort? I expected such a transformation on raising the lid, but I'm better pleased that it should not commence till I share it. Besides, unless I had received a distinct impression of her passionless features, that strange feeling would hardly have been removed. It began oddly. You know, I was wild after she died, and eternally, from dawn to dawn, praying her to return to me – her spirit – I have a strong faith in ghosts; I have a conviction that they can, and do exist, among us!

'The day she was buried there came a fall of snow. In the evening I went to the churchyard. It blew bleak as winter – all round was solitary: I didn't fear that her fool of a husband would wander up the den so late – and no one else had business to bring them there.

'Being alone, and conscious two yards of loose earth was the sole barrier between us, I said to myself –

' "I'll have her in my arms again! If she be cold, I'll think it is this north wind that chills me; and if she be motionless, it is sleep."

'I got a spade from the toolhouse, and began to delve with all my might – it scraped the coffin; I fell to work with my hands; the wood commenced cracking about the screws, I was on the point of attaining my object, when it seemed that I heard a sigh from some one above, close at the edge of the grave, and bending down. "If I can only get this off," I muttered, "I wish they may shovel in the earth over us both!" and I wrenched more desperately still. There was another sigh, close at my ear. I appeared to feel the warm breath of it displacing the sleet-laden wind. I knew no living thing in flesh and blood was by – but as certainly as you perceive the approach to some substantial body in the dark, though it cannot be discerned, so certainly I felt that Cathy was there, not under me, but on the earth.

'A sudden sense of relief flowed, from my heart, through every limb. I relinquished my labour of agony, and turned consoled at once, unspeakably consoled. Her presence was with me; it remained while I re-filled the grave, and led me home. You may laugh, if you will, but I was sure I should see her there. I was sure she was with me, and I could not help talking to her.

'Having reached the Heights, I rushed eagerly to the door. It was fastened; and, I remember, that accursed Earnshaw and my wife opposed my entrance. I remember stopping to kick the breath out of him, and then hurrying upstairs, to my room, and hers – I looked round impatiently – I felt her by me – I could *almost* see her, and yet I *could not*! I ought to have sweat blood then, from the anguish of my yearning, from the fervour of my supplications to have but one glimpse! I had not one. She showed herself, as she often was in life, a devil to

me! And, since then, sometimes more and sometimes less, I've been the sport of that intolerable torture! Infernal – keeping my nerves at such a stretch, that, if they had not resembled catgut, they would, long ago, have relaxed to the feebleness of Linton's.

'When I sat in the house with Hareton, it seemed that on going out, I should meet her; when I walked on the moors I should meet her coming in. When I went from home, I hastened to return, she *must* be somewhere at the Heights, I was certain! And when I slept in her chamber – I was beaten out of that – I couldn't lie there; for the moment I closed my eyes, she was either outside the window, or sliding back the panels, or entering the room, or even resting her darling head on the same pillow as she did when a child. And I must open my lids to see. And so I opened and closed them a hundred times a night – to be always disappointed! It racked me! I've often groaned aloud, till that old rascal Joseph, no doubt, believed that my conscience was playing the fiend inside of me.

'Now since I've seen her, I'm pacified – a little. It was a strange way of killing, not by inches, but by fractions of hair-breadths, to beguile me with the spectre of a hope, through eighteen years!'

Mr Heathcliff paused and wiped his forehead – his hair clung to it, wet with perspiration; his eyes were fixed on the red embers of the fire; the brows not contracted, but raised next the temples, diminishing the grim aspect of his countenance, but imparting a peculiar look of trouble, and a painful appearance of mental tension towards one absorbing subject. He only half addressed me, and I maintained silence – I didn't like to hear him talk!

After a short period, he resumed his meditation on the picture, took it down, and leant it against the sofa to contemplate it at better advantage; and while so occupied Catherine entered, announcing that she was ready, when her pony should be saddled.

'Send that over to-morrow,' said Heathcliff to me, then turning to her he added, 'You may do without your pony – it is a fine evening, and you'll need no ponies at Wuthering Heights, for what journeys you take, your own feet will serve you – Come along.'

'Goodbye, Ellen!' whispered my dear little mistress. As she kissed me, her lips felt like ice. 'Come and see me, Ellen, don't forget.'

'Take care you do no such thing, Mrs Dean!' said her new father. 'When I wish to speak to you I'll come here. I want none of your prying at my house!'

He signed her to precede him; and casting back a look that cut my heart, she obeyed.

I watched them, from the window, walk down the garden, Heathcliff fixed Catherine's arm under his, though she disputed the act, at first, evidently; and with rapid strides, he hurried her into the alley, whose trees concealed them.

# Chapter 30

have paid a visit to the Heights, but I have not seen her since she left! Joseph held the door in his hand, when I called to ask after her, and wouldn't let me pass. He said Mrs Linton was 'thrang,' and the master was not in. Zillah has told me something of the way they go on, otherwise I should hardly know who was dead, and who living.

She thinks Catherine haughty, and does not like her, I can guess by her talk. My young lady asked some aid of her, when she first came, but Mr Heathcliff told her to follow her own business, and let his daughter-in-law look after herself, and Zillah willingly acquiesced, being a narrow-minded selfish woman. Catherine evinced a child's annoyance at this neglect; repaid it with contempt, and thus enlisted my informant among her enemies, as securely as if she had done her some great wrong.

I had a long talk with Zillah, about six weeks ago, a little before you came, one day, when we foregathered on the moor; and this is what she told me.

'The first thing Mrs Linton did,' she said, 'on her arrival at the Heights, was to run upstairs without even wishing good-evening to me and Joseph; she shut herself into Linton's room, and remained till morning – then, while the master and Earnshaw were at breakfast, she entered the house and asked all in a quiver if the doctor might be sent for? her cousin was very ill.

' "We know that!" answered Heathcliff, "but his life is not worth a farthing, and I won't spend a farthing on him."

' "But I cannot tell how to do," she said; "and if nobody will help me, he'll die!"

' "Walk out of the room!" cried the master, "and let me never hear a word more about him! None here care what becomes of him; if you do, act the nurse; if you do not, lock him up and leave him."

'Then she began to bother me, and I said I'd had enough plague with the tiresome thing; we each had our tasks, and hers was to wait on Linton, Mr Heathcliff bid me leave that labour to her.

'How they managed together, I can't tell. I fancy he fretted a great deal, and moaned hisseln, night and day; and she had precious little rest, one could guess by her white face, and heavy eyes – she sometimes came into the kitchen all wildered like, and looked as if she would fain beg assistance; but I was not going to disobey the master – I never dare disobey him, Mrs Dean, and though I thought it wrong that Kenneth should not be sent for, it was no concern of mine, either to advise or complain; and I always refused to meddle.

'Once or twice, after we had gone to bed, I've happened to open my door again, and seen her sitting crying, on the stairs' top; and then I've shut myself

# Wuthering Heights

in, quick, for fear of being moved to interfere. I did pity her then, I'm sure; still I didn't want to lose my place, you know!

'At last, one night she came boldly into my chamber, and frightened me out of my wits, by saying –

' "Tell Mr Heathcliff that his son is dying – I'm sure he is, this time – Get up, instantly, and tell him!"

'Having uttered this speech, she vanished again. I lay a quarter of an hour listening and trembling – Nothing stirred – the house was quiet.

' "She's mistaken," I said to myself. "He's got over it. I needn't disturb them." And I began to dose. But my sleep was marred a second time, by a sharp ringing of the bell – the only bell we have, put up on purpose for Linton, and the master called to me, to see what was the matter, and inform them that he wouldn't have that noise repeated.

'I delivered Catherine's message. He cursed to himself, and in a few minutes, came out with a lighted candle, and proceeded to their room. I followed – Mrs Heathcliff was seated by the bedside, with her hands folded on her knees. Her father-in-law went up, held the light to Linton's face, looked at him, and touched him, afterwards he turned to her.

' "Now – Catherine," he said, "how do you feel?"

'She was dumb.

' "How do you feel, Catherine?" he repeated.

' "He's safe, and I'm free," she answered, "I should feel well – but," she continued with a bitterness she couldn't conceal, "you have left me so long to struggle against death, alone, that I feel and see only death! I feel like death!"

'And she looked like it, too! I gave her a little wine. Hareton and Joseph, who had been wakened by the ringing, and the sound of feet, and heard our talk from outside, now entered. Joseph was fain, I believe, of the lad's removal: Hareton seemed a thought bothered, though he was more taken up with staring at Catherine than thinking of Linton. But the master bid him get off to bed again – we didn't want his help. He afterwards made Joseph remove the body to his chamber, and told me to return to mine, and Mrs Heathcliff remained by herself.

'In the morning, he sent me to tell her she must come down to breakfast – she had undressed, and appeared going to sleep; and said she was ill; at which I hardly wondered. I informed Mr Heathcliff, and he replied –

' "Well, let her be till after the funeral; and go up now and then to get her what is needful; and as soon as she seems better, tell me." '

Cathy stayed upstairs a fortnight, according to Zillah, who visited her twice a-day, and would have been rather more friendly, but her attempts at increasing kindness were proudly and promptly repelled.

Heathcliff went up at once, to show her Linton's will. He had bequeathed the whole of his, and what had been her moveable property to his father. The poor creature was threatened, or coaxed, into that act during her week's absence, when his uncle died. The lands, being a minor, he could not meddle with. However, Mr Heathcliff has claimed and kept them in his wife's right, and his also – I suppose legally – at any rate, Catherine, destitute of cash and friends, cannot disturb his possession.

'Nobody,' said Zillah, 'ever approached her door, except that once, but I . . .

# Wuthering Heights

and nobody asked anything about her. The first occasion of her coming down into the house, was on a Sunday afternoon.

'She had cried out, when I carried up her dinner, that she couldn't bear any longer being in the cold; and I told her the master was going to Thrushcross Grange; and Earnshaw and I needn't hinder her from descending; so, as soon as she heard Heathcliff's horse trot off, she made her appearance, donned in black, and her yellow curls combed back behind her ears, as plain as a quaker, she couldn't comb them out.

'Joseph and I generally go to chapel on Sundays,' (the Kirk, you know, has no minister, now, explained Mrs Dean; and they call the Methodists' or Baptists' place, I can't say which it is, at Gimmerton, a chapel). 'Joseph had gone,' she continued, 'but I thought proper to bide at home. Young folks are always the better for an elder's over-looking, and Hareton, with all his bashfulness, isn't a model of nice behaviour. I let him know that his cousin would very likely sit with us, and she had been always used to see the Sabbath respected, so he had as good leave his guns, and bits of indoor work alone, while she stayed.

'He coloured up at the news; and cast his eyes over his hands and clothes. The trainoil and gunpowder were shoved out of sight in a minute. I saw he meant to give her his company; and I guessed, by his way, he wanted to be presentable; so, laughing, as I durst not laugh when the master is by, I offered to help him, if he would, and joked at his confusion. He grew sullen, and began to swear.

'Now, Mrs Dean,' she went on, seeing me not pleased by her manner, 'you happen think your young lady too fine for Mr Hareton, and happen you're right – but, I own, I should love well to bring her pride a peg lower. And what will all her learning and her daintiness do for her, now? She's as poor as you, or I – poorer – I'll be bound, you're saving – and I'm doing my little all, that road.'

Hareton allowed Zillah to give him her aid; and she flattered him into a good humour; so, when Catherine came, half forgetting her former insults, he tried to make himself agreeable, by the housekeeper's account.

'Missis walked in,' she said, 'as chill as an icicle, and as high as a princess. I got up and offered her my seat in the armchair. No, she turned up her nose at my civility. Earnshaw rose too, and bid her come to the settle, and sit close by the fire; he was sure she was starved.

' "I've been starved a month and more," she answered, resting on the word, as scornful as she could.

'And she got a chair for herself, and placed it at a distance from both of us.

'Having sat till she was warm, she began to look round, and discovered a number of books in the dresser; she was instantly upon her feet again, stretching to reach them, but they were too high up.

'Her cousin, after watching her endeavours à while, at last summoned courage to help her; she held her frock, and he filled it with the first that came to hand.

'That was a great advance for the lad – she didn't thank him; still, he felt gratified that she had accepted his assistance, and ventured to stand behind as she examined them, and even to stoop and point out what struck his fancy in certain old pictures which they contained – nor was he daunted by the saucy style in which she jerked the page from his finger; he contented himself with going a bit farther back, and looking at her instead of the book.

# Wuthering Heights

'She continued reading, or seeking for something to read. His attention became, by degrees, quite centred in the study of her thick, silky curls – her face he couldn't see, and she couldn't see him. And, perhaps, not quite awake to what he did, but attracted like a child to a candle, at last, he proceeded from staring to touching; he put out his hand and stroked one curl, as gently as if it were a bird. He might have stuck a knife into her neck, she started round in such a taking.

' "Get away, this moment! How dare you touch me? Why are you stopping there?" she cried, in a tone of disgust. "I can't endure you! I'll go upstairs again, if you come near me."

'Mr Hareton recoiled, looking as foolish as he could do; he sat down in the settle, very quiet, and she continued turning over her volumes, another half hour; finally, Earnshaw crossed over, and whispered to me.

' "Will you ask her to read to us, Zillah? I'm stalled of doing naught – and I do like – I could like to hear her! Dunnot say I wanted it, but ask of yourseln."

' "Mr Hareton wishes you would read to us, ma'am," I said, immediately. "He'd take it very kind – he'd be much obliged."

'She frowned; and, looking up, answered –

' "Mr Hareton, and the whole set of you, will be good enough to understand that I reject any pretence at kindness you have the hypocrisy to offer! I despise you, and will have nothing to say to any of you! When I would have given my life for one kind word, even to see one of your faces, you all kept off. But I won't complain to you! I'm driven down here by the cold, not either to amuse you, or enjoy your society."

' "What could I ha' done?" began Earnshaw. "How was I to blame?"

' "Oh! you are an exception," answered Mrs Heathcliff. "I never missed such a concern as you."

' "But, I offered more than once, and asked," he said, kindling up at her pertness, "I asked Mr Heathcliff to let me wake for you – "

' "Be silent! I'll go out of doors, or anywhere, rather than have your disagreeable voice in my ear!" said my lady.

'Hareton muttered, she might go to hell, for him! and unslinging his gun, restrained himself from his Sunday occupations no longer.

'He talked now, freely enough; and she presently saw fit to retreat to her solitude: but the frost had set in, and, in spite of her pride, she was forced to condescend to our company, more and more. However, I took care there should be no further scorning at my good nature – ever since, I've been as stiff as herself – and she has no lover, or liker among us – and she does not deserve one – for, let them say the least word to her, and she'll curl back without respect of anyone! She'll snap at the master himself, and as good as dares him to thrash her; and the more hurt she gets, the more venomous she grows.'

At first, on hearing this account from Zillah, I determined to leave my situation, take a cottage, and get Catherine to come and live with me; but Mr Heathcliff would as soon permit that, as he would set up Hareton in an independent house; and I can see no remedy, at present, unless she could marry again; and that scheme, it does not come within my province to arrange.

Thus ended Mrs Dean's story. Notwithstanding the doctor's prophecy, I am rapidly recovering strength, and, though it be only the second week in January, I propose getting out on horseback, in a day or two, and riding over to Wuthering

Heights, to inform my landlord that I shall spend the next six months in London; and, if he likes, he may look out for another tenant to take the place, after October – I would not pass another winter here, for much.

# Chapter 31

Yesterday was bright, calm, and frosty. I went to the Heights as I proposed; my housekeeper entreated me to bear a little note from her to her young lady, and I did not refuse, for the worthy woman was not conscious of anything odd in her request.

The front door stood open, but the jealous gate was fastened, as at my last visit; I knocked and invoked Earnshaw from among the garden beds; he unchained it, and I entered. The fellow is as handsome a rustic as need be seen. I took particular notice of him this time; but then, he does his best, apparently, to make the least of his advantages.

I asked if Mr Heathcliff were at home. He answered, no; but he would be in at dinner-time. It was eleven o'clock, and I announced my intention of going in, and waiting for him, at which he immediately flung down his tools and accompanied me, in the office of watchdog, not as a substitute for the host.

We entered together; Catherine was there, making herself useful in preparing some vegetables for the approaching meal; she looked more sulky, and less spirited than when I had seen her first. She hardly raised her eyes to notice me, and continued her employment with the same disregard to common forms of politeness, as before; never returning my bow and good-morning by the slightest acknowledgment.

'She does not seem so amiable,' I thought, 'as Mrs Dean would persuade me to believe. She's a beauty, it is true; but not an angel.'

Earnshaw surlily bid her remove her things to the kitchen.

'Remove them yourself,' she said, pushing them from her as soon as she had done; and retiring to a stool by the window, where she began to carve figures of birds and beasts, out of the turnip parings in her lap.

I approached her, pretending to desire a view of the garden; and, as I fancied, adroitly dropped Mrs Dean's note onto her knee, unnoticed by Hareton – but she asked aloud –

'What is that?' And chucked it off.

'A letter from your old acquaintance, the housekeeper at the Grange,' I answered, annoyed at her exposing my kind deed, and fearful lest it should be imagined a missive of my own.

She would gladly have gathered it up, at this information, but Hareton beat her; he seized, and put it in his waistcoat, saying Mr Heathcliff should look at it first.

# Wuthering Heights

Thereat, Catherine silently turned her face from us, and, very stealthily, drew out her pocket-handkerchief and applied it to her eyes; and her cousin, after struggling a while to keep down his softer feelings, pulled out the letter and flung it on the floor beside her as ungraciously as he could.

Catherine caught and perused it eagerly; then she put a few questions to me concerning the inmates, rational and irrational, of her former home; and gazing towards the hills, murmured in soliloquy.

'I should like to be riding Minny down there! I should like to be climbing up there – Oh! I'm tired – I'm *stalled*, Hareton!'

And she leant her pretty head back against the sill, with half a yawn and half a sigh, and lapsed into an aspect of abstracted sadness, neither caring nor knowing whether we remarked her.

'Mrs Heathcliff,' I said, after sitting some time mute, 'you are not aware that I am an acquaintance of yours? so intimate, that I think it strange you won't come and speak to me. My housekeeper never wearies of talking about and praising you; and she'll be greatly disappointed if I return with no news of, or from you, except that you received her letter and said nothing!'

She appeared to wonder at this speech and asked,

'Does Ellen like you?'

'Yes, very well,' I replied unhesitatingly.

'You must tell her,' she continued, 'that I would answer her letter, but I have no materials for writing, not even a book from which I might tear a leaf.'

'No books!' I exclaimed. 'How do you contrive to live here without them? if I may take the liberty to inquire – Though provided with a large library, I'm frequently very dull at the Grange – take my books away, and I should be desperate!'

'I was always reading, when I had them,' said Catherine, 'and Mr Heathcliff never reads; so he took it into his head to destroy my books. I have not had a glimpse of one, for weeks. Only once, I searched through Joseph's store of theology, to his great irritation; and once, Hareton, I came upon a secret stock in your room ... some Latin and Greek, and some tales and poetry; all old friends – I brought the last here – and you gathered them, as a magpie gathers silver spoons, for the mere love of stealing! They are of no use to you – or else you concealed them in bad spirit, that you cannot enjoy them, nobody else shall. Perhaps *your* envy counselled Mr Heathcliff to rob me of my treasures? But I've most of them written on my brain and printed in my heart, and you cannot deprive me of those!'

Earnshaw blushed crimson, when his cousin made this revelation of his private literary accumulations, and stammered an indignant denial of her accusations.

'Mr Hareton is desirous of increasing his amount of knowledge,' I said, coming to his rescue. 'He is not *envious* but *emulous* of your attainments – He'll be a clever scholar in a few years!'

'And he wants *me* to sink into a dunce, meantime,' answered Catherine. 'Yes, I hear him trying to spell and read to himself, and pretty blunders he makes! I wish you would repeat Chevy Chase as you did yesterday – it was extremely funny! I heard you ... and I heard you turning over the dictionary, to seek out the hard words, and then cursing, because you couldn't read their explanations!'

The young man evidently thought it too bad that he should be laughed at for

# Wuthering Heights

his ignorance, and then laughed at for trying to remove it. I had a similar notion, and, remebering Mrs Dean's anecdotes of his first attempt at enlightening the darkness in which he had been reared, I observed –

'But, Mrs Heathcliff, we have each had a commencement, and each stumbled and tottered on the threshold, and had our teachers scorned, instead of aiding us, we should stumble and totter yet.'

'Oh! she replied, 'I don't wish to limit his acquirements ... still, he has no right to appropriate what is mine, and make it ridiculous to me with his vile mistakes and mispronunciations! Those books, both prose and verse, were consecrated to me by other associations, and I hate to have them debased and profaned in his mouth! Besides, of all, he has selected my favourite pieces that I love the most to repeat, as if out of deliberate malice!'

Hareton's chest heaved in silence a minute; he laboured under a severe sense of mortification and wrath, which it was no easy task to suppress.

I rose, and from a gentlemanly idea of relieving his embarrassment, took up my station in the doorway, surveying the external prospect, as I stood.

He followed my example, and left the room, but presently reappeared, bearing half a dozen volumes in his hands, which he threw into Catherine's lap, exclaiming –

'Take them! I never want to hear, or read, or think of them again!'

'I won't have them, now,' she answered. 'I shall connect them with you, and hate them.'

She opened one that had obviously been often turned over, and read a portion in the drawling tone of a beginner; then laughed, and threw it from her.

'And listen,' she continued provokingly, commencing a verse of an old ballad in the same fashion.

But his self-love would endure no further torment – I heard, and not altogether disapprovingly, a manual check given to her saucy tongue – The little wretch had done her utmost to hurt her cousin's sensitive though uncultivated feelings, and a physical argument was the only mode he had of balancing the account, and repaying its effects on the inflicter.

He afterwards gathered the books and hurled them on the fire. I read in his countenance what anguish it was to offer that sacrifice to spleen – I fancied that as they consumed, he recalled the pleasure they had already imparted; and the triumph and ever-increasing pleasure he had anticipated from them – and I fancied, I guessed the incitement to his secret studies, also. He had been content with daily labour and rough animal enjoyments, till Catherine crossed his path – Shame at her scorn, and hope of her approval were his first prompters to higher pursuits; and instead of guarding him from one, and winning him the other, his endeavours to raise himself had produced just the contrary result.

'Yes, that's all the good that such a brute as you can get from them!' cried Catherine, sucking her damaged lip, and watching the conflagration with indignant eyes.

'You'd *better* hold your tongue, now!' he answered fiercely.

And his agitation precluding further speech, he advanced hastily to the entrance, where I made way for him to pass. But, ere he had crossed the door-stones, Mr Heathcliff, coming up the causeway, encountered him, and laying hold of his shoulder asked –

'What's to do now, my lad?'

'Naught, naught!' he said, and broke away, to enjoy his grief and anger in solitude.

Heathcliff gazed after him, and sighed.

'It will be odd, if I thwart myself!' he muttered, unconscious that I was behind him. 'But, when I look for his father in his face, I find *her* every day more! How the devil is he so like? I can hardly bear to see him.'

He bent his eyes to the ground, and walked moodily in. There was a restless, anxious expression in his countenance, I had never remarked there before, and he looked sparer in person.

His daughter-in-law, on perceiving him through the window, immediately escaped to the kitchen, so that I remained alone.

'I'm glad to see you out of doors again, Mr Lockwood,' he said in reply to my greeting, 'from selfish motives partly; I don't think I could readily supply your loss in this desolation. I've wondered, more than once, what brought you here.'

'An idle whim, I fear, sir,' was my answer, 'or else an idle whim is going to spirit me away – I shall set out for London, next week, and I must give you warning, that I feel no disposition to retain Thrushcross Grange, beyond the twelve-months I agreed to rent it. I believe I shall not live there any more.'

'Oh, indeed! you're tired of being banished from the world, are you?' he said. 'But, if you be coming to plead off paying for a place you won't occupy, your journey is useless – I never relent in exacting my due, from anyone.'

'I'm coming to plead off nothing about it!' I exclaimed, considerably irritated. 'Should you wish it, I'll settle with you now,' and I drew my note-book from my pocket.

'No, no,' he replied coolly, 'you'll leave sufficient behind to cover your debts, if you fail to return . . . I'm not in such a hurry – sit down and take your dinner with us – a guest that is safe from repeating his visit, can generally be made welcome – Catherine! bring the things in – where are you?'

Catherine re-appeared, bearing a tray of knives and forks.

'You may get your dinner with Joseph,' muttered Heathcliff aside, 'and remain in the kitchen till he is gone.'

She obeyed his directions very punctually – perhaps she had no temptation to transgress. Living among clowns and misanthropists, she probably cannot appreciate a better class of people, when she meets them.

With Mr Heathcliff, grim and saturnine, on one hand, and Hareton, absolutely dumb, on the other, I made a somewhat cheerless meal, and bid adieu early. I would have departed by the back way, to get a last glimpse of Catherine, and annoy old Joseph; but Hareton received orders to lead up my horse, and my host himself escorted me to the door, so I could not fulfil my wish.

'How dreary life gets over in that house!' I reflected, while riding down the road. 'What a realization of something more romantic than a fairy tale it would have been for Mrs Linton Heathcliff, had she and I struck up an attachment, as her good nurse desired, and migrated together, into the stirring atmosphere of the town!'

# Chapter 32

*1802.* – This September, I was invited to devastate the moors of a friend, in the North; and, on my journey to his abode, I unexpectedly came within fifteen miles of Gimmerton. The hostler, at a roadside public-house, was holding a pail of water to refresh my horses, when a cart of very green oats, newly reaped, passed by, and he remarked –

'Yon's frough Gimmerton, nah! They're allas three wick' after other folk wi' ther harvest.'

'Gimmerton?' I repeated – my residence in that locality had already grown dim and dreamy. 'Ah! I know! How far is it from this?'

'Happen fourteen mile' o'er th' hills, and a rough road,' he answered.

A sudden impulse seized me to visit Thrushcross Grange. It was scarcely noon, and I conceived that I might as well pass the night under my own roof, as in an inn. Besides, I could spare a day easily, to arrange matters with my landlord, and thus save myself the trouble of invading the neighbourhood again.

Having rested a while, I directed my servant to inquire the way to the village; and, with great fatigue to our beasts, we managed the distance in some three hours.

I left him there, and proceeded down the valley alone. The grey church looked greyer, and the lonely churchyard lonelier. I distinguished a moor sheep cropping the short turf on the graves. It was sweet, warm weather – too warm for travelling; but the heat did not hinder me from enjoying the delightful scenery above and below; had I seen it nearer August, I'm sure it would have tempted me to waste a month among its solitudes. In winter, nothing more dreary, in summer, nothing more divine, than those glens shut in by hills, and those bluff, bold swells of heath.

I reached the Grange before sunset, and knocked for admittance; but the family had retreated into the back premises, I judged by one thin, blue wreath curling from the kitchen chimney, and they did not hear.

I rode into the court. Under the porch, a girl of nine or ten sat knitting, and an old woman reclined on the horse-steps, smoking a meditative pipe.

'Is Mrs Dean within?' I demanded of the dame.

'Mistress Dean? Nay!' she answered, 'shoo doesn't bide here; shoo's up at th' Heights.'

'Are you the housekeeper, then?' I continued.

'Eea, Aw keep th' hause,' she replied.

'Well, I'm Mr Lockwood, the master – Are there any rooms to lodge me in, I wonder? I wish to stay here all night.'

'T' maister!' she cried in astonishment. 'Whet, whoiver knew yah wur coming?

# Wuthering Heights

Yah sud ha' send word! They's nowt norther dry – nor mensful abaht t' place – nowt there isn't!'

She threw down her pipe and bustled in, the girl followed, and I entered too; soon perceiving that her report was true, and, moreover, that I had almost upset her wits by my unwelcome apparition.

I bid her be composed – I would go out for a walk; and, meantime, she must try to prepare a corner of a sitting-room for me to sup in, and a bed-room to sleep in. No sweeping and dusting, only good fires and dry sheets were necessary.

She seemed willing to do her best; though she thrust the hearthbrush into the grates in mistake for the poker; and malappropriated several other articles of her craft; but I retired, confiding in her energy for a resting-place against my return.

Wuthering Heights was the goal of my proposed excursion. An after-thought brought me back, when I had quitted the court.

'All well at the Heights?' I inquired of the woman.

'Ea, f'r owt Ee knaw!' she answered, scurrying away with a pan of hot cinders.

I would have asked why Mrs Dean had deserted the Grange; but it was impossible to delay her at such a crisis, so I turned away and made my exit, rambling leisurely along, with the glow of a sinking sun behind, and the mild glory of a rising moon in front; one fading, and the other brightening, as I quitted the park, and climbed the stony by-road branching off to Mr Heathcliff's dwelling.

Before I arrived in sight of it, all that remained of day was a beamless, amber light along the west; but I could see every pebble on the path, and every blade of grass, by that splendid moon.

I had neither to climb the gate, nor to knock – it yielded to my hand.

This is an improvement! I thought. And I noticed another, by the aid of my nostrils; a fragrance of stocks and wall flowers, wafted on the air, from amongst the homely fruit trees.

Both doors and lattices were open; and, yet, as is usually the case in a coal district, a fine, red fire illumined the chimney; the comfort which the eye derives from it, renders the extra heat endurable. But the house of Wuthering Heights is so large, that the inmates have plenty of space for withdrawing out of its influence; and, accordingly, what inmates there were had stationed themselves not far from one of the windows. I could both see them and hear them talk before I entered, and looked and listened in consequence, being moved thereto by a mingled sense of curiosity, and envy that grew as I lingered.

'Con-*trary*!' said a voice, as sweet as a silver bell – 'That for the third time, you dunce! I'm not going to tell you, again – Recollect, or I pull your hair!'

'Contrary, then,' answered another, in deep, but softened tones. 'And now, kiss me, for minding so well.'

'No, read it over first correctly, without a single mistake.'

The male speaker began to read – he was a young man, respectably dressed, and seated at a table, having a book before him. His handsome features glowed with pleasure, and his eyes kept impatiently wandering from the page to a small white hand over his shoulder, which recalled him by a smart slap on the cheek, whenever its owner detected such signs of inattention.

Its owner stood behind; her light shining ringlets blending at intervals, with

his brown locks, as she bent to superintend his studies; and her face – it was lucky he could not see her face, or he would never have been so steady – I could, and I bit my lip, in spite, at having thrown away the chance I might have had, of doing something besides staring at its smiting beauty.

The task was done, not free from further blunders, but the pupil claimed a reward and received at least fives kisses, which, however, he generously returned. Then, they came to the door, and from their conversation, I judged they were about to issue out and have a walk on the moors. I supposed I should be condemned in Hareton Earnshaw's heart, if not by his mouth, to the lowest pit in the infernal regions if I showed my unfortunate person in his neighbourhood then, and feeling very mean and malignant, I skulked round to seek refuge in the kitchen.

There was unobstructed admittance on that side also; and, at the door, sat my old friend, Nelly Dean, sewing and singing a song, which was often interrupted from within, by harsh words of scorn and intolerance, uttered in far from musical accents.

'Aw'd rayther, by th' hauf, hev' em swearing i' my lugs frough morn tuh neeght, nur hearken yah, hahsiver!' said the tenant of the kitchen, in answer to an unheard speech of Nelly's. 'It's a blazing shaime, ut Aw cannut oppen t' Blessed Book, bud yah set up them glories tuh sattan, un' all t' flaysome wickednesses ut iver wer born intuh t'warld! Oh! yah're a raight nowt; un' shoo's another; un' that poor lad 'ull be lost atween ye. Poor lad!' he added, with a groan; 'he's witched, Aw'm sartin on 't! O, Lord, judge 'em, fur they's norther law nur justice amang wer rullers!'

'No! or we should be sitting in flaming fagots, I suppose,' retorted the singer. 'But whisht, old man, and read your Bible like a christian, and never mind me. This is "Fairy Annie's Wedding" – a bonny tune – it goes to a dance.'

Mrs Dean was about to recommence, when I advanced, and recognizing me directly, she jumped to her feet, crying –

'Why bless you, Mr Lockwood! How could you think of returning in this way? All's shut up at Thrushcross Grange. You should have given us notice!'

'I've arranged to be accommodated there, for as long as I shall stay,' I answered. 'I depart again to-morrow. And how are you transplanted here, Mrs Dean? tell me that.'

'Zillah left, and Mr Heathcliff wished me to come, soon after you went to London, and stay till you returned. But, step in, pray! Have you walked from Gimmerton this evening?'

'From the Grange,' I replied; 'and, while they make me lodging room there, I want to finish my business with your master, because I don't think of having another opportunity in a hurry.'

'What business, sir?' said Nelly, conducting me into the house. 'He's gone out at present, and won't return soon.'

'About the rent,' I answered.

'Oh! then it is with Mrs Heathcliff you must settle,' she observed, 'or rather with me. She has not learnt to manage her affairs yet, and I act for her; there's nobody else.'

I looked surprised.

'Ah! you have not heard of Heathcliff's death, I see!' she continued.

'Heathcliff dead?' I exclaimed, astonished. 'How long ago?'

# Wuthering Heights

'Three months since – but, sit down, and let me take your hat, and I'll tell you all about it. Stop, you have had nothing to eat, have you?'

'I want nothing. I have ordered supper at home. You sit down too. I never dreamt of his dying! Let me hear how it came to pass. You say you don't expect them back for some time – the young people?'

'No – I have to scold them every evening, for their late rambles – but they don't care for me. At least, have a drink of our old ale – it will do you good – you seem weary.'

She hastened to fetch it, before I could refuse, and I heard Joseph asking, whether 'it warn't a crying scandal that she should have fellies at her time of life? And then, to get them jocks out uh't' Maister's cellar! He fair shaamed to 'bide still and see it.'

She did not stay to retaliate, but re-entered, in a minute, bearing a reaming, silver pint, whose contents I lauded with becoming earnestness. And afterwards she furnished me with the sequel of Heathcliff's history. He had a 'queer' end, as she expressed it.

I was summoned to Wuthering Heights, within a fortnight of your leaving us, she said; and I obeyed joyfully, for Catherine's sake.

My first interview with her grieved and shocked me! she had altered so much since our separation. Mr Heathcliff did not explain his reasons for taking a new mind about my coming here; he only told me he wanted me, and he was tired of seeing Catherine; I must make the little parlour my sitting room, and keep her with me. It was enough if he were obliged to see her once or twice a day.

She seemed pleased at this arrangement; and, by degrees, I smuggled over a great number of books, and other articles, that had formed her amusement at the Grange; and flattered myself we should get on in tolerable comfort.

The delusion did not last long. Catherine, contented at first, in a brief space grew irritable and restless. For one thing, she was forbidden to move out of the garden, and it fretted her sadly to be confined to its narrow bounds, as Spring drew on – for another, in following the house, I was forced to quit her frequently, and she complained of loneliness; she preferred quarrelling with Joseph in the kitchen, to sitting at peace in her solitude.

I did not mind her skirmishes; but Hareton was often obliged to seek the kitchen also, when the master wanted to have the house to himself; and, though, in the beginning, she either left it at his approach, or quietly joined in my occupations, and shunned remarking, or addressing him – and though he was always as sullen and silent, as possible – after a while, she changed her behaviour, and became incapable of letting him alone. Talking at him; commenting on his stupidity and idleness; expressing her wonder how he could endure the life he lived – how he could sit a whole evening staring into the fire, and dozing.

'He's just like a dog, is he not, Ellen?' she once observed, 'or a cart-horse? He does his work, eats his food, and sleeps, eternally! What a blank, dreary mind he must have! Do you ever dream, Hareton? And, if you do, what is it about? But you can't speak to me!'

Then she looked at him; but he would neither open his mouth, nor look again.

'He's perhaps, dreaming now,' she continued. 'He twitched his shoulder as Juno twitches hers. Ask him, Ellen.'

'Mr Hareton will ask the master to send you upstairs, if you don't behave!'

I said. He had not only twitched his shoulder, but clenched his fist, as if tempted to use it.

'I know why Hareton never speaks, when I am in the kitchen,' she exclaimed, on another occasion. 'He is afraid I shall laugh at him. Ellen, what do you think? He began to teach himself to read once; and, because I laughed, he burned his books, and dropped it – was he not a fool?'

'Were not you naughty?' I said; 'answer me that.'

'Perhaps I was,' she went on, 'but I did not expect him to be so silly. Hareton, if I gave you a book, would you take it now? I'll try!'

She placed one she had been perusing on his hand; he flung it off, and muttered, if she did not give over, he would break her neck.

'Well, I shall put it here,' she said, 'in the table drawer, and I'm going to bed.'

Then she whispered me to watch whether he touched it, and departed. But he would not come near it, and so I informed her in the morning, to her great disappointment. I saw she was sorry for his persevering sulkiness and indolence – her conscience reproved her for frightening him off improving himself – she had done it effectually.

But her ingenuity was at work to remedy the injury; while I ironed, or pursued other stationary employments I could not well do in the parlour – she would bring some pleasant volume, and read it aloud to me. When Hareton was there, she generally paused in an interesting part, and left the book lying about – that she did repeatedly; but he was as obstinate as a mule, and, instead of snatching at her bait, in wet weather he took to smoking with Joseph, and they sat like automatons, one on each side of the fire, the elder happily too deaf to understand her wicked nonsense, as he would have called it, the younger doing his best to seem to disregard it. On fine evenings the latter followed his shooting expeditions, and Catherine yawned and sighed, and teased me to talk to her, and ran off into the court or garden, the moment I began; and, as a last resource, cried, and said, she was tired of living, her life was useless.

Mr Heathcliff, who grew more and more disinclined to society, had almost banished Earnshaw out of his apartment. Owing to an accident, at the commencement of March, he became for some days a fixture in the kitchen. His gun burst, while out on the hills, by himself; a splinter cut his arm, and he lost a good deal of blood before he could reach home. The consequence was, that, perforce, he was condemned to the fire-side and tranquillity, till he made it up again.

It suited Catherine to have him there: at any rate, it made her hate her room upstairs more than ever; and she would compel me to find out business below, that she might accompany me.

On Easter Monday, Joseph went to Gimmerton fair with some cattle; and, in the afternoon, I was busy getting up linen in the kitchen, Earnshaw sat, morose as usual, at the chimney corner, and my little mistress was beguiling an idle hour with drawing pictures on the window panes, varying her amusement by smothered bursts of songs, and whispered ejaculations, and quick glances of annoyance and impatience in the direction of her cousin, who steadfastly smoked, and looked into the grate.

At a notice that I could do with her no longer intercepting my light, she

# Wuthering Heights

removed to the hearthstone. I bestowed little attention on her proceedings, but, presently, I heard her begin –

'I've found out, Hareton, that I want – that I'm glad – that I should like you to be my cousin, now, if you had not grown so cross to me, and so rough.'

Hareton returned no answer.

'Hareton, Hareton, Hareton! do you hear?' she continued.

'Get off wi' ye!' he growled, with uncompromising gruffness.

'Let me take that pipe,' she said, cautiously advancing her hand, and abstracting it from his mouth.

Before he could attempt to recover it, it was broken, and behind the fire. He swore at her and seized another.

'Stop,' she cried, 'you must listen to me, first; and I can't speak while those clouds are floating in my face.'

'Will you go to the devil!' he exclaimed, ferociously, 'and let me be!'

'No,' she persisted, 'I won't – I can't tell what to do to make you talk to me, and you are determined not to understand. When I call you stupid, I don't mean anything – I don't mean that I despise you. Come, you shall take notice of me, Hareton – you are my cousin, and you shall own me.'

'I shall have naught to do wi' you, and your mucky pride, and your damned, mocking tricks!' he answered. 'I'll go to hell, body and soul, before I look sideways after you again! Side out of t' gait, now; this minute!'

Catherine frowned, and retreated to the window-seat, chewing her lip, and endeavouring, by humming an eccentric tune, to conceal a growing tendency to sob.

'You should be friends with your cousin, Mr Hareton,' I interrupted, 'since she repents of her sauciness! it would do you a great deal of good – it would make you another man, to have her for a companion.'

'A companion?' he cried; 'when she hates me, and does not think me fit to wipe her shoon! Nay, if it made me a king, I'd not be scorned for seeking her good will any more.'

'It is not I who hate you, it is you who hate me!' wept Cathy, no longer disguising her trouble. 'You hate me as much as Mr Heathcliff does, and more.'

'You're a damned liar,' began Earnshaw; 'why have I made him angry, by taking your part then, a hundred times? and that, when you sneered at, and despised me, and – Go on plaguing me, and I'll step in yonder, and say you worried me out of the kitchen!'

'I didn't know you took my part,' she answered, drying her eyes; 'and I was miserable and bitter at everybody; but now I thank you, and beg you to forgive me, what can I do besides?'

She returned to the hearth, and frankly extended her hand.

He blackened, and scowled like a thunder-cloud, and kept his fists resolutely clenched, and his gaze fixed on the ground.

Catherine, by instinct, must have divined it was obdurate perversity, and not dislike, that prompted this dogged conduct; for, after remaining an instant, undecided, she stooped, and impressed on his cheek a gentle kiss.

The little rogue thought I had not seen her, and, drawing back, she took her former station by the window, quite demurely.

I shook my head reprovingly; and then she blushed and whispered –

'Well, what should I have done, Ellen? He wouldn't shake hands, and he

wouldn't look – I must show him someway that I like him, that I want to be friends.'

Whether the kiss convinced Hareton, I cannot tell; he was very careful, for some minutes, that his face should not be seen; and when he did raise it, he was sadly puzzled where to turn his eyes.

Catherine employed herself in wrapping a handsome book neatly in white paper; and having tied it with a bit of ribband, and addressed it to 'Mr Hareton Earnshaw,' she desired me to be her ambassadress, and convey the present to its destined recipient.

'And tell him, if he'll take it, I'll come and teach him to read it right,' she said, 'and, if he refuse it, I'll go upstairs, and never tease him again.'

I carried it, and repeated the message, anxiously watched by my employer. Hareton would not open his fingers, so I laid it on his knee. He did not strike it off either. I returned to my work: Catherine leaned her head and arms on the table, till she heard the slight rustle of the covering being removed; then she stole away, and quietly seated herself beside her cousin. He trembled, and his face glowed – all his rudeness, and all his surly harshness had deserted him – he could not summon courage, at first, to utter a syllable, in reply to her questioning look, and her murmured petition.

'Say you forgive me, Hareton, do! You can make me so happy, by speaking that little word.'

He muttered something inaudible.

'And you'll be my friend?' added Catherine interrogatively.

'Nay! you'll be ashamed of me every day of your life,' he answered. 'And the more, the more you know me, and I cannot bide it.'

'So, you won't be my friend?' she said, smiling as sweet as honey, and creeping close up.

I overheard no further distinguishable talk; but on looking round again, I perceived two such radiant countenances bent over the page of the accepted book, that I did not doubt the treaty had been ratified, on both sides, and the enemies were, thenceforth, sworn allies.

The work they studied was full of costly pictures; and those, and their position, had charm enough to keep them unmoved, till Joseph came home. He, poor man, was perfectly aghast at the spectacle of Catherine seated on the same bench with Hareton Earnshaw, leaning her hand on his shoulder; and confounded at his favourite's endurance of her proximity. It affected him too deeply to allow an observation on the subject that night. His emotion was only revealed by the immense sighs he drew, as he solemnly spread his large Bible on the table, and overlaid it with dirty bank-notes from his pocket-book, the produce of the day's transactions. At length, he summoned Hareton from his seat.

'Tak' these un tuh t' maister, lad,' he said, 'un' bide theare; Aw's gang up tuh my awn rahm. This hoile's norther mensful, nor seemly fur us – we mun side aht, and seearch another!'

'Come, Catherine,' I said, 'we must "side out," too – I've done my ironing, are you ready to go?'

'It is not eight o'clock!' she answered, rising unwillingly. 'Hareton, I'll leave this book upon the chimney-piece, and I'll bring some more to-morrow.'

'Ony books ut yah leave, Aw suall tak' intuh th' hahse,' said Joseph, 'un' it 'ull be mitch if ya find 'em agean; soa, yah muh plase youseln!'

# Wuthering Heights

Cathy threatened that his library should pay for hers; and, smiling as she passed Hareton, went singing upstairs, lighter of heart, I venture to say, than ever she had been under that roof before; except, perhaps, during her earliest visits to Linton.

The intimacy thus commenced, grew rapidly; though it encountered temporary interruptions. Earnshaw was not to be civilized with a wish; and my young lady was no philosopher, and no paragon of patience; but both their minds tending to the same point – one loving and desiring to esteem; and the other loving and desiring to be esteemed – they contrived in the end, to reach it.

You see, Mr Lockwood, it was easy enough to win Mrs Heathcliff's heart; but now, I'm glad you did not try – the crown of all my wishes will be the union of those two; I shall envy no one on their wedding day – there won't be a happier woman than myself in England!

# Chapter 33

On the morrow of that Monday, Earnshaw being still unable to follow his ordinary employments, and, therefore, remaining about the house, I speedily found it would be impracticable to retain my charge beside me, as heretofore.

She got downstairs before me, and out into the garden, where she had seen her cousin performing some easy work; and when I went to bid them come to breakfast, I saw she had persuaded him to clear a large space of ground from currant and gooseberry bushes, and they were busy planning together an importation of plants from the Grange.

I was terrified at the devastation which had been accomplished in a brief half hour; the black currant trees were the apple of Joseph's eye, and she had just fixed her choice of a flower bed in the midst of them!

'There! That will be all shewn to the master,' I exclaimed, 'the minute it is discovered. And what excuse have you to offer for taking such liberties with the garden? We shall have a fine explosion on the head of it: see if we don't! Mr Hareton, I wonder you should have no more wit, than to go and make the mess at her bidding!'

'I'd forgotten they were Joseph's,' answered Earnshaw, rather puzzled, 'but I'll tell him I did it.'

We always ate our meals with Mr Heathcliff. I held the mistress's post in making tea and carving; so I was indispensable at table. Catherine usually sat by me; but to-day, she stole nearer to Hareton, and I presently saw she would have no more discretion in her friendship, than she had in her hostility.

'Now, mind you don't talk with and notice your cousin too much,' were my

whispered instructions, as we entered the room. 'It will certainly annoy Mr Heathcliff, and he'll be mad at you both.'

'I'm not going to,' she answered.

The minute after, she had sidled to him, and was sticking primroses in his plate of porridge.

He dared not speak to her, there; he dared hardly look; and yet she went on teasing, till he was twice on the point of being provoked to laugh; and I frowned, and then she glanced towards the master, whose mind was occupied on other subjects than his company, as his countenance evinced, and she grew serious for an instant, scrutinizing him with deep gravity. Afterwards she turned, and re-commenced her nonsense; at last, Hareton uttered a smothered laugh.

Mr Heathcliff started; his eyes rapidly surveyed our faces. Catherine met it with her accustomed look of nervousness, and yet defiance, which he abhorred.

'It is well you are out of my reach,' he exclaimed. 'What fiend possesses you to stare back at me, continually, with those infernal eyes? Down with them! and don't remind me of your existence again. I thought I had cured you of laughing!'

'It was me,' muttered Hareton.

'What do you say?' demanded the master.

Hareton looked at his plate, and did not repeat the confession.

Mr Heathcliff looked at him a bit, and then silently resumed his breakfast, and his interrupted musing.

We had nearly finished, and the two young people prudently shifted wider asunder, so I anticipated no further disturbance during that sitting; when Joseph appeared at the door, revealing by his quivering lip, and furious eyes, that the outrage committed on his precious shrubs was detected.

He must have seen Cathy and her cousin about the spot, before he examined it, for while his jaws worked like those of a cow chewing its cud, and rendered his speech difficult to understand, he began:

'Aw mun hev my wage, and Aw mun goa! Aw *hed* aimed tuh dee, wheare Aw'd sarved fur sixty years; un' Aw thowt Aw'd lug my books up intuh t' garret, 'un all my bits uh stuff, un' they sud hev t' kitchen tuh theirseln; fur t' sake uh quietness. It wur hard tuh gie up my awn heathstun, bud Aw thowt Aw *could* do that! Bud, nah, shoo's taan my garden frough me, un' by th' heart! Maister, Aw cannot stand it! Yah muh bend tuh th' yoak, an ye will – Aw' noan used to 't and an ow'd man doesn't sooin get used tuh new barthens – Aw'd rayther arn my bite, an' my sup, wi' a hammer in th' road!'

'Now, now, idiot!' interrupted Heathcliff, 'cut it short! What's your grievance? I'll interfere in no quarrels between you and Nelly – She may thrust you into the coal-hole for anything I care.'

'It's noan Nelly!' answered Joseph. 'Aw sudn't shift fur Nelly – Nasty, ill nowt as shoo is, Thank God! *shoo* cannot stale t' sowl uh nob'dy! Shoo wer niver soa handsome, bud whet a body mud look at her 'baht winking. It's yon flaysome, graceless quean, ut's witched ahr lad, wi' her bold een, un' her forrard ways – till – Nay! it fair brusts my heart! He's forgotten all E done for him, un made on him, un' goan un' riven up a whole row ut t' grandest currant trees, i' t' garden!' And here he lamented outright, unmanned by a sense of his bitter injuries, and Earnshaw's ingratitude and dangerous condition.

'Is the fool drunk?' asked Mr Heathcliff. 'Hareton, is it you he's finding fault with?'

'I've pulled up two or three bushes,' replied the young man, 'but I'm going to set 'em again.'

'And why have you pulled them up?' said the master.

Catherine wisely put in her tongue.

'We want to plant some flowers there,' she cried. 'I'm the only person to blame, for I wished him to do it.'

'And who the devil gave *you* leave to touch a stick about the place?' demanded her father-in-law, much surprised. 'And who ordered *you* to obey her?' he added, turning to Hareton.

The latter was speechless; his cousin replied –

'You shouldn't grudge a few yards of earth, for me to ornament, when you have taken all my land!'

'Your land, insolent slut? You never had any!' said Heathcliff.

'And my money,' she continued, returning his angry glare, and meantime, biting a piece of crust, the remnant of her breakfast.

'Silence!' he exclaimed. 'Get done, and begone!'

'And Hareton's land, and his money,' pursued the reckless thing. 'Hareton and I are friends now; and I shall tell him all about you!'

The master seemed confounded a moment; he grew pale, and rose up, eyeing her all the while, with an expression of mortal hate.

'If you strike me, Hareton will strike you!' she said; 'so you may as well sit down.'

'If Hareton does not turn you out of the room, I'll strike him to Hell,' thundered Heathcliff. 'Damnable witch! dare you pretend to rouse him against me? Off with her! Do you hear? Fling her into the kitchen! I'll kill her, Ellen Dean, if you let her come into my sight again!'

Hareton tried under his breath to persuade her to go.

'Drag her away!' he cried savagely. 'Are you staying to talk?' And he approached to execute his own command.

'He'll not obey you, wicked man, any more!' said Catherine; 'and he'll soon detest you, as much as I do!'

'Wisht! wisht!' muttered the young man reproachfully. 'I will not hear you speak so to him – Have done.'

'But you won't let him strike me?' she cried.

'Come then!' he whispered earnestly.

It was too late – Heathcliff had caught hold of her.

'Now *you* go!' he said to Earnshaw. 'Accursed witch! this time she has provoked me, when I could not bear it; and I'll make her repent it for ever!'

He had his hand in her hair; Hareton attempted to release the locks, entreating him not to hurt her that once. His black eyes flashed, he seemed ready to tear Catherine in pieces, and I was just worked up to risk coming to the rescue, when of a sudden, his fingers relaxed, he shifted his grasp from her head, to her arm, and gazed intently in her face – Then, he drew his hand over his eyes, stood a moment to collect himself apparently, and turning anew to Catherine, said with assumed calmness,

'You must learn to avoid putting me in a passion, or I shall really murder you, some time! Go with Mrs Dean, and keep with her, and confine your insolence to her ears. As to Hareton Earnshaw, if I see him listen to you, I'll

send him seeking his bread where he can get it! Your love will make him an
outcast, and a beggar – Nelly, take her, and leave me, all of you! Leave me!'

I led my young lady out; she was too glad of her escape, to resist; the other
followed, and Mr Heathcliff had the room to himself, till dinner.

I had counselled Catherine to get hers upstairs; but, as soon as he perceived
her vacant seat, he sent me to call her. He spoke to none of us, eat very little,
and went out directly afterwards, intimating that he should not return before
evening.

The two friends established themselves in the house, during his absence,
where I heard Hareton sternly check his cousin, on her offering a revelation of
her father-in-law's conduct to his father.

He said he wouldn't suffer a word to be uttered to him, in his disparagement;
if he were the devil, it didn't signify; he would stand by him; and he'd rather
she would abuse himself, as she used to, than begin on Mr Heathcliff.

Catherine was waxing cross at this; but he found means to make her hold her
tongue, by asking, how she would like *him* to speak ill of her father? and then
she comprehended that Earnshaw took the master's reputation home to himself:
and was attached by ties stronger than reason could break – chains, forged by
habit, which it would be cruel to attempt to loosen.

She showed a good heart, thenceforth, in avoiding both complaints and
expressions of antipathy concerning Heathcliff; and confessed to me her sorrow
that she had endeavoured to raise a bad spirit between him and Hareton –
indeed, I don't believe she has ever breathed a syllable, in the latter's hearing,
against her oppressor, since.

When this slight disagreement was over, they were thick again, and as busy
as possible, in their several occupations, of pupil and teacher. I came in to sit
with them, after I had done my work, and I felt so soothed and comforted to
watch them, that I did not notice how time got on. You know, they both
appeared, in a measure, my children: I had long been proud of one; and now,
I was sure, the other would be a source of equal satisfaction. His honest, warm,
and intelligent nature shook off rapidly the clouds of ignorance and degradation
in which it had been bred; and Catherine's sincere commendations acted as a
spur to his industry. His brightening mind brightened his features, and added
spirit and nobility to their aspect – I could hardly fancy it the same individual
I had beheld on the day I discovered my little lady at Wuthering Heights, after
her expedition to the Crags.

While I admired, and they laboured, dusk grew on, and with it returned the
master. He came upon us quite unexpectedly, entering by the front way, and
had a full view of the whole three, ere we could raise our heads to glance at him.

Well, I reflected, there was never a pleasanter, or more harmless sight; and
it will be a burning shame to scold them. The red fire-light glowed on their two
bonny heads, and revealed their faces, animated with the eager interest of
children; for, though he was twenty-three, and she eighteen, each had so much
of novelty to feel, and learn, that neither experienced nor evinced the sentiments
of sober disenchanted maturity.

They lifted their eyes together, to encounter Mr Heathcliff – perhaps, you
have never remarked that their eyes are precisely similar, and they are those of
Catherine Earnshaw. The present Catherine has no other likeness to her, except
a breadth of forehead, and a certain arch of the nostril that makes her appear

rather haughty, whether she will, or not. With Hareton the resemblance is carried farther; it is singular, at all times – then it was particularly striking: because his senses were alert, and his mental faculties wakened to unwonted activity.

I suppose this resemblance disarmed Mr Heathcliff: he walked to the hearth in evident agitation, but it quickly subsided, as he looked at the young man; or, I should say, altered its character; for it was there yet.

He took the book from his hand, and glanced at the open page, then returned it without any observation; merely signing Catherine away – her companion lingered very little behind her, and I was about to depart also, but he bid me sit still.

'It is a poor conclusion, is it not,' he observed, having brooded a while on the scene he had just witnessed. 'An absurd termination to my violent exertions? I get levers and mattocks to demolish the two houses, and train myself to be capable of working like Hercules, and when everything is ready, and in my power, I find the will to lift a slate off either roof has vanished! My old enemies have not beaten me – now would be the precise time to revenge myself on their representatives – I could do it; and none could hinder me – But where is the use? I don't care for striking, I can't take the trouble to raise my hand! That sounds as if I had been labouring the whole time, only to exhibit a fine trait of magnanimity. It is far from being the case – I have lost the faculty of enjoying their destruction, and I am too idle to destroy for nothing.

'Nelly, there is a strange change approaching – I'm in its shadow at present – I take so little interest in my daily life, that I hardly remember to eat, and drink – Those two who have left the room are the only objects which retain a distinct material appearance to me; and, that appearance causes me pain, amounting to agony. About *her* I won't speak; and I don't desire to think; but I earnestly wish she were invisible – her presence invokes only maddening sensations. *He* moves me differently; and yet if I could do it without seeming insane, I'd never see him again! You'll perhaps think me rather inclined to become so,' he added, making an effort to smile, 'if I try to describe the thousand forms of past associations, and ideas he awakens, or embodies – But you'll not talk of what I tell you, and my mind is so eternally secluded in itself, it is tempting, at last, to turn it out to another.

'Five minutes ago, Hareton seemed a personification of my youth, not a human being – I felt to him in such a variety of ways, that it would have been impossible to have accosted him rationally.

'In the first place, his startling likeness to Catherine connected him fearfully with her – That however which you may suppose the most potent to arrest my imagination, is actually the least – for what is not connected with her to me? and what does not recall her? I cannot look down to this floor, but her features are shaped on the flags! In every cloud, in every tree – filling the air at night, and caught by glimpses in every object, by day I am surrounded with her image! The most ordinary faces of men, and women – my own features mock me with a resemblance. The entire world is a dreadful collection of memoranda that she did exist, and that I have lost her!

'Well, Hareton's aspect was the ghost of my immortal love, of my wild endeavours to hold my right, my degradation, my pride, my happiness, and my anguish –

'But it is frenzy to repeat these thoughts to you; only it will let you know, why, with a reluctance to be always alone, his society is no benefit, rather an aggravation of the constant torment I suffer – and it partly contributes to render me regardless how he and his cousin go on together. I can give them no attention, any more.'

'But what do you mean by a *change*, Mr Heathcliff?' I said, alarmed at his manner, though he was neither in danger of losing his senses, nor dying, according to my judgment he was quite strong and healthy; and, as to his reason, from childhood, he had a delight in dwelling on dark things, and entertaining odd fancies – he might have had a monomania on the subject of his departed idol; but on every other point his wits were as sound as mine.

'I shall not know that, till it comes,' he said, 'I'm only half conscious of it now.'

'You have no feelings of illness, have you?' I asked.

'No, Nelly, I have not,' he answered.

'Then, you are not afraid of death?' I pursued.

'Afraid? No!' he replied. 'I have neither a fear, nor a presentiment, nor a hope of death – Why should I? With my hard constitution, and temperate mode of living, and unperilous occupations, I ought to, and probably *shall* remain above ground, till there is scarcely a black hair on my head – And yet I cannot continue in this condition! – I have to remind myself to breathe – almost to remind my heart to beat! And it is like bending back a stiff spring . . . it is by compulsion, that I do the slightest act, not promoted by one thought, and by compulsion, that I notice anything alive or dead, which is not associated with one universal idea . . . I have a single wish, and my whole being and faculties are yearning to attain it. They have yearned towards it so long, and so unwaveringly, that I'm convinced it *will* be reached – and *soon* – because it has devoured my existence – I am swallowed in the anticipation of its fulfilment.

'My confessions have not relieved me – but, they may account for some otherwise unaccountable phases of humour which I show. O God! It is a long fight, I wish it were over!'

He began to pace the room, muttering terrible things to himself; till I was inclined to believe, as he said Joseph did, that conscience had turned his heart to an earthly hell – I wondered greatly how it would end.

Though he seldom before had revealed this state of mind, even by looks, it was his habitual mood, I had no doubt: he asserted it himself – but not a soul, from his general bearing, would have conjectured the fact. You did not, when you saw him Mr Lockwood – and at the period of which I speak, he was just the same as then, only fonder of continued solitude, and perhaps still more laconic in company.

# Chapter 34

For some days after that evening, Mr Heathcliff shunned meeting us at meals; yet he would not consent, formally, to exclude Hareton and Cathy. He had an aversion to yielding so completely to his feelings, choosing, rather, to absent himself – and eating once in twenty-four hours seemed sufficient sustenance for him.

One night, after the family were in bed, I heard him go downstairs, and out at the front door: I did not hear him re-enter, and, in the morning, I found he was still away.

We were in April then, the weather was sweet and warm, the grass as green as showers and sun could make it, and the two dwarf apple trees, near the southern wall, in full bloom.

After breakfast, Catherine insisted on my bringing a chair, and sitting, with my work, under the fir trees, at the end of the house; and she beguiled Hareton, who had perfectly recovered from his accident, to dig and arrange her little garden, which was shifted to that corner by the influence of Joseph's complaints.

I was comfortably revelling in the spring fragrance around, and the beautiful soft blue overhead, when my young lady, who had run down near the gate to procure some primrose roots for a border, returned only half laden, and informed us that Mr Heathcliff was coming in.

'And he spoke to me,' she added, with a perplexed countenance.

'What did he say?' asked Hareton.

'He told me to begone as fast as I could,' she answered. 'But he looked so different from his usual look that I stopped a moment to stare at him.'

'How?' he inquired.

'Why, almost bright and cheerful – No, almost nothing – *very much* excited, and wild and glad!' she replied.

'Night-walking amuses him, then,' I remarked, affecting a careless manner. In reality, as surprised as she was; and, anxious to ascertain the truth of her statement, for to see the master looking glad would not be an everyday spectacle, I framed an excuse to go in.

Heathcliff stood at the open door; he was pale, and he trembled; yet, certainly, he had a strange joyful glitter in his eyes, that altered the aspect of his whole face.

'Will you have some breakfast?' I said. 'You must be hungry, rambling about all night!'

I wanted to discover where he had been; but I did not like to ask directly.

'No, I'm not hungry,' he answered, averting his head, and speaking rather

contemptuously, as if he guessed I was trying to divine the occasion of his good humour.

I felt perplexed – I didn't know whether it were not a proper opportunity to offer a bit of admonition.

'I don't think it right to wander out of doors,' I observed, 'instead of being in bed; it is not wise, at any rate, this moist season. I dare say you'll catch a bad cold, or fever – you have something the matter with you now!'

'Nothing but what I can bear,' he replied, 'and with the greatest pleasure, provided you'll leave me alone – get in, and don't annoy me.'

I obeyed; and, in passing, I noticed he breathed as fast as a cat.

'Yes!' I reflected to myself, 'we shall have a fit of illness. I cannot conceive what he has been doing!'

That noon, he sat down to dinner with us, and received a heaped-up plate from my hands, as if he intended to make amends for previous fasting.

'I've neither cold nor fever, Nelly,' he remarked, in allusion to my morning's speech. 'And I'm ready to do justice to the food you give me.'

He took his knife and fork, and was going to commence eating, when the inclination appeared to become suddenly extinct. He laid them on the table, looked eagerly towards the window, then rose and went out.

We saw him walking, to and fro, in the garden, while we concluded our meal; and Earnshaw said he'd go and ask why he would not dine; he thought we had grieved him some way.

'Well, is he coming?' cried Catherine, when her cousin returned.

'Nay,' he answered; 'but he's not angry; he seemed rare and pleased indeed; only I made him impatient by speaking to him twice; and then he bid me be off to you; he wondered how I could want the company of any body else.'

I set his plate, to keep warm, on the fender: and after an hour or two, he re-entered, when the room was clear, in no degree calmer – the same unnatural – it was unnatural – appearance of joy under his black brows; the same bloodless hue; and his teeth visible, now and then, in a kind of smile; his frame shivering, not as one shivers with chill or weakness, but as a tight-stretched cord vibrates – a strong thrilling, rather than trembling.

I will ask what is the matter, I thought, or who should? And I exclaimed –

'Have you heard any good news, Mr Heathcliff? You look uncommonly animated.'

'Where should good news come from, to me?' he said. 'I'm animated with hunger; and, seemingly, I must not eat.'

'Your dinner is here,' I returned; 'why won't you get it?'

'I don't want it now,' he muttered, hastily. 'I'll wait till supper. And, Nelly, once for all, let me beg you to warn Hareton and the other away from me. I wish to be troubled by nobody – I wish to have this place to myself.'

'Is there some new reason for this banishment?' I inquired. 'Tell me why you are so queer, Mr Heathcliff? Where were you last night? I'm not putting the question through idle curiosity, but –'

'You are putting the question through very idle curiosity,' he interrupted, with a laugh. 'Yet, I'll answer it. Last night, I was on the threshold of hell. To-day, I am within sight of my heaven – I have my eyes on it – hardly three feet to sever me! And now you'd better go – You'll neither see nor hear anything to frighten you, if you refrain from prying.'

# Wuthering Heights

Having swept the hearth, and wiped the table, I departed more perplexed than ever.

He did not quit the house again that afternoon, and no one intruded on his solitude, till, at eight o'clock, I deemed it proper, though unsummoned, to carry a candle, and his supper, to him.

He was leaning against the ledge of an open lattice, but not looking out; his face was turned to the interior gloom. The fire had smouldered to ashes; the room was filled with the damp, mild air of the cloudy evening, and so still, that not only the murmur of the beck down Gimmerton was distinguishable, but its ripples and its gurgling over the pebbles, or through the large stones which it could not cover.

I uttered an ejaculation of discontent at seeing the dismal grate, and commenced shutting the casements, one after another, till I came to his.

'Must I close this?' I asked, in order to rouse him, for he would not stir.

The light flashed on his features, as I spoke. Oh, Mr Lockwood, I cannot express what a terrible start I got, by the momentary view! Those deep black eyes! That smile, and ghastly paleness! It appeared to me, not Mr Heathcliff, but a goblin; and, in my terror, I let the candle bend towards the wall, and it left me in darkness.

'Yes, close it,' he replied, in his familiar voice. 'There, that is pure awkwardness! Why did you hold the candle horizontally? Be quick, and bring another.'

I hurried out in a foolish state of dread, and said to Joseph –

'The master wishes you to take him a light, and re-kindle the fire.' For I dared not go in myself again just then.

Joseph rattled some fire into the shovel, and went; but he brought it back, immediately, with the supper-tray in his other hand, explaining that Mr Heathcliff was going to bed, and he wanted nothing to eat till morning.

We heard him mount the stairs directly; he did not proceed to his ordinary chamber, but turned into that with the panelled bed – its window, as I mentioned before, is wide enough for anybody to get through, and it struck me, that he plotted another midnight excursion, which he had rather we had no suspicion of.

'Is he a ghoul or a vampire?' I mused. I had read of such hideous, incarnate demons. And then, I set myself to reflect, how I had tended him in infancy; and watched him grow to youth; and followed him almost through his whole course; and what absurd nonsense it was to yield to that sense of horror.

'But, where did he come from, the little dark thing, harboured by a good man to his bane?' muttered superstition, as I dozed into unconsciousness. And I began, half dreaming, to weary myself with imaging some fit parentage for him; and repeating my waking meditations, I tracked his existence over again, with grim variations; at last, picturing his death and funeral; of which, all I can remember is, being exceedingly vexed at having the task of dictating an inscription for his monument, and consulting the sexton about it; and, as he had no surname, and we could not tell his age, we were obliged to content ourselves with the single word, 'Heathcliff.' That came true; we were. If you enter the kirkyard, you'll read on his headstone, only that, and the date of his death.

Dawn restored me to common sense. I rose, and went into the garden, as soon

215

as I could see, to ascertain if there were any footmarks under his window. There were none.

'He stayed at home,' I thought, 'and he'll be all right, to-day!'

I prepared breakfast for the household, as was my usual custom, but told Hareton and Catherine to get theirs ere the master came down, for he lay late. They preferred taking it out of doors, under the trees, and I set a little table to accommodate them.

On my re-entrance, I found Mr Heathcliff below. He and Joseph were conversing about some farming business; he gave clear, minute directions concerning the matter discussed, but he spoke rapidly, and turned his head continually aside, and had the same excited expression, even more exaggerated.

When Joseph quitted the room, he took his seat in the place he generally chose, and I put a basin of coffee before him. He drew it nearer, and then rested his arms on the table, and looked at the opposite wall, as I supposed, surveying one particular portion, up and down, with glittering, restless eyes, and with such eager interest, that he stopped breathing, during half a minute together.

'Come now,' I exclaimed, pushing some bread against his hand. 'Eat and drink that, while it is hot. It has been waiting near an hour.'

He didn't notice me, and yet he smiled. I'd rather have seen him gnash his teeth than smile so.

'Mr Heathcliff! master!' I cried. 'Don't, for God's sake, stare as if you saw an unearthly vision.'

'Don't, for God's sake, shout so loud,' he replied. 'Turn round, and tell me, are we by ourselves?'

'Of course,' was my answer, 'of course we are!'

Still, I involuntarily obeyed him, as if I were not quite sure.

With a sweep of his hand, he cleared a vacant space in front among the breakfast things, and leant forward to gaze more at his ease.

Now, I perceived he was not looking at the wall, for when I regarded him alone, it seemed, exactly, that he gazed at something within two yards distance. And, whatever it was, it communicated, apparently, both pleasure and pain, in exquisite extremes; at least, the anguished, yet raptured expression of his countenance suggested that idea.

The fancied object was not fixed, either; his eyes pursued it with unwearied vigilance; and, even in speaking to me, were never weaned away.

I vainly reminded him of his protracted abstinence from food; if he stirred to touch anything in compliance with my entreaties, if he stretched his hand out to get a piece of bread, his fingers clenched, before they reached it, and remained on the table, forgetful of their aim.

I sat a model of patience, trying to attract his absorbed attention from its engrossing speculation; till he grew irritable, and got up, asking, why I would not allow him to have his own time in taking his meals? and saying that, on the next occasion, I needn't wait, I might set the things down, and go.

Having uttered these words, he left the house, slowly sauntered down the garden path, and disappeared through the gate.

The hours crept anxiously by: another evening came. I did not retire to rest till late, and when I did, I could not sleep. He returned after midnight, and, instead of going to bed, shut himself into the room beneath. I listened, and tossed

about; and, finally, dressed, and descended. It was too irksome to lie up there, harassing my brain with a hundred idle misgivings.

I distinguished Mr Heathcliff's step, restlessly measuring the floor; and he frequently broke the silence, by a deep inspiration, resembling a groan. He muttered detached words, also; the only one, I could catch, was the name of Catherine, coupled with some wild term of endearment, or suffering; and spoken as one would speak to a person present – low and earnest, and wrung from the depth of his soul.

I had not courage to walk straight into the apartment; but I desired to divert him from his reverie, and, therefore, fell foul of the kitchen fire, stirred it, and began to scrape the cinders. It drew him forth sooner than I expected. He opened the door immediately, and said –

'Nelly come here – is it morning? Come in with your light.'

'It is striking four,' I answered; 'you want a candle to take upstairs – you might have lit one at this fire.'

'No, I don't wish to go upstairs,' he said. 'Come in, and kindle *me* a fire, and do anything there is to do about the room.'

'I must blow the coals red first, before I can carry any,' I replied, getting a chair and the bellows.

He roamed to and fro, meantime, in a state approaching distraction; his heavy sighs succeeding each other so thick as to leave no space for common breathing between.

When day breaks I'll send for Green,' he said. 'I wish to make some legal inquiries of him while I can bestow a thought on those matters, and while I can act calmly. I have not written my will yet, and how to leave my property, I cannot determine! I wish I could annihilate it from the face of the earth.'

'I would not talk so, Mr Heathcliff,' I interposed. 'Let your will be, a while – you'll be spared to repent of your many injustices, yet! I never expected that your nerves would be disordered – they are, at present, marvellously so, however; and, almost entirely, through your own fault. The way you've passed these three last days might knock up a Titan. Do take some food, and some repose. You need only look at yourself, in a glass, to see how you require both. Your cheeks are hollow, and your eyes bloodshot, like a person starving with hunger, and going blind with loss of sleep.'

'It is not my fault, that I cannot eat or rest,' he replied. 'I assure you it is through no settled designs. I'll do both, as soon as I possibly can. But you might as well bid a man struggling in the water, rest within arm's length of the shore! I must reach it first, and then I'll rest. Well, never mind Mr Green; as to repenting of my injustices, I've done no injustice, and I repent of nothing – I'm too happy, and yet I'm not happy enough. My soul's bliss kills my body, but does not satisfy itself.'

'Happy, master?' I cried. 'Strange happiness! If you would hear me without being angry, I might offer some advice that would make you happier.'

'What is that?' he asked. 'Give it.'

'You are aware, Mr Heathcliff,' I said, 'that from the time you were thirteen years old, you have lived a selfish, unchristian life; and probably hardly had a Bible in your hands, during all that period. You must have forgotten the contents of the book, and you may not have space to search it now. Could it be hurtful to send for some one – some minister of any denomination, it does not matter

# Wuthering Heights

which, to explain it, and show you how very far you have erred from its precepts, and how unfit you will be for its heaven, unless a change takes place before you die?'

'I'm rather obliged than angry, Nelly,' he said, 'for you remind me of the manner that I desire to be buried in – It is to be carried to the churchyard, in the evening. You and Hareton may, if you please, accompany me – and mind, particularly to notice that the sexton obeys my directions concerning the two coffins! No minister need come; nor need anything be said over me – I tell you I have nearly attained *my* heaven; and that of others is altogether unvalued, and uncoveted by me!'

'And supposing you persevered in your obstinate fast, and died by that means, and they refused to bury you in the precincts of the Kirk?' I said, shocked at his godless indifference. 'How would you like it?'

'They won't do that,' he replied; 'if they did, you must have me removed secretly; and if you neglect it, you shall prove, practically, that the dead are not annihilated!'

As soon as he heard the other members of the family stirring he retired to his den, and I breathed freer. But in the afternoon, while Joseph and Hareton were at their work, he came into the kitchen again, and with a wild look, bid me come, and sit in the house – he wanted somebody with him.

I declined, telling him plainly, that his strange talk and manner frightened me, and I had neither the nerve nor the will to be his companion, alone.

'I believe you think me a fiend!' he said, with his dismal laugh, 'something too horrible to live under a decent roof!'

Then turning to Catherine, who was there, and who drew behind me at his approach, he added, half sneeringly –

'Will *you* come, chuck? I'll not hurt you. No! to you, I've made myself worse than the devil. Well, there is *one* who won't shrink from my company! By God; she's relentless. Oh, damn it! It's unutterably too much for flesh and blood to bear, even mine.'

He solicited the society of no one more. At dusk, he went into his chamber – through the whole night, and far into the morning, we heard him groaning, and murmuring to himself. Hareton was anxious to enter, but I bid him fetch Mr Kenneth, and he should go in, and see him.

When he came, and I requested admittance and tried to open the door, I found it locked; and Heathcliff bid us be damned. He was better, and would be left alone; so the doctor went away.

The following evening was very wet; indeed, it poured down, till day-dawn; and, as I took my morning walk round the house, I observed the master's window swinging open, and the rain driving straight in.

'He cannot be in bed,' I thought, 'those showers would drench him through! He must either be up, or out. But I'll make no more ado, I'll go boldly, and look!'

Having succeeded in obtaining entrance with another key, I ran to unclose the panels, for the chamber was vacant – quickly pushing them aside, I peeped in. Mr Heathcliff was there – laid on his back. His eyes met mine so keen, and fierce, I started; and then he seemed to smile.

I could not think him dead – but his face and throat were washed with rain; the bed-clothes dripped, and he was perfectly still. The lattice, flapping to and

fro, had grazed one hand that rested on the sill – no blood trickled from the broken skin, and when I put my fingers to it, I could doubt no more – he was dead and stark!

I hasped the window; I combed his black long hair from his forehead; I tried to close his eyes – to extinguish, if possible, that frightful, life-like gaze of exultation, before any one else beheld it. They would not shut – they seemed to sneer at my attempts, and his parted lips, and sharp, white teeth sneered too! Taken with another fit of cowardice, I cried for Joseph. Joseph shuffled up, and made a noise, but resolutely refused to meddle with him.

'Th' divil's harried off his soul,' he cried, 'and he muh hev his carcass intuh t' bargain, for ow't Aw care! Ech! what a wicked un he looks grinning at death!' and the old sinner grinned in mockery.

I thought he intended to cut a caper round the bed; but suddenly composing himself, he fell on his knees, and raised his hands, and returned thanks that the lawful master and the ancient stock were restored to their rights.

I felt stunned by the awful event; and my memory unavoidably recurred to former times with a sort of oppressive sadness. But poor Hareton, the most wronged, was the only one that really suffered much. He sat by the corpse all night, weeping in bitter earnest. He pressed his hand, and kissed the sarcastic, savage face that every one else shrank from contemplating; and bemoaned him with that strong grief which springs naturally from a generous heart, though it be tough as tempered steel.

Kenneth was perplexed to pronounce of what disorder the master died. I concealed the fact of his having swallowed nothing for four days, fearing it might lead to trouble, and then, I am persuaded he did not abstain on purpose; it was the consequence of his strange illness, not the cause.

We buried him, to the scandal of the whole neighbourhood, as he had wished. Earnshaw, and I, the sexton and six men to carry the coffin, comprehended the whole attendance.

The six men departed when they had let it down into the grave: we stayed to see it covered. Hareton, with a streaming face, dug green sods, and laid them over the brown mould himself, at present it is as smooth and verdant as its companion mounds – and I hope its tenant sleeps as soundly. But the country folks, if you asked them, would swear on their Bible that he *walks*. There are those who speak of having met him near the church, and on the moor, and even within this house – Idle tales, you'll say, and so say I. Yet that old man by the kitchen fire affirms he has seen two on 'em looking out of his chamber window, on every rainy night since his death – and an odd thing happened to me about a month ago.

I was going to the Grange one evening – a dark evening threatening thunder – and, just at the turn of the Heights, I encountered a little boy with a sheep and two lambs before him, he was crying terribly, and I supposed the lambs were skittish, and would not be guided.

'What is the matter, my little man?' I asked.

'They's Heathcliff, and a woman, yonder, under t' Nab,' he blubbered, 'un' Aw darnut pass 'em.'

I saw nothing; but neither the sheep nor he would go on, so I bid him take the road lower down.

He probably raised the phantoms from thinking, as he traversed the moors

alone, on the nonsense he had heard his parents and companions repeat – yet still I don't like being out in the dark, now – and I don't like being left by myself in this grim house – I cannot help it, I shall be glad when they leave it, and shift to the Grange!

'They are going to the Grange then?' I said.

'Yes,' answered Mrs Dean, 'as soon as they are married; and that will be on New Year's day.'

'And who will live here then?'

'Why, Joseph will take care of the house, and, perhaps, a lad to keep him company. They will live in the kitchen, and the rest will be shut up.'

'For the use of such ghosts as choose to inhabit it,' I observed.

'No, Mr Lockwood,' said Nelly, shaking her head. 'I believe the dead are at peace, but it is not right to speak of them with levity.'

At that moment the garden gate swung to; the ramblers were returning.

'*They* are afraid of nothing,' I grumbled, watching their approach through the window. 'Together they would brave satan and all his legions.'

As they stepped onto the door-stones, and halted to take a last look at the moon, or, more correctly, at each other, by her light, I felt irresistibly impelled to escape them again; and, pressing a remembrance into the hand of Mrs Dean, and disregarding her expostulations at my rudeness, I vanished through the kitchen, as they opened the house-door, and so, should have confirmed Joseph in his opinion of his fellow-servant's gay indiscretions, had he not, fortunately, recognized me for a respectable character, by the sweet ring of a sovereign at his feet.

My walk home was lengthened by a diversion in the direction of the kirk. When beneath its walls, I perceived decay had made progress, even in seven months – many a window showed black gaps deprived of glass; and slates jutted off, here and there, beyond the right line of the roof, to be gradually worked off in coming autumn storms.

I sought, and soon discovered, the three head-stones on the slope next the moor – the middle one, grey, and half buried in heath – Edgar Linton's only harmonized by the turf and moss, creeping up its foot – Heathcliff's still bare.

I lingered round them, under that benign sky; watched the moths fluttering among the heath and hare-bells; listened to the soft wind breathing through the grass; and wondered how anyone could ever imagine unquiet slumbers, for the sleepers in that quiet earth.

ANNE
BRONTË

# The Tenant of Wildfell Hall

# Chapter 1

You must go back with me to the autumn of 1827. My father, as you know, was a sort of gentleman farmer in —shire; and I, by his express desire, succeeded him in the same quiet occupation, not very willingly, for ambition urged me to higher aims, and self-conceit assured me that, in disregarding its voice, I was burying my talent in the earth, and hiding my light under a bushel. My mother had done her utmost to persuade me that I was capable of great achievements; but my father, who thought ambition was the surest road to ruin, and change but another word for destruction, would listen to no scheme for bettering either my own condition, or that of my fellow mortals. He assured me it was all rubbish, and exhorted me, with his dying breath, to continue in the good old way, to follow his steps, and those of his father before him, and let my highest ambition be, to walk honestly through the world, looking neither to the right hand nor to the left, and to transmit the paternal acres to my children in, at least, as flourishing a condition as he left them to me.

'Well! – an honest and industrious farmer is one of the most useful members of society; and if I devote my talents to the cultivation of my farm, and the improvement of agriculture in general, I shall thereby benefit, not only my own immediate connections and dependents, but, in some degree, mankind at large: – hence I shall not have lived in vain.'

With such reflections as these, I was endeavouring to console myself, as I plodded home from the fields, one cold, damp, cloudy evening towards the close of October. But the gleam of a bright red fire through the parlour window had more effect in cheering my spirits, and rebuking my thankless repinings, than all the sage reflections and good resolutions I had forced my mind to frame; for I was young then, remember – only four and twenty – and had not acquired half the rule over my own spirit, that I now possess – trifling as that may be.

However, that haven of bliss must not be entered till I had exchanged my miry boots for a clean pair of shoes, and my rough surtout for a respectable coat, and made myself generally presentable before decent society; for my mother, with all her kindness, was vastly particular on certain points.

In ascending to my room, I was met upon the stairs by a smart, pretty girl of nineteen, with a tidy, dumpy figure, a round face, bright, blooming cheeks, glossy, clustering curls, and little merry brown eyes. I need not tell you this was my sister Rose. She is, I know, a comely matron still, and, doubtless, no less lovely – in your eyes – than on the happy day you first beheld her. Nothing told me then, that she, a few years hence, would be the wife of one entirely unknown to me as yet, but destined, hereafter, to become a closer friend than even herself, more intimate than that unmannerly lad of seventeen, by whom I was collared

in the passage, on coming down, and well-nigh jerked off my equilibrium, and who, in correction for his impudence, received a resounding whack over the sconce, which, however, sustained no serious injury from the infliction; as, besides being more than commonly thick, it was protected by a redundant shock of short, reddish curls, that my mother called auburn.

On entering the parlour, we found that honoured lady seated in her arm-chair at the fireside, working away at her knitting, according to her usual custom, when she had nothing else to do. She had swept the hearth, and made a bright blazing fire for our reception; the servant had just brought in the tea-tray; and Rose was producing the sugar-basin and tea-caddy, from the cupboard in the black, oak sideboard, that shone like polished ebony, in the cheerful parlour twilight.

'Well! here they both are,' cried my mother, looking round upon us without retarding the motion of her nimble fingers, and glittering needles. 'Now shut the door, and come to the fire, while Rose gets the tea ready; I'm sure you must be starved; – and tell me what you've been about all day; – I like to know what my children have been about.'

'I've been breaking in the grey colt – no easy business that – directing the ploughing of the last wheat stubble – for the ploughboy has not the sense to direct himself – and carrying out a plan for the extensive and efficient draining of the low meadowlands.'

'That's my brave boy! – and Fergus – what have you been doing?'

'Badger-baiting.'

And here he proceeded to give a particular account of his sport, and the respective traits of prowess evinced by the badger and the dogs; my mother, pretending to listen with deep attention, and watching his animated countenance with a degree of maternal admiration I thought highly disproportioned to its object.

'It's time you should be doing something else, Fergus,' said I, as soon as a momentary pause in his narration allowed me to get in a word.

'What can I do?' replied he; 'my mother won't let me go to sea or enter the army; and I'm determined to do nothing else – except make myself such a nuisance to you all, that you will be thankful to get rid of me on any terms.'

Our parent soothingly stroked his stiff, short curls. He growled, and tried to look sulky, and then we all took our seats at the table, in obedience to the thrice-repeated summons of Rose.

'Now take your tea,' said she; 'and I'll tell you what I've been doing. I've been to call on the Wilsons; and it's a thousand pities you didn't go with me, Gilbert, for Eliza Millward was there!'

'Well! what of her?'

'Oh, nothing! – I'm not going to tell you about her; – only that she's a nice, amusing little thing, when she is in a merry humour, and I shouldn't mind calling her' –

'Hush, hush, my dear! your brother has no such idea!' whispered my mother earnestly, holding up her finger.

'Well,' resumed Rose; 'I was going to tell you an important piece of news I heard there – I've been bursting with it ever since. You know it was reported a month ago, that somebody was going to take Wildfell Hall – and – what do you think? It has actually been inhabited above a week! – and we never knew!'

# The Tenant of Wildfell Hall

'Impossible!' cried my mother.

'Preposterous!!!' shrieked Fergus.

'It has indeed! – and by a single lady!'

'Good gracious, my dear! The place is in ruins!'

'She has had two or three rooms made habitable; and there she lives, all alone – except an old woman for a servant!'

'Oh dear! – that spoils it – I'd hoped she was a witch,' observed Fergus, while carving his inch-thick slice of bread and butter.

'Nonsense, Fergus! But isn't it strange, mamma?'

'Strange! I can hardly believe it.'

'But you may believe it; for Jane Wilson has seen her. She went with her mother, who, of course, when she heard of a stranger being in the neighbourhood, would be on pins and needles till she had seen her and got all she could out of her. She is called Mrs Graham, and she is in mourning – not widow's weeds, but slightish mourning – and she is quite young, they say, – not above five or six and twenty, – but so reserved! They tried all they could to find out who she was, and where she came from, and all about her, but neither Mrs Wilson, with her pertinacious and impertinent home-thrusts, nor Miss Wilson, with her skilful manoeuvring, could manage to elicit a single satisfactory answer, or even a casual remark, or chance expression calculated to allay their curiosity, or throw the faintest ray of light upon her history, circumstances, or connections. Moreover, she was barely civil to them, and evidently better pleased to say "good-bye", than "how do you do". But Eliza Millward says her father intends to call upon her soon, to offer some pastoral advice, which he fears she needs, as, though she is known to have entered the neighbourhood early last week, she did not make her appearance at church on Sunday; and she – Eliza, that is – will beg to accompany him, and is sure she can succeed in wheedling something out of her – you know Gilbert, she can do anything. And we should call some time, mamma; it's only proper, you know.'

'Of course, my dear. Poor thing! how lonely she must feel!'

'And pray, be quick about it; and mind you bring me word how much sugar she puts in her tea, and what sort of caps and aprons she wears, and all about it; for I don't know how I can live till I know,' said Fergus, very gravely.

But if he intended the speech to be hailed as a master-stroke of wit, he signally failed, for nobody laughed. However, he was not much disconcerted at that; for when he had taken a mouthful of bread and butter, and was about to swallow a gulp of tea, the humour of the thing burst open him with such irresistible force, that he was obliged to jump up from the table, and rush snorting and choking from the room; and a minute after, was heard screaming in fearful agony in the garden.

As for me, I was hungry, and contented myself with silently demolishing the tea, ham, and toast, while my mother and sister went on talking, and continued to discuss the apparent or non-apparent circumstances, and probable or improbable history of the mysterious lady; but I must confess that, after my brother's misadventure, I once or twice raised the cup to my lips, and put it down again without daring to taste the contents, lest I should injure my dignity by a similar explosion.

The next day, my mother and Rose hastened to pay their compliments to the fair recluse; and came back but little wiser than they went; though my mother

declared she did not regret the journey, for if she had not gained much good, she flattered herself she had imparted some, and that was better: she had given some useful advice, which, she hoped, would not be thrown away; for Mrs Graham, though she said little to any purpose, and appeared somewhat self-opinionated, seemed not incapable of reflection, – though she did not know where she had been all her life, poor thing, for she betrayed a lamentable ignorance on certain points, and had not even the sense to be ashamed of it.

'On what points, mother?' asked I.

'On household matters, and all the little niceties of cookery, and such things, that every lady ought to be familiar with, whether she be required to make a practical use of her knowledge or not. I gave her some useful pieces of information, however, and several excellent receipts, the value of which she evidently could not appreciate, for she begged I would not trouble myself, as she lived in such a plain, quiet way, that she was sure she should never make use of them. "No matter, my dear," said I; "it is what every respectable female ought to know; – and besides, though you are alone now, you will not be always so; you have been married, and probably – I might say almost certainly – will be again." "You are mistaken there, ma'am," said she, almost haughtily; "I am certain I never shall." – But I told her I knew better.'

'Some romantic young widow, I suppose,' said I, 'come there to end her days in solitude, and mourn in secret for the dear departed – but it won't last long.'

'No, I think not,' observed Rose; 'for she didn't seem very disconsolate after all; and she's excessively pretty – handsome rather – you must see her, Gilbert; you will call her a perfect beauty, though you could hardly pretend to discover a resemblance between her and Eliza Millward.'

'Well, I can imagine many faces more beautiful than Eliza's, though not more charming. I allow she has small claims to perfection; but then, I maintain, that, if she were more perfect, she would be less interesting.'

'And so you prefer her faults to other people's perfections?'

'Just so – saving my mother's presence.'

'Oh, my dear Gilbert, what nonsense you talk! – I know you don't mean it; it's quite out of the question,' said my mother, getting up, and bustling out of the room, under pretence of household business, in order to escape the contradiction that was trembling on my tongue.

After that, Rose favoured me with further particulars respecting Mrs Graham. Her appearance, manners, and dress, and the very furniture of the room she inhabited, were all set before me, with rather more clearness and precision than I cared to see them; but, as I was not a very attentive listener, I could not repeat the description if I would.

The next day was Saturday; and on Sunday, everybody wondered whether or not the fair unknown would profit by the vicar's remonstrance and come to church. I confess, I looked with some interest myself towards the old family pew, appertaining to Wildfell Hall, where the faded crimson cushions and lining had been unpressed and unrenewed so many years, and the grim escutcheons, with their lugubrious borders of rusty black cloth, frowned so sternly from the wall above.

And there I beheld a tall, lady-like figure, clad in black. Her face was towards me, and there was something in it, which, once seen, invited me to look again. Her hair was raven black, and disposed in long glossy ringlets, a style of coiffure

rather unusual in those days, but always graceful and becoming; her complexion was clear and pale; her eyes I could not see, for being bent upon her prayer-book they were concealed by their drooping lids and long black lashes, but the brows above were expressive and well defined; the forehead was lofty and intellectual, the nose a perfect aquiline, and the features in general unexceptionable – only there was a slight hollowness about the cheeks and eyes, and the lips, though finely formed, were a little too thin, a little too firmly compressed, and had something about them that betokened, I thought, no very soft or amiable temper; and I said in my heart—

'I would rather admire you from this distance, fair lady, than be the partner of your home.'

Just then, she happened to raise her eyes, and they met mine; I did not choose to withdraw my gaze, and she turned again to her book, but with a momentary, indefinable expression of quiet scorn, that was inexpressibly provoking to me.

'She thinks me an impudent puppy,' thought I. 'Humph! – she shall change her mind before long, if I think it worth while.'

But then it flashed upon me that these were very improper thoughts for a place of worship, and that my behaviour, on the present occasion, was anything but what it ought to be. Previous, however, to directing my mind to the service, I glanced round the church to see if any one had been observing me; – but no, – all, who were not attending to their prayer books, were attending to the strange lady, – my good mother and sister among the rest, and Mrs Wilson and her daughter; and even Eliza Millward was slily glancing from the corners of her eyes towards the object of general attraction. Then, she glanced at me, simpered a little, and blushed, modestly looked at her prayer-book, and endeavoured to compose her features.

Here I was transgressing again; and this time I was made sensible of it by a sudden dig in the ribs, from the elbow of my pert brother. For the present, I could only resent the insult by pressing my foot upon his toes, deferring further vengeance till we got out of church.

Now, Halford, before I close this letter, I'll tell you who Eliza Millward was; she was the vicar's younger daughter, and a very engaging little creature, for whom I felt no small degree of partiality; – and she knew it, though I had never come to any direct explanation, and had no definite intention of so doing, for my mother, who maintained there was no one good enough for me within twenty miles round, could not bear the thoughts of my marrying that insignificant little thing, who, in addition to her numerous other disqualifications, had not twenty pounds to call her own. Eliza's figure was at once slight and plump, her face small, and nearly as round as my sister's, – complexion something similar to hers, but more delicate and less decidedly blooming – nose, retroussé – features, generally, irregular; – and, altogether, she was rather charming than pretty. But her eyes – I must not forget those remarkable features, for therein her chief attraction lay – in outward aspect at least; they were long and narrow in shape, the irids black, or very dark brown, the expression various, and ever changing, but always either preternaturally – I had almost said diabolically – wicked, or irresistibly bewitching – often both. Her voice was gentle and childish, her tread light and soft as that of a cat; – but her manners more frequently resembled those of a pretty playful kitten, that is now pert and roguish, now timid and demure, according to its own sweet will.

# The Tenant of Wildfell Hall

Her sister, Mary, was several years older, several inches taller, and of a larger, coarser build – a plain, quiet, sensible girl, who had patiently nursed their mother through her last long, tedious illness, and been the housekeeper, and family drudge, from thence to the present time. She was trusted and valued by her father, loved and courted by all dogs, cats, children, and poor people, and slighted and neglected by everybody else.

The Reverend Michael Millward, himself, was a tall, ponderous, elderly gentleman, who placed a shovel-hat above his large, square, massive-featured face, carried a stout walking-stick in his hand, and encased his still powerful limbs in knee-breeches and gaiters, – or black silk stockings on state occasions. He was a man of fixed principles, strong prejudices, and regular habits, intolerant of dissent in any shape, acting under a firm conviction that his opinions were always right, and whoever differed from them must be either most deplorably ignorant, or wilfully blind.

In childhood, I had always been accustomed to regard him with a feeling of reverential awe – but lately, even now, surmounted, for, though he had a fatherly kindness for the well-behaved, he was a strict disciplinarian, and had often sternly reproved our juvenile failings and peccadilloes; and moreover, in those days whenever he called upon our parents, we had to stand up before him, and say our catechism, or repeat 'How doth the little busy bee,' or some other hymn, or – worse than all – be questioned about his last test, and the heads of the discourse, which we never could remember. Sometimes, the worthy gentleman would reprove my mother for being over-indulgent to her sons, with a reference to old Eli, or David and Absalom, which was particularly galling to her feelings; and, very highly as she respected him, and all his sayings, I once heard her exclaim, 'I wish to goodness he had a son himself! He wouldn't be so ready with his advice to other people then; – he'd see what it is to have a couple of boys to keep in order.'

He had a laudable care for his own bodily health – kept very early hours, regularly took a walk before breakfast, was vastly particular about warm and dry clothing, had never been known to preach a sermon without previously swallowing a raw egg – albeit he was gifted with good lungs and a powerful voice, – and was, generally, extremely particular about what he ate and drank, though by no means abstemious, and having a mode of dietary peculiar to himself, – being a great despiser of tea and such slops, and a patron of malt liquors, bacon and eggs, ham, hung beef, and other strong meats, which agreed well enough with his digestive organs, and therefore were maintained by him to be good and wholesome for everybody, and confidently recommended to the most delicate convalescents or dyspeptics, who, if they failed to derive the promised benefit from his prescriptions, were told it was because they had not persevered, and if they complained of inconvenient results therefrom, were assured it was all fancy.

I will just touch upon two other persons whom I have mentioned, and then bring this long letter to a close. These are Mrs Wilson and her daughter. The former was the widow of a substantial farmer, a narrow-minded, tattling old gossip, whose character is not worth describing. She had two sons, Robert, a rough countrified farmer, and Richard, a retiring, studious young man, who was studying the classics with the vicar's assistance, preparing for college, with a view to enter the Church.

Their sister Jane was a young lady of some talents, and more ambition. She had, at her own desire, received a regular boarding-school education, superior to what any member of the family had obtained before. She had taken the polish well, acquired considerable elegance of manners, quite lost her provinical accent, and could boast of more accomplishments than the vicar's daughters. She was considered a beauty besides; but never for a moment could she number me amongst her admirers. She was about six and twenty, rather tall, and very slender, her hair was neither chestnut nor auburn, but a most decided, bright, light red, her complexion was remarkably fair and brilliant, her head small, her neck long, chin well turned, but very short, lips thin and red, eyes clear hazel, quick and penetrating, but entirely destitute of poetry or feeling. She had, or might have had, many suitors in her own rank of life, but scornfully repulsed or rejected them all; for none but a gentleman could please her refined taste, and none but a rich one could satisfy her soaring ambition. One gentleman there was, from whom she had lately received some rather pointed attentions, and upon whose heart, name, and fortune, it was whispered, she had serious designs. This was Mr Lawrence, the young squire, whose family had formerly occupied Wildfell Hall, but had deserted it, some fifteen years ago, for a more modern and commodious mansion in the neighbouring parish.

Now, Halford, I bid you adieu for the present. This is the first instalment of my debt. If the coin suits you, tell me so, and I'll send you the rest at my leisure: if you would rather remain my creditor than stuff your purse with such ungainly heavy pieces, – tell me still, and I'll pardon your bad taste, and willingly keep the treasure to myself. – Yours, immutably,

GILBERT MARKHAM.

# Chapter 2

I perceive with joy, my most valued friend, that the cloud of your displeasure has passed away; the light of your countenance blesses me once more, and you desire the continuation of my story; therefore, without more ado, you shall have it.

I think the day I last mentioned was a certain Sunday, the latest in the October of 1827. On the following Tuesday I was out with my dog and gun, in pursuit of such game as I could find within the territory of Linden-Car; but finding none at all, I turned my arms against the hawks and carrion-crows, whose depredations, as I suspected, had deprived me of better prey. To this end I left the more frequented regions, the wooded valleys, the corn-fields and the meadow-lands, and proceeded to mount the steep acclivity of Wildfell, the wildest and the loftiest eminence in our neighbourhood, where, as you ascend, the hedges,

as well as the trees, become scanty and stunted, the former, at length, giving place to rough stone fences, partly greened over with ivy and moss, the latter to larches and Scotch fir-trees, or isolated blackthorns. The fields, being rough and stony, and wholly unfit for the plough, were mostly devoted to the pasturing of sheep and cattle; the soil was thin and poor: bits of grey rock here and there peeped out from the grassy hillocks; bilberry plants and heather – relics of more savage wildness – grew under the walls; and in many of the enclosures, ragweeds and rushes usurped supremacy over the scanty herbage; – but these were not my property.

Near the top of this hill, about two miles from Linden-Car, stood Wildfell Hall, a superannuated mansion of the Elizabethan era, built of dark grey stone, – venerable and picturesque to look at, but, doubtless, cold and gloomy enough to inhabit, with its thick stone mullions and little latticed panes, its time-eaten air-holes, and its too lonely, too unsheltered situation, – only shielded from the war of wind and weather by a group of Scotch firs, themselves half blighted with storms, and looking as stern and gloomy as the Hall itself. Behind it lay a few desolate fields, and then, the brown heath-clad summit of the hill; before it (enclosed by stone walls, and entered by an iron gate with large balls of grey granite – similar to those which decorated the roof and gables – surmounting the gate-posts) was a garden, – once stocked with such hardy plants and flowers as could best brook the soil and climate, and such trees and shrubs as could best endure the gardener's torturing shears, and most readily assume the shapes he chose to give them, – now, having been left so many years, untilled and untrimmed, abandoned to the weeds and the grass, to the frost and the wind, the rain and the drought, it presented a very singular appearance indeed. The close green walls of privet, that had bordered the principal walk, were two-thirds withered away, and the rest grown beyond all reasonable bounds; the old boxwood swan, that sat beside the scraper, had lost its neck and half its body: the castellated towers of laurel in the middle of the garden, the gigantic warrior that stood on one side of the gateway, and the lion that guarded the other, were sprouted into such fantastic shapes as resembled nothing either in heaven or earth, or in the waters under the earth; but, to my young imagination, they presented all of them a goblinish appearance, that harmonized well with the ghostly legends and dark traditions our old nurse had told us respecting the haunted hall and its departed occupants.

I had succeeded in killing a hawk and two crows when I came within sight of the mansion; and then, relinquishing further depredations, I sauntered on, to have a look at the old place, and see what changes had been wrought in it by its new inhabitant. I did not like to go quite to the front and stare in at the gate; but I paused beside the garden wall, and looked, and saw no change – except in one wing, where the broken windows and dilapidated roof had evidently been repaired, and where a thin wreath of smoke was curling up from the stack of chimneys.

While I thus stood, leaning on my gun, and looking up at the dark gables, sunk in an idle reverie, weaving a tissue of wayward fancies, in which old associations and the fair young hermit, now within those walls, bore a nearly equal part, I heard a slight rustling and scrambling just within the garden; and, glancing in the direction whence the sound proceeded, I beheld a tiny hand elevated above the wall: it clung to the topmost stone, and then another little

hand was raised to take a firmer hold, and then appeared a small white forehead, surmounted with wreaths of light brown hair, with a pair of deep blue eyes beneath, and the upper portion of a diminutive ivory nose.

The eyes did not notice me, but sparkled with glee on beholding Sancho, my beautiful black and white setter, that was coursing about the field with its muzzle to the ground. The little creature raised its face and called aloud to the dog. The good-natured animal paused, looked up, and wagged his tail, but made no further advances. The child (a little boy, apparently about five years old) scrambled up to the top of the wall and called again and again; but finding this of no avail, apparently made up his mind, like Mahomet, to go to the mountain, since the mountain would not come to him, and attempted to get over; but a crabbed old cherry tree, that grew hard by, caught him by the frock in one of its crooked scraggy arms that stretched over the wall. In attempting to disengage himself, his foot slipped, and down he tumbled – but not to the earth; – the tree still kept him suspended. There was a silent struggle, and then a piercing shriek; – but, in an instant, I had dropped my gun on the grass, and caught the little fellow in my arms.

I wiped his eyes with his frock, told him he was all right, and called Sancho to pacify him. He was just putting his little hand on the dog's neck and beginning to smile through his tears, when I heard, behind me, a click of the iron gate, and a rustle of female garments, and lo! Mrs Graham darted upon me, – her neck uncovered, her black locks streaming in the wind.

'Give me the child!' she said, in a voice scarce louder than a whisper, but with a tone of startling vehemence, and, seizing the boy, she snatched him from me, as if some dire contamination were in my touch, and then stood with one hand firmly clasping his, the other on his shoulder, fixing upon me her large, luminous, dark eyes – pale, breathless, quivering with agitation.

'I was not harming the child, madam,' said I, scarce knowing whether to be most astonished or displeased; 'he was tumbling off the wall there; and I was so fortunate as to catch him, while he hung suspended headlong from that tree, and prevent I know not what catastrophe.'

'I beg your pardon, sir,' stammered she; – suddenly calming down, – the light of reason seeming to break upon her beclouded spirit, and a faint blush mantling her cheek— 'I did not know you; – and I thought'—

She stooped to kiss the child, and fondly clasped her arm round his neck.

'You thought I was going to kidnap your son, I suppose?'

She stroked his head with a half-embarrassed laugh, and replied—

'I did not know he had attempted to climb the wall. – I have the pleasure of addressing Mr Markham, I believe?' she added, somewhat abruptly.

I bowed, but ventured to ask her how she knew me.

'You sister called here, a few days ago, with Mrs Markham.'

'Is the resemblance so strong then?' I asked, in some surprise, and not so greatly flattered at the idea as I ought to have been.

'There is a likeness about the eyes and complexion, I think,' replied she, somewhat dubiously surveying my face: – 'and I think I saw you at church on Sunday.'

I smiled. – There was something either in that smile or the recollections it awakened that was particularly displeasing to her, for she suddenly assumed again that proud, chilly look that had so unspeakably roused my corruption at

church – a look of repellent scorn, so easily assumed, and so entirely without the least distortion of a single feature, that, while there, it seemed like the natural expression of the face, and was the more provoking to me, because I could not think it affected.

'Good morning, Mr Markham,' said she; and without another word or glance, she withdrew, with her child, into the garden; and I returned home, angry and dissatisfied – I could scarcely tell you why – and therefore will not attempt it.

I only stayed to put away my gun and powder-horn, and give some requisite directions to one of the farming-men, and then repaired to the vicarage, to solace my spirit and soothe my ruffled temper with the company and conversation of Eliza Millward.

I found her as usual, busy with some piece of soft embroidery (the mania for Berlin wools had not yet commenced), while her sister was seated at the chimney corner, with the cat on her knee, mending a heap of stockings.

'Mary – Mary, put them away!' Eliza was hastily saying just as I entered the room.

'Not I, indeed!' was the phlegmatic reply; and my appearance prevented further discussion.

'You're so unfortunate, Mr Markham!' observed the younger sister, with one of her arch, sidelong glances. 'Papa's just gone out into the parish, and not likely to be back for an hour!'

'Never mind; I can manage to spend a few minutes with his daughters, if they'll allow me,' said I, bringing a chair to the fire, and seating myself therein, without waiting to be asked.

'Well, if you'll be very good and amusing, we shall not object.'

'Let your permission be unconditional, pray; for I came not to give pleasure, but to seek it,' I answered.

However, I thought it but reasonable to make some slight exertion to render my company agreeable; and what little effort I made, was apparently pretty successful, for Miss Eliza was never in a better humour. We seemed, indeed, to be mutually pleased with each other, and managed to maintain between us a cheerful and animated, though not very profound conversation. It was little better than a *tête-à-tête*, for Miss Millward never opened her lips, except occasionally to correct some random assertion or exaggerated expression of her sister's, and once to ask her to pick up the ball of cotton, that had rolled under the table. I did this myself, however, as in duty bound.

'Thank you, Mr Markham,' said she, as I presented it to her. 'I would have picked it up myself; only I did not want to disturb the cat.'

'Mary, dear, that won't excuse you in Mr Markham's eyes,' said Eliza; 'he hates cats, I dare say, as cordially as he does old maids – like all other gentlemen. Don't you, Mr Markham?'

'I believe it is natural for our unamiable sex to dislike the creatures,' replied I: 'for you ladies lavish so many caresses upon them.'

'Bless them – little darlings!' cried she, in a sudden burst of enthusiasm, turning round, and overwhelming her sister's pet with a shower of kisses.

'Don't, Eliza!' said Miss Millward, somewhat gruffly, as she impatiently pushed her away.

But it was time for me to be going: make what haste I would, I should still be too late for tea; and my mother was the soul of order and punctuality.

My fair friend was evidently unwilling to bid me adieu. I tenderly squeezed her little hand at parting; and she repaid me with one of her softest smiles and most bewitching glances. I went home, very happy, with a heart brimful of complacency for myself and overflowing with love for Eliza.

# Chapter 3

wo days after, Mrs Graham called at Linden-Car, contrary to the expectation of Rose, who entertained an idea that the mysterious occupant of Wildfell Hall would wholly disregard the common observances of civilized life, – in which opinion she was supported by the Wilsons, who testified that neither their call nor the Millwards' had been returned as yet. Now, however, the cause of that omission was explained, though not entirely to the satisfaction of Rose. Mrs Graham had brought her child with her, and on my mother's expressing surprise that he could walk so far, she replied—

'It is a long walk for him; but I must have either taken him with me, or relinquished the visit altogether; for I never leave him alone; and I think, Mrs Markham, I must beg you to make my excuses to the Millwards and Mrs Wilson, when you see them, as I fear I cannot do myself the pleasure of calling upon them till my little Arthur is able to accompany me.'

'But you have a servant,' said Rose; 'could you not leave him with her?'

'She has her own occupations to attend to; and, besides, she is too old to run after a child, and he is too mercurial to be tied to an elderly woman.'

'But you left him to come to church.'

'Yes, once; but I would not have left him for any other purpose; and I think, in future, I must contrive to bring him with me, or stay at home.'

'Is he so mischievous?' asked my mother, considerably shocked.

'No,' replied the lady, sadly smiling, as she stroked the wavy locks of her son, who was seated on a low stool at her feet, 'but he is my only treasure; and I am his only friend, so we don't like to be separated.'

'But, my dear, I call that doting,' said my plain-spoken parent. 'You should try to suppress such foolish fondness, as well to save your son from ruin as yourself from ridicule.'

'Ruin! Mrs Markham?'

'Yes; it is spoiling the child. Even at his age, he ought not to be always tied to his mother's apron-string; he should learn to be ashamed of it.'

'Mrs Markham, I beg you will not say such things in his presence at least. I trust my son will never be ashamed to love his mother!' said Mrs Graham, with a serious energy that startled the company.

My mother attempted to appease her by an explanation; but she seemed to think enough had been said on the subject, and abruptly turned the conversation.

'Just as I thought,' said I to myself. 'The lady's temper is none of the mildest, notwithstanding her sweet, pale face and lofty brow, where thought and suffering seem equally to have stamped their impress.'

All this time, I was seated at a table on the other side of the room, apparently immersed in the perusal of a volume of the *Farmer's Magazine*, which I happened to have been reading at the moment of our visitor's arrival; and, not choosing to be over civil, I had merely bowed as she entered, and continued my occupation as before.

In a little while, however, I was sensible that some one was approaching me, with a light, but slow and hesitating, tread. It was little Arthur, irresistibly attracted by my dog Sancho, that was lying at my feet. On looking up, I beheld him standing about two yards off, with his clear blue eyes wistfully gazing on the dog, transfixed to the spot, not by fear of the animal, but by a timid disinclination to approach its master. A little encouragement, however, induced him to come forward. The child, though shy, was not sullen. In a minute he was kneeling on the carpet, with his arms round Sancho's neck, and in a minute or two more, the little fellow was seated on my knee, surveying with eager interest the various specimens of horses, cattle, pigs, and model farms portrayed in the volume before me. I glanced at his mother now and then, to see how she relished the new-sprung intimacy; and I saw, by the unquiet aspect of her eye, that for some reason or other she was uneasy at the child's position.

'Arthur,' she said, at length, 'come here. You are troublesome to Mr Markham: he wishes to read.'

'By no means, Mrs Graham; pray let him stay. I am as much amused as he is,' pleaded I. But still, with hand and eye, she silently called him to her side.

'No, mamma,' said the child; 'let me look at these pictures first; and then I'll come, and tell you all about them.'

'We are going to have a small party on Monday, the 5th of November,' said my mother; 'and I hope you will not refuse to make one, Mrs Graham. You can bring your little boy with you, you know – I dare say we shall be able to amuse him; – and then you can make your own apologies to the Millwards and Wilsons – they will all be here, I expect.'

'Thank you, I never go to parties.'

'Oh! but this will be quite a family concern – early hours, and nobody here but ourselves, and just the Millwards and Wilsons, most of whom you already know, and Mr Lawrence, your landlord, with whom you ought to make acquaintance.'

'I do know something of him – but you must excuse me this time; for the evenings, now, are dark and damp, and Arthur, I fear, is too delicate to risk exposure to their influence with impunity. We must defer the enjoyment of your hospitality, till the return of longer days and warmer nights.'

Rose, now, at a hint from my mother, produced a decanter of wine, with accompaniments of glasses and cake, from the cupboard and the oak sideboard, and the refreshment was duly presented to the guests. They both partook of the cake, but obstinately refused the wine, in spite of their hostess's hospitable attempts to force it upon them. Arthur, especially, shrank from the ruby nectar as if in terror and disgust, and was ready to cry when urged to take it.

'Never mind, Arthur,' said his mamma, 'Mrs Markham thinks it will do you good, as you were tired with your walk; but she will not oblige you to take it!

# The Tenant of Wildfell Hall

– I dare say you will do very well without. He detests the very sight of wine,' she added, 'and the smell of it almost makes him sick. I have been accustomed to make him swallow a little wine or weak spirits-and-water, by way of medicine when he was sick, and, in fact, I have done what I could to make him hate them.'

Everybody laughed except the young widow and her son.

'Well, Mrs Graham,' said my mother, wiping the tears of merriment from her bright blue eyes— 'well, you surprise me! I really give you credit for having more sense.— The poor child will be the veriest milksop that ever was sopped! Only think what a man you will make of him, if you persist in'—

'I think it a very excellent plan,' interrupted Mrs Graham with imperturbable gravity. 'By that means I hope to save him from one degrading vice at least. I wish I could render the incentives to every other equally innoxious in his case.'

'But by such means,' said I, 'you will never render him virtuous.— What is it that constitutes virtue, Mrs Graham! Is it the circumstance of being able and willing to resist temptation; or that of having no temptations to resist? Is he a strong man that overcomes great obstacles and performs surprising achievements, though by dint of great muscular exertion, and at the risk of some subsequent fatigue, or he that sits in his chair all day, with nothing to do more laborious than stirring the fire, and carrying his food to his mouth? If you would have your son to walk honourably through the world, you must not attempt to clear the stones from his path, but teach him to walk firmly over them – not insist upon leading him by the hand, but let him learn to go alone.'

'I will lead him by the hand, Mr Markham, till he has strength to go alone; and I will clear as many stones from his path as I can, and teach him to avoid the rest – or walk firmly over them, as you say; – for when I have done my utmost, in the way of clearance, there will still be plenty left to exercise all the agility, steadiness, and circumspection he will ever have. – It is all very well to talk about noble resistance, and trials of virtue; but for fifty – or five hundred men that have yielded to temptation, show me one that has had virtue to resist. And why should I take it for granted that my son will be one in a thousand? – and not rather prepare for the worst, and suppose he will be like his – like the rest of mankind, unless I take care to prevent it?'

'You are very complimentary to us all,' I observed.

'I know nothing about you – I speak of those I do know – and when I see the whole race of mankind (with a few rare exceptions) stumbling and blundering along the path of life, sinking into every pitfall, and breaking their shins over every impediment that lies in their way, shall I not use all the means in my power to insure for him a smoother and a safer passage?'

'Yes, but the surest means will be to endeavour to fortify him against temptation, not to remove it out of his way.'

'I will do both, Mr Markham. God knows he will have temptations enough to assail him, both from within and without, when I have done all I can to render vice as uninviting to him, as it is abominable in its own nature – I myself have had, indeed, but few incentives to what the world calls vice, but yet I have experienced temptations and trials of another kind, that have required, on many occasions, more watchfulness and firmness to resist, than I have hitherto been able to muster against them. And this, I believe, is what most others would

acknowledge, who are accustomed to reflection, and wishful to strive against their natural corruptions.'

'Yes,' said my mother, but half apprehending her drift; 'but you would not judge of a boy by yourself – and my dear Mrs Graham, let me warn you in good time against the error – the fatal error, I may call it – of taking that boy's education upon yourself. Because you are clever in some things; and well-informed, you may fancy yourself equal to the task; but indeed you are not; and if you persist in the attempt, believe me you will bitterly repent it when the mischief is done.

'I am to send him to school, I suppose, to learn to despise his mother's authority and affection!' said the lady, with rather a bitter smile.

'Oh, no!— But if you would have a boy to despise his mother, let her keep him at home, and spend her life in petting him up, and slaving to indulge his follies and caprices.'

'I perfectly agree with you, Mrs Markham; but nothing can be further from my principles and practice than such criminal weakness as that.'

'Well, but you will treat him like a girl – you'll spoil his spirit, and make a mere Miss Nancy of him – you will, indeed, Mrs Graham, whatever you may think. But I'll get Mr Millward to talk to you about it: – he'll tell you the consequences; he'll set it before you as plain as the day; – and tell you what you ought to do, and all about it; and, I don't doubt, he'll be able to convince you in a minute.'

'No occasion to trouble the vicar,' said Mrs Graham, glancing at me – I suppose I was smiling at my mother's unbounded confidence in that worthy gentleman— 'Mr Markham here, thinks his powers of conviction at least equal to Mr Millward's. If I hear not him, neither should I be convinced though one rose from the dead. Well, Mr Markham, you that maintain that a boy should not be shielded from evil, but sent out to battle against it, alone and unassisted – not taught to avoid the snares of life, but boldly to rush into them, or over them, as he may – to seek danger rather than shun it, and feed his virtue by temptation, – would you'—

'I beg your pardon, Mrs Graham – but you get on too fast. I have not yet said that a boy should be taught to rush into the snares of life, – or even wilfully to seek temptation for the sake of exercising his virtue by overcoming it; – I only say that it is better to arm and strengthen your hero, than to disarm and enfeeble the foe; – and if you were to rear an oak sapling in a hothouse, tending it carefully night and day, and shielding it from every breath of wind, you could not expect it to become a hardy tree, like that which has grown up on the mountain-side, exposed to all the action of the elements, and not even sheltered from the shock of the tempest.'

'Granted; – but would you use the same arguments with regard to a girl?'

'Certainly not.'

'No; you would have her to be tenderly and delicately nurtured, like a hot-house plant – taught to cling to others for direction and support, and guarded, as much as possible, from the very knowledge of evil. But will you be so good as to inform me why you make this distinction? Is it that you think she has no virtue?'

'Assuredly not.'

'Well, but you affirm that virtue is only elicited by temptation; – and you

think that a woman cannot be too little exposed to temptation, or too little acquainted with vice, or anything connected therewith. It must be, either, that you think she is essentially so vicious, or so feeble-minded that she cannot withstand temptation, – and though she may be pure and innocent as long as she is kept in ignorance and restraint, yet, being destitude of real virtue, to teach her how to sin, is at once to make her a sinner, and the greater her knowledge, the wider her liberty, the deeper will be her depravity, – whereas, in the nobler sex, there is natural tendency to goodness, guarded by a superior fortitude, which, the more it is exercised by trials and dangers, is only the further developed'—

'Heaven forbid that I should think so!' I interrupted her at last.

'Well then, it must be that you think they are both weak and prone to err, and the slightest error, the nearest shadow of pollution, will ruin the one, while the character of the other will be strengthened and embellished – his education properly finished by a little practical acquaintance with forbidden things. Such experience, to him (to use a trite simile), will be like the storm to the oak, which, though it may scatter the leaves, and snap the smaller branches, serves but to rivet the roots, and to harden and condense the fibres of the tree. You would have us encourage our sons to prove all things by their own experience, while our daughters must not even profit by the experience of others. Now I would have both so to benefit by the experience of others, and the precepts of a higher authority, that they should know beforehand to refuse the evil and choose the good, and require no experimental proofs to teach them the evil of transgression. I would not send a poor girl into the world, unarmed against her foes, and ignorant of the snares that beset her path; nor would I watch and guard her, till, deprived of self-respect and self-reliance, she lost the power or the will to watch and guard herself; – and as for my son – if I thought he would grow up to be what you call a man of the world – one that has "seen life", and glories in his experience, even though he should so far profit by it as to sober down, at length, into a useful and respected member of society – I would rather that he died tomorrow! – rather a thousand times!' she earnestly repeated, pressing her darling to her side and kissing his forehead with intense affection. He had, already, left his new companion, and been standing for some time beside his mother's knee, looking up into her face, and listening in silent wonder to her incomprehensible discourse.

'Well! you ladies must always have the last word, I suppose,' said I, observing her rise, and begin to take leave of my mother.

'You may have as many words as you please, – only I can't stay to hear them.'

'No: that is the way: you hear just as much of an argument as you please; and the rest may be spoken to the wind.'

'If you are anxious to say anything more on the subject,' replied she, as she shook hands with Rose, 'you must bring your sister to see me some fine day, and I'll listen, as patiently as you could wish, to whatever you please to say. I would rather be lectured by you than the vicar, because I should have less remorse in telling you, at the end of the discourse, that I preserve my own opinion precisely the same as at the beginning – as would be the case, I am persuaded, with regard to either logician.'

'Yes, of course,' replied I, determined to be as provoking as herself; 'for when a lady does consent to listen to an argument against her own opinions, she is

always predetermined to withstand it – to listen only with her bodily ears, keeping the mental organs resolutely closed against the strongest reasoning.'

'Good morning, Mr Markham,' said my fair antagonist, with a pitying smile; and deigning no further rejoinder, she slightly bowed, and was about to withdraw; but her son, with childish impertinence, arrested her by exclaiming—

'Mamma, you have not shaken hands with Mr Markham!'

She laughingly turned round, and held out her hand. I gave it a spiteful squeeze; for I was annoyed at the continual injustice she had done me from the very dawn of our acquaintance. Without knowing anything about my real disposition and principles, she was evidently prejudiced against me, and seemed bent upon showing me that her opinions respecting me, on every particular, fell far below those I entertained of myself. I was naturally touchy, or it would not have vexed me so much. Perhaps, too, I was a little bit spoiled by my mother and sister, and some other ladies of my acquaintance; and yet I was by no means a fop – of that I am fully convinced, whether you are or not.

# Chapter 4

Our party, on the 5th of November, passed off very well, in spite of Mrs Graham's refusal to grace it with her presence. Indeed, it is probable that, had she been there, there would have been less cordiality, freedom, and frolic amongst us than there was without her.

My mother, as usual, was cheerful and chatty, full of activity and good-nature, and only faulty in being too anxious to make her guests happy, thereby forcing several of them to do what their soul abhorred, in the way of eating or drinking, sitting opposite the blazing fire, or talking when they would be silent. Nevertheless, they bore it very well, being all in their holiday humours.

Mr Millward was mighty in important dogmas and sententious jokes, pompous anecdotes and oracular discourses, dealt out for the edification of the whole assembly in general, and of the admiring Mrs Markham, the polite Mr Lawrence, the sedate Mary Millward, the quiet Richard Wilson, and the matter-of-fact Robert, in particular, – as being the most attentive listeners.

Mrs Wilson was more brilliant than ever, with her budgets of fresh news and old scandal, strung together with trivial questions and remarks, and oft-repeated observations, uttered apparently for the sole purpose of denying a moment's rest to her inexhaustible organs of speech. She had brought her knitting with her, and it seemed as if her tongue had laid a wager with her fingers, to outdo them in swift and ceaseless motion.

Her daughter Jane was, of course, as graceful and elegant, as witty and seductive, as she could possibly manage to be; for here were all the ladies to outshine, and all the gentlemen to charm, – and Mr Lawrence, especially, to

# The Tenant of Wildfell Hall

capture and subdue. Her little arts to effect his subjugation were too subtle and impalpable to attract my observation; but I thought there was a certain refined affectation of superiority, and an ungenial self-consciousness about her, that negatived all her advantages; and after she was gone, Rose interpreted to me her various looks, words, and actions with a mingled acuteness and asperity that made me wonder, equally, at the lady's artifice and my sister's penetration, and ask myself if she too had an eye to the squire – but never mind, Halford; she had not.

Richard Wilson, Jane's younger brother, sat in a corner, apparently good-tempered, but silent and shy, desirous to escape observation, but willing enough to listen and observe; and although somewhat out of his element, he would have been happy enough in his own quiet way, if my mother could only have let him alone; but in her mistaken kindness, she would keep persecuting him with her attentions – pressing upon him all manner of viands, under the notion that he was too bashful to help himself, and obliging him to shout across the room his monosyllabic replies to the numerous questions and observations by which she vainly attempted to draw him into conversation.

Rose informed me that he never would have favoured us with his company, but for the importunities of his sister Jane, who was most anxious to show Mr Lawrence that she had at least one brother more gentlemanly and refined than Robert. That worthy individual she had been equally solicitous to keep away; but he affirmed that he saw no reason why he should not enjoy a crack with Markham and the old lady (my mother was not old, really), and bonny Miss Rose and the parson, as well as the best; – and he was in the right of it too. So he talked commonplace with my mother and Rose, and discussed parish affairs with the vicar, farming matters with me, and politics with us both.

Mary Millward was another mute, – not so much tormented with cruel kindness as Dick Wilson, because she had a certain short, decided way of answering and refusing, and was supposed to be rather sullen than diffident. However that might be, she certainly did not give much pleasure to the company; – nor did she appear to derive much from it. Eliza told me she had only come because her father insisted upon it, having taken it into his head that she devoted herself too exclusively to her household duties, to the neglect of such relaxations and innocent enjoyments as were proper to her age and sex. She seemed to be good-humoured enough on the whole. Once or twice she was provoked to laughter by the wit or the merriment of some favoured individual amongst us; and then I observed she sought the eye of Richard Wilson, who sat over against her. As he studied with her father, she had some acquaintance with him, in spite of the retiring habits of both, and I suppose there was a kind of fellow-feeling established between them.

My Eliza was charming beyond description, coquettish without affectation, and evidently more desirous to engage my attention than that of all the room besides. Her delight in having me near her, seated or standing by her side, whispering in her ear, or pressing her hand in the dance, was plainly legible in her glowing face and heaving bosom, however belied by saucy words and gestures. But I had better hold my tongue: if I boast of these things now, I shall have to blush hereafter.

To proceed, then, with the various individuals of our party; Rose was simple and natural as usual, and full of mirth and vivacity.

# The Tenant of Wildfell Hall

Fergus was impertinent and absurd; but his impertinence and folly served to make others laugh, if they did not raise himself in their estimation.

And finally (for I omit myself), Mr Lawrence was gentlemanly and inoffensive to all, and polite to the vicar and the ladies, especially his hostess and her daughter, and Miss Wilson – misguided man; he had not the taste to prefer Eliza Millward. Mr Lawrence and I were on tolerably intimate terms. Essentially of reserved habits, and but seldom quitting the secluded place of his birth, where he had lived in solitary state since the death of his father, he had neither the opportunity nor the inclination for forming many acquaintances; and, of all he had ever known, I (judging by the results) was the companion most agreeable to his taste. I liked the man well enough, but he was too cold, and shy, and self-contained, to obtain my cordial sympathies. A spirit of candour and frankness, when wholly unaccompanied with coarseness, he admired in others, but he could not acquire it himself. His excessive reserve upon all his own concerns was, indeed, provoking and chilly enough; but I forgave it, from a conviction that it originated less in pride and want of confidence in his friends, than in a certain morbid feeling of delicacy, and a peculiar diffidence, that he was sensible of, but wanted energy to overcome. His heart was like a sensitive plant, that opens for a moment in the sunshine, but curls up and shrinks into itself at the slightest touch of the finger, or the lightest breath of wind. And, upon the whole, our intimacy was rather a mutual predilection than a deep and solid friendship, such as has since arisen between myself and you, Halford, whom, in spite of your occasional crustiness, I can liken to nothing so well as an old coat, unimpeachable in texture, but easy and loose – that has conformed itself to the shape of the wearer, and which he may use as he pleases, without being bothered with the fear of spoiling it; – whereas Mr Lawrence was like a new garment, all very neat and trim to look at, but so tight in the elbows, that you would fear to split the seams by the unrestricted motion of your arms, and so smooth and fine in surface that you scruple to expose it to a single drop of rain.

Soon after the arrival of the guests, my mother mentioned Mrs Graham, regretted she was not there to meet them, and explained to the Millwards and Wilsons the reasons she had given for neglecting to return their calls, hoping they would excuse her, as she was sure she did not mean to be uncivil, and would be glad to see them at any time—

'But she is a very singular lady, Mr Lawrence,' added she; 'we don't know what to make of her – but I dare say you can tell us something about her, for she is your tenant, you know, – and she said she knew you a little.'

All eyes were turned to Mr Lawrence. I thought he looked unnecessarily confused at being so appealed to.

'I, Mrs Markham!' said he; 'you are mistaken – I don't – that is – I have seen her, certainly; but I am the last person you should apply to for information respecting Mrs Graham.'

He then immediately turned to Rose, and asked her to favour the company with a song, or a tune on the piano.

'No,' said she, 'you must ask Miss Wilson: she outshines us all in singing and music too.'

Miss Wilson demurred.

'She'll sing readily enough,' said Fergus, 'if you'll undertake to stand by her, Mr Lawrence, and turn over the leaves for her.'

# The Tenant of Wildfell Hall

'I shall be most happy to do so, Miss Wilson; will you allow me?'

She bridled her long neck and smiled, and suffered him to lead her to the instrument, where she played and sang, in her very best style, one piece after another, while he stood patiently by, leaning one hand on the back of her chair, and turning over the leaves of her book with the other. Perhaps he was as much charmed with her performance as she was. It was all very fine in its way; but I cannot say that it moved me very deeply. There was plenty of skill and execution, but precious little feeling.

But we had not done with Mrs Graham yet.

'I don't take wine, Mrs Markham,' said Mr Millward, upon the introduction of that beverage; 'I'll take a little of your home-brewed ale. I always prefer your home-brewed to anything else.'

Flattered at this compliment, my mother rang the bell, and a china jug of our best ale was presently brought and set before the worthy gentleman who so well knew how to appreciate its excellences.

'Now THIS is the thing!' cried he, pouring out a glass of the same in a long stream, skilfully directed from the jug to the tumbler, so as to produce much foam without spilling a drop; and, having surveyed it for a moment opposite the candle, he took a deep draught, and then smacked his lips, drew a long breath, and refilled his glass, my mother looking on with the greatest satisfaction.

'There's nothing like this, Mrs Markham!' said he. 'I always maintain that there's nothing to compare with your home-brewed ale.'

'I'm sure I'm glad you like it, sir. I always look after the brewing myself, as well as the cheese and the butter – I like to have things well done, while we're about it.'

'Quite right, Mrs Markham!'

'But then, Mr Millward, you don't think it wrong to take a little wine now and then – or a little spirits either!' said my mother, as she handed a smoking tumbler of gin-and-water to Mrs Wilson, who affirmed that wine sat heavy on her stomach, and whose son Robert was at the moment helping himself to a pretty stiff glass of the same.

'By no means!' replied the oracle, with a Jove-like nod; 'these things are all blessings and mercies, if we only knew how to make use of them.'

'But Mrs Graham doesn't think so. You shall just hear now what she told us the other day – I told her I'd tell you.'

And my mother favoured the company with a particular account of that lady's mistaken ideas and conduct regarding the matter in hand, concluding with, 'Now, don't you think it is wrong?'

'Wrong!' repeated the vicar, with more than common solemnity – 'criminal, I should say – criminal! – Not only is it making a fool of the boy, but it is despising the gifts of Providence, and teaching him to trample them under his feet.'

He then entered more fully into the question, and explained at large the folly and impiety of such a proceeding. My mother heard him with profoundest reverence; and even Mrs Wilson vouchsafed to rest her tongue for a moment, and listen in silence, while she complacently sipped her gin-and-water. Mr Lawrence sat with his elbow on the table, carelessly playing with his half-empty wine-glass, and covertly smiling to himself.

'But don't you think, Mr Millward,' suggested he, when at length that

gentleman paused in his discourse, 'that when a child may be naturally prone to intemperance – by the fault of its parents or ancestors, for instance – some precautions are advisable?' (Now it was generally believed that Mr Lawrence's father had shortened his days by intemperance.)

'Some precautions, it may be; but temperance, sir, is one thing, and abstinence another.'

'But I have heard that, with some persons, temperance – that is, moderation – is almost impossible; and if abstinence be an evil (which some have doubted), no one will deny that excess is a greater. Some parents have entirely prohibited their children from tasting intoxicating liquors; but a parent's authority cannot last for ever: children are naturally prone to hanker after forbidden things; and a child, in such a case, would be likely to have a strong curiosity to taste, and try the effect of what has been so lauded and enjoyed by others, so strictly forbidden to himself – which curiosity would generally be gratified on the first convenient opportunity; and the restraint once broken, serious consequences might ensure. I don't pretend to be a judge of such matters, but it seems to me, that this plan of Mrs Graham's, as you describe it, Mrs Markham, extraordinary as it may be, is not without its advantages; for here you see the child is delivered at once from temptation; he has no secret curiosity, no hankering desire; he is as well acquainted with the tempting liquors as he ever wishes to be; and is thoroughly disgusted with them, without having suffered from their effects.'

'And is that right, sir? Have I not proven to you how wrong it is – how contrary to Scripture and to reason to teach a child to look with contempt and disgust upon the blessings of Providence, instead of to use them aright?'

'You may consider laudanum a blessing of Providence, sir,' replied Mr Lawrence, smiling; 'and yet, you will allow that most of us had better abstain from it, even in moderation, but,' added he, 'I would not desire you to follow out my simile too closely – in witness whereof I finish my glass.'

'And take another, I hope, Mr Lawrence,' said my mother, pushing the bottle towards him.

He politely declined, and pushing his chair a little away from the table, leant back towards me – I was seated a trifle behind on the sofa beside Eliza Millward – and carelessly asked me if I knew Mrs Graham.

'I have met her once or twice,' I replied.

'What do you think of her?'

'I cannot say that I like her much. She is handsome – or rather I should say distinguished and interesting – in her appearance, but by no means amiable – a woman liable to take strong prejudices, I should fancy, and stick to them through thick and thin, twisting everything into conformity with her own preconceived opinions – too hard, too sharp, too bitter for my taste.'

He made no reply, but looked down and bit his lip, and shortly after rose and sauntered up to Miss Wilson, as much repelled by me, I fancy, as attracted by her. I scarcely noticed it at the time, but afterwards, I was led to recall this and other trifling facts, of a similar nature, to my remembrance, when – but I must not anticipate.

We wound up the evening with dancing – our worthy pastor thinking it no scandal to be present on the occasion, though one of the village musicians was engaged to direct our evolutions with his violin. But Mary Millward obstinately

refused to join us; and so did Richard Wilson, though my mother earnestly entreated him to do so, and even offered to be his partner.

We managed very well without them, however. With a single set of quadrilles, and several country dances, we carried it on to a pretty late hour; and at length, having called upon our musician to strike up a waltz, I was just about to whirl Eliza round in that delightful dance, accompanied by Lawrence and Jane Wilson, and Fergus and Rose, when Mr Millward interposed with—

'No, no, I don't allow that! Come, it's time to be going home.'

'Oh, no, papa!' pleaded Eliza.

'High time, my girl – high time! Moderation in all things, remember! That's the plan— "Let your moderation be known unto all men!"'

But in revenge, I followed Eliza into the dimly-lighted passage, where, under pretence of helping her on with her shawl, I fear I must plead guilty to snatching a kiss behind her father's back, while he was enveloping his throat and chin in the folds of a mighty comforter. But alas! in turning round, there was my mother close beside me. The consequence was, that no sooner were the guests departed, than I was doomed to a very serious remonstrance, which unpleasantly checked the galloping course of my spirits, and made a disagreeable close to the evening.

'My dear Gilbert,' said she, 'I wish you wouldn't do so! You know how deeply I have your advantage at heart, how I love you and prize you above everything else in the world, and how much I long to see you well settled in life – and how bitterly it would grieve me to see you married to that girl – or any other in the neighbourhood. What you see in her I don't know. It isn't only the want of money that I think about – nothing of the kind – but there's neither beauty, nor cleverness, nor goodness, nor anything else that's desirable. If you knew your own value, as I do, you wouldn't dream of it. Do wait awhile and see! If you bind yourself to her, you'll repent it all your lifetime when you look round and see how many better there are. Take my word for it, you will.'

'Well, mother, do be quiet! – I hate to be lectured! – I'm not going to marry yet, I tell you! but – dear me! mayn't I enjoy myself at all?'

'Yes, my dear boy, but not in that way. Indeed, you shouldn't do such things. You would be wronging the girl, if she were what she ought to be; but I assure you she is as artful a little hussy as anybody need wish to see; and you'll get entangled in her snares before you know where you are. And if you marry her, Gilbert, you'll break my heart! – so there's an end of it.'

'Well, don't cry about it, mother,' said I, for the tears were gushing from her eyes; 'there, let that kiss efface the one I gave Eliza; don't abuse her any more, and set your mind at rest; for I'll promise never – that is, I'll promise to think twice before I take any important step you seriously disapprove of.'

So saying, I lighted my candle, and went to bed, considerably quenched in spirit.

# Chapter 5

t was about the close of the month, that, yielding at length to the urgent importunities of Rose, I accompanied her in a visit to Wildfell Hall. To our surprise we were ushered into a room where the first object that met the eye was a painter's easel, with a table beside it covered with rolls of canvas, bottles of oil and varnish, palette, brushes, paints, etc. Leaning against the wall were several sketches in various stages of progression, and a few finished paintings – mostly of landscapes and figures.

'I must make you welcome to my studio,' said Mrs Graham, 'there is no fire in the sitting-room today, and it is rather too cold to show you into a place with an empty grate.'

And disengaging a couple of chairs from the artistical lumber that usurped them, she bid us be seated, and resumed her place beside the easel – not facing it exactly, but now and then glancing at the picture upon it while she conversed, and giving it an occasional touch with her brush, as if she found it impossible to wean her attention entirely from her occupation to fix it upon her guests. It was a view of Wildfell Hall, as seen at early morning from the field below, rising in dark relief against a sky of clear silvery blue, with a few red streaks on the horizon, faithfully drawn and coloured, and very elegantly and artistically handled.

'I see your heart is in your work, Mrs Graham,' observed I: 'I must beg you to go on with it; for if you suffer our presence to interrupt you, we shall be constrained to regard ourselves as unwelcome intruders.'

'Oh, no!' replied she, throwing her brush on to the table, as if startled into politeness. I am not so beset with visitors, but that I can readily spare a few minutes to the few that do favour me with their company.'

'You have almost completed your painting,' said I, approaching to observe it more closely, and surveying it with a greater degree of admiration and delight than I cared to express. 'A few more touches in the foreground will finish it, I should think. But why have you called it Fernley Manor, Cumberland, instead of Wildfell Hall, —shire?' I asked, alluding to the name she had traced in small characters at the bottom of the canvas.

But immediately I was sensible of having committed an act of impertinence in so doing; for she coloured and hesitated; but after a moment's pause, with a kind of desperate frankness, she replied—

'Because I have friends – acquaintances at least – in the world, from whom I desire my present abode to be concealed; and as they might see the picture, and might possibly recognize the style, in spite of the false initials I have put in the

corner, I take the precaution to give a false name to the place also, in order to put them on a wrong scent, if they should attempt to trace me out by it.'

'Then you don't intend to keep the picture?' said I, anxious to say anything to change the subject.

'No; I cannot afford to paint for my own amusement.'

'Mamma sends all her pictures to London,' said Arthur; 'and somebody sells them for her there, and sends us the money.'

In looking round upon the other pieces, I remarked a pretty sketch of Lindenhope from the top of the hill; another view of the old hall, basking in the sunny haze of a quiet summer afternoon; and a simple but striking little picture of a child brooding with looks of silent but deep and sorrowful regret, over a handful of withered flowers, with glimpses of dark low hills and autumnal fields behind it, and a dull beclouded sky above.

'You see there is a sad dearth of subjects,' observed the fair artist. 'I took the old hall once on a moonlight night, and I suppose I must take it again on a snowy winter's day, and then again on a dark cloudy evening; for I really have nothing else to paint. I have been told that you have a fine view of the sea, somewhere in the neighbourhood – Is it true? – and is it within walking distance?'

'Yes, if you don't object to walking four miles – or nearly so – little short of eight miles, there and back – and over a somewhat rough, fatiguing road.'

'In what direction does it lie?'

I described the situation as well as I could, and was entering upon an explanation of the various roads, lanes, and fields to be traversed in order to reach it, the goings straight on, and turnings to the right and to the left, when she checked me with—

'Oh, stop! – don't tell me now: I shall forget every word of your directions before I require them. I shall not think about going till next spring; and then, perhaps, I may trouble you. At present we have the winter before us, and'—

She suddenly paused, with a suppressed exclamation, started up from her seat, and saying, 'Excuse me one moment,' hurried from the room, and shut the door behind her.

Curious to see what had startled her so, I looked towards the window – for her eyes had been carelessly fixed upon it the moment before – and just beheld the skirts of a man's coat vanishing behind a large holly-bush that stood between the window and the porch.

'It's mamma's friend,' said Arthur.

Rose and I looked at each other.

'I don't know what to make of her at all,' whispered Rose.

The child looked at her in grave surprise. She straightway began to talk to him on indifferent matters, while I amused myself with looking at the pictures. There was one in an obscure corner that I had not before observed. It was a little child, seated on the grass with its lap full of flowers. The tiny features and large blue eyes, smiling through a shock of light brown curls, shaken over the forehead as it bent above its treasure, bore sufficient resemblance to those of the young gentleman before me, to proclaim it a portrait of Arthur Graham in his early infancy.

In taking this up to bring it to the light, I discovered another behind it, with its face to the wall. I ventured to take that up too. It was the portrait of a

gentleman in the full prime of youthful manhood – handsome enough, and not badly executed, but, if done by the same hand as the others, it was evidently some years before; for there was far more careful minuteness of detail, and less of that freshness of colouring and freedom of handling, that delighted and surprised me in them. Nevertheless, I surveyed it with considerable interest. There was a certain individuality in the features and expression that stamped it, at once, a successful likeness. The bright blue eyes regarded the spectator with a kind of lurking drollery – you almost expected to see them wink; the lips – a little too voluptuously full – seemed ready to break into a smile; the warmly-tinted cheeks were embellished with a luxuriant growth of reddish whiskers; while the bright chestnut hair, clustering in abundant, wavy curls, trespassed too much upon the forehead, and seemed to intimate that the owner thereof was prouder of his beauty than his intellect – as, perhaps, he had reason to be; – and yet he looked no fool.

I had not had the portrait in my hands two minutes before the fair artist returned.

'Only some one come about the pictures,' said she, in apology for her abrupt departure. 'I told him to wait.'

'I fear it will be considered an act of impertinence,' said I, 'to presume to look at a picture that the artist has turned to the wall; but may I ask'—

'It is an act of very great impertinence, sir; and therefore I beg you will ask nothing about it, for your curiosity will not be gratified,' replied she, attempting to cover the tartness of her rebuke with a smile; but I could see, by her flushed cheek and kindling eye, that she was seriously annoyed.

'I was only going to ask if you had painted it yourself,' said I, sulkily resigning the picture into her hands; for without a grain of ceremony she took it from me; and quickly restoring it to the dark corner, with its face to the wall, placed the other against it as before, and then turned to me and laughed.

But I was in no humour for jesting. I carelessly turned to the window, and stood looking out upon the desolate garden, leaving her to talk to Rose for a minute or two; and then, telling my sister it was time to go, shook hands with the little gentleman, coolly bowed to the lady, and moved towards the door. But having bid adieu to Rose, Mrs Graham presented her hand to me, saying, with a soft voice, and by no means a disagreeable smile —

'Let not the sun go down upon your wrath, Mr Markham. I'm sorry I offended you by my abruptness.'

When a lady condescends to apologize, there is no keeping one's anger of course; so we parted good friends for once; and this time I squeezed her hand with a cordial, not a spiteful pressure.

# Chapter 6

uring the next four months I did not enter Mrs Graham's house, nor she mine; but still the ladies continued to talk about her, and still our acquaintance continued, though slowly, to advance. As for their talk, I paid little attention to that (when it related to the fair hermit, I mean), and the only information I derived from it was, that, one fine frosty day, she had ventured to take her little boy as far as the vicarage, and that, unfortunately, nobody was at home but Miss Millward; nevertheless, she had sat a long time, and, by all accounts, they had found a good deal to say to each other, and parted with a mutual desire to meet again. But Mary liked children, and fond mammas like those who can duly appreciate their treasures.

But sometimes I saw her myself, not only when she came to church, but when she was out on the hills with her son, whether taking a long, purpose-like walk, or – on special fine days – leisurely rambling over the moor or the bleak pasture-lands surrounding the old hall, herself with a book in her hand, her son gambolling about her;·and on any of these occasions, when I caught sight of her in my solitary walks or rides, or while following my agricultural pursuits, I generally contrived to meet or overtake her, for I rather liked to see Mrs Graham, and to talk to her, and I decidedly liked to talk to her little companion, whom, when once the ice of his shyness was fairly broken, I found to be a very amiable, intelligent, and entertaining little fellow; and we soon became excellent friends – how much to the gratification of his mamma I cannot undertake to say. I suspected at first that she was desirous of throwing cold water on this growing intimacy – to quench, as it were, the kindling flame of our friendship – but discovering, at length, in spite of her prejudice against me, that I was perfectly harmless, and even well-intentioned, and that, between myself and my dog, her son derived a great deal of pleasure from the acquaintance that he would not otherwise have known, she ceased to object, and even welcomed my coming with a smile.

As for Arthur, he would shout his welcome from afar, and run to meet me fifty yards from his mother's side. If I happened to be on horseback, he was sure to get a canter or a gallop; or, if there was one of the draught horses within an available distance, he was treated to a steady ride upon that, which served his turn almost as well; but his mother would always follow and trudge beside him – not so much, I believe, to ensure his safe conduct, as to see that I instilled no objectionable notions into his infant mind, for she was ever on the watch, and never would allow him to be taken out of her sight. What pleased her best of all was to see him romping and racing with Sancho, while I walked by her side – not, I fear, for love of my company (though I sometimes deluded myself with

that idea), so much as for the delight she took in seeing her son thus happily engaged in the enjoyment of those active sports so invigorating to his tender frame, yet so seldom exercised for want of playmates suited to his years; and, perhaps, her pleasure was sweetened not a little by the fact of my being with her instead of with him, and therefore incapable of doing him any injury directly or indirectly, designedly or otherwise, small thanks to her for that same.

But sometimes, I believe, she really had some little gratification in conversing with me; and one bright February morning, during twenty minutes' stroll along the moor, she laid aside her usual asperity and reserve, and fairly entered into conversation with me, discoursing with so much eloquence and depth of thought and feeling on a subject happily coinciding with my own ideas, and looking so beautiful withal, that I went home enchanted; and on the way (morally) started to find myself thinking that, after all, it would, perhaps, be better to spend one's day with such a woman than with Eliza Millward; and then, I (figuratively) blushed for my inconstancy.

On entering the parlour I found Eliza there with Rose, and no one else. The surprise was not altogether so agreeable as it ought to have been. We chatted together a long time, but I found her rather frivolous, and even a little insipid, compared with the more matured and earnest Mrs Graham. Alas for human constancy!

'However,' thought I, 'I ought not to marry Eliza, since my mother so strongly objects to it, and I ought not to delude the girl with the idea that I intended to do so. Now, if this mood continue, I shall have less difficulty in emancipating my affections from her soft yet unrelenting sway; and, though Mrs Graham might be equally objectionable, I may be permitted, like the doctors, to cure a greater evil by a less, for I shall not fall seriously in love with the young widow, I think, nor she with me – that's certain – but if I find a little pleasure in her society I may surely be allowed to seek it; and if the star of her divinity be bright enough to dim the lustre of Eliza's, so much the better, but I scarcely can think it.'

And thereafter I seldom suffered a fine day to pass without paying a visit to Wildfell about the time my new acquaintance usually left her hermitage; but so frequently was I balked in my expectations of another interview, so changeable was she in her times of coming forth and in her places of resort, so transient were the occasional glimpses I was able to obtain, that I felt half inclined to think she took as much pains to avoid my company as I to seek hers; but this was too disagreeable a supposition to be entertained a moment after it could conveniently be dismissed.

One calm, clear afternoon, however, in March, as I was superintending the rolling of the meadow-land, and the repairing of a hedge in the valley, I saw Mrs Graham down by the brook, with a sketch-book in her hand, absorbed in the exercise of her favourite art, while Arthur was putting on the time with constructing dams and breakwaters in the shallow, stony stream. I was rather in want of amusement, and so rare an opportunity was not to be neglected; so, leaving both meadow and hedge, I quickly repaired to the spot, but not before Sancho, who, immediately upon perceiving his young friend, scoured at full gallop the intervening space, and pounced upon him with an impetuous mirth that precipitated the child almost into the middle of the beck; but, happily, the

stones preserved him from any serious wetting, while their smoothness prevented his being too much hurt to laugh at the untoward event.

Mrs Graham was studying the distinctive characters of the different varieties of trees in their winter nakedness, and copying, with a spirited, though delicate touch, their various ramifications. She did not talk much, but I stood and watched the progress of her pencil: it was a pleasure to behold it so dexterously guided by those fair and graceful fingers. But ere long their dexterity became impaired, they began to hesitate, to tremble slightly and make false strokes, and then suddenly came to a pause, while their owner laughingly raised her face to mine, and told me that her sketch did not profit by my superintendence.

'Then,' said I, 'I'll talk to Arthur till you've done.'

'I should like to have a ride, Mr Markham, if mamma will let me,' said the child.

'What on, my boy?'

'I think there's a horse in that field,' replied he, pointing to where the strong black mare was pulling the roller.

'No, no, Arthur; it's too far,' objected his mother.

But I promised to bring him back safe after a turn or two up and down the meadow; and when she looked at his eager face she smiled and let him go. It was the first time she had even allowed me to take him so much as half a field's length from her side.

Enthroned upon his monstrous steed, and solemnly proceeding up and down the wide, steep field, he looked the very incarnation of quiet, gleeful satisfaction and delight. The rolling, however, was soon completed; but when I dismounted the gallant horseman, and restored him to his mother, she seemed rather displeased at my keeping him so long. She had shut up her sketch-book, and been, probably, for some minutes impatiently waiting his return.

It was now high time to go home, she said, and would have bid me good evening, but I was not going to leave her yet: I accompanied her half way up the hill. She became more sociable, and I was beginning to be very happy; but, on coming within sight of the grim old hall, she stood still and turned towards me while she spoke, as if expecting I should go no further, that the conversation would end here, and I should now take leave and depart – as, indeed, it was time to do, for 'the clear, cold eve' was fast 'declining', the sun had set, and the gibbous moon was visibly brightening in the pale grey sky; but a feeling almost of compassion riveted me to the spot. It seemed hard to leave her to such a lonely, comfortless home. I looked up at it. Silent and grim it frowned before us. A faint, red light was gleaming from the lower windows of one wing, but all the other windows were in darkness, and many exhibited their black, cavernous gulfs, entirely destitute of glazing or framework.

'Do you not find it a desolate place to live in?' said I, after a moment of silent contemplation.

'I do, sometimes,' replied she. 'On winter evenings, when Arthur is in bed, and I am sitting there alone, hearing the bleak wind moaning round me and howling through the ruinous old chambers, no books or occupations can repress the dismal thoughts and apprehensions that come crowding in – but it is folly to give way to such weakness, I know. If Rachel is satisfied with such a life, why should not I? – Indeed I cannot be too thankful for such an asylum, while it is left me.'

# The Tenant of Wildfell Hall

The closing sentence was uttered in an undertone, as if spoken rather to herself than to me. She then bid me good evening and withdrew.

I had not proceeded many steps on my way homewards, when I perceived Mr Lawrence, on his pretty grey pony, coming up the rugged lane that crossed over the hill-top. I went a little out of my way to speak to him; for we had not met for some time.

'Was that Mrs Graham you were speaking to just now?' said he, after the first few words of greeting had passed between us.

'Yes.'

'Humph! I thought so.' He looked contemplatively at his horse's mane, as if he had some serious cause of dissatisfaction with it, or something else.

'Well! what then?'

'Oh, nothing!' replied he. 'Only, I thought you disliked her,' he quietly added, curling his classic lip with a slightly sarcastic smile.

'Suppose I did; mayn't a man change his mind on further acquaintance?'

'Yes, of course,' returned he, nicely reducing an entanglement in the pony's redundant hoary mane. Then suddenly turning to me, and fixing his shy, hazel eyes upon me with a steady, penetrating gaze, he added, 'then you have changed your mind?'

'I can't say that I have exactly. No, I think I hold the same opinion respecting her as before – but slightly ameliorated.'

'Oh!' He looked round for something else to talk about; and glancing up at the moon, made some remark upon the beauty of the evening, which I did not answer, as being irrelevant to the subject.

'Lawrence,' said I, calmly looking him in the face, 'are you in love with Mrs Graham?'

Instead of his being deeply offended at this, as I more than half expected he would, the first start of surprise at the audacious question was followed by a tittering laugh, as if he was highly amused at the idea.

'I in love with her!' repeated he. 'What makes you dream of such a thing?'

'From the interest you take in the progress of my acquaintance with the lady, and the changes of my opinion concerning her. I thought you might be jealous.'

He laughed again. 'Jealous! no – but I thought you were going to marry Eliza Millward?'

'You thought wrong then; I am not going to marry either one or the other – that I know of.'

'Then I think you'd better let them alone.'

'Are you going to marry Jane Wilson?'

He coloured, and played with the mane again, but answered:

'No, I think not.'

'Then you had better let her alone.'

She won't let me alone – he might have said; but he only looked silly and said nothing for the space of half a minute, and then made another attempt to turn the conversation; and this time, I let it pass; for he had borne enough: another word on the subject would have been like the last atom that breaks the camel's back.

I was too late for tea; but my mother had kindly kept the teapot and muffin warm upon the hob, and, though she scolded me a little, readily admitted my excuses; and when I complained of the flavour of the overdrawn tea, she poured

the remainder into the slop-basin, and bade Rose put some fresh into the pot, and reboil the kettle, which offices were performed with great commotion, and certain remarkable comments.

'Well! – if it had been me now, I should have had no tea at all – if it had been Fergus, even, he would have to put up with such as there was, and been told to be thankful, for it was far too good for him; but you, we can't do too much for you. It's always so – if there's anything particularly nice at table, mamma winks and nods at me, to abstain from it, and if I don't attend to that, she whispers, "don't eat so much of that, Rose; Gilbert will like it for his supper" – I'm nothing at all. In the parlour, it's "Come, Rose, put away your things, and let's have the room nice and tidy against they come in; and keep up a good fire; Gilbert likes a cheerful fire." In the kitchen – "Make that pie a large one, Rose; I dare say the boys'll be hungry; – and don't put so much pepper in, they'll not like it, I'm sure" – or, "Rose, don't put so many spices in the pudding, Gilbert likes it plain," – or, "Mind you put plenty of currants in the cake, Fergus likes plenty." If I say, "Well, mamma, I don't," I'm told I ought not to think of myself — "You know, Rose, in all household matters, we have only two things to consider, first, what's proper to be done, and, secondly, what's most agreeable to the gentlemen of the house – anything will do for the ladies."'

'And very good doctrine too,' said my mother. 'Gilbert thinks so, I'm sure.'

'Very convenient doctrine for us, at all events' said I; 'but if you would really study my pleasure, mother, you must consider your own comfort and convenience a little more than you do – as for Rose, I have no doubt she'll take care of herself; and whenever she does make a sacrifice or perform a remarkable act of devotedness, she'll take good care to let me know the extent of it. But for you, I might sink into the grossest condition of self-indulgence and carelessness about the wants of others, from the mere habit of being constantly cared for myself, and having all my wants anticipated or immediately supplied, while left in total ignorance of what is done for me, – if Rose did not enlighten me now and then; and I should receive all your kindness as a matter of course, and never know how much I owe you.'

'Ah! and you never will know, Gilbert, till you're married. Then, when you've got some trifling, self-conceited girl like Eliza Millward, careless of everything but her own immediate pleasure and advantage, or some misguided, obstinate woman like Mrs Graham, ignorant of her principal duties, and clever only in what concerns her least to know – then you'll find the difference.'

'It will do me good, mother; I was not sent into the world merely to exercise the good capacities and good feelings of others – was I? – but to exert my own towards them; and when I marry I shall expect to find more pleasure in making my wife happy and comfortable, than in being made so by her: I would rather give than receive.'

'Oh! that's all nonsense, my dear. It's mere boy's talk that! You'll soon tire of petting and humouring your wife, be she ever so charming, and then comes the trial.'

'Well, then, we must bear one another's burdens.'

'Then you must fall each into your proper place. You'll do your business, and she, if she's worthy of you, will do hers; but it's your business to please yourself, and hers to please you. I'm sure your poor, dear father was as good a husband as ever lived, and after the first six months or so were over, I should as soon

have expected him to fly, as to put himself out of his way to pleasure me. He always said I was a good wife, and did my duty; and he always did his – bless him! – he was steady and punctual, seldom found fault without a reason, always did justice to my good dinners, and hardly ever spoiled my cookery by delay – and that's as much as any woman can expect of any man.'

Is it so, Halford? Is that the extent of your domestic virtues; and does your happy wife exact no more?

# Chapter 7

Not many days after this, on a mild sunny morning – rather soft under foot; for the last fall of snow was only just wasted away, leaving yet a thin ridge, here and there, lingering on the fresh green grass beneath the hedges; but beside them already, the young primroses were peeping from among their moist, dark foliage, and the lark above was singing of summer, and hope, and love, and every heavenly thing – I was out on the hillside, enjoying those delights, and looking after the well-being of my young lambs and their mothers, when, on glancing round me, I beheld three persons ascending from the vale below. They were Eliza Millward, Fergus, and Rose; so I crossed the field to meet them; and, being told they were going to Wildfell Hall, I declared myself willing to go with them, and offering my arm to Eliza, who readily accepted it in lieu of my brother's, told the latter he might go back, for I would accompany the ladies.

'I beg your pardon!' exclaimed he. 'It's the ladies that are accompanying me, not I them. You had all had a peep at this wonderful stranger but me, and I could endure my wretched ignorance no longer – come what would, I must be satisfied; so I begged Rose to go with me to the hall, and introduce me to her at once. She swore she would not, unless Miss Eliza would go too; so I ran to the vicarage and fetched her; and we've come hooked all the way, as fond as a pair of lovers – and now you've taken her from me; and you want to deprive me of my walk and my visit besides. Go back to your fields and your cattle, you lubberly fellow; you're not fit to associate with ladies and gentlemen, like us, that have nothing to do but to run snooking about to our neighbours' houses, peeping into their private corners, and scenting out their secrets, and picking holes in their coats, when we don't find them ready-made to our hands – you don't understand such refined sources of enjoyment.'

'Can't you both go?' suggested Eliza, disregarding the latter half of the speech.

'Yes, both, to be sure!' cried Rose; 'the more the merrier – and I'm sure we shall want all the cheerfulness we can carry with us to that great, dark, gloomy room with its narrow latticed windows, and its dismal old furniture – unless she shows us into her studio again.'

# The Tenant of Wildfell Hall

So we went all in a body; and the meagre old maid-servant that opened the door, ushered us into an apartment, such as Rose had described to me as the scene of her first introduction to Mrs Graham, a tolerably spacious and lofty room, but obscurely lighted by the old-fashioned windows, the ceiling, panels, and chimney-piece of grim black oak – the latter elaborately but not very tastefully carved, – with tables and chairs to match, an old bookcase on one side of the fireplace, stocked with a motley assemblage of books, and an elderly cabinet piano on the other.

The lady was seated in a stiff, high-backed, arm-chair, with a small, round table, containing a desk and a work-basket, on one side of her, and her little boy on the other, who stood leaning his elbow on her knee, and reading to her, with wonderful fluency, from a small volume that lay in her lap; while she rested her hand on his shoulder, and abstractedly played with the long, wavy curls that fell on his ivory neck. They struck me as forming a pleasing contrast to all the surrounding objects; but of course their position was immediately changed on our entrance. I could only observe the picture during the few brief seconds that Rachel held the door for our admittance.

I do not think Mrs Graham was particularly delighted to see us; there was something indescribably chilly in her quiet, calm civility, but I did not talk much to her. Seating myself near the window, a little back from the circle, I called Arthur to me, and he and I and Sancho amused ourselves very pleasantly together, while the two young ladies baited his mother with small talk, and Fergus sat opposite, with his legs crossed, and his hands in his breeches' pockets, leaning back in his chair, and staring now up at the ceiling, now straight forward at his hostess (in a manner that made me strongly inclined to kick him out of the room), now whistling sotto voce to himself a snatch of a favourite air, now interrupting the conversation, or filling up a pause (as the case might be) with some most impertinent question or remark. At one time it was —

'It amazes me, Mrs Graham, how you could choose such a dilapidated, rickety old place as this to live in. If you couldn't afford to occupy the whole house, and have it mended up, why couldn't you take a neat little cottage?'

'Perhaps I was too proud, Mr Fergus,' replied she, smiling; 'perhaps I took a particular fancy for this romantic, old-fashioned place – but, indeed, it has many advantages over a cottage. In the first place, you see, the rooms are larger and more airy; in the second place, the unoccupied apartments, which I don't pay for, may serve as lumber-rooms, if I have anything to put in them; and they are very useful for my little boy to run about in on rainy days when he can't go out; and then there is the garden for him to play in, and for me to work in. You see I have effected some little improvement already,' continued she, turning to the window. 'There is a bed of young vegetables in that corner, and here are some snowdrops and primroses already in bloom – and there, too, is a yellow crocus just opening in the sunshine.'

'But then how can you bear such a situation – your nearest neighbours two miles distant, and nobody looking in or passing by? – Rose would go stark mad in such a place. She can't put on life unless she sees half-a-dozen fresh gowns and bonnets a day – not to speak of the faces within; but you might sit watching at these windows all day long, and never see so much as an old woman carrying her eggs to market.'

'I am not sure the loneliness of the place was not one of its chief recommen-

dations. I take no pleasure in watching people pass the windows; and I like to be quiet.'

'Oh! as good as to say, you wish we would all of us mind our own business, and let you alone.'

'No, I dislike an extensive acquaintance; but if I have a few friends, of course I am glad to see them occasionally. No one can be happy in eternal solitude. Therefore, Mr Fergus, if you choose to enter my house as a friend, I will make you welcome; if not, I must confess, I would rather you kept away.' She then turned and addressed some observation to Rose or Eliza.

'And Mrs Graham,' said he again, five minutes after, 'we were disputing, as we came along, a question that you can readily decide for us, as it mainly regarded yourself – and, indeed, we often hold discussions about our neighbours' concerns, and we, the indigenous plants of the soil, have known each other so long, and talked each other over so often, that we are quite sick of that game; so that a stranger coming amongst us makes an invaluable addition to our exhausted sources of amusement. Well, the question, or questions, you are requested to solve'—

'Hold your tongue, Fergus!' cried Rose, in a fever of apprehension and wrath.

'I won't, I tell you. The questions you are requested to solve are these:– First, concerning your birth, extraction, and previous residence. Some will have it that you are a foreigner, and some an Englishwoman; some a native of the north country, and some of the south; some say'—

'Well, Mr Fergus, I'll tell you. I'm an Englishwoman – and I don't see why any one should doubt it – and I was born in the country neither in the extreme north, nor south of our happy isle; and in the country I have chiefly passed my life, and now, I hope, you are satisfied; for I am not disposed to answer any more questions at present.'

'Except this'—

'No, not one more!' laughed she, and instantly quitting her seat, she sought refuge at the window by which I was seated, and, in very desperation, to escape my brother's persecutions, endeavoured to draw me into the conversation.

'Mr Markham,' said she, her rapid utterance and heightened colour too plainly evincing her disquietude; 'have you forgotten the fine sea-view we were speaking of some time ago? I think I must trouble you, now, to tell me the nearest way to it; for if this beautiful weather continue, I shall, perhaps, be able to walk there, and take my sketch; I have exhausted every other subject for painting; and I long to see it.'

I was about to comply with her request, but Rose would not suffer me to proceed.

'Oh, don't tell her, Gilbert!' cried she; 'she shall go with us. It's —— Bay you are thinking about, I suppose, Mrs Graham? It is a very long walk, too far for you, and out of the question for Arthur. But we were thinking about making a picnic to see it, some fine day; and, if you will wait till the settled fine weather comes, I'm sure we shall all be delighted to have you amongst us.'

Poor Mrs Graham looked dismayed, and attempted to make excuses, but Rose, either compassionating her lonely life, or anxious to cultivate her acquaintance, was determined to have her; and every objection was overruled. She was told it would only be a small party, and all friends, and that the best view of all was from —— Cliffs, full five miles distant.

# The Tenant of Wildfell Hall

'Just a nice walk for the gentlemen,' continued Rose; 'but the ladies will drive and walk by turns; for we shall have our pony-carriage, which will be plenty large enough to contain little Arthur and three ladies, together with your sketching apparatus, and our provisions.'

So the proposal was finally acceded to; and, after some further discussion respecting the time and manner of the projected excursion, we rose, and took our leave.

But this was only March: a cold, wet April, and two weeks of May passed over before we could venture forth on our expedition with the reasonable hope of obtaining that pleasure we sought in pleasant prospects, cheerful society, fresh air, good cheer and exercise, without the alloy of bad roads, cold winds, or threatening clouds. Then, on a glorious morning, we gathered our forces and set forth. The company consisted of Mrs and Master Graham, Mary and Eliza Millward, Jane and Richard Wilson, and Rose, Fergus, and Gilbert Markham.

Mr Lawrence had been invited to join us, but, for some reason best known to himself, had refused to give us his company. I had solicited the favour myself. When I did so, he hesitated, and asked who were going. Upon my naming Miss Wilson among the rest, he seemed half inclined to go, but when I mentioned Mrs Graham, thinking it might be a further inducement, it appeared to have a contrary effect, and he declined it altogether, and, to confess the truth, the decision was not displeasing to me, though I could scarcely tell you why.

It was about mid-day when we reached the place of our destination. Mrs Graham walked all the way to the cliffs; and little Arthur walked the greater part of it too; for he was now much more hardy and active than when he first entered the neighbourhood, and he did not like being in the carriage with strangers, while all his four friends, mamma, and Sancho, and Mr Markham, and Miss Millward, were on foot, journeying far behind, or passing through distant fields and lanes.

I have a very pleasant recollection of that walk, along the hard, white, sunny road, shaded here and there with bright green trees, and adorned with flowery banks, and blossoming hedges of delicious fragrance; or through pleasant fields and lanes, all glorious in the sweet flowers and brilliant verdure of delightful May. It was true, Eliza was not beside me; but she was with her friends in the pony-carriage, as happy, I trusted, as I was; and even when we pedestrians, having forsaken the highway for a short cut across the fields, beheld the little carriage far away, disappearing amid the green, embowering trees, I did not hate those trees for snatching the dear little bonnet and shawl from my sight, nor did I feel that all those intervening objects lay between my happiness and me; for, to confess the truth, I was too happy in the company of Mrs Graham to regret the absence of Eliza Millward.

The former, it is true, was most provokingly unsociable at first – seemingly bent upon talking to no one but Mary Millward and Arthur. She and Mary journeyed along together, generally with the child between them; – but where the road permitted, I always walked on the other side of her, Richard Wilson taking the other side of Miss Millward, and Fergus roving here and there according to his fancy; and after a while she became more friendly, and at length I succeeded in securing her attention almost entirely to myself – and then I was happy indeed; for whenever she did condescend to converse, I liked to listen. Where her opinions and sentiments tallied with mine, it was her extreme good

# The Tenant of Wildfell Hall

sense, her exquisite taste and feeling, that delighted me; where they differed it was still her uncompromising boldness in the avowal or defence of that difference, her earnestness and keenness, that piqued my fancy: and even when she angered me by her unkind words or looks, and her uncharitable conclusions respecting me, it only made me the more dissatisfied with myself for having so unfavourably impressed her, and the more desirous to vindicate my character and disposition in her eyes, and, if possible, to win her esteem.

At length our walk was ended. The increasing height and boldness of the hills had for some time intercepted the prospect; but, on gaining the summit of a steep acclivity, and looking downward, an opening lay before us – and the blue sea burst upon our sight! – deep violet blue – not deadly calm, but covered with glinting breakers – diminutive white specks twinkling on its bosom, and scarcely to be distinguished, by the keenest vision, from the little sea-mews that sported above, their white wings glittering in the sunshine: only one or two vessels were visible: and those were far away.

I looked at my companion to see what she thought of this glorious scene. She said nothing: but she stood still, and fixed her eyes upon it with a gaze that assured me she was not disappointed. She had very fine eyes, by-the-bye – I don't know whether I've told before, but they were full of soul, large, clear, and nearly black – not brown, but very dark grey. A cool, reviving breeze blew from the sea – soft, pure, salubrious: it waved her drooping ringlets, and imparted a livelier colour to her usually too pallid lip and cheek. She felt its exhilarating influence, and so did I – I felt it tingling through my frame, but dared not give way to it while she remained so quiet. There was an aspect of subdued exhilaration in her face, that kindled into almost a smile of exalted, glad intelligence as her eye met mine. Never had she looked so lovely: never had my heart so warmly cleaved to her as now. Had we been left two minutes longer, standing there alone, I cannot answer for the consequences. Happily for my discretion, perhaps for my enjoyment during the remainder of the day, we were speedily summoned to the repast – a very respectable collation, which Rose, assisted by Miss Wilson and Eliza, who, having shared her seat in the carriage, had arrived with her a little before the rest, had set out upon an elevated platform overlooking the sea, and sheltered from the hot sun by a shelving rock and overhanging trees.

Mrs Graham seated herself at a distance from me. Eliza was my nearest neighbour. She exerted herself to be agreeable, in her gentle, unobtrusive way, and was, no doubt, as fascinating and charming as ever, if I could only have felt it. But soon, my heart began to warm towards her once again; and we were all very merry and happy together – as far as I could see – throughout the protracted, social meal.

When that was over, Rose summoned Fergus to help her to gather up the fragments, and the knives, dishes, etc., and restore them to the baskets; and Mrs Graham took her camp stool and drawing materials; and having begged Miss Millward to take charge of her precious son, and strictly enjoined him not to wander from his new guardian's side, she left us, and proceeded along the steep, stony hill, to a loftier, more precipitous eminence at some distance, whence a still finer prospect was to be had, where she preferred taking her sketch, though some of the ladies told her it was a frightful place, and advised her not to attempt it.

258

# The Tenant of Wildfell Hall

When she was gone, I felt as if there was to be no more fun – though it was difficult to say what she had contributed to the hilarity of the party. No jests, and little laughter, had escaped her lips; but her smile had animated my mirth, a keen observation or a cheerful word from her had insensibly sharpened my wits, and thrown an interest over all that was done and said by the rest. Even my conversation with Eliza had been enlivened by her presence, though I knew it not; and now that she was gone, Eliza's playful nonsense ceased to amuse me – nay, grew wearisome to my soul, and I grew weary of amusing her: I felt myself drawn by an irresistible attraction to that distant point where the fair artist sat and plied her solitary task – and not long did I attempt to resist it: while my little neighbour was exchanging a few words with Miss Wilson, I rose and cannily slipped away. A few rapid strides, and a little active clambering, soon brought me to the place where she was seated – a narrow ledge of rock at the very verge of the cliff, which descended with a steep, precipitous slant, quite down to the rocky shore.

She did not hear me coming: the falling of my shadow across her paper gave her an electric start; and she looked hastily round – any other lady of my acquaintance would have screamed under such a sudden alarm.

'Oh! I didn't know it was you. – Why did you startle me so?' said she, somewhat testily. 'I hate anybody to come upon me so unexpectedly.'

'Why, what did you take me for?' said I: 'if I had known you were so nervous, I would have been more cautious; but'—

'Well, never mind. What did you come for? are they all coming?'

'No; this little ledge could scarcely contain them all.'

'I'm glad, for I'm tired of talking.'

'Well, then, I won't talk. I'll only sit and watch your drawing.'

'Oh, but you know I don't like that.'

'Then I'll content myself with admiring this magnificent prospect.'

She made no objection to this; and, for some time, sketched away in silence. But I could not help stealing a glance, now and then, from the splendid view at our feet to the elegant white hand that held the pencil, and the graceful neck and glossy raven curls that drooped over the paper.

'Now,' thought I, 'if I had but a pencil and a morsel of paper, I could make a lovelier sketch than hers, admitting I had the power to delineate faithfully what is before me.'

But though this satisfaction was denied me, I was very well content to sit beside her there, and say nothing.

'Are you there still, Mr Markham?' said she at length, looking round upon me – for I was seated a little behind on a mossy projection of the cliff.– 'Why don't you go and amuse yourself with your friends?'

'Because I am tired of them, like you; and I shall have enough of them tomorrow – or at any time hence; but you I may not have the pleasure of seeing again for I know not how long.'

'What was Arthur doing when you came away?'

'He was with Miss Millward where you left him – all right, but hoping mamma would not be long away. You didn't entrust him to me, by-the-bye,' I grumbled, 'though I had the honour of a much longer acquaintance; but Miss Millward has the art of conciliating and amusing children,' I carelessly added, 'if she is good for nothing else.'

# The Tenant of Wildfell Hall

'Miss Millward has many estimable qualities, which such as you cannot be expected to perceive or appreciate. Will you tell Arthur that I shall come in a few minutes?'

'If that be the case, I will wait, with your permission, till those few minutes are past; and then I can assist you to descend this difficult path.'

'Thank you – I always manage best, on such occasions, without assistance.'

'But, at least, I can carry your stool and sketch-book.'

She did not deny me this favour; but I was rather offended at her evident desire to be rid of me, and was beginning to repent of my pertinacity, when she somewhat appeased me by consulting my taste and judgment about some doubtful matter in her drawing. My opinion, happily, met her approbation, and the improvement I suggested was adopted without hesitation.

'I have often wished in vain,' said she, 'for another's judgment to appeal to when I could scarcely trust the direction of my own eye and head, they having been so long occupied with the contemplation of a single object, as to become almost incapable of forming a proper idea respecting it.'

'That,' replied I, 'is only one of the many evils to which a solitary life exposes us.'

'True,' said she; and again we relapsed into silence.

About two minutes after, however, she declared her sketch complete, and closed the book.

On returning to the scene of our repast, we found all the company had deserted it, with the exception of three – Mary Millward, Richard Wilson, and Arthur Graham. The younger gentleman lay fast asleep with his head pillowed on the lady's lap; the other was seated beside her with a pocket edition of some classic author in his hand. He never went anywhere without such a companion wherewith to improve his leisure moments: all time seemed lost that was not devoted to study, or exacted, by his physical nature, for the bare support of life. Even now, he could not abandon himself to the enjoyment of that pure air and balmy sunshine – that splendid prospect, and those soothing sounds, the music of the waves and of the soft wind in the sheltering trees above him – not even with a lady by his side (though not a very charming one, I will allow) – he must pull out his book and make the most of his time while digesting his temperate meal, and reposing his weary limbs, unused to so much exercise.

Perhaps, however, he spared a moment to exchange a word or a glance with his companion now and then – at any rate, she did not appear at all resentful of his conduct; for her homely features wore an expression of unusual cheerfulness and serenity, and she was studying his pale, thoughtful face with great complacency when we arrived.

The journey homeward was by no means so agreeable, to me, as the former part of the day; for now Mrs Graham was in the carriage, and Eliza Millward was the companion of my walk. She had observed my preference for the young widow, and evidently felt herself neglected. She did not manifest her chagrin by keen reproaches, bitter sarcasms, or pouting sullen silence – any or all of these I could easily have endured, or lightly laughed away; but she showed it by a kind of gentle melancholy, a mild, reproachful sadness that cut me to the heart. I tried to cheer her up, and apparently succeeded in some degree, before the walk was over; but in the very act my conscience reproved me, knowing, as I

did, that, sooner or later, the tie must be broken, and this was only nourishing false hopes, and putting off the evil day.

When the pony-carriage had approached as near Wildfell Hall as the road would permit – unless, indeed, it proceeded up the long rough lane, which Mrs Graham would not allow – the young widow and her son alighted, relinquishing the latter's seat to Rose; and I persuaded Eliza to take the driver's place. Having put her comfortably in, bid her take care of the evening air, and wished her a kind good-night, I felt considerably relieved, and hastened to offer my services to Mrs Graham to carry her apparatus up the fields, but she had already hung her camp-stool on her arm and taken her sketch-book in her hand; and insisted upon bidding me adieu then and there, with the rest of the company. But this time, she declined my proffered aid in so kind and friendly a manner that I almost forgave her.

# Chapter 8

Six weeks had passed away. It was a splendid morning about the close of June. Most of the hay was cut, but the last week had been very unfavourable; and now that fine weather was come at last, being determined to make the most of it, I had gathered all hands together into the hayfield, and was working away myself, in the midst of them, in my shirtsleeves, with a light, shady straw hat on my head, catching up armfuls of moist, reeking grass, and shaking it out to the four winds of heaven, at the head of a goodly file of servants and hirelings – intending so to labour, from morning to night, with as much zeal and assiduity as I could look for from any of them, as well to prosper the work by my own exertion as to animate the workers by my example – when lo! my resolutions were overthrown in a moment, by the simple fact of my brother's running up to me and putting into my hand a small parcel, just arrived from London, which I had been for some time expecting. I tore off the cover, and disclosed and elegant and portable edition of *Marmion*.

'I guess I know who that's for,' said Fergus, who stood looking on while I complacently examined the volume. 'That's for Miss Eliza, now.'

He pronounced this with a tone and look so prodigiously knowing, that I was glad to contradict him.

'You're wrong, my lad,' said I; and taking up my coat, I deposited the book in one of its pockets, and then put it on (*i.e.*, the coat). 'Now come here, you idle dog, and make yourself useful for once,' I continued – 'Pull off your coat, and take my place in the field till I come back.'

'Till you come back? – and where are you going, pray?'

'No matter where – the when is all that concerns you; and I shall be back by dinner, at least.'

# The Tenant of Wildfell Hall

'Oh, ho! and I'm to labour away till then, am I? – and to keep all these fellows hard at it besides? Well, well! I'll submit – for once in a way. – Come, my lads, you must look sharp: I'm come to help you now: – and woe be to that man, or woman either, that pauses for a moment amongst you – whether to stare about him, to scratch his head, or blow his nose – no pretext will serve – nothing but work, work, work in the sweat of your face,' etc., etc.

Leaving him thus haranguing the people, more to their amusement than edification, I returned to the house, and having made some alteration in my toilet, hastened away to Wildfell Hall with the book in my pocket; for it was destined for the shelves of Mrs Graham.

'What, then, had she and you got on so well together as to come to the giving and receiving of presents?' – Not precisely, old buck; this was my first experiment in that line; and I was very anxious to see the result of it.

We had met several times since the —— Bay excursion, and I had found she was not averse to my company, provided I confined my conversation to the discussion of abstract matters or topics of common interest; – the moment I touched upon the sentimental or the complimentary, or made the slightest approach to tenderness in word or look, I was not only punished by an immediate change in her manner at the time, but doomed to find her more cold and distant, if not entirely inaccessible, when next I sought her company. This circumstance did not greatly disconcert me, however, because I attributed it, not so much to any dislike of my person, as to some absolute resolution against a second marriage formed prior to the time of our acquaintance, whether from excess of affection for her late husband, or because she had had enough of him and the matrimonial state together. At first, indeed, she had seemed to take a pleasure in mortifying my vanity and crushing my presumption – relentlessly nipping off bud by bud as they ventured to appear; and then, I confess, I was deeply wounded, though, at the same time, stimulated to seek revenge; – but latterly, finding, beyond a doubt, that I was not that empty-headed coxcomb she had at first supposed me, she had repulsed my modest advances in quite a different spirit. It was a kind of serious, almost sorrowful displeasure, which I soon learnt carefully to avoid awakening.

'Let me first establish my position as a friend,' thought I, – 'the patron and playfellow of her son, the sober, solid, plain-dealing friend of herself, and then, when I have made myself fairly necessary to her comfort and enjoyment in life (as I believe I can), we'll see what next may be effected.

So we talked about painting, poetry, and music, theology, geology, and philosophy: once or twice I lent her a book, and once she lent me one in return: I met her in her walks as often as I could; I came to her house as often as I dared. My first pretext for invading the sanctum was to bring Arthur a little waddling puppy of which Sancho was the father, and which delighted the child beyond expression, and, consequently, could not fail to please his mamma. My second was to bring him a book, which, knowing his mother's particularity, I had carefully selected, and which I submitted for her approbation before presenting it to him. Then, I brought her some plants for her garden, in my sister's name – having previously persuaded Rose to send them. Each of these times I inquired after the picture she was painting from the sketch taken on the cliff, and was admitted into the studio, and asked my opinion or advice respecting its progress.

# The Tenant of Wildfell Hall

My last visit had been to return the book she had lent me; and then it was, that, in casually discussing the poetry of Sir Walter Scott, she had expressed a wish to see *Marmion*, and I had conceived the presumptuous idea of making her a present of it, and, on my return home, instantly sent for the smart little volume I had this morning received. But an apology for invading the hermitage was still necessary; so I had furnished myself with a blue morocco collar for Arthur's little dog; and that being given and received, with much more joy and gratitude, on the part of the receiver, than the worth of the gift or the selfish motive of the giver deserved, I ventured to ask Mrs Graham for one more look at the picture, if it was still there.

'Oh, yes! come in,' said she (for I had met them in the garden). 'It is finished and framed, all ready for sending away; but give me your last opinion, and, if you can suggest any further improvement, it shall be – duly considered, at least.'

The picture was strikingly beautiful: it was the very scene itself, transferred as if by magic to the canvas; but I expressed my approbation in guarded terms, and few words, for fear of displeasing her. She however, attentively watched my looks, and her artist's pride was gratified, no doubt, to read my heartfelt admiration in my eyes. But, while I gazed, I thought upon the book, and wondered how it was to be presented. My heart failed me; but I determined not to be such a fool as to come away without having made the attempt. It was useless waiting for an opportunity, and useless trying to concoct a speech for the occasion. The more plainly and naturally the thing was done, the better, I thought; so I just looked out of the window to screw up my courage, and then pulled out the book, turned round, and put it into her hand, with this short explanation—

'You were wishing to see *Marmion*, Mrs Graham; and here it is, if you will be so kind as to take it.'

A momentary blush suffused her face – perhaps a blush of sympathetic shame for such an awkward style of presentation: she gravely examined the volume on both sides; then silently turned over the leaves, knitting her brows the while, in serious cogitation; then closed the book, and turning from it to me, quietly asked the price of it – I felt the hot blood rush to my face.

'I'm sorry to offend you, Mr Markham,' said she, 'but unless I pay for the book, I cannot take it.' And she laid it on the table.

'Why cannot you?'

'Because' – she paused, and looked at the carpet.

'Why cannot you?' I repeated, with a degree of irascibility that roused her to lift her eyes, and look me steadily in the face.

'Because I don't like to put myself under obligations that I can never repay – I am obliged to you already for your kindness to my son; but his grateful affection and your own good feelings must reward you for that.'

'Nonsense!' ejaculated I.

She turned her eyes on me again, with a look of quiet, grave surprise, that had the effect of a rebuke, whether intended for such or not.

'Then you won't take the book?' I asked, more mildly than I had yet spoken.

'I will gladly take it, if you will let me pay for it.'

I told her the exact price, and the cost of the carriage besides, in as calm a tone as I could command – for, in fact, I was ready to weep with disappointment and vexation.

She produced her purse, and coolly counted out the money, but hesitated to put it into my hand. Attentively regarding me, in a tone of soothing softness, she observed—

'You think yourself insulted, Mr Markham – I wish I could make you understand that – that I'—

'I do understand you, perfectly,' I said. 'You think that if you were to accept that trifle from me now, I should presume upon it hereafter; but you are mistaken: – if you will only oblige me by taking it, believe me, I shall build no hopes upon it, and consider this no precedent for future favours: – and it is nonsense to talk about putting yourself under obligations to me when you must know that in such a case the obligation is entirely on my side, – the favour on yours.'

'Well, then, I'll take you at your word,' she answered, with a most angelic smile, returning the odious money to her purse – 'but remember!'

'I will remember – what I have said; – but do not you punish my presumption by withdrawing your friendship entirely from me, – or expect me to atone for it by being more distant than before,' said I, extending my hand to take leave, for I was too much excited to remain.

'Well then! let us be as we were,' replied she, frankly placing her hand in mine; and while I held it there, I had much difficulty to refrain from pressing it to my lips; – but that would be suicidal madness; I had been bold enough already, and this premature offering had well-nigh given the death-blow to my hopes.

It was with an agitated burning heart and brain that I hurried homewards, regardless of that scorching noonday sun – forgetful of everything but her I had just left – regretting nothing but her impenetrability, and my own precipitancy and want of tact – fearing nothing but her hateful resolution and my inability to overcome it – hoping nothing– But halt, – I will not bore you with my conflicting hopes and fears – my serious cogitations and resolves.

# Chapter 9

Though my affections might now be said to be fairly weaned from Eliza Millward, I did not yet entirely relinquish my visits to the vicarage, because I wanted, as it were, to let her down easy; without raising much sorrow, or incurring much resentment, – or making myself the talk of the parish; and besides, if I had wholly kept away, the vicar, who looked upon my visits as paid chiefly, if not entirely, to himself, would have felt himself decidedly affronted by the neglect. But when I called there the day after my interview with Mrs Graham, he happened to be from home – a circumstance by no means so agreeable to me now as it had been on former occasions. Miss Millward was

there, it is true, but she, of course, would be little better than a nonentity. However, I resolved to make my visit a short one, and to talk to Eliza in a brotherly, friendly sort of way, such as our long acquaintance might warrant me in assuming, and which, I thought, could neither give offence nor serve to encourage false hopes.

It was never my custom to talk about Mrs Graham either to her or to any one else; but I had not been seated three minutes, before she brought that lady on to the carpet herself, in a rather remarkable manner.

'Oh, Mr Markham!' said she, with a shocked expression and voice subdued almost to a whisper, 'what do you think of these shocking reports about Mrs Graham? – can you encourage us to disbelieve them?'

'What reports?'

'Ah, now! you know!' she slyly smiled and shook her head.

'I know nothing about them. What in the world do you mean, Eliza?'

'Oh, don't ask me! *I* can't explain it.' She took up the cambric handkerchief which she had been beautifying with a deep lace border, and began to be very busy.

'What is it, Miss Millward? What does she mean?' said I, appealing to her sister, who seemed to be absorbed in the hemming of a large, coarse sheet.

'I don't know,' replied she. 'Some idle slander somebody has been inventing, I suppose. I never heard it till Eliza told me the other day, – but if all the parish dinned it in my ears, I shouldn't believe a word of it – I know Mrs Graham too well!'

'Quite right, Miss Millward! – and so do I – whatever it may be.'

'Well!' observed Eliza, with a gentle sigh, 'it's well to have such a comfortable assurance regarding the worth of those we love. I only wish you may not find your confidence misplaced.'

And she raised her face, and gave me such a look of sorrowful tenderness as might have melted my heart, but within those eyes there lurked a something that I did not like; and I wondered how I ever could have admired them; her sister's honest face and small grey optics appeared far more agreeable; but I was out of temper with Eliza, at that moment, for her insinuations against Mrs Graham, which were false, I was certain, whether she knew it or not.

I said nothing more on the subject, however, at the time, and but little on any other; for, finding I could not well recover my equanimity, I presently rose and took leave, excusing myself under the plea of business at the farm; and to the farm I went, not troubling my mind one whit about the possible truth of these mysterious reports, but only wondering what they were, by whom originated, and on what foundations raised, and how they could the most effectually be silenced or disproved.

A few days after this, we had another of our quiet little parties, to which the usual company of friends and neighbours had been invited, and Mrs Graham among the number. She could not now absent herself under the plea of dark evenings or inclement weather, and, greatly to my relief, she came. Without her I should have found the whole affair an intolerable bore; but the moment of her arrival brought new life to the house, and though I must not neglect the other guests for her, or expect to engross much of her attention and conversation to myself alone, I anticipated an evening of no common enjoyment.

Mr Lawrence came too. He did not arrive till some time after the rest were

# The Tenant of Wildfell Hall

assembled. I was curious to see how he would comport himself to Mrs Graham. A slight bow was all that passed between them on his entrance; and having politely greeted the other members of the company, he seated himself quite aloof from the young widow, between my mother and Rose.

'Did you ever see such art?' whispered Eliza, who was my nearest neighbour. 'Would you not say they were perfect strangers?'

'Almost; but what then?'

'What then! why, you can't pretend to be ignorant?'

'Ignorant of what?' demanded I, so sharply that she started and replied—

'Oh, hush! don't speak so loud.'

'Well, tell me then,' I answered in a lower tone, 'what is it you mean? I hate enigmas.'

'Well, you know, I don't vouch for the truth of it – indeed, far from it – but haven't you heard'—

'I've heard nothing, except from you.'

'You must be wilfully deaf then, for any one will tell you that; but I shall only anger you by repeating it, I see, so I had better hold my tongue.'

She closed her lips and folded her hands before her with an air of injured meekness.

'If you had wished not to anger me, you should have held your tongue from the beginning; or else spoken out plainly and honestly all you had to say.'

She turned aside her face, pulled out her handkerchief, rose and went to the window, where she stood for some time, evidently dissolved in tears. I was astounded, provoked, ashamed – not so much of my harshness as for her childish weakness. However, no one seemed to notice her, and shortly after we were summoned to the tea-table; in those parts it was customary to sit to the table at tea-time, on all occasions, and make a meal of it, for we dined early. On taking my seat, I had Rose on one side of me, and an empty chair on the other.

'May I sit by you?' said a soft voice at my elbow.

'If you like,' was the reply; and Eliza slipped into the vacant chair; then looking up into my face with a half-sad, half-playful smile, she whispered—

'You're so stern, Gilbert.'

I handed down her tea with a slightly contemptuous smile, and said nothing, for I had nothing to say.

'What have I done to offend you?' said she, more plaintively. 'I wish I knew.'

'Come, take your tea, Eliza, and don't be foolish,' responded I, handing her the sugar and cream.

Just then, there arose a slight commotion on the other side of me, occasioned by Miss Wilson's coming to negotiate an exchange of seats with Rose.

'Will you be so good as to exchange places with me, Miss Markham?' said she, 'for I don't like to sit by Mrs. Graham. If your mamma thinks proper to invite such persons to her house, she cannot object to her daughter's keeping company with them.'

This latter clause was added in a sort of soliloquy when Rose was gone; but I was not polite enough to let it pass.

'Will you be so good as to tell me what you mean, Miss Wilson?' said I.

The question startled her a little, but not much.

'Why, Mr Markham,' replied she coolly, having quickly recovered her self-possession, 'it surprises me rather that Mrs Markham should invite such a

# The Tenant of Wildfell Hall

person as Mrs Graham to her house; but, perhaps, she is not aware that the lady's character is considered scarcely respectable.'

'She is not, nor am I; and therefore you will oblige me by explaining your meaning a little further.'

'This is scarcely the time or the place for such explanations; but I think you can hardly be so ignorant as you pretend, you must know her as well as I do.'

'I think I do, perhaps a little better; and therefore, if you will inform me what you have heard or imagined against her, I shall perhaps be able to set you right.'

'Can you tell me, then, who was her husband, or if she ever had any?'

Indignation kept me silent. At such a time and place I could not trust myself to answer.

'Have you never observed,' said Eliza, 'what a striking likeness there is between that child of hers and'—

'And whom?' demanded Miss Wilson, with an air of cold, but keen severity.

Eliza was startled; the timidly spoken suggestion had been intended for my ear alone.

'Oh, I beg your pardon!' pleaded she, 'I may be mistaken – perhaps I was mistaken.' But she accompanied the words with a sly glance of derision directed to me from the corner of her disingenuous eye.

'There's no need to ask my pardon,' replied her friend, 'but I see no one here that at all resembles that child, except his mother; and when you hear ill-natured reports, Miss Eliza, I will thank you, that is, I think you will do well, to refrain from repeating them. I presume the person you allude to is Mr Lawrence; but I think I can assure you that your suspicions, in that respect, are utterly misplaced; and if he has any particular connection with the lady at all (which no one has a right to assert), as least he has (what cannot be said of some others) sufficient sense of propriety to withhold him from acknowledging anything more than a bowing acquaintance in the presence of respectable persons; he was evidently both surprised and annoyed to find her here.'

'Go it!' cried Fergus, who sat on the other side of Eliza, and was the only individual who shared that side of the table with us, 'go it like bricks! mind you don't leave her one stone upon another.'

Miss Wilson drew herself up with a look of freezing scorn, but said nothing. Eliza would have replied, but I interrupted her by saying as calmly as I could, though in a tone which betrayed, no doubt, some little of what I felt within—

'We have had enough of this subject; if we can only speak to slander our betters, let us hold our tongues.'

'I think you'd better,' observed Fergus, 'and so does our good parson; he has been addressing the company in his richest vein all the while, and eyeing you from time to time, with looks of stern distaste, while you sat there, irreverently whispering and muttering together; and once he paused in the middle of a story or a sermon, I don't know which, and fixed his eyes upon you, Gilbert, as much as to say, "When Mr Markham has done flirting with those two ladies I will proceed."'

What more was said at the tea-table I cannot tell, nor how I found patience to sit till the meal was over. I remember, however, that I swallowed with difficulty the remainder of the tea that was in my cup and ate nothing: and that the first thing I did was to stare at Arthur Graham, who sat beside his mother on the opposite side of the table, and the second to stare at Mr Lawrence, who

sat below; and, first, it struck me that there was a likeness; but, on further contemplation, I concluded it was only in imagination. Both, it is true, had more delicate features and smaller bones than commonly fall to the lot of individuals of the rougher sex, and Lawrence's complexion was pale and clear, and Arthur's delicately fair; but Arthur's tiny, somewhat snubby nose could never become so long and straight as Mr Lawrence's; and the outline of his face, though not full enough to be round, and too finely converging to the small, dimpled chin to be square, could never be drawn out to the long oval of the other's, while the child's hair was evidently of a lighter, warmer tint than the elder gentleman's had ever been, and his large, clear, blue eyes, though prematurely serious at times, were utterly dissimilar to the shy hazel eyes of Mr Lawrence, whence the sensitive soul looked so distrustfully forth, as ever ready to retire within, from the offences of a too rude, too uncongenial world. Wretch that I was to harbour that detestable idea for a moment! Did I not know Mrs Graham? Had I not seen her, conversed with her time after time? Was I not certain that she, in intellect, in purity and elevation of soul, was immeasurably superior to any of her detractors; that she was, in fact, the noblest, the most adorable, of her sex I had ever beheld, or even imagined to exist? Yes, and I would say with Mary Millward (sensible girl as she was), that if all the parish, say, or all the world, should din these horrible lies in my ears, I would not believe them, for I knew her better than they.

Meantime my brain was on fire with indignation, and my heart seemed ready to burst from its prison with conflicting passions. I regarded my two fair neighbours with a feeling of abhorrence and loathing I scarcely endeavoured to conceal. I was rallied from several quarters for my abstraction and ungallant neglect of the ladies; but I cared little for that: all I cared about, besides that one grand subject of my thoughts, was to see the cups travel up to the tea-tray, and not come down again. I thought Mr Millward never would cease telling us that he was no tea-drinker, and that it was highly injurious to keep loading the stomach with slops to the exclusion of more wholesome sustenance, and so give himself time to finish his fourth cup.

At length it was over; and I rose and left the table and the guests without a word of apology – I could endure their company no longer. I rushed out to cool my brain in the balmy evening air, and to compose my mind or indulge my passionate thoughts in the solitude of the garden.

To avoid being seen from the windows I went down a quiet little avenue that skirted one side of the enclosure, at the bottom of which was a seat embowered in roses and honeysuckles. Here I sat down to think over the virtues and wrongs of the lady of Wildfell Hall; but I had not been so occupied two minutes, before voices and laughter, and glimpses of moving objects through the trees, informed me that the whole company had turned out to take an airing in the garden too. However, I nestled up in a corner of the bower, and hoped to retain possession of it, secure alike from observation and intrusion. But no – confound it – there was some one coming down the avenue! Why couldn't they enjoy the flowers and sunshine of the open garden, and leave that sunless nook to me, and the gnats and midges.

But, peeping through my fragrant screen of the interwoven branches to discover who the intruders were (for a murmur of voices told me it was more than one), my vexation instantly subsided, and far other feelings agitated my still unquiet soul; for there was Mrs Graham, slowly moving down the walk

# The Tenant of Wildfell Hall

with Arthur by her side, and no one else. Why were they alone? Had the poison of detracting tongues already spread through all; and had they all turned their backs upon her? I now recollected having seen Mrs Wilson, in the early part of the evening, edging her chair close up to my mother, and bending forward, evidently in the delivery of some important, confidential intelligence; and from the incessant wagging of her head, the frequent distortions of her wrinkled physiognomy, and the winking and malicious twinkle of her little ugly eyes, I judged it was some spicy piece of scandal that engaged her powers; and from the cautious privacy of the communication I supposed some person then present was the luckless object of her calumnies; and from all these tokens, together with my mother's looks and gestures of mingled horror and incredulity, I now concluded that object to have been Mrs Graham. I did not emerge from my place of concealment till she had nearly reached the bottom of the walk, lest my appearance should drive her away; and when I did step forward she stood still and seemed inclined to turn back as it was.

'Oh, don't let us disturb you, Mr Markham'! said she. 'We came here to seek retirement ourselves, not to intrude on your seclusion.'

'I am no hermit, Mrs Graham – though I own it looks rather like it to absent myself in this uncourteous fashion from my guests.'

'I feared you were unwell,' said she, with a look of real concern.

'I was rather, but it's over now. Do sit here a little and rest, and tell me how you like this arbour,' said I, and lifting Arthur by the shoulders, I planted him in the middle of the seat by way of securing his mamma, who, acknowledging it to be a tempting place of refuge, threw herself back in one corner while I took possession of the other.

But that word refuge disturbed me. Had their unkindness then really driven her to seek for peace in solitude?

'Why have they left you alone?' I asked.

'It is I who have left them,' was the smiling rejoinder. 'I was wearied to death with small talk – nothing wears me out like that. I cannot imagine how they go on as they do.'

I could not help smiling at the serious depth of her wonderment.

'Is it that they think it a duty to be continually talking,' pursued she, 'and so never pause to think, but fill up with aimless trifles and vain repetitions when subjects of real interest fail to present themselves? Or do they really take a pleasure in such discourse?'

'Very likely they do,' said I: 'their shallow minds can hold no great ideas, and their light heads are carried away by trivialities that would not move a better-furnished skull: and their only alternative to such discourse is to plunge over head and ears into the slough of scandal – which is their chief delight.'

'Not all of them, surely?' cried the lady, astonished at the bitterness of my remark.

'No, certainly; I exonerate my sister from such degraded tastes and my mother, too, if you included her in your animadversions.'

'I meant no animadversions against any one, and certainly intended no disrespectful allusions to your mother. I have known some sensible persons adepts in that style of conversation when circumstances impelled them to it; but it is a gift I cannot boast the possession of. I kept up my attention on this occasion as long as I could, but when my powers were exhausted I stole away to seek a

few minutes' repose in this quiet walk. I hate talking where there is no exchange of ideas or sentiments, and no good given or received.'

'Well,' said I, 'if ever I trouble you with my loquacity tell me so at once, and I promise not to be offended; for I possess the faculty of enjoying the company of those I— of my friends as well in silence as in conversation.'

'I don't quite believe you; but if it were so you would exactly suit me for a companion.'

'I am all you wish, then, in other respects?'

'No, I don't mean that. How beautiful those little clusters of foliage look, where the sun comes through behind them!' said she, on purpose to change the subject.

And they did look beautiful, where at intervals the level rays of the sun penetrating the thickness of trees and shrubs on the opposite side of the path before us, relieved their dusky verdure by displaying patches of semi-transparent leaves of resplendent golden green.

'I almost wish I were not a painter,' observed my companion.

'Why so! one would think at such a time you would most exult in your privilege of being able to imitate the various brilliant and delightful touches of nature.'

'No; for instead of delivering myself up to the full enjoyment of them as others do, I am always troubling my head about how I could produce the same effect upon canvas; and as that can never be done, it is mere vanity and vexation of spirit.'

'Perhaps you cannot do it to satisfy yourself, but you may and do succeed in delighting others with the result of your endeavours.'

'Well, after all I should not complain: perhaps few people gain their livelihood with so much pleasure in their toil as I do. Here is some one coming.'

She seemed vexed at the interruption.

'It is only Mr Lawrence and Miss Wilson,' said I, 'coming to enjoy a quiet stroll. They will not disturb us.'

I could not quite decipher the expression on her face; but I was satisfied there was no jealousy therein. What business had I to look for it?

'What sort of a person is Miss Wilson?' she asked.

'She is elegant and accomplished above the generality of her birth and station; and some say she is lady-like and agreeable.'

'I thought her somewhat frigid, and rather supercilious in her manner today.'

'Very likely she might be so to you. She has possibly taken a prejudice against you, for I think she regards you in the light of a rival.'

'Me! Impossible, Mr Markham!' said she, evidently astonished and annoyed.

'Well, I know nothing about it,' returned I, rather doggedly; for I thought her annoyance was chiefly against myself.

The pair had now approached within a few paces of us. Our arbour was set snugly back in a corner before which the avenue at its termination turned off into the more airy walk along the bottom of the garden. As they approached this, I saw, by the aspect of Jane Wilson, that she was directing her companion's attention to us; and, as well by her cold, sarcastic smile as by the few isolated words of her discourse that reached me, I knew full well that she was impressing him with the idea that we were strongly attached to each other. I noticed that

he coloured up to the temples, gave us one furtive glance in passing, and walked on, looking grave, but seemingly offering no reply to her remarks.

It was true, then, that he had some designs upon Mrs Graham; and, were they honourable, he would not be so anxious to conceal them. She was blameless, of course, but he was detestable beyond all count.

While these thoughts flashed through my mind, my companion abruptly rose, and calling her son, said they would now go in quest of the company, and departed up the avenue. Doubtless she had heard or guessed something of Miss Wilson's remarks, and therefore it was natural enough she should choose to continue the *tête-à-tête* no longer, especially as at that moment my cheeks were burning with indignation against my former friend, the token of which she might mistake for a blush of stupid embarrassment. For this I owed Miss Wilson yet another grudge; and still the more I thought upon her conduct the more I hated her.

It was late in the evening before I joined the company. I found Mrs Graham already equipped for departure, and taking leave of the rest, who were now returned to the house. I offered, nay, begged to accompany her home. Mr Lawrence was standing by at the time conversing with some one else. He did not look at us, but, on hearing my earnest request, he paused in the middle of a sentence to listen for her reply, and went on, with a look of quiet satisfaction, the moment he found it was to be a denial.

A denial it was, decided, though not unkind. She could not be persuaded to think there was danger for herself or her child in traversing those lonely lanes and fields without attendance. It was daylight still, and she should meet no one; or if she did, the people were quiet and harmless she was well assured. In fact, she would not hear of any one's putting himself out of the way to accompany her, though Fergus vouchsafed to offer his services in case they should be more acceptable than mine and my mother begged she might send one of the farming-men to escort her.

When she was gone the rest was all a blank or worse. Lawrence attempted to draw me into conversation, but I snubbed him and went to another part of the room. Shortly after the party broke up and he himself took leave. When he came to me I was blind to his extended hand, and deaf to his goodnight till he repeated it a second time; and then, to get rid of him, I muttered an inarticulate reply accompanied by a sulky nod.

'What is the matter, Markham?' whispered he.

I replied by a wrathful and contemptuous stare.

'Are you angry because Mrs Graham would not let you go home with her?' he asked, with a faint smile that nearly exasperated me beyond control.

But swallowing down all fierce answers, I merely demanded—

'What business is it of yours?'

'Why, none,' replied he, with provoking quietness; 'only', and he raised his eyes to my face, and spoke with unusual solemnity, 'only let me tell you, Markham, that if you have any designs in that quarter they will certainly fail; and it grieves me to see you cherishing false hope, and wasting your strength in useless efforts, for'—

'Hypocrite!' I exclaimed; and he held his breath, and looked very blank, turned white about the gills, and went away without another word.

I had wounded him to the quick; and I was glad of it.

# Chapter 10

hen all were gone, I learned that the vile slander had indeed been circulated throughout the company, in the very presence of the victim. Rose, however, vowed she did not and would not believe it, and my mother made the same declaration, though not, I fear, with the same amount of real, unwavering incredulity. It seemed to dwell continually on her mind, and she kept irritating me from time to time by such expressions as— 'Dear, dear, who would have thought it!— Well! I always thought there was something odd about her.— You see what it is for women to affect to be different to other people.' And once it was—

'I misdoubted that appearance of mystery from the very first – I thought there would no good come of it; but this is a sad, sad business to be sure!'

'Why, mother, you said you didn't believe these tales,' said Fergus.

'No more I do, my dear; but then, you know, there must be some foundation.'

'The foundation is in the wickedness and falsehood of the world,' said I, 'and in the fact that Mr Lawrence has been seen to go that way once or twice of an evening – and the village gossips say he goes to pay his addresses to the strange lady, and the scandalmongers have greedily seized the rumour, to make it the basis of their own infernal structure.'

'Well, but Gilbert, there must be something in her manner to countenance such reports.'

'Did you see anything in her manner?'

'No, certainly; but then you know, I always said there was something strange about her.'

I believe it was on that very evening that I ventured on another invasion of Wildfell Hall. From the time of our party, which was upwards of a week ago, I had been making daily efforts to meet its mistress in her walks; and always disappointed (she must have managed it so on purpose), had nightly kept revolving in my mind some pretext for another call. At length, I concluded that the separation could be endured no longer (by this time, you will see, I was pretty far gone); and, taking from the book-case an old volume that I thought she might be interested in, though, from its unsightly and somewhat dilapidated condition, I had not yet ventured to offer it for perusal, I hastened away, – but not without sundry misgivings as to how she would receive me, or how I could summon courage to present myself with so slight an excuse. But, perhaps, I might see her in the field or the garden, and then there would be no great difficulty: it was the formal knocking at the door, with the prospect of being gravely ushered in by Rachel, to the presence of a surprised, uncordial mistress, that so greatly disturbed me.

# The Tenant of Wildfell Hall

My wish, however, was not gratified. Mrs Graham, herself, was not to be seen; but there was Arthur playing with his frolicsome little dog in the garden. I looked over the gate and called him to me. He wanted me to come in; but I told him I could not without his mother's leave.

'I'll go and ask her,' said the child.

'No, no, Arthur, you mustn't do that, – but if she's not engaged, just ask her to come here a minute: tell her I want to speak to her.'

He ran to perform my bidding, and quickly returned with his mother. How lovely she looked with her dark ringlets streaming in the light summer breeze, her fair cheek slightly flushed and her countenance radiant with smiles! – Dear Arthur! what did I not owe to you for this and every other happy meeting? – Through him, I was at once delivered from all formality, and terror, and constraint. In love affairs, there is no mediator like a merry, simple-hearted child – ever ready to cement divided hearts, to span the unfriendly gulf of custom, to melt the ice of cold reserve, and overthrow the separating walls of dread formality and pride.

'Well, Mr Markham, what is it?' said the young mother, accosting me with a pleasant smile.

'I want you to look at this book, and, if you please, to take it, and peruse it at your leisure. I make no apology for calling you out on such a lovely evening, though it be for a matter of no greater importance.'

'Tell him to come in mamma,' said Arthur.

'Would you like to come in?' asked the lady.

'Yes; I should like to see your improvements in the garden.'

'And how your sister's roots have prospered in my charge,' added she, as she opened the gate.

And we sauntered through the garden, and talked of the flowers, the trees, and the book, – and then of other things. The evening was kind and genial, and so was my companion. By degrees, I waxed more warm and tender than, perhaps, I had ever been before; but still, I said nothing tangible, and she attempted no repulse; until, in passing a moss rose-tree that I had brought her some weeks since, in my sister's name, she plucked a beautiful half-open bud and bade me give it to Rose.

'May I not keep it myself?' I asked.

'No; but here is another for you.'

Instead of taking it quietly, I likewise took the hand that offered it, and looked into her face. She let me hold it for a moment, and I saw a flash of ecstatic brilliance in her eye, a glow of glad excitement on her face – I thought my hour of victory was come – but instantly a painful recollection seemed to flash upon her; a cloud of anguish darkened her brow, a marble paleness blanched her cheek and lip; there seemed a moment of inward conflict, – and with a sudden effort, she withdrew her hand, and retreated a step or two back.

'Now, Mr Markham,' said she, with a kind of desperate calmness, 'I must tell you plainly, that I cannot do with this. I like your company, because I am alone here, and your conversation pleases me more than that of any other person; but if you cannot be content to regard me as a friend – a plain, cold, motherly, or sisterly friend, I must beg you to leave me now, and let me alone hereafter – in fact, we must be strangers for the future.'

'I will, then – be your friend, – or brother, or anything you wish, if you will only let me continue to see you; but tell me why I cannot be anything more.'

There was a perplexed and thoughtful pause.

'Is it in consequence of some rash vow?'

'It is something of the kind,' she answered – 'some day I may tell you, but at present you had better leave me; and never, Gilbert, put me to the painful necessity of repeating what I have just now said to you!' – she earnestly added, giving me her hand in serious kindness. How sweet, how musical my own name sounded in her mouth!

'I will not,' I replied. 'But you pardon this offence?'

'On condition that you never repeat it.'

'And may I come to see you now and then?'

'Perhaps, – occasionally; provided you never abuse the privilege.'

'I make no empty promises, but you shall see.'

'The moment you do, our intimacy is at an end, that's all.'

'And will you always call me Gilbert? – it sounds more sisterly, and it will serve to remind me of our contract.'

She smiled, and once more bid me go – and, at length, I judged it prudent to obey; and she re-entered the house, and I went down the hill. But as I went, the tramp of horses' hoofs fell on my ear, and broke the stillness of the dewy evening; and, looking towards the lane, I saw a solitary equestrian coming up. Inclining to dusk as it was, I knew him at a glance: it was Mr Lawrence on his grey pony. I flew across the field – leaped the stone fence – and then walked down the lane to meet him. On seeing me, he suddenly drew in his little steed, and seemed inclined to turn back, but on second thought, apparently judged it better to continue his course as before. He accosted me with a slight bow, and, edging close to the wall, endeavoured to pass on – but I was not so minded: seizing his horse by the bridle, I exclaimed—

'Now, Lawrence, I will have this mystery explained! Tell me where you are going, and what you mean to do – at once, and distinctly!'

'Will you take your hand off the bridle?' said he quietly – 'you're hurting my pony's mouth.'

'You and your pony be—'

'What makes you so coarse and brutal, Markham? I'm quite ashamed of you.'

'You answer my questions – before you leave this spot! I will know what you mean by this perfidious duplicity!'

'I shall answer no questions till you let go the bridle, – if you stand till morning.'

'Now then,' said I, unclosing my hand, but still standing before him.

'Ask me some other time, when you can speak like a gentleman,' returned he, and he made an effort to pass me again; but I quickly re-captured the pony, scarce less astonished than its master at such uncivil usage.

'Really, Mr Markham, this is too much!' said the latter. 'Can I not go to see my tenant on matters of business, without being assaulted in this manner by'—

'This is no time for business, sir! – I'll tell you, now, what I think of your conduct.'

'You'd better defer your opinion to a more convenient season,' interrupted he in a low tone – 'here's the vicar.'

And in truth, the vicar was just behind me, plodding homeward from some remote corner of his parish. I immediately released the squire; and he went on his way, saluting Mr Millward as he passed.

'What, quarrelling, Markham?' cried the latter, addressing himself to me, – 'and about that young widow I doubt,' he added, reproachfully shaking his head. 'But let me tell you, young man' (here he put his face into mine with an important, confidential air), 'she's not worth it!' and he confirmed the assertion by a solemn nod.

'MR MILLWARD!' I exclaimed, in a tone of wrathful menace that made the reverend gentleman look round – aghast – astounded at such unwonted insolence, and stare me in the face with a look that plainly said: 'What, this to me?' But I was too indignant to apologize, or to speak another word to him: I turned away, and hastened homewards, descending with rapid strides the steep, rough lane, and leaving him to follow as he pleased.

# Chapter 11

You must suppose about three weeks passed over. Mrs Graham and I were not established friends – or brother and sister as we rather chose to consider ourselves. She called me Gilbert, by my express desire, and I called her Helen, for I had seen that name written in her books. I seldom attempted to see her above twice a week; and still I made our meetings appear the result of accident as often as I could – for I found it necessary to be extremely careful – and, altogether, I behaved with such exceeding propriety that she never had occasion to reprove me once. Yet I could not but perceive that she was at times unhappy and dissatisfied with herself or her position, and truly I myself was not quite contented with the latter: this assumption of brotherly nonchalance was very hard to sustain, and I often felt myself a most confounded hypocrite with it all: I saw too, or rather I felt, that, in spite of herself, 'I was not indifferent to her,' as the novel heroes modestly express it, and while I thankfully enjoyed my present good fortune, I could not fail to wish and hope for something better in future; but, of course, I kept such dreams entirely to myself.

'Where are you going, Gilbert?' said Rose, one evening, shortly after tea, when I had been busy with the farm all day.

'To take a walk,' was the reply.

'Do you always brush your hat so carefully, and do your hair so nicely, and put on such smart new gloves when you take a walk?'

'Not always!'

'You're going to Wildfell Hall, aren't you?'

'What makes you think so?'

'Because you look as if you were – but I wish you wouldn't go so often.'

'Nonsense, child! I don't go once in six weeks – what do you mean?'

'Well, but if I were you, I wouldn't have so much to do with Mrs Graham.'

'Why, Rose, are you, too, giving in to the prevailing opinion?'

'No,' returned she hesitatingly – 'but I've heard so much about her lately, both at the Wilsons' and the vicarage; – and besides, mamma says, if she were a proper person she would not be living there by herself – and don't you remember last winter, Gilbert, all that about the false name to the picture; and how she explained it – saying she had friends or acquaintances from whom she wished her present residence to be concealed, and that she was afraid of their tracing her out; – and then, how suddenly she started up and left the room when that person came – whom she took good care not to let us catch a glimpse of, and who Arthur, with such an air of mystery, told us was his mamma's friend?'

'Yes, Rose, I remember it all; and I can forgive your uncharitable conclusions; for perhaps, if I did not know her myself, I should put all these things together, and believe the same as you do; but thank God, I do know her; and I should be unworthy the name of a man, if I could believe anything that was said against her, unless I heard it from her own lips. – I should as soon believe such things of you, Rose.'

'Oh, Gilbert!'

'Well, do you think I could believe anything of the kind, – whatever the Wilsons and Millwards dared to whisper?'

'I should hope not indeed!'

'And why not? – Because I know you. – Well, and I know her just as well.'

'Oh, no; you know nothing of her former life; and last year at this time, you did not know that such a person existed.'

'No matter. There is such a thing as looking through a person's eyes into the heart, and learning more of the height and breadth, and depth of another's soul in one hour, than it might take you a lifetime to discover, if he or she were not disposed to reveal it, or if you had not the sense to understand it.'

'Then you are going to see her this evening?'

'To be sure I am!'

'But what would mamma say, Gilbert?'

'Mamma needn't know.'

'But she must know some time, if you go on.'

'Go on! – there's no going on in the matter. Mrs Graham and I are two friends – and will be; and no man breathing shall hinder it, – or has a right to interfere between us.'

'But if you knew how they talk, you would be more careful, for her sake as well as for your own. Jane Wilson thinks your visits to the old hall but another proof of her depravity' –

'Confound Jane Wilson!'

'And Eliza Millward is quite grieved about you.'

'I hope she is.'

'But I wouldn't, if I were you.'

'Wouldn't what? How do they know that I go there?'

'There's nothing hid from them, they spy out everything.'

'Oh, I never thought of this! – and so they dare to turn my friendship into

# The Tenant of Wildfell Hall

food for further scandal against her! – That proves the falsehood of their other lies, at all events, if any proof were wanting. – Mind you contradict them, Rose, whenever you can.'

'But they don't speak openly to me about such things: it is only by hints and innuendoes, and by what I hear others say, that I know what they think.'

'Well then, I won't go today, as it's getting latish. But oh, deuce take their cursed envenomed tongues!' I muttered, in the bitterness of my soul.

And just at that moment the vicar entered the room: we had been too much absorbed in our conversation to observe his knock. After his customary, cheerful, and fatherly greeting of Rose, who was rather a favourite with the old gentleman, he turned somewhat sternly to me—

'Well, sir,' said he, 'you're quite a stranger. It is – let – me – see,' he continued slowly, as he deposited his ponderous bulk in the arm-chair that Rose officiously brought towards him, 'it is just – six – weeks – by my reckoning, since you darkened – my – door!' He spoke it with emphasis, and struck his stick on the floor.

'Is it, sir?' said I.

'Ay! It is so!' He added an affirmatory nod, and continued to gaze upon me with a kind of irate solemnity, holding his substantial stick between his knees, with his hands clasped upon his head.

'I have been busy,' I said, for an apology was evidently demanded.

'Busy,' repeated he derisively.

'Yes, you know I've been getting in my hay; and now the harvest is beginning.'

'Humph.'

Just then my mother came in, and created a diversion in my favour by her loquacious and animated welcome of the reverend guest. She regretted deeply that he had not come a little earlier, in time for tea, but offered to have some immediately prepared, if he would do her the favour to partake of it.

'Not any for me, I thank you,' replied he; 'I shall be at home in a few minutes.'

'Oh, but do stay and take a little! it will be ready in five minutes.'

But he rejected the offer, with a majestic wave of his hand.

'I'll tell you what I'll take, Mrs Markham,' said he: 'I'll take a glass of your excellent ale.'

'With pleasure!' cried my mother, proceeding with alacrity to pull the bell and order the favoured beverage.

'I thought,' continued he, 'I'd just look in upon you as I passed, and taste your home-brewed ale. I've been to call on Mrs Graham.'

'Have you, indeed?'

He nodded gravely, and added with awful emphasis—

'I thought it incumbent upon me to do so.'

'Really!' ejaculated my mother.

'Why so, Mr Millward?' asked I. He looked at me with some severity, and turning again to my mother, repeated—

'I thought it incumbent upon me!' and struck his stick on the floor again. My mother sat opposite, an awe-struck but admiring auditor.

' "Mrs Graham," said I,' he continued, shaking his head as he spoke, ' "these are terrible reports!" "What, sir?" says she, affecting to be ignorant of my meaning. "It is my – duty – as – your pastor," said I, "to tell you both everything

that I myself see reprehensible in your conduct, and all I have reason to suspect, and what others tell me concerning you." – So I told her!'

'You did, sir?' cried I, starting from my seat, and striking my fist on the table. He merely glanced towards me, and continued, addressing his hostess—

'It was a painful duty, Mrs Markham – but I told her!'

'And how did she take it?' asked my mother.

'Hardened, I fear – hardened!' he replied, with a despondent shake of the head; 'and, at the same time, there was a strong display of unchastened, misdirected passions. She turned white in the face, and drew her breath through her teeth in a savage sort of way; – but she offered no extenuation or defence; and with a kind of shameless calmness – shocking indeed to witness in one so young – as good as told me that my remonstrance was unavailing, and my pastoral advice quite thrown away upon her – nay, that my very presence was displeasing while I spoke such things. And I withdrew at length, too plainly seeing that nothing could be done – and sadly grieved to find her case so hopeless. But I am fully determined, Mrs Markham, that my daughters – shall – not – consort with her. Do you adopt the same resolution with regard to yours! – As for your sons – as for you, young man,' he continued, sternly turning to me—

'As for ME, sir,' I began, but checked by some impediment in my utterance, and finding that my whole frame trembled with fury, I said no more, but took the wiser part of snatching up my hat and bolting from the room, slamming the door behind me, with a bang that shook the house to its foundations, and made my mother scream, and give a momentary relief to my excited feelings.

The next minute saw me hurrying with rapid strides in the direction of Wildfell Hall – to what intent or purpose I could scarcely tell, but I must be moving somewhere, and no other goal would do – I must see her too, and speak to her – that was certain; but what to say, or how to act, I had no definite idea. Such stormy thoughts – so many different resolutions crowded in upon me, that my mind was little better than a chaos of conflicting passions.

# Chapter 12

n little more than twenty minutes, the journey was accomplished. I paused at the gate to wipe my streaming forehead, and recover my breath and some degree of composure. Already the rapid walking had somewhat mitigated my excitement; and with a firm and steady tread, I paced the garden walk. In passing the inhabited wing of the building, I caught a sight of Mrs Graham, through the open window, slowly pacing up and down her lonely room.

She seemed agitated, and even dismayed at my arrival, as if she thought I too was coming to accuse her. I had entered her presence intending to condole with

her upon the wickedness of the world, and help her to abuse the vicar and his vile informants, but now I felt positively ashamed to mention the subject, and determined not to refer to it, unless she led the way.

'I am come at an unseasonable hour' said I, assuming a cheerfulness I did not feel, in order to reassure her; 'but I won't stay many minutes.'

She smiled upon me, faintly it is true, but most kindly – I had almost said thankfully, as her apprehensions were removed.

'How dismal you are, Helen! Why have you no fire?' I said, looking round on the gloomy apartment.

'It is summer yet,' she replied.

'But we always have a fire in the evenings, if we can bear it; and you especially require one in this cold house and dreary room.'

'You should have come a little sooner, and I would have had one lighted for you; but it is not worth while now, you won't stay many minutes, you say, and Arthur is gone to bed.'

'But I have a fancy for a fire, nevertheless. Will you order one, if I ring?'

'Why, Gilbert, you don't look cold?' said she smilingly regarding my face, which no doubt seemed warm enough.

'No,' replied I, 'but I want to see you comfortable before I go.'

'Me comfortable!' repeated she, with a bitter laugh, as if there was something amusingly absurd in the idea. 'It suits me better as it is,' she added, in a tone of mournful resignation.

But determined to have my own way, I pulled the bell.

'There now, Helen!' I said, as the approaching steps of Rachel were heard in answer to the summons. There was nothing for it but to turn round and desire the maid to light the fire.

I owe Rachel a grudge to this day, for the look she cast upon me ere she departed on her mission, the sour, suspicious, inquisitorial look that plainly demanded, 'What are you here for, I wonder?' Her mistress did not fail to notice it, and a shade of uneasiness darkened her brow.

'You must not stay long, Gilbert,' said she, when the door was closed upon us.

'I'm not going to,' said I, somewhat testily, though without a grain of anger in my heart against any one but the meddling old woman. 'But, Helen, I've something to say to you before I go.'

'What is it?'

'No, not now – I don't know yet precisely what it is, or how to say it,' replied I, with more truth than wisdom; and then, fearing lest she should turn me out of the house, I began talking about indifferent matters in order to gain time. Meanwhile Rachel came in to kindle the fire, which was soon effected by thrusting a red-hot poker between the bars of the grate, where the fuel was already disposed for ignition. She honoured me with another of her hard, inhospitable looks in departing, but, little moved thereby, I went on talking; and setting a chair for Mrs Graham on one side of the hearth, and one for myself on the other, I ventured to sit down, though half suspecting she would rather see me go.

In a little while we both relapsed into silence, and continued for several minutes gazing abstractedly into the fire – she intent upon her own sad thoughts, and I reflecting how delightful it would be to be seated thus beside her with no

other presence to restrain our intercourse – not even that of Arthur, our mutual friend, without whom we had never met before – if only I could venture to speak my mind, and disburden my full heart of the feelings that had so long oppressed it, and which it now struggled to retain, with an effort that it seemed impossible to continue much longer, – and revolving the pros and cons for opening my heart to her there and then, and imploring a return of affection, the permission to regard her thenceforth as my own, and the right and the power to defend her from the calumnies of malicious tongues. On the one hand, I felt a new-born confidence in my powers of persuasion – a strong conviction that my own fervour of spirit would grant me eloquence – that my very determination – the absolute necessity for succeeding, that I felt must win me what I sought; while on the other, I feared to lose the ground I had already gained with so much toil and skill, and destroy all future hope by one rash effort, when time and patience might have won success. It was like setting my life upon the cast of a die; and yet I was ready to resolve upon the attempt. At any rate, I would entreat the explanation she had half promised to give me before; I would demand the reason of this hateful barrier, this mysterious impediment to my happiness, and, as I trusted, to her own.

But while I considered in what manner I could best frame my request, my companion wakened from her reverie with a scarcely audible sigh, and looking towards the window where the blood-red harvest moon, just rising over one of the grim, fantastic evergreens, was shining in upon us, said—

'Gilbert, it is getting late.'

'I see,' said I. 'You want me to go, I suppose.'

'I think you ought. If my kind neighbours get to know of this visit – as no doubt they will – they will not turn it much to my advantage.'

It was with what the vicar would doubtless have called a savage sort of smile that she said this.

'Let them turn it as they will,' said I. 'What are their thoughts to you or me, so long as we are satisfied with ourselves – and each other. Let them go to the deuce with their vile constructions, and their lying inventions!'

This outburst brought a flush of colour to her face.

'You have heard, then, what they say of me?'

'I heard some detestable falsehoods; but none but fools would credit them for a moment, Helen, so don't let them trouble you.'

'I did not think Mr Millward a fool, and he believes it all; but however little you may value the opinions of those about you – however little you may esteem them as individuals, it is not pleasant to be looked upon as a liar and a hypocrite, to be thought to practise what you abhor, and to encourage the vices you would discountenance, to find your good intentions frustrated, and your hands crippled by your supposed unworthiness, and to bring disgrace on the principles you profess.'

'True; and if I, by my thoughtlessness and selfish disregard to appearances, have at all assisted to expose you to these evils, let me entreat you not only to pardon me, but to enable me to make reparation; authorize me to clear your name from every imputation: give me the right to identify your honour with my own, and to defend your reputation as more precious than my life!'

'Are you hero enough to unite yourself to one whom you know to be suspected

and despised by all around you, and identify your interests and your honour with hers? Think! it is a serious thing.'

'I should be proud to do it, Helen! – most happy – delighted beyond expression! and if that be all the obstacle to our union, it is demolished, and you must – you shall be mine!'

And starting from my seat in a frenzy of ardour, I seized her hand and would have pressed it to my lips, but she as suddenly caught it away, exclaiming in the bitterness of intense affliction:

'No, no, it is not all!'

'What is it then? You promised I should know some time, and'—

'You shall know some time – but not now – my head aches terribly,' she said, pressing her hand to her forehead, 'and I must have some repose – and surely, I have had misery enough today!' she added, almost wildly.

'But it could not harm you to tell it,' I persisted: 'it would ease your mind; and I should then know how to comfort you.'

She shook her head despondingly. 'If you knew all, you, too, would blame me – perhaps even more than I deserve – though I have cruelly wronged you,' she added in a low murmur, as if she mused aloud.

'You, Helen? Impossible!'

'Yes, not willingly; for I did not know the strength and depth of your attachment. I thought – at least I endeavoured to think – your regard for me was as cold and fraternal as you professed it to be.'

'Or as yours?'

'Or as mine – ought to have been – of such a light and selfish, superficial nature that'—

'There, indeed, you wronged me.'

'I know I did; and sometimes, I suspected it then; but I thought, upon the whole, there could be no great harm in leaving your fancies and your hopes to dream themselves to nothing – or flutter away to some more fitting object, while your friendly sympathies remained with me; but if I had known the depth of your regard, the generous disinterested affection you seem to feel'—

'Seem, Helen?'

'That you do feel, then, I would have acted differently.'

'How? You would not have given me less encouragement, or treated me with greater severity than you did! And if you think you have wronged me by giving me your friendship, and occasionally admitting me to the enjoyment of your company and conversation, when all hopes of close intimacy were vain – as indeed you always gave me to understand – if you think you have wronged me by this, you are mistaken; for such favours, in themselves alone, are not only delightful to my heart, but purifying, exalting, ennobling to my soul; and I would rather have your friendship than the love of any other woman in the world!'

Little comforted by this, she clasped her hands upon her knee, and glancing upward, seemed, in silent anguish, to implore divine assistance; then turning to me, she calmly said—

'To-morrow, if you meet me on the moor about mid-day, I will tell you all you seek to know; and perhaps you will then see the necessity of discontinuing our intimacy – if, indeed, you do not willingly resign me as one no longer worthy of regard.'

'I can safely answer no, to that: you cannot have such grave confessions to make – you must be trying my faith, Helen.'

'No, no, no,' she earnestly repeated – 'I wish it were so! Thank heaven!' she added, 'I have no great crime to confess: but I have more than you will like to hear, or, perhaps, can readily excuse, – and more than I can tell you now; so let me entreat you to leave me!'

'I will; but answer me this one question first; – do you love me?'

'I will not answer it!'

'Then I will conclude you do; and so good-night.'

She turned from me to hide the emotion she could not quite control; but I took her hand and fervently kissed it.

'Gilbert, do leave me!' she cried, in a tone of such thrilling anguish that I felt it would be cruel to disobey.

But I gave one look back before I closed the door, and saw her leaning forward on the table, with her hands pressed against her eyes, sobbing convulsively; yet I withdrew in silence. I felt that to obtrude my consolations on her then would only serve to aggravate her sufferings.

To tell you all the questionings and conjectures – the fears, and hopes, and wild emotions that jostled and chased each other through my mind as I descended the hill, would almost fill a volume in itself. But before I was half way down a sentiment of strong sympathy for her I had left behind me had displaced all other feelings, and seemed imperatively to draw me back: I began to think, 'Why am I hurrying so fast in this direction? Can I find comfort or consolation – peace, certainty, contentment, all – or anything that I want at home? and can I leave all perturbation, sorrow, and anxiety behind me there?'

And I turned round to look at the old hall. There was little besides the chimneys visible above my contracted horizon. I walked back to get a better view of it. When it rose in sight, I stood still a moment to look, and then continued moving towards the gloomy object of attraction. Something called me nearer – nearer still – and why not, pray? Might I not find more benefit in the contemplation of that venerable pile with the full moon in the cloudless heaven shining so calmly above it – with that warm yellow lustre peculiar to an August night – and the mistress of my soul within, than in returning to my home where all comparatively was light, and life, and cheerfulness, and therefore inimical to me in my present frame of mind, and the more so that its inmates all were more or less imbued with that detestable belief the very thought of which made my blood boil in my veins – and how could I endure to hear it openly declared – or cautiously insinuated – which was worse? – I had had trouble enough already, with some babbling fiend that would keep whispering in my ear, 'It may be true,' till I had shouted aloud, 'It is false! I defy you to make me suppose it!'

I could see the red firelight dimly gleaming from her parlour window. I went up to the garden wall, and stood leaning over it, with my eyes fixed upon the lattice, wondering what she was doing, thinking, or suffering now, and wishing I could speak to her but one word, or even catch one glimpse of her, before I went.

I had not thus looked, and wished, and wondered long, before I vaulted over the barrier, unable to resist the temptation of taking one glance through the window, just to see if she were more composed than when we parted; – and if

# The Tenant of Wildfell Hall

I found her still in deep distress, perhaps I might venture to attempt a word of comfort – to utter one of the many things I should have said before, instead of aggravating her sufferings by my stupid impetuosity. I looked. Her chair was vacant: so was the room. But at that moment someone opened the outer door, and a voice – her voice – said—

'Come out – I want to see the moon, and breathe the evening air: they will do me good – if anything will.'

Here, then, were she and Rachel coming to take a walk in the garden. I wished myself back over the wall. I stood, however, in the shadow of the tall holly-bush, which, standing between the window and the porch, at present screened me from observation, but did not prevent me from seeing two figures come forth into the moonlight: Mrs Graham followed by another – not Rachel, but a young man, slender and rather tall. Oh, heavens, how my temples throbbed! Intense anxiety darkened my sight; but I thought – yes, and the voice confirmed it – it was Mr Lawrence.

'You should not let it worry you so much, Helen,' said he; 'I will be more cautious in the future; and in time'—

I did not hear the rest of the sentence; for he walked close beside her and spoke so gently that I could not catch the words. My heart was splitting with hatred; but I listened intently for her reply. I heard it plainly enough.

'But I must leave this place, Frederick,' she said – 'I never can he happy here, – nor anywhere else, indeed,' she added, with a mirthless laugh, – 'but I cannot rest here.'

'But where could you find a better place?' replied he, 'so secluded – so near me, if you think anything of that.'

'Yes,' interrupted she, 'it is all I could wish, if they could only have left me alone.'

'But wherever you go, Helen, there will be the same sources of annoyance. I cannot consent to lose you: I must go with you, or come to you; and there are meddling fools elsewhere, as well as here.'

While thus conversing, they had sauntered slowly past me, down the walk, and I heard no more of their discourse; but I saw him put his arm round her waist, while she lovingly rested her hand on his shoulder; – and then, a tremulous darkness obscured my sight, my heart sickened and my head burned like fire. I half rushed, half staggered from the spot where horror had kept me rooted, and leaped or tumbled over the wall – I hardly know which – but I know that, afterwards, like a passionate child, I dashed myself on the ground and lay there in a paroxysm of anger and despair – how long, I cannot undertake to say; but it must have been a considerable time; for when, having partially relieved myself by a torrent of tears, and looked up at the moon, shining so calmly and carelessly on, as little influenced by my misery as I was by its peaceful radiance, and earnestly prayed for death or forgetfulness, I had risen and journeyed homewards – little regarding the way, but carried instinctively by my feet to the door, I found it bolted against me, and everyone in bed except my mother, who hastened to answer my impatient knocking, and received me with a shower of questions and rebukes.

'Oh, Gilbert, how could you do so? Where have you been? Do come in and take your supper – I've got it all ready, though you don't deserve it, for keeping me in such a fright, after the strange manner you left the house this evening.

Mr Millward was quite— Bless the boy! how ill he looks! Oh, gracious! what is the matter?'

'Nothing, nothing – give me a candle.'

'But won't you take some supper?'

'No, I want to go to bed,' said I, taking a candle and lighting it at the one she held in her hand.

'Oh, Gilbert, how you tremble!' exclaimed my anxious parent. 'How white you look! – Do tell me what it is? Has anything happened?'

'It's nothing!' cried I, ready to stamp with vexation because the candle would not light. Then, suppressing my irritation, I added, 'I've been walking too fast, that's all. Good night,' and marched off to bed, regardless of the 'Walking too fast! where have you been?' that was called after me from below.

My mother followed me to the very door of my room, with her questionings and advice concerning my health and my conduct; but I implored her to let me alone till morning; and she withdrew, and at length I had the satisfaction to hear her close her own door. There was no sleep for me, however, that night, as I thought; and instead of attempting to solicit it, I employed myself in rapidly pacing the chamber – having first removed my boots lest my mother should hear me. But the boards creaked, and she was watchful. I had not walked above a quarter of an hour before she was at the door again.

'Gilbert, why are you not in bed – you said you wanted to go?'

'Confound it! I'm going,' said I.

'But why are you so long about it? you must have something on your mind'—

'For heaven's sake, let me alone, and get to bed yourself!'

'Can it be that Mrs Graham that distresses you so?'

'No, no, I tell you – it's nothing!'

'I wish to goodness it mayn't!' murmured she, with a sigh, as she returned to her own apartment, while I threw myself on the bed, feeling most undutifully disaffected towards her for having deprived me of what seemed the only shadow of a consolation that remained, and chained me to that wretched couch of thorns.

Never did I endure so long, so miserable a night as that. And yet, it was not wholly sleepless: towards morning my distracting thoughts began to lose all pretensions to coherency, and shape themselves into confused and feverish dreams, and, at length, there followed an interval of unconscious slumber. But then the dawn of bitter recollection that succeeded – the waking to find life a blank, and worse than a blank – teeming with torment and misery – not a mere barren wilderness, but full of thorns and briars – to find myself deceived, duped, hopeless, my affections trampled upon, my angel not an angel, and my friend a fiend incarnate – it was worse than if I had not slept at all.

It was a dull, gloomy morning, the weather had changed like my prospects, and the rain was pattering against the window. I rose, nevertheless, and went out; not to look after the farm, though that would serve as my excuse, but to cool my brain, and regain, if possible, a sufficient degree of composure to meet the family at the morning meal without exciting inconvenient remarks. If I get a wetting, that, in conjunction with a pretended over-exertion before breakfast, might excuse my sudden loss of appetite; and if a cold ensued, the severer the better, it would help to account for the sullen moods and moping melancholy likely to cloud my brow for long enough.

# Chapter 13

'My dear Gilbert! I wish you would try to be a little more amiable,' said my mother, one morning after some display of unjustifiable ill-humour on my part. 'You say there is nothing the matter with you, and nothing has happened to grieve you, and yet, I never saw any one so altered as you within these last few days: you haven't a good word for anybody – friends and strangers, equals and inferiors – it's all the same. I do wish you'd try to check it.'

'Check what?'

'Why, your strange temper. You don't know how it spoils you. I'm sure a finer disposition than yours by nature, could not be, if you'd let it have fair play; so you've no excuse that way.'

While she thus remonstrated, I took up a book, and laying it open on the table before me, pretended to be deeply absorbed in its perusal; for I was equally unable to justify myself, and unwilling to acknowledge my errors; and I wished to have nothing to say on the matter. But my excellent parent went on lecturing, and then came to coaxing, and began to stroke my hair; and I was getting to feel quite a good boy, but my mischievous brother, who was idling about the room, revived my corruption by suddenly calling out—

'Don't touch him, mother! he'll bite! He's a very tiger in human form. I've given him up for my part – fairly disowned him – cast him off, root and branch. It's as much as my life is worth to come within six yards of him. The other day he nearly fractured my skull for singing a pretty, inoffensive love song, on purpose to amuse him.'

'Oh, Gilbert! how could you?' exclaimed my mother.

'I told you to hold your noise first, you know, Fergus,' said I.

'Yes, but when I assured you it was no trouble, and went on with the next verse, thinking you might like it better, you clutched me by the shoulder and dashed me away, right against the wall there, with such force, that I thought I had bitten my tongue in two, and expected to see the place plastered with my brains; and when I put my hand to my head and found my skull was not broken, I thought it was a miracle and no mistake. But poor fellow!' added he, with a sentimental sigh – 'his heart's broken – that's the truth of it – and his head's'—

'Will you be silent NOW?' cried I, starting up, and eyeing the fellow so fiercely that my mother, thinking I meant to inflict some grievous bodily injury, laid her hand on my arm, and besought me to let him alone, and he walked leisurely out, with his hands in his pockets, singing provokingly—'Shall I, because a woman's fair,' etc.

# The Tenant of Wildfell Hall

'I'm not going to defile my fingers with him,' said I, in answer to the maternal intercession. 'I wouldn't touch him with the tongs.'

I now recollected that I had business with Robert Wilson, concerning the purchase of a certain field adjoining my farm – a business I had been putting off from day to day; for I had no interest in anything now; and besides, I was misanthropically inclined, and, moreover, had a particular objection to meeting Jane Wilson or her mother; for though I had too good reason, now, to credit their reports concerning Mrs Graham, I did not like them a bit better for it – or Eliza Millward either – and the thought of meeting them was the more repugnant to me, that I could not, now, defy their seeming calumnies and triumph in my own convictions as before. But today, I determined to make an effort to return to my duty. Though I found no pleasure in it, it would be less irksome than idleness – at all events it would be more profitable. If life promised no enjoyment within my vocation, at least it offered no allurements out of it; and henceforth, I would put my shoulder to the wheel and toil away, like any poor drudge of a cart-horse that was fairly broken in to its labour, and plod through life, not wholly useless if not agreeable, and uncomplaining if not contented with my lot.

Thus resolving, with a kind of sullen resignation, if such a term may be allowed, I wended my way to Ryecote Farm scarcely expecting to find its owner within at this time of day, but hoping to learn in what part of the premises he was most likely to be found.

Absent he was, but expected home in a few minutes; and I was desired to step into the parlour and wait. Mrs Wilson was busy in the kitchen, but the room was now empty; and I scarcely checked an involuntary recoil as I entered it; for there sat Miss Wilson chattering with Eliza Millward. However, I determined to be cool and civil. Eliza seemed to have made the same resolution on her part. We had not met since the evening of the tea-party; but there was no visible emotion either of pleasure or pain, no attempt at pathos, no display of injured pride: she was cool in temper, civil in demeanour. There was even an ease and cheerfulness about her air and manner that I made no pretension to: but there was a depth of malice in her too expressive eye, that plainly told me I was not forgiven; for, though she no longer hoped to win me to herself, she still hated her rival, and evidently delighted to wreak her spite on me. On the other hand, Miss Wilson was as affable and courteous as heart could wish, and though I was in no very conversible humour myself, the two ladies between them managed to keep up a pretty continuous fire of small talk. But Eliza took advantage of the first convenient pause to ask if I had lately seen Mrs Graham, in a tone of merely casual inquiry, but with a sidelong glance – intended to be playfully mischievous – really, brimful and running over with malice.

'Not lately,' I replied in a careless tone, but sternly repelling her odious glances with my eyes; for I was vexed to feel the colour mounting to my forehead, despite my strenuous efforts to appear unmoved.

'What! are you beginning to tire already? I thought so noble a creature would have power to attach you for a year at least!'

'I would rather not speak of her, now.'

'Ah! then you are convinced, at last, of your mistake – you have at length discovered that your divinity is not quite the immaculate'—

'I desired you not to speak of her, Miss Eliza.'

# The Tenant of Wildfell Hall

'Oh, I beg your pardon! I perceive Cupid's arrows have been too sharp for you: the wounds being more than skin deep, are not yet healed, and bleed afresh at every mention of the loved one's name.'

'Say, rather,' interposed Miss Wilson, 'that Mr Markham feels that name is unworthy to be mentioned in the presence of right-minded females. I wonder, Eliza, you should think of referring to that unfortunate person – you might know the mention of her would be anything but agreeable to any one here present.'

How could this be borne? I rose and was about to clap my hat upon my head and burst away, in wrathful indignation, from the house; but recollecting – just in time to save my dignity – the folly of such a proceeding, and how it would only give my fair tormentors a merry laugh at my expense, for the sake of one I acknowledged in my own heart to be unworthy of the slightest sacrifice – though the ghost of my former reverence and love so hung about me still, that I could not bear to hear her name aspersed by others – I merely walked to the window, and having spent a few seconds in vengibly biting my lips, and sternly repressing the passionate heavings of my chest, I observed to Miss Wilson that I could see nothing of her brother, and added that, as my time was precious, it would perhaps be better to call again tomorrow, at some time when I should be sure to find him at home.

'Oh, no!' said she, 'if you wait a minute, he will be sure to come; for he has business at L—' (that was our market town) 'and will require a little refreshment before he goes.'

I submitted accordingly, with the best grace I could; and, happily, I had not long to wait. Mr Wilson soon arrived, and, indisposed for business as I was at that moment, and little as I cared for the field or its owner, I forced my attention to the matter in hand, with very creditable determination, and quickly concluded the bargain – perhaps more to the thrifty farmer's satisfaction than he cared to acknowledge. Then, leaving him to the discussion of his substantial 'refreshment', I gladly quitted the house, and went to look after my reapers.

Leaving them busy at work on the side of the valley, I ascended the hill, intending to visit a cornfield in the more elevated regions, and see when it would be ripe for the sickle. But I did not visit it that day; for, as I approached, I beheld at no great distance Mrs Graham and her son coming down in the opposite direction. They saw me; and Arthur already was running to meet me; but I immediately turned back and walked steadily homeward; for I had fully determined never to encounter his mother again; and regardless of the shrill voice in my ear, calling upon me to 'wait a moment', I pursued the even tenor of my way; and he soon relinquished the pursuit as hopeless, or was called away by his mother. At all events, when I looked back, five minutes after, not a trace of either was to be seen.

This incident agitated and disturbed me most unaccountably – unless you would account for it by saying that Cupid's arrows not only had been too sharp for me, but they were barbed and deeply rooted, and I had not yet been able to wrench them from my heart. However that be, I was rendered doubly miserable for the remainder of the day.

# Chapter 14

Next morning, I bethought me, I, too, had business at L—; so I mounted my horse and set forth on the expedition, soon after breakfast. It was a dull, drizzly day; but that was no matter: it was all the more suitable to my frame of mind. It was likely to be a lonely journey; for it was no market day, and the road I traversed was little frequented at any other time; but that suited me all the better too.

As I trotted along, however, chewing the cud of bitter fancies, I heard another horse at no great distance behind me; but I never conjectured who the rider might be, or troubled my head about him, till, on slackening my pace to ascend a gentle acclivity – or rather suffering my horse to slacken his pace into a lazy walk; for, lost in my own reflections, I was letting it jog on as leisurely as it thought proper – I lost ground and my fellow traveller overtook me. He accosted me by name; for it was no stranger – it was Mr Lawrence! Instinctively the fingers of my whip hand tingled, and grasped their charge with convulsive energy; but I restrained the impulse, and answering his salutation with a nod, attempted to push on; but he pushed on beside me and began to talk about the weather and the crops. I gave the briefest possible answers to his queries and observations, and fell back. He fell back, too, and asked if my horse was lame. I replied with a look – at which he placidly smiled.

I was as much astonished as exasperated at this singular pertinacity and imperturbable assurance on his part. I had thought the circumstances of our last meeting would have left such an impression on his mind as to render him cold and distant ever after: instead of that, he appeared not only to have forgotten all former offences, but to be impenetrable to all present incivilities. Formerly, the slightest hint, or mere fancied coldness in tone or glance, had sufficed to repulse him: now, positive rudeness could not drive him away. Had he heard of my disappointment; and was he come to witness the result, and triumph in my despair? I grasped my whip with more determined energy than before – but still forbore to raise it, and rode on in silence, waiting for some more tangible cause of offence, before I opened the floodgates of my soul, and poured out the dammed-up fury that was foaming and swelling within.

'Markham,' said he, in his usual quiet tone, 'why do you quarrel with your friends, because you have been disappointed in one quarter? You have found your hopes defeated; but how am I to blame for it? I warned you beforehand, you know, but you would not'—

He said no more; for impelled by some fiend at my elbow, I had seized my whip by the small end, and – swift and sudden as a flash of lightning – brought the other down upon his head. It was not without a feeling of savage satisfaction

# The Tenant of Wildfell Hall

that I beheld the instant, deadly pallor that overspread his face, and the few red drops that trickled down his forehead, while he reeled a moment in the saddle, and then fell backward to the ground. The pony, surprised to be so strangely relieved of its burden, started and capered, and kicked a little, and then made use of its freedom to go and crop the grass of the hedge bank; while its master lay as still and silent as a corpse. Had I killed him? – an icy hand seemed to grasp my heart and check its pulsation, as I bent over him, gazing with breathless intensity upon the ghastly, upturned face. But no; he moved his eyelids and uttered a slight groan. I breathed again – he was only stunned by the fall. It served him right – it would teach him better manners in future. Should I help him to his horse! No. For any other combination of offences I would; but his were too unpardonable. He might mount it himself, if he liked – in a while: already he was beginning to stir and look about him – and there it was for him, quietly browsing on the roadside.

So with a muttered execration I left the fellow to his fate, and clapping spurs to my own horse, galloped away, excited by a combination of feelings it would not be easy to analyse; and perhaps, if I did so, the result would not be very creditable to my disposition; for I am not sure that a species of exultation in what I had done was not one principal concomitant.

Shortly, however, the effervescence began to abate, and not many minutes elapsed before I had turned and gone back to look after the fate of my victim. It was no generous impulse – no kind relentings that led me to this – nor even the fear of what might be the consequences to myself, if I finished my assault upon the squire by leaving him thus neglected, and exposed to further injury; it was, simply, the voice of conscience; and I took great credit to myself for attending so promptly to its dictates – and judging the merit of the deed by the sacrifice it cost, I was not far wrong.

Mr Lawrence and his pony had both altered their positions in some degree. The pony had wandered eight to ten yards further away; and he had managed, somehow, to remove himself from the middle of the road: I found him seated in a recumbent position on the bank, – looking very white and sickly still, and holding his cambric handkerchief (now more red than white) to his head. It must have been a powerful blow; but half the credit – or the blame for it (which you please) must be attributed to the whip, which was garnished with a massive horse's head of plated metal. The grass, being sodden with rain, afforded the young gentleman a rather inhospitable couch; his clothes were considerably bemired; and his hat was rolling in the mud, on the other side of the road. But his thoughts seemed chiefly bent upon his pony, on which he was wistfully gazing – half in helpless anxiety, and half in hopeless abandonment to his fate.

I dismounted, however, and having fastened my own animal to the nearest tree, picked up his hat, intending to clap it on his head; but either he considered his head unfit for a hat, or the hat, in its present condition, unfit for his head; for shrinking away the one, he took the other from my hand, and scornfully cast it aside.

'It's good enough for you,' I muttered.

My next good office was to catch his pony and bring it to him, which was soon accomplished; for the beast was quiet enough in the main, and only winced and flirted a trifle till I got hold of the bridle – but then, I must see him in the saddle.

# The Tenant of Wildfell Hall

'Here, you fellow – scoundrel – dog – give me your hand, and I'll help you to mount.'

No; he turned from me in disgust. I attempted to take him by the arm. He shrank away as if there had been contamination in my touch.

'What, you won't? Well! you may sit there till doomsday, for what I care. But I suppose you don't want to lose all the blood in your body – I'll just condescend to bind that up for you.'

'Let me alone, if you please.'

'Humph! with all my heart. You may go to the d—l, if you choose – and say I sent you.'

But before I abandoned him to his fate, I flung his pony's bridle over a stake in the hedge, and threw him my handkerchief, as his own was now saturated with blood. He took it and cast it back to me, in abhorrence and contempt, with all the strength he could muster. It wanted but this to fill the measure of his offences. With execrations not loud but deep, I left him to live or die as he could, well satisfied that I had done my duty in attempting to save him – but forgetting how I had erred in bringing him into such a condition, and how insultingly my after services had been offered – and sullenly prepared to meet the consequences if he should choose to say I had attempted to murder him – which I thought not unlikely, as it seemed probable he was actuated by such spiteful motives in so perseveringly refusing my assistance.

Having remounted my horse, I just looked back to see how he was getting on, before I rode away. He had risen from the ground, and grasping his pony's mane, was attempting to resume his seat in the saddle; but scarcely had he put his foot in the stirrup, when a sickness or dizziness seemed to overpower him: he leant forward a moment, with his head drooped on the animal's back, and then made one more effort, which proving ineffectual, he sank back on the bank where I left him, reposing his head on the oozy turf, and, to all appearance, as calmly reclining as if he had been taking his rest on his sofa at home.

I ought to have helped him in spite of himself – to have bound up the wound he was unable to staunch, and insisted upon getting him on his horse and seeing him safe home; but, beside my bitter indignation against himself, there was the question what to say to his servants – and what to my own family. Either I should have to acknowledge the deed, which would set me down as a madman, unless I acknowledged the motive too – and that seemed impossible – or I must get up a lie, which seemed equally out of the question – especially as Mr Lawrence would probably reveal the whole truth, and thereby bring me to tenfold disgrace – unless I were villain enough, presuming on the absence of witnesses, to persist in my own version of the case, and make him out a still greater scoundrel than he was. No; he had only received a cut above the temple, and perhaps, a few bruises from the fall, or the hoofs of his own pony: that could not kill him if he lay there half the day; and, if he could not help himself, surely some one would be coming by: it would be impossible that a whole day should pass and no one traverse the road but ourselves. As for what he might choose to say hereafter, I would take my chance about it: if he told lies, I would contradict him; if he told the truth, I would bear it as best I could. I was not obliged to enter into explanations, further than I thought proper. Perhaps, he might choose to be silent on the subject, for fear of raising inquiries as to the cause of the quarrel, and drawing the public attention to his connection with

Mrs Graham, which, whether for her sake or his own, he seemed so very desirous to conceal.

Thus reasoning, I trotted away to the town, where I duly transacted my business, and performed various little commissions for my mother and Rose, with very laudable exactitude, considering the different circumstances of the case. In returning home, I was troubled with sundry misgivings about the unfortunate Lawrence. The question, what if I should find him lying still on the damp earth, fairly dying of cold and exhaustion – or already stark and chill? thrust itself most unpleasantly upon my mind, and the appalling possibility pictured itself with painful vividness to my imagination as I approached the spot where I had left him. But no; thank Heaven, both man and horse were gone, and nothing was left to witness against me but two objects – unpleasant enough in themselves, to be sure, and presenting a very ugly, not to say murderous, appearance – in one place, the hat saturated with rain and coated with mud, indented and broken above the brim by that villainous whip-handle: in another, the crimson handkerchief, soaking in a deeply tinctured pool of water – for much rain had fallen in the interim.

Bad news flies fast: it was hardly four o'clock when I got home, but my mother gravely accosted me with—

'Oh, Gilbert! – such an accident! Rose has been shopping in the village, and she's heard that Mr. Lawrence has been thrown from his horse and brought home dying!'

This shocked me a trifle, as you may suppose; but I was comforted to hear that he had frightfully fractured his skull and broken a leg; for, assured of the falsehood of this, I trusted the rest of the story was equally exaggerated; and when I heard my mother and sister so feelingly deploring his condition, I had considerable difficulty in preventing myself from telling them the real extent of the injuries, as far as I knew them.

'You must go and see him tomorrow,' said my mother.

'Or today,' suggested Rose; 'there's plenty of time; and you can have the pony, as your horse is tired. Won't you, Gilbert – as soon as you've had something to eat?'

'No, no – How can we tell that it isn't all a false report? It's highly im'—

'Oh, I'm sure it isn't; for the village is all alive about it; and I saw two people that had seen others that had seen the man that found him. That sounds far-fetched; but it isn't so, when you think of it.'

'Well, but Lawrence is a good rider; it is not likely he would fall from his horse at all; and if he did, it is highly improbable he would break his bones in that way. It must be a gross exaggeration at least.'

'No, but the horse kicked him – or something.'

'What, his quiet little pony?'

'How do you know it was that?'

'He seldom rides any other.'

'At any rate,' said my mother, 'you will call tomorrow. Whether it be true or false, exaggerated or otherwise, we shall like to know how he is.'

'Fergus may go.'

'Why not you?'

'He has more time: I am busy just now.'

'Oh! but Gilbert, how can you be so composed about it! You won't mind

business, for an hour or two, in a case of this sort – when your friend is at the point of death!'

'He is not, I tell you!'

'For anything you know, he may be! you can't tell till you have seen him. At all events, he must have met with some terrible accident, and you ought to see him: he'll take it very unkind if you don't.'

'Confound it! I can't. He and I have not been on good terms of late.'

'Oh, my dear boy! Surely, surely, you are not so unforgiving as to carry your little differences to such a length as'—

'Little differences, indeed!' I muttered.

'Well, but only remember the occasion! Think how'—

'Well, well, don't bother me now – I'll see about it,' I replied.

And my seeing about it, was to send Fergus next morning, with my mother's compliments, to make the requisite inquiries; for, of course, my going was out of the question – or sending a message either. He brought back intelligence that the young squire was laid up with the complicated evils of a broken head and certain contusions (occasioned by a fall – of which he did not trouble himself to relate the particulars – and the subsequent misconduct of his horse), and a severe cold, the consequence of lying on the wet ground in the rain; but there were no broken bones, and no immediate prospects of dissolution.

It was evident then, that, for Mrs Graham's sake, it was not his intention to criminate me.

# Chapter 15

That day was rainy like its predecessor; but towards evening it began to clear up a little, and the next morning was fair and promising. I was out on the hill with the reapers. A light wind swept over the corn; and all nature laughed in the sunshine. The lark was rejoicing among the silvery floating clouds. The late rain had so sweetly freshened and cleared the air, and washed the sky, and left such glittering gems on branch and blade, that not even the farmers could have the heart to blame it. But no ray of sunshine could reach my heart, no breeze could freshen it; nothing could fill the void my faith, and hope, and joy in Helen Graham had left, or drive away the keen regrets, and bitter dregs of lingering love that still oppressed it.

While I stood, with folded arms, abstractedly gazing on the undulating swell of the corn not yet disturbed by the reapers, something gently pulled my skirts, and a small voice, no longer welcome to my ears, aroused me with the startling words—

'Mr Markham, mamma wants you.'

'Wants me, Arthur?'

# The Tenant of Wildfell Hall

'Yes. Why do you look so queer?' said he, half laughing, half frightened at the unexpected aspect of my face in suddenly turning towards him – 'and why have you kept so long away? – Come! – Won't you come?'

'I'm busy just now,' I replied, scarce knowing what to answer.

He looked up in childish bewilderment; but before I could speak again, the lady herself was at my side.

'Gilbert, I must speak with you!' said she, in a tone of suppressed vehemence.

I looked at her pale cheek and glittering eye, but answered nothing.

'Only for a moment,' pleaded she. 'Just step aside into this other field,' she glanced at the reapers, some of whom were directing looks of impertinent curiosity towards her – 'I won't keep you a minute.'

I accompanied her through the gap.

'Arthur, darling, run and gather those blue-bells,' said she, pointing to some that were gleaming, at some distance, under the hedge along which we walked. The child hesitated, as if unwilling to quit my side. 'Go love!' repeated she, more urgently, and in a tone, which, though not unkind, demanded prompt obedience, and obtained it.

'Well, Mrs Graham?' said I, calmly and coldly; for, though I saw she was miserable, and pitied her, I felt glad to have it in my power to torment her.

She fixed her eyes upon me with a look that pierced me to the heart; and yet, it made me smile.

'I don't ask the reason for this change, Gilbert,' said she, with bitter calmness. 'I know it too well; but though I could see myself suspected and condemned by every one else, and bear it with calmness, I cannot endure it from you. – Why did you not come to hear my explanation on the day I appointed to give it?'

'Because I happened, in the interim, to learn all you would have told me – and a trifle more, I imagine.'

'Impossible, for I would have told you all!' cried she passionately – 'but I won't now, for I see you are not worthy of it!'

And her pale lips quivered with agitation.

'Why not, may I ask?'

She repelled my mocking smile with a glance of scornful indignation.

'Because you never understood me, or you would not soon have listened to my traducers – my confidence would be misplaced in you – you are not the man I thought you – Go! I won't care what you think of me.'

She turned away, and I went; for I thought that would torment her as much as anything; and I believe I was right; for, looking back a minute after, I saw her half turn round, as if hoping or expecting to find me still beside her; and then she stood still, and cast one look behind. It was a look less expressive of anger than of bitter anguish and despair: but I immediately assumed an aspect of indifference, and affected to be gazing carelessly round me, and I suppose she went on; for after lingering awhile to see if she would come back or call, I ventured one more glance, and saw her a good way off, moving rapidly up the field with little Arthur running by her side and apparently talking as he went; but she kept her face averted from him, as if to hide some uncontrollable emotion. And I returned to my business.

But I soon began to regret my precipitancy in leaving her so soon. It was evident she loved me – probably, she was tired of Mr Lawrence, and wished to exchange him for me; and if I had loved and reverenced her less to begin with,

the preference might have gratified and amused me; but now, the contrast between her outward seeming and her inward mind, as I supposed, – between my former and my present opinion of her, was so harrowing – so distressing to my feelings, that it swallowed up every lighter consideration.

But still, I was curious to know what sort of an explanation she would have given me, – or would give now, if I pressed her for it – how much she would confess, and how she would endeavour to excuse herself. I longed to know what to despise, and what to admire in her; how much to pity, and how much to hate; – and, what was more, I would know. I would see her once more, and fairly satisfy myself in what light to regard her, before we parted. Lost to me she was, for ever, of course; but still, I could not bear to think that we had parted, for the last time, with so much unkindesss and misery on both sides. That last look of hers had sunk into my heart; I could not forget it. But what a fool I was! Had she not deceived me, injured me – blighted my happiness for life? 'Well, I'll see her, however,' was my concluding resolve, – 'but not today: today and tonight, she may think upon her sins, and be as miserable as she will: tomorrow, I will see her once again, and know something more about her. The interview may be serviceable to her, or it may not. At any rate, it will give a breath of excitement to the life she has doomed to stagnation, and may calm with certainty some agitating thoughts.'

I did go on the morrow; but not till towards evening, after the business of the day was concluded, that is, between six and seven; and the westering sun was gleaming redly on the old hall, and flaming in the latticed windows, as I reached it, imparting to the place a cheerfulness not its own. I need not dilate upon the feelings with which I approached the shrine of my former divinity – that spot teeming with a thousand delightful recollections and glorious dreams – all darkened now, by one disastrous truth.

Rachel admitted me into the parlour, and went to call her mistress, for she was not there; but there was her desk left open on the little round table beside the high-backed chair, with a book laid upon it. Her limited but choice collection of books was almost as familiar to me as my own; but this volume I had not seen before. I took it up. It was Sir Humphry Davy's *Last Days of a Philosopher*, and on the first leaf was written,— 'Frederick Lawrence.' I closed the book, but kept it in my hand, and stood facing the door, with my back to the fireplace, calmly waiting her arrival; for I did not doubt she would come. And soon I heard her step in the hall. My heart was beginning to throb, but I checked it with an internal rebuke, and maintained my composure – outwardly, at least. She entered, calm, pale, collected.

'To what am I indebted for this favour, Mr Markham?' said she, with such severe but quiet dignity as almost disconcerted me; but I answered with a smile, and impudently enough—

'Well, I am come to hear your explanation.'

'I told you I would not give it,' said she. 'I said you were unworthy of my confidence.'

'Oh, very well,' replied I, moving to the door.

'Stay a moment,' said she. 'This is the last time I shall see you: don't go just yet.'

I remained awaiting her further commands.

# The Tenant of Wildfell Hall

'Tell me,' resumed she, 'on what grounds you believe those things against me; who told you; and what did they say?'

I paused a moment. She met my eyes as unflinchingly as if her bosom had been steeled with conscious innocence. She was resolved to know the worst, and determined to dare it too. 'I can crush that bold spirit,' thought I. But while I secretly exulted in my power, I felt disposed to dally with my victim like a cat. Showing her the book that I still held in my hand, and pointing to the name on the fly-leaf, but fixing my eye upon her face, I asked—

'Do you know that gentleman?'

'Of course I do,' replied she; and a sudden flush suffused her features – whether of shame or anger I could not tell: it rather resembled the latter. 'What next, sir?'

'How long is it since you saw him?'

'Who gave you the right to catechize me, on this or any other subject?'

'Oh, no one! – it's quite at your option whether to answer or not. And now, let me ask – have you heard what has lately befallen this friend of yours? – because, if you have not'—

'I will not be insulted, Mr Markham!' cried she, almost infuriated at my manner. 'So you had better leave the house at once, if you came only for that.'

'I did not come to insult you: I came to hear your explanation.'

'And I tell you I won't give it!' retorted she, pacing the room in a state of strong excitement, with her hands clasped tightly together, breathing short, and flashing fires of indignation from her eyes. 'I will not condescend to explain myself to one that can make a jest of such horrible suspicions, and be so easily led to entertain them.'

'I do not make a jest of them, Mrs Graham,' returned I, dropping at once my tone of taunting sarcasm. 'I heartily wish I could find them a jesting matter! And as to being easily led to suspect, God only knows what a blind incredulous fool I have hitherto been, perseveringly shutting my eyes and stopping my ears against everything that threatened to shake my confidence in you, till proof itself confounded my infatuation!'

'What proof, sir?'

'Well, I'll tell you. You remember that evening when I was here last?'

'I do.'

'Even then, you dropped some hints that might have opened the eyes of a wiser man; but they had no such effect upon me: I went on trusting and believing, hoping against hope, and adoring where I could not comprehend. It so happened, however, that after I left you, I turned back – drawn by pure depth of sympathy, and ardour of affection – not daring to intrude my presence openly upon you, but unable to resist the temptation of catching one glimpse through the window, just to see how you were; for I had left you apparently in great affliction, and I partly blamed my own want of forbearance and discretion as the cause of it. If I did wrong, love alone was my incentive, and the punishment was severe enough; for it was just as I had reached that tree, that you came out into the garden with your friend. Not choosing to show myself, under the circumstances, I stood still, in the shadow, till you had both passed by.

'And how much of our conversation did you hear?'

'I heard quite enough, Helen. And it was well for me that I did hear it; for nothing less could have cured my infatuation. I always said and thought, that

# The Tenant of Wildfell Hall

I would never believe a word against you, unless I heard it from your own lips. All the hints and affirmations of others I treated as malignant, baseless slanders; your own self-accusations I believed to be overstrained; and all that seemed unaccountable in your position, I trusted that you could account for if you chose.'

Mrs Graham had discontinued her walk. She leant against one end of the chimney-piece, opposite that near which I was standing, with her chin resting on her closed hand, her eyes – no longer burning with anger, but gleaming with restless excitement – sometimes glancing at me while I spoke, then coursing the opposite wall, or fixed upon the carpet.

'You should have come to me, after all,' said she, 'and heard what I had to say in my own justification. It was ungenerous and wrong to withdraw yourself so secretly and suddenly, immediately after such ardent protestations of attachment, without ever assigning a reason for the change. You should have told me all – no matter how bitterly. It would have been better than this silence.'

'To what end should I have done so? You could not have enlightened me further, on the subject which alone concerned me; nor could you have made me discredit the evidence of my senses. I desired our intimacy to be discontinued at once, as you yourself had acknowledged would probably be the case if I knew all; but I did not wish to upbraid you, – though (as you also acknowledged) you had deeply wronged me. Yes; you have done me an injury you can never repair – or any other either – you have blighted the freshness and promise of youth, and made my life a wilderness! I might live a hundred years, but I could never recover from the effects of this withering blow – and never forget it! Hereafter— You smile, Mrs Graham,' said I, suddenly stopping short, checked in my passionate declamation by unutterable feelings to behold her actually smiling at the picture of the ruin she had wrought.

'Did I?' replied she, looking seriously up; 'I was not aware of it. If I did, it was not for pleasure at the thoughts of the harm I had done you. Heaven knows I have had torment enough at the bare possibility of that; – it was for joy to find that you had some depth of soul and feeling after all, and to hope that I had not been utterly mistaken in your worth. But smiles and tears are so alike with me; they are neither of them confined to particular feelings: I often cry when I am happy, and smile when I am sad.'

She looked at me again, and seemed to expect a reply; but I continued silent.

'Would you be very glad,' resumed she, 'to find that you were mistaken in your conclusions?'

'How can you ask it, Helen?'

'I don't say I can clear myself altogether,' said she, speaking low and fast, while her heart beat visibly and her bosom heaved with excitement, – 'but would you be glad to discover I was better than you think me?'

'Anything, that could, in the least degree, tend to restore my former opinion of you, to excuse the regard I still feel for you, and alleviate the pangs of unutterable regret that accompany it, would be only too gladly – too eagerly received!'

Her cheeks burned and her whole frame trembled, now, with excess of agitation. She did not speak, but flew to her desk, and snatching thence what seemed a thick album or manuscript volume, hastily tore away a few leaves from the end, and thrust the rest into my hand, saying, 'You needn't read it all; but take it home with you,' and hurried from the room. But when I had left the

house, and was proceeding down the walk, she opened the window and called me back. It was only to say—

'Bring it back when you have read it; and don't breathe a word of what it tells you to any living being. I trust to your honour.'

Before I could answer, she had closed the casement and turned away. I saw her cast herself back in the old oak chair, and cover her face with her hands. Her feelings had been wrought to a pitch that rendered it necessary to seek relief in tears.

Panting with eagerness, and struggling to suppress my hopes, I hurried home, and rushed upstairs to my room, having first provided myself with a candle, though it was scarcely twilight yet – then, shut and bolted the door, determined to tolerate no interruption; and sitting down before the table, opened out my prize and delivered myself up to its perusal – first, hastily turning over the leaves, and snatching a sentence here and there, and then, setting myself steadily to read it through.

I have it now before me; and though you could not, of course, peruse it with half the interest that I did, I know you would not be satisfied with an abbreviation of its contents, and you shall have the whole, save, perhaps, a few passages here and there of merely temporal interest to the writer, or such as would serve to encumber the story rather than elucidate it. It begins somewhat abruptly, thus – but we will reserve its commencement for another chapter, and call it—

# Chapter 16

*June 1st, 1821*

 e have just returned to Staningly – that is, we returned some days ago, and I am not yet settled, and feel as if I never should be. We left town sooner than was intended, in consequence of my uncle's indisposition – I wonder what would have been the result if we had stayed the full time. I am quite ashamed of my new-sprung distaste for country life. All my former occupations seem so tedious and dull, my former amusements so insipid and unprofitable. I cannot enjoy my music, because there is no one to hear it. I cannot enjoy my walks, because there is no one to meet. I cannot enjoy my books, because they have not power to arrest my attention – my head is so haunted with the recollections of the last few weeks, that I cannot attend to them. My drawing suits me best, for I can draw and think at the same time; and if my productions cannot now be seen by any one but myself and those who do not care about them, they, possibly, may always be, hereafter. But then, there is one face I am trying to paint or to sketch, and always without success; and that vexes me. As for the owner of that face, I cannot get him out of my mind – and, indeed, I never try. I wonder whether he ever thinks of me; and I wonder

whether I shall ever see him again. And then might follow a train of other wonderments – questions for time and fate to answer – concluding with: – supposing all the rest be answered in the affirmative, I wonder whether I shall ever repent it – as my aunt would tell me I should, if she knew what I was thinking about. How distinctly I remember our conversation that evening before our departure for town, when we were sitting together over the fire, my uncle having gone to bed with a slight attack of the gout.

'Helen,' said she, after a thoughtful silence, 'do you ever think about marriage?'

'Yes, aunt, often.'

'And do you ever contemplate the possibility of being married yourself, or engaged, before the season is over?'

'Sometimes; but I don't think it at all likely that I ever shall.'

'Why so?'

'Because, I imagine there must be only a very, very few men in the world, that I should like to marry; and of those few, it is ten to one I may never be acquainted with one: or if I should, it is twenty to one, he may not happen to be single, or to take a fancy to me.'

'That is no argument at all. It may be very true – and I hope is true, that there are very few men whom you would choose to marry, of yourself. It is not, indeed, to be supposed, that you would wish to marry any one, till you were asked: a girl's affections should never be won unsought. But when they are sought – when the citadel of the heart is fairly besieged – it is apt to surrender sooner than the owner is aware of, and often against her better judgment, and in opposition to all her preconceived ideas of what she could have loved, unless she be extremely careful and discreet. Now, I want to warn you, Helen, of these things, and to exhort you to be watchful and circumspect from the very commencement of your career, and not to suffer your heart to be stolen from you by the first foolish or unprincipled person that covets the possession of it. – You know, my dear, you are only just eighteen; there is plenty of time before you, and neither your uncle nor I are in any hurry to get you off our hands, and I may venture to say, there will be no lack of suitors; for you can boast a good family, a pretty considerable fortune and expectations, and, I may as well tell you likewise – for, if I don't, others will – that you have a fair share of beauty, besides – and I hope you may never have cause to regret it!'

'I hope not, aunt; but why should you fear it?'

'Because, my dear, beauty is that quality which, next to money, is generally the most attractive to the worst kinds of men; and therefore, it is likely to entail a great deal of trouble on the possessor.'

'Have you been troubled in that way, aunt?'

'No, Helen,' said she, with reproachful gravity, 'but I know many that have; and some, through carelessness, have been the wretched victims of deceit; and some, through weakness, have fallen into snares and temptations, terrible to relate.'

'Well, I shall be neither careless nor weak.'

'Remember Peter, Helen! Don't boast, but watch. Keep a guard over your eyes and ears as the inlets of your heart, and over your lips as the outlet, lest they betray you in a moment of unwariness. Receive, coldly and dispassionately, every attention, till you have ascertained and duly considered the worth of the aspirant; and let your affections be consequent upon approbation alone. First

study; then approve; then love. Let your eyes be blind to all external attractions, your ears deaf to all the fascinations of flattery and light discourse. – These are nothing – and worse than nothing – snares and wiles of the tempter, to lure the thoughtless to their own destruction. Principle is the first thing, after all; and next to that, good sense, respectability, and moderate wealth. If you should marry the handsomest, and most accomplished and superficially agreeable man in the world, you little know the misery that would overwhelm you, if, after all, you should find him to be a worthless reprobate, or even an impracticable fool.'

'But what are all the poor fools and reprobates to do, aunt? If everybody followed your advice, the world would soon come to an end.'

'Never fear, my dear! the male fools and reprobates will never want for partners, while there are so many of the other sex to match them; but do you follow my advice. And this is no subject for jesting, Helen – I am sorry to see you treat the matter in that light way. Believe me, matrimony is a serious thing.' And she spoke it so seriously, that one might have fancied she had known it to her cost; but I asked no more impertinent questions and merely answered—

'I know it is; and I know there is truth and sense in what you say; but you need not fear for me, for I not only should think it wrong to marry a man that was deficient in sense or in principle, but I should never be tempted to do it; for I could not like him, if he were ever so handsome, and ever so charming, in other respects; I should hate him – despise him – pity him – anything but love him. My affections not only ought to be founded on approbation, but they will and must be so: for, without approving, I cannot love. It is needless to say, I ought to be able to respect and honour the man I marry, as well as love him, for I cannot love him without. So set your mind at rest.'

'I hope it may be so,' answered she.

'I know it is so,' persisted I.

'You have not been tried yet, Helen – we can but hope,' said she, in her cold, cautious way.

I was vexed at her incredulity; but I am not sure her doubts were entirely without sagacity; I fear I have found it much easier to remember her advice than to profit by it; – indeed I have sometimes been led to question the soundness of her doctrines on those subjects. Her counsels may be good as far as they go – in the main points, at least; but there are some things she has overlooked in her calculations. I wonder if she was ever in love.

I commenced my career – or my first campaign, as my uncle calls it – kindling with bright hopes and fancies – chiefly raised by this conversation – and full of confidence in my own discretion. At first, I was delighted with the novelty and excitement of our London life; but soon I began to weary of its mingled turbulence and constraint, and sigh for the freshness and freedom of home. My new acquaintances, both male and female, disappointed my expectations, and vexed and depressed me by turns for I soon grew tired of studying their peculiarities, and laughing at their foibles – particularly as I was obliged to keep my criticisms to myself, for my aunt would not hear them – and they – the ladies especially – appeared so provokingly mindless, and heartless, and artificial. The gentlemen seemed better, but, perhaps, it was because I knew them less – perhaps, because they flattered me; but I did not fall in love with any of them; and, if their attentions pleased me one moment, they provoked me the next,

# The Tenant of Wildfell Hall

because they put me out of humour with myself, by revealing my vanity, and making me fear I was becoming like some of the ladies I so heartily despised.

There was one elderly gentleman that annoyed me very much; a rich old friend of my uncle's, who, I believe, thought I could not do better than marry him; but, besides being old, he was ugly and disagreeable, – and wicked, I am sure, though my aunt scolded me for saying so; but she allowed he was no saint. And there was another, less hateful, but still more tiresome, because she favoured him, and was always thrusting him upon me, and sounding his praises in my ears, Mr Boarham, by name, Bore'em, as I prefer spelling it, for a terrible bore he was: I shudder still, at the remembrance of his voice, drone, drone, drone, in my ear, while he sat beside me, prosing away by the half-hour together, and beguiling himself with the notion that he was improving my mind by useful information, or impressing his dogmas upon me, and reforming my errors of judgment, or perhaps, that he was talking down to my level, and amusing me with entertaining discourse. Yet he was a decent man enough, in the main, I dare say; and if he had kept his distance, I never would have hated him. As it was, it was almost impossible to help it; for he not only bothered me with the infliction of his own presence, but he kept me from the enjoyment of more agreeable society.

One night, however, at a ball, he had been more than usually tormenting, and my patience was quite exhausted. It appeared as if the whole evening was fated to be insupportable: I had just had one dance with an empty-headed coxcomb, and then Mr Boarham had come upon me and seemed determined to cling to me for the rest of the night. He never danced himself, and there he sat, poking his head in my face, and impressing all beholders with the idea that he was a confirmed, acknowledged lover; my aunt looking complacently on, all the time, and wishing him God-speed. In vain I attempted to drive him away by giving a loose to my exasperated feelings, even to positive rudeness: nothing could convince him that his presence was disagreeable. Sullen silence was taken for rapt attention, and gave him greater room to talk; sharp answers were received as smart sallies of girlish vivacity, that only required an indulgent rebuke; and flat contradictions were but as oil to the flames, calling forth new strains of argument to support his dogmas, and bringing down upon me endless floods of reasoning to overwhelm me with conviction.

But there was one present who seemed to have better appreciation of my frame of mind. A gentleman stood by, who had been watching our conference for some time, evidently much amused at my companion's remorseless pertinacity and my manifest annoyance, and laughing to himself at the asperity and uncompromising spirit of my replies. At length, however, he withdrew, and went to the lady of the house, apparently for the purpose of asking an introduction to me, for, shortly after, they both came up, and she introduced him as Mr Huntingdon, the son of a late friend of my uncle's. He asked me to dance. I gladly consented, of course; and he was my companion during the remainder of my stay, which was not long, for my aunt, as usual, insisted upon an early departure.

I was sorry to go, for I had found my new acquaintance a very lively and entertaining companion. There was a certain graceful ease and freedom about all he said and did, that gave a sense of repose and expansion to the mind, after so much constraint and formality as I had been doomed to suffer. There might

# The Tenant of Wildfell Hall

be, it is true, a little too much careless boldness in his manner and address, but I was in so good a humour, and so grateful for my late deliverance from Mr Boarham, that it did not anger me.

'Well, Helen, how do you like Mr Boarham now?' said my aunt as we took our seats in the carriage and drove away.

'Worse than ever,' I replied.

She looked displeased, but said no more on that subject.

'Who was the gentleman you danced with last,' resumed she after a pause – 'that was so officious in helping you on with your shawl?'

'He was not officious at all, aunt: he never attempted to help me, till he saw Mr Boarham coming to do so; and then he stepped laughingly forward and said, "Come, I'll preserve you from that infliction."'

'Who was it, I ask?' said she, with frigid gravity.

'It was Mr Huntingdon, the son of uncle's old friend.'

'I have heard your uncle speak of young Mr Huntingdon. I've heard him say, "He's a fine lad, that young Huntingdon, but a bit wildish, I fancy." So I'd have you beware.'

'What does "a bit wildish" mean?' I inquired.

'It means destitute of principle, and prone to every vice that is common to youth.'

'But I've heard uncle say he was a sad wild fellow himself, when he was young.'

She sternly shook her head.

'He was jesting then, I suppose,' said I, 'and here he was speaking at random – at least, I cannot believe there is any harm in those laughing blue eyes.'

'False reasoning, Helen!' said she, with a sigh.

'Well, we ought to be charitable, you know, aunt – besides, I don't think it is false: I am an excellent physiognomist, and I always judge of people's characters by their looks – not by whether they are handsome or ugly, but by the general cast of the countenance. For instance, I should know by your countenance that you were not of a cheerful, sanguine disposition; and I should know by Mr Wilmot's that he was a worthless old reprobate, and by Mr Boarham's that he was not an agreeable companion, and by Mr Huntingdon's that he was neither a fool nor a knave, though, possibly, neither a sage nor a saint – but that is no matter to me, as I am not likely to meet him again – unless as an occasional partner in the ballroom.'

It was not so, however, for I met him again next morning. He came to call upon my uncle, apologizing for not having done so before, by saying he was only lately returned from the Continent, and had not heard, till the previous night, of my uncle's arrival in town; and after that, I often met him; sometimes in public, sometimes at home; for he was very assiduous in paying his respects to his old friend, who did not, however, consider himself greatly obliged by the attention.

'I wonder what the deuce the lad means by coming so often?' he would say, – 'can you tell, Helen? – Hey? He wants none o' my company, nor I his – that's certain.'

'I wish you'd tell him so, then,' said my aunt.

'Why, what for? If I don't want him, somebody does mayhap (winking at me). Besides, he's a pretty tidy fortune, Peggy, you know – not such a catch as

# The Tenant of Wildfell Hall

Wilmot, but then Helen won't hear of that match; for, somehow, these old chaps don't go down with the girls – with all their money – and their experience to boot. I'll bet anything she'd rather have this young fellow without a penny, than Wilmot with his house full of gold – Wouldn't you, Nell?'

'Yes, uncle; but that's not saying much for Mr Huntingdon, for I'd rather be an old maid and a pauper, than Mrs Wilmot.'

'And Mrs Huntingdon? What would you rather be than Mrs Huntingdon? eh?'

'I'll tell you when I've considered the matter.'

'Ah! it needs consideration then. But come, now – would you rather be an old maid – let alone the pauper?'

'I can't tell till I'm asked.'

And I left the room immediately, to escape further examination. But five minutes after, in looking from my window, I beheld Mr Boarham, coming up to the door. I waited nearly half-an-hour in uncomfortable suspense, expecting every minute to be called, and vainly longing to hear him go. Then, footsteps were heard on the stairs, and my aunt entered the room with a solemn countenance, and closed the door behind her.

'Here is Mr Boarham, Helen,' said she. 'He wishes to see you.'

'Oh, aunt! Can't you tell him I'm indisposed? I'm sure I am – to see him.'

'Nonsense, my dear! this is no trifling matter. He is come on a very important errand – to ask your hand in marriage of your uncle and me.'

'I hope my uncle and you told him it was not in your power to give it. What right had he to ask any one before me?'

'Helen!'

'What did my uncle say?'

'He said he would not interfere in the matter; if you liked to accept Mr Boarham's obliging offer, you'—

'Did he say obliging offer?'

'No; he said if you liked to take him you might; and if not, you might please yourself.'

'He said right; and what did you say?'

'It is no matter what I said. What will you say? – that is the question. He is now waiting to ask you himself; but consider well before you go; and if you intend to refuse him, give me your reasons.'

'I shall refuse him, of course, but you must tell me how, for I want to be civil and yet decided – and when I've got rid of him I'll give you my reasons afterwards.'

'But stay, Helen; sit down a little, and compose yourself. Mr Boarham is in no particular hurry, for he has little doubt of your acceptance; and I want to speak with you. Tell me, my dear, what are your objections to him? Do you deny that he is an upright, honourable man?'

'No.'

'Do you deny that he is sensible, sober, respectable?'

'No; he may be all this, but'—

'But, Helen! How many such men do you expect to meet with in the world! Upright, honourable, sensible, sober, respectable! – Is this such an everyday character, that you should reject the possessor of such noble qualities, without a moment's hesitation? – Yes, noble, I may call them; for, think of the full

meaning of each, and how many inestimable virtues they include (and I might add many more to the list), and consider that all this is laid at your feet; it is in your power to secure this inestimable blessing for life – a worthy and excellent husband, who loves you tenderly, but not too fondly so as to blind him to your faults, and will be your guide throughout life's pilgrimage, and your partner in eternal bliss! Think how'—

'But I hate him, aunt,' said I, interrupting this unusual flow of eloquence.

'Hate him, Helen! Is this a Christian spirit? – you hate him? – and he so good a man!'

'I don't hate him as a man, but as a husband. As a man, I love him so much, that I wish him a better wife than I – one as good as himself, or better – if you think that possible – provided, she could like him; but I never could, and therefore'—

'But why not? What objection do you find?'

'Firstly, he is, at least, forty years old – considerably more I should think, and I am but eighteen; secondly, he is narrow-minded and bigoted in the extreme; thirdly, his tastes and feelings are wholly dissimilar to mine; fourthly, his looks, voice, and manner are particularly displeasing to me; and finally, I have an aversion to his whole person that I never can surmount.'

'Then you ought to surmount it! And please to compare him for a moment with Mr Huntingdon, and, good looks apart (which contribute nothing to the merit of the man, or to the happiness of married life, and which you have so often professed to hold in light esteem), tell me which is the better man.'

'I have no doubt Mr Huntingdon is a much better man than you think him – but we are not talking about him, but about Mr Boarham; and as I would rather grow, live and die in single blessedness than be his wife, it is but right that I should tell him so at once, and put him out of suspense – so let me go.'

'But don't give him a flat denial; he has no idea of such a thing, and it would offend him greatly: say you have no thoughts of matrimony, at present'—

'But I have thoughts of it.'

'Or that you desire a further acquaintance.'

'But I don't desire a further acquaintance – quite the contrary.'

And without waiting for further admonitions, I left the room, and went to seek Mr Boarham. He was walking up and down the drawing-room, humming snatches of tunes, and nibbling the end of his cane.

'My dear young lady,' said he, bowing and smirking with great complacency, 'I have your kind guardian's permission'—

'I know, sir,' said I, wishing to shorten the scene as much as possible, 'and I am greatly obliged for your preference, but must beg to decline the honour you wish to confer; for I think, we were not made for each other – as you yourself would shortly discover if the experiment were tried.'

My aunt was right: it was quite evident he had had little doubt of my acceptance, and no idea of a positive denial. He was amazed – astounded at such an answer, but too incredulous to be much offended; and after a little humming and hawing he returned to the attack.

'I know, my dear, that there exists a considerable disparity between us in years, in temperament, and perhaps some other things; but let me assure you, I shall not be severe to mark the faults and foibles of a young and ardent nature such as yours, and while I acknowledge them to myself, and even rebuke them

with all a father's care, believe me, no youthful lover could be more tenderly indulgent towards the object of his affections, than I to you; and, on the other hand, let me hope that my more experienced years and graver habits of reflection will be no disparagement in your eyes, as I shall endeavour to make them all conducive to your happiness. Come now! What do you say? – Let us have no young lady's affectations and caprices, but speak out at once!'

'I will, but only to repeat what I said before, that I am certain we were not made for each other.'

'You really think so?'

'I do.'

'But, you don't know me – you wish for a further acquaintance – a longer time to'—

'No, I don't. I know you as well as I ever shall, and better than you know me, or you would never dream of uniting yourself to one so incongruous – so utterly unsuitable to you in every way.'

'But, my dear young lady, I don't look for perfection, I can excuse'—

'Thank you, Mr Boarham, but I won't trespass upon your goodness. You may save your indulgence and consideration for some more worthy object, that won't tax them so heavily.'

'But let me beg you to consult your aunt; that excellent lady, I am sure, will'—

'I have consulted her; and I know her wishes coincide with yours; but in such important matters, I take the liberty of judging for myself; and no persuasion can alter my inclinations, or induce me to believe that such a step would be conducive to my happiness, or yours – and I wonder that a man of your experience and discretion should think of choosing such a wife.'

'Ah, well!' said he, 'I have sometimes wondered at that myself. I have sometimes said to myself, "Now, Boarham, what is this you're after? Take care, man – look before you leap! This is a sweet, bewitching creature, but remember, the brightest attractions to the lover, too often prove the husband's greatest torments!" I assure you my choice has not been made without much reasoning and reflection. The seeming imprudence of the match has cost me many an anxious thought by day, and many a sleepless hour by night; but at length, I satisfied myself, that it was not, in very deed, imprudent. I saw my sweet girl was not without her faults, but of these, her youth, I trusted, was not one, but rather an earnest of virtues yet unblown – a strong ground of presumption that her little defects of temper, and errors of judgment, opinion, or manner were not irremediable, but might easily be removed or mitigated by the patient efforts of a watchful and judicious adviser, and where I failed to enlighten and control, I thought I might safety undertake to pardon, for the sake of her many excellences. Therefore, my dearest girl, since I am satisfied, why should you object – on my account, at least?'

'But to tell you the truth, Mr Boarham, it is on my own account I principally object; so let us – drop the subject,' I would have said, 'for it is worse than useless to pursue it any further,' but he pertinaciously interrupted me with—

'But why so? I would love you, cherish you, protect you,' etc., etc.

I shall not trouble myself to put down all that passed between us. Suffice it to say, that I found him very troublesome, and very hard to convince that I really meant what I said, and really was so obstinate and blind to my own

interests, that there was no shadow of a chance that either he or my aunt would ever be able to overcome my objections. Indeed, I am not sure that I succeeded after all, though, wearied with his so pertinaciously returning to the same point and repeating the same arguments over and over again, forcing me to reiterate the same replies, I at length turned short and sharp upon him, and my last words were—

'I tell you plainly, that it cannot be. No consideration can induce me to marry against my inclinations. I respect you – at least, I would respect you, if you would behave like a sensible man – but I cannot love you, and never could – and the more you talk the further you repel me; so pray don't say any more about it.'

Whereupon, he wished me a good morning and withdrew, disconcerted and offended, no doubt; but surely it was not my fault.

# Chapter 17

The next day, I accompanied my uncle and aunt to a dinner-party at Mr Wilmot's. He had two ladies staying with him, his niece Annabella, a fine dashing girl, or rather young woman, of some five-and-twenty, too great a flirt to be married, according to her own assertion, but greatly admired by the gentlemen, who universally pronounced her a splendid woman, – and her gentle cousin Milicent Hargrave, who had taken a violent fancy to me, mistaking me for something vastly better than I was. And I, in return, was very fond of her. I should entirely exclude poor Milicent in my general animadversions against the ladies of my acquaintance. But it was not on her account, or her cousin's, that I have mentioned the party: it was for the sake of another of Mr Wilmot's guests, to wit Mr Huntingdon. I have good reason to remember his presence there, for this was the last time I saw him.

He did not sit near me at dinner; for it was his fate to hand in a capacious old dowager, and mine to be handed in by Mr Grimsby, a friend of his, but a man I very greatly disliked: there was a sinister cast in his countenance, and a mixture of lurking ferocity and fulsome insincerity in his demeanour, that I could not away with. What a tiresome custom that is, by-the-bye – one among the many sources of factitious annoyance of this ultra-civilized life. If the gentlemen must lead the ladies into the dining-room, why cannot they take those they like best?

'I am not sure, however, that Mr Huntingdon would have taken me, if he had been at liberty to make his own selection. It is quite possible he might have chosen Miss Wilmot; for she seemed bent upon engrossing his attention to herself, and he seemed nothing loath to pay the homage she demanded. I thought so, at least, when I saw how they talked and laughed, and glanced across the

table to the neglect and evident umbrage of their respective neighbours – and afterwards, as the gentlemen joined us in the drawing-room, when she, immediately upon his entrance, loudly called upon him to be the arbiter of a dispute between herself and another lady, and he answered the summons with alacrity, and decided the question without a moment's hesitation in her favour – though, to my thinking she was obviously in the wrong – and then stood chatting familiarly with her and a group of other ladies; while I sat with Milicent Hargrave at the opposite end of the room, looking over the latter's drawings, and aiding her with my critical observations and advice, at her particular desire. But in spite of my efforts to remain composed, my attention wandered from the drawings to the merry group, and against my better judgment my wrath rose, and doubtless my countenance lowered; for Milicent observing that I must be tired of her daubs and scratches, begged I would join the company now, and defer the examination of the remainder to another opportunity. But while I was assuring her that I had no wish to join them, and was not tired, Mr Huntingdon himself came up to the little round table at which we sat.

'Are these yours?' said he, carelessly taking up one of the drawings.

'No, they are Miss Hargrave's.'

'Oh! well, let's have a look at them.'

And, regardless of Miss Hargrave's protestations that they were not worth looking at, he drew a chair to my side, and receiving the drawings, one by one, from my hand, successively scanned them over, and threw them on the table, but said not a word about them, though he was talking all the time. I don't know what Milicent Hargrave thought of such conduct, but I found his conversation extremely interesting, though, as I afterwards discovered, when I came to analyse it, it was chiefly confined to quizzing the different members of the company present; and albeit he made some clever remarks, and some excessively droll ones, I do not think the whole would appear anything very particular, if written here, without the adventitious aids of look, and tone, and gesture, and that ineffable but indefinite charm, which cast a halo over all he did and said, and which would have made it a delight to look in his face, and hear the music of his voice, if he had been talking positive nonsense – and which, moreover, made me feel so bitter against my aunt when she put a stop to this enjoyment, by coming composedly forward, under pretence of wishing to see the drawings, that she cared and knew nothing about, and while making believe to examine them, addressing herself to Mr Huntingdon, with one of her coldest and most repellent aspects, and beginning a series of the most commonplace and formidably formal questions and observations, on purpose to wrest his attention from me – on purpose to vex me, as I thought: and having now looked through the portfolio, I left them to their *tête-à-tête*, and seated myself on a sofa, quite apart from the company – never thinking how strange such conduct would appear, but merely to indulge, at first the vexation of the moment, and subsequently to enjoy my private thoughts.

But I was not left long alone, for Mr Wilmot, of all men the least welcome, took advantage of my isolated position to come and plant himself beside me. I had flattered myself that I had so effectually repulsed his advances on all former occasions, that I had nothing more to apprehend from his unfortunate predilection; but it seems I was mistaken: so great was his confidence, either in his wealth or his remaining powers of attraction, and so firm his conviction of

# The Tenant of Wildfell Hall

feminine weakness, that he thought himself warranted to return to the siege, which he did with renovated ardour, enkindled by the quantity of wine he had drunk – a circumstance that rendered him infinitely the more disgusting; but greatly as I abhorred him at that moment, I did not like to treat him with rudeness, as I was now his guest and had just been enjoying his hospitality; and I was no hand at a polite but determined rejection, nor would it have greatly availed me if I had; for he was too coarse-minded to take any repulse that was not as plain and positive as his own effrontery. The consequence was, that he waxed more fulsomely tender, and more repulsively warm, and I was driven to the very verge of desperation, and about to say, I know not what, when I felt my hand, that hung over the arm of the sofa, suddenly taken by another and gently but fervently pressed. Instinctively, I guessed who it was, and, on looking up, was less surprised than delighted to see Mr Huntingdon smiling upon me. It was like turning from some purgatorial fiend to an angel of light, come to announce that the season of torment was past.

'Helen,' said he (he frequently called me Helen, and I never resented the freedom), 'I want you to look at this picture; Mr Wilmot will excuse you a moment, I'm sure.'

I rose with alacrity. He drew my arm within his, and led me across the room to a splendid painting of Vandyke's that I had noticed before, but not sufficiently examined. After a moment of silent contemplation, I was beginning to comment on its beauties and peculiarities, when, playfully pressing the hand he still retained within his arm, he interrupted me with—

'Never mind the picture, it was not for that I brought you here; it was to get you away from that scoundrelly old profligate yonder, who is looking as if he would like to challenge me for the affront.'

'I am very much obliged to you,' said I. 'This is twice you have delivered me from such unpleasant companionship.'

'Don't be too thankful,' he answered: 'it is not all kindness to you; it is partly from a feeling of spite to your tormentors that makes me delighted to do the old fellows a bad turn, though I don't think I have any great reason to dread them as rivals. Have I, Helen?'

'You know I detest them both.'

'And me?'

'I have no reason to detest you.'

'But what are your sentiments towards me? Helen? – Speak! How do you regard me?'

And again he pressed my hand; but I feared there was more of conscious power than tenderness in his demeanour, and I felt he had no right to extort a confession of attachment from me when he had made no correspondent avowal himself, and knew not what to answer. At last I said—

'How do you regard me?'

'Sweet angel, I adore you! I'—

'Helen, I want you a moment,' said the distinct, low voice of my aunt, close beside us. And I left him muttering maledictions against his evil angel.

'Well, aunt, what is it? What do you want?' said I, following her to the embrasure of the window.

'I want you to join the company, when you are fit to be seen,' returned she, severely regarding me; 'but please to stay here a little till that shocking colour

is somewhat abated, and your eyes have recovered something of their natural expression. I should be ashamed for any one to see you in your present state.'

Of course, such a remark had no effect in reducing the 'shocking colour'; on the contrary, I felt my face glow with redoubled fires kindled by a complication of emotions, of which indignant, swelling anger was the chief. I offered no reply, however, but pushed aside the curtain and looked into the night – or rather into the lamp-lit square.

'Was Mr Huntingdon proposing to you, Helen?' inquired my too watchful relative.

'No.'

'What was he saying then? I heard something very like it.'

'I don't know what he would have said, if you hadn't interrupted him.'

'And would you have accepted him, Helen, if he had proposed?'

'Of course not – without consulting uncle and you.'

'Oh! I'm glad, my dear, you have so much prudence left. Well, now,' she added, after a moment's pause, 'you have made yourself conspicuous enough for one evening. The ladies are directing inquiring glances towards us at this moment I see. I shall join them. Do you come too, when you are sufficiently composed to appear as usual.'

'I am so now.'

'Speak gently then; and don't look so malicious,' said my calm, but provoking aunt. 'We shall return home shortly, and then,' she added, with solemn significance, 'I have much to say to you.'

So I went home prepared for a formidable lecture. Little was said by either party in the carriage during our short transit homewards; but when I had entered my room and thrown myself into an easy-chair to reflect on the events of the day, my aunt followed me thither, and having dismissed Rachel, who was carefully stowing away my ornaments, closed the door; and placing a chair beside me, or rather at right angles with mine, sat down. With due deference I offered her my more commodious seat. She declined it, and thus opened the conference—

'Do you remember, Helen, our conversation the night but one before we left Staningly?'

'Yes, aunt.'

'And do you remember how I warned you against letting your heart be stolen from you by those unworthy of its possession; and fixing you affections where approbation did not go before, and where reason and judgment withheld their sanction?'

'Yes, but my reason'—

'Pardon me – and do you remember assuring me that there was no occasion for uneasiness on your account; for you should never be tempted to marry a man who was deficient in sense or principle, however handsome or charming in other respects he might be, for you could not love him, you should hate – despise – pity – anything but love him – were not those your words?'

'Yes, but'—

'And did you not say that your affection must be founded on approbation; and that unless you could approve and honour and respect, you could not love?'

'Yes, but I do approve and honour, and respect'—

'How so, my dear? Is Mr Huntingdon a good man?'

'He is a much better man than you think him.'

'That is nothing to the purpose. Is he a good man?'

'Yes – in some respects. He has a good disposition.'

'Is he a man of principle?'

'Perhaps not, exactly; but it is only for want of thought: if he had some one to advise him, and remind him of what is right'—

'He would soon learn, you think – and you yourself would willingly undertake to be his teacher? But, my dear, he is, I believe, full ten years older than you – how is it that you are so before-hand in moral acquirements?'

'Thanks to you, aunt, I have been well brought up, and had good examples always before me, which he, most likely, has not; and besides, he is of a sanguine temperament, and a gay, thoughtless temper, and I am naturally inclined to reflection.'

'Well, now you have made him out to be deficient in both sense and principle, by your own confession'—

'Then, my sense and my principle are at his service!'

'That sounds presumptuous, Helen! Do you think you have enough for both; and do you imagine your merry, thoughtless profligate would allow himself to be guided by a young girl like you?'

'No; I should not wish to guide him; but I think I might have influence sufficient to save him from some errors, and I should think my life well spent in the effort to preserve so noble a nature from destruction. He always listens attentively now, when I speak seriously to him (and I often venture to reprove his random way of talking), and sometimes he says that if he had me always by his side he should never do or say a wicked thing, and that a little daily talk with me would make him quite a saint. It may be partly jest and partly flattery, but still'—

'But still you think it may be truth?'

'If I do think there is any mixture of truth in it, it is not from confidence in my own powers, but in his natural goodness. And you have no right to call him a profligate, aunt; he is nothing of the kind.'

'Who told you so, my dear? What was that story about his intrigue with a married lady – Lady who was it – Miss Wilmot herself was telling you the other day?'

'It was false – false!' I cried. 'I don't believe a word of it.'

'You think, then, that he is a virtuous, well-conducted young man?'

'I know nothing positive respecting his character. I only know that I have heard nothing definite against it – nothing that could be proved, at least; and till people can prove their slanderous accusations, I will not believe them. And I know this, that if he has committed errors, they are only such as are common to youth, and such as nobody thinks anything about; for I see that everybody likes him, and all the mammas smile upon him, and their daughters – and Miss Wilmot herself – are only too glad to attract his attention.'

'Helen, the world may look upon such offences as venial; a few unprincipled mothers may be anxious to catch a young man of fortune without reference to his character; and thoughtless girls may be glad to win the smiles of so handsome a gentleman, without seeking to penetrate beyond the surface; but you, I trusted, were better informed than to see with their eyes, and judge with their perverted judgment. I did not think you would call these venial errors!'

'Nor do I, aunt; but if I hate the sins I love the sinner, and would do much for his salvation, even supposing your suspicions to be mainly true – which I do not and will not believe.'

'Well, my dear, ask your uncle what sort of company he keeps, and if he is not banded with a set of loose, profligate young men, whom he calls his friends – his jolly companions, and whose chief delight is to wallow in vice, and vie with each other who can run fastest and furthest down the headlong road to the place prepared for the devil and his angels.'

'Then, I will save him from them.'

'Oh, Helen, Helen! you little know the misery of uniting your fortunes to such a man!'

'I have such confidence in him, aunt, notwithstanding all you say, that I would willingly risk my happiness for the chance of securing his. I will leave better men to those who only consider their own advantage. If he has done amiss, I shall consider my life well spent in saving him from the consequences of his early errors, and striving to recall him to the path of virtue. God grant me success!'

Here the conversation ended, for at this juncture my uncle's voice was heard, from his chamber, loudly calling upon my aunt to come to bed. He was in a bad humour that night; for his gout was worse. It had been gradually increasing upon him ever since we came to town; and my aunt took advantage of the circumstance, next morning, to persuade him to return to the country immediately, without waiting for the close of the season. His physician supported and enforced her arguments; and contrary to her usual habits, she so hurried the preparations for removal (as much for my sake as my uncle's, I think), that in a very few days we departed; and I saw no more of Mr Huntingdon. My aunt flatters herself I shall soon forget him – perhaps, she thinks I have forgotten him, already, for I never mention his name; and she may continue to think so, till we meet again – if ever that should be. I wonder if it will.

# Chapter 18

*August 25th*

I am now quite settled down to my usual routine of steady occupations and quiet amusements – tolerably contented and cheerful, but still looking forward to spring with the hope of returning to town, not for its gaieties and dissipations, but for the chance of meeting Mr Huntingdon once again; for still, he is always in my thoughts and in my dreams. In all my employments, whatever I do, or see, or hear, has an ultimate reference to him; whatever skill or knowledge I acquire is some day to be turned to his advantage or amusement; whatever new beauties in nature or art I discover, are to be

depicted to meet his eye, or stored in my memory to be told him at some future period. This, at least, is the hope that I cherish, the fancy that lights me on my lonely way. It may be only an *ignis fatuus*, after all, but it can do no harm to follow it with my eyes and rejoice in its lustre, as long as it does not lure me from the path I ought to keep; and I think it will not, for I have thought deeply on my aunt's advice, and I see clearly, now, the folly of throwing myself away on one that is unworthy of all the love I have to give, and incapable of responding to the best and deepest feelings of my inmost heart – so clearly, that even if I should see him again, and if he should remember me and love me still (which, alas! is too little probable, considering how he is situated, and by whom surrounded), and if he should ask me to marry him – I am determined not to consent until I know for certain whether my aunt's opinion of him or mine is nearest the truth; for if mine is altogether wrong, it is not he that I love; it is a creature of my own imagination. But I think it is not wrong – no, no – there is a secret something – an inward instinct that assures me I am right. There is essential goodness in him; – and what delight to unfold it! If he has wandered, what bliss to recall him! If he is now exposed to the· baneful influence of corrupting and wicked companions, what glory to deliver him from them! Oh! If I could but believe that Heaven has designed me for this!

Today is the 1st of September; but my uncle has ordered the gamekeeper to spare the partridges till the gentlemen come. 'What gentlemen?' I asked when I heard it – a small party he had invited to shoot. His friend Mr Wilmot was one, and my aunt's friend Mr Boarham another. This struck me as terrible news, at the moment, but all regret and apprehension vanished like a dream when I heard that Mr Huntingdon was actually to be a third! My aunt is greatly against his coming, of course: she earnestly endeavoured to dissuade my uncle from asking him; but he, laughing at her objections, told her it was no use talking, for the mischief was already done: he had invited Huntingdon and his friend Lord Lowborough before we left London, and nothing now remained but to fix the day for their coming. So he is safe, and I am sure of seeing him. I cannot express my joy. I find it very difficult to conceal it from my aunt; but I don't wish to trouble her with my feelings till I know whether I ought to indulge them or not. If I find it my absolute duty to suppress them, they shall trouble no one but myself; and if I can really feel myself justified in indulging this attachment, I can dare anything, even the anger and grief of my best friend, for its object – surely, I shall soon know. But they are not coming till about the middle of the month.

We are to have two lady visitors also: Mr Wilmot is to bring his niece and her cousin Milicent. I suppose, my aunt thinks the latter will benefit me by her society and the salutary example of her gentle deportment, and lowly and tractable spirit; and of the former, I suspect, she intends as a species of counter attraction to win Mr Huntingdon's attention from me. I don't thank her for this; but I shall be glad of Milicent's company: she is a sweet, good girl, and I wish I were like her – more like her, at least, than I am.

*19th.* – They are come. They came the day before yesterday. The gentlemen are all gone out to shoot, and the ladies are with my aunt, at work, in the drawing-room I have retired to the library, for I am very unhappy, and I want

to be alone. Books cannot divert me; so having opened my desk, I will try what may be done by detailing the cause of my uneasiness. This paper will serve instead of a confidential friend into whose ear I might pour forth the overflowings of my heart. It will not sympathize with my distresses, but then, it will not laugh at them, and, if I keep it close, it cannot tell again; so it is, perhaps, the best friend I could have for the purpose.

First, let me speak of his arrival – how I sat at my window, and watched for nearly two hours, before his carriage entered the park gates – for they all came before him, – and how deeply I was disappointed at every arrival, because it was not his. First came Mr Wilmot and the ladies. When Milicent had got into her room, I quitted my post a few minutes, to look in upon her, and have a little private conversation, for she was now my intimate friend, several long epistles having passed between us since our parting. On returning to my window, I beheld another carriage at the door. Was it his? No; it was Mr Boarham's plain, dark chariot; and there stood he upon the steps, carefully superintending the dislodging of his various boxes and packages. What a collection! one would have thought he projected a visit of six months at least. A considerable time after, came Lord Lowborough in his barouche. Is he one of the profligate friends, I wonder? I should think not; for no one could call him a jolly companion, I'm sure, – and besides, he appears too sober and gentlemanly in his demeanour, to merit such suspicions. He is a tall, thin, gloomy-looking man, apparently between thirty and forty, and of a somewhat sickly, careworn aspect.

At last, Mr Huntingdon's light phaeton came bowling merrily up the lawn. I had but a transient glimpse of him, for the moment it stopped, he sprang out over the side on to the portico steps, and disappeared into the house.

I now submitted to be dressed for dinner – a duty which Rachel had been urging upon me for the last twenty minutes; and when that important business was completed, I repaired to the drawing-room, where I found Mr and Miss Wilmot, and Milicent Hargrave, already assembled. Shortly after, Lord Lowborough entered, and then Mr Boarham, who seemed quite willing to forget and forgive my former conduct, and to hope that a little conciliation and steady perseverance on his part might yet succeed in bringing me to reason. While I stood at the window, conversing with Milicent, he came up to me, and was beginning to talk in nearly his usual strain, when Mr Huntingdon entered the room.

'How will he greet me, I wonder?' said my bounding heart; and, instead of advancing to meet him, I turned to the window to hide or subdue my emotion. But having saluted his host and hostess, and the rest of the company, he came to me, ardently squeezed my hand, and murmured he was glad to see me once again. At that moment dinner was announced, my aunt desired him to take Miss Hargrave into the dining-room, and odious Mr Wilmot, with unspeakable grimaces, offered his arm to me; and I was condemned to sit between himself and Mr Boarham. But, afterwards, when we were all again assembled in the drawing-room, I was indemnified for so much suffering by a few delightful minutes of conversation with Mr Huntingdon.

In the course of the evening, Miss Wilmot was called upon to sing and play for the amusement of the company, and I to exhibit my drawings, and, though he likes music, and she is an accomplished musician, I think I am right in affirming, that he paid more atttention to my drawings than to her music.

# The Tenant of Wildfell Hall

So far, so good; – but, hearing him pronounce, *sotto voce*, but with peculiar emphasis, concerning one of the pieces, 'This is better than all!' – I looked up, curious to see which it was, and, to my horror, beheld him complacently gazing at the back of the picture: – it was his own face that I had sketched there, and forgotten to rub out! To make matters worse, in the agony of the moment, I attempted to snatch it from his hand; but he prevented me, and exclaiming, 'No – by George, I'll keep it!' placed it against his waistcoat, and buttoned his coat upon it with a delighted chuckle.

Then, drawing a candle close to his elbow, he gathered all the drawings to himself, as well what he had seen as the others, and muttering, 'I must look at both sides now', he eagerly commenced an examination, which I watched, at first, with tolerable composure, in the confidence that his vanity would not be gratified by any further discoveries; for, though I must plead guilty to having disfigured the backs of several with abortive attempts to delineate that too fascinating physiognomy, I was sure that, with the one unfortunate exception, I had carefully obliterated all such witnesses of my infatuation. But the pencil frequently leaves an impression upon card-board, that no amount of rubbing can efface. Such, it seems, was the case with most of those; and, I confess, I trembled, when I saw him holding them so close to the candle, and poring so intently over the seeming blanks; but still, I trusted, he would not be able to make out these dim traces to his own satisfaction. I was mistaken, however – having ended his scrutiny, he quietly remarked—

'I perceive the backs of young ladies' drawings, like the postscripts of their letters, are the most important and interesting part of the concern.'

Then, leaning back in his chair, he reflected a few minutes in silence, complacently smiling to himself, and, while I was concocting some cutting speech wherewith to check his gratification, he rose, and passing over to where Annabella Wilmot sat vehemently coquetting with Lord Lowborough, seated himself on the sofa beside her, and attached himself to her for the rest of the evening.

'So then!' thought I – 'he despises me, because he knows I love him.'

And the reflection made me so miserable – I knew not what to do. Milicent came and began to admire my drawings, and made remarks upon them; but I could not talk to her – I could talk to no one; and, upon the introduction of tea, I took advantage of the open door and the slight diversion caused by its entrance, to slip out – for I was sure I could not take any – and take refuge in the library. My aunt sent Thomas in quest of me, to ask if I were not coming to tea; but I bade him say, I should not take any tonight; and, happily, she was too much occupied with her guests, to make any further inquiries at the time.

As most of the company had travelled far that day, they retired early to rest; and having heard them all, as I thought, go upstairs, I ventured out, to get my candlestick from the drawing-room side-board. But Mr Huntingdon had lingered behind the rest: he was just at the foot of the stairs, when I opened the door; and, hearing my step in the hall – though I could hardly hear it myself – he instantly turned back.

'Helen, is that you?' said he; 'why did you run away from us?'

'Good-night, Mr Huntingdon,' said I coldly, not choosing to answer the question. And I turned away to enter the drawing-room.

'But you'll shake hands, won't you?' said he, placing himself in the doorway, before me. And he seized my hand, and held it much against my will.

# The Tenant of Wildfell Hall

'Let me go, Mr Huntingdon!' said I – 'I want to get a candle.'

'The candle will keep,' returned he.

I made a desperate effort to free my hand from his grasp.

'Why are you in such a hurry to leave me, Helen?' he said, with a smile of the most provoking self-sufficiency – 'you don't hate me, you know.'

'Yes, I do – at this moment.'

'Not you! It is Annabella Wilmot you hate, not me.'

'I have nothing to do with Annabella Wilmot,' said I, burning with indignation.

'But I have, you know,' returned he, with peculiar emphasis.

'That is nothing to me, sir!' I retorted.

'Is it nothing to you, Helen? – Will you swear it? – Will you?'

'No, I won't, Mr Huntingdon! and I will go!' cried I, not knowing whether to laugh, or to cry, or to break out into a tempest of fury.

'Go, then, you vixen!' he said; but the instant he released my hand, he had the audacity to put his arm round my neck, and kiss me.

Trembling with anger and agitation – and I don't know what besides, I broke away, and got my candle, and rushed upstairs to my room. He would not have done so, but for that hateful picture! And there he had it still in his possession, an eternal monument to his pride and my humiliation!

It was but little sleep I got that night; and, in the morning, I rose perplexed and troubled with the thoughts of meeting him at breakfast. I knew not how it was to be done – an assumption of dignified, cold indifference would hardly do, after what he knew of my devotion – to his face, at least. Yet something must be done to check his presumption – I would not submit to be tyrannized over by those bright, laughing eyes. And, accordingly, I received his cheerful morning salutation as calmly and coldly as my aunt could have wished, and defeated with brief answers his one or two attempts to draw me into conversation; while I comported myself with unusual cheerfulness and complaisance towards every other member of the party, especially Annabella Wilmot, and even her uncle and Mr Boarham were treated with an extra amount of civility on the occasion, not from any motives of coquetry, but just to show him that my particular coolness and reserve arose from no general ill-humour or depression of spirits.

He was not, however, to be repelled by such acting as this. He did not talk much to me, but when he did speak it was with a degree of freedom and openness – and kindliness too – that plainly seemed to intimate he knew his words were music to my ears; and when his looks met mine it was with a smile – presumptuous it might be – but oh, so sweet, so bright, so genial, that I could not possibly retain my anger; every vestige of displeasure soon melted away beneath it like morning clouds before the summer sun.

Soon after breakfast all the gentlemen save one, with boyish eagerness, set out on their expedition against the hapless partridges; my uncle and Mr Wilmot on their shooting ponies, Mr Huntingdon and Lord Lowborough on their legs: the one exception being Mr Boarham, who, in consideration of the rain that had fallen during the night, thought it prudent to remain behind a little and join them in a while when the sun had dried the grass. And he favoured us all with a long and minute disquisition upon the evils and dangers attendant upon damp feet, delivered with the most imperturbable gravity, amid the jeers and laughter of Mr Huntingdon and my uncle, who, leaving the prudent sportsman to entertain the ladies with his medical discussions, sallied forth with their guns,

314

bending their steps to the stables first to have a look at the horses, and let out the dogs.

Not desirous of sharing Mr Boarham's company for the whole of the morning, I betook myself to the library, and there brought forth my easel and began to paint. The easel and the painting apparatus would serve as an excuse for abandoning the drawing-room if my aunt should come to complain of the desertion, and besides I wanted to finish the picture. It was one I had taken great pains with, and I intended it to be my masterpiece, though it was somewhat presumptuous in the design. By the bright azure of the sky, and by the warm and brilliant lights and deep long shadows, I had endeavoured to convey the idea of a sunny morning. I had ventured to give more of the bright verdure of spring or early summer to the grass and foliage than is commonly attempted in painting. The scene represented was an open glade in a wood. A group of dark Scotch firs was introduced in the middle distance to relieve the prevailing freshness of the rest; but in the foreground were part of the gnarled trunk and of the spreading boughs of a large forest tree, whose foliage was of a brilliant golden green – not golden from autumnal mellowness, but from the sunshine and the very immaturity of the scarce expanded leaves. Upon this bough, that stood out in bold relief against the sombre firs, were seated an amorous pair of turtle doves, whose soft sad-coloured plumage afforded a contrast of another nature; and beneath it a young girl was kneeling on the daisy-spangled turf with head thrown back and masses of fair hair falling on her shoulders, her hands clasped, lips parted, and eyes intently gazing upward in pleased yet earnest contemplation of those feathered lovers – too deeply absorbed in each other to notice her.

I had scarcely settled to my work, which, however, wanted but a few touches to the finishing, when the sportsmen passed the window on their return from the stables. It was partly open, and Mr Huntingdon must have seen me as he went by, for in half a minute he came back, and setting his gun against the wall threw up the sash and sprang in and set himself before my picture.

'Very pretty, i'faith;' said he, after attentively regarding it for a few seconds; 'and a very fitting study for a young lady. Spring just opening into summer – morning just approaching noon – girlhood just ripening into womanhood, and hope just verging on fruition. She's a sweet creature! but why didn't you make her black hair?'

'I thought light hair would suit her better. You see I have made her blue-eyed and plump, and fair and rosy.'

'Upon my word – a very Hebe! I should fall in love with her if I hadn't the artist before me. Sweet innocent! she's thinking there will come a time when she will be wooed and won like that pretty hen-dove by as fond and fervent a lover; and she's thinking how pleasant it will be, and how tender and faithful he will find her.'

'And perhaps,' suggested I, 'how tender and faithful she shall find him.'

'Perhaps, for there is no limit to the wild extravagance of Hope's imaginings at such an age.'

'Do you call that, then, one of her wild, extravagant delusions?'

'No; my heart tells me it is not. I might have thought so once, but now, I say, give me the girl I love, and I will swear eternal constancy to her and her alone,

# The Tenant of Wildfell Hall

through summer and winter, through youth and age, and life and death! if age and death must come.'

He spoke this in such serious earnest that my heart bounded with delight; but the minute after he changed his tone, and asked, with a significant smile, if I had 'any more portraits'.

'No,' replied I, reddening with confusion and wrath. But my portfolio was on the table: he took it up, and coolly sat down to examine its contents.

'Mr Huntingdon, those are my unfinished sketches,' cried I, 'and I never let any one see them.'

And I placed my hand on the portfolio to wrest it from him, but he maintained his hold, assuring me that he 'liked unfinished sketches of all things.'

'But I hate them to be seen,' returned I. 'I can't let you have it, indeed!'

'Let me have its bowels then,' said he; and just as I wrenched the portfolio from his hand he deftly abstracted the greater part of its contents, and after turning them over a moment he cried out—

'Bless my stars, here's another!' and slipped a small oval of ivory paper into his waistcoat pocket – a complete miniature portrait that I had sketched with such tolerable success as to be induced to colour it with great pains and care. But I was determined he should not keep it.

'Mr Huntingdon,' cried I, 'I insist upon having that back! It is mine, and you have no right to take it. Give it me, directly – I'll never forgive you if you don't!'

But the more vehemently I insisted, the more he aggravated my distress by his insulting gleeful laugh. At length, however, he restored it to me, saying—

'Well, well, since you value it so much, I'll not deprive you of it.'

To show him how I valued it I tore it in two and threw it into the fire. He was not prepared for this. His merriment suddenly ceasing, he stared in mute amazement at the consuming treasure; and then with a careless 'Humph! I'll go and shoot now,' he turned on his heel, and vacated the apartment by the window as he came, and setting on his hat with an air, took up his gun and walked away, whistling as he went - and leaving me not too much agitated to finish my picture, for I was glad, at the moment, that I had vexed him.

When I returned to the drawing-room, I found Mr Boarham had ventured to follow his comrades to the field; and shortly after lunch, to which they did not think of returning, I volunteered to accompany the ladies in a walk, and show Annabella and Milicent the beauties of the country. We took a long ramble and re-entered the park just as the sportsmen were returning from their expedition. Toil-spent and travel-stained, the main body of them crossed over the grass to avoid us, but Mr Huntingdon, all spattered and splashed as he was, and stained with the blood of his prey – to the no small offence of my aunt's strict sense of propriety – came out of his way to meet us with cheerful smiles and words for all but me, and placing himself between Annabella Wilmot and myself walked up the road and began to relate the various exploits and disasters of the day, in a manner that would have convulsed me with laughter if I had been on good terms with him; but he addressed himself entirely to Annabella, and I, of course, left all the laughter and all the badinage to her, and affecting the utmost indifference to whatever passed between them, walked along a few paces apart, and looking every way but theirs, while my aunt and Milicent went before, linked arm in arm, and gravely discoursing together. At length Mr Huntingdon turned to me, and addressing me in a confidential whisper, said—

# The Tenant of Wildfell Hall

'Helen, why did you burn my picture?'

'Because I wished to destroy it,' I answered, with an asperity it is useless now to lament.

'Oh, very good!' was the reply, 'if you don't value me, I must turn to somebody that will.'

I thought it was partly in jest – a half-playful mixture of mock resignation and pretended indifference: but immediately he resumed his place beside Miss Wilmot, and from that hour to this – during all the evening, and all the next day, and the next, and the next, and all this morning (the 22nd), he has never given me one kind word or one pleasant look – never spoken to me, but from pure necessity – never glanced towards me but with a cold unfriendly look I thought him quite incapable of assuming.

My aunt observes the change, and though she has not inquired the cause or made any remark to me on the subject, I see it gives her pleasure. Miss Wilmot observes it, too, and triumphantly ascribes it to her own superior charms and blandishments; but I am truly miserable – more so than I like to acknowledge to myself. Pride refuses to aid me. It has brought me into the scrape, and will not help me out of it.

He meant no harm – it was only his joyous, playful spirit; and I, by my acrimonious resentment – so serious, so disproportioned to the offence – have so wounded his feelings – so deeply offended him, that I fear he will never forgive me – and all for a mere jest! He thinks I dislike him, and he must continue to think so. I must lose him for ever, and Annabella may win him, and triumph as she will.

But it is not my loss nor her triumph that I deplore so greatly as the wreck of my fond hopes for his advantage, and her unworthiness of his affection, and the injury he will do himself by trusting his happiness to her. She does not love him: she thinks only of herself. She cannot appreciate the good that is in him: she will neither see it, nor value it, nor cherish it. She will neither deplore his faults nor attempt their amendment, but rather aggravate them by her own. And I doubt whether she will not deceive him after all, I see she is playing double between him and Lord Lowborough, and while she amuses herself with the lively Huntingdon she tries her utmost to enslave his moody friend; and should she succeed in bringing both to her feet, the fascinating commoner will have but little chance against the lordly peer. If he observes her artful by-play it gives him no uneasiness, but rather adds new zest to his diversion by opposing a stimulating check to his otherwise too easy conquest.

Messrs Wilmot and Boarham have severally taken occasion by his neglect of me to renew their advances; and if I were like Annabella and some others I should take advantage of their perseverance to endeavour to pique him into a revival of affection; but, justice and honesty apart, I could not bear to do it; I am annoyed enough by their present persecutions without encouraging them further; and even if I did it would have precious little effect upon him. He sees me suffering under the condescending attentions and prosaic discourses of the one, and the repulsive obtrusions of the other, without so much as a shadow of commiseration for me, or resentment against my tormentors. He never could have loved me, or he would not have resigned me so willingly, and he would not go on talking to everybody else so cheerfully as he does – laughing and jesting with Lord Lowborough and my uncle, teasing Milicent Hargrave, and flirting

with Annabella Wilmot – as if nothing were on his mind. Oh, why can't I hate him? I must be infatuated, or I should scorn to regret him as I do! But I must rally all the powers I have remaining, and try to tear him from my heart. There goes the dinner bell, and here comes my aunt to scold me for sitting here at my desk all day instead of staying with the company: wish the company were – gone.

# Chapter 19

wenty-second. Night. – What have I done? and what will be the end of it? I cannot calmly reflect upon it; I cannot sleep. I must have recourse to my diary again; I will commit it to paper tonight, and see what I shall think of it tomorrow.

I went down to dinner resolving to be cheerful and well-conducted, and kept my resolution very creditably, considering how my head ached, and how internally wretched I felt – I don't know what is come over me of late; my very energies, both mental and physical, must be strangely impaired, or I should not have acted so weakly in many respects as I have done; – but I have not been well this last day or two: I suppose it is with sleeping and eating so little, and thinking so much, and being so continually out of humour. But to return: I was exerting myself to sing and play for the amusement, and at the request of my aunt and Milicent, before the gentlemen came into the drawing-room (Miss Wilmot never likes to waste her musical efforts on ladies' ears alone): Milicent had asked for a little Scotch song, and I was just in the middle of it when they entered. The first thing Mr Huntingdon did, was to walk up to Annabella.

'Now, Miss Wilmot, won't you give us some music tonight?' said he. 'Do now! I know you will, when I tell you that I have been hungering and thirsting all day for the sound of your voice. Come! the piano's vacant.'

It was; for I had quitted it immediately upon hearing his petition. Had I been endowed with a proper degree of self-possession, I should have turned to the lady myself, and cheerfully joined my entreaties to his; whereby I should have disappointed his expectations, if the affront had been purposely given, or made him sensible of the wrong, if it had only arisen from thoughtlessness; but I felt it too deeply to do anything but rise from the music-stool, and throw myself back on the sofa, suppressing with difficulty the audible expression of the bitterness I felt within. I knew Annabella's musical talents were superior to mine, but there was no reason why I should be treated as a perfect nonentity. The time and the manner of his asking her, appeared like a gratuitous insult to me; and I could have wept with pure vexation.

Meantime, she exultingly seated herself at the piano, and favoured him with two of his favourite songs, in such superior style that even I soon lost my anger

in admiration, and listened with a sort of gloomy pleasure to the skilful modulations of her full-toned and powerful voice, so judiciously aided by her rounded and spirited touch; and while my ears drank in the sound, my eyes rested on the face of her principal auditor, and derived an equal or superior delight from the contemplation of his speaking countenance, as he stood beside her – that eye and brow lighted up with keen enthusiasm, and that sweet smile passing and appearing like gleams of sunshine on an April day. No wonder he should hunger and thirst to hear her sing. I now forgave him, from my heart, his reckless slight of me, and I felt ashamed at my pettish resentment of such a trifle – ashamed too of those bitter envious pangs that gnawed my inmost heart, in spite of all this admiration and delight.

'There now!' said she, playfully running her fingers over the keys, when she had concluded the second song. 'What shall I give you next?'

But in saying this, she looked back at Lord Lowborough, who was standing a little behind, leaning against the back of a chair, an attentive listener too, experiencing, to judge by his countenance, much the same feelings of mingled pleasure and sadness as I did. But the look she gave him plainly said, 'Do you choose for me now. I have done enough for him, and will gladly exert myself to gratify you; and thus encouraged, his lordship came forward, and turning over the music, presently set before her a little song that I had noticed before, and read more than once, with an interest arising from the circumstance of my connecting it in my mind with the reigning tyrant of my thoughts. And now with my nerves already excited and half unstrung, I could not hear those words so sweetly warbled forth, without some symptoms of emotion I was not able to suppress. Tears rose unbidden to my eyes, and I buried my face in the sofa-pillow that they might flow unseen while I listened. The air was simple, sweet, and sad, it is still running in my head, – and so are the words—

> *Farewell to thee! but not farewell*
> *To all my fondest thoughts of thee:*
> *Within my heart they still shall dwell;*
> *And they shall cheer and comfort me.*
>
> *Oh, beautiful, and full of grace!*
> *If thou hadst never met mine eye,*
> *I had not dreamed a living face*
> *Could fancied charms so far outvie.*
>
> *If I may ne'er behold again*
> *That form and face so dear to me,*
> *Nor hear thy voice, still would I fain*
> *Preserve, for aye, their memory.*
>
> *That voice the magic of whose tone*
> *Can wake an echo in my breast,*
> *Creating feelings that, alone,*
> *Can make my tranced spirit blest.*

# The Tenant of Wildfell Hall

*That laughing eye, whose sunny beam*
*My memory would not cherish less:–*
*And oh, that smile! whose joyous gleam*
*No mortal language can express.*

*Adieu! but let me cherish, still,*
*The hope with which I cannot part.*
*Contempt may wound, and coldness chill,*
*But still it lingers in my heart.*

*And who can tell but Heaven, at last,*
*May answer all my thousand prayers,*
*And bid the future pay the past*
*With joy for anguish, smiles for tears!*

When it ceased, I longed for nothing so much as to be out of the room. The sofa was not far from the door, but I did not dare to raise my head, for I knew Mr Huntingdon was standing near me, and I knew by the sound of his voice, as he spoke in answer to some remark of Lord Lowborough's, that his face was turned towards me. Perhaps a half-suppressed sob had caught his ear, and caused him to look round – Heaven forbid! But, with a violent effort, I checked all further signs of weakness, dried my tears, and, when I thought he had turned away again, rose, and instantly left the apartment, taking refuge in my favourite resort, the library.

There was no light there but the faint red glow of the neglected fire; – but I did not want a light; I only wanted to indulge my thoughts, unnoticed and undisturbed; and sitting down on a low stool before the easy-chair, I sunk my head upon its cushioned seat, and thought, and thought, until the tears gushed out again, and I wept like any child. Presently, however, the door was gently opened and some one entered the room. I trusted it was only a servant, and did not stir. The door was closed again – but I was not alone; a hand gently touched my shoulder, and a voice said softly—

'Helen, what is the matter?'

I could not answer at the moment.

'You must, and shall tell me,' was added, more vehemently, and the speaker threw himself on his knees beside me on the rug, and forcibly possessed himself of my hand; but I hastily caught it away, and replied—

'It is nothing to you, Mr Huntingdon.'

'Are you sure it is nothing to me?' he returned; 'can you swear that you were not thinking of me while you wept?'

This was unendurable. I made an effort to rise, but he was kneeling on my dress.

'Tell me,' continued he – 'I want to know, – because, if you were, I have something to say to you, – and if not, I'll go.'

'Go then!' I cried; but fearing he would obey too well, and never come again, I hastily added – 'Or say what you have to say, and have done with it!'

'But which?' said he – 'for I shall only say it if you really were thinking of me. So tell me, Helen.'

'You're excessively impertinent, Mr Huntingdon!'

'Not at all – too pertinent, you mean – so you won't tell me? – Well, I'll spare

# The Tenant of Wildfell Hall

your woman's pride, and construing your silence into "Yes," I'll take it for granted that I was the subject of your thoughts, and the cause of your affliction'—

'Indeed, sir'—

'If you deny it, I won't tell you my secret,' threatened he; and I did not interrupt him again – or even attempt to repulse him, though he had taken my hand once more, and half embraced me with his other arm – I was scarcely conscious of it at the time.

'It is this,' resumed he; 'that Annabella Wilmot, in comparison with you, is like a flaunting peony compared with a sweet, wild rosebud gemmed with dew – and I love you to distraction! – Now, tell me if that intelligence gives you any pleasure. Silence again? That means yes – Then let me add, that I cannot live without you, and if you answer, No, to this last question, you will drive me mad. – Will you bestow yourself upon me? – you will!' he cried, nearly squeezing me to death in his arms.

'No, no!' I exclaimed, struggling to free myself from him – 'you must ask my uncle and aunt.'

'They won't refuse me, if you don't.'

'I'm not so sure of that – my aunt dislikes you.'

'But you don't, Helen – say you love me, and I'll go.'

'I wish you would go!' I replied.

'I will, this instant, – if you'll only say you love me.'

'You know I do,' I answered. And again he caught me in his arms, and smothered me with kisses.

At that moment, my aunt opened wide the door, and stood before us, candle in hand, in shocked and horrified amazement, gazing alternately at Mr Huntingdon and me, – for we had both started up, and now stood wide enough asunder. But his confusion was only for a moment. Rallying in an instant, with the most enviable assurance, he began—

'I beg ten thousand pardons, Mrs Maxwell! don't be too severe upon me. I've been asking your sweet niece to take me for better, for worse; and she, like a good girl, informs me she cannot think of it without her uncle's and aunt's consent. So let me implore you not to condemn me to eternal wretchedness: if you favour my cause, I am safe; for Mr Maxwell, I am certain, can refuse you nothing.'

'We will talk of this tomorrow, sir,' said my aunt coldly. 'It is a subject that demands mature and serious deliberation. At present, you had better return to the drawing-room.'

'But meantime,' pleaded he, 'let me commend my cause to your most indulgent'—

'No indulgence for you, Mr Huntingdon, must come between me and the consideration of my niece's happiness.'

'Ah, true! I know she is an angel, and I am a presumptuous dog to dream of possessing such a treasure; but, nevertheless, I would sooner die than relinquish her in favour of the best man that ever went to heaven – and as for her happiness, I would sacrifice my body and soul'—

'Body and soul, Mr Huntingdon – sacrifice your soul?'

'Well, I would lay down life'—

'You would not be required to lay it down.'

'I would spend it, then – devote my life – and all its powers, to the promotion and preservation'—

'Another time, sir, we will talk of this – and I should have felt disposed to judge more favourably of your pretensions, if you too had chosen another time and place, and let me add – another manner for your declaration.'

'Why, you see, Mrs Maxwell,' – he began.

'Pardon me, sir,' said she, with dignity – 'The company are inquiring for you in the other room.' And she turned to me.

'Then you must plead for me, Helen,' said he, and at length withdrew.

'You had better retire to your room, Helen,' said my aunt gravely. 'I will discuss this matter with you, too, tomorrow.'

'Don't be angry, aunt,' said I.

'My dear, I am not angry,' she replied: 'I am surprised. If it is true that you told him you could not accept his offer without our consent'—

'It is true,' interrupted I.

'Then how could you permit'—

'I couldn't help it, aunt,' I cried, bursting into tears. They were not altogether the tears of sorrow, or of fear for her displeasure, but rather the outbreak of the general tumultuous excitement of my feelings. But my good aunt was touched at my agitation. In a softer tone, she repeated her recommendation to retire, and, gently kissing my forehead, bade me good-night, and put her candle in my hand; and I went; but my brain worked so, I could not think of sleeping. I feel calmer now that I have written all this; and I will go to bed, and try to win tired nature's sweet restorer.

# Chapter 20

*September 24th*

In the morning I rose, light and cheerful, nay, intensely happy. The hovering cloud cast over me by my aunt's views, and by the fear of not obtaining her consent, was lost in the bright effulgence of my own hopes, and the too delightful consciousness of requited love. It was a splendid morning; and I went out to enjoy it, in a quiet ramble in company with my own blissful thoughts. The dew was on the grass and ten thousand gossamers were waving in the breeze; the happy red-breast was pouring out its little soul in song, and my heart overflowed with silent hymns of gratitude and praise to Heaven.

But I had not wandered far before my solitude was interrupted by the only person that could have disturbed my musings, at that moment, without being looked upon as an unwelcome intruder: Mr Huntingdon came suddenly upon me. So unexpected was the apparition, that I might have thought it the creation of an over-excited imagination, had the sense of sight alone borne witness to his

presence; but immediately I felt his strong arm round my waist and his warm kiss on my cheek, while his keen and gleeful salutation, 'My own Helen!' was ringing in my ear.

'Not yours yet,' said I, hastily swerving aside from this too presumptuous greeting – 'remember my guardians. You will not easily obtain my aunt's consent. Don't you see she is prejudiced against you?'

'I do, dearest; and you must tell me why, that I may best know how to combat her objections. I suppose she thinks I am a prodigal,' pursued he, observing that I was unwilling to reply, 'and concludes that I shall have but little worldly goods wherewith to endow my better half? If so, you must tell her that my property is mostly entailed, and I cannot get rid of it. There may be a few mortgages on the rest – a few trifling debts and incumbrances here and there, but nothing to speak of; and though I acknowledge I am not so rich as I might be – or have been – still, I think, we could manage pretty comfortably on what's left. My father, you know, was something of a miser, and, in his latter days especially, saw no pleasure in life but to amass riches; and so it is no wonder that his son should make it his chief delight to spend them, which was accordingly the case, until my acquaintance with you, dear Helen, taught me other views and nobler aims. And the very idea of having you to care for under my roof, would force me to moderate my expenses and live like a Christian – not to speak of all the prudence and virtue you would instil into my mind by your wise counsels and sweet, attractive goodness.'

'But it is not that,' said I, 'it is not money my aunt thinks about. She knows better than to value worldly wealth above its price.'

'What is it then?'

'She wishes me to – to marry none but a really good man.'

'What, a man of "decided" piety? – ahem! – Well, come, I'll manage that too! It's Sunday today, isn't it? I'll go to church morning, afternoon, and evening, and comport myself in such a godly sort that she shall regard me with admiration and sisterly love, as a brand plucked from the burning. I'll come home sighing like a furnace, and full of the savour and unction of dear Mr Blatant's discourse'—

'Mr Leighton,' said I dryly.

'Is Mr Leighton a "sweet preacher", Helen – a "dear, delightful, heavenly-minded man"?'

'He is a good man, Mr Huntingdon. I wish I could say half as much for you.'

'Oh, I forgot, you are a saint, too. I crave your pardon, dearest – but don't call me Mr Huntingdon, my name is Arthur.'

'I'll call you nothing – for I'll have nothing at all to do with you if you talk in that way any more. If you really mean to deceive my aunt as you say, you are very wicked; and if not, you are very wrong to jest on such a subject.'

'I stand corrected,' said he, concluding his laugh with a sorrowful sigh. 'Now,' resumed he, after a momentary pause, 'let us talk about something else. And come nearer to me, Helen, and take my arm; and then I'll let you alone. I can't be quiet while I see you walking there.'

I complied; but said we must soon return to the house.

'No one will be down to breakfast, yet, for long enough,' he answered. 'You spoke of your guardians, just now, Helen, but is not your father still living?'

'Yes, but I always look upon my uncle and aunt as my guardians, for they

are so, in deed, though not in name. My father has entirely given me up to their care. I have never seen him since dear mamma died when I was a very little girl, and my aunt, at her request, offered to take charge of me, and took me away to Staningley, where I have remained ever since; and I don't think he would object to anything for me, that she thought proper to sanction.'

'But would he sanction anything to which she thought proper to object?'

'No, I don't think he cares enough about me.'

'He is very much to blame – but he doesn't know what an angel he has for his daughter – which is all the better for me, as, if he did, he would not be willing to part with such a treasure.'

'And Mr Huntingdon,' said I; 'I suppose you know I am not an heiress?'

He protested he had never given it a thought, and begged I would not disturb his present enjoyment by the mention of such uninteresting subjects. I was glad of this proof of disinterested affection; for Annabella Wilmot is the probable heiress to all her uncle's wealth, in addition to her late father's property, which she has already in possession.

I now insisted upon retracing our steps to the house; but we walked slowly, and went on talking as we proceeded. I need not repeat all we said: let me rather refer to what passed between my aunt and me, after breakfast, when Mr Huntingdon called my uncle aside, no doubt to make his proposals, and she beckoned me into another room, where she once more commenced a solemn remonstrance, which, however, entirely failed to convince me that her view of the case was preferable to my own.

'You judge him uncharitably, aunt, I know,' said I. 'His very friends are not half so bad as you represent them. There is Walter Hargrave, Milicent's brother, for one; he is but a little lower than the angels, if half she says of him is true. She is continually talking to me about him, and lauding his many virtues to the skies.'

'You will form a very inadequate estimate of a man's character,' replied she, 'if you judge by what a fond sister says of him. The worst of them generally know how to hide their misdeeds from their sisters' eyes, and their mothers' too.'

'And there is Lord Lowborough,' continued I, 'quite a decent man.'

'Who told you so? Lord Lowborough is a desperate man. He has dissipated his fortune in gambling and other things, and is now seeking an heiress to retrieve it. I told Miss Wilmot so; but you're all alike: she haughtily answered she was very much obliged to me, but she believed she knew when a man was seeking her for her fortune, and when for herself; she flattered herself she had had experience enough in those matters, to be justified in trusting to her own judgment – and as for his lordship's lack of fortune, she cared nothing about that, as she hoped her own would suffice for both; and as for his wildness, she supposed he was no worse than others – besides, he was reformed now. Yes, they can all play the hypocrite when they want to take in a fond, misguided woman!'

'Well, I think he's about as good as she is,' said I. 'But when Mr Huntingdon is married, he won't have many opportunities of consorting with his bachelor friends; – and the worse they are, the more I long to deliver him from them.'

'To be sure, my dear; and the worse he is, I suppose, the more you long to deliver him from himself.'

'Yes, provided he is not incorrigible – that is, the more I long to deliver him

from his faults – to give him an opportunity of shaking off the adventitious evil got from contact with others worse than himself, and shining out in the unclouded light of his own genuine goodness – to do my utmost to help his better self against his worse, and make him what he would have been if he had not, from the beginning, had a bad, selfish, miserly father, who, to gratify his own sordid passions, restricted him in the most innocent enjoyments of childhood and youth, and so disgusted him with every kind of restraint; – and a foolish mother who indulged him to the top of his bent, deceiving her husband for him, and doing her utmost to encourage those germs of folly and vice it was her duty to suppress, – and then, such a set of companions as you represent his friends to be'—

'Poor man!' said she sarcastically, 'his kind have greatly wronged him!'

'They have,' cried I – 'and they shall wrong him no more – his wife shall undo what his mother did!'

'Well,' said she, after a short pause, 'I must say, Helen, I thought better of your judgment than this – and your taste too. How you can love such a man I cannot tell, or what pleasure you can find in his company; for "What fellowship hath light with darkness; or he that believeth with an infidel?"'

'He is not an infidel; – and I am not light, and he is not darkness; his worst and only vice is thoughtlessness.'

'And thoughtlessness,' pursued my aunt, 'may lead to every crime, and will but poorly excuse our errors in the sight of God, Mr Huntingdon, I suppose, is not without the common faculties of men; he is not so light-headed as to be irresponsible: his Maker has endowed him with reason and conscience as well as the rest of us; the Scriptures are open to him as well as to others; – and "If he hear not them, neither will he hear though one rose from the dead." And, remember, Helen,' continued she solemnly. '"The wicked shall be turned into hell, and they shall forget God!" And suppose, even, that he should continue to love you, and you him, and that you should pass through life together with tolerable comfort, – how will it be in the end, when you see yourselves parted for ever; you, perhaps, taken into eternal bliss, and he cast into the lake that burneth with unquenchable fire – there for ever to'—

'Not for ever,' I exclaimed, 'only "till he has paid the uttermost farthing"; for "if any man's work abide not the fire, he shall suffer loss, yet himself shall be saved, but so as by fire"; and He that "is able to subdue all things to Himself will have all men to be saved," and "will in the fulness of time, gather together in one all things in Christ Jesus, who tasted death for every man, and in whom God will reconcile all things to Himself, whether they be things in earth or things in heaven."'

'Oh, Helen! where did you learn all this?'

'In the Bible, aunt. I have searched it through, and found nearly thirty passages, all tending to support the same theory.'

'And is that the use you make of your Bible? And did you find no passages tending to prove the danger and falsity of such a belief?'

'No: I found, indeed, some passages that, taken by themselves, might seem to contradict that opinion; but they will all bear a different construction to that which is commonly given, and in most the only difficulty is in the word which we translate "everlasting" or "eternal." I don't know the Greek, but I believe it strictly means for ages, and might signify either endless or long-enduring. And as for the danger of the belief, I would not publish it abroad, if I thought

# The Tenant of Wildfell Hall

any poor wretch would be likely to presume upon it to his own destruction, but it is a glorious thought to cherish in one's own heart, and I would not part with it for all the world can give!'

Here our conference ended, for it was now high time to prepare for church. Every one attended the morning service, except my uncle, who hardly ever goes, and Mr Wilmot, who stayed at home with him to enjoy a quiet game of cribbage. In the afternoon Miss Wilmot and Lord Lowborough likewise excused themselves from attending; but Mr Huntingdon vouchsafed to accompany us again. Whether it was to ingratiate himself with my aunt I cannot tell, but, if so, he certainly should have behaved better. I must confess, I did not like his conduct during service at all. Holding his Prayer-book upside down, or open at any place but the right, he did nothing but stare about him, unless he happened to catch my aunt's eye or mine, and then he would drop his own on his book, with a puritanical air of mock solemnity that would have been ludicrous, if it had not been too provoking. Once, during the sermon, after attentively regarding Mr Leighton for a few minutes, he suddenly produced his gold pencil-case and snatched up a Bible. Perceiving that I observed this movement, he whispered that he was going to make a note of the sermon; but instead of that – as I sat next him I could not help seeing that he was making a caricature of the preacher, giving to the respectable, pious, elderly gentleman, the air and aspect of a most absurd old hypocrite. And yet, upon his return, he talked to my aunt about the sermon with a degree of modest, serious discrimination that tempted me to believe he had really attended and profited by the discourse.

Just before dinner my uncle called me into the library for the discussion of a very important matter, which was dismissed in few words.

'Now, Nell,' said he, 'this young Huntingdon has been asking for you: what must I say about it? Your aunt would answer "No" – but what say you?'

'I say yes, uncle,' replied I, without a moment's hesitation; for I had thoroughly made up my mind on the subject.

'Very good!' cried he, 'Now that's a good honest answer – wonderful for a girl! – Well, I'll write to your father tomorrow. He's sure to give his consent; so you may look on the matter as settled. You'd have done a deal better if you'd taken Wilmot, I can tell you; but that you won't believe. At your time of life, it's love that rules the roost: at mine, it's solid, serviceable gold. I suppose now, you'd never dream of looking into the state of your husband's finances, or troubling your head about settlements, or anything of that sort?'

'I don't think I should.'

'Well, be thankful, then, that you've wiser heads to think for you. I haven't had time, yet, to examine thoroughly into this young rascal's affairs, but I see that a great part of his father's fine property has been squandered away; – but still, I think there's a pretty share of it left, and a little careful nursing may make a handsome thing of it yet; and then we must persuade your father to give you a decent fortune, as he has only one besides yourself to care for; and, if you behave well, who knows but what I may be induced to remember you in my will?' continued he, putting his fingers to his nose, with a knowing wink.

'Thanks, uncle, for that and all your kindness,' replied I.

'Well, and I questioned this young spark on the matter of settlements,' continued he; 'and he seemed disposed to be generous enough on that point'—

'I knew he would!' said I. 'But pray don't trouble your head – or his, or mine

about that; for all I have will be his, and all he has will be mine; and what more could either of us require?' And I was about to make my exit, but he called me back.

'Stop, stop!' cried he— 'We haven't mentioned the time yet. When must it be? Your aunt would put it off till the Lord knows when, but he is anxious to be bound as soon as may be: he won't hear of waiting beyond next month; and you, I guess, will be of the same mind, so'—

'Not at all, uncle; on the contrary, I should like to wait till after Christmas, at least.'

'Oh! pooh, pooh! never tell me that tale – I know better,' cried he; and he persisted in his incredulity. Nevertheless, it is quite true. I am in no hurry at all. How can I be, when I think of the momentous change that awaits me, and of all I have to leave? It is happiness enough, to know that we are to be united; and that he really loves me, and I may love him as devotedly, and think of him as often as I please. However, I insisted upon consulting my aunt about the time of the wedding, for I determined her counsels should not be utterly disregarded; and no conclusions on that particular are come to yet.

# Chapter 21

*October 1st*

All is settled now. My father has given his consent, and the time is fixed for Christmas, by a sort of compromise between the respective advocates for hurry and delay. Milicent Hargrave is to be one bridesmaid, and Annabella Wilmot the other – not that I am particularly fond of the latter, but she is an intimate of the family, and I have not another friend.

When I told Milicent of my engagement, she rather provoked me by her manner of taking it. After staring a moment in mute surprise, she said—

'Well, Helen, I suppose I ought to congratulate you – and I am glad to see you so happy; but I did not think you would take him; and I can't help feeling surprised that you should like him so much.'

'Why so?'

'Because you are so superior to him in every way, and there's something so bold – and reckless about him – so, I don't know how – but I always feel a wish to get out of his way, when I see him approach.'

'You are timid, Milicent, but that's no fault of his.'

'And then his look,' continued she. 'People say he's handsome, and of course he is, but I don't like that kind of beauty; and I wonder that you should.'

'Why so?'

'Well, you know, I think there's nothing noble or lofty in his appearance.'

'In fact you wonder that I can like anyone so unlike the stilted heroes of

# The Tenant of Wildfell Hall

romance! Well! give me my flesh and blood lover, and I'll leave all the Sir Herberts and Valentines to you – if you can find them.'

'I don't want them,' said she. 'I'll be satisfied with flesh and blood too – only the spirit must shine through and predominate. But don't you think Mr Huntingdon's face is too red?'

'No!' cried I indignantly. 'It is not red at all. There is just a pleasant glow – a healthy freshness in his complexion, the warm, pinky tint of the whole harmonizing with the deeper colour of the cheeks, exactly as it ought to do. I hate a man to be red and white, like a painted doll – or all sickly white, or smoky black, or cadaverous yellow!'

'Well, tastes differ – but I like pale or dark,' replied she. 'But to tell you the truth, Helen, I had been deluding myself with the hope that you would one day be my sister. I expected Walter would be introduced to you next season; and I thought you would like him, and was certain he would like you; and I flattered myself I should thus have the felicity of seeing the two persons I liked best in the world – except mamma – united in one. He mayn't be exactly what you would call handsome, but he's far more distinguished-looking, and nicer and better than Mr Huntingdon; – and I'm sure you would say so, if you knew him.'

'Impossible, Milicent! You think so, because you're his sister; and, on that account, I'll forgive you; but nobody else should so disparage Arthur Huntingdon to me, with impunity.'

Miss Wilmot expressed her feelings on the subject, almost as openly.

'And so, Helen,' said she, coming up to me with a smile of no amiable import, 'you are to be Mrs Huntingdon, I suppose?'

'Yes,' replied I. 'Don't you envy me?'

'Oh, dear no!' she exclaimed. 'I shall probably be Lady Lowborough some day, and then you know, dear, I shall be in a capacity to inquire, "Don't you envy me?"'

'Henceforth, I shall envy no one,' returned I.

'Indeed! Are you so happy then?' said she thoughtfully; and something very like a cloud of disappointment shadowed her face. 'And does he love you – I mean, does he idolize you as much as you do him?' she added, fixing her eyes upon me with ill-disguised anxiety for the reply.

'I don't want to be idolized,' I answered, 'but I am well assured that he loves me more than anybody else in the world – as I do him.'

'Exactly,' said she, with a nod. 'I wish'— she paused.

'What do you wish?' asked I, annoyed at the vindictive expression of her countenance.

'I wish,' returned she, with a short laugh, 'that all the attractive points and desirable qualifications of the two gentlemen were united in one – that Lord Lowborough had Huntingdon's handsome face and good temper, and all his wit, and mirth, and charm, or else that Huntingdon had Lowborough's pedigree, and title, and delightful old family seat, and I had him; and you might have the other and welcome.'

'Thank you, dear Annabella, I am better satisfied with things as they are, for my own part; and for you, I wish you were as well content with your intended as I am with mine,' said I; and it was true enough; for, though vexed at first at

her unamiable spirit, her frankness touched me, and the contrast between our situations was such, that I could well afford to pity her and wish her well.

Mr Huntingdon's acquaintances appear to be no better pleased with our approaching union than mine. This morning's post brought him letters from several of his friends, during the perusal of which, at the breakfast-table, he excited the attention of the company, by the singular variety of his grimaces. But he crushed them all into his pocket, with a private laugh, and said nothing till the meal was concluded. Then, while the company were hanging over the fire or loitering through the room, previous to settling to their various morning's avocations, he came and leant over the back of my chair, with his face in contact with my curls, and commencing with a quiet little kiss, poured forth the following complaints into my ear—

'Helen, you witch, do you know that you've entailed upon me the curses of all my friends? I wrote to them the other day, to tell them of my happy prospects, and now, instead of a bundle of congratulations, I've got a pocketful of bitter execrations and reproaches. There's not one kind wish for me, or one good word for you, among them all. They say there'll be no more fun now, no more merry days and glorious nights – and all my fault – I am the first to break up the jovial band, and others, in pure despair, will follow my example. I was the very life and prop of the community, they do me the honour to say, and I have shamefully betrayed my trust'—

'You may join them again, if you like,' said I, somewhat piqued at the sorrowful tone of his discourse. 'I should be sorry to stand between any man – or body of men, and so much happiness; and perhaps I can manage to do without you, as well as your poor deserted friends.'

'Bless you; no,' murmured he. 'It's "all for love or the world well lost," with me. Let them go to – where they belong, to speak politely. But if you saw how they abuse me, Helen, you would love me all the more, for having ventured so much for your sake.'

He pulled out his crumpled letters. I thought he was going to show them to me, and told him I did not wish to see them.

'I'm not going to show them to you, love,' said he. 'They're hardly fit for a lady's eyes – the most part of them. But look here. This is Grimsby's scrawl – only three lines, the sulky dog! He doesn't say much, to be sure, but his very silence implies more than all the others' words, and the less he says, the more he thinks – and this is Hargrave's missive. He is particularly grieved at me, because, forsooth, he had fallen in love with you from his sister's reports, and meant to have married you himself, as soon as he had sown his wild oats.'

'I'm vastly obliged to him,' observed I.

'And so am I,' said he. 'And look at this. This is Hattersley's – every page stuffed full of railing accusations, bitter curses, and lamentable complaints, ending up with swearing that he'll get married himself in revenge; he'll throw himself away on the first old maid that chooses to set her cap at him, – as if I cared what he did with himself.'

'Well,' said I, 'if you do give up your intimacy with these men, I don't think you will have much cause to regret the loss of their society; for it's my belief they never did you much good.'

'Maybe not; but we'd a merry time of it, too, though mingled with sorrow and pain, as Lowborough knows to his cost - Ha! ha!' and while he was

laughing at the recollections of Lowborough's troubles, my uncle came and slapped him on the shoulder.

'Come, my lad!' said he. 'Are you too busy making love to my niece to make war with the pheasants? – First of October, remember! – Sun shines out – rain ceased – even Boarham's not afraid to venture in his waterproof boots; and Wilmot and I are going to beat you all. I declare, we old 'uns are the keenest sportsmen of the lot!'

'I'll show you what I can do today, however,' said my companion. 'I'll murder your birds by wholesale, just for keeping me away from better company than either you or them.'

And so saying he departed; and I saw no more of him till dinner. It seemed a weary time; I wonder what I shall do without him.

It is very true that the three elder gentlemen had proved themselves much keener sportsmen than the two younger ones; for both Lord Lowborough and Arthur Huntingdon have of late almost daily neglected the shooting excursions, to accompany us in our various rides and rambles. But these merry times are fast drawing to a close. In less than a fortnight the party break up, much to my sorrow, for every day I enjoy it more and more – now that Messrs Boarham and Wilmot have ceased to tease me, and my aunt has ceased to lecture me, and I have ceased to be jealous of Annabella – and even to dislike her – and now that Mr Huntingdon is become my Arthur, and I may enjoy his society without restraint – What shall I do without him, I repeat?

# Chapter 22

## October 5th

My cup of sweets is not unmingled: it is dashed with a bitterness that I cannot hide from myself, disguise it as I will. I may try to persuade myself that the sweetness overpowers it; I may call it a pleasant aromatic flavour; but say what I will, it is still there, and I cannot but taste it. I cannot shut my eyes to Arthur's faults; and the more I love him the more they trouble me. His very heart, that I trusted so, is, I fear, less warm and generous than I thought it. At least, he gave me a specimen of his character today, that seemed to merit a harder name than thoughtlessness. He and Lord Lowborough were accompanying Annabella and me in a long, delightful ride; he was riding by my side, as usual, and Annabella and Lord Lowborough were a little before us, the latter bending towards his companion as if in tender and confidential discourse.

'Those two will get the start of us, Helen, if we don't look sharp,' observed Huntingdon. 'They'll make a match of it, as sure as can be. That Lowborough's fairly besotted. But he'll find himself in a fix when he's got her, I doubt.'

# The Tenant of Wildfell Hall

'And she'll find herself in a fix when she's got him,' said I, 'if what I have heard of him is true.'

'Not a bit of it. She knows what she's about; but he, poor fool, deludes himself with the notion that she'll make him a good wife, and because she has amused him with some rodomontade about despising rank and wealth in matters of love and marriage, he flatters himself that she's devotedly attached to him; that she will not refuse him for his poverty, and does not court him for his rank, but loves him for himself alone.'

'But is not he courting her for her fortune?'

'No, not he. That was the first attraction, certainly; but now he has quite lost sight of it: it never enters his calculations, except merely as an essential without which, for the lady's own sake, he could not think of marrying her. No; he's fairly in love. He thought he never could be again, but he's in for it once more. He was to have been married before, some two or three years ago; but he lost his bride by losing his fortune. He got into a bad way among us in London: he had an unfortunate taste for gambling; and surely the fellow was born under an unlucky star, for he always lost thrice where he gained once. That's a mode of self-torment I never was much addicted to. When I spend my money I like to enjoy the full value of it: I see no fun in wasting it on thieves and blacklegs; and as for gaining money, hitherto, I have always had sufficient; it's time enough to be clutching for more, I think, when you begin to see the end of what you have. But I have sometimes frequented the gaming-houses just to watch the on-goings of those mad votaries of chance – a very interesting study, I assure you, Helen, and sometimes very diverting: I've had many a laugh at the boobies and bedlamites. Lowborough was quite infatuated – not willingly, but of necessity, – he was always resolving to give it up, and always breaking his resolutions. Every venture was the "just once more": if he gained a little, he hoped to gain a little more next time, and if he lost, it would not do to leave off at that juncture; he must go on till he had retrieved that last misfortune, at least: bad luck could not last for ever; and every lucky hit was looked upon as the dawn of better times, till experience proved the contrary. At length he grew desperate, and we were daily on the look-out for a case of *felo de se* – no great matter, some of us whispered, as his existence had ceased to be an acquisition to our club. At last, however, he came to a check. He made a large stake which he determined should be the last, whether he lost or won. He had often so determined before, to be sure, and as often broken his determination; and so it was this time. He lost; and while his antagonist smilingly swept away the stakes, he turned chalky white, drew back in silence, and wiped his forehead. I was present at the time; and while he stood with folded arms and eyes fixed on the ground, I knew well enough what was passing in his mind.

' "Is it to be the last Lowborough?" said I, stepping up to him.

' "The last but one," he answered, with a grim smile; and then, rushing back to the table, he struck his hand upon it, and, raising his voice high above all the confusion of jingling coins and muttered oaths and curses in the room, he swore a deep and solemn oath, that, come what would, this trial should be the last, and imprecated unspeakable curses on his head, if ever he should shuffle a card, or rattle a dice-box again. He then doubled his former stake, and challenged any one present to play against him. Grimsby instantly presented himself. Lowborough glared fiercely at him, for Grimsby was almost as celebrated for his

luck as he was for his ill-fortune. However, they fell to work. But Grimsby had much skill and little scruple, and whether he took advantage of the other's trembling, blinded eagerness to deal unfairly by him, I cannot undertake to say; but Lowborough lost again, and fell dead sick.

' "You'd better try once more," said Grimsby, leaning across the table. And then he winked at me.

' "I've nothing to try with," said the poor devil, with a ghastly smile.

' "Oh, Huntingdon will lend you what you want," said the other.

' "No; you heard my oath," answered Lowborough, turning away in quiet despair. And I took him by the arm, and led him out.

' "Is it to be the last, Lowborough?" I asked, when I got him into the street.

' "The last," he answered, somewhat against my expectation. And I took him home – that is, to our club – for he was as submissive as a child, and plied him with brandy-and-water till he began to look rather brighter – rather more alive, at least.

' "Huntingdon. I'm ruined!" said he, taking the third glass from my hand – he had drunk the others in dead silence.

' "Not you!" said I. "You'll find a man can live without his money as merrily as a tortoise without its head, or a wasp without its body."

' "But I'm in debt," said he – "deep in debt! And I can never, never get out of it!"

' "Well, what of that? many a better man than you has lived and died in debt, and they can't put you in prison, you know because you're a peer." And I handed him his fourth tumbler.

' "But I hate to be in debt!" he shouted. "I wasn't born for it, and I cannot bear it!"

' "What can't be cured must be endured," said I, beginning to mix the fifth.

' "And then, I've lost my Caroline." And he began to snivel then, for the brandy had softened his heart.

' "No matter," I answered, "there are more Carolines in the world than one."

' "There's only one for me," he replied, with a dolorous sigh. "And if there were fifty more, who's to get them, I wonder, without money?"

' "Oh, somebody will take you for your title; and then you've your family estate yet; that's entailed, you know."

' "I wish to God I could sell it to pay my debts," he muttered.

' "And then," said Grimsby, who had just come in, "you can try again, you know. I would have more than one chance, if I were you. I'd never stop here."

' "I won't, I tell you!" shouted he. And he started up, and left the room – walking rather unsteadily, for the liquor had got into his head. He was not so much used to it then, but after that, he took to it kindly to solace his cares.

'He kept his oath about gambling (not a little to the surprise of us all), though Grimsby did his utmost to tempt him to break it; but now he had got hold of another habit that bothered him nearly as much, for he soon discovered that the demon of drink was as black as the demon of play, and nearly as hard to get rid of – especially as his kind friends did all they could to second the promptings of his own insatiable cravings.'

'Then, they were demons themselves,' cried I, unable to contain my indignation. 'And you, Mr Huntingdon, it seems, were the first to tempt him.'

'Well, what could we do?' replied he deprecatingly. – 'We meant it in kindness

– we couldn't bear to see the poor fellow so miserable: – and besides, he was such a damper upon us, sitting there, silent and glum, when he was under the threefold influence of the loss of his sweetheart, the loss of his fortune, and the reaction of the last night's debauch; whereas, when he had something in him, if he was not merry himself, he was an unfailing source of merriment to us. Even Grimsby could chuckle over his odd sayings: they delighted him far more than my merry jests, or Hattersley's riotous mirth. But, one evening, when we were sitting over our wine, after one of our club dinners, and all had been hearty together, – Lowborough giving us mad toasts, and hearing our wild songs, and bearing a hand in the applause, if he did not help us to sing them himself – he suddenly relapsed into silence, sinking his head on his hand, and never lifting his glass to his lips; but this was nothing new; so we let him alone, and went on with our jollification, till, suddenly raising his head, he interrupted us in the middle of a roar of laughter, by exclaiming—

' "Gentlemen, where is all this to end? – Will you just tell me that now? – Where is it all to end?" He rose.

' "A speech, a speech!" shouted we. "Hear, hear! Lowborough's going to give us a speech!"

'He waited calmly till the thunder of applause and jingling of glasses had ceased, and then proceeded—

' "It's only this, gentlemen, – that I think we'd better go no further. We'd better stop while we can."

' "Just so," cried Hattersley—

> Stop, poor sinner, stop and think
> Before you further go,
> No longer sport upon the brink
> Of everlasting woe.

' "Exactly!" replied his lordship, with the utmost gravity. "And if you choose to visit the bottomless pit, I won't go with you – we must part company, for I swear I'll not move another step towards it! – What's this?" he said, taking up his glass of wine.

' "Taste it," suggested I.

' "This is hell broth!" he exclaimed. "I renounce it for ever!" And he threw it out into the middle of the table.

' "Fill again!" said I, handing him the bottle – "and let us drink to your renunciation."

' "It's rank poison," said he, grasping the bottle by the neck, "and I forswear it! I've given up gambling, and I'll give up this too." He was on the point of deliberately pouring the whole contents of the bottle on to the table, but Hargrave wrested it from him. "On you be the curse then!" said he. And, backing from the room, he shouted, "Farewell, ye tempters!" and vanished among shouts of laughter and applause.

'We expected him back among us the next day; but, to our surprise, the place remained vacant; we saw nothing of him for a whole week; and we really began to think he was going to keep his word. At last, one evening, when we were most of us assembled together again, he entered, silent and grim as a ghost, and would have quietly slipped into his usual seat at my elbow, but we all rose to welcome

him, and several voices were raised to ask what he would have, and several hands were busy with bottle and glass to serve him; but I knew a smoking tumbler of brandy-and-water would comfort him best, and had nearly prepared it, when he peevishly pushed it away, saying—

' "Do let me alone, Huntingdon! Do be quiet, all of you! I'm not come to join you: I'm only come to be with you awhile, because I can't bear my own thoughts." And he folded his arms, and leant back in his chair; so we let him be. But I left the glass by him; and, after a while, Grimsby directed my attention towards it, by a significant wink; and, on turning my head, I saw it was drained to the bottom. He made me a sign to replenish, and quietly pushed up the bottle. I willingly complied: but Lowborough detected the pantomime, and nettled at the intelligent grins that were passing between us, snatched the glass from my hand, dashed the contents of it in Grimsby's face, threw the empty tumbler at me, and then bolted from the room.'

'I hope he broke your head,' said I.

'No, love,' replied he, laughing immoderately at the recollection of the whole affair, 'he would have done so, – and, perhaps, spoilt my face, too, but providentially, this forest of curls' (taking off his hat, and showing his luxuriant chestnut locks) 'saved my skull, and prevented the glass from breaking, till it reached the table.

'After that,' he continued, 'Lowborough kept aloof from us a week or two longer. I used to meet him occasionally in the town; and then, as I was too good-natured to resent his unmannerly conduct, and he bore no malice against me, – he was never unwilling to talk to me; on the contrary, he would cling to me, and follow me anywhere, – but to the club, and the gaming-houses, and such like dangerous places of resort – he was so weary of his own moping, melancholy mind. At last, I got him to come in with me to the club, on condition that I would not tempt him to drink; and, for some time, he continued to look in upon us pretty regularly of an evening, – still abstaining, with wonderful perseverance, from the "rank poison" he had so bravely forsworn. But some of our members protested against this conduct. They did not like to have him sitting there like a skeleton at a feast, instead of contributing his quota to the general amusement, casting a cloud over all, and watching, with greedy eyes, every drop they carried to their lips – they vowed it was not fair; and some of them maintained, that he should either be compelled to do as others did, or expelled from the society; and swore that, next time he showed himself, they would tell him as much, and, if he did not take the warning, proceed to active measures. However, I befriended him on this occasion, and recommended them to let him be for a while, intimating that, with a little patience on our parts, he would soon come round again. But, to be sure, it was rather provoking; for, though he refused to drink like an honest Christian, it was well known to me that he kept a private bottle of laudanum about him, which he was continually soaking at – or rather, holding off and on with, abstaining one day, and exceeding the next – just like the spirits.

'One night, however, during one of our orgies – one of our high festivals, I mean – he glided in, like the ghost in Macbeth, and seated himself, as usual, a little back from the table, in the chair we always placed for "the spectre", whether it chose to fill it or not. I saw by his face that he was suffering from the effects of an overdose of his insidious comforter; but nobody spoke to him,

and he spoke to nobody. A few sidelong glances, and a whispered observation, that "the ghost was come," was all the notice he drew by his appearance, and we went on with our merry carousals as before, till he startled us all, by suddenly drawing in his chair, and leaning forward with his elbows on the table, and exclaiming with portentous solemnity—

' "Well! it puzzles me what you can find to be so merry about. What you see in life I don't know – I see only the blackness of darkness, and a fearful looking for of judgment and fiery indignation!"

'All the company simultaneously pushed up their glasses to him, and I set them before him in a semicircle, and, tenderly patting him on the back, bid him drink, and he would soon see as bright a prospect as any of us; but he pushed them back, muttering—

' "Take them away! I won't taste it, I tell you. I won't – I won't!" So I handed them down again to the owners; but I saw that he followed them with a glare of hungry regret as they departed. Then, he clasped his hands before his eyes to shut out the sight, and two minutes after, lifted his head again, and said, in a hoarse but vehement whisper—

' "And yet I must! Huntingdon, get me a glass!"

' "Take the bottle, man!" said I, thrusting the brandy-bottle into his hand – but stop, I'm telling too much,' muttered the narrator, startled at the look I turned upon him. 'But no matter,' he recklessly added, and thus continued his relation. 'In his desperate eagerness, he seized the bottle and sucked away, till he suddenly dropped from his chair, disappearing under the table amid a tempest of applause. The consequence of this imprudence was something like an apoplectic fit, followed by a rather severe brain fever'—

'And what did you think of yourself, sir?' said I quickly.

'Of course I was very penitent,' he replied. 'I went to see him once or twice – nay, twice or thrice – or by'r lady, some four times – and when he got better, I tenderly brought him back to the fold.'

'What do you mean?'

'I mean, I restored him to the bosom of the club, and compassionating the feebleness of his health and extreme lowness of his spirits, I recommended him to "take a little wine for his stomach's sake," and, when he was sufficiently re-established, to embrace the *media-via, ni-jamais-ni-toujours* plan – not to kill himself like a fool, and not to abstain like a ninny – in a word, to enjoy himself like a rational creature, and do as I did; for don't think, Helen, that I'm a tippler; I'm nothing at all of the kind, and never was, and never shall be. I value my comfort far too much. I see that a man cannot give himself up to drinking without being miserable one half his days and mad the other; besides, I like to enjoy my life at all sides and ends, which cannot be done by one that suffers himself to be the slave of a single propensity – and, moreover, drinking spoils one's good looks,' he concluded, with a most conceited smile that ought to have provoked me more than it did.

'And did Lord Lowborough profit by your advice?' I asked.

'Why, yes, in a manner. For a while, he managed very well: indeed he was a model of moderation and prudence – something too much so for the tastes of our wild community; but, somehow, Lowborough had not the gift of moderation: if he stumbled a little to one side, he must go down before he could right himself: if he overshot the mark one night, the effects of it rendered him so miserable the

next day that he must repeat the offence to mend it; and so on from day to day, till his clamorous conscience brought him to a stand. And then, in his sober moments, he so bothered his friends with his remorse and his terrors and woes, that they were obliged, in self-defence, to get him to drown his sorrows in wine, or any more potent beverage that came to hand; and when his first scruples of conscience were overcome, he would need no more persuading, he would often grow desperate, and be as great a blackguard as any of them could desire – but only to lament his own unutterable wickedness and degradation the more when the fit was over.

'At last, one day, when he and I were alone together, after pondering awhile in one of his gloomy, abstracted moods, with his arms folded and his head sunk on his breast, he suddenly woke up, and vehemently grasping my arm, said—

' 'Huntingdon, this won't do! I'm resolved to have done with it."

' "What, are you going to shoot yourself?" said I.

' "No; I'm going to reform."

' "Oh, that's nothing new! You've been going to reform these twelve months and more."

' "Yes, but you wouldn't let me; and I was such a fool I couldn't live without you. But now I see what it is that keeps me back, and what's wanted to save me; and I'd compass sea and land to get it – only I'm afraid there's no chance." And he sighed as if his heart would break.

' "What is it, Lowborough?" said I, thinking he was fairly cracked at last.

' "A wife," he answered; "for I can't live alone, because my own mind distracts me, and I can't live with you, because you take the devil's part against me."

' "Who – I?"

' "Yes – all of you do – and you more than any of them, you know. But if I could get a wife, with fortune enough to pay off my debts and set me straight in the world"—

' "To be sure," said I.

' "And sweetness and goodness enough," he continued, "to make home tolerable, and to reconcile me to myself, I think I should do, yet. I shall never be in love again, that's certain; but perhaps that would be no great matter, it would enable me to choose with my eyes open – and I should make a good husband in spite of it; but could any one be in love with me? – that's the question. With your good looks and powers of fascination" (he was pleased to say), "I might hope; but as it is, Huntingdon, do you think anybody would take me – ruined and wretched as I am?"

' "Yes, certainly."

' "Who?"

' "Why, any neglected old maid, fast sinking in despair, would be delighted to"—

' "No, no," said he – "it must be somebody that I can love."

' "Why, you just said you never could be in love again!"

' "Well, love is not the word – but somebody that I can like. I'll search all England through, at all events!" he cried, with a sudden burst of hope or desperation. "Succeed or fail, it will be better than rushing headlong to destruction at that d—d club: so farewell to it and you. Whenever I meet you on honest ground or under a Christian roof, I shall be glad to see you; but never more shall you entice me to that devil's den!"

# The Tenant of Wildfell Hall

'This was shameful language, but I shook hands with him, and we parted. He kept his word; and from that time forward, he has been a pattern of propriety, as far as I can tell; but till lately, I have not had very much to do with him. He occasionally sought my company, but as frequently shrunk from it, fearing lest I should wile him back to destruction, and I found his not very entertaining, especially, as he sometimes attempted to awaken my conscience and draw me from the perdition he considered himself to have escaped; but when I did happen to meet him, I seldom failed to ask after the progress of his matrimonial efforts and researches, and, in general, he could give me but a poor account. The mothers were repelled by his empty coffers and his reputation for gambling, and the daughters by his cloudy brow and melancholy temper – besides, he didn't understand them; he wanted the spirit and assurance to carry his point.

'I left him at it when I went to the Continent; and on my return, at the year's end, I found him still a disconsolate bachelor – though, certainly, looking somewhat less like an unblest exile from the tomb than before. The young ladies had ceased to be afraid of him, and were beginning to think him quite interesting; but the mammas were still unrelenting. It was about this time, Helen, that my good angel brought me into conjunction with you; and then I had eyes and ears for nobody else. But, meantime, Lowborough became acquainted with our charming friend Miss Wilmot – through the intervention of his good angel, no doubt he would tell you, though he did not dare to fix his hopes on one so courted and admired, till after they were brought into closer contact here at Staningley, and she, in the absence of her other admirers, indubitably courted his notice and held out every encouragement to his timid advances. Then, indeed, he began to hope for a dawn of brighter days; and if, for a while, I darkened his prospects by standing between him and his sun – and so, nearly plunged him again into the abyss of despair – it only intensified his ardour and strengthened his hopes when I chose to abandon the field in the pursuit of a brighter treasure. In a word, as I told you, he is fairly besotted. At first, he could dimly perceive her faults, and they gave him considerable uneasiness; but now his passion and her art together have blinded him to everything, but her perfections and his amazing good fortune. Last night, he came to me brimful of his new-found felicity—

' "Huntingdon, I am not a cast-away!" said he, seizing my hand and squeezing it like a vice. "There is happiness in store for me, yet – even in this life – she loves me!"

' "Indeed!" said I. "Has she told you so?"

' "No, but I can no longer doubt it. Do you not see how pointedly kind and affectionate she is? And she knows the utmost extent of my poverty, and cares nothing about it! She knows all the folly and all the wickedness of my former life, and is not afraid to trust me – and my rank and title are no allurements to her; for them she utterly disregards. She is the most generous, high-minded being that can be conceived of. She will save me, body and soul, from destruction. Already, she has ennobled me in my own estimation, and made me three times better, wiser, greater than I was. Oh! if I had but known her before, how much degradation and misery I should have been spared! But what have I done to deserve so magnificent a creature?"

'And the cream of the jest,' continued Mr Huntingdon, laughing, 'is, that the

artful minx loves nothing about him but his title and pedigree, and "that delightful old family seat."'

'How do you know?' said I.

'She told me so herself; she said, "As for the man himself, I thoroughly despise him; but then, I suppose, it is time to be making my choice, and if I waited for some one capable of eliciting my esteem and affection, I should have to pass my life in single blessedness, for I detest you all!" Ha, ha! I suspect she was wrong there; but however, it is evident she has no love for him, poor fellow.'

'Then you ought to tell him so.'

'What! and spoil all her plans and prospects, poor girl? No, no: that would be a breach of confidence, wouldn't it, Helen? Ha, ha! Besides, it would break his heart.' And he laughed again.

'Well, Mr Huntingdon, I don't know what you see so amazingly diverting in the matter; I see nothing to laugh at.'

'I'm laughing at you, just now, love,' said he, redoubling his cachinnations.

And leaving him to enjoy his merriment alone, I touched Ruby with the whip and cantered on to rejoin our companions; for we had been walking our horses all this time, and were consequently a long way behind. Arthur was soon at my side again; but not disposed to talk to him, I broke into a gallop. He did the same; and we did not slacken our pace till we came up with Miss Wilmot and Lord Lowborough, which was within half a mile of the park gates. I avoided all further conversation with him, till we came to the end of our ride, when I meant to jump off my horse and vanish into the house, before he could offer his assistance; but while I was disengaging my habit from the crutch, he lifted me off, and held me by both hands, asserting that he would not let me go till I had forgiven him.

'I have nothing to forgive,' said I. 'You have not injured me.'

'No, darling – God forbid that I should! but you are angry, because it was to me that Annabella confessed her lack of esteem for her lover.'

'No, Arthur, it is not that that displeases me: it is the whole system of your conduct towards your friend; and if you wish me to forget it, go, now, and tell him what sort of a woman it is that he adores so madly, and on whom he has hung his hopes of future happiness.'

'I tell you, Helen, it would break his heart – it would be the death of him – besides being a scandalous trick to poor Annabella. There is no help for him now; he is past praying for. Besides, she may keep up the deception to the end of the chapter; and then he will be just as happy in the illusion as if it were reality; or perhaps he will only discover his mistake when he has ceased to love her; and if not, it is much better that the truth should dawn gradually upon him. So now, my angel, I hope I have made out a clear case, and fully convinced you that I cannot make the atonement you require. What other requisition have you to make? Speak, and I will gladly obey.'

'I have none but this,' said I, as gravely as before; 'that, in future, you will never make a jest of the sufferings of others, and always use your influence with your friends for their own advantage against their evil propensities, instead of seconding their evil propensities against themselves.'

'I will do my utmost,' said he, 'to remember and perform the injunction of my angel monitress'; and after kissing both my gloved hands, he let me go.

When I entered my room, I was surprised to see Annabella Wilmot standing

before my toilet table, composedly surveying her features in the glass, with one hand flirting her gold-mounted whip, and the other holding up her long habit.

'She certainly is a magnificent creature!' thought I, as I beheld that tall, finely-developed figure, and the reflection of the handsome face in the mirror before me, with the glossy dark hair, slightly and not ungracefully disordered by the breezy ride, the rich brown complexion glowing with exercise, and the black eyes sparkling with unwonted brilliance. On perceiving me, she turned round, exclaiming, with a laugh that savoured more of malice than of mirth—

'Why, Helen! what have you been doing so long? I came to tell you my good fortune,' she continued, regardless of Rachel's presence. 'Lord Lowborough has proposed, and I have been graciously pleased to accept him. Don't you envy me, dear?'

'No, love,' said I – 'or him either,' I mentally added. 'And do you like him, Annabella?'

'Like him! yes, to be sure – over head and ears in love!'

'Well, I hope you'll make him a good wife.'

'Thank you, my dear. And what besides do you hope?'

'I hope you will both love each other, and both be happy.'

'Thanks; and I hope you will make a very good wife to Mr Huntingdon!' said she, with a queenly bow, and retired.

'Oh, miss! how could you say so to her!' cried Rachel.

'Say what?' replied I.

'Why, that you hoped she would make him a good wife. I never heard such a thing!'

'Because, I do hope it – or rather, I wish it – she's almost past hope.'

'Well!' said she, 'I'm sure I hope he'll make her a good husband. They tell queer things about him downstairs. They were saying'—

'I know, Rachel. I've heard all about him; but he's reformed now. And they have no business to tell tales about their masters.'

'No, mum – or else, they have said some things about Mr Huntingdon, too.'

'I won't hear them, Rachel; they tell lies.'

'Yes, mum,' said she quietly, as she went on arranging my hair.

'Do you believe them, Rachel?' I asked, after a short pause.

'No, miss, not all. You know when a lot of servants gets together they like to talk about their betters; and some, for a bit of swagger, likes to make it appear as though they knew more than they do, and to throw out hints and things just to astonish the others. But I think if I was you, Miss Helen, I'd look very well before I leaped. I do believe a young lady can't be too careful who she marries.'

'Of course not,' said I; 'but be quick, will you, Rachel; I want to be dressed.'

And indeed, I was anxious to be rid of the good woman, for I was in such a melancholy frame I could hardly keep the tears out of my eyes while she dressed me. It was not for Lord Lowborough – it was not for Annabella – it was not for myself – it was for Arthur Huntingdon that they rose.

*13th* – They are gone – and he is gone. We are to be parted for more than two months – above ten weeks! a long, long time to live and not to see him. But he has promised to write often, and made me promise to write still oftener, because he will be busy settling his affairs, and I shall have nothing better to do. Well, I think I shall always have plenty to say. But oh! for the time when

we shall be always together, and can exchange our thoughts without the intervention of these cold go-betweens, pen, ink, and paper!

*22nd* – I have had several letters from Arthur, already. They are not long, but passing sweet, and just like himself – full of ardent affection, and playful lively humour; but – there is always a 'but' in this imperfect world – and I do wish he would sometimes be serious. I cannot get him to write or speak in real, solid earnest. I don't much mind it now, but if it be always so, what shall I do with the serious part of myself?

# Chapter 23

## *Feb. 18th, 1822*

Early this morning, Arthur mounted his hunter and set off in high glee to meet the — hounds. He will be away all day, and so I will amuse myself with my neglected diary, if I can give that name to such an irregular composition. It is exactly four months since I opened it last.

I am married now, and settled down as Mrs Huntingdon of Grassdale Manor. I have had eight weeks' experience of matrimony. And do I regret the step I have taken? No, though I must confess, in my secret heart, that Arthur is not what I thought him at first, and if I had known him in the beginning as thoroughly as I do now, I probably never should have loved him, and if I loved him first, and then made the discovery, I fear I should have thought it my duty not to have married him. To be sure I might have known him, for every one was willing enough to tell me about him, and he himself was no accomplished hypocrite, but I was wilfully blind, and now, instead of regretting that I did not discern his full character before I was indissolubly bound to him, I am glad, for it has saved me a great deal of battling with my conscience, and a great deal of consequent trouble and pain; and, whatever I ought to have done, my duty now is plainly to love him and to cleave to him, and this just tallies with my inclination.

He is very fond of me – almost too fond. I could do with less caressing and more rationality. I should like to be less of a pet and more of a friend if I might choose, but I won't complain of that! I am only afraid his affection loses in depth where it gains in ardour. I sometimes liken it to a fire of dry twigs and branches compared with one solid coal – very bright and hot; but if it should burn itself out and leave nothing but ashes behind, what shall I do? But it won't – it shan't, I am determined – and surely I have power to keep it alive. So let me dismiss that thought at once. But Arthur is selfish; I am constrained to acknowledge that; and, indeed, the admission gives me less pain than might be expected, for, since I love him so much, I can easily forgive him for loving himself: he likes

to be pleased, and it is my delight to please him, and when I regret this tendency of his it is for his own sake, not for mine.

The first instance he gave was on the occasion of our bridal tour. He wanted to hurry it over, for all the Continental scenes were already familiar to him: many had lost their interest in his eyes, and others had never had anything to lose. The consequence was, that after a flying transit, through part of France and part of Italy, I came back nearly as ignorant as I went, having made no acquaintance with persons and manners, and very little with things, my head swarming with a motley confusion of objects and scenes – some, it is true, leaving a deeper and more pleasing impression than others, but these embittered by the recollection that my emotions had not been shared by my companion, but that, on the contrary, when I had expressed a particular interest in anything that I saw or desired to see, it had been displeasing to him, inasmuch as it proved that I could take delight in anything disconnected with himself.

As for Paris, we only just touched at that, and he would not give me time to see one-tenth of the beauties and interesting objects of Rome. He wanted to get me home, he said, to have me all to himself, and to see me safely installed as the mistress of Grassdale Manor, just as single-minded, as naïve, and piquant as I was; and, as if I had been some frail butterfly, he expressed himself fearful of rubbing the silver off my wings by bringing me into contact with society, especially that of Paris and Rome; and, moreover, he did not scruple to tell me that there were ladies in both places that would tear his eyes out if they happened to meet him with me.

Of course I was vexed at all this; but, still, it was less the disappointment to myself that annoyed me, than the disappointment in him, and the trouble I was at to frame excuses to my friends for having seen and observed so little, without imputing one particle of blame to my companion. But when we got home – to my new, delightful home – I was so happy and he was so kind that I freely forgave him all; and I was beginning to think my lot too happy, and my husband actually too good for me, if not too good for this world, when, on the second Sunday after our arrival, he shocked and horrified me by another instance of his unreasonable exaction. We were walking home from the morning service, for it was a fine frosty day, and, as we are so near the church, I had requested the carriage should not be used.

'Helen,' said he, with unusual gravity, 'I am not quite satisfied with you.'

I desired to know what was wrong.

'But will you promise to reform if I tell you?'

'Yes, if I can, and without offending a higher authority.'

'Ah! there it is, you see, you don't love me with all your heart.'

'I don't understand you, Arthur (at least I hope I don't): pray tell me what I have done or said amiss?'

'It is nothing you have done or said; it is something that you are – you are too religious. Now I like a woman to be religious, and I think your piety one of your greatest charms, but then, like all other good things, it may be carried too far. To my thinking, a woman's religion ought not to lessen her devotion to her earthly lord. She should have enough to purify and etherealize her soul, but not enough to refine away her heart, and raise her above all human sympathies.'

'And am I above all human sympathies?' said I.

'No, darling; but you are making more progress towards that saintly condition

than I like; for all these two hours I have been thinking of you and wanting to catch your eye, and you were so absorbed in your devotions that you had not even a glance to spare for me – I declare it is enough to make one jealous of one's Maker – which is very wrong, you know; so don't excite such wicked passions again for my soul's sake.'

'I will give my whole heart and soul to my Maker if I can,' I answered, 'and not one atom more of it to you than He allows. What are you, sir, that you should set yourself up as a god, and presume to dispute possession of my heart with Him to whom I owe all I have and all I am, every blessing I ever did or ever can enjoy – and yourself among the rest – if you are a blessing, which I am half inclined to doubt.'

'Don't be so hard upon me, Helen; and don't pinch my arm so, you're squeezing your fingers into the bone.'

'Arthur,' continued I, relaxing my hold of his arm, 'you don't love me half as much as I do you; and yet, if you loved me far less than you do I would not complain, provided you loved your Maker more. I should rejoice to see you at any time so deeply absorbed in your devotions that you had not even a glance to spare for me. But, indeed, I should lose nothing by the change, for the more you loved your God the more deep and pure and true would be your love to me.'

At this he only laughed and kissed my hand, calling me a sweet enthusiast. Then taking off his hat, he added—

'But look here, Helen – what can a man do with such a head as this?'

The head looked right enough, but when he placed my hand on the top of it, it sunk in a bed of curls, rather alarmingly low, especially in the middle.

'You see I was not made to be a saint,' said he, laughing. 'If God meant me to be religious, why didn't He give me a proper organ of veneration?'

'You are like the servant,' I replied, 'who, instead of employing his one talent in his master's service, restored it to him unimproved, alleging, as an excuse, that he knew him "to be a hard man, reaping where he had not sown, and gathering where he had not strawed". Of him to whom less is given, less will be required, but our utmost exertions are required of us all. You are not without the capacity of veneration, and faith and hope, and conscience and reason, and every other requisite to our Christian's character if you choose to employ them; but all our talents increase in the using, and every faculty, both good and bad, strengthens by exercise: therefore, if you choose to use the bad, or those which tend to evil, till they become your masters, and neglect the good till they dwindle away, you have only yourself to blame. But you have talents, Arthur, natural endowments both of heart and mind and temper, such as many a better Christian would be glad to possess, if you would only employ them in God's service. I should never expect to see you a devotee, but it is quite possible to be a good Christian without ceasing to be a happy, merry-hearted man.'

'You speak like an oracle, Helen, and all you say is indisputably true; but listen here: I am hungry, and I see before me a good substantial dinner; I am told that if I abstain from this today I shall have a sumptuous feast tomorrow, consisting of all manner of dainties and delicacies. Now in the first place, I should be loath to wait till tomorrow when I have the means of appeasing my hunger already before me: in the second place, the solid viands of today are more to my taste than the dainties that are promised me; in the third place, I don't see tomorrow's banquet, and how can I tell that it is not all a fable, got

up by the greasy-faced fellow that is advising me to abstain in order that he may
have all the good victuals to himself? in the fourth place, this table must be
spread for somebody, and, as Solomon says, "Who can eat, or who else can
hasten hereunto more than I?" and finally, with your leave, I'll sit down and
satisfy my cravings of today, and leave tomorrow to shift for itself – who knows
but what I may secure both this and that?'

'But you are not required to abstain from the substantial dinner of today: you
are only advised to partake of these coarser viands in such moderation as not to
incapacitate you from enjoying the choicer banquet of tomorrow. If, regardless
of that counsel, you choose to make a beast of yourself now, and over-eat and
over-drink yourself till you turn the good victuals into poison, who is to blame
if, hereafter, while you are suffering the torments of yesterday's gluttony and
drunkenness, you see more temperate men sitting down to enjoy themselves at
that splendid entertainment which you are unable to taste?'

'Most true, my patron saint; but again, our friend Solomon says, "There is
nothing better for a man than to eat and to drink and to be merry."'

'And again,' returned I, 'he says, "Rejoice, O young man, in thy youth; and
walk in the ways of thine heart, and in the sight of thine eyes: but know thou,
that for all these things, God will bring thee into judgment."'

'Well but, Helen, I'm sure I've been very good these last few weeks. What
have you seen amiss in me, and what would you have me to do?'

'Nothing more than you do, Arthur: your actions are all right so far; but I
would have your thoughts changed: I would have you to fortify yourself against
temptation, and not to call evil good, and good evil; I should wish you to think
more deeply, to look further, and aim higher than you do.'

# Chapter 24

*March 25th*

Arthur is getting tired – not of me, I trust, but
of the idle, quiet life he leads – and no wonder,
for he has so few sources of amusement: he
never reads anything but newspapers and sporting magazines; and when he sees
me occupied with a book he won't let me rest till I close it. In fine weather he
generally manages to get through the time pretty well, but on rainy days, of
which we have had a good many of late, it is quite painful to witness his ennui.
I do all I can to amuse him, but it is impossible to get him to feel interested in
what I most like to talk about, while, on the other hand, he likes to talk about
things that cannot interest me – or even that annoy me – and these please him
the most of all; for his favourite amusement is to sit or loll beside me on the sofa,
and tell me stories of his former amours, always turning upon the ruin of some
confiding girl or the cozening of some unsuspecting husband; and when I express

# The Tenant of Wildfell Hall

my horror and indignation then lays it all to the charge of jealousy, and laughs till the tears run down his cheeks. I used to fly into passions or melt into tears at first, but seeing that his delight increased in proportion to my anger and agitation, I have since endeavoured to suppress my feelings and receive his revelations in the silence of calm contempt; but still he reads the inward struggle in my face, and misconstrues my bitterness of soul for his unworthiness into the pangs of wounded jealousy; and when he has sufficiently diverted himself with that, or fears my displeasure will become too serious for his comfort, he tries to kiss and soothe me into smiles again – never were his caresses so little welcome as then! This is double selfishness displayed to me and to the victims of his former love. There are times when, with a momentary pang – a flash of wild dismay, I ask myself, 'Helen, what have you done?' But I rebuke the inward questioner, and repel the obtrusive thoughts that crowd upon me; for were he ten times as sensual and impenetrable to good and lofty thoughts, I well know I have no right to complain. And I don't and won't complain. I do and will love him still; and I do not and will not regret that I have linked my fate with his.

*April 4th* – We have had a downright quarrel. The particulars are as follows:
– Arthur had told me, at different intervals, the whole story of his intrigue with Lady F—, which I would not believe before. It was some consolation, however, to find that in this instance the lady had been more to blame than he, for he was very young at the time, and she had decidedly made the first advances, if what he said was true. I hated her for it, for it seemed as if she had chiefly contributed to his corruption, and when he was beginning to talk about her the other day, I begged he would not mention her, for I detested the very sound of her name.

'Not because you loved her, Arthur, mind, but because she injured you and deceived her husband, and was altogether a very abominable woman, whom you ought to be ashamed to mention.'

But he defended her by saying that she had a doting old husband, whom it was impossible to love.

'Then why did she marry him?' said I.

'For his money,' was the reply.

'Then that was another crime, and her solemn promise to love and honour him was another, that only increased the enormity of the last.'

'You are too severe upon the poor lady,' laughed he. 'But never mind, Helen, I don't care for her now; and I never loved any of them half as much as I do you, so you needn't fear to be forsaken like them.'

'If you had told me these things before, Arthur, I never should have given you the chance.'

'Wouldn't you, my darling?'

'Most certainly not!'

He laughed incredulously.

'I wish I could convince you of it now!' cried I, starting up from beside him; and for the first time in my life, and I hope the last, I wished I had not married him.

'Helen,' said he, more gravely, 'do you know that if I believed you now I should be very angry? but thank Heaven I don't. Though you stand there with your white face and flashing eyes, looking at me like a very tigress, I know the heart within you perhaps a trifle better than you know it yourself.'

Without another word I left the room and locked myself up in my own

# The Tenant of Wildfell Hall

chamber. In about half-an-hour he came to the door, and first he tried the handle, then he knocked.

'Won't you let me in, Helen?' said he.

'No; you have displeased me,' I replied, 'and I don't want to see your face or hear your voice again till the morning.'

He paused a moment as if dumbfounded or uncertain how to answer such a speech, and then turned and walked away. This was only an hour after dinner: I knew he would find it very dull to sit alone all the evening; and this considerably softened my resentment, though it did not make me relent. I was determined to show him that my heart was not his slave, and I could live without him if I chose; and I sat down and wrote a long letter to my aunt – of course telling her nothing of all this. Soon after ten o'clock I heard him come up again, but he passed my door and went straight to his own dressing-room, where he shut himself in for the night.

I was rather anxious to see how he would meet me in the morning, and not a little disappointed to behold him enter the breakfast-room with a careless smile.

'Are you still cross, Helen?' said he, approaching as if to salute me. I coldly turned to the table, and began to pour out the coffee, observing that he was rather late.

He uttered a low whistle and sauntered away to the window, where he stood for some minutes looking out upon the pleasing prospect of sullen, grey clouds, streaming rain, soaking lawn, and dripping, leafless trees, and muttering execrations on the weather, and then sat down to breakfast. While taking his coffee he muttered it was 'd—d cold.'

'You should not have left it so long,' said I.

He made no answer, and the meal was concluded in silence. It was a relief to both when the letter-bag was brought in. It contained upon examination a newspaper and one or two letters for him, and a couple of letters for me, which he tossed across the table without a remark. One was from my brother, the other from Milicent Hargrave, who is now in London with her mother. His, I think, were business letters, and apparently not much to his mind, for he crushed them into his pocket with some muttered expletives that I should have reproved him for at any other time. The paper, he set before him, and pretended to be deeply absorbed in its contents during the remainder of breakfast, and a considerable time after.

The reading and answering of my letters, and the direction of household concerns, afforded me ample employment for the morning: after lunch I got my drawing, and from dinner till bed-time I read. Meanwhile, poor Arthur was sadly at a loss for something to amuse him or to occupy his time. He wanted to appear as busy and as unconcerned as I did: had the weather at all permitted he would doubtless have ordered his horse and set off to some distant region – no matter where – immediately after breakfast, and not returned till night: had there been a lady anywhere within reach, of any age between fifteen and forty-five, he would have sought revenge and found employment in getting up, or trying to get up, a desperate flirtation with her; but being, to my private satisfaction, entirely cut off from both these sources of diversion, his sufferings were truly deplorable. When he had done yawning over his paper and scribbling short answers to his shorter letters, he spent the remainder of the morning and

the whole of the afternoon in fidgeting about from room to room, watching the clouds, cursing the rain, alternately petting and teasing and abusing his dogs, sometimes lounging on the sofa with a book that he could not force himself to read, and very often fixedly gazing at me when he thought I did not perceive it, with the vain hope of detecting some traces of tears, or some tokens of remorseful anguish in my face. But I managed to preserve an undisturbed though grave serenity throughout the day. I was not really angry: I felt for him all the time, and longed to be reconciled; but I determined he should make the first advances, or at least show some signs of an humble and contrite spirit first; for, if I began, it would only minister to his self-conceit, increase his arrogance, and quite destroy the lesson I wanted to give him.

He made a long stay in the dining-room after dinner, and I fear, took an unusual quantity of wine, but not enough to loosen his tongue, for when he came in and found me quietly occupied with my book, too busy to lift my head on his entrance, he merely murmured an expression of suppressed disapprobation, and, shutting the door with a bang, went and stretched himself at full length on the sofa, and composed himself to sleep. But his favourite cocker, Dash, that had been lying at my feet, took the liberty of jumping upon him and beginning to lick his face. He struck it off with a smart blow, and the poor dog squeaked, and ran cowering back to me. When he woke up, about half-an-hour after, he called it to him again, but Dash only looked sheepish and wagged the tip of his tail. He called again more sharply, but Dash only clung the closer to me, and licked my hand as if imploring protection. Enraged at this, his master snatched up a heavy book and hurled it at his head. The poor dog set up a piteous outcry and ran to the door. I let him out, and then quietly took up the book.

'Give that book to me,' said Arthur, in no very courteous tone. I gave it to him.

'Why did you let the dog out?' he asked. 'You knew I wanted him.'

'By what token?' I replied; 'by your throwing the book at him? but perhaps, it was intended for me?'

'No; but I see you've got a taste of it,' said he, looking at my hand, that had also been struck, and was rather severely grazed.

I returned to my reading, and he endeavoured to occupy himself in the same manner; but, in a little while, after several portentous yawns, he pronounced his book to be 'cursed trash', and threw it on the table. Then followed eight or ten minutes of silence, during the greater part of which, I believe, he was staring at me. At last his patience was tired out.

'What is that book, Helen?' he exclaimed.

I told him.

'Is it interesting?'

'Yes, very.'

I went on reading, or pretending to read, at least – I cannot say there was much communication between my eyes and my brain; for, while the former ran over the pages, the latter was earnestly wondering when Arthur would speak next, and what he would say, and what I should answer. But he did not speak again till I rose to make the tea, and then it was only to say he should not take any. He continued lounging on the sofa, and alternately closing his eyes and

looking at his watch and at me, till bed-time, when I rose, and took my candle and retired.

'Helen!' cried he, the moment I had left the room. I turned back, and stood awaiting his commands.

'What do you want, Arthur?' I said at length.

'Nothing,' replied he. 'Go!'

I went, but hearing him mutter something as I was closing the door, I turned again. It sounded very like 'confounded slut', but I was quite willing it should be something else.

'Were you speaking, Arthur?' I asked.

'No,' was the answer, and I shut the door and departed. I saw nothing more of him till the following morning at breakfast, when he came down a full hour after his usual time.

'You're very late,' was my morning's salutation.

'You needn't have waited for me,' was his; and he walked up to the window again. It was just such weather as yesterday.

'Oh, this confounded rain!' he muttered. But, after studiously regarding it for a minute or two, a bright idea seemed to strike him, for he suddenly exclaimed, 'But I know what I'll do!' and then returned and took his seat at the table. The letter-bag was already there, waiting to be opened. He unlocked it and examined the contents, but said nothing about them.

'Is there anything for me?' I asked.

'No.'

He opened the newspaper and began to read.

'You'd better take your coffee,' suggested I; 'it will be cold again.'

'You may go,' said he, 'if you've done. I don't want you.'

I rose and withdrew to the next room, wondering if we were to have another such miserable day as yesterday, and wishing intensely for an end of these mutually inflicted torments. Shortly after I heard him ring the bell and give some orders about his wardrobe that sounded as if he meditated a long journey. He then sent for the coachman, and I heard something about the carriage and the horses, and London, and seven o'clock tomorrow morning, that startled and disturbed me not a little.

'I must not let him go to London, whatever comes of it,' said I to myself; 'he will run into all kinds of mischief, and I shall be the cause of it. But the question is, how am I to alter his purpose? – Well, I will wait awhile, and see if he mentions it.'

I waited most anxiously, from hour to hour; not a word was spoken, on that or any other subject, to me. He whistled and talked to his dogs, and wandered from room to room, much the same as on the previous day. At last I began to think I must introduce the subject myself, and was pondering how to bring it about, when John unwittingly came to my relief with the following message from the coachman—

'Please, sir, Richard says one of the horses has got a very bad cold, and he thinks, sir, if you could make it convenient to go the day after tomorrow, instead of tomorrow, he could physic it today so as'—

'Confound his impudence!' interjected the master.

'Please, sir, he says it would be a deal better if you could,' persisted John,

# The Tenant of Wildfell Hall

'for he hopes there'll be a change in the weather shortly, and he says it's not likely, when a horse is so bad with a cold, and physicked and all'—

'Devil take the horse!' cried the gentleman – 'Well, tell him I'll think about it,' he added, after a moment's reflection. He cast a searching glance at me, as the servant withdrew, expecting to see some token of deep astonishment and alarm; but, being previously prepared, I preserved an aspect of stoical indifference. His countenance fell as he met my steady gaze, and he turned away in very obvious disappointment, and walked up to the fireplace, where he stood in an attitude of undisguised dejection, leaning against the chimney-piece with his forehead sunk upon his arm.

'Where do you want to go, Arthur?' said I.

'To London,' replied he gravely.

'What for?' I asked.

'Because I cannot be happy here.'

'Why not?'

'Because my wife doesn't love me.'

'She would love you with all her heart, if you deserved it.'

'What must I do to deserve it?'

This seemed humble and earnest enough; and I was so much affected, between sorrow and joy, that I was obliged to pause a few seconds before I could steady my voice to reply.

'If she gives you her heart.' said I, 'you must take it thankfully, and use it well, and not pull it in pieces, and laugh in her face, because she cannot snatch it away.'

He now turned round and stood facing me, with his back to the fire.

'Come then, Helen, are you going to be a good girl?' said he.

This sounded rather too arrogant, and the smile that accompanied it did not please me. I therefore hesitated to reply. Perhaps my former answer had implied too much: he had heard my voice falter, and might have seen me brush away a tear.

'Are you going to forgive me, Helen?' he resumed more humbly.

'Are you penitent?' I replied, stepping up to him and smiling in his face.

'Heart-broken!' he answered, with a rueful countenance, yet with a merry smile just lurking within his eyes and about the corners of his mouth; but this could not repulse me, and I flew into his arms. He fervently embraced me, and though I shed a torrent of tears, I think I never was happier in my life than at that moment.

'Then you won't go to London, Arthur?' I said, when the first transport of tears and kisses had subsided.

'No, love, – unless you will go with me.'

'I will, gladly,' I answered, 'if you think the change will amuse you, and if you will put off the journey till next week.'

He readily consented, but said there was no need of much preparation, as he should not be for staying long, for he did not wish me to be Londonized, and to lose my country freshness and originality by too much intercourse with the ladies of the world. I thought this folly; but I did not wish to contradict him now: I merely said that I was of very domestic habits, as he well knew, and had no particular wish to mingle with the world.

So we are to go to London on Monday, the day after tomorrow. It is now four

days since the termination of our quarrel, and I'm sure it has done us both good: it has made me like Arthur a great deal better, and made him behave a great deal better to me. He has never once attempted to annoy me since, by the most distant allusion to Lady F—, or any of those disagreeable reminiscences of his former life – I wish I could blot them from my memory, or else get him to regard such matters in the same light as I do. Well! it is something, however, to have made him see that they are not fit subjects for a conjugal jest. He may see further some time – I will put no limits to my hopes; and, in spite of my aunt's forebodings and my own unspoken fears, I trust we shall be happy yet.

# Chapter 25

On the eighth of April, we went to London; on the eighth of May I returned, in obedience to Arthur's wish; very much against my own, because I left him behind. If he had come with me, I should have been very glad to get home again, for he led me such a round of restless dissipation while there, that, in that short space of time, I was quite tired out. He seemed bent upon displaying me to his friends and acquaintances in particular, and the public in general, on every possible occasion, and to the greatest possible advantage. It was something to feel that he considered me a worthy object of pride; but I paid dear for the gratification, for, in the first place, to please him, I had to violate my cherished predilections – my almost rooted principles in favour of a plain, dark, sober style of dress; I must sparkle in costly jewels, and deck myself out like a painted butterfly, just as I had, long since, determined I would never do – and this was no trifling sacrifice; – in the second place, I was continually straining to satisfy his sanguine expectations and do honour to his choice, by my general conduct and deportment, and fearing to disappoint him by some awkward misdemeanour, or some trait of inexperienced ignorance about the customs of society, especially when I acted the part of hostess, which I was not unfrequently called upon to do; and in the third place, as I intimated before, I was wearied of the throng and bustle, the restless hurry and ceaseless change of a life so alien to all my previous habits. At last, he suddenly discovered that the London air did not agree with me, and I was languishing for my country home, and must immediately return to Grassdale.

I laughingly assured him that the case was not so urgent as he appeared to think it, but I was quite willing to go home if he was. He replied that he should be obliged to remain a week or two longer, as he had business that required his presence.

'Then I will stay with you,' said I.

'But I can't do with you, Helen,' was his answer: 'as long as you stay, I shall attend to you and neglect my business.'

'But I won't let you,' I returned: 'Now that I know you have business to attend to, I shall insist upon your attending to it, and letting me alone – and, to tell the truth, I shall be glad of a little rest. I can take my rides and walks in the park as usual; and your business cannot occupy all your time; I shall see you at meal-times and in the evenings, at least, and that will be better than being leagues away and never seeing you at all.'

'But, my love, I cannot let you stay. How can I settle my affairs when I know that you are here, neglected'—

'I shall not feel myself neglected: while you are doing your duty, Arthur, I shall never complain of neglect. If you had told me before, that you had anything to do, it would have been half done before this; and now you must make up for lost time by redoubled exertions. Tell me what it is; and I will be your taskmaster, instead of being a hindrance.'

'No, no,' persisted the impracticable creature; 'you must go home, Helen; I must have the satisfaction of knowing that you are safe and well, though far away. Your bright eyes are faded, and that tender, delicate bloom has quite deserted your cheek.'

'That is only with too much gaiety and fatigue.'

'It is not, I tell you; it is the London air: you are pining for the fresh breezes of your country home – and you shall feel them, before you are two days older. And remember your situation, dearest Helen; on your health, you know, depends the health, if not the life, of our future hope.'

'Then you really wish to get rid of me?'

'Positively, I do; and I will take you down myself to Grassdale, and then return. I shall not be absent above a week – or fortnight at most.'

'But if I must go, I will go alone: if you must stay, it is needless to waste your time in the journey there and back.'

But he did not like the idea of sending me alone.

'Why, what helpless creature do you take me for,' I replied, 'that you cannot trust me to go a hundred miles in our own carriage with our own footman and a maid to attend me? If you come with me I shall assuredly keep you. But tell me, Arthur, what is this tiresome business; and why did you never mention it before?'

'It is only a little business with my lawyer,' said he; and he told me something about a piece of property he wanted to sell in order to pay off a part of the incumbrances on his estate; but either the account was a little confused, or I was rather dull of comprehension, for I could not clearly understand how that should keep him in town a fortnight after me. Still less can I now comprehend how it should keep him a month – for it is nearly that time since I left him, and no signs of his return as yet. In every letter he promises to be with me in a few days, and every time deceives me – or deceives himself. His excuses are vague and insufficient. I cannot doubt that he is got among his former companions again – Oh, why did I leave him! I wish – I do intensely wish he would return!

*June 29th* – No Arthur yet; and for many days I have been looking and longing in vain for a letter. His letters, when they come, are kind – if fair words and endearing epithets can give them a claim to the title – but very short, and full of trivial excuses and promises that I cannot trust; and yet how anxiously I look forward to them! how eagerly I open and devour one of those little,

hastily-scribbled returns for the three or four long letters, hitherto unanswered, he has had from me!

Oh, it is cruel to leave me so long alone! He knows I have no one but Rachel to speak to, for we have no neighbours here, except the Hargraves, whose residence I can dimly descry from these upper windows embosomed among those low, woody hills beyond the Dale. I was glad when I learned that Milicent was so near us; and her company would be soothing solace to me now, but she is still in town with her mother: there is no one at the Grove but little Esther and her French governess, for Walter is always away. I saw that paragon of manly perfections in London: he seemed scarcely to merit the eulogiums of his mother and sister, though he certainly appeared more conversable and agreeable than Lord Lowborough, more candid and high-minded than Mr Grimsby, and more polished and gentlemanly than Mr Hattersley, Arthur's only other friend whom he judged fit to introduce to me. – Oh, Arthur, why won't you come! why won't you write to me at least! You talked about my health – how can you expect me to gather bloom and vigour here; pining in solitude and restless anxiety from day to day? – It would serve you right to come back and find my good looks entirely wasted away. I would beg my uncle and aunt, or my brother, to come and see me, but I do not like to complain of my loneliness to them, – and indeed, loneliness is the least of my sufferings; but what is he doing – what is it that keeps him away? It is this ever-recurring question and the horrible suggestions it raises that distract me.

*July 3rd* – My last bitter letter has wrung from him an answer at last, – and a rather longer one than usual; but still I don't know what to make of it. He playfully abuses me for the gall and vinegar of my latest effusion, tells me I can have no conception of the multitudinous engagements that keep him away, but avers that, in spite of them all, he will assuredly be with me before the close of next week; though it is impossible for a man, so circumstanced as he is, to fix the precise day of his return: meantime he exhorts me to the exercise of patience, 'that first of woman's virtues', and desires me to remember the saying, 'Absence makes the heart grow fonder', and comfort myself with the assurance that the longer he stays away, the better he shall love me when he returns; and till he does return, he begs I will continue to write to him constantly, for, though he is sometimes too idle and often too busy to answer my letters as they come, he likes to receive them daily, and if I fulfil my threat of punishing his seeming neglect by ceasing to write, he shall be so angry that he will do his utmost to forget me. He adds this piece of intelligence respecting poor Milicent Hargrave—

'Your little friend Milicent is likely, before long, to follow your example, and take upon her the yoke of matrimony in conjunction with a friend of mine. Hattersley, you know, has not yet fulfilled his direful threat of throwing his precious person away on the first old maid that chose to evince a tenderness for him; but he still preserves a resolute determination to see himself a married man before the year is out: "Only," said he to me, "I must have somebody that will let me have my own way in everything – not like your wife, Huntingdon; she is a charming creature, but she looks as if she had a will of her own, and could play the vixen, upon occasion" (I thought "you're right there, man," but I didn't say so). "I must have some good, quiet soul that will let me just do what I like and go where I like, keep at home or stay away, without a word of reproach or complaint; for I can't do with being bothered," "Well," said I, "I know somebody

# The Tenant of Wildfell Hall

that will suit you to a tee, if you don't care for money, and that's Hargrave's sister, Milicent." He desired to be introduced to her forthwith, for he said he had plenty of the needful himself – or should have, when his old governor chose to quit the stage. So you see, Helen, I have managed pretty well, both for your friend and mine.'

Poor Milicent! But I cannot imagine she will ever be led to accept such a suitor – one so repugnant to all her ideas of a man to be honoured and loved.

*5th* – Alas! I was mistaken. I have got a long letter from her this morning, telling me she is already engaged, and expects to be married before the close of the month.

'I hardly know what to say about it,' she writes, 'or what to think. To tell you the truth, Helen, I don't like the thoughts of it at all. If I am to be Mr Hattersley's wife, I must try to love him; and I do try with all my might; but I have made very little progress yet; and the worst symptom of the case is, that the further he is from me the better I like him: he frightens me with his abrupt manners and strange hectoring ways, and I dread the thoughts of marrying him. "Then why have you accepted him?" you will ask; and I didn't know I had accepted him; but mamma tells me I have, and he seems to think so too. I certainly didn't mean to do so; but I did not like to give him a flat refusal for fear mamma should be grieved and angry (for I knew she wished me to marry him) and I wanted to talk to her first about it, so I gave him what I thought was an evasive, half negative answer; but she says it was as good as an acceptance, and he would think me very capricious if I were to attempt to draw back – and indeed, I was so confused and frightened at the moment, I can hardly tell what I said. And next time I saw him, he accosted me in all confidence as his affianced bride, and immediately began to settle matters with mamma. I had not courage to contradict them then, and how can I do it now? I cannot: they would think me mad. Besides, mamma is so delighted with the idea of the match; she thinks she has managed so well for me; and I cannot bear to disappoint her. I do object sometimes, and tell her what I feel, but you don't know how she talks. Mr Hattersley, you know, is the son of a rich banker, and as Esther and I have no fortunes, and Walter very little, our dear mamma is very anxious to see us all well married, that is, united to rich partners – it is not my idea of being well married, but she means it all for the best. She says when I am safe off her hands it will be such a relief to her mind; and she assures me it will be a good thing for the family as well as for me. Even Walter is pleased at the prospect, and when I confessed my reluctance to him, he said it was all childish nonsense. Do you think it nonsense, Helen? I should not care if I could see any prospect of being able to love and admire him, but I can't. There is nothing about him to hang one's esteem and affection upon: he is so diametrically opposite to what I imagined my husband should be. Do write to me, and say all you can to encourage me. Don't attempt to dissuade me, for my fate is fixed: preparations for the important event are already going on around me; and don't say a word against Mr Hattersley, for I want to think well of him; and though I have spoken against him myself, it is for the last time; hereafter, I shall never permit myself to utter a word in his dispraise, however he may seem to deserve it; and whoever ventures to speak slightingly of the man I have promised to love, to honour, and obey, must expect my serious displeasure. After all, I think he is quite as good as Mr Huntingdon, if not better; and yet, you love him, and seem

to be happy and contented; and perhaps I may manage as well. You must tell me, if you can, that Mr Hattersley is better than he seems – that he is upright, honourable, and open-hearted – in fact, a perfect diamond in the rough. He may be all this, but I don't know him. I know only the exterior and what I trust is the worst part of him.'

She concludes with 'Good-bye, dear Helen, I am waiting anxiously for your advice – but mind you let it be all on the right side.'

Alas! poor Milicent, what encouragement can I give you? or what advice – except that it is better to make a bold stand now, though at the expense of disappointing and angering both mother and brother, and lover, than to devote your whole life, hereafter, to misery and vain regret?

*Saturday, 13th* – The week is over, and he is not come. All the sweet summer is passing away without one breath of pleasure to me or benefit to him. And I had all along been looking forward to this season with the fond, delusive hope that we should enjoy it so sweetly together; and that, with God's help and my exertions, it would be the means of elevating his mind, and refining his taste to a due appreciation of the salutary and pure delights of nature and peace, and holy love. But now – at evening, when I see the round, red sun sink quietly down behind those woody hills, leaving them sleeping in a warm, red, golden haze, I only think another lovely day is lost to him and me; and at morning, when roused by the flutter and chirp of the sparrows, and the gleeful twitter of the swallows – all intent upon feeding their young, and full of life and joy in their own little frames – I open the window to inhale the balmy, soul-reviving air, and look out upon the lovely landscape, laughing in dew and sunshine – I too often shame that glorious scene with tears of thankless misery, because he cannot feel its freshening influence; and when I wander in the ancient woods, and meet the little wild-flowers smiling in my path, or sit in the shadow of our noble ash-trees by the water-side, with their branches gently swaying in the light summer breeze that murmurs through their feathery foliage – my ears full of that low music mingled with the dreamy hum of insects, my eyes abstractedly gazing on the glassy surface of the little lake before me, with the trees that crowd about its bank, some gracefully bending to kiss its waters, some rearing their stately heads high above, but stretching their wide arms over its margin, all faithfully mirrored far, far down in its glassy depth – though sometimes the images are partially broken by the sport of aquatic insects, and sometimes, for a moment, the whole is shivered into trembling fragments by a transient breeze that swept the surface too roughly – still I have no pleasure; for the greater the happiness that nature sets before me, the more I lament that he is not here to taste it: the greater the bliss we might enjoy together, the more I feel our present wretchedness apart (yes, ours; he must be wretched though he may not know it); and the more my senses are pleased, the more my heart is oppressed, for he keeps it with him confined amid the dust and smoke of London – perhaps, shut up within the walls of his own abominable club.

But most of all, at night, when I enter my lonely chamber, and look out upon the summer moon, 'sweet regent of the sky', floating above me in the 'black blue vault of heaven', shedding a flood of silver radiance over park, and wood, and water, so pure, so peaceful, so divine – and think, Where is he now? – what is he doing at this moment? wholly unconscious of this heavenly scene – perhaps,

revelling with his boon companions, perhaps – God help me, it is too – too much!

*23rd* – Thank Heaven, he is come at last! But how altered! flushed and feverish, listless and languid, his beauty strangely diminished, his vigour and vivacity quite departed. I have not upbraided him by word or look; I have not even asked him what he has been doing. I have not the heart to do it, for I think he is ashamed of himself – he must be so indeed, and such inquiries could not fail to be painful to both. My forbearance pleases him – touches him even, I am inclined to think. He says he is glad to be home again, and God knows how glad I am to get him back, even as he is. He lies on the sofa nearly all day long; and I play and sing to him for hours together. I write his letters for him, and get him everything he wants; and sometimes I read to him, and sometimes I talk, and sometimes only sit by him and soothe him with silent caresses. I know he does not deserve it; and I fear I am spoiling him; but this once, I will forgive him, freely and entirely, I will shame him into virtue if I can, and I will never let him leave me again.

He is pleased with my attentions – it may be, grateful for them. He likes to have me near him; and though he is peevish and testy with his servants and his dogs, he is gentle and kind to me. What he would be, if I did not so watchfully anticipate his wants, and so carefully avoid, or immediately desist from doing anything that has a tendency to irritate or disturb him, with however little reason, I cannot tell. How intensely I wish he were worthy of all this care! Last night as I sat beside him, with his head in my lap, passing my fingers through his beautiful curls, this thought made my eyes overflow with sorrowful tears – as it often does; but this time, a tear fell on his face and made him look up. He smiled, but not insultingly.

'Dear Helen!' he said – 'Why do you cry? you know that I love you' (and he pressed my hand to his feverish lips), 'and what more could you desire?'

'Only, Arthur, that you would love yourself, as truly and as faithfully as you are loved by me.'

'That would be hard, indeed!' he replied, tenderly squeezing my hand.

*August 24th* – Arthur is himself again, as lusty and reckless, as light of heart and head as ever, and as restless and hard to amuse as a spoilt child, and almost as full of mischief too, especially when wet weather keeps him within doors. I wish he had something to do, some useful trade, or profession, or employment – anything to occupy his head or his hands for a few hours a day, and give him something besides his own pleasure to think about. If he would play the country gentleman, and attend to the farm – but that he knows nothing about, and won't give his mind to consider, – or if he would take up with some literary study, or learn to draw or to play – as he is so fond of music, I often try to persuade him to learn the piano, but he is far too idle for such an undertaking: he has no more idea of exerting himself to overcome obstacles than he has of restraining his natural appetites; and these two things are the ruin of him. I lay them both to the charge of his harsh yet careless father, and his madly indulgent mother. If ever I am a mother I will zealously strive against this crime of over-indulgence. I can hardly give it a milder name when I think of the evils it brings.

Happily, it will soon be the shooting season, and then, if the weather permit, he will find occupation enough in the pursuit and destruction of the partridges and pheasants: we have no grouse, or he might have been similarly occupied at

this moment, instead of lying under the acacia tree pulling poor Dash's ears. But he says it is dull work shooting alone; he must have a friend or two to help him.

'Let them be tolerably decent then, Arthur,' said I. The word 'friend', in his mouth, makes me shudder: I know it was some of his 'friends' that induced him to stay behind me in London, and kept him away so long – indeed, from what he has unguardedly told me, or hinted from time to time, I cannot doubt that he frequently showed them my letters, to let them see how fondly his wife watched over his interests, and how keenly she regretted his absence; and that they induced him to remain week after week, and to plunge into all manner of excesses to avoid being laughed at for a wife-ridden fool, and, perhaps, to show how far he could venture to go without danger of shaking the fond creature's devoted attachment. It is a hateful idea, but I cannot believe it is a false one.

'Well,' replied he, 'I thought of Lord Lowborough for one; but there is no possibility of getting him without his better half, our mutual friend, Annabella; so we must ask them both. You're not afraid of her, are you, Helen?' he asked, with a mischievous twinkle in his eyes.

'Of course not,' I answered: 'Why should I? – And who besides?'

'Hargrave for one – he will be glad to come, though his own place is so near, for he has little enough land of his own to shoot over, and we can extend our depredations into it, if we like; – and he is thoroughly respectable, you know, Helen, quite a lady's man: – and I think Grimsby for another: he's a decent, quiet fellow enough – you'll not object to Grimsby?'

'I hate him: but, however, if you wish it, I'll try to endure his presence for a while.'

'All a prejudice, Helen – a mere woman's antipathy.'

'No; I have solid grounds for my dislike. And is that all?'

'Why, yes, I think so. Hattersley will be too busy billing and cooing with his bride to have much time to spare for guns and dogs, at present,' he replied. And that reminds me, that I have had several letters from Milicent since her marriage, and that she either is, or pretends to be, quite reconciled to her lot. She professes to have discovered numberless virtues and perfections in her husband, some of which, I fear, less partial eyes would fail to distinguish, though they sought them carefully with tears; and now that she is accustomed to his loud voice, and abrupt, uncourteous manners, she affirms she finds no difficulty in loving him as a wife should do, and begs I will burn that letter wherein she spoke so unadvisedly against him. So that I trust she may yet be happy; but, if she is, it will be entirely the reward of her own goodness of heart; for had she chosen to consider herself the victim of fate, or of her mother's worldly wisdom, she might have been thoroughly miserable; and if, for duty's sake, she had not made every effort to love her husband, she would, doubtless, have hated him to the end of her days.

# Chapter 26

*September 23rd*

Our guests arrived three weeks ago. Lord and Lady Lowborough have now been married above eight months; and I will do the lady the credit to say that her husband is quite an altered man; his looks, his spirits, and his temper, are all perceptibly changed for the better since I last saw him. But there is room for improvement still. He is not always cheerful, not always contented, and she often complains of his ill-humour, which, however, of all persons, she ought to be the last to accuse him of, as he never displays it against her, except for such conduct as would provoke a saint. He adores her still, and would go to the world's end to please her. She knows her power, and she uses it too; but well knowing, that to wheedle and coax is safer than to command, she judiciously tempers her despotism with flattery and blandishments enough to make him deem himself a favoured and a happy man.

But she has a way of tormenting him, in which I am a fellow-sufferer, or might be, if I chose to regard myself as such. This is by openly, but not too glaringly, coquetting with Mr Huntingdon, who is quite willing to be her partner in the game; but I don't care for it, because, with him, I know there is nothing but personal vanity, and a mischievous desire to excite my jealousy, and, perhaps, to torment his friend; and she, no doubt, is actuated by much the same motives; only there is more of malice, and less of playfulness, in her manoeuvres. It is, obviously, therefore, my interest to disappoint them both, as far as I am concerned, by preserving a cheerful, undisturbed serenity throughout; and, accordingly, I endeavour to show the fullest confidence in my husband, and the greatest indifference to the arts of my attractive guest. I have never reproached the former but once, and that was for laughing at Lord Lowborough's depressed and anxious countenance one evening, when they had both been particularly provoking; and then, indeed, I said a good deal on the subject, and rebuked him sternly enough; but he only laughed, and said—

'You can feel for him, Helen – can't you?'

'I can feel for anyone that is unjustly treated,' I replied, 'and I can feel for those that injure them too.'

'Why Helen, you are as jealous as he is!' cried he, laughing still more; and I found it impossible to convince him of his mistake. So, from that time, I have carefully refrained from any notice of the subject whatever, and left Lord Lowborough to take care of himself. He either has not the sense or the power to follow my example, though he does try to conceal his uneasiness as well as he can; but still, it will appear in his face, and his ill-humour will peep out at intervals, though not in the expression of open resentment – they never go far

enough for that. But, I confess, I do feel jealous at times – most painfully, bitterly so – when she sings and plays to him, and he hands over the instrument, and dwells upon her voice with no affected interest; for then, I know he is really delighted, and I have no power to awaken similar fervour. I can amuse and please him with my simple songs, but not delight him thus.

28th – Yesterday, we all went to the Grove, Mr Hargrave's much-neglected home. His mother frequently asks us over, that she may have the pleasure of her dear Walter's company; and this time she had invited us to a dinner-party, and got together as many of the country gentry as were within reach to meet us. The entertainment was very well got up; but I could not help thinking about the cost of it all the time. I don't like Mrs Hargrave; she is a hard, pretentious, worldly-minded woman. She has money enough to live very comfortably, if she only knew how to use it judiciously, and had taught her son to do the same; but she is ever straining to keep up appearances, with that despicable pride that shuns the semblance of poverty as of a shameful crime. She grinds her dependents, pinches her servants, and deprives even her daughters and herself of the real comforts of life, because she will not consent to yield the palm in outward show to those who have three times her wealth; and, above all, because she is determined her cherished son shall be enabled to 'hold up his head with the highest gentleman in the land'. This same son, I imagine, is a man of expensive habits – no reckless spendthrift, and no abandoned sensualist, but one who likes to have 'everything handsome about him', and to go to a certain length in youthful indulgences – not so much to gratify his own tastes as to maintain his reputation as a man of fashion in the world, and a respectable fellow among his own lawless companions; while he is too selfish to consider how many comforts might be obtained for his fond mother and sisters with the money he thus wastes upon himself as long as they can contrive to make a respectable appearance once a year, when they come to town, he gives himself little concern about their private stintings and struggles at home. This is a harsh judgment to form of 'dear, noble-minded, generous-hearted Walter', but I fear it is too just.

Mrs Hargrave's anxiety to make good matches for her daughters is partly the cause, and partly the result, of these errors: by making a figure in the world and showing them off to advantage, she hopes to obtain better chances for them; and by thus living beyond her legitimate means, and lavishing so much on their brother, she renders them portionless, and makes them burdens on her hands. Poor Milicent, I fear, has already fallen a sacrifice to the manoeuvrings of this mistaken mother, who congratulates herself on having so satisfactorily discharged her maternal duty, and hopes to do as well for Esther. But Esther is a child as yet – a little merry romp of fourteen: as honest-hearted, and as guileless and simple as her sister; but with a fearless spirit of her own, that I fancy her mother will find some difficulty in bending to her purposes.

# Chapter 27

*October 9th*

t was on the night of the 4th, a little after tea, that Annabella had been singing and playing, with Arthur as usual at her side: she had ended her song, but still she sat at the instrument; and he stood leaning on the back of her chair, conversing in scarcely audible tones, with his face in very close proximity with hers. I looked at Lord Lowborough. He was at the other end of the room, talking with Messrs. Hargrave and Grimsby; but I saw him dart towards his lady and his host a quick, impatient glance, expressive of intense disquietude, at which Grimsby smiled. Determined to interrupt the *tête-à-tête*, I rose, and, selecting a piece of music from the music-stand, stepped up to the piano, intending to ask the lady to play it; but I stood transfixed and speechless on seeing her seated there, listening, with what seemed an exultant smile on her flushed face, to his soft murmurings, with her hand quietly surrendered to his clasp. The blood rushed first to my heart, and then to my head; for there was more than this; almost at the moment of my approach, he cast a hurried glance over his shoulder towards the other occupants of the room, and then ardently pressed the unresisting hand to his lips. On raising his eyes, he beheld me, and dropped them again, confounded and dismayed. She saw me too, and confronted me with a look of hard defiance. I laid the music on the piano, and retired. I felt ill; but I did not leave the room: happily, it was getting late, and could not be long before the company dispersed. I went to the fire, and leant my head against the chimneypiece. In a minute or two, some one asked me if I felt unwell. I did not answer; indeed, at the time, I knew not what was said; but I mechanically looked up, and saw Mr Hargrave standing beside me on the rug.

'Shall I get you a glass of wine?' said he.

'No, thank you,' I replied; and, turning from him, I looked round. Lady Lowborough was beside her husband, bending over him as he sat, with her hand on his shoulder, softly talking and smiling in his face; and Arthur was at the table, turning over a book of engravings. I seated myself in the nearest chair; and Mr Hargrave, finding his services were not desired, judiciously withdrew. Shortly after, the company broke up, and, as the guests were retiring to their rooms, Arthur approached me, smiling with the utmost assurance.

'Are you very angry, Helen?' murmured he.

'This is no jest, Arthur,' said I seriously, but as calmly as I could – 'unless you think it is a jest to lose my affection for ever.'

'What! so bitter?' he exclaimed laughingly, clasping my hand between both his; but I snatched it away, in indignation – almost in disgust, for he was obviously affected with wine.

# The Tenant of Wildfell Hall

'Then I must go down on my knees,' said he; and kneeling before me, with clasped hands, uplifted in mock humiliation, he continued imploringly – 'Forgive me, Helen! – dear Helen, forgive me, and I'll never do it again!' and, burying his face in his handkerchief, he affected to sob aloud.

Leaving him thus employed, I took my candle, and, slipping quietly from the room, hastened upstairs as fast as I could. But he soon discovered that I had left him, and, rushing up after me, caught me in his arms, just as I had entered the chamber and was about to shut the door in his face.

'No, no, by heaven, you shan't escape me so!' he cried. Then, alarmed at my agitation, he begged me not to put myself in such a passion, telling me I was white in the face, and should kill myself if I did so.

'Let me go, then,' I murmured; and immediately he released me – and it was well he did, for I was really in a passion. I sank into the easy-chair and endeavoured to compose myself, for I wanted to speak to him calmly. He stood beside me, but did not venture to touch me or to speak, for a few seconds; then approaching a little nearer, he dropped on one knee – not in mock humility, but to bring himself nearer my level, and leaning his hand on the arm of the chair, he began in a low voice—

'It is all nonsense, Helen – a jest, a mere nothing – not worth a thought. Will you never learn,' he continued more boldly, 'that you have nothing to fear from me? that I love you wholly and entirely? – or if,' he added with a lurking smile, 'I ever give a thought to another you may well spare it, for those fancies are here and gone like a flash of lightning, while my love for you burns on steadily, and for ever like the sun. You little exorbitant tyrant, will not that'—

'Be quiet a moment, will you, Arthur,' said I, 'and listen to me – and don't think I'm in a jealous fury: I am perfectly calm. Feel my hand.' And I gravely extended it towards him – but closed it upon his with an energy that seemed to disprove the assertion and made him smile. 'You needn't smile, sir,' said I, still tightening my grasp, and looking steadfastly on him till he almost quailed before me. 'You may think it all very fine, Mr Huntingdon, to amuse yourself with rousing my jealousy; but take care you don't rouse my hate instead. And when you have once extinguished my love, you will find it no easy matter to kindle it again.'

'Well, Helen, I won't repeat the offence. But I meant nothing by it, I assure you. I had taken too much wine, and I was scarcely myself at the time.'

'You often take too much wine; and that is another practice I detest.' He looked up astonished at my warmth. 'Yes, I continued. 'I never mentioned it before, because I was ashamed to do so; but now I'll tell you that it distresses me, and may disgust me, if you go on and suffer the habit to grow upon you, as it will if you don't check it in time. But the whole system of your conduct to Lady Lowborough is not referable to wine; and this night you knew perfectly well what you were doing.'

'Well, I am sorry for it,' replied he, with more of sulkiness than contrition: 'what more would you have?'

'You are sorry that I saw you, no doubt,' I answered coldly.

'If you had not seen me,' he muttered, fixing his eyes on the carpet, 'it would have done no harm.'

My heart felt ready to burst; but I resolutely swallowed back my emotion, and answered calmly, 'You think not?'

'No,' replied he boldly. 'After all, what have I done? It's nothing – except as you choose to make it a subject of accusation and distress.'

'What would Lord Lowborough, your friend, think, if he knew all? or what would you yourself think, if he or any other had acted the same part to me, throughout, as you have to Annabella?'

'I would blow his brains out.'

'Well, then, Arthur, how can you call it nothing – an offence for which you would think yourself justified in blowing another man's brains out? Is it nothing to trifle with your friends's feelings and mine – to endeavour to steal a woman's affections from her husband – what he valued more than his gold, and therefore what it is more dishonest to take? Are the marriage vows a jest; and is it nothing to make it your sport to break them, and to tempt another to do the same? Can I love a man that does such things, and coolly maintains it is nothing?'

'You are breaking your marriage vows yourself,' said he, indignantly rising and pacing to and fro. 'You promised to honour and obey me, and now you attempt to hector over me, and threaten and accuse me and call me worse than a highwayman. If it were not for your situation, Helen, I would not submit to it so tamely. I won't be dictated to by a woman, though she be my wife.'

'What will you do then? Will you go on till I hate you; and then accuse me of breaking my vows?'

He was silent a moment, and then replied—

'You never will hate me.' Returning and resuming his former position at my feet, he repeated more vehemently – 'You cannot hate me, as long as I love you.'

'But how can I believe that you love me, if you continue to act in this way? Just imagine yourself in my place: would you think I loved you, if I did so? Would you believe my protestations, and honour and trust me under such circumstances?'

'The cases are different,' he replied. 'It is a woman's nature to be constant – to love one and one only, blindly, tenderly, and for ever – bless them, dear creatures! and you above them all – but you must have some commiseration for us, Helen; you must give us a little more licence, for as Shakespeare has it—

> However we do praise ourselves,
> Our fancies are more giddy and unfirm,
> More longing, wavering, sooner lost and won
> Than women's are.'

'Do you mean by that, that your fancies are lost to me, and won by Lady Lowborough?'

'No; Heaven is my witness that I think her mere dust and ashes in comparison with you, – and shall continue to think so, unless you drive me from you by too much severity. She is a daughter of earth; you are an angel of heaven; only be not too austere in your divinity, and remember that I am a poor, fallible mortal. Come now, Helen; wont you forgive me?' he said, gently taking my hand, and looking up with an innocent smile.

'If I do, you will repeat the offence.'

'I swear by—'

'Don't swear; I'll believe your word as well as your oath. I wish I could have confidence in either.'

# The Tenant of Wildfell Hall

'Try me, then, Helen: only trust and pardon me this once, and you shall see! Come, I am in hell's torments till you speak the word.'

I did not speak it, but I put my hand on his shoulder and kissed his forehead, and then burst into tears. He embraced me tenderly; and we have been good friends ever since. He has been decently temperate at table, and well conducted towards Lady Lowborough. The first day, he held himself aloof from her, as far as he could without any flagrant breach of hospitality: since that, he has been friendly and civil, but nothing more – in my presence, at least, nor, I think, at any other time; for she seems haughty and displeased, and Lord Lowborough is manifestly more cheerful, and more cordial towards his host than before. But I shall be glad when they are gone, for I have so little love for Annabella that is it quite a task to be civil to her, and as she is the only woman here besides myself, we are necessarily thrown so much together. Next time Mrs Hargrave calls, I shall hail her advent as quite a relief. I have a good mind to ask Arthur's leave to invite the old lady to stay with us till our guests depart. I think I will. She will take it as a kind attention, and, though I have little relish for her society, she will be truly welcome as a third to stand between Lady Lowborough and me.

The first time the latter and I were alone together, after that unhappy evening, was an hour or two after breakfast on the following day, when the gentlemen were gone out after the usual time spent in the writing of letters, the reading of newspapers, and desultory conversation. We sat silent for two or three minutes. She was busy with her work, and I was running over the columns of the paper from which I had extracted all the pith some twenty minutes before. It was a moment of painful embarrassment to me, and I thought it must be infinitely more so to her; but it seems I was mistaken. She was the first to speak; and, smiling with the coolest assurance, she began—

'Your husband was merry last night, Helen: is he often so?'

My blood boiled in my face; but it was better she should seem to attribute his conduct to this than to anything else.

'No,' replied I, 'and never will be so again, I trust.'

'You gave him a curtain lecture, did you?'

'No; but I told him I disliked such conduct, and he promised me not to repeat it.'

'I thought he looked rather subdued this morning,' she continued; 'and you, Helen; you've been weeping I see – that's our grand resource, you know – but doesn't it make your eyes smart? – and do you always find it to answer?'

'I never cry for effect; nor can I conceive how any one can.'

'Well, I don't know: I never had occasion to try it; but I think if Lowborough were to commit such improprieties I'd make him cry. I don't wonder at your being angry, for I'm sure I'd give my husband a lesson he would not soon forget for a lighter offence than that. But then he will never do anything of the kind; for I keep him in too good order for that.'

'Are you sure you don't arrogate too much of the credit to yourself? Lord Lowborough was quite as remarkable for his abstemiousness for some time before you married him, as he is now, I have heard.'

'Oh, about the wine you mean – yes, he's safe enough for that. And as to looking askance to another woman – he's safe enough for that too, while I live, for he worships the very ground I tread on.'

'Indeed – and are you sure you deserve it?'

'Why, as to that, I can't say: you know we're all fallible creatures, Helen; we none of us deserve to be worshipped. But are you sure your darling Huntingdon deserves all the love you give to him?'

I knew not what to answer to this. I was burning with anger; but I suppressed all outward manifestations of it, and only bit my lip and pretended to arrange my work.

'At any rate,' resumed she, pursuing her advantage, 'you can console yourself with the assurance that you are worthy of all the love he gives to you.'

'You flatter me,' said I, 'but, at least, I can try to be worthy of it.' And then I turned the conversation.

# Chapter 28

*December 25th*

Last Christmas I was a bride, with a heart overflowing with present bliss, and full of ardent hopes for the future – though not unmingled with foreboding fears. Now I am a wife: my bliss is sobered, but not destroyed; my hopes diminished, but not departed; my fears increased, but not yet thoroughly confirmed; and, thank Heaven, I am a mother too. God sent me a soul to educate for heaven, and given me a new and calmer bliss, and stronger hopes to comfort me.

*December 25th, 1823.* – Another year is gone. My little Arthur lives and thrives. He is healthy but not robust, full of gentle playfulness and vivacity, already affectionate, and susceptible of passions and emotions it will be long ere he can find words to express. He has won his father's heart at last; and now my constant terror is, lest he should be ruined by that father's thoughtless indulgence. But I must beware of my own weakness too, for I never knew till now how strong are a parent's temptations to spoil an only child.

I have need of consolation in my son, for (to this silent paper I may confess it) I have but little in my husband. I love him still; and he loves me, in his own way – but oh, how different from the love I could have given, and once had hoped to receive! how little real sympathy there exists between us; how many of my thoughts and feelings are gloomily cloistered within my own mind; how much of my higher and better self is indeed unmarried – doomed either to harden and sour in the sunless shade of solitude, or to quite degenerate and fall away for lack of nutriment in this unwholesome soil! But, I repeat, I have no right to complain; only let me state the truth – some of the truth at least, – and see hereafter if any darker truths will blot these pages. We have now been full two years united – the 'romance' of our attachment must be worn away. Surely I have now got down to the lowest gradation in Arthur's affection, and discovered

all the evils of his nature: if there by any further change, it must be for the better, as we become still more accustomed to each other: surely we shall find no lower depth than this. And, if so, I can bear it well – as well, at least, as I have borne it hitherto.

Arthur is not what is commonly called a bad man: he has many good qualities; but he is a man without self-restraint or lofty aspirations – a lover of pleasure, given up to animal enjoyments: he is not a bad husband, but his notions of matrimonial duties and comforts are not my notions. Judging from appearances, his idea of a wife is a thing to love one devotedly and to stay at home – to wait upon her husband, and amuse him and minister to his comfort in every possible way, while he chooses to stay with her; and, when he is absent, to attend to his interests, domestic or otherwise, and patiently wait his return; no matter how he may be occupied in the meantime.

Early in spring, he announced his intention of going to London: his affairs there demanded his attendance, he said, and he could refuse it no longer. He expressed his regret at having to leave me, but hoped I would amuse myself with the baby till he returned.

'But why leave me?' I said. 'I can go with you: I can be ready at any time.'

'You would not take that child to town?'

'Yes – why not?'

The thing was absurd: the air of the town would be certain to disagree with him, and with me as a nurse; the late hours and London habits would not suit me under such circumstances; and altogether he assured me that it would be excessively troublesome, injurious, and unsafe. I overruled his objections as well as I could, for I trembled at the thoughts of his going alone, and would sacrifice almost anything for myself, much even for my child, to prevent it; but at length he told me plainly, and somewhat testily, that he could not do with me: he was worn out with the baby's restless nights, and must have some repose. I proposed separate apartments; but it would not do.

'The truth is, Arthur,' I said at last, 'you are weary of my company, and determined not to have me with you. You might as well have said so at once.'

He denied it; but I immediately left the room, and flew to the nursery to hide my feelings, if I could not soothe them, there.

I was too much hurt to express any further dissatisfaction with his plans, or at all to refer to the subject again, except for the necessary arrangements concerning his departure and the conduct of affairs, during his absence, till the day before he went, when I earnestly exhorted him to take care of himself and keep out of the way of temptation. He laughed at my anxiety, but assured me there was no cause for it, and promised to attend to my advice.

'I suppose it is no use asking you to fix a day for your return?' said I.

'Why, no; I hardly can, under the circumstances; but be assured, love, I shall not be long away.'

'I don't wish to keep you a prisoner at home,' I replied. 'I should not grumble at your staying whole months away – if you can be happy so long without me – provided I knew you were safe; but I don't like the idea of your being there among your friends, as you call them.'

'Pooh, pooh, you silly girl! Do you think I can't take care of myself?'

'You didn't last time. – But THIS time, Arthur,' I added earnestly, 'show me that you can, and teach me that I need not fear to trust you!'

He promised fair, but in such a manner as we seek to soothe a child. And did he keep his promise? No; – and, henceforth, I can never trust his word. Bitter, bitter confession! Tears blind me while I write. It was early in March that he went, and he did not return till July. This time he did not trouble himself to make excuses as before, and his letters were less frequent, and shorter, and less affectionate, especially after the first few weeks: they came slower and slower, and more terse and careless every time. But still, when I omitted writing he complained of my neglect. When I wrote sternly and coldly, as I confess I frequently did at the last, he blamed my harshness, and said it was enough to scare him from his home; when I tried mild persuasion, he was a little more gentle in his replies, and promised to return; but I had learnt, at last, to disregard his promises.

# Chapter 29

Those were four miserable months, alternating between intense anxiety, despair, and indignation; pity for him, and pity for myself. And yet, through all, I was not wholly comfortless; I had my darling, sinless, inoffensive little one to console me, but even this consolation was embittered by the constantly recurring thought, 'How shall I teach him hereafter to respect his father, and yet to avoid his example?'

But I remembered that I had brought all these afflictions in a manner, wilfully, upon myself; and I determined to bear them without a murmur. At the same time I resolved not to give myself up to misery for the transgressions of another, and endeavoured to divert myself as much as I could; and besides the companionship of my child, and my dear, faithful Rachel, who evidently guessed my sorrows and felt for them, though she was too discreet to allude to them, – I had my books and pencil, my domestic affairs, and the welfare and comfort of Arthur's poor tenants and labourers to attend to; and I sometimes sought and obtained amusement in the company of my young friend Esther Hargrave: occasionally I rode over to see her, and once or twice I had her to spend the day with me at the manor. Mrs Hargrave did not visit London that season; having no daughter to marry, she thought it as well to stay at home and economize; and, for a wonder, Walter came down to join her in the beginning of June and stayed till near the close of August.

The first time I saw him was on a sweet warm evening, when I was sauntering in the park with little Arthur and Rachel, who is head-nurse and lady's-maid in one – for, with my secluded life and tolerably active habits, I require but little attendance, and as she had nursed me and coveted to nurse my child, and was moreover so very trustworthy, I preferred committing the important charge to her, with a young nursery-maid under her directions, to engaging any one else:

# The Tenant of Wildfell Hall

besides, it saves money; and since I have made acquaintance with Arthur's affairs, I have learnt to regard that as no trifling recommendation; for, by my own desire, nearly the whole of the income of my fortune is devoted, for years to come, to the paying off of his debts, and the money he contrives to squander away in London is incomprehensible. – But to return to Mr Hargrave: – I was standing with Rachel beside the water, amusing the laughing baby in her arms with a twig of willow laden with golden catkins, when, greatly to my surprise, he entered the park, mounted on his costly black hunter, and crossed over the grass to meet me. He saluted me with a very fine compliment, delicately worded, and modestly delivered withal, which he had doubtless concocted as he rode along. He told me he had brought a message from his mother, who, as he was riding that way, had desired him to call at the manor and beg the pleasure of my company to a friendly family dinner tomorrow.

'There is no one to meet but ourselves,' said he; 'but Esther is very anxious to see you; and my mother fears you will feel solitary in this great house so much alone, and wishes she could persuade you to give her the pleasure of your company more frequently, and make yourself at home in our humble dwelling, till Mr Huntingdon's return shall render this a little more conducive to your comfort.'

'She is very kind,' I answered, 'but I am not alone, you see; – and those whose time is fully occupied seldom complain of solitude.'

'Will you not come tomorrow, then? She will be sadly disappointed if you refuse.'

I did not relish being thus compassionated for my loneliness; but, however, I promised to come.

'What a sweet evening this is!' observed he, looking round upon the sunny park, with its imposing swell and slope, its placid water, and majestic clumps of trees. 'And what a paradise you live in!'

'It is a lovely evening,' answered I; and I sighed to think how little I had felt its loveliness, and how little of a paradise sweet Grassdale was to me – how still less to the voluntary exile from its scenes. Whether Mr Hargrave divined my thoughts, I cannot tell, but with a half-hesitating, sympathizing seriousness of tone and manner, he asked if I had lately heard from Mr Huntingdon.

'Not lately,' I replied.

'I thought not,' he muttered, as if to himself, looking thoughtfully on the ground.

'Are you not lately returned from London?' I asked.

'Only yesterday.'

'And did you see him there?'

'Yes – I saw him.'

'Was he well?'

'Yes – that is,' said he, with increasing hesitation and an appearance of suppressed indignation, 'he was as well as – as he deserved to be, but under circumstances I should have deemed incredible for a man so favoured as he is.' He here looked up and pointed the sentence with a serious bow to me. I suppose my face was crimson.

'Pardon me, Mrs Huntingdon,' he continued, 'but I cannot suppress my indignation when I behold such infatuated blindness and perversion of taste; – but, perhaps you are not aware—' He paused.

'I am aware of nothing, sir – except that he delays his coming longer than I expected; and if, at present, he prefers the society of his friends to that of his wife, and the dissipations of the town to the quiet of country life, I suppose I have those friends to thank for it. Their tastes and occupations are similar to his, and I don't see why his conduct should awaken either their indignation or surprise.'

'You wrong me cruelly,' answered he. 'I have shared but little of Mr Huntingdon's society for the last few weeks; and as for his tastes and occupations, they are quite beyond me – lonely wanderer as I am. Where I have but sipped and tasted, he drains the cup to the dregs; and if ever for a moment I have sought to drown the voice of reflection in madness and folly, or if I have wasted too much of my time and talents among reckless and dissipated companions, God knows I would gladly renounce them entirely and for ever, if I had but half the blessings that man so thanklessly casts behind his back – but half the inducements to virtue and domestic orderly habits that he despises – but such a home, and such a partner to share it! It is infamous!' he muttered, between his teeth. 'And don't think, Mrs Huntingdon,' he added aloud, 'that I could be guilty of inciting him to persevere in his present pursuits: on the contrary, I have remonstrated with him again and again, I have frequently expressed my surprise at his conduct, and reminded him of his duties and his privileges – but to no purpose; he only—'

'Enough, Mr Hargrave; you ought to be aware that whatever my husband's faults may be, it can only aggravate the evil for me to hear them from a stranger's lips.'

'Am I then a stranger?' said he in a sorrowful tone. 'I am your nearest neighbour, your son's godfather, and your husband's friend; may I not be yours also?'

'Intimate acquaintance must precede real friendship; I know but little of you, Mr Hargrave, except from report.'

'Have you then forgotton the six or seven weeks I spent under your roof last autumn? I have not forgotten them. And I know enough of you, Mrs Huntingdon, to think that your husband is the most enviable man in the world, and I should be the next if you would deem me worthy of your friendship.'

'If you knew more of me, you would not think it, or if you did you would not say it, and expect me to be flattered by the compliment.'

I stepped backward as I spoke. He saw that I wished the conversation to end; and immediately taking the hint, he gravely bowed, wished me good evening, and turned his horse towards the road. He appeared grieved and hurt at my unkind reception of his sympathizing overtures. I was not sure that I had done right in speaking so harshly to him; but at the time, I had felt irritated – almost insulted by his conduct; it seemed as if he was presuming upon the absence and neglect of my husband, and insinuating even more than the truth against him.

Rachel had moved on, during our conversation, to some yards distance. He rode up to her, and asked to see the child. He took it carefully into his arms, looked upon it with an almost paternal smile, and I heard him say, as I approached—

'And this, too, he has forsaken!'

He then tenderly kissed it, and restored it to the gratified nurse.

# The Tenant of Wildfell Hall

'Are you fond of children, Mr Hargrave?' said I, a little softened towards him.

'Not in general,' he replied, 'but that is such a sweet child, and so like its mother,' he added in a lower tone.

'You are mistaken there; it is its father it resembles.'

'Am I not right, nurse?' said he, appealing to Rachel.

'I think, sir, there's a bit of both,' she replied.

He departed; and Rachel pronounced him a very nice gentleman. I had still my doubts on the subject.

In the course of the following six weeks, I met him several times, but always, save once, in company with his mother, or his sister, or both. When I called on them, he always happened to be at home, and, when they called on me, it was always he that drove them over in the phaeton. His mother, evidently, was quite delighted with his dutiful attentions, and newly-acquired domestic habits.

The time that I met him alone was on a bright, but not oppressively hot, day, in the beginning of July: I had taken little Arthur into the wood that skirts the park, and there seated him on the moss-cushioned roots of an old oak; and, having gathered a handful of bluebells and wild roses, I was kneeling before him, and presenting them, one by one, to the grasp of his tiny fingers; enjoying the heavenly beauty of the flowers, through the medium of his smiling eyes; forgetting, for the moment, all my cares, laughing at his gleeful laughter, and delighting myself with his delight, – when a shadow suddenly eclipsed the little space of sunshine on the grass before us; and looking up, I beheld Walter Hargrave standing and gazing upon us.

'Excuse me, Mrs Huntingdon,' said he, 'but I was spell-bound; I had neither the power to come forward, and interrupt you, nor to withdraw from the contemplation of such a scene. How vigorous my little godson grows! and how merry he is this morning!' He approached the child, and stooped to take his hand; but, on seeing that his caresses were likely to produce tears and lamentations, instead of a reciprocation of friendly demonstrations, he prudently drew back.

'What a pleasure and comfort that little creature must be to you, Mrs Huntingdon!' he observed, with a touch of sadness in his intonation, as he admiringly contemplated the infant.

'It is,' replied I; and then I asked after his mother and sister.

He politely answered my inquiries, and then returned again to the subject I wished to avoid; though with a degree of timidity that witnessed his fear to offend.

'You have not heard from Huntingdon lately?' he said.

'Not this week,' I replied. Not this three weeks, I might have said.

'I had a letter from him this morning. I wish it were such a one as I could show to his lady.' He half drew from his waistcoat pocket a letter with Arthur's still-beloved hand on the address, scowled at it, and put it back again, adding – 'But he tells me he is about to return next week.'

'He tells me so every time he writes.'

'Indeed! – Well, it is like him. But to me he always avowed it his intention to stay till the present month.'

It struck me like a blow, this proof of premeditated transgression and systematic disregard of truth.

'It is only of a piece with the rest of his conduct,' observed Mr Hargrave, thoughtfully regarding me, and reading, I suppose, my feelings in my face.

'Then he is really coming next week?' said I, after a pause.

'You may rely upon it, if the assurance can give you any pleasure. And is it possible, Mrs Huntingdon, that you can rejoice at his return?' he exclaimed, attentively perusing my features again.

'Of course, Mr Hargrave; is he not my husband?'

'Oh, Huntingdon; you know not what you slight!' he passionately murmured.

I took up my baby, and, wishing him good morning, departed to indulge my thoughts unscrutinized, within the sanctum of my home.

And was I glad? Yes, delighted; though I was angered by Arthur's conduct, and though I felt that he had wronged me, and was determined he should feel it too.

# Chapter 30

On the following morning, I received a few lines from him myself, confirming Hargrave's intimations respecting his approaching return. And he did come next week, but in a condition of body and mind even worse than before. I did not, however, intend to pass over his derelictions this time without a remark: – I found it would not do. But the first day he was weary with his journey, and I was glad to get him back: I would not upbraid him then; I would wait till tomorrow. Next morning he was weary still; I would wait a little longer. But at dinner, when, after breakfasting at twelve o'clock on a bottle of soda-water and a cup of strong coffee, and lunching at two on another bottle of soda-water mingled with brandy, he was finding fault with everything on the table, and declaring we must change our cook – I thought the time was come.

'It is the same cook as we had before you went, Arthur,' said I. 'You were generally pretty well satisfied with her then.'

'You must have been letting her get into slovenly habits then, while I was away. It is enough to poison one, eating such a disgusting mess?' And he pettishly pushed away his plate, and leant back despairingly in his chair.

'I think it is you that are changed, not she,' said I, but with the utmost gentleness, for I did not wish to irritate him.

'It may be so,' he replied carelessly, as he seized a tumbler of wine and water, adding, when he had tossed it off, 'for I have an infernal fire in my veins, that all the waters of the ocean cannot quench!'

'What kindled it?' I was about to ask, but at that moment the butler entered and began to take away the things.

'Be quick, Benson; do have done with that infernal clatter!' cried his master. 'And don't bring the cheese, unless you want to make me sick outright!'

# The Tenant of Wildfell Hall

Benson, in some surprise, removed the cheese, and did his best to effect a quiet and speedy clearance of the rest, but, unfortunately, there was a rumple in the carpet, caused by the hasty pushing back of his master's chair, at which he tripped and stumbled, causing a rather alarming concussion with the tray full of crockery in his hands, but no positive damage, save the falling and breaking of a sauce tureen; but, to my unspeakable shame and dismay, Arthur turned furiously around upon him, and swore at him with savage coarseness. The poor man turned pale, and visibly trembled as he stooped to pick up the fragments.

'He couldn't help it, Arthur,' said I; 'the carpet caught his foot, and there's no great harm done. Never mind the pieces now, Benson, you can clear them away afterwards.'

Glad to be released, Benson expeditiously set out the dessert and withdrew.

'What could you mean, Helen, by taking the servant's part against me,' said Arthur, as soon as the door was closed, 'when you knew I was distracted!'

'I did not know you were distracted, Arthur, and the poor man was quite frightened and hurt at your sudden explosion.'

'Poor man, indeed! and do you think I could stop to consider the feelings of an insensate brute like that, when my own nerves were racked and torn to pieces by his confounded blunders?'

'I never heard you complain of your nerves before.'

'And why shouldn't I have nerves as well as you?'

'Oh, I don't dispute your claim to their possession, but I never complain of mine.'

'No – how should you, when you never do anything to try them?'

'Then why do you try yours, Arthur?'

'Do you think I have nothing to do but to stay at home and take care of myself like a woman?'

'Is it impossible then, to take care of yourself like a man when you go abroad? You told me that you could – and would too; and you promised—'

'Come, come, Helen, don't begin with that nonsense now; I can't bear it.'

'Can't bear what? – to be reminded of the promises you have broken?'

'Helen, you are cruel. If you knew how my heart throbbed, and how every nerve thrilled through me while you spoke, you would spare me. You can pity a dolt of a servant for breaking a dish; but you have no compassion for me, when my head is split in two and all on fire with this consuming fever.'

He leant his head on his hand and sighed. I went to him and put my hand on his forehead. It was burning indeed.

'Then come with me into the drawing-room, Arthur; and don't take any more wine; you have taken several glasses since dinner, and eaten next to nothing all day. How can that make you better?'

With some coaxing and persuasion, I got him to leave the table. When the baby was brought I tried to amuse him with that; but poor little Arthur was cutting his teeth, and his father could not bear his complaints; sentence of immediate banishment was passed upon him on the first indication of fretfulness; and because, in the course of the evening, I went to share his exile for a little while, I was reproached, on my return, for preferring my child to my husband. I found the latter reclining on the sofa just as I had left him.

'Well!' exclaimed the injured man, in a tone of pseudo-resignation. 'I thought

I wouldn't send for you; I thought I'd just see – how long it would please you to leave me alone.'

'I have not been very long, have I, Arthur? I have not been an hour, I'm sure.'

'Oh, of course, an hour is nothing to you, so pleasantly employed; but to me—'

'It has not been pleasantly employed,' interrupted I. 'I have been nursing our poor little baby, who is very far from well, and I could not leave him till I got him to sleep.'

'Oh, to be sure, you're overflowing with kindness and pity for everything but me.'

'And why should I pity you? what is the matter with you?'

'Well! that passes everything! After all the wear and tear that I've had, when I come home sick and weary, longing for comfort, and expecting to find attention and kindness, at least, from my wife, – she calmly asks what is the matter with me!'

'There is nothing the matter with you,' returned I, 'except what you have wilfully brought upon yourself against my earnest exhortation and entreaty.'

'Now, Helen,' said he emphatically, half rising from his recumbent posture, 'if you bother me with another word, I'll ring the bell and order six bottles of wine – and, by Heaven, I'll drink them dry before I stir from this place!'

I said no more, but sat down before the table and drew a book towards me.

'Do let me have quietness at least!' continued he, 'if you deny me every other comfort,' and sinking back into his former position, with an impatient expiration between a sigh and a groan, he languidly closed his eyes as if to sleep.

What the book was, that lay open on the table before me, I cannot tell, for I never looked at it. With an elbow on each side of it, and my hands clasped before my eyes, I delivered myself up to silent weeping. But Arthur was not asleep; at the first slight sob, he raised his head and looked round, impatiently exclaiming—

'What are you crying for, Helen? What the deuce is the matter now?'

'I'm crying for you, Arthur,' I replied, speedily drying my tears; and starting up, I threw myself on my knees before him, and, clasping his nerveless hand between my own, continued: 'Don't you know that you are a part of myself? And do you think you can injure and degrade yourself, and I not feel it?'

'Degrade myself, Helen?'

'Yes, degrade! What have you been doing all this time?'

'You'd better not ask,' said he, with a faint smile.

'And you had better not tell; but you cannot deny that you have degraded yourself miserably. You have shamefully wronged yourself, body and soul, and me too; and I can't endure it quietly – and I won't!'

'Well, don't squeeze my hand so frantically, and don't agitate me so, for heaven's sake! Oh, Hattersley! you were right; this woman will be the death of me, with her keen feelings and her interesting force of character. There, there, do spare me a little.'

'Arthur, you must repent!' cried I, in a frenzy of desperation, throwing my arms around him and burying my face in his bosom. 'You shall say you are sorry for what you have done!'

'Well, well, I am.'

# The Tenant of Wildfell Hall

'You are not! you'll do it again.'

'I shall never live to do it again, if you treat me so savagely,' replied he, pushing me from him. 'You've nearly squeezed the breath out of my body.' He pressed his hand to his heart, and looked really agitated and ill.

'Now get me a glass of wine,' said he, 'to remedy what you've done, you she-tiger! I'm almost ready to faint.'

I flew to get the required remedy. It seemed to revive him considerably.

'What a shame it is,' said I, as I took the empty glass from his hand, 'for a strong young man like you to reduce yourself to such a state!'

'If you knew all, my girl, you'd say rather, "What a wonder it is you can bear it so well as you do!" I've lived more in these four months, Helen, than you have in the whole course of your existence, or will to the end of your days, if they numbered a hundred years; so I must expect to pay for it in some shape.'

'You will have to pay a higher price than you anticipate, if you don't take care: there will be the total loss of your own health, and of my affection too, if that is of any value to you.'

'What, you're at that game of threatening me with the loss of your affection again, are you? I think it couldn't have been very genuine stuff to begin with, if it's so easily demolished. If you don't mind, my pretty tyrant, you'll make me regret my choice in good earnest, and envy my friend Hattersley his meek little wife; she's quite a pattern to her sex, Helen. He had her with him in London all the season, and she was no trouble at all. He might amuse himself just as he pleased, in regular bachelor style, and she never complained of neglect; he might come home at any hour of the night or morning, or not come home at all; be sullen, sober, or glorious drunk; and play the fool or the madman to his own heart's desire without any fear or botheration. She never gives him a word of reproach or complaint, do what he will. He says there's not such a jewel in all England, and swears he wouldn't take a kingdom for her.'

'But he makes her life a curse to her.'

'Not he! She has no will but his, and is always contented and happy as long as he is enjoying himself.'

'In that case she is as great a fool as he is; but it is not so. I have several letters from her, expressing the greatest anxiety about his proceedings, and complaining that you incite him to commit those extravagances – one especially, in which she implores me to use my influence with you to get you away from London, and affirms that her husband never did such things before you came, and would certainly discontinue them as soon as you departed and left him to the guidance of his own good sense.'

'The detestable little traitor! Give me the letter, and he shall see it as sure as I'm a living man.'

'No, he shall not see it without her consent; but if he did, there is nothing there to anger him – nor in any of the others. She never speaks a word against him; it is only anxiety for him that she expresses. She only alludes to his conduct in the most delicate terms, and makes every excuse for him that she can possibly think of – and as for her own misery, I rather feel it than see it expressed in her letters.'

'But she abuses me; and no doubt you helped her.'

'No; I told her she over-rated my influence with you, that I would gladly draw you away from the temptations of the town if I could, but had little hope

of success, and that I thought she was wrong in supposing that you enticed Mr Hattersley or any one else into error. I had myself held the contrary opinion at one time, but I now believed that you mutually corrupted each other; and, perhaps, if she used a little gentle but serious remonstrance with her husband, it might be of some service; as, though he was more rough-hewn than mine, I believed he was of a less impenetrable material.'

'And so that is the way you go on – heartening each other up to mutiny, and abusing each other's partners, and throwing out implications against your own, to the mutual gratification of both!'

'According to your own account,' said I, 'my evil counsel has had but little effect upon her. And as to abuse and aspersions, we are both of us far too deeply ashamed of the errors and vices of our other halves, to make them the common subjects of our correspondence. Friends as we are, we would willingly keep your failings to ourselves – even from ourselves if we could, unless by knowing them we could deliver you from them.'

'Well, well! don't worry me about them: you'll never effect any good by that. Have patience with me, and bear with my languor and crossness a little while, till I get this cursed low fever out of my veins, and then you'll find me cheerful and kind as ever. Why can't you be gentle and good as you were last time? – I'm sure I was very grateful for it.'

'And what good did your gratitude do? I deluded myself with the idea that you were ashamed of your transgressions, and hoped you would never repeat them again; but now, you have left me nothing to hope!'

'My case is quite desperate, is it? A very blessed consideration, if it will only secure me from the pain and worry of my dear anxious wife's efforts to convert me, and her from the toil and trouble of such exertions, and her sweet face and silver accents from the ruinous effects of the same. A burst of passion is a fine rousing thing upon occasion, Helen, and a flood of tears is marvellously affecting, but, when indulged too often, they are both deuced plaguy things for spoiling one's beauty and tiring out one's friends.'

Thenceforth, I restrained my tears and passions as much as I could. I spared him my exhortations and fruitless efforts at conversion too, for I saw it was all in vain: God might awaken that heart, supine and stupefied with self-indulgence, and remove the film of sensual darkness from his eyes, but I could not. His injustice and ill-humour towards his inferiors, who could not defend themselves, I still resented and withstood, but when I alone was their object, as was frequently the case, I endured it with calm forbearance, except at times when my temper, worn out by repeated annoyances, or stung to distraction by some new instance or irrationality, gave way in spite of myself, and exposed me to the imputations of fierceness, cruelty, and impatience. I attended carefully to his wants and amusements, but not, I own, with the same devoted fondness as before, becaue I could not feel it; besides, I had now another claimant on my time and care – my ailing infant, for whose sake I frequently braved and suffered the reproaches and complaints of his unreasonably exacting father.

But Arthur is not naturally a peevish or irritable man – so far from it, that there was something almost ludicrous in the incongruity of this adventitious fretfulness and nervous irritability, rather calculated to excite laughter than anger, if it were not for the intensely painful considerations attendant upon those symptoms of a disordered frame, – and his temper gradually improved as

his bodily health was restored, which was much sooner than would have been the case, but for my strenuous exertions; for there was still one thing about him that I did not give up in despair, and one effort for his preservation that I would not remit. His appetite for the stimulus of wine had increased upon him, as I had too well foreseen. It was now something more to him than an accessory to social enjoyment: it was an important source of enjoyment in itself. In this time of weakness and depression he would have made it his medicine and support, his comforter, his recreation, and his friend, – and thereby sunk deeper and deeper – and bound himself down for ever in the bathos whereinto he had fallen. But I determined this should never be, as long as I had any influence left; and though I could not prevent him from taking more than was good for him, still, by incessant perseverance, by kindness and firmness, and vigilance, by coaxing, and daring, and determination, – I succeeded in preserving him from absolute bondage to that detestable propensity, so insidious in its advances, so inexorable in its tyranny, so disastrous in its effects.

And here, I must not forget that I am not a little indebted to his friend, Mr Hargrave. About that time he frequently called at Grassdale, and often dined with us, on which occasions, I fear, Arthur would willingly have cast prudence and decorum to the winds, and made 'a night of it', as often as his friend would have consented to join him in that exalted pastime; and if the latter had chosen to comply, he might, in a night or two, have ruined the labour of weeks, and overthrown with a touch the frail bulwark it had cost me such trouble and toil to construct. I was so fearful of this at first, that I humbled myself to intimate to him in private, my apprehensions of Arthur's proneness to these excesses, and to express a hope that he would not encourage it. He was pleased with this mark of confidence, and certainly did not betray it. On that and every subsequent occasion, his presence served rather as a check upon his host, than an incitement to further acts of intemperance; and he always succeeded in bringing him from the dining-room in good time, and in tolerably good condition; for if Arthur disregarded such intimations, as 'Well, I must not detain you from your lady,' or, 'We must not forget that Mrs Huntingdon is alone,' he would insist upon leaving the table himself, to join me, and his host, however unwillingly, was obliged to follow.

Hence, I learned to welcome Mr Hargrave as a real friend to the family, a harmless companion for Arthur, to cheer his spirits and preserve him from the tedium of absolute idleness, and a total isolation from all society but mine, and a useful ally to me. I could not but feel grateful to him under such circumstances; and I did not scruple to acknowledge my obligation on the first convenient opportunity; yet, as I did so, my heart whispered all was not right, and brought a glow to my face, which he heightened by his steady, serious gaze, while, by his manner of receiving those acknowledgements, he more than doubled my misgivings. His high delight at being able to serve me, was chastened by sympathy for me and commiseration for himself – about, I know not what, for I would not stay to inquire, or suffer him to unburden his sorrows to me. His sighs and intimations of suppressed afflictions seemed to come from a full heart; but either he must contrive to retain them within it, or breathe them forth in other ears than mine: there was enough of confidence between us already. It seemed wrong that there should exist a secret understanding between my

# The Tenant of Wildfell Hall

husband's friend and me, unknown to him, of which he was the object. But my afterthought was, 'If it is wrong, surely Arthur's is the fault, not mine.'

And indeed, I know not whether, at the time, it was not for him rather than myself that I blushed? for, since he and I are one, I so identify myself with him, that I feel his degradation, his failings, and transgressions, as my own; I blush for him, I fear for him; I repent for him, weep, pray, and feel for him as for myself; but I cannot act for him; and hence, I must be, and I am, debased, contaminated by the union, both in my own eyes, and in the actual truth. I am so determined to love him – so intensely anxious to excuse his errors, that I am continually dwelling upon them, and labouring to extenuate the loosest of his principles, and the worst of his practices, till I am familiarized with vice, and almost a partaker in his sins. Things that formerly shocked and disgusted me, now seem only natural. I know them to be wrong, because reason and God's Word declare them to be so; but I am gradually losing that instinctive horror and repulsion which were given me by nature, or instilled into me by the precepts and example of my aunt. Perhaps, then, I was too severe in my judgments, for I abhorred the sinner as well as the sin; now, I flatter myself I am more charitable and considerate; but am I not becoming more indifferent and insensate too? Fool that I was, to dream that I had strength and purity enough to save myself and him! Such vain presumption would be rightly served, if I should perish with him in the gulf from which I sought to save him! – Yet, God preserve me from it! – and him too. Yes, poor Arthur, I will still hope and pray for you; and though I write as if you were some abandoned wretch, past hope, and past reprieve, it is only my anxious fears – my strong desires that make me do so; one who loved you less would be less bitter – less dissatisfied.

His conduct has, of late, been what the world calls irreproachable; but then I know his heart is still unchanged; – and I know that spring is approaching, and deeply dread the consequences.

As he began to recover the tone and vigour of his exhausted frame, and with it something of his former impatience of retirement and repose, I suggested a short residence by the seaside, for his recreation and further restoration, and for the benefit of our little one as well. But no; watering-places were so intolerably dull – besides, he had been invited by one of his friends to spend a month or two in Scotland for the better recreation of grouse-shooting and deer-stalking, and had promised to go.

'Then you will leave me again, Arthur?' said I.

'Yes, dearest, but only to love you the better when I come back, and make up for all past offences and shortcomings; and you needn't fear me this time; there are no temptations on the mountains. And during my absence you may pay a visit to Staningley, if you like: your uncle and aunt have long been wanting us to go there, you know; but somehow, there's such a repulsion between the good lady and me, that I never could bring myself up to the scratch.'

About the third week in August, Arthur set out for Scotland, and Mr Hargrave accompanied him thither, to my private satisfaction. Shortly after, I, with little Arthur and Rachel, went to Staningley, my dear old home, which, as well as my dear old friends its inhabitants, I saw again with mingled feelings of pleasure and pain so intimately blended that I could scarcely distinguish the one from the other, or tell to which to attribute the various tears, and smiles, and sighs awakened by those old familiar scenes, and tones, and faces.

Arthur did not come home till several weeks after my return to Grassdale; but I did not feel so anxious about him now: to think of him engaged in active sports among the wild hills of Scotland, was very different from knowing him to be immersed amid the corruptions and temptations of London. His letters now, though neither long nor lover-like, were more regular than ever they had been before; and when he did return, to my great joy, instead of being worse than when he went, he was more cheerful and vigorous, and better in every respect. Since that time, I have had little cause to complain. He still has an unfortunate predilection for the pleasures of the table, against which I have to struggle and watch; but he has begun to notice his boy, and that is an increasing source of amusement to him within doors, while his fox-hunting and coursing are a sufficient occupation for him without, when the ground is not hardened by frost; so that he is not wholly dependent on me for entertainment. But it is now January: spring is approaching; and I repeat, I dread the consequences of its arrival. That sweet season, I once so joyously welcomed as the time of hope and gladness, awakens, now, far other anticipations by its return.

# Chapter 31

*March 20th, 1824*

The dreaded time is come, and Arthur is gone, as I expected. This time he announced it his intention to make but a short stay in London, and pass over to the Continent, where he should probably stay a few weeks; but I shall not expect him till after the lapse of many weeks: I now know that, with him, days signify weeks, and weeks months.

*July 30th* – He returned about three weeks ago, rather better in health, certainly, than before, but still worse in temper. And yet, perhaps, I am wrong: it is I that am less patient and forbearing. I am tired out with his injustice, his selfishness, and hopeless depravity. I wish a milder word would do: – I am no angel, and my corruption rises against it. My poor father died last week: Arthur was vexed to hear of it, because he saw that I was shocked and grieved, and he feared the circumstance would mar his comfort. When I spoke of ordering my mourning, he exclaimed—

'Oh, I hate black! But, however, I suppose you must wear it awhile, for form's sake; but I hope, Helen, you won't think it your bounden duty to compose your face and manners into conformity with your funereal garb. Why should you sigh and groan, and I be made uncomfortable because an old gentleman in —shire, a perfect stranger to us both, has thought proper to drink himself to death? There, now, I declare you're crying! Well, it must be affectation.'

He would not hear of my attending the funeral, or going for a day or two to cheer poor Frederick's solitude. It was quite unnecessary, he said, and I was

# The Tenant of Wildfell Hall

unreasonable to wish it. What was my father to me? I had never seen him, but once since I was a baby, and I well knew he had never cared a stiver about me; – and my brother, too, was little better than a stranger. 'Besides, dear Helen,' said he, embracing me with flattering fondness, 'I cannot spare you for a single day.'

'Then how have you managed without me these many days?' said I.

'Ah! then I was knocking about the world, now I am at home; and home without you, my household deity, would be intolerable.'

'Yes, as long as I am necessary to your comfort; but you did not say so before, when you urged me to leave you, in order that you might get away from your home without me,' retorted I; but before the words were well out of my mouth, I regretted having uttered them. It seemed so heavy a charge: if false, too gross an insult; if truth, too humiliating a fact to be thus openly cast in his teeth. But I might have spared myself that momentary pang of self-reproach. The accusation awoke neither shame nor indignation in him: he attempted neither denial nor excuse, but only answered with a long, low chuckling laugh, as if he viewed the whole transaction as a clever, merry jest from beginning to end. Surely that man will make me dislike him at least!

> Sine as ye brew, my maiden fair,
> Keep mind that ye maun drink the yill.

Yes; and I will drink it to the very dregs: and none but myself shall know how bitter I find it!

*August 20th* – We are shaken down again to about our usual position. Arthur has returned to nearly his former condition and habits; and I have found it my wisest plan to shut my eyes against the past and future, as far as he, at least, is concerned, and live only for the present; to love him when I can; to smile (if possible) when he smiles, be cheerful when he is cheerful, and pleased when he is agreeable; and when he is not, to try to make him so – and if that won't answer, to bear with him, to excuse him, and forgive him as well as I can, and restrain my own evil passions from aggravating his; and yet, while I thus yield and minister to his more harmless propensities to self-indulgence, to do all in my power to save him from the worse.

But we shall not be long alone together. I shall shortly be called upon to entertain the same select body of friends as we had the autumn before last, with the addition of Mr Hattersley, and, at my special request, his wife and child. I long to see Milicent – and her little girl too. The latter is now above a year old; she will be a charming playmate for my little Arthur.

*September 30th* – Our guests have been here a week or two; but I have had no leisure to pass any comments upon them till now. I cannot get over my dislike to Lady Lowborough. It is not founded on mere personal pique; it is the woman herself that I dislike, because I so thoroughly disapprove of her. I always avoid her company as much as I can without violating the laws of hospitality; but when we do speak or converse together, it is with the utmost civility – even apparent cordiality on her part; but preserve me from such cordiality! It is like handling briar-roses and may-blossoms – bright enough to the eye, and outwardly soft to the touch, but you know there are thorns beneath, and every now and then you feel them too; and perhaps resent the injury by crushing them in till

you have destroyed their power, though somewhat to the detriment of your own fingers.

Of late, however, I have seen nothing in her conduct towards Arthur to anger or alarm me. During the first few days I thought she seemed very solicitous to win his admiration. Her efforts were not unnoticed by him; I frequently saw him smiling to himself at her artful manoeuvres: but, to his praise be it spoken, her shafts fell powerless by his side. Her most bewitching smiles, her haughtiest frowns were ever received with the same immutable, careless, good-humour; till, finding he was indeed impenetrable, she suddenly remitted her efforts, and became, to all appearance, as perfectly indifferent as himself. Nor have I since witnessed any symptom of pique on his part, or renewed attempts at conquest upon hers.

This is as it should be: but Arthur never will let me be satisfied with him. I have never, for a single hour since I married him, known what it is to realize that sweet idea, 'In quietness and confidence shall be your rest.' Those two detestable men, Grimsby and Hattersley, have destroyed all my labour against his love of wine. They encourage him daily to overstep the bounds of moderation, and, not unfrequently, to disgrace himself by positive excess. I shall not soon forget the second night after their arrival. Just as I had retired from the dining-room, with the ladies, before the door was closed upon us, Arthur exclaimed—

'Now then, my lads, what say you to a regular jollification?'

Milicent glanced at me with a half-reproachful look, as if I could hinder it; but her countenance changed when she heard Hattersley's voice shouting through door and wall—

'I'm your man! Send for more wine: here isn't half enough!'

We had scarcely entered the drawing-room before we were joined by Lord Lowborough.

'What can induce you to come so soon?' exclaimed his lady, with a most ungracious air of dissatisfaction.

'You know I never drink, Annabella,' replied he seriously.

'Well, but you might stay with them a little: it looks so silly to be always dangling after the women; I wonder you can!'

He reproached her with a look of mingled bitterness and surprise, and, sinking into a chair, suppressed a heavy sigh, bit his pale lips and fixed his eyes upon the floor.

'You did right to leave them, Lord Lowborough,' said I. 'I trust you will always continue to honour us so early with your company. And if Annabella knew the value of true wisdom, and the misery of folly and – and intemperance, she would not talk such nonsense – even in jest.'

He raised his eyes while I spoke, and gravely turned them upon me, with a half-surprised, half-abstracted look, and then bent them on his wife.

'At least,' said she, 'I know the value of a warm heart, and a bold, manly spirit.'

'Well, Annabella,' said he, in a deep and hollow tone, 'since my presence is disagreeable to you, I will relieve you of it.'

'Are you going back to them, then?' said she carelessly.

'No,' exclaimed he, with harsh and startling emphasis; 'I will not go back to them! And I will never stay with them one moment longer than I think right,

for you or any other tempter! But you needn't mind that; I shall never trouble you again, by intruding my company upon you so unseasonably.'

He left the room, I heard the hall door open and shut, and, immediately after, on putting aside the curtain, I saw him pacing down the park, in the comfortless gloom of the damp, cloudy twilight.

'It would serve you right, Annabella,' said I, at length, 'if Lord Lowborough were to return to his old habits, which had so nearly effected his ruin, and which it cost him such an effort to break: you would then see cause to repent such conduct as this.'

'Not at all, my dear! I should not mind, if his lordship were to see fit to intoxicate himself every day: I should only the sooner be rid of him.'

'Oh, Annabella!' cried Milicent. 'How can you say such wicked things! It would, indeed, be a just punishment, as far as you are concerned, if Providence should take you at your word, and make you feel what others feel that—' She paused as a sudden burst of loud talking and laughter reached us from the dining-room, in which the voice of Hattersley was pre-eminently conspicuous, even to my unpractised ear.

'What you feel at this moment, I suppose?' said Lady Lowborough, with a malicious smile, fixing her eyes upon her cousin's distressed countenance.

The latter offered no reply, but averted her face and brushed away a tear. At that moment the door opened and admitted Mr Hargrave; just a little flushed, his dark eyes sparkling with unwonted vivacity.

'Oh, I'm glad you're come, Walter!' cried his sister – 'But I wish you could have got Ralph to come too.'

'Utterly impossible, dear Milicent,' replied he gaily. 'I had much ado to get away myself. Ralph attempted to keep me by violence; Huntingdon threatened me with the eternal loss of his friendship; and Grimsby, worse than all, endeavoured to make me ashamed of my virtue, by such galling sarcasms and innuendos as he knew would wound me the most. So you see, ladies, you ought to make me welcome when I have braved and suffered so much for the favour of your sweet society.' He smilingly turned to me and bowed as he finished the sentence.

'Isn't he handsome now, Helen?' whispered Milicent, her sisterly pride overcoming, for the moment, all other considerations.

'He would be,' I returned, 'if that brilliance of eye, and lip, and cheek were natural to him; but look again, a few hours hence.'

Here the gentleman took a seat near me at the table, and petitioned for a cup of coffee.

'I consider this an apt illustration of Heaven taken by storm,' said he, as I handed one to him. 'I am in paradise now; but I have fought my way through flood and fire to win it. Ralph Hattersley's last resource was to set his back against the door, and swear I should find no passage but through his body (a pretty substantial one too). Happily, however, that was not the only door, and I effected my escape by the side entrance, through the butler's pantry, to the infinite amazement of Benson, who was cleaning the plate.'

Mr Hargrave laughed, and so did his cousin; but his sister and I remained silent and grave.

'Pardon my levity, Mrs Huntingdon,' murmured he, more seriously, as he raised his eyes to my face. 'You are not used to these things: you suffer them to

# The Tenant of Wildfell Hall

affect your delicate mind too sensibly. But I thought of you in the midst of those lawless roisterers; and I endeavoured to persuade Mr Huntingdon to think of you too; but to no purpose: I fear he is fully determined to enjoy himself this night; and it will be no use keeping the coffee waiting for him or his companions; it will be much if they join us at tea. Meantime, I earnestly wish I could banish the thoughts of them from your mind – and my own too, for I hate to think of them – yes – even of my dear friend Huntingdon, when I consider the power he possesses over the happiness of one so immeasurably superior to himself, and the use he makes of it – I positively detest the man!'

'You had better not say so to me, then,' said I; 'for, bad as he is, he is part of myself, and you cannot abuse him without offending me.'

'Pardon me, then, for I would sooner die than offend you. But let us say no more of him for the present, if you please.'

At last they came; but not till after ten, when tea, which had been delayed for more than half an hour, was nearly over. Much as I had longed for their coming, my heart failed me at the riotous uproar of their approach; and Milicent turned pale and almost started from her seat as Mr Hattersley burst into the room with a clamorous volley of oaths in his mouth, which Hargrave endeavoured to check by entreating him to remember the ladies.

'Ah! you do well to remind me of the ladies, you dastardly deserter,' cried he, shaking his formidable fist at his brother-in-law; 'If it were not for them, you well know, I'd demolish you in the twinkling of an eye, and give your body to the fowls of heaven and the lilies of the field!' Then, planting a chair by Lady Lowborough's side, he stationed himself in it, and began to talk to her, with a mixture of absurdity and impudence that seemed rather to amuse than to offend her; though she affected to resent his insolence, and to keep him at bay with sallies of smart and spirited repartee.

Meantime, Mr Grimsby seated himself by me, in the chair vacated by Hargrave as they entered, and gravely stated that he would thank me for a cup of tea; and Arthur placed himself beside poor Milicent, confidentially pushing his head into her face, and drawing closer to her as she shrunk away from him. He was not so noisy as Hattersley, but his face was exceedingly flushed, he laughed incessantly, and while I blushed for all I saw and heard of him, I was glad that he chose to talk to his companion in so low a tone that no one could hear what he said but herself.

'What fools they are!' drawled Mr Grimsby, who had been talking away, at my elbow, with sententious gravity all the time; but I had been too much absorbed in contemplating the deplorable state of the other two – especially Arthur – to attend to him.

'Did you ever hear such nonsense as they talk, Mrs Huntingdon?' he continued. 'I'm quite ashamed of them, for my part: they can't take so much as a bottle between them without its getting into their heads—'

'You are pouring the cream into your saucer, Mr Grimsby.'

'Ah! yes, I see, but we're almost in darkness here. Hargrave, snuff those candles, will you?'

'They're wax: they don't require snuffing,' said I.

' "The light of the body is the eye," ' observed Hargrave, with a sarcastic smile. ' "If thine eye be single, thy whole body shall be full of light." '

Grimsby repulsed him with a solemn wave of the hand, and then, turning to

me, continued, with the same drawling tones and strange uncertainty of utterance and heavy gravity of aspect as before. 'But, as I was saying, Mrs Huntingdon, they have no head at all: they can't take half a bottle without being affected some way; whereas I – well, I've taken three times as much as they have tonight, and you see I'm perfectly steady. Now that may strike you as very singular, but I think I can explain it: – you see their brains – I mention no names, but you'll understand to whom I allude – their brains are light to begin with, and the fumes of the fermented liquor render them lighter still, and produce an entire light-headedness, or giddiness, resulting in intoxication; whereas my brains being composed of more solid materials, will absorb a considerable quantity of this alcoholic vapour without the production of any sensible result—'

'I think you will find a sensible result produced on that tea,' interrupted Mr Hargrave, 'by the quantity of sugar you have put into it. Instead of your usual complement of one lump, you have put in six.'

'Have I so?' replied the philosopher, diving with his spoon into the cup, and bringing up several half-dissolved pieces in confirmation of the assertion. 'Um! I perceive. Thus, madam, you see the evil of absence of mind – of thinking too much while engaged in the common concerns of life. Now, if I had had my wits about me, li. : ordinary men, instead of within me like a philosopher, I should not have spoiled this cup of tea, and been constrained to trouble you for another.'

'That is the sugar-basin, Mr Grimsby. Now you have spoiled the sugar too; and I'll thank you to ring for some more – for here is Lord Lowborough, at last; and I hope his lordship will condescend to sit down with us, such as we are, and allow me to give him some tea.'

His lordship gravely bowed in answer to my appeal, but said nothing. Meantime, Hargrave volunteered to ring for the sugar, while Grimsby lamented his mistake, and attempted to prove that it was owing to the shadow of the urn and the badness of the lights.

Lord Lowborough had entered a minute or two before, unobserved by any one but me, and had been standing before the door, grimly surveying the company. He now stepped up to Annabella, who sat with her back towards him, with Hattersley still beside her, though not now attending to her, being occupied in vociferously abusing and bullying his host.

'Well, Annabella,' said her husband, as he leant over the back of her chair, 'which of these three "bold, manly spirits" would you have me to resemble?'

'By heaven and earth, you shall resemble us all!' cried Hattersley, starting up and rudely seizing him by the arm. 'Hallo, Huntingdon!' he shouted – 'I've got him! Come, man, and help me! And d—n me if I don't make him drunk before I let him go! He shall make up for all past delinquencies, as sure as I'm a living soul!'

There followed a disgraceful contest; Lord Lowborough, in desperate earnest, and pale with anger, silently struggling to release himself from the powerful madman that was striving to drag him from the room. I attempted to urge Arthur to interfere in behalf of his outraged guest, but he could do nothing but laugh.

'Huntingdon, you fool, come and help me, can't you!' cried Hattersley, himself somewhat weakened by his excesses.

'I'm wishing you God-speed, Hattersley,' cried Arthur, 'and aiding you with my prayers: I can't do anything else if my life depended on it! I'm quite used

# The Tenant of Wildfell Hall

up. Oh, ho!' and leaning back in his seat, he clapped his hands on his sides and groaned aloud.

'Annabella, give me a candle!' said Lowborough, whose antagonist had now got him round the waist and was endeavouring to root him from the door-post, to which he madly clung with all the energy of desperation.

'I shall take no part in your rude sports!' replied the lady, coldly drawing back; 'I wonder you can expect it.'

But I snatched up a candle and brought it to him. He took it and held the flame to Hattersley's hands, till, roaring like a wild beast, the latter unclasped them and let him go. He vanished, I suppose to his own apartment, for nothing more was seen of him till the morning. Swearing and cursing like a maniac, Hattersley threw himself on to the ottoman beside the window. The door being now free, Milicent attempted to make her escape from the scene of her husband's disgrace; but he called her back, and insisted upon her coming to him.

'What do you want, Ralph?' murmured she, reluctantly approaching him.

'I want to know what's the matter with you,' said he, pulling her on to his knee like a child. 'What are you crying for, Milicent? – Tell me!'

'I'm not crying.'

'You are,' persisted he, rudely pulling her hands from her face. 'How dare you tell such a lie?'

'I'm not crying now,' pleaded she.

'But you have been – and just this minute too; and I will know what for. Come now, you shall tell me.!'

'Do let me alone, Ralph! remember, we are not at home.'

'No matter: you shall answer my question!' exclaimed her tormentor; and he attempted to extort the confession by shaking her, and remorselessly crushing her slight arms in the grip of his powerful fingers.

'Don't let him treat your sister in that way,' said I to Mr Hargrave.

'Come now, Hattersley, I can't allow that,' said that gentleman, stepping up to the ill-assorted couple. 'Let my sister alone, if you please.' And he made an effort to unclasp the ruffian's fingers from her arm, but was suddenly driven backward, and nearly laid upon the floor by a violent blow in the chest accompanied with the admonition—

'Take that for your insolence! – and learn not to interfere between me and mine again.'

'If you were not drunk, I'd have satisfaction for that!' gasped Hargrave, white and breathless as much from passion as from the immediate effects of the blow.

'Go to the devil!' responded his brother-in-law. 'Now, Milicent, tell me what you were crying for.'

'I'll tell you some other time,' murmured she, 'when we are alone.'

'Tell me now!' said he, with another shake and a squeeze that made her draw in her breath and bite her lip to suppress a cry of pain.

'I'll tell you, Mr Hattersley,' said I. 'She was crying from pure shame and humiliation for you! because she could not bear to see you conduct yourself so disgracefully.'

'Confound you, madam!' muttered he, with a stare of stupid amazement at my 'impudence'. 'It was not that – was it, Milicent?'

She was silent.

'Come, speak up, child!'

# The Tenant of Wildfell Hall

'I can't tell now,' sobbed she.

'But you can say "yes" or "no" as well as "I can't tell". – Come!'

'Yes,' she whispered, hanging her head, and blushing at the awful acknowledgment.

'Curse you for an impertinent hussy, then!' cried he, throwing her from him with such violence that she fell on her side; but she was up again before either I or her brother could come to her assistance, and made the best of her way out of the room, and I suppose, upstairs, without loss of time.

The next object of assault was Arthur, who sat opposite, and had, no doubt, richly enjoyed the whole scene.

'Now, Huntingdon!' exclaimed his irascible friend, 'I will not have you sitting there and laughing like an idiot!'

'Oh, Hattersley!' cried he, wiping his swimming eyes – 'You'll be the death of me.'

'Yes, I will, but not as you suppose: I'll have the heart out of your body, man, if you irritate me with any more of that imbecile laughter! – What! – are you at it yet? There! see if that'll settle you!' cried Hattersley, snatching up a footstool and hurling it at the head of his host; but he missed his aim, and the latter still sat collapsed and quaking with feeble laughter, with the tears running down his face; a deplorable spectacle indeed.

Hattersley tried cursing and swearing, but it would not do; he then took a number of books from the table beside him, and threw them, one by one, at the object of his wrath, but Arthur only laughed the more; and finally, Hattersley rushed upon him in a frenzy, and, seizing him by the shoulders, gave him a violent shaking, under which he laughed and shrieked alarmingly. But I saw no more: I thought I had witnessed enough of my husband's degradation; and, leaving Annabella and the rest to follow when they pleased, I withdrew, but not to bed. Dismissing Rachel to her rest, I walked up and down my room, in an agony of misery, for what had been done, and suspense, not knowing what might further happen, or how, or when, that unhappy creature would come up to bed.

At last he came slowly, and stumblingly, ascending the stairs, supported by Grimsby and Hattersley, who neither of them walked quite steadily themselves, but were both laughing and joking at him, and making noise enough for all the servants to hear. He himself was no longer laughing now, but sick and stupid. I will write no more about that.

Such disgraceful scenes (or nearly such) have been repeated more than once. I don't say much to Arthur about it, for, if I did, it would do more harm than good; but I let him know that I intensely dislike such exhibitions: and each time he has promised they should never again be repeated; but I fear he is losing the little self-command and self-respect he once possessed; formerly, he would have been ashamed to act thus – at least, before any other witnesses than his boon companions, or such as they. His friend, Hargrave, with a prudence and self-government that I envy for him, never disgraced himself by taking more than sufficient to render him a little 'elevated', and is always the first to leave the table, after Lord Lowborough, who, wiser still, perseveres in vacating the dining-room immediately after us: but never once, since Annabella offended him so deeply, has he entered the drawing-room before the rest; always spending the interim in the library, which I take care to have lighted for his accommodation; or, on fine moonlight nights, in roaming about the grounds. But I think she

382

regrets her misconduct, for she has never repeated it since, and of late she has comported herself with wonderful propriety towards him, treating him with more uniform kindness and consideration than ever I have observed her do before. I date the time of this improvement from the period when she ceased to hope and strive for Arthur's admiration.

# Chapter 32

*October 5th*

Esther Hargrave is getting a fine girl. She is not out of the school-room yet, but her mother frequently brings her over to call in the mornings when the gentlemen are out, and sometimes she spends an hour or two in company with her sister and me and the children; and when we go to the Grove, I always contrive to see her, and talk more to her than to any one else, for I am very much attached to my little friend, and so is she to me. I wonder what she can see to like in me though, for I am no longer the happy, lively girl I used to be; but she has no other society – save that of her uncongenial mother, and her governess (as artificial and conventional a person as that prudent mother could procure to rectify the pupil's natural qualities), and, now and then, her subdued, quiet sister. I often wonder what will be her lot in life – and so does she; but her speculations on the future are full of buoyant hope – so were mine once. I shudder to think of her being awakened, like me, to a sense of their delusive vanity. It seems as if I should feel her disappointment, even more deeply than my own. I feel, almost as if I were born for such a fate, but she is so joyous and fresh, so light of heart and free of spirit, and so guileless and unsuspecting too. Oh, I would be cruel to make her feel as I feel now, and know what I have known!

Her sister trembles for her too. Yesterday morning, one of October's brightest, loveliest days, Milicent and I were in the garden enjoying a brief half hour together with our children, while Annabella was lying on the drawing-room sofa, deep in the last new novel. We had been romping with the little creatures, almost as merry and wild as themselves, and now paused in the shade of the tall copper beech, to recover breath, and rectify our hair, disordered by the rough play and the frolicsome breeze – while they toddled together along the broad, sunny walk; my Arthur supporting the feebler steps of her little Helen, and sagaciously pointing out to her the brightest beauties of the border as they passed, with semi-articulate prattle, that did as well for her as any other mode of discourse. From laughing at the pretty sight, we began to talk of the children's future life; and that made us thoughtful. We both relapsed into silent musing as we slowly proceeded up the walk; and I suppose Milicent, by a train of associations, was led to think of her sister.

'Helen,' said she, 'you often see Esther, don't you?'

'Not very often.'

'But you have more frequent opportunities of meeting her than I have; and she loves you, I know, and reverences you too; there is nobody's opinion she thinks so much of; and she says you have more sense than mamma.'

'That is because she is self-willed, and my opinions more generally coincide with her own than your mamma's. But what then, Milicent?'

'Well, since you have so much influence with her, I wish you would seriously impress it upon her, never, on any account, or for anybody's persuasion, to marry for the sake of money, or rank, or establishment, or any earthly thing but true affection and well-grounded esteem.'

'There is no necessity for that,' said I, 'for we have had some discourse on that subject already, and I assure you her ideas of love and matrimony are as romantic as any one could desire.'

'But romantic notions will not do: I want her to have true notions.'

'Very right; but in my judgment, what the world stigmatizes as romantic, is often more nearly allied to the truth than is commonly supposed; for, if the generous ideas of youth are too often overclouded by the sordid views of after-life, that scarcely proves them to be false.'

'Well, but if you think her ideas are what they ought to be, strengthen them, will you? and confirm them, as far as you can; for I had romantic notions once – I don't mean to say that I regret my lot, for I am quite sure I don't – but—'

'I understand you,' said I; 'you are contented for yourself, but you would not have your sister to suffer the same as you.'

'No – or worse. She might have far worse to suffer than I – for I am really contented, Helen, though you mayn't think it: I speak the solemn truth in saying that I would not exchange my husband for any man on earth, if I might do it by the plucking of this leaf.'

'Well, I believe you: now that you have him, you would not exchange him for another; but then you would gladly exchange some of his qualities for those of better men.'

'Yes; just as I would gladly exchange some of my own qualities for those of better women; for neither he nor I are perfect, and I desire his improvement as earnestly as my own. And he will improve – don't you think so, Helen? – he's only six-and-twenty yet.'

'He may,' I answered.

'He will – he WILL!' repeated she.

'Excuse the faintness of my acquiescence, Milicent; I would not discourage your hopes for the world, but mine have been so often disappointed, that I am become as cold and doubtful in my expectations as the flattest of octogenarians.'

'And yet you do hope, still – even for Mr Huntingdon?'

'I do, I confess – "even" for him; for it seems as if life and hope must cease together. And is he so much worse, Milicent, than Mr Hattersley?'

'Well, to give you my candid opinion, I think there is no comparison between them. But you mustn't be offended, Helen, for you know I always speak my mind, and you may speak yours too; I shan't care.'

'I am not offended, love; and my opinion is, that if there be a comparison made between the two, the difference, for the most part, is certainly in Hattersley's favour.'

# The Tenant of Wildfell Hall

Milicent's own heart told her how much it cost me to make this acknowledg-
ment; and, with a childlike impulse, she expressed her sympathy by suddenly
kissing my cheek, without a word of reply, and then turning quickly away,
caught up her baby, and hid her face in its frock. How odd it is that we so often
weep for each other's distresses, when we shed not a tear for our own! Her heart
had been full enough of her own sorrows, but it overflowed at the idea of mine;
– and I, too, shed tears, at the sight of her sympathetic emotion, though I had
not wept for myself for many a week.

It was one rainy day last week; most of the company were killing time in the
billiard-room, but Milicent and I were with little Arthur and Helen in the
library, and between our books, our children, and each other, we expected to
make out a very agreeable morning. We had not been thus secluded above two
hours, however, when Mr Hattersley came in, attracted, I suppose, by the voice
of his child, as he was crossing the hall, for he is prodigiously fond of her, and
she of him.

He was redolent of the stables, where he had been regaling himself with the
company of his fellow-creatures, the horses, ever since breakfast. But that was
no matter to my little namesake: as soon as the colossal person of her father
darkened the door, she uttered a shrill scream of delight, and, quitting her
mother's side, ran crowing towards him – balancing her course with out-stretched
arms, – and embracing his knee, threw back her head and laughed in his face.
He might well look smilingly down upon those small, fair features, radiant with
innocent mirth, those clear, blue shining eyes, and that soft flaxen hair cast back
upon the little ivory neck and shoulders. Did he not think how unworthy he was
of such a possession? I fear no such idea crossed his mind. He caught her up,
and there followed some minutes of very rough play, during which it is difficult
to say whether the father or the daughter laughed and shouted the loudest. At
length, however, the boisterous pastime terminated – suddenly, as might be
expected: the little one was hurt, and began to cry; and the ungentle playfellow
tossed it into its mother's lap, bidding her 'make all straight'. As happy to return
to that gentle comforter as it had been to leave her, the child nestled in her arms,
and hushed its cries in a moment; and, sinking its weary head on her bosom,
soon dropped asleep.

Meantime, Mr Hattersley strode up to the fire, and, interposing his height
and breadth between us and it, stood, with arms akimbo, expanding his chest,
and gazing round him as if the house and all its appurtenances and contents
were his own undisputed possessions.

'Deuced bad weather this!' he began. 'There'll be no shooting today, I guess.'
Then, suddenly lifting up his voice, he regaled us with a few bars of a rollicking
song, which abruptly ceasing, he finished the tune with a whistle, and then
continued, – 'I say, Mrs Huntingdon, what a fine stud your husband has! – not
large, but good. – I've been looking at them a bit this morning; and upon my
word, Black Bess, and Grey Tom, and that young Nimrod, are the finest animals
I've seen for many a day!' Then followed a particular discussion of their various
merits, succeeded by a sketch of the great things he intended to do in the horse-
jockey line, when his old governor thought proper to quit the stage. 'Not that
I wish him to close his accounts,' added he; 'the old Trojan is welcome to keep
his books open as long as he pleases for me.'

'I hope so, indeed, Mr Hattersley.'

# The Tenant of Wildfell Hall

'Oh yes! It's only my way of talking. The event must come some time, and so I look to the bright side of it – that's the right plan, isn't it, Mrs H.? What are you two doing here, by-the-bye – where's Lady Lowborough?'

'In the billiard-room.'

'What a splendid creature she is!' continued he, fixing his eyes on his wife, who changed colour, and looked more and more disconcerted as he proceeded. 'What a noble figure she has! and what magnificent black eyes; and what a fine spirit of her own; – and what a tongue of her own, too, when she likes to use it – I perfectly adore her! But never mind, Milicent: I wouldn't have her for my wife – not if she'd a kingdom for her dowry! I'm better satisfied with the one I have. Now then! what do you look so sulky for? don't you believe me?'

'Yes, I believe you,' murmured she, in a tone of half-sad, half-sullen resignation, as she turned away to stroke the hair of her sleeping infant, that she had laid on the sofa beside her.

'Well then, what makes you so cross? Come here, Milly, and tell me why you can't be satisfied with my assurance.'

She went, and putting her little hand within his arm, looked up in his face, and said softly—

'What does it amount to, Ralph? Only to this, that though you admire Annabella so much, and for qualities that I don't possess, you would still rather have me than her for your wife, which merely proves that you don't think it necessary to love your wife; you are satisfied if she can keep your house, and take care of your child. But I'm not cross; I'm only sorry; for,' added she, in a low tremulous accent, withdrawing her hand from his arm, and bending her looks on the rug, 'if you don't love me, you don't, and it can't be helped.'

'Very true; but who told you I didn't? Did I say I loved Annabella?'

'You said you adored her.'

'True, but adoration isn't love. I adore Annabella, but I don't love her; and I love thee, Milicent, but I don't adore thee.' In proof of his affection, he clutched a handful of her light brown ringlets, and appeared to twist them unmercifully.

'Do you really, Ralph?' murmured she, with a faint smile beaming through her tears, just putting up her hand to his, in token that he pulled rather too hard.

'To be sure I do,' responded he; 'only you bother me rather, sometimes.'

'I bother you!' cried she in very natural surprise.

'Yes, you – but only by your exceeding goodness – when a boy has been eating raisins and sugar-plums all day, he longs for a squeeze of sour orange by way of a change. And did you never, Milly, observe the sands on the sea-shore: how nice and smooth they look, and how soft and easy they feel to the foot? But if you plod along for half an hour over this soft, easy carpet – giving way at every step, yielding the more the harder you press – you'll find it wearisome work, and be glad enough to come to a bit of good, firm rock, that won't budge an inch whether you stand, walk, or stamp upon it; and, though it be hard as the nether millstone, you'll find it the easier footing after all.'

'I know what you mean, Ralph,' said she, nervously playing with her watch-guard and tracing the figure on the rug with the point of her tiny foot. 'I know what you mean, but I thought you always liked to be yielded to; and I can't alter now.'

'I do like it,' replied he, bringing her to him by another tug at her hair. 'You

mustn't mind my talk, Milly. A man must have something to grumble about; and if he can't complain that his wife harries him to death with her perversity and ill-humour, he must complain that she wears him out with her kindness and gentleness.'

'But why complain at all, unless because you are tired and dissatisfied?'

'To excuse my own failings, to be sure. Do you think I'll bear all the burden of my sins on my own shoulders, as long as there's another ready to help me, with none of her own to carry?'

'There is no such one on earth,' said she, seriously; and then, taking his hand from her head, she kissed it with an air of genuine devotion, and tripped away to the door.

'What now?' said he. 'Where are you going?'

'To tidy my hair,' she answered, smiling through her disordered locks: 'you've made it all come down.'

'Off with you then! – An excellent little woman,' he remarked when she was gone, 'but a thought too soft – she almost melts in one's hands. I positively think I ill-use her sometimes when I've taken too much – but I can't help it, for she never complains, either at the time or after. I suppose she doesn't mind it.'

'I can enlighten you on that subject, Mr Hattersley,' said I: 'she does mind it; and some other things she minds still more, which yet you may never hear her complain of.'

'How do you know? – does she complain to you?' demanded he, with a sudden spark of fury ready to burst into a flame if I should answer 'Yes'.

'No,' I replied; 'but I have known her longer and studied her more closely than you have done. – And I can tell you, Mr Hattersley, that Milicent loves you more than you deserve, and that you have it in your power to make her very happy, instead of which you are her evil genius, and, I will venture to say, there is not a single day passes in which you do not inflict upon her some pang that you might spare her if you would.'

'Well, it's not my fault,' said he, gazing carelessly up at the ceiling and plunging his hands into his pockets: 'if my ongoings don't suit her, she should tell me so.'

'Is she not exactly the wife you wanted? Did you not tell Mr Huntingdon you must have one that would submit to anything without a murmur, and never blame you, whatever you did?'

'True, but we shouldn't always have what we want: it spoils the best of us, doesn't it? How can I help playing the deuce when I see it's all one to her whether I behave like a Christian or like a scoundrel such as nature made me? – and how can I help teasing her when she's so invitingly meek and mim – when she lies down like a spaniel at my feet and never so much as squeaks to tell me that's enough!'

'If you are a tyrant by nature, the temptation is strong, I allow; but no generous mind delights to oppress the weak, but rather to cherish and protect.'

'I don't oppress her; but it's so confounded flat to be always cherishing and protecting; – and then how can I tell that I am oppressing her when she "melts away and makes no sign"? I sometimes think she has no feeling at all; and then I go on till she cries – and that satisfies me.'

'Then you do delight to oppress her?'

'I don't, I tell you! – only when I'm in a bad humour – or a particularly good

one, and want to afflict for the pleasure of comforting; or when she looks flat and wants shaking up a bit. And sometimes she provokes me by crying for nothing, and won't tell me what it's for; and then, I allow, it enrages me past bearing – especially when I'm not my own man.'

'As is no doubt generally the case on such occasions,' said I. 'But in future, Mr Hattersley, when you see her looking flat, or crying for "nothing" (as you call it), ascribe it all to yourself: be assured it is something you have done amiss, or your general misconduct, that distresses her.'

'I don't believe it. If it were, she should tell me so: I don't like that way of moping and fretting in silence, and saying nothing – it's not honest. How can she expect me to mend my ways at that rate?'

Perhaps she gives you credit for having more sense than you possess, and deludes herself with the hope that you will one day see your own errors and repair them, if left to your own reflection.'

'None of your sneers, Mrs Huntingdon. I have the sense to see that I'm not always quite correct; but sometimes I think that's no great matter, as long as I injure nobody but myself—'

'It is a great matter,' interrupted I, 'both to yourself (as you will hereafter find to your cost) and to all connected with you – most especially your wife. But, indeed, it is nonsense to talk about injuring no one but yourself; it is impossible to injure yourself – especially by such acts as we allude to – without injuring hundreds, if not thousands, besides, in a greater or less degree, either by the evil you do or the good you leave undone.'

'And as I was saying,' continued he – 'or would have said if you hadn't taken me up so short – I sometimes think I should do better if I were joined to one that would always remind me when I was wrong, and give me a motive for doing good and eschewing evil by decidedly showing her approval of the one and disapproval of the other.'

'If you had no higher motive than the approval of your fellow-mortal, it would do you little good.'

'Well, but if I had a mate that would not always be yielding, and always equally kind, but that would have the spirit to stand at bay now and then, and honestly tell me her mind at all times – such a one as yourself, for instance. – Now if I went on with you as I do with her when I'm in London, you'd make the house too hot to hold me at times, I'll be sworn.'

'You mistake me: I am no termagant.'

'Well, all the better for that, for I can't stand contradiction – in a general way – and I'm as fond of my own will as another: only I think too much of it doesn't answer for any man.'

'Well, I would never contradict you without a cause, but certainly I would always let you know what I thought of your conduct; and if you oppressed me in body, mind, or estate, you should at least have no reason to suppose "I didn't mind it." '

'I know that, my lady; and I think if my little wife were to follow the same plan, it would be better for us both.'

'I'll tell her.'

'No, no, let her be; there's much to be said on both sides – and, now I think upon it, Huntingdon often regrets that you are not more like her – scoundrelly dog that he is – and you see, after all, you can't reform him; he's ten times worse

than I. He's afraid of you, to be sure – that is, he's always on his best behaviour in your presence – but—'

'I wonder what his worst behaviour is like, then?' I could not forbear observing.

'Why, to tell you the truth, it's very bad indeed – isn't it, Hargrave?' said he, addressing that gentleman, who had entered the room unperceived by me, for I was now standing near the fire with my back to the door. 'Isn't Huntingdon,' he continued, 'as great a reprobate as ever was d—d?'

'His lady will not hear him censured with impunity,' replied Mr Hargrave, coming forward; 'but I must say, I thank God I am not such another.'

'Perhaps it would become you better,' said I, 'to look at what you are, and say, "God be merciful to me a sinner." '

'You are severe,' returned he, bowing slightly and drawing himself up with a proud yet injured air. Hattersley laughed, and clapped him on the shoulder. Moving from under his hand with a gesture of insulted dignity, Mr Hargrave took himself away to the other end of the rug.

'Isn't it a shame, Mrs Huntingdon?' cried his brother-in-law. 'I struck Walter Hargrave when I was drunk, the second night after we came, and he's turned a cold shoulder on me ever since; though I asked his pardon the very morning after it was done!'

'Your manner of asking it,' returned the other, ' and the clearness with which you remembered the whole transaction, showed you were not too drunk to be fully conscious of what you were about, and quite responsible for the deed.'

'You wanted to interfere between me and my wife,' grumbled Hattersley, 'and that is enough to provoke any man.'

'You justify it, then?' said his opponent, darting upon him a most vindictive glance.

'No, I tell you I wouldn't have done it if I hadn't been under excitement; and if you choose to bear malice for it after all the handsome things I've said, do so and be d—d!'

'I would refrain from such language in a lady's presence, at least,' said Mr Hargrave, hiding his anger under a mask of disgust.

'What have I said?' returned Hattersley. 'Nothing but heaven's truth – he will be damned, won't he, Mrs Huntingdon, if he doesn't forgive his brother's trespasses.'

'You ought to forgive him, Mr Hargrave, since he asks you,' said I.

'Do you say so? Then I will!' And, smiling almost frankly, he stepped forward and offered his hand. It was immediately clasped in that of his relative, and the reconciliation was apparently cordial on both sides.

'The affront,' continued Hargrave, turning to me, 'owed half its bitterness to the fact of its being offered in your presence; and since you bid me forgive it, I will, and forget it too.'

'I guess the best return I can make will be to take myself off,' muttered Hattersley, with a broad grin. His companion smiled, and he left the room. This put me on my guard. Mr Hargrave turned seriously to me, and earnestly began—

'Dear Mrs Huntingdon, how I have longed for, yet dreaded, this hour! Do not be alarmed,' he added, for my face was crimson with anger; 'I am not about to offend you with any useless entreaties or complaints. I am not going to

presume to trouble you with the mention of my own feelings or your perfections, but I have something to reveal to you which you ought to know, and which, yet it pains me inexpressibly—'

'Then don't trouble yourself to reveal it!'

'But it is of importance—'

'If so, I shall hear it soon enough, especially if it is bad news, as you seem to consider it. At present I am going to take the children to the nursery.'

'But can't you ring and send them?'

'No; I want the exercise of a run to the top of the house. – Come, Arthur.'

'But you will return?'

'Not yet; don't wait.'

'Then when may I see you again?'

'At lunch,' said I, departing with little Helen in one arm and leading Arthur by the hand.

He turned away muttering some sentence of impatient censure or complaint, in which 'heartless' was the only distinguishable word.

'What nonsense is this, Mr Hargrave?' said I, pausing in the doorway. 'What do you mean?'

'Oh, nothing – I did not intend you should hear my soliloquy. But the fact is, Mrs Huntingdon, I have a disclosure to make – painful for me to offer as for you to hear – and I want you to give me a few minutes of your attention in private at any time and place you like to appoint. It is from no selfish motive that I ask it, and not for any cause that could alarm your superhuman purity; therefore you need not kill me with that look of cold and pitiless disdain. I know too well the feelings with which the bearers of bad tidings are commonly regarded not to—'

'What is this wonderful piece of intelligence?' said I, impatiently interrupting him. 'If it is anything of real importance, speak it in three words before I go.'

'In three words I cannot. Send those children away and stay with me.'

'No: keep your bad tidings to yourself. I know it is something I don't want to hear, and something you would displease me by telling.'

'You have divined too truly, I fear; but still, since I know it, I feel it my duty to disclose it to you.'

'Oh, spare us both the infliction, and I will exonerate you from the duty. You have offered to tell; I have refused to hear: my ignorance will not be charged on you.'

'Be it so – you shall not hear it from me. But if the blow falls too suddenly upon you when it comes, remember I wished to soften it!'

I left him. I was determined his words should not alarm me. What could he of all men have to reveal that was of importance for me to hear? It was no doubt some exaggerated tale about my unfortunate husband that he wished to make the most of to serve his own bad purposes.

6th – He has not alluded to this momentous mystery since, and I have seen no reason to repent of my unwillingness to hear it. The threatened blow has not been struck yet, and I do not greatly fear it. At present I am pleased with Arthur: he has not positively disgraced himself for upwards of a fortnight, and all this last week has been so very moderate in his indulgence at table that I can perceive a marked difference in his general temper and appearance. Dare I hope this will continue?

# Chapter 33

## *Seventh*

Yes, I will hope! Tonight I heard Grimsby and Hattersley grumbling together about the inhospitality of their host. They did not know I was near, for I happened to be standing behind the curtain in the bow of the window, watching the moon rising over the clump of tall, dark elm-trees below the lawn, and wondering why Arthur was so sentimental as to stand without, leaning against the outer pillar of the portico, apparently watching it too.

'So, I suppose we've seen the last of our merry carousals in this house,' said Mr Hattersley; 'I thought his good fellowship wouldn't last long. But,' added he, laughing, 'I didn't expect it would meet its end this way. I rather thought our pretty hostess would be setting up her porcupine quills, and threatening to turn us out of the house if we didn't mind our manners.'

'You didn't foresee this, then?' answered Grimsby with a guttural chuckle. 'But he'll change again when he's sick of her. If we come here a year or two hence, we shall have all our own way, you'll see.'

'I don't know,' replied the other: 'she's not the style of woman you soon tire of; but be that as it may, it's devilish provoking now that we can't be jolly, because he chooses to be on his good behaviour.'

'It's all these cursed women!' muttered Grimsby. 'They're the very bane of the world! They bring troubles and discomfort wherever they come, with their false, fair faces and their deceitful tongues.'

At this juncture I issued from my retreat, and smiling on Mr Grimsby as I passed, left the room and went out in search of Arthur. Having seen him bend his course towards the shrubbery, I followed him thither, and found him just entering the shadowy walk. I was so light of heart, so overflowing with affection, that I sprang upon him and clasped him in my arms. This startling conduct had a singular effect upon him: first, he muttered, 'Bless you, darling!' and returned my close embrace with a fervour like old times, and then he started, and, in a tone of absolute terror, exclaimed—

'Helen!' What the devil is this?' and I saw, by the faint light gleaming through the overshadowing tree, that he was positively pale with the shock.

How strange that the instinctive impulse of affection should come first, and then the shock of surprise! It shows, at least, that the affection is genuine: he is not sick of me yet.

'I startled you, Arthur,' said I, laughing in my glee. 'How nervous you are!'

'What the deuce did you do it for?' cried he, quite testily, extricating himself from my arms, and wiping his forehead with his handkerchief. 'Go back, Helen – go back directly! You'll get your death of cold!'

'I won't – till I've told you what I came for. They are blaming you, Arthur, for your temperance and sobriety, and I'm come to thank you for it. They say it is all "these cursed women," and that we are the bane of the world; but don't let them laugh or grumble you out of your good resolutions, or your affection for me.'

He laughed. I squeezed him in my arms again, and cried in tearful earnest—

'Do – do persevere! and I'll love you better than ever I did before!'

'Well, well, I will!' said he, hastily kissing me. 'There now, go. You mad creature, how could you come out in your light evening-dress this autumn night?'

'It is a glorious night,' said I.

'It is a night that will give you your death in another minute. Run away, do!'

'Do you see my death among those trees, Arthur?' said I, for he was gazing intently at the shrubs, as if he saw it coming, and I was reluctant to leave him, in my new-found happiness and revival of hope and love. But he grew angry at my delay; so I kissed him and ran back to the house.

I was in such a good-humour that night: Milicent told me I was the life of the party, and whispered she had never seen me so brilliant. Certainly, I talked enough for twenty, and smiled upon them all. Grimsby, Hattersley, Hargrave, Lady Lowborough – all shared my sisterly kindness. Grimsby stared and wondered; Hattersley laughed and jested (in spite of the little wine he had been suffered to imbibe), but still behaved as well as he knew how; Hargrave and Annabella, from different motives and in different ways, emulated me, and doubtless both surpassed me, the former in his discursive versatility and eloquence, the latter in boldness and animation at least. Milicent, delighted to see her husband, her brother, and her over-estimated friend acquitting themselves so well, was lively and gay too, in her quiet way. Even Lord Lowborough caught the general contagion: his dark, greenish eyes were lighted up beneath his moody brows; his sombre countenance was beautified by smiles; all traces of gloom, and proud or cold reserve had vanished for the time; and he astonished us all, not only by his general cheerfulness and animation, but by the positive flashes of true force and brilliance he emitted from time to time. Arthur did not talk much, but he laughed, and listened to the rest, and was in perfect good-humour, though not excited by wine. So that, altogether we made a very merry, innocent, and entertaining party.

*9th* – Yesterday, when Rachel came to dress me for dinner, I saw that she had been crying. I wanted to know the cause of it, but she seemed reluctant to tell. Was she unwell? No. Had she heard bad news from her friends? No. Had any of the servants vexed her?

'Oh, no, ma'am!' she answered – 'it's not for myself.'

'What then, Rachel? Have you been reading novels?'

'Bless you, no!' said she with a sorrowful shake of the head; and then she sighed and continued, 'but to tell you the truth, ma'am, I don't like master's ways of going on.'

'What do you mean, Rachel? – He's going on very properly – at present.'

'Well, ma'am, if you think so, it's right.'

And she went on dressing my hair in a hurried way, quite unlike her usual calm, collected manner – murmuring, half to herself, she was sure it was

beautiful hair, she 'could like to see 'em match it.' When it was done, she fondly stroked it, and gently patted my head.

'Is that affectionate ebullition intended for my hair or myself, nurse?' said I, laughingly turning round upon her; – but a tear was even now in her eye.

'What do you mean, Rachel?' I exclaimed.

'Well, ma'am, I don't know, – but if—'

'If what?'

'Well, if I was you, I wouldn't have that Lady Lowborough in the house another minute – not another minute I wouldn't!'

I was thunderstruck; but before I could recover from the shock sufficiently to demand an explanation, Milicent entered my room, as she frequently does when she is dressed before me; and she stayed with me till it was time to go down. She must have found me a very unsociable companion this time, for Rachel's last words rang in my ears. But still, I hoped – I trusted they had no foundation but in some idle rumours of the servants from what they had seen in Lady Lowborough's manner last month – or perhaps, from something that had passed between their master and her during her former visit. At dinner, I narrowly observed both her and Arthur and saw nothing extraordinary in the conduct of either – nothing calculated to excite suspicion, except in distrustful minds which mine was not, and therefore I would not suspect.

Almost immediately after dinner, Annabella went out with her husband to share his moonlight ramble, for it was a splendid evening like the last. Mr Hargrave entered the drawing-room a little before the others, and challenged me to a game of chess. He did it without any of that sad but proud humility he usually assumes in addressing me, unless he is excited with wine. I looked at his face to see if that was the case now. His eyes met mine keenly but steadily: there was something about him I did not understand, but he seemed sober enough. Not choosing to engage with him, I referred him to Milicent.

'She plays badly,' said he; 'I want to match my skill with yours. Come now! – you can't pretend you are reluctant to lay down your work – I know you never take it up except to pass an idle hour, when there is nothing better you can do.'

'But chess-players are so unsociable,' I objected; 'they are no company for any but themselves.'

'There is no one here but Milicent, and she—'

'Oh, I shall be delighted to watch you!' cried our mutual friend. 'Two such players – it will be quite a treat! I wonder which will conquer.'

I consented.

'Now, Mrs Huntingdon,' said Hargrave, as he arranged the men on the board, speaking distinctly, and with a peculiar emphasis, as if he had a double meaning to all his words, 'you are a good player' – but I am a better: we shall have a long game and you will give me some trouble; but I can be as patient as you, and, in the end, I shall certainly win.' He fixed his eyes upon me with a glance I did not like – keen, crafty, bold and almost impudent; already half triumphant in his anticipated success.

'I hope not, Mr Hargrave!' returned I with vehemence that must have startled Milicent at least; but he only smiled and murmured—

'Time will show!'

We set to work; he, sufficiently interested in the game, but calm and fearless in the consciousness of superior skill; I, intensely eager to disappoint his

expectations, for I considered this the type of a more serious contest – as I imagined he did – and I felt an almost superstitious dread of being beaten: at all events, I could ill endure that present success should add one title to his conscious power (his insolent self-confidence, I ought to say), or encourage for a moment his dream of future conquest. His play was cautious and deep, but I struggled hard against him. For some time the combat was doubtful; at length, to my joy, the victory seemed inclining to my side: I had taken several of his best pieces, and manifestly baffled his projects. He put his hand to his brow and paused, in evident perplexity. I rejoiced in my advantage, but dared not glory in it yet. At length he lifted his head, and quietly making his move, looked at me and said, calmly—

'Now, you think you will win, don't you?'

'I hope so,' replied I, taking his pawn that he had pushed into the way of my bishop with so careless an air that I thought it was an oversight, but was not generous enough, under the circumstances, to direct his attention to it, and too heedless, at the moment, to foresee the after consequences of my move.

'It is those bishops that trouble me,' said he; 'but the bold knight can overleap the reverend gentleman,' taking my last bishop with his knight; 'and now, those sacred persons once removed, I shall carry all before me.'

'Oh, Walter, how you talk!' cried Milicent; 'she has far more pieces than you still.'

'I intend to give you some trouble yet,' said I; 'and perhaps, sir, you will find yourself checkmated before you are aware. Look to your queen.'

The combat deepened. The game was a long one, and I did give him some trouble; but he was a better player than I.

'What keen gamesters you are!' said Mr Hattersley, who had now entered, and been watching us for some time. 'Why, Mrs Huntingdon, your hand trembles as if you had staked your all upon it! and Walter – you dog – you look as deep and cool as if you were certain of success, and as keen and cruel as if you would drain her heart's blood! But if I were you, I wouldn't beat her for very fear: she'll hate you if you do – she will, by Heaven! I see it in her eye.'

'Hold your tongue, will you?' said I – his talk distracted me, for I was driven to extremities. A few more moves, and I was inextricably entangled in the snare of my antagonist.

'Check,' cried he: I sought in agony some means of escape – 'mate!' he added quietly, but with evident delight. He had suspended the utterance of that last fatal syllable the better to enjoy my dismay. I was foolishly disconcerted by the event. Hattersley laughed; Milicent was troubled to see me so disturbed. Hargrave placed his hand on mine that rested on the table, and squeezing it with a firm but gentle pressure, murmured, 'Beaten – beaten!' but gazed into my face with a look where exultation was blended with an expression of ardour and tenderness yet more insulting.

'No, never, Mr Hargrave!' exclaimed I, quickly withdrawing my hand.

'Do you deny?' replied he, smilingly pointing to the board.

'No, no,' I answered, recollecting how strange my conduct must appear: 'you have beaten me in that game.'

'Will you try another, then?'

'No.'

'You acknowledge my superiority?'

'Yes – as a chess-player.'

I rose to resume my work.

'Where is Annabella?' said Hargrave gravely, after glancing round the room.

'Gone out with Lord Lowborough,' answered I, for he looked at me for a reply.

'And not yet returned!' he said seriously.

'I suppose not.'

'Where is Huntingdon?' looking round again.

'Gone out with Grimsby, as you know,' said Hattersley, suppressing a laugh, which broke forth as he concluded the sentence.

Why did he laugh? Why did Hargrave connect them thus together? Was it true, then? And was this the dreadful secret he had wished to reveal to me? I must know, and that quickly. I instantly rose and left the room to go in search of Rachel, and demand an explanation of her words; but Mr Hargrave followed me into the ante-room, and before I could open its outer door, gently laid his hand upon the lock.

'May I tell you something, Mrs Huntingdon?' said he, in a subdued tone, with serious downcast eyes.

'If it be anything worth hearing,' replied I, struggling to be composed, for I trembled in every limb.

He quietly pushed a chair towards me. I merely leant my hand upon it, and bid him go on.

'Do not be alarmed,' said he; 'what I wish to say is nothing in itself; and I will leave you to draw your own inferences from it. You say that Annabella is not yet returned?'

'Yes, yes – go on!' said I impatiently, for I feared my forced calmness would leave me before the end of his disclosure, whatever it might be.

'And you hear,' continued he, 'that Huntingdon is gone out with Grimsby?'

'Well?'

'I heard the latter say to your husband – or the man who calls himself so—'

'Go on, sir!'

He bowed submissively, and continued, 'I heard him say, – "I shall manage it, you'll see! They're gone down by the water; I shall meet them there, and tell him I want a bit of talk with him about some things that we needn't trouble the lady with; and she'll say she can be walking back to the house; and then I shall apologize, you know, and all that, and tip her a wink to take the way of the shrubbery. I'll keep him talking there, about those matters I mentioned, and anything else I can think of, as long as I can, and then bring him round the other way, stopping to look at the trees, the fields, and anything else I can find to discourse of." ' Mr Hargrave paused, and looked at me.

Without a word of comment or further questioning, I rose, and darted from the room and out of the house. The torment of suspense was not to be endured. I would not suspect my husband falsely on this man's accusation, and I would not trust him unworthily – I must know the truth at once. I flew to the shrubbery. Scarcely had I reached it, when a sound of voices arrested my breathless speed.

'We have lingered too long; he will be back,' said Lady Lowborough's voice.

'Surely not, dearest,' was his reply; 'but you can run across the lawn, and get in as quietly as you can: I'll follow in a while.'

My knees trembled under me; my brain swam round: I was ready to faint.

# The Tenant of Wildfell Hall

She must not see me thus. I shrunk among the bushes, and leant against the trunk of a tree to let her pass.

'Ah, Huntingdon!' said she reproachfully, pausing where I had stood with him the night before, 'it was here you kissed that woman!' she looked back into the leafy shade. Advancing thence, he answered, with a careless laugh—

'Well, dearest, I couldn't help it. You know I must keep straight with her as long as I can. Haven't I seen you kiss your dolt of a husband scores of times? – and do I ever complain?'

'But tell me, don't you love her still – a little?' said she, placing her hand on his arm, looking earnestly into his face – for I could see them plainly, the moon shining full upon them from between the branches of the tree that sheltered me.

'Not one bit, by all that's sacred!' he replied, kissing her glowing cheek.

'Good heavens, I must be gone!' cried she, suddenly breaking from him, and away she flew.

There he stood before me; but I had not strength to confront him now; my tongue cleaved to the roof of my mouth, I was wellnigh sinking to the earth, and I almost wondered he did not hear the beating of my heart above the low sighing of the wind, and the fitful rustle of the falling leaves. My senses seemed to fail me, but still I saw his shadowy form pass before me, and through the rushing sound in my ears I distinctly heard him say, as he stood looking up the lawn—

'There goes the fool! Run, Annabella, run! There – in with you! Ah, he didn't see! That's right, Grimsby, keep him back!' And even his low laugh reached me as he walked away.

'God help me now!' I murmured, sinking on my knees among the damp weeds and brushwood that surrounded me, and looking up at the moonlit sky through the scant foliage above. It seemed all dim and quivering now to my darkened sight. My burning, bursting heart strove to pour forth its agony to God, but could not frame its anguish into prayer, until a gust of wind swept over me, which, while it scattered the dead leaves like blighted hopes around, cooled my forehead, and seemed a little to revive my sinking frame. Then, while I lifted up my soul in speechless, earnest supplication, some heavenly influence seemed to strengthen me within: I breathed more freely; my vision cleared; I saw distinctly the pure moon shining on, and the light clouds skimming the clear, dark sky; and then I saw the eternal stars twinkling down upon me; I knew their God was mine, and He was strong to save and swift to hear. 'I will never leave thee, nor forsake thee,' seemed whispered from above their myriad orbs. No, no; I felt He would not leave me comfortless: in spite of earth and hell, I should have strength for all my trials, and win a glorious rest at last!

Refreshed, invigorated, if not composed, I rose and returned to the house. Much of my new-born strength and courage forsook me, I confess, as I entered it, and shut out the fresh wind and the glorious sky: everything I saw and heard seemed to sicken my heart – the hall, the lamp, the staircase, the doors of the different apartments, the social sound of talk and laughter from the drawing-room. How could I bear my future life! In this house, among those people – O how could I endure to live! John just then entered the hall, and seeing me, told me he had been sent in search of me, adding that he had taken the tea, and master wished to know if I were coming.

'Ask Mrs Hattersley to be so kind as to make the tea, John,' said I. 'Say I am not well tonight, and wish to be excused.'

# The Tenant of Wildfell Hall

I retired into the large, empty dining-room, where all was silence and darkness, but for the soft sighing of the wind without, and the faint gleam of moonlight that pierced the blinds and curtains; and there I walked rapidly up and down, thinking of my bitter thoughts alone. How different was this from the evening of yesterday! That, it seems, was the last expiring flash of my life's happiness. Poor, blinded fool that I was, to be so happy! I could now see the reason of Arthur's strange reception of me in the shrubbery; the burst of kindness was for his paramour, the start of horror for his wife. Now, too, I could better understand the conversation between Hattersley and Grimsby; it was doubtless of his love for her they spoke, not for me.

I heard the drawing-room door open; a light quick step came out of the ante-room, crossed the hall, and ascended the stairs. It was Milicent, poor Milicent, gone to see how I was – no one else cared for me; but still she was kind. I shed no tears before, but now they came, fast and free. Thus she did me good, without approaching me. Disappointed in her search, I heard her come down, more slowly than she had ascended. Would she come in there and find me out? No, she turned in the opposite direction and re-entered the drawing-room. I was glad, for I knew not how to meet her or what to say. I wanted no confidante in my distress. I deserved none, and I wanted none. I had taken the burden upon myself; let me bear it alone.

As the usual hour of retirement approached, I dried my eyes, and tried to clear my voice and calm my mind. I must see Arthur tonight, and speak to him; but I would do it calmly: there should be no scene – nothing to complain or to boast of to his companions – nothing to laugh at with his lady-love. When the company were retiring to their chambers I gently opened the door, and just as he passed I beckoned him in.

'What's to do with you, Helen?' said he. 'Why couldn't you come to make tea for us? and what the deuce are you here for, in the dark! What ails you, young woman; you look like a ghost!' he continued, surveying me by the light of his candle.

'No matter,' I answered, 'to you; you have no longer any regard for me, it appears; and I have no longer any for you.'

'Hal-low! what the devil is this!' he muttered.

'I would leave you tomorrow,' continued I, 'And never again come under this roof, but for my child' – I paused a moment to steady my voice.

'What in the devil's name is this, Helen?' he cried. 'What can you be driving at?'

'You know perfectly well. Let us waste no time in useless explanation, but tell me, will you—'

He vehemently swore he knew nothing about it, and insisted upon hearing what poisonous old woman had been blackening his name, and what infamous lies I had been fool enough to believe.

'Spare yourself the trouble of forswearing yourself and racking your brains to stifle truth with falsehood,' I coldly replied. 'I have trusted to the testimony of no third person. I was in the shrubbery this evening, and I saw and heard for myself.'

This was enough. He uttered a suppressed exclamation of consternation and dismay, and muttering, 'I shall catch it now!' set down his candle on the nearest

chair, and rearing his back against the wall, stood confronting me with folded arms.

'Well, what then?' said he, with the calm insolence of mingled shamelessness and desperation.

'Only this,' returned I: 'Will you let me take our child and what remains of my fortune, and go?'

'Go where?'

'Anywhere, where he will be safe from your contaminating influence, and I shall be delivered from your presence, and you from mine.'

'No.'

'Will you let me have the child then, without the money?'

'No, nor yourself without the child. Do you think I'm going to be made the talk of the country for your fastidious caprices?'

'Then I must stay here, to be hated and despised. But henceforth we are husband and wife only in the name.'

'Very good.'

'I am your child's mother, and your housekeeper, nothing more. So you need not trouble yourself any longer to feign the love you cannot feel. I will exact no more heartless caresses from you, nor offer nor endure them either. I will not be mocked with the empty husk of conjugal endearments, when you have given the substance to another!'

'Very good, if you please. We will see who will tire first, my lady.'

'If I tire, it will be of living in the world with you: not of living without your mockery of love. When you tire of your sinful ways, and show yourself truly repentant, I will forgive you, and, perhaps, try to love you again, though that will be hard indeed.'

'Humph! and meantime you will go and talk me over to Mrs Hargrave, and write long letters to Aunt Maxwell to complain of the wicked wretch you have married?'

'I shall complain to no one. Hitherto I have struggled hard to hide your vices from every eye, and invest you with virtues you never possessed; but now you must look to yourself.'

I left him muttering bad language to himself, and went upstairs.

'You are poorly, ma'am,' said Rachel, surveying me with deep anxiety.

'It is too true, Rachel,' said I, answering her sad looks rather than her words. 'I knew it, or I wouldn't have mentioned such a thing.'

'But don't you trouble yourself about it,' said I, kissing her pale, time-wasted cheek; 'I can bear it better than you imagine.'

'Yes, you were always for "bearing". But if I was you I wouldn't bear it: I'd give way to it, and cry right hard! and I'd talk too, I just would – I'd let him know what it was to—'

'I have talked,' said I: 'I've said enough.'

'Then I'd cry,' persisted she. 'I wouldn't look so white and so calm, and burst my heart with keeping it in.'

'I have cried,' said I, smiling, in spite of my misery; 'and I am calm now, really, so don't discompose me again, nurse: let us say no more about it, and don't mention it to the servants. There, you may go now. Goodnight; and don't disturb your rest for me: I shall sleep well – if I can.'

Notwithstanding this resolution, I found my bed so intolerable that, before

two o'clock, I rose, and lighting my candle by the rushlight that was still burning, I got my desk and sat down in my dressing-gown to recount the events of the past evening. It was better to be so occupied than to be lying in bed torturing my brain with recollections of the far past and anticipations of the dreadful future. I have found relief in describing the very circumstances that have destroyed my peace, as well as the little trivial details attendant upon their discovery. No sleep I could have got this night would have done so much towards composing my mind, and preparing me to meet the trials of the day – I fancy so, at least; and yet, when I cease writing, I find my head aches terribly; and when I look into the glass I am startled at my haggard, worn appearance.

Rachel has been to dress me, and says I have had a sad night of it, she can see. Milicent has just looked in to ask me how I was. I told her I was better, but, to excuse my appearance, admitted I had had a restless night. I wish this day were over! I shudder at the thoughts of going down to breakfast. How shall I encounter them all? Yet let me remember it is not I that am guilty: I have no cause to fear; and if they scorn me as the victim of their guilt, I can pity their folly and despise their scorn.

# Chapter 34

*Evening*

Breakfast passed well over; I was calm and cool throughout. I answered composedly all inquiries respecting my health; and whatever was unusual in my look or manner was generally attributed to the trifling indisposition that had occasioned my early retirement last night. But how am I to get over the ten or twelve days that must yet elapse before they go? Yet why so long for their departure? When they are gone, how shall I get through the months or years of my future life in company with that man – my greatest enemy? for none could injure me as he has done. Oh! when I think how fondly, how foolishly I have loved him, how madly I have trusted him, how constantly I have laboured, and studied, and prayed, and struggled for his advantage; and how cruelly he has trampled on my love, betrayed my trust, scorned my prayers and tears, and efforts for his preservation, crushed my hopes, destroyed my youth's best feelings, and doomed me to a life of hopeless misery – as far as man can do it – it is not enough to say that I no longer love my husband – I HATE him! The word stares me in the face like a guilty confession, but it is true: I hate him – I hate him! But God have mercy on his miserable soul! and make him see and feel his guilt – I ask no other vengeance! if he could but fully know and truly feel my wrongs, I should be well avenged, and I could freely pardon all; but he is so lost, so hardened in his heartless depravity, that in this life I believe he never will. But

it is useless dwelling on this theme: let me seek once more to dissipate reflection in the minor details of passing events.

Mr Hargrave has annoyed me all day long with his serious, sympathizing, and (as he thinks) unobtrusive politeness. If it were more obtrusive it would trouble me less, for then I could snub him; but, as it is, he contrives to appear so really kind and thoughtful, that I cannot do so without rudeness and seeming ingratitude. I sometimes think I ought to give him credit for the good feeling he simulates so well; and then again, I think it is my duty to suspect him under the peculiar circumstances in which I am placed. His kindness may not all be feigned, but still, let not the purest impulse of gratitude to him induce me to forget myself; let me remember the game of chess, the expressions he used on the occasion, and those indescribable looks of his, that so justly roused my indignation, and I think I shall be safe enough. I have done well to record them so minutely.

I think he wishes to find an opportunity of speaking to me alone: he has seemed to be on the watch all day, but I have taken care to disappoint him; not that I fear anything he could say, but I have trouble enough without the addition of his insulting consolations, condolences, or whatever else he might attempt; and, for Milicent's sake, I do not wish to quarrel with him. He excused himself from going out to shoot with the other gentlemen in the morning, under the pretext of having letters to write; and instead of retiring for that purpose into the library, he sent for his desk into the morning-room, where I was seated with Milicent and Lady Lowborough. They had betaken themselves to their work; I, less to divert my mind than to deprecate conversation, had provided myself with a book. Milicent saw that I wished to be quiet, and accordingly let me alone. Annabella, doubtless, saw it too; but that was no reason why she should restrain her tongue, or curb her cheerful spirits: she accordingly chatted away, addressing herself almost exclusively to me, and with the utmost assurance and familiarity, growing the more animated and friendly, the colder and brief my answers became. Mr Hargrave saw that I could ill endure it; and looking up from his desk, he answered her questions and observations for me, as far as he could, and attempted to transfer her social attentions from me to himself; but it would not do. Perhaps, she thought I had a headache and could not bear to talk – at any rate, she saw that her loquacious vivacity annoyed me, as I could tell by the malicious pertinacity with which she persisted. But I checked it effectually, by putting into her hand the book I had been trying to read, on the fly-leaf of which I had hastily scribbled—

'I am too well acquainted with your character and conduct to feel any real friendship for you, and, as I am without your talent for dissimulation, I cannot assume the appearance of it. I must, therefore, beg that hereafter all familiar intercourse may cease between us, and if I still continue to treat you with civility, as if you were a woman worthy of consideration and respect, understand that it is out of regard for your cousin Milicent's feelings, not for yours.'

Upon perusing this, she turned scarlet, and bit her lip. Covertly tearing away the leaf, she crumpled it up and put it in the fire, and then employed herself in turning over the pages of the book, and, really or apparently, perusing its contents. In a little while Milicent announced it her intention to repair to the nursery, and asked if I would accompany her.

'Annabella will excuse us,' said she, 'she's busy reading.'

'No, I won't,' cried Annabella, suddenly looking up, and throwing her book on the table. 'I want to speak to Helen a minute. You may go, Milicent, and she'll follow in a while.' (Milicent went.) 'Will you oblige me, Helen?' continued she.

Her impudence astounded me; but I complied, and followed her into the library. She closed the door, and walked up to the fire.

'Who told you this?' said she.

'No one: I am not incapable of seeing for myself.'

'Ah, you are suspicious!' cried she, smiling with a gleam of hope – hitherto, there had been a kind of desperation in her hardihood; now she was evidently relieved.

'If I were suspicious,' I replied, 'I should have discovered your infamy long before. No, Lady Lowborough, I do not found my charge upon suspicion.'

'On what do you found it then?' said she, throwing herself into an arm chair, and stretching out her feet to the fender, with an obvious effort to appear composed.

'I enjoy a moonlight ramble as well as you,' I answered, steadily fixing my eyes upon her: 'And the shrubbery happens to be one of my favourite resorts.'

She coloured again, excessively, and remained silent, pressing her finger against her teeth, and gazing into the fire. I watched her a few moments with a feeling of malevolent gratification; then, moving towards the door, I calmly asked if she had anything more to say.

'Yes, yes!' cried she eagerly, starting up from her reclining posture. 'I want to know if you will tell Lord Lowborough?'

'Suppose I do?'

'Well, if you are disposed to publish the matter, I cannot dissuade you, of course – but there will be terrible work if you do – and if you don't, I shall think you the most generous of mortal beings – and if there is anything in the world I can do for you – anything short of—' she hesitated.

'Short of renouncing your guilty connection with my husband, I suppose you mean,' said I.

She paused, in evident disconcertion and perplexity, mingled with anger she dared not show.

'I cannot renounce what is dearer than life,' she muttered, in a low, hurried tone. Then, suddenly raising her head and fixing her gleaming eyes upon me, she continued earnestly, 'But Helen – or Mrs Huntingdon, or whatever you would have me call you – will you tell him? If you are generous, here is a fitting opportunity for the exercise of your magnanimity: if you are proud, here am I – your rival – ready to acknowledge myself your debtor for an act of the most noble forbearance.'

'I shall not tell him.'

'You will not!', cried she delightedly. 'Accept my sincere thanks, then!'

She sprang up, and offered me her hand. I drew back.

'Give me no thanks; it is not for your sake that I refrain. Neither is it an act of any forbearance: I have no wish to publish your shame. I should be sorry to distress your husband with the knowledge of it.'

'And Milicent? will you tell her?'

'No, on the contrary I shall do my utmost to conceal it from her. I would not for much that she should know the infamy and disgrace of her relation!'

'You use hard words, Mrs Huntingdon – but I can pardon you.'

'And now, Lady Lowborough,' continued I, 'let me counsel you to leave this house as soon as possible. You must be aware that your continuance here is excessively disagreeable to me – not for Mr Huntingdon's sake,' said I observing the dawn of a malicious smile of triumph on her face – 'You are welcome to him, if you like him, as far as I am concerned – but because it is painful to be always disguising my true sentiments respecting you, and straining to keep up an appearance of civility and respect towards one for whom I have not the most distant shadow of esteem; and because, if you stay, your conduct cannot possibly remain concealed much longer from the only two persons in the house who do not know it already. And, for your husband's sake, Annabella, and even for your own, I wish – I earnestly advise and entreat you to break off this unlawful connection at once, and return to your duty while you may, before the dreadful consequences—'

'Yes, yes, of course,' said she, interrupting me with a gesture of impatience. – 'But I cannot go, Helen, before the time appointed for our departure. What possible pretext could I frame for such a thing? Whether I proposed going back alone – which Lowborough would not hear of – or taking him with me, the very circumstance itself would be certain to excite suspicion – and when our visit is so nearly at an end too – little more than a week – surely, you can endure my presence so long! I will not annoy you with any more of my friendly impertinences.'

'Well, I have nothing more to say to you.'

'Have you mentioned this affair to Huntingdon?' asked she, as I was leaving the room.

'How dare you mention his name to me!' was the only answer I gave.

No words have passed between us since, but such as outward decency or pure necessity demanded.

# Chapter 35

*Nineteenth*

In proportion as Lady Lowborough finds she has nothing to fear from me, and as the time of departure draws nigh, the more audacious and insolent she becomes. She does not scruple to speak to my husband with affectionate familiarity in my presence, when no one else is by, and is particularly fond of displaying her interest in his health and welfare, or in anything that concerns him, as if for the purpose of contrasting her kind solicitude with my cold indifference. And he rewards her by such smiles and glances, such whispered words, or boldly spoken insinuations, indicative of his sense of her goodness and my neglect, as makes the blood rush into my face, in spite of myself – for I

would be utterly regardless of it all – deaf and blind to everything that passes between them, since the more I show myself sensible of their wickedness, the more she triumphs in her victory, and the more he flatters himself that I love him devotedly still, in spite of my pretended indifference. On such occasions I have sometimes been startled by a subtle, fiendish suggestion inciting me to show him the contrary by a seeming encouragement of Hargrave's advances; but such ideas are banished in a moment with horror and self-abasement; and then I hate him tenfold more than ever for having brought me to this! – God pardon me for it – and all my sinful thoughts! Instead of being humbled and purified by my afflictions, I feel that they are turning my nature into gall. This must be my fault as much as theirs that wrong me. No true Christian could cherish such bitter feelings as I do against him and her – especially the latter: him, I still feel that I could pardon – freely, gladly, – on the slightest token of repentance; but she – words cannot utter my abhorrence. Reason forbids, but passion urges strongly; and I must pray and struggle long ere I subdue it.

It is well that she is leaving tomorrow, for I could not well endure her presence for another day. This morning, she rose earlier than usual. I found her in the room alone, when I went down to breakfast.

'Oh Helen! is it you?' said she, turning as I entered.

I gave an involuntary start back on seeing her, at which she uttered a short laugh, observing—

'I think we are both disappointed.'

I came forward and busied myself with the breakfast things.

'This is the last day I shall burden your hospitality,' said she, as she seated herself at the table. 'Ah, here comes one that will not rejoice at it!' she murmured, half to herself, as Arthur entered the room.

He shook hands with her and wished her good morning: then, looking lovingly in her face, and still retaining her hand in his, murmured pathetically—

'The last – last day!'

'Yes,' said she with some asperity; 'and I rose early to make the best of it – I have been here alone this half hour, and you, you lazy creature—'

'Well, I thought I was early too,' said he – 'but,' dropping his voice almost to a whisper, 'you see we are not alone.'

'We never are,' returned she. But they were almost as good as alone, for I was now standing at the window, watching the clouds, and struggling to suppress my wrath.

Some more words passed between them, which, happily, I did not overhear; but Annabella had the audacity to come and place herself beside me, and even to put her hand upon my shoulder, and say softly—

'You need not grudge him to me, Helen, for I love him more than ever you could do.'

This put me beside myself. I took her hand and violently dashed it from me, with an expression of abhorrence and indignation that could not be suppressed. Startled, almost appalled, by this sudden outbreak, she recoiled in silence. I would have given way to my fury, and said more, but Arthur's low laugh recalled me to myself. I checked the half-uttered invective, and scornfully turned away, regretting that I had given him so much amusement. He was still laughing when Mr Hargrave made his appearance. How much of the scene he had witnessed I do not know, for the door was ajar when he entered. He greeted his

host and his cousin both coldly, and me with a glance intended to express the deepest sympathy mingled with high admiration and esteem.

'How much allegiance do you owe to that man?' he asked below his breath, as he stood beside me at the window, affecting to be making observations on the weather.

'None,', I answered. And immediately returning to the table, I employed myself in making the tea. He followed, and would have entered into some kind of conversation with me, but the other guests were now beginning to assemble, and I took no more notice of him, except to give him his coffee.

After breakfast, determined to pass as little of the day as possible in company with Lady Lowborough, I quietly stole away from the company and retired to the library. Mr Hargrave followed me thither, under pretence of coming for a book; and first, turning to the shelves, he selected a volume; and then, quietly, but by no means timidly, approaching me, he stood beside me, resting his hand on the back of my chair, and said softly—

'And so you consider yourself free, at last?'

'Yes,' said I, without moving, or raising my eyes from my book, – 'free to do anything but offend God and my conscience.'

There was a momentary pause.

'Very right,' said he; 'provided your conscience be not too morbidly tender, and your ideas of God not too erroneously severe; but can you suppose it would offend that benevolent Being to make the happiness of one who would die for yours? – to raise a devoted heart from purgatorial torments to a state of heavenly bliss, when you could do it without the slightest injury to yourself, or any other?'

This was spoken in a low, earnest, melting tone as he bent over me. I now raised my head; and steadily confronting his gaze, I answered calmly—

'Mr Hargrave, do you mean to insult me?'

He was not prepared for this. He paused a moment to recover the shock; then, drawing himself up and removing his hand from my chair, he answered, with proud sadness—

'That was not my intention.'

I just looked towards the door, with a slight movement of the head, and then returned to my book. He immediately withdrew. This was better than if I had answered with more words, and in the passionate spirit to which my first impulse would have prompted. What a good thing it is to be able to command one's temper! I must labour to cultivate this inestimable quality: God only knows how often I shall need it in this rough, dark road that lies before me.

In the course of the morning, I drove over to the Grove with the two ladies, to give Milicent an opportunity for bidding farewell to her mother and sister. They persuaded her to stay with them the rest of the day, Mrs Hargrave promising to bring her back in the evening and remain till the party broke up on the morrow. Consequently, Lady Lowborough and I had the pleasure of returning *tête-à-tête* in the carriage together. For the first mile or two, we kept silence. I looking out of my window, and she leaning back in her corner. But I was not going to restrict myself to any particular position for her: when I was tired of leaning forward, with the cold, raw wind in my face, and surveying the russet hedges, and the damp, tangled grass of their banks, I gave it up, and leant back too. With her usual impudence, my companion then made some attempts to get up a conversation; but the monosyllables 'yes', or 'no', or 'humph', were

# The Tenant of Wildfell Hall

the utmost her several remarks could elicit from me. At last, on her asking my opinion upon some immaterial point of discussion, I answered—

'Why do you wish to talk to me, Lady Lowborough? - you must know what I think of you.'

'Well, if you will be so bitter against me,' replied she, 'I can't help it; but I'm not going to sulk for anybody.'

Our short drive was now at an end. As soon as the carriage door was opened, she sprang out, and went down the park to meet the gentlemen, who were just returning from the woods. Of course I did not follow.

But I had not done with her impudence yet: - after dinner I retired to the drawing-room, as usual, and she accompanied me, but I had the two children with me, and I gave them my whole attention, and determined to keep them till the gentlemen came, or till Milicent arrived with her mother. Little Helen, however, was soon tired of playing, and insisted upon going to sleep; and while I sat on the sofa with her on my knee, and Arthur seated beside me, gently playing with her soft flaxen hair, - Lady Lowborough composedly came and placed herself on the other side.

'Tomorrow, Mrs Huntingdon,' said she, 'you will be delivered from my presence, which, no doubt, you will be very glad of - it is natural you should: but do you know I have rendered you a great service? - Shall I tell you what it is?'

'I shall be glad to hear of any service you have rendered me,' said I, determined to be calm, for I knew by the tone of her voice she wanted to provoke me.

'Well,' resumed she, 'have you not observed the salutary change in Mr Huntingdon? Don't you see what a sober, temperate man he is become? You saw with regret the sad habits he was contracting, I know; and I know you did your utmost to deliver him from them, - but without success, until I came to your assistance. I told him in a few words that I could not bear to see him degrade himself so, and that I should cease to - no matter what I told him, - but you see the reformation I have wrought; and you ought to thank me for it.'

I rose, and rang for the nurse.

'But I desire no thanks,' she continued; 'all the return I ask is, that you will take care of him when I am gone, and not, by harshness and neglect, drive him back to his old courses.'

I was almost sick with passion, but Rachel was now at the door: I pointed to the children, for I could not trust myself to speak: she took them away, and I followed.

'Will you, Helen?' continued the speaker.

I gave her a look that blighted the malicious smile on her face - or checked it, at least for a moment - and departed. In the ante-room I met Mr Hargrave. He saw I was in no humour to be spoken to, and suffered me to pass without a word; but when, after a few minutes, seclusion in the library, I had regained my composure, and was returning to join Mrs Hargrave and Milicent, whom I had just heard come downstairs and go into the drawing-room, I found him there still, lingering in the dimly-lighted apartment, and evidently waiting for me.

'Mrs Huntingdon,' said he as I passed, 'will you allow me one word?'

'What is it then? - be quick if you please.'

'I offended you this morning; and I cannot live under your displeasure.'

'Then go, and sin no more,' replied I, turning away.

'No, no!' said he hastily, setting himself before me – 'Pardon me, but I must have your forgiveness. I leave you tomorrow, and I may not have an opportunity of speaking to you again. I was wrong to forget myself – and you, as I did; but let me implore you to forget and forgive my rash presumption, and think of me as if those words had never been spoken; for, believe me, I regret them deeply, and the loss of your esteem is too severe a penalty – I cannot bear it.'

'Forgetfulness is not to be purchased with a wish; and I cannot bestow my esteem on all who desire it, unless they deserve it too.'

'I shall think my life well spent in labouring to deserve it, if you will but pardon this offence – Will you?'

'Yes.'

'Yes! but that is coldly spoken. Give me your hand and I'll believe you. You won't? Then, Mrs Huntingdon, you do not forgive me!'

'Yes – here it is, and my forgiveness with it: only – *sin no more.*'

He pressed my cold hand with sentimental fervour, but said nothing, and stood aside to let me pass into the room, where all the company were now assembled. Mr Grimsby was seated near the door: on seeing me enter, almost immediately followed by Hargrave, he leered at me, with a glance of intolerable significance, as I passed. I looked him in the face, till he sullenly turned away, if not ashamed, at least confounded for the moment. Meantime, Hattersley had seized Hargrave by the arm, and was whispering something in his ear – some coarse joke, no doubt, for the latter neither laughed nor spoke in answer, but, turning from him with a slight curl of the lip, disengaged himself and went to his mother, who was telling Lord Lowborough how many reasons she had to be proud of her son.

Thank Heaven, they are all going tomorrow.

# Chapter 36

*December 20th, 1824*

his is the third anniversary of our felicitous union. It is now two months since our guests left us to the enjoyment of each other's society; and I have had nine weeks' experience of this new phase of conjugal life – two persons living together, as master and mistress of the house, and father and mother of a winsome, merry little child, with the mutual understanding that there is no love, friendship, or sympathy between them. As far as in me lies, I endeavour to live peaceably with him: I treat him with unimpeachable civility, give up my convenience to his, wherever it may reasonably be done, and consult him in a business-like way on household affairs, deferring to his pleasure and judgment, even when I know the latter to be inferior to my own.

As for him: for the first week or two, he was peevish and low – fretting, I

suppose, over his dear Annabella's departure – and particularly ill-tempered to me: everything I did was wrong; I was cold hearted, hard, insensate; my sour, pale face was perfectly repulsive; my voice made him shudder; he knew not how he could live through the winter with me, I should kill him by inches. Again I proposed a separation, but it would not do: he was not going to be the talk of all the old gossips in the neighbourhood; he would not have it said that he was such a brute his wife could not live with him; – no; he must contrive to bear with me.

'I must contrive to bear with you, you mean,' said I; 'for so long as I discharge my functions of steward and housekeeper, so conscientiously and well, without pay and without thanks, you cannot afford to part with me. I shall therefore remit these duties when my bondage becomes intolerable.' This threat, I thought, would serve to keep him in check, if anything would.

I believe he was much disappointed that I did not feel his offensive sayings more acutely, for when he had said anything particularly well calculated to hurt my feelings, he would stare me searchingly in the face, and then grumble against my 'marble heart', or my 'brutal insensibility'. If I had bitterly wept and deplored his lost affection, he would, perhaps, have condescended to pity me, and taken me into favour for a while, just to comfort his solitude and console him for the absence of his beloved Annabella, until he could meet her again, or some more fitting substitute. Thank Heaven, I am not so weak as that! I was infatuated once with a foolish besotted affection, that clung to him in spite of his unworthiness, but it is fairly gone now – wholly crushed and withered away; and he has none but himself and his vices to thank for it.

At first (in compliance with his sweet lady's injunctions, I suppose), he abstained wonderfully well from seeking to solace his cares in wine; but at length, he began to relax his virtuous efforts, and now and then exceeded a little, and still continues to do so – nay, sometimes, not a little. When he is under the exciting influence of these excesses, he sometimes fires up and attempts to play the brute; and then I take little pains to suppress my scorn and disgust; when he is under the depressing influence of the after consequences, he bemoans his sufferings and his errors, and charges them both upon me; he knows such indulgence injures his health, and does him more harm than good; but he says I drive him to it by my unnatural, unwomanly conduct; it will be the ruin of him in the end, but it is all my fault; – and then I am roused to defend myself, sometimes, with bitter recrimination. This is a kind of injustice I cannot patiently endure. Have I not laboured long and hard to save him from this very vice? would I not labour still to deliver him from it, if I could? But could I do so by fawning upon him and caressing him when I know that he scorns me? Is it my fault that I have lost my influence with him, or that he has forfeited every claim to my regard? And should I seek a reconciliation with him, when I feel that I abhor him, and that he despises me? – and while he continues still to correspond with Lady Lowborough, as I know he does? No, never, never, never! – he may drink himself dead, but it is NOT my fault!

Yet I do my part to save him still: I give him to understand that drinking makes his eyes dull, and his face red and bloated; and that tends to render him imbecile in body and mind; and if Annabella were to see him as often as I do, she would speedily be disenchanted; and that she certainly will withdraw her favour from him, if he continues such courses. Such a mode of admonition wins

only coarse abuse for me – and, indeed, I almost feel as if I deserved it, for I hate to use such arguments, but they sink into his stupefied heart, and make him pause, and ponder, and abstain, more than anything else I could say.

At present, I am enjoying a temporary relief from his presence: he is gone with Hargrave to join a distant hunt, and will probably not be back before tomorrow evening. How differently I used to feel his absence!

Mr Hargrave is still at the Grove. He and Arthur frequently meet to pursue their rural sports together: he often calls upon us here, and Arthur not unfrequently rides over to him. I do not think either of these *soi-disant* friends is overflowing with love for the other; but such intercourse serves to get the time on, and I am very willing it should continue, as it saves me some hours of discomfort in Arthur's society, and gives him some better employment than the sottish indulgence of his sensual appetites. The only objection I have to Mr Hargrave's being in the neighbourhood, is that the fear of meeting him at the Grove prevents me from seeing his sister so often as I otherwise should; for, of late, he has conducted himself towards me with such unerring propriety, that I have almost forgotten his former conduct. I suppose he is striving to 'win my esteem'. If he continues to act in this way, he may win it; – but what then? The moment he attempts to demand anything more, he will lose it again.

*February 10th.* – It is a hard, embittering thing to have one's kind feelings and good intentions cast back in one's teeth. I was beginning to relent towards my wretched partner – to pity his forlorn, comfortless condition, unalleviated as it is by the consolations of intellectual resources and the answer of a good conscience towards God – and to think I ought to sacrifice my pride, and renew my efforts once again to make his home agreeable and lead him back to the path of virtue; not by false professions of love, and not by pretended remorse, but by mitigating my habitual coldness of manner, and commuting my frigid civility into kindness wherever an opportunity occurred; and not only was I beginning to think so, but I had already begun to act upon the thought – and what was the result? No answering spark of kindness – no awakening penitence, but an unappeasable ill-humour, and a spirit of tyrannous exaction that increased with indulgence, and a lurking gleam of self-complacent triumph, at every detection of relenting softness in my manner, that congealed me to marble again as often as it recurred; and this morning he finished the business: – I think the petrifaction is so completely effected at last, that nothing can melt me again. Among his letters was one which he perused with symptoms of unusual gratification, and then threw it across the table to me, with the admonition—

'There! read that, and take a lesson by it!'

It was in the free, dashing hand of Lady Lowborough. I glanced at the first page; it seemed full of extravagant protestations of affection; impetuous longings for a speedy re-union; and impious defiance of God's mandates, and railings against His providence for having cast their lot asunder, and doomed them both to the hateful bondage of alliance with those they could not love. He gave a slight titter on seeing me change colour. I folded up the letter, rose, and returned it to him, with no remark, but—

'Thank you – I will take a lesson by it!'

My little Arthur was standing between his knees, delightedly playing with the bright, ruby ring on his finger. Urged by a sudden, imperative impulse to deliver my son from that contaminating influence, I caught him up in my arms

and carried him with me out of the room. Not liking this abrupt removal, the child began to pout and cry. This was a new stab to my already tortured heart. I would not let him go; but, taking him with me into the library, I shut the door, and kneeling on the floor beside him, I embraced him, kissed him, wept over him with passionate fondness. Rather frightened than consoled by this, he turned struggling from me and cried out aloud for his papa. I released him from my arms, and never were more bitter tears than those that now concealed him from my blinded, burning eyes. Hearing his cries the father came to the room. I instantly turned away lest he should see and misconstrue my emotion. He swore at me, and took the now pacified child away.

It is hard that my little darling should love him more than me; and that, when the well-being and culture of my son is all I have to live for, I should see my influence destroyed by one whose selfish affection is more injurious than the coldest indifference or the harshest tyranny could be. If I, for his good, deny him some trifling indulgence, he goes to his father, and the latter, in spite of his selfish indolence, will even give himself some trouble to meet the child's desires: if I attempt to curb his will, or look gravely on him for some act of childish disobedience, he knows his other parent will smile and take his part against me. Thus, not only have I the father's spirit in the son to contend against, the germs of his evil tendencies to search out and eradicate, and his corrupting intercourse and example in after-life to counteract, but already he counteracts my arduous labour for the child's advantage, destroys my influence over his tender mind, and robs me of his very love; I had no earthly hope but this, and he seems to take a diabolical delight in tearing it away.

But it is wrong to despair; I will remember the counsel of the inspired writer to him 'that feareth the Lord and obeyeth the voice of his servant, that sitteth in darkness and hath no light; let him trust in the name of the Lord, and stay upon his God!'

# Chapter 37

*December 20th, 1825*

nother year is past; and I am weary of this life. And yet I cannot wish to leave it: whatever afflictions assail me here, I cannot wish to go and leave my darling in this dark and wicked world alone, without a friend to guide him through its weary mazes, to warm him of its thousand snares, and guard him from the perils that beset him on every hand. I am not well fitted to be his only companion, I know; but there is no other to supply my place. I am too grave to minister to his amusements and enter into his infantile sports as a nurse or a mother ought to do, and often his bursts of gleeful merriment trouble and alarm me; I see in them his father's spirit and temperament, and I tremble

for the consequences; and, too often, damp the innocent mirth I ought to share. That father, on the contrary, has no weight of sadness on his mind – is troubled with no fears, no scruples concerning his son's future welfare; and at evenings especially, the times when the child sees him the most and the oftenest, he is always particularly jocund and open-hearted: ready to laugh and to jest with anything or anybody – but me – and I am particularly silent and sad: therefore, of course, the child dotes upon his seemingly joyous, amusing, ever-indulgent papa, and will at any time gladly exchange my company for his. This disturbs me greatly; not so much for the sake of my son's affection (though I do prize that highly, and though I feel it is my right, and I know I have done much to earn it) as for that influence over him which for his own advantage I would strive to purchase and retain, and which for very spite his father delights to rob me of, and, from motives of mere idle egotism, is pleased to win to himself; making no use of it but to torment me and ruin the child. My only consolation is, that he spends comparatively little of his time at home, and, during the months he passes in London or elsewhere, I have a chance of recovering the ground I had lost, and overcoming with good the evil he has wrought by his wilful mismanagement. But then it is a bitter trial to behold him, on his return, doing his utmost to subvert my labours and transform my innocent, affectionate, tractable darling into a selfish, disobedient, and mischievous boy; thereby preparing the soil for those vices he has so successfully cultivated in his perverted nature.

Happily, there were none of Arthur's 'friends' invited to Grassdale last autumn: he took himself off to visit some of them instead. I wish he would always do so, and I wish his friends were numerous and loving enough to keep him amongst them all the year round. Mr Hargrave, considerably to my annoyance, did not go with him; but I think I have done with that gentleman at last.

For seven or eight months, he behaved so remarkably well, and managed so skilfully too, that I was almost completely off my guard, and was really beginning to look upon him as a friend, and even to treat him as such, with certain prudent restrictions (which I deemed scarcely necessary); when, presuming upon my unsuspecting kindness, he thought he might venture to overstep the bounds of decent moderation and propriety that had so long restrained him. It was on a pleasant evening at the close of May: I was wandering in the park, and he, on seeing me there as he rode past, made bold to enter and approach me, dismounting and leaving his horse at the gate. This was the first time he had ventured to come within its enclosure since I had been left alone, without the sanction of his mother's or sister's company, or at least the excuse of a message from them. But he managed to appear so calm and easy, so respectful and self-possessed in his friendliness, that, though a little surprised, I was neither alarmed nor offended at the unusual liberty, and he walked with me under the ash-trees and by the water-side, and talked, with considerable animation, good taste, and intelligence, on many subjects, before I began to think about getting rid of him. Then, after a pause, during which we both stood gazing on the calm, blue water; I revolving in my mind the best means of politely dismissing my companion, he, no doubt, pondering other matters equally alien to the sweet sights and sounds that alone were present to his senses, – he suddenly electrified me by beginning, in a peculiar tone, low, soft, but perfectly distinct, to pour forth the most unequivocal

expressions of earnest and passionate love; pleading his cause with all the bold yet artful eloquence he could summon to his aid. But I cut short his appeal, and repulsed him so determinately, so decidedly, and with such a mixture of scornful indignation, tempered with cool, dispassionate sorrow and pity for his benighted mind, that he withdrew, astonished, mortified, and discomforted; and, a few days after, I heard that he had departed for London. He returned, however, in eight or nine weeks – and did not entirely keep aloof from me, but comported himself in so remarkable a manner that his quick-sighted sister could not fail to notice the change.

'What have you done to Walter, Mrs Huntingdon?' said she one morning, when I had called at the Grove, and he had just left the room after exchanging a few words of the coldest civility. 'He has been so extremely ceremonious and stately of late, I can't imagine what it is all about, unless you have desperately offended him. Tell me what it is, that I may be your mediator, and make you friends again.'

'I have done nothing willingly to offend him,' said I. 'If he is offended, he can best tell you himself what it is about.'

'I'll ask him,' cried the giddy girl, springing up and putting her head out of the window; 'He's only in the garden – Walter!'

'No, no, Esther! you will seriously displease me if you do; and I shall leave you immediately, and not come again for months – perhaps years.'

'Did you call, Esther?' said her brother, approaching the window from without.

'Yes; I wanted to ask you'—

'Good morning, Esther,' said I, taking her hand and giving it a severe squeeze.

'To ask you,' continued she, 'to get me a rose for Mrs Huntingdon.' He departed. 'Mrs Huntingdon,' she exclaimed, turning to me and still holding me fast by the hand. 'I'm quite shocked at you – you're just as angry, and distant, and cold as he is: and I'm determined you shall be as good friends as ever before you go.'

'Esther, how can you be so rude?' cried Mrs Hargrave, who was seated gravely knitting in her easy chair. 'Surely, you never will learn to conduct yourself like a lady!'

'Well, mamma, you said, yourself'— But the young lady was silenced by the uplifted finger of her mamma, accompanied with a very stern shake of the head.

'Isn't she cross?' whispered she to me; but before I could add my share of reproof, Mr Hargrave reappeared at the window with a beautiful moss-rose in his hand.

'Here, Esther, I've brought you the rose,' said he, extending it towards her.

'Give it her yourself, you blockhead!' cried she, recoiling with a spring from between us.

'Mrs Huntingdon would rather receive it from you,' replied he, in a very serious tone, but lowering his voice that his mother might not hear. His sister took the rose and gave it to me.

'My brother's compliments, Mrs Huntingdon, and he hopes you and he will come to a better understanding by-and-by. Will that do, Walter?' added the saucy girl, turning to him and putting her arm round his neck, as he stood leaning upon the sill of the window – 'or should I have said that you are sorry you were so touchy? or that you hope she will pardon your offence?'

'You silly girl! you don't know what you are talking about,' replied he gravely.

'Indeed I don't: for I'm quite in the dark!'

'Now, Esther,' interposed Mrs Hargrave, who, if equally benighted on the subject of our estrangement, saw at least that her daughter was behaving very improperly, 'I must insist upon your leaving the room!'

'Pray don't, Mrs Hargrave, for I'm going to leave it myself,' said I, and immediately made my adieux.

About a week after, Mr Hargrave brought his sister to see me. He conducted himself, at first, with his usual cold, distant, half-stately, half-melancholy, altogether injured air; but Esther made no remark upon it this time: she had evidently been schooled into better manners. She talked to me, and laughed and romped with little Arthur, her loved and loving playmate. He, somewhat to my discomfort, enticed her from the room to have a run in the hall, and thence into the garden. I got up to stir the fire. Mr Hargrave asked if I felt cold, and shut the door – a very unseasonable piece of officiousness, for I had meditated following the noisy play-fellows if they did not speedily return. He then took the liberty of walking up to the fire himself, and asking me if I were aware that Mr Huntingdon was now at the seat of Lord Lowborough, and likely to continue there some time.

'No; but it's no matter,' I answered carelessly; and if my cheek glowed like fire, it was rather at the question than the information it conveyed.

'You don't object to it?' he said.

'Not at all, if Lord Lowborough likes his company.'

'You have no love left for him, then?'

'Not the least.'

'I knew that – I knew you were too high-minded and pure in your own nature to continue to regard one so utterly false and polluted with any feelings but those of indignation and scornful abhorrence!'

'Is he not your friend?' said I, turning my eyes from the fire to his face with perhaps a slight touch of those feelings he assigned to another.

'He was,' replied he, with the same calm gravity as before, 'but do not wrong me by supposing that I could continue my friendship and esteem to a man who could so infamously, so impiously forsake and injure one so transcendently – well, I won't speak of it. But tell me, do you never think of revenge?'

'Revenge! No – what good would that do? – it would make him no better, and me no happier.'

'I don't know how to talk to you, Mrs Huntingdon,' said he, smiling; 'you are only half a woman – your nature must be half human, half angelic. Such goodness overawes me; I don't know what to make of it.'

'Then, sir, I fear you must be very much worse than you should be, if I, a mere ordinary mortal, am, by your own confession, so vastly your superior; and since there exists so little sympathy between us, I think we had better each look out for some more congenial companion.' And forthwith moving to the window, I began to look out for my little son and his gay young friend.

'No, I am the ordinary mortal, I maintain,' replied Mr Hargrave. 'I will not allow myself to be worse than my fellows; but you, madam, I equally maintain there is nobody like you. But are you happy?' he asked in a serious tone.

'As happy as some others, I suppose.'

'Are you as happy as you desire to be?'

'No one is so blest as that comes to on this side eternity.'

'One thing I know,' returned he, with a deep, sad sigh; 'you are immeasurably happier than I am.'

'I am very sorry for you' then,' I could not help replying.

'Are you, indeed? No, for if you were you would be glad to relieve me.'

'And so I should if I could do so without injuring myself or any other.'

'And can you suppose that I should wish you to injure yourself? No, on the contrary, it is your own happiness I long for more than mine. You are miserable now, Mrs Huntingdon,' continued he, looking me boldly in the face. 'You do not complain, but I see – and feel – and know that you are miserable – and must remain so as long as you keep those walls of impenetrable ice about your still warm and palpitating heart; and I am miserable too. Deign to smile on me and I am happy: trust me and you shall be happy also, for if you are a woman I can make you so – and I will do it in spite of yourself!' he muttered between his teeth; 'and as for others, the question is between ourselves alone: you cannot injure your husband, you know, and no one else has any concern in the matter.'

'I have a son, Mr Hargrave, and you have a mother,' said I, retiring from the window, whither he had followed me.

'They need not know,' he began; but before anything more could be said on either side Esther and Arthur re-entered the room. The former glanced at Walter's flushed, excited countenance and then at mine – a little flushed and excited too, I dare say, though from far different causes. She must have thought we had been quarrelling desperately, and was evidently perplexed and disturbed at the circumstance; but she was too polite or too much afraid of her brother's anger to refer to it. She seated herself on the sofa, and putting back her bright, golden ringlets, that were scattered in wild profusion over her face, she immediately began to talk about the garden and her little playfellow, and continued to chatter away in her usual strain till her brother summoned her to depart.

'If I have spoken too warmly, forgive me,' he murmured on taking his leave, 'or I shall never forgive myself.'

Esther smiled and glanced at me: I merely bowed, and her countenance fell. She thought it a poor return for Walter's generous concession, and was disappointed in her friend. Poor child, she little knows the world she lives in!

Mr Hargrave had not an opportunity of meeting me again in private for several weeks after this; but when he did meet me there was less of pride and more of touching melancholy in his manner than before. Oh, how he annoyed me! I was obliged at last almost entirely to remit my visits to the Grove, at the expense of deeply offending Mrs Hargrave and seriously afflicting poor Esther, who really values my society for want of better, and who ought not to suffer for the fault of her brother. But that indefatigable foe was not yet vanquished: he seemed to be always on the watch. I frequently saw him riding lingeringly past the premises, looking searchingly round him as he went – or, if I did not, Rachel did. That sharp-sighted woman soon guessed how matters stood between us, and descrying the enemy's movements from her elevation at the nursery-window, she would give me a quiet intimation if she saw me preparing for a walk when she had reason to believe he was about or to think it likely that he would meet or overtake me in the way I meant to traverse. I would then defer my ramble, or confine myself for that day to the park and gardens, or, if the proposed

# The Tenant of Wildfell Hall

excursion was a matter of importance, such as a visit to the sick or afflicted, I would take Rachel with me, and then I was never molested.

But one mild, sunshiny day, early in November, I had ventured forth alone to visit the village school and a few of the poor tenants, and on my return I was alarmed at the clatter of a horse's feet behind me approaching at a rapid, steady trot. There was no stile or gap at hand by which I could escape into the fields, so I walked quietly on, saying to myself—

'It may not be he after all; and if it is, and if he do annoy me, it shall be for the last time, I am determined, if there is power in words and looks against cool impudence and mawkish sentimentality so inexhaustible as his.'

The horse soon overtook me, and was reined up close beside me. It was Mr Hargrave. He greeted me with a smile intended to be soft and melancholy, but his triumphant satisfaction at having caught me at last so shone through that it was quite a failure. After briefly answering his salutation and inquiring after the ladies at the Grove, I turned away and walked on; but he followed and kept his horse at my side: it was evident he intended to be my companion all the way.

'Well! I don't much care. If you want another rebuff take it – and welcome,' was my inward remark. 'Now, sir, what next?'

This question, though unspoken, was not long unanswered: after a few passing observations upon indifferent subjects, he began in solemn tones the following appeal to my humanity—

'It will be four years next April since I first saw you, Mrs Huntingdon – you may have forgotten the circumstance, but I never can. I admired you then most deeply, but I dared not love you: in the following autumn I saw so much of your perfections that I could not fail to love you, though I dared not show it. For upwards of three years I have endured a perfect martyrdom. From the anguish of suppressed emotions, intense and fruitless longings, silent sorrow, crushing hopes, and trampled affections, I have suffered more than I can tell, or you imagine – and you were the cause of it, and not altogether the innocent cause. My youth is wasting away; my prospects are darkened; my life is a desolate blank; I have no rest day or night: I am become a burden to myself and others, and you might save me by a word – a glance, and will not do it – is this right?'

'In the first place I don't believe you,' answered I: 'In the second, if you will be such a fool I can't hinder it.'

'If you affect,' replied he earnestly, 'to regard as folly, the best, the strongest, the most godlike impulses of our nature, – I don't believe you; I know you are not the heartless, icy being you pretend to be – you had a heart once and gave it to your husband. When you found him utterly unworthy of the treasure, you reclaimed it: and you will not pretend that you loved that sensual, earthly-minded profligate so deeply, so devotedly, that you can never love another. I know that there are feelings in your nature that have never yet been called forth – I know, too, that in your present neglected lonely state you are and must be miserable. You have it in your power to raise two human beings from a state of actual suffering to such unspeakable beatitude as only generous, noble, self-forgetting love can give (for you can love me if you will); you may tell me that you scorn and detest me, but – since you have set me the example of plain speaking – I will answer that I do not believe you! but you will not do it! you choose rather to leave us miserable; and you coolly tell me it is the will of God that we should remain so. You may call this religion, but I call it wild fanaticism!'

# The Tenant of Wildfell Hall

'There is another life both for you and for me,' said I. 'If it be the will of God that we should sow in tears now, it is only that we may reap in joy hereafter. It is His will that we should not injure others by the gratification of our own earthly passions; and you have a mother, and sisters, and friends, who would be seriously injured by your disgrace; and I, too, have friends, whose peace of mind shall never be sacrificed to my enjoyment – or yours either, with my consent – and if I were alone in the world, I have still my God and my religion, and I would sooner die than disgrace my calling and break my faith with Heaven to obtain a few brief years of false and fleeting happiness – happiness sure to end in misery, even here – for myself or any other!'

'There need be no disgrace – no misery or sacrifice in any quarter,' persisted he. 'I do not ask you to leave your home or defy the world's opinion.' – But I need not repeat all his arguments. I refuted them to the best of my power: but that power was provokingly small, at the moment, for I was too much flurried with indignation – and even shame – that he should thus dare to address me, to retain sufficient command of thought and language to enable me adequately to contend against his powerful sophistries. Finding, however, that he could not be silenced by reason, and even covertly exulted in his seeming advantage, and ventured to deride those assertions I had not the coolness to prove, I changed my course and tried another plan.

'Do you really love me?' said I seriously, pausing and looking him calmly in the face.

'Do I love you?' cried he.

'Truly?' I demanded.

His countenance brightened; he thought his triumph was at hand. He commenced a passionate protestation of the truth and fervour of his attachment, which I cut short by another question—

'But is it not a selfish love? – have you enough disinterested affection to enable you to sacrifice your own pleasure to mine?'

'I would give my life to serve you.'

'I don't want your life – but have you enough real sympathy for my afflictions to induce you to make an effort to relieve them, at the risk of a little discomfort to yourself?'

'Try me, and see!'

'If you have – never mention this subject again. You cannot recur to it in any way, without doubling the weight of those sufferings you so feelingly deplore. I have nothing left me but the solace of a good conscience and a hopeful trust in Heaven, and you labour continually to rob me of these. If you persist, I must regard you as my deadliest foe.'

'But hear me a moment'—

'No, sir! you said you would give your life to serve me: I only ask your silence on one particular point. I have spoken plainly; and what I say I mean. If you torment me in this way any more, I must conclude that your protestations are entirely false, and that you hate me in your heart as fervently as you profess to love me!'

He bit his lip and bent his eyes upon the ground in silence for a while.

'Then I must leave you,' said he at length, looking steadily upon me, as if with the last hope of detecting some token of irrepressible anguish or dismay

awakened by those solemn words, 'I must leave you. I cannot live here, and be for ever silent on the all-absorbing subject of my thoughts and wishes.'

'Formerly, I believe, you spent but little of your time at home,' I answered; 'it will do you no harm to absent yourself again, for a while – if that be really necessary.'

'If that be really possible,' he muttered – 'and can you bid me go so coolly? Do you really wish it?'

'Most certainly I do. If you cannot see me without tormenting me as you have lately done, I would gladly say farewell and never see you more.'

He made no answer, but, bending from his horse, held out his hand toward me. I looked up at his face, and saw therein such a look of genuine agony of soul that, whether bitter disappointment, or wounded pride, or lingering love, or burning wrath were uppermost, I could not hesitate to put my hand in his as frankly as if I bade a friend farewell. He grasped it very hard, and immediately put spurs to his horse and galloped away. Very soon after, I learned that he was gone to Paris, where he still is; and the longer he stays there the better for me.

I thank God for this deliverance!

# Chapter 38

*December 20th, 1826*

The fifth anniversary of my wedding day, and, I trust, the last I shall spend under this roof. My resolution is formed, my plan concocted, and already partly put in execution. My conscience does not blame me, but while the purpose ripens, let me beguile a few of these long winter evenings in stating the case for my own satisfaction – a dreary amusement enough, but having the air of a useful occupation, and being pursued as a task, it will suit me better than a lighter one.

In September, quiet Grassdale was again alive with a party of ladies and gentlemen (so called) consisting of the same individuals as those invited the year before last, with the addition of two or three others, among whom were Mrs Hargrave and her younger daughter. The gentlemen and Lady Lowborough were invited for the pleasure and convenience of the host, the other ladies, I suppose for the sake of appearances, and to keep me in check, and make me discreet and civil in my demeanour. But the ladies stayed only three weeks, the gentlemen, with two exceptions, above two months, for their hospitable entertainer was loath to part with them and be left alone with his bright intellect, his stainless conscience, and his loved and loving wife.

On the day of Lady Lowborough's arrival, I followed her into her chamber, and plainly told her that, if I found reason to believe that she still continued her criminal connection with Mr Huntingdon, I should think it my absolute duty

to inform her husband of the circumstance – or awaken his suspicions at least – however painful it might be, or however dreadful the consequences. She was startled at first by the declaration, so unexpected, and so determinately yet calmly delivered; but rallying in a moment, she coolly replied that if I saw anything at all reprehensible or suspicious in her conduct, she would freely give me leave to tell his lordship all about it. Willing to be satisfied with this, I left her; and certainly I saw nothing thenceforth particularly reprehensible or suspicious in her demeanour towards her host; but then I had the other guests to attend to, and I did not watch them narrowly – for to confess the truth, I feared to see anything between them. I no longer regarded it as any concern of mine, and if it was my duty to enlighten Lord Lowborough, it was a painful duty, and I dreaded to be called to perform it.

But my fears were brought to an end, in a manner I had not anticipated. One evening, about a fortnight after the visitors' arrival, I had retired into the library to snatch a few minutes' respite from forced cheerfulness and wearisome discourse – for after so long a period of seclusion, dreary indeed as I had often found it, I could not always bear to be doing violence to my feelings, and goading my powers to talk, and smile and listen, and play the attentive hostess, or even the cheerful friend: – I had just ensconced myself within the bow of the window, and was looking out upon the west where the darkening hills rose sharply defined against the clear amber light of evening, that gradually blended and faded away into the pure, pale blue of the upper sky, where one bright star was shining through, as if to promise – 'When that dying light is gone, the world will not be left in darkness, and they who trust in God – whose minds are unbeclouded by the mists of unbelief and sin – are never wholly comfortless,' – when I heard a hurried step approaching, and Lord Lowborough entered – this room was still his favourite resort. He flung the door to with unusual violence, and cast his hat aside regardless where it fell. What could be the matter with him? His face was ghastly pale; his eyes were fixed upon the ground; his teeth clenched; his forehead glistened with the dews of agony. It was plain he knew his wrongs at last!

Unconscious of my presence, he began to pace the room in a state of fearful agitation, violently wringing his hands and uttering low groans and incoherent ejaculations. I made a movement to let him know that he was not alone; but he was too preoccupied to notice it. Perhaps, while his back was towards me, I might cross the room and slip away unobserved. I rose to make the attempt, but then he perceived me. He started and stood still a moment; then wiped his streaming forehead, and, advancing towards me, with a kind of unnatural composure, said in a deep, almost sepulchral tone—

'Mrs Huntingdon, I must leave you tomorrow.'

'Tomorrow!' I repeated. 'I do not ask the cause.'

'You know it then – and you can be so calm!' said he, surveying me with profound astonishment, not unmingled with a kind of resentful bitterness, as it appeared to me.

'I have so long been aware of'— I paused in time, and added, 'of my husband's character, that nothing shocks me.'

'But this – how long have you been aware of this?' demanded he, laying his clenched hand on the table beside him, and looking me keenly and fixedly in the face.

# The Tenant of Wildfell Hall

I felt like a criminal.

'Not long,' I answered.

'You knew it!' cried he, with bitter vehemence – 'and you did not tell me! You helped to deceive me!'

'My lord, I did not help to deceive you.'

'Then why did you not tell me?'

'Because I knew it would be painful to you – I hoped she would return to her duty, and then there would be no need to harrow your feelings with such'—

'Oh God! how long has this been going on? how long has it been, Mrs Huntingdon? – Tell me – I must know!' he exclaimed, with intense and fearful eagerness.

'Two years, I believe.'

'Great Heaven! and she has duped me all this time!' He turned away with a suppressed groan of agony, and paced the room again, in a paroxysm of renewed agitation. My heart smote me; but I would try to console him, though I knew not how to attempt it.

'She is a wicked woman,' I said. 'She had basely deceived and betrayed you. She is as little worthy of your regret as she was of your affection. Let her injure you no further; abstract yourself from her, and stand alone.'

'And you, madam,' said he sternly, arresting himself, and turning round upon me – 'you have injured me too, by this ungenerous concealment!'

There was a sudden revulsion in my feelings. Something rose within me, and urged me to resent this harsh return for my heartfelt sympathy, and defend myself with answering severity. Happily, I did not yield to the impulse. I saw his anguish as, suddenly smiting his forehead, he turned abruptly to the window, and, looking upward at the placid sky, murmured passionately, 'O God, that I might die!' – and felt that to add one drop of bitterness to that already overflowing cup, would be ungenerous indeed. And yet, I fear there was more coldness than gentleness in the quiet tone of my reply—

'I might offer many excuses that some would admit to be valid, but I will not attempt to enumerate them'—

'I know them,' said he hastily, 'you would say that it was no business of yours – that I ought to have taken care of myself – that if my own blindness has led me into this pit of hell, I have no right to blame another for giving me credit for a larger amount of sagacity than I possessed'—

'I confess I was wrong,' continued I, without regarding this bitter interruption; 'but whether want of courage or mistaken kindness was the cause of my error, I think you blame me too severely. I told Lady Lowborough two weeks ago, the very hour she came, that I should certainly think it my duty to inform you if she continued to deceive you: she gave me full liberty to do so if I should see anything reprehensible or suspicious in her conduct – I have seen nothing; and I trusted she had altered her course.'

He continued gazing from the window while I spoke, and did not answer, but stung by the recollections my words awakened, stamped his foot upon the floor, ground his teeth, and corrugated his brow, like one under the influence of acute physical pain.

'It was wrong – it was wrong!' he muttered at length. 'Nothing can excuse it – nothing can atone for it, – nothing can recall those years of cursed credulity

– nothing obliterate them! – nothing, nothing!' he repeated in a whisper whose despairing bitterness precluded all resentment.

'When I put the case to myself, I own it was wrong,' I answered; 'but I can only now regret that I did not see it in this light before, and that, as you say, nothing can recall the past.'

Something in my voice or in the spirit of this answer seemed to alter his mood. Turning towards me, and attentively surveying my face by the dim light, he said, in a milder tone than he had yet employed—

'You, too, have suffered, I suppose.'

'I suffered much at first.'

'When was that?'

'Two years ago; and two years hence you will be as calm as I am now, – and far, far happier, I trust, for you are a man, and free to act as you please.'

Something like a smile, but a very bitter one, crossed his face for a moment.

'You have not been happy lately?' he said, with a kind of effort to regain composure, and a determination to waive the further discussion of his own calamity.

'Happy!' I repeated, almost provoked at such a question. 'Could I be so, with such a husband?'

'I have noticed a change in your appearance since the first years of your marriage,' pursued he: 'I observed it to – to that infernal demon,' he muttered between his teeth – 'and he said it was your own sour temper that was eating away your bloom: it was making you old and ugly before your time, and had already made his fireside as comfortless as a convent cell. You smile, Mrs Huntingdon – nothing moves you. I wish my nature were as calm as yours.'

'My nature was not originally calm,' said I. 'I have learned to appear so by dint of hard lessons and many repeated efforts.'

At this juncture Mr Hattersely burst into the room.

'Hallo, Lowborough!' he began – 'Oh! I beg your pardon,' he exclaimed on seeing me; 'I didn't know it was a *tête-à-tête*. Cheer up, man,' he continued, giving Lord Lowborough a thump on the back, which caused the latter to recoil from him with looks of ineffable disgust and irritation. 'Come, I want to speak with you a bit.'

'Speak, then.'

'But I'm not sure it would be quite agreeable to the lady, what I have to say.'

'Then it would not be agreeable to me,' said his lordship, turning to leave the room.

'Yes, it would,' cried the other, following him into the hall. 'If you've the heart of a man it would be the very ticket for you. It's just this, my lad,' he continued, rather lowering his voice, but not enough to prevent me from hearing every word he said, though the half-closed door stood between us. 'I think you're an ill-used man – nay, now, don't flare up – I don't want to offend you: it's only my rough way of talking. I must speak right out, you know, or else not at all; – and I'm come – stop now! let me explain – I'm come to offer you my services, for though Huntingdon is my friend, he's a devilish scamp, as we all know, and I'll be your friend for the nonce. I know what it is you want, to make matters straight: it's just to exchange a shot with him, and then you'll feel yourself all right again; and if an accident happens – why, that'll be all right too, I dare say,

to a desperate fellow like you. Come now, give me your hand, and don't look so black upon it. Name time and place, and I'll manage the rest.'

'That,' answered the more low, deliberate voice of Lord Lowborough, 'is just the remedy my own heart – or the devil within it, suggested – to meet him, and not to part without blood. Whether I or he should fall – or both, it would be an inexpressible relief to me, if'—

'Just so! Well then'—

'No!' exclaimed his lordship, with deep, determined emphasis. 'Though I hate him from my heart, and should rejoice at any calamity that could befall him – I'll leave him to God; and though I abhor my own life, I'll leave that, too, to Him that gave it.'

'But you see in this case' – pleaded Hattersely.

'I'll not hear you!' exlaimed his companion, hastily turning away. 'Not another word! I've enough to do against the fiend within me.'

'Then you're a white-livered fool, and I wash my hands of you,' grumbled the tempter, as he swung himself round and departed.

'Right, right, Lord Lowborough,' cried I, darting out and clasping his burning hand, as he was moving away to the stairs. 'I begin to think the world is not worthy of you!'

Not understanding this sudden ebullition, he turned upon me with a stare of gloomy, bewildered amazement, that made me ashamed of the impulse to which I had yielded; but soon a more humanized expression dawned upon his countenance, and, before I could withdraw my hand, he pressed it kindly, while a gleam of genuine feeling flashed from his eyes as he murmured—

'God help us both!'

'Amen!' responded I; and we parted.

I returned to the drawing-room, where, doubtless my presence would be expected by most, desired by one or two. In the ante-room was Mr Hattersley, railing against Lord Lowborough's poltroonery before a select audience, viz., Mr. Huntingdon, who was lounging against the table, exulting in his own treacherous villainy, and laughing his victim to scorn, and Mr Grimsby, standing by, quietly rubbing his hands, and chuckling with fiendish satisfaction.

In the drawing-room I found Lady Lowborough, evidently in no very enviable state of mind, and struggling hard to conceal her discomposure by an overstrained affectation of unusual cheerfulness and vivacity, very uncalled for under the circumstances, for she had herself given the company to understand that her husband had received unpleasant intelligence from home, which necessitated his immediate departure, and that he had suffered it so to bother his mind, that it had brought on a bilious headache, owing to which, and the preparations he judged necessary to hasten his departure, she believed they would not have the pleasure of seeing him tonight. However, she asserted, it was only a business concern, and so she did not intend it should trouble her. She was just saying this as I entered, and she darted upon me such a glance of hardihood and defiance as at once astonished and revolted me.

'But I am troubled,' continued she, 'and vexed too, for I think it my duty to accompany his lordship, and of course I am very sorry to part with all my kind friends so unexpectedly and so soon.'

'And yet, Annabella,' said Esther, who was sitting beside her, 'I never saw you in better spirits in my life.'

# The Tenant of Wildfell Hall

'Precisely so, my love; because I wish to make the best of your society, since it appears this is to be the last night I am to enjoy it till Heaven knows when; and I wish to leave a good impression on you all,' – she glanced round, and seeing her aunt's eye fixed upon her, rather too scrutinizingly, as she probably thought, she started up and continued, 'to which end I'll give you a song – shall I, aunt? shall I, Mrs Huntingdon? shall I, ladies and gentlemen – all? Very well, I'll do my best to amuse you.'

She and Lord Lowborough occupied the apartments next to mine. I know not how she passed the night, but I lay awake the greater part of it listening to his heavy step pacing monotonously up and down his dressing-room, which was nearest my chamber. Once I heard him pause and throw something out of the window with a passionate ejaculation; and in the morning, after they were gone, a keen-bladed clasp-knife was found on the grass-plot below; a razor, likewise, was snapped in two and thrust deep into the cinders of the grate, but partially corroded by the decaying embers. So strong had been the temptation to end his miserable life, so determined his resolution to resist it.

My heart bled for him as I lay listening to that ceaseless tread. Hitherto I had thought too much of myself, too little of him: now I forgot my own afflictions, and thought only of his – of the ardent affection so miserably wasted, the fond faith so cruelly betrayed, the – no, I will not attempt to enumerate his wrongs – but I hated his wife and my husband more intensely than ever, and not for my sake, but for his.

They departed early in the morning, before any one else was down, except myself, and just as I was leaving my room, Lord Lowborough was descending to take his place in the carriage where his lady was already ensconced; and Arthur (or Mr Huntingdon as I prefer calling him, for the other is my child's name) had the gratuitous insolence to come out in his dressing-gown to bid his 'friend' good-bye.

'What, going already, Lowborough?' said he, 'Well, good morning.' He smilingly offered his hand.

I think the other would have knocked him down, had he not instinctively started back before that bony fist quivering with rage and clenched till the knuckles gleamed white and glistening through the skin. Looking upon him with a countenance livid with furious hate, Lord Lowborough muttered between his closed teeth a deadly execration he would not have uttered had he been calm enough to choose his words, and departed.

'I call that an unchristian spirit now,' said the villain. 'But I'd never give up an old friend for the sake of a wife. You may have mine if you like, and I call that handsome – I can do no more than offer restitution, can I?'

But Lowborough had gained the bottom of the stairs, and was now crossing the hall; and Mr Huntingdon, leaning over the banisters, called out, 'Give my love to Annabella! and I wish you both a happy journey,' and withdrew laughing to his chamber.

He subsequently expressed himself rather glad she was gone: 'She was so deuced imperious and exacting,' said he, 'now I shall be my own man again, and feel rather more at my ease.'

# Chapter 39

y greatest source of uneasiness, in this time of trial, was my son, whom his father and his father's friends delighted to encourage in all the embryo vices a little child can show, and to instruct in all the evil habits he could acquire – in a word, to 'make a man of him' was one of their staple amusements; and I need say no more to justify my alarm on his account, and my determination to deliver him at any hazard from the hands of such instructors. I first attempted to keep him always with me or in the nursery, and gave Rachel particular injunctions never to let him come down to dessert as long as these 'gentlemen' stayed; but it was no use; these orders were immediately counter-manded and overruled by his father; he was not going to have the little fellow moped to death between an old nurse and a cursed fool of a mother. So the little fellow came down every evening in spite of his cross mamma, and learned to tipple wine like papa, to swear like Mr Hattersley, and to have his own way like a man, and sent mamma to the devil when she tried to prevent him. To see such things done with the roguish naïveté of that pretty little child, and hear such things spoken by that small infantile voice, was as peculiarly piquant and irresistibly droll to them as it was inexpressibly distressing and painful to me; and when he had set the table in a roar he would look round delightedly upon them all, and add his shrill laugh to theirs. But if that beaming blue eye rested on me, its light would vanish for a moment, and he would say, in some concern – 'Mamma, why don't you laugh? Make her laugh, papa – she never will.'

Hence was I obliged to stay among these human brutes, watching an opportunity to get my child away from them, instead of leaving them immediately after the removal of the cloth, as I should always otherwise have done. He was never willing to go, and I frequently had to carry him away by force, for which he thought me very cruel and unjust; and sometimes his father would insist upon my letting him remain; and then I would leave him to his kind friends, and retire to indulge my bitterness and despair alone, or to rack my brains for a remedy to this great evil.

But here again I must do Mr Hargrave the justice to acknowledge that I never saw him laugh at the child's misdemeanours, nor heard him utter a word of encouragement to his aspirations after manly accomplishments. But when anything very extraordinary was said or done by the infant profligate, I noticed, at times, a peculiar expression in his face that I could neither interpret nor define – a slight twitching about the muscles of the mouth – a sudden flash in the eye, as he darted a sudden glance at the child and then at me: and then I could fancy there arose a gleam of hard, keen, sombre satisfaction in his countenance at the look of impotent wrath and anguish he was too certain to

behold in mine. But on one occasion, when Arthur had been behaving particularly ill, and Mr Huntingdon and his guests had been particularly provoking and insulting to me in their encouragement of him, and I particularly anxious to get him out of the room, and on the very point of demeaning myself by a burst of uncontrollable passion – Mr Hargrave suddenly rose from his seat with an aspect of stern determination, lifted the child from his father's knee where he was sitting half tipsy, cocking his head and laughing at me, and execrating me with words he little knew the meaning of – handed him out of the room, and, setting him down in the hall, held the door open for me, gravely bowed as I withdrew, and closed it after me. I heard high words exchanged between him and his already half-inebriated host as I departed, leading away my bewildered and disconcerted boy.

But this should not continue: my child must not be abandoned to this corruption: better far that he should live in poverty and obscurity with a fugitive mother, than in luxury and affluence with such a father. These guests might not be with us long, but they would return again: and he, the most injurious of the whole, his child's worst enemy, would still remain. I could endure it for myself, but for my son it must be borne no longer: the world's opinion and the feelings of my friends must be alike unheeded here, at least, alike unable to deter me from my duty. But where should I find an asylum, and how obtain subsistence for us both? Oh, I would take my precious charge at early dawn, take the coach to M—, flee to the port of —, cross the Atlantic, and seek a quiet, humble home in New England, where I would support myself and him by the labour of my hands. The palette and the easel, my darling playmates once, must be my sober toil-fellows now. But was I sufficiently skilful as an artist to obtain my livelihood in a strange land, without friends and without recommendation? No; I must wait a little; I must labour hard to improve my talent, and to produce something worth while as a specimen of my powers, something to speak favourably for me, whether as an actual painter or a teacher. Brilliant success, of course, I did not look for, but some degree of security from positive failure was indispensable – I must not take my son to starve. And then I must have money for the journey, the passage, and some little to support us in our retreat in case I should be unsuccessful at first: and not too little either, for who could tell how long I might have to struggle with the indifference or neglect of others, or my own inexperience or inability to suit their tastes?

What should I do then? Apply to my brother and explain my circumstances and my resolves to him? No, no: even if I told him all my grievances, which I should be very reluctant to do, he would be certain to disapprove of the step: it would seem like madness to him, as it would to my uncle and aunt, or to Milicent. No; I must have patience and gather a hoard of my own. Rachel should be my only confidante – I thought I could persuade her into the scheme; and she should help me, first, to find out a picture-dealer in some distant town; then, through her means, I would privately sell what pictures I had on hand that would do for such a purpose, and some of those I should thereafter paint. Besides this, I would contrive to dispose of my jewels – not the family jewels, but the few I brought with me from home, and those my uncle gave me on my marriage. A few months' arduous toil might well be borne by me with such an end in view; and in the interim my son could not be much more injured than he was already.

# The Tenant of Wildfell Hall

Having formed this resolution, I immediately set to work to accomplish it. I might possibly have been induced to wax cool upon it afterwards, or perhaps to keep weighing the pros and cons in my mind till the latter overbalanced the former, and I was driven to relinquish the project altogether, or delay the execution of it to an indefinite period, – had not something occurred to confirm me in that determination to which I still adhere, which I still think I did well to form, and shall do better to execute.

Since Lord Lowborough's departure, I had regarded the library as entirely my own, a secure retreat at all hours of the day. None of our gentlemen had the smallest pretensions to a literary taste except Mr Hargrave; and, he, at present, was quite contented with the newspapers and periodicals of the day. And if, by any chance, he should look in here, I felt assured he would soon depart on seeing me, for, instead of becoming less cool and distant towards me, he had become decidedly more so since the departure of his mother and sisters, which was just what I wished. Here, then, I set up my easel, and here I worked at my canvas from daylight till dusk, with very little intermission saving when pure necessity, or my duties to little Arthur, called me away – for I still thought proper to devote some portion of every day exclusively to his instruction and amusement. But, contrary to my expectation, on the third morning, while I was thus employed, Mr Hargrave did look in, and did not immediately withdraw on seeing me. He apologized for his intrusion, and said he was only come for a book; but when he had got it, he condescended to cast a glance over my picture. Being a man of taste, he had something to say on this subject as well as another, and having modestly commented on it, without much encouragement from me, he proceeded to expatiate on the art in general. Receiving no encouragement in that either, he dropped it, but did not depart.

'You don't give us much of your company, Mrs Huntingdon,' observed he, after a brief pause, during which I went on coolly mixing and tempering my colours; 'and I cannot wonder at it, for you must be heartily sick of us all. I myself am so thoroughly ashamed of my companions, and so weary of their irrational conversation and pursuits – now that there is no one to humanize them and keep them in check, since you have justly abandoned us to our own devices – that I think I shall presently withdraw from amongst them – probably within this week – and I cannot suppose you will regret my departure.'

He paused. I did not answer.

'Probably,' he added, with a smile, 'your only regret on the subject will be, that I do not take all my companions along with me. I flatter myself, at times, that though among them, I am not of them; but it is natural that you should be glad to get rid of me. I may regret this, but I cannot blame you for it.'

'I shall not rejoice at your departure, for you can conduct yourself like a gentleman,' said I, thinking it but right to make some acknowledgment for his good behaviour, 'but I must confess I shall rejoice to bid adieu to the rest, inhospitable as it may appear.'

'No one can blame you for such an avowal,' replied he gravely; 'not even the gentlemen themselves, I imagine. I'll just tell you,' he continued, as if actuated by a sudden resolution, 'what was said last night in the dining-room, after you left us – perhaps you will not mind it, as you're so very philosophical on certain points,' he added with a slight sneer. 'They were talking about Lord Lowborough and his delectable lady, the cause of whose sudden departure is no secret amongst

them; and her character is so well known to them all, that, nearly related to me as she is, I could not attempt to defend it. – Curse me,' he muttered, *par parenthèse*, 'If I don't have vengeance for this! If the villain must disgrace the family, must he blazon it abroad to every low-bred knave of his acquaintance? – I beg your pardon, Mrs Huntingdon. Well, they were talking of these things, and some of them remarked that, as she was separated from her husband, he might see her again when he pleased.

' "Thank you," said he; "I've had enough of her for the present: I'll not trouble to see her, unless she comes to me."

' "Then what do you mean to do, Huntingdon, when we're gone?"', said Ralph Hattersley. "Do you mean to turn from the error of your ways, and be a good husband, a good father, and so forth – as I do, when I get shut of you and all these rollicking devils you call your friends? I think it's time; and your wife is fifty times too good for you, you know"—

'And he added some praise of you, which you would not thank me for repeating – nor him for uttering; proclaiming it aloud, as he did, without delicacy or discrimination, in an audience where it seemed profanation to utter your name – himself utterly incapable of understanding or appreciating your real excellences. Huntingdon, meanwhile, sat quietly drinking his wine, or looking smilingly into his glass and offering no interruption or reply, till Hattersley shouted out—

' "Do you hear me, man?"

' "Yes, go on," said he.

' "Nay, I've done," replied the other: "I only want to know if you intend to take my advice."

' "What advice?"

' "To turn over a new leaf, you double-dyed scoundrel," shouted Ralph, "and beg your wife's pardon, and be a good boy for the future."

' "My wife: what wife? I have no wife," replied Huntingdon, looking innocently up from his glass – "or if I have, look you, gentlemen, I value her so highly, that any one among you, that can fancy her, may have her and welcome – you may, by Jove, and my blessing into the bargain!"

'I – hem – some one asked if he really meant what he said, upon which, he solemnly swore he did, and no mistake. – What do you think of that, Mrs Huntingdon?' asked Mr Hargrave, after a short pause, during which I had felt he was keenly examining my half-averted face.

'I say,' replied I calmly, 'that what he prizes so lightly, will not be long in his possession.'

'You cannot mean that you will break your heart and die for the detestable conduct of an infamous villain like that!'

'By no means: my heart is too thoroughly dried to be broken in a hurry, and I mean to live as long as I can.'

'Will you leave him then?'

'Yes.'

'When – and how?' asked he eagerly.

'When I am ready, and how I can manage it most effectually.'

'But your child?'

'My child goes with me.'

'He will not allow it.'

'I shall not ask him.'

'Ah, then, it is a secret flight you meditate! – but with whom, Mrs Huntingdon?'

'With my son – and, possibly, his nurse.'

'Alone – and unprotected! But where can you go? what can you do? He will follow you and bring you back.'

'I have laid my plans too well for that. Let me once get clear of Grassdale, and I shall consider myself safe.'

Mr Hargrave advanced one step towards me, looked me in the face, and drew in his breath to speak; but that look, that heightened colour, that sudden sparkle of the eye, made my blood rise in wrath: I abruptly turned away and, snatching up my brush, began to dash away at my canvas with rather too much energy for the good of the picture.

'Mrs Huntingdon,' said he with bitter solemnity, 'you are cruel – cruel to me – cruel to yourself.'

'Mr Hargrave, remember your promise.'

'I must speak – my heart will burst if I don't! I have been silent long enough – and you must hear me!' cried he, boldly intercepting my retreat to the door. 'You tell me you owe no allegiance to your husband; he openly declares himself weary of you, and calmly gives you up to anybody that will take you; you are about to leave him; no one will believe that you go alone – all the world will say, "She has left him at last, and who can wonder at it? Few can blame her, fewer still can pity him; but who is the companion of her flight?" Thus you will have no credit for your virtue (if you call it such): even your best friends will not believe in it; because it is monstrous, and not to be credited – but by those who suffer, from the effects of it, such cruel torments that they know it to be indeed reality. But what can you do in the cold, rough world alone? you, a young and inexperienced woman, delicately nurtured, and utterly'—

'In a word, you would advise me to stay where I am,' interrupted I. 'Well, I'll see about it.'

'By all means, leave him!' cried he earnestly, 'but NOT alone! Helen! let me protect you!'

'Never! while heaven spares my reason,' replied I, snatching away the hand he had presumed to seize and press between his own. But he was in for it now; he had fairly broken the barrier: he was completely roused, and determined to hazard all for victory.

'I must not be denied!' exclaimed he vehemently; and seizing both my hands, he held them very tight, but dropped upon his knee, and looked up in my face with a half-imploring, half imperious gaze. 'You have no reason now: you are flying in the face of heaven's decrees. God has designed me to be your comfort and protector – I feel it – I know it as certainly as if a voice from heaven declared "Ye twain shall be one flesh" – and you spurn me from you'—

'Let me go, Mr Hargrave!' said I sternly. But he only tightened his grasp.

'Let me go!' I repeated, quivering with indignation.

His face was almost opposite the window as he knelt. With a slight start, I saw him glance towards it; and then a gleam of malicious triumph lit up his countenance. Looking over my shoulder, I beheld a shadow just retiring round the corner.

'That is Grimsby,' said he deliberately. 'He will report what he has seen to

Huntingdon and all the rest, with such embellishments as he thinks proper. He has no love for you, Mrs Huntingdon – no reverence for your sex – no belief in virtue – no admiration for its image. He will give such a version of this story as will leave no doubt at all, about your character, in the minds of those who hear it. Your fair fame is gone; and nothing that I or you can say can ever retrieve it. But give me the power to protect you, and show me the villain that dares to insult!'

'No one has ever dared to insult me as you are doing now!' said I, at length releasing my hands, and recoiling from him.

'I do not insult you,' cried he: 'I worship you. You are my angel – my divinity! I lay my powers at your feet – and you must and shall accept them!' he exclaimed, impetuously starting to his feet – 'I will be your consoler and defender! and if your conscience upbraid you for it, say I overcame you, and you could not choose but yield!'

I never saw a man so terribly excited. He precipitated himself towards me. I snatched up my palette-knife and held it against him. This startled him; he stood and gazed at me in astonishment; I dare say I looked as fierce and resolute as he. I moved to the bell, and put my hand upon the cord. This tamed him still more. With a half-authoritative half-deprecating wave of the hand, he sought to deter me from ringing.

'Stand off, then!' said I – he stepped back – 'And listen to me. – I don't like you,' I continued, as deliberately and emphatically as I could, to give the greater efficacy to my words; 'and if I were divorced from my husband – or if he were dead, I would not marry you. There now! I hope you're satisfied.'

His face grew blanched with anger.

'I am satisfied,' he replied, with bitter emphasis, 'that you are the most cold-hearted, unnatural, ungrateful woman I ever yet beheld!'

'Ungrateful, sir?'

'Ungrateful.'

'No, Mr Hargrave; I am not. For all the good you ever did me, or ever wished to do, I most sincerely thank you: for all the evil you have done me, and all you would have done, I pray God to pardon you, and make you of a better mind.'

Here the door was thrown open, and Messrs. Huntingdon and Hattersley appeared without. The latter remained in the hall, busy with his ramrod and his gun; the former walked in, and stood with his back to the fire, surveying Mr Hargrave and me, particularly the former, with a smile of insupportable meaning, accompanied as it was by the impudence of his brazen brow, and the sly, malicious twinkle of his eye.

'Well, sir?' said Hargrave interrogatively, and with the air of one prepared to stand on the defensive.

'Well, sir,' returned his host.

'We want to know if you're at liberty to join us in a go at the pheasant, Walter,' interposed Hattersley from without. 'Come! there shall be nothing shot besides, except a puss or two; I'll vouch for that.'

Walter did not answer, but walked to the window to collect his faculties. Arthur uttered a low whistle, and followed him with his eyes. A slight flush of anger rose to Hargrave's cheek; but in a moment, he turned calmly round, and said carelessly—

# The Tenant of Wildfell Hall

'I came here to bid farewell to Mrs Huntingdon, and tell her I must go tomorrow.'

'Humph! You're mighty sudden in your resolution. What takes you off so soon, may I ask?'

'Business,' returned he, repelling the other's incredulous sneer with a glance of scornful defiance.

'Very good,' was the reply; and Hargrave walked away. Thereupon, Mr Huntingdon, gathering his coat-laps under his arms, and setting his shoulder against the mantelpiece, turned to me, and, addressing me in a low voice, scarcely above his breath, poured forth a volley of the vilest and grossest abuse it was possible for the imagination to conceive or the tongue to utter. I did not attempt to interrupt him; but my spirit kindled within me, and when he had done I replied—

'If your accusation were true, Mr Huntingdon, how dare you blame me?'

'She's hit it, by Jove!' cried Hattersley, rearing his gun against the wall; and stepping into the room, he took his precious friend by the arm, and attempted to drag him away. 'Come, my lad,' he muttered; 'true or false, you've no right to blame her, you know – nor him either, after what you said last night. So come along.'

There was something implied here that I could not endure.

'Dare you suspect me, Mr Hattersley?' said I, almost beside myself with fury.

'Nay, nay, I suspect nobody. It's all right – it's all right. So come along, Huntingdon, you blackguard.'

'She can't deny it!' cried the gentleman thus addressed, grinning in mingled rage and triumph. 'She can't deny it if her life depended on it!' and muttering some more abusive language, he walked into the hall, and took up his hat and gun from the table.

'I scorn to justify myself to you!' said I. 'But you,' turning to Hattersley, 'if you presume to have any doubts on the subject, ask Mr Hargrave.'

At this, they simultaneously burst into a rude laugh that made my whole frame tingle to the fingers' ends.

'Where is he? I'll ask him myself!' said I, advancing towards them.

Suppressing a new burst of merriment, Hattersley pointed to the outer door. It was half open. His brother-in-law was standing on the front without.

'Mr Hargrave, will you please to step this way?' said I.

He turned and looked at me in grave surprise.

'Step this way, if you please!' I repeated, in so determined a manner that he could not, or did not choose to resist its authority. Somewhat reluctantly he ascended the steps and advanced a pace or two into the hall.

'And tell those gentlemen, ' I continued – 'these men, whether or not I yielded to your solicitations.'

'I don't understand you, Mrs Huntingdon.'

'You do understand me, sir; I charge you upon your honour as a gentleman (if you have any), to answer truly. Did I, or did I not?'

'No,' muttered he, turning away.

'Speak up, sir; they can't hear you. Did I grant your request?'

'You did not.'

'No, I'll be sworn she didn't,' said Hattersley, 'or he'd never look so black.'

'I'm willing to grant you the satisfaction of a gentleman, Huntingdon,' said

Mr Hargrave, calmly addressing his host, but with a bitter sneer upon his countenance.

'Go to the deuce!' replied the latter, with an impatient jerk of the head. Hargrave withdrew with a look of cold disdain, saying—

'You know where to find me, should you feel disposed to send a friend.'

Muttered oaths and curses were all the answer this intimation obtained.

'Now, Huntingdon, you see!' said Hattersley, 'clear as the day.'

'I don't care what he sees,' said I, 'or what he imagines; but you, Mr Hattersley, when you hear my name belied and slandered, will you defend it?'

'I will.'

I instantly departed, and shut myself into the library. What could possess me to make such a request of such a man? I cannot tell, but drowning men catch at straws: they had driven me desperate between them; I hardly knew what I said. There was no other to preserve my name from being blackened and aspersed among this nest of boon companions, and through them, perhaps, into the world; and beside my abandoned wretch of a husband, the base, malignant Grimsby, and the false villain Hargrave, this boorish ruffian, coarse and brutal as he was, shone like a glow-worm in the dark, among its fellow-worms.

What a scene was this! Could I ever have imagined that I should be doomed to bear such insults under my own roof – to hear such things spoken in my presence – nay, spoken to me and of me – and by those who arrogated to themselves the name of gentlemen? And could I have imagined that I should have been able to endure it as calmly, and to repel their insults as firmly and as boldly as I had done? A hardness such as this, is taught by rough experience and despair alone.

Such thoughts as these chased one another through my mind, as I paced to and fro the room, and longed – oh, how I longed – to take my child and leave them now, without an hour's delay! But it could not be; there was work before me – hard work, that must be done.

'Then let me do it,' said I, 'and lose not a moment in vain repinings, and idle chafings against my fate, and those who influence it.'

And conquering my agitation with a powerful effort, I immediately resumed my task, and laboured hard all day.

Mr Hargrave did depart on the morrow; and I have never seen him since. The others stayed on for two or three weeks longer; but I kept aloof from them as much as possible, and still continued my labour, and have continued it, with almost unabated ardour, to the present day. I soon acquainted Rachel with my design, confiding all my motives and intentions to her ear, and, much to my agreeable surprise, found little difficulty in persuading her to enter into my views. She is a sober, cautious woman, but she so hates her master, and so loves her mistress and her nursling, that after several ejaculations, a few faint objections, and many tears and lamentations that I should be brought to such a pass, she applauded my resolution and consented to aid me with all her might – on one condition only – that she might share my exile: otherwise, she was utterly inexorable, regarding it as perfect madness for me and Arthur to go alone. With touching generosity, she modestly offered to aid me with her little hoard of savings, hoping I would 'excuse her for the liberty, but really, if I would do her the favour to accept it as a loan, she would be very happy.' Of course I could not think of such a thing; – but now, thank heaven, I have

gathered a little hoard of my own, and my preparations are so far advanced, that I am looking forward to a speedy emancipation. Only let the stormy severity of this winter weather be somewhat abated, and then, some morning, Mr Huntingdon will come down to a solitary breakfast-table, and perhaps be clamouring through the house for his invisible wife and child, when they are some fifty miles on their way to the western world – or it may be more, for we shall leave him hours before the dawn, and it is not probable he will discover the loss of both, until the day is far advanced.

I am fully alive to the evils that may and must result upon the step I am about to take; but I never waver in my resolution, because I never forget my son. It was only this morning – while I pursued my usual employment, he was sitting at my feet quietly playing with the shreds of canvas I had thrown upon the carpet – but his mind was otherwise occupied, for, in a while, he looked up wistfully in my face, and gravely asked—

'Mamma, why are you wicked?'

'Who told you I was wicked, love?'

'Rachel.'

'No, Arthur, Rachel never said so, I am certain.'

'Well, then, it was papa,' replied he thoughtfully. Then, after a reflective pause, he added, 'At least I'll tell you how it was I got to know: when I'm with papa, if I say mamma wants me, or mamma says I'm not to do something that he tells me to do – he always says, "Mamma be damned," – and Rachel says it's only wicked people that are damned. So, mamma, that's why I think you must be wicked – and I wish you wouldn't.'

'My dear child, I am not. Those are bad words, and wicked people often say them of others better than themselves. Those words cannot make people be damned, nor show that they deserve it. God will judge us by our own thoughts and deeds, not by what others say about us. And when you hear such words spoken, Arthur, remember never to repeat them: it is wicked to say such things of others, not to have them said against you.'

'Then it's papa that's wicked,' said he ruefully.

'Papa is wrong to say such things, and you will be very wrong to imitate him now that you know better.'

'What is imitate?'

'To do as he does.'

'Does he know better?'

'Perhaps he does; but that is nothing to you.'

'If he doesn't, you ought to tell him, mamma.'

'I have told him.'

The little moralist paused and pondered. I tried in vain to divert his mind from the subject.

'I'm sorry papa's wicked,' said he mournfully, at length, 'for I don't want him to go to hell.' And so saying he burst into tears.

I consoled him with the hope that perhaps his papa would alter and become good before he died – but is it not time to deliver him from such a parent?

# Chapter 40

*January 10th, 1827*

hile writing the above, yesterday evening, I sat in the drawing-room. Mr Huntingdon was present, but, as I thought, asleep on the sofa behind me. He had risen, however, unknown to me, and, actuated by some base spirit of curiosity, been looking over my shoulder for I know not how long; for when I had laid aside my pen, and was about to close the book, he suddenly placed his hand upon it, and saying – 'With your leave, my dear, I'll have a look at this,' forcibly wrested it from me, and, drawing a chair to the table, composedly sat down to examine it – turning back leaf after leaf to find an explanation of what he had read. Unluckily for me, he was more sober that night than he usually is at such an hour.

Of course I did not leave him to pursue this occupation in quiet: I made several attempts to snatch the book from his hands, but he held it too firmly for that; I upbraided him in bitterness and scorn for his mean and dishonourable conduct, but that had no effect upon him; and finally, I extinguished both the candles, but he only wheeled round to the fire, and raising a blaze sufficient for his purposes, calmly continued the investigation. I had serious thoughts of getting a pitcher of water and extinguishing that light too; but it was evident his curiosity was too keenly excited to be quenched by that, and the more I manifested my anxiety to baffle his scrutiny, the greater would be his determination to persist in it – besides, it was too late.

'It seems very interesting, love,' said he, lifting his head and turning to where I stood wringing my hands in silent rage and anguish; 'but it's rather long; I'll look at it some other time; – and meanwhile, I'll trouble you for your keys, my dear.'

'What keys?'

'The keys of your cabinet, desk, drawers, and whatever else you possess,' said he, rising and holding out his hand.

'I've not got them,' I replied. The key of my desk, in fact, was, at that moment, in the lock, and the others were attached to it.

'Then you must send for them,' said he; 'and if that old devil, Rachel, doesn't immediately deliver them up, she tramps bag and baggage tomorrow.'

'She doesn't know where they are,' I answered, quietly placing my hand upon them, and taking them from the desk, as I thought, unobserved. 'I know, but I shall not give them up without a reason.'

'And I know, too,' said he, suddenly seizing my closed hand and rudely abstracting them from it. He then took up one of the candles and relighted it by

431

thrusting it into the fire. 'Now, then,' sneered he, 'we must have a confiscation of property. But, first, let us take a peep into the studio.'

And putting the keys into his pocket, he walked into the library. I followed, whether with the dim idea of preventing mischief, or only to know the worst, I can hardly tell. My painting materials were laid together on the corner table, ready for tomorrow's use, and only covered with a cloth. He soon spied them out, and putting down the candle, deliberately proceeded to cast them into the fire – palette, paints, bladders, pencils, brushes, varnish – I saw them all consumed – the palette-knives snapped in two – the oil and turpentine sent hissing and roaring up the chimney. He then rang the bell.

'Benson, take those things away,' said he, pointing to the easel, canvas, and stretcher; 'and tell the housemaid she may kindle the fire with them: your mistress won't want them any more.'

Benson paused aghast and looked at me.

'Take them away, Benson,' said I; and his master muttered an oath.

'And this and all, sir?' said the astonished servant, referring to the half-finished picture.

'That and all,' replied the master; and the things were cleared away.

Mr Huntingdon then went upstairs. I did not attempt to follow him, but remained seated in the armchair, speechless, tearless, and almost motionless, till he returned about half-an-hour after, and walking up to me, held the candle in my face and peered into my eyes with looks and laughter too insulting to be borne. With a sudden stroke of my hand, I dashed the candle to the floor.

'Hal-lo!' muttered he, starting back – 'She's the very devil for spite! Did ever any mortal see such eyes? – they shine in the dark like a cat's. Oh, you're a sweet one!' – so saying, he gathered up the candle and the candlestick. The former being broken as well as extinguished, he rang for another.

'Benson, your mistress has broken the candle; bring another.'

'You expose yourself finely,' observed I as the man departed.

'I didn't say I'd broken it, did I?' returned he. He then threw my keys into my lap, saying, – 'There! you'll find nothing gone but your money, and the jewels – and a few little trifles I thought it advisable to take into my own possession, lest your mercantile spirit should be tempted to turn them into gold. I've left you a few sovereigns in your purse, which I expect to last you through the month – at all events, when you want more you will be so good as to give me an account of how that's spent. I shall put you upon a small monthly allowance, in future, for your own private expenses; and you needn't trouble yourself any more about my concerns; I shall look out for a steward, my dear; I won't expose you to the temptation. And as for the household matters, Mrs Greaves must be very particular in keeping her accounts: we must go upon an entirely new plan'—

'What great discovery have you made now, Mr Huntingdon? Have I attempted to defraud you?'

'Not in money matters, exactly, it seems, but it's best to keep out of the way of temptation.'

Here Benson entered with the candles, and there followed a brief interval of silence; I sitting still in my chair, and he standing with his back to the fire, silently triumphing in my despair.

'And so,' said he at length, 'you thought to disgrace me, did you, by running

away and turning artist, and supporting yourself by the labour of your hands, forsooth? And you thought to rob me of my son too, and bring him up to be a dirty Yankee tradesman, or a low, beggarly painter?'

'Yes, to obviate his becoming such a gentleman as his father.'

'It's well you couldn't keep your own secret – ha, ha! It's well these women must be blabbing – if they haven't a friend to talk to, they must whisper their secrets to the fishes, or write them on the sand, or something; and it's well too I wasn't over full tonight, now I think of it, or I might have snoozed away and never dreamt of looking what my sweet lady was about – or I might have lacked the sense or the power to carry my point like a man as I have done.'

Leaving him to his self-congratulations, I rose to secure my manuscript, for I now remembered it had been left upon the drawing-room table, and I determined, if possible, to save myself the humiliation of seeing it in his hands again. I could not bear the idea of his amusing himself over my secret thoughts and recollections; though, to be sure, he would find little good of himself therein indited, except in the former part – and oh, I would sooner burn it all than he should read what I had written when I was such a fool as to love him!

'And by-the-bye,' cried he as I was leaving the room, 'you'd better tell that d—d old sneak of a nurse to keep out of my way for a day or two – I'd pay her her wages and send her packing to-morrow, but I know she'd do more mischief out of the house than in it.'

And as I departed, he went on cursing and abusing my faithful friend and servant with epithets I will not defile this paper with repeating. I went to her as soon as I had put away my book, and told her how our project was defeated. She was as much distressed and horrified as I was – and more so than I was that night, for I was partly stunned by the blow, and partly excited and supported against it by the bitterness of my wrath. But in the morning, when I woke without that cheering hope that had been my secret comfort and support so long, and all this day, when I have wandered about restless and objectless, shunning my husband, shrinking even from my child – knowing that I am unfit to be his teacher or companion, hoping nothing for his future life, and fervently wishing he had never been born – I felt the full extent of my calamity – and I feel it now. I know that day after day such feelings will return upon me: I am a slave – a prisoner – but that is nothing; if it were myself only, I would not complain, but I am forbidden to rescue my son from ruin, and what was once my only consolation, is become the crowning source of my despair.

Have I no faith in God? I try to look to Him and raise my heart to heaven, but it will cleave to the dust: I can only say – 'He hath hedged me about, that I cannot get out: He hath made my chain heavy. He hath filled me with bitterness, He hath made me drunken with wormwood': – I forget to add – 'But though He cause grief, yet will He have compassion according to the multitude of His mercies. For He doth not afflict willingly nor grieve the children of men.' I ought to think of this; and if there be nothing but sorrow for me in this world, what is the longest life of misery to a whole eternity of peace? And for my little Arthur – has he no friend but me? Who was it said, 'It is not the will of your Father which is in heaven that one of these little ones should perish'?

# Chapter 41

## *March 20th*

Having now got rid of Mr Huntingdon for a season, my spirits begin to revive. He left me early in February; and the moment he was gone, I breathed again, and felt my vital energy return; not with the hope of escape – he has taken care to leave me no visible chance of that – but with a determination to make the best of existing circumstances. Here was Arthur left to me at last; and rousing from my despondent apathy, I exerted all my powers to eradicate the weeds that had been fostered in his infant mind, and sow again the good seed they had rendered unproductive. Thank heaven, it is not a barren or a stony soil; if weeds spring fast there, so do better plants. His apprehensions are more quick, his heart more overflowing with affection than ever his father's could have been; and it is no hopeless task to bend him to obedience and win him to love and know his own true friend, as long as there is no one to counteract my efforts.

I had much trouble at first in breaking him off those evil habits his father had taught him to acquire, but already that difficulty is nearly vanquished now: bad language seldom defiles his mouth, and I have succeeded in giving him an absolute disgust of all intoxicating liquors, which I hope not even his father or his father's friends will be able to overcome. He was inordinately fond of them for so young a creature, and, remembering my unfortunate father as well as his, I dreaded the consequences of such taste. But if I had stinted him in his usual quantity of wine, or forbidden him to taste it altogether, that would only have increased his partiality for it, and made him regard it as a greater treat than ever. I therefore gave him quite as much as his father was accustomed to allow him – as much, indeed, as he desired to have, but into every glass I surreptitiously introduced a small quantity of tartar-emetic – just enough to produce inevitable nausea and depression without positive sickness. Finding such disagreeable consequences invariably to result from this indulgence, he soon grew weary of it, but the more he shrank from the daily treat, the more I pressed it upon him, till his reluctance was strengthened to perfect abhorrence. When he was thoroughly disgusted with every kind of wine, I allowed him, at his own request, to try brandy and water, and then gin and water; for the little toper was familiar with them all, and I was determined that all should be equally hateful to him. This I have now effected; and since he declares that the taste, the smell, the sight of any one of them is sufficient to make him sick, I have given up teasing him about them, except now and then as objects of terror in cases of misbehaviour: 'Arthur, if you're not a good boy I shall give you a glass of wine,' or, 'Now, Arthur, if you say that again you shall have some brandy and water,' is as good

as any other threat; and, once or twice, when he was sick, I have obliged the poor child to swallow a little wine and water without the tartar-emetic, by way of medicine; and this practice I intend to continue for some time to come; not that I think it of any real service in a physical sense, but because I am determined to enlist all the powers of association in my service: I wish this aversion to be so deeply grounded in his nature that nothing in after life may be able to overcome it.

Thus, I flatter myself I shall secure him from this one vice; and for the rest, if on his father's return I find reason to apprehend that my good lessons will be all destroyed – if Mr Huntingdon commence again the game of teaching the child to hate and despise his mother and emulate his father's wickedness, I will yet deliver my son from his hands. I have devised another scheme that might be resorted to in such a case, and if I could but obtain my brother's consent and assistance, I should not doubt of its success. The old Hall where he and I were born, and where our mother died, is not now inhabited, nor yet quite sunk into decay, as I believe. Now if I could persuade him to have one or two rooms made habitable, and to let them to me as a stranger, I might live there, with my child, under an assumed name, and still support myself by my favourite art. He should lend me the money to begin with, and I would pay him back and live in lowly independence and strict seclusion, for the house stands in a lonely place, and the neighbourhood is thinly inhabited, and he himself should negotiate the sale of my pictures for me. I have arranged the whole plan in my head; and all I want, is to persuade Frederick to be of the same mind as myself. He is coming to see me soon, and then I will make the proposal to him, having first enlightened him upon my circumstances sufficiently to excuse the project.

Already, I believe, he knows much more of my situation than I have told him. I can tell this by the air of tender sadness pervading his letters; and by the fact of his so seldom mentioning my husband, and generally evincing a kind of covert bitterness when he does refer to him; as well as by the circumstance of his never coming to see me when Mr Huntingdon is at home. But he has never openly expressed any disapprobation of him or sympathy for me; he has never asked any questions, or said anything to invite my confidence. Had he done so, I should probably have had but few concealments from him. Perhaps he feels hurt at my reserve. He is a strange being – I wish we knew each other better. He used to spend a month at Staningley every year, before I was married; but, since our father's death, I have only seen him once, when he came for a few days while Mr Huntingdon was away. He shall stay many days this time, and there shall be more candour and cordiality between us than ever there was before, since our early childhood: my heart clings to him more than ever; and my soul is sick of solitude.

*April 16th* – He is come and gone. He would not stay above a fortnight. The time passed quicky, but very, very happily, and it has done me good. I must have a bad disposition, for my misfortunes have soured and embittered me exceedingly: I was beginning insensibly to cherish very unamiable feelings against my fellow-mortals – the male part of them especially; but it is a comfort to see there is at least one among them worthy to be trusted and esteemed; and doubtless there are more, though I have never known them – unless I except poor Lord Lowborough, and he was bad enough in his day; but what would Frederick have been, if he had lived in the world, and mingled from his childhood

with such men as these of my acquaintance? and what will Arthur be, with all his natural sweetness of disposition, if I do not save him from that world and those companions? I mentioned my fears to Frederick, and introduced the subject of my plan of rescue on the evening after his arrival, when I presented my little son to his uncle.

'He is like you, Frederick,' said I, 'in some of his moods I sometimes think he resembles you more than his father; and I am glad of it.'

'You flatter me, Helen,' replied he, stroking the child's soft, wavy locks.

'No, – will you think it no compliment when I tell you I would rather have him to resemble Benson than his father.'

He slightly elevated his eyebrows, but said nothing.

'Do you know what sort of man Mr Huntingdon is?' said I.

'I think I have an idea.'

'Have you so clear an idea that you can hear, without surprise or disapproval, that I meditate escaping with that child to some secret asylum where we can live in peace and never see him again?'

'Is it really so?'

'If you have not,' continued I, 'I'll tell you something more about him,' – and I gave a sketch of his general conduct, and a more particular account of his behaviour with regard to his child, and explained my apprehensions on the latter's account, and my determination to deliver him from his father's influence.

Frederick was exceedingly indignant against Mr Huntingdon, and very much grieved for me; but still he looked upon my project as wild and impracticable; he deemed my fears for Arthur disproportioned to the circumstances, and opposed so many objections to my plans, and devised so many milder methods for ameliorating my condition, that I was obliged to enter into further details to convince him that my husband was utterly incorrigible, and that nothing could persuade him to give up his son, whatever became of me, he being as fully determined the child should not leave him, as I was not to leave the child; and that, in fact, nothing would answer but this, unless I fled the country, as I had intended before. To obviate that, he at length consented to have one wing of the old Hall put into a habitable condition, as a place of refuge against a time of need; but hoped I would not take advantage of it, unless circumstances should render it really necessary, which I was ready enough to promise; for though, for my own sake, such a hermitage appears like paradise itself, compared with my present situation, yet for my friends' sakes – for Milicent and Esther, my sisters in heart and affection, for the poor tenants of Grassdale, and above all for my aunt – I will stay if I possibly can.

*July 29th* – Mrs Hargrave and her daughter are come back from London. Esther is full of her first season in town; but she is still heart-whole and unengaged. Her mother sought out an excellent match for her, and even brought the gentleman to lay his heart and fortune at her feet; but Esther had the audacity to refuse the noble gifts. He was a man of good family and large possessions, but the naughty girl maintained he was as old as Adam, ugly as sin, and hateful as – one who shall be nameless.

'But, indeed, I had a hard time of it,' said she: 'mamma was very greatly disappointed at the failure of her darling project, and very, very angry at my obstinate resistance to her will, and is so still; but I can't help it. And Walter, too, is so seriously displeased at my perversity and absurd caprice, as he calls

it, that I fear he will never forgive me – I did not think he could be so unkind as he has lately shown himself. But Milicent begged me not to yield, and I'm sure, Mrs Huntingdon, if you had seen the man they wanted to palm upon me, you would have advised me not to take him too.'

'I should have done so whether I had seen him or not,' said I. 'It is enough that you dislike him.'

'I knew you would say so; though mamma affirmed you would be quite shocked at my undutiful conduct – you can't imagine how she lectures me – I am disobedient and ungrateful; I am thwarting her wishes, wronging my brother, and making myself a burden on her hands – I sometimes fear she'll overcome me after all. I have a strong will, but so has she, and when she says such bitter things, it provokes me to such a pass that I feel inclined to do as she bids me, and then break my heart and say, "There, mamma, it's all your fault!"'

'Pray don't!' said I. 'Obedience from such a motive would be positive wickedness, and certain to bring the punishment it deserves. Stand firm, and your mamma will soon relinquish her persecution; – and the gentleman himself will cease to pester you with his addresses if he finds them steadily rejected.'

'Oh, no! mamma will weary all about her before she tires herself with her exertions; and as for Mr Oldfield, she has given him to understand that I have refused his offer, not from any dislike of his person, but merely because I am giddy and young, and cannot at present reconcile myself to the thoughts of marriage under any circumstances: but, by next season, she has no doubt, I shall have more sense, and hopes my girlish fancies will be worn away. So she has brought me home, to school me into a proper sense of my duty, against the time comes round again – indeed, I believe she will not put herself to the expense of taking me up to London again, unless I surrender: she cannot afford to take me to town for pleasure and nonsense, she says, and it is not every rich gentleman that will consent to take me without a fortune, whatever exalted ideas I may have of my own attractions.'

'Well, Esther, I pity you; but still, I repeat, stand firm. You might as well sell yourself to slavery at once, as marry a man you dislike. If your mother and brother are unkind to you, you may leave them, but remember you are bound to your husband for life.'

'But I cannot leave them unless I get married, and I cannot get married if nobody sees me. I saw one or two gentlemen in London that I might have liked, but they were younger sons, and mamma would not let me get to know them – one especially, who I believe rather liked me, but she threw every possible obstacle in the way of our better acquaintance – wasn't it provoking?'

'I have no doubt you would feel it so, but it is possible that if you married him, you might have more reason to regret it hereafter, than if you married Mr Oldfield. When I tell you not to marry without love, I do not advise you to marry for love alone – there are many, many other things to be considered. Keep both heart and hand in your own possession, till you see good reason to part with them; and if such an occasion should never present itself, comfort your mind with this reflection – that, though in single life your joys may not be very many, your sorrows, at least, will not be more than you can bear. Marriage may change your circumstances for the better, but in my private opinion, it is far more likely to produce a contrary result.'

'So thinks Milicent; but allow me to say, I think otherwise. If I thought myself

doomed to old maidenhood, I should cease to value my life. The thoughts of living on, year after year, at the Grove – a hanger-on upon mamma and Walter – a mere cumberer of the ground (now that I know in what light they would regard it), is perfectly intolerable – I would rather run away with the butler.'

'Your circumstances are peculiar, I allow; but have patience, love; do nothing rashly. Remember you are not yet nineteen, and many years are yet to pass before any one can set you down as an old maid: you cannot tell what providence may have in store for you. And meantime, remember you have a right to the protection and support of your mother and brother, however they may seem to grudge it.'

'You are so grave, Mrs Huntingdon,' said Esther, after a pause. 'When Milicent uttered the same discouraging sentiments concerning marriage, I asked if she was happy; she said she was; but I only half believed her; and now I must put the same question to you.'

'It is a very impertinent question,' laughed I, 'from a young girl to a married woman so many years her senior – and I shall not answer it.'

'Pardon me, dear madam,' said she, laughingly throwing herself into my arms, and kissing me with playful affection; but I felt a tear on my neck, as she dropped her head on my bosom and continued, with an odd mixture of sadness and levity, timidity and audacity – 'I know you are not so happy as I mean to be, for you spend half your life alone at Grassdale, while Mr Huntingdon goes about enjoying himself where and how he pleases – I shall expect my husband to have no pleasure but what he shares with me; and if his greatest pleasure of all is not the enjoyment of my company – why – it will be the worse for him – that's all.'

'If such are your expectations of matrimony, Esther, you must, indeed, be careful whom you marry – or rather, you must avoid it altogether.'

# Chapter 42

*September 1st*

No Mr Huntingdon yet. Perhaps he will stay among his friends till Christmas; and then, next spring, he will be off again. If he continue this plan, I shall be able to stay at Grassdale well enough – that is, I shall be able to stay, and that is enough; even an occasional bevy of friends at the shooting season may be borne, if Arthur gets so firmly attached to me, so well established in good sense and principles before they come, that I shall be able, by reason and affection, to keep him pure from their contaminations. Vain hope, I fear! but still, till such a time of trial comes, I will forbear to think of my quiet asylum in the beloved old Hall.

Mr and Mrs Hattersley have been staying at the Grove a fortnight; and as

# The Tenant of Wildfell Hall

Mr Hargrave is still absent, and the weather was remarkably fine, I never passed a day without seeing my two friends, Milicent and Esther, either there or here. On one occasion, when Mr Hattersley had driven them over to Grassdale in the phaeton, with little Helen and Ralph, and we were all enjoying ourselves in the garden – I had a few minutes' conversation with that gentleman, while the ladies were amusing themselves with the children.

'Do you want to hear anything of your husband, Mrs Huntingdon?' said he.

'No, unless you can tell me when to expect him home.'

'I can't. – You don't want him, do you?' said he, with a broad grin.

'No.'

'Well, I think you're better without him, sure enough – for my part, I'm downright weary of him. I told him I'd leave him if he didn't mend his manners – and he wouldn't; so I left him – you see I'm a better man than you think me; and, what's more, I have serious thoughts of washing my hands of him entirely, and the whole set of 'em, and comporting myself from this day forward, with all decency and sobriety, as a Christian and the father of a family should do. What do you think of that?'

'It is a resolution you ought to have formed long ago.'

'Well, I'm not thirty yet; it isn't too late, is it?'

'No; it is never too late to reform, as long as you have the sense to desire it, and the strength to execute your purpose.'

'Well, to tell you the truth, I've thought of it often and often before, but he's such devilish good company is Huntingdon, after all – you can't imagine what a jovial good fellow he is when he's not fairly drunk, only just primed or half seas over – we all have a bit of a liking for him at the bottom of our hearts, though we can't respect him.'

'But should you wish yourself to be like him?'

'No, I'd rather be like myself, bad as I am.'

'You can't continue as bad as you are without getting worse, and more brutalized every day – and therefore more like him.'

I could not help smiling at the comical, half-angry half-confounded look he put on at this rather unusual mode of address.

'Never mind my plain speaking,' said I; 'it is from the best motives. But, tell me, should you wish your sons to be like Mr Huntingdon – even like yourself?'

'Hang it, no.'

'Should you wish your daughter to despise you – or, at least, to feel no vestige of respect for you, and no affection but what is mingled with the bitterest regret.'

'Oh, no! I couldn't stand that.'

'And finally, should you wish your wife to be ready to sink into the earth when she hears you mentioned; and to loathe the very sound of your voice, and shudder at your approach?'

'She never will; she likes me all the same, whatever I do.'

'Impossible, Mr Hattersley! you mistake her quiet submission for affection.'

'Fire and fury'—

'Now don't burst into a tempest at that – I don't mean to say she does not love you – she does, I know, a great deal better than you deserve; but I am quite sure, that if you behave better, she will love you more, and if you behave worse, she will love you less and less, till all is lost in fear, aversion, and bitterness of soul, if not in secret hatred and contempt. But, dropping the subject of affection,

should you wish to be the tyrant of her life – to take away all the sunshine from her existence, and make her thoroughly miserable?'

'Of course not; and I don't, and I'm not going to.'

'You have done more towards it than you suppose.'

'Pooh, pooh! she's not the susceptible, anxious, worriting creature you imagine: she's a little meek, peaceable, affectionate body; apt to be rather sulky at times, but quiet and cool in the main, and ready to take things as they come.'

'Think of what she was five years ago, when you married her, and what she is now.'

'I know – she was a little plump lassie then, with a pretty pink and white face: now she's a poor little bit of a creature, fading and melting away like a snow-wreath – but hang it! – that's not my fault.'

'What is the cause of it then? Not years, for she's only five-and-twenty.'

'It's her own delicate health, and – confound it, madam! what would you make of me? – and the children, to be sure, that worry her to death between them.'

'No, Mr Hattersley, the children give her more pleasure than pain: they are fine, well-dispositioned children'—

'I know they are – bless them!'

'Then why lay the blame on them? – I'll tell you what it is: it's silent fretting and constant anxiety on your account, mingled, I suspect, with something of bodily fear on her own. When you behave well, she can only rejoice with trembling; she has no security, no confidence in your judgments or principles; but is continually dreading the close of such short-lived felicity; when you behave ill, her causes of terror and misery are more than any one can tell but herself. In patient endurance of evil, she forgets it is our duty to admonish our neighbours of their transgressions. Since you will mistake her silence for indifference, come with me, and I'll show you one or two of her letters – no breach of confidence, I hope, since you are her other half.'

He followed me into the library. I sought out and put into his hands two of Milicent's letters; one dated from London, and written during one of his wildest seasons of reckless dissipation; the other in the country during a lucid interval. The former was full of trouble and anguish; not accusing him, but deeply regretting his connection with his profligate companions, abusing Mr Grimsby and others, insinuating bitter things against Mr Huntingdon, and most ingeniously throwing the blame of her husband's misconduct on to other men's shoulders. The latter was full of hope and joy, yet with a trembling consciousness that this happiness would not last; praising his goodness to the skies, but with an evident, though but half-expressed wish, that it were based on a surer foundation than the natural impulses of the heart, and a half-prophetic dread of the fall of that house so founded on the sand, – which fall had shortly after taken place, as Hattersley must have been conscious while he read.

Almost at the commencement of the first letter I had the unexpected pleasure of seeing him blush; but he immediately turned his back to me, and finished the perusal at the window. At the second, I saw him, once or twice, raise his hand, and hurriedly pass it across his face. Could it be to dash away a tear? When he had done, there was an interval spent in clearing his throat, and staring out of the window, and then, after whistling a few bars of a favourite air, he turned round, gave me back the letters, and silently shook me by the hand.

'I've been a cursed rascal, God knows,' said he, as he gave it a hearty squeeze, 'but you see if I don't make amends for it – d—n me, if I don't!'

'Don't curse yourself, Mr Hattersley; if God had heard half your invocations of that kind, you would have been in hell long before now – and you cannot make amends for the past by doing your duty for the future, inasmuch as your duty is only what you owe to your Maker, and you cannot do more than fulfil it – another must make amends for your past delinquencies. If you intend to reform, invoke God's blessing, His mercy, and His aid; not His curse.'

'God help me, then – for I'm sure I need it – Where's Milicent?'

'She's there, just coming in with her sister.'

He stepped out at the glass door, and went to meet them. I followed at a little distance. Somewhat to his wife's astonishment, he lifted her off from the ground, and saluted her with a hearty kiss and a strong embrace; then, placing his two hands on her shoulders, he gave her, I suppose, a sketch of the great things he meant to do, for she suddenly threw her arms round him, and burst into tears, exclaiming—

'Do, do, Ralph – we shall be so happy! How very, very good you are!'

'Nay, not I,' said he, turning her round, and pushing her towards me. 'Thank her; it's her doing.'

Milicent flew to thank me, overflowing with gratitude. I disclaimed all title to it, telling her her husband was predisposed to amendment before I added my mite of exhortation and encouragement, and that I had only done what she might – and ought to – have done herself.

'Oh, no!' cried she, 'I couldn't have influenced him, I'm sure, by anything that I could have said. I should only have bothered him by my clumsy efforts at persuasion, if I had made the attempt.'

'You never tried me, Milly,' said he.

Shortly after, they took their leave. They are now gone on a visit to Hattersley's father. After that, they will repair to their country home. I hope his good resolutions will not fall through, and poor Milicent will not be again disappointed. Her last letter was full of present bliss, and pleasing anticipations for the future; but no particular temptation has yet occurred to put his virtue to the test. Henceforth, however, she will doubtless be somewhat less timid and reserved, and he more kind and thoughtful. – Surely, then, her hopes are not unfounded; and I have one bright spot, at least, whereon to rest my thoughts.

# Chapter 43

*October 10th*

**M**r Huntingdon returned about three weeks ago. His appearance, his demeanour and conversation, and my feelings with regard to him, I shall not trouble myself to describe. The day after his arrival, however, he surprised me by the announcement of an intention to procure a governess for little Arthur: I told him it was quite unnecessary, not to say ridiculous, at the present season: I thought I was fully competent to the task of teaching him myself – for some years to come, at least the child's education was the only pleasure and business of my life; and since he had deprived me of every other occupation, he might surely leave me that.

He said I was not fit to teach children, or to be with them: I had already reduced the boy to little better than an automaton, I had broken his fine spirit with my rigid severity; and I should freeze all the sunshine out of his heart, and make him as gloomy an ascetic as myself, if I had the handling of him much longer. And poor Rachel, too, came in for her share of abuse, as usual; he cannot endure Rachel, because he knows she has a proper appreciation of him.

I calmly defended our several qualifications as nurse and governess, and still resisted the proposed addition to our family; but he cut me short by saying, it was no use bothering about the matter, for he had engaged a governess already, and she was coming next week; so that all I had to do was to get things ready for her reception. This was a rather startling piece of intelligence. I ventured to inquire her name and address, by whom she had been recommended, or how he had been led to make choice of her.

'She is a very estimable, pious young person,' said he; 'you needn't be afraid. Her name is Myers, I believe; and she was recommended to me by a respectable old dowager – a lady of high repute in the religious world. I have not seen her myself, and therefore cannot give you a particular account of her person and conversation, and so forth; but, if the old lady's eulogies are correct, you will find her to possess all desirable qualifications for her position – an inordinate love of children among the rest.'

All this was gravely and quietly spoken, but there was a laughing demon in his half-averted eye that boded no good I imagined. However, I thought of my asylum in —shire, and made no further objections.

When Miss Myers arrived, I was not prepared to give her a very cordial reception. Her appearance was not particularly calculated to produce a favourable impression at first sight, nor did her manners and subsequent conduct, in any degree, remove the prejudice I had already conceived against her. Her attainments were limited, her intellect no ways above mediocrity. She had a fine

voice, and could sing like a nightingale, and accompany herself sufficiently well on the piano; but these were her only accomplishments. There was a look of guile and subtlety in her face, a sound of it in her voice. She seemed afraid of me, and would start if I suddenly approached her. In her behaviour, she was respectful and complaisant, even to servility: she attempted to flatter and fawn upon me at first, but I soon checked that. Her fondness for her little pupil was overstrained, and I was obliged to remonstrate with her on the subject of over-indulgence and injudicious praise; but she could not gain his heart. Her piety consisted in an occasional heaving of sighs, and uplifting of eyes to the ceiling, and the utterance of a few cant phrases. She told me she was a clergyman's daughter, and had been left an orphan from her childhood, but had had the good fortune to obtain a situation in a very pious family; and then she spoke so gratefully of the kindness she had experienced from its different members, that I reproached myself for my uncharitable thoughts and unfriendly conduct, and relented for a time – but not for long; my causes of dislike were too rational, my suspicions too well founded for that; and I knew it was my duty to watch and scrutinize till those suspicions were either satisfactorily removed or confirmed.

I asked the name and residence of the kind and pious family. She mentioned a common name, and an unknown and distant place of abode, but told me they were now on the Continent, and their present address was unknown to her. I never saw her speak much to Mr Huntingdon; but he would frequently look into the schoolroom to see how little Arthur got on with his new companion, when I was not there. In the evening, she sat with us in the drawing-room, and would sing and play to amuse him – or us, as she pretended – and was very attentive to his wants, and watchful to anticipate them, though she only talked to me – indeed, he was seldom in a condition to be talked to. Had she been other than she was, I should have felt her presence a great relief to come between us thus, except, indeed, that I should have been thoroughly ashamed for any decent person to see him as he often was.

I did not mention my suspicions to Rachel; but she, having sojourned for half a century in this land of sin and sorrow, has learned to be suspicious herself. She told me from the first she was 'down of that new governess,' and I soon found she watched her quite as narrowly as I did; and I was glad of it, for I longed to know the truth; the atmosphere of Grassdale seemed to stifle me, and I could only live by thinking of Wildfell Hall.

At last, one morning, she entered my chamber with such intelligence that my resolution was taken before she had ceased to speak. While she dressed me I explained to her my intentions and what assistance I should require from her, and told her which of my things she was to pack up, and what she was to leave behind for herself, as I had no other means of recompensing her for this sudden dismissal after her long and faithful service – a circumstance I most deeply regretted, but could not avoid.

'And what will you do, Rachel?' said I; 'will you go home, or seek another place?'

'I have no home, ma'am, but with you,' she replied; 'and if I leave you I'll never go into place again as long as I live.'

'But I can't afford to live like a lady now,' returned I: 'I must be my own maid and my child's nurse.'

'What signifies?' replied she in some excitement. 'You'll want somebody to

clean and wash, and cook, won't you? I can do all that; and never mind the wages – I've my bits o' savings yet, and if you wouldn't take me I should have to find my own board and lodging out of 'em somewhere, or else work among strangers – and it's what I'm not used to – so you can please yourself, ma'am.' Her voice quavered as she spoke, and the tears stood in her eyes.

'I should like it above all things, Rachel, and I'd give you such wages as I could afford – such as I should give to any servant-of-all-work I might employ; but don't you see I should be dragging you down with me when you have done nothing to deserve it?'

'Oh, fiddle!' ejaculated she.

'And, besides, my future way of living will be so widely different to the past – so different to all you have been accustomed to'—

'Do you think, ma'am, I can't bear what my missis can? surely I'm not so proud and so dainty as that comes to – and my little master, too, God bless him!'

'But I'm young, Rachel; I shan't mind it; and Arthur is young too – it will be nothing to him.'

'Nor me either: I'm not so old but what I can stand hard fare and hard work, if it's only to help and comfort them as I've loved like my own bairns – for all I'm too old to bide the thoughts o' leaving 'em in trouble and danger, and going amongst strangers myself.'

'Then you shan't, Rachel!' cried I, embracing my faithful friend. 'We'll all go together, and you shall see how the new life suits you.'

'Bless you, honey!' cried she, affectionately returning my embrace. 'Only let us get shut of this wicked house, and we'll do right enough, you'll see.'

'So think I,' was my answer; and so that point was settled.

By that morning's post, I despatched a few hasty lines to Frederick, beseeching him to prepare my asylum for my immediate reception – for I should probably come to claim it within a day after the receipt of that note, – and telling him, in few words, the cause of my sudden resolution. I then wrote three letters of adieu: the first to Esther Hargrave, in which I told her that I found it impossible to stay any longer at Grassdale, or to leave my son under his father's protection; and, as it was of the last importance that our future abode should be unknown to him and his acquaintance, I should disclose it to no one but my brother, through the medium of whom I hoped still to correspond with my friends. I then gave her his address, exhorted her to write frequently, reiterated some of my former admonitions regarding her own concerns, and bade her a fond farewell.

The second was to Milicent; much to the same effect, but a little more confidential, as befitted our longer intimacy, and her greater experience and better acquaintance with my circumstances.

The third was to my aunt – a much more difficult and painful undertaking, and therefore I had left it to the last; but I must give her some explanation of that extraordinary step I had taken, – and that quickly, for she and my uncle would no doubt hear of it within a day or two after my disappearance, as it was probable that Mr Huntingdon would speedily apply to them to know what was become of me. At last, however, I told her I was sensible of my error: I did not complain of its punishment, and I was sorry to trouble my friends with its consequences; but in duty to my son, I must submit no longer; it was absolutely necessary that he should be delivered from his father's corrupting influence. I should not disclose my place of refuge even to her, in order that she and my

uncle might be able, with truth, to deny all knowledge concerning it; but any communications addressed to me under cover to my brother would be certain to reach me. I hoped she and my uncle would pardon the step I had taken, for if they knew all, I was sure they would not blame me; and I trusted they would not afflict themselves on my account, for if I could only reach my retreat in safety and keep it unmolested, I should be very happy, but for the thoughts of them; and should be quite contented to spend my life in obscurity, devoting myself to the training up of my child, and teaching him to avoid the errors of both his parents.

These things were done yesterday: I have given two whole days to the preparation for our departure, that Frederick may have more time to prepare the rooms, and Rachel to pack up the things – for the latter task must be done with the utmost caution and secrecy, and there is no one but me to assist her: I can help to get the articles together, but I do not understand the art of stowing them into the boxes, so as to take up the smallest possible space; and there are her own things to do, as well as mine and Arthur's. I can ill afford to leave anything behind, since I have no money, except a few guineas in my purse; – and besides, as Rachel observed, whatever I left would most likely become the property of Miss Myers, and I should not relish that.

But what trouble I have had throughout these two days struggling to appear calm and collected – to meet him and her as usual, when I was obliged to meet them, and forcing myself to leave my little Arthur in her hands for hours together! But I trust these trials are over now: I have laid him in my bed for better security, and never more, I trust, shall his innocent lips be defiled by their contaminating kisses, or his young ears polluted by their words. But shall we escape in safety? Oh, that the morning were come, and we were on our way at least! This evening, when I had given Rachel all the assistance I could and had nothing left me but to wait, and wish and tremble, I became so greatly agitated, that I knew not what to do. I went down to dinner, but I could not force myself to eat. Mr Huntingdon remarked the circumstance.

'What's to do with you now?' said he, when the removal of the second course gave him time to look about him.

'I am not well,' I replied: 'I think I must lie down a little – you won't miss me much!'

'Not the least if you leave your chair, it'll do just as well – better a trifle,' he muttered, as I left the room, 'for I can fancy somebody else fills it.'

'Somebody else may fill it tomorrow,' I thought – but did not say. 'There! I've seen the last of you, I hope,' I muttered as I closed the door upon him.

Rachel urged me to seek repose, at once, to recruit my strength for tomorrow's journey, as we must be gone before the dawn, but in my present state of nervous excitement that was entirely out of the question. It was equally out of the question to sit, or wander about my room, counting the hours and the minutes between me and the appointed time of action, straining my ears and trembling at every sound, lest some one should discover and betray us after all. I took up a book and tried to read. My eyes wandered over the pages, but it was impossible to bind my thoughts to their contents. Why not have recourse to the old expedient, and add this last event to my chronicle? I opened its pages once more, and wrote the above account – with difficulty, at first, but gradually my mind became more calm and steady. Thus several hours have passed away: the time is drawing

near; – and now my eyes feel heavy, and my frame exhausted: I will commend my cause to God, and then lie down and gain an hour or two of sleep; and then!—

Little Arthur sleeps soundly. All the house is still: there can be no one watching. The boxes were all corded by Benson, and quietly conveyed down the back stairs after dusk, and sent away in a cart to the M— coach-office. The name upon the cards was Mrs Graham, which appellation I mean henceforth to adopt. My mother's maiden name was Graham, and therefore I fancy I have some claim to it, and prefer it to any other, except my own, which I dare not resume.

# Chapter 44

## *October 24th*

Thank Heaven, I am free and safe at last! – Early we rose, swiftly and quietly dressed, slowly and stealthily descended to the hall, where Benson stood ready with a light to open the door and fasten it after us. We were obliged to let one man into our secret on account of the boxes, etc. All the servants were but too well acquainted with their master's conduct, and either Benson or John would have been willing to serve me, but as the former was more staid and elderly, and a crony of Rachel's besides, I of course directed her to make choice of him as her assistant and confidant on the occasion, as far as necessity demanded. I only hope he may not be brought into trouble thereby, and only wish I could reward him for the perilous service he was so ready to undertake. I slipped two guineas into his hand, by way of remembrance, as he stood in the doorway, holding the candle to light our departure, with a tear in his honest grey eye and a host of good wishes depicted on his solemn countenance. Alas! I could offer not more: I had barely sufficient remaining for the probable expenses of the journey.

What trembling joy it was when the little wicket closed behind us as we issued from the park! Then, for one moment, I paused, to inhale one draught of that cool, bracing air, and venture one look back upon the house. All was dark and still; no light glimmered in the windows; no wreath of smoke obscured the stars that sparkled above it in the frosty sky. As I bade farewell for ever to that place, the scene of so much guilt and misery, I felt glad that I had not left it before, for now there was no doubt about the propriety of such a step – no shadow of remorse for him I left behind: there was nothing to disturb my joy but the fear of detection; and every step removed us further from the chance of that.

We had left Grassdale many miles behind us, before the round, red sun arose to welcome our deliverance, and if any inhabitant of its vicinity had chanced to

# The Tenant of Wildfell Hall

see us then, as we bowled along on the top of the coach, I scarcely think they would have suspected our identity. As I intend to be taken for a widow I thought it advisable to enter my new abode in mourning: I was therefore attired in a plain black silk dress and mantle, a black veil (which I kept carefully over my face for the first twenty or thirty miles of the journey), and a black silk bonnet, which I had been constrained to borrow of Rachel for want of such an article myself – it was not in the newest fashion, of course; but none the worse for that, under present circumstances. Arthur was clad in his plainest clothes, and wrapped in a coarse woollen shawl; and Rachel was muffled in a grey cloak and hood that had seen better days, and gave her more the appearance of an ordinary though decent old woman, than of a lady's maid.

Oh, what delight it was to be thus seated aloft, rumbling along the broad, sunshiny road, with the fresh morning breeze in my face, surrounded by an unknown country all smiling – cheerfully, gloriously smiling in the yellow lustre of those early beams, – with my darling child in my arms, almost as happy as myself, and my faithful friend beside me; a prison and despair behind me, receding further, further back at every clatter of the horse's feet, – and liberty and hope before! I could hardly refrain from praising God aloud for my deliverance, or astonishing my fellow-passengers by some surprising outburst of hilarity.

But the journey was a very long one, and we were all weary enough before the close of it. It was far into the night when we reached the town of L—, and still we were seven miles from our journey's end; and there was no more coaching – nor any conveyance – to be had, except a common cart – and that with the greatest difficulty, for half the town was in bed. And a dreary ride we had of it that last stage of the journey, cold and weary as we were; sitting on our boxes, with nothing to cling to, nothing to lean against, slowly dragged and cruelly shaken over the rough, hill roads. But Arthur was asleep in Rachel's lap, and between us we managed pretty well to shield him from the cold night air.

At last we began to ascend a terribly steep and stony lane, which, in spite of the darkness, Rachel said she remembered well: she had often walked there with me in her arms, and little thought to come again so many years after, under such circumstances as the present. Arthur being now awakened by the jolting and the stoppages, we all got out and walked. We had not far to go; but what if Frederick should not have received my letter? or if he should not have had time to prepare the rooms for our reception; and we should find them all dark, damp, and comfortless; destitute of food, fire, and furniture, after all our toil?

At length the grim dark pile appeared before us. The lane conducted us round by the back way. We entered the desolate court, and in breathless anxiety surveyed the ruinous mass. Was it all blackness and desolation? No; one faint red glimmer cheered us from a window where the lattice was in good repair. The door was fastened, but after due knocking and waiting, and some parleying with a voice from an upper window, we were admitted by an old woman who had been commissioned to air and keep the house till our arrival, into a tolerably snug little apartment, formerly the scullery of the mansion, which Frederick had now fitted up as a kitchen. Here she procured us a light, roused the fire to a cheerful blaze, and soon prepared a simple repast for our refreshment; while we disencumbered ourselves of our travelling gear, and took a hasty survey of our new abode. Besides the kitchen there were two bedrooms, a good-sized

447

parlour and another smaller one, which I destined for my studio, all well aired and seemingly in good repair, but only partly furnished with a few old articles, chiefly of ponderous black oak – the veritable ones that had been there before, and which had been kept as antiquarian relics in my brother's present residence, and now, in all haste, transported back again.

The old woman brought my supper and Arthur's into the parlour, and told me, with all due formality that 'The master desired his compliments to Mrs Graham, and he had prepared the rooms as well as he could upon so short a notice, but he would do himself the pleasure of calling upon her tomorrow, to receive her further commands.'

I was glad to ascend the stern-looking stone staircase, and lie down in the gloomy old-fashioned bed, beside my little Arthur. He was asleep in a minute; but, weary as I was, my excited feelings and restless cogitations kept me awake till dawn began to struggle with the darkness; but sleep was sweet and refreshing when it came, and the waking was delightful beyond expression. It was little Arthur that roused me, with his gentle kisses: – He was here, then – safely clasped in my arms, and many leagues away from his unworthy father! Broad daylight illumined the apartment, for the sun was high in heaven, though obscured by rolling masses of autumnal vapour.

The scene, indeed, was not remarkably cheerful in itself, either within or without. The large bare room, with its grim old furniture, the narrow, latticed window revealing the dull, grey sky above and the desolate wilderness below, where the dark stone walls and iron gate, the rank growth of grass and weeds, and the hardy evergreens of preternatural forms, alone remained to tell that there had been once a garden, – and the bleak and barren fields beyond might have struck me as gloomy enough at another time, but now each separate object seemed to echo back my own exhilarating sense of hope and freedom: indefinite dreams of the far past and bright anticipations of the future seemed to greet me at every turn. I should rejoice with more security, to be sure, had the broad sea rolled between my present and my former hopes, but surely in this lonely spot I might remain unknown; and then, I had my brother here to cheer my solitude with his occasional visits.

He came that morning; and I have had several interviews with him alone; but he is obliged to be very cautious when and how he comes; not even his servants or his best friends must know of his visits to Wildfell – except on such occasions as a landlord might be expected to call upon a stranger tenant – lest suspicion should be excited against me, whether of the truth or of some slanderous falsehood.

I have now been here nearly a fortnight, and, but for one disturbing care, the haunting dread of discovery, I am comfortably settled in my new home: Frederick has supplied me with all requisite furniture and painting materials: Rachel has sold most of my clothes for me, in a distant town, and procured me a wardrobe more suitable to my present position: I have a secondhand piano, and a tolerably well-stocked bookcase in my parlour; and my other room has assumed quite a professional, business-like appearance already. I am working hard to repay my brother for all his expenses on my account; not that there is the slightest necessity for anything of the kind, but it pleases me to do so: I shall have so much more pleasure in my labour, my earnings, my frugal fare, and household economy, when I know that I am paying my way honestly, and that what little I possess

is legitimately all my own; and that no one suffers for my folly – in a pecuniary way at least. I shall make him take the last penny I owe him, if I can possibly effect it without offending him too deeply. I have a few pictures already done, for I told Rachel to pack up all I had; and she executed her commission but too well, for among the rest, she put up a portrait of Mr Huntingdon that I had painted in the first year of my marriage. It struck me with dismay, at the moment, when I took it from the box and beheld those eyes fixed upon me in their mocking mirth, as if exulting, still, in his power to control my fate and deriding my efforts to escape.

How widely different had been my feelings in painting that portrait to what they now were in looking upon it! How I had studied and toiled to produce something, as I thought, worthy of the original! what mingled pleasure and dissatisfaction I had had in the result of my labours! – pleasure for the likeness I had caught; dissatisfaction, because I had not made it handsome enough. Now, I see no beauty in it – nothing pleasing in any part of its expression; and yet it is far handsomer and far more agreeable – far less repulsive I should rather say – than he is now; for these six years have wrought almost as great a change upon himself as on my feelings regarding him. The frame, however, is handsome enough; it will serve for another painting. The picture itself I have not destroyed, as I had first intended; I have put it aside; not, I think, from any lurking tenderness for the memory of past affection, nor yet to remind me of my former folly but chiefly that I may compare my son's features and countenance with this, as he grows up, and thus be enabled to judge how much or how little he resembles his father – if I may be allowed to keep him with me still, and never to behold that father's face again – a blessing I hardly dare to reckon upon.

It seems Mr Huntingdon is making every exertion to discover the place of my retreat. He has been in person to Staningley, seeking redress for his grievances – expecting to hear of his victims, if not to find them there – and has told so many lies, and with such unblushing coolness, that my uncle more than half believes him, and strongly advocates my going back to him and being friends again; but my aunt knows better, she is too cool and cautious, and too well acquainted with both my husband's character and my own to be imposed upon by any specious falsehoods the former could invent. But he does not want me back; he wants my child; and gives my friends to understand that if I prefer living apart from him, he will indulge the whim and let me do so unmolested, and even settle a reasonable allowance on me, provided I will immediately deliver up his son. But, Heaven help me! I am not going to sell my child for gold, though it were to save both him and me from starving: it would be better that he should die with me, than that he should live with his father.

Frederick showed me a letter he had received from that gentleman, full of cool impudence such as would astonish any one who did not know him, but such as, I am convinced, none would know better how to answer than my brother. He gave me no account of his reply, except to tell me that he had not acknowledged his acquaintance with my place of refuge, but rather left it to be inferred that it was quite unknown to him, by saying it was useless to apply to him, or any other of my relations, for information on the subject, as it appeared I had been driven to such extremity, that I had concealed my retreat even from my best friends; but that if he had known it, or should at any time be made aware of it, most certainly Mr Huntingdon would be the last person to whom

# The Tenant of Wildfell Hall

he should communicate the intelligence; and that he need not trouble himself to bargain for the child, for he (Frederick) fancied he knew enough of his sister to enable him to declare, that wherever she might be, or however, situated, no consideration would induce her to deliver him up.

*30th.* – Alas! my kind neighbours will not let me alone. By some means they have ferreted me out, and I have had to sustain visits from three different families, all more or less bent upon discovering who and what I am, whence I came, and why I have chosen such a home as this. Their society is unnecessary to me, to say the least, and their curiosity annoys and alarms me: if I gratify it, it may lead to the ruin of my son, and if I am too mysterious, it will only excite their suspicions, invite conjecture, and rouse them to greater exertions – and perhaps by the means of spreading my fame from parish to parish, till it reach the ears of some one who will carry it to the lord of Grassdale Manor.

I shall be expected to return their calls, but if, upon inquiry, I find that any of them live too far away for Arthur to accompany me, they must expect in vain for a while, for I cannot bear to leave him, unless it be to go to church; and I have not attempted that yet, for – it may be foolish weakness, but I am under such constant dread of his being snatched away, that I am never easy when he is not by my side; and I fear these nervous terrors would so entirely disturb my devotions, that I should obtain no benefit from the attendance. I mean, however, to make the experiment next Sunday, and oblige myself to leave him in charge of Rachel for a few hours. It will be a hard task, but surely no imprudence; and the vicar has been to scold me for my neglect of the ordinances of religion. I had no sufficient excuse to offer, and I promised, if all were well, he should see me in my pew next Sunday; for I do not wish to be set down as an infidel; and, besides, I know I should derive great comfort and benefit from an occasional attendance at public worship, if I could only have faith and fortitude to compose my thoughts in conformity with the solemn occasion, and forbid them to be for ever dwelling on my absent child, and on the dreadful possibility of finding him gone when I return; and surely God in His mercy will preserve me from so severe a trial: for my child's own sake, if not for mine, He will not suffer him to be torn away.

*November 3rd.* – I have made some further acquaintance with my neighbours. The fine gentleman, and beau of the parish and its vicinity (in his own estimation, at least), is a young . . .

Here it ended. The rest was torn away. How cruel – just when she was going to mention me! for I could not doubt it was your humble servant she was about to mention, though not very favourably of course – I could tell that, as well by those few words as by the recollection of her whole aspect and demeanour towards me in the commencement of our acquaintance. Well! I could readily forgive her prejudice against me, and her hard thoughts of our sex in general, when I saw to what brilliant specimens her experience had been limited.

Respecting me, however, she had long since seen her error, and perhaps fallen into another in the opposite extreme; for if, at first her opinion of me had been lower than I deserved, I was convinced that now my deserts were lower than her opinion; and if the former part of this continuation had been torn away to avoid wounding my feelings, perhaps the latter portion had been removed for

fear of ministering too much to my self-conceit. At any rate, I would have given much to have seen it all – to have witnessed the gradual friendship for me, – and whatever warmer feeling she might have – to have seen how much love there was in her regard, and how it had grown upon her in spite of her virtuous resolutions and strenuous exertions to – but no, I had no right to see it: all this was too sacred for any eyes but her own, and she had done well to keep it from me.

# Chapter 45

ell, Halford, what do you think of all this? and while you read it, did you ever picture to yourself what my feelings would probably be during its perusal? Most likely not; but I am not going to descant upon them now: I will only make this acknowledgment, little honourable as it may be to human nature, and especially to myself – that the former half of the narrative was, to me, more painful than the latter; not that I was at all insensible to Mrs Huntingdon's wrongs or unmoved by her sufferings, but, I must confess, I felt a kind of selfish gratification in watching her husband's gradual decline in her good graces, and seeing how completely he extinguished all her affection at last. The effect of the whole, however, in spite of all my sympathy for her, and my fury against him, was to relieve my mind of an intolerable burden, and fill my heart with joy, as if some friend had roused me from a dreadful nightmare.

It was now near eight o'clock in the morning, for my candle had expired in the midst of my perusal, leaving me no alternative but to get another, at the expense of alarming the house, or to go to bed and wait the return of daylight. On my mother's account, I chose the latter; but how willingly I sought my pillow, and how much sleep it brought me, I leave you to imagine.

At the first appearance of dawn, I rose, and I brought the manuscript to the window, but it was impossible to read it yet; I devoted half-an-hour to dressing, and then returned to it again. Now, with a little difficulty, I could manage; and with intense and eager interest, I devoured the remainder of its contents. When it was ended, and my transient regret at its abrupt conclusion was over, I opened the window and put out my head to catch the cooling breeze, and imbibe deep draughts of the pure morning air. A splendid morning it was; the half-frozen dew lay thick on the grass, the swallows were twittering round me, the rooks cawing, and cows lowing in the distance; and early frost and summer sunshine mingled their sweetness in the air. But I did not think of that; a confusion of countless thoughts and varied emotions crowded upon me while I gazed abstract-edly on the lovely face of nature. Soon, however, this chaos of thoughts and passions cleared away, giving place to two distinct emotions; joy unspeakable that my adored Helen was all I wished to think her – that through the noisome

# The Tenant of Wildfell Hall

vapours of the world's aspersions and my own fancied convictions, her character shone bright, and clear, and stainless as that sun I could not bear to look on; and shame and deep remorse for my own conduct.

Immediately after breakfast, I hurried over to Wildfell Hall. Rachel had risen many degrees in my estimation since yesterday. I was ready to greet her quite as an old friend; but every kindly impulse was checked by the look of cold distrust she cast upon me on opening the door. The old virgin had constituted herself the guardian of her lady's honour, I supposed, and doubtless she saw in me another Mr Hargrave, only the more dangerous in being more esteemed and trusted by her mistress.

'Missis can't see any one today, sir – she's poorly,' said she, in answer to my inquiry for Mrs Graham.

'But I must see her, Rachel,' said I, placing my hand on the door to prevent it being shut against me.

'Indeed, sir, you can't,' replied she, settling her countenance in still more iron frigidity than before.

'Be so good as to announce me.'

'It's no manner of use, Mr Markham; she's poorly, I tell you.'

Just in time to prevent me from committing the impropriety of taking the citadel by storm, and pushing forward unannounced, an inner door opened, and little Arthur appeared with his frolicsome playfellow, the dog. He seized my hand between both his, and smilingly drew me forward.

'Mamma says you're to come in, Mr Markham,' said he, 'and I am to go out and play with Rover.'

Rachel retired with a sigh, and I stepped into the parlour and shut the door. There, before the fireplace, stood the tall, graceful figure, wasted with many sorrows. I cast the manuscript on the table, and looked in her face. Anxious and pale, it was turned towards me; her clear, dark eyes were fixed on mine with a gaze so intensely earnest that they bound me like a spell.

'Have you looked it over?' she murmured. The spell was broken.

'I've read it through,' said I, advancing into the room, – 'and I want to know if you'll forgive me – if you can forgive me?'

She did not answer, but her eyes glistened, and a faint red mantled on her lip and cheek. As I approached, she abruptly turned away, and went to the window. It was not in anger, I was well assured, but only to conceal or control her emotion. I therefore ventured to follow and stand beside her there, – but not to speak. She gave me her hand, without turning her head, and murmured in a voice she strove in vain to steady—

'Can you forgive me?'

It might be seemed a breach of trust, I thought, to convey that lily hand to my lips, so I only gently pressed it between my own, and smilingly replied—

'I hardly can. You should have told me this before. It shows a want of confidence'—

'Oh, no,' cried she, eagerly interrupting me, 'it was not that! It was no want of confidence in you; but if I had told you anything of my history, I must have told you all, in order to excuse my conduct; and I might well shrink from such a disclosure, till necessity obliged me to make it. But you forgive me? – I have done very, very wrong, I know; but, as usual, I have reaped the bitter fruits of my own error, – and must reap them to the end.'

452

# The Tenant of Wildfell Hall

Bitter, indeed, was the tone of anguish, repressed by resolute firmness, in which this was spoken. Now, I raised her hand to my lips, and fervently kissed it again and again; for tears prevented any other reply. She suffered these wild caresses without resistance or resentment: then, suddenly turning from me, she paced twice or thrice through the room. I knew by the contraction of her brow, the tight compression of her lips, and wringing of her hands, that meantime a violent conflict between reason and passion was silently passing within. At length she paused before the empty fireplace, and turning to me, said calmly – if that might be called calmness, which was so evidently the result of a violent effort—

'Now, Gilbert, you must leave me – not this moment, but soon – and you must never come again.'

'Never again, Helen? just when I love you more than ever!'

'For that very reason, if it be so, we should not meet again. I thought this interview was necessary – at least, I persuaded myself it was so – that we might severally ask and receive each other's pardon for the past; but there can be no excuse for another. I shall leave this place, as soon as I have means to seek another asylum; but our intercourse must end here.'

'End here!' echoed I; and approaching the high, carved chimney-piece, I leant my hand against its heavy mouldings, and dropped my forehead upon it in silent, sullen despondency.

'You must not come again,' continued she. There was a slight tremor in her voice, but I thought her whole manner was provokingly composed, considering the dreadful sentence she pronounced. 'You must know why I tell you so,' she resumed; 'and you must see that it is better to part at once – if it be hard to say adieu for ever, you ought to help me.' She paused. I did not answer. 'Will you promise not to come? – If you won't, and if you do come here again, you will drive me away before I know where to find another place of refuge – or how to seek it.'

'Helen,' said I, turning impatiently towards her, 'I cannot discuss the matter of eternal separation, calmly and dispassionately as you can do. It is no question of mere expedience with me; it is a question of life and death!'

She was silent. Her pale lips quivered, and her fingers trembled with agitation, as she nervously entwined them in the hair chain to which was appended her small gold watch – the only thing of value she had permitted herself to keep. I had said an unjust and cruel thing; but I must needs follow it up with something worse.

'But, Helen!' I began in a soft, low tone, not daring to raise my eyes to her face – 'that man is not your husband: in the sight of Heaven he has forfeited all claim to'— She seized my arm with a grasp of startling energy.

'Gilbert, don't!' she cried, in a tone that would have pierced a heart of adamant. For God's sake, don't you attempt these arguments! No fiend could torture me like this!'

'I won't, I won't!' said I, gently laying my hand on hers; almost as much alarmed at her vehemence, as ashamed of my own misconduct.

'Instead of acting like a true friend,' continued she, breaking from me, and throwing herself into the old arm-chair – 'and helping me with all your might – or rather taking your own part in the struggle of right against passion – you leave all the burden to me; – and not satisfied with that, you do your utmost to

453

fight against me – when you know that I' – she paused, and hid her face in her handkerchief.

'Forgive me, Helen!' pleaded I, 'I will never utter another word on the subject. But may we not still meet as friends?'

'It will not do,' she replied, mournfully shaking her head; and then she raised her eyes to mine, with a mildly reproachful look that seemed to say, 'You must know that as well as I.'

'Then what must we do?' cried I passionately. But immediately I added in a quieter tone – 'I'll do whatever you desire; only don't say that this meeting is to be our last.'

'And why not? Don't you know that every time we meet, the thoughts of the final parting will become more painful? Don't you feel that every interview makes us dearer to each other than the last?'

The utterance of this last question was hurried and low, and the downcast eyes and burning blush too plainly showed that she, at least, had felt it. It was scarcely prudent to make such an admission, or to add – as she presently did – 'I have power to bid you go, now; another time it might be different,' – but I was not base enough to attempt to take advantage of her candour.

'But we may write,' I timidly suggested – 'you will not deny me that consolation?'

'We can hear of each other through my brother.'

'Your brother!' A pang of remorse and shame shot through me. She had not heard of the injury he had sustained at my hands; and I had not the courage to tell her. 'Your brother will not help us,' I said: 'he would have all communion between us to be entirely at an end.'

'And he would be right, I suppose. As a friend of both, he would wish us both well; and every friend would tell us it was our interest, as well as our duty, to forget each other, though we might not see it ourselves. But don't be afraid, Gilbert,' she added, smiling sadly at my manifest discomposure, 'there is little chance of my forgetting you. But I did not mean that Frederick should be the means of transmitting messages between us, only that each might know, through him, of the other's welfare; – and more than this ought not to be; for you are young, Gilbert, and you ought to marry – and will some time, though you may think it impossible now: and though I hardly can say I wish you to forget me, I know it is right that you should, both for your own happiness, and that of your future wife; – and therefore I must and will wish it,' she added resolutely.

'And you are young too, Helen,' I boldly replied, 'and when that profligate scoundrel has run through his career, you will give your hand to me – I'll wait till then.'

But she would not leave me this support. Independently of the moral evil of basing our hopes upon the death of another, who, if unfit for this world, was at least no less so for the next, and whose amelioration would thus become our bane and his greatest transgression our greatest benefit, – she maintained it to be madness: many men of Mr Huntingdon's habits had lived to a ripe though miserable old age; – 'and if I,' said she, 'am young in years I am old in sorrow; but even if trouble should fail to kill me before vice destroys him, think, if he reached but fifty years or so, would you wait twenty or fifteen – in vague uncertainty and suspense – through all the prime of youth and manhood – and marry at last a woman faded and worn as I shall be – without ever having seen

# The Tenant of Wildfell Hall

me from this day to that? – You would not,' she continued, interrupting my earnest protestations of unfailing constancy, – 'or if you would you should not. Trust me, Gilbert; in this matter I know better than you. You think me cold and stony-hearted, and you may, but'—

'I don't, Helen.'

'Well, never mind; you might if you would – but I have not spent my solitude in utter idleness, and I am not speaking now from the impulse of the moment as you do: I have thought of all these matters again and again; I have argued these questions with myself, and pondered well our past, and present, and future career; and, believe me, I have come to the right conclusion at last. Trust my words rather than your own feelings, now, and in a few years you will see that I was right – though at present I hardly can see it myself,' she murmured with a sigh, as she rested her head on her hand. 'And don't argue against me any more: all you can say has been already said by my own heart and refuted by my reason. It was hard enough to combat those suggestions as they were whispered within me; in your mouth they are ten times worse, and if you knew how much they pain me you would cease at once, I know. If you knew my present feelings, you would even try to relieve them at the expense of your own.'

'I will go – in a minute, if that can relieve you – and NEVER return!' said I, with bitter emphasis. 'But, if we may never meet, and never hope to meet again, is it a crime to exchange our thoughts by letter? May not kindred spirits meet, and mingle in communion, whatever be the fate and circumstances of their earthly tenements?'

'They may, they may!' cried she, with a momentary burst of glad enthusiasm. 'I thought of that too, Gilbert, but I feared to mention it, because I feared you would not understand my views upon the subject – I fear it even now – I fear any kind friend would tell us we are both deluding ourselves with the idea of keeping up a spiritual intercourse without hope or prospect of anything further – without fostering vain regrets and hurt aspirations, and feeding thoughts that should be sternly and pitilessly left to perish of inanition'—

'Never mind our kind friends: if they can part our bodies, it is enough; but in God's name, let them not sunder our souls!' cried I, in terror lest she should deem it her duty to deny us this last remaining consolation.

'But no letters can pass between us here,' said she, 'without giving fresh food for scandal; and when I departed, I had intended that my new abode should be unknown to you as to the rest of the world; not that I should doubt your word if you promised not to visit me, but I thought you would be more tranquil in your own mind if you knew you could not do it; and likely to find less difficulty in abstracting yourself from me if you could not picture my situation to your mind. But listen,' said she, smilingly putting up her finger to check my impatient reply: 'in six months you shall hear from Frederick precisely where I am; and if you still retain your wish to write to me, and think you can maintain a correspondence all thought, all spirit – such as disembodied souls or unimpassioned friends, at least, might hold, – write, and I will answer you.'

'Six months!'

'Yes, to give your present ardour time to cool, and try the truth and constancy of your soul's love for mine. And now, enough has been said between us. Why can't we part at once?' exclaimed she almost wildly, after a moment's pause, as she suddenly rose from her chair with her hands resolutely clasped together. I

thought it was my duty to go without delay; and I approached and half extended my hand as if to take leave – she grasped it in silence. But this thought of final separation was too intolerable: it seemed to squeeze the blood out of my heart; and my feet were glued to the floor.

'And must we never meet again?' I murmured, in the anguish of my soul.

'We shall meet in heaven. Let us think of that,' said she in a tone of desperate calmness; but her eyes glittered wildly, and her face was deadly pale.

'But not as we are now,' I could not help replying. 'It gives me little consolation to think I shall next behold you as a disembodied spirit, or an altered being, with a frame perfect and glorious, but not like this! – and a heart, perhaps, entirely estranged from me.'

'No, Gilbert, there is perfect love in heaven!'

'So perfect, I suppose, that it soars above distinctions, and you will have no closer sympathy with me than with any one of the ten thousand angels and the innumerable multitude of happy spirits round us.'

'Whatever I am, you will be the same, and, therefore, cannot possibly regret it; and whatever that change may be, we know it must be for the better.'

'But if I am to be so changed that I shall cease to adore you with my whole heart and soul, and love you beyond every other creature, I shall not be myself; and, though, if ever I win heaven at all, I must, I know, be infinitely better and happier than I am now, my earthly nature cannot rejoice in the anticipation of such beatitude, from which itself and its chief joy must be excluded.'

'Is your love all earthly then?'

'No, but I am supposing we shall have no more intimate communion with each other, than with the rest.'

'If so, it will be because we love them more and not each other less. Increase of love brings increase of happiness, when it is mutual, and pure as that will be.'

'But can you, Helen, contemplate with delight this prospect of losing me in a sea of glory?'

'I own I cannot; but we know not that it will be so; – and I do know that to regret the exchange of earthly pleasures for the joys of heaven, is as if the grovelling caterpillar should lament that it must one day quit the nibbled leaf to soar aloft and flutter through the air, roving at will from flower to flower, sipping sweet honey from their cups, or basking in their sunny petals. If these little creatures knew how great a change awaited them, no doubt they would regret it; but would not all such sorrow be misplaced? And if that illustration will not move you, here is another: – We are children now; we feel as children, and we understand as children; and when we are told that men and women do not play with toys, and that our companions will one day weary of the trivial sports and occupations that interest them and us so deeply now, we cannot help being saddened at the thoughts of such an alteration, because we cannot conceive that as we grow up, our minds will become so enlarged and elevated that we ourselves shall then regard as trifling those subjects and pursuits we now so fondly cherish, and that, though our companions will no longer join us in those childish pastimes, they will drink with us at other fountains of delight, and mingle their souls with ours in higher aims and nobler occupations beyond our present comprehension, but not less deeply relished or less truly good for that, while yet both we and they remain essentially the same individuals as before. But Gilbert, can you really derive no consolation from the thought that we may

# The Tenant of Wildfell Hall

meet together where there is no more pain and sorrow, no more striving against sin, and struggling of the spirit against the flesh; where both will behold the same glorious truths, and drink exalted and supreme felicity from the same fountain of light and goodness – that Being whom both will worship with the same intensity of holy ardour, and where poor and happy creatures both will love with the same divine affection? If you cannot, never write to me!'

'Helen, I can! if faith would never fail.'

'Now, then,' exclaimed she, 'while this hope is strong within us'—

'We will part,' I cried. 'You shall not have the pain of another effort to dismiss me: I will go at once; but'—

I did not put my request in words: she understood it instinctively, and this time she yielded too – or rather, there was nothing so deliberate as requesting or yielding in the matter: there was a sudden impulse that neither could resist. One moment I stood and looked into her face, the next I held her to my heart, and we seemed to grow together in a close embrace from which no physical or mental force could rend us. A whispered 'God bless you!' and 'Go – go!' was all she said; but while she spoke, she held me so fast that, without violence, I could not have obeyed her. At length, however, by some heroic effort, we tore ourselves apart, and I rushed from the house.

I have a confused remembrance of seeing little Arthur running up the garden walk to meet me, and of bolting over the wall to avoid him – and subsequently running down the steep fields, clearing the stone fences and hedges as they came in my way, till I got completely out of sight of the old Hall and down to the bottom of the hill; and then of long hours spent in bitter tears and lamentations, and melancholy musings in the lonely valley, with the eternal music in my ears, of the west wind rushing through the over-shadowing trees, and the brook babbling and gurgling along its stony bed – my eyes, for the most part, vacantly fixed on the deep, checkered shades restlessly playing over the bright sunny grass at my feet, where now and then a withered leaf or two would come dancing to share the revelry, but my heart was away up in the hill in that dark room where she was weeping desolate and alone – she whom I was not to comfort, not to see again, till years or suffering had overcome us both, and torn our spirits from their perishing abodes of clay.

There was little business done that day, you may be sure. The farm was abandoned to the labourers, and the labourers were left to their own devices. But one duty must be attended to: I had not forgotten my assault upon Frederick Lawrence; and I must see him to apologize for the unhappy deed. I would fain have put it off till the morrow; but what if he should denounce me to his sister in the meantime? No, no, I must ask his pardon today, and entreat him to be lenient in his accusation, if the revelation must be made. I deferred it, however, till the evening, when my spirits were more composed, and when – oh, wonderful perversity of human nature? – some faint germs of indefinite hopes were beginning to rise in my mind; not that I intended to cherish them after all that had been said on the subject, but there they must lie for awhile, uncrushed though not encouraged, till I had learnt to live without them.

Arrived at Woodford, the young squire's abode, I found no little difficulty in obtaining admission to his presence. The servant that opened the door told me his master was very ill, and seemed to think it doubtful whether he would be able to see me. I was not going to be balked, however. I waited calmly in the

# The Tenant of Wildfell Hall

hall to be announced, but inwardly determined to take no denial. The message was such as I expected – a polite intimation that Mr Lawrence could see no one; he was feverish and must not be disturbed.

'I shall not disturb him long,' said I; 'but I must see him for a moment: it is on business of importance that I wish to speak to him.'

'I'll tell him, sir,' said the man. And I advanced further into the hall and followed him nearly to the door of the apartment where his master was – for it seemed he was not in bed. The answer returned, was that Mr Lawrence hoped I would be so good as to leave a message or a note with the servant, as he could attend to no business at present.

'He may as well see me as you,' said I; and, stepping past the astonished footman, I boldly rapped at the door, entered, and closed it behind me. The room was spacious and handsomely furnished – very comfortably, too, for a bachelor. A clear, red fire was burning in the polished grate: a superannuated greyhound, given up to idleness and good living, lay basking before it on the thick, soft rug, on one corner of which, beside the sofa, sat a smart young springer, looking wistfully up in its master's face; perhaps, asking permission to share his couch, or, it might be, only soliciting a caress from his hand or a kind word from his lips. The invalid himself looked very interesting as he lay reclining there, in his elegant dressing-gown, with a silk handkerchief bound across his temples. His usually pale face was flushed and feverish; his eyes were half-closed, until he became sensible of my presence – and then he opened them wide enough; – one hand was thrown listlessly over the back of the sofa, and held a small volume with which, apparently, he had been vainly attempting to beguile the weary hours. He dropped it, however, in his start of indignant surprise as I advanced into the room and stood before him on the rug. He raised himself on his pillows, and gazed upon me with equal degrees of nervous horror, anger, and amazement depicted on his countenance.

'Mr Markham, I scarcely expected this!' he said; and the blood left his cheek as he spoke.

'I know you didn't,' answered I; 'but be quiet a minute, and I'll tell you what I came for.' Unthinkingly I advanced a step or two nearer. He winced at my approach, with an expression of aversion and instinctive physical fear anything but conciliatory to my feelings. I stepped back, however.

'Make your story a short one,' said he, putting his hand on the small silver bell that stood on the table beside him, – 'or I shall be obliged to call for assistance. I am in no state to bear your brutalities now, or your presence either.' And in truth the moisture started from his pores and stood on his pale forehead like dew.

Such a reception was hardly calculated to diminish the difficulties of my unenviable task. It must be performed, however, in some fashion: and so I plunged into it at once, and floundered through it as I could.

'The truth is, Lawrence,' said I, 'I have not acted quite correctly towards you of late – especially on this last occasion; and I'm come to – in short, to express my regret for what has been done, and to beg your pardon. – If you don't choose to grant it,' I added hastily, not liking the aspect of his face, 'it's no matter – only, I've done my duty – that's all.'

'It's easily done,' replied he, with a faint smile, bordering on a sneer: 'to abuse your friend and knock him on the head, without any assignable cause,

and then tell him the deed was not quite correct, but it's no matter whether he pardons it or not.'

'I forgot to tell you that it was in consequence of a mistake,' muttered I. 'I should have made a very handsome apology, but you provoked me so profoundly with your— Well, I suppose it's my fault. The fact is, I didn't know that you were Mrs Graham's brother, and I saw and heard some things respecting your conduct towards her, which were calculated to awaken unpleasant suspicions, that, allow me to say, a little candour and confidence on your part might have removed; and at last, I chanced to overhear a part of a conversation between you and her that made me think I had a right to hate you.'

'And how came you to know that I was her brother?' asked he in some anxiety.

'She told me herself. She told me all. She knew I might be trusted. But you needn't disturb yourself about that, Mr Lawrence, for I've seen the last of her!'

'The last! is she gone then?'

'No, but she has bid adieu to me; and I have promised never to go near that house again while she inhabits it.' I could have groaned aloud at the bitter thoughts awakened by this turn in the discourse. But I only clenched my hands and stamped my foot upon the rug. My companion, however, was evidently relieved.

'You have done right!' he said, in a tone of unqualified approbation, while his face brightened into almost a sunny expression. 'And as for the mistake, I am sorry for both our sakes that it should have occurred. Perhaps you can forgive my want of candour, and remember, as some partial mitigation of the offence, how little encouragement to friendly confidence you have given me of late.'

'Yes, yes, I remember it all: nobody can blame me more than I blame myself in my own heart – at any rate, nobody can regret more sincerely than I do the result of my brutality, as you rightly term it.'

'Never mind that,' said he, faintly smiling; 'let us forget all unpleasant words on both sides, as well as deeds, and consign to oblivion everything that we have cause to regret. Have you any objection to take my hand – or you'd rather not?' It trembled through weakness, as he held it out, and dropped before I had time to catch it and give it a hearty squeeze, which he had not the strength to return.

'How dry and burning your hand is, Lawrence,' said I. 'You are really ill, and I have made you worse by all this talk.'

'Oh, it is nothing: only a cold got by the rain.'

'My doing, too.'

'Never mind that – but tell me, did you mention this affair to my sister?'

'To confess the truth, I had not the courage to do so; but when you tell her, will you just say that I deeply regret it, and'—

'Oh, never fear! I shall say nothing against you, as long as you keep your good resolution of remaining aloof from her. She has not heard of my illness then, that you are aware of?'

'I think not.'

'I'm glad of that, for I have been all this time tormenting myself with the fear that somebody would tell her I was dying, or desperately ill, and she would be either distressing herself on account of her inability to hear from me or do me any good, or perhaps committing the madness of coming to see me. I must contrive to let her know something about it, if I can,' continued he reflectively,

'or she will be hearing some such story. Many would be glad to tell her such news, just to see how she would take it; and then she might expose herself to fresh scandal.'

'I wish I had told her,' said I. 'If it were not for my promise, I would tell her now.'

'By no means! I am not dreaming of that; – but if I were to write a short note, now – not mentioning you, Markham, but just giving a slight account of my illness, by way of excuse for my not coming to see her, and to put her on her guard against any exaggerated reports she may hear, – and address it in a disguised hand – would you do me the favour to slip it into the post-office as you pass? for I dare not trust any of the servants in such a case.'

Most willingly I consented, and immediately brought him his desk. There was little need to disguise his hand, for the poor fellow seemed to have considerable difficulty in writing at all, so as to be legible. When the note was done, I thought it time to retire and took leave after asking if there was anything in the world I could do for him, little or great, in the way of alleviating his sufferings, and repairing the injury I had done.

'No,' said he; 'you have already done much towards it; you have done more for me than the most skilful physician could do; for you have relieved my mind of two great burdens – anxiety on my sister's account, and deep regret upon your own, for I do believe these two sources of torment have had more effect in working me up into a fever, than anything else; and I am persuaded I shall soon recover now. There is one more thing you can do for me, and that is, come and see me now and then – for you see I am very lonely here, and I promise your entrance shall not be disputed again.'

I engaged to do so, and departed with a cordial pressure of the hand. I posted the letter on my way home, most manfully resisting the temptation of dropping in a word for myself at the same time.

# Chapter 46

I felt strongly tempted, at times, to enlighten my mother and sister on the real character and circumstances of the persecuted tenant of Wildfell Hall, and at first I greatly regretted having omitted to ask that lady's permission to do so; but, on due reflection, I considered that if it were known to them, it could not long remain a secret to the Millwards and Wilsons, and such was my present appreciation of Eliza Millward's disposition, that, if once she got a clue to the story, I should fear she would soon find means to enlighten Mr Huntingdon upon the place of his wife's retreat. I would therefore wait patiently till these weary six months were over, and then, when the fugitive had found another home, and I was permitted to write to her, I would beg to be

allowed to clear her name from these vile calumnies: at present I must content myself with simply asserting that I knew them to be false, and would prove it some day, to the shame of those who slandered her. I don't think anybody believed me, but everybody soon learned to avoid insinuating a word against her, or even mentioning her name in my presence. They thought I was so madly infatuated by the seductions of that unhappy lady that I was determined to support her in the very face of reason; and meantime I grew insupportably morose and misanthropical from the idea that every one I met was harbouring unworthy thoughts of the supposed Mrs Graham, and would express them if he dared. My poor mother was quite distressed about me; but I couldn't help it – at least I thought I could not, though sometimes I felt a pang of remorse for my undutiful conduct to her, and made an effort to amend, attended with some partial success; and indeed I was generally more humanized in my demeanour to her than to anyone else, Mr Lawrence excepted. Rose and Fergus usually shunned my presence; and it was well they did, for I was not fit company for them, nor they for me, under the present circumstances.

Mrs Huntingdon did not leave Wildfell Hall till above two months after our farewell interview. During that time she never appeared at church, and I never went near the house: I only knew she was still there by her brother's brief answers to my many and varied inquiries respecting her. I was a very constant and attentive visitor to him throughout the whole period of his illness and convalescence; not only from the interest I took in his recovery, and my desire to cheer him up and make the utmost possible amends for my former 'brutality', but from my growing attachment to himself, and the increasing pleasure I found in his society – partly from his increased cordiality to me, but chiefly on account of his close connection, both in blood and in affection, with my adored Helen. I loved him for it better than I liked to express; and I took a secret delight in pressing those slender white fingers, so marvellously like her own, considering he was not a woman, and in watching the passing changes in his fair pale features, and observing the intonations of his voice, detecting resemblances which I wondered had never struck me before. He provoked me at times, indeed, by his evident reluctance to talk to me about his sister, though I did not question the friendliness of his motives in wishing to discourage my remembrance of her.

His recovery was not quite so rapid as he had expected it to be: he was not able to mount his pony till a fortnight after the date of our reconciliation; and the first use he made of his returning strength, was to ride over by night to Wildfell Hall, to see his sister. It was a hazardous enterprise both for him and for her, but he thought it necessary to consult with her on the subject of her projected departure, if not to calm her apprehensions respecting his health, and the worst result was a slight relapse of his illness, for no one knew of the visit but the inmates of the old Hall, except myself; and I believe it had not been his intention to mention it to me, for when I came to see him the next day, and observed he was not so well as he ought to have been, he merely said he had caught cold by being out too late in the evening.

'You'll never be able to see your sister, if you don't take care of yourself,' said I, a little provoked at the circumstance on her account, instead of commiserating him.

'I've seen her already,' said he quietly.

'You've seen her?' cried I, in astonishment.

'Yes.' And then he told me what considerations had impelled him to make the venture, and with what precautions he had made it.

'And how was she?' I eagerly asked.

'As usual,' was the brief though sad reply.

'As usual – that is, far from happy and far from strong.'

'She is not positively ill,' returned he; 'and she will recover her spirits in a while, I have no doubt – but so many trials have been almost too much for her. – How threatening those clouds look', continued he, turning towards the window. 'We shall have thunder showers before night, I imagine, and they are just in the midst of stacking my corn. Have you got yours all in yet?'

'No. – And, Lawrence, did she – did your sister mention me?'

'She asked if I had seen you lately.'

'And what else did she say?'

'I cannot tell you all she said,' replied he, with a slight smile, 'for we talked a good deal, though my stay was but short; but our conversation was chiefly on the subject of her intended departure, which I begged her to delay till I was better able to assist her in her search after another home.'

'But did she say no more about me?'

'She did not say much about you, Markham. I should not have encouraged her to do so, had she been inclined; but happily she was not: she only asked a few questions concerning you, and seemed satisfied with my brief answers, wherein she showed herself wiser than her friend; and I may tell you, too, that she seemed to be far more anxious lest you should think too much of her, than lest you should forget her.'

'She was right.'

'But I fear your anxiety is quite the other way respecting her.'

'No, it is not: I wish her to be happy; but I don't wish her to forget me altogether. She knows it is impossible that I should forget her; and she is right to wish me not to remember her too well. I should not desire her to regret me too deeply; but I can scarcely imagine she will make herself very unhappy about me, because I know I am not worthy of it, except in my appreciation of her.'

'You are neither of you worthy of a broken heart, – nor of all the sighs, and tears, and sorrowful thoughts that have been, and I fear will be, wasted upon you both; but, at present, each has a more exalted opinion of the other than, I fear, he or she deserves; and my sister's feelings are naturally full as keen as yours, and I believe more constant; but she has the good sense and fortitude to strive against them in this particular; and I trust she will not rest till she has entirely weaned her thoughts—' he hesitated.

'From me,' said I.

'And I wish you would make the like exertions,' continued he.

'Did she tell you that that was her intention?'

'No; the question was not broached between us: there was no necessity for it, for I had no doubt that such was her determination.'

'To forget me?'

'Yes, Markham! Why not?'

'Oh! well,' was my only audible reply; but I internally answered, – 'No Lawrence, you're wrong there, she is not determined to forget me. It would be wrong to forget one so deeply and fondly devoted to her, who can so thoroughly appreciate her excellences, and sympathize with all her thoughts, as I can do,

and it would be wrong in me to forget so excellent and divine a piece of God's creation as she, when I have once so truly loved and known her.' But I said no more to him on that subject. I instantly started a new topic of conversation, and soon took leave of my companion, with a feeling of less cordiality towards him than usual. Perhaps I had no right to be annoyed at him, but I was so nevertheless.

In little more than a week after this, I met him returning from a visit to the Wilsons; and I now resolved to do him a good turn, though at the expense of his feelings, and, perhaps, at the risk of incurring that displeasure which is so commonly the reward of those who give disagreeable information, or tender their advice unasked. In this, believe me, I was actuated by no motives of revenge for the occasional annoyances I had lately sustained from him, – nor yet by any feeling of malevolent enmity towards Miss Wilson, but purely the fact that I could not endure that such a woman should be Mrs Huntingdon's sister, and that, as well for his own sake as for hers, I could not bear to think of his being deceived into a union with one so unworthy of him, and so utterly unfitted to be the partner of his quiet home, and the companion of his life. He had had uncomfortable suspicions on that head himself I imagined; but such was his inexperience, and such were the lady's powers of attraction, and her skill in bringing them to bear upon his young imagination, that they had not disturbed him long, and I believe the only effectual causes of the vacillating indecision that had preserved him hitherto from making an actual declaration of love, was the consideration of her connections, and especially of her mother, whom he could not abide. Had they lived at a distance, he might have surmounted the objection, but within two or three miles of Woodford, it was really no light matter.

'You've been to call on the Wilsons, Lawrence,' said I, as I walked beside his pony.

'Yes,' replied he, slightly averting his face: 'I thought it but civil to take the first opportunity of returning their kind attentions, since they have been so very particular and constant in their inquiries throughout the whole course of my illness.'

'It's all Miss Wilson's doing.'

'And if it is,' returned he, with a very perceptible blush, 'is that any reason why I should not make a suitable acknowledgment?'

'It is a reason why you should not make the acknowledgment she looks for.'

'Let us drop that subject if you please,' said he, in evident displeasure.

'No, Lawrence, with your leave we'll continue it a while longer; and I'll tell you something, now we're about it, which you may believe or not as you choose – only please to remember that it is not my custom to speak falsely, and that in this case, I can have no motive for misrepresenting the truth'—

'Well, Markham! what now?'

'Miss Wilson hates your sister. It may be natural enough that, in her ignorance of the relationship, she should feel some degree of enmity against her, but no good or amiable woman would be capable of evincing that bitter, cold-blooded, designing malice towards a fancied rival that I have observed in her.'

'Markham!!'

'Yes – and it is my belief that Eliza Millward and she, if not the very originators of the slanderous reports that have been propagated, were designedly the encouragers and chief disseminators of them. She was not desirous to mix

up your name in the matter, of course, but her delight was, and still is, to blacken your sister's character, to the utmost of her power, without risking too greatly the exposure of her own malevolence!'

'I cannot believe it,' interrupted my companion, his face burning with indignation.

'Well, as I cannot prove it, I must content myself with asserting that it is so to the best of my belief; but as you would not willingly marry Miss Wilson if it were so, you will do well to be cautious, till you have proved it to be otherwise.'

'I never told you, Markham, that I intended to marry Miss Wilson,' said he proudly.

'No, but whether you do or not, she intends to marry you.'

'Did she tell you so?'

'No, but'—

'Then you have no right to make such an assertion respecting her.' He slightly quickened his pony's pace, but I laid my hand on its mane, determined he should not leave me yet.

'Wait a moment, Lawrence, and let me explain myself; and don't be so very – I don't know what to call it – inaccessible as you are. – I know what you think of Jane Wilson; and I believe I know how far you are mistaken in your opinion, you think she is singularly charming, elegant, sensible, and refined: you are not aware that she is selfish, cold-hearted, ambitious, artful, shallow-minded'—

'Enough, Markham, enough.'

'No; let me finish – you don't know that if you married her, your home would be rayless and comfortless; and it would break your heart at last to find yourself united to one so wholly incapable of sharing your tastes, feelings, and ideas – so utterly destitute of sensibility, good feeling, and true nobility of soul.'

'Have you done?' asked my companion quietly.

'Yes: – I know you hate me for my impertinence, but I don't care if it only conduces to preserve you from that fatal mistake.'

'Well!' returned he, with a rather wintry smile – 'I'm glad you have overcome or forgotten your own afflictions, so far as to be able to study so deeply the affairs of others, and trouble your head, so unnecessarily, about the fancied or possible calamities of their future life.'

We parted – somewhat coldly again; but still we did not cease to be friends; and my well-meant warning, though it might have been more judiciously delivered, as well as more thankfully received, was not wholly unproductive of the desired effect: his visit to the Wilsons was not repeated, and though, in our subsequent interviews, he never mentioned her name to me, nor I to him, – I have reason to believe he pondered my words in his mind, eagerly though covertly sought information respecting the fair lady from other quarters, secretly compared my character of her with what he had himself observed and what he heard from others, and finally came to the conclusion that, all things considered, she had much better remain Miss Wilson of Ryecote Farm, than be transmuted into Mrs Lawrence of Woodford Hall. I believe, too, that he soon learned to contemplate with secret amazement his former predilection, and to congratulate himself on the lucky escape he had made; but he never confessed it to me, or hinted one word of acknowledgment for the part I had had in his deliverance – but this was not surprising to anyone that knew him as I did.

As for Jane Wilson, she, of course, was disappointed and embittered by the

sudden cold neglect and ultimate desertion of her former admirer. Had I done wrong to blight her cherished hopes? I think not; and certainly my conscience has never accused me, from that day to this, of any evil design in the matter.

# Chapter 47

ne morning, about the beginning of November, while I was inditing some business letters, shortly after breakfast, Eliza Millward came to call upon my sister. Rose had neither the discrimination nor the virulence to regard the little demon as I did, and they still preserved their former intimacy. At the moment of her arrival, however, there was no one in the room but Fergus and myself, my mother and sister being both of them absent, 'on household cares intent'; so I was not going to lay myself out for her amusement, whoever else might so incline: I merely honoured her with a careless salutation and a few words of course, and then went on with my writing, leaving my brother to be more polite if he chose. But she wanted to tease me.

'What a pleasure it is to find you at home, Mr Markham!' said she, with a disingenuously malicious smile. 'I so seldom see you now, for you never come to the vicarage. Papa is quite offended I can tell you,' she added playfully, looking into my face with an impertinent laugh, as she seated herself, half beside and half before my desk, off the corner of the table.

'I have had a good deal to do of late,' said I, without looking up from my letter.

'Have you indeed! Somebody said you had been strangely neglecting your business these last few months.'

'Somebody said wrong, for, these last two months especially, I have been particularly plodding and diligent.'

'Ah! Well, there's nothing like active employment, I suppose, to console the afflicted; – and, excuse me, Mr Markham, but you look so very far from well, and have been, by all accounts, so moody and thoughtful of late, – I could almost think you have some secret care preying on your spirits. Formerly,' said she timidly, 'I could have ventured to ask you what it was, and what I could do to comfort you: I dare not do it now.'

'You're very kind, Miss Eliza. When I think you can do anything to comfort me, I'll make bold to tell you.'

'Pray do! – I suppose I mayn't guess what it is that troubles you?'

'There's no necessity, for I'll tell you plainly. The thing that troubles me the most at present, is a young lady sitting at my elbow, and preventing me from finishing my letter, and, thereafter, repairing to my daily business.'

Before she could reply to this ungallant speech, Rose entered the room; and Miss Eliza rising to greet her, they both seated themselves near the fire, where

# The Tenant of Wildfell Hall

that idle lad, Fergus, was standing, leaning his shoulder against the corner of the chimney-piece, with his legs crossed and his hands in his breeches-pockets.

'Now Rose, I'll tell you a piece of news – I hope you've not heard it before, for good, bad, or indifferent, one always likes to be the first to tell – It's about that sad Mrs Graham—'

'Hush-sh-sh!' whispered Fergus, in a tone of solemn import. 'We never mention her; her name is never heard.' And glancing up, I caught him with his eye askance on me, and his finger pointing to his forehead; then, winking at the young lady with a doleful shake of the head, he whispered – 'A monomania – but don't mention it – all right but that.'

'I should be sorry to injure any one's feelings,' returned she, speaking below her breath; 'another time, perhaps.'

'Speak out, Miss Eliza!' said I, not deigning to notice the other's buffooneries, 'you needn't fear to say anything in my presence.'

'Well,' answered she, 'perhaps you know already that Mrs Graham's husband is not really dead, and that she had run away from him?' I started, and felt my face glow; but I bent it over my letter, and went on folding it up as she proceeded. 'But perhaps you did not know that she is now gone back to him again, and that a perfect reconciliation has taken place between them? Only think,' she continued, turning to the confounded Rose, 'what a fool the man must be!'.

'And who gave you this piece of intelligence, Miss Eliza?' said I, interrupting my sister's exclamation.

'I had it from a very authentic source, sir.'

'From whom, may I ask?'

'From one of the servants at Woodford.'

'Oh! I was not aware that you were on such intimate terms with Mr Lawrence's household.'

'It was not from the man himself, that I heard it; but he told it in confidence to our maid Sarah, and Sarah told it to me.'

'In confidence, I suppose; and you tell it in confidence to us; but I can tell you that it is but a lame story after all, and scarcely one-half of it true.'

While I spoke, I completed the sealing and direction of my letters, with a somewhat unsteady hand, in spite of all my efforts to retain composure, and in spite of my firm conviction that the story was a lame one – that the supposed Mrs Graham most certainly had not voluntarily gone back to her husband, or dreamt of a reconciliation. Most likely, she was gone away, and the tale-bearing servant, not knowing what was become of her, had conjectured that such was the case, and our fair visitor had detailed it as a certainty, delighted with such an opportunity of tormenting me. But it was possible – barely possible, that some one might have betrayed her, and she had been taken away by force. Determined to know the worst, I hastily pocketed my two letters, and muttering something about being too late for the post, left the room, rushed into the yard, and vociferously called for my horse. No one being there, I dragged him out of the stable myself, strapped the saddle on to his back and the bridle on to his head, mounted, and speedily galloped away to Woodford. I found its owner pensively strolling in the grounds.

'Is your sister gone?' were my first words as I grasped his hand, instead of the usual inquiry after his health.

# The Tenant of Wildfell Hall

'Yes, she's gone,' was his answer, so calmly spoken, that my terror was at once removed.

'I suppose I mayn't know where she is?' said I, as I dismounted and relinquished my horse to the gardener, who, being the only servant within call, had been summoned by his master, from his employment of raking up the dead leaves on the lawn, to take him to the stables.

My companion gravely took my arm, and leading me away to the garden, thus answered my question—

'She is at Grassdale Manor, in—shire.'

'Where?' cried I, with a convulsive start.

'At Grassdale Manor.'

'How was it?' I gasped. 'Who betrayed her?'

'She went of her own accord.'

'Impossible, Lawrence! She could not be so frantic!' exclaimed I, vehemently grasping his arm, as if to force him to unsay those hateful words.

'She did,' persisted he, in the same grave collected manner as before; 'and not without reason,' he continued, gently disengaging himself from my grasp: 'Mr Huntingdon is ill.'

'And so she went to nurse him?'

'Yes.'

'Fool!' I could not help exclaiming – and Lawrence looked up with a rather reproachful glance. 'Is he dying, then?'

'I think not, Markham.'

'And how many more nurses has he? – how many ladies are there besides, to take care of him?'

'None! he was alone, or she would not have gone.'

'Oh, confound it! this is intolerable!'

'What is? that he should be alone?'

I attempted no reply, for I was not sure that this circumstance did not partly conduce to my distraction. I therefore continued to pace the walk in silent anguish, with my hand pressed to my forehead; then suddenly pausing and turning to my companion, I impatiently exclaimed—

'Why did she take this infatuated step? What fiend persuaded her to it?'

'Nothing persuaded her but her own sense of duty.'

'Humbug!'

'I was half inclined to say so myself, Markham, at first. I assure you it was not by my advice that she went, for I detest that man as fervently as you can do – except, indeed, that his reformation would give me much greater pleasure than his death; but all I did was to inform her of the circumstance of his illness (the consequence of a fall from his horse in hunting), and to tell her that unhappy person, Miss Myers, had left him some time ago.'

'It was ill done! Now, when he finds the convenience of her presence, he will make all manner of lying speeches and false, fair promises for the future, and she will believe him, and then her condition will be ten times worse and ten times more irremediable than before.'

'There does not appear to be much ground for such apprehensions at present,' said he, producing a letter from his pocket: 'From the account I received this morning, I should say—'

It was her writing! By an irresistible impulse, I held out my hand, and the

words – 'Let me see it,' involuntarily passed my lips. He was evidently reluctant to grant the request, but while he hesitated, I snatched it from his hand. Recollecting myself, however, the minute after, I offered to restore it.

'Here, take it,' said I, 'if you don't want me to read it.'

'No,' replied he, 'you may read it if you like.'

I read it, and so may you.

Grassdale, *November 4th.*

'DEAR FREDERICK, – *I know you will be anxious to hear from me, and I will tell you all I can. Mr Huntingdon is very ill, but not dying, or in any immediate danger; and he is rather better at present than he was when I came. I found the house in sad confusion: Mrs Greaves, Benson, every decent servant had left, and those that were come to supply their places were a negligent, disorderly set, to say no worse – I must change them again, if I stay. A professional nurse, a grim, hard old woman, had been hired to attend the wretched invalid. He suffers much, and has no fortitude to bear him through. The immediate injuries he sustained from the accident, however, were not very severe, and would, as the doctor says, have been but trifling to a man of temperate habits, but with him it is very different. On the night of my arrival, when I first entered his room, he was lying in a kind of half delirium. He did not notice me till I spoke, and then he mistook me for another.*

' *"Is it you, Alice, come again?" he murmured. "What did you leave me for?"*

' *"It is I, Arthur – it is Helen, your wife," I replied.*

' *"My wife!" said he, with a start. "For heaven's sake, don't mention her! – I have none. Devil take her," he cried, a moment after, "and you too! What did you do it for?"*

' *I said no more; but observing that he kept gazing towards the foot of the bed, I went and sat there, placing the light so as to shine full upon me, for I thought he might be dying, and I wanted him to know me. For a long time he lay silently looking upon me, first with a vacant stare, then with a fixed gaze of strange growing intensity. At last he startled me by suddenly raising himself on his elbow and demanding in a horrified whisper, with his eyes still fixed on me – "Who is it?"*

' *"It is Helen Huntingdon," said I, quietly rising at the same time, and removing to a less conspicuous position.*

' *"I must be going mad," cried he, "or something – delirious perhaps; but leave me, whoever you are – I can't bear that white face, and those eyes; for God's sake go, and send me somebody else, that doesn't look like that!"*

' *I went at once, and sent the hired nurse; but next morning I ventured to enter his chamber again; and, taking the nurse's place by his bedside, I watched him and waited on him for several hours, showing myself as little as possible, and only speaking when necessary, and then not above my breath. At first he addressed me as the nurse, but, on my crossing the room to draw up the window-blinds, in obedience to his directions, he said—*

' *"No, it isn't nurse; it's Alice. Stay with me – do! that old hag will be the death of me."*

' *"I mean to stay with you," said I. And after that he would call me Alice, or some other name almost equally repugnant to my feelings. I forced myself to endure it for a while, fearing a contradiction might disturb him too much, but*

# The Tenant of Wildfell Hall

*when, having asked for a glass of water, while I held it to his lips, he murmured,*
*"Thanks, dearest!" I could not help distinctly observing – "You would not say*
*so if you knew me," intending to follow that up with another declaration of my*
*identity, but he merely muttered an incoherent reply, so I dropped it again, till*
*some time after, when, as I was bathing his forehead and temples with vinegar*
*and water to relieve the heat and pain in his head, he observed – after looking*
*earnestly upon me for some minute – "I have such strange fancies – I can't get*
*rid of them, and they won't let me rest; and the most singular and pertinacious*
*of them all is your face and voice; they seem just like hers. I could swear at this*
*moment, that she was by my side."*

' *"She is," said I.*

' *"That seems comfortable," continued he, without noticing my words; "and*
*while you do it, the other fancies fade away – but this only strengthens. Go on*
*– go on, till it vanishes too. I can't stand such a mania as this; it would kill me!"*

' *"It never will vanish," said I distinctly, "for it is the truth."*

' *"The truth!" he cried, starting as if an asp had stung him. "You don't mean*
*to say that you are really she?"*

' *"I do; but you needn't shrink away from me, as if I were your greatest enemy:*
*I am come to take care of you, and do what none of them would do."*

' *"For God's sake, don't torment me now!" cried he in pitiable agitation; and*
*then he began to mutter bitter curses against me, or the evil fortune that had*
*brought me there; while I put down the sponge and basin, and resumed my seat*
*at the bed-side.*

' *"Where are they?" said he – "have they all left me – servants and all?"*

' *"There are servants within call if you want them; but you had better lie*
*down now and be quiet: none of them could or would attend you as carefully as*
*I shall do."*

' *"I can't understand it at all," said he, in bewildered perplexity. "Was it a*
*dream that" – and he covered his eyes with his hands, as if trying to unravel the*
*mystery.*

' *"No, Arthur, it was not a dream, that your conduct was such as to oblige me*
*to leave you; but I heard that you were ill and alone, and I am come back to*
*nurse you. You need not fear to trust me: tell me all your wants, and I will try*
·to satisfy them. There is no one else to care for you; and I shall not upbraid you*
*now."*

' *"Oh! I see," said he, with a bitter smile, "it's an act of Christian charity,*
*whereby you hope to gain a higher seat in heaven for yourself, and scoop a deeper*
*pit in hell for me."*

' *"No; I came to offer you that comfort and assistance your situation required;*
*and if I could benefit your soul as well as your body, and awaken some sense of*
*contrition and"*—

' *"Oh, yes; if you could overwhelm me with remorse and confusion of face,*
*now's the time. What have you done with my son?"*

' *"He is well, and you may see him some time if you will compose yourself,*
*but not now."* ·

' *"Where is he?"*

' *"He is safe."*

' *"Is he here?"*

' *"Wherever he is, you will not see him till you have promised to leave him*

*entirely under my care and protection, and to let me take him away whenever and wherever I please, if I should hereafter judge it necessary to remove him again. But we will talk of that tomorrow: you must be quiet now."*

' "No, let me see him now. I promise, if it must be so."

' "No"—

' "I swear it, as God is in heaven! Now then, let me see him."

' "But I cannot trust your oaths and promises; I must have a written agreement, and you must sign it in presence of a witness – but not today, tomorrow."

' "No, today – now," *persisted he: and he was in such a state of feverish excitement, and so bent upon the immediate gratification of his wish, that I thought it better to grant it at once, as I saw he would not rest till I did. But I was determined my son's interest should not be forgotten and, having clearly written out the promise I wished Mr. Huntingdon to give upon a slip of paper, I deliberately read it over to him, and made him sign it in the presence of Rachel. He begged I would not insist upon this: it was a useless exposure of my want of faith in his word to the servant. I told him I was sorry, but since he had forfeited my confidence, he must take the consequence. He next pleaded inability to hold the pen.* "Then we must wait until you can hold it," *said I. Upon which he said he would try; but then he could not see to write. I placed my finger where the signature was to be, and told him he might write his name in the dark, if he only knew where to put it. But he had not power to form the letters.* "In that case, you must be too ill to see the child," *said I; and finding me inexorable, he at length managed to ratify the agreement; and I bade Rachel send the boy.*

'All this may strike you as harsh, but I felt I must not lose my present advantage, and my son's future welfare should not be sacrificed to any mistaken tenderness for this man's feelings. Little Arthur had not forgotten his father, but thirteen months of absence, during which he had seldom been permitted to hear a word about him, or hardly to whisper his name, had rendered him somewhat shy; and when he was ushered into the darkened room where the sick man lay, so altered from his former self, with fiercely-flushed face and wildly-gleaming eyes – he instinctively clung to me, and stood looking on his father with a countenance expressive of far more awe than pleasure.

' "Come here, Arthur," *said the latter, extending his hand towards him. The child went, and timidly touched that burning hand, but almost started in alarm, when his father suddenly clutched his arm and drew him nearer to his side.*

' "Do you know me?" *asked Mr. Huntingdon, intently perusing his features.*

' "Yes."

' "Who am I?"

' "Papa."

' "Are you glad to see me?"

' "Yes."

' "You're not!' *replied the disappointed parent, relaxing his hold, and darting a vindictive glance at me.*

'Arthur, thus released, crept back to me, and put his hand in mine. His father swore I had made the child hate him, and abused and cursed me bitterly. The instant he began I sent our son out of the room; and when he paused to breathe, I calmly assured him that he was entirely mistaken; I had never once attempted to prejudice his child against him.

' "I did indeed desire him to forget you," I said, "and especially to forget the

*lessons you taught him; and for that cause, and to lessen the danger of discovery, I own I have generally discouraged his inclination to talk about you; but no one can blame me for that, I think."*

*'The invalid only replied by groaning aloud, and rolling his head on a pillow in a paroxysm of impatience.*

*' "I am in hell, already!" cried he. 'This cursed thirst is burning my heart to ashes! Will nobody –"*

*'Before he could finish the sentence, I had poured out a glass of some acidulated, cooling drink that was on the table, and brought it to him. He drank it greedily, but muttered, as I took away the glass—*

*' "I suppose you're heaping coals of fire on my head – you think."*

*'Not noticing this speech, I asked if there was anything else I could do for him.*

*' "Yes; I'll give you another opportunity of showing your Christian magnaminity," sneered he: – "set my pillow straight, – and those confounded bedclothes," I did so. "There – now get me another glass of that slop." I complied. "This is delightful! isn't it?" said he, with a malicious grin, as I held it to his lips "you never hoped for such a glorious opportunity?"*

*' "Now, shall I stay with you?" said I, as I replaced the glass on the table – "or will you be more quiet if I go and send the nurse?"*

*' "Oh, yes, you're wondrous gentle and obliging! – But you've driven me mad with it all!" responded he, with an impatient toss.*

*' "I'll leave you, then," said I; and I withdrew, and did not trouble him with my presence again that day, except for a minute or two at a time, just to see how he was and what he wanted.*

*'Next morning, the doctor ordered him to be bled; and after that, he was more subdued and tranquil. I passed half the day in his room at different intervals. My presence did not appear to agitate or irritate him as before, and he accepted my services quietly, without any bitter remarks – indeed he scarcely spoke at all, except to make known his wants, and hardly then. But on the morrow – that is, today – in proportion as he recovered from the state of exhaustion and stupefaction – his ill-nature appeared to revive.*

*' "Oh, this sweet revenge!" cried he, when I had been doing all I could to make him comfortable and to remedy the carelessness of his nurse. "And you can enjoy it with such a quiet conscience too, because it's all in the way of duty."*

*' "It is well for me that I am doing my duty," said I, with a bitterness I could not repress, "for it is the only comfort I have; and the satisfaction of my own conscience, it seems, is the only reward I need look for!"*

*'He looked rather surprised at the earnestness of my manner.*

*' "What reward did you look for?" he asked.*

*' "You will think me a liar if I tell you – but I did hope to benefit you: as well to better your mind as to alleviate your present sufferings; but it appears I am to do neither – your own bad spirit will not let me. As far as you are concerned, I have sacrificed my own feelings, and all the little earthly comfort that was left me, to no purpose – and every little thing I do for you is ascribed to self-righteous malice and refined revenge!"*

*' "It's all very fine, I dare say," said he, eyeing me with stupid amazement; "and of course I ought to be melted to tears of penitence and admiration at the sight of so much generosity and superhuman goodness, – but you see I can't manage it. However, pray do me all the good you can, if you do really find any*

*pleasure in it; for you perceive I am almost as miserable just now as you need wish to see me. Since you came, I confess, I have had better attendance than before, for these wretches neglected me shamefully, and all my old friends seem to have fairly forsaken me. I've had a dreadful time of it, I assure you: I sometimes thought I should have died – do you think there's any chance?"*

*' "There's always a chance of death; and it is always well to live with such a chance in view."*

*' "Yes, yes – but do you think there's any likelihood that this illness will have a fatal termination?"*

*' "I cannot tell; but, supposing it should, how are you prepared to meet the event?"*

*' "Why, the doctor told me I wasn't to think about it, for I was sure to get better, if I stuck to his regimen and prescriptions."*

*' "I hope you may, Arthur; but neither the doctor nor I can speak with certainty in such a case; there is internal injury, and it is difficult to know to what extent."*

*' "There now! you want to scare me to death."*

*' "No; but I don't want to lull you to false security. If a consciousness of the uncertainty of life can dispose you to serious and useful thoughts, I would not deprive you of the benefit of such reflections, whether you do eventually recover or not. Does the idea of death appal you very much?"*

*' "It's just the only thing I can't bear to think of; so if you've any—"*

*' "But it must come some time," interrupted I; "and if it be years hence, it will as certainly overtake you as if it came today, – and no doubt be as unwelcome then as now, unless you—"*

*' "Oh, hang it! don't torment me with your preachments now, unless you want to kill me outright – I can't stand it, I tell you, I've sufferings enough without that. If you think there's danger, save me from it; and then, in gratitude, I'll hear whatever you like to say."*

*'I accordingly dropped the unwelcome topic. And now, Frederick, I think I may bring my letter to a close. From these details you may form your own judgment of the state of my patient, and of my own position and future prospects. Let me hear from you soon, and I will write again to tell you how we get on; but now that my presence is tolerated, and even required, in the sick-room, I shall have but little time to spare between my husband and my son, – for I must not entirely neglect the latter: it would not do to keep him always with Rachel, and I dare not leave him for a moment with any of the other servants, or suffer him to be alone, lest he should meet him. If his father get worse, I shall ask Esther Hargrave to take charge of him for a time, till I have re-organized the household at least; but I greatly prefer keeping him under my own eye.*

*'I find myself in rather a singular position: I am exerting my utmost endeavours to promote the recovery and reformation of my husband, and if I succeed, what shall I do? My duty, of course, – but how? – No matter; I can perform the task that is before me now, and God will give me strength to do whatever He requires hereafter. – Good-bye, dear Frederick.*

'HELEN HUNTINGDON'

'What do you think of it?' said Lawrence, as I silently refolded the letter.

'It seems to me,' returned I, 'that she is casting her pearls before swine. May they be satisfied with trampling them under their feet, and not turn again and

rend her! But I shall say no more against her: I see that she was actuated by the best and noblest motives in what she has done; and if the act is not a wise one, may Heaven protect her from its consequences! May I keep this letter, Lawrence? – you see she has never once mentioned me throughout – or made the most distant allusion to me; therefore, there can be no impropriety or harm in it.'

'And therefore, why should you wish to keep it?'

'Were not these characters written by her hand? and were not these words conceived in her mind, and many of them spoken by her lips?'

'Well,' said he. And so I kept it; otherwise, Halford, you could never have become so thoroughly acquainted with its contents.

'And when you write,' said I, 'will you have the goodness to ask her if I may be permitted to enlighten my mother and sister of her real history and circumstances, just so far as is necessary to make the neighbourhood sensible of the shameful injustice they have done her? I want no tender messages, but just ask her that, and tell her it is the greatest favour she could do me; and tell her – no, nothing more. – You see I know the address, and I might write to her myself, but I am so virtuous as to refrain.'

'Well, I'll do this for you, Markham.'

'And as soon as you receive an answer, you'll let me know?'

'If all be well, I'll come myself and tell you immediately.'

# Chapter 48

Five or six days after this, Mr Lawrence paid us the honour of a call; and when he and I were alone together – which I contrived as soon as possible, by bringing him out to look at my cornstacks – he showed me another letter from his sister. This one he was quite willing to submit to my longing gaze; he thought, I suppose, it would do me good. The only answer it gave to my message was this—

'Mr Markham is at liberty to make such revelations concerning me as he judges necessary. He will know that I should wish but little to be said on the subject. I hope he is well; but tell him he must not think of me.'

I can give you a few extracts from the rest of the letter, for I was permitted to keep this also – perhaps, as an antidote to all pernicious hopes and fancies.

*'He is decidedly better, but very low from the depressing effects of his severe illness and the strict regimen he is obliged to observe – so opposite to all his previous habits. It is deplorable to see how completely his past life has degenerated his once noble constitution, and vitiated the whole system of his organization. But the doctor says he may now be considered out of danger, if he will only continue to observe the necessary restrictions. Some stimulating cordials he must*

# The Tenant of Wildfell Hall

*have, but they should be judiciously diluted and sparingly used; and I find it very difficult to keep him to this. At first, his extreme dread of death rendered the task an easy one; but in proportion as he feels his acute suffering abating, and sees the danger receding, the more intractable he becomes. Now, also, his appetite for food is beginning to return; and here, too, his long habits of self-indulgence are greatly against him. I watch and restrain him as well as I can, and often get bitterly abused for my rigid severity; and sometimes he contrives to elude my vigilance, and sometimes acts in opposition to my will. But now he is so completely reconciled to my attendance in general that he is never satisfied when I am not by his side. I am obliged to be a little stiff with him sometimes, or he would make a complete slave of me; and I know it would be unpardonable weakness to give up all other interests for him. I have the servants to overlook, and my little Arthur to attend to, – and my own health too, all of which would be entirely neglected were I to satisfy his exorbitant demands. I do not generally sit up at night, for I think the nurse who has made it her business, is better qualified for such undertakings than I am; but still, an unbroken night's rest is what I but seldom enjoy, and never can venture to reckon upon; for my patient makes no scruple of calling me up at any hour when his wants or his fancies require my presence. But he is manifestly afraid of my displeasure; and if at one time he tries my patience by his unreasonable exactions, and fretful complaints and reproaches, at another he depresses me by his abject submission and deprecatory self-abasement when he fears he has gone too far. But all this I can readily pardon; I know it is chiefly the result of his enfeebled frame and disordered nerves – what annoys me the most, is his occasional attempts at affectionate fondness that I can neither credit nor return; not that I hate him: his sufferings and my own laborious care have given him some claim to my regard – to my affection even, if he could only be quiet and sincere, and content to let things remain as they are; but the more he tries to conciliate me, the more I shrink from him and from the future.*

'"Helen, what do you mean to do when I get well?" he asked this morning. "Will you run away again?"

'"It entirely depends upon your own conduct."

'"Oh, I'll be very good."

'"But if I find it necessary to leave you, Arthur, I shall not 'run away': you know I have your own promise that I may go whenever I please, and take my son with me."

'"Oh, but you shall have no cause." And then followed a variety of professions, which I rather coldly checked.

'"Will you not forgive me then?" said he.

'"Yes, – I have forgiven you; but I know you cannot love me as you once did – and I should be very sorry if you were to, for I could not pretend to return it; so let us drop the subject and never recur to it again. By what I have done for you, you may judge of what I will do – if it be not incompatible with the higher duty I owe to my son (higher, because he never forfeited his claims, and because I hope to do more good to him than I can ever do to you); and if you wish me to feel kindly towards you, it is deeds, not words, which must purchase my affection and esteem."

'His sole reply to this was a slight grimace, and a scarcely perceptible shrug. Alas, unhappy man! words, with him, are so much cheaper than deeds; it was

474

*as if I had said, "Pounds, not pence, must buy the article you want." And then he sighed a querulous, half-commiserating sigh, as if in pure regret that he, the loved and courted of so many worshippers, should be now abandoned to the mercy of a harsh, exacting, cold-hearted woman like that, and even glad of what kindness she chose to bestow.*

*' "It's a pity, isn't it?" said I; and whether I rightly divined his musings or not, the observation chimed in with his thoughts, for he answered – "It can't be helped," with a rueful smile at my penetration.*

*'I have seen Esther Hargrave twice. She is a charming creature, but her blithe spirit is almost broken, and her sweet temper almost spoiled, by the still unremitting persecutions of her mother in behalf of her rejected suitor – not violent, but wearisome and unremitting like a continual dropping. The unnatural parent seems determined to make her daughter's life a burden, if she will not yield to her desires.*

*' "Mamma does all she can," said she, "to make me feel myself a burden and encumbrance to the family, and the most ungrateful, selfish, and undutiful daughter that ever was born; and Walter, too, is as stern and cold and haughty as if he hated me outright. I believe I should have yielded at once if I had known from the beginning how much resistance would have cost me; but now, for very obstinacy's sake, I will stand out!"*

*' "A bad motive for a good resolve," I answered. "But, however, I know you have better motives, really, for your perseverance: and I counsel you to keep them still in view."*

*' "Trust me I will. I threaten mamma sometimes, that I'll run away, and disgrace the family by earning my own livelihood, if she torments me any more; and then that frightens her a little. But I will do it, in good earnest, if they don't mind."*

*' "Be quiet and patient awhile," said I, "and better times will come."*

*'Poor girl! I wish somebody that was worthy to possess her would come and take her away – don't you, Frederick?'*

If the perusal of this letter filled me with dismay for Helen's future life and mine, there was one great source of consolation: it was now in my power to clear her name from every foul aspersion. The Millwards and the Wilsons should see with their own eyes the bright sun bursting from the cloud – and they should be scorched and dazzled by its beams; – and my own friends too should see it – they whose suspicions had been such gall and wormwood to my soul. To effect this, I had only to drop the seed into the ground, and it would soon become a stately, branching herb: a few words to my mother and sister, I knew, would suffice to spread the news throughout the whole neighbourhood, without any further exertion on my part.

Rose was delighted; and as soon as I had told her all I thought proper – which was all I affected to know – she flew with alacrity to put on her bonnet and shawl, and hasten to carry the glad tidings to the Millwards and Wilsons – glad tidings, I suspect, to none but herself and Mary Millward – that steady, sensible girl, whose sterling worth had been so quickly perceived and duly valued by the supposed Mrs Graham, in spite of her plain outside; and who, on her

part, had been better able to see and appreciate that lady's true character and qualities than the brightest genius among them.

As I may never have occasion to mention her again, I may as well tell you here, that she was at this time privately engaged to Richard Wilson – a secret, I believe, to every one but themselves. That worthy student was now at Cambridge, where his most exemplary conduct and his diligent perseverance in the pursuit of learning carried him safely through, and eventually brought him with hard-earned honours, and an untarnished reputation, to the close of his collegiate career. In due time, he became Mr Millward's first and only curate – for that gentleman's declining years forced him at last to acknowledge that the duties of his extensive parish were a little too much for those vaunted energies which he was wont to boast over his younger and less active brethren of the cloth. This was what the patient, faithful lovers had privately planned, and quietly waited for years ago; and in due time they were united, to the astonishment of the little world they lived in, that had long since declared them born to single blessedness; affirming it impossible that the pale, retiring bookworm should ever summon courage to seek a wife, or be able to obtain one if he did, and equally impossible that the plain looking, plain dealing, unattractive, unconciliating Miss Millward should ever find a husband.

They still continued to live at the vicarage, the lady dividing her time between her father, her husband, and their poor parishioners, – and subsequently her rising family; and now that the Reverend Michael Millward has been gathered to his fathers, full of years and honours, the Reverend Richard Wilson has succeeded him to the vicarage of Lindenhope, greatly to the satisfaction of its inhabitants, who had so long tried and fully proved his merits, and those of his excellent and well-loved partner.

If you are interested in the after-fate of the lady's sister, I can only tell you – what perhaps you have heard from another quarter – that some twelve or thirteen years ago she relieved the happy couple of her presence by marrying a wealthy tradesman of L—; and I don't envy him his bargain. I fear she leads him a rather uncomfortable life, though, happily, he is too dull to perceive the extent of his misfortune. I have little enough to do with her myself: we have not met for many years; but I am well assured, she has not yet forgotten or forgiven either her former lover, or the lady whose superior qualities first opened his eyes to the folly of his boyish attachment.

As for Richard Wilson's sister, she, having been wholly unable to re-capture Mr Lawrence, or obtain any partner rich and elegant enough to suit her ideas of what the husband of Jane Wilson ought to be, is yet in single blessedness. Shortly after the death of her mother, she withdrew the light of her presence from Ryecote Farm, finding it impossible any longer to endure the rough manners and unsophisticated habits of her honest brother Robert and his worthy wife, or the idea of being identified with such vulgar people in the eyes of the world, – and took lodgings in —, the county town, where she lived, and still lives, I suppose, in a kind of close-fisted, cold, uncomfortable gentility, doing no good to others, and but little to herself; spending her days in fancy work and scandal; referring frequently to her 'brother, the vicar,' and her 'sister, the vicar's lady,' but never to her brother, the farmer, and her sister, the farmer's wife; seeing as much company as she can without too much expense, but loving no

one and beloved by none – a cold-hearted, supercilious, keenly insidious, censorious old maid.

# Chapter 49

Though Mr Lawrence's health was now quite re-established, my visits to Woodford were as unremitting as ever; though often less protracted than before. We seldom talked about Mrs Huntingdon; but yet we never met without mentioning her, for I never sought his company but with the hope of hearing something about her, and he never sought mine at all, because he saw me often enough without. But I always began to talk of other things, and waited first to see if he would introduce the subject. If he did not, I would casually ask, 'Have you heard from your sister lately?' If he said 'No,' the matter was dropped: if he said 'Yes,' I would venture to inquire, 'How is she?' but never 'How is her husband?' though I might be burning to know; because I had not the hypocrisy to profess an anxiety for his recovery, and I had not the face to express any desire for a contrary result. Had I any such desire? – I fear I must plead guilty; but since you have heard my confession, you must hear my justification as well – a few of the excuses, at least, wherewith I sought to pacify my own accusing conscience.

In the first place, you see his life did harm to others, and evidently no good to himself; and though I wished it to terminate I would not have hastened its close, if, by the lifting of a finger I could have done so, or if a spirit had whispered in my ear that a single effort of the will would be enough, – unless, indeed, I had the power to exchange him for some other victim of the grave, whose life might be of service to his race, and whose death would be lamented by his friends. But was there any harm in wishing that, among the many thousands whose souls would certainly be required of them before the year was over, this wretched mortal might be one? I thought not; and therefore I wished with all my heart that it might please Heaven to remove him to a better world, or if that might not be, still, to take him out of this; for if he were unfit to answer the summons now, after a warning sickness, and with such an angel by his side, it seemed but too certain that he never would be – that, on the contrary, returning health would bring returning lust and villainy, and as he grew more certain of recovery, more accustomed to her generous goodness, his feelings would become more callous, his heart more flinty and impervious to her persuasive arguments – but God knew best. Meantime, however, I could not but be anxious for the result of His decrees; knowing, as I did, that (leaving myself entirely out of the question) however Helen might feel interested in her husband's welfare, however she might deplore his fate, still while he lived she must be miserable.

# The Tenant of Wildfell Hall

A fortnight passed away, and my inquiries were always answered in the negative. At length a welcome 'yes' drew from me the second question. Lawrence divined my anxious thoughts, and appreciated my reserve. I feared, at first, he was going to torture me by unsatisfactory replies, and either leave me quite in the dark concerning what I wanted to know, or force me to drag the information out of him, morsel by morsel, by direct inquiries – 'and serve you right,' you will say; but he was more merciful; and in a little while, he put his sister's letter into my hand. I silently read it, and restored it to him without comment or remark. This mode of procedure suited him so well, that thereafter he always pursued the plan of showing me her letters at once, when I inquired after her, if there were any to show – it was so much less trouble than to tell me their contents; and I received such confidences so quietly and discreetly that he was never induced to discontinue them.

But I devoured those precious letters with my eyes, and never let them go till their contents were stamped upon my mind; and when I got home, the most important passages were entered in my diary among the remarkable events of the day.

The first of these communications brought intelligence of a serious relapse in Mr Huntingdon's illness, entirely the result of his own infatuation in persisting in the indulgence of his appetite for stimulating drink. In vain had she remonstrated, in vain she had mingled his wine with water: her arguments and entreaties were a nuisance, her interference was an insult so intolerable, that, at length, on finding she had covertly diluted the pale port that was brought him, he threw the bottle out of the window, swearing he would not be cheated like a baby, ordered the butler, on pain of instant dismissal, to bring a bottle of the strongest wine in the cellar, and affirming that he should have been well long ago if he had been let to have his own way, but she wanted to keep him weak in order that she might have him under her thumb – but by the Lord Harry, he would have no more humbug – seized a glass in one hand, and a bottle in the other, and never rested till he had drunk it dry. Alarming symptoms were the immediate result of his 'imprudence', as she mildly termed it – symptoms which had rather increased than diminished since; and this was the cause of her delay in writing to her brother. Every former feature of his malady had returned with augmented virulence; the slight external wound, half healed, had broken out afresh; internal inflammation had taken place, which might terminate fatally if not soon removed. Of course, the wretched sufferer's temper was not improved by his calamity – in fact, I suspect it was wellnigh insupportable, though his kind nurse did not complain; but she said she had been obliged at last to give her son in charge to Esther Hargrave, as her presence was so constantly required in the sick-room that she could not possibly attend to him herself; and though the child had begged to be allowed to continue with her there, and to help her to nurse his papa, and though she had no doubt he would have been very good and quiet – she could not think of subjecting his young and tender feelings to the sight of so much suffering, or of allowing him to witness his father's impatience or hear the dreadful language he was wont to use in his paroxysms of pain or irritation.

'The latter,' continued she, 'most deeply regrets the step that has occasioned his relapse, – but, as usual, he throws the blame upon me. If I had reasoned with him like a rational creature, he says, it never would have happened; but

# The Tenant of Wildfell Hall

to be treated like a baby or a fool, was enough to put any man past his patience, and drive him to assert his independence even at the sacrifice of his own interest – he forgets how often I had reasoned him "past his patience" before. He appears to be sensible of his danger; but nothing can induce him to behold it in the proper light. The other night while I was waiting on him, and just as I had brought him a draught to assuage his burning thirst – he observed, with a return of his former sarcastic bitterness—

' "Yes, you're mighty attentive now! – I suppose there's nothing you wouldn't do for me now?'

' "You know," said I, a little surprised at his manner, "that I am willing to do anything I can to relieve you."

' "Yes, now, my immaculate angel; but when once you have secured your reward, and find yourself safe in heaven, and me howling in hell-fire, catch you lifting a finger to serve me then! – No, you'll look complacently on, and not so much as dip the tip of your finger in water to cool my tongue!"

' "If so, it will be because of the great gulf over which I cannot pass; and if I could look complacently on in such a case, it would be only from the assurance that you were being purified from your sins, and fitted to enjoy the happiness I felt. – But are you determined, Arthur, that I shall not meet you in heaven?"

' "Humph! What should I do there, I should like to know?"

' "Indeed, I cannot tell; and I fear it is too certain that your tastes and feelings must be widely altered before you can have any enjoyment there. But do you prefer sinking, without an effort, into the state of torment you picture to yourself?"

' "Oh, it's all a fable," said he contemptuously.

' "Are you sure, Arthur? are you quite sure? Because if there is any doubt, and if you should find yourself mistaken after all, when it is too late to turn"—

' "It would be rather awkward to be sure," said he: "but don't bother me now – I'm not going to die yet. I can't and won't," he added vehemently, as if suddenly struck with the appalling aspect of that terrible event. "Helen, you must save me!" And he earnestly seized my hand, and looked into my face with such imploring eagerness that my heart bled for him, and I could not speak for tears.'

The next letter brought intelligence that the malady was fast increasing; and the poor sufferer's horror of death was still more distressing than his impatience of bodily pain. All his friends had not forsaken him, for Mr Hattersley, hearing of his danger, had come to see him from his distant home in the north. His wife had accompanied him, as much for the pleasure of seeing her dear friend from whom she had been parted so long, as to visit her mother and sister.

Mrs Huntingdon expressed herself glad to see Milicent once more, and pleased to behold her so happy and well. 'She is now at the Grove,' continued the letter, 'but she often calls to see me. Mr Hattersley spends much of his time at Arthur's bedside. With more good feeling than I gave him credit for, he evinces considerable sympathy for his unhappy friend, and is far more willing than able to comfort him. Sometimes he tries to joke and laugh with him, but that will not do: sometimes he endeavours to cheer him with talk about old times; and this at one time may serve to divert the sufferer from his own sad thoughts; at another, it will only plunge him into deeper melancholy than before;

and then Hattersley is confounded, and knows not what to say, – unless it be a timid suggestion that the clergyman might be sent for. But Arthur will never consent to that: he knows he has rejected the clergyman's well-meant admonitions with scoffing levity at other times, and cannot dream of turning to him for consolation now.

'Mr Hattersley sometimes offers his services instead of mine, but Arthur will not let me go: that strange whim still increases as his strength declines – the fancy to have me always by his side. I hardly ever leave him, except to go into the next room, where I sometimes snatch an hour or so of sleep when he is quiet; but even then, the door is left ajar that he may know me to be within call. I am with him now, while I write; and I fear my occupation annoys him; though I frequently break off to attend him, and though Mr Hattersley is also by his side. That gentleman came, as he said, to beg a holiday for me, that I might have a run in the park, this fine, frosty morning, with Milicent, and Esther, and little Arthur, whom he had driven over to see me. Our poor invalid evidently felt it a heartless proposition, and would have felt it still more heartless in me to accede to it. I therefore said I would only go and speak to them a minute, and then come back. I did but exchange a few words with them, just outside the portico – inhaling the fresh bracing air as I stood – and then, resisting the earnest and eloquent entreaties of all three to stay a little longer, and join them in a walk round the garden, I tore myself away and returned to my patient. I had not been absent five minutes, but he reproached me bitterly for my levity and neglect. His friend espoused my cause—

' "Nay, nay, Huntingdon," said he, "you're too hard upon her – she must have food and sleep, and a mouthful of fresh air now and then, or she can't stand it, I tell you. Look at her man, she's worn to a shadow already."

' "What are her sufferings to mine?" said the poor invalid. "You don't grudge me these attentions, do you, Helen?"

' "No, Arthur, if I could really serve you by them. I would give my life to save you, if I might."

' "Would you, indeed? – No?"

' "Most willingly, I would."

' "Ah! that's because you think yourself more fit to die!"

'There was a painful pause. He was evidently plunged in gloomy reflections, but while I pondered for something to say, that might benefit without alarming him, Hattersley, whose mind had been pursuing almost the same course, broke silence with—

' "I say, Huntingdon, I would send for a parson of some sort. – If you didn't like the vicar, you know, you could have his curate or somebody else."

' "No; none of them can benefit me if she can't," was the answer. And the tears gushed from his eyes as he earnestly exclaimed – "Oh, Helen, if I had listened to you, it never would have come to this! And if I had heard you long ago – Oh, God! how different it would have been!"

' "Hear me now, then, Arthur," said I, gently pressing his hand.

' "It's too late, now," said he despondingly. And after that another paroxysm of pain came on; and then his mind began to wander, and we feared his death was approaching; but an opiate was administered, his sufferings began to abate, he gradually became more composed, and at length sank into a kind of slumber.

He has been quieter since; and now Hattersley has left him, expressing a hope that he shall find him better when he calls tomorrow.

' "Perhaps I may recover," he replied, "who knows? – this may have been the crisis. What do you think, Helen?"

'Unwilling to depress him, I gave the most cheering answer I could, but still recommended him to prepare for the possibility of what I only feared was too certain. But he was determined to hope. Shortly after, he relapsed into a kind of doze – but now he groans again.

'There is a sudden change. Suddenly he called me to his side, with such a strange excited manner that I feared he was delirious – but he was not. "That was the crisis, Helen!" said he delightedly – "I had an infernal pain here – it is quite gone now; I never was so easy since the fall – Quite gone, by heaven!" and he clasped and kissed my hand in the very fulness of his heart; but, finding I did not participate his joy, he quickly flung it from him, and bitterly cursed my coldness and insensibility. How could I reply? Kneeling beside him, I took his hand and fondly pressed it to my lips – for the first time since our separation – and told him as well as tears would let me speak, that it was not that that kept me silent; it was the fear that this sudden cessation of pain was not so favourable a symptom as he supposed. I immediately sent for the doctor. We are now anxiously awaiting him. I will tell you what he says. There is still the same freedom from pain – the same deadness to all sensation where the suffering was most acute.

'My worst fears are realized – moritification has commenced. The doctor has told him there is no hope – no words can describe his anguish. I can write no more.'

The next was still more distressing in the tenor of its contents. The sufferer was fast approaching dissolution – dragged almost to the verge of that awful chasm he trembled to contemplate, from which no agony of prayers or tears could save him. Nothing could comfort him now; Hattersley's rough attempts at consolation were utterly in vain. The world was nothing to him: life and all its interests, its petty cares and transient pleasures, were a cruel mockery. To talk of the past, was to torture him with vain remorse: to refer to the future, was to increase his anguish; and yet to be silent, was to leave him a prey to his own regrets and apprehensions. Often he dwelt with shuddering minuteness on the fate of his perishing clay – the slow, piecemeal dissolution already invading his frame: the shroud, the coffin, the dark, lonely grave, and all the horrors of corruption.

'If I try,' said his afflicted wife, 'to divert him from these things – to raise his thoughts to higher themes, it is no better – "Worse and worse!" he groans. "If there be really life beyond the tomb, and judgment after death, how can I face it?" – I cannot do him any good; he will neither be enlightened, nor roused, nor comforted by anything I say; and yet he clings to me with unrelenting pertinacity – with a kind of childish desperation, as if I could save him from the fate he dreads. He keeps me night and day beside him. He is holding my left hand now, while I write; he has held it thus for hours: sometimes clutching my arm with violence – the big drops starting from his forehead, at the thoughts of what he sees, or thinks he sees before him. If I withdraw my hand for a moment, it distresses him—

' "Stay with me, Helen," he says; "let me hold you so: it seems as if harm could not reach me while you are here. But death will come – it is coming now – fast, fast! – and – Oh, if I could believe there was nothing after!"

' "Don't try to believe it, Arthur; there is joy and glory after, if you will but try to reach it!"

' "What, for me?" he said, with something like a laugh. "Are we not to be judged according to the deeds done in the body? Where's the use of a probationary existence, if a man may spend it as he pleases, just contrary to God's decrees, and then go to heaven with the best – if the vilest sinner may win the reward of the holiest saint, by merely saying, 'I repent'?"

' "But if you sincerely repent—"

' "I can't repent; I only fear."

' "You only regret the past for its consequences to yourself?"

' "Just so – except that I'm sorry to have wronged you, Nell, because you're so good to me."

' "Think of the goodness of God, and you cannot but be grieved to have offended Him."

' "What is God – I cannot see Him or hear Him? – God is only an idea."

' "God is Infinite Wisdom, and Power, and Goodness – and LOVE; but if this idea is too vast for your human faculties – if your mind loses itself in its overwhelming infinitude, fix it on Him who condescended to take our nature upon Him, who was raised to heaven even in His glorified human body, in whom the fulness of the Godhead shines."

'But he only shook his head and sighed. Then, in another paroxysm of shuddering horror, he tightened his grasp on my hand and arm, and groaning and lamenting, still clung to me with that wild, desperate earnestness so harrowing to my soul, because I know I cannot help him. I did my best to soothe and comfort him.

' "Death is so terrible," he cried, "I cannot bear it! You don't know, Helen – you can't imagine what it is, because you haven't it before you; and when I'm buried, you'll return to your old ways and be as happy as ever, and all the world will go on just as busy and merry as if I had never been; while I—' He burst into tears.

' "You needn't let that distress you," I said: "we shall all follow you soon enough."

' "I wish to God I could take you with me now!" he exclaimed, "you should plead for me."

' "No man can deliver his brother, nor make agreement unto God for him," I replied: "it cost more to redeem their souls – it cost the blood of an incarnate God, perfect and sinless in Himself, to redeem us from the bondage of the evil one:– let Him plead for you."

'But I seem to speak in vain. He does not now, as formerly, laugh these blessed truths to scorn: but still he cannot trust, or will not comprehend them. He cannot linger long. He suffers dreadfully, and so do those that wait upon him – but I will not harass you with further details: I have said enough, I think, to convince you that I did well to go to him.'

Poor, poor Helen! dreadful indeed her trials must have been! And I could do nothing to lessen them – nay, it almost seemed as if I had brought them upon

her myself, by my own secret desires; and whether I looked at her husband's sufferings or her own, it seemed almost like a judgment upon myself for having cherished such a wish.

The next day but one there came another letter. That too was put into my hands without a remark, and these are its contents–

*Dec. 5th*

'*He is gone at last. I sat beside him all night, with my hand fast locked in his, watching the changes of his features and listening to his failing breath. He had been silent for a long time, and I thought he would never speak again, when he murmured, faintly but distinctly –*

'*"Pray for me, Helen!"*

'*"I do pray for you – every hour and every minute, Arthur; but you must pray for yourself."*

'*His lips moved, but emitted no sound; – then his looks became unsettled; and, from the incoherent half-uttered words that escaped him from time to time, supposing him to be now unconscious, I gently disengaged my hand from his, intending to steal away for a breath of air, for I was almost ready to faint; but a convulsive movement of the fingers, and a faintly whispered "Don't leave me!" immediately recalled me: I took his hand again, and held it till he was no more – and then I fainted: it was not grief; it was exhaustion, that, till then, I had been enabled successfully to combat. Oh, Frederick! none can imagine the miseries, bodily and mental, of that death-bed! How could I endure to think that poor trembling soul was hurried away to everlasting torment? it would drive me mad! But, thank God, I have hope – not only from a vague dependence on the possibility that penitence and pardon might have reached him at the last, but from the blessed confidence that, through whatever purging fires the erring spirit may be doomed to pass – whatever fate awaits it, still, it is not lost, and God, who hateth nothing that He hath made, will bless it in the end!*

'*His body will be consigned on Thursday to that dark grave he so much dreaded; but the coffin must be closed as soon as possible. If you will attend the funeral come quickly, for I need help.*

'HELEN HUNTINGDON.'

# Chapter 50

n reading this, I had no reason to disguise my joy and hope from Frederick Lawrence, for I had none to be ashamed of. I felt no joy but that his sister was at length released from her afflictive, overwhelming toil – no hope but that she would in time recover from the effects of it, and be suffered to rest in peace and quietness, at least, for the remainder of her life. I experienced

a painful commiseration for her unhappy husband (though fully aware that he had brought every particle of his sufferings upon himself, and but too well deserved them all), and a profound sympathy for her own afflictions, and deep anxiety for the consequences of those harassing cares, those dreadful vigils, that incessant and deleterious confinement beside a living corpse – for I was persuaded she had not hinted half the sufferings she had had to endure.

'You will go to her, Lawrence?' said I, as I put the letter into his hand.

'Yes, immediately.'

'That's right! I'll leave you, then, to prepare for your departure.'

'I've done that already, while you were reading the letter, and before you came; and the carriage is now coming round to the door.'

Inly approving his promptitude, I bade him good morning, and withdrew. He gave me a searching glance as we pressed each other's hands at parting; but whatever he sought in my countenance, he saw there nothing but the most becoming gravity – it might be, mingled with a little sternness in momentary resentment at what I suspected to be passing in his mind.

Had I forgotten my own prospects, my ardent love, my pertinacious hopes? It seemed like sacrilege to revert to them now, but I had not forgotten them. It was, however, with a gloomy sense of the darkness of those prospects, the fallacy of those hopes, and the vanity of that affection, that I reflected on those things as I remounted my horse and slowly journeyed homewards. Mrs Huntingdon was free now; it was no longer a crime to think of her – but did she ever think of me? – not now – of course it was not to be expected – but would she, when this shock was over? – In all the course of her correspondence with her brother (our mutual friend, as she herself had called him), she had never mentioned me but once – and that was from necessity. This, alone, afforded strong presumption that I was already forgotten; yet this was not the worst: it might have been her sense of duty that kept her silent, she might be only trying to forget; but in addition to this, I had a gloomy conviction that the awful realities she had seen and felt, her reconciliation with the man she had once loved, his dreadful sufferings and death, must eventually efface from her mind all traces of her passing love for me. She might recover from these horrors so far as to be restored to her former health, her tranquillity, her cheerfulness even – but never to those feelings which would appear to her, henceforth, as a fleeting fancy, a vain, illusive dream; especially as there was no one to remind her of my existence – no means of assuring her of my fervent constancy, now that we were so far apart, and delicacy forbade me to see her or to write to her, for months to come at least. And how could I engage her brother in my behalf? how could I break that icy crust of shy reserve? Perhaps he would disapprove of my attachment now, as highly as before; perhaps he would think me too poor – too lowly born, to match with his sister? Yes, there was another barrier: doubtless there was a wide distinction between the rank and circumstances of Mrs Huntingdon, the lady of Grassdale Manor, and those of Mrs Graham the artist, the tenant of Wildfell Hall; and it might be deemed presumption in me to offer my hand to the former – by the world, by her friends – if not by herself – a penalty I might brave, if I were certain she loved me; but otherwise, how could I? And, finally, her deceased husband, with his usual selfishness, might have so constructed his will as to place restrictions upon her marrying again. So that you see I had reasons enough for despair if I chose to indulge it.

# The Tenant of Wildfell Hall

Nevertheless, it was with no small degree of impatience that I looked forward to Mr Lawrence's return from Grassdale – impatience that increased in proportion as his absence was prolonged. He stayed away some ten or twelve days. All very right that he should remain to comfort and help his sister, but he might have written to tell me how she was, – or at least to tell me when to expect his return; for he might have known I was suffering tortures of anxiety for her, and uncertainty for my own future prospects. And when he did return, all he told me about her was that she had been greatly exhausted and worn by her unremitting exertions in behalf of that man who had been the scourge of her life, and had dragged her with him nearly to the portals of the grave, and was still much shaken and depressed by his melancholy end and the circumstances attendant upon it; but no word in reference to me – no intimation that my name had ever passed her lips, or even been spoken in her presence. To be sure, I asked no questions on the subject: I could not bring my mind to do so, believing, as I did, that Lawrence was indeed averse to the idea of my union with his sister.

I saw that he expected to be further questioned concerning his visit, and I saw too, with the keen perception of awakened jealousy, or alarmed self-esteem – or by whatever name I ought to call it – that he rather shrank from that impending scrutiny, and was no less pleased than surprised to find it did not come. Of course, I was burning with anger, but pride obliged me to suppress my feelings, and preserve a smooth face – or at least a stoic calmness – throughout the interview. It was well it did, for, reviewing the matter in my sober judgment, I must say it would have been highly absurd and improper to have quarrelled with him on such an occasion: I must confess too that I wronged him in my heart: the truth was, he liked me very well, but he was fully aware that a union between Mrs Huntingdon and me would be what the world calls a mesalliance; and it was not in his nature to set the world at defiance; – especially in such a case as this, for its dread laugh, or ill-opinion, would be far more terrible to him directed against his sister than himself. Had he believed that a union was necessary to the happiness of both, or of either, or had he known how fervently I loved her, he would have acted differently; but seeing me so calm and cool, he would not for the world disturb my philosophy; and though refraining entirely from any active opposition to the match, he would yet do nothing to bring it about, and would much rather take the part of prudence, in aiding us to overcome our mutual predilections, than that of feeling, to encourage them. 'And he was in the right of it,' you will say. Perhaps he was – at any rate, I had no business to feel so bitterly against him as I did; but I could not then regard the matter in such a moderate light; and, after a brief conversation upon indifferent topics, I went away, suffering all the pangs of wounded pride and injured friendship, in addition to those resulting from the fear that I was indeed forgotten, and the knowledge that she I loved was alone and afflicted, suffering from injured health and dejected spirits, and I was forbidden to console or assist her – forbidden even to assure her of my sympathy, for the transmission of any such message through Mr Lawrence was now completely out of the question.

But what should I do? I would wait, and see if she would notice me, which of course she would not, unless by some kind message entrusted to her brother, that, in all probability, he would not deliver, and then – dreadful thought! – she would think me cooled and changed for not returning it, or, perhaps, he had

# The Tenant of Wildfell Hall

already given her to understand that I had ceased to think of her. I would wait, however, till the six months after our parting were fairly passed (which would be about the close of February), and then I would send her a letter modestly reminding her of her former permission to write to her at the close of that period, and hoping I might avail myself of it, at least to express my heartfelt sorrow for her late afflictions, my just appreciation of her generous conduct, and my hope that her health was now completely re-established, and that she would, some time, be permitted to enjoy those blessings of a peaceful happy life, which had been denied her so long, but which none could more truly be said to merit than herself, – adding a few words of kind remembrance to my little friend, Arthur, with a hope that he had not forgotten me, and, perhaps, a few more in reference to bygone times, to the delightful hours I had passed in her society, and my unfading recollection of them, which was the salt and solace of my life, and a hope that her recent troubles had not entirely banished me from her mind. If she did not answer this, of course I should write no more: if she did (as surely she would, in some fashion), my future proceedings should be regulated by her reply.

Ten weeks was long to wait in such a miserable state of uncertainty, but courage! it must be endured; and meantime I would continue to see Lawrence now and then, though not so often as before, and I would still pursue my habitual inquiries after his sister, if he had lately heard from her, and how she was, and nothing more.

I did so, and the answers I received were always provokingly limited to the letter of the inquiry: she was much as usual: she made no complaints, but the tone of her last letter evinced great depression of mind, she said she was better, and, finally, she said she was well, and very busy with her son's education, and with the management of her late husband's property, and the regulation of his affairs. The rascal had never told me how that property was disposed, or whether Mr Huntingdon had died intestate or not; and I would sooner die than ask him, lest he should misconstrue into covetousness my desire to know. He never offered to show me his sister's letters now, and I never hinted a wish to see them. February, however, was approaching; December was past; January, at length, was almost over – a few more weeks, and then, certain despair or renewal of hope would put an end to this long agony of suspense.

But alas! it was just about that time she was called to sustain another blow in the death of her uncle, a worthless old fellow enough in himself, I dare say, but he had always shown more kindness and affection to her than to any other creature, and she had always been accustomed to regard him as a parent. She was with him when he died, and had assisted her aunt to nurse him during the last stage of his illness. Her brother went to Staningley to attend the funeral, and told me, upon his return, that she was still there, endeavouring to cheer her aunt with her presence, and likely to remain some time. This was bad news for me, for while she continued there I could not write to her, as I did not know the address, and would not ask it of him. But week followed week, and every time I inquired about her she was still at Staningley.

'Where is Staningley?' I asked at last.

'In —shire,' was the brief reply; and there was something so cold and dry in the manner of it, that I was effectually deterred from requesting a more definite account.

'When will she return to Grassdale?' was my next question.

'I don't know.'

'Confound it!' I muttered.

'Why, Markham?' asked my companion, with an air of innocent surprise. But I did not deign to answer him, save by a look of silent sullen contempt, at which he turned away, and contemplated the carpet with a slight smile, half pensive, half amused; but quickly looking up, he began to talk of other subjects, trying to draw me into a cheerful and friendly conversation, but I was too much irritated to discourse with him, and soon took leave.

You see Lawrence and I somehow could not manage to get on very well together. The fact is, I believe, we were both of us a little too touchy. It is a troublesome thing, Halford, this susceptibility to affronts where none are intended. I am no martyr to it now, as you can bear me witness: I have learned to be merry and wise, to be more easy with myself and more indulgent to my neighbours, and I can afford to laugh at both Lawrence and you.

Partly from accident, partly from wilful negligence on my part (for I was really beginning to dislike him), several weeks elapsed before I saw my friend again. When we did meet, it was he that sought me out. One bright morning, early in June, he came into the field where I was just commencing my hay harvest.

'It is long since I saw you, Markham,' said he, after the first few words had passed between us. 'Do you never mean to come to Woodford again?'

'I called once, and you were out.'

'I was sorry, but that was long since; I hoped you would call again, and now I have called, and you were out, which you generally are, or I would do myself the pleasure of calling more frequently; but being determined to see you this time, I have left my pony in the lane, and come over hedge and ditch to join you; for I am about to leave Woodford for a while, and may not have the pleasure of seeing you again for a month or two.'

'Where are you going?'

'To Grassdale first,' said he, with a half-smile he would willingly have suppressed if he could.

'To Grassdale! Is she there, then?'

'Yes, but in a day or two she will leave it to accompany Mrs Maxwell to F— for the benefit of the sea air, and I shall go with them.' (F— was at that time a quiet but respectable watering-place: it is considerably more frequented now.)

Lawrence seemed to expect me to take advantage of this circumstance to entrust him with some sort of a message to his sister; and I believe he would have undertaken to deliver it without any material objections, if I had had the sense to ask him, though of course he would not offer to do so, if I was content to let it alone. But I could not bring myself to make the request; and it was not till after he was gone, that I saw how fair an opportunity I had lost; and then, indeed, I deeply regretted my stupidity and my foolish pride, but it was now too late to remedy the evil.

He did not return till towards the latter end of August. He wrote to me twice or thrice from F—, but his letters were most provokingly unsatisfactory, dealing in generalities or in trifles that I cared nothing about, or replete with fancies and reflections equally unwelcome to me at the time, saying next to nothing about his sister, and little more about himself. I would wait, however, till he came

back; perhaps I could get something more out of him then. At all events, I would not write to her now, while she was with him and her aunt, who doubtless would be still more hostile to my presumptuous aspirations than himself. When she was returned to the silence and solitude of her own home it would be my fittest opportunity.

When Lawrence came, however, he was as reserved as ever on the subject of my keen anxiety. He told me that his sister had derived considerable benefit from her stay at F—, that her son was quite well, and – alas! that both of them were gone with Mrs Maxwell, back to Staningley, and there they stayed at least three months. But instead of boring you with my chagrin, my expectations and disappointments, my fluctuations of dull despondency and flickering hope, my varying resolutions, now to drop it, and now to persevere – now to make a bold push, and now to let things pass and patiently abide my time, – I will employ myself in settling the business of one or two of the characters, introduced in the course of this narrative, whom I may not have occasion to mention again.

Some time before Mr Huntingdon's death, Lady Lowborough eloped with another gallant to the Continent, where, having lived awhile in reckless gaiety and dissipation, they quarrelled and parted. She went dashing on for a season, but years came and money went: she sunk, at length, in difficulty and debt, disgrace and misery; and died at last, as I have heard, in penury, neglect, and utter wretchedness. But this might be only a report: she may be living yet for anything I or any of her relatives or former acquaintances can tell; for they have all lost sight of her long years ago, and would as thoroughly forget her if they could. Her husband, however, upon this second misdemeanour, immediately sought and obtained a divorce, and, not long after married again. It was well he did, for Lord Lowborough, morose and moody as he seemed, was not the man for a bachelor's life. No public interests, no ambitious projects, or active pursuits, – or ties of friendship even (if he had had any friends), could compensate to him for the absence of domestic comforts and endearments. He had a son and a nominal daughter, it is true, but they too painfully reminded him of their mother, and the unfortunate little Annabella was a source of perpetual bitterness to his soul. He had obliged himself to treat her with paternal kindness: he had forced himself not to hate her, and even, perhaps, to feel some degree of kindly regard for her, at last, in return for her artless and unsuspecting attachment to himself; but the bitterness of his self-condemnation for his inward feelings towards that innocent being, his constant struggles to subdue the evil promptings of his nature (for it was not a generous one), though partly guessed at by those who knew him, could be known to God and his own heart alone; – so also was the hardness of his conflicts with the temptation to return to the vice of his youth, and seek oblivion for past calamities, and deadness to the present misery of a blighted heart, a joyless, friendless life, and a morbidly disconsolate mind, by yielding again to that insidious foe to health, and sense, and virtue, which had so deplorably enslaved and degraded him before.

The second object of his choice was widely different from the first. Some wondered at his taste; some even ridiculed it – but in this their folly was more apparent than his. The lady was about his own age – i.e., between thirty and forty – remarkable neither for beauty, nor wealth, nor brilliant accomplishments; nor any other thing that I ever heard of, except genuine good sense, unswerving integrity, active piety, warm-hearted benevolence, and a fund of cheerful spirits.

These qualities, however, as you may readily imagine, combined to render her an excellent mother to the children, and an invaluable wife to his lordship. He, with his usual self-depreciation, thought her a world too good for him, and while he wondered at the kindness of Providence in conferring such a gift upon him, and even at her taste in preferring him to other men, he did his best to reciprocate the good she did him, and so far succeeded, that she was, and I believe still is, one of the happiest and fondest wives in England; and all who question the good taste of either partner, may be thankful if their respective selections afford them half the genuine satisfaction in the end, or repay their preference with affection half as lasting and sincere.

If you are at all interested in the fate of that low scoundrel, Grimsby, I can only tell you that he went from bad to worse, sinking from bathos to bathos of vice and villainy, consorting only with the worst members of his club and the lowest dregs of society – happily for the rest of the world – and at last met his end in a drunken brawl, from the hands, it is said, of some brother scoundrel he had cheated at play.

As for Mr Hattersley, he had never wholly forgotten his resolution to 'come out from among them,' and behave like a man and a Christian, and the last illness and death of his once jolly friend Huntingdon so deeply and seriously impressed him with the evil of their former practices, that he never needed another lesson of the kind. Avoiding the temptations of the town, he continued to pass his life in the country, immersed in the usual pursuits of a hearty, active, country gentleman; his occupations being those of farming, and breeding horses and cattle, diversified with a little hunting and shooting, and enlivened by the occasional companionship of his friends (better friends than those of his youth), and the society of his happy little wife (now cheerful and confiding as heart could wish), and his fine family of stalwart sons and blooming daughters. His father, the banker, having died some years ago and left him all his riches, he has now full scope for the exercise of his prevailing tastes, and I need not tell you that Ralph Hattersley, Esq., is celebrated throughout the country for his noble breed of horses.

# Chapter 51

We will now turn to a certain still, cold, cloudy afternoon about the commencement of December, when the first fall of snow lay thinly scattered over the blighted fields and frozen roads, or stored more thickly in the hollows of the deep cart-ruts and footsteps of men and horses impressed in the now petrified mire of last month's drenching rains. I remember it well, for I was walking home from the vicarage, with no less remarkable a personage than Miss Eliza Millward by my side. I had been to call upon her father, – a sacrifice to

civility undertaken entirely to please my mother, not myself, for I hated to go near the house; not merely on account of my antipathy to the once so bewitching Eliza, but because I had not half forgiven the old gentleman himself for his ill opinion of Mrs Huntingdon; for though now constrained to acknowledge himself mistaken in his former judgment, he still maintained that she had done wrong to leave her husband; it was a violation of her sacred duties as a wife, and a tempting of Providence by laying herself open to temptation; and nothing short of bodily ill-usage (and that of no trifling nature) could excuse such a step – not even that, for in such a case she ought to appeal to the laws for protection. But it was not of him I intended to speak; it was of his daughter Eliza. Just as I was taking leave of the vicar, she entered the room, ready equipped for a walk.

'I was just coming to see your sister, Mr Markham,' said she; 'and so, if you have no objection, I'll accompany you home. I like company when I'm walking out – don't you?'

'Yes, when its agreeable.'

'That of course,' rejoined the young lady, smiling archly. So we proceeded together.

'Shall I find Rose at home, do you think?' said she, as we closed the garden gate, and set our faces towards Linden-Car.

'I believe so.'

'I trust I shall, for I've a little bit of news for her – if you haven't forestalled me?'

'I?'

'Yes: do you know what Mr Lawrence has gone for?' She looked up anxiously for my reply.

'Is he gone?' said I; and her face brightened.

'Ah! then he hasn't told you about his sister?'

'What of her?' I demanded, in terror lest some evil should have befallen her.

'Oh, Mr Markham, how you blush!' cried she, with a tormenting laugh. 'Ha, ha, you have not forgotten her yet! But you had better be quick about it, I can tell you, for – alas, alas! – she's going to be married next Thursday!'

'No, Miss Eliza! that's false.'

'Do you charge me with a falsehood, sir?'

'You are misinformed.'

'Am I? Do you know better then?'

'I think I do.'

'What makes you look so pale then?' said she, smiling with delight at my emotion. 'Is it anger at poor me for telling such a fib? Well, I only "tell the tale as 'twas told to me"; I don't vouch for the truth of it; but at the same time, I don't see what reason Sarah should have for deceiving me, or her informant for deceiving her; and that was what she told me the footman told her: – that Mrs Huntingdon was going to be married on Thursday, and Mr Lawrence was going to the wedding. She did tell me the name of the gentleman, but I've forgotten that. Perhaps you can assist me to remember it. Is there not some one that lives near – or frequently visits the neighbourhood, that has long been attached to her? a Mr – oh dear! – Mr' –

'Hargrave?' suggested I, with a bitter smile.

'You're right!' cried she, 'that was the very name.'

'Impossible, Miss Eliza!' I exclaimed, in a tone that made her start.

# The Tenant of Wildfell Hall

'Well, you know, that's what they told me,' said she, composedly staring me in the face. And then she broke out into a long shrill laugh that put me to my wits' end with fury.

'Really you must excuse me,' cried she: 'I know it's very rude, but ha, ha, ha! – did you think to marry her yourself? Dear, dear, what a pity! ha, ha, ha! – Gracious, Mr Markham! are you going to faint? O mercy! shall I call this man? Here, Jacob' – But checking the word on her lips, I seized her arm and gave it, I think, a pretty severe squeeze, for she shrank into herself with a faint cry of pain or terror; but the spirit within her was not subdued: instantly rallying, she continued, with well-feigned concern–

'What can I do for you? Will you have some water – some brandy? – I dare say they have some in the public-house down here, if you'll let me run.'

'Have done with this nonsense!' cried I sternly. She looked confounded – almost frightened again, for a moment. 'You know I hate such jests,' I continued.

'Jests indeed! I wasn't jesting!'

'You were laughing, at all events; and I don't like to be laughed at,' returned I, making violent efforts to speak with proper dignity and composure, and to say nothing but what was coherent and sensible. 'And since you are in such a merry mood, Miss Eliza, you must be good enough company for yourself; and therefore I shall leave you to finish your walk alone – for, now I think of it, I have business elsewhere; so good evening.'

With that I left her (smothering her malicious laughter) and turned aside into the fields, springing up the bank, and pushing through the nearest gap in the hedge. Determined at once to prove the truth – or rather the falsehood – of her story, I hastened to Woodford as fast as my legs could carry me – first, veering round by a circuitous course, but the moment I was out of sight of my fair tormentor, cutting away across the country, just as a bird might fly – over pasture-land and fallow, and stubble and lane – clearing hedges and ditches, and hurdles, till I came to the young squire's gates. Never till now had I known the full fervour of my love – the full strength of my hopes, not wholly crushed even in my hours of deepest despondency, always tenaciously clinging to the thought that one day she might be mine – or if not that, at least that something of my memory, some light remembrance of our friendship and our love would be for ever cherished in her heart. I marched up to the door, determined, if I saw the master, to question him boldly concerning his sister, to wait and hesitate no longer but cast false delicacy and stupid pride behind my back, and know my fate at once.

'Is Mr Lawrence at home?' I eagerly asked of the servant that opened the door.

'No, sir, master went yesterday,' replied he, looking very alert.

'Went where?'

'To Grassdale, sir – wasn't you aware, sir? He's very close, is master,' said the fellow, with a foolish, simpering grin. 'I suppose, sir'—

But I turned and left him, without waiting to hear what he supposed. I was not going to stand there to expose my tortured feelings to the insolent laughter and impertinent curiosity of a fellow like that.

But what was to be done now? Could it be possible that she had left me for that man? I could not believe it. Me she might forsake, but not to give herself to him! Well, I would know the truth – to no concerns of daily life could I attend

while this tempest of doubt and dread, of jealousy and rage, distracted me. I would take the morning coach from L— (the evening one would be already gone), and fly to Grassdale – I must be there before the marriage. And why? Because a thought struck me that perhaps I might prevent it – that if I did not she and I might both lament it to the latest moment of our lives. It struck me that some one might have belied me to her: perhaps her brother – yes, no doubt her brother had persuaded her that I was false and faithless, and taking advantage of her natural indignation, and perhaps her desponding carelessness about her future life, had urged her, artfully, cruelly, on to this other marriage in order to secure her from me. If this was the case, and if she should only discover her mistake when too late to repair it – to what a life of misery and vain regret might she be doomed as well as me! and what remorse for me, to think my foolish scruples had induced it all! Oh, I must see her – she must know my truth even if I told it at the church door! I might pass for a madman or an impertinent fool – even she might be offended at such an interruption, or at least might tell me it was now too late – but if I could save her! if she might be mine – it was too rapturous a thought!

Winged by this hope, and goaded by these fears, I hurried homewards to prepare for my departure on the morrow. I told my mother that urgent business which admitted no delay, but which I could not then explain, called me away.

My deep anxiety and serious pre-occupation could not be concealed from her maternal eyes; and I had much ado to calm her apprehensions of some disastrous mystery.

That night there came a heavy fall of snow, which so retarded the progress of the coaches on the following day, that I was almost driven to distraction. I travelled all night, of course, for this was Wednesday: tomorrow morning, doubtless, the marriage would take place. But the night was long and dark: the snow heavily clogged the wheels and balled the horses' feet; the animals were consumedly lazy; the coachmen most execrably cautious; the passengers confoundedly apathetic in their supine indifference to the rate of our progression. Instead of assisting me to bully the several coachmen and urge them forward, they merely stared and grinned at my impatience: one fellow even ventured to rally me upon it – but I silenced him with a look that quelled him for the rest of the journey; – and when, at the last stage, I would have taken the reins into my own hands, they all with one accord opposed it.

It was broad daylight when we entered M— and drew up at the 'Rose and Crown'. I alighted and called aloud for a post-chaise to Grassdale. There was none to be had: the only one in the town was under repair. 'A gig then – a fly – car – anything – only be quick!' There was a gig, but not a horse to spare. I sent into the town to seek one; but they were such an intolerable time about it that I could wait no longer: I thought my own feet could carry me sooner; and bidding them send the conveyance after me, if it were ready within an hour, I set off as fast as I could walk. The distance was little more than six miles, but the road was strange, and I had to keep stopping to inquire my way – hallooing to carters and clodhoppers, and frequently invading the cottages, for there were few abroad that winter's morning, – sometimes knocking up the lazy people from their beds, for where so little work was to be done, perhaps so little food and fire to be had, they cared not to curtail their slumbers. I had no time to think of them, however; aching with weariness and desperation, I hurried on.

# The Tenant of Wildfell Hall

The gig did not overtake me: and it was well I had not waited for it – vexatious, rather, that I had been fool enough to wait so long.

At length, however, I entered the neighbourhood of Grassdale. I approached the little rural church – but lo! there stood a train of carriages before it – it needed not the white favours bedecking the servants and horses, nor the merry voices of the village idlers assembled to witness the show, to apprise me that there was a wedding within. I ran in among them, demanding, with breathless eagerness, had the ceremony long commenced? They only gaped and stared. In my desperation, I pushed past them, and was about to enter the churchyard gate, when a group of ragged urchins, that had been hanging like bees to the windows, suddenly dropped off and made a rush for the porch, vociferating in the uncouth dialect of their country something which signified, 'It's over – they're coming out!'

If Eliza Millward had seen me then, she might indeed have been delighted. I grasped the gate-post for support, and stood intently gazing towards the door to take my last look on my soul's delight, my first on that detested mortal who had torn her from my heart, and doomed her, I was certain, to a life of misery and hollow, vain repining – for what happiness could she enjoy with him? I did not wish to shock her with my presence now, but I had not power to move away. Forth came the bride and bridegroom. Him I saw not; I had eyes for none but her. A long veil shrouded half her graceful form, but did not hide it; I could see that, while she carried her head erect, her eyes were bent upon the ground, and her face and neck were suffused with a crimson blush; but every feature was radiant with smiles, and gleaming through the misty whiteness of her veil were clusters of golden ringlets! Oh, heavens! it was not my Helen! The first glimpse made me start – but my eyes were darkened with exhaustion and despair – dare I trust them? Yes – it is not she! It was a younger, slighter, rosier beauty – lovely, indeed, but with far less dignity and depth of soul – without that indefinable grace, that keenly spiritual yet gentle charm, that ineffable power to attract and subjugate the heart – my heart at least. I looked at the bridegroom – it was Frederick Lawrence! I wiped away the cold drops that were trickling down my forehead, and stepped back as he approached; but his eyes fell upon me, and he knew me, altered as my appearance must have been.

'Is that you, Markham?' said he, startled and confounded at the apparition – perhaps, too, at the wildness of my looks.

'Yes, Lawrence – is that you?' I mustered the presence of mind to reply.

He smiled and coloured, as if half-proud and half-ashamed of his identity; and if he had reason to be proud of the sweet lady on his arm, he had no less cause to be ashamed of having concealed his good fortune so long.

'Allow me to introduce you to my bride,' said he, endeavouring to hide his embarrassment by an assumption of careless gaiety. 'Esther, this is Mr Markham; my friend Markham, Mrs Lawrence, late Miss Hargrave.'

I bowed to the bride, and vehemently wrung the bridegroom's hand.

'Why did you not tell me of this?' I said reproachfully, pretending a resentment I did not feel (for in truth I was almost wild with joy to find myself so happily mistaken, and overflowing with affection to him for this and for the base injustice I felt that I had done him in my mind – he might have wronged me, but not to that extent; and as I had hated him like a demon for the last forty hours, the

# The Tenant of Wildfell Hall

reaction from such a feeling was so great that I could pardon all offences for the moment – and love him in spite of them too).

'I did tell you,' said he, with an air of guilty confusion; 'you received my letter?'

'What letter?'

'The one announcing my intended marriage.'

'I never received the most distant hint of such an intention.'

'It must have crossed you on your way then – it should have reached you yesterday morning – it was rather late, I acknowledge. But what brought you here then, if you received no information?'

It was now my turn to be confounded; but the young lady, who had been busily patting the snow with her foot during our short *sotto voce* colloquy, very opportunely came to my assistance by pinching her companion's arm and whispering a suggestion that his friend should be invited to step into the carriage and go with them; it being scarcely agreeable to stand there among so many gazers, and keeping their friends waiting into the bargain.

'And so cold as it is too!' said he, glancing with dismay at her slight drapery, and immediately handing her into the carriage. 'Markham, will you come? We are going to Paris, but we can drop you anywhere between this and Dover.'

'No, thank you. Good-bye – I needn't wish you a pleasant journey; but I shall expect a very handsome apology, some time, mind, and scores of letters, before we meet again.'

He shook my hand, and hastened to take his place beside his lady. This was no time or place for explanation or discourse: we had already stood long enough to excite the wonder of the village sight-seers and perhaps the wrath of the attendant bridal party; though, of course, all this passed in a much shorter time than I have taken to relate, or even than you will take to read it. I stood beside the carriage, and the window being down, I saw my happy friend fondly encircle his companion's waist with his arm, while she rested her glowing cheek on his shoulder, looking the very impersonation of loving, trusting bliss. In the interval between the footman's closing the door and taking his place behind, she raised her smiling brown eyes to his face, observing, playfully—

'I fear you must think me very insensible, Frederick: I know it is the custom for ladies to cry on these occasions, but I couldn't squeeze a tear for my life.'

He only answered with a kiss, and pressed her still closer to his bosom.

'But what is this?' he murmured. 'Why, Esther you're crying now!'

'Oh, its nothing – It's only too much happiness – and the wish,' sobbed she, 'that our dear Helen were as happy as ourselves.'

'Bless you for that wish!' I inwardly responded as the carriage rolled away – 'and Heaven grant it be not wholly vain!'

I thought a cloud had suddenly darkened her husband's face as she spoke. What did he think? Could he grudge such happiness to his dear sister and his friend as he now felt himself? At such a moment it was impossible. The contrast between her fate and his must darken his bliss for a time. Perhaps, too, he thought of me: perhaps he regretted the part he had had in preventing our union, by omitting to help us, if not by actually plotting against us – I exonerated him from that charge, now, and deeply lamented my former ungenerous suspicions; but he had wronged us, still – I hoped, I trusted that he had. He had not attempted to check the course of our love by actually damming up the

streams in their passage, but he had passively watched the two currents wandering through life's arid wilderness, declining to clear away the obstructions that divided them, and secretly hoping that both would lose themselves in the sand before they could be joined in one. And meantime he had been quietly proceeding with his own affairs: perhaps his heart and head had been so full of his fair lady that he had had but little thought to spare for others. Doubtless he had made his first acquaintance with her – his first intimate acquaintance at least – during his three months' sojourn at F—, for I now recollected that he had once casually let fall an intimation that his aunt and sister had a young friend staying with them at the time, and this accounted for at least one-half his silence about all transactions there. Now, too, I saw a reason for many little things that had slightly puzzled me before; among the rest, for sundry departures from Woodford, and absences more or less prolonged, for which he never satisfactorily accounted, and concerning which he hated to be questioned on his return. Well might the servant say his master was 'very close'. But why this strange reserve to me? Partly, from that remarkable idiosyncrasy to which I have before alluded; partly, perhaps, from tenderness to my feelings, or fear to disturb my philosophy by touching upon the infectious theme of love.

# Chapter 52

he tardy gig had overtaken me at last. I entered it, and bade the man who brought it to drive to Grassdale Manor – I was too busy with my own thoughts to care to drive it myself. I would see Mrs Huntingdon – there could be no impropriety in that now that her husband had been dead above a year – and by her indifference or her joy at my unexpected arrival, I could soon tell whether her heart was truly mine. But my companion, a loquacious, forward fellow, was not disposed to leave me to the indulgence of my private cogitations.

'There they go!' said he, as the carriage filed away before us. 'There'll be brave doings on yonder today, as what come tomorra. – Know anything of that family, sir? or you're a stranger in these parts?'

'I know them by report.'

'Humph! There's the best of 'em gone, anyhow. And I suppose the old missis is agoing to leave after this stir's gotten overed, and take herself off, somewhere, to live on her bit of a jointure; and the young 'un – at least the new 'un (she's none so very young) is coming down to live at the Grove.'

'Is Mr Hargrave married, then?'

'Ay, sir, a few months since. He should a been wed afore to a widow lady, but they couldn't agree over the money: she'd a rare long purse, and Mr Hargrave wanted it all to his-self; but she wouldn't let it go, and so then they fell out. This one isn't quite as rich – nor as handsome either, but she hasn't

been married before. She's very plain, they say, and getting on to forty or past, and so, you know, if she didn't jump at this opportunity, she thought she'd never get a better. I guess she thought such a handsome young husband was worth all 'at ever she had, and he might take it and welcome; but I lay she'll rue her bargain afore long. They say she begins already to see 'at he isn't not altogether that nice generous, perlite, delightful gentleman 'at she thought him afore marriage – he begins a being careless, and masterful already. Ay, and she'll find him harder and carelesser nor she thinks on.'

'You seem to be well acquainted with him,' I observed.

'I am, sir; I've known him since he was quite a young gentleman; and a proud 'un he was, and a wilful. I was servant yonder for several years; but I couldn't stand their niggardly ways – she got ever longer and worse did missis, with her nipping and screwing, and watching and grudging; so I thought I'd find another place.'

'Are we not near the house?' said I, interrupting him.

'Yes, sir; yon's the park.'

My heart sank within me to behold that stately mansion in the midst of its expansive grounds – the park as beautiful now, in its wintry garb, as it could be in its summer glory: the majestic sweep, the undulating swell and fall, displayed to full advantage in that robe of dazzling purity, stainless and printless – save one long, winding track left by the trooping deer – the stately timber-trees with their heavy laden branches gleaming white against the dull, grey sky; the deep encircling woods; the broad expanse of water sleeping in frozen quiet; and the weeping ash and willow drooping their snow-clad boughs above it – all presented a picture striking indeed, and pleasing to an unencumbered mind, but by no means encouraging to me. There was one comfort, however, – all this was entailed upon little Arthur, and could not under any circumstances, strictly speaking, be his mother's. But how was she situated! Overcoming with a sudden effort my repugnance to mention her name to my garrulous companion, I asked him if he knew whether her late husband had left a will, and how the property had been disposed of. Oh, yes, he knew all about it; and I was quickly informed that to her had been left the full control and management of the estate during her son's minority, besides the absolute, unconditional possession of her own fortune (but I knew that her father had not given her much), and the small additional sum that had been settled upon her before marriage.

Before the close of the explanation, we drew up at the park gates. Now for the trial – if I should find her within – but alas! she might be still at Staningley: her brother had given me no intimation to the contrary. I inquired at the porter's lodge if Mrs Huntingdon were at home. No, she was with her aunt in —shire, but was expected to return before Christmas. She usually spent most of her time at Staningley, only coming to Grassdale occasionally, when the management of affairs, or the interest of her tenants and dependants, required her presence.

'Near what town is Staningley situated?' I asked. The requisite information was soon obtained. 'Now then, my man, give me the reins, and we'll return to M—. I must have some breakfast at the 'Rose and Crown,' and then away to Staningley by the first coach for —.'

At M— I had time before the coach started to replenish my forces with a hearty breakfast, and to obtain the refreshment of my usual morning's ablutions, and the amelioration of some slight change in my toilet, – and also to despatch

# The Tenant of Wildfell Hall

a short note to my mother (excellent son that I was) to assure her that I was still in existence, and to excuse my non-appearance at the expected time. It was a long journey to Staningley for those slow travelling days; but I did not deny myself needful refreshment on the road, nor even a night's rest at a wayside inn; choosing rather to brook a little delay than to present myself worn, wild, and weather-beaten before my mistress and her aunt, who would be astonished enough to see me without that. Next morning, therefore, I not only fortified myself with as substantial a breakfast as my excited feelings would allow me to swallow, but I bestowed a little more than usual time and care upon my toilet; and, furnished with a change of linen from my small carpet-bag, well brushed clothes, well polished boots, and neat new gloves, I mounted 'The Lightning,' and resumed my journey. I had nearly two stages yet before me, but the coach, I was informed, passed through the neighbourhood of Staningley, and having desired to be set down as near the Hall as possible, I had nothing to do but to sit with folded arms and speculate upon the coming hour.

It was a clear, frosty morning. The very fact of sitting exalted aloft, surveying the snowy landscape, and sweet, sunny sky, inhaling the pure, bracing air, and crunching away over the crisp, frozen snow, was exhilarating enough in itself; but add to this the idea of to what goal I was hastening, and whom I expected to meet, and you may have some faint conception of my frame of mind at the time – only a faint one, though, for my heart swelled with unspeakable delight, and my spirits rose almost to madness, in spite of my prudent endeavours to bind them down to a reasonable platitude by thinking of all the undeniable difference between Helen's rank and mine; of all that she had passed through since our parting; of her long, unbroken silence; and, above all, of her cool, cautious aunt, whose counsels she would doubtless be careful not to slight again. These considerations made my heart flutter with anxiety, and my chest heave with impatience to get the crisis over, but they could not dim her image in my mind, or mar the vivid recollection of what had been said and felt between us – or destroy the keen anticipation of what was to be – in fact, I could not realize their terrors now. Towards the close of the journey, however, a couple of my fellow-passengers kindly came to my assistance, and brought me low enough.

'Fine land this,' said one of them, pointing with his umbrella to the wide fields on the right, conspicuous for their compact hedgerows, deep, well-cut ditches, and fine timber-trees, growing sometimes on the borders, sometimes in the midst of the enclosure; – 'very fine land, if you saw it in the summer or spring.'

'Ay,' responded the other – a gruff, elderly man, with a drab greatcoat buttoned up to the chin and a cotton umbrella between his knees. 'It's old Maxwell's, I suppose?'

'It was his, sir, but he's dead now, you're aware, and has left it all to his niece.'

'All?'

'Every rood of it, – and the mansion-house and all, – every hatom of his worldly goods! – except just a trifle, by way of remembrance, to his nephew down in —shire and an annuity to his wife.'

'It's strange, sir.'

'It is, sir. And she wasn't his own niece neither; but he had no near relations of his own - none but a nephew he'd quarrelled with – and he always had a

partiality for this one. And then his wife advised him to it, they say: she'd brought most of the property, and it was her wish that this lady should have it.'

'Humph! – she'll be a fine catch for somebody.'

'She will so. She's a widow, but quite young yet, and uncommon handsome – a fortune of her own, besides, and only one child – and she's nursing a fine estate for him in —. There'll be lots to speak for her! – 'fraid there's no chance of uz – (facetiously jogging me with his elbow, as well as his companion) – ha, ha, ha! No offence, sir, I hope?' (to me) 'Ahem! – I should think she'll marry none but a nobleman, myself. Look ye, sir,' resumed he, turning to his other neighbour, and pointing past me with his umbrella, 'that's the hall – grand park, you see – and all them woods – plenty of timber there, and lots of game – hallo – what now?'

This exclamation was occasioned by the sudden stoppage of the coach at the park gates.

'Gen'leman for Staningley Hall?' cried the coachman; and I rose and threw my carpet-bag on to the ground, preparatory to dropping myself down after it.

'Sickly, sir?' asked my talkative neighbour, staring me in the face (I dare say it was white enough).

'No. Here, coachman.'

'Thank'ee sir. – All right!'

The coachman pocketed his fee and drove away, leaving me not walking up the park, but pacing to and fro before its gates, with folded arms and eyes fixed upon the ground – an overwhelming force of images, thoughts, impressions, crowding on my mind, and nothing tangibly distinct but this: – My love had been cherished in vain; my hope was gone for ever; I must tear myself away at once, and banish or suppress all thoughts of her like the remembrance of a wild, mad dream. Gladly would I have lingered round the place for hours, in the hope of catching, at least, one distant glimpse of her before I went, but it must not be: I must not suffer her to see me; for what could have brought me hither but the hope of reviving her attachment, with a view, hereafter, to obtain her hand? And could I bear that she should think me capable of such a thing? – or presuming upon the acquaintance – the love if you will – accidentally contracted, or rather forced upon her against her will, when she was an unknown fugitive, toiling for her own support, apparently without fortune, family, or connections – to come upon her now, when she was reinstated in her proper sphere, and claim a share in her prosperity, which, had it never failed her, would most certainly have kept her unknown to me for ever? and this too when we had parted sixteen months ago, and she had expressly forbidden me to hope for a reunion in this world – and never sent me a line or a message from that day to this? No! The very idea was intolerable.

And even if she should have a lingering affection for me still, ought I to disturb her peace by awakening those feelings? to subject her to the struggles of conflicting duty and inclination – to whichsoever side the latter might allure, or the former imperatively call her – whether she should deem it her duty to risk the slights and censures of the world, the sorrow and displeasure of those she loved, for a romantic idea of truth and constancy to me, or to sacrifice her individual wishes to the feelings of her friends and her own sense of prudence and the fitness of things? No – and I would not! I would go at once, and she should never know that I had approached the place of her abode; for though I

might disclaim all idea of ever aspiring to her hand, or even of soliciting a place in her friendly regard, her peace should not be broken by my presence, nor her heart afflicted by the sight of my fidelity.

'Adieu then, dear Helen, for ever! For ever adieu!'

So said I – and yet I could not tear myself away. I moved a few paces, and then looked back, for one last view of her stately home, that I might have its outward form, at least, impressed upon my mind as indelibly as her own image, which, alas! I must not see again – then walked a few steps further; and then, lost in melancholy musings, paused again and leant my back against a rough old tree that grew beside the road.

# Chapter 53

While standing thus, absorbed in my gloomy reverie, a gentleman's carriage came round the corner of the road. I did not look at it; and had it rolled quietly by me, I should not have remembered the fact of its appearance at all; but a tiny voice from within it roused me by exclaiming—

I did not hear the reply, but presently the same voice answered—

'It is, indeed, mamma – look for yourself.'

'Mamma, mamma, here's Mr. Markham!'

I did not raise my eyes, but I suppose mamma looked, for a clear, melodious voice, whose tones thrilled through my nerves, exclaimed—

'Oh, aunt, here's Mr Markham – Arthur's friend! – Stop, Richard!'

There was such evidence of joyous though suppressed excitement in the utterance of those few words – especially that tremulous 'Oh, aunt' – that it threw me almost off my guard. The carriage stopped immediately, and I looked up and met the eye of a pale, grave, elderly lady surveying me from the open window. She bowed and so did I, and then she withdrew her head, while Arthur screamed to the footman to let him out; but before that functionary could descend from his box, a hand was silently put forth from the carriage window. I knew that hand, though a black glove concealed its delicate whiteness and half its fair proportions, and quickly seizing it, I pressed it in my own – ardently for a moment, but instantly recollecting myself, I dropped it, and it was immediately withdrawn.

'Were you coming to see us, or only passing by?' asked the low voice of its owner, who, I felt, was attentively surveying my countenance from behind the thick, black veil which, with the shadowing panels, entirely concealed her own from me.

'I – I came to see the place,' faltered I.

'The place,' repeated she, in a tone which betokened more displeasure or disappointment than surprise.

'Will you not enter it then?'

'If you wish it.'

'Can you doubt?'

'Yes, yes! he must enter,' cried Arthur, running round from the other door; and seizing my hand in both his, he shook it heartily.

'Do you remember me, sir?' said he.

'Yes, full well, my little man, altered though you are,' replied I, surveying the comparatively tall, slim young gentleman with his mother's image visibly stamped upon his fair, intelligent features, in spite of the blue eyes beaming with gladness, and the bright locks clustering beneath his cap.

'Am I not grown?' said he, stretching himself up to his full height.

'Grown! three inches, upon my word!'

'I was seven last birthday,' was the proud rejoinder. 'In seven years more I shall be as tall as you, nearly.'

'Arthur,' said his mother, 'tell him to come in. Go on, Richard,'

There was a touch of sadness as well as coldness in her voice, but I knew not to what to ascribe it. The carriage drove on and entered the gates before us. My little companion led me up the park, discoursing merrily all the way. Arrived at the hall door, I paused on the steps and looked round me, waiting to recover my composure, if possible – or, at any rate, to remember my new-formed resolutions and the principles on which they were founded; and it was not till Arthur had been for some time gently pulling my coat, and repeating his invitations to enter, that I at length consented to accompany him into the apartment where the ladies awaited us.

Helen eyed me as I entered with a kind of gentle, serious scrutiny, and politely asked after Mrs Markham and Rose. I respectfully answered her inquiries. Mrs Maxwell begged me to be seated, observing it was rather cold, but she supposed I had not travelled far that morning.

'Not quite twenty miles,' I answered.

'Not on foot?'

'No, madam, by coach.'

'Here's Rachel, sir,' said Arthur, the only truly happy one amongst us, directing my attention to that worthy individual, who had just entered to take her mistress's things. She vouchsafed me an almost friendly smile of recognition – a favour that demanded, at least, a civil salutation on my part, which was accordingly given and respectfully returned – she had seen the error of her former estimation of my character.

When Helen was divested of her lugubrious bonnet and veil, her heavy winter cloak, etc., she looked so like herself that I knew not how to bear it. I was particularly glad to see her beautiful black hair unstinted still and unconcealed in its glossy luxuriance.

'Mamma has left off her widow's cap in honour of uncle's marriage,' observed Arthur, reading my looks with a child's mingled simplicity and quickness of observation. Mamma looked grave, and Mrs Maxwell shook her head. 'And Aunt Maxwell is never going to leave off hers,' persisted the naughty boy; but when he saw that his pertness was seriously displeasing and painful to his aunt, he went and silently put his arm round her neck, kissed her cheek, and withdrew to the recess of one of the great bay-windows, where he quietly amused himself with his dog while Mrs Maxwell gravely discussed with me the interesting

topics of the weather, the season, and the roads. I considered her presence very useful as a check upon my natural impulses – an antidote to those emotions of tumultuous excitement which would otherwise have carried me away against my reason and my will, but just then I felt the restrain almost intolerable, and I had the greatest difficulty in forcing myself to attend to her remarks and answer them with ordinary politeness; for I was sensible that Helen was standing within a few feet of me beside the fire. I dared not look at her, but I felt her eye was upon me, and from one hasty, furtive glance I thought her cheek was slightly flushed, and that her fingers, as she played with her watch-chain, were agitated with that restless, trembling motion which betokens high excitement.

'Tell me,' said she, availing herself of the first pause in the attempted conversion between her aunt and me, and speaking fast and low, with her eyes bent on the gold chain – for I now ventured another glance, – 'Tell me how you all are at Lindenhope – has nothing happened since I left you?'

'I believe not.'

'Nobody dead? nobody married?'

'No.'

'Or – or expecting to marry? – No old ties dissolved or new ones formed? No old friends forgotten or supplanted?'

She dropped her voice so low in the last sentence that no one could have caught the concluding words but myself, and at the same time turned her eyes upon me with a dawning smile, most sweetly melancholy, and a look of timid though keen inquiry that made my cheeks tingle with inexpressible emotions.

'I believe not,' I answered – 'Certainly not, if others are as little changed as I.' Her face glowed in sympathy with mine.

'And you really did not mean to call?' she exclaimed.

'I feared to intrude.'

'To intrude!' cried she, with an impatient gesture. – 'What' – but as if suddenly recollecting her aunt's presence, she checked herself, and, turning to that lady, continued – 'Why aunt, this man is my brother's close friend, and was my own intimate acquaintance (for a few short months at least), and professed a great attachment to my boy – and when he passes the house, so many scores of miles from his home, he declines to look in for fear of intruding!'

'Mr Markham is over modest,' observed Mrs Maxwell.

'Over ceremonious rather,' said her niece – 'over – well, it's no matter.' And turning from me, she seated herself in a chair beside the table, and, pulling a book to her by the cover, began to turn over the leaves in an energetic kind of abstraction.

'If I had known,' said I, 'that you would have honoured me by remembering me as an intimate acquaintance, I most likely should not have denied myself the pleasure of calling upon you, but I thought you had forgotten me long ago.'

'You judged of others by yourself,' muttered she without raising her eyes from the book, but reddening as she spoke, and hastily turning over a dozen leaves at once.

There was a pause, of which Arthur thought he might venture to avail himself to introduce his handsome young setter, and show me how wonderfully it was grown and improved, and to ask after the welfare of its father Sancho. Mrs Maxwell then withdrew to take off her things. Helen immediately pushed the book from her, and after silently surveying her son, his friend, and his dog for

a few moments, she dismissed the former from the room under the pretence of wishing him to fetch his last new book to show me. The child obeyed with alacrity; but I continued caressing the dog. The silence might have lasted till its master's return had it depended on me to break it, but, in half a minute or less, my hostess impatiently rose, and, taking her former station on the rug between me and the chimney corner, earnestly exclaimed—

'Gilbert, what is the matter with you? - why are you so changed? - It is a very indiscreet question, I know,' she hastened to add: 'perhaps a very rude one - don't answer it if you think so - but I hate mysteries and concealments.'

'I am not changed, Helen - unfortunately I am as keen and passionate as ever - it is not I, it is circumstances that are changed.'

'What circumstances? Do tell me!' Her cheek was blanched with the very anguish of anxiety - could it be with the fear that I had rashly pledged my faith to another?

'I'll tell you at once,' said I. 'I will confess that I came here for the purpose of seeing you (not without some monitory misgivings at my own presumption, and fears that I should be as little welcome as expected when I came), but I did not know that this estate was yours, until enlightened on the subject of your inheritance by the conversation of two fellow-passengers in the last stage of my journey; and then I saw at once the folly of the hopes I had cherished and the madness of retaining them a moment longer; and though I alighted at your gates I determined not to enter within them; I lingered a few minutes to see the place, but was fully resolved to return to M— without seeing its mistress.'

'And if my aunt and I had not been just returning from our morning drive, I should have seen and heard no more of you?'

'I thought it would be better for both that we should not meet,' replied I, as calmly as I could, but not daring to speak above my breath, from conscious inability to steady my voice, and not daring to look in her face lest my firmness should forsake me altogether: 'I thought an interview would only disturb your peace and madden me. But I am glad, now, of this opportunity of seeing you once more and knowing that you have not forgotten me, and of assuring you that I shall never cease to remember you.'

There was a moment's pause. Mrs Huntingdon moved away, and stood in the recess of the window. Did she regard this as an intimation that modesty alone prevented me from asking her hand? and was she considering how to repulse me with the smallest injury to my feelings? Before I could speak to relieve her from such a perplexity, she broke the silence herself by suddenly turning towards me and observing—

'You might have had such an opportunity before - as far, I mean, as regards assuring me of your kindly recollections, and yourself of mine, if you had written to me.'

'I would have done so, but I did not know your address, and did not like to ask your brother, because I thought he would object to my writing - but this would not have deterred me for a moment, if I could have ventured to believe that you expected to hear from me, or even wasted a thought upon your unhappy friend; but your silence naturally led me to conclude myself forgotten.'

'Did you expect me to write to you, then?'

'No, Helen - Mrs Huntingdon,' said I, blushing at the implied inputation,

'certainly not; but if you had sent me a message through your brother, or even asked him about me now and then'—

'I did ask about you frequently. I was not going to do more,' continued she, smiling, 'so long as you continued to restrict yourself to a few polite inquiries about my health.'

'Your brother never told me that you had mentioned my name.

'Did you ever ask him?'

'No – for I saw he did not wish to be questioned about you, or to afford the slightest encouragement or assistance to my too obstinate attachment.' Helen did not reply. 'And he was perfectly right,' added I. But she remained in silence, looking out upon the snowy lawn. 'Oh, I will relieve her of my presence,' thought I; and immediately I rose and advanced to take leave, with a most heroic resolution – but pride was at the bottom of it, or it could not have carried me through.

'Are you going already?' said she, taking the hand I offered, and not immediately letting it go.

'Why should I stay any longer?'

'Wait till Arthur comes, at least.'

Only too glad to obey, I stood and leant against the opposite side of the window.

'You told me you were not changed,' said my companion: 'you are – very much so.'

'No, Mrs Huntingdon, I only ought to be.'

'Do you mean to maintain that you have the same regard for me that you had when last we met?'

'I have; but it would be wrong to talk of it now.'

'It was wrong to talk of it then, Gilbert; it would not now – unless to do so would be to violate the truth.'

I was too much agitated to speak; but, without waiting for an answer, she turned away her glistening eye and crimson cheek, and threw up the window and looked out, whether to calm her own excited feelings or to relieve her embarrassment, or only to pluck that beautiful half-blown Christmas rose that grew upon the little shrub without, just peeping from the snow that had hitherto, no doubt, defended it from the frost, and was now melting away in the sun. Pluck it, however, she did, and having gently dashed the glittering powder from its leaves, approached it to her lips and said—

'This rose is not so fragrant as a summer flower, but it has stood through hardships none of them could bear: the cold rain of winter has sufficed to nourish it, and its faint sun to warm it; the bleak winds have not blanched it, or broken its stem, and the keen frost has not blighted it. Look, Gilbert, it is still fresh and blooming as a flower can be, with the cold snow even now on its petals. Will you have it?'

I held out my hand: I dared not speak lest my emotion should overmaster me. She laid the rose across my palm, but I scarcely closed my fingers upon it, so deeply was I absorbed in thinking what might be the meaning of her words, and what I ought to do or say upon the occasion; whether to give way to my feelings or restrain them still. Misconstruing this hesitation into indifference – or reluctance even – to accept her gift, Helen suddenly snatched it from my hand,

threw it out on to the snow, shut down the window with an emphasis, and withdrew to the fire.

'Helen! what means this? I cried, electrified at this startling change in her demeanour.

'You did not understand my gift,' said she – 'or, what is worse, you despised it: I'm sorry I gave it you; but since I did make such a mistake, the only remedy I could think of was to take it away.'

'You misunderstand me, cruelly,' I replied, and in a minute I had opened the window again, leaped out, picked up the flower, brought it in, and presented it to her, imploring her to give it me again, and I would keep it for her sake, and prize it more highly than anything in the world I possessed.

'And will this content you?' said she, as she took it in her hand.

'It shall,' I answered.

'There, then; take it.'

I pressed it earnestly to my lips, and put it in my bosom, Mrs Huntingdon looking on with a half-sarcastic smile.

'Now, are you going?' said she.

'I will if – I must.'

'You are changed,' persisted she – 'you are grown either very proud or very indifferent.'

'I am neither, Helen – Mrs Huntingdon. If you could see my heart'—

'You must be one, – if not both. And why Mrs Huntingdon? – why not Helen, as before?'

'Helen, then – dear Helen!' I murmured. I was in an agony of mingled love, hope, delight, uncertainty, and suspense.

'The rose I gave you was an emblem of my heart,' said she; 'would you take it away and leave me here alone?'

'Would you give me your hand too, if I asked it?'

'Have I not said enough?' she answered, with a most enchanting smile. I snatched her hand, and would have fervently kissed it, but suddenly checked myself and said—

'But have you considered the consequences?'

'Hardly, I think, or I should not have offered myself to one too proud to take me, or too indifferent to make his affection outweigh my worldy goods.'

Stupid blockhead that I was! – I trembled to clasp her in my arms, but dared not believe in so much joy, and yet restrained myself to say—

'But if you should repent?'

'It would be your fault,' she replied: 'I never shall, unless you bitterly disappoint me. If you have not sufficient confidence in my affection to believe this, let me alone.'

'My darling angel – my own Helen,' cried I, now passionately kissing the hand I still retained, and throwing my left arm around her, 'you never shall repent if it depend on me alone. But have you thought of your aunt?' I trembled for the answer, and clasped her closer to my heart in the instinctive dread of losing my new-found treasure.

'My aunt must not know of it yet,' said she. 'She would think it a rash, wild step, because she could not imagine how well I know you but she must know you herself, and learn to like you. You must leave us now, after lunch, and come

again in spring, and make a longer stay, and cultivate her acquaintance, and I know you will like each other.'

'And then you will be mine,' said I, printing a kiss upon her lips, and another, and another; for I was as daring and impetuous now as I had been backward and constrained before.

'No – in another year,' replied she, gently disengaging herself from my embrace, but still fondly clasping my hand.

'Another year! O Helen, I could not wait so long!'

'Where is your fidelity?'

'I mean I could not endure the misery of so long a separation.'

'It would not be a separation: we will write every day; my spirit shall be always with you, and sometimes you shall see me with your bodily eye. I will not be such a hypocrite as to pretend that I desire to wait so long myself, but as my marriage is to please myself alone, I ought to consult my friends about the time of it.'

'Your friends will disapprove.'

'They will not greatly disapprove, dear Gilbert,' said she, earnestly kissing my hand; 'they cannot, when they know you, or, if they could, they would not be true friends – I should not care for their estrangement. Now are you satisfied?' She looked up in my face with a smile of ineffable tenderness.

'Can I be otherwise, with your love? And you do love me, Helen?' said I, not doubting the fact, but wishing to hear it confirmed by her own acknowledgment.

'If you loved as I do,' she earnestly replied, 'you would not have so nearly lost me – these scruples of false delicacy and pride would never thus have troubled you – you would have seen that the greatest worldly distinctions and discrepancies of rank, birth, and fortune are as dust in the balance compared with the unity of accordant thoughts and feelings, and truly loving, sympathizing hearts and souls.'

'But this is too much happiness,' said I, embracing her again; 'I have not deserved it, Helen – I dare not believe in such felicity and the longer I have to wait, the greater will be my dread that something will intervene to snatch you from me – and think, a thousand things may happen in a year! – I shall be in one long fever of restless terror and impatience all the time. And besides, winter is such a dreary season.'

'I thought so too,' replied she gravely: 'I would not be married in winter – in December, at least,' she added, with a shudder – for in that month had occurred both the ill-starred marriage that had bound her to her former husband and the terrible death that released her – 'and therefore I said another year, in spring.'

'Next spring?'

'No, no – next autumn, perhaps.'

'Summer, then.'

'Well, the close of summer. There now! be satisfied.'

While she was speaking, Arthur re-entered the room – good boy for keeping out so long.

'Mamma, I couldn't find the book in either of the places you told me to look for it' (there was a conscious something in mamma's smile that seemed to say, 'no, dear, I knew you could not'), 'but Rachel got it for me at last. Look, Mr

Markham, a natural history with all kinds of birds and beasts in it, and the reading as nice as the pictures!'

In great good-humour, I sat down to examine the book, and drew the little fellow between my knees. Had he come a minute before, I should have received him less graciously, but now I affectionately stroked his curling locks, and even kissed his ivory forehead: he was my own Helen's son, and therefore mine; and as such I have ever since regarded him. That pretty child is now a fine young man: he has realized his mother's brightest expectations, and is at present residing in Grassdale Manor with his young wife, the merry little Helen Hattersley of yore.

I had not looked through half the book before Mrs Maxwell appeared to invite me into the other room to lunch. That lady's cool, distant manners rather chilled me at first; but I did my best to propitiate her, and not entirely without success, I think, even in that first short visit; for when I talked cheerfully to her, she gradually became more kind and cordial, and when I departed she bade me a gracious adieu, hoping ere long to have the pleasure of seeing me again.

'But you must not go till you have seen the conservatory, my aunt's winter garden,' said Helen, as I advanced to take leave of her, with as much philosophy and self-command as I could summon to my aid.

I gladly availed myself of such a respite, and followed her into a large and beautiful conservatory, plentifully furnished with flowers considering the season – but, of course, I had little attention to spare for them. It was not, however, for any tender colloquy that my companion had brought me there—

'My aunt is particularly fond of flowers,' she observed, 'and she is fond of Staningley too: I brought you here to offer a petition in her behalf, that this may be her home as long as she lives, and – if it be not our home likewise – that I may often see her and be with her; for I fear she will be sorry to lose me; and though she leads a retired and contemplative life, she is apt to get low-spirited if left too much alone.'

'By all means, dearest Helen! – do what you will with your own. I should not dream of wishing your aunt to leave the place under any circumstances; and we will live either here or elsewhere as you and she may determine, and you shall see her as often as you like. I know she must be pained to part with you, and I am willing to make any reparation in my power. I love her for your sake, and her happiness shall be as dear to me as that of my own mother.'

'Thank you darling! you shall have a kiss for that. Goodbye. There now – there, Gilbert – let me go – here's Arthur, don't astonish his infantile brain with your madness.'

But it is time to bring my narrative to a close – any one but you would say I had made it too long already; but for your satisfaction, I will add a few words more; because I know you will have a fellow-feeling for the old lady, and will wish to know the last of her history. I did come again in spring, and, agreeably to Helen's injunctions, did my best to cultivate her acquaintance. She received me very kindly, having been, doubtless, already prepared to think highly of my character by her niece's too favourable report. I turned my best side out, of course, and we got along marvellously well together. When my ambitious intentions were made known to her, she took it more sensibly than I had ventured to hope. Her only remark on the subject, in my hearing, was—

# The Tenant of Wildfell Hall

'And so, Mr Markham, you are going to rob me of my niece, I understand. Well! I hope God will prosper your union, and make my dear girl happy at last. Could she have been contented to remain single, I own I should have been better satisfied; but if she must marry again, I know of no one, now living and of a suitable age, to whom I would more willingly resign her than yourself, or who would be more likely to appreciate her worth and make her truly happy, as far as I can tell.'

Of course I was delighted with the compliment, and hoped to show her that she was not mistaken in her favourable judgment.

'I have, however, one request to offer,' continued she. 'It seems I am still to look on Staningley as my home: I wish you to make it yours likewise, for Helen is attached to the place and to me – as I am to her. There are painful associations connected with Grassdale, which she cannot easily overcome; and I shall not molest you with my company or interference here: I am a very quiet person, and shall keep my own apartments, and attend to my own concerns, and only see you now and then.'

Of course I most readily consented to this; and we lived in the greatest harmony with our dear aunt until the day of her death, which melancholy event took place a few years after – melancholy, not to herself (for it came quietly upon her, and she was glad to reach her journey's end), but only to the few loving friends and grateful dependants she left behind.

To return, however, to my own affairs: I was married in summer, on a glorious August morning. It took the whole eight months, and all Helen's kindness and goodness to boot, to overcome my mother's prejudices against my bride-elect, and to reconcile her to the idea of my leaving Linden Grange and living so far away. Yet she was gratified at her son's good fortune after all, and proudly attributed it all to his own superior merits and endowments. I bequeathed the farm to Fergus, with better hopes of its prosperity than I should have had a year ago under similar circumstances; for he had lately fallen in love with the vicar of L—'s eldest daughter, a lady whose superiority had roused his latent virtues, and stimulated him to the most surprising exertion not only to gain her affection and esteem, and to obtain a fortune sufficient to aspire to her hand, but to render himself worthy of her, in his own eyes, as well as in those of her parents; and in the end he was successful, as you already know. As for myself, I need not tell you how happily my Helen and I have lived together, and how blessed we still are in each other's society, and in the promising young scions that are growing up about us. We are just now looking forward to the advent of you and Rose, for the time of your annual visit draws nigh, when you must leave your dusty, smoky, noisy, toiling, striving city for a season of invigorating relaxation and social retirement with us.

<div align="center">Till then, farewell,</div>

<div align="right">GILBERT MARKHAM.</div>

STANINGLEY, *June 10th, 1847.*

# Shirley

# Chapter 1

## Levitical

f late years, an abundant shower of curates has fallen upon the north of England: they lie very thick on the hills; every parish has one or more of them; they are young enough to be very active, and ought to be doing a great deal of good. But not of late years are we about to speak; we are going back to the beginning of this century: late years – present years are dusty, sun-burnt, hot, arid; we will evade the noon, forget it in siesta, pass the mid-day in slumber, and dream of dawn.

If you think, from this prelude, that anything like a romance is preparing for you, reader, you never were more mistaken. Do you anticipate sentiment, and poetry, and reverie? Do you expect passion, and stimulus, and melodrama? Calm your expectations; reduce them to a lowly standard. Something real, cool, and solid, lies before you; something unromantic as Monday morning, when all who have work wake with the consciousness that they must rise and betake themselves thereto. It is not positively affirmed that you shall not have a taste of the exciting, perhaps towards the middle and close of the meal, but it is resolved that the first dish set upon the table shall be one that a Catholic – ay, even an Anglo-Catholic – might eat on Good Friday in Passion Week: it shall be cold lentils and vinegar without oil; it shall be unleavened bread with bitter herbs, and no roast lamb.

Of late years, I say, an abundant shower of curates has fallen upon the north of England: but in eighteen-hundred-eleven-twelve that affluent rain had not descended: curates were scarce then: there was no Pastoral Aid – no Additional Curates' Society to stretch a helping hand to worn-out old rectors and incumbents, and give them the wherewithal to pay a vigorous young colleague from Oxford or Cambridge. The present successors of the apostles, disciples of Dr Pusey and tools of the Propaganda, were at that time being hatched under cradle-blankets, or undergoing regeneration by nursery-baptism in wash-hand-basins. You could not have guessed by looking at any one of them that the Italian-ironed double frills of its net-cap surrounded the brows of a preordained, specially sanctified successor of St Paul, St Peter, or St John; nor could you have foreseen in the folds of its long night-gown the white surplice in which it was hereafter cruelly to exercise the souls of its parishioners, and strangely to nonplus its old-fashioned vicar by flourishing aloft in a pulpit the shirt-like raiment which had never before waved higher than the reading-desk.

Yet even in those days of scarcity there were curates: the precious plant was rare, but it might be found. A certain favoured district in the West Riding of Yorkshire could boast three rods of Aaron blossoming within a circuit of twenty

# Shirley

miles. You shall see them, reader. Step into this neat garden-house on the skirts of Whinbury, walk forward into the little parlour – there they are at dinner. Allow me to introduce them to you: – Mr Donne, curate of Whinbury; Mr Malone, curate of Briarfield; Mr Sweeting, curate of Nunnely. These are Mr Donne's lodgings, being the habitation of one John Gale, a small clothier. Mr Donne has kindly invited his brethren to regale with him. You and I will join the party, see what is to be seen, and hear what is to be heard. At present, however, they are only eating; and while they eat we will talk aside.

These gentlemen are in the bloom of youth; they possess all the activity of that interesting age – an activity which their moping old vicars would fain turn into the channel of their pastoral duties, often expressing a wish to see it expended in a diligent superintendence of the schools, and in frequent visits to the sick of their respective parishes. But the youthful Levites feel this to be dull work; they prefer lavishing their energies on a course of proceeding, which, though to other eyes it appear more heavy with ennui, more cursed with monotony, than the toil of the weaver at his loom, seems to yield them an unfailing supply of enjoyment and occupation.

I allude to a rushing backwards and forwards, amongst themselves, to and from their respective lodgings: not a round – but a triangle of visits, which they keep up all the year through, in winter, spring, summer, and autumn. Season and weather make no difference; with unintelligible zeal they dare snow and hail, wind and rain, mire and dust, to go and dine, or drink tea, or sup with each other. What attracts them, it would be difficult to say. It is not friendship; for whenever they meet they quarrel. It is not religion; the thing is never named amongst them: theology they may discuss occasionally, but piety – never. It is not the love of eating and drinking; each might have as good a joint and pudding, tea as potent, and toast as succulent, at his own lodgings, as is served to him at his brother's. Mrs Gale, Mrs Hogg, and Mrs Whipp – their respective landladies – affirm that 'it is just for naught else but to give folk trouble.' By 'folk,' the good ladies of course mean themselves; for indeed they are kept in a continual 'fry' by this system of mutual invasion.

Mr Donne and his guests, as I have said, are at dinner; Mrs Gale waits on them, but a spark of the hot kitchen fire is in her eye. She considers that the privilege of inviting a friend to a meal occasionally, without additional charge (a privilege included in the terms on which she lets her lodgings), has been quite sufficiently exercised of late. The present week is yet but at Thursday, and on Monday, Mr Malone, the curate of Briarfield, came to breakfast and stayed dinner; on Tuesday, Mr Malone and Mr Sweeting of Nunnely, came to tea, remained to supper, occupied the spare bed, and favoured her with their company to breakfast on Wednesday morning; now, on Thursday, they are both here at dinner, and she is almost certain they will stay all night. 'C'en est trop,' she would say, if she could speak French.

Mr Sweeting is mincing the slice of roast-beef on his plate, and complaining that it is very tough; Mr Donne says the beer is flat. Ay! that is the worst of it: if they would only be civil, Mrs Gale wouldn't mind it so much; if they would only seem satisfied with what they get, she wouldn't care, but 'these young parsons is so high and so scornful, they set everybody beneath their "fit;" they treat her with less than civility, just because she doesn't keep a servant, but does the work of the house herself, as her mother did afore her: then they are always

speaking against Yorkshire ways and Yorkshire folk,' and by that very token Mrs Gale does not believe one of them to be a real gentleman, or come of gentle kin. 'The old parsons is worth the whole lump of college lads; they know what belangs good manners, and is kind to high and low.'

'More bread!' cries Mr Malone, in a tone which, though prolonged but to utter two syllables, proclaims him at once a native of the land of shamrocks and potatoes. Mrs Gale hates Mr Malone more than either of the other two; but she fears him also, for he is a tall, strongly-built personage, with real Irish legs and arms, and a face as genuinely national; not the Milesian face – not Daniel O'Connell's style, but the high-featured, North-American-Indian sort of visage, which belongs to a certain class of the Irish gentry, and has a petrified and proud look, better suited to the owner of an estate of slaves, than to the landlord of a free peasantry. Mr Malone's father termed himself a gentleman: he was poor and in debt, and besottedly arrogant; and his son was like him.

Mrs Gale offered the loaf.

'Cut it, woman,' said her guest; and the 'woman' cut it accordingly. Had she followed her inclinations, she would have cut the parson also; her Yorkshire soul revolted absolutely from his manner of command.

The curates had good appetites, and though the beef was 'tough,' they ate a great deal of it. They swallowed, too, a tolerable allowance of the 'flat beer,' while a dish of Yorkshire pudding, and two tureens of vegetables, disappeared like leaves before locusts. The cheese, too, received distinguished marks of their attention; and a 'spice-cake,' which followed by way of dessert, vanished like a vision, and was no more found. Its elegy was chanted in the kitchen by Abraham, Mrs Gale's son and heir, a youth of six summers; he had reckoned upon the reversion thereof, and when his mother brought down the empty platter, he lifted up his voice and wept sore.

The curates, meantime, sat and sipped their wine; a liquor of unpretending vintage, moderately enjoyed. Mr Malone, indeed, would much rather have had whisky; but Mr Donne, being an Englishman, did not keep the beverage. While they sipped, they argued; not on politics, nor on philosophy, nor on literature – these topics were now as ever totally without interest for them – not even on theology, practical or doctrinal; but on minute points of ecclesiastical discipline, frivolities which seemed empty as bubbles to all save themselves. Mr Malone, who contrived to secure two glasses of wine, when his brethren contented themselves with one, waxed by degrees hilarious after his fashion; that is, he grew a little insolent, said rude things in a hectoring tone, and laughed clamorously at his own brilliancy.

Each of his companions became in turn his butt. Malone had a stock of jokes at their service, which he was accustomed to serve out regularly on convivial occasions like the present, seldom varying his wit; for which, indeed, there was no necessity, as he never appeared to consider himself monotonous, and did not at all care what others thought. Mr Donne, he favoured with hints about his extreme meagreness, allusions to his turned-up nose, cutting sarcasms on a certain threadbare chocolate surtout, which that gentleman was accustomed to sport whenever it rained, or seemed likely to rain, and criticisms on a choice set of cockney phrases, and modes of pronunciation, Mr Donne's own property, and certainly deserving of remark for the elegance and finish they communicated to his style.

# Shirley

Mr Sweeting was bantered about his stature – he was a little man, a mere boy in height and breadth compared with the athletic Malone – rallied on his musical accomplishments – he played the flute and sang hymns like a seraph (some young ladies of his parish thought), sneered at as 'the lady's pet,' teased about his mamma and sisters; for whom poor Mr Sweeting had some lingering regard, and of whom he was foolish enough now and then to speak in the presence of the priestly Paddy, from whose anatomy the bowels of natural affection had somehow been omitted.

The victims met these attacks each in his own way: Mr Donne with a stilted self-complacency, and half-sullen phlegm, the sole props of his otherwise somewhat rickety dignity; Mr Sweeting, with the indifference of a light, easy disposition, which never professed to have any dignity to maintain.

When Malone's raillery became rather too offensive, which it soon did, they joined in an attempt to turn the tables on him, by asking him how many boys had shouted 'Irish Peter!' after him, as he came along the road that day (Malone's name was Peter – the Rev. Peter Augustus Malone); requesting to be informed whether it was the mode in Ireland for clergymen to carry loaded pistols in their pockets, and a shillelagh in their hands, when they made pastoral visits; inquiring the signification of such words, as vele, firrum, hellum, storrum (so Mr Malone invariably pronounced veil, firm, helm, storm), and employing such other methods of retaliation as the innate refinement of their minds suggested.

This, of course, would not do. Malone, being neither good-natured nor phlegmatic, was presently in a towering passion. He vociferated, gesticulated; Donne and Sweeting laughed. He reviled them as Saxons and snobs at the very top pitch of his high Celtic voice; they taunted him with being the native of a conquered land. He menaced rebellion in the name of his 'counthry,' vented bitter hatred against English rule; they spoke of rags, beggary, and pestilence. The little parlour was in an uproar; you would have thought a duel must follow such virulent abuse; it seemed a wonder that Mr and Mrs Gale did not take alarm at the noise, and send for a constable to keep the peace. But they were accustomed to such demonstrations; they well knew that the curates never dined or took tea together without a little exercise of the sort, and were quite easy as to consequences; knowing that these clerical quarrels were as harmless as they were noisy; that they resulted in nothing; and that, on whatever terms the curates might part to-night, they would be sure to meet the best friends in the world to-morrow morning.

As the worthy pair were sitting by their kitchen fire, listening to the repeated and sonorous contact of Malone's fist with the mahogany plane of the parlour table, and to the consequent start and jingle of decanters and glasses following each assault, to the mocking laughter of the allied English disputants, and the stuttering declamation of the isolated Hibernian, – as they thus sat, a foot was heard on the outer door-step, and the knocker quivered to a sharp appeal.

Mr Gale went and opened.

'Whom have you up-stairs in the parlour?' asked a voice; a rather remarkable voice, nasal in tone, abrupt in utterance.

'Oh! Mr Helstone, is it you, sir? I could hardly see you for the darkness; it is so soon dark now. Will you walk in, sir?'

'I want to know first whether it is worth my while walking in. Whom have you up-stairs?'

# Shirley

'The curates, sir.'

'What! all of them?'

'Yes, sir.'

'Been dining here?'

'Yes, sir.'

'That will do.'

With these words a person entered, – a middle-aged man, in black. He walked straight across the kitchen to an inner door, opened it, inclined his head forward, and stood listening. There was something to listen to, for the noise above was just then louder than ever.

'Hey!' he ejaculated to himself; then, turning to Mr Gale, – 'Have you often this sort of work?'

Mr Gale had been a churchwarden, and was indulgent to the clergy.

'They're young, you know, sir, – they're young,' said he, deprecatingly.

'Young! They want caning. Bad boys! – bad boys! and if you were a Dissenter, John Gale, instead of being a good Churchman, they'd do the like; – they'd expose themselves: but I'll –'

By way of finish to this sentence, he passed through the inner door, drew it after him, and mounted the stair. Again he listened a few minutes when he arrived at the upper room. Making entrance without warning, he stood before the curates.

And they were silent; they were transfixed; and so was the invader. He, – a personage short of stature, but straight of port, and bearing on broad shoulders a hawk's head, beak, and eye, the whole surmounted by a Rehoboam, or shovel-hat, which he did not seem to think it necessary to lift or remove before the presence in which he then stood, – *he* folded his arms on his chest and surveyed his young friends – if friends they were – much at his leisure.

'What!' he began, delivering his words in a voice no longer nasal, but deep, – more than deep, – a voice made purposely hollow and cavernous; 'What! has the miracle of Pentecost been renewed? Have the cloven tongues come down again? Where are they? The sound filled the whole house just now. I heard the seventeen languages in full action: – Parthians, and Medes, and Elamites, the dwellers in Mesopotamia, and in Judaea, and Cappadocia, in Pontus and Asia, Phrygia and Pamphylia, in Egypt and in the parts of Libya about Cyrene, strangers of Rome, Jews and proselytes, Cretes and Arabians; – every one of these must have had its representative in this room two minutes since.'

'I beg your pardon, Mr Helstone,' began Mr Donne; 'take a seat, pray, sir. Have a glass of wine?'

His civilities received no answer: the falcon in the black coat proceeded: –

'What do I talk about the gift of tongues? Gift, indeed! I mistook the chapter, and book, and testament: – Gospel for law, Acts for Genesis, the city of Jerusalem for the plain of Shinar. It was no gift, but the confusion of tongues which has gabbled me deaf as a post. *You*, apostles? What! – you three? Certainly not: – three presumptuous Babylonish masons, – neither more nor less!'

'I assure you, sir, we were only having a little chat together over a glass of wine, after a friendly dinner: – settling the Dissenters.'

'Oh! settling the Dissenters – were you? Was Malone settling the Dissenters? It sounded to me much more like settling his co-apostles. You were quarrelling together; making almost as much noise – you three alone – as Moses Barraclough,

the preaching tailor, and all his hearers, are making in the methodist chapel down yonder, where they are in the thick of a revival. I know whose fault it is – it is yours, Malone.'

'Mine! sir?'

'Yours, sir. Donne and Sweeting were quiet before you came, and would be quiet if you were gone. I wish when you crossed the Channel, you had left your Irish habits behind you. Dublin student ways won't do here: the proceedings which might pass unnoticed in a wild bog and mountain district in Connaught will, in a decent English parish, bring disgrace on those who indulge in them, and, what is far worse, on the sacred institution of which they are merely the humble appendages.'

There was a certain dignity in the little elderly gentleman's manner of rebuking these youths; though it was not, perhaps, quite the dignity most appropriate to the occasion. Mr Helstone – standing straight as a ramrod – looking keen as a kite, presented, despite his clerical hat, black coat, and gaiters, more the air of a veteran officer chiding his subalterns, than of a venerable priest exhorting his sons in the faith. Gospel mildness – apostolic benignity, never seemed to have breathed their influence over that keen brown visage; but firmness had fixed the features, and sagacity had carved her own lines about them.

'I met Supplehough,' he continued, 'plodding through the mud this wet night, going to preach at Milldean opposition shop. As I told you, I heard Barraclough bellowing in the midst of a conventicle like a possessed bull; and I find *you*, gentlemen, tarrying over your half pint of muddy port-wine, and scolding like angry old women. No wonder Supplehough should have dipped sixteen adult converts in a day – which he did a fortnight since; no wonder Barraclough, scamp and hypocrite as he is, should attract all the weaver-girls, in their flowers and ribbons, to witness how much harder are his knuckles than the wooden brim of his tub, as little wonder that *you*, when you are left to yourselves, without your rectors – myself, and Hall, and Boultby – to back you, should too often perform the holy service of our church to bare walls, and read your bit of a dry discourse to the clerk, and the organist, and the beadle. But enough of the subject: I came to see Malone – I have an errand unto thee, O captain!'

'What is it?' inquired Malone, discontentedly; 'there can be no funeral to take at this time of day.'

'Have you any arms about you?'

'Arms, sir? – yes, and legs:' and he advanced the mighty members.

'Bah! weapons, I mean.'

'I have the pistols you gave me yourself; I never part with them: I lay them ready cocked on a chair by my bedside at night. I have my blackthorn.'

'Very good. Will you go to Hollow's-mill?'

'What is stirring at Hollow's-mill?'

'Nothing as yet, nor perhaps will be; but Moore is alone there: he has sent all the workmen he can trust to Stilbro'; there are only two women left about the place. It would be a nice opportunity for any of his well-wishers to pay him a visit, if they knew how straight the path was made before them.'

'I am none of his well-wishers, sir: I don't care for him.'

'Soh! Malone, you are afraid.'

'You know me better than that. If I really thought there was a chance of a

# Shirley

row, I would go: but Moore is a strange, shy man, whom I never pretend to understand; and for the sake of his sweet company only, I would not stir a step.'

'But there *is* a chance of a row; if a positive riot does not take place – of which, indeed, I see no signs – yet it is unlikely this night will pass quite tranquilly. You know Moore has resolved to have the new machinery, and he expects two waggon loads of frames and shears from Stilbro' this evening. Scott, the overlooker, and a few picked men, are gone to fetch them.'

'They will bring them in safely and quietly enough, sir.'

'Moore says so, and affirms he wants nobody: some one, however, he must have, if it were only to bear evidence in case anything should happen. I call him very careless. He sits in the counting-house with the shutters unclosed; he goes out here and there after dark, wanders right up the hollow, down Fieldhead-lane, among the plantations, just as if he were the darling of the neighbourhood, or – being, as he is, its detestation – bore a "charmed life" as they say in tale-books. He takes no warning from the fate of Pearson, nor from that of Armitage – shot, one in his own house and the other on the moor.'

'But he should take warning, sir, and use precautions too,' interposed Mr Sweeting; 'and I think he would, if he heard what I heard the other day.'

'What did you hear, Davy?'

'You know Mike Hartley, sir?'

'The Antinomian weaver? Yes.'

'When Mike has been drinking for a few weeks together, he generally winds up by a visit to Nunnely vicarage, to tell Mr Hall a piece of his mind about his sermons, to denounce the horrible tendency of his doctrine of works, and warn him that he and all his hearers are sitting in outer darkness.'

'Well – that has nothing to do with Moore.'

'Besides being an Antinomian, he is a violent Jacobin and leveller, sir.'

'I know. When he is very drunk, his mind is always running on regicide. Mike is not unacquainted with history, and it is rich to hear him going over the list of tyrants of whom, as he says, "the revenger of blood has obtained satisfaction." The fellow exults strangely in murder done on crowned heads, or on any head for political reasons. I have already heard it hinted that he seems to have a queer hankering after Moore: is that what you allude to, Sweeting?'

'You use the proper term, sir. Mr Hall thinks Mike has no personal hatred of Moore; Mike says he even likes to talk to him, and run after him, but he has a *hankering* that Moore should be made an example of: he was extolling him to Mr Hall the other day as the mill-owner with the most brains in Yorkshire, and for that reason he affirms Moore should be chosen as a sacrifice, an oblation of a sweet savour. Is Mike Hartley in his right mind, do you think, sir?' inquired Sweeting, simply.

'Can't tell, Davy: he may be crazed or he may be only crafty – or, perhaps, a little of both.'

'He talks of seeing visions, sir.'

'Ay! He is a very Ezekiel or Daniel for visions. He came just when I was going to bed, last Friday night, to describe one that had been revealed to him in Nunnely Park that very afternoon.'

'Tell it, sir – what was it?' urged Sweeting.

'Davy, thou hast an enormous organ of Wonder in thy cranium; Malone, you

see, has none; neither murders nor visions interest him: see what a big vacant Saph, he looks at this moment.'

'Saph! Who was Saph, sir?'

'I thought you would not know: you may find it out: it is biblical. I know nothing more of him than his name and race; but from a boy upwards, I have always attached a personality to Saph. Depend on it he was honest, heavy, and luckless; he met his end at Gob, by the hand of Sibbechai.'

'But the vision, sir?'

'Davy, thou shalt hear. Donne is biting his nails, and Malone yawning; so I will tell it but to thee. Mike is out of work, like many others, unfortunately; Mr Grame, Sir Philip Nunnely's steward, gave him a job about the priory; according to his account, Mike was busy hedging rather late in the afternoon, but before dark, when he heard what he thought was a band at a distance, bugles, fifes, and the sound of a trumpet; it came from the forest, and he wondered that there should be music there. He looked up: all amongst the trees he saw moving objects, red, like poppies, or white, like May-blossom; the wood was full of them; they poured out and filled the park. He then perceived they were soldiers – thousands and tens of thousands; but they made no more noise than a swarm of midges on a summer evening. They formed in order, he affirmed, and marched, regiment after regiment, across the park; he followed them to Nunnely Common; the music still played soft and distant. On the common he watched them go through a number of evolutions, a man clothed in scarlet stood in the centre and directed them; they extended, he declared, over fifty acres; they were in sight half an hour; then they marched away quite silently: the whole time he heard neither voice nor tread – nothing but the faint music playing a solemn march.'

'Where did they go, sir?'

'Towards Briarfield. Mike followed them; they seemed passing Fieldhead, when a column of smoke, such as might be vomited by a park of artillery, spread noiseless over the fields, the road, the common, and rolled, he said, blue and dim to his very feet. As it cleared away he looked again for the soldiers, but they were vanished; he saw them no more. Mike, like a wise Daniel as he is, not only rehearsed the vision, but gave the interpretation thereof: it signifies, he intimated, bloodshed and civil conflict.'

'Do you credit it, sir?' asked Sweeting.

'Do you, Davy? But come, Malone, why are you not off?'

'I am rather surprised, sir, you did not stay with Moore yourself: you like this kind of thing.'

'So I should have done, had I not unfortunately happened to engage Boultby to sup with me on his way home from the Bible Society meeting at Nunnely. I promised to send you as my substitute; for which, by-the-by, he did not thank me: he would much rather have had me than you, Peter. Should there be any real need of help, I shall join you: the mill-bell will give warning. Meantime, go; unless (turning suddenly to Messrs Sweeting and Donne), – unless Davy Sweeting or Joseph Donne prefers going. What do you say, gentlemen? The commission is an honourable one, not without the seasoning of a little real peril; for the country is in a queer state, as you all know, and Moore and his mill, and his machinery, are held in sufficient odium. There are chivalric sentiments, there is high-beating courage under those waistcoats of yours, I doubt not. Perhaps

I am too partial to my favourite, Peter; little David shall be the champion, or spotless Joseph. Malone, you are but a great floundering Saul after all, good only to lend your armour: out with your firearms, fetch your shillelagh; it is there – in the corner.'

With a significant grin, Malone produced his pistols, offering one to each of his brethren. They were not readily seized on: with graceful modesty, each gentleman retired a step from the presented weapon.

'I never touch them: I never did touch anything of the kind,' said Mr Donne.

'I am almost a stranger to Mr Moore,' murmured Sweeting.

'If you never touched a pistol, try the feel of it now, great satrap of Egypt. As to the little minstrel, he probably prefers encountering the Philistines with no other weapon than his flute. Get their hats, Peter; they'll both of 'em go.'

'No, sir; no, Mr Helstone; my mother wouldn't like it,' pleaded Sweeting.

'And I make it a rule never to get mixed up in affairs of the kind,' observed Donne.

Helstone smiled sardonically; Malone laughed a horse-laugh. He then replaced his arms, took his hat and cudgel, and saying that 'he never felt more in tune for a shindy in his life, and that he wished a score of greasy cloth-dressers might beat up Moore's quarters that night,' he made his exit; clearing the stairs at a stride or two, and making the house shake with the bang of the front-door behind him.

# Chapter 2

## The Waggons

The evening was pitch-dark: star and moon were quenched in gray rain-clouds – gray they would have been by day, by night they looked sable. Malone was not a man given to close observation of Nature; her changes passed, for the most part, unnoticed by him: he could walk miles on the most varying April day, and never see the beautiful dallying of earth and heaven; never mark when a sunbeam kissed the hill-tops, making them smile clear in green light, or when a shower wept over them, hiding their crests with the low-hanging, dishevelled tresses of a cloud. He did not, therefore, care to contrast the sky as it now appeared – a muffled, streaming vault, all black, save where, towards the east, the furnaces of Stilbro' iron-works threw a tremulous lurid shimmer on the horizon – with the same sky on an unclouded frosty night. He did not trouble himself to ask where the constellations and the planets were gone, or to regret the 'black-blue' serenity of the air-ocean which those white islets stud; and which another ocean, of heavier and denser element, now rolled below and concealed. He just doggedly pursued his way, leaning a little forward as he walked, and wearing his hat on the back of his head, as his Irish manner

was. 'Tramp, tramp,' he went along the causeway, where the road boasted the privilege of such an accommodation; 'splash, splash,' through the mire-filled cart-ruts, where the flags were exchanged for soft mud. He looked but for certain landmarks: the spire of Briarfield church; further on, the lights of Redhouse. This was an inn; and when he reached it, the glow of a fire through a half-curtained window, a vision of glasses on a round table, and of revellers on an oaken settle, had nearly drawn aside the curate from his course. He thought longingly of a tumbler of whisky-and-water: in a strange place, he would instantly have realized the dream; but the company assembled in that kitchen were Mr Helstone's own parishioners; they all knew him. He sighed, and passed on.

The high road was now to be quitted, as the remaining distance to Hollow's-mill might be considerably reduced by a short cut across fields. These fields were level and monotonous; Malone took a direct course through them, jumping hedge and wall. He passed but one building here, and that seemed large and hall-like, though irregular: you could see a high gable, then a long front, then a low gable, then a thick, lofty stack of chimneys: there were some trees behind it. It was dark; not a candle shone from any window; it was absolutely still: the rain running from the eaves, and the rather wild, but very low whistle of the wind round the chimneys and through the boughs, were the sole sounds in its neighbourhood.

This building passed, the fields, hitherto flat, declined in a rapid descent: evidently a vale lay below, through which you could hear the water run. One light glimmered in the depth: for that beacon Malone steered.

He came to a little white house – you could see it was white even through this dense darkness – and knocked at the door. A fresh-faced servant opened it; by the candle she held was revealed a narrow passage, terminating in a narrow stair. Two doors covered with crimson baize, a strip of crimson carpet down the steps, contrasted with light-coloured walls and white floor, made the little interior look clean and fresh.

'Mr Moore is at home, I suppose?'

'Yes, sir, but he is not in.'

'Not in! Where is he then?'

'At the mill – in the counting-house.'

Here one of the crimson doors opened.

'Are the waggons come, Sarah?' asked a female voice, and a female head at the same time was apparent. It might not be the head of a goddess – indeed a screw of curl-paper on each side the temples quite forbade that supposition – but neither was it the head of a Gorgon; yet Malone seemed to take it in the latter light. Big as he was, he shrank bashfully back into the rain at the view thereof; and saying, 'I'll go to him,' hurried in seeming trepidation down a short lane, across an obscure yard, towards a huge black mill.

The work-hours were over; the 'hands' were gone; the machinery was at rest; the mill shut up. Malone walked round it; somewhere in its great sooty flank he found another clink of light; he knocked at another door, using for the purpose the thick end of his shillelagh, with which he beat a rousing tattoo. A key turned; the door unclosed.

'Is it Joe Scott? What news of the waggons, Joe?'

'No, – it's myself. Mr Helstone would send me.'

# Shirley

'Oh! Mr Malone.' The voice in uttering this name had the slightest possible cadence of disappointment. After a moment's pause, it continued, politely, but a little formally: –

'I beg you will come in, Mr Malone. I regret extremely Mr Helstone should have thought it necessary to trouble you so far; there was no necessity: – I told him so; – and on such a night – but walk forwards.'

Through a dark apartment, of aspect undistinguishable, Malone followed the speaker into a light and bright room within: very light and bright indeed it seemed to eyes which for the last hour had been striving to penetrate the double darkness of night and fog; but except for its excellent fire, and for a lamp of elegant design and vivid lustre burning on a table, it was a very plain place. The boarded floor was carpetless; the three or four stiff-backed green-painted chairs seemed once to have furnished the kitchen of some farm-house; a desk of strong, solid formation, the table aforesaid, and some framed sheets on the stone-coloured walls, bearing plans for building, for gardening, designs of machinery, &c., completed the furniture of the place.

Plain as it was, it seemed to satisfy Malone; who, when he had removed and hung up his wet surtout and hat, drew one of the rheumatic-looking chairs to the hearth, and set his knees almost within the bars of the red grate.

'Comfortable quarters you have here, Mr Moore; and all snug to yourself.'

'Yes; but my sister would be glad to see you, if you would prefer stepping into the house.'

'Oh, no! the ladies are best alone. I never was a lady's man. You don't mistake me for my friend Sweeting, do you, Mr Moore?'

'Sweeting! – which of them is that? The gentleman in the chocolate over-coat, or the little gentleman?'

'The little one; – he of Nunnely; – the cavalier of the Misses Sykes, with the whole six of whom he is in love, ha! ha!'

'Better be generally in love with all than specially with one, I should think, in that quarter.'

'But he *is* specially in love with one besides, for when I and Donne urged him to make a choice amongst the fair bevy, he named – which do you think?'

With a queer, quiet smile, Mr Moore replied, 'Dora, of course, or Harriet.'

'Ha! ha! you've an excellent guess; but what made you hit on those two?'

'Because they are the tallest, the handsomest; and Dora, at least, is the stoutest; and as your friend Mr Sweeting is but a little, slight figure, I concluded that, according to a frequent rule in such cases, he preferred his contrast.'

'You are right; Dora it is: but he has no chance, has he, Moore?'

'What has Mr Sweeting, besides his curacy?'

This question seemed to tickle Malone amazingly; he laughed for full three minutes before he answered it.

'What has Sweeting? Why David has his harp, or flute, which come to the same thing. He has a sort of pinchbeck watch; ditto, ring; ditto, eye-glass: that's what he has.'

'How would he propose to keep Miss Sykes in gowns only?'

'Ha! ha! Excellent! I'll ask him that next time I see him. I'll roast him for his presumption: but no doubt he expects old Christopher Sykes would do something handsome. He is rich, is he not? They live in a large house.'

'Sykes carries on an extensive concern.'

# Shirley

'Therefore he must be wealthy, eh?'

'Therefore he must have plenty to do with his wealth; and in these times would be about as likely to think of drawing money from the business to give dowries to his daughters as I should be to dream of pulling down the cottage there, and constructing on its ruins a house as large as Fieldhead.'

'Do you know what I heard, Moore, the other day?'

'No: perhaps that I *was* about to effect some such change. Your Briarfield gossips are capable of saying that or sillier things.'

'That you were going to take Fieldhead on a lease – I thought it looked a dismal place, by-the-by, to-night, as I passed it – and that it was your intention to settle a Miss Sykes there as mistress; to be married, in short, ha! ha! Now, which is it? Dora – I am sure: you said she was the handsomest.'

'I wonder how often it has been settled that I was to be married since I came to Briarfield! They have assigned me every marriageable single woman by turns in the district. Now it was the two Misses Wynns – first the dark, then the light one. Now the red-haired Miss Armitage, then the mature Ann Pearson; at present you throw on my shoulders all the tribe of the Misses Sykes. On what grounds this gossip rests, God knows. I visit nowhere – I seek female society about as assiduously as you do, Mr Malone. If ever I go to Whinbury, it is only to give Sykes or Pearson a call in their counting-house; where our discussions run on other topics than matrimony, and our thoughts are occupied with other things than courtships, establishments, dowries: the cloth we can't sell, the hands we can't employ, the mills we can't run, the perverse course of events generally, which we cannot alter, fill our hearts, I take it, pretty well at present, to the tolerably complete exclusion of such figments as love-making, &c.'

'I go along with you completely, Moore. If there is one notion I hate more than another, it is that of marriage: I mean marriage in the vulgar weak sense, as a mere matter of sentiment; two beggarly fools agreeing to unite their indigence by some fantastic tie of feeling – humbug! But an advantageous connexion, such as can be formed in consonance with dignity of views, and permanency of solid interests, is not so bad – eh?'

'No,' responded Moore, in an absent manner; the subject seemed to have no interest for him: he did not pursue it. After sitting for some time gazing at the fire with a preoccupied air, he suddenly turned his head.

'Hark!' said he: 'did you hear wheels?'

Rising, he went to the window, opened it, and listened. He soon closed it. 'It is only the sound of the wind rising,' he remarked, 'and the rivulet a little swollen, rushing down the hollow. I expected those waggons at six; it is near nine now.'

'Seriously, do you suppose that the putting up of this new machinery will bring you into danger?' inquired Malone. 'Helstone seems to think it will.'

'I only wish the machines – the frames were safe here, and lodged within the walls of this mill. Once put up, I defy the framebreakers: let them only pay me a visit, and take the consequences: my mill is my castle.'

'One despises such low scoundrels,' observed Malone, in a profound vein of reflection. 'I almost wish a party would call upon you to-night; but the road seemed extremely quiet as I came along: I saw nothing astir.'

'You came by the Redhouse?'

'Yes.'

# Shirley

'There would be nothing on that road: it is in the direction of Stilbro' the risk lies.'

'And you think there is risk?'

'What these fellows have done to others, they may do to me. There is only this difference: most of the manufacturers seem paralysed when they are attacked. Sykes, for instance, when his dressing-shop was set on fire and burned to the ground, when the cloth was torn from his tenters and left in shreds in the field, took no steps to discover or punish the miscreants: he gave up as tamely as a rabbit under the jaws of a ferret. Now I, if I know myself, should stand by my trade, my mill, and my machinery.'

'Helstone says these three are your gods; that the "Orders in Council" are with you another name for the seven deadly sins; that Castlereagh is your Antichrist, and the war-party his legions.'

'Yes; I abhor all these things because they ruin me: they stand in my way: I cannot get on. I cannot execute my plans because of them: I see myself baffled at every turn by their untoward effects.'

'But you are rich and thriving, Moore?'

'I am very rich in cloth, I cannot sell: you should step into my warehouse yonder, and observe how it is piled to the roof with pieces. Roakes and Pearson are in the same condition: America used to be their market, but the Orders in Council have cut that off.'

Malone did not seem prepared to carry on briskly a conversation of this sort; he began to knock the heels of his boots together, and to yawn.

'And then to think,' continued Mr Moore, who seemed too much taken up with the current of his own thoughts to note the symptoms of his guest's *ennui*, – 'to think that these ridiculous gossips of Whinbury and Briarfield will keep pestering one about being married! As if there was nothing to be done in life but to "pay attention," as they say, to some young lady, and then to go to church with her, and then to start on a bridal tour, and then to run through a round of visits, and then, I suppose, to be "having a family." – Oh, que le diable emporte!' – He broke off the aspiration into which he was launching with a certain energy, and added, more calmly – 'I believe women talk and think only of these things, and they naturally fancy men's minds similarly occupied.'

'Of course – of course,' assented Malone; 'but never mind them.' And he whistled, looked impatiently round, and seemed to feel a great want of something. This time Moore caught, and, it appeared, comprehended his demonstrations.

'Mr Malone,' said he, 'you must require refreshment after your wet walk: I forget hospitality.'

'Not at all,' rejoined Malone; but he looked as if the right nail was at last hit on the head, nevertheless. Moore rose and opened a cupboard.

'It is my fancy,' said he, 'to have every convenience within myself, and not to be dependent on the feminity in the cottage yonder for every mouthful I eat or every drop I drink. I often spend the evening and sup here alone, and sleep with Joe Scott in the mill. Sometimes I am my own watchman; I require little sleep, and it pleases me on a fine night to wander for an hour or two with my musket about the hollow. – Mr Malone, can you cook a mutton-chop?'

'Try me: I've done it hundreds of times at college.'

'There's a dishful, then, and there's the gridiron. Turn them quickly; you know the secret of keeping the juices in?'

# Shirley

'Never fear me – you shall see. Hand a knife and fork, please.'

The curate turned up his coat-cuffs, and applied himself to the cookery with vigour. The manufacturer placed on the table, plates, a loaf of bread, a black bottle, and two tumblers. He then produced a small copper kettle – still from the same well-stored recess, his cupboard – filled it with water from a large stone jar in a corner, set it on the fire beside the hissing gridiron, got lemons, sugar, and a small china punch-bowl; but while he was brewing the punch, a tap at the door called him away.

'Is it you, Sarah?'

'Yes, sir. Will you come to supper, please sir?'

'No; I shall not be in to-night: I shall sleep in the mill. So lock the doors, and tell your mistress to go to bed.' He returned.

'You have your household in proper order,' observed Malone approvingly, as, with his fine face ruddy as the embers over which he bent, he assiduously turned the mutton-chops. 'You are not under petticoat-government, like poor Sweeting; a man – whew! – how the fat spits! – it has burnt my hand – destined to be ruled by women. Now you and I, Moore – there's a fine brown one for you, and full of gravy – you and I will have no grey mares in our stables when we marry.

'I don't know – I never think about it: if the grey mare is handsome and tractable, why not?'

'The chops are done: is the punch brewed?'

'There is a glassful: taste it. When Joe Scott and his minions return they shall have a share of this, provided they bring home the frames intact.'

Malone waxed very exultant over the supper: he laughed aloud at trifles; made bad jokes and applauded them himself; and, in short, grew unmeaningly noisy. His host, on the contrary, remained quiet as before. It is time, reader, that you should have some idea of the appearance of this same host: I must endeavour to sketch him as he sits at table.

He is what you would probably call, at first view, rather a strange-looking man; for he is thin, dark, sallow; very foreign of aspect, with shadowy hair carelessly streaking his forehead: it appears that he spends but little time at his toilette, or he would arrange it with more taste. He seems unconscious that his features are fine, that they have a southern symmetry, cleanness, regularity in their chiseling; nor does a spectator become aware of this advantage till he has examined him well, for an anxious countenance, and a hollow, somewhat haggard, outline of face disturb the idea of beauty with one of care. His eyes are large, and grave, and gray; their expression is intent and meditative, rather searching than soft, rather thoughtful than genial. When he parts his lips in a smile, his physiognomy is agreeable: not that it is frank or cheerful even then, but you feel the influence of a certain sedate charm, suggestive, whether truly or delusively, of a considerate, perhaps a kind nature; of feelings that may wear well at home; patient, forbearing, possibly faithful feelings. He is still young – not more than thirty; his stature is tall, his figure slender. His manner of speaking displeases: he has an outlandish accent, which, notwithstanding a studied carelessness of pronunciation and diction, grates on a British, and especially on a Yorkshire ear.

Mr Moore, indeed, was but half a Briton, and scarcely that. He came of a foreign ancestry by the mother's side, and was himself born, and partly reared, on a foreign soil. A hybrid in nature, it is probable he had a hybrid's feeling on

many points – patriotism for one; it is likely that he was unapt to attach himself to parties, to sects, even to climes and customs; it is not impossible that he had a tendency to isolate his individual person from any community amidst which his lot might temporarily happen to be thrown, and that he felt it to be his best wisdom to push the interests of Robert Gérard Moore, to the exclusion of philanthropic consideration for general interests: with which he regarded the said Gérard Moore as in a great measure disconnected. Trade was Mr Moore's hereditary calling: the Gérards of Antwerp had been merchants for two centuries back. Once they had been wealthy merchants; but the uncertainties, the involvements of business had come upon them; disastrous speculations had loosened by degrees the foundations of their credit; the house had stood on a tottering base for a dozen years; and at last, in the shock of the French Revolution, it had rushed down a total ruin. In its fall was involved the English and Yorkshire firm of Moore, closely connected with the Antwerp house; and of which one of the partners, resident in Antwerp, Robert Moore, had married Hortense Gérard, with the prospect of his bride inheriting her father Constantine Gérard's share in the business. She inherited, as we have seen, but his share in the liabilities of the firm; and these liabilities, though duly set aside by a composition with creditors, some said her son Robert accepted, in his turn, as a legacy; and that he aspired one day to discharge them, and to rebuild the fallen house of Gérard and Moore on a scale at least equal to its former greatness. It was even supposed that he took bypast circumstances much to heart; and if a childhood passed at the side of a saturnine mother, under foreboding of coming evil, and a manhood drenched and blighted by the pitiless descent of the storm, could painfully impress the mind, *his* probably was impressed in no golden characters.

If, however, he had a great end of restoration in view, it was not in his power to employ great means for its attainment; he was obliged to be content with the day of small things. When he came to Yorkshire, he – whose ancestors had owned warehouses in this seaport, and factories in that inland town, had possessed their town-house and their country-seat – saw no way open to him but to rent a cloth-mill, in an out-of-the-way nook of an out-of-the-way district; to take a cottage adjoining it for his residence, and to add to his possessions, as pasture for his horse, and space for his cloth-tenters, a few acres of the steep rugged land that lined the hollow through which his mill-stream brawled. All this he held at a somewhat high rent (for these war times were hard, and everything was dear), of the trustees of the Fieldhead estate, then the property of a minor.

At the time this history commences, Robert Moore had lived but two years in the district; during which period he had at least proved himself possessed of the quality of activity. The dingy cottage was converted into a neat, tasteful residence. Of part of the rough land he had made garden-ground, which he cultivated with singular, even with Flemish, exactness and care. As to the mill, which was an old structure, and fitted up with old machinery, now become inefficient and out of date, he had from the first evinced the strongest contempt for all its arrangements and appointments: his aim had been to effect a radical reform, which he had executed as fast as his very limited capital would allow; and the narrowness of that capital, and consequent check on his progress, was a restraint which galled his spirit sorely. Moore ever wanted to push on: 'Forward' was the device stamped upon his soul; but poverty curbed him:

sometimes (figuratively) he foamed at the mouth when the reins were drawn very tight.

In this state of feeling, it is not to be expected that he would deliberate much as to whether his advance was or was not prejudicial to others. Not being a native, nor for any length of time a resident of the neighbourhood, he did not sufficiently care when the new inventions threw the old work-people out of employ: he never asked himself where those to whom he no longer paid weekly wages found daily bread; and in this negligence he only resembled thousands besides, on whom the starving poor of Yorkshire seemed to have a closer claim.

The period of which I write was an overshadowed one in British history, and especially in the history of the northern provinces. War was then at its height. Europe was all involved therein. England, if not weary, was worn with long resistance: yes, and half her people were weary too, and cried out for peace on any terms. National honour was become a mere empty name, of no value in the eyes of many, because their sight was dim with famine; and for a morsel of meat they would have sold their birthright.

The 'Orders in Council,' provoked by Napoleon's Milan and Berlin decrees, and forbidding neutral powers to trade with France, had, by offending America, cut off the principal market of the Yorkshire woollen trade, and brought it consequently to the verge of ruin. Minor foreign markets were glutted, and would receive no more: the Brazils, Portugal, Sicily, were all overstocked by nearly two years' consumption. At this crisis, certain inventions in machinery were introduced into the staple manufacturers of the north, which, greatly reducing the number of hands necessary to be employed, threw thousands out of work, and left them without legitimate means of sustaining life. A bad harvest supervened. Distress reached its climax. Endurance, overgoaded, stretched the hand of fraternity to sedition. The throes of a sort of moral earthquake were felt heaving under the hills of the northern counties. But, as is usual in such cases, nobody took much notice. When a food-riot broke out in a manufacturing town, when a gig-mill was burnt to the ground, or a manufacturer's house was attacked, the furniture thrown into the streets, and the family forced to flee for their lives, some local measures were or were not taken by the local magistracy; a ringleader was detected, or more frequently suffered to elude detection; newspaper paragraphs were written on the subject, and there the thing stopped. As to the sufferers, whose sole inheritance was labour, and who had lost that inheritance – who could not get work, and consequently could not get wages, and consequently could not get bread – they were left to suffer on; perhaps inevitably left: it would not do to stop the progress of invention, to damage science by discouraging its improvements; the war could not be terminated, efficient relief could not be raised: there was no help then; so the unemployed underwent their destiny – ate the bread and drank the waters of affliction.

Misery generates hate: these sufferers hated the machines which they believed took their bread from them; they hated the buildings which contained those machines; they hated the manufacturers who owned those buildings. In the parish of Briarfield, with which we have at present to do, Hollow's-mill was the place held most abominable; Gérard Moore, in his double character of semi-foreigner and thorough-going progressist, the man most abominated. And it perhaps rather agreed with Moore's temperament than otherwise to be generally hated; especially when he believed the thing for which he was hated a right and

# Shirley

an expedient thing; and it was with a sense of warlike excitement he, on this night, sat in his counting-house waiting the arrival of his frame-laden waggons. Malone's coming and company were, it may be, most unwelcome to him: he would have preferred sitting alone; for he liked a silent, sombre, unsafe solitude: his watchman's musket would have been company enough for him; the full-flowing beck in the den would have delivered continuously the discourse most genial to his ear.

With the queerest look in the world, had the manufacturer for some ten minutes been watching the Irish curate, as the latter made free with the punch; when suddenly that steady gray eye changed, as if another vision came between it and Malone. Moore raised his hand.

'Chut!' he said, in his French fashion, as Malone made a noise with his glass. He listened a moment, then rose, put his hat on, and went out at the counting-house door.

The night was still, dark, and stagnant; the water yet rushed on full and fast: its flow almost seemed a flood in the utter silence. Moore's ear, however, caught another sound – very distant, but yet dissimilar – broken, and rugged: in short, a sound of heavy wheels crunching a stony road. He returned to the counting-house and lit a lantern, with which he walked down the mill-yard, and proceeded to open the gates. The big waggons were coming on; the dray-horses' huge hoofs were heard splashing in the mud and water. Moore hailed them.

'Hey, Joe Scott! Is all right?'

Probably Joe Scott was yet at too great a distance to hear the inquiry; he did not answer it.

'Is all right, I say?' again asked Moore, when the elephant-like leader's nose almost touched his.

Some one jumped out from the foremost waggon into the road; a voice cried aloud, 'Ay, ay, divil, all's raight! We've smashed 'em.'

And there was a run. The waggons stood still: they were now deserted.

'Joe Scott!' No Joe Scott answered, 'Murgatroyd! Pighills! Sykes!' No reply. Mr Moore lifted his lantern, and looked into the vehicles; there was neither man nor machinery: they were empty and abandoned.

Now Mr Moore loved his machinery: he had risked the last of his capital on the purchase of these frames and shears which to-night had been expected; speculations most important to his interests depended on the results to be wrought by them: where were they?

The words 'we've smashed 'em!' rung in his ears. How did the catastrophe affect him? By the light of the lantern he held, were his features visible, relaxing to a singular smile: the smile the man of determined spirit wears when he reaches a juncture in his life where this determined spirit is to feel a demand on its strength: when the strain is to be made, and the faculty must bear or break. Yet he remained silent, and even motionless; for at the instant he neither knew what to say nor what to do. He placed the lantern on the ground, and stood with his arms folded, gazing down and reflecting.

An impatient trampling of one of the horses made him presently look up; his eye, in the moment, caught the gleam of something white attached to a part of

527

the harness. Examined by the light of the lantern, this proved to be a folded paper – a billet. It bore no address without; within was the superscription: –
'To the Divil of Hollow's-miln.'

We will not copy the rest of the orthography, which was very peculiar, but translate it into legible English. It ran thus: –

'Your hellish machinery is shivered to smash on Stilbro' Moor, and your men are lying bound hand and foot in a ditch by the roadside. Take this as a warning from men that are starving, and have starving wives and children to go home to when they have done this deed. If you get new machines, or if you otherwise go on as you have done, you shall hear from us again. Beware!'

'Hear from you again? Yes; I'll hear from you again, and you shall hear from me. I'll speak to you directly: on Stilbro' Moor you shall hear from me in a moment.'

Having led the waggons within the gates, he hastened towards the cottage. Opening the door, he spoke a few words quickly, but quietly, to two females who ran to meet him in the passage. He calmed the seeming alarm of one by a brief palliative account of what had taken place; to the other he said, 'Go into the mill, Sarah – there is the key – and ring the mill-bell as loud as you can: afterwards you will get another lantern and help me to light up the front.'

Returning to his horses, he unharnessed, fed, and stabled them with equal speed and care, pausing occasionally, while so occupied, as if to listen for the mill-bell. It clanged out presently, with irregular but loud and alarming din: the hurried agitated peal seemed more urgent than if the summons had been steadily given by a practised hand. On that still night, at that unusual hour, it was heard a long way round: the guests in the kitchen of the Redhouse were startled by the clangor; and, declaring that 'there must be summat more nor common to do at Hollow's-miln,' they called for lanterns, and hurried to the spot in a body. And scarcely had they thronged into the yard with their gleaming lights, when the tramp of horses was heard, and a little man in a shovel hat, sitting erect on the back of a shaggy pony, 'rode lightly in,' followed by an aide-de-camp mounted on a larger steed.

Mr Moore, meantime, after stabling his dray-horses, had saddled his hackney; and, with the aid of Sarah, the servant, lit up his mill; whose wide and long front now glared one great illumination, throwing a sufficient light on the yard to obviate all fear of confusion arising from obscurity. Already a deep hum of voices became audible. Mr Malone had at length issued from the counting-house, previously taking the precaution to dip his head and face in the stone water-jar; and this precaution, together with the sudden alarm, had nearly restored to him the possession of those senses which the punch had partially scattered. He stood with his hat on the back of his head, and his shillelagh grasped in his dexter fist, answering much at random the questions of the newly-arrived party from the Redhouse. Mr Moore now appeared, and was immediately confronted by the shovel hat and the shaggy pony.

'Well, Moore, what is your business with us? I thought you would want us tonight: me and the hetman here (patting his pony's neck), and Tom and his charger. When I heard your mill-bell, I could sit still no longer, so I left Boultby to finish his supper alone: but where is the enemy? I do not see a mask or a smutted face present; and there is not a pane of glass broken in your windows. Have you had an attack, or do you expect one?'

'Oh, not at all! I have neither had one nor expect one,' answered Moore, coolly. 'I only ordered the bell to be rung because I want two or three neighbours to stay here in the Hollow, while I and a couple or so more go over to Stilbro' Moor.'

'To Stilbro' Moor! What to do? To meet the waggons?'

'The waggons are come home an hour ago.'

'Then all's right. What more would you have?'

'They came home empty; and Joe Scott and Company are left on the moor, and so are the frames. Read that scrawl.'

Mr Helstone received and perused the document of which the contents have before been given.

'Hum! They've only served you as they serve others. But, however, the poor fellows in the ditch will be expecting help with some impatience: this is a wet night for such a berth. I and Tom will go with you; Malone may stay behind and take care of the mill: what is the matter with him? His eyes seem starting out of his head.'

'He has been eating a mutton-chop.'

'Indeed! Peter Augustus, be on your guard. Eat no more mutton-chops to-night. You are left here in command of these premises: an honourable post!'

'Is anybody to stay with me?'

'As many of the present assemblage as choose. My lads, how many of you will remain here, and how many will go a little way with me and Mr Moore on the Stilbro'-road, to meet some men who have been waylaid and assaulted by frame-breakers?'

The small number of three volunteered to go; the rest preferred staying behind. As Mr Moore mounted his horse, the rector asked him in a low voice, whether he had locked up the mutton-chops, so that Peter Augustus could not get at them? The manufacturer nodded an affirmative, and the rescue-party set out.

# Chapter 3

## Mr Yorke

Cheerfulness, it would appear, is a matter which depends fully as much on the state of things within, as on the state of things without and around us. I make this trite remark, because I happen to know that Messrs Helstone and Moore trotted forth from the mill-yard gates, at the head of their very small company, in the best possible spirits. When a ray from a lantern (the three pedestrians of the party carried each one) fell on Mr Moore's face, you could see an unusual, because a lively, spark dancing in his eyes, and a new-found vivacity mantling on his dark physiognomy; and when the rector's visage

was illuminated, his hard features were revealed all agrin and ashine with glee. Yet a drizzling night, a somewhat perilous expedition, you would think were not circumstances calculated to enliven those exposed to the wet and engaged in the adventure. If any member or members of the crew who had been at work on Stilbro' Moor had caught a view of this party, they would have had great pleasure in shooting either of the leaders from behind a wall: and the leaders knew this; and, the fact is, being both men of steely nerves and steady-beating hearts, were elate with the knowledge.

I am aware, reader, and you need not remind me, that it is a dreadful thing for a parson to be warlike: I am aware that he should be a man of peace. I have some faint outline of an idea of what a clergyman's mission is amongst mankind, and I remember distinctly whose servant he is; whose message he delivers, whose example he should follow; yet, with all this, if you are a parson-hater, you need not expect me to go along with you every step of your dismal, downward-tending, unchristian road; you need not expect me to join in your deep anathemas, at once so narrow and so sweeping – in your poisonous rancour so intense and so absurd, against 'the cloth;' to lift up my eyes and hands with a Supplehough, or to inflate my lungs with a Barraclough, in horror and denunciation of the diabolical rector of Briarfield.

He was not diabolical àt all. The evil simply was – he had missed his vocation: he should have been a soldier, and circumstances had made him a priest. For the rest, he was a conscientious, hard-headed, hard-handed, brave, stern, implacable, faithful little man: a man almost without sympathy, ungentle, prejudiced, and rigid; but a man true to principle, – honourable, sagacious, and sincere. It seems to me, reader, that you cannot always cut out men to fit their profession, and that you ought not to curse them because that profession sometimes hangs on them ungracefully: nor will I curse Helstone, clerical Cossack as he was. Yet he *was* cursed, and by many of his own parishioners, as by others he was adored: which is the frequent fate of men who show partiality in friendship, and bitterness in enmity; who are equally attached to principles and adherent to prejudices.

Helstone and Moore, being both in excellent spirits, and united for the present in one cause, you would expect that, as they rode side by side, they would converse amicably. Oh, no! These two men, of hard bilious natures both, rarely came into contact but they chafed each other's moods. Their frequent bone of contention was the war. Helstone was a high Tory (there were Tories in those days) and Moore was a bitter Whig – a Whig, at least, as far as opposition to the war-party was concerned: that being the question which affected his own interest; and only on that question did he profess any British politics at all. He liked to infuriate Helstone by declaring his belief in the invincibility of Bonaparte; by taunting England and Europe with the impotence of their efforts to withstand him; and by coolly advancing the opinion that it was as well to yield to him soon as late, since he must in the end crush every antagonist, and reign supreme.

Helstone could not bear these sentiments: it was only on the consideration of Moore being a sort of outcast and alien, and having but half measure of British blood to temper the foreign gall which corroded his veins, that he brought himself to listen to them without indulging the wish he felt to cane the speaker. Another thing, too, somewhat allayed his disgust; namely, a fellow-feeling for

# Shirley

the dogged tone with which these opinions were asserted, and a respect for the consistency of Moore's crabbed contumacy.

As the party turned into the Stilbro' road, they met what little wind there was; the rain dashed in their faces. Moore had been fretting his companion previously, and now, braced up by the raw breeze, and perhaps irritated by the sharp drizzle, he began to goad him.

'Does your Peninsular news please you still?' he asked.

'What do you mean?' was the surly demand of the Rector.

'I mean have you still faith in that Baal of a Lord Wellington?'

'And what do you mean now?'

'Do you still believe that this wooden-faced and pebble-hearted idol of England has power to send fire down from heaven to consume the French holocaust you want to offer up?'

'I believe Wellington will flog Bonaparte's marshals into the sea, the day it pleases him to lift his arm.'

'But, my dear sir, you can't be serious in what you say. Bonaparte's marshals are great men, who act under the guidance of an omnipotent master-spirit; your Wellington is the most humdrum of common-place martinets, whose slow mechanical movements are further cramped by an ignorant home-government.'

'Wellington is the soul of England. Wellington is the right champion of a good cause; the fit representative of a powerful, a resolute, a sensible, and an honest nation.'

'Your good cause, as far as I understand it, is simply the restoration of that filthy, feeble Ferdinand, to a throne which he disgraced; your fit representative of an honest people is a dull-witted drover, acting for a duller-witted farmer; and against these are arrayed victorious supremacy and invincible genius.'

'Against legitimacy is arrayed usurpation; against modest, single-minded, righteous, and brave resistance to encroachment, is arrayed boastful, double-tongued, selfish, and treacherous ambition to possess. God defend the right!'

'God often defends the powerful.'

'What! I suppose the handful of Israelites standing dry-shod on the Asiatic side of the Red Sea, was more powerful than the host of the Egyptians drawn up on the African side? Were they more numerous? Were they better appointed? Were they more mighty, in a word – eh? Don't speak, or you'll tell a lie, Moore; you know you will. They were a poor over-wrought band of bondsmen. Tyrants had oppressed them through four hundred years; a feeble mixture of women and children diluted their thin ranks; their masters, who roared to follow them through the divided flood, were a set of pampered Ethiops, about as strong and brutal as the lions of Libya. They were armed, horsed, and charioted, the poor Hebrew wanderers were afoot; few of them, it is likely, had better weapons than their shepherds' crooks, or their masons' building-tools; their meek and mighty leader himself had only his rod. But bethink you, Robert Moore, right was with them; the God of battles was on their side. Crime and the lost archangel generalled the ranks of Pharaoh, and which triumphed? We know that well: "The Lord saved Israel that day out of the hand of the Egyptians, and Israel saw the Egyptians dead upon the seashore;" yea, "the depths covered them, they sank to the bottom as a stone." The right hand of the Lord became glorious in power; the right hand of the Lord dashed in pieces the enemy!'

'You are all right; only you forget the true parallel: France is Israel, and

Napoleon is Moses. Europe, with her old over-gorged empires and rotten dynasties, is corrupt Egypt; gallant France is the Twelve Tribes, and her fresh and vigorous Usurper the Shepherd of Horeb.'

'I scorn to answer you.'

Moore accordingly answered himself; at least he subjoined to what he had just said an additional observation in a lower voice.

'Oh, in Italy he was as great as any Moses! He was the right thing there; fit to head and organize measures for the regeneration of nations. It puzzles me to this day how the conqueror of Lodi should have condescended to become an emperor, a vulgar, stupid humbug; and still more how a people, who had once called themselves republicans, should have sunk again to the grade of mere slaves. I despise France! If England had gone as far on the march of civilization as France did, she would hardly have retreated so shamelessly.'

'You don't mean to say that besotted imperial France is any worse than bloody republican France?' demanded Helstone, fiercely.

'I mean to say nothing: but I can think what I please, you know, Mr Helstone, both about France and England; and about revolutions, and regicides, and restorations in general; and about the divine right of kings, which you often stickle for in your sermons, and the duty of non-resistance, and the sanity of war, and –'

Mr Moore's sentence was here cut short by the rapid rolling up of a gig, and its sudden stoppage in the middle of the road; both he and the Rector had been too much occupied with their discourse to notice its approach till it was close upon them.

'Nah, maister, did th' waggons hit home?' demanded a voice from the vehicle.

'Can that be Joe Scott?'

'Ay, ay!' returned another voice; for the gig contained two persons, as was seen by the glimmer of its lamp: the men with the lanterns had now fallen into the rear, or rather the equestrians of the rescue-party had outridden the pedestrians. 'Ay, Mr Moore, it's Joe Scott. I'm bringing him back to you in a bonny pickle. I fand him on the top of the moor yonder, him and three others. What will you give me for restoring him to you?'

'Why, my thanks, I believe; for I could better have afforded to lose a better man. That is you, I suppose, Mr Yorke, by your voice?'

'Ay, lad, it's me. I was coming home from Stilbro' market, and just as I got to the middle of the moor, and was whipping on as swift as the wind (for these, they say, are not safe times, thanks to a bad government!) I heard a groan. I pulled up: some would have whipt on faster; but I've naught to fear, that I know of. I don't believe there's a lad in these parts would harm me: at least I'd give them as good as I got if they offered to do it. I said, "Is there aught wrong anywhere?" – "'Deed is there," somebody says; speaking out of the ground, like. "What's to do? be sharp, and tell me," I ordered. – "Nobbut four on us ligging in a ditch," says Joe, as quiet as could be. I tell'd 'em, more shame to 'em, and bid them get up and move on, or I'd lend them a lick of the gig-whip; for my notion was, they were all fresh. – "We'd ha' done that an hour sin'; but we're teed wi' a bit o' band," says Joe. So in a while I got down and loosed 'em wi' my penknife; and Scott would ride wi' me, to tell me all how it happened; and t'others are coming on as fast as their feet will bring them.'

'Well, I am greatly obliged to you, Mr Yorke.'

'Are you, my lad? you know you're not. However, here are the rest approaching. And here, by the Lord! is another set with lights in their pitchers, like the army of Gideon; and as we've th' parson wi' us, – good-evening, Mr Helstone, – we'se do.'

Mr Helstone returned the salutation of the individual in the gig very stiffly indeed. That individual proceeded: –

'We're eleven strong men, and there's both horses and chariots amang us. If we could only fall in wi' some of these starved ragamuffins of frame-breakers, we could win a grand victory; we could iv'ry one be a Wellington, – that would please ye, Mr Helstone; and sich paragraphs as we could contrive for t' papers! Briarfield suld be famous: but we'se hev a column and a half i' th' *Stilbro' Courier* ower this job, as it is, I daresay: I'se expect no less.'

'And I'll promise you no less, Mr Yorke, for I'll write the article myself,' returned the Rector.

'To be sure! sartainly! And mind ye recommend weel that them 'at brake t' bits o' frames, and teed Joe Scott's legs wi' band, suld be hung without benefit o' clergy. It's a hanging matter, or suld be; no doubt o' that.'

'If I judged them, I'd give them short shrift!' cried Moore; 'but I mean to let them quite alone this bout, to give them rope enough, certain that in the end they will hang themselves.'

'Let them alone, will ye, Moore? Do you promise that?'

'Promise? No. All I mean to say is, I shall give myself no particular trouble to catch them; but if one falls in my way –'

'You'll snap him up, of course: only you would rather they would do something worse than merely stop a waggon before you reckon with them. Well, we'll say no more on the subject at present. Here we are at my door, gentlemen, and I hope you and the men will step in: you will none of you be the worse of a little refreshment.'

Moore and Helstone opposed this proposition as unnecessary; it was, however, pressed on them so courteously, and the night, besides, was so inclement, and the gleam from the muslin-curtained windows of the house before which they had halted, looked so inviting, that at length they yielded. Mr Yorke, after having alighted from his gig, which he left in charge of a man who issued from an outbuilding on his arrival, led the way in.

It will have been remarked that Mr Yorke varied a little in his phraseology; now he spoke broad Yorkshire, and anon he expressed himself in very pure English. His manner seemed liable to equal alternations; he could be polite and affable, and he could be blunt and rough. His station then you could not easily determine by his speech or demeanour; perhaps the appearance of his residence may decide it.

The men he recommended to take the kitchen way, saying that he would 'see them served wi' summat to taste presently.' The gentlemen were ushered in at the front entrance. They found themselves in a matted hall, lined almost to the ceiling with pictures; through this they were conducted to a large parlour, with a magnificent fire in the grate; the most cheerful of rooms it appeared as a whole, and when you came to examine details, the enlivening effect was not diminished. There was no splendour, but there was taste everywhere, – unusual taste, – the taste, you would have said, of a travelled man, a scholar, and a gentleman. A series of Italian views decked the walls; each of these was a

specimen of true art; a connoisseur had selected them: they were genuine and valuable. Even by candlelight, the bright clear skies, the soft distances, with blue air quivering between the eye and the hills, the fresh tints and well massed lights and shadows charmed the view. The subjects were all pastoral, the scenes were all sunny. There was a guitar and some music on a sofa; there were cameos, beautiful miniatures; a set of Grecian-looking vases on the mantelpiece; there were books well arranged in two elegant bookcases.

Mr Yorke bade his guests be seated; he then rang for wine; to the servant who brought it he gave hospitable orders for the refreshment of the men in the kitchen. The Rector remained standing; he seemed not to like his quarters; he would not touch the wine his host offered him.

'E'en as you will,' remarked Mr Yorke. 'I reckon you're thinking of Eastern customs, Mr Helstone, and you'll not eat nor drink under my roof, feared we suld be forced to be friends; but I'm not so particular or superstitious. You might sup the contents of that decanter, and you might give me a bottle of the best in your own cellar, and I'd hold myself free to oppose you at every turn still, – in every vestry-meeting and justice-meeting where we encountered one another.'

'It is just what I should expect of you, Mr Yorke.'

'Does it agree wi' ye now, Mr Helstone, to be riding out after rioters, of a wet night, at your age?'

'It always agrees with me to be doing my duty; and in this case my duty is a thorough pleasure. To hunt down vermin is a noble occupation, – fit for an Archbishop.'

'Fit for ye, at ony rate: but where's t' curate? He's happen gone to visit some poor body in a sick gird, or he's happen hunting down vermin in another direction.'

'He is doing garrison duty at Hollow's-mill.'

'You left him a sup o' wine, I hope, Bob (turning to Mr Moore), to keep his courage up?'

He did not pause for an answer, but continued, quickly – still addressing Moore, who had thrown himself into an old-fashioned chair by the fireside, – 'Move it, Robert! Get up, my lad! That place is mine. Take the sofa, or three other chairs, if you will, but not this; it belangs to me, and nob'dy else.'

'Why are you so particular to that chair, Mr Yorke?' asked Moore, lazily vacating the place, in obedience to orders.

'My father war afore me, and that's all t' answer I sall gie thee; and it's as good a reason as Mr Helstone can give for the main feck o' his notions.'

'Moore, are you ready to go?' inquired the Rector.

'Nay; Robert's not ready; or rather, I'm not ready to part wi' him: he's an ill lad, and wants correcting.'

'Why, sir? What have I done?'

'Made thyself enemies on every hand.'

'What do I care for that? What difference does it make to me whether your Yorkshire louts hate me or like me?'

'Ay, there it is. The lad is a mak' of an alien amang us: his father would never have talked i' that way. Go back to Antwerp, where you were born and bred, mauvaise tête!'

# Shirley

'Mauvaise tête vous-même; je ne fais que mon devoir: quant à vos lourdauds de paysans, je m'en moque!'

'En revanche, mon garçon, nos lourdauds de paysans se moqueront de toi; sois en certain,' replied Yorke, speaking with nearly as pure a French accent as Gérard Moore.

'C'est bon! c'est bon! Et puisque cela m'est égal, que mes amis ne s'en inquiètent pas.'

'Tes amis! Où sont-ils, tes amis?'

'Je fais écho, où sont-ils? et je suis fort aise que l'écho seul y répond. Au diable les amis! Je me souviens encore du moment où mon père et mes oncles Gérard appellèrent autour d'eux leurs amis, et Dieu sait si les amis se sont empressés d'accourir à leur secours! Tenez, M. Yorke, ce mot, ami, m'irrite trop; ne m'en parlez plus.'

'Comme tu voudras.'

And here Mr Yorke held his peace; and while he sits leaning back in his three-cornered, carved oak chair, I will snatch my opportunity to sketch the portrait of this French-speaking Yorkshire gentleman.

# Chapter 4

## Mr Yorke *(continued)*

 Yorkshire gentleman he was par excellence, in every point. About fifty-five years old, but looking at first sight still older, for his hair was silver white. His forehead was broad, not high; his face fresh and hale; the harshness of the north was seen in his features, as it was heard in his voice: every trait was thoroughly English, not a Norman line anywhere; it was an inelegant, unclassic, unaristocratic mould of visage. Fine people would perhaps have called it vulgar; sensible people would have termed it characteristic; shrewd people would have delighted in it for the pith, sagacity, intelligence – the rude, yet real originality marked in every lineament, latent in every furrow. But it was an indocile, a scornful, and a sarcastic face; the face of a man difficult to lead, and impossible to drive. His stature was rather tall, and he was well-made and wiry, and had a stately integrity of port; there was not a suspicion of the clown about him anywhere.

I did not find it easy to sketch Mr Yorke's person, but it is more difficult to indicate his mind. If you expect to be treated to a Perfection, reader, or even to a benevolent, philanthropic old gentleman in him, you are mistaken. He has spoken with some sense, and with some good feeling, to Mr Moore; but you are not thence to conclude that he always spoke and thought justly and kindly.

Mr Yorke, in the first place, was without the organ of Veneration – a great want, and which throws a man wrong on every point where veneration is

535

# Shirley

required. Secondly, he was without the organ of Comparison – a deficiency which strips a man of sympathy; and, thirdly, he had too little of the organs of Benevolence and Ideality, which took the glory and softness from his nature, and for him diminished those divine qualities throughout the universe.

The want of veneration made him intolerant to those above him: kings and nobles and priests, dynasties and parliaments and establishments, with all their doings, most of their enactments, their forms, their rights, their claims, were to him an abomination – all rubbish; he found no use or pleasure in them, and believed it would be clear gain, and no damage to the world, if its high places were razed, and their occupants crushed in the fall. The want of veneration, too, made him dead at heart to the electric delight of admiring what is admirable; it dried up a thousand pure sources of enjoyment; it withered a thousand vivid pleasures. He was not irreligious, though a member of no sect; but his religion could not be that of one who knows how to venerate. He believed in God and heaven; but his God and heaven were those of a man in whom awe, imagination, and tenderness lack.

The weakness of his powers of comparison made him inconsistent; while he professed some excellent general doctrines of mutual toleration and forbearance, he cherished towards certain classes a bigoted antipathy: he spoke of 'parsons' and all who belonged to parsons, of 'lords' and the appendages of lords, with a harshness, sometimes an insolence, as unjust as it was insufferable. He could not place himself in the position of those he vituperated; he could not compare their errors with their temptations, their defects with their disadvantages; he could not realize the effect of such and such circumstances on himself similarly situated, and he would often express the most ferocious and tyrannical wishes regarding those who had acted, as he thought, ferociously and tyrannically. To judge by his threats, he would have employed arbitrary, even cruel, means to advance the cause of freedom and equality. Equality – yes, Mr Yorke talked about equality, but at heart he was a proud man: very friendly to his work-people, very good to all who were beneath him, and submitted quietly to be beneath him, but haughty as Beelzebub to whomsoever the world deemed (for he deemed no man) his superior. Revolt was in his blood: he could not bear control; his father, his grandfather before him, could not bear it, and his children after him never could.

The want of general benevolence made him very impatient of imbecility, and of all faults which grated on his strong, shrewd nature: it left no check to his cutting sarcasm. As he was not merciful, he would sometimes wound and wound again, without noticing how much he hurt, or caring how deep he thrust.

As to the paucity of ideality in his mind, that can scarcely be called a fault: a fine ear for music, a correct eye for colour and form, left him the quality of taste; and who cares for imagination? Who does not think it a rather dangerous, senseless attribute – akin to weakness – perhaps partaking of frenzy – a disease rather than a gift of the mind?

Probably all think it so, but those who possess – or fancy they possess – it. To hear them speak, you would believe that their hearts would be cold if that elixir did not flow about them; that their eyes would be dim if that flame did not refine their vision; that they would be lonely if this strange companion abandoned them. You would suppose that it imparted some glad hope to spring, some fine charm to summer, some tranquil joy to autumn, some consolation to

winter, which you do not feel. All illusion, of course; but the fanatics cling to their dream, and would not give it for gold.

As Mr Yorke did not possess poetic imagination himself, he considered it a most superfluous quality in others. Painters and musicians he could tolerate, and even encourage, because he could relish the results of their art; he could see the charm of a fine picture, and feel the pleasure of good music; but a quiet poet – whatever force struggled, whatever fire glowed, in his breast – if he could not have played the man in the counting-house, or the tradesman in the Piece Hall, might have lived despised, and died scorned, under the eyes of Hiram Yorke.

And as there are many Hiram Yorkes in the world, it is well that the true poet, quiet externally though he may be, has often a truculent spirit under his placidity, and is full of shrewdness in his meekness, and can measure the whole stature of those who look down on him, and correctly ascertain the weight and value of the pursuits they disdain him for not having followed. It is happy that he can have his own bliss, his own society with his great friend and goddess, Nature, quite independent of those who find little pleasure in him, and in whom he finds no pleasure at all. It is just, that while the world and circumstances often turn a dark, cold side to him – and properly, too, because he first turns a dark, cold, careless side to them – he should be able to maintain a festal brightness and cherishing glow in his bosom, which makes all bright and genial for him; while strangers, perhaps, deem his existence a Polar winter never gladdened by a sun. The true poet is not one whit to be pitied; and he is apt to laugh in his sleeve, when any misguided sympathizer whines over his wrongs. Even when utilitarians sit in judgment on him, and pronounce him and his art useless, he hears the sentence with such a hard derision, such a broad, deep, comprehensive, and merciless contempt of the unhappy Pharisees who pronounce it, that he is rather to be chidden than condoled with. These, however, are not Mr Yorke's reflections; and it is with Mr Yorke we have at present to do.

I have told you some of his faults, reader; as to his good points, he was one of the most honourable and capable men in Yorkshire: even those who disliked him were forced to respect him. He was much beloved by the poor, because he was thoroughly kind and very fatherly to them. To his workmen he was considerate and cordial: when he dismissed them from an occupation, he would try to set them on to something else; or, if that was impossible, help them to remove with their families to a district where work might possibly be had. It must also be remarked that if, as sometimes chanced, any individual amongst his 'hands' showed signs of insubordination, Yorke – who, like many who abhor being controlled, knew how to control with vigour – had the secret of crushing rebellion in the germ, of eradicating it like a bad weed, so that it never spread or developed within the sphere of his authority. Such being the happy state of his own affairs, he felt himself at liberty to speak with the utmost severity of those who were differently situated; to ascribe whatever was unpleasant in their position entirely to their own fault, to sever himself from the masters, and advocate freely the cause of the operatives.

Mr Yorke's family was the first and oldest in the district; and he, though not the wealthiest, was one of the most influential men. His education had been good; in his youth, before the French Revolution, he had travelled on the continent: he was an adept in the French and Italian languages. During a two years' sojourn in Italy, he had collected many good paintings and tasteful rarities,

with which his residence was now adorned. His manners, when he liked, were those of a finished gentleman of the old school; his conversation, when he was disposed to please, was singularly interesting and original; and if he usually expressed himself in the Yorkshire dialect, it was because he chose to do so, preferring his native Doric to a more refined vocabulary. 'A Yorkshire burr,' he affirmed, 'was as much better than a Cockney's lisp, as a bull's bellow than a ratton's squeak.'

Mr Yorke knew every one, and was known by every one for miles round; yet his intimate acquaintance were very few. Himself thoroughly original, he had no taste for what was ordinary: a racy, rough character, high or low, ever found acceptance with him; a refined, insipid personage, however exalted in station, was his aversion. He would spend an hour any time in talking freely with a shrewd workman of his own, or with some queer, sagacious old woman amongst his cottagers, when he would have grudged a moment to a commonplace fine gentleman, or to the most fashionable and elegant, if frivolous, lady. His preferences on these points he carried to an extreme, forgetting that there may be amiable and even admirable characters amongst those who cannot be original. Yet he made exceptions to his own rule: there was a certain order of mind, plain, ingenuous, neglecting refinement, almost devoid of intellectuality, and quite incapable of appreciating what was intellectual in him; but which, at the same time, never felt disgust at his rudeness, was not easily wounded by his sarcasm, did not closely analyse his sayings, doings, or opinions; with which he was peculiarly at ease, and, consequently, which he peculiarly preferred. He was lord amongst such characters. They, while submitting implicitly to his influence, never acknowledged, because they never reflected on, his superiority; they were quite tractable, therefore, without running the smallest danger of being servile; and their unthinking, easy, artless insensibility was as acceptable, because as convenient to Mr Yorke, as that of the chair he sat on, or of the floor he trod.

It will have been observed that he was not quite uncordial with Mr Moore; he had two or three reasons for entertaining a faint partiality to that gentleman. It may sound odd, but the first of these was that Moore spoke English with a foreign, and French with a perfectly pure accent; and that his dark, thin face, with its fine though rather wasted lines, had a most anti-British and anti-Yorkshire look. These points seem frivolous, unlikely to influence a character like Yorke's; but, the fact is, they recalled old, perhaps pleasurable associations: they brought back his travelling, his youthful days. He had seen, amidst Italian cities and scenes, faces like Moore's; he had heard, in Parisian cafés, and theatres, voices like his; he was young then, and when he looked at and listened to the alien, he seemed young again.

Secondly, he had known Moore's father, and had had dealings with him: that was a more substantial, though by no means a more agreeable tie;' for, as his firm had been connected with Moore's in business, it had also, in some measure, been implicated in its losses.

Thirdly, he had found Robert himself a sharp man of business. He saw reason to anticipate that he would in the end, by one means or another, make money; and he respected both his resolution and acuteness; perhaps, also, his hardness. A fourth circumstance which drew them together was that of Mr Yorke being one of the guardians of the minor on whose estate Hollow's mill was situated;

consequently Moore, in the course of his alterations, and improvements, had frequent occasion to consult him.

As to the other guest now present in Mr Yorke's parlour, Mr Helstone, between him and his host there existed a double antipathy: the antipathy of nature and that of circumstances. The free-thinker hated the formalist; the lover of liberty detested the disciplinarian: besides, it was said that in former years they had been rival suitors of the same lady.

Mr Yorke, as a general rule, was, when young, noted for his preference of sprightly and dashing women: a showy shape and air, a lively wit, a ready tongue, chiefly seemed to attract him. He never, however, proposed to any of these brilliant belles, whose society he sought; and all at once he seriously fell in love with, and eagerly wooed a girl who presented a complete contrast to those he had hitherto noticed: a girl with the face of a Madonna; a girl of living marble; stillness personified. No matter that, when he spoke to her, she only answered him in monosyllables; no matter that his sighs seemed unheard, that his glances were unreturned, that she never responded to his opinions, rarely smiled at his jests, paid him no respect and no attention; no matter that she seemed the opposite of everything feminine he had ever, in his whole life, been known to admire: for him Mary Cave was perfect, because somehow, for some reason – no doubt he had a reason – he loved her.

Mr Helstone, at that time curate of Briarfield, loved Mary too; or, at any rate, he fancied her. Several others admired her, for she was beautiful as a monumental angel; but the clergyman was preferred for his office's sake: that office probably investing him with some of the illusion necessary to allure to the commission of matrimony, and which Miss Cave did not find in any of the young wool-staplers, her other adorers. Mr Helstone neither had, nor professed to have, Mr Yorke's absorbing passion for her: he had known of the humble reverence which seemed to subdue most of her suitors; he saw her more as she really was than the rest did; he was, consequently, more master of her and himself. She accepted him at the first offer, and they were married.

Nature never intended Mr Helstone to make a very good husband, especially to a quiet wife. He thought, so long as a woman was silent, nothing ailed her, and she wanted nothing. If she did not complain of solitude, solitude, however continued, could not be irksome to her. If she did not talk and put herself forward, express a partiality for this, an aversion to that, she had no partialities or aversions, and it was useless to consult her tastes. He made no pretence of comprehending women, or comparing them with men: they were a different, probably a very inferior order of existence; a wife could not be her husband's companion, much less his confidant, much less his stay. *His* wife, after a year or two, was of no great importance to him in any shape; and when she one day, as he thought, suddenly – for he had scarcely noticed her decline – but as others thought gradually, took her leave of him and of life, and there was only a still beautiful-featured mould of clay left, cold and white, in the conjugal couch, he felt his bereavement – who shall say how little? Yet, perhaps, more than he seemed to feel it; for he was not a man from whom grief easily wrung tears.

His dry-eyed and sober mourning scandalized an old housekeeper, and likewise a female attendant, who had waited upon Mrs Helstone in her sickness; and who, perhaps, had had opportunities of learning more of the deceased lady's nature, of her capacity for feeling and loving, than her husband knew: they

# Shirley

gossiped together over the corpse, related anecdotes, with embellishments of her lingering decline, and its real or supposed cause; in short, they worked each other up to some indignation against the austere little man, who sat examining papers in an adjoining room, unconscious of what opprobrium he was the object.

Mrs Helstone was hardly under the sod when rumours began to be rife in the neighbourhood that she had died of a broken heart; these magnified quickly into reports of hard usage, and, finally, details of harsh treatment on the part of her husband: reports grossly untrue, but not the less eagerly received on that account. Mr Yorke heard them, partly believed them. Already, of course, he had no friendly feeling to his successful rival; though himself a married man now, and united to a woman who seemed a complete contrast to Mary Cave in all respects, he could not forget the great disappointment of his life; and when he heard that what would have been so precious to him had been neglected, perhaps abused by another, he conceived for that other a rooted and bitter animosity.

Of the nature and strength of this animosity, Mr Helstone was but half aware: he neither knew how much Yorke had loved Mary Cave, what he had felt on losing her, nor was he conscious of the calumnies concerning his treatment of her, familiar to every ear in the neighbourhood but his own. He believed political and religious differences alone separated him and Mr Yorke; had he known how the case really stood, he would hardly have been induced by any persuasion to cross his former rival's threshold.

Mr Yorke did not resume his lecture of Robert Moore; the conversation erelong recommenced in a more general form, though still in a somewhat disputative tone. The unquiet state of the country, the various depredations lately committed on mill-property in the district, supplied abundant matter for disagreement; especially as each of the three gentlemen present differed more or less in his views on these subjects. Mr Helstone thought the masters aggrieved, the workpeople unreasonable; he condemned sweepingly the widespread spirit of disaffection against constituted authorities, the growing indisposition to bear with patience evils he regarded as inevitable: the cures he prescribed were vigorous government interference, strict magisterial vigilance; when necessary, prompt military coercion.

Mr Yorke wished to know whether this interference, vigilance and coercion would feed those who were hungry, give work to those who wanted work and whom no man would hire. He scouted the idea of inevitable evils; he said public patience was a camel, on whose back the last atom that could be borne had already been laid, and that resistance was now a duty: the wide-spread spirit of disaffection against constituted authorities, he regarded as the most promising sign of the times; the masters, he allowed, were truly aggrieved, but their main grievances had been heaped on them by a 'corrupt, base, and bloody' government (these were Mr Yorke's epithets). Madmen like Pitt, demons like Castlereagh, mischievous idiots like Perceval, were the tyrants, the curses of the country, the destroyers of her trade. It was their infatuated perseverance in an unjustifiable, a hopeless, a ruinous war, which had brought the nation to its present pass. It was their monstrously oppressive taxation, it was the infamous 'Orders in Council' – the originators of which deserved impeachment and the scaffold, if ever public men did – that hung a millstone about England's neck.

'But where was the use of talking?' he demanded – 'What chance was there

of reason being heard in a land that was king-ridden, priest-ridden, peer-ridden – where a lunatic was the nominal monarch, an unprincipled debauchee the real ruler; where such an insult to common sense as hereditary legislators were tolerated – where such a humbug as a bench of bishops – such an arrogant abuse as a pampered, persecuting established Church was endured and venerated – where a standing army was maintained, and a host of lazy parsons and their pauper families were kept on the fat of the land?'

Mr Helstone, rising up and putting on his shovel-hat, observed in reply, 'That in the course of his life he had met with two or three instances where sentiments of this sort had been very bravely maintained so long as health, strength, and worldly prosperity had been the allies of him who professed them; but there came a time,' he said, 'to all men, "when the keepers of the house should tremble; when they should be afraid of that which is high, and fear should be in the way;" and that time was the test of the advocate of anarchy and rebellion, the enemy of religion and order. Erenow,' – he affirmed, 'he had been called upon to read those prayers our Church has provided for the sick, by the miserable dying-bed of one of her most rancorous foes; he had seen such a one stricken with remorse, solicitous to discover a place for repentance, and unable to find any, though he sought it carefully with tears. He must forewarn Mr Yorke, that blasphemy against God and the king was a deadly sin, and that there was such a thing as "judgement to come." '

Mr Yorke 'believed fully that there was such a thing as judgement to come. If it were otherwise, it would be difficult to imagine how all the scoundrels who seemed triumphant in this world, who broke innocent hearts with impunity, abused unmerited privileges, were a scandal to honourable callings, took the bread out of the mouths of the poor, browbeat the humble, and truckled meanly to the rich and proud – were to be properly paid off, in such coin as they had earned. But,' he added, 'whenever he got low-spirited about such like goings-on, and their seeming success in this mucky lump of a planet, he just reached down t' owd book (pointing to a great Bible in the bookcase), opened it like at a chance, and he was sure to light of a verse blazing wi' a blue brimstone low that set all straight. He knew,' he said, 'where some folk war bound for, just as weel as if an angel wi' great white wings had come in ower t' door-stone and told him.'

'Sir,' said Mr Helstone, collecting all his dignity, 'Sir – the great knowledge of man is to know himself, and the bourne whither his own steps tend.'

'Ay, ay! you'll recollect, Mr Helstone, that Ignorance was carried away from the very gates of heaven, borne through the air, and thrust in at a door in the side of the hill which led down to hell.'

'Nor have I forgotten, Mr Yorke, that Vain-Confidence, not seeing the way before him, fell into a deep pit, which was on purpose there made by the prince of the grounds, to catch vain-glorious fools withal, and was dashed to pieces with his fall.'

'Now,' interposed Mr Moore, who had hitherto sat a silent but amused spectator of this wordy combat, and whose indifference to the party politics of the day, as well as to the gossip of the neighbourhood, made him an impartial, if apathetic judge of the merits of such an encounter – 'you have both sufficiently black-balled each other, and proved how cordially you detest each other, and how wicked you think each other. For my part, my hate is still running in such

a strong current against the fellows who have broken my frames, that I have none to spare for my private acquaintance, and still less for such a vague thing as a sect or a government: but really, gentlemen, you both seem very bad, by your own showing; worse than ever I suspected you to be. I dare not stay all night with a rebel and blasphemer, like you, Yorke: and I hardly dare ride home with a cruel and tyrannical ecclesiastic, like Mr Helstone.'

'I am going, however, Mr Moore,' said the Rector sternly: 'come with me or not, as you please.'

'Nay, he shall not have the choice – he *shall* go with you,' responded Yorke. 'It's midnight, and past: and I'll have nob'dy staying up i' my house any longer. Ye mun all go.'

He rang the bell.

'Deb,' said he to the servant who answered it, 'clear them folk out o' t' kitchen, and lock t' doors, and be off to bed. Here is your way, gentlemen,' he continued to his guests; and, lighting them through the passage, he fairly put them out at his front-door.

They met their party hurrying out pell-mell by the back way; their horses stood at the gate; they mounted, and rode off – Moore laughing at their abrupt dismissal, Helstone deeply indignant thereat.

# Chapter 5

## Hollow's Cottage

Moore's good spirits were still with him when he rose next morning. He and Joe Scott had both spent the night in the mill, availing themselves of certain sleeping accommodations producible from recesses in the front and back counting-houses: the master, always an early riser, was up somewhat sooner even than usual; he awoke his man by singing a French song as he made his toilet.

'Ye 're not custen dahm, then, maister?' cried Joe.

'Not a stiver, mon garçon – which means, my lad: – get up, and we'll take a turn through the mill before the hands come in, and I'll explain my future plans. We'll have the machinery yet, Joseph: you never heard of Bruce, perhaps?'

'And th' arrand (spider)? Yes, but I hev: I've read th' history o' Scotland, and happen knaw as mich on't as ye; and I understand ye to mean to say ye'll persevere.'

'I do.'

'Is there mony o' your mak' i' your country?' inquired Joe, as he folded up his temporary bed, and put it away.

'In my country! Which is my country?'

'Why, France – isn't it?'

'Not it, indeed! The circumstance of the French having seized Antwerp, where I was born, does not make me a Frenchman.'

'Holland, then?'

'I am not a Dutchman: now you are confounding Antwerp with Amsterdam.'

'Flanders?'

'I scorn the insinuation, Joe! I, a Flamand! Have I a Flemish face? – the clumsy nose standing out – the mean forehead falling back – the pale blue eyes "à fleur de tête?" Am I all body and no legs, like a Flamand? But you don't know what they are like – those Netherlanders. Joe, I'm an Anversois: my mother was an Anversoise, though she came of French lineage, which is the reason I speak French.'

'But your father war Yorkshire, which maks ye a bit Yorkshire too; and onybody may see ye're akin to us, ye're so keen o' making brass, and getting forrards.'

'Joe, you're an impudent dog; but I've always been accustomed to a boorish sort of insolence from my youth up: the "classe ouvrière" – that is, the working people, in Belgium – bear themselves brutally towards their employers; and by *brutally*, Joe, I mean *brutalement* – which, perhaps, when properly translated, should be *roughly*.'

'We allus speak our minds i' this country; and them young parsons and grand folk fro' London is shocked at wer *"incivility,"* and we like weel enow to gi'e 'em summat to be shocked at, 'cause it's sport to us to watch 'em turn up the whites o' their een, and spreed out their bits o' hands, like as they're flayed wi' boggards, and then to hear 'em say, nipping off their words short, like – "Dear! dear! Whet seveges! How very corse!"'

'You *are* savages, Joe; you don't suppose you're civilized, do you?'

'Middling, middling, maister. I reckon 'at us manufacturing lads i' th' north is a deal more intelligent, and knaws a deal more nor th' farming folk i' th' south. Trade sharpens wer wits; and them that's mechanics, like me, is forced to think. Ye know, what wi' looking after machinery and sich like, I've getten into that way that when I see an effect, I look straight out for a cause, and I oft lig hold on't to purpose; and then I like reading, and I'm curious to knaw what them that reckons to govern us aims to do for us and wi' us: and there's many 'cuter nor me; there's many a one amang them greasy chaps 'at smells o' oil, and amang them dyers wi' blue and black skins, that has a long head, and that can tell what a fooil of a law is, as well as ye or old Yorke, and a deal better nor soft uns like Christopher Sykes o' Whinbury, and greet hectoring nowts like yond' Irish Peter, Helstone's curate.'

'You think yourself a clever fellow, I know, Scott.'

'Ay, I'm fairish; I can tell cheese fro' chalk, and I'm varry weel aware that I've improved sich opportunities as I have had, a deal better nor some 'at reckons to be aboon me; but there's thousands i' Yorkshire that's as good as me, and a two-three that's better.'

'You're a great man – you're a sublime fellow; but you're a prig, a conceited noodle with it all, Joe! You need not to think that because you've picked up a little knowledge of practical mathematics, and because you have found some scantling of the elements of chemistry at the bottom of a dyeing vat, that therefore you're a neglected man of science; and you need not to suppose that because the course of trade does not always run smooth, and you, and such as you, are

sometimes short of work and of bread, that therefore your class are martyrs, and that the whole form of government under which you live is wrong. And, moreover, you need not for a moment to insinuate that the virtues have taken refuge in cottages and wholly abandoned slated houses. Let me tell you, I particularly abominate that sort of trash, because I know so well that human nature is human nature everywhere, whether under tile or thatch, and that in every specimen of human nature that breathes, vice and virtue are ever found blended, in smaller or greater proportions, and that the proportion is not determined by station. I have seen villains who were rich, and I have seen villains who were poor, and I have seen villains who were neither rich nor poor, but who had realized Agar's wish, and lived in fair and modest competency. The clock is going to strike six: away with you, Joe, and ring the mill bell.'

It was now the middle of the month of February; by six o'clock, therefore, dawn was just beginning to steal on night, to penetrate with a pale ray its brown obscurity, and give a demi-translucence to its opaque shadows. Pale enough that ray was on this particular morning; no colour tinged the east, no flush warmed it. To see what a heavy lid day slowly lifted, what a wan glance she flung along the hills, you would have thought the sun's fire quenched in last night's floods. The breath of this morning was chill as its aspect; a raw wind stirred the mass of night-cloud, and showed, as it slowly rose – leaving a colourless, silver-gleaming ring all round the horizon – not blue sky, but a stratum of paler vapour beyond. It had ceased to rain, but the earth was sodden, and the pools and rivulets were full.

The mill-windows were alight, the bell still rung loud, and now the little children came running in, in too great a hurry, let us hope, to feel very much nipped by the inclement air; and, indeed, by contrast, perhaps the morning appeared rather favourable to them than otherwise; for they had often come to their work that winter through snow-storms, through heavy rain, through hard frost.

Mr Moore stood at the entrance to watch them pass: he counted them as they went by; to those who came rather late he said a word of reprimand, which was a little more sharply repeated by Joe Scott when the lingerers reached the work-rooms. Neither master nor overlooker spoke savagely; they were not savage men either of them, though it appeared both were rigid, for they fined a delinquent who came considerably too late: Mr Moore made him pay his penny down ere he entered, and informed him that the next repetition of the fault would cost him twopence.

Rules, no doubt, are necessary in such cases, and coarse and cruel masters will make coarse and cruel rules, which, at the time we treat of at least, they used sometimes to enforce tyrannically; but, though I describe imperfect characters (every character in this book will be found to be more or less imperfect, my pen refusing to draw anything in the model line), I have not undertaken to handle degraded or utterly infamous ones. Child-torturers, slave masters and drivers, I consign to the hands of jailers; the novelist may be excused from sullying his page with the record of their deeds.

Instead, then, of harrowing up my reader's soul, and delighting his organ of Wonder, with effective descriptions of stripes and scourgings, I am happy to be able to inform him that neither Mr Moore nor his overlooker ever struck a child in their mill. Joe had, indeed, once very severely flogged a son of his own for

# Shirley

telling a lie and persisting in it; but, like his employer, he was too phlegmatic, too calm, as well as too reasonable a man, to make corporeal chastisement other than the exception to his treatment of the young.

Mr Moore haunted his mill, his mill-yard, his dye-house, and his warehouse, till the sickly dawn strengthened into day. The sun even rose, – at least a white disk, clear, tintless, and almost chill-looking as ice, – peeped over the dark crest of a hill, changed to silver the livid edge of the cloud above it, and looked solemnly down the whole length of the den, or narrow dale, to whose strait bounds we are at present limited. It was eight o'clock; the mill lights were all extinguished; the signal was given for breakfast; the children, released for half an hour from toil, betook themselves to the little tin cans which held their coffee, and to the small baskets which contained their allowance of bread. Let us hope they have enough to eat; it would be a pity were it otherwise.

And now, at last, Mr Moore quitted the mill-yard, and bent his steps to his dwelling-house. It was only a short distance from the factory, but the hedge and high bank on each side of the lane which conducted to it seemed to give it something of the appearance and feeling of seclusion. It was a small, white-washed place, with a green porch over the door; scanty brown stalks showed in the garden soil near this porch, and likewise beneath the windows, – stalks budless and flowerless now, but giving dim prediction of trained and blooming creepers for summer days. A grass plat and borders fronted the cottage; the borders presented only black mould yet, except where, in sheltered nooks, the first shoots of snowdrop or crocus peeped, green as emerald, from the earth. The spring was late; it had been a severe and prolonged winter; the last deep snow had but just disappeared before yesterday's rains; on the hills, indeed, white remnants of it yet gleamed, flecking the hollows and crowning the peaks: the lawn was not verdant, but bleached, as was the grass on the bank, and under the hedge in the lane. Three trees, gracefully grouped, rose beside the cottage; they were not lofty, but having no rivals near, they looked well and imposing where they grew. Such was Mr Moore's home; a snug nest for content and contemplation, but one within which the wings of action and ambition could not long lie folded.

Its air of modest comfort seemed to possess no particular attraction for its owner; instead of entering the house at once, he fetched a spade from a little shed and began to work in the garden. For about a quarter of an hour he dug on uninterrupted; at length, however, a window opened, and a female voice called to him: –

'Eh, bien! Tu ne déjeûnes pas ce matin?'

The answer and the rest of the conversation was in French, but as this is an English book, I shall translate it into English.

'Is breakfast ready, Hortense?'

'Certainly; it has been ready half an hour.'

'Then I am ready, too: I have a canine hunger.'

He threw down his spade and entered the house: the narrow passage conducted him to a small parlour, where a breakfast of coffee and bread and butter, with the somewhat un-English accompaniment of stewed pears, was spread on the table. Over these viands presided the lady who had spoken from the window. I must describe her before I go any further.

She seemed a little older than Mr Moore, perhaps she was thirty-five, tall,

# Shirley

and proportionately stout; she had very black hair, for the present twisted up in curl-papers; a high colour in her cheeks, a small nose, a pair of little black eyes. The lower part of her face was large in proportion to the upper; her forehead was small and rather corrugated; she had a fretful though not an ill-natured expression of countenance; there was something in her whole appearance one felt inclined to be half provoked with, and half amused at. The strangest point was her dress: a stuff petticoat and a striped cotton camisole. The petticoat was short, displaying well a pair of feet and ankles which left much to be desired in the article of symmetry.

You will think I have depicted a remarkable slattern, reader; – not at all. Hortense Moore (she was Mr Moore's sister) was a very orderly, economical person; the petticoat, camisole, and curl-papers were her morning costume, in which, of forenoons, she had always been accustomed to 'go her household ways' in her own country. She did not choose to adopt English fashions because she was obliged to live in England; she adhered to her old Belgian modes, quite satisfied that there was a merit in so doing.

Mademoiselle had an excellent opinion of herself, an opinion not wholly undeserved, for she possessed some good and sterling qualities; but she rather over-estimated the kind and degree of these qualities, and quite left out of the account sundry little defects which accompanied them. You could never have persuaded her that she was a prejudiced and narrow-minded person, that she was too susceptible on the subject of her own dignity and importance, and too apt to take offence about trifles; yet all this was true. However, where her claims to distinction were not opposed, and where her prejudices were not offended, she could be kind and friendly enough. To her two brothers (for there was another Gérard Moore besides Robert), she was very much attached. As the sole remaining representatives of their decayed family, the persons of both were almost sacred in her eyes; of Louis, however, she knew less than of Robert; he had been sent to England when a mere boy, and had received his education at an English school. His education not being such as to adapt him for trade, perhaps, too, his natural bent not inclining him to mercantile pursuits, he had, when the blight of hereditary prospects rendered it necessary for him to push his own fortune, adopted the very arduous and very modest career of a teacher; he had been usher in a school, and was said now to be tutor in a private family. Hortense, when she mentioned Louis, described him as having what she called 'des moyens,' but as being too backward and quiet: her praise of Robert was in a different strain, less qualified; she was very proud of him; she regarded him as the greatest man in Europe: all he said and did was remarkable in her eyes, and she expected others to behold him from the same point of view; nothing could be more irrational, monstrous, and infamous, than opposition from any quarter to Robert, unless it were opposition to herself.

Accordingly, as soon as the said Robert was seated at the breakfast table, and she had helped him to a portion of stewed pears, and cut him a good-sized Belgian tartine, she began to pour out a flood of amazement and horror at the transaction of last night, the destruction of the frames.

'Quelle idée! to destroy them. Quelle action honteuse! On voyait bien que les ouvriers de ce pays étaient à la fois bêtes et méchants. C'était absolument comme les domestiques Anglais, les servantes surtout: rien d'insupportable comme cette Sara, par exemple!'

# Shirley

'She looks clean and industrious,' Mr Moore remarked.

'Looks! I don't know how she looks; and I do not say that she is altogether dirty or idle: mais elle est d'une insolence! She disputed with me a quarter of an hour yesterday about the cooking of the beef; she said I boiled it to rags, that English people would never be able to eat such a dish as our bouilli, that the bouillon was no better than greasy warm water, and as to the choucroute, she affirms she cannot touch it! That barrel we have in the cellar – delightfully prepared by my own hands – she termed a tub of hog-wash, which means food for pigs. I am harassed with the girl, and yet I cannot part with her lest I should get a worse. You are in the same position with your workmen, – pauvre cher frère!'

'I am afraid you are not very happy in England, Hortense.'

'It is my duty to be happy where you are, brother; but otherwise, there are certainly a thousand things which make me regret our native town. All the world here appears to me ill-bred (mal-élevé). I find my habits considered ridiculous: if a girl out of your mill chances to come into the kitchen and find me in my jupon and camisole preparing dinner (for you know I cannot trust Sarah to cook a single dish), she sneers. If I accept an invitation out to tea, which I have done once or twice, I perceive I am put quite into the background; I have not that attention paid me which decidedly is my due. Of what an excellent family are the Gérards, as we know, and the Moores also! They have a right to claim a certain respect, and to feel wounded when it is withheld from them. In Antwerp, I was always treated with distinction; here, one would think that when I open my lips in company, I speak English with a ridiculous accent, whereas I am quite assured that I pronounce it perfectly.'

'Hortense, in Antwerp we were known rich; in England we were never known but poor.'

'Precisely, and thus mercenary are mankind. Again, dear brother, last Sunday, if you recollect, was very wet; accordingly, I went to church in my neat black sabots, objects one would not indeed wear in a fashionable city; but which in the country I have ever been accustomed to use for walking in dirty roads. Believe me, as I paced up the aisle, composed and tranquil, as I am always, four ladies, and as many gentlemen, laughed and hid their faces behind their prayer-books.'

'Well, well! don't put on the sabots again. I told you before I thought they were not quite the thing for this country.'

'But, brother, they are not common sabots, such as the peasantry wear. I tell you, they are sabots noirs, très propres, très convenables. At Mons and Leuze – cities not very far removed from the elegant capital of Brussels – it is very seldom that the respectable people wear anything else for walking in winter. Let any one try to wade the mud of the Flemish chaussées in a pair of Paris brodequins, on m'en dirait des nouvelles!'

'Never mind Mons and Leuze, and the Flemish chaussées; do at Rome as the Romans do; and as to the camisole and jupon, I am not quite sure about them either. I never see an English lady dressed in such garments. Ask Caroline Helstone.'

'Caroline! I ask Caroline? I consult her about my dress? It is *she* who on all points should consult *me*; she is a child.'

'She is eighteen, or at the least seventeen; old enough to know all about gowns, petticoats, and chaussures.'

# Shirley

'Do not spoil Caroline, I entreat you, brother; do not make her of more consequence than she ought to be. At present she is modest and unassuming: let us keep her so.'

'With all my heart. Is she coming this morning?'

'She will come at ten, as usual, to take her French lesson.'

'You don't find that she sneers at you, do you?'

'She does not, she appreciates me better than any one else here; but then she has more intimate opportunities of knowing me: she sees that I have education, intelligence, manner, principles; all, in short, which belongs to a person well born and well bred.'

'Are you at all fond of her?'

'For *fond* – I cannot say: I am not one who is prone to take violent fancies, and, consequently, my friendship is the more to be depended on. I have a regard for her as my relative; her position also inspires interest, and her conduct as my pupil has hitherto been such as rather to enhance than diminish the attachment that springs from other causes.'

'She behaves pretty well at lessons?'

'To *me* she behaves very well; but you are conscious, brother, that I have a manner calculated to repel over-familiarity, to win esteem, and to command respect. Yet, possessed of penetration, I perceive clearly that Caroline is not perfect; that there is much to be desired in her.'

'Give me a last cup of coffee, and while I am drinking it amuse me with an account of her faults.'

'Dear brother, I am happy to see you eat your breakfast with relish, after the fatiguing night you have passed. Caroline, then, is defective; but, with my forming hand and almost motherly care, she may improve. There is about her an occasional something – a reserve, I think – which I do not quite like, because it is not sufficiently girlish and submissive; and there are glimpses of an unsettled hurry in her nature, which put me out. Yet she is usually most tranquil, too dejected and thoughtful indeed sometimes. In time, I doubt not, I shall make her uniformly sedate and decorous, without being unaccountably pensive. I ever disapprove what is not intelligible.'

'I don't understand your account in the least; what do you mean by "unsettled hurries," for instance?'

'An example will, perhaps, be the most satisfactory explanation. I sometimes, you are aware, make her read French poetry by way of practice in pronunciation. She has, in the course of her lessons, gone through much of Corneille and Racine, in a very steady, sober spirit, such as I approve. Occasionally she showed, indeed, a degree of languor in the perusal of those esteemed authors, partaking rather of apathy than sobriety, and apathy is what I cannot tolerate in those who have the benefit of my instructions; besides, one should not be apathetic in studying standard works. The other day I put into her hands a volume of short fugitive pieces. I sent her to the window to learn one by heart, and when I looked up I saw her turning the leaves over impatiently, and curling her lip, absolutely with scorn, as she surveyed the little poems cursorily. I chid her "Ma cousine," said she, "tout cela m'ennuie à la mort." I told her this was improper language. – "Dieu!" she exclaimed, "Il n'y a donc pas deux lignes de poësie dans toute la littérature française?" I inquired what she meant. She begged my pardon with proper submission Erelong she was still; I saw her smiling to

# Shirley

herself over the book; she began to learn assiduously. In half an hour she came and stood before me, presented the volume, folded her hands, as I always require her to do, and commenced the repetition of that short thing by Chénier, "La Jeune Captive." If you had heard the manner in which she went through this, and in which she uttered a few incoherent comments when she had done, you would have known what I meant by the phrase "unsettled hurry." One would have thought Chénier was more moving than all Racine and all Corneille. You, brother, who have so much sagacity, will discern that this disproportionate preference argues an ill-regulated mind; but she is fortunate in a preceptress. I will give her a system, a method of thought, a set of opinions; I will give her the perfect control and guidance of her feelings.'

'Be sure you do, Hortense: here she comes. That was her shadow passed the window, I believe.'

'Ah! truly. She is too early – half an hour before her time. – My child, what brings you here before I have breakfasted?'

This question was addressed to an individual who now entered the room, a young girl, wrapped in a winter mantle, the folds of which were gathered with some grace round an apparently slender figure.

'I came in haste to see how you were, Hortense, and how Robert was, too. I was sure you would be both grieved by what happened last night. I did not hear till this morning: my uncle told me at breakfast.'

'Ah! it is unspeakable. You sympathize with us? Your uncle sympathizes with us?'

'My uncle is very angry; but he was with Robert, I believe: was he not? Did he not go with you to Stilbro' Moor?'

'Yes: we set out in very martial style, Caroline: but the prisoners we went to rescue met us half-way.'

'Of course, nobody was hurt?'

'Why, no; only Joe Scott's wrists were a little galled with being pinioned too tightly behind his back.'

'You were not there? You were not with the waggons when they were attacked?'

'No: one seldom has the fortune to be present at occurrences at which one would particularly wish to assist.'

'Where are you going this morning? I saw Murgatroyd saddling your horse in the yard.'

'To Whinbury: it is market-day.'

'Mr Yorke is going too: I met him in his gig. Come home with him.'

'Why?'

'Two are better than one, and nobody dislikes Mr Yorke; at least, poor people do not dislike him.'

'Therefore he would be a protection to me, who am hated?'

'Who are *misunderstood*: that, probably, is the word. Shall you be late? – Will he be late, cousin Hortense?'

'It is too probable: he has often much business to transact at Whinbury. Have you brought your exercise-book, child?'

'Yes. What time will you return, Robert?'

'I generally return at seven. Do you wish me to be at home earlier?'

# Shirley

'Try rather to be back by six. It is not absolutely dark at six now; but by seven daylight is quite gone.'

'And what danger is to be apprehended, Caroline, when daylight *is* gone? What peril do you conceive comes as the companion of darkness, for me?'

'I am not sure that I can define my fears; but we all have a certain anxiety at present about our friends. My uncle calls these times dangerous: he says, too, that mill-owners are unpopular.'

'And I one of the most unpopular? Is not that the fact? You are reluctant to speak out plainly, but at heart you think me liable to Pearson's fate, who was shot at – not, indeed, from behind a hedge, but in his own house, through his staircase-window, as he was going to bed.'

'Anne Pearson showed me the bullet in the chamber-door,' remarked Caroline, gravely, as she folded her mantle, and arranged it and her muff on a side-table. 'You know,' she continued, 'there is a hedge all the way along the road from here to Whinbury, and there are the Fieldhead plantations to pass; but you will be back by six – or before?'

'Certainly he will,' affirmed Hortense. 'And now, my child, prepare your lessons for repetition, while I put the pease to soak for the purée at dinner.'

With this direction, she left the room.

'You suspect I have many enemies then, Caroline?' said Mr Moore; 'and, doubtless, you know me to be destitute of friends?'

'Not destitute, Robert. There is your sister, your brother Louis – whom I have never seen – there is Mr Yorke, and there is my uncle; besides, of course, many more.'

Robert smiled. 'You would be puzzled to name your "many more," ' said he. 'But show me your exercise-book. What extreme pains you take with the writing! My sister, I suppose, exacts this care: she wants to form you in all things after the model of a Flemish school-girl. What life are you destined for, Caroline? What will you do with your French, drawing, and other accomplishments when they are acquired?'

'You may well say, when they are acquired; for, as you are aware, till Hortense began to teach me, I knew precious little. As to the life I am destined for, I cannot tell: I suppose, to keep my uncle's house, till – ' she hesitated.

'Till what? Till he dies?'

'No. How harsh to say that! I never think of his dying: he is only fifty-five. But till – in short, till events offer other occupations for me.'

'A remarkably vague prospect! Are you content with it?'

'I used to be, formerly. Children, you know, have little reflection, or rather their reflections run on ideal themes. There are moments *now* when I am not quite satisfied.'

'Why?'

'I am making no money – earning nothing.'

'You come to the point, Lina: you too, then, wish to make money?'

'I do: I should like an occupation; and if I were a boy, it would not be so difficult to find one. I see such an easy, pleasant way of learning a business, and making my way in life.'

'Go on: let us hear what way.'

'I could be apprenticed to your trade – the cloth-trade: I could learn it of you, as we are distant relations. I would do the counting-house work, keep the books,

550

# Shirley

and write the letters, while you went to market. I know you greatly desire to be rich, in order to pay your father's debts; perhaps I could help you to get rich.'

'Help *me*? You should think of yourself.'

'I do think of myself; but must one for ever think only of oneself?'

'Of whom else do I think? Of whom else *dare* I think? The poor ought to have no large sympathies; it is their duty to be narrow.'

'No, Robert –'

'Yes, Caroline. Poverty is necessarily selfish, contracted, grovelling, anxious. Now and then a poor man's heart, when certain beams and dews visit it, may swell like the budding vegetation in yonder garden on this spring-day, may feel ripe to evolve in foliage – perhaps blossom; but he must not encourage the pleasant impulse; he must invoke Prudence to check it, with that frosty breath of hers, which is as nipping as any north wind.'

'No cottage would be happy then.'

'When I speak of poverty, I do not so much mean the natural, habitual poverty of the working-man, as the embarrassed penury of the man in debt; my grub-worm is always a straitened, struggling, care-worn tradesman.'

'Cherish hope, not anxiety. Certain ideas have become too fixed in your mind. It may be presumptuous to say it, but I have the impression that there is something wrong in your notions of the best means of attaining happiness; as there is in –' Second hesitation.

'I am all ear, Caroline.'

'In – (courage! let me speak the truth) – in your manner – mind, I say only *manner* – to these Yorkshire workpeople.'

'You have often wanted to tell me that, have you not?'

'Yes; often – very often.'

'The faults of my manner are, I think, only negative. I am not proud: what has a man in my position to be proud of? I am only taciturn, phlegmatic, and joyless.'

'As if your living cloth-dressers were all machines like your frames and shears: in your own house you seem different.'

'To those of my own house I am no alien, which I am to these English clowns. I might act the benevolent with them, but acting is not my *forte*. I find them irrational, perverse; they hinder me when I long to hurry forward. In treating them justly, I fulfil my whole duty towards them.'

'You don't expect them to love you, of course?'

'Nor wish it.'

'Ah! said the monitress, shaking her head, and heaving a deep sigh. With this ejaculation, indicative that she perceived a screw to be loose somewhere, but that it was out of her reach to set it right, she bent over her grammar, and sought the rule and exercise for the day.

'I suppose I am not an affectionate man, Caroline; the attachment of a very few suffices me.'

'If you please, Robert, will you mend me a pen or two before you go?'

'First, let me rule your book, for you always contrive to draw the lines aslant ... There now ... And now for the pens: you like a fine one, I think?'

'Such as you generally make for me and Hortense; not your own broad points.'

'If I were of Louis's calling, I might stay at home and dedicate this morning to you and your studies; whereas I must spend it in Sykes' wool-warehouse.'

# Shirley

'You will be making money.'

'More likely losing it.'

As he finished mending the pens, a horse, saddled and bridled, was brought up to the garden-gate.

'There, Fred. is ready for me; I must go. I'll take one look to see what the spring has done in the south border, too, first.'

He quitted the room, and went out into the garden-ground behind the mill. A sweet fringe of young verdure and opening flowers – snowdrops, crocus, even primrose – bloomed in the sunshine under the hot wall of the factory. Moore plucked here and there a blossom and leaf, till he had collected a little bouquet; he returned to the parlour, pilfered a thread of silk from his sister's work-basket, tied the flowers, and laid them on Caroline's desk.

'Now, good-morning.'

'Thank you, Robert; it is pretty; it looks, as it lies there, like sparkles of sunshine and blue sky: good-morning.'

He went to the door – stopped – opened his lips as if to speak – said nothing, and moved on. He passed through the wicket, and mounted his horse: in a second, he had flung himself from the saddle again, transferred the reins to Murgatroyd, and re-entered the cottage.

'I forgot my gloves,' he said, appearing to take something from the side-table; then, as an impromptu thought, he remarked, 'You have no binding engagement at home, perhaps, Caroline?'

'I never have: some children's socks, which Mrs Ramsden has ordered, to knit for the Jew's basket; but they will keep.'

'Jew's basket be – sold! Never was utensil better named. Anything more Jewish than it – its contents, and their prices – cannot be conceived: but I see something, a very tiny curl, at the corners of your lip, which tells me that you know its merits as well as I do. Forget the Jew's basket, then, and spend the day here as a change. Your uncle won't break his heart at your absence?'

She smiled. 'No.'

'The old Cossack! I daresay not,' muttered Moore. 'Then stay and dine with Hortense; she will be glad of your company; I shall return in good time. We will have a little reading in the evening: the moon rises at half-past eight, and I will walk up to the Rectory with you at nine. Do you agree?'

She nodded her head; and her eyes lit up.

Moore lingered yet two minutes: he bent over Caroline's desk and glanced at her grammar, he fingered her pen, he lifted her bouquet and played with it; his horse stamped impatient; Fred. Murgatroyd hemmed and coughed at the gate, as if he wondered what in the world his master was doing. 'Good-morning,' again said Moore, and finally vanished.

Hortense, coming in ten minutes after, found to her surprise, that Caroline had not yet commenced her exercise.

# Chapter 6

## Coriolanus

ademoiselle Moore had that morning a somewhat absent-minded pupil. Caroline forgot, again and again, the explanations which were given to her; however, she still bore with unclouded mood the chidings her inattention brought upon her. Sitting in the sunshine, near the window, she seemed to receive with its warmth a kind influence, which made her both happy and good. Thus disposed, she looked her best, and her best was a pleasing vision.

To her had not been denied the gift of beauty; it was not absolutely necessary to know her in order to like her; she was fair enough to please, even at the first view. Her shape suited her age; it was girlish, light, and pliant; every curve was neat, every limb proportionate: her face was expressive and gentle; her eyes were handsome, and gifted at times with a winning beam that stole into the heart, with a language that spoke softly to the affections. Her mouth was very pretty; she had a delicate skin, and a fine flow of brown hair, which she knew how to arrange with taste; curls became her, and she possessed them in picturesque profusion. Her style of dress announced taste in the wearer; very unobtrusive in fashion, far from costly in material, but suitable in colour to the fair complexion with which it contrasted, and in make to the slight form which it draped. Her present winter garb was of merino, the same soft shade of brown as her hair; the little collar round her neck lay over a pink ribbon, and was fastened with a pink knot: she wore no other decoration.

So much for Caroline Helstone's appearance; as to her character or intellect, if she had any, they must speak for themselves in due time.

Her connections are soon explained. She was the child of parents separated soon after her birth, in consequence of disagreement of disposition. Her mother was the half-sister of Mr Moore's father; thus – though there was no mixture of blood – she was, in a distant sense, the cousin of Robert, Louis, and Hortense. Her father was the brother of Mr Helstone – a man of the character friends desire not to recall, after death has once settled all earthly accounts. He had rendered his wife unhappy: the reports which were known to be true concerning him, had given an air of probability to those which were falsely circulated respecting his better-principled brother. Caroline had never known her mother, as she was taken from her in infancy, and had not since seen her; her father died comparatively young, and her uncle, the Rector, had for some years been her sole guardian. He was not, as we are aware, much adapted, either by nature or habits, to have the charge of a young girl: he had taken little trouble about her education; probably, he would have taken none if she, finding herself neglected, had not grown anxious on her own account, and asked, every now and then, for

# Shirley

a little attention, and for the means of acquiring such amount of knowledge as could not be dispensed with. Still, she had a depressing feeling that she was inferior, that her attainments were fewer than were usually possessed by girls of her age and station; and very glad was she to avail herself of the kind offer made by her cousin Hortense, soon after the arrival of the latter at Hollow's mill, to teach her French and fine needlework. Mdlle Moore, for her part, delighted in the task, because it gave her importance; she liked to lord it a little over a docile yet quick pupil. She took Caroline precisely at her own estimate, as an irregularly taught, even ignorant girl; and when she found that she made rapid and eager progress, it was to no talent, no application in the scholar, she ascribed the improvement, but entirely to her own superior method of teaching; when she found that Caroline, unskilled in routine, had a knowledge of her own – desultory but varied, the discovery caused her no surprise, for she still imagined that from her conversation had the girl unawares gleaned these treasures: she thought it even when forced to feel that her pupil knew much on subjects whereof she knew little: the idea was not logical, but Hortense had perfect faith in it.

Mademoiselle, who prided herself on possessing 'un esprit positif,' and on entertaining a decided preference for dry studies, kept her young cousin to the same as closely as she could. She worked her unrelentingly at the grammar of the French language, assigning her, as the most improving exercise she could devise, interminable 'analyses logiques.' These 'analyses' were by no means a source of particular pleasure to Caroline; she thought she could have learned French just as well without them, and grudged excessively the time spent in pondering over 'propositions, principales, et incidents;' in deciding the 'incidente determinative' and the 'incidente applicative;' in examining whether the proposition was 'pleine,' 'elliptique,' or 'implicite.' Sometimes she lost herself in the maze, and when so lost, she would, now and then (while Hortense was rummaging her drawers up-stairs, – an unaccountable occupation in which she spent a large portion of each day, arranging, disarranging, rearranging and counter-arranging) – carry her book to Robert in the counting-house, and get the rough place made smooth by his aid. Mr Moore possessed a clear, tranquil brain of his own; almost as soon as he looked at Caroline's little difficulties they seemed to dissolve beneath his eye: in two minutes he would explain all; in two words give the key to the puzzle. She thought if Hortense could only teach like him, how much faster she might learn! Repaying him by an admiring and grateful smile, rather shed at his feet than lifted to his face, she would leave the mill reluctantly to go back to the cottage, and then, while she completed the exercise, or worked out the sum (for Mdlle Moore taught her arithmetic, too,) she would wish nature had made her a boy instead of a girl, that she might ask Robert to let her be his clerk, and sit with him in the counting-house, instead of sitting with Hortense in the parlour.

Occasionally – but this happened very rarely – she spent the evening at Hollow's cottage. Sometimes during these visits, Moore was away, attending a market; sometimes he was gone to Mr Yorke's; often he was engaged with a male visitor in another room; but sometimes, too, he was at home, disengaged, free to talk with Caroline. When this was the case, the evening hours passed on wings of light; they were gone before they were counted. There was no room in England so pleasant as that small parlour when the three cousins occupied

554

# Shirley

it. Hortense, when she was not teaching, or scolding, or cooking, was far from ill-humoured; it was her custom to relax towards evening, and to be kind to her young English kinswoman. There was a means, too, of rendering her delightful, by inducing her to take her guitar and sing and play; she then became quite good-natured; and as she played with skill, and had a well-toned voice, it was not disagreeable to listen to her: it would have been absolutely agreeable, except that her formal and self-important character modulated her strains, as it impressed her manners and moulded her countenance.

Mr Moore, released from the business-yoke, was, if not lively himself, a willing spectator of Caroline's liveliness, a complacent listener to her talk, a ready respondent to her questions. He was something agreeable to sit near, to hover round, to address and look at. Sometimes he was better than this, – almost animated, quite gentle and friendly.

The drawback was, that by the next morning he was sure to be frozen up again; and however much he seemed, in his quiet way, to enjoy these social evenings, he rarely contrived their recurrence. This circumstance puzzled the inexperienced head of his cousin. 'If I had a means of happiness at my command,' she thought, 'I would employ that means often; I would keep it bright with use, and not let it lie for weeks aside, till it gets rusty.'

Yet she was careful not to put in practice her own theory. Much as she liked an evening visit to the cottage, she never paid one unasked. Often, indeed, when pressed by Hortense to come, she would refuse, because Robert did not second, or but slightly seconded the request. This morning was the first time he had ever, of his own unprompted will, given her an invitation; and then he had spoken so kindly, that in hearing him she had received a sense of happiness sufficient to keep her glad for the whole day.

The morning passed as usual. Mademoiselle, ever breathlessly busy, spent it in bustling from kitchen to parlour – now scolding Sarah, now looking over Caroline's exercise or hearing her repetition-lesson. However faultlessly these tasks were achieved, she never commended: it was a maxim with her that praise is inconsistent with a teacher's dignity, and that blame, in more or less unqualified measure, is indispensable to it. She thought incessant reprimand, severe or slight, quite necessary to the maintenance of her authority; and if no possible error was to be found in the lesson, it was the pupil's carriage, or air, or dress, or mien, which required correction.

The usual affray took place about the dinner, which meal, when Sarah at last brought it into the room, she almost flung upon the table, with a look that expressed quite plainly: 'I never dished such stuff i' my life afore; it's not fit for dogs.' Notwithstanding Sarah's scorn, it was a savoury repast enough. The soup was a sort of purée of dried pease, which Mademoiselle had prepared amidst bitter lamentations that in this desolate country of England no haricot beans were to be had. Then came a dish of meat – nature unknown, but supposed to be miscellaneous – singularly chopped up with crumbs of bread, seasoned uniquely though not unpleasantly, and baked in a mould; a queer, but by no means unpalatable dish. Greens, oddly bruised, formed the accompanying vegetable; and a pâté of fruit, conserved after a receipt devised by Madam Gérard Moore's 'grand'mère,' and from the taste of which it appeared probable that 'mélasse' had been substituted for sugar, completed the dinner.

Caroline had no objection to this Belgian cookery: indeed, she rather liked it

# Shirley

for a change, and it was well she did so, for had she evinced any disrelish thereof, such manifestation would have injured her in Mademoiselle's good graces for ever; a positive crime might have been more easily pardoned than a symptom of distaste for the foreign comestibles.

Soon after dinner Caroline coaxed her governess-cousin upstairs to dress: this manoeuvre required management. To have hinted that the jupon, camisole, and curl-papers were odious objects, or indeed other than quite meritorious points, would have been a felony. Any premature attempt to urge their disappearance was therefore unwise, and would be likely to issue in the persevering wear of them during the whole day. Carefully avoiding rocks and quicksands, however, the pupil, on pretence of requiring a change of scene, contrived to get the teacher aloft, and, once in the bed-room, she persuaded her that it was not worth while returning thither, and that she might as well make her toilette now; and while Mademoiselle delivered a solemn homily on her own surpassing merit in disregarding all frivolities of fashion, Caroline denuded her of the camisole, invested her with a decent gown, arranged her collar, hair, &c., and made her quite presentable. But Hortense would put the finishing touches herself, and these finishing touches consisted in a thick handkerchief tied round the throat, and a large, servant-like black apron, which spoiled everything. On no account would Mademoiselle have appeared in her own house without the thick handkerchief and the voluminous apron: the first was a positive matter of morality – it was quite improper not to wear a fichu; the second was the ensign of a good housewife – she appeared to think that by means of it she somehow effected a large saving in her brother's income. She had, with her own hands, made and presented to Caroline similar equipments; and the only serious quarrel they had ever had, and which still left a soreness in the elder cousin's soul, had arisen from the refusal of the younger one to accept of and profit by these elegant presents.

'I wear a high dress and a collar,' said Caroline, 'and I should feel suffocated with a handkerchief in addition; and my short aprons do quite as well as that very long one: I would rather make no change.'

Yet Hortense, by dint of perseverance, would probably have compelled her to make a change, had not Mr Moore chanced to overhear a dispute on the subject, and decided that Caroline's little aprons would suffice, and that, in his opinion, as she was still but a child, she might for the present dispense with the fichu, especially as her curls were long, and almost touched her shoulders.

There was no appeal against Robert's opinion, therefore his sister was compelled to yield: but she disapproved entirely of the piquant neatness of Caroline's costume, and the lady-like grace of her appearance: something more solid and homely, she would have considered 'beaucoup plus convenable.'

The afternoon was devoted to sewing. Mademoiselle, like most Belgian ladies, was specially skilful with her needle. She by no means thought it waste of time to devote unnumbered hours to fine embroidery, sight-destroying lace-work, marvellous netting and knitting, and, above all, to most elaborate stocking-mending. She would give a day to the mending of two holes in a stocking any time, and think her 'mission' nobly fulfilled when she had accomplished it. It was another of Caroline's troubles to be condemned to learn this foreign style of darning, which was done stitch by stitch so as exactly to imitate the fabric of the stocking itself; a wearifu' process, but considered by Hortense Gérard, and

# Shirley

by her ancestresses before her for long generations back, as one of the first 'duties of woman.' She herself had had a needle, cotton, and a fearfully torn stocking put into her hand while she yet wore a child's coif on her little black head: her 'hauts faits' in the darning line had been exhibited to company ere she was six years old, and when she first discovered that Caroline was profoundly ignorant of this most essential of attainments, she could have wept with pity over her miserably neglected youth.

No time did she lose in seeking up a hopeless pair of hose, of which the heels were entirely gone, and in setting the ignorant English girl to repair the deficiency: this task had been commenced two years ago, and Caroline had the stockings in her work-bag yet. She did a few rows every day, by way of penance for the expiation of her sins: they were a grievous burden to her; she would much have liked to put them in the fire; and once Mr Moore, who had observed her sitting and sighing over them, had proposed a private incremation in the counting-house, but to this proposal Caroline knew it would have been impolitic to accede – the result could only be a fresh pair of hose, probably in worse condition: she adhered, therefore, to the ills she knew.

All the afternoon, the two ladies sat and sewed, till the eyes and fingers, and even the spirits of one of them were weary. The sky since dinner had darkened; it had begun to rain again, to pour fast; secret fears began to steal on Caroline that Robert would be persuaded by Mr Sykes or Mr Yorke to remain at Whinbury till it cleared, and of that there appeared no present change. Five o'clock struck, and time stole on; still the clouds streamed: a sighing wind whispered in the roof-trees of the cottage; day seemed already closing; the parlour-fire shed on the clear hearth a glow ruddy as at twilight.

'It will not be fair till the moon rises,' pronounced Mademoiselle Moore; 'consequently, I feel assured that my brother will not return till then: indeed, I should be sorry if he did. We will have coffee; it would be vain to wait for him.'

'I am tired – may I leave my work now, cousin?'

'You may, since it grows too dark to see to do it well. Fold it up; put it carefully in your bag; then step into the kitchen, and desire Sarah to bring in the goûter, or tea, as you call it.'

'But it has not yet struck six: he may still come.'

'He will not, I tell you. I can calculate his movements. I understand my brother.'

Suspense is irksome, disappointment bitter. All the world has, some time or other, felt that. Caroline, obedient to orders, passed into the kitchen. Sarah was making a dress for herself at the table.

'You are to bring in coffee,' said the young lady, in a spiritless tone; and then she leaned her arm and head against the kitchen mantelpiece, and hung listlessly over the fire.

'How low you seem, Miss! But it's all because your cousin keeps you so close to work. It's a shame!'

'Nothing of the kind, Sarah,' was the brief reply.

'Oh! but I know it is. You're fit to cry just this minute, for nothing else but because you've sat still the whole day. It would make a kitten dull to be mewed up so.'

'Sarah, does your master often come home early from market when it is wet?'

# Shirley

'Never, hardly; but just today, for some reason, he has made a difference.'

'What do you mean?'

'He is come: I am certain I saw Murgatroyd lead his horse into the yard by the back-way, when I went to get some water at the pump five minutes since. He was in the counting-house with Joe Scott, I believe.'

'You are mistaken.'

'What should I be mistaken for? I know his horse surely?'

'But you did not see himself?'

'I heard him speak, though. He was saying something to Joe Scott about having settled all concerning ways and means, and that there would be a new set of frames in the mill before another week passed; and that this time he would get four soldiers from Stilbro' barracks to guard the waggon.'

'Sarah, are you making a gown?'

'Yes: is it a handsome one?'

'Beautiful! Get the coffee ready. I'll finish cutting out that sleeve for you; and I'll give you some trimming for it. I have some narrow satin ribbon of a colour that will just match it.'

'You're very kind, Miss.'

'Be quick, there's a good girl; but first put your master's shoes on the hearth: he will take his boots off when he comes in. I hear him—he is coming.'

'Miss! you're cutting the stuff wrong.'

'So I am; but it is only a snip: there is no harm done.'

The kitchen-door opened; Mr Moore entered, very wet and cold. Caroline half turned from her dressmaking occupation, but renewed it for a moment, as if to gain a minute's time for some purpose. Bent over the dress, her face was hidden; there was an attempt to settle her features and veil their expression, which failed: when she at last met Mr Moore, her countenance beamed.

'We had ceased to expect you: they asserted you would not come,' she said.

'But I promised to return soon: *you* expected me, I suppose?'

'No, Robert: I dared not when it rained so fast. And you are wet and chilled – change everything: if you took cold, I should – we should blame ourselves in some measure.'

'I am not wet through: my riding-coat is water-proof. Dry shoes are all I require. – There . . . the fire is pleasant after facing the cold wind and rain for a few miles.'

He stood on the kitchen-hearth; Caroline stood beside him. Mr Moore, while enjoying the genial glow, kept his eyes directed towards the glittering brasses on the shelf above. Chancing for an instant to look down, his glance rested on an uplifted face, flushed, smiling, happy, shaded with silky curls, lit with fine eyes. Sarah was gone into the parlour with the tray: a lecture from her mistress detained her there. Moore placed his hand a moment on his young cousin's shoulder, stooped, and left a kiss on her forehead.

'Oh!' said she, as if the action had unsealed her lips, 'I was miserable when I thought you would not come: I am almost too happy now. Are you happy, Robert? Do you like to come home?'

'I think I do; to-night, at least.'

'Are you certain you are not fretting about your frames, and your business, and the war?'

'Not just now.'

# Shirley

'Are you positive you don't feel Hollow's cottage too small for you and narrow and dismal?'

'At this moment, no.'

'Can you affirm that you are not bitter at heart because rich and great people forget you?'

'No more questions. You are mistaken if you think I am anxious to curry favour with rich and great people. I only want means – a position – a career.'

'Which your own talent and goodness shall win you. You were made to be great – you *shall* be great.'

'I wonder now, if you spoke honestly out of your heart, what receipt you would give me for acquiring this same greatness; but I know it – better than you know it yourself. Would it be efficacious? would it work? Yes – poverty, misery, bankruptcy. Oh! life is not what you think it, Lina!'

'But you are what I think you.'

'I am not.'

'You are better, then?'

'Far worse.'

'No; far better. I know you are good.'

'How do you know it?'

'You look so; and I feel you *are* so.'

'Where do you feel it?'

'In my heart.'

'Ah! you judge me with your heart, Lina; you should judge me with your head.'

'I do; and then I am quite proud of you. Robert, you cannot tell all my thoughts about you.'

Mr Moore's dark face mustered colour; his lips smiled, and yet were compressed; his eyes laughed, and yet he resolutely knit his brow.

'Think meanly of me, Lina,' said he. 'Men, in general, are a sort of scum, very different to anything of which you have an idea; I make no pretension to be better than my fellows.'

'If you did, I should not esteem you so much; it is because you are modest that I have such confidence in your merit.'

'Are you flattering me?' he demanded, turning sharply upon her, and searching her face with an eye of acute penetration.

'No,' she said, softly, laughing at his sudden quickness. She seemed to think it unnecessary to proffer any eager disavowal of the charge.

'You don't care whether I think you flatter me or not?'

'No.'

'You are so secure of your own intentions?'

'I suppose so.'

'What are they, Caroline?'

'Only to ease my mind by expressing for once part of what I think; and then to make you better satisfied with yourself.'

'By assuring me that my kinswoman is my sincere friend?'

'Just so; I am your sincere friend, Robert.'

'And I am – what chance and change shall make me, Lina.'

'Not my enemy, however?'

The answer was cut short by Sarah and her mistress entering the kitchen

# Shirley

together in some commotion. They had been improving the time which Mr Moore and Miss Helstone had spent in dialogue by a short dispute on the subject of 'café au lait,' which Sarah said was the queerest mess she ever saw, and a waste of God's good gifts, as it was 'the nature of coffee to be boiled in water;' and which Mademoiselle affirmed to be 'un breuvage royal,' a thousand times too good for the mean person who objected to it.

The former occupants of the kitchen now withdrew into the parlour. Before Hortense followed them thither, Caroline had only time again to question, 'Not my enemy, Robert?' And Moore, quaker-like, had replied with another query, 'Could I be?' and then, seating himself at the table, had settled Caroline at his side.

Caroline scarcely heard Mademoiselle's explosion of wrath when she rejoined them; the long declamation about the 'conduite indigne de cette méchante créature,' sounded in her ear as confusedly as the agitated rattling of the china. Robert laughed a little at it, in very subdued sort, and then, politely and calmly entreating his sister to be tranquil, assured her that if it would yield her any satisfaction, she should have her choice of an attendant amongst all the girls in his mill; only he feared they would scarcely suit her, as they were most of them, he was informed, completely ignorant of household work; and pert and self-willed as Sarah was, she was perhaps no worse than the majority of the women of her class.

Mademoiselle admitted the truth of this conjecture: according to her, 'ces paysannes Anglaises étaient tout insupportables.' What would she not give for some 'bonne cuisinière Anversoise,' with the high cap, short petticoat, and decent sabots proper to her class: something better, indeed, than an insolent coquette in a flounced gown, and absolutely without cap! (for Sarah, it appears, did not partake the opinion of St Paul, that 'it is a shame for a woman to go with her head uncovered;' but, holding rather a contrary doctrine, resolutely refused to imprison in linen or muslin the plentiful tresses of her yellow hair, which it was her wont to fasten up smartly with a comb behind, and on Sundays to wear curled in front.)

'Shall I try and get you an Antwerp girl?' asked Mr Moore, who – stern in public – was on the whole very kind in private.

'Merci du cadeau!' was the answer. 'An Antwerp girl would not stay here ten days, sneered at as she would be by all the young coquines in your factory;' then softening, 'You are very good, dear brother – excuse my petulance – but truly, my domestic trials are severe, yet they are probably my destiny; for I recollect that our revered mother experienced similar sufferings, though she had the choice of all the best servants in Antwerp: domestics are in all countries a spoiled and unruly set.'

Mr Moore had also certain reminiscences about the trials of his revered mother. A good mother she had been to him, and he honoured her memory, but he recollected that she kept a hot kitchen of it in Antwerp, just as his faithful sister did here in England. Thus, therefore, he let the subject drop, and when the coffee-service was removed, proceeded to console Hortense by fetching her music-book and guitar; and, having arranged the ribbon of the instrument round her neck with a quiet fraternal kindness he knew to be all-powerful in soothing her most ruffled moods, he asked her to give him some of their mother's favourite songs.

# Shirley

Nothing refines like affection. Family jarring vulgarizes – family union elevates. Hortense, pleased with her brother, and grateful to him, looked, as she touched her guitar, almost graceful, almost handsome; her every-day fretful look was gone for a moment, and was replaced by a 'sourire plein de bonté.' She sang the songs he asked for, with feeling; they reminded her of a parent to whom she had been truly attached; they reminded her of her young days. She observed, too, that Caroline listened with naïve interest; this augmented her good-humour, and the exclamation at the close of the song, 'I wish I could sing and play like Hortense!' achieved the business, and rendered her charming for the evening.

It is true, a little lecture to Caroline followed, on the vanity of *wishing*, and the duty of *trying*. 'As Rome,' it was suggested, 'had not been built in a day, so neither had Mademoiselle Gérard Moore's education been completed in a week, or by merely *wishing* to be clever. It was effort that had accomplished that great work: she was ever remarkable for her perseverance, for her industry: her masters had remarked that it was as delightful as it was uncommon to find so much talent united with so much solidity, and so on.' Once on the theme of her own merits, Mademoiselle was fluent.

Cradled at last in blissful self-complacency, she took her knitting and sat down tranquil. Drawn curtains, a clear fire, a softly shining lamp, gave now to the little parlour its best – its evening charm. It is probable that the three there present felt this charm: they all looked happy.

'What shall we do now, Caroline?' asked Mr Moore, returning to his seat beside his cousin.

'What shall we do, Robert?' repeated she playfully. 'You decide.'

'Not play at chess?'

'No.'

'Nor draughts, nor backgammon?'

'No – no; we both hate silent games that only keep one's hands employed, don't we?'

'I believe we do: then, shall we talk scandal?'

'About whom? Are we sufficiently interested in anybody to take pleasure in pulling their character to pieces?'

'A question that comes to the point. For my part – unamiable as it sounds – I must say, no.'

'And I, too. But it is strange – though we want no third – fourth, I mean (she hastily and with contrition glanced at Hortense), living person among us – so selfish we are in our happiness – though we don't want to think of the present existing world, it would be pleasant to go back to the past; to hear people that have slept for generations in graves that are perhaps no longer graves now, but gardens and fields, speak to us and tell us their thoughts, and impart their ideas.'

'Who shall be the speaker? What language shall he utter? French?'

'Your French forefathers don't speak so sweetly, nor so solemnly, nor so impressively as your English ancestors, Robert. To-night you shall be entirely English: you shall read an English book.'

'An old English book?'

'Yes, an old English book, one that you like; and I will choose a part of it that is toned quite in harmony with something in you. It shall waken your nature, fill your mind with music: it shall pass like a skilful hand over your heart, and make its strings sound. Your heart is a lyre, Robert; but the lot of your life has

# Shirley

not been a minstrel to sweep it, and it is often silent. Let glorious William come near and touch it; you will see how he will draw the English power and melody out of its chords.'

'I must read Shakspeare?'

'You must have his spirit before you; you must hear his voice with your mind's ear; you must take some of his soul into yours.'

'With a view to making me better; is it to operate like a sermon?'

'It is to stir you; to give you new sensations. It is to make you feel your life strongly, not only your virtues, but your vicious, perverse points.'

'Dieu! que dit-elle?' cried Hortense, who hitherto had been counting stitches in her knitting, and had not much attended to what was said, but whose ear these two strong words caught with a tweak.

'Never mind her, sister: let her talk; now just let her say anything she pleases to-night. She likes to come down hard upon your brother sometimes; it amuses me, so let her alone.'

Caroline, who, mounted on a chair, had been rummaging the book-case, returned with a book.

'Here's Shakspeare,' she said, 'and there's Coriolanus. Now, read, and discover by the feelings the reading will give you at once how low and how high you are.'

'Come then, sit near me, and correct when I mispronounce.'

'I am to be the teacher then, and you my pupil?'

'Ainsi, soit-il!'

'And Shakspeare is our science, since we are going to study?'

'It appears so.'

'And you are not going to be French, and sceptical, and sneering? You are not going to think it a sign of wisdom to refuse to admire?'

'I don't know.'

'If you do, Robert, I'll take Shakspeare away; and I'll shrivel up within myself, and put on my bonnet and go home.'

'Sit down; here I begin.'

'One minute, if you please, brother,' interrupted Mademoiselle, 'when the gentleman of a family reads, the ladies should always sew. Caroline, dear child, take your embroidery; you may get three sprigs done to-night.'

Caroline looked dismayed. 'I can't see by lamp-light; my eyes are tired and I can't do two things well at once. If I sew, I cannot listen; if I listen, I cannot sew.'

'Fi, donc! Quel enfantillage!' began Hortense. Mr Moore, as usual, suavely interposed.

'Permit her to neglect the embroidery for this evening. I wish her whole attention to be fixed on my accent, and to ensure this, she must follow the reading with her eyes; she must look at the book.'

He placed it between them, reposed his arm on the back of Caroline's chair, and thus began to read.

The very first scene in 'Coriolanus' came with smart relish to his intellectual palate, and still as he read he warmed. He delivered the haughty speech of Caius Marcius to the starving citizens with unction; he did not say he thought his irrational pride right, but he seemed to feel it so. Caroline looked up at him with a singular smile.

'There's a vicious point hit already,' she said; 'you sympathize with that proud

patrician who does not sympathize with his famished fellow-men, and insults them: there, go on.' He proceeded. The war-like portions did not rouse him much; he said all that was out of date, or should be; the spirit displayed was barbarous, yet the encounter single-handed between Marcius and Tullus Aufidius, he delighted in. As he advanced, he forgot to criticize; it was evident he appreciated the power, the truth of each portion; and, stepping out of the narrow line of private prejudices, began to revel in the large picture of human nature, to feel the reality stamped upon the characters who were speaking from that page before him.

He did not read the comic scenes well, and Caroline, taking the book out of his hand, read these parts for him. From her he seemed to enjoy them, and indeed she gave them with a spirit no one could have expected of her, with a pithy expression with which she seemed gifted on the spot, and for that brief moment only. It may be remarked, in passing, that the general character of her conversation that evening, whether serious or sprightly, grave or gay, was as of something untaught, unstudied, intuitive, fitful; when once gone, no more to be reproduced as it had been, than the glancing ray of the meteor, than the tints of the dew-gem, than the colour or form of the sun-set cloud, than the fleeting and glittering ripple varying the flow of a rivulet.

Coriolanus in glory; Coriolanus in disaster; Coriolanus banished, followed like giant-shades one after the other. Before the vision of the banished man, Moore's spirit seemed to pause. He stood on the hearth of Aufidius's hall, facing the image of greatness fallen, but greater than ever in that low estate. He saw 'the grim appearance,' the dark face 'bearing command in it,' 'the noble vessel with its tackle torn.' With the revenge of Caius Marcius, Moore perfectly sympathized; he was not scandalized by it; and again Caroline whispered, 'There I see another glimpse of brotherhood in error.'

The march on Rome, the mother's supplication, the long resistance, the final yielding of bad passions to good, which ever must be the case in a nature worthy the epithet of noble, the rage of Aufidius at what he considered his ally's weakness, the death of Coriolanus, the final sorrow of his great enemy; all scenes made of condensed truth and strength, came on in succession, and carried with them in their deep, fast flow, the heart and mind of reader and listener.

'Now, have you felt Shakspeare?' asked Caroline, some ten minutes after her cousin had closed the book.

'I think so.'

'And have you felt anything in Coriolanus like you?'

'Perhaps I have.'

'Was he not faulty as well as great?'

Moore nodded. 'And what was his fault? What made him hated by the citizens? What caused him to be banished by his countrymen?'

'What do you think it was?'

'I ask again –

> "Whether was it pride,
> Which out of daily fortune ever taints
> The happy man? whether defect of judgment,
> To fail in the disposing of those chances

# Shirley

*Which he was lord of? or whether nature,*
*Not to be other than one thing; not moving*
*From the casque to the cushion, but commanding peace*
*Even with the same austerity and garb*
*As he controlled the war?"'*

'Well, answer yourself, Sphynx.'

'It was a spice of all: and you must not be proud to your workpeople; you must not neglect chances of soothing them, and you must not be of an inflexible nature, uttering a request as austerely as if it were a command.'

'That is the moral you tack to the play. What puts such notions into your head?'

'A wish for your good, a care for your safety, dear Robert, and a fear caused by many things which I have heard lately, that you will come to harm.'

'Who tells you these things?'

'I hear my uncle talk about you: he praises your hard spirit, your determined cast of mind, your scorn of low enemies, your resolution not "to truckle to the mob" as he says.'

'And would you have me truckle to them?'

'No, not for the world: I never wish you to lower yourself; but somehow, I cannot help thinking it unjust to include all poor working people under the general and insulting name of "the mob," and continually to think of them and treat them haughtily.'

'You are a little democrat, Caroline: if your uncle knew, what would he say?'

'I rarely talk to my uncle, as you know, and never about such things: he thinks everything but sewing and cooking above women's comprehension, and out of their line.'

'And do you fancy you comprehend the subjects on which you advise me?'

'As far as they concern you, I comprehend them. I know it would be better for you to be loved by your workpeople than to be hated by them, and I am sure that kindness is more likely to win their regard than pride. If you were proud and cold to me and Hortense, should we love you? When you are cold to me, as you *are* sometimes, can I venture to be affectionate in return?'

'Now, Lina, I've had my lesson both in languages and ethics, with a touch on politics; it is your turn. Hortense tells me you were much taken by a little piece of poetry you learned the other day, a piece by poor André Chénier– "La Jeune Captive;" do you remember it still?'

'I think so.'

'Repeat it, then. Take your time and mind your accent: especially let us have no English u's.'

Caroline, beginning in a low, rather tremulous voice, but gaining courage as she proceeded, repeated the sweet verses of Chénier; the last three stanzas she rehearsed well.

*'Mon beau voyage encore est si loin de sa fin!*
*Je pars, et des ormeaux qui bordent le chemin*
*J'ai passé le premiers à peine.*

# Shirley

*Au banquet de la vie à peine commencé,*
*Un instant seulement mes lèvres ont pressé*
   *La coupe en mes mains encore pleine.*
*'Je ne suis qu'au printemps – je veux voir la moisson;*
*Et comme le soleil, de saison en saison,*
   *Je veux achever mon année.*
*Brillante sur ma tige, et l'honneur du jardin*
*Je n'ai vu luire encore que les feux du matin,*
   *Je veux achever ma journée!'*

Moore listened at first with his eyes cast down, but soon he furtively raised them: leaning back in his chair, he could watch Caroline without her perceiving where his gaze was fixed. Her cheek had a colour, her eyes a light, her countenance an expression, this evening, which would have made even plain features striking; but there was not the grievous defect of plainness to pardon in her case. The sunshine was not shed on rough barrenness; it fell on soft bloom. Each lineament was turned with grace; the whole aspect was pleasing. At the present moment – animated, interested, touched – she might be called beautiful. Such a face was calculated to awaken not only the calm sentiment of esteem, the distant one of admiration; but some feeling more tender, genial, intimate: friendship, perhaps – affection, interest. When she had finished, she turned to Moore, and met his eye.

'Is that pretty well repeated?' she inquired, smiling like any happy, docile child.

'I really don't know.'

'Why don't you know? Have you not listened?'

'Yes – and looked. You are fond of poetry, Lina?'

'When I meet with *real* poetry, I cannot rest till I have learned it by heart, and so made it partly mine.'

Mr Moore now sat silent for several minutes. It struck nine o'clock: Sarah entered, and said that Mr Helstone's servant was come for Miss Caroline.

'Then the evening is gone already,' she observed; 'and it will be long, I suppose, before I pass another here.'

Hortense had been for some time nodding over her knitting; fallen into a doze now, she made no response to the remark.

'You would have no objection to come here oftener of an evening?' inquired Robert, as he took her folded mantle from the side-table, where it still lay, and carefully wrapped it round her.

'I like to come here; but I have no desire to be intrusive. I am not hinting to be asked: you must understand that.'

'Oh! I understand thee, child. You sometimes lecture me for wishing to be rich, Lina; but if I *were* rich, you should live here always: at any rate, you should live with me wherever my habitation might be.'

'That would be pleasant; and if you were poor – ever so poor – it would still be pleasant. Good-night, Robert.'

'I promised to walk with you up to the Rectory.'

'I know you did; but I thought you had forgotten, and I hardly knew how to remind you, though I wished to do it. But would you like to go? It is a cold night; and, as Fanny is come, there is no necessity–'

# Shirley

'Here is your muff – don't wake Hortense – come.'

The half-mile to the Rectory was soon traversed. They parted in the garden without kiss, scarcely with a pressure of hands; yet Robert sent his cousin in excited and joyously troubled. He had been singularly kind to her that day: not in phrase, compliment, profession; but in manner, in look, and in soft and friendly tones.

For himself, he came home grave, almost morose. As he stood leaning on his own yard-gate, musing in the watery moonlight, all alone – the hushed, dark mill before him, the hill-environed hollow round – he exclaimed, abruptly:–

'This won't do! There's weakness – there's downright ruin in all this. However,' he added, dropping his voice, 'the frenzy is quite temporary. I know it very well: I have had it before. It will be gone to-morrow.'

# Chapter 7

## The Curates at Tea

Caroline Helstone was just eighteen years old; and at eighteen the true narrative of life is yet to be commenced. Before that time, we sit listening to a tale, a marvellous fiction; delightful sometimes, and sad sometimes; almost always unreal. Before that time, our world is heroic; its inhabitants half-divine or semi-demon; its scenes are dream-scenes: darker woods, and stranger hills; brighter skies, more dangerous waters; sweeter flowers, more tempting fruits; wider plains, drearier deserts, sunnier fields than are found in nature, over-spread our enchanted globe. What a moon we gaze on before that time! How the trembling of our hearts at her aspect bears witness to its unutterable beauty! As to our sun, it is a burning heaven – the world of gods.

At that time – at eighteen, drawing near the confines of illusive, void dreams, Elf-land lies behind us, the shores of Reality rise in front. These shores are yet distant: they look so blue, soft, gentle, we long to reach them. In sunshine we see a greenness beneath the azure, as of spring meadows; we catch glimpses of silver lines, and imagine the roll of living waters. Could we but reach this land, we think to hunger and thirst no more; whereas many a wilderness, and often the flood of Death, or some stream of sorrow as cold and almost as black as Death, is to be crossed ere true bliss can be tasted. Every joy that life gives must be earned ere it is secured; and how hardly earned, those only know who have wrestled for great prizes. The heart's blood must gem with red beads the brow of the combatant, before the wreath of victory rustles over it.

At eighteen, we are not aware of this. Hope, when she smiles on us, and

566

# Shirley

promises happiness to-morrow, is implicitly believed; – Love, when he comes wandering like a lost angel to our door, is at once admitted, welcomed, embraced: his quiver is not seen; if his arrows penetrate, their wound is like a thrill of new life: there are no fears of poison, none of the barb which no leech's hand can extract: that perilous passion – an agony ever in some of its phases; with many, an agony throughout – is believed to be an unqualified good: in short, at eighteen, the school of Experience is to be entered, and her humbling, crushing, grinding, but yet purifying and invigorating lessons are yet to be learnt.

Alas, Experience! No other mentor has so wasted and frozen a face as yours: none wears a robe so black, none bears a rod so heavy, none with hand so inexorable draws the novice so sternly to his task, and forces him with authority so resistless to its acquirement. It is by your instructions alone that man or woman can ever find a safe track through life's wilds: without it, how they stumble, how they stray! On what forbidden grounds do they intrude, down what dread declivities are they hurled!

Caroline, having been conveyed home by Robert, had no wish to pass what remained of the evening with her uncle; the room in which he sat was very sacred ground to her; she seldom intruded on it, and to-night she kept aloof till the bell rung for prayers. Part of the evening church service was the form of worship observed in Mr Helstone's household: he read it in his usual nasal voice, clear, loud, and monotonous. The rite over, his niece, according to her wont, stepped up to him.

'Good-night, uncle.'

'Hey! You've been gadding abroad all day – visiting, dining out, and what not!'

'Only at the cottage.'

'And have you learnt your lessons?'

'Yes.'

'And made a shirt?'

'Only part of one.'

'Well, that will do: stick to the needle – learn shirt-making and gown-making, and pie-crust-making, and you'll be a clever woman some day. Go to bed now: I'm busy with a pamphlet here.'

Presently the niece was enclosed in her small bed-room; the door bolted, her white dressing-gown assumed, her long hair loosened and falling thick, soft, and wavy to her waist; and as, resting from the task of combing it out, she leaned her cheek on her hand and fixed her eyes on the carpet, before her rose, and close around her drew, the visions we see at eighteen years.

Her thoughts were speaking with her: speaking pleasantly, as it seemed, for she smiled as she listened. She looked pretty, meditating thus: but a brighter thing than she was in that apartment – the spirit of youthful Hope. According to this flattering prophet, she was to know disappointment, to feel chill no more: she had entered on the dawn of a summer day – no false dawn, but the true spring of morning – and her sun would quickly rise. Impossible for her now to suspect that she was the sport of delusion: her expectations seemed warranted, the foundation on which they rested appeared solid.

'When people love, the next step is they marry,' was her argument. 'Now, I love Robert, and I feel sure that Robert loves me: I have thought so many a time before; to-day I *felt* it. When I looked up at him after repeating Chénier's poem,

# Shirley

his eyes (what handsome eyes he has!) sent the truth through my heart. Sometimes I am afraid to speak to him, lest I should be too frank, lest I should seem forward: for I have more than once regretted bitterly, overflowing, superfluous words, and feared I had said more than he expected me to say, and that he would disapprove what he might deem my indiscretion; now, to-night, I could have ventured to express any thought, he was so indulgent. How kind he was, as we walked up the lane! He does not flatter or say foolish things; his love-making (friendship, I mean: of course I don't yet account him my lover, but I hope he will be so some day) is not like what we read of in books – it is far better – original, quiet, manly, sincere. I *do* like him: I would be an excellent wife to him if he did marry me: I would tell him of his faults (for he has a few faults), but I would study his comfort, and cherish him, and do my best to make him happy. Now, I am sure he will not be cold to-morrow: I feel almost certain that to-morrow evening he will either come here, or ask me to go there.'

She recommenced combing her hair, long as a mermaid's; turning her head, as she arranged it, she saw her own face and form in the glass. Such reflections are soberizing to plain people: their own eyes are not enchanted with the image; they are confident then that the eyes of others can see in it no fascination; but the fair must naturally draw other conclusions: the picture is charming, and must charm. Caroline saw a shape, a head, that, daguerreotyped in that attitude and with that expression, would have been lovely: she could not choose but derive from the spectacle confirmation to her hopes: it was then in undiminished gladness she sought her couch.

And in undiminished gladness she rose the next day: as she entered her uncle's breakfast-room, and with soft cheerfulness wished him good-morning, even that little man of bronze himself thought, for an instant, his niece was growing 'a fine girl.' Generally she was quiet and timid with him: very docile, but not communicative; this morning, however, she found many things to say. Slight topics alone might be discussed between them; for with a woman – a girl – Mr Helstone would touch on no other. She had taken an early walk in the garden, and she told him what flowers were beginning to spring there; she inquired when the gardener was to come and trim the borders; she informed him that certain starlings were beginning to build their nests in the church-tower (Briarfield church was close to Briarfield rectory); she wondered the tolling of the bells in the belfry did not scare them.

Mr Helstone opined that 'they were like other fools who had just paired; insensible to inconvenience just for the moment.' Caroline, made perhaps a little too courageous by her temporary good spirits, here hazarded a remark of a kind she had never before ventured to make on observations dropped by her revered relative.

'Uncle,' said she, 'whenever you speak of marriage, you speak of it scornfully: do you think people shouldn't marry?'

'It is decidedly the wisest plan to remain single, especially for women.'

'Are all marriages unhappy?'

'Millions of marriages are unhappy: if everybody confessed the truth, perhaps all are more or less so.'

'You are always vexed when you are asked to come and marry a couple – why?'

# Shirley

'Because one does not like to act as accessory to the commission of a piece of pure folly.'

Mr Helstone spoke so readily, he seemed rather glad of the opportunity to give his niece a piece of his mind on this point. Emboldened by the impunity which had hitherto attended her questions, she went a little further:–

'But why,' said she, 'should it be pure folly? If two people like each other, why shouldn't they consent to live together?'

'They tire of each other – they tire of each other in a month. A yokefellow is not a companion; he or she is a fellow-sufferer.'

It was by no means naïve simplicity which inspired Caroline's next remark: it was a sense of antipathy to such opinions, and of displeasure at him who held them.

'One would think you had never been married, uncle: one would think you were an old bachelor.'

'Practically, I am so.'

'But you have been married. Why were you so inconsistent as to marry?'

'Every man is mad once or twice in his life.'

'So you tired of my aunt, and my aunt of you, and you were miserable together?'

Mr Helstone pushed out his cynical lip, wrinkled his brown forehead, and gave an inarticulate grunt.

'Did she not suit you? Was she not good-tempered? Did you not get used to her? Were you not sorry when she died?'

'Caroline,' said Mr Helstone, bringing his hand slowly down to within an inch or two of the table, and then smiting it suddenly on the mahogany, 'understand this: it is vulgar and puerile to confound generals with particulars: in every case, there is the rule, and there are the exceptions. Your questions are stupid and babyish. Ring the bell, if you have done breakfast.'

The breakfast was taken away, and that meal over, it was the general custom of uncle and niece to separate, and not to meet again till dinner; but to-day the niece, instead of quitting the room, went to the window-seat, and sat down there. Mr Helstone looked round uneasily once or twice, as if he wished her away, but she was gazing from the window, and did not seem to mind him; so he continued the perusal of his morning paper – a particularly interesting one it chanced to be, as new movements had just taken place in the Peninsula, and certain columns of the journal were rich in long despatches from General Lord Wellington. He little knew, meantime, what thoughts were busy in his niece's mind – thoughts the conversation of the past half-hour had revived, but not generated; tumultuous were they now, as disturbed bees in a hive; but it was years since they had first made their cells in her brain.

She was reviewing his character, his disposition, repeating his sentiments on marriage. Many a time has she reviewed them before, and sounded the gulf between her own mind and his; and then, on the other side of the wide and deep chasm, she had seen, and she now saw, another figure standing beside her uncle's – a strange shape; dim, sinister, scarcely earthly: the half-remembered image of her own father, James Helstone, Matthewson Helstone's brother.

Rumours had reached her ear of what that father's character was; old servants had dropped hints: she knew, too, that he was not a good man, and that he was never kind to her. She recollected – a dark recollection it was – some weeks that

# Shirley

she had spent with him in a great town somewhere, when she had had no maid to dress her or take care of her; when she had been shut up, day and night, in a high garret-room, without a carpet, with a bare uncurtained bed, and scarcely any other furniture; when he went out early every morning, and often forgot to return and give her her dinner during the day, and at night, when he came back, was like a madman, furious, terrible; or – still more painful – like an idiot, imbecile, senseless. She knew she had fallen ill in this place, and that one night when she was very sick, he had come raving into the room, and said he would kill her, for she was a burden to him; her screams had brought aid, and from the moment she was then rescued from him she had never seen him, except as a dead man in his coffin.

That was her father: also she had a mother; though Mr Helstone never spoke to her of that mother; though she could not remember having seen her: but that she was alive she knew. This mother was then the drunkard's wife: what had *their* marriage been? Caroline, turning from the lattice whence she had been watching the starlings (though without seeing them), in a low voice, and with a sad bitter tone, thus broke the silence of the room: –

'You term marriage miserable, I suppose, from what you saw of my father and mother's. If my mother suffered what I suffered when I was with papa, she must have had a dreadful life.'

Mr Helstone, thus addressed, wheeled about in his chair, and looked over his spectacles at his niece: he was taken aback.

Her father and mother! What had put it into her head to mention her father and mother, of whom he had never, during the twelve years she had lived with him, spoken to her? That the thoughts were self-matured; that she had any recollections or speculations about her parents, he could not fancy.

'Your father and mother? Who has been talking to you about them?'

'Nobody; but I remember something of what papa was, and I pity mamma. Where is she?'

This 'Where is she?' had been on Caroline's lips hundreds of times before; but till now she had never uttered it.

'I hardly know,' returned Mr Helstone; 'I was little acquainted with her. I have not heard from her for years: but wherever she is, she thinks nothing of you; she never inquires about you; I have reason to believe she does not wish to see you. Come, it is schooltime: you go to your cousin at ten, don't you? The clock has struck.'

Perhaps Caroline would have said more; but Fanny coming in, informed her master that the churchwardens wanted to speak to him in the vestry. He hastened to join them, and his niece presently set out for the cottage.

The road from the Rectory to Hollow's mill inclined downwards; she ran, therefore, almost all the way. Exercise, the fresh air, the thought of seeing Robert, at least of being on his premises, in his vicinage, revived her somewhat depressed spirits quickly. Arriving in sight of the white house, and within hearing of the thundering mill and its rushing water-course, the first thing she saw was Moore at his garden-gate. There he stood; in his belted Holland blouse, a light cap covering his head, which undress costume suited him: he was looking down the lane, not in the direction of his cousin's approach. She stopped, withdrawing a little behind a willow, and studied his appearance.

'He has not his peer,' she thought; 'he is as handsome as he is intelligent.

# Shirley

What a keen eye he has! What clearly cut, spirited features – thin and serious, but graceful! I do like his face – I do like his aspect – I do like him so much! Better than any of those shuffling curates, for instance, – better than anybody: bonnie Robert!'

She sought 'bonnie Robert's' presence speedily. For his part, when she challenged his sight, I believe he would have passed from before her eyes like a phantom, if he could; but being a tall fact, and no fiction, he was obliged to stand the greeting. He made it brief: it was cousin-like, brother-like, friend-like, anything but lover-like. The nameless charm of last night had left his manner: he was no longer the same man; or, at any rate, the same heart did not beat in his breast. Rude disappointment! sharp cross! At first the eager girl would not believe in the change, though she saw and felt it. It was difficult to withdraw her hand from his, till he had bestowed at least something like a kind pressure; it was difficult to turn her eyes from his eyes, till his looks had expressed something more and fonder than that cool welcome.

A lover masculine so disappointed can speak and urge explanation; a lover feminine can say nothing: if she did, the result would be shame and anguish, inward remorse for self-treachery. Nature would brand such demonstration as a rebellion against her instincts, and would vindictively repay it afterwards by the thunderbolt of self-contempt smiting suddenly in secret. Take the matter as you find it: ask no questions; utter no remonstrances: it is your best wisdom. You expected bread, and you have got a stone; break your teeth on it, and don't shriek because the nerves are martyrized: do not doubt that your mental stomach – if you have such a thing – is strong as an ostrich's – the stone will digest. You held out your hand for an egg, and fate put into it a scorpion. Show no consternation: close your fingers firmly upon the gift; let it sting through your palm. Never mind: in time, after your hand and arm have swelled and quivered long with torture, the squeezed scorpion will die, and you will have learned the great lesson how to endure without a sob. For the whole remnant of your life, if you survive the test – some, it is said, die under it – you will be stronger, wiser, less sensitive. This you are not aware of, perhaps, at the time, and so cannot borrow courage of that hope. Nature, however, as has been intimated, is an excellent friend in such cases; sealing the lips, interdicting utterance, commanding a placid dissimulation: a dissimulation often wearing an easy and gay mien at first, settling down to sorrow and paleness in time, then passing away and leaving a convenient stoicism, not the less fortifying because it is half-bitter.

Half-bitter! Is that wrong? No – it should be bitter: bitterness is strength – it is a tonic. Sweet mild force following acute suffering, you find nowhere: to talk of it is delusion. There may be apathetic exhaustion after the rack; if energy remains, it will be rather a dangerous energy – deadly when confronted with injustice.

Who has read the ballad of 'Puir Mary Lee?' – that old Scotch ballad, written I know not in what generation nor by what hand. Mary had been ill used – probably in being made to believe that truth which was falsehood: she is not complaining, but she is sitting alone in the snow-storm, and you hear her thoughts. They are not the thoughts of a model-heroine under her circumstances, but they are those of a deeply-feeling, strongly-resentful peasant-girl. Anguish has driven her from the ingle-nook of home, to the white-shrouded and icy hills:

# Shirley

crouched under the 'cauld drift,' she recalls every image of horror, – 'the yellow-wymed ask,' 'the hairy adder,' 'the auld moon-bowing tyke,' 'the ghaist at e'en,' 'the sour bullister,' 'the milk on the taed's back:' she hates these, but 'waur she hates Robin-a-Ree!'

> 'Oh! ance I lived happily by yon bonny burn –
> The warld was in love wi' me;
> But now I maun sit 'neath the cauld drift and mourn,
> And curse black Robin-a-Ree!
>
> 'Then whudder awa' thou bitter biting blast,
> And sough through the scrunty tree,
> And smoor me up in the snaw fu' fast,
> And ne'er let the sun me see!
>
> 'Oh, never melt awa, thou wreath o' snaw,
> That's sae kind in graving me;
> But hide me frae the scorn and guffaw
> O' villains like Robin-a-Ree!'

But what has been said in the last page or two is not germane to Caroline Helstone's feelings, or to the state of things between her and Robert Moore. Robert had done her no wrong: he had told her no lie; it was she that was to blame, if any one was: what bitterness her mind distilled should and would be poured on her own head. She had loved without being asked to love, – a natural, sometimes an inevitable chance, but big with misery.

Robert, indeed, had sometimes seemed to be fond of her – but why? Because she had made herself so pleasing to him, he could not, in spite of all his efforts, help testifying a state of feeling his judgment did not approve, nor his will sanction. He was about to withdraw decidedly from intimate communication with her, because he did not choose to have his affections inextricably entangled, nor to be drawn, despite his reason, into a marriage he believed imprudent. Now, what was she to do? – to give way to her feelings, or to vanquish them? To pursue him, or to turn upon herself? If she is weak, she will try the first expedient, – will lose his esteem and win his aversion: if she has sense, she will be her own governor, and resolve to subdue and bring under guidance the disturbed realm of her emotions. She will determine to look on life steadily, as it is; to begin to learn its severe truths seriously, and to study its knotty problems closely, conscientiously.

It appeared she had a little sense, for she quitted Robert quietly, without complaint or question – without the alteration of a muscle or the shedding of a tear – betook herself to her studies under Hortense as usual, and at dinner-time went home without lingering.

When she had dined, and found herself in the Rectory drawing-room alone, having left her uncle over his temperate glass of port wine, the difficulty that occurred to and embarrassed her, was – 'How am I to get through this day?'

Last night she had hoped it would be spent as yesterday was, – that the evening would be again passed with Happiness and Robert: she had learned her mistake this morning, and yet she could not settle down, convinced that no

chance would occur to recall her to Hollow's cottage, or to bring Moore again into her society.

He had walked up after tea, more than once, to pass an hour with her uncle: the door-bell had rung, his voice had been heard in the passage just at twilight, when she little expected such a pleasure; and this had happened twice after he had treated her with peculiar reserve; and, though he rarely talked to her in her uncle's presence, he had looked at her relentingly, as he sat opposite her work-table during his stay: the few words he had spoken to her were comforting; his manner on bidding her good-night was genial. Now, he might come this evening, said False Hope: she almost knew it was False Hope which breathed the whisper, and yet she listened.

She tried to read – her thoughts wandered; she tried to sew – every stitch she put in was an ennui, the occupation was insufferably tedious; she opened her desk, and attempted to write a French composition – she wrote nothing but mistakes.

Suddenly the door-bell sharply rang – her heart leaped – she sprang to the drawing-room door, opened it softly, peeped through the aperture: Fanny was admitting a visitor – a gentleman – a tall man – just the height of Robert. For one second she thought it was Robert – for one second she exulted; but the voice asking for Mr Helstone undeceived her: that voice was an Irish voice, conse-quently not Moore's but the curate's – Malone's. He was ushered into the dining-room, where, doubtless, he speedily helped his Rector to empty the decanters.

It was a fact to be noted, that at whatever house in Briarfield, Whinbury, or Nunnely, one curate dropped in to a meal – dinner or tea, as the case might be – another presently followed; often two more. Not that they gave each other the rendezvous, but they were usually all on the run at the same time; and when Donne, for instance, sought Malone at his lodgings and found him not, he inquired whither he had posted, and having learned of the landlady his destination, hastened with all speed after him: the same causes operated in the same way with Sweeting. Thus it chanced on that afternoon that Caroline's ears were three times tortured with the ringing of the bell, and the advent of undesired guests: for Donne followed Malone, and Sweeting followed Donne; and more wine was ordered up from the cellar into the dining-room (for though old Helstone chid the inferior priesthood when he found them 'carousing,' as he called it, in their own tents, yet at his hierarchical table he ever liked to treat them to a glass of his best), and through the closed doors Caroline heard their boyish laughter, and the vacant cackle of their voices. Her fear was lest they should stay to tea; for she had no pleasure in making tea for that particular trio. What distinctions people draw! These three were men – young men – educated men, like Moore: yet, for her, how great the difference! Their society was a bore – his a delight.

Not only was she destined to be favoured with their clerical company, but Fortune was at this moment bringing her four other guests – lady-guests, all packed in a pony-phaeton now rolling somewhat heavily along the road from Whinbury: an elderly lady, and three of her buxom daughters, were coming to see her 'in a friendly way,' as the custom of that neighbourhood was. Yes, a fourth time the bell clanged: Fanny brought the present announcement to the drawing-room –

# Shirley

'Mrs Sykes and the three Misses Sykes.'

When Caroline was going to receive company, her habit was to wring her hands very nervously, to flush a little, and come forward hurriedly yet hesitatingly, wishing herself meantime at Jericho. She was, at such crises, sadly deficient in finished manner, though she had once been at school a year. Accordingly, on this occasion, her small white hands sadly maltreated each other, while she stood up, waiting the entrance of Mrs Sykes.

In stalked that lady, a tall bilious gentlewoman, who made an ample and not altogether insincere profession of piety, and was greatly given to hospitality towards the clergy; in sailed her three daughters, a showy trio, being all three well grown, and more or less handsome.

In English country ladies there is this point to be remarked. Whether young or old, pretty or plain, dull or sprightly, they all (or almost all) have a certain expression stamped on their features, which seems to say, 'I know – I do not boast of it – but I *know* that I am the standard of what is proper; let every one therefore whom I approach, or who approaches me, keep a sharp look-out, for wherein they differ from me – be the same in dress, manner, opinion, principle, or practice – therein they are wrong.'

Mrs and Misses Sykes, far from being exceptions to this observation, were pointed illustrations of its truth. Miss Mary – a well-looked, well-meant, and, on the whole, well-dispositioned girl – wore her complacency with some state, though without harshness; Miss Harriet – a beauty – carried it more overbearingly: she looked high and cold; Miss Hannah, who was conceited, dashing, pushing, flourished hers consciously and openly; the mother evinced it with the gravity proper to her age and religious fame.

The reception was got through somehow. Caroline 'was glad to see them' (an unmitigated fib), hoped they were well, hoped Mrs Sykes's cough was better (Mrs Sykes had had a cough for the last twenty years), hoped the Misses Sykes had left their sisters at home well; to which inquiry, the Misses Sykes, sitting on three chairs opposite the music-stool, whereon Caroline had undesignedly come to anchor, after wavering for some seconds between it and a large armchair, into which she at length recollected she ought to induct Mrs Sykes: and indeed that lady saved her the trouble by depositing herself therein; the Misses Sykes replied to Caroline by one stimultaneous bow, very majestic and mighty awful. A pause followed: this bow was of a character to ensure silence for the next five minutes, and it did. Mrs Sykes then inquired after Mr Helstone, and whether he had had any return of rheumatism, and whether preaching twice on a Sunday fatigued him, and if he was capable of taking a full service now; and on being assured he was, she and all her daughters, combining in chorus, expressed their opinion that he was a 'wonderful man of his years.'

Pause second.

Miss Mary, getting up the steam in her turn, asked whether Caroline had attended the Bible Society Meeting which had been held at Nunnely last Thursday night: the negative answer which truth compelled Caroline to utter – for last Thursday evening she had been sitting at home, reading a novel which Robert had lent her – elicited a simultaneous expression of surprise from the lips of the four ladies.

'We were all there,' said Miss Mary; 'mamma and all of us; we even persuaded papa to go: Hannah would insist upon it; but he fell asleep while Mr

574

# Shirley

Langweilig, the German Moravian minister, was speaking: I felt quite ashamed, he nodded so.'

'And there was Dr Broadbent,' cried Hannah, 'such a beautiful speaker! You couldn't expect it of him, for he is almost a vulgar-looking man.'

'But such a dear man,' interrupted Mary.

'And such a good man, such a useful man,' added her mother.

'Only like a butcher in appearance,' interposed the fair, proud Harriet. 'I couldn't bear to look at him: I listened with my eyes shut.'

Miss Helstone felt her ignorance and incompetency; not having seen Dr Broadbent, she could not give her opinions. Pause third came on. During its continuance, Caroline was feeling at her heart's core what a dreaming fool she was; what an unpractical life she led; how little fitness there was in her for ordinary intercourse with the ordinary world. She was feeling how exclusively she had attached herself to the white cottage in the Hollow; how in the existence of one inmate of that cottage she had pent all her universe: she was sensible that this would not do, and that some day she would be forced to make an alteration: it could not be said that she exactly wished to resemble the ladies before her, but she wished to become superior to her present self, so as to feel less scared by their dignity.

The sole means she found of reviving the flagging discourse, was by asking them if they would all stay to tea; and a cruel struggle it cost her to perform this piece of civility. Mrs Sykes had begun – 'We are much obliged to you, but –' when in came Fanny once more.

'The gentlemen will stay the evening, ma'am,' was the message she brought from Mr Helstone.

'What gentlemen have you?' now inquired Mrs Sykes. Their names were specified; she and her daughters interchanged glances: the curates were not to them what they were to Caroline. Mr Sweeting was quite a favourite with them; even Mr Malone rather so, because he was a clergyman. 'Really, since you have company already, I think we will stay,' remarked Mrs Sykes. 'We shall be quite a pleasant little party: I always like to meet the clergy.'

And now Caroline had to usher them up-stairs, to help them to unshawl, smooth their hair and make themselves smart; to reconduct them to the drawing-room, to distribute amongst them books of engravings, or odd things purchased from the Jew-basket: she was obliged to be a purchaser, though she was but a slack contributor; and if she had possessed plenty of money, she would rather, when it was brought to the Rectory – an awful incubus! – have purchased the whole stock, than contributed a single pincushion.

It ought perhaps to be explained in passing, for the benefit of those who are not 'au fait' to the mysteries of the 'Jew-basket' and 'Missionary-basket,' that these 'meubles' are willow-repositories, of the capacity of a good-sized family clothes-basket, dedicated to the purpose of conveying from house to house a monster collection of pin-cushions, needle-books, card-racks, work-bags, articles of infant-wear, &c. &c. &c., made by the willing or reluctant hands of the Christian ladies of a parish, and sold per force to the heathenish gentlemen thereof, at prices unblushingly exorbitant. The proceeds of such compulsory sales are applied to the conversion of the Jews, the seeking up of the ten missing tribes, or to the regeneration of the interesting coloured population of the globe. Each lady-contributor takes it in her turn to keep the basket a month, to sew

# Shirley

for it, and to foist off its contents on a shrinking male public. An exciting time it is when that turn comes round: some active-minded women, with a good trading spirit, like it, and enjoy exceedingly the fun of making hard-handed worsted-spinners cash up, to the tune of four or five hundred per cent. above cost price, for articles quite useless to them; other – feebler – souls object to it, and would rather see the prince of darkness himself at their door any morning, than that phantom-basket, brought with 'Mrs Rouse's compliments, and please, ma'am, she says it's your turn now.'

Miss Helstone's duties of hostess performed, more anxiously than cheerily, she betook herself to the kitchen, to hold a brief privy council with Fanny and Eliza about the tea.

'What a lot on 'em!' cried Eliza, who was cook. 'And I put off the baking to-day because I thought there would be bread plenty to fit while morning: we shall never have enow.'

'Are there any tea-cakes?' asked the young mistress.

'Only three and a loaf. I wish these fine folk would stay at home till they're asked: and I want to finish trimming my hat' (bonnet she meant).

'Then,' suggested Caroline, to whom the importance of the emergency gave a certain energy, 'Fanny must run down to Briarfield and buy some muffins and crumpets, and some biscuits: and don't be cross, Eliza, we can't help it now.'

'And which tea-things are we to have?'

'Oh, the best, I suppose: I'll get out the silver service,' and she ran up-stairs, to the plate-closet, and presently brought down tea-pot, cream-ewer, and sugar-basin.

'And mun we have th' urn?'

'Yes; and now get it ready as quickly as you can, for the sooner we have tea over, the sooner they will go – at least, I hope so. Heigho! I wish they were gone,' she sighed as she returned to the drawing-room. 'Still,' she thought, as she paused at the door ere opening it, 'if Robert would but come even now how bright all would be! How comparatively easy the task of amusing these people, if he were present! There would be an interest in hearing him talk (though he never says much in company) and in talking in his presence: there can be no interest in hearing any of them, or in speaking to them. How they will gabble when the curates come in, and how weary I shall grow with listening to them! But I suppose I am a selfish fool: these are very respectable gentlefolks; I ought no doubt to be proud of their countenance: I don't say they are not as good as I am – far from it – but they are different from me.'

She went in.

Yorkshire people, in those days, took their tea round the table; sitting well into it, with their knees duly introduced under the mahogany. It was essential to have a multitude of plates of bread and butter, varied in sorts and plentiful in quantity: it was thought proper, too, that on the centre-plate should stand a glass dish of marmalade; among the viands was expected to be found a small assortment of cheesecakes and tarts; if there was also a plate of thin slices of pink ham garnished with green parsley, so much the better.

Eliza, the Rector's cook, fortunately knew her business as provider: she had been put out of humour a little at first, when the invaders came so unexpectedly in such strength; but it appeared that she regained her cheerfulness with action,

576

# Shirley

for in due time the tea was spread forth in handsome style; and neither ham, tarts, nor marmalade were wanting among its accompaniments.

The curates, summoned to this bounteous repast, entered joyous; but at once, on seeing the ladies, of whose presence they had not been forewarned, they came to a stand in the door-way. Malone headed the party; he stopped short and fell back, almost capsizing Donne, who was behind him. Donne, staggering three paces in retreat, sent little Sweeting into the arms of old Helstone, who brought up the rear. There was some expostulation, some tittering: Malone was desired to mind what he was about, and urged to push forward; which at last he did, though colouring to the top of his peaked forehead a bluish purple. Helstone, advancing, set the shy curates aside, welcomed all his fair guests, shook hands and passed a jest with each, and seated himself snugly between the lovely Harriet and the dashing Hannah; Miss Mary he requested to move to the seat opposite to him, that he might see her if he couldn't be near her. Perfectly easy and gallant, in his way, were his manners always to young ladies; and most popular was he amongst them: yet, at heart, he neither respected nor liked the sex, and such of them as circumstances had brought into intimate relation with him had ever feared rather than loved him.

The curates were left to shift for themselves. Sweeting, who was the least embarrassed of the three, took refuge beside Mrs Sykes; who, he knew, was almost as fond of him as if he had been her son. Donne, after making his general bow with a grace all his own, and saying in a high pragmatical voice, 'How d'ye do, Miss Helstone?' dropped into a seat at Caroline's elbow: to her unmitigated annoyance, for she had a peculiar antipathy to Donne, on account of his stultified and unmovable self-conceit, and his incurable narrowness of mind. Malone, grinning most unmeaningly, inducted himself into the corresponding seat on the other side: she was thus blessed in a pair of supporters; neither of whom, she knew, would be of any mortal use, whether for keeping up the conversation, handing cups, circulating the muffins, or even lifting the plate from the slop-basin. Little Sweeting, small and boyish as he was, would have been worth twenty of them.

Malone, though a ceaseless talker when there were only men present, was usually tongue-tied in the presence of ladies: three phrases, however, he had ready cut and dried, which he never failed to produce: –

1stly. – 'Have you had a walk to-day, Miss Helstone?'

2dly. – 'Have you seen your cousin, Moore, lately?'

3dly. – 'Does your class at the Sunday-school keep up its number?'

These three questions being put and responded to, between Caroline and Malone reigned silence.

With Donne it was otherwise: he was troublesome, exasperating. He had a stock of small-talk on hand, at once the most trite and perverse than can well be imagined: abuse of the people of Briarfield; of the natives of Yorkshire generally; complaints of the want of high society; of the backward state of civilization in these districts; murmurings against the disrespectful conduct of the lower orders in the north toward their betters; silly ridicule of the manner of living in these parts, – the want of style, the absence of elegance, as if he, Donne, had been accustomed to very great doings indeed: an insinuation which his somewhat underbred manner and aspect failed to bear out. These strictures he seemed to think must raise him in the estimation of Miss Helstone, or of any

# Shirley

other lady who heard him; whereas with her, at least, they brought him to a level below contempt: though sometimes, indeed, they incensed her; for, a Yorkshire girl herself, she hated to hear Yorkshire abused by such a pitiful prater; and when wrought up to a certain pitch, she would turn and say something of which neither the matter nor the manner recommended her to Mr Donne's good-will. She would tell him it was no proof of refinement to be ever scolding others for vulgarity; and no sign of a good pastor to be eternally censuring his flock. She would ask him what he had entered the church for, since he complained there were only cottages to visit, and poor people to preach to? – whether he had been ordained to the ministry merely to wear soft clothing, and sit in kings' houses? These questions were considered by all the curates as, to the last degree, audacious and impious.

Tea was a long time in progress: all the guests gabbled as their hostess had expected they would. Mr Helstone, being in excellent spirits, – when, indeed, was he ever otherwise in society, attractive female society? – it being only with the one lady of his own family that he maintained a grim taciturnity, – kept up a brilliant flow of easy prattle with his right-hand and left-hand neighbours, and even with his *vis-à-vis*, Miss Mary: though as Mary was the most sensible, the least coquettish of the three, to her the elderly widower was the least attentive. At heart, he could not abide sense in women: he liked to see them as silly, as light-headed, as vain, as open to ridicule as possible; because they were then in reality what he held them to be, and wished them to be, – inferior: toys to play with, to amuse a vacant hour and to be thrown away.

Hannah was his favourite. Harriet, though beautiful, egotistical, and self-satisfied, was not quite weak enough for him: she had some genuine self-respect amidst much false pride, and if she did not talk like an oracle, neither would she babble like one crazy: she would not permit herself to be treated quite as a doll, a child, a plaything; she expected to be bent to like a queen.

Hannah, on the contrary, demanded no respect; only flattery: if her admirers only *told* her that she was an angel, she would let them *treat* her like an idiot. So very credulous and frivolous was she; so very silly did she become when besieged with attention, flattered and admired to the proper degree, that there were moments when Helstone actually felt tempted to commit matrimony a second time, and to try the experiment of taking her for his second helpmeet: but, fortunately, the salutary recollection of the ennuis of his first marriage, the impression still left on him of the weight of the millstone he had once worn round his neck, the fixity of his feelings respecting the insufferable evils of conjugal existence, operated as a check to his tenderness, suppressed the sigh heaving his old iron lungs, and restrained him from whispering to Hannah proposals it would have been high fun and great satisfaction to her to hear.

It is probable she would have married him if he had asked her; her parents would have quite approved the match: to them his fifty-five years, his bend-leather heart, could have presented no obstacles; and, as he was a rector, held an excellent living, occupied a good house, and was supposed even to have private property (though in that the world was mistaken: every penny of the £5000 inherited by him from his father had been devoted to the building and endowing of a new church at his native village in Lancashire – for he could show a lordly munificence when he pleased, and, if the end was to his liking, never hesitated about making a grand sacrifice to attain it), – her parents, I say,

# Shirley

would have delivered Hannah over to his loving-kindness and his tender mercies without one scruple; and the second Mrs Helstone, inversing the natural order of insect existence, would have fluttered through the honeymoon a bright, admired butterfly, and crawled the rest of her days a sordid, trampled worm.

Little Mr Sweeting, seated between Mrs Sykes and Miss Mary, both of whom were very kind to him, and having a dish of tarts before him, and marmalade and crumpet upon his plate, looked and felt more content than any monarch. He was fond of all the Misses Sykes; they were all fond of him: he thought them magnificent girls, quite proper to mate with one of his inches. If he had a cause of regret at this blissful moment, it was that Miss Dora happened to be absent; Dora being the one whom he secretly hoped one day to call Mrs David Sweeting, with whom he dreamt of taking stately walks, leading her like an empress through the village of Nunnely: and an empress she would have been, if size could make an empress. She was vast, ponderous: seen from behind, she had the air of a very stout lady of forty; but withal she possessed a good face, and no unkindly character.

The meal at last drew to a close: it would have been over long ago, if Mr Donne had not persisted in sitting with his cup half full of cold tea before him, long after the rest had finished, and after he himself had discussed such allowance of viands as he felt competent to swallow – long, indeed, after signs of impatience had been manifested all round the board: till chairs were pushed back; till the talk flagged; till silence fell. Vainly did Caroline inquire repeatedly if he would have another cup; if he would take a little hot tea, as that must be cold, &c.: he would neither drink it nor leave it. He seemed to think that this isolated position of his gave him somehow a certain importance: that it was dignified and stately to be the last; that it was grand to keep all the others waiting. So long did he linger, that the very urn died: it ceased to hiss. At length, however, the old Rector himself, who had hitherto been too pleasantly engaged with Hannah to care for the delay, got impatient.

'For whom are we waiting?' he asked.

'For me, I believe,' returned Donne, complacently; appearing to think it much to his credit that a party should thus be kept dependent on his movements.

'Tut!' cried Helstone; then standing up, 'Let us return thanks,' said he; which he did forthwith, and all quitted the table. Donne, nothing abashed, still sat ten minutes quite alone, whereupon Mr Helstone rang the bell for the things to be removed; the curate at length saw himself forced to empty his cup, and to relinquish the *rôle* which, he thought, had given him such a felicitous distinction, drawn upon him such flattering general notice.

And now, in the natural course of events (Caroline, knowing how it would be, had opened the piano, and produced music-books in readiness) music was asked for. This was Mr Sweeting's chance for showing off: he was eager to commence; he undertook, therefore, the arduous task of persuading the young ladies to favour the company with an air – a song. Con amore, he went through the whole business of begging, praying, resisting excuses, explaining away difficulties, and at last succeeded in persuading Miss Harriet to allow herself to be led to the instrument. Then out came the pieces of his flute (he always carried them in his pocket, as unfailingly as he carried his handkerchief). They were screwed and arranged: Malone and Donne meantime herding together, and sneering at him, which the little man, glancing over his shoulder, saw, but

did not heed at all: he was persuaded their sarcasm all arose from envy; they could not accompany the ladies as he could; he was about to enjoy a triumph over them.

The triumph began. Malone, much chagrined at hearing him pipe up in most superior style, determined to earn distinction, too, if possible, and all at once assuming the character of a swain (which character he had endeavoured to enact once or twice before, but in which he had not hitherto met with the success he doubtless opined his merits deserved), approached a sofa on which Miss Helstone was seated, and depositing his great Irish frame near her, tried his hand (or rather tongue) at a fine speech or two, accompanied by grins the most extraordinary and incomprehensible. In the course of his efforts to render himself agreeable, he contrived to possess himself of the two long sofa cushions and a square one; with which, after rolling them about for some time with strange gestures, he managed to erect a sort of barrier between himself and the object of his attentions. Caroline, quite willing that they should be sundered, soon devised an excuse for stepping over to the opposite side of the room, and taking up a position beside Mrs Sykes; of which good lady she entreated some instruction in a new stitch in ornamental knitting, a favour readily granted; and thus Peter Augustus was thrown out.

Very sullenly did his countenance lower when he saw himself abandoned, – left entirely to his own resources, on a large sofa, with the charge of three small cushions on his hands. The fact was, he felt disposed seriously to cultivate acquaintance with Miss Helstone; because he thought, in common with others, that her uncle possessed money, and concluded, that since he had no children, he would probably leave it to his niece. Gérard Moore was better instructed on this point: he had seen the neat church that owed its origin to the Rector's zeal and cash, and more than once, in his inmost soul, had cursed an expensive caprice which crossed his wishes.

The evening seemed long to one person in that room. Caroline at intervals dropped her knitting on her lap, and gave herself up to a sort of brain-lethargy – closing her eyes and depressing her head – caused by what seemed to her the unmeaning hum round her: the inharmonious, tasteless rattle of the piano keys, the squeaking and gasping notes of the flute, the laughter and mirth of her uncle and Hannah and Mary, she could not tell whence originating, for she heard nothing comic or gleeful in their discourse; and, more than all, by the interminable gossip of Mrs Sykes murmured close at her ear; gossip which rang the changes on four subjects: her own health and that of the various members of her family; the Missionary and Jew baskets and their contents; the late meeting at Nunnely, and one which was expected to come off next week at Whinbury.

Tired at length to exhaustion, she embraced the opportunity of Mr Sweeting coming up to speak to Mrs Sykes, to slip quietly out of the apartment, and seek a moment's respite in solitude. She repaired to the dining-room, where the clear but now low remnant of a fire still burnt in the grate. The place was empty and quiet, glasses and decanters were cleared from the table, the chairs were put back in their places, all was orderly. Caroline sank into her uncle's large easy chair, half shut her eyes, and rested herself – rested at least her limbs, her senses, her hearing, her vision – weary with listening to nothing, and gazing on vacancy. As to her mind, that flew directly to the Hollow: it stood on the threshold of the parlour there, then it passed to the counting-house, and wondered

# Shirley

which spot was blessed by the presence of Robert. It so happened that neither locality had that honour; for Robert was half a mile away from both, and much nearer to Caroline than her deadened spirit suspected: he was at this moment crossing the churchyard, approaching the Rectory garden-gate: not, however, coming to see his cousin, but intent solely on communicating a brief piece of intelligence to the Rector.

Yes, Caroline; you hear the wire of the bell vibrate: it rings again for the fifth time this afternoon: you start, and you are certain now that this must be him of whom you dream. Why you are so certain you cannot explain to yourself, but you know it. You lean forward, listening eagerly as Fanny opens the door: right! that is *the* voice – low – with the slight foreign accent, but so sweet, as you fancy: you half rise: 'Fanny will tell him Mr Helstone is with company, and then he will go away.' Oh! she cannot let him go: in spite of herself – in spite of her reason she walks half across the room; she stands ready to dart out in case the step should retreat: but he enters the passage. 'Since your master is engaged,' he says, 'just show me into the dining-room; bring me pen and ink: I will write a short note and leave it for him.'

Now, having caught these words, and hearing him advance, Caroline, if there was a door within the dining-room, would glide through it and disappear. She feels caught, hemmed in; she dreads her unexpected presence may annoy him. A second since, she would have flown to him; that second passed, she would flee from him. She cannot; there is no way to escape; the dining-room has but one door, through which now enters her cousin. The look of troubled surprise she expected to see in his face appeared there, has shocked her, and is gone. She has stammered a sort of apology: –

'I only left the drawing-room a minute for a little quiet.'

There was something so diffident and downcast in the air and tone with which she said this, any one might perceive that some saddening change had lately passed over her prospects, and that the faculty of cheerful self-possession had left her. Mr Moore, probably, remembered how she had formerly been accustomed to meet him with gentle ardour and hopeful confidence; he must have seen how the check of this morning had operated: here was an opportunity for carrying out his new system with effect, if he chose to improve it. Perhaps he found it easier to practise that system in broad daylight, in his mill-yard, amidst busy occupations, than in a quiet parlour, disengaged, at the hour of eventide. Fanny lit the candles, which before had stood unlit on the table, brought writing materials, and left the room: Caroline was about to follow her. Moore, to act consistently, should have let her go; whereas he stood in the doorway, and, holding out his hand, gently kept her back: he did not ask her to stay, but he would not let her go.

'Shall I tell my uncle you are here?' asked she, still in the same subdued voice.

'No: I can say to you all I had to say to him. You will be my messenger?'

'Yes, Robert.'

'Then you may just inform him that I have got a clue to the identity of one, at least, of the men who broke my frames; that he belongs to the same gang who attacked Sykes and Pearson's dressing-shop; and that I hope to have him in custody to-morrow. You can remember that?'

'Oh! yes.' These two monosyllables were uttered in a sadder tone than ever;

and, as she said them, she shook her head slightly, and sighed. 'Will you prosecute him?'

'Doubtless.'

'No, Robert.'

'And why no, Caroline?'

'Because it will set all the neighbourhood against you more than ever.'

'That is no reason why I should not do my duty, and defend my property. This fellow is a great scoundrel, and ought to be incapacitated from perpetrating further mischief.'

'But his accomplices will take revenge on you. You do not know how the people of this country bear malice: it is the boast of some of them that they can keep a stone in their pocket seven years, turn it at the end of that time, keep it seven years longer, and hurl it, and hit their mark "at last." '

Moore laughed.

'A most pithy vaunt,' said he; 'one that redounds vastly to the credit of your dear Yorkshire friends. But don't fear for me, Lina: I am on my guard against these lamb-like compatriots of yours: don't make yourself uneasy about me.'

'How can I help it? You are my cousin. If anything happened –' she stopped.

'Nothing will happen, Lina. To speak in your own language, there is a Providence above all – is there not?'

'Yes, dear Robert. May He guard you!'

'And if prayers have efficacy, yours will benefit me: you pray for me sometimes?'

'Not *sometimes*, Robert: you, and Louis, and Hortense are *always* remembered.'

'So I have often imagined: it has occurred to me, when, weary and vexed, I have myself gone to bed like a heathen, that another had asked forgiveness for my day, and safety for my night. I don't suppose such vicarial piety will avail much; but the petitions come out of a sincere breast, from innocent lips: they should be acceptable as Abel's offering; and doubtless would be, if the object deserved them.'

'Annihilate that doubt: it is groundless.'

'When a man has been brought up only to make money, and lives to make it, and for nothing else, and scarcely breathes any other air than that of mills and markets, it seems odd to utter his name in a prayer, or to mix his idea with anything divine; and very strange it seems, that a good, pure heart should take him in and harbour him, as if he had any claim to that sort of nest. If I could guide that benignant heart, I believe I should counsel it to exclude one who does not profess to have any higher aim in life than that of patching up his broken fortune, and wiping clean from his bourgeois scutcheon the foul stain of bankruptcy.'

The hint, though conveyed thus tenderly and modestly (as Caroline thought), was felt keenly and comprehended clearly.

'Indeed, I only think – or I *will only* think – of you as my cousin,' was the quick answer. 'I am beginning to understand things better than I did, Robert, when you first came to England: better than I did, a week – a day ago. I know it is your duty to try to get on, and that it won't do for you to be romantic; but in future you must not misunderstand me, if I seem friendly. You misunderstood me this morning, did you not?'

'What made you think so?'

'Your look – your manner.'

'But look at me now –'

'Oh! you are different now: at present, I dare speak to you.'

'Yet I am the same, except that I have left the tradesman behind me in the Hollow: your kinsman alone stands before you.'

'My cousin, Robert; not Mr Moore.'

'Not a bit of Mr Moore. Caroline –'

Here the company was heard rising in the other room; the door was opened; the pony-carriage was ordered; shawls and bonnets were demanded; Mr Helstone called for his niece.

'I must go, Robert.'

'Yes, you must go, or they will come in, and find us here; and I, rather than meet all that host in the passage, will take my departure through the window: luckily, it opens like a door. One minute only – put down the candle an instant – good-night! I kiss you because we are cousins; and, being cousins – one – two – three kisses are allowable. Caroline, good-night!'

# Chapter 8

## Noah and Moses

The next day, Moore had risen before the sun, and had taken a ride to Whinbury and back ere his sister had made the café au lait, or cut the tartines for his breakfast. What business he transacted there, he kept to himself. Hortense asked no questions: it was not her wont to comment on his movements, nor his to render an account of them. The secrets of business – complicated and often dismal mysteries – were buried in his breast, and never came out of their sepulchre, save now and then to scare Joe Scott, or give a start to some foreign correspondent: indeed, a general habit of reserve on whatever was important seemed bred in his mercantile blood.

Breakfast over, he went to his counting-house. Henry, Joe Scott's boy, brought in the letters and the daily papers; Moore seated himself at his desk, broke the seals of the documents, and glanced them over. They were all short, but not – it seemed – sweet; probably rather sour on the contrary, for as Moore laid down the last, his nostrils emitted a derisive and defiant snuff; and, though he burst into no soliloquy, there was a glance in his eye which seemed to invoke the devil, and lay charges on him to sweep the whole concern to Gehenna. However, having chosen a pen and stripped away the feathered top in a brief spasm of finger-fury – only finger-fury, his face was placid – he dashed off a batch of answers, sealed them, and then went out and walked through the mill; on coming back, he sat down to read his newspaper.

# Shirley

The contents seemed not absorbingly interesting; he more than once laid it across his knee, folded his arms, and gazed into the fire; he occasionally turned his head towards the window; he looked at intervals at his watch: in short, his mind appeared preoccupied. Perhaps he was thinking of the beauty of the weather – for it was a fine and mild morning for the season – and wishing to be out in the fields enjoying it. The door of his counting-house stood wide open, the breeze and sunshine entered freely; but the first visitant brought no spring perfume on its wings, only an occasional sulphur-puff from the soot-thick column of smoke rushing sable from the gaunt mill-chimney.

A dark blue apparition (that of Joe Scott, fresh from a dyeing vat) appeared momentarily at the open door, uttered the words 'He's comed, sir,' and vanished.

Mr Moore raised not his eyes from the paper. A large man, broad-shouldered and massive-limbed, clad in fustian garments and grey-worsted stockings, entered, who was received with a nod, and desired to take a seat; which he did, making the remark – as he removed his hat (a very bad one), stowed it away under his chair, and wiped his forehead with a spotted cotton handkerchief extracted from the hat-crown – that it was 'raight dahn warm for Febewerry.' Mr Moore assented: at least he uttered some slight sound, which, though inarticulate, might pass for an assent. The visiter now carefully deposited in the corner beside him an official-looking staff which he bore in his hand; this done, he whistled, probably by way of appearing at his ease.

'You have what is necessary, I suppose,' said Mr Moore.

'Ay! ay! all's raight.'

He renewed his whistling, Mr Moore his reading: the paper apparently had become more interesting. Presently, however, he turned to his cupboard, which was within reach of his long arm, opened it without rising, took out a black bottle – the same he had produced for Malone's benefit – a tumbler, and a jug, placed them on the table, and said to his guest, –

'Help yourself; there's water in that jar in the corner.'

'I dunnut knaw that there's mich need, for all a body is dry (thirsty) in a morning,' said the fustian gentleman, rising and doing as requested.

'Will you tak' naught yourseln, Mr Moore?' he inquired, as with skilled hand he mixed a portion, and having tested it by a deep draught, sank back satisfied and bland in his seat. Moore – chary of words – replied by a negative movement and murmur.

'Yah'd as good,' continued his visitor; 'it 'uld set ye up, wald a sup o' this stuff. Uncommon good Hollands! ye get it fro' furrin' parts, I'se think?'

'Ay!'

'Tak' my advice, and try a glass on 't; them lads 'at 's coming 'll keep ye talking, nob'dy knows how long: ye'll need propping.'

'Have you seen Mr Sykes this morning?' inquired Moore.

'I seed him a hauf hour – nay – happen a quarter of an hour sin', just afore I set off: he said he aimed to come here, and I sudn't wonder but ye'll have old Helstone too; I seed 'em saddling his little nag as I passed at back o' t' Rectory.'

The speaker was a true prophet, for the trot of a little nag's hoofs were, five minutes after, heard in the yard; it stopped, and a well-known nasal voice cried aloud – 'Boy (probably addressing Harry Scott, who usually hung about the premises from nine a.m. to five p.m.), take my horse and lead him into the stable.'

# Shirley

Helstone came in marching nimbly and erect, looking browner, keener, and livelier than usual.

'Beautiful morning, Moore: how do, my boy? Ha! Whom have we here (turning to the personage with the staff)? Sugden! What! you're going to work directly? On my word, you lose no time: but I come to ask explanations: your message was delivered to me; are you sure you are on the right scent? How do you mean to set about the business? Have you got a warrant?'

'Sugden has.'

'Then you are going to seek him now? I'll accompany you.'

'You will be spared that trouble, sir; he is coming to seek me. I'm just now sitting in state, waiting his arrival.'

'And who is it? One of my parishioners?'

Joe Scott had entered unobserved; he now stood, a most sinister phantom, half his person being dyed of the deepest tint of indigo, leaning on the desk. His master's answer to the Rector's question was a smile; Joe took the word; putting on a quiet but pawky look, he said, –

'It's a friend of yours, Mr Helstone; a gentleman you often speak of.'

'Indeed! His name, Joe? – You look well this morning.'

'Only the Rev. Moses Barraclough: t' tub orator you call him sometimes, I think.'

'Ah!' said the Rector, taking out his snuff-box, and administering to himself a very long pinch – 'Ah! couldn't have supposed it. Why, the pious man never was a workman of yours, Moore? He's a tailor by trade.'

'And so much the worse grudge I owe him, for interfering, and setting my discarded men against me.'

'And Moses was actually present at the battle of Stilbro' Moor? He went there – wooden leg and all?'

'Ay, sir,' said Joe; 'he went there on horseback, that his leg mightn't be noticed: he was the captain and wore a mask; the rest only had their faces blacked.'

'And how was he found out?'

'I'll tell you, sir,' said Joe: 't' maister 's not so fond of talking; I've no objections. He courted Sarah, Mr Moore's sarvant lass, and so it seems she would have nothing to say to him; she either didn't like his wooden leg, or she'd some notion about his being a hypocrite. Happen (for women is queer hands – we may say that amang werseln when there none of 'em nigh) she'd have encouraged him, in spite of his leg and his deceit – just to pass time like; I've known some on 'em do as mich, and some o' t' bonniest and mimmest-looking too – ay! I've seen clean, trim young things, that looked as denty and pure as daisies, and wi' time a body fun' 'em out to be nowt but stinging, venomed nettles.'

'Joe's a sensible fellow,' interjected Helstone.

'Howsiver, Sarah had another string to her bow: Fred. Murgatroyd, one of our lads, is for her, and as women judge men by their faces – and Fred. has a middling face, while Moses is none so handsome, as we all knaw – the lass took on wi' Fred. A two-three months sin', Murgatroyd and Moses chanced to meet one Sunday night; they'd both come lurking about these premises wi' the notion of counselling Sarah to tak' a bit of a walk wi' them; they fell out, had a tussel, and Fred. was worsted: for he's young and small, and Barraclough, for all he

585

has only one leg, is almost as strong as Sugden there; indeed, anybody that hears him roaring at a revival or a love-feast, may be sure he's no weakling.'

'Joe, you're insupportable,' here broke in Mr Moore. 'You spin out your explanation as Moses spins out his sermons. The long and short of it is, Murgatroyd was jealous of Barraclough; and last night, as he and a friend took shelter in a barn from a shower, they heard and saw Moses conferring with some associates within. From their discourse, it was plain he had been the leader, not only at Stilbro' Moor, but in the attack on Sykes's property: moreover they planned a deputation to wait on me this morning, which the tailor is to head, and which, in the most religious and peaceful spirit, is to entreat me to put the accursed thing out of my tent. I rode over to Whinbury this morning, got a constable and a warrant, and I am now waiting to give my friend the reception he deserves: here, meantime, comes Sykes: Mr Helstone, you must spirit him up; he feels timid at the thoughts of prosecuting.'

A gig was heard to roll into the yard: Mr Sykes entered; a tall stout man of about fifty, comely of feature, but feeble of physiognomy: he looked anxious.

'Have they been? Are they gone? Have you got him? Is it over?' he asked.

'Not yet,' returned Moore with phlegm. 'We are waiting for them.'

'They'll not come; it's near noon: better give it up; it will excite bad feeling – make a stir – cause perhaps fatal consequences.'

'*You* need not appear,' said Moore. 'I shall meet them in the yard when they come; *you* can stay here.'

'But my name must be seen in the law proceedings: a wife and family, Mr Moore – a wife and family make a man cautious.'

Moore looked disgusted. 'Give way, if you please,' said he; 'leave me to myself; I have no objection to act alone: only be assured you will not find safety in submission; your partner, Pearson, gave way, and conceded, and forbore – well, that did not prevent them from attempting to shoot him in his own house.'

'My dear sir, take a little wine and water,' recommended Mr Helstone. The wine and water was Hollands and water, as Mr Sykes discovered when he had compounded and swallowed a brimming tumbler thereof: it transfigured him in two minutes, brought the colour back to his face, and made him at least *word*-valiant. He now announced that he hoped he was above being trampled on by the common people; he was determined to endure the insolence of the working-classes no longer; he had considered of it and made up his mind to go all lengths; if money and spirit could put down these rioters, they should be put down; Mr Moore might do as he liked, but *he* – Christie Sykes – would spend his last penny in law before he would be beaten: he'd settle them, or he'd see.

'Take another glass,' urged Moore.

Mr Sykes didn't mind if he did; this was a cold morning (Sugden had found it a warm one); it was necessary to be careful at this season of the year – it was proper to take something to keep the damp out; he had a little cough already (here he coughed in attestation of the fact); something of this sort (lifting the black bottle) was excellent taken medicinally (he poured the physic into his tumbler); he didn't make a practice of drinking spirits in a morning, but occasionally it really was prudent to take precautions.

'Quite prudent, and take them by all means,' urged the host.

Mr Sykes now addressed Mr Helstone, who stood on the hearth, his shovel-hat on his head, watching him significantly with his little keen eyes.

# Shirley

'You, sir, as a clergyman,' said he, 'may feel it disagreeable to be present amidst scenes of hurry and flurry, and, I may say, peril: I dare say your nerves won't stand it; you're a man of peace, sir, but we manufacturers, living in the world and always in turmoil, get quite belligerent. Really there's an ardour excited by the thoughts of danger that makes my heart pant. When Mrs Sykes is afraid of the house being attacked and broke open – as she is every night – I get quite excited. I couldn't describe to you, sir, my feelings: really, if anybody was to come – thieves or anything – I believe I should enjoy it, such is my spirit.'

The hardest of laughs, though brief and low, and by no means insulting, was the response of the Rector. Moore would have pressed upon the heroic mill-owner a third tumbler, but the clergyman, who never transgressed, nor would suffer others in his presence to transgress the bounds of decorum, checked him.

'Enough is as good as a feast, is it not, Mr Sykes?' he said, and Mr Sykes assented; and then sat and watched Joe Scott remove the bottle at a sign from Helstone, with a self-satisfied simper on his lips, and a regretful glisten in his eye. Moore looked as if he should have liked to fool him to the top of his bent. What would a certain young kinswoman of his have said, could she have seen her dear, good, great Robert – her Coriolanus – just now? Would she have acknowledged in that mischievous sardonic visage the same face to which she had looked up with such love, which had bent over her with such gentleness last night? Was that the man who had spent so quiet an evening with his sister and his cousin – so suave to one, so tender to the other – reading Shakspeare and listening to Chénier?

Yes, it was the same man, only seen on a different side; a side Caroline had not yet fairly beheld, though perhaps she had enough sagacity faintly to suspect its existence. Well, Caroline had, doubtless, her defective side too: she was human, she must then have been very imperfect, and had she seen Moore on his very worst side, she would probably have said this to herself and excused him. Love can excuse anything except Meanness; but Meanness kills Love, cripples even Natural Affection: without Esteem, True Love cannot exist. Moore with all his faults might be esteemed; for he had no moral scrofula in his mind, no hopeless polluting taint, such, for instance, as that of falsehood; neither was he the slave of his appetites; the active life to which he had been born and bred had given him something else to do than to join the futile chase of the pleasure-hunter: he was a man undegraded, the disciple of Reason, *not* the votary of Sense. The same might be said of old Helstone: neither of these two would look, think, or speak a lie; for neither of them had the wretched black bottle, which had just been put away, any charms; both might boast a valid claim to the proud title of 'lord of the creation,' for no animal vice was lord of them: they looked and were superior beings to poor Sykes.

A sort of gathering and trampling sound was heard in the yard, and then a pause. Moore walked to the window, Helstone followed; both stood on one side, the tall junior behind the under-sized senior, looking forth carefully, so that they might not be visible from without, their sole comment on what they saw was a cynical smile flashed into each other's stern eyes.

A flourishing oratical cough was now heard, followed by the interjection, 'Whisht!' designed, as it seemed, to still the hum of several voices. Moore opened his casement an inch or two to admit sound more freely.

'Joseph Scott,' began a snuffling voice – Scott was standing sentinel at the

counting-house door – 'might we inquire if your master be within, and is to be spoken to?'

'He's within, ay!' said Joe, nonchalantly.

'Would you, then, if *you* please (emphasis on "you"), have the goodness to tell *him* that twelve gentlemen wants to see him.'

'He'd happen ax what for,' suggested Joe. 'I mught as weel tell him that at t' same time.'

'For a purpose,' was the answer. Joe entered.

'Please, sir, there's twelve gentlemen wants to see ye "for a purpose."'

'Good, Joe; I'm their man. Sugden, come when I whistle.'

Moore went out, chuckling drily. He advanced into the yard, one hand in his pocket, the other in his waistcoat, his cap brim over his eyes, shading in some measure their deep dancing ray of scorn. Twelve men waited in the yard, some in their shirt-sleeves, some in blue aprons: two figured conspicuously in the van of the party. One, a little dapper strutting man, with a turned-up nose; the other, a broad-shouldered fellow, distinguished no less by his demure face and cat-like, trustless eyes, than by a wooden leg and stout crutch: there was a kind of leer about his lips, he seemed laughing in his sleeve at some person or thing, his whole air was anything but that of a true man.

'Good-morning, Mr Barraclough,' said Moore debonnairly, for him.

'Peace be unto you!' was the answer: Mr Barraclough entirely closing his naturally half-shut eyes as he delivered it.

'I'm obliged to you: peace is an excellent thing; there's nothing I more wish for myself; but that is not all you have to say to me, I suppose? I imagine peace is not your purpose?'

'As to our purpose,' began Barraclough, 'it's one that may sound strange, and perhaps foolish to ears like yours, for the childer of this world is wiser in their generation than the childer of light.'

'To the point, if you please, and let me hear what it is.'

'Ye 'se hear, sir; if I cannot get it off, there's eleven behint can help me. It is a grand purpose, and (changing his voice from a half-sneer to a whine) it's the Looard's own purpose, and that's better.'

'Do you want a subscription to a new Ranter's chapel, Mr Barraclough? Unless your errand be something of that sort, I cannot see what you have to do with it.'

'I hadn't that duty on my mind, sir; but as Providence has led ye to mention the subject, I'll make it i' my way to tak' ony trifle ye may have to spare; the smallest contribution will be acceptable.'

With that he doffed his hat, and held it out as a begging-box; a brazen grin at the same time crossing his countenance.

'If I gave you sixpence, you would drink it.'

Barraclough uplifted the palms of his hands and the whites of his eyes, evincing in the gesture a mere burlesque of hypocrisy.

'You seem a fine fellow,' said Moore, quite coolly and drily; 'you don't care for showing me that you are a double-dyed hypocrite, that your trade is fraud: you expect indeed to make me laugh at the cleverness with which you play your coarsely farcical part, while at the same time you think you are deceiving the men behind you.'

Moses' countenance lowered; he saw he had gone too far: he was going to

# Shirley

answer, when the second leader, impatient of being hitherto kept in the background, stepped forward. This man did not look like a traitor, though he had an exceedingly self-confident and conceited air.

'Mr Moore,' commenced he, speaking also in his throat and nose, and enunciating each word very slowly, as if with a view to giving his audience time to appreciate fully the uncommon elegance of the phraseology; 'it might, perhaps, justly be said that reason rather than peace is our purpose. We come, in the first place, to request you to hear reason, and should *you* refuse, it is my duty to warn *you*, in very decided terms, that measures will be had resort to (he meant recourse), which will probably terminate in – in bringing *you* to a sense of the unwisdom, of the – the foolishness, which seems to guide and guard your perceedings as a tradesman in this – this manufacturing part of the country. Hem! . . . sir, I would beg to allude that as a furriner, coming from a distant coast, another quarter and hemisphere of this globe, thrown, as I may say, a perfect outcast on these shores – the cliffs of Albion – you have not that understanding of huz and wer ways which might conduce to the benefit of the working-classes. If, to come at once to partic'lars, you'd consider to give up this here miln, and go without further protractions straight home to where you belong, it 'ud happen be as well. I can see naught ageean such a plan. What hev ye to say tull 't, lads?' turning round to the other members of the deputation, who responded unanimously. 'Hear! hear!'

'Brayvo, Noah o' Tim's!' murmured Joe Scott, who stood behind Mr Moore. 'Moses'll niver beat that – Cliffs o' Albion, and t' other hemisphere! my certy! Did ye come fro' th' Antarctic Zone, maister? Moses is dished.'

Moses, however, refused to be dished; he thought he would try again. Casting a somewhat ireful glance at 'Noah o' Tim's,' he launched out in his turn: and now he spoke in a serious tone, relinquishing the sarcasm which he found had not answered.

'Or iver you set up the pole o' your tent amang us, Mr Moore, we lived i' peace and quietness; yea, I may say, in all loving-kindness. I am not myself an aged person as yet, but I can remember as far back as maybe some twenty year, when hand-labour were encouraged and respected, and no mischief-maker had ventured to introduce these here machines, which is so pernicious. Now, I'm not a cloth-dresser myself, but by trade a tailor; howsiver, my heart is of a softish natur': I'm a very feeling man, and when I see my brethren oppressed like my great namesake of old, I stand up for 'em; for which intent, I this day speak with you face to face, and advises you to part wi' your infernal machinery, and tak' on more hands.'

'What if I don't follow your advice, Mr Barraclough?'

'The Looard pardon you! The Looard soften your heart, sir!'

'Are you in connexion with the Wesleyans now, Mr Barraclough?'

'Praise God! Bless His Name! I'm a joined Methody!'

'Which in no respect prevents you from being at the same time a drunkard and a swindler. I saw you one night a week ago laid dead-drunk by the roadside, as I returned from Stilbro' market; and while you preach peace, you make it the business of your life to stir up dissension. You no more sympathize with the poor who are in distress, than you sympathize with me: you incite them to outrage for bad purposes of your own; so does the individual called Noah o' Tim's. You two are restless, meddling, impudent scoundrels, whose chief motive-

principle is a selfish ambition, as dangerous as it is puerile. The persons behind you are some of them honest though misguided men; but you two I count altogether bad.'

Barraclough was going to speak.

'Silence! You have had your say, and now I will have mine. As to being dictated to by you, or any Jack, Jem, or Jonathan on earth, I shall not suffer it for a moment. You desire me to quit the country; you request me to part with my machinery; in case I refuse, you threaten me. I *do* refuse – point-blank! Here I stay; and by this mill I stand; and into it will I convey the best machinery inventors can furnish. What will you do? The utmost you *can* do – and this you will never *dare* to do – is to burn down my mill, destroy its contents, and shoot me. What then? Suppose that building was a ruin and I was a corpse, what then? – you lads behind these two scamps, would that stop invention or exhaust science? – Not for the fraction of a second of time! Another and better gig-mill would rise on the ruins of this, and perhaps a more enterprising owner come in my place. Hear me! – I'll make my cloth as I please, and according to the best lights I have. In its manufacture I will employ what means I choose. Whoever, after hearing this, shall dare to interfere with me, may just take the consequences. An example shall prove I'm in earnest.'

He whistled shrill and loud. Sugden, his staff and warrant, came on to the scene.

Moore turned sharply to Barraclough: 'You were at Stilbro',' said he; 'I have proof of that. You were on the moor, – you wore a mask, – you knocked down one of my men with your own hand, – you! a preacher of the Gospel! Sugden, arrest him!'

Moses was captured. There was a cry and a rush to rescue, but the right hand which all this while had lain hidden in Moore's breast, reappearing, held out a pistol.

'Both barrels are loaded,' said he. 'I'm quite determined! – keep off!'

Stepping backwards, facing the foe as he went, he guarded his prey to the counting-house. He ordered Joe Scott to pass in with Sugden and the prisoner, and to bolt the door inside. For himself, he walked backwards and forwards along the front of the mill, looking meditatively on the ground, his hand hanging carelessly by his side, but still holding the pistol. The eleven remaining deputies watched him some time, talking under their breath to each other: at length one of them approached. This man looked very different from either of the two who had previously spoken: he was hard-favoured, but modest, and manly-looking.

'I've not much faith i' Moses Barraclough,' said he; 'and I would speak a word to you myseln, Mr Moore. It's out o' no ill-will that I'm here, for my part; it's just to mak' a effort to get things straightened, for they're sorely a crooked. Ye see we're ill off, – varry ill off: wer families is poor and pined. We're thrown out o' work wi' these frames: we can get nought to do: we can earn nought. What is to be done? Mun we say, wisht! and lig us down and dee? Nay: I've no grand words at my tongue's end, Mr Moore, but I feel that it would be a low principle for a reasonable man to starve to death like a dumb cratur': – I will n't do 't. I'm not for shedding blood: I'd neither kill a man nor hurt a man; and I'm not for pulling down mills and breaking machines: for, as ye say, that way o' going on 'll niver stop invention; but I'll talk, – I'll mak' as big a din as ever I can. Invention may be all right, but I know it isn't right for poor folks to

starve. Them that governs mun find a way to help us: they mun mak' fresh orderations. Ye'll say that's hard to do: – so mich louder mun we shout out then, for so much slacker will t' Parliament-men be to set on to a tough job.'

'Worry the Parliament-men as much as you please,' said Moore; 'but to worry the mill-owners is absurd; and I, for one, won't stand it.'

'Ye're a raight hard 'un!' returned the workman. 'Will n't ye gie us a bit o' time? – Will n't ye consent to mak' your changes rather more slowly?'

'Am I the whole body of clothiers in Yorkshire? Answer me that!'

'Ye're yourseln.'

'And only myself; and if I stopped by the way an instant, while others are rushing on, I should be trodden down. If I did as you wish me to do, I should be bankrupt in a month: and would my bankruptcy put bread into your hungry children's mouths? William Farren, neither to your dictation, nor to that of any other, will I submit. Talk to me no more about machinery; I will have my own way. I shall get new frames in to-morrow: – If you broke these, I would still get more. *I'll never give in.*'

Here the mill-bell rang twelve o'clock: it was the dinner hour. Moore abruptly turned from the deputation and re-entered his counting-house.

His last words had left a bad, harsh impression: he, at least, had 'failed in the disposing of a chance he was lord of.' By speaking kindly to William Farren, – who was a very honest man, without envy or hatred of those more happily circumstanced than himself; thinking it no hardship and no injustice to be forced to live by labour; disposed to be honourably content if he could but get work to do, – Moore might have made a friend. It seemed wonderful how he could turn from such a man without a conciliatory or a sympathizing expression. The poor fellow's face looked haggard with want: he had the aspect of a man who had not known what it was to live in comfort and plenty for weeks, perhaps months past; and yet there was no ferocity, no malignity in his countenance: it was worn, dejected, austere, but still patient. How could Moore leave him thus, with the words 'I'll never give in,' and not a whisper of good-will, or hope, or aid?

Farren, as he went home to his cottage, – once, in better times, a decent, clean, pleasant place, but now, though still clean, very dreary, because so poor – asked himself this question. He concluded that the foreign mill-owner was a selfish, an unfeeling, and, he thought, too, a foolish man. It appeared to him that emigration, had he only the means to emigrate, would be preferable to service under such a master. He felt much cast down, – almost hopeless.

On his entrance, his wife served out, in orderly sort, such dinner as she had to give him and the bairns: it was only porridge, and too little of that. Some of the younger children asked for more when they had done their portion – an application which disturbed William much: while his wife quieted them as well as she could, he left his seat, and went to the door. He whistled a cheery stave, which did not, however, prevent a broad drop or two (much more like the 'first of a thunder-shower' than those which oozed from the wound of the gladiator) from gathering on the lids of his grey eyes, and plashing thence to the threshold. He cleared his vision with his sleeve, and the melting mood over, a very stern one followed.

He still stood brooding in silence, when a gentleman in black came up – a clergyman, it might be seen at once; but neither Helstone, nor Malone, nor Donne, nor Sweeting. He might be forty years old; he was plain-looking, dark-

complexioned, and already rather grey-haired. He stooped a little in walking. His countenance, as he came on, wore an abstracted and somewhat doleful air; but, in approaching Farren, he looked up, and then a hearty expression illuminated the preoccupied, serious face.

'Is it you, William? How are you?' he asked.

'Middling, Mr Hall: how are *ye*? Will ye step in and rest ye?'

Mr Hall, whose name the reader has seen mentioned before, (and who, indeed, was vicar of Nunnely, of which parish Farren was a native, and from whence he had removed but three years ago to reside in Briarfield, for the convenience of being near Hollow's mill, where he had obtained work) entered the cottage, and, having greeted the goodwife and the children, sat down. He proceeded to talk very cheerfully about the length of time that had elapsed since the family quitted his parish, the changes which had occurred since; he answered questions touching his sister Margaret, who was inquired after with much interest; he asked questions in his turn, and at last, glancing hastily and anxiously round through his spectacles (he wore spectacles, for he was short-sighted) at the bare room, and at the meagre and wan faces of the circle about him – for the children had come round his knee, and the father and mother stood before him – he said, abruptly, –

'And how are you all? How do you get on?'

Mr Hall, be it remarked, though an accomplished scholar, not only spoke with a strong northern accent, but, on occasion, used freely north-country expressions.

'We get on poorly,' said William: 'we're all out of work. I've selled most o' t' household stuff, as ye may see; and what we're to do next, God knows.'

'Has Mr Moore turned you off?'

'He has turned us off; and I've sich an opinion of him now, that I think, if he'd tak' me on again to-morrow, I wouldn't work for him.'

'It is not like you to say so, William.'

'I know it isn't; but I'm getting different to mysel': I feel I am changing. I wad n't heed, if t' bairns and t' wife had enough to live on; but they're pinched – they're pined –'

'Well, my lad, and so are you; I see you are. These are grievous times; I see suffering wherever I turn. William, sit down; Grace, sit down; let us talk it over.'

And in order the better to talk it over, Mr Hall lifted the least of the children on to his knee, and placed his hand on the head of the next least; but when the small things began to chatter to him, he bid them 'Whisht!' and, fixing his eyes on the grate, he regarded the handful of embers which burnt there very gravely.

'Sad times!' he said, 'and they last long. It is the will of God: His will be done! but He tries us to the utmost.'

Again he reflected.

'You've no money, William, and you've nothing you could sell to raise a small sum?'

'No; I've selled t' chest o' drawers, and t' clock, and t' bit of a mahogany stand, and t' wife's bonny tea-tray and set o' cheeney 'at she brought for a portion when we were wed.'

'And if somebody lent you a pound or two, could you make any good use of it? Could you get into a new way of doing something?'

Farren did not answer; but his wife said quickly, 'Ay, I'm sure he could, sir; he's a very contriving chap, is our William. If he'd two or three pounds, he could begin selling stuff.'

'Could you, William?'

'Please God,' returned William, deliberately, 'I could buy groceries, and bits o' tapes, and thread, and what I thought would sell, and I could begin hawking at first.'

'And you know, sir,' interposed Grace, 'you're sure William would neither drink, nor idle, nor waste in any way. He's my husband, and I shouldn't praise him; but I *will* say, there's not a soberer, honester man i' England nor he is.'

'Well, I'll speak to one or two friends, and I think I can promise to let him have £5 in a day or two: as a loan, ye mind, not a gift: he must pay it back.'

'I understand, sir: I'm quite agreeable to that.'

'Meantime, there's a few shillings for you, Grace, just to keep the pot boiling till custom comes. Now, bairns, stand up in a row and say your catechism, while your mother goes and buys some dinner: for you've not had much to-day, I'll be bound. You begin, Ben. What is your name?'

Mr Hall stayed till Grace came back; then he hastily took his leave, shaking hands with both Farren and his wife: just at the door, he said to them a few brief but very earnest words of religious consolation and exhortation: with a mutual 'God bless you, sir!' 'God bless you, my friends!' they separated.

# Chapter 9

## Briarmains

essrs Helstone and Sykes began to be extremely jocose and congratulatory with Mr Moore when he returned to them after dismissing the deputation; he was so quiet, however, under their compliments upon his firmness, &c., and wore a countenance so like a still, dark day, equally beamless and breezeless, that the Rector, after glancing shrewdly into his eyes, buttoned up his felicitations with his coat, and said to Sykes, whose senses were not acute enough to enable him to discover unassisted where his presence and conversation were a nuisance: –

'Come, sir; your road and mine lie partly together: had we not better bear each other company? We'll bid Moore good-morning, and leave him to the happy fancies he seems disposed to indulge.'

'And where is Sugden?' demanded Moore, looking up.

'Ah, ha!' cried Helstone. 'I've not been quite idle while you were busy. I've been helping you a little: I flatter myself, not injudiciously. I thought it better not to lose time; so, while you were parleying with that down-looking gentleman – Farren, I think his name is – I opened this back window, shouted to

# Shirley

Murgatroyd, who was in the stable, to bring Mr Sykes's gig round; then I smuggled Sugden and brother Moses – wooden leg and all – through the aperture, and saw them mount the gig (always with our good friend Sykes's permission, of course). Sugden took the reins – he drives like Jehu, and in another quarter of an hour, Barraclough will be safe in Stilbro' jail.'

'Very good: thank you,' said Moore, 'and good-morning, gentlemen,' he added, and so politely conducted them to the door and saw them clear of his premises.

He was a taciturn, serious man the rest of the day: he did not even bandy a repartee with Joe Scott; who, for his part, said to his master only just what was absolutely necessary to the progress of business, but looked at him a good deal out of the corners of his eyes, frequently came to poke the counting-house fire for him, and once, as he was locking up for the day (the mill was then working short time, owing to the slackness of trade), observed that it was a grand evening, and he 'could wish Mr Moore to tak' a bit of a walk up th' Hollow; it would do him good.'

At this recommendation, Mr Moore burst into a short laugh, and after demanding of Joe what all this solicitude meant, and whether he took him for a woman or a child, seized the keys from his hand, and shoved him by the shoulders out of his presence. He called him back, however, ere he had reached the yard-gate.

'Joe, do you know those Farrens? They are not well off, I suppose?'

'They cannot be well off, sir, when they've not had work as a three month. Ye'd see yoursel' 'at William's sorely changed, – fair pared: they've selled most o' t' stuff out o' th' house.'

'He was not a bad workman?'

'Ye never had a better, sir, sin' ye began trade.'

'And decent people – the whole family?'

'Niver dacenter: th' wife's a raight cant body, and as clean –! ye mught eat your porridge off th' house floor: they're sorely comed down. I wish William could get a job as gardener or summat i' that way; he understands gardening weel. He once lived wi' a Scotchman that tached him the mysteries o' that craft, as they say.'

'Now, then, you can go, Joe; you need not stand there staring at me.'

'Ye've no orders to give, sir?'

'None, but for you to take yourself off.'

Which Joe did accordingly.

Spring evenings are often cold and raw, and though this had been a fine day, warm even in the morning and meridian sunshine, the air chilled at sunset, the ground crisped, and ere dusk a hoar frost was insidiously stealing over growing grass and unfolding bud. It whitened the pavement in front of Briarmains (Mr Yorke's residence), and made silent havoc among the tender plants in his garden, and on the mossy level of his lawn. As to that great tree, strong-trunked and broad-armed, which guarded the gable nearest the road, it seemed to defy a spring-night frost to harm its still bare boughs; and so did the leafless grove of walnut-trees rising tall behind the house.

In the dusk of the moonless if starry night, lights from windows shone vividly: this was no dark or lonely scene, nor even a silent one. Briarmains stood near

the highway; it was rather an old place, and had been built ere that highway was cut, and when a lane winding up through fields was the only path conducting to it. Briarfield lay scarce a mile off: its hum was heard, its glare distinctly seen. Briar-chapel, a large, new, raw, Wesleyan place of worship, rose but a hundred yards distant; and, as there was even now a prayer-meeting being held within its walls, the illumination of its windows cast a bright reflection on the road, while a hymn of a most extraordinary description, such as a very Quaker might feel himself moved by the spirit to dance to, roused cheerily all the echoes of the vicinage. The words were distinctly audible by snatches: here is a quotation or two from different strains; for the singers passed jauntily from hymn to hymn and from tune to tune, with an ease and buoyancy all their own.

*'Oh! who can explain*
*This struggle for life,*
*This travail and pain,*
*This trembling and strife?*
*Plague, earthquake, and famine,*
*And tumult and war,*
*The wonderful coming*
*Of Jesus declare!*

*'For every fight*
*Is dreadful and loud, –*
*The warrior's delight*
*Is slaughter and blood;*
*His foes overturning,*
*Till all shall expire, –*
*And this is with burning,*
*And fuel, and fire!'*

Here followed an interval of clamorous prayer, accompanied by fearful groans. A shout of 'I've found liberty!' 'Doad o' Bill's has fun' liberty!' rung from the chapel, and out all the assembly broke again.

*'What a mercy is this!*
*What a heaven of bliss!*
*How unspeakably happy am I!*
*Gather'd into the fold,*
*With thy people enroll'd,*
*With thy people to live and to die!*

*'Oh, the goodness of God*
*In employing a clod*
*His tribute of glory to raise;*
*His standard to bear,*
*And with triumph declare*
*His unspeakable riches of grace!*

# Shirley

*'Oh, the fathomless love,*
*    That has deign'd to approve*
*And prosper the work of my hands;*
*    With my pastoral crook,*
*    I went over the brook,*
*And behold I am spread into bands!*

*'Who, I ask in amaze,*
*    Hath begotten me these?*
*And inquire from what quarter they came;*
*    My full heart it replies,*
*    They are born from the skies,*
*And gives glory to God and the Lamb!'*

The stanza which followed this, after another and longer interregnum of shouts, yells, ejaculations, frantic cries, agonized groans, seemed to cap the climax of noise and zeal.

*'Sleeping on the brink of sin,*
*    Tophet gaped to take us in;*
*Mercy to our rescue flew, –*
*    Broke the snare, and brought us through.*

*'Here, as in a lion's den,*
*    Undevour'd we still remain;*
*Pass secure the watery flood,*
*    Hanging on the arm of God.*

*'Here'* –

(Terrible, most distracting to the ear was the strained shout in which the last stanza was given).

*'Here we raise our voices higher,*
*    Shout in the refiner's fire;*
*Clap our hands amidst the flame,*
*    Glory give to Jesus' name!'*

The roof of the chapel did *not* fly off; which speaks volumes in praise of its solid slating.

But if Briar-chapel seemed alive, so also did Briarmains: though certainly the mansion appeared to enjoy a quieter phase of existence than the temple; some of its windows too were a-glow: the lower casements opened upon the lawn, curtains concealed the interior, and partly obscured the ray of the candles which lit it, but they did not entirely muffle the sound of voice and laughter. We are privileged to enter that front-door, and to penetrate to the domestic sanctum.

It is not the presence of company which makes Mr Yorke's habitation lively, for there is none within it save his own family, and they are assembled in that farthest room to the right, the back-parlour.

This is the usual sitting-room of an evening. Those windows would be seen

# Shirley

by daylight to be of brilliantly-stained glass – purple and amber the predominant hues, glittering round a gravely tinted medallion in the centre of each, representing the suave head of William Shakspeare, and the serene one of John Milton. Some Canadian views hang on the walls – green forest and blue water-scenery – and in the midst of them blazes a night-eruption of Vesuvius; very ardently it glows, contrasted with the cool foam and azure of cataracts, and the dusky depths of woods.

The fire illuminating this room, reader, is such as, if you be a southern, you do not often see burning on the hearth of a private apartment; it is a clear, hot, coal fire, heaped high in the ample chimney. Mr Yorke *will* have such fires even in warm summer weather: he sits beside it with a book in his hand, a little round stand at his elbow supporting a candle – but he is not reading, he is watching his children. Opposite to him sits his lady – a personage whom I might describe minutely, but I feel no vocation to the task. I see her, though, very plainly before me: a large woman of the gravest aspect, care on her front and on her shoulders – but not overwhelming, inevitable care – rather the sort of voluntary, exemplary cloud and burden people ever carry who deem it their duty to be gloomy. Ah, well-a-day! Mrs Yorke had that notion, and grave as Saturn she was, morning, noon, and night; and hard things she thought of any unhappy wight – especially of the female sex – who dared in her presence to show the light of a gay heart on a sunny countenance. In her estimation, to be mirthful was to be profane; to be cheerful was to be frivolous; she drew no distinctions. Yet she was a very good wife, a very careful mother, looked after her children unceasingly, was sincerely attached to her husband; only, the worst of it was, if she could have had her will, she would not have permitted him to have any friend in the world beside herself: all his relations were insupportable to her, and she kept them at arm's length.

Mr Yorke and she agreed perfectly well; yet he was naturally a social, hospitable man – an advocate for family unity – and in his youth, as has been said, he liked none but lively cheerful women. Why he chose her – how they contrived to suit each other, is a problem puzzling enough, but which might soon be solved if one had time to go into the analysis of the case. Suffice it here to say, that Yorke had a shadowy as well as a sunny side to his character, and that his shadowy side found sympathy and affinity in the whole of his wife's uniformly overcast nature. For the rest, she was a strong-minded woman; never said a weak or a trite thing: took stern, democratic views of society, and rather cynical ones of human nature; considered herself perfect and safe, and the rest of the world all wrong. Her main fault was a brooding, eternal, immitigable suspicion of all men, things, creeds, and parties; this suspicion was a mist before her eyes, a false guide in her path, wherever she looked, wherever she turned.

It may be supposed that the children of such a pair were not likely to turn out quite ordinary, common-place beings; and they were not. You see six of them, reader: the youngest is a baby on the mother's knee; it is all her own yet – and that one she has not yet begun to doubt, suspect, condemn; it derives its sustenance from her, it hangs on her, it clings to her, it loves her above everything else in the world: she is sure of that, because, as it lives by her, it cannot be otherwise, therefore she loves it.

The two next are girls, Rose and Jessy; they are both now at their father's knee; they seldom go near their mother, except when obliged to do so. Rose, the

# Shirley

elder, is twelve years old; she is like her father, – the most like him of the whole group, – but it is a granite head copied in ivory; all is softened in colour and line. Yorke himself has a harsh face; his daughter's is not harsh, neither is it quite pretty; it is simple, – childlike in feature; the round cheeks bloom: as to the grey eyes, they are otherwise than childlike, – a serious soul lights them, – a young soul yet, but it will mature, if the body lives; and neither father nor mother have a spirit to compare with it. Partaking of the essence of each, it will one day be better than either, – stronger, much purer, more aspiring. Rose is a still, sometimes a stubborn girl now: her mother wants to make of her such a woman as she is herself, – a woman of dark and dreary duties, – and Rose has a mind full-set, thick-sown with the germs of ideas her mother never knew. It is agony to her often to have these ideas trampled on and repressed. She has never rebelled yet; but if hard driven, she will rebel one day, and then it will be once for all. Rose loves her father: her father does not rule her with a rod of iron; he is good to her. He sometimes fears she will not live, so bright are the sparks of intelligence which, at moments, flash from her glance, and gleam in her language. This idea makes him often sadly tender to her.

He has no idea that little Jessy will die young, she is so gay and chattering, arch – original even now; passionate when provoked, but most affectionate if caressed; by turns gentle and rattling; exacting yet generous; fearless – of her mother for instance, whose irrationally hard and strict rule she has often defied – yet reliant on any who will help her. Jessy, with her little piquant face, engaging prattle, and winning ways, is made to be a pet; and her father's pet she accordingly is. It is odd that the doll should resemble her mother feature by feature, as Rose resembles her father, and yet the physiognomy – how different!

Mr Yorke, if a magic mirror were now held before you, and if therein were shown you your two daughters as they will be twenty years from this night, what would you think? The magic mirror is here: you shall learn their destinies – and first that of your little life, Jessy.

Do you know this place? No, you never saw it; but you recognize the nature of these trees, this foliage, – the cypress, the willow, the yew. Stone crosses like these are not unfamiliar to you, nor are these dim garlands of everlasting flowers. Here is the place; green sod and a grey marble headstone – Jessy sleeps below. She lived through an April day; much loved was she, much loving. She often, in her brief life, shed tears, she had frequent sorrows; she smiled between, gladdening whatever saw her. Her death was tranquil and happy in Rose's guardian arms, for Rose had been her stay and defence through many trials: the dying and the watching English girls were at that hour alone in a foreign country, and the soil of that country gave Jessy a grave.

Now, behold Rose, two years later. The crosses and garlands looked strange, but the hills and woods of this landscape look still stranger. This, indeed, is far from England; remote must be the shores which wear that wild, luxuriant aspect. This is some virgin solitude: unknown birds flutter round the skirts of that forest; no European river this, on whose banks Rose sits thinking. The little, quiet Yorkshire girl is a lonely emigrant in some region of the southern hemisphere. Will she ever come back?

The three eldest of the family are all boys: Matthew, Mark and Martin. They are seated together in that corner, engaged in some game. Observe their three heads: much alike at a first glance; at a second, different; at a third,

# Shirley

contrasted. Dark-haired, dark-eyed, red-cheeked, are the whole trio; small English features they all possess; all own a blended resemblance to sire and mother, and yet a distinctive physiognomy, mark of a separate character, belongs to each.

I shall not say much about Matthew, the first-born of the house; though it is impossible to avoid gazing at him long, and conjecturing what qualities that visage hides or indicates. He is no plain-looking boy: that jet-black hair, white brow, high-coloured cheek, those quick, dark eyes, are good points in their way. How is it that, look as long as you will, there is but one object in the room, and that the most sinister, to which Matthew's face seems to bear an affinity, and which, ever and anon, it reminds you strangely – the eruption of Vesuvius. Flame and shadow seem the component parts of that lad's soul: no daylight in it, and no sunshine, and no pure cool moonbeam ever shone there. He has an English frame, but, apparently, not an English mind: you would say, an Italian stiletto in a sheath of British workmanship. He is crossed in the game – look at his scowl. Mr Yorke sees it, and what does he say? In a low voice, he pleads: 'Mark and Martin, don't anger your brother.' And this is ever the tone adopted by both parents. Theoretically, they decry partiality; no rights of primogeniture are to be allowed in that house; but Matthew is never to be vexed, never to be opposed: they avert provocation from him as assiduously as they would avert fire from a barrel of gunpowder. 'Concede, conciliate,' is their motto wherever he is concerned. The republicans are fast making a tyrant of their own flesh and blood. This the younger scions know and feel, and at heart they all rebel against the injustice: they cannot read their parents' motives; they only see the difference of treatment. The dragon's teeth are already sown amongst Mr Yorke's young olive-branches: discord will one day be the harvest.

Mark is a bonnie-looking boy, the most regular-featured of the family; he is exceedingly calm; his smile is shrewd; he can say the driest, most cutting things in the quietest of tones. Despite his tranquillity, a somewhat heavy brow speaks temper, and reminds you that the smoothest waters are not always the safest. Besides, he is too still, unmoved, phlegmatic, to be happy. Life will never have much joy in it for Mark: by the time he is five-and-twenty, he will wonder why people ever laugh, and think all fools who seem merry. Poetry will not exist for Mark, either in literature or in life; its best effusions will sound to him mere rant and jargon: enthusiasm will be his aversion and contempt. Mark will have no youth: while he looks juvenile and blooming, he will be already middle-aged in mind. His body is now fourteen years of age, but his soul is already thirty.

Martin, the youngest of the three, owns another nature. Life may, or may not, be brief for him; but it will certainly be brilliant: he will pass through all its illusions, half believe in them, wholly enjoy them, then outlive them. That boy is not handsome – not so handsome as either of his brothers: he is plain; there is a husk upon him, a dry shell, and he will wear it till he is near twenty; then he will put it off: about that period, he will make himself handsome. He will wear uncouth manners till that age, perhaps homely garments; but the chrysalis will retain the power of transfiguring itself into the butterfly, and such transfiguration will, in due season, take place. For a space, he will be vain, probably a downright puppy, eager for pleasure, and desirous of admiration; athirst, too, for knowledge. He will want all that the world can give him, both of enjoyment and lore; he will, perhaps, take deep draughts at each fount. That

thirst satisfied – what next? I know not. Martin might be a remarkable man: whether he will or not, the seer is powerless to predict: on that subject, there has been no open vision.

Take Mr Yorke's family in the aggregate, there is as much mental power in those six young heads, as much originality, as much activity and vigour of brain, as – divided amongst half a dozen common-place broods – would give to each rather more than an average amount of sense and capacity. Mr Yorke knows this and is proud of his race. Yorkshire has such families here and there amongst her hills and wolds – peculiar, racy, vigorous; of good blood and strong brain; turbulent somewhat in the pride of their strength, and intractable in the force of their native powers; wanting polish, wanting consideration, wanting docility, but sound, spirited, and true-bred as the eagle on the cliff or the steed in the steppe.

A low tap is heard at the parlour door; the boys have been making such a noise over their game, and little Jessy, besides, has been singing so sweet a Scotch song to her father – who delights in Scotch and Italian songs, and has taught his musical little daughter some of the best – that the ring at the outer door was not observed.

'Come in,' says Mrs Yorke, in that conscientiously constrained and solemnized voice of hers, which ever modulates itself to a funeral dreariness of tone, though the subject it is exercised upon be but to give orders for the making of a pudding in the kitchen, to bid the boys hang up their caps in the hall, or to call the girls to their sewing: 'Come in!' And in came Robert Moore.

Moore's habitual gravity, as well as his abstemiousness (for the case of spirit-decanters is never ordered up when he pays an evening visit), has so far recommended him to Mrs Yorke, that she has not yet made him the subject of private animadversions with her husband: she has not yet found out that he is hampered by a secret intrigue which prevents him from marrying, or that he is a wolf in sheep's clothing; discoveries which she made at an early date after marriage concerning most of her husband's bachelor friends, and excluded them from her board accordingly: which part of her conduct, indeed, might be said to have its just and sensible, as well as its harsh side.

'Well, is it you?' she says to Mr Moore, as he comes up to her and gives his hand. 'What are you roving about at this time of night for? You should be at home.'

'Can a single man be said to have a home, madam?' he asks.

'Pooh!' says Mrs Yorke, who despises conventional smoothness quite as much as her husband does, and practices it as little, and whose plain speaking, on all occasions, is carried to a point calculated, sometimes, to awaken admiration, but oftener alarm – 'Pooh! you need not talk nonsense to me; a single man can have a home if he likes. Pray, does not your sister make a home for you?'

'Not she,' joined in Mr Yorke. 'Hortense is an honest lass; but when I was Robert's age, I had five or six sisters, all as decent and proper as she is; but you see, Hesther, for all that, it did not hinder me from looking out for a wife.'

'And sorely he has repented marrying me,' added Mrs Yorke, who liked occasionally to crack a dry jest against matrimony, even though it should be at her own expense. 'He has repented it in sackcloth and ashes, Robert Moore, as you may well believe when you see his punishment (here she pointed to her children). Who would burden themselves with such a set of great, rough lads

as those, if they could help it? It is not only bringing them into the world, though that is bad enough, but they are all to feed, to clothe, to rear, to settle in life. Young sir, when you feel tempted to marry, think of our four sons and two daughters, and look twice before you leap.'

'I am not tempted now, at any rate: I think these are not times for marrying or giving in marriage.'

A lugubrious sentiment of this sort was sure to obtain Mrs Yorke's approbation: she nodded and groaned acquiescence; but in a minute she said: –

'I make little account of the wisdom of a Solomon of your age; it will be upset by the first fancy that crosses you. Meantime, sit down, sir: you can talk, I suppose, as well sitting as standing?'

This was her way of inviting her guest to take a chair; he had no sooner obeyed her, than little Jessy jumped from her father's knee, and ran into Mr Moore's arms, which were very promptly held out to receive her.

'You talk of marrying him,' said she to her mother, quite indignantly, as she was lifted lightly to his knee, 'and he is married now, or as good: he promised that I should be his wife last summer, the first time he saw me in my new white frock and blue sash. Didn't he, father?' (These children were not accustomed to say papa and mamma; their mother would allow no such 'namby-pamby.')

'Ay, my little lassie, he promised; I'll bear witness. But make him say it over again now, Jessy: such as he are only false loons.'

'He is not false: he is too bonnie to be false,' said Jessy, looking up to her tall sweetheart with the fullest confidence in his faith.

'Bonnie!' cried Mr Yorke; 'that's the reason that he should be, and proof that he is – a scoundrel.'

'But he looks too sorrowful to be false,' here interposed a quiet voice from behind the father's chair. 'If he were always laughing, I should think he forgot promises soon, but Mr Moore never laughs.'

'Your sentimental buck is the greatest cheat of all, Rose,' remarked Mr Yorke.

'He's not sentimental,' said Rose.

Mr Moore turned to her with a little surprise, smiling at the same time.

'How do you know I am not sentimental, Rose?'

'Because I heard a lady say you were not.'

'Voilà, qui devient intéressant!' exclaimed Mr Yorke, hitching his chair nearer the fire. 'A lady! That has quite a romantic twang: we must guess who it is. Rosy, whisper the name low to your father: don't let *him* hear.'

'Rose, don't be too forward to talk,' here interrupted Mrs Yorke, in her usual kill-joy fashion; 'nor Jessy either: it becomes all children, especially girls, to be silent in the presence of their elders.'

'Why have we tongues, then?' asked Jessy, pertly; while Rose only looked at her mother with an expression that seemed to say, she should take that maxim in, and think it over at her leisure. After two minutes' grave deliberation, she asked, –

'And why especially girls, mother?'

'Firstly, because I say so; and, secondly, because discretion and reserve is a girl's best wisdom.'

'My dear madam,' observed Moore, 'what you say is excellent: it reminds me, indeed, of my dear sister's observations; but really it is not applicable to these

# Shirley

little ones. Let Rose and Jessy talk to me freely, or my chief pleasure in coming here is gone. I like their prattle: it does me good.'

'Does it not?' asked Jessy. 'More good than if the rough lads came round you: you call them rough, mother, yourself.'

'Yes, mignonne, a thousand times more good: I have rough lads enough about me all day long, poulet.'

'There are plenty of people,' continued she, 'who take notice of the boys: all my uncles and aunts seem to think their nephews better than their nieces; and when gentlemen come here to dine, it is always Matthew, and Mark, and Martin, that are talked to, and never Rose and me. Mr Moore is *our* friend, and we'll keep him: but mind, Rose, he's not so much your friend as he is mine: he is my *particular acquaintance*; remember that!' And she held up her small hand with an admonitory gesture.

Rose was quite accustomed to be admonished by that small hand; her will daily bent itself to that of the impetuous little Jessy: she was guided – overruled by Jessy in a thousand things. On all occasions of show and pleasure, Jessy took the lead, and Rose fell quietly into the background; whereas, when the disagreeables of life – its work and privations were in question, Rose instinctively took upon her, in addition to her own share, what she could of her sister's. Jessy had already settled it in her mind that she, when she was old enough, was to be married; Rose, she decided, must be an old maid, to live with her, look after her children, keep her house. This state of things is not uncommon between two sisters, where one is plain and the other pretty; but in this case, if there *was* a difference in external appearance, Rose had the advantage: her face was more regular-featured than that of the piquant little Jessy. Jessy, however, was destined to possess, along with sprightly intelligence and vivacious feeling, the gift of fascination, the power to charm when, where, and whom she would. Rose was to have a fine, generous soul, a noble intellect profoundly cultivated, a heart as true as steel, but the manner to attract was not to be hers.

'Now, Rose, tell me the name of this lady who denied that I was sentimental,' urged Mr Moore.

Rose had no idea of tantalization, or she would have held him a while in doubt; she answered briefly: –

'I can't: I don't know her name.'

'Describe her to me: what was she like? Where did you see her?'

'When Jessy and I went to spend the day at Whinbury with Kate and Susan Pearson, who were just come home from school, there was a party at Mrs Pearson's, and some grown-up ladies were sitting in a corner of the drawing-room talking about you.'

'Did you know none of them?'

'Hannah, and Harriet, and Dora, and Mary Sykes.'

'Good. Were they abusing me, Rosy?'

'Some of them were: they called you a misanthrope: I remember the word – I looked for it in the dictionary when I came home: it means a man-hater.'

'What besides?'

'Hannah Sykes said you were a solemn puppy.'

'Better!' cried Mr Yorke, laughing. 'Oh! excellent! Hannah – that's the one with the red hair: a fine girl, but half-witted.'

'She has wit enough for me, it appears,' said Moore. 'A solemn puppy, indeed! Well, Rose, go on.'

'Miss Pearson said she believed there was a good deal of affectation about you, and that with your dark hair and pale face, you looked to her like some sort of a sentimental noodle.'

Again Mr Yorke laughed: Mrs Yorke even joined in this time. 'You see in what esteem you are held behind your back,' said she; 'yet I believe *that* Miss Pearson would like to catch you: she set her cap at you when you first came into the country, old as she is.'

'And who contradicted her, Rosy?' inquired Moore.

'A lady whom I don't know, because she never visits here, though I see her every Sunday at church; she sits in the pew near the pulpit. I generally look at her, instead of looking at my prayer-book; for she is like a picture in our dining-room, that woman with the dove in her hand: at least she has eyes like it, and a nose too, a straight nose, that makes all her face look, somehow, what I call clear.'

'And you don't know her!' exclaimed Jessy, in a tone of exceeding surprise. 'That's so like Rose. Mr Moore, I often wonder in what sort of a world my sister lives; I am sure she does not live all her time in this: one is continually finding out that she is quite ignorant of some little matter which everybody else knows. To think of her going solemnly to church every Sunday, and looking all service-time at one particular person, and never so much as asking that person's name! She means Caroline Helstone, the Rector's niece: I remember all about it. Miss Helstone was quite angry with Anne Pearson: she said, "Robert Moore is neither affected nor sentimental; you mistake his character utterly, or rather not one of you here knows anything about it." Now, shall I tell you what she is like? I can tell what people are like, and how they are dressed, better than Rose can.'

'Let us hear.'

'She is nice; she is fair; she has a pretty white slender throat; she has long curls, not stiff ones, they hang loose and soft, their colour is brown but not dark; she speaks quietly, with a clear tone; she never makes a bustle in moving; she often wears a grey silk dress; she is neat all over: her gowns, and her shoes, and her gloves always fit her. She is what I call a lady, and when I am as tall as she is, I mean to be like her. Shall I suit you if I am? Will you really marry me?'

Moore stroked Jessy's hair: for a minute he seemed as if he would draw her nearer to him, but instead he put her a little farther off.

'Oh! you won't have me? You push me away.'

'Why, Jessy, you care nothing about me: you never come to see me now at the Hollow.'

'Because you don't ask me.'

Hereupon Mr Moore gave both the little girls an invitation to pay him a visit next day, promising, that as he was going to Stilbro' in the morning, he would buy them each a present, of what nature he would not then declare, but they must come and see. Jessy was about to reply, when one of the boys unexpectedly broke in.

'I know that Miss Helstone you have all been palavering about: she's an ugly girl. I hate her! I hate all womenites. I wonder what they were made for.'

'Martin!' said his father – for Martin it was – the lad only answered by

# Shirley

turning his cynical young face, half-arch, half-truculent, towards the paternal chair. 'Martin, my lad, thou'rt a swaggering whelp, now; thou wilt some day be an outrageous puppy: but stick to those sentiments of thine. See, I'll write down the words now i' my pocket book. (The senior took out a morocco-covered book, and deliberately wrote therein.) Ten years hence, Martin, if thou and I be both alive at that day, I'll remind thee of that speech.'

'I'll say the same then: I mean always to hate women; they're such dolls: they do nothing but dress themselves finely, and go swimming about to be admired. I'll never marry: I'll be a bachelor.'

'Stick to it! stick to it! Hesther (addressing his wife) I was like him when I was his age, a regular misogamist; and behold! by the time I was three-and-twenty, – being then a tourist in France and Italy, and the Lord knows where! – I curled my hair every night before I went to bed, and wore a ring i' my ear, and would have worn one i' my nose if it had been the fashion – and all that I might make mysel' pleasing and charming to the ladies. Martin will do the like.'

'Will I? Never! I've more sense. What a Guy you were, father! As to dressing, I make this vow: I'll never dress more finely than as you see me at present. Mr Moore, I'm clad in blue cloth from top to toe, and they laugh at me, and call me sailor at the grammar-school. I laugh louder at them, and say they are all magpies and parrots, with their coats one colour, and their waistcoats another, and their trousers a third. I'll always wear blue cloth, and nothing but blue cloth: it is beneath a human being's dignity to dress himself in parti-coloured garments.'

'Ten years hence, Martin, no tailor's shop will have choice of colours varied enough for thy exacting taste; no perfumer's stores essences exquisite enough for thy fastidious senses.'

Martin looked disdain, but vouchsafed no further reply. Meantime Mark, who for some minutes had been rummaging amongst a pile of books on a side-table, took the word. He spoke in a peculiarly slow, quiet voice, and with an expression of still irony in his face not easy to describe.

'Mr Moore,' said he, 'you think perhaps it was a compliment on Miss Caroline Helstone's part to say you were not sentimental. I thought you appeared confused when my sisters told you the words, as if you felt flattered: you turned red, just like a certain vain little lad at our school, who always thinks proper to blush when he gets a rise in the class. For your benefit, Mr Moore, I've been looking up the word "sentimental" in the dictionary, and I find it to mean "tinctured with sentiment." On examining further, "sentiment" is explained to be, thought, idea, notion. A sentimental man, then, is one who has thoughts, ideas, notions; an unsentimental man is one destitute of thought, idea, or notion.'

And Mark stopped: he did not smile, he did not look round for admiration: he had said his say, and was silent.

'Ma foi! mon ami,' observed Mr Moore to Yorke; 'ce sont vraiment des enfants terribles, que les vôtres!'

Rose, who had been listening attentively to Mark's speech, replied to him:–

'There are different kinds of thoughts, ideas, and notions,' said she, 'good and bad: sentimental must refer to the bad, or Miss Helstone must have taken it in that sense, for she was not blaming Mr Moore; she was defending him.'

# Shirley

'That's my kind little advocate!' said Moore, taking Rose's hand.

'She was defending him,' repeated Rose, 'as I should have done had I been in her place, for the other ladies seemed to speak spitefully.'

'Ladies always do speak spitefully,' observed Martin; 'it is the nature of womenites to be spiteful.'

Matthew now, for the first time, opened his lips: –

'What a fool Martin is, to be always gabbling about what he does not understand.'

'It is my privilege, as a freeman, to gabble on whatever subject I like,' responded Martin.

'You use it, or rather abuse it, to such an extent,' rejoined the elder brother, 'that you prove you ought to have been a slave.'

'A slave! a slave! That to a Yorke, and from a Yorke! This fellow,' he added, standing up at the table, and pointing across it to Matthew, – 'this fellow forgets, what every cottier in Briarfield knows, that all born of our house have that arched instep under which water can flow – proof that there has not been a slave of the blood for three hundred years.'

'Mountebank!' said Matthew.

'Lads, be silent!' exclaimed Mr Yorke. 'Martin, you are a mischief-maker: there would have been no disturbance, but for you.'

'Indeed! Is that correct? Did I begin, or did Matthew? Had I spoken to him when he accused me of gabbling like a fool?'

'A presumptuous fool!' repeated Matthew.

Here Mrs Yorke commenced rocking herself – rather a portentous movement with her, as it was occasionally followed, especially when Matthew was worsted in a conflict, by a fit of hysterics.

'I don't see why I should bear insolence from Matthew Yorke, or what right he has to use bad language to me,' observed Martin.

'He has no right, my lad; but forgive your brother until seventy and seven times,' said Mr Yorke soothingly.

'Always alike, and theory and practice always adverse!' murmured Martin as he turned to leave the room.

'Where art thou going, my son?' asked the father.

'Somewhere where I shall be safe from insult: if in this house I can find any such place.'

Matthew laughed very insolently: Martin threw a strange look at him, and trembled through all his slight lad's frame, but he restrained himself.

'I suppose there is no objection to my withdrawing?' he inquired.

'No; go, my lad: but remember not to bear malice.'

Martin went, and Matthew sent another insolent laugh after him. Rose, lifting her fair head from Moore's shoulder, against which, for a moment, it had been resting, said, as she directed a steady gaze to Matthew – 'Martin is grieved, and you are glad; but I would rather be Martin than you: I dislike your nature.'

Here Mr Moore, by way of averting, or at least escaping, a scene – which a sob from Mrs Yorke warned him was likely to come on – rose, and putting Jessy off his knee, he kissed her and Rose; reminding them, at the same time, to be sure and come to the Hollow in good time to-morrow afternoon: then, having taken leave of his hostess, he said to Mr Yorke – 'May I speak a word

# Shirley

with you?' and was followed by him from the room. Their brief conference took place in the hall.

'Have you employment for a good workman?' asked Moore.

'A nonsense question in these times, when you know that every master has many good workmen to whom he cannot give full employment.'

'You must oblige me by taking on this man, if possible.'

'My lad, I can take on no more hands to oblige all England.'

'It does not signify; I must find him a place somewhere.'

'Who is he?'

'William Farren.'

'I know William; a right-down honest man is William.'

'He has been out of work three months; he has a large family: we are sure they cannot live without wages: he was one of a deputation of cloth-dressers who came to me this morning to complain and threaten. William did not threaten: he only asked me to give them rather more time, – to make my changes more slowly. You know I cannot do that: straitened on all sides as I am, I have nothing for it but to push on. I thought it would be idle to palaver long with them. I sent them away, after arresting a rascal amongst them, whom I hope to transport – a fellow who preaches at the chapel yonder sometimes.'

'Not Moses Barraclough?'

'Yes.'

'Ah! you've arrested him? Good! Then out of a scoundrel you're going to make a martyr: you've done a wise thing.'

'I've done a right thing. Well, the short and the long of it is, I'm determined to get Farren a place, and I reckon on you to give him one.'

'This is cool, however!' exclaimed Mr Yorke. 'What right have you to reckon on me to provide for your dismissed workmen? What do I know about your Farrens and your Williams? I've heard he's an honest man; but am I to support all the honest men in Yorkshire? You may say that would be no great charge to undertake; but great or little I'll none of it.'

'Come, Mr Yorke, what can you find for him to do?'

'I find! You'll make me use language I'm not accustomed to use. I wish you would go home – here is the door – set off.'

Moore sat down on one of the hall chairs.

'You can't give him work in your mill – good – but you have land: find him some occupation on your land, Mr Yorke.'

'Bob, I thought you cared nothing about our "lourdauds de paysans:" I don't understand this change.'

'I do: the fellow spoke to me nothing but truth and sense. I answered him just as roughly as I did the rest, who jabbered mere gibberish. I couldn't make distinctions there and then: his appearance told what he had gone through lately clearer than his words: but where is the use of explaining? Let him have work.'

'Let him have it yourself. If you are so very much in earnest, strain a point.'

'If there was a point left in my affairs to strain, I would strain it till it cracked again; but I received letters this morning which show me pretty nearly where I stand, and it is not far off the end of the plank. My foreign market, at any rate, is gorged. If there is no change – if there dawns no prospect of peace – if the Orders in Council are not, at least, suspended, so as to open our way in the West—I do not know where I am to turn. I see no more light than if I were

606

sealed in a rock; so that for me to pretend to offer a man a livelihood would be to do a dishonest thing.'

'Come, let us take a turn on the front: it is a starlight night,' said Mr Yorke.

They passed out, closing the front-door after them, and, side by side, paced the frost-white pavement to and fro.

'Settle about Farren at once,' urged Mr Moore. 'You have large fruit-gardens at Yorke Mills: he is a good gardener: give him work there.'

'Well, so be it. I'll send for him to-morrow, and we'll see. And now, my lad, you're concerned about the condition of your affairs?'

'Yes: a second failure – which I may delay, but which, at this moment, I see no way finally to avert – would blight the name of Moore completely; and you are aware I had fine intentions of paying off every debt, and re-establishing the old firm on its former basis.'

'You want capital – that's all you want.'

'Yes; but you might as well say that breath is all a dead man wants to live.'

'I know – I know capital is not to be had for the asking; and if you were a married man, and had a family, like me, I should think your case pretty nigh desperate; but the young and unencumbered have chances peculiar to themselves. I hear gossip now and then about your being on the eve of marriage with this miss and that; but I suppose it is none of it true?'

'You may well suppose that: I think I am not in a position to be dreaming of marriage. Marriage! I cannot bear the word: it sounds so silly and utopian. I have settled it decidedly that marriage and love are superfluities, intended only for the rich, who live at ease, and have no need to take thought for the morrow; or desperations, the last and reckless joy of the deeply wretched, who never hope to rise out of the slough of their utter poverty.'

'I should not think so if I were circumstanced as you are: I should think I could very likely get a wife with a few thousands, who would suit both me and my affairs.'

'I wonder where?'

'Would you try, if you had a chance?'

'I don't know: it depends on – in short, it depends on many things.'

'Would you take an old woman?'

'I'd rather break stones on the road.'

'So would I. Would you take an ugly one?'

'Bah! I hate ugliness and delight in beauty: my eyes and heart, Yorke, take pleasure in a sweet, young, fair face, as they are repelled by a grim, rugged, meagre one: soft delicate lines and hues please – harsh ones prejudice me. I won't have an ugly wife.'

'Not if she were rich?'

'Not if she were dressed in gems. I could not love – I could not fancy – I could not endure her. My taste must have satisfaction, or disgust would break out in despotism – or worse – freeze to utter iciness.'

'What, Bob, if you married an honest, good-natured, and wealthy lass, though a little hard-favoured, couldn't you put up with the high cheek-bones, the rather wide mouth, and reddish hair?'

'I'll never try, I tell you. Grace at least I *will* have, and youth and symmetry – yes, and what I call beauty.'

'And poverty, and a nursery full of bairns you can neither clothe nor feed,

and very soon an anxious faded mother – and then bankruptcy, discredit – a life-long struggle.'

'Let me alone, Yorke.'

'If you are romantic, Robert, and especially if you are already in love, it is of no use talking.'

'I am not romantic. I am stript of romance as bare as the white tenters in that field are of cloth.'

'Always use such figures of speech, lad; I can understand them: and there is no love-affair to disturb your judgment?'

'I thought I had said enough on that subject before. Love for me? Stuff!'

'Well, then; if you are sound both in heart and head, there is no reason why you should not profit by a good chance if it offers: therefore, wait and see.'

'You are quite oracular, Yorke.'

'I think I am a bit i' that line. I promise ye naught and I advise ye naught; but I bid ye keep your heart up, and be guided by circumstances.'

'My namesake the physician's almanack could not speak more guardedly.'

'In the mean time, I care naught about ye, Robert Moore: ye are nothing akin to me or mine, and whether ye lose or find a fortune it mak's no difference to me. Go home, now: it has stricken ten. Miss Hortense will be wondering where ye are.'

# Chapter 10

## Old Maids

ime wore on, and spring matured. The surface of England began to look pleasant: her fields grew green, her hills fresh, her gardens blooming; but at heart she was no better: still her poor were wretched, still their employers were harassed: commerce, in some of its branches, seemed threatened with paralysis, for the war continued; England's blood was shed and her wealth lavished: all, it seemed, to attain most inadequate ends. Some tidings there were indeed occasionally of successes in the Peninsula, but these came in slowly; long intervals occurred between, in which no note was heard but the insolent self-felicitations of Bonaparte on his continued triumphs. Those who suffered from the results of the war felt this tedious, and – as they thought – hopeless, struggle against what their fears or their interests taught them to regard as an invincible power, most insufferable: they demanded peace on any terms: men like Yorke and Moore – and there were thousands whom the war placed where it placed them, shuddering on the verge of bankruptcy – insisted on peace with the energy of desperation.

They held meetings; they made speeches; they got up petitions to extort this boon: on what terms it was made, they cared not.

# Shirley

All men, taken singly, are more or less selfish; and taken in bodies they are intensely so. The British merchant is no exception to this rule: the mercantile classes illustrate it strikingly. These classes certainly think too exclusively of making money: they are too oblivious of every national consideration but that of extending England's (*i.e.* their own) commerce. Chivalrous feeling, disinterestedness, pride in honour, is too dead in their hearts. A land ruled by them alone would too often make ignominious submission – not at all from the motives Christ teaches, but rather from those Mammon instils. During the late war, the tradesmen of England would have endured buffets from the French on the right cheek and on the left; their cloak they would have given to Napoleon, and then have politely offered him their coat also, nor would they have withheld their waistcoat if urged: they would have prayed permission only to retain their one other garment, for the sake of the purse in its pocket. Not one spark of spirit, not one symptom of resistance would they have shown till the hand of the Corsican bandit had grasped that beloved purse; *then*, perhaps, transfigured at once into British bull-dogs, they would have sprung at the robber's throat, and there they would have fastened, and there hung – inveterate, insatiable, till the treasure had been restored. Tradesmen, when they speak against war, always profess to hate it because it is a bloody and barbarous proceeding: you would think, to hear them talk, that they are peculiarly civilized – especially gentle and kindly of disposition to their fellow-men. This is not the case. Many of them are extremely narrow and cold-hearted, have no good feeling for any class but their own, are distant – even hostile to all others; call them useless; seem to question their right to exist; seem to grudge them the very air they breathe, and to think the circumstance of their eating, drinking, and living in decent houses, quite unjustifiable. They do not know what others do in the way of helping, pleasing, or teaching their race; they will not trouble themselves to inquire: whoever is not in trade is accused of eating the bread of idleness, of passing a useless existence. Long may it be ere England really becomes a nation of shopkeepers!

We have already said that Moore was no self-sacrificing patriot, and we have also explained what circumstances rendered him specially prone to confine his attention and efforts to the furtherance of his individual interest; accordingly, when he felt himself urged a second time to the brink of ruin, none struggled harder than he against the influences which would have thrust him over. What he *could* do towards stirring agitation in the north against the war, he did, and he instigated others whose money and connexions gave them more power than he possessed. Sometimes, by flashes, he felt there was little reason in the demands his party made on Government: when he heard of all Europe threatened by Bonaparte, and of all Europe arming to resist him; when he saw Russia menaced, and beheld Russia rising, incensed and stern, to defend her frozen soil, her wild provinces of serfs, her dark native despotism, from the tread, the yoke, the tyranny of a foreign victor, he knew that England, a free realm, could not *then* depute her sons to make concessions and propose terms to the unjust, grasping French leader. When news came from time to time of the movements of that MAN then representing England in the Peninsula; of his advance from success to success – that advance so deliberate but so unswerving, so circumspect but so certain, so 'unhasting' but so 'unresting;' when he read Lord Wellington's own despatches in the columns of the newspapers, documents written by Modesty to the dictation of Truth – Moore confessed at heart that a power was with the

troops of Britain, of that vigilant, enduring, genuine, unostentatious sort, which must win victory to the side it led, in the end. In the end! but that end, he thought, was yet far off; and meantime he, Moore, as an individual, would be crushed, his hopes ground to dust: it was himself he had to care for, his hopes he had to pursue, and he would fulfil his destiny.

He fulfilled it so vigorously that erelong he came to a decisive rupture with his old Tory friend the Rector. They quarrelled at a public meeting, and afterwards exchanged some pungent letters in the newspapers. Mr Helstone denounced Moore as a Jacobin, ceased to see him, would not even speak to him when they met: he intimated also to his niece, very distinctly, that her communications with Hollow's cottage must for the present cease; she must give up taking French lessons. The language, he observed, was a bad and frivolous one at the best, and most of the works it boasted were bad and frivolous, highly injurious in their tendency to weak female minds. He wondered (he remarked parenthetically) what noodle first made it the fashion to teach women French: nothing was more improper for them; it was like feeding a rickety child on chalk and water-gruel: Caroline must give it up, and give up her cousins too: they were dangerous people.

Mr Helstone quite expected opposition to this order: he expected tears. Seldom did he trouble himself about Caroline's movements, but a vague idea possessed him that she was fond of going to Hollow's cottage: also he suspected that she liked Robert Moore's occasional presence at the Rectory. The Cossack had perceived that whereas if Malone stepped in of an evening to make himself sociable and charming, by pinching the ears of an aged black cat, which usually shared with Miss Helstone's feet the accommodation of her footstool, or by borrowing a fowlingpiece, and banging away at a tool-shed door in the garden while enough of daylight remained to show that conspicuous mark – keeping the passage and sitting-room doors meantime uncomfortably open, for the convenience of running in and out to announce his failures and successes with noisy brusquerie – he had observed that under such entertaining circumstances, Caroline had a trick of disappearing, tripping noiselessly up-stairs, and remaining invisible till called down to supper. On the other hand, when Robert Moore was the guest, though he elicited no vivacities from the cat, did nothing to it, indeed, beyond occasionally coaxing it from the stool to his knee, and there letting it purr, climb to his shoulder and rub its head against his cheek; though there was no ear-splitting cracking off of firearms, no diffusion of sulphurous gunpowder perfume, no noise, no boasting during his stay, that still Caroline sat in the room, and seemed to find wondrous content in the stitching of Jew-basket pincushions, and the knitting of Missionary-basket socks.

She was very quiet, and Robert paid her little attention, scarcely ever addressing his discourse to her; but Mr Helstone, not being one of those elderly gentlemen who are easily blinded, on the contrary, finding himself on all occasions extremely wide-awake, had watched them when they bade each other good-night: he had just seen their eyes meet once – only once. Some natures would have taken pleasure in the glance then surprised, because there was no harm and some delight in it. It was by no means a glance of mutual intelligence, for mutual love-secrets existed not between them: there was nothing then of craft and concealment to offend; only Mr Moore's eyes, looking into Caroline's, felt they were clear and gentle, and Caroline's eyes encountering Mr Moore's,

confessed they were manly and searching: each acknowledged the charm in his or her own way. Moore smiled slightly, and Caroline coloured as slightly. Mr Helstone could, on the spot, have rated them both: they annoyed him; why? – impossible to say. If you had asked him what Moore merited at that moment, he would have said 'a horsewhip;' if you had inquired into Caroline's deserts, he would have adjudged her a box on the ear; if you had further demanded the reason of such chastisements, he would have stormed against flirtation and love-making, and vowed he would have no such folly going on under his roof.

These private considerations, combined with political reasons, fixed his resolution of separating the cousins. He announced his will to Caroline one evening, as she was sitting at work near the drawing-room window: her face was turned towards him, and the light fell full upon it. It had struck him a few minutes before that she was looking paler and quieter than she used to look; it had not escaped him either that Robert Moore's name had never, for some three weeks past, dropped from her lips; nor during the same space of time had that personage made his appearance at the Rectory. Some suspicion of clandestine meetings haunted his mind; having but an indifferent opinion of women, he always suspected them: he thought they needed constant watching. It was in a tone drily significant he desired her to cease her daily visits to the Hollow; he expected a start, a look of deprecation: the start he saw, but it was a very slight one; no look whatever was directed to him.

'Do you hear me?' he asked.

'Yes, uncle.'

'Of course, you mean to attend to what I say.'

'Yes, certainly.'

'And there must be no letter-scribbling to your cousin Hortense: no intercourse whatever. I do not approve of the principles of the family; they are Jacobinical.'

'Very well,' said Caroline quietly. She acquiesced then: there was no vexed flushing of the face, no gathering tears: the shadowy thoughtfulness which had covered her features ere Mr Helstone spoke remained undisturbed: she was obedient.

Yes, perfectly; because the mandate coincided with her own previous judgment; because it was now become pain to her to go to Hollow's cottage; nothing met her there but disappointment: hope and love had quitted that little tenement, for Robert seemed to have deserted its precincts. Whenever she asked after him – which she very seldom did, since the mere utterance of his name made her face grow hot – the answer was, he was from home, or he was quite taken up with business: Hortense feared he was killing himself by application: he scarcely ever took a meal in the house; he lived in the counting-house.

At church only Caroline had the chance of seeing him, and there she rarely looked at him: it was both too much pain and too much pleasure to look: it excited too much emotion; and that it was all wasted emotion, she had learned well to comprehend.

Once, on a dark, wet Sunday, when there were few people at church, and when especially certain ladies were absent, of whose observant faculties and tomahawk tongues Caroline stood in awe, she had allowed her eye to seek Robert's pew, and to rest a while on its occupant. He was there alone: Hortense had been kept at home by prudent considerations relative to the rain and a new spring 'chapeau.' During the sermon, he sat with folded arms and eyes cast

# Shirley

down, looking very sad and abstracted. When depressed, the very hue of his face seemed more dusk than when he smiled, and to-day cheek and forehead wore their most tintless and sober olive. By instinct Caroline knew, as she examined that clouded countenance, that his thoughts were running in no familiar or kindly channel; that they were far away, not merely from her, but from all which she could comprehend, or in which she could sympathize. Nothing that they had ever talked of together was now in his mind: he was wrapt from her by interests and responsibilities in which it was deemed such as she could have no part.

Caroline meditated in her own way on the subject; speculated on his feelings, on his life, on his fears, on his fate; mused over the mystery of 'business,' tried to comprehend more about it than had ever been told her – to understand its perplexities, liabilities, duties, exactions; endeavoured to realize the state of mind of a 'man of business,' to enter into it, feel what he would feel, aspire to what he would aspire. Her earnest wish was to see things as they were, and not to be romantic. By dint of effort she contrived to get a glimpse of the light of truth here and there, and hoped that scant ray might suffice to guide her.

'Different, indeed,' she concluded, 'is Robert's mental condition to mine: I think only of him; he has no room, no leisure to think of me. The feeling called love is and has been for two years the predominant emotion of my heart; always there, always awake, always astir: quite other feelings absorb his reflections, and govern his faculties. He is rising now, going to leave the church, for service is over. Will he turn his head towards this pew? – no – not once – he has not one look for me: that is hard: a kind glance would have made me happy till to-morrow: I have not got it; he would not give it; he is gone. Strange that grief should now almost choke me, because another human being's eye has failed to greet mine.'

That Sunday evening, Mr Malone coming, as usual, to pass it with his Rector, Caroline withdrew after tea to her chamber. Fanny, knowing her habits, had lit her a cheerful little fire, as the weather was so gusty and chill. Closeted there, silent and solitary, what could she do but think? She noiselessly paced too and fro the carpeted floor; her head drooped, her hands folded: it was irksome to sit: the current of reflection ran rapidly through her mind: to-night she was mutely excited.

Mute was the room, – mute the house. The double-door of the study muffled the voices of the gentlemen: the servants were quiet in the kitchen, engaged with books their young mistress had lent them; books which she had told them were 'fit for Sunday reading.' And she herself had another of the same sort open on the table, but she could not read it: its theology was incomprehensible to her, and her own mind was too busy, teeming, wandering, to listen to the language of another mind.

Then, too, her imagination was full of pictures: images of Moore; scenes where he and she had been together; winter fireside sketches; a glowing landscape of a hot summer afternoon passed with him in the bosom of Nunnely wood: divine vignettes of mild spring or mellow autumn moments, when she had sat at his side in Hollow's copse, listening to the call of the May cuckoo, or sharing the September treasure of nuts and ripe blackberries – a wild dessert which it was her morning's pleasure to collect in a little basket, and cover with green

612

# Shirley

leaves and fresh blossoms, and her afternoon's delight to administer to Moore, berry by berry, and nut by nut, like a bird feeding its fledgling.

Robert's features and form were with her; the sound of his voice was quite distinct in her ear; his few caresses seemed renewed. But these joys being hollow, were, erelong, crushed in: the pictures faded, the voice failed, the visionary clasp melted chill from her hand, and where the warm seal of lips had made impress on her forehead, it felt now as if a sleety rain-drop had fallen. She returned from an enchanted region to the real world: for Nunnely wood in June, she saw her narrow chamber; for the songs of birds in alleys, she heard the rain on her casement; for the sigh of the south wind, came the sob of the mournful east; and for Moore's manly companionship, she had the thin illusion of her own dim shadow on the wall. Turning from the pale phantom which reflected herself in its outline, and her reverie in the drooped attitude of its dim head and colourless tresses, she sat down – inaction would suit the frame of mind into which she was now declining – she said to herself: –

'I have to live, perhaps, till seventy years. As far as I know, I have good health: half a century of existence may lie before me. How am I to occupy it? What am I to do to fill the interval of time which spreads between me and the grave?'

She reflected.

'I shall not be married, it appears,' she continued. 'I suppose, as Robert does not care for me, I shall never have a husband to love, nor little children to take care of. Till lately I had reckoned securely on the duties and affections of wife and mother to occupy my existence. I considered, somehow, as a matter of course, that I was growing up to the ordinary destiny, and never troubled myself to seek any other; but now, I perceive plainly, I may have been mistaken. Probably I shall be an old maid. I shall live to see Robert married to some one else, some rich lady: I shall never marry. What was I created for, I wonder? Where is my place in the world?'

She mused again.

'Ah! I see,' she pursued presently; 'that is the question which most old maids are puzzled to solve, other people solve it for them by saying, "Your place is to do good to others, to be helpful whenever help is wanted." That is right in some measure, and a very convenient doctrine for the people who hold it; but I perceive that certain sets of human beings are very apt to maintain that other sets should give up their lives to them and their service, and then they requite them by praise: they call them devoted and virtuous. Is this enough? Is it to live? Is there not a terrible hollowness, mockery, want, craving, in that existence which is given away to others, for want of something of your own to bestow it on? I suspect there is. Does virtue lie in abnegation of self? I do not believe it. Undue humility makes tyranny; weak concession creates selfishness. The Romish religion especially teaches renunciation of self, submission to others, and nowhere are found so many grasping tyrants as in the ranks of the Romish priesthood. Each human being has his share of rights. I suspect it would conduce to the happiness and welfare of all, if each knew his allotment, and held to it as tenaciously as the martyr to his creed. Queer thoughts these, that surge in my mind: are they right thoughts? I am not certain.

'Well, life is short at the best: seventy years, they say, pass like a vapour, like a dream when one awaketh; and every path trod by human feet terminates in

one bourne – the grave: the little chink in the surface of this great globe – the furrow where the mighty husbandman with the scythe deposits the seed he has shaken from the ripe stem; and there it falls, decays, and thence it springs again, when the world has rolled round a few times more. So much for the body: the soul meantime wings its long flight upward, folds its wings on the brink of the sea of fire and glass, and gazing down through the burning clearness, finds there mirrored the vision of the Christian's triple Godhead: the Sovereign Father; the Mediating Son; the Creator Spirit. Such words, at least, have been chosen to express what is inexpressible: to describe what baffles description. The soul's real hereafter, who shall guess?'

Her fire was decayed to its last cinder; Malone had departed; and now the study-bell rang for prayers.

The next day Caroline had to spend altogether alone, her uncle being gone to dine with his friend Dr Boultby, vicar of Whinbury. The whole time she was talking inwardly in the same strain: looking forwards, asking what she was to do with life. Fanny, as she passed in and out of the room occasionally, intent on housemaid errands, perceived that her young mistress sat very still. She was always in the same place, always bent industriously over a piece of work: she did not lift her head to speak to Fanny, as her custom was; and when the latter remarked that the day was fine, and she ought to take a walk, she only said – 'It is cold.'

'You are very diligent at that sewing, Miss Caroline,' continued the girl, approaching her little table.

'I am tired of it, Fanny.'

'Then why do you go on with it? Put it down: read, or do something to amuse you.'

'It is solitary in this house, Fanny: don't you think so?'

'I don't find it so, Miss. Me and Eliza are company for one another; but you are quite too still – you should visit more. Now, be persuaded; go up stairs and dress yourself smart, and go and take tea, in a friendly way, with Miss Mann or Miss Ainley: I am certain either of those ladies would be delighted to see you.'

'But their houses are dismal: they are both old maids. I am certain old maids are a very unhappy race.'

'Not they, Miss: they can't be unhappy; they take such care of themselves. They are all selfish.'

'Miss Ainley is not selfish, Fanny: she is always doing good. How devotedly kind she was to her stepmother, as long as the old lady lived; and now when she is quite alone in the world, without brother or sister, or any one to care for her, how charitable she is to the poor, as far as her means permit! Still nobody thinks much of her, or has pleasure in going to see her: and how gentlemen always sneer at her!'

'They shouldn't, Miss; I believe she is a good woman: but gentlemen think only of ladies' looks.'

'I'll go and see her,' exclaimed Caroline, starting up: 'and if she asks me to stay to tea, I'll stay. How wrong it is to neglect people because they are not pretty, and young, and merry! And I will certainly call to see Miss Mann, too: she may not be amiable; but what has made her unamiable? What has life been to her?'

# Shirley

Fanny helped Miss Helstone to put away her work, and afterwards assisted her to dress.

'*You*'ll not be an old maid, Miss Caroline,' she said, as she tied the sash of her brown-silk frock, having previously smoothed her soft, full, and shining curls; 'there are no signs of an old maid about you.'

Caroline looked at the little mirror before her, and she thought there were some signs. She could see that she was altered within the last month; that the hues of her complexion were paler, her eyes changed – a wan shade seemed to circle them, her countenance was dejected: she was not, in short, so pretty or so fresh as she used to be. She distantly hinted this to Fanny, from whom she got no direct answer, only a remark that people did vary in their looks; but that at her age a little falling away signified nothing, – she would soon come round again, and be plumper and rosier than ever. Having given this assurance, Fanny showed singular zeal in wrapping her up in warm shawls and handkerchiefs, till Caroline, nearly smothered with the weight, was fain to resist further additions.

She paid her visits: first to Miss Mann, for this was the most difficult point: Miss Mann was certainly not quite a lovable person. Till now, Caroline had always unhesitatingly declared she disliked her, and more than once she had joined her cousin Robert in laughing at some of her peculiarities. Moore was not habitually given to sarcasm, especially on anything humbler or weaker than himself; but he had once or twice happened to be in the room when Miss Mann had made a call on his sister, and after listening to her conversation and viewing her features for a time, he had gone out into the garden where his little cousin was tending some of his favourite flowers, and while standing near and watching her, he had amused himself with comparing fair youth – delicate and attractive – with shrivelled eld, livid and loveless, and in jestingly repeating to a smiling girl the vinegar discourse of a cankered old maid. Once on such an occasion, Caroline had said to him, looking up from the luxuriant creeper she was binding to its frame, –

'Ah! Robert, you do not like old maids. I, too, should come under the lash of your sarcasm, if I were an old maid.'

'You an old maid!' he had replied. 'A piquant notion suggested by lips of that tint and form. I can fancy you, though, at forty, quietly dressed, pale and sunk, but still with that straight nose, white forehead, and those soft eyes. I suppose, too, you will keep your voice, which has another "timbre" than that hard, deep organ of Miss Mann's. Courage, Cary! – even at fifty you will not be repulsive.'

'Miss Mann did not make herself, or tune her voice, Robert.'

'Nature made her in the mood in which she makes her briars and thorns; whereas for the creation of some women, she reserves the May morning hours, when with light and dew she woos the primrose from the turf, and the lily from the wood-moss.'

Ushered into Miss Mann's little parlour, Caroline found her, as she always found her, surrounded by perfect neatness, cleanliness, and comfort; (after all, is it not a virtue in old maids that solitude rarely makes them negligent or disorderly?) no dust on her polished furniture, none on her carpet, fresh flowers in the vase on her table, a bright fire in the grate. She herself sat primly and somewhat grimly-tidy in a cushioned rocking-chair, her hands busied with some

# Shirley

knitting: this was her favourite work, as it required the least exertion. She scarcely rose as Caroline entered; to avoid excitement was one of Miss Mann's aims in life: she had been composing herself ever since she came down in the morning, and had just attained a certain lethargic state of tranquillity when the visitor's knock at the door startled her, and undid her day's work. She was scarcely pleased, therefore, to see Miss Helstone: she received her with reserve, bade her be seated with austerity, and when she had got her placed opposite, she fixed her with her eye.

This was no ordinary doom – to be fixed with Miss Mann's eye. Robert Moore had undergone it once, and had never forgotten the circumstance.

He considered it quite equal to anything Medusa could do: he professed to doubt whether, since that infliction, his flesh had been quite what it was before, – whether there was not something stony in its texture. The gaze had had such an effect on him as to drive him promptly from the apartment and house; it had even sent him straightway up to the Rectory, where he had appeared in Caroline's presence with a very queer face, and amazed her by demanding a cousinly salute on the spot, to rectify a damage that had been done him.

Certainly Miss Mann had a formidable eye for one of the softer sex: it was prominent, and showed a great deal of the white, and looked as steadily, as unwinkingly, at you as if it were a steel ball soldered in her head; and when, while looking, she began to talk in an indescribably dry monotonous tone – a tone without vibration or inflection – you felt as if a graven image of some bad spirit were addressing you. But it was all a figment of fancy, a matter of surface. Miss Mann's goblin-grimness scarcely went deeper than the angel-sweetness of hundreds of beauties. She was a perfectly honest, conscientious woman, who had performed duties in her day from whose severe anguish many a human Peri, gazelle-eyed, silken-tressed, and silver-tongued, would have shrunk appalled: she had passed alone through protracted scenes of suffering, exercised rigid self-denial, made large sacrifices of time, money, health, for those who had repaid her only by ingratitude, and now her main – almost her sole – fault was, that she was censorious.

Censorious she certainly was. Caroline had not sat five minutes ere her hostess, still keeping her under the spell of that dread and Gorgon gaze, began flaying alive certain of the families in the neighbourhood. She went to work at this business in a singularly cool, deliberate manner, like some surgeon practising with his scalpel on a lifeless subject: she made few distinctions; she allowed scarcely any one to be good; she dissected impartially almost all her acquaintance. If her auditress ventured now and then to put in a palliative word, she set it aside with a certain disdain. Still, though thus pitiless in moral anatomy, she was no scandal-monger: she never disseminated really malignant or dangerous reports: it was not her heart so much as her temper that was wrong.

Caroline made this discovery for the first time to-day; and, moved thereby to regret divers unjust judgments she had more than once passed on the crabbed old maid, she began to talk to her softly, not in sympathizing words, but with a sympathizing voice. The loneliness of her condition struck her visitor in a new light; as did also the character of her ugliness, – a bloodless pallor of complexion, and deeply worn lines of feature. The girl pitied the solitary and afflicted woman; her looks told what she felt: a sweet countenance is never so sweet as when the moved heart animates it with compassionate tenderness. Miss Mann, seeing such

a countenance raised to her, was touched in her turn: she acknowledged her sense of the interest thus unexpectedly shown in her, who usually met with only coldness and ridicule, by replying to her candidly. Communicative on her own affairs she usually was not, because no one cared to listen to her; but to-day she became so, and her confidant shed tears as she heard her speak: for she told of cruel, slow-wasting, obstinate sufferings. Well might she be corpse-like; well might she look grim, and never smile; well might she wish to avoid excitement, to gain and retain composure! Caroline, when she knew all, acknowledged that Miss Mann was rather to be admired for fortitude than blamed for moroseness. Reader! when you behold an aspect for whose constant gloom and frown you cannot account, whose unvarying cloud exasperates you by its apparent cause-lessness, be sure that there is a canker somewhere, and a canker not the less deeply corroding because concealed.

Miss Mann felt that she was understood partly, and wished to be understood further; for however old, plain, humble, desolate, afflicted we may be, so long as our hearts preserve the feeblest spark of life, they preserve also, shivering near that pale ember, a starved, ghostly longing for appreciation and affection. To this extenuated spectre, perhaps, a crumb is not thrown once a-year; but when ahungered and athirst to famine – when all humanity has forgotten the dying tenant of a decaying house – Divine Mercy remembers the mourner, and a shower of manna falls for lips that earthly nutriment is to pass no more. Biblical promises, heard first in health, but then unheeded, come whispering to the couch of sickness: it is felt that a pitying God watches what all mankind have forsaken; the tender compassion of Jesus is recalled and relied on: the faded eye, gazing beyond Time, sees a Home, a Friend, a Refuge in Eternity.

Miss Mann, drawn on by the still attention of her listener, proceeded to allude to circumstances in her past life. She spoke like one who tells the truth – simply, and with a certain reserve: she did not boast, nor did she exaggerate. Caroline found that the old maid had been a most devoted daughter and sister, an unwearied watcher by lingering deathbeds; that to prolonged and unrelaxing attendance on the sick the malady that now poisoned her own life owed its origin; that to one wretched relative she had been a support and succour in the depths of self-earned degradation, and that it was still her hand which kept him from utter destitution. Miss Helstone stayed the whole evening, omitting to pay her other intended visit; and when she left Miss Mann, it was with the determination to try in future to excuse her faults, never again to make light of her peculiarities or to laugh at her plainness; and, above all things, not to neglect her, but to come once a-week, and to offer her, from one human heart at least, the homage of affection and respect: she felt she could now sincerely give her a small tribute of each feeling.

Caroline, on her return, told Fanny she was very glad she had gone out, as she felt much better for the visit. The next day she failed not to seek Miss Ainley. This lady was in narrower circumstances than Miss Mann, and her dwelling was more humble: it was, however, if possible, yet more exquisitely clean; though the decayed gentlewoman could not afford to keep a servant, but waited on herself, and had only the occasional assistance of a little girl who lived in a cottage near.

Not only was Miss Ainley poorer, but she was even plainer than the other old maid. In her first youth she must have been ugly; now, at the age of fifty,

# Shirley

she was *very* ugly. At first sight, all but peculiarly well-disciplined minds were apt to turn from her with annoyance: to conceive against her a prejudice, simply on the ground of her unattractive look. Then she was prim in dress and manner: she looked, spoke, and moved the complete old maid.

Her welcome to Caroline was formal, even in its kindness – for it was kind; but Miss Helstone excused this. She knew something of the benevolence of the heart which beat under that starched kerchief; all the neighbourhood – at least all the female neighbourhood – knew something of it: no one spoke against Miss Ainley except lively young gentlemen, and inconsiderate old ones, who declared her hideous.

Caroline was soon at home in that tiny parlour; a kind hand took from her her shawl and bonnet, and installed her in the most comfortable seat near the fire. The young and the antiquated woman were presently deep in kindly conversation, and soon Caroline became aware of the power a most serene, unselfish, and benignant mind could exercise over those to whom it was developed. She talked never of herself – always of others. Their faults she passed over; her theme was their wants, which she sought to supply; their sufferings, which she longed to alleviate. She was religious – a professor of religion – what some would call 'a saint,' and she referred to religion often in sanctioned phrase – in phrase which those who possess a perception of the ridiculous, without owning the power of exactly testing and truly judging character, would certainly have esteemed a proper subject for satire – a matter for mimicry and laughter. They would have been hugely mistaken for their pains. Sincerity is never ludicrous; it is always respectable. Whether truth – be it religious or moral truth – speak eloquently and in well-chosen language or not, its voice should be heard with reverence. Let those who cannot nicely, and with certainty, discern the difference between the tones of hypocrisy and those of sincerity, never presume to laugh at all, lest they should have the miserable misfortune to laugh in the wrong place, and commit impiety when they think they are achieving wit.

Not from Miss Ainley's own lips did Caroline hear of her good works; but she knew much of them nevertheless: her beneficence was the familiar topic of the poor in Briarfield. They were not works of almsgiving: the old maid was too poor to give much, though she straitened herself to privation that she might contribute her mite when needful: they were the works of a Sister of Charity, far more difficult to perform than those of a Lady Bountiful. She would watch by any sickbed: she seemed to fear no disease; she would nurse the poorest whom none else would nurse: she was serene, humble, kind and equable through everything.

For this goodness she got but little reward in this life. Many of the poor became so accustomed to her services that they hardly thanked her for them: the rich heard them mentioned with wonder, but were silent, from a sense of shame at the difference between her sacrifices and their own. Many ladies, however, respected her deeply: they could not help it; one gentleman – one only – gave her his friendship and perfect confidence: this was Mr Hall, the vicar of Nunnely. He said, and said truly, that her life came nearer the life of Christ, than that of any other human being he had ever met with. You must not think, reader, that in sketching Miss Ainley's character, I depict a figment of imagination – no – we seek the originals of such portraits in real life only.

Miss Helstone studied well the mind and heart now revealed to her. She

found no high intellect to admire: the old maid was merely sensible; but she discovered so much goodness, so much usefulness, so much mildness, patience, truth, that she bent her own mind before Miss Ainley's in reverence. What was her love of nature, what was her sense of beauty, what were her more varied and fervent emotions, what was her deeper power of thought, what her wider capacity to comprehend, compared to the practical excellence of this good woman? Momently, they seemed only beautiful forms of selfish delight; mentally, she trod them under foot.

It is true, she still felt with pain that the life which made Miss Ainley happy could not make her happy: pure and active as it was, in her heart she deemed it deeply dreary because it was so loveless – to her ideas, so forlorn. Yet, doubtless, she reflected, it needed only habit to make it practicable and agreeable to any one: it was despicable, she felt, to pine sentimentally, to cherish secret griefs, vain memories; to be inert, to waste youth in aching languor, to grow old doing nothing.

'I will bestir myself,' was her resolution, 'and try to be wise if I cannot be good.'

She proceeded to make inquiry of Miss Ainley, if she could help her in anything. Miss Ainley, glad of an assistant, told her that she could, and indicated some poor families in Briarfield that it was desirable she should visit; giving her likewise, at her further request, some work to do for certain poor women who had many children, and who were unskilled in using the needle for themselves.

Caroline went home, laid her plans, and took a resolve not to swerve from them. She allotted a certain portion of her time for her various studies, and a certain portion for doing anything Miss Ainley might direct her to do; the remainder was to be spent in exercise; not a moment was to be left for the indulgence of such fevered thoughts as had poisoned last Sunday evening.

To do her justice, she executed her plans conscientiously, perseveringly. It was very hard work at first – it was even hard work to the end, but it helped her to stem and keep down anguish: it forced her to be employed; it forbade her to brood; and gleams of satisfaction chequered her grey life here and there when she found she had done good, imparted pleasure, or allayed suffering.

Yet I must speak truth; these efforts brought her neither health of body nor continued peace of mind: with them all, she wasted, grew more joyless and more wan; with them all, her memory kept harping on the name of Robert Moore: an elegy over the past still rung constantly in her ear; a funereal inward cry haunted and harassed her: the heaviness of a broken spirit, and of pining and palsifying faculties, settled slow on her buoyant youth. Winter seemed conquering her spring: the mind's soil and its treasures were freezing gradually to barren stagnation.

# Chapter 11

## Fieldhead

Yet Caroline refused tamely to succumb: she had native strength in her girl's heart, and she used it. Men and women never struggle so hard as when they struggle alone, without witness, counsellor, or confidant; unencouraged, unadvised, and unpitied.

Miss Helstone was in this position. Her sufferings were her only spur; and being very real and sharp, they roused her spirit keenly. Bent on victory over a mortal pain, she did her best to quell it. Never had she been seen so busy, so studious, and above all, so active. She took walks in all weathers – long walks in solitary directions. Day by day she came back in the evening, pale and wearied-looking, yet seemingly not fatigued; for still, as soon as she had thrown off her bonnet and shawl, she would, instead of resting, begin to pace her apartment: sometimes she would not sit down till she was literally faint. She said she did this to tire herself well, that she might sleep soundly at night. But if that was her aim it was unattained, for at night, when others slumbered, she was tossing on her pillow, or sitting at the foot of her couch in the darkness, forgetful apparently of the necessity of seeking repose. Often, unhappy girl! she was crying – crying in a sort of intolerable despair; which, when it rushed over her, smote down her strength, and reduced her to childlike helplessness.

When thus prostrate, temptations besieged her: weak suggestions whispered in her weary heart to write to Robert, and say that she was unhappy because she was forbidden to see him and Hortense, and that she feared he would withdraw his friendship (not love) from her, and forget her entirely, and begging him to remember her, and sometimes to write to her. One or two such letters she actually indited, but she never sent them: shame and good sense forbade.

At last the life she led reached the point when it seemed she could bear it no longer; that she must seek and find a change somehow, or her heart and head would fail under the pressure which strained them. She longed to leave Briarfield, to go to some very distant place. She longed for something else: the deep, secret, anxious yearning to discover and know her mother strengthened daily; but with the desire was coupled a doubt, a dread – if she knew her, could she love her? There was cause for hesitation, for apprehension on this point: never in her life had she heard that mother praised: whoever mentioned her, mentioned her coolly. Her uncle seemed to regard his sister-in-law with a sort of tacit antipathy; an old servant, who had lived with Mrs James Helstone for a short time after her marriage, whenever she referred to her former mistress, spoke with chilling reserve: sometimes she called her 'queer,' sometimes she said she did not understand her. These expressions were ice to the daughter's heart; they

# Shirley

suggested the conclusion that it was perhaps better never to know her parent, than to know her and not like her.

But one project could she frame whose execution seemed likely to bring her a hope of relief; it was to take a situation, to be a governess – she could do nothing else. A little incident brought her to the point, when she found courage to break her design to her uncle.

Her long and late walks lay always, as has been said, on lonely roads; but in whatever direction she had rambled, whether along the drear skirts of Stilbro' Moor, or over the sunny stretch of Nunnely Common, her homeward path was still so contrived as to lead her near the Hollow. She rarely descended the den, but she visited its brink at twilight almost as regularly as the stars rose over the hillcrests. Her resting-place was at a certain stile under a certain old thorn: thence she could look down on the cottage, the mill, the dewy garden-ground, the still, deep dam; thence was visible the well-known counting-house window, from whose panes at a fixed hour shot, suddenly bright, the ray of the well-known lamp. Her errand was to watch for this ray: her reward to catch it, sometimes sparkling bright in clear air, sometimes shimmering dim through mist, and anon flashing broken between slant lines of rain – for she came in all weathers.

There were nights when it failed to appear: she knew then that Robert was from home, and went away doubly sad; whereas its kindling rendered her elate, as though she saw in it the promise of some indefinite hope. If, while she gazed, a shadow bent between the light and lattice, her heart leaped – that eclipse was Robert: she had seen him. She would return home comforted, carrying in her mind a clearer vision of his aspect, a distincter recollection of his voice, his smile, his bearing; and, blent with these impressions, was often a sweet persuasion that, if she could get near him, his heart might welcome her presence yet: that at this moment he might be willing to extend his hand and draw her to him, and shelter her at his side as he used to do. That night, though she might weep as usual, she would fancy her tears less scalding; the pillow they watered seemed a little softer; the temples pressed to that pillow ached less.

The shortest path from the Hollow to the Rectory wound near a certain mansion, the same under whose lone walls Malone passed on that night-journey mentioned in an early chapter of this work – the old and tenantless dwelling yclept Fieldhead. Tenantless by the proprietor it had been for ten years, but it was no ruin: Mr Yorke had seen it kept in good repair, and an old gardener and his wife had lived in it, cultivated the grounds, and maintained the house in habitable condition.

If Fieldhead had few other merits as a building, it might at least be termed picturesque: its irregular architecture, and the grey and mossy colouring communicated by time, gave it a just claim to this epithet. The old latticed windows, the stone porch, the walls, the roof, the chimney-stacks, were rich in crayon touches and sepia lights and shades. The trees behind were fine, bold, and spreading; the cedar on the lawn in front was grand, and the granite urns on the garden wall, the fretted arch of the gateway, were, for an artist, as the very desire of the eye.

One mild May evening, Caroline passing near about moonrise, and feeling, though weary, unwilling yet to go home, where there was only the bed of thorns and the night of grief to anticipate, sat down on the mossy ground near the gate,

# Shirley

and gazed through towards cedar and mansion. It was a still night – calm, dewy, cloudless: the gables, turned to the west, reflected the clear amber of the horizon they faced; the oaks behind were black; the cedar was blacker; under its dense, raven boughs a glimpse of sky opened gravely blue: it was full of the moon, which looked solemnly and mildly down on Caroline from beneath that sombre canopy.

She felt this night and prospect mournfully lovely. She wished she could be happy: she wished she could know inward peace: she wondered Providence had no pity on her, and would not help or console her. Recollections of happy trysts of lovers, commemorated in old ballads, returned on her mind: she thought such tryst in such scene would be blissful. Where now was Robert? she asked: not at the Hollow: she had watched for his lamp long, and had not seen it. She questioned within herself whether she and Moore were ever destined to meet and speak again. Suddenly the door within the stone porch of the Hall opened, and two men came out; one elderly and white-headed, the other young, dark-haired, and tall. They passed across the lawn, out through a portal in the garden wall: Caroline saw them cross the road, pass the stile, descend the fields; she saw them disappear. Robert Moore had passed before her with his friend Mr Yorke: neither had seen her.

The apparition had been transient – scarce seen ere gone; but its electric passage left her veins kindled, her soul insurgent. It found her despairing: it left her desperate – two different states.

'Oh! had he but been alone! Had he but seen me!' was her cry, 'he would have said something; he would have given me his hand. He *does*, he *must* love me a little: he would have shown some token of affection: in his eye, on his lips, I should have read comfort: but the chance is lost. The wind – the cloud's shadow does not pass more silently, more emptily than he. I have been mocked, and Heaven is cruel!'

Thus, in the utter sickness of longing and disappointment, she went home.

The next morning at breakfast, where she appeared white-cheeked and miserable-looking as one who had seen a ghost, she inquired of Mr Helstone, –

'Have you any objection, uncle, to my inquiring for a situation in a family?'

Her uncle, ignorant as the table supporting his coffee-cup of all his niece had undergone and was undergoing, scarcely believed his ears.

'What whim now?' he asked. 'Are you bewitched? What can you mean?'

'I am not well, and need a change,' she said.

He examined her. He discovered she had *experienced* a change, at any rate. Without his being aware of it, the rose had dwindled and faded to a mere snow drop: bloom had vanished, flesh wasted; she sat before him drooping, colourless, and thin. But for the soft expression of her brown eyes, the delicate lines of her features, and the flowing abundance of her hair, she would no longer have possessed a claim to the epithet – pretty.

'What on earth is the matter with you?' he asked. 'What is wrong? How are you ailing?'

No answer, only the brown eyes filled, the faintly-tinted lips trembled.

'Look out for a situation, indeed! For what situation are you fit? What have you been doing with yourself? You are not well.'

'I should be well if I went from home.'

'These women are incomprehensible. They have the strangest knack of

startling you with unpleasant surprises. To-day you see them bouncing, buxom, red as cherries, and round as apples; to-morrow they exhibit themselves effete as dead weeds, blanched and broken down. And the reason of it all? that's the puzzle. She has her meals, her liberty, a good house to live in, and good clothes to wear, as usual: a while since that sufficed to keep her handsome and cheery, and there she sits now a poor, little, pale, puling chit enough. Provoking! Then comes the question, what is to be done? I suppose I must send for advice. Will you have a doctor, child?'

'No, uncle; I don't want one: a doctor could do me no good. I merely want change of air and scene.'

'Well, if that be the caprice, it shall be gratified. You shall go to a watering-place. I don't mind the expense: Fanny shall accompany you.'

'But, uncle, some day I must do something for myself: I have no fortune. I had better begin now.'

'While I live, you shall not turn out as a governess, Caroline. I will not have it said that my niece is a governess.'

'But the later in life one makes a change of that sort, uncle, the more difficult and painful it is. I should wish to get accustomed to the yoke before any habits of ease and independence are formed.'

'I beg you will not harass me, Caroline. I mean to provide for you. I have always meant to provide for you: I will purchase an annuity. Bless me! I am but fifty-five; my health and constitution are excellent: there is plenty of time to save and take measures. Don't make yourself anxious respecting the future: is that what frets you?'

'No, uncle; but I long for a change.'

He laughed. 'There speaks the woman!' cried he, 'the very woman! A change! a change! Always fantastical and whimsical! Well, it's in her sex.'

'But it is no fantasy and whim, uncle.'

'What is it then?'

'Necessity, I think. I feel weaker than formerly, I believe I should have more to do.'

'Admirable! She feels weak, and *therefore* she should be set to hard labour – "clair comme le jour" – as Moore – confound Moore! You shall go to Cliff-bridge; and there are two guineas to buy a new frock. Come, Cary, never fear; we'll find balm in Gilead.'

'Uncle, I wish you were less generous, and more –'

'More what?'

Sympathizing was the word on Caroline's lips, but it was not uttered: she checked herself in time: her uncle would indeed have laughed if that namby-pamby word had escaped her. Finding her silent, he said, –

'The fact is, you don't know precisely what you want.'

'Only to be a governess.'

'Pooh! mere nonsense! I'll not hear of governessing. Don't mention it again. It is rather too feminine a fancy. I have finished breakfast, ring the bell: put all crotchets out of your head, and run away and amuse yourself.'

'What with? My doll?' asked Caroline to herself as she quitted the room.

A week or two passed; her bodily and mental health neither grew worse nor better. She was now precisely in that state, when, if her constitution had contained the seeds of consumption, decline, or slow fever, those diseases would

# Shirley

have been rapidly developed, and would soon have carried her quietly from the world. People never die of love or grief alone; though some die of inherent maladies, which the tortures of those passions prematurely force into destructive action. The sound by nature undergo these tortures, and are racked, shaken, shattered: their beauty and bloom perish, but life remains untouched. They are brought to a certain point of dilapidation; they are reduced to pallor, debility, and emaciation. People think, as they see them gliding languidly about, that they will soon withdraw to sickbeds, perish there, and cease from among the healthy and happy. This does not happen: they live on; and though they cannot regain youth and gaiety, they may regain strength and serenity. The blossom which the March wind nips, but fails to sweep away, may survive to hang a withered apple on the tree late into autumn: having braved the last frosts of spring, it may also brave the first of winter.

Every one noticed the change in Miss Helstone's appearance, and most people said she was going to die. She never thought so herself: she felt in no dying case; she had neither pain nor sickness. Her appetite was diminished; she knew the reason: it was because she wept so much at night. Her strength was lessened; she could account for it; sleep was coy and hard to be won; dreams were distressing and baleful. In the far future she still seemed to anticipate a time when this passage of misery should be got over, and when she should once more be calm, though perhaps never again happy.

Meanwhile her uncle urged her to visit; to comply with the frequent invitations of their acquaintance: this she evaded doing; she could not be cheerful in company: she felt she was observed there with more curiosity than sympathy. Old ladies were always offering her their advice, recommending this or that nostrum; young ladies looked at her in a way she understood, and from which she shrank. Their eyes said they knew she had been 'disappointed,' as custom phrases it: by whom, they were not certain.

Commonplace young ladies can be quite as hard as commonplace young gentlemen, – quite as worldly and selfish. Those who suffer should always avoid them; grief and calamity they despise: they seem to regard them as the judgments of God on the lowly. With them to 'love' is merely to contrive a scheme for achieving a good match: to be 'disappointed' is to have their scheme seen through and frustrated. They think the feelings and projects of others on the subject of love, similar to their own, and judge them accordingly.

All this Caroline knew, partly by instinct, partly by observation: she regulated her conduct by her knowledge, keeping her pale face and wasted figure as much out of sight as she could. Living thus in complete seclusion, she ceased to receive intelligence of the little transactions of the neighbourhood.

One morning her uncle came into the parlour, where she sat endeavouring to find some pleasure in painting a little group of wild flowers, gathered under a hedge at the top of the Hollow fields, and said to her in his abrupt manner: –

'Come, child, you are always stooping over palette, or book, or sampler: leave that tinting work. By-the-by, do you put your pencil to your lips when you paint?'

'Sometimes, uncle, when I forget.'

'Then it is that which is poisoning you. The paints are deleterious, child: there is white lead, and red lead, and verdigris, and gamboge, and twenty other

poisons in those colour cakes. Lock them up! lock them up! Get your bonnet on: I want you to make a call with me.'

'With *you*, uncle?'

This question was asked in a tone of surprise. She was not accustomed to make calls with her uncle: she never rode or walked out with him on any occasion.

'Quick! quick! I am always busy, you know: I have no time to lose.'

She hurriedly gathered up her materials, asking, meantime, where they were going.

'To Fieldhead.'

'Fieldhead! What, to see old James Booth, the gardener? Is he ill?'

'We are going to see Miss Shirley Keeldar.'

'Miss Keeldar! Is she come to Yorkshire! Is she at Fieldhead?'

'She is. She has been there a week. I met her at a party last night: – that party to which you would not go. I was pleased with her: I choose that you shall make her acquaintance: it will do you good.'

'She is now come of age, I suppose?'

'She is come of age, and will reside for a time on her property. I lectured her on the subject: I showed her her duty: she is not intractable: she is rather a fine girl; she will teach you what it is to have a sprightly spirit: nothing lackadaisical about *her*.'

'I don't think she will want to see me, or to have me introduced to her. What good can I do her? How can I amuse her?'

'Pshaw! Put your bonnet on.'

'Is she proud, uncle?'

'Don't know. You hardly imagine she would show her pride to me, I suppose? A chit like that would scarcely presume to give herself airs with the Rector of her parish, however rich she might be.'

'No, – but how did she behave to other people?'

'Didn't observe. She holds her head high, and probably can be saucy enough where she dare, – she wouldn't be a woman otherwise. There, – away now for your bonnet at once!'

Not naturally very confident, a failure of physical strength and a depression of spirits had not tended to increase Caroline's presence of mind and ease of manner, or to give her additional courage to face strangers, and she quailed, in spite of self-remonstrance, as she and her uncle walked up the broad, paved approach leading from the gateway of Fieldhead to its porch. She followed Mr Helstone reluctantly through that porch into the sombre old vestibule beyond.

Very sombre it was; long, vast, and dark: one latticed window lit it but dimly; the wide old chimney contained now no fire, for the present warm weather needed it not; it was filled instead with willow-boughs. The gallery on high, opposite the entrance, was seen but in outline, so shadowy became this hall towards its ceiling; carved stags' heads, with real antlers, looked down grotesquely from the walls. This was neither a grand nor a comfortable house: within as without it was antique, rambling, and incommodious. A property of a thousand a-year belonged to it; which property had descended, for lack of male heirs, on a female. There were mercantile families in the district boasting twice the income, but the Keeldars, by virtue of their antiquity, and their distinction of lords of the manor, took the precedence of all.

# Shirley

Mr and Miss Helstone were ushered into a parlour: of course, as was to be expected in such a gothic old barrack, this parlour was lined with oak: fine dark, glossy panels compassed the walls gloomily and grandly. Very handsome, reader, these shining, brown panels are: very mellow in colouring and tasteful in effect, but – if you know what a 'Spring-clean' is – very execrable and inhuman. Whoever, having the bowels of humanity, has seen servants scrubbing at these polished wooden walls with bees-waxed cloths on a warm May day, must allow that they are 'tolerable and not to be endured;' and I cannot but secretly applaud the benevolent barbarian who had painted another and larger apartment of Fieldhead – the drawing-room to-wit, formerly also an oak-room – of a delicate pinky white; thereby earning for himself the character of a Hun, but mightily enhancing the cheerfulness of that portion of his abode, and saving future housemaids a world of toil.

The brown-panelled parlour was furnished all in old style, and with real old furniture. On each side of the high mantelpiece stood two antique chairs of oak, solid as sylvan thrones, and in one of these sat a lady. But if this were Miss Keeldar, she must have come of age at least some twenty years ago: she was of matronly form, and though she wore no cap, and possessed hair of quite an undimmed auburn, shading small and naturally young-looking features, she had no youthful aspect, nor apparently the wish to assume it. You could have wished her attire of a newer fashion: in a well-cut, well-made gown, hers would have been no uncomely presence. It puzzled you to guess why a garment of handsome materials should be arranged in such scanty folds, and devised after such an obsolete mode: you felt disposed to set down the wearer as somewhat eccentric at once.

This lady received the visitors with a mixture of ceremony and diffidence quite English: no middle-aged matron who was not an Englishwoman *could* evince precisely the same manner; a manner so uncertain of herself, of her own merits, of her power to please; and yet so anxious to be proper, and, if possible, rather agreeable than otherwise. In the present instance, however, more embarrassment was shown than is usual even with diffident Englishwomen: Miss Helstone felt this, sympathized with the stranger, and knowing by experience what was good for the timid, took a seat quietly near her, and began to talk to her with a gentle ease, communicated for the moment by the presence of one less self-possessed than herself.

She and this lady would, if alone, have at once got on extremely well together. The lady had the clearest voice imaginable: infinitely softer and more tuneful than could have been reasonably expected from forty years, and a form decidedly inclined to embonpoint. This voice Caroline liked; it atoned for the formal, if correct, accent and language: the lady would soon have discovered she liked it and her, and in ten minutes they would have been friends. But Mr Helstone stood on the rug looking at them both; looking especially at the strange lady with his sarcastic, keen eye, that clearly expressed impatience of her chilly ceremony, and annoyance at her want of aplomb. His hard gaze and rasping voice discomfited the lady more and more; she tried, however, to get up little speeches about the weather, the aspect of the country, &c., but the impracticable Mr Helstone presently found himself somewhat deaf: whatever she said, he affected not to hear distinctly, and she was obliged to go over each elaborately constructed nothing twice. The effort soon became too much for her; she was

just rising in a perplexed flutter, nervously murmuring that she knew not what detained Miss Keeldar – that she would go and look for her, when Miss Keeldar saved her the trouble by appearing: it was to be presumed at least that she who now came in through a glass-door from the garden owned that name.

There is real grace in ease of manner, and so old Helstone felt when an erect, slight girl walked up to him, retaining with her left hand her little silk apron full of flowers, and, giving him her right hand, said pleasantly: –

'I knew you would come to see me, though you *do* think Mr Yorke has made me a Jacobin. Good-morning.'

'But we'll not have you a Jacobin,' returned he. 'No, Miss Shirley, they shall not steal the flower of my parish from me: now that you are amongst us, you shall be my pupil in politics and religion: I'll teach you sound doctrine on both points.'

'Mrs Pryor has anticipated you,' she replied, turning to the elder lady. 'Mrs Pryor, you know, was my governess, and is still my friend; and of all the high and rigid Tories, she is queen; of all the staunch churchwomen, she is chief. I have been well drilled both in theology and history, I assure you, Mr Helstone.'

The Rector immediately bowed very low to Mrs Pryor, and expressed himself obliged to her.

The ex-governess disclaimed skill either in political or religious controversy, explained that she thought such matters little adapted for female minds, but avowed herself in general terms the advocate of order and loyalty, and, of course, truly attached to the Establishment. She added, she was ever averse to change under any circumstances; and something scarcely audible about the extreme danger of being too ready to take up new ideas, closed her sentence.

'Miss Keeldar thinks as you think, I hope, madam.'

'Difference of age and difference of temperament occasion difference of sentiment,' was the reply. 'It can scarcely be expected that the eager and young should hold the opinions of the cool and middle-aged.'

'Oh! oh! we are independent: we think for ourselves!' cried Mr Helstone. 'We are a little Jacobin, for anything I know: a little free-thinker, in good earnest. Let us have a confession of faith on the spot.'

And he took the heiress's two hands – causing her to let fall her whole cargo of flowers – and seated her by him on the sofa.

'Say your creed,' he ordered.

'The Apostles' Creed?'

'Yes.'

She said it like a child.

'Now for St Athanasius's: that's the test!'

'Let me gather up my flowers: here is Tartar coming, he will tread upon them.'

Tartar was a rather large, strong, and fierce-looking dog, very ugly, being of a breed between mastiff and bull-dog, who at this moment entered through the glass door, and posting directly to the rug, snuffed the fresh flowers scattered there. He seemed to scorn them as food; but probably thinking their velvety petals might be convenient as litter, he was turning round preparatory to depositing his tawny bulk upon them, when Miss Helstone and Miss Keeldar simultaneously stooped to the rescue.

'Thank you,' said the heiress, as she again held out her little apron for

# Shirley

Caroline to heap the blossoms into it. 'Is this your daughter, Mr Helstone?' she asked.

'My niece, Caroline.'

Miss Keeldar shook hands with her, and then looked at her. Caroline also looked at her hostess.

Shirley Keeldar (she had no Christian name but Shirley: her parents, who had wished to have a son, finding that, after eight years of marriage, Providence had granted them only a daughter, bestowed on her the same masculine family cognomen they would have bestowed on a boy, if with a boy they had been blessed) – Shirley Keeldar was no ugly heiress: she was agreeable to the eye. Her height and shape were not unlike Miss Helstone's: perhaps in stature she might have the advantage by an inch or two; she was gracefully made, and her face, too, possessed a charm as well described by the word grace as any other. It was pale naturally, but intelligent, and of varied expression. She was not a blonde, like Caroline: clear and dark were the characteristics of her aspect as to colour: her face and brow were clear, her eyes of the darkest grey: no green lights in them, – transparent, pure, neutral grey; and her hair of the darkest brown. Her features were distinguished; by which I do not mean that they were high, bony, and Roman, being indeed rather small and slightly marked than otherwise; but only that they were, to use a few French words, 'fins, gracieux, spirituels:' mobile they were and speaking; but their changes were not to be understood, nor their language interpreted all at once. She examined Caroline seriously, inclining her head a little to one side, with a thoughtful air.

'You see she is only a feeble chick,' observed Mr Helstone.

'She looks young – younger than I. How old are you?' she inquired, in a manner that would have been patronizing if it had not been extremely solemn and simple.

'Eighteen years and six months.'

'And I am twenty-one.'

She said no more; she had now placed her flowers on the table, and was busied in arranging them.

'And St Athanasius's creed?' urged the Rector; 'you believe it all – don't you?'

'I can't remember it quite all. I will give you a nosegay, Mr Helstone, when I have given your niece one.'

She had selected a little bouquet of one brilliant and two or three delicate flowers, relieved by a spray of dark verdure: she tied it with silk from her workbox, and placed it on Caroline's lap; and then she put her hands behind her, and stood, bending slightly towards her guest, still regarding her, in the attitude and with something of the aspect of a grave but gallant little cavalier. This temporary expression of face was aided by the style in which she wore her hair, parted on one temple and brushed in a glossy sweep above the forehead, whence it fell in curls that looked natural, so free were their wavy undulations.

'Are you tired with your walk?' she inquired.

'No – not in the least; it is but a short distance – but a mile.'

'You look pale. Is she always so pale? she asked, turning to the Rector.

'She used to be as rosy as the reddest of your flowers.'

'Why is she altered? What has made her pale? Has she been ill?'

'She tells me she wants a change.'

# Shirley

'She ought to have one: you ought to give her one: you should send her to the seacoast.'

'I will, ere summer is over. Meantime, I intend her to make acquaintance with you, if you have no objection.'

'I am sure Miss Keeldar will have no objection,' here observed Mrs Pryor. 'I think I may take it upon me to say that Miss Helstone's frequent presence at Fieldhead will be esteemed a favour.'

'You speak my sentiments precisely, ma'am,' said Shirley, 'and I thank you for anticipating me. Let me tell you,' she continued, turning again to Caroline, 'that you also ought to thank my governess; it is not every one she would welcome as she has welcomed you: you are distinguished more than you think. This morning, as soon as you are gone, I shall ask Mrs Pryor's opinion of you. I am apt to rely on her judgment of character, for hitherto I have found it wondrous accurate. Already I foresee a favourable answer to my inquiries: do I not guess rightly, Mrs Pryor?'

'My dear – you said but now you would ask my opinion when Miss Helstone was gone; I am scarcely likely to give it in her presence.'

'No – and perhaps it will be long enough before I obtain it. I am sometimes sadly tantalized, Mr Helstone, by Mrs Pryor's extreme caution: her judgments ought to be correct when they come, for they are often as tardy of delivery as a lord-chancellor's: on some people's characters I cannot get her to pronounce sentence, entreat as I may.'

Mrs Pryor here smiled.

'Yes,' said her pupil, 'I know what that smile means: you are thinking of my gentleman-tenant. Do you know Mr Moore of the Hollow?' she asked Mr Helstone.

'Ay! ay! your tenant – so he is: you have seen a good deal of him, no doubt, since you came?'

'I have been obliged to see him: there was business to transact. Business! Really the word makes me conscious that I am indeed no longer a girl, but quite a woman and something more. I am an esquire: Shirley Keeldar, Esquire, ought to be my style and title. They gave me a man's name; I hold a man's position: it is enough to inspire me with a touch of manhood; and when I see such people as that stately Anglo-Belgian – that Gérard Moore before me, gravely talking to me of business, really I feel quite gentlemanlike. You must choose me for your churchwarden, Mr Helstone, the next time you elect new ones: they ought to make me a magistrate and a captain of yeomanry: Tony Lumpkin's mother was a colonel, and his aunt a justice of the peace – why shouldn't I be?'

'With all my heart. If you choose to get up a requisition on the subject, I promise to head the list of signatures with my name. But you were speaking of Moore?'

'Ah! yes. I find it a little difficult to understand Mr Moore – to know what to think of him: whether to like him or not. He seems a tenant of whom any proprietor might be proud – and proud of him I am, in that sense – but as a neighbour, what is he? Again and again I have entreated Mrs Pryor to say what she thinks of him, but she still evades returning a direct answer. I hope you will be less oracular, Mr Helstone, and pronounce at once: do you like him?'

'Not at all, just now: his name is entirely blotted from my good books.'

'What is the matter? What has he done?'

# Shirley

'My uncle and he disagree on politics,' interposed the low voice of Caroline. She had better not have spoken just then: having scarcely joined in the conversation before, it was not apropos to do it now: she felt this, with nervous acuteness, as soon as she had spoken, and coloured to the eyes.

'What are Moore's politics?' inquired Shirley.

'Those of a tradesman,' returned the Rector; 'narrow, selfish, and unpatriotic. The man is eternally writing and speaking against the continuance of the war: I have no patience with him.'

'The war hurts his trade. I remember he remarked that only yesterday. But what other objection have you to him?'

'That is enough.'

'He looks the gentleman, in my sense of the term,' pursued Shirley, 'and it pleases me to think he is such.'

Caroline rent the Tyrian petals of the one brilliant flower in her bouquet, and answered in distinct tones – 'Decidedly he is.' Shirley, hearing this courageous affirmation, flashed an arch, searching glance at the speaker from her deep, expressive eyes.

'*You* are his friend, at any rate,' she said: 'you defend him in his absence.'

'I am both his friend and his relative,' was the prompt reply. 'Robert Moore is my cousin.'

'Oh, then, you can tell me all about him. Just give me a sketch of his character.'

Insuperable embarrassment seized Caroline when this demand was made: she could not, and did not attempt to comply with it. Her silence was immediately covered by Mrs Pryor, who proceeded to address sundry questions to Mr Helstone regarding a family or two in the neighbourhood, with whose connexions in the south she said she was acquainted. Shirley soon withdrew her gaze from Miss Helstone's face. She did not renew her interrogations, but returning to her flowers, proceeded to choose a nosegay for the Rector. She presented it to him as he took leave, and received the homage of a salute on the hand in return.

'Be sure you wear it for my sake,' said she.

'Next my heart, of course,' responded Helstone. 'Mrs Pryor, take care of this future magistrate, this churchwarden in perspective, this captain of yeomanry, this young squire of Briarfield, in a word: don't let him exert himself too much: don't let him break his neck in hunting: especially, let him mind how he rides down that dangerous hill near the Hollow.'

'I like a descent,' said Shirley – 'I like to clear it rapidly; and especially I like that romantic Hollow, with all my heart.'

'Romantic – with a mill in it?'

'Romantic with a mill in it. The old mill and the white cottage are each admirable in its way.'

'And the counting-house, Mr Keeldar?'

'The counting-house is better than my bloom-coloured drawing-room: I adore the counting-house.'

'And the trade? The cloth – the greasy wool – the polluting dyeing-vats?'

'The trade is to be thoroughly respected.'

'And the tradesman is a hero? Good!'

'I am glad to hear you say so: I thought the tradesman looked heroic.'

Mischief, spirit, and glee sparkled all over her face as she thus bandied words with the old Cossack, who almost equally enjoyed the tilt.

'Captain Keeldar, you have no mercantile blood in your veins: why are you so fond of trade?'

'Because I am a mill-owner, of course. Half my income comes from the works in that Hollow.'

'Don't enter into partnership, that's all.'

'You've put it into my head! you've put it into my head!' she exclaimed, with a joyous laugh. 'It will never get out: thank you.' And waving her hand, white as a lily and fine as a fairy's, she vanished within the porch, while the Rector and his niece passed out through the arched gateway.

# Chapter 12

## Shirley and Caroline

Shirley showed she had been sincere in saying she should be glad of Caroline's society, by frequently seeking it: and, indeed, if she had not sought it, she would not have had it; for Miss Helstone was slow to make fresh acquaintance. She was always held back by the idea that people could not want her, – that she could not amuse them; and a brilliant, happy, youthful creature, like the heiress of Fieldhead, seemed to her too completely independent of society so uninteresting as hers, ever to find it really welcome.

Shirley might be brilliant, and probably happy likewise, but no one is independent of genial society; and though in about a month she had made the acquaintance of most of the families round, and was on quite free and easy terms with all the Misses Sykes, and all the Misses Pearson, and the two superlative Misses Wynne of Walden Hall; yet, it appeared, she found none amongst them very genial: she fraternized with none of them, to use her own words. If she had had the bliss to be really Shirley Keeldar, Esq., Lord of the Manor of Briarfield, there was not a single fair one in this and the two neighbouring parishes, whom she should have felt disposed to request to become Mrs Keeldar, lady of the manor. This declaration she made to Mrs Pryor, who received it very quietly, as she did most of her pupil's off-hand speeches, responding, –

'My dear, do not allow that habit of alluding to yourself as a gentleman to be confirmed: it is a strange one. Those who do not know you, hearing you speak thus, would think you affected masculine manners.'

Shirley never laughed at her former governess: even the little formalities and harmless peculiarities of that lady were respectable in her eyes: had it been otherwise, she would have proved herself a weak character at once: for it is only the weak who make a butt of quiet worth; therefore she took her remonstrance

in silence. She stood quietly near the window, looking at the grand cedar on her lawn, watching a bird on one of its lower boughs. Presently she began to chirrup to the bird: soon her chirrup grew clearer; erelong she was whistling; the whistle struck into a tune, and very sweetly and deftly it was executed.

'My dear!' expostulated Mrs Pryor.

'Was I whistling?' said Shirley; 'I forgot. I beg your pardon, ma'am. I had resolved to take care not to whistle before you.'

'But, Miss Keeldar, where did you learn to whistle? You must have got the habit since you came down into Yorkshire. I never knew you guilty of it before.'

'Oh! I learned to whistle a long while ago.'

'Who taught you?'

'No one: I took it up by listening, and I had laid it down again; but lately yesterday evening, as I was coming up our lane, I heard a gentleman whistling that very tune in the field on the other side of the hedge, and that reminded me.'

'What gentleman was it?'

'We have only one gentleman in this region, ma'am, and that is Mr Moore; at least he is the only gentleman who is not grey-haired: my two venerable favourites, Mr Helstone and Mr Yorke, it is true, are fine old beaux; infinitely better than any of the stupid young ones.'

Mrs Pryor was silent.

'You do not like Mr Helstone, ma'am?'

'My dear, Mr Helstone's office secures him from criticism.'

'You generally contrive to leave the room when he is announced.'

'Do you walk out this morning, my dear?'

'Yes, I shall go to the Rectory, and seek and find Caroline Helstone, and make her take some exercise: she shall have a breezy walk over Nunnely Common.'

'If you go in that direction, my dear, have the goodness to remind Miss Helstone to wrap up well, as there is a fresh wind, and she appears to me to require care.'

'You shall be minutely obeyed, Mrs Pryor: meantime, will you not accompany us yourself?'

'No, my love; I should be a restraint upon you: I am stout, and cannot walk so quickly as you would wish to do.'

Shirley easily persuaded Caroline to go with her: and when they were fairly out on the quiet road, traversing the extensive and solitary sweep of Nunnely Common, she as easily drew her into conversation. The first feelings of diffidence overcome, Caroline soon felt glad to talk with Miss Keeldar. The very first interchange of slight observations sufficed to give each an idea of what the other was. Shirley said she liked the green sweep of the common turf, and, better still, the heath on its ridges, for the heath reminded her of moors: she had seen moors when she was travelling on the borders near Scotland. She remembered particularly a district traversed one long afternoon, on a sultry but sunless day in summer: they journeyed from noon till sunset, over what seemed a boundless waste of deep heath, and nothing had they seen but wild sheep; nothing heard but the cries of wild birds.

'I know how the heath would look on such a day,' said Caroline; 'purple-black: a deeper shade of the sky-tint, and that would be livid.'

'Yes – quite livid, with brassy edges to the clouds, and here and there a white

# Shirley

gleam, more ghastly than the lurid tinge, which, as you looked at it, you momentarily expected would kindle into blinding lightning.'

'Did it thunder?'

'It muttered distant peals, but the storm did not break till evening, after we had reached our inn: that inn being an isolated house at the foot of a range of mountains.'

'Did you watch the clouds come down over the mountains?'

'I did: I stood at the window an hour watching them. The hills seemed rolled in a sullen mist, and when the rain fell in whitening sheets, suddenly they were blotted from the prospect: they were washed from the world.'

'I have seen such storms in hilly districts in Yorkshire; and at their riotous climax, while the sky was all cataract, the earth all flood, I have remembered the Deluge.'

'It is singularly reviving after such hurricanes to feel calm return, and from the opening clouds to receive a consolatory gleam, softly testifying that the sun is not quenched.'

'Miss Keeldar, just stand still now, and look down at Nunnely dale and wood.'

They both halted on the green brow of the Common: they looked down on the deep valley robed in May raiment; on varied meads, some pearled with daisies, and some golden with king-cups: today all this young verdure smiled clear in sunlight; transparent emerald and amber gleams played over it. On Nunnwood – the sole remnant of antique British forest in a region whose lowlands were once all sylvan chase, as its highlands were breast-deep heather – slept the shadow of a cloud; the distant hills were dappled, the horizon was shaded and tinted like mother-of-pearl; silvery blues, soft purples, evanescent greens and rose-shades, all melting into fleeces of white cloud, pure as azury snow, allured the eye as with a remote glimpse of heaven's foundations. The air blowing on the brow was fresh, and sweet, and bracing.

'Our England is a bonnie island,' said Shirley, 'and Yorkshire is one of her bonniest nooks.'

'You are a Yorkshire girl too?'

'I am – Yorkshire in blood and birth. Five generations of my race sleep under the aisles of Briarfield Church: I drew my first breath in the old black hall behind us.'

Hereupon Caroline presented her hand, which was accordingly taken and shaken. 'We are compatriots,' said she.

'Yes,' agreed Shirley, with a grave nod.

'And that,' asked Miss Keeldar, pointing to the forest, – 'that is Nunnwood?'

'It is.'

'Were you ever there?'

'Many a time.'

'In the heart of it?'

'Yes.'

'What is it like?'

'It is like an encampment of forest sons of Anak. The trees are huge and old. When you stand at their roots, the summits seem in another region: the trunks remain still and firm as pillars, while the boughs sway to every breeze. In the deepest calm their leaves are never quite hushed, and in high wind a flood rushes – a sea thunders above you.'

# Shirley

'Was it not one of Robin Hood's haunts?'

'Yes, and there are mementos of him still existing. To penetrate into Nunn-wood, Miss Keeldar, is to go far back into the dim days of eld. Can you see a break in the forest, about the centre?'

'Yes, distinctly.'

'That break is a dell; a deep, hollow cup, lined with turf as green and short as the sod of this Common: the very oldest of the trees, gnarled mighty oaks, crowd about the brink of this dell: in the bottom lie the ruins of a nunnery.'

'We will go – you and I alone, Caroline – to that wood, early some fine summer morning, and spend a long day there. We can take pencils and sketch-books, and any interesting reading-book we like; and of course we shall take something to eat. I have two little baskets, in which Mrs Gill, my housekeeper, might pack our provisions, and we could each carry our own. It would not tire you too much to walk so far?'

'Oh, no; especially if we rested the whole day in the wood, and I know all the pleasantest spots: I know where we could get nuts in nutting time; I know where wild strawberries abound; I know certain lonely, quite untrodden glades, carpeted with strange mosses, some yellow as if gilded, some a sober grey, some gem-green. I know groups of trees that ravish the eye with their perfect, picture-like effects: rude oak, delicate birch, glossy beech, clustered in contrast; and ash trees stately as Saul, standing isolated, and superannuated wood-giants clad in bright shrouds of ivy. Miss Keeldar, I could guide you.'

'You would be dull with me alone?'

'I should not. I think we should suit: and what third person is there whose presence would not spoil our pleasure?'

'Indeed, I know of none about our own ages – no lady at least, and as to gentlemen –'

'An excursion becomes quite a different thing when there are gentlemen of the party,' interrupted Caroline.

'I agree with you – quite a different thing to what we were proposing.'

'We were going simply to see the old trees, the old ruins; to pass a day in old times, surrounded by olden silence, and above all by quietude.'

'You are right; and the presence of gentlemen dispels the last charm, I think. If they are of the wrong sort, like your Malones, and your young Sykes, and Wynnes, irritation takes the place of serenity. If they are of the right sort, there is still a change – I can hardly tell what change, one easy to feel, difficult to describe.'

'We forget Nature, imprimis.'

'And then Nature forgets us; covers her vast, calm brow with a dim veil, conceals her face, and withdraws the peaceful joy with which, if we had been content to worship her only, she would have filled our hearts.'

'What does she give us instead?'

'More elation and more anxiety: an excitement that steals the hours away fast, and a trouble that ruffles their course.'

'Our power of being happy lies a good deal in ourselves, I believe,' remarked Caroline, sagely. 'I have gone to Nunnwood with a large party, all the curates and some other gentry of these parts, together with sundry ladies; and I found the affair insufferably tedious and absurd: and I have gone quite alone, or accompanied but by Fanny, who sat in the woodman's hut and sewed, or talked

# Shirley

to the goodwife, while I roamed about and made sketches, or read; and I have enjoyed much happiness of a quiet kind all day long. But that was when I was young – two years ago.'

'Did you ever go with your cousin, Robert Moore?'

'Yes; once.'

'What sort of a companion is he on these occasions?'

'A cousin, you know, is different to a stranger.'

'I am aware of that; but cousins, if they are stupid, are still more insupportable than strangers, because you cannot so easily keep them at a distance. But your cousin is not stupid?'

'No; but –'

'Well?'

'If the company of fools irritates, as you say, the society of clever men leaves its own peculiar pain also. Where the goodness or talent of your friend is beyond and above all doubt, your own worthiness to be his associate often becomes a matter of question.'

'Oh! there I cannot follow you: that crotchet is not one I should choose to entertain for an instant. I consider myself not unworthy to be the associate of the best of them – of gentlemen, I mean: though that is saying a great deal. Where they are good, they are very good, I believe. Your uncle, by-the-by, is not a bad specimen of the elderly gentleman: I am always glad to see his brown, keen, sensible old face, either in my own house or any other. Are you fond of him? Is he kind to you? Now, speak the truth.'

'He has brought me up from childhood, I doubt not, precisely as he would have brought up his own daughter, if he had had one; and that is kindness; but I am not fond of him: I would rather be out of his presence than in it.'

'Strange! when he has the art of making himself so agreeable.'

'Yes, in company; but he is stern and silent at home. As he puts away his cane and shovel-hat in the Rectory-hall, so he locks his liveliness in his book-case and study-desk: the knitted brow and brief word for the fireside; the smile, the jest, the witty sally, for society.'

'Is he tyrannical?'

'Not in the least: he is neither tyrannical nor hypocritical: he is simply a man who is rather liberal than good-natured, rather brilliant than genial, rather scrupulously equitable than truly just, – if you can understand such superfine distinctions?'

'Oh! yes: good-nature implies indulgence, which he has not; geniality, warmth of heart, which he does not own; and genuine justice is the offspring of sympathy and considerateness, of which, I can well conceive, my bronzed old friend is quite innocent.'

'I often wonder, Shirley, whether most men resemble my uncle in their domestic relations; whether it is necessary to be new and unfamiliar to them, in order to seem agreeable or estimable in their eyes; and whether it is impossible to their natures to retain a constant interest and affection for those they see every day.'

'I don't know: I can't clear up your doubts. I ponder over similar ones myself sometimes. But, to tell you a secret, if I were convinced that they are necessarily and universally different from us – fickle, soon petrifying, unsympathizing – I would never marry. I should not like to find out that what I loved did not love

me, that it was weary of me, and that whatever effort I might make to please would hereafter be worse than useless, since it was inevitably in its nature to change and become indifferent. That discovery once made, what should I long for? To go away – to remove from a presence where my society gave no pleasure.'

'But you could not, if you were married.'

'No, I could not, – there it is. I could never be my own mistress more. A terrible thought! – it suffocates me! Nothing irks me like the idea of being a burden and a bore, – an inevitable burden, – a ceaseless bore! Now, when I feel my company superfluous, I can comfortably fold my independence round me like a mantle, and drop my pride like a veil, and withdraw to solitude. If married, that could not be.'

'I wonder we don't all make up our minds to remain single,' said Caroline: 'we should if we listened to the wisdom of experience. My uncle always speaks of marriage as a burden; and I believe whenever he hears of a man being married, he invariably regards him as a fool, or, at any rate, as doing a foolish thing.'

'But, Caroline, men are not all like your uncle: surely not – I hope not.'

She paused and mused.

'I suppose we each find an exception in the one we love, till we *are* married,' suggested Caroline.

'I suppose so: and this exception we believe to be of sterling materials; we fancy it like ourselves; we imagine a sense of harmony. We think his voice gives the softest, truest promise of a heart that will never harden against us: we read in his eyes that faithful feeling – affection. I don't think we should trust to what they call passion at all, Caroline. I believe it is a mere fire of dry sticks, blazing up and vanishing: but we watch him, and see him kind to animals, to little children, to poor people. He is kind to us likewise – good – considerate: he does not flatter women, but he is patient with them, and he seems to be easy in their presence, and to find their company genial. He likes them not only for vain and selfish reasons, but as *we* like him – because we like him. Then we observe that he is just – that he always speaks the truth – that he is conscientious. We feel joy and peace when he comes into a room: we feel sadness and trouble when he leaves it. We know that this man has been a kind son, that he is a kind brother: will any one dare to tell me that he will not be a kind husband?'

'My uncle would affirm it unhesitatingly. "He will be sick of you in a month," he would say.'

'Mrs Pryor would seriously intimate the same.'

'Mrs Yorke and Miss Mann would darkly suggest ditto.'

'If they are true oracles, it is good never to fall in love.'

'Very good, if you can avoid it.'

'I choose to doubt their truth.'

'I am afraid that proves you are already caught.'

'Not I: but if I were, do you know what soothsayers I would consult?'

'Let me hear.'

'Neither man nor woman, elderly nor young: – the little Irish beggar that comes barefoot to my door; the mouse that steals out of the cranny in the wainscot; the bird that in frost and snow pecks at my window for a crumb; the dog that licks my hand and sits beside my knee.'

'Did you ever see any one who was kind to such things?'

# Shirley

'Did you ever see any one whom such things seemed instinctively to follow, like, rely on?'

'We have a black cat and an old dog at the Rectory. I know somebody to whose knee that black cat loves to climb; against whose shoulder and cheek it likes to purr. The old dog always comes out of his kennel and wags his tail, and whines affectionately when somebody passes.'

'And what does that somebody do?'

'He quietly strokes the cat, and lets her sit while he conveniently can, and when he must disturb her by rising, he puts her softly down, and never flings her from him roughly; he always whistles to the dog and gives him a caress.'

'Does he? It is not Robert?'

'But it is Robert.'

'Handsome fellow!' said Shirley, with enthusiasm: her eyes sparkled.

'Is he not handsome? Has he not fine eyes and well-cut features, and a clear, princely forehead?'

'He has all that, Caroline. Bless him! he is both graceful and good.'

'I was sure you would see that he was: when I first looked at your face I knew you would.'

'I was well inclined to him before I saw him. I liked him when I did see him: I admire him now. There is charm in beauty for itself, Caroline; when it is blent with goodness, there is a powerful charm.'

'When mind is added, Shirley?'

'Who can resist it?'

'Remember my uncle, Mesdames Pryor, Yorke, and Mann.'

'Remember the croaking of the frogs of Egypt! He is a noble being. I tell you when they *are* good, they are the lords of the creation, – they are the sons of God. Moulded in their Maker's image, the minutest spark of His spirit lifts them almost above mortality. Indisputably, a great, good, handsome man is the first of created things.'

'Above us?'

'I would scorn to contend for empire with him, – I would scorn it. Shall my left hand dispute for precedence with my right? – shall my heart quarrel with my pulse? – shall my veins be jealous of the blood which fills them?'

'Men and women, husbands and wives quarrel horribly, Shirley.'

'Poor things! – poor, fallen, degenerate things! God made them for another lot – for other feelings.'

'But are we men's equals, or are we not?'

'Nothing ever charms me more than when I meet my superior – one who makes me sincerely feel that he is my superior.'

'Did you ever meet him?'

'I should be glad to see him any day: the higher above me, so much the better: it degrades to stoop – it is glorious to look up. What frets me is, that when I try to esteem, I am baffled: when religiously inclined, there are but false gods to adore. I disdain to be a Pagan.'

'Miss Keeldar, will you come in? We are here at the Rectory gates.'

'Not to-day; but to-morrow I shall fetch you to spend the evening with me. Caroline Helstone – if you really are what at present to me you seem – you and I will suit. I have never in my whole life been able to talk to a young lady as I have talked to you this morning. Kiss me – and good-bye.'

# Shirley

Mrs Pryor seemed as well-disposed to cultivate Caroline's acquaintance as Shirley. She, who went nowhere else, called on an early day at the Rectory. She came in the afternoon, when the Rector happened to be out. It was rather a close day; the heat of the weather had flushed her, and she seemed fluttered, too, by the circumstance of entering a strange house; for it appeared her habits were most retiring and secluded. When Miss Helstone went to her in the dining-room, she found her seated on the sofa, trembling, fanning herself with her handkerchief, and seeming to contend with a nervous discomposure that threatened to become hysterical.

Caroline marvelled somewhat at this unusual want of self-command in a lady of her years, and also at the lack of real strength in one who appeared almost robust: for Mrs Pryor hastened to allege the fatigue of her walk, the heat of the sun etc., as reasons for her temporary indisposition; and still as, with more hurry than coherence, she again and again enumerated these causes of exhaustion, Caroline gently sought to relieve her by opening her shawl and removing her bonnet. Attentions of this sort, Mrs Pryor would not have accepted from every one: in general, she recoiled from touch or close approach, with a mixture of embarrassment and coldness far from flattering to those who offered her aid: to Miss Helstone's little light hand, however, she yielded tractàbly, and seemed soothed by its contact. In a few minutes she ceased to tremble, and grew quiet and tranquil.

Her usual manner being resumed, she proceeded to talk of ordinary topics. In a miscellaneous company, Mrs Pryor rarely opened her lips; or, if obliged to speak, she spoke under restraint, and consequently not well; in dialogue, she was a good converser: her language, always a little formal, was well chosen; her sentiments were just; her information was varied and correct. Caroline felt it pleasant to listen to her: more pleasant than she could have anticipated.

On the wall opposite the sofa where they sat, hung three pictures: the centre one, above the mantelpiece, that of a lady; the two others, male portraits.

'That is a beautiful face,' said Mrs Pryor, interrupting a brief pause which had followed half an hour's animated conversation: 'the features may be termed perfect; no statuary's chisel could improve them: it is a portrait from the life, I presume?'

'It is a portrait of Mrs Helstone.'

'Of Mrs Matthewson Helstone? Of your uncle's wife?'

'It is, and is said to be a good likeness: before her marriage, she was accounted the beauty of the district.'

'I should say she merited the distinction: what accuracy in all the lineaments! It is, however, a passive face: the original could not have been, what is generally termed, "a woman of spirit." '

'I believe she was a remarkably still, silent person.'

'One would scarcely have expected, my dear, that your uncle's choice should have fallen on a partner of that description. Is he not fond of being amused by lively chat?'

'In company he is; but he always says he could never do with a talking wife: he must have quiet at home. You go out to gossip, he affirms; you come home to read and reflect.'

'Mrs Matthewson lived but a few years after her marriage, I think I have heard?'

# Shirley

'About five years.'

'Well, my dear,' pursued Mrs Pryor, rising to go, 'I trust it is understood that you will frequently come to Fieldhead: I hope you will. You must feel lonely here, having no female relative in the house: you must necessarily pass much of your time in solitude.'

'I am inured to it: I have grown up by myself. May I arrange your shawl for you?'

Mrs Pryor submitted to be assisted.

'Should you chance to require help in your studies,' she said, 'you may command me.'

Caroline expressed her sense of such kindness.

'I hope to have frequent conversations with you. I should wish to be of use to you.'

Again Miss Helstone returned thanks. She thought what a kind heart was hidden under her visitor's seeming chilliness. Observing that Mrs Pryor again glanced with an air of interest towards the portraits, as she walked down the room, Caroline casually explained: –

'The likeness that hangs near the window, you will see, is my uncle, taken twenty years ago; the other, to the left of the mantelpiece, is his brother James, my father.'

'They resemble each other in some measure,' said Mrs Pryor; 'yet a difference of character may be traced in the different mould of the brow and mouth.'

'What difference?' inquired Caroline, accompanying her to the door. 'James Helstone – that is, my father – is generally considered the best-looking of the two: strangers, I remark, always exclaim, What a handsome man! Do you think his picture handsome, Mrs Pryor?'

'It is much softer or finer featured than that of your uncle.'

'But where or what is the difference of character to which you alluded? Tell me: I wish to see if you guess right.'

'My dear, your uncle is a man of principle: his forehead and his lips are firm, and his eye is steady.'

'Well, and the other? Do not be afraid of offending me: I always like the truth.'

'Do you like the truth? It is well for you: adhere to that preference – never swerve thence. The other, my dear, if he had been living now, would probably have furnished little support to his daughter. It is, however, a graceful head – taken in youth, I should think. My dear (turning abruptly), you acknowledge an inestimate value in principle?'

'I am sure no character can have true worth without it.'

'You feel what you say? You have considered the subject?'

'Often. Circumstances early forced it upon my attention.'

'The lesson was not lost, then, though it came so prematurely. I suppose the soil is not light nor stony, otherwise seed falling in that season never would have borne fruit. My dear, do not stand in the air of the door, you will take cold: good-afternoon.'

Miss Helstone's new acquaintance soon became of value to her: their society was acknowledged a privilege. She found she would have been in error indeed to have let slip this chance of relief – to have neglected to avail herself of this happy change: a turn was thereby given to her thoughts; a new channel was

# Shirley

opened for them, which, diverting a few of them at least from the one direction in which all had hitherto tended, abated the impetuosity of their rush, and lessened the force of their pressure on one worn-down point.

Soon she was content to spend whole days at Fieldhead, doing by turns whatever Shirley or Mrs Pryor wished her to do: and now one would claim her, now the other. Nothing could be less demonstrative than the friendship of the elder lady; but also nothing could be more vigilant, assiduous, untiring. I have intimated that she was a peculiar personage; and in nothing was her peculiarity more shown than in the nature of the interest she evinced for Caroline. She watched all her movements: she seemed as if she would have guarded all her steps: it gave her pleasure to be applied to by Miss Helstone for advice and assistance; she yielded her aid, when asked, with such quiet yet obvious enjoyment, that Caroline erelong took delight in depending on her.

Shirley Keeldar's complete docility with Mrs Pryor had at first surprised Miss Helstone, and not less the fact of the reserved ex-governess being so much at home and at ease in the residence of her young pupil, where she filled with such quiet independency a very dependent post; but she soon found that it needed but to know both ladies to comprehend fully the enigma. Every one, it seemed to her, must like, must love, must prize Mrs Pryor when they knew her. No matter that she perseveringly wore old-fashioned gowns; that her speech was formal, and her manner cool; that she had twenty little ways such as nobody else had – she was still such a stay, such a counsellor, so truthful, so kind in her way, that, in Caroline's idea, none once accustomed to her presence could easily afford to dispense with it.

As to dependency or humiliation, Caroline did not feel it in her intercourse with Shirley, and why should Mrs Pryor? The heiress was rich – very rich – compared with her new friend: one possessed a clear thousand a-year – the other not a penny; and yet there was a safe sense of equality experienced in her society, never known in that of the ordinary Briarfield and Whinbury gentry.

The reason was, Shirley's head ran on other things than money and position. She was glad to be independent as to property: by fits she was even elated at the notion of being lady of the manor, and having tenants and an estate: she was especially tickled with an agreeable complacency when reminded of 'all that property' down in the Hollow, 'comprising an excellent cloth-mill, dyehouse, warehouse, together with the messuage, gardens, and outbuildings, termed Hollow's cottage;' but her exultation being quite undisguised was singularly inoffensive; and, for her serious thoughts, they tended elsewhere. To admire the great, reverence the good, and be joyous with the genial, was very much the bent of Shirley's soul: she mused therefore on the means of following this bent far oftener than she pondered on her social superiority.

In Caroline, Miss Keeldar had first taken an interest because she was quiet, retiring, looked delicate, and seemed as if she needed some one to take care of her. Her predilection increased greatly when she discovered that her own way of thinking and talking was understood and responded to by this new acquaintance. She had hardly expected it. Miss Helstone, she fancied, had too pretty a face, manners and voice too soft, to be anything out of the common way in mind and attainments; and she very much wondered to see the gentle features light up archly to the reveillé of a dry sally or two risked by herself; and more did she wonder to discover the self-won knowledge treasured, and the untaught

# Shirley

speculations working in that girlish, curl-veiled head. Caroline's instinct of taste, too, was like her own: such books as Miss Keeldar had read with the most pleasure, were Miss Helstone's delight also. They held many aversions too in common, and could have the comfort of laughing together over works of false sentimentality and pompous pretension.

Few, Shirley conceived, men or women have the right taste in poetry: the right sense for discriminating between what is real and what is false. She had again and again heard very clever people pronounce this or that passage, in this or that versifier, altogether admirable, which, when she read, her soul refused to acknowledge as anything but cant, flourish, and tinsel, or at the best, elaborate wordiness; curious, clever, learned perhaps; haply even tinged with the fascinating hues of fancy, but, God knows, as different from real poetry as the gorgeous and massy vase of mosaic is from the little cup of pure metal; or, to give the reader a choice of similes, as the milliner's artificial wreath is from the fresh-gathered lily of the field.

Caroline, she found, felt the value of the true ore, and knew the deception of the flashy dross. The minds of the two girls being toned in harmony, often chimed very sweetly together.

One evening, they chanced to be alone in the oak-parlour. They had passed a long wet day together without ennui; it was now on the edge of dark; candles were not yet brought in; both, as twilight deepened, grew meditative and silent. A western wind roared high round the hall, driving wild clouds and stormy rain up from the far-remote ocean: all was tempest outside the antique lattices, all deep peace within. Shirley sat at the window, watching the rack in heaven, the mist on earth, listening to certain notes of the gale that plained like restless spirits – notes which, had she not been so young, gay, and healthy, would have swept her trembling nerves like some omen, some anticipatory dirge: in this her prime of existence and bloom of beauty, they but subdued vivacity to pensiveness. Snatches of sweet ballads haunted her ear; now and then she sang a stanza: her accents obeyed the fitful impulse of the wind; they swelled as its gusts rushed on, and died as they wandered away. Caroline, withdrawn to the farthest and darkest end of the room, her figure just discernible by the ruby shine of the flameless fire, was pacing to and fro, murmuring to herself fragments of well-remembered poetry. She spoke very low, but Shirley heard her; and while singing softly, she listened. This was the strain: –

> 'Obscurest night involved the sky,
>   The Atlantic billows roar'd,
> When such a destined wretch as I,
>   Washed headlong from on board,
> Of friends, of hope, of all bereft,
> His floating home for ever left.'

Here the fragment stopped; because Shirley's song, erewhile somewhat full and thrilling, had become delicately faint.

'Go on,' said she.

'Then you go on, too. I was only repeating, "The Castaway." '

'I know: if you can remember it all, say it all.'

And as it was nearly dark, and, after all, Miss Keeldar was no formidable

641

# Shirley

auditor, Caroline went through it. She went through it as she should have gone through it. The wild sea, the drowning mariner, the reluctant ship swept on in the storm, you heard were realized by her; and more vividly was realized the heart of the poet, who did not weep for the 'Castaway,' but who, in an hour of tearless anguish, traced a semblance to his own God-abandoned misery in the fate of that man-forsaken sailor, and cried from the depths where he struggled: –

> *'No voice divine the storm allayed,*
> *No light propitious shone,*
> *When, snatch'd from all effectual aid,*
> *We perish'd – each alone!*
> *But I – beneath a rougher sea,*
> *And whelm'd in deeper gulfs than he.'*

'I hope William Cowper is safe and calm in heaven now,' said Caroline.

'Do you pity what he suffered on earth?' asked Miss Keeldar.

'Pity him, Shirley? What can I do else? He was nearly broken-hearted when he wrote that poem, and it almost breaks one's heart to read it. But he found relief in writing it – I know he did; and that gift of poetry – the most divine bestowed on man – was, I believe, granted to allay emotions when their strength threatens harm. It seems to me, Shirley, that nobody should write poetry to exhibit intellect or attainment. Who cares for that sort of poetry? Who cares for learning – who cares for fine words in poetry? And who does not care for feeling – real feeling – however simply, even rudely expressed?'

'It seems you care for it, at all events: and certainly, in hearing that poem, one discovers that Cowper was under an impulse strong as that of the wind which drove the ship – an impulse which, while it would not suffer him to stop to add ornament to a single stanza, filled him with force to achieve the whole with consummate perfection. You managed to recite it with a steady voice, Caroline: I wonder thereat.'

'Cowper's hand did not tremble in writing the lines: why should my voice falter in repeating them? Depend on it, Shirley, no tear blistered the manuscript of "The Castaway," I hear in it no sob of sorrow, only the cry of despair; but, that cry uttered, I believe the deadly spasm passed from his heart; that he wept abundantly, and was comforted.'

Shirley resumed her ballad minstrelsy. Stopping short, she remarked erelong:

'One could have loved Cowper, if it were only for the sake of having the privilege of comforting him.'

'You never would have loved Cowper,' rejoined Caroline promptly: 'he was not made to be loved by woman.'

'What do you mean?'

'What I say. I know there is a kind of natures in the world – and very noble, elevated natures, too – whom love never comes near. You might have sought Cowper with the intention of loving him; and you would have looked at him, pitied him, and left him: forced away by a sense of the impossible, the incongruous, as the crew were borne from their drowning comrade by "the furious blast." '

'You may be right. Who told you this?'

'And what I say of Cowper, I should say of Rousseau. Was Rousseau ever

loved? He loved passionately; but was his passion ever returned? I am certain, never. And if there were any female Cowpers and Rousseaus, I should assert the same of them.'

'Who told you this, I ask? Did Moore?'

'Why should anybody have told me? Have I not an instinct? Can I not divine by analogy? Moore never talked to me either about Cowper, or Rousseau, or love. The voice we hear in solitude told me all I know on these subjects.'

'Do you like characters of the Rousseau order, Caroline?'

'Not at all, as a whole. I sympathize intensely with certain qualities they possess: certain divine sparks in their nature dazzle my eyes, and make my soul glow. Then, again, I scorn them. They are made of clay and gold. The refuse and the ore make a mass of weakness: taken altogether, I feel them unnatural, unhealthy, repulsive.'

'I dare say I should be more tolerant of a Rousseau than you would, Cary: submissive and contemplative yourself, you like the stern and the practical. By-the-way, you must miss that Cousin Robert of yours very much, now that you and he never meet?'

'I do.'

'And he must miss you?'

'That he does not.'

'I cannot imagine,' pursued Shirley, who had lately got a habit of introducing Moore's name into the conversation, even when it seemed to have no business there, – 'I cannot imagine but that he was fond of you, since he took so much notice of you, talked to you, and taught you so much.'

'He never was fond of me: he never professed to be fond of me. He took pains to prove that he only just tolerated me.'

Caroline, determined not to err on the flattering side in estimating her cousin's regard for her, always now habitually thought of it and mentioned it in the most scanty measure. She had her own reasons for being less sanguine than ever in hopeful views of the future: less indulgent to pleasurable retrospections of the past.

'Of course, then,' observed Miss Keeldar, 'you only just tolerated him, in return?'

'Shirley, men and women are so different: they are in such a different position. Women have so few things to think about – men so many: you may have a friendship for a man, while he is almost indifferent to you. Much of what cheers your life may be dependent on him, while not a feeling or interest of moment in his eyes may have reference to you. Robert used to be in the habit of going to London, sometimes for a week or a fortnight together; well, while he was away, I found his absence a void: there was something wanting; Briarfield was duller. Of course, I had my usual occupations; still I missed him. As I sat by myself in the evenings, I used to feel a strange certainty of conviction I cannot describe: that if a magician or a genius had, at that moment, offered me Prince Ali's tube (you remember it in the Arabian Nights?), and if, with its aid, I had been enabled to take a view of Robert – to see where he was, how occupied – I should have learned, in a startling manner, the width of the chasm which gaped between such as he and such as I. I knew that, however my thoughts might adhere to him, his were effectually sundered from me.'

# Shirley

'Caroline,' demanded Miss Keeldar, abruptly, 'don't you wish you had a profession – a trade?'

'I wish it fifty times a-day. As it is, I often wonder what I came into the world for. I long to have something absorbing and compulsory to fill my head and hands, and to occupy my thoughts.'

'Can labour alone make a human happy?'

'No; but it can give varieties of pain, and prevent us from breaking our hearts with a single tyrant master-torture. Besides, successful labour has its recompense; a vacant, weary, lonely, hopeless life has none.'

'But hard labour and learned professions, they say, make women masculine, coarse, unwomanly.'

'And what does it signify, whether unmarried and never-to-be-married women are unattractive and inelegant, or not? – provided only they are decent, decorous, and neat, it is enough. The utmost which ought to be required of old maids, in the way of appearance, is that they should not absolutely offend men's eyes as they pass them in the street; for the rest, they should be allowed, without too much scorn, to be as absorbed, grave, plain-looking, and plain-dressed as they please.'

'You might be an old maid yourself, Caroline, you speak so earnestly.'

'I shall be one: it is my destiny. I will never marry a Malone or a Sykes – and no one else will ever marry me.'

Here fell a long pause: Shirley broke it. Again the name by which she seemed bewitched was almost the first on her lips.

'Lina – did not Moore call you Lina sometimes?'

'Yes: it is sometimes used as the abbreviation of Caroline in his native country.'

'Well, Lina, do you remember my one day noticing an inequality in your hair – a curl wanting on that right side – and your telling me that it was Robert's fault, as he had once cut therefrom a long lock?'

'Yes.'

'If he is, and always was, as indifferent to you as you say, why did he steal your hair?'

'I don't know – yes, I do: it was my doing, not his. Everything of that sort always was my doing. He was going from home, to London, as usual; and the night before he went, I had found in his sister's work-box a lock of black hair – a short, round curl: Hortense told me it was her brother's and a keepsake. He was sitting near the table; I looked at his head – he has plenty of hair; on the temples were many such round curls. I thought he could spare me one: I knew I should like to have it and I asked for it. He said, on condition that he might have his choice of a tress from my head; so he got one of my long locks of hair, and I got one of his short ones. I keep his, but, I dare say, he has lost mine. It was my doing, and one of those silly deeds it distresses the heart and sets the face on fire to think of: one of those small but sharp recollections that return, lacerating your self-respect like tiny penknives, and forcing from your lips, as you sit alone, sudden insane-sounding interjections.'

'Caroline!'

'I *do* think myself a fool, Shirley, in some respects: I *do* despise myself. But I said I would not make you my confessor; for you cannot reciprocate foible for foible: you are not weak. How steadily you watch me now! turn aside your clear, strong, she-eagle eye: it is an insult to fix it on me thus.'

'What a study of character you are! Weak, certainly; but not in the sense you think. – Come in!'

This was said in answer to a tap at the door. Miss Keeldar happened to be near it at the moment, Caroline at the other end of the room: she saw a note put into Shirley's hands, and heard the words –

'From Mr Moore, ma'am.'

'Bring candles,' said Miss Keeldar.

Caroline sat expectant.

'A communication on business,' said the heiress; but when candles were brought, she neither opened nor read it. The Rector's Fanny was presently announced, and the Rector's niece went home.

# Chapter 13

## Further Communications on Business

n Shirley's nature prevailed at times an easy indolence: there were periods when she took delight in perfect vacancy of hand and eye – moments when her thoughts, her simple existence, the fact of the world being around – and heaven above her, seemed to yield her such fullness of happiness, that she did not need to lift a finger to increase the joy. Often, after an active morning, she would spend a sunny afternoon in lying stirless on the turf, at the foot of some tree of friendly umbrage: no society did she need but that of Caroline, and it sufficed if she were within call; no spectacle did she ask but that of the deep blue sky, and such cloudlets as sailed afar and aloft across its span; no sound but that of the bee's hum, the leaf's whisper. Her sole book in such hours was the dim chronicle of memory, or the sibyl page of anticipation; from her young eyes fell on each volume a glorious light to read by; round her lips at moments played a smile which revealed glimpses of the tale or prophecy: it was not sad, not dark. Fate had been benign to the blissful dreamer, and promised to favour her yet again. In her past were sweet passages; in her future rosy hopes.

Yet one day when Caroline drew near to rouse her, thinking she had lain long enough, behold, as she looked down, Shirley's cheek was wet as if with dew: those fine eyes of hers shone humid and brimming.

'Shirley, why do *you* cry?' asked Caroline, involuntarily laying stress on *you*.

Miss Keeldar smiled, and turned her picturesque head towards the questioner. 'Because it pleases me mightily to cry,' she said; 'my heart is both sad and glad: but why, you good, patient child – why do you not bear me company? I only weep tears, delightful and soon wiped away: you might weep gall, if you choose.'

'Why should I weep gall?'

'Mateless, solitary bird!' was the only answer.

# Shirley

'And are not you, too, mateless, Shirley?'

'At heart – no.'

'Oh! who nestles there, Shirley?'

But Shirley only laughed gaily at this question, and alertly started up.

'I have dreamed,' she said: 'a mere day-dream; certainly bright, probably baseless!'

Miss Helstone was by this time free enough from illusions: she took a sufficiently grave view of the future, and fancied she knew pretty well how her own destiny and that of some others were tending. Yet old associations retained their influence over her, and it was these, and the power of habit, which still frequently drew her of an evening to the field-stile and the old thorn overlooking the Hollow.

One night, the night after the incident of the note, she had been at her usual post, watching for her beacon – watching vainly; that evening no lamp was lit. She waited till the rising of certain constellations warned her of lateness, and signed her away. In passing Fieldhead, on her return, its moonlight beauty attracted her glance, and stayed her step an instant. Tree and hall rose peaceful under the night sky and clear full orb; pearly paleness gilded the building; mellow brown gloom bosomed it round; shadows of deep green brooded above its oak-wreathed roof. The broad pavement in front shone pale also; it gleamed as if some spell had transformed the dark granite to glistering Parian: on the silvery space slept two sable shadows, thrown sharply defined from two human figures. These figures when first seen were motionless and mute; presently they moved in harmonious step, and spoke low in harmonious key. Earnest was the gaze that scrutinized them as they emerged from behind the trunk of the cedar. 'Is it Mrs Pryor and Shirley?'

Certainly it is Shirley. Who else has a shape so lithe, and proud, and graceful? And her face, too, is visible: her countenance careless and pensive, and musing and mirthful, and mocking and tender. Not fearing the dew, she has not covered her head; her curls are free: they veil her neck and caress her shoulder with their tendril rings. An ornament of gold gleams through the half-closed folds of the scarf she has wrapped across her bust, and a large bright gem glitters on the white hand which confines it. Yes, that is Shirley.

Her companion then is, of course, Mrs Pryor?

Yes, if Mrs Pryor owns six feet of stature, and if she has changed her decent widow's weeds for masculine disguise. The figure walking at Miss Keeldar's side is a man – a tall, young, stately man – it is her tenant, Robert Moore.

The pair speak softly, their words are not distinguishable: to remain a moment to gaze is not to be an eavesdropper; and as the moon shines so clearly and their countenances are so distinctly apparent, who can resist the attraction of such interest? Caroline it seems cannot, for she lingers.

There was a time when, on summer nights, Moore had been wont to walk with his cousin, as he was now walking with the heiress. Often had she gone up the Hollow with him after sunset, to scent the freshness of the earth, where a growth of fragrant herbage carpeted a certain narrow terrace, edging a deep ravine, from whose rifted gloom was heard a sound like the spirit of the lonely

watercourse, moaning amongst its wet stones, and between its weedy banks, and under its dark bower of alders.

'But I used to be closer to him,' thought Caroline: 'he felt no obligation to treat me with homage; I needed only kindness. He used to hold my hand: he does not touch hers. And yet Shirley is not proud where she loves. There is no haughtiness in her aspect now, only a little in her port; what is natural to and inseparable from her: what she retains in her most careless as in her most guarded moments. Robert must think as I think, that he is at this instant looking down on a fine face; and he must think it with a man's brain, not with mine. She has such generous, yet soft fire in her eyes. She smiles – what makes her smile so sweet? I saw that Robert felt its beauty, and he must have felt it with his man's heart, not with my dim woman's perceptions. They look to me like two great happy spirits: yonder silvered pavement reminds me of that white shore we believe to be beyond the death-flood: they have reached it, they walked there united. And what am I – standing here in shadow, shrinking into concealment, my mind darker than my hiding-place? I am one of this world, no spirit – a poor, doomed mortal, who asks, in ignorance and hopelessness, wherefore she was born, to what end she lives; whose mind for ever runs on the question, how she shall at last encounter, and by whom be sustained through death?

'This is the worst passage I have come to yet: still I was quite prepared for it. I gave Robert up, and gave him up to Shirley, the first day I heard she was come: the first moment I saw her – rich, youthful, and lovely. She has him now: he is her lover; she is his darling: she will be far more his darling yet when they are married: the more Robert knows of Shirley, the more his soul will cleave to her. They will both be happy, and I do not grudge them their bliss; but I groan under my own misery: some of my suffering is very acute. Truly, I ought not to have been born: they should have smothered me at the first cry.'

Here, Shirley stepping aside to gather a dewy flower, she and her companion turned into a path that lay nearer the gate: some of their conversation became audible. Caroline would not stay to listen: she passed away noiselessly, and the moonlight kissed the wall which her shadow had dimmed. The reader is privileged to remain, and try what he can make of the discourse.

'I cannot conceive why Nature did not give you a bulldog's head, for you have all a bulldog's tenacity,' said Shirley.

'Not a flattering idea: am I so ignoble?'

'And something also you have of the same animal's silent ways of going about its work: you give no warning; you come noiselessly behind, seize fast, and hold on.'

'This is guess-work; you have witnessed no such feat on my part: in your presence I have been no bulldog.'

'Your very silence indicates your race. How little you talk in general, yet how deeply you scheme! You are far-seeing; you are calculating.'

'I know the ways of these people. I have gathered information of their intentions. My note last night informed you that Barraclough's trial had ended in his conviction and sentence to transportation: his associates will plot vengeance: I shall lay my plans so as to counteract, or, at least, be prepared for theirs; that is all. Having now given you as clear an explanation as I can, am I to understand that for what I propose doing I have your approbation?'

'I shall stand by you so long as you remain on the defensive. Yes.'

'Good! Without any aid – even opposed or disapproved by you – I believe I should have acted precisely as I now intend to act; but in another spirit. I now feel satisfied. On the whole, I relish the position.'

'I dare say you do; that is evident: you relish the work which lies before you still better than you would relish the execution of a government order for army-cloth.'

'I certainly feel it congenial.'

'So would old Helstone. It is true there is a shade of difference in your motives: many shades, perhaps. Shall I speak to Mr Helstone? I will, if you like.'

'Act as you please: your judgment, Miss Keeldar, will guide you accurately. I could rely on it myself, in a more difficult crisis; but I should inform you, Mr Helstone is somewhat prejudiced against me at present.'

'I am aware, I have heard all about your differences: depend upon it they will melt away; he cannot resist the temptation of an alliance under present circumstances.'

'I should be glad to have him: he is of true metal.'

'I think so also.'

'An old blade, and rusted somewhat; but the edge and temper still excellent.'

'Well, you shall have him, Mr Moore: that is, if I can win him.'

'Whom can you not win?'

'Perhaps not the Rector; but I will make the effort.'

'Effort! He will yield for a word – a smile.'

'By no means. It will cost me several cups of tea, some toast and cake, and an ample measure of remonstrances, expostulations, and persuasions. It grows rather chill.'

'I perceive you shiver. Am I acting wrongly to detain you here? Yet it is so calm: I even feel it warm; and society such as yours is a pleasure to me so rare. – If you were wrapped in a thicker shawl –'

'I might stay longer, and forget how late it is, which would chagrin Mrs Pryor. We keep early and regular hours at Fieldhead, Mr Moore; and so, I am sure, does your sister at the cottage.'

'Yes; but Hortense and I have an understanding the most convenient in the world, that we shall each do as we please.'

'How do you please to do?'

'Three nights in the week I sleep in the mill: but I require little rest; and when it is moonlight and mild, I often haunt the Hollow till daybreak.'

'When I was a very little girl, Mr Moore, my nurse used to tell me tales of fairies being seen in that Hollow. That was before my father built the mill, when it was a perfectly solitary ravine: you will be falling under enchantment.'

'I fear it is done,' said Moore, in a low voice.

'But there are worse things than fairies to be guarded against,' pursued Miss Keeldar.

'Things more perilous,' he subjoined.

'Far more so. For instance, how would you like to meet Michael Hartley, that mad Calvinist and Jacobin weaver? They say he is addicted to poaching, and often goes abroad at night with his gun.'

'I have already had the luck to meet him. We held a long argument together one night. A strange little incident it was: I liked it.'

# Shirley

'Liked it? I admire your taste! Michael is not sane. Where did you meet him?'

'In the deepest, shadiest spot in the glen, where the water runs low, under brushwood. We sat down near that plank bridge. It was moonlight, but clouded, and very windy. We had a talk.'

'On politics?'

'And religion. I think the moon was at the full, and Michael was as near crazed as possible: he uttered strange blasphemy in his Antinomian fashion.'

'Excuse me, but I think you must have been nearly as mad as he, to sit listening to him.'

'There is a wild interest in his ravings. The man would be half a poet, if he were not wholly a maniac; and perhaps a prophet, if he were not a profligate. He solemnly informed me that hell was fore-ordained my inevitable portion; that he read the mark of the beast on my brow; that I had been an outcast from the beginning. God's vengeance, he said, was preparing for me, and affirmed that in a vision of the night he had beheld the manner and the instrument of my doom. I wanted to know further, but he left me with these words, "The end is not yet." '

'Have you ever seen him since?'

'About a month afterwards, in returning from market, I encountered him and Moses Barraclough both in an advanced stage of inebriation: they were praying in frantic sort at the roadside. They accosted me as Satan, bid me avaunt, and clamoured to be delivered from temptation. Again, but a few days ago, Michael took the trouble of appearing at the counting-house door, hatless, in his shirt-sleeves, – his coat and castor having been detained at the public-house in pledge: he delivered himself of the comfortable message that he could wish Mr Moore to set his house in order, as his soul was likely shortly to be required of him.'

'Do you make light of these things?'

'The poor man had been drinking for weeks, and was in a state bordering on delirium tremens.'

'What then? He is the more likely to attempt the fulfilment of his own prophecies.'

'It would not do to permit incidents of this sort to affect one's nerves.'

'Mr Moore, go home!'

'So soon?'

'Pass straight down the fields, not round by the lane and plantations.'

'It is early yet.'

'It is late: for my part I am going in. Will you promise me not to wander in the Hollow to-night?'

'If you wish it.'

'I do wish it. May I ask whether you consider life valueless?'

'By no means: on the contrary, of late I regard my life as invaluable.'

'Of late?'

'Existence is neither aimless nor hopeless to me now; and it was both three months ago. I was then drowning, and rather wished the operation over. All at once a hand was stretched to me, – such a delicate hand, I scarcely dared trust it: – its strength, however, has rescued me from ruin.'

'Are you really rescued?'

'For the time: your assistance has given me another chance.'

# Shirley

'Live to make the best of it. Don't offer yourself as a target to Michael Hartley, and good-night!'

Miss Helstone was under a promise to spend the evening of the next day at Fieldhead: she kept her promise. Some gloomy hours had she spent in the interval. Most of the time had been passed shut up in her own apartment; only issuing from it, indeed, to join her uncle at meals, and anticipating inquiries from Fanny by telling her that she was busy altering a dress, and preferred sewing up-stairs, to avoid interruption.

She did sew: she plied her needle continuously, ceaselessly; but her brain worked faster than her fingers. Again, and more intensely than ever, she desired a fixed occupation, – no matter how onerous, how irksome. Her uncle must be once more entreated, but first she would consult Mrs Pryor. Her head laboured to frame projects as diligently as her hands to plait and stitch the thin texture of the muslin summer dress spread on the little white couch at the foot of which she sat. Now and then, while thus doubly occupied, a tear would fill her eyes and fall on her busy hands; but this sign of emotion was rare, and quickly effaced: the sharp pang passed, the dimness cleared from her vision; she would re-thread her needle, re-arrange tuck and trimming, and work on.

Late in the afternoon she dressed herself: she reached Fieldhead, and appeared in the oak parlour just as tea was brought in. Shirley asked her why she came so late.

'Because I have been making my dress,' said she. 'These fine sunny days began to make me ashamed of my winter merino; so I have furbished up a lighter garment.'

'In which you look as I like to see you,' said Shirley. 'You are a lady-like little person, Caroline: is she not, Mrs Pryor?'

Mrs Pryor never paid compliments, and seldom indulged in remarks, favourable or otherwise, on personal appearance. On the present occasion she only swept Caroline's curls from her cheek as she took a seat near her, caressed the oval outline, and observed, –

'You get somewhat thin, my love, and somewhat pale. Do you sleep well? Your eyes have a languid look;' and she gazed at her anxiously.

'I sometimes dream melancholy dreams,' answered Caroline; 'and if I lie awake for an hour or two in the night, I am continually thinking of the Rectory as a dreary old place. You know it is very near the churchyard: the back part of the house is extremely ancient, and it is said that the out-kitchens there were once enclosed in the churchyard, and that there are graves under them. I rather long to leave the Rectory.'

'My dear! You are surely not superstitious?'

'No, Mrs Pryor; but I think I grow what is called nervous. I see things under a darker aspect than I used to do. I have fears I never used to have – not of ghosts, but of omens and disastrous events; and I have an inexpressible weight on my mind which I would give the world to shake off, and I cannot do it.'

'Strange!' cried Shirley. 'I never feel so.' Mrs Pryor said nothing.

'Fine weather, pleasant days, pleasant scenes are powerless to give me pleasure,' continued Caroline. 'Calm evenings are not calm to me: moonlight,

which I used to think mild, now only looks mournful. Is this weakness of mind, Mrs Pryor, or what is it? I cannot help it: I often struggle against it: I reason; but reason and effort make no difference.'

'You should take more exercise,' said Mrs Pryor.

'Exercise! I exercise sufficiently: I exercise till I am ready to drop.'

'My dear, you should go from home.'

'Mrs Pryor, I should like to go from home, but not on any purposeless excursion or visit. I wish to be a governess as you have been. It would oblige me greatly if you would speak to my uncle on the subject.'

'Nonsense!' broke in Shirley. 'What an idea! Be a governess! Better be a slave at once. Where is the necessity of it? Why should you dream of such a painful step?'

'My dear,' said Mrs Pryor, 'you are very young to be a governess, and not sufficiently robust: the duties a governess undertakes are often severe.'

'And I believe I want severe duties to occupy me.'

'Occupy you?' cried Shirley. 'When are you idle? I never saw a more industrious girl than you: you are always at work. Come,' she continued, – 'Come and sit by my side, and take some tea to refresh you. You don't care much for my friendship, then, that you wish to leave me?'

'Indeed I do, Shirley; and I don't wish to leave you. I shall never find another friend so dear.'

At which words Miss Keeldar put her hand into Caroline's with an impulsively affectionate movement, which was well seconded by the expression of her face.

'If you think so, you had better make much of me,' she said, 'and not run away from me. I hate to part with those to whom I am become attached. Mrs Pryor there sometimes talks of leaving me, and says I might make a more advantageous connexion than herself. I should as soon think of exchanging an old-fashioned mother for something modish and stylish. As for you – why I began to flatter myself we were thoroughly friends; that you liked Shirley almost as well as Shirley likes you: and she does not stint her regard.'

'I *do* like Shirley: I like her more and more every day; but that does not make me strong or happy.'

'And would it make you strong or happy to go and live as a dependant amongst utter strangers? It would not; and the experiment must not be tried. I tell you it would fail: it is not in your nature to bear the desolate life governesses generally lead; you would fall ill: I won't hear of it.'

And Miss Keeldar paused, having uttered this prohibition very decidedly. Soon she recommenced, still looking somewhat 'courroucée:' –

'Why, it is my daily pleasure now to look out for the little cottage bonnet and the silk scarf glancing through the trees in the lane, and to know that my quiet, shrewd, thoughtful companion and monitress is coming back to me: that I shall have her sitting in the room to look at, to talk to, or to let alone, as she and I please. This may be a selfish sort of language – I know it is; but it is the language which naturally rises to my lips; therefore I utter it.'

'I would write to you, Shirley.'

'And what are letters? Only a sort of pis-aller. Drink some tea, Caroline: eat something – you eat nothing; laugh and be cheerful, and stay at home.'

Miss Helstone shook her head and sighed. She felt what difficulty she would have to persuade any one to assist or sanction her in making that change in her

life which she believed desirable. Might she only follow her own judgment, she thought she should be able to find, perhaps a harsh, but an effectual cure for her sufferings. But this judgment, founded on circumstances she could fully explain to none, least of all to Shirley, seemed, in all eyes but her own, incomprehensible and fantastic, and was opposed accordingly.

There really was no present pecuniary need for her to leave a comfortable home and 'take a situation;' and there was every probability that her uncle might in some way permanently provide for her. So her friends thought, and, as far as their lights enabled them to see, they reasoned correctly: but of Caroline's strange sufferings, which she desired so eagerly to overcome or escape, they had no idea, – of her racked nights and dismal days, no suspicion. It was at once impossible and hopeless to explain: to wait and endure was her only plan. Many that want food and clothing have cheerier lives and brighter prospects than she had; many, harassed by poverty, are in a strait less afflictive.

'Now, is your mind quieted?' inquired Shirley. 'Will you consent to stay at home?'

'I shall not leave it against the approbation of my friends,' was the reply; 'but I think in time they will be obliged to think as I do.'

During this conversation Mrs Pryor looked far from easy. Her extreme habitual reserve would rarely permit her to talk freely, or to interrogate others closely. She could think a multitude of questions she never ventured to put; give advice in her mind which her tongue never delivered. Had she been alone with Caroline, she might possibly have said something to the point: Miss Keeldar's presence, accustomed as she was to it, sealed her lips. Now, as on a thousand other occasions, inexplicable nervous scruples kept her back from interfering. She merely showed her concern for Miss Helstone in an indirect way, by asking her if the fire made her too warm, placing a screen between her chair and the hearth, closing a window whence she imagined a draught proceeded, and often and restlessly glancing at her. Shirley resumed, –

'Having destroyed your plan,' she said, 'which I hope I have done, I shall construct a new one of my own. Every summer I make an excursion. This season I propose spending two months either at the Scotch lochs or the English lakes: that is, I shall go there, provided you consent to accompany me: if you refuse, I shall not stir a foot.'

'You are very good, Shirley.'

'I would be very good, if you would let me: I have every disposition to be good. It is my misfortune and habit, I know, to think of myself paramount to anybody else: but who is not like me in that respect? However, when Captain Keeldar is made comfortable, accommodated with all he wants, including a sensible genial comrade, it gives him a thorough pleasure to devote his spare efforts to making that comrade happy. And should we not be happy, Caroline, in the Highlands? We will go to the Highlands. We will, if you can bear a sea-voyage, go to the Isles, – the Hebrides, the Shetland, the Orkney Islands. Would you not like that? I see you would: Mrs Pryor, I call you to witness; her face is all sunshine at the bare mention of it.'

'I should like it much,' returned Caroline; to whom, indeed, the notion of such a tour was not only pleasant, but gloriously reviving. Shirley rubbed her hands.

'Come, I can bestow a benefit,' she exclaimed. 'I can do a good deed with my

# Shirley

cash. My thousand a-year is not merely a matter of dirty bank-notes and jaundiced guineas (let me speak respectfully of both though, for I adore them); but, it may be, health to the drooping, strength to the weak, consolation to the sad. I was determined to make something of it better than a fine old house to live in, than satin gowns to wear; better than deference from acquaintance, and homage from the poor. Here is to begin. This summer – Caroline, Mrs Pryor, and I go out into the North Atlantic, beyond the Shetland – perhaps to the Faroe Isles. We will see seals in Suderoe, and, doubtless, mermaids in Stromoe. Caroline is laughing, Mrs Pryor: *I* made her laugh; *I* have done her good.'

'I shall like to go, Shirley,' again said Miss Helstone. 'I long to hear the sound of waves – ocean-waves, and to see them as I have imagined them in dreams, like tossing banks of green light, strewed with vanishing and re-appearing wreaths of foam, whiter than lilies. I shall delight to pass the shores of those lone rock-islets where the sea-birds live and breed unmolested. We shall be on the track of the old Scandinavians – of the Norsemen: we shall almost see the shores of Norway. This is a very vague delight that I feel, communicated by your proposal, but it *is* a delight.'

'Will you think of Fitful-Head now, when you lie awake at night; of gulls shrieking round it, and waves tumbling in upon it, rather than of the graves under the Rectory back-kitchen?'

'I will try; and instead of musing about remnants of shrouds, and fragments of coffins, and human bones and mould, I will fancy seals lying in the sunshine on solitary shores, where neither fisherman nor hunter ever come: of rock-crevices full of pearly eggs bedded in sea-weed; of unscared birds covering white sands in happy flocks.'

'And what will become of that inexpressible weight you said you had on your mind?'

'I will try to forget it in speculation on the sway of the whole Great Deep above a herd of whales rushing through the livid and liquid thunder down from the frozen zone: a hundred of them, perhaps, wallowing, flashing, rolling in the wake of a patriarch bull, huge enough to have been spawned before the Flood: such a creature as poor Smart had in his mind when he said, –

> *"Strong against tides, the enormous whale*
> *Emerges as he goes."* '

'I hope our bark will meet with no such shoal, or herd, as you term it, Caroline: (I suppose you fancy the sea-mammoths pasturing about the bases of the "everlasting hills," devouring strange provender in the vast valleys through and above which sea-billows roll). I should not like to be capsized by the patriarch bull.'

'I suppose you expect to see mermaids, Shirley?'

'One of them at any rate: I do not bargain for less: and she is to appear in some such fashion as this. I am to be walking by myself on deck, rather late of an August evening, watching and being watched by a full harvest-moon: something is to rise white on the surface of the sea, over which that moon mounts silent, and hangs glorious: the object glitters and sinks. It rises again. I think I hear it cry with an articulate voice: I call you up from the cabin: I show you an image, fair as alabaster, emerging from the dim wave. We both see the long

# Shirley

hair, the lifted and foam-white arm, the oval mirror brilliant as a star. It glides
nearer: a human face is plainly visible; a face in the style of yours, whose
straight, pure (excuse the word, it is appropriate), – whose straight, pure
lineaments, paleness does not disfigure. It looks at us, but not with your eyes.
I see a preternatural lure in its wily glance: it beckons. Were we men, we should
spring at the sign, the cold billow would be dared for the sake of the colder
enchantress; being women, we stand safe, though not dreadless. She comprehends
our unmoved gaze; she feels herself powerless; anger crosses her front; she cannot
charm, but she will appal us: she rises high, and glides all revealed, on the dark
wave-ridge. Temptress-terror! monstrous likeness of ourselves! Are you not glad,
Caroline, when at last, and with a wild shriek, she dives?'

'But, Shirley, she is not like us: we are neither temptresses, nor terrors, nor
monsters.'

'Some of our kind, it is said, are all three. There are men who ascribe to
"woman," in general, such attributes.'

'My dears,' here interrupted Mrs Pryor, 'does it not strike you that your
conversation for the last ten minutes has been rather fanciful?'

'But there is no harm in our fancies: is there ma'am?'

'We are aware that mermaids do not exist: why speak of them as if they did?
How can you find interest in speaking of a nonentity?'

'I don't know,' said Shirley.

'My dear, I think there is an arrival. I heard a step in the lane, while you
were talking; and is not that the garden-gate which creaks?'

Shirley stepped to the window.

'Yes, there is some one,' said she, turning quietly away; and, as she resumed
her seat, a sensitive flush animated her face, while a trembling ray at once
kindled and softened her eye. She raised her hand to her chin, cast her gaze
down, and seemed to think as she waited.

The servant announced Mr Moore, and Shirley turned round when Mr
Moore appeared at the door. His figure seemed very tall as he entered, and
stood in contrast with the three ladies, none of whom could boast a stature much
beyond the average. He was looking well, better than he had been known to
look for the past twelve months: a sort of renewed youth glowed in his eye and
colour, and an invigorated hope and settled purpose sustained his bearing:
firmness his countenance still indicated, but not austerity: it looked as cheerful
as it was earnest.

'I am just returned from Stilbro',' he said to Miss Keeldar, as he greeted her;
'and I thought I would call to impart to you the result of my mission.'

'You did right not to keep me in suspense,' she said; 'and your visit is well-
timed. Sit down: we have not finished tea. Are you English enough to relish tea;
or do you faithfully adhere to coffee?'

Moore accepted tea.

'I am learning to be a naturalized Englishman,' said he; 'my foreign habits
are leaving me one by one.'

And now he paid his respects to Mrs Pryor, and paid them well, with a grave
modesty that became his age, compared with hers. Then he looked at Caroline
– not, however, for the first time – his glance had fallen upon her before: he bent
towards her as she sat, gave her his hand, and asked her how she was. The light
from the window did not fall upon Miss Helstone, her back was turned towards

it: a quiet though rather low reply, a still demeanour, and the friendly protection of early twilight, kept out of view each traitorous symptom. None could affirm that she had trembled or blushed, that her heart had quaked, or her nerves thrilled: none could prove emotion: a greeting showing less effusion was never interchanged. Moore took the empty chair near her, opposite Miss Keeldar. He had placed himself well: his neighbour, screened by the very closeness of his vicinage from his scrutiny, and sheltered further by the dusk which deepened each moment, soon regained, not merely *seeming*, but *real* mastery of the feelings which had started into insurrection at the first announcement of his name.

He addressed his conversation to Miss Keeldar.

'I went to the barracks,' he said, 'and had an interview with Colonel Ryde: he approved my plans, and promised the aid I wanted: indeed, he offered a more numerous force than I require – half a dozen will suffice. I don't intend to be swamped by red-coats: they are needed for appearance rather than anything else; my main reliance is on my own civilians.'

'And on their captain,' interposed Shirley.

'What, Captain Keeldar?' inquired Moore, slightly smiling, and not lifting his eyes: the tone of raillery in which he said this was very respectful and suppressed.

'No,' returned Shirley, answering the smile; 'Captain Gérard Moore, who trusts much to the prowess of his own right arm, I believe.'

'Furnished with his counting-house ruler,' added Moore. Resuming his usual gravity, he went on: 'I received by this evening's post a note from the Home-Secretary in answer to mine: it appears they are uneasy at the state of matters here in the north; they especially condemn the supineness and pusillanimity of the mill-owners; they say, as I have always said, that inaction, under present circumstances, is criminal, and that cowardice is cruelty, since both can only encourage disorder, and lead finally to sanguinary outbreaks. There is the note: I brought it for your perusal; and there is a batch of newspapers, containing further accounts of proceedings in Nottingham, Manchester, and elsewhere.'

He produced letters and journals, and laid them before Miss Keeldar. While she perused them, he took his tea quietly; but, though his tongue was still, his observant faculties seemed by no means off duty. Mrs Pryor, sitting in the background, did not come within the range of his glance, but the two younger ladies had the full benefit thereof.

Miss Keeldar, placed directly opposite, was seen without effort: she was the object his eyes, when lifted, naturally met first; and, as what remained of daylight – the gilding of the west – was upon her, her shape rose in relief from the dark panelling behind. Shirley's clear cheek was tinted yet with the colour which had risen into it a few minutes since: the dark lashes of her eyes looking down as she read, the dusk yet delicate line of her eyebrows, the almost sable gloss of her curls, made her heightened complexion look fine as the bloom of a red wild-flower, by contrast. There was natural grace in her attitude, and there was artistic effect in the ample and shining folds of her silk dress – an attire simply fashioned, but almost splendid from the shifting brightness of its dye, warp and woof being of tints deep and changing as the hue on a pheasant's neck. A glancing bracelet on her arm produced the contrast of gold and ivory: there was something brilliant in the whole picture. It is to be supposed that Moore thought so, as his eye dwelt long on it, but he seldom permitted his feelings or his

opinions to exhibit themselves in his face: his temperament boasted a certain amount of phlegm, and he preferred an undemonstrative, not ungentle, but serious aspect, to any other.

He could not, by looking straight before him, see Caroline, as she was close at his side; it was necessary, therefore, to manoeuvre a little to get her well within the range of his observation: he leaned back in his chair, and looked down on her. In Miss Helstone, neither he nor any one else could discover brilliancy. Sitting in the shade, without flowers or ornaments, her attire the modest muslin dress, colourless but for its narrow stripe of pale azure, her complexion unflushed, unexcited, the very brownness of her hair and eyes invisible by this faint light, she was, compared with the heiress, as a graceful pencil-sketch compared with a vivid painting. Since Robert had seen her last, a great change had been wrought in her; whether he perceived it, might not be ascertained: he said nothing to that effect.

'How is Hortense?' asked Caroline, softly.

'Very well; but she complains of being unemployed: she misses you.'

'Tell her that I miss her, and that I write and read a portion of French every day.'

'She will ask if you sent your love: she is always particular on that point. You know she likes attention.'

'My best love – my very best; and say to her, that whenever she has time to write me a little note, I shall be glad to hear from her.'

'What if I forget? I am not the surest messenger of compliments.'

'No, don't forget, Robert: it is no compliment – it is in good earnest.'

'And must therefore be delivered punctually?'

'If you please.'

'Hortense will be ready to shed tears. She is tender-hearted on the subject of her pupil; yet she reproaches you sometimes for obeying your uncle's injunctions too literally. Affection, like love, will be unjust now and then.'

And Caroline made no answer to this observation; for indeed her heart was troubled, and to her eyes she would have raised her handkerchief, if she had dared. If she had dared, too, she would have declared how the very flowers in the garden of Hollow's cottage were dear to her; how the little parlour of that house was her earthly paradise; how she longed to return to it, as much almost as the First Woman, in her exile, must have longed to revisit Eden. Not daring, however, to say these things, she held her peace: she sat quiet at Robert's side, waiting for him to say something more. It was long since this proximity had been hers – long since his voice had addressed her: could she, with any show of probability, even of possibility, have imagined that the meeting gave him pleasure, to her it would have given deep bliss. Yet, even in doubt that it pleased – in dread that it might annoy him – she received the boon of the meeting as an imprisoned bird would the admission of sunshine to its cage: it was of no use arguing – contending against the sense of present happiness: to be near Robert was to be revived.

Miss Keeldar laid down the papers.

'And are you glad or sad for all these menacing tidings?' she inquired of her tenant.

'Not precisely either; but I certainly am instructed. I see that our only plan

is to be firm. I see that efficient preparation and a resolute attitude are the best means of averting bloodshed.'

He then inquired if she had observed some particular paragraph, to which she replied in the negative, and he rose to show it to her: he continued the conversation standing before her. From the tenor of what he said, it appeared evident that they both apprehended disturbances in the neighbourhood of Briarfield, though in what form they expected them to break out was not specified. Neither Caroline nor Mrs Pryor asked questions: the subject did not appear to be regarded as one ripe for free discussion; therefore the lady and her tenant were suffered to keep details to themselves, unimportuned by the curiosity of their listeners.

Miss Keeldar, in speaking to Mr Moore, took a tone at once animated and dignified, confidential and self-respecting. When, however, the candles were brought in, and the fire was stirred up, and the fullness of light thus produced rendered the expression of her countenance legible, you could see that she was all interest, life, and earnestness: there was nothing coquettish in her demeanour: whatever she felt for Moore, she felt it seriously. And serious, too, were his feelings, and settled were his views, apparently; for he made no petty effort to attract, dazzle, or impress. He contrived, notwithstanding, to command a little; because the deeper voice, however mildly modulated, the somewhat harder mind, now and then, though involuntarily and unintentionally, bore down by some peremptory phrase or tone the mellow accents and susceptible, if high, nature of Shirley. Miss Keeldar looked happy in conversing with him, and her joy seemed twofold, – a joy of the past and present, of memory and of hope.

What I have just said are Caroline's ideas of the pair: she felt what has just been described. In thus feeling, she tried not to suffer; but suffered sharply, nevertheless. She suffered, indeed, miserably: a few minutes before, her famished heart had tasted a drop and crumb of nourishment that, if freely given, would have brought back abundance of life where life was failing; but the generous feast was snatched from her, spread before another, and she remained but a bystander at the banquet.

The clock struck nine: it was Caroline's time for going home: she gathered up her work, put the embroidery, the scissors, the thimble into her bag: she bade Mrs Pryor a quiet good-night, receiving from that lady a warmer pressure of the hand than usual: she stepped up to Miss Keeldar.

'Good-night, Shirley!'

Shirley started up. 'What! – so soon? Are you going already?'

'It is past nine.'

'I never heard the clock. You will come again to-morrow; and you will be happy to-night, will you not? Remember our plans.'

'Yes,' said Caroline; 'I have not forgotten.'

Her mind misgave her that neither those plans nor any other could permanently restore her mental tranquillity. She turned to Robert, who stood close behind her: as he looked up, the light of the candles on the mantelpiece fell full on her face: all its paleness, all its change, all its forlorn meaning were clearly revealed. Robert had good eyes, and might have seen it, if he would: whether he did see it, nothing indicated.

'Good-night!' she said, shaking like a leaf, offering her thin hand hastily, anxious to part from him quickly.

'You are going home?' he asked, not touching her hand.

'Yes.'

'Is Fanny coming for you?'

'Yes.'

'I may as well accompany you a step of the way: not up to the Rectory, though, lest my old friend, Helstone, should shoot me from the window.'

He laughed and took his hat. Caroline spoke of unnecessary trouble: he told her to put on her bonnet and shawl. She was quickly ready, and they were soon both in the open air. Moore drew her hand under his arm, just in his old manner, – that manner which she ever felt to be so kind.

'You may run on, Fanny,' he said to the housemaid; 'we shall overtake you:' and when the girl had got a little in advance, he enclosed Caroline's hand in his, and said he was glad to find she was a familiar guest at Fieldhead: he hoped her intimacy with Miss Keeldar would continue; such society would be both pleasant and improving.

Caroline replied that she liked Shirley.

'And there is no doubt the liking is mutual,' said Moore: 'if she professes friendship, be certain she is sincere: she cannot feign; she scorns hypocrisy. And, Caroline, are we never to see you at Hollow's cottage again?'

'I suppose not, unless my uncle should change his mind.'

'Are you much alone now?'

'Yes; a good deal. I have little pleasure in any society but Miss Keeldar's.'

'Have you been quite well lately?'

'Quite.'

'You must take care of yourself. Be sure not to neglect exercise. Do you know I fancied you somewhat altered; – a little fallen away, and pale. Is your uncle kind to you?'

'Yes; he is just as he always is.'

'Not too tender, that is to say; not too protective and attentive. And what ails you, then? – tell me, Lina.'

'Nothing, Robert,' but her voice faltered.

'That is to say, nothing that you will tell me: I am not to be taken into confidence. Separation is then quite to estrange us, is it?'

'I do not know: sometimes I almost fear it is.'

'But it ought not to have that effect. "Should auld acquaintance be forgot, and days o' lang syne?" '

'Robert, I don't forget.'

'It is two months, I should think, Caroline, since you were at the cottage.'

'Since I was *within* it – yes.'

'Have you ever passed that way in your walk?'

'I have come to the top of the fields sometimes of an evening, and looked down. Once I saw Hortense in the garden watering her flowers, and I know at what time you light your lamp in the counting-house: I have waited for it to shine out now and then; and I have seen you bend between it and the window: I knew it was you – I could almost trace the outline of your form.'

'I wonder I never encountered you: I occasionally walk to the top of the Hollow's fields after sunset.'

'I know you do: I had almost spoken to you one night, you passed so near me.'

'Did I? I passed near you, and did not see you! Was I alone?'

# Shirley

'I saw you twice, and neither time were you alone.'

'Who was my companion? Probably nothing but Joe Scott, or my own shadow by moonlight.'

'No; neither Joe Scott nor your shadow, Robert. The first time you were with Mr Yorke; and the second time what you call your shadow was a shape with a white forehead and dark curls, and a sparkling necklace round its neck; but I only just got a glimpse of you and that fairy shadow: I did not wait to hear you converse.'

'It appears you walk invisible. I noticed a ring on your hand this evening; can it be the ring of Gyges? Henceforth, when sitting in the counting-house by myself, perhaps at dead of night, I shall permit myself to imagine that Caroline may be leaning over my shoulder reading with me from the same book, or sitting at my side engaged in her own particular task, and now and then raising her unseen eyes to my face to read there my thoughts.'

'You need fear no such infliction: I do not come near you: I only stand afar off, watching what may become of you.'

'When I walk out along the hedgerows in the evening after the mill is shut – or at night, when I take the watchman's place – I shall fancy the flutter of every little bird over its nest, the rustle of every leaf, a movement made by you; tree-shadows will take your shape; in the white sprays of hawthorn, I shall imagine glimpses of you. Lina, you will haunt me.'

'I will never be where you would not wish me to be, nor see nor hear what you would wish unseen and unheard.'

'I shall see you in my very mill in broad daylight: indeed, I have seen you there once. But a week ago, I was standing at the top of one of my long rooms, girls were working at the other end, and amongst half a dozen of them, moving to and fro, I seemed to see a figure resembling yours. It was some effect of doubtful light or shade, or of dazzling sunbeam. I walked up to this group; what I sought had glided away: I found myself between two buxom lasses in pinafores.'

'I shall not follow you into your mill, Robert, unless you call me there.'

'Nor is that the only occasion on which imagination has played me a trick. One night, when I came home late from market, I walked into the cottage parlour thinking to find Hortense; but instead of her, I thought I found you. There was no candle in the room: my sister had taken the light up-stairs with her; the window-blind was not drawn, and broad moonbeams poured through the panes: there you were, Lina, at the casement, shrinking a little to one side in an attitude not unusual with you. You were dressed in white, as I have seen you dressed at an evening party. For half a second, your fresh, living face seemed turned towards me, looking at me; for half a second, my idea was to go and take your hand, to chide you for your long absence, and welcome your present visit. Two steps forward broke the spell: the drapery of the dress changed outline; the tints of the complexion dissolved, and were formless: positively, as I reached the spot, there was nothing left but the sweep of a white muslin curtain, and a balsam plant in a flower-pot, covered with a flush of bloom – "sic transit," et cetera.'

'It was not my wraith, then? I almost thought it was.'

'No; only gauze, crockery, and pink blossom; a sample of earthly illusions.'

'I wonder you have time for such illusions, occupied as your mind must be.'

'So do I. But I find in myself, Lina, two natures; one for the world and

business, and one for home and leisure. Gérard Moore is a hard dog, brought up to mill and market: the person you call your cousin Robert is sometimes a dreamer, who lives elsewhere than in Cloth-hall and counting-house.'

'Your two natures agree with you: I think you are looking in good spirits and health: you have quite lost that harassed air which it often pained one to see in your face a few months ago.'

'Do you observe that? Certainly, I am disentangled of some difficulties: I have got clear of some shoals, and have more sea-room.'

'And, with a fair wind, you may now hope to make a prosperous voyage?'

'I may *hope* it – yes – but hope is deceptive: there is no controlling wind or wave: gusts and swells perpetually trouble the mariner's course; he dare not dismiss from his mind the expectation of tempest.'

'But you are ready for a breeze – you are a good seaman – an able commander: you are a skilful pilot, Robert; you will weather the storm.'

'My kinswoman always thinks the best of me, but I will take her words for a propitious omen: I will consider that in meeting her to-night, I have met with one of those birds whose appearance is to the sailor the harbinger of good-luck.'

'A poor harbinger of good-luck is she who can do nothing – who has no power. I feel my incapacity: it is of no use saying I have the will to serve you, when I cannot prove it; yet I have that will. I wish you success; I wish you high fortune and true happiness.'

'When did you ever wish me anything else? What is Fanny waiting for – I told her to walk on? Oh! we have reached the churchyard; then, we are to part here, I suppose: we might have sat a few minutes in the church-porch, if the girl had not been with us. It is so fine a night, so summer-mild and still, I have no particular wish to return yet to the Hollow.'

'But we cannot sit in the porch now, Robert.'

Caroline said this because Moore was turning her round towards it.

'Perhaps not, but tell Fanny to go in; say we are coming, a few minutes will make no difference.'

The church-clock struck ten.

'My uncle will be coming out to take his usual sentinel round, and he always surveys the church and churchyard.'

'And if he does? If it were not for Fanny, who knows we are here, I should find pleasure in dodging and eluding him. We could be under the east window when he is at the porch; as he came round to the north side, we could wheel off to the south; we might at a pinch hide behind some of the monuments: that tall erection of the Wynnes would screen us completely.'

'Robert, what good spirits you have! Go – go!' added Caroline hastily, 'I hear the front door –'

'I don't want to go; on the contrary, I want to stay.'

'You know my uncle will be terribly angry: he forbade me to see you because you are a Jacobin.'

'A queer Jacobin!'

'Go, Robert, he is coming; I hear him cough.'

'Diable! It is strange – what a pertinacious wish I feel to stay!'

'You remember what he did to Fanny's –' began Caroline, and stopped abruptly short. Sweetheart was the word that ought to have followed, but she could not utter it; it seemed calculated to suggest ideas she had no intention to

suggest; ideas delusive and disturbing. Moore was less scrupulous; 'Fanny's sweetheart?' he said at once. 'He gave him a shower-bath under the pump – did he not? He'd do as much for me, I daresay, with pleasure. I should like to provoke the old Turk – not however against *you*: but he would make a distinction between a cousin and a lover, would he not?'

'Oh! he would not think of you in that way, of course not; his quarrel with you is entirely political; yet I should not like the breach to be widened, and he is so testy. Here he is at the garden-gate – for your own sake and mine, Robert, go!'

The beseeching words were aided by a beseeching gesture and a more beseeching look. Moore covered her clasped hands an instant with his, answered her upward by a downward gaze, said 'Good-night!' and went.

Caroline was in a moment at the kitchen-door behind Fanny; the shadow of the shovel-hat at that very instant fell on a moonlit tomb; the Rector emerged, erect as a cane, from his garden, and proceeded in slow march, his hands behind him, down the cemetery. Moore was almost caught: he had to 'dodge' after all, to coast round the church, and finally to bend his tall form behind the Wynnes' ambitious monument. There he was forced to hide full ten minutes, kneeling with one knee on the turf, his hat off, his curls bare to the dew, his dark eye shining, and his lips parted with inward laughter at his position; for the Rector meantime stood coolly star-gazing, and taking snuff within three feet of him.

It happened, however, that Mr Helstone had no suspicion whatever on his mind; for being usually but vaguely informed of his niece's movements, not thinking it worth while to follow them closely, he was not aware that she had been out at all that day, and imagined her then occupied with book or work in her chamber: where, indeed, she was by this time; though not absorbed in the tranquil employment he ascribed to her, but standing at her window with fast-throbbing heart, peeping anxiously from behind the blind, watching for her uncle to re-enter and her cousin to escape; and at last she was gratified: she heard Mr Helstone come in; she saw Robert stride the tombs and vault the wall; she then went down to prayers. When she returned to her chamber, it was to meet the memory of Robert. Slumber's visitation was long averted: long she sat at her lattice, long gazed down on the old garden and older church, on the tombs laid out all grey and calm, and clear in moonlight. She followed the steps of the night, on its pathway of stars, far into the 'wee sma' hours ayont the twal':' she was with Moore in spirit, the whole time: she was at his side: she heard his voice: she gave her hand into his hand; it rested warm in his fingers. When the church-clock struck, when any other sound stirred, when a little mouse familiar to her chamber, an intruder for which she would never permit Fanny to lay a trap, came rattling among the links of her locket-chain, her one ring, and another trinket or two, on the toilette-table, to nibble a bit of biscuit laid ready for it, she looked up, recalled momentarily to the real. Then she said half aloud, as if deprecating the accusation of some unseen and unheard monitor, –

'I am not cherishing love-dreams: I am only thinking because I cannot sleep: of course, I know he will marry Shirley.'

With returning silence, with the lull of the chime, and the retreat of her small untamed and unknown protégé, she still resumed the dream, nestling to the vision's side, – listening to, conversing with it. It paled at last: as dawn approached, the setting stars and breaking day dimmed the creation of Fancy:

the wakened song of birds hushed her whispers. The tale full of fire, quick with interest, borne away by the morning wind, became a vague murmur. The shape that, seen in a moonbeam, lived, had a pulse, had movement, wore health's glow and youth's freshness, turned cold and ghostly grey, confronted with the red of sunrise. It wasted. She was left solitary at last: she crept to her couch, chill and dejected.

# Chapter 14

## Shirley Seeks to be Saved by Works

'Of course, I know he will marry Shirley,' were her first words when she rose in the morning. 'And he ought to marry her: she can help him,' she added firmly. 'But I shall be forgotten when they *are* married,' was the cruel succeeding thought. 'Oh! I shall be wholly forgotten! And what – *what* shall I do when Robert is taken quite from me? Where shall I turn? *My* Robert! I wish I could justly call him mine: but I am poverty and incapacity; Shirley is wealth and power: and she is beauty too, and love – I cannot deny it. This is no sordid suit: she loves him – not with inferior feelings: she loves, or *will* love, as he must feel proud to be loved. Not a valid objection can be made. Let them be married then: but afterwards I shall be nothing to him. As for being his sister, and all that stuff, I despise it. I will either be all or nothing to a man like Robert: no feeble shuffling, or false cant, is endurable. Once let that pair be united, and I will certainly leave them. As for lingering about, playing the hypocrite, and pretending to calm sentiments of friendship, when my soul will be wrung with other feelings, I shall not descend to such degradation. As little could I fill the place of their mutual friend as that of their deadly foe: as little could I stand between them as trample over them. Robert is a first-rate man – in my eyes: I *have* loved, *do* love, and *must* love him. I would be his wife, if I could; as I cannot, I must go where I shall never see him. There is but one alternative – to cleave to him as if I were a part of him, or to be sundered from him wide as the two poles of a sphere. Sunder me then, Providence. Part us speedily.'

Some such aspirations as these were again working in her mind late in the afternoon, when the apparition of one of the personages haunting her thoughts passed the parlour window. Miss Keeldar sauntered slowly by: her gait, her countenance wearing that mixture of wistfulness and carelessness which, when quiescent, was the wonted cast of her look, and character of her bearing. When animated, the carelessness quite vanished, the wistfulness became blent with a genial gaiety, seasoning the laugh, the smile, the glance, with an unique flavour of sentiment, so that mirth from her never resembled 'the crackling of thorns under a pot.'

# Shirley

'What do you mean by not coming to see me this afternoon, as you promised?' was her address to Caroline as she entered the room.

'I was not in the humour,' replied Miss Helstone, very truly.

Shirley had already fixed on her a penetrating eye.

'No,' she said; 'I see you are not in the humour for loving me: you are in one of your sunless, inclement moods, when one feels a fellow-creature's presence is not welcome to you. You have such moods: are you aware of it?'

'Do you mean to stay long, Shirley?'

'Yes: I am come to have my tea, and must have it before I go. I shall take the liberty then of removing my bonnet, without being asked.'

And this she did, and then stood on the rug with her hands behind her.

'A pretty expression you have in your countenance,' she went on, still gazing keenly, though not inimically, rather indeed pityingly at Caroline. 'Wonderfully self-supported you look, you solitude-seeking, wounded deer. Are you afraid Shirley will worry you, if she discovers that you are hurt, and that you bleed?'

'I never do fear Shirley.'

'But sometimes you dislike her: often you avoid her. Shirley can feel when she is slighted and shunned. If you had not walked home in the company you did last night, you would have been a different girl to-day. What time did you reach the Rectory?'

'By ten.'

'Humph! You took three-quarters of an hour to walk a mile. Was it you, or Moore, who lingered so?'

'Shirley, you talk nonsense.'

'*He* talked nonsense – that I doubt not: or he looked it, which is a thousand times worse: I see the reflection of his eyes on your forehead at this moment. I feel disposed to call him out, if I could only get a trustworthy second: I feel desperately irritated: I felt so last night, and have felt it all day.

'You don't ask me why,' she proceeded, after a pause, 'you little, silent, over-modest thing; and you don't deserve that I should pour out my secrets into your lap without an invitation. Upon my word, I could have found it in my heart to have dogged Moore yesterday evening with dire intent: I have pistols, and can use them.'

'Stuff, Shirley! Which would you have shot – me or Robert?'

'Neither, perhaps – perhaps myself – more likely a bat or a tree-bough. He is a puppy – your cousin: a quiet, serious, sensible, judicious, ambitious puppy. I see him standing before me, talking his half-stern, half-gentle talk, bearing me down (as I am very conscious he does) with his fixity of purpose, &c.; and then – I have no patience with him!'

Miss Keeldar started off on a rapid walk through the room, repeating energetically that she had no patience with men in general, and with her tenant in particular.

'You are mistaken,' urged Caroline, in some anxiety: 'Robert is no puppy or male flirt; I can vouch for that.'

'*You* vouch for it! Do you think I'll take your word on the subject? There is no one's testimony I would not credit sooner than yours. To advance Moore's fortune, you would cut off your right hand.'

'But not tell lies; and if I speak the truth, I must assure you that he was just civil to me last night – that was all.'

# Shirley

'I never asked what he was – I can guess: I saw him from the window take your hand in his long fingers, just as he went out at my gate.'

'That is nothing. I am not a stranger, you know: I am an old acquaintance, and his cousin.'

'I feel indignant; and that is the long and short of the matter,' responded Miss Keeldar. 'All my comfort,' she added presently, 'is broken up by his manoeuvres. He keeps intruding between you and me: without him we should be good friends; but that six feet of puppyhood makes a perpetually recurring eclipse of our friendship. Again and again he crosses and obscures the disk I want always to see clear: ever and anon he renders me to you a mere bore and nuisance.'

'No, Shirley; no.'

'He does. You did not want my society this afternoon, and I feel it hard: you are naturally somewhat reserved, but I am a social personage, who cannot live alone. If we were but left unmolested, I have that regard for you that I could bear you in my presence for ever, and not for the fraction of a second do I ever wish to be rid of you. You cannot say as much respecting me.'

'Shirley, I can say anything you wish: Shirley, I like you.'

'You will wish me at Jericho to-morrow, Lina.'

'I shall not. I am every day growing more accustomed to – fonder of you. You know I am too English to get up a vehement friendship all at once; but you are so much better than common – you are so different to everyday young ladies – I esteem you – I value you: you are never a burden to me – never. Do you believe what I say?'

'Partly,' replied Miss Keeldar, smiling rather incredulously; 'but you are a peculiar personage: quiet as you look, there is both a force and a depth somewhere within, not easily reached or appreciated: then you certainly are not happy.'

'And unhappy people are rarely good – is that what you mean?'

'Not at all: I mean rather that unhappy people are often preoccupied, and not in the mood for discoursing with companions of my nature. Moreover, there is a sort of unhappiness which not only depresses, but corrodes – and that, I fear, is your portion. Will pity do you any good, Lina? If it will, take some from Shirley: she offers largely, and warrants the article genuine.'

'Shirley, I never had a sister – you never had a sister; but it flashes on me at this moment how sisters feel towards each other. Affection twined with their life, which no shocks of feeling can uproot, which little quarrels only trample an instant that it may spring more freshly when the pressure is removed; affection that no passion can ultimately outrival, with which even love itself cannot do more than compete in force and truth. Love hurts us so, Shirley: it is so tormenting, so racking, and it burns away our strength with its flame; in affection is no pain and no fire, only sustenance and balm. I am supported and soothed when you – that is, *you only* – are near, Shirley. Do you believe me now?'

'I am always easy of belief when the creed pleases me. We really are friends then, Lina, in spite of the black eclipse?'

'We really are,' returned the other, drawing Shirley towards her, and making her sit down, 'chance what may.'

'Come, then, we will talk of something else than the Troubler.' But at this moment the Rector came in, and the 'something else' of which Miss Keeldar

was about to talk was not again alluded to till the moment of her departure; she then delayed a few minutes in the passage to say–

'Caroline, I wish to tell you that I have a great weight on my mind: my conscience is quite uneasy, as if I had committed, or was going to commit, a crime. It is not my *private* conscience, you must understand, but my landed-proprietor and lord-of-the-manor conscience. I have got into the clutch of an eagle with iron talons. I have fallen under a stern influence, which I scarcely approve, but cannot resist. Something will be done erelong, I fear, which it by no means pleases me to think of. To ease my mind, and to prevent harm as far as I can, I mean to enter on a series of good works. Don't be surprised, therefore, if you see me all at once turn outrageously charitable. I have no idea how to begin, but you must give me some advice: we will talk more on the subject to-morrow; and just ask that excellent person, Miss Ainley, to step up to Fieldhead: I have some notion of putting myself under her tuition – won't she have a precious pupil? Drop a hint to her, Lina, that, though a well-meaning, I am rather a neglected character, and then she will feel less scandalized at my ignorance about clothing societies, and such things.'

On the morrow, Caroline found Shirley sitting gravely at her desk, with an account-book, a bundle of bank-notes, and a well-filled purse before her. She was looking mighty serious, but a little puzzled. She said she had been 'casting an eye' over the weekly expenditure in housekeeping at the Hall, trying to find out where she could retrench; that she had also just given audience to Mrs Gill, the cook, and had sent that person away with a notion that her (Shirley's) brain was certainly crazed. 'I have lectured her on the duty of being careful,' said she, 'in a way quite new to her. So eloquent was I on the text of economy, that I surprised myself; for, you see, it is altogether a fresh idea: I never thought, much less spoke, on the subject till lately. But it is all theory; for when I came to the practical part I could retrench nothing. I had not firmness to take off a single pound of butter, or to prosecute to any clear result an inquest into the destiny of either dripping, lard, bread, cold meat, or other kitchen perquisite whatever. I know we never get up illuminations at Fieldhead, but I could not ask the meaning of sundry quite unaccountable pounds of candles: we do not wash for the parish, yet I viewed in silence items of soap and bleaching powder calculated to satisfy the solicitude of the most anxious inquirer after our position in reference to those articles: carnivorous I am not, nor is Mrs Pryor, nor is Mrs Gill herself, yet I only hemmed and opened my eyes a little wide when I saw butchers' bills whose figure seemed to prove that fact – falsehood, I mean. Caroline, you may laugh at me, but you can't change me. I am a poltroon on certain points – I feel it. There is a base alloy of moral cowardice in my composition. I blushed and hung my head before Mrs Gill, when she ought to have been faltering confessions to me. I found it impossible to get up the spirit even to hint, much less to prove, to her that she was a cheat. I have no calm dignity – no true courage about me.'

'Shirley, what fit of self-injustice is this? My uncle, who is not given to speak well of women, says there are not ten thousand men in England as genuinely fearless as you.'

'I am fearless, physically: I am never nervous about danger. I was not startled from self-possession when Mr Wynne's great red bull rose with a bellow before my face, as I was crossing the cowslip-lea alone, stooped his begrimed, sullen

head, and made a run at me; but I was afraid of seeing Mrs Gill brought to shame and confusion of face. You have twice – ten times my strength of mind on certain subjects, Caroline: you, whom no persuasions can induce to pass a bull, however quiet he looks, would have firmly shown my housekeeper she had done wrong; then you would have gently and wisely admonished her; and at last, I daresay, provided she had seemed penitent, you would have very sweetly forgiven her. Of this conduct I am incapable. However, in spite of exaggerated imposition, I still find we live within our means; I have money in hand, and I really must do some good with it. The Briarfield poor are badly off; they must be helped. What ought I to do, think you, Lina? Had I not better distribute the cash at once?'

'No, indeed, Shirley; you will not manage properly. I have often noticed that your notion of charity is to give shillings and half-crowns in a careless, freehanded sort of way, which is liable to continual abuse. You must have a prime minister, or you will get yourself into a series of scrapes. You suggested Miss Ainley yourself: to Miss Ainley I will apply; and, meantime, promise to keep quiet, and not begin throwing away your money. What a great deal you have, Shirley! – you must feel very rich with all that?'

'Yes; I feel of consequence. It is not an immense sum, but I feel responsible for its disposal; and really this responsibility weighs on my mind more heavily than I could have expected. They say that there are some families almost starving to death in Briarfield: some of my own cottagers are in wretched circumstances: I must and will help them.'

'Some people say we shouldn't give alms to the poor, Shirley.'

'They are great fools for their pains. For those who are not hungry, it is easy to palaver about the degradation of charity, and so on; but they forget the brevity of life, as well as its bitterness. We have none of us long to live: let us help each other through seasons of want and woe, as well as we can, without heeding in the least the scruples of vain philosophy.'

'But you do help others, Shirley: you give a great deal as it is.'

'Not enough: I must give more, or, I tell you, my brother's blood will some day be crying to Heaven against me. For, after all, if political incendiaries come here to kindle conflagration in the neighbourhood, and my property is attacked, I shall defend it like a tigress – I know I shall. Let me listen to Mercy as long as she is near me: her voice once drowned by the shout of ruffian defiance, and I shall be full of impulses to resist and quell. If once the poor gather and rise in the form of the mob, I shall turn against them as an aristocrat: if they bully me, I must defy; if they attack, I must resist, – and I will.'

'You talk like Robert.'

'I feel like Robert, only more fireily. Let them meddle with Robert, or Robert's mill, or Robert's interests, and I shall hate them. At present I am no patrician, nor do I regard the poor round me as plebeians; but if once they violently wrong me or mine, and then presume to dictate to us, I shall quite forget pity for their wretchedness and respect for their poverty, in scorn of their ignorance and wrath at their insolence.'

'Shirley – how your eyes flash!'

'Because my soul burns. Would you, any more than me, let Robert be borne down by numbers?'

'If I had your power to aid Robert, I would use it as you mean to use it. If

# Shirley

I could be such a friend to him as you can be, I would stand by him as you mean
to stand by him – till death.'

'And now, Lina, though your eyes don't flash, they glow. You drop your lids;
but I saw a kindled spark. However, it is not yet come to fighting. What I want
to do is to *prevent* mischief. I cannot forget, either day or night, that these
imbittered feelings of the poor against the rich have been generated in suffering:
they would neither hate nor envy us if they did not deem us so much happier
than themselves. To allay this suffering, and thereby lessen this hate, let me, out
of my abundance, give abundantly; and that the donation may go farther, let it
be made wisely. To that intent, we must introduce some clear, calm, practical
sense into our councils: so go, and fetch Miss Ainley.'

Without another word, Caroline put on her bonnet and departed. It may,
perhaps, appear strange that neither she nor Shirley thought of consulting Mrs
Pryor on their scheme; but they were wise in abstaining. To have consulted her
– and this they knew by instinct – would only have been to involve her in painful
embarrassment. She was far better informed, better read, a deeper thinker than
Miss Ainley, but of administrative energy, of executive activity, she had none.
She would subscribe her own modest mite to a charitable object willingly, –
secret almsgiving suited her; but in public plans, on a large scale, she could take
no part: as to originating them, that was out of the question. This Shirley knew,
and therefore she did not trouble Mrs Pryor by unavailing conferences, which
could only remind her of her own deficiencies, and do no good.

It was a bright day for Miss Ainley, when she was summoned to Fieldhead
to deliberate on projects so congenial to her; when she was seated with all honour
and deference at a table with paper, pen, ink and – what was best of all – cash
before her, and requested to draw up a regular plan for administering relief to
the destitute poor of Briarfield. She, who knew them all, had studied their wants,
had again and again felt in what way they might best be succoured, could the
means of succour only be found, was fully competent to the undertaking, and
a meek exultation gladdened her kind heart as she felt herself able to answer
clearly and promptly the eager questions put by the two young girls; as she
showed them in her answers how much and what serviceable knowledge she
had acquired of the condition of her fellow-creatures round her.

Shirley placed at her disposal £300, and at sight of the money Miss Ainley's
eyes filled with joyful tears; for she already saw the hungry fed, the naked
clothed, the sick comforted thereby. She quickly drew up a simple, sensible plan
for its expenditure; and she assured them brighter times would now come round,
for she doubted not the lady of Fieldhead's example would be followed by others:
she should try to get additional subscriptions, and to form a fund; but first she
must consult the clergy: yes, on that point, she was peremptory: Mr Helstone,
Dr Boultby, Mr Hall, *must* be consulted – (for not only must Briarfield be
relieved, but Whinbury and Nunnely) – it would, she averred, be presumption
in her to take a single step unauthorized by them.

The clergy were sacred beings in Miss Ainley's eyes: no matter what might
be the insignificance of the individual, his station made him holy. The very
curates – who, in their trivial arrogance, were hardly worthy to tie her patten-
strings, or carry her cotton umbrella, or check woollen-shawl – she, in her pure,
sincere enthusiasm, looked upon as sucking saints. No matter how clearly their
little vices and enormous absurdities were pointed out to her, she could not see

# Shirley

them: she was blind to ecclesiastical defects: the white surplice covered a multitude of sins.

Shirley, knowing this harmless infatuation on the part of her recently chosen prime minister, stipulated expressly that the curates were to have no voice in the disposal of the money; that their meddling fingers were not to be inserted into the pie. The rectors, of course, must be paramount, and they might be trusted: they had some experience, some sagacity, and Mr Hall, at least, had sympathy and loving-kindness for his fellow-men; but as for the youth under them, they must be set aside, kept down, and taught that subordination and silence best became their years and capacity.

It was with some horror Miss Ainley heard this language: Caroline, however, interposing with a mild word or two in praise of Mr Sweeting, calmed her again. Sweeting was, indeed, her own favourite: she endeavoured to respect Messrs Malone and Donne; but the slices of spunge-cake, and glasses of cowslip or primrose wine, she had at different times administered to Sweeting, when he came to see her in her little cottage, were ever offered with sentiments of truly motherly regard. The same innocuous collation she had once presented to Malone; but that personage evinced such open scorn of the offering, she had never ventured to renew it. To Donne she always served the treat, and was happy to see his approbation of it proved beyond a doubt, by the fact of his usually eating two pieces of cake, and putting a third in his pocket.

Indefatigable in her exertions where good was to be done, Miss Ainley would immediately have set out on a walk of ten miles round to the three rectors, in order to show her plan, and humbly solicit their approval: but Miss Keeldar interdicted this, and proposed as an amendment, to collect the clergy in a small select reunion that evening at Fieldhead. Miss Ainley was to meet them, and the plan was to be discussed in full privy council.

Shirley managed to get the senior priesthood together accordingly; and before the old maid's arrival she had, further, talked all the gentlemen into the most charming mood imaginable. She herself had taken in hand Dr Boultby and Mr Helstone. The first was a stubborn old Welshman, hot, opinionated, and obstinate, but withal a man who did a great deal of good, though not without making some noise about it: the latter, we know. She had rather a friendly feeling for both; especially for old Helstone; and it cost her no trouble to be quite delightful to them. She took them round the garden; she gathered them flowers; she was like a kind daughter to them. Mr Hall she left to Caroline – or rather, it was to Caroline's care Mr Hall consigned himself.

He generally sought Caroline in every party where she and he happened to be. He was not in general a lady's man, though all ladies liked him: something of a book-worm he was, near-sighted, spectacled, now and then abstracted. To old ladies he was kind as a son. To men of every occupation and grade he was acceptable: the truth, simplicity, frankness of his manners, the nobleness of his integrity, the reality and elevation of his piety, won him friends in every grade: his poor clerk and sexton delighted in him; the noble patron of his living esteemed him highly. It was only with young, handsome, fashionable, and stylish ladies he felt a little shy: being himself a plain man – plain in aspect, plain in manners, plain in speech – he seemed to fear their dash, elegance, and airs. But Miss Helstone had neither dash nor airs, and her native elegance was of a very quiet order – quiet as the beauty of a ground-loving hedge-flower. He was a fluent,

# Shirley

cheerful, agreeable talker. Caroline could talk, too, in a *tête-à-tête*: she liked Mr Hall to come and take the seat next her in a party, and thus secure her from Peter Augustus Malone, Joseph Donne, or John Sykes; and Mr Hall never failed to avail himself of this privilege when he possibly could. Such preference shown by a single gentleman to a single lady would certainly, in ordinary cases, have set in motion the tongues of the gossips; but Cyril Hall was forty-five years old, slightly bald, and slightly grey, and nobody ever said or thought he was likely to be married to Miss Helstone. Nor did he think so himself: he was wedded already to his books and his parish: his kind sister Margaret, spectacled and learned like himself, made him happy in his single state; he considered it too late to change. Besides, he had known Caroline as a pretty little girl: she had sat on his knee many a time; he had bought her toys and given her books; he felt that her friendship for him was mixed with a sort of filial respect; he could not have brought himself to attempt to give another colour to her sentiments, and his serene mind could glass a fair image without feeling its depths troubled by the reflection.

When Miss Ainley arrived, she was made kindly welcome by every one: Mrs Pryor and Margaret Hall made room for her on the sofa between them; and when the three were seated, they formed a trio which the gay and thoughtless would have scorned, indeed, as quite worthless and unattractive – a middle-aged widow and two plain spectacled old maids – yet which had its own quiet value, as many a suffering and friendless human being knew.

Shirley opened the business and showed the plan.

'I know the hand which drew up that,' said Mr Hall, glancing at Miss Ainley, and smiling benignantly: his approbation was won at once. Boultby heard and deliberated with bent brow and protruded under lip: his consent he considered too weighty to be given in a hurry. Helstone glanced sharply round with an alert, suspicious expression, as if he apprehended that female craft was at work, and that something in petticoats was somehow trying underhand to acquire too much influence, and make itself of too much importance. Shirley caught and comprehended the expression:–

'This scheme is nothing,' said she, carelessly; 'it is only an outline – a mere suggestion; you, gentlemen, are requested to draw up rules of your own.'

And she directly fetched her writing-case, smiling queerly to herself as she bent over the table where it stood: she produced a sheet of paper, a new pen, drew an arm-chair to the table, and presenting her hand to old Helstone, begged permission to instal him in it. For a minute he was a little stiff, and stood wrinkling his copper-coloured forehead strangely. At last he muttered:–

'Well – you are neither my wife nor my daughter, so I'll be led for once; but mind – I know I *am* led: your little female manoeuvres don't blind me.'

'Oh!' said Shirley, dipping the pen in the ink, and putting it into his hand, 'you must regard me as Captain Keeldar to-day. This is quite a gentleman's affair – yours and mine entirely, Doctor (so she had dubbed the Rector). The ladies there are only to be our aides-de-camp, and at their peril they speak, till we have settled the whole business.'

He smiled a little grimly, and began to write. He soon interrupted himself to ask questions, and consult his brethren, disdainfully lifting his glance over the curly heads of the two girls, and the demure caps of the elder ladies, to meet the winking glasses and grey pates of the priests. In the discussion which ensued,

# Shirley

all three gentlemen, to their infinite credit, showed a thorough acquaintance with the poor of their parishes, – an even minute knowledge of their separate wants. Each rector knew where clothing was needed, where food would be most acceptable, where money could be bestowed with a probability of it being judiciously laid out. Wherever their memories fell short, Miss Ainley or Miss Hall, if applied to, could help them out; but both ladies took care not to speak unless spoken to. Neither of them wanted to be foremost, but each sincerely desired to be useful, and useful the clergy consented to make them: with which boon they were content.

Shirley stood behind the rectors, leaning over their shoulders now and then to glance at the rules drawn up, and the list of cases making out, listening to all they said, and still at intervals smiling her queer smile – a smile not ill-natured, but significant: too significant to be generally thought amiable. Men rarely like such of their fellows as read their inward nature too clearly and truly. It is good for women, especially, to be endowed with a soft blindness: to have mild, dim eyes, that never penetrate below the surface of things – that take all for what it seems: thousands, knowing this, keep their eyelids drooped, on system; but the most downcast glance has its loophole, through which it can, on occasion, take its sentinel-survey of life. I remember once seeing a pair of blue eyes, that were usually thought sleepy, secretly on the alert, and I knew by their expression – an expression which chilled my blood, it was in that quarter so wondrously unexpected – that for years they had been accustomed to silent soul-reading. The world called the owner of these blue eyes 'bonne petite femme' (she was not an Englishwoman): I learned her nature afterwards – got it off by heart – studied it in its farthest, most hidden recesses – she was the finest, deepest, subtlest schemer in Europe.

When all was at length settled to Miss Keeldar's mind, and the clergy had entered so fully into the spirit of her plans as to head the subscription-list with their signatures for £50 each, she ordered supper to be served; having previously directed Mrs Gill to exercise her utmost skill in the preparation of this repast. Mr Hall was no bon-vivant: he was naturally an abstemious man, indifferent to luxury; but Boultby and Helstone both liked good cookery; the recherché supper consequently put them into excellent humour: they did justice to it, though in a gentlemanly way – not in the mode Mr Donne would have done, had he been present. A glass of fine wine was likewise tasted, with discerning though most decorous relish. Captain Keeldar was complimented on his taste; the compliment charmed him: it had been his aim to gratify and satisfy his priestly guests: he had succeeded, and was radiant with glee.

# Chapter 15

## Mr Donne's Exodus

The next day Shirley expressed to Caroline how delighted she felt that the little party had gone off so well.

'I rather like to entertain a circle of gentlemen,' said she: 'it is amusing to observe how they enjoy a judiciously concocted repast. For ourselves, you see, these choice wines and these scientific dishes are of no importance to us; but gentlemen seem to retain something of the naïveté of children about food, and one likes to please them: that is, when they show the becoming, decent self-government of our admirable rectors. I watch Moore sometimes, to try and discover how he can be pleased; but he has not that child's simplicity about him. Did you ever find out his accessible point, Caroline? You have seen more of him than I.'

'It is not, at any rate, that of my uncle and Dr Boultby,' returned Caroline, smiling. She always felt a sort of shy pleasure in following Miss Keeldar's lead respecting the discussion of her cousin's character: left to herself, she would never have touched on the subject; but when invited, the temptation of talking about him of whom she was ever thinking was irresistible. 'But,' she added, 'I really don't know what it is; for I never watched Robert in my life but my scrutiny was presently baffled by finding he was watching me.'

'There it is!' exclaimed Shirley: 'you can't fix your eyes on him but his presently flash on you. He is never off his guard: he won't give you an advantage: even when he does not look at you, his thoughts seem to be busy amongst your own thoughts, tracing your words and actions to their source, contemplating your motives at his ease. Oh! I know that sort of character, or something in the same style: it is one that piques me singularly – how does it affect you?'

This question was a specimen of one of Shirley's sharp, sudden turns: Caroline used to be fluttered by them at first, but she had now got into the way of parrying these home-thrusts like a little quakeress.

'Pique you? In what way does it pique you?' she said.

'Here he comes!' suddenly exclaimed Shirley, breaking off, starting up and running to the window. 'Here comes a diversion. I never told you of a superb conquest I have made lately – made at those parties to which I can never persuade you to accompany me; and the thing has been done without effort or intention on my part: that I aver. There is the bell – and, by all that's delicious! there are two of them. Do they never hunt, then, except in couples? You may have one, Lina, and you may take your choice: I hope I am generous enough. Listen to Tartar!'

The black-muzzled, tawny dog, a glimpse of which was seen in the chapter

# Shirley

which first introduced its mistress to the reader, here gave tongue in the hall, amidst whose hollow space the deep bark resounded formidably. A growl, more terrible than the bark – menacing as muttered thunder – succeeded.

'Listen!' again cried Shirley, laughing. 'You would think that the prelude to bloody onslaught: they will be frightened: they don't know old Tartar as I do: they are not aware his uproars are all sound and fury, signifying nothing.'

Some bustle was heard. 'Down, sir! – down!' exclaimed a high-toned, imperious voice, and then came a crack of a cane or whip. Immediately there was a yell – a scutter – a run – a positive tumult.

'Oh! Malone! Malone!'

'Down! down! down!' cried the high voice.

'He really is worrying them!' exclaimed Shirley. 'They have struck him: a blow is what he is not used to, and will not take.'

Out she ran: a gentleman was fleeing up the oak staircase, making for refuge in the gallery or chambers in hot haste; another was backing fast to the stair-foot, wildly flourishing a knotty stick, at the same time reiterating, 'Down! down! down!' while the tawny dog bayed, bellowed, howled at him, and a group of servants came bundling from the kitchen. The dog made a spring; the second gentleman turned tail and rushed after his comrade: the first was already safe in a bed-room: he held the door against his fellow; – nothing so merciless as terror; – but the other fugitive struggled hard: the door was about to yield to his strength.

'Gentlemen,' was uttered in Miss Keeldar's silvery but vibrating tones, 'spare my locks, if you please. Calm yourselves! – come down! Look at Tartar, – he won't harm a cat.'

She was caressing the said Tartar: he lay crouched at her feet, his fore-paws stretched out, his tail still in threatening agitation, his nostrils snorting, his bulldog eyes conscious of a dull fire. He was an honest, phlegmatic, stupid, but stubborn canine character: he loved his mistress, and John – the man who fed him, – but was mostly indifferent to the rest of the world: quiet enough he was, unless struck or threatened with a stick, and that put a demon into him at once.

'Mr Malone, how do you do!' continued Shirley, lifting up her mirth-lit face to the gallery. 'That is not the way to the oak-parlour: that is Mrs Pryor's apartment. Request your friend Mr Donne to evacuate: I shall have the greatest pleasure in receiving him in a lower room.'

'Ha! ha!' cried Malone, in hollow laughter, quitting the door, and leaning over the massive balustrade. 'Really that animal alarmed Donne. He is a little timid,' he proceeded, stiffening himself, and walking trimly to the stair-head. 'I thought it better to follow, in order to reassure him.'

'It appears you did: well, come down, if you please. John' (turning to her man-servant), 'go up-stairs and liberate Mr Donne. Take care, Mr Malone, the stairs are slippery.'

In truth they were; being of polished oak. The caution came a little late for Malone: he had slipped already in his stately descent, and was only saved from falling by a clutch at the banisters, which made the whole structure creak again.

Tartar seemed to think the visitor's descent effected with unwarranted éclat, and accordingly he growled once more. Malone, however, was no coward: the spring of the dog had taken him by surprise; but he passed him now in suppressed fury rather than fear: if a look could have strangled Tartar, he would have

# Shirley

breathed no more. Forgetting politeness, in his sullen rage, Malone pushed into the parlour before Miss Keeldar. He glanced at Miss Helstone; he could scarcely bring himself to bend to her. He glared on both the ladies: he looked as if, had either of them been his wife, he would have made a glorious husband at the moment: in each hand he seemed as if he would have liked to clutch one and gripe her to death.

However, Shirley took pity: she ceased to laugh; and Caroline was too true a lady to smile even at any one under mortification. Tartar was dismissed; Peter Augustus was soothed: for Shirley had looks and tones that might soothe a very bull: he had sense to feel that, since he could not challenge the owner of the dog, he had better be civil; and civil he tried to be; and his attempts being well received, he grew presently *very* civil and quite himself again. He had come, indeed, for the express purpose of making himself charming and fascinating: rough portents had met him on his first admission to Fieldhead; but that passage got over, charming and fascinating he resolved to be. Like March, having come in like a lion, he purposed to go out like a lamb.

For the sake of air, as it appeared, or perhaps for that of ready exit in case of some new emergency arising, he took his seat – not on the sofa, where Miss Keeldar offered him enthronization, nor yet near the fireside, to which Caroline, by a friendly sign, gently invited him, – but on a chair close to the door. Being no longer sullen or furious, he grew, after his fashion, constrained and embarrassed. He talked to the ladies by fits and starts, choosing for topics whatever was most intensely commonplace: he sighed deeply, significantly, at the close of every sentence; he sighed in each pause; he sighed ere he opened his mouth. At last, finding it desirable to add ease to his other charms, he drew forth to aid him an ample silk pocket-handkerchief. This was to be the graceful toy with which his unoccupied hands were to trifle. He went to work with a certain energy: he folded the red and yellow square cornerwise; he whipped it open with a waft: again he folded it in narrower compass: he made of it a handsome band. To what purpose would he proceed to apply the ligature? Would he wrap it about his throat – his head? Should it be a comforter or a turban? Neither. Peter Augustus had an inventive – an original genius: he was about to show the ladies graces of action possessing at least the charm of novelty. He sat on the chair with his athletic Irish legs crossed, and these legs, in that attitude, he circled with the bandana and bound firmly together. It was evident he felt this device to be worth an encore: he repeated it more than once. The second performance sent Shirley to the window to laugh her silent but irrepressible laugh unseen: it turned Caroline's head aside, that her long curls might screen the smile mantling on her features. Miss Helstone, indeed, was amused by more than one point in Peter's demeanour: she was edified at the complete though abrupt diversion of his homage from herself to the heiress: the £5000 he supposed her likely one day to inherit, were not to be weighed in the balance against Miss Keeldar's estate and hall. He took no pains to conceal his calculations and tactics: he pretended to no gradual change of views; he wheeled about at once: the pursuit of the lesser fortune was openly relinquished for that of the greater. On what grounds he expected to succeed in his chase, himself best knew: certainly not by skilful management.

From the length of time that elapsed, it appeared that John had some difficulty in persuading Mr Donne to descend. At length, however, that gentleman

appeared: nor, as he presented himself at the oak-parlour door, did he seem in the slightest degree ashamed or confused – not a whit. Donne, indeed, was of that coldly phlegmatic, immovably complacent, densely self-satisfied nature which is insensible to shame. He had never blushed in his life: no humiliation could abash him: his nerves were not capable of sensation enough to stir his life, and make colour mount to his cheek: he had no fire in his blood, and no modesty in his soul: he was a frontless, arrogant, decorous slip of the commonplace; conceited, inane, insipid: and this gentleman had a notion of wooing Miss Keeldar! He knew no more, however, how to set about the business than if he had been an image carved in wood: he had no idea of a taste to be pleased, a heart to be reached in courtship: his notion was, when he should have formally visited her a few times, to write a letter proposing marriage; then he calculated she would accept him for love of his office, then they would be married, then he should be master of Fieldhead, and he should live very comfortably, have servants at his command, eat and drink of the best, and be a great man. You would not have suspected his intentions when he addressed his intended bride in an impertinent injured tone:–

'A very dangerous dog that, Miss Keeldar. I wonder you should keep such an animal.'

'Do you, Mr Donne? Perhaps you will wonder more when I tell you I am very fond of him.'

'I should say you are not serious in the assertion. Can't fancy a lady fond of that brute – 'tis so ugly – a mere carter's dog – pray hang him.'

'Hang what I am fond of?'

'And purchase in his stead some sweetly pooty pug or poodle: something appropriate to the fair sex: ladies generally like lap-dogs.'

'Perhaps I am an exception.'

'Oh! you can't be, you know. All ladies are alike in those matters: that is universally allowed.'

'Tartar frightened you terribly, Mr Donne. I hope you won't take any harm.'

'That I shall, no doubt. He gave me a turn I shall not soon forget. When I *sor* him (such was Mr Donne's pronunciation) about to spring, I thought I should have fainted.'

'Perhaps you did faint in the bed-room – you were a long time there?'

'No; I bore up that I might hold the door fast: I was determined not to let any one enter: I thought I would keep a barrier between me and the enemy.'

'But what if your friend Mr Malone had been worried?'

'Malone must take care of himself. Your man persuaded me to come out at last by saying the dog was chained up in his kennel: if I had not been assured of this, I would have remained all day in the chamber. But what is that? I declare the man has told a falsehood! The dog is there!

And indeed Tartar walked past the glass-door opening to the garden, stiff, tawny, and black-muzzled as ever. He still seemed in bad humour; he was growling again, and whistling a half-strangled whistle, being an inheritance from the bulldog side of his ancestry.

'There are other visitors coming,' observed Shirley, with that provoking coolness which the owners of formidable-looking dogs are apt to show while their animals are all bristle and bay. Tartar sprang down the pavement towards the gate, bellowing 'avec explosion.' His mistress quietly opened the glass-door,

and stepped out chirruping to him. His bellow was already silence, and he was lifting up his huge, blunt, stupid head to the new callers to be patted.

'What – Tartar, Tartar!' said a cheery, rather boyish voice: 'don't you know us? Good-morning, old boy!'

And little Mr Sweeting, whose conscious good-nature made him comparatively fearless of man, woman, child, or brute, came through the gate, caressing the guardian. His vicar, Mr Hall, followed: he had no fear of Tartar either, and Tartar had no ill-will to him: he snuffed both the gentlemen round, and then, as if concluding that they were harmless, and might be allowed to pass, he withdrew to the sunny front of the hall, leaving the archway free. Mr Sweeting followed, and would have played with him, but Tartar took no notice of his caresses: it was only his mistress's hand whose touch gave him pleasure; to all others he showed himself obstinately insensible.

Shirley advanced to meet Messrs Hall and Sweeting, shaking hands with them cordially: they were come to tell her of certain successes they had achieved that morning in applications for subscriptions to the fund. Mr Hall's eyes beamed benignantly through his spectacles: his plain face looked positively handsome with goodness, and when Caroline, seeing who was come, ran out to meet him, and put both her hands into his, he gazed down on her with a gentle, serene, affectionate expression, that gave him the aspect of a smiling Melancthon.

Instead of re-entering the house, they strayed through the garden, the ladies walking one on each side of Mr Hall. It was a breezy sunny day; the air freshened the girls' cheeks, and gracefully dishevelled their ringlets: both of them looked pretty, – one, gay: Mr Hall spoke oftenest to his brilliant companion, looked most frequently at the quiet one. Miss Keeldar gathered handfuls of the profusely blooming flowers, whose perfume filled the enclosure; she gave some to Caroline, telling her to choose a nosegay for Mr Hall; and with her lap filled with delicate and splendid blossoms, Caroline sat down on the steps of a summer-house: the Vicar stood near her, leaning on his cane.

Shirley, who could not be inhospitable, now called out the neglected pair in the oak-parlour: she convoyed Donne past his dread enemy Tartar, who, with his nose on his fore-paws, lay snoring under the meridian sun. Donne was not grateful: he never *was* grateful for kindness and attention; but he was glad of the safeguard. Miss Keeldar, desirous of being impartial, offered the curates flowers: they accepted them with native awkwardness. Malone seemed specially at a loss, when a bouquet filled one hand, while his shillelagh occupied the other. Donne's 'Thank you!' was rich to hear: it was the most fatuous and arrogant of sounds, implying that he considered this offering an homage to his merits, and an attempt on the part of the heiress to ingratiate herself into his priceless affections. Sweeting alone received the posy like a smart, sensible, little man, as he was; putting it gallantly and nattily into his button-hole.

As a reward for his good manners, Miss Keeldar beckoning him apart, gave him some commission, which made his eyes sparkle with glee. Away he flew, round by the courtyard to the kitchen: no need to give him directions; he was always at home everywhere. Erelong he re-appeared, carrying a round table, which he placed under the cedar; then he collected six garden-chairs from various nooks and bowers in the grounds, and placed them in a circle. The parlour-maid – Miss Keeldar kept no footman – came out, bearing a napkin-covered tray. Sweeting's nimble fingers aided in disposing glasses, plates, knives and

forks: he assisted her too in setting forth a neat luncheon, consisting of cold chicken, ham, and tarts.

This sort of impromptu regale, it was Shirley's delight to offer any chance guests; and nothing pleased her better than to have an alert, obliging little friend, like Sweeting, to run about her hand, cheerily receive and briskly execute her hospitable hints. David and she were on the best terms in the world; and his devotion to the heiress was quite disinterested, since it prejudiced in nothing his faithful allegiance to the magnificent Dora Sykes.

The repast turned out a very merry one. Donne and Malone, indeed, contributed but little to its vivacity, the chief part they played in it being what concerned the knife, fork, and wine-glass; but where four such natures as Mr Hall, David Sweeting, Shirley, and Caroline, were assembled in health and amity, on a green lawn, under a sunny sky, amidst a wilderness of flowers, there could not be ungenial dullness.

In the course of conversation, Mr Hall reminded the ladies that Whitsuntide was approaching, when the grand United Sunday-School tea-drinking and procession of the three parishes of Briarfield, Whinbury, and Nunnely were to take place. Caroline he knew would be at her post as teacher, he said, and he hoped Miss Keeldar would not be wanting: he hoped she would make her first public appearance amongst them at that time. Shirley was not the person to miss an occasion of this sort: she liked festive excitement, a gathering of happiness, a concentration and combination of pleasant details, a throng of glad faces, a muster of elated hearts: she told Mr Hall they might count on her with security: she did not know what she would have to do, but they might dispose of her as they pleased.

'And,' said Caroline, 'you will promise to come to my table, and to sit near me, Mr Hall?'

'I shall not fail, Deo volente,' said he. 'I have occupied the place on her right hand at these monster tea-drinkings for the last six years,' he proceeded, turning to Miss Keeldar. 'They made her a Sunday-school teacher when she was a little girl of twelve: she is not particularly self-confident by nature, as you may have observed; and the first time she had to "take a tray," as the phrase is, and make tea in public, there was some piteous trembling and flushing. I observed the speechless panic, the cups shaking in the little hand, and the overflowing teapot filled too full from the urn. I came to her aid, took a seat near her, managed the urn and the slop-basin, and in fact made the tea for her like any old woman.'

'I was very grateful to you,' interposed Caroline.

'You were: you told me so with an earnest sincerity that repaid me well; inasmuch as it was not like the majority of little ladies of twelve, whom you may help and caress for ever without their evincing any quicker sense of the kindness done and meant than if they were made of wax and wood, instead of flesh and nerves. She kept close to me, Miss Keeldar, the rest of the evening, walking with me over the grounds where the children were playing; she followed me into the vestry when all were summoned into church: she would, I believe, have mounted with me to the pulpit, had I not taken the previous precaution of conducting her to the Rectory-pew.'

'And he has been my friend ever since,' said Caroline.

'And always sat at her table, near her tray, and handed the cups, – that is the extent of my services. The next thing I do for her will be to marry her some day

# Shirley

to some curate or mill-owner: but mind, Caroline, I shall inquire about the bridegroom's character, and if he is not a gentleman likely to render happy the little girl who walked with me hand in hand over Nunnely Common, I will not officiate: so take care.'

'The caution is useless: I am not going to be married. I shall live single like your sister Margaret, Mr Hall.'

'Very well – you might do worse – Margaret is not unhappy: she has her books for a pleasure, and her brother for a care, and is content. If ever you want a home; if the day should come when Briarfield Rectory is yours no longer, come to Nunnely Vicarage. Should the old maid and bachelor be still living, they will make you tenderly welcome.'

'There are your flowers. Now,' said Caroline, who had kept the nosegay she had selected for him till this moment, '*you* don't care for a bouquet, but you must give it to Margaret: only – to be sentimental for once – keep that little forget-me-not, which is a wild-flower I gathered from the grass; and – to be still more sentimental – let me take two or three of the blue blossoms and put them in my souvenir.'

And she took out a small book with enamelled cover and silver clasp, wherein, having opened it, she inserted the flowers, writing round them in pencil – 'To be kept for the sake of the Rev. Cyril Hall, my friend. May — 18—.'

The Rev. Cyril Hall, on his part also, placed a sprig in safety between the leaves of a pocket Testament: he only wrote on the margin – 'Caroline.'

'Now,' said he, smiling, 'I trust we are romantic enough. Miss Keeldar,' he continued (the curates, by-the-by, during this conversation, were too much occupied with their own jokes to notice what passed at the other end of the table), 'I hope you are laughing at this trait of "*exaltation*" in the old greyheaded Vicar; but, the fact is, I am so used to comply with the requests of this young friend of yours, I don't know how to refuse her when she tells me to do anything. You would say it is not much in my way to traffic with flowers and forget-me-nots; but, you see, when requested to be sentimental, I am obedient.'

'He is naturally rather sentimental,' remarked Caroline: 'Margaret told me so, and I know what pleases him.'

'That you should be good and happy? Yes; that is one of my greatest pleasures. May God long preserve to you the blessings of peace and innocence! By which phrase, I mean *comparative* innocence; for in His sight, I am well aware *none* are pure. What, to our human perceptions, looks spotless as we fancy angels, is to Him but frailty, needing the blood of His Son to cleanse, and the strength of His Spirit to sustain. Let us each and all cherish humility – I, as you, my young friends; and we may well do it when we look into our own hearts, and see there temptations, inconsistencies, propensities, even we blush to recognize. And it is not youth, nor good looks, nor grace, nor any gentle outside charm which makes either beauty or goodness in God's eyes. Young ladies, when your mirror or men's tongues flatter you, remember that, in the sight of her Maker, Mary Anne Ainley – a woman whom neither glass nor lips have ever panegyrized – is fairer and better than either of you. She is, indeed,' he added, after a pause – 'she is, indeed. You young things – wrapt up in yourselves and in earthly hopes – scarcely live as Christ lived: perhaps you cannot do it yet, while existence is so sweet and earth so smiling to you; it would be too much to expect: she, with meek heart and due reverence, treads close in her Redeemer's steps.'

# Shirley

Here the harsh voice of Donne broke in on the mild tones of Mr Hall: –

'Ahem!' he began, clearing his throat evidently for a speech of some importance. 'Ahem! Miss Keeldar, your attention an instant, if you please.'

'Well,' said Shirley, nonchalantly. 'What is it? I listen: all of me is ear that is not eye.'

'I hope part of you is hand also,' returned Donne, in his vulgarly presumptuous and familiar style, 'and part purse: it is to the hand and purse I propose to appeal. I came here this morning with a view to beg of you' –

'You should have gone to Mrs Gill: she is my almoner.'

'To beg of you a subscription to a school. I and Dr Boultby intend to erect one in the hamlet of Ecclefigg which is under our vicarage of Whinbury. The Baptists have got possession of it: they have a chapel there, and we want to dispute the ground.'

'But I have nothing to do with Ecclefigg: I possess no property there.'

'What does that signify? You're a Churchwoman, ain't you?'

'Admirable creature!' muttered Shirley, under her breath: 'exquisite address: fine style! What raptures he excites in me!' then, aloud, 'I am a Churchwoman, certainly.'

'Then you can't refuse to contribute in this case. The population of Ecclefigg are a parcel of brutes – we want to civilize them.'

'Who is to be the missionary?'

'Myself, probably.'

'You won't fail through lack of sympathy with your flock.'

'I hope not – I expect success; but we must have money. There is the paper – pray give a handsome sum.'

When asked for money, Shirley rarely held back. She put down her name for £5: after the £300 she had lately given, and the many smaller sums she was giving constantly, it was as much as she could at present afford. Donne looked at it, declared the subscription 'shabby,' and clamorously demanded more. Miss Keeldar flushed up with some indignation and more astonishment.

'At present, I shall give no more,' said she.

'Not give more! Why, I expected you to head the list with a cool hundred. With your property, you should never put down a signature for less.'

She was silent.

'In the south,' went on Donne, 'a lady with a thousand a-year would be ashamed to give five pounds for a public object.'

Shirley, so rarely haughty, looked so now. Her slight frame became nerved; her distinguished face quickened with scorn.

'Strange remarks!' said she: 'most inconsiderate! Reproach in return for bounty is misplaced.'

'Bounty! Do you call five pounds bounty?'

'I do: and bounty which, had I not given it to Dr Boultby's intended school, of the erection of which I approve, and in no sort to his curate, who seems ill-advised in his manner of applying for – or rather extorting subscriptions, – bounty, I repeat, which, but for this consideration, I should instantly reclaim.'

Donne was thick-skinned: he did not feel all or half that the tone, air, glance of the speaker expressed: he knew not on what ground he stood.

'Wretched place – this Yorkshire,' he went on. 'I could never have formed an

678

# Shirley

idea*r* of the country had I not seen it; and the people – rich and poor – what a set! How *corse* and uncultivated! They would be scouted in the south.'

Shirley leaned forwards on the table, her nostrils dilating a little, her taper fingers interlaced and compressing each other hard.

'The rich,' pursued the infatuated and unconscious Donne, 'are a parcel of misers – never living as persons with their incomes ought to live: you scarsley – (you must excuse Mr Donne's pronunciation, reader; it was very choice; he considered it genteel, and prided himself on his southern accent; northern ears received with singular sensations his utterance of certain words); you scarsley ever see a fam'ly where a propa carriage or a reg'la butla is kep; and as to the poor – just look at them when they come crowding about the church-doors on the occasion of a marriage or a funeral, clattering in clogs; the men in their shirt-sleeves and wool-combers' aprons, the women in mob-caps and bed-gowns. They pos'tively deserve that one should turn a mad cow in amongst them to rout their rabble-ranks – he! he! What fun it would be!'

'There, – you have reached the climax,' said Shirley, quietly. 'You have reached the climax,' she repeated, turning her glowing glance towards him. 'You cannot go beyond it, and,' she added with emphasis, 'you *shall* not, in my house.'

Up she rose: nobody could control her now, for she was exasperated; straight she walked to her garden-gates, wide she flung them open.

'Walk through,' she said austerely, 'and pretty quickly, and set foot on this pavement no more.'

Donne was astounded. He had thought all the time he was showing himself off to high advantage, as a lofty-souled person of the first 'ton;' he imagined he was producing a crushing impression. Had he not expressed disdain of everything in Yorkshire? What more conclusive proof could be given that he was better than anything there? And yet here was he about to be turned like a dog out of a Yorkshire garden! Where, under such circumstances, was the 'concatenation accordingly?'

'Rid me of you instantly – instantly!' reiterated Shirley, as he lingered.

'Madam – a clergyman! Turn out a clergyman?'

'Off! Were you an archbishop: you have proved yourself no gentleman, and must go. Quick!'

She was quite resolved: there was no trifling with her: besides, Tartar was again rising; he perceived symptoms of a commotion: he manifested a disposition to join in; there was evidently nothing for it but to go, and Donne made his Exodus; the heiress sweeping him a deep curtsy as she closed the gates on him.

'How dare the pompous priest abuse his flock? How dare the lisping cockney revile Yorkshire?' was her sole observation on the circumstance, as she returned to the table.

Erelong, the little party broke up: Miss Keeldar's ruffled and darkened brow, curled lip, and incensed eye, gave no invitation to further social enjoyment.

# Chapter 16

## Whitsuntide

The fund prospered. By dint of Miss Keeldar's example, the three rectors' vigorous exertions, and the efficient though quiet aid of their spinster and spectacled lieutenants, Mary Ann Ainley and Margaret Hall, a handsome sum was raised; and this being judiciously managed, served for the present greatly to alleviate the distress of the unemployed poor. The neighbourhood seemed to grow calmer: for a fortnight past no cloth had been destroyed; no outrage on mill or mansion had been committed in the three parishes. Shirley was sanguine that the evil she wished to avert was almost escaped; that the threatened storm was passing over: with the approach of summer she felt certain that trade would improve – it always did; and then this weary war could not last for ever; peace must return one day: with peace what an impulse would be given to commerce!

Such was the usual tenor of her observations to her tenant, Gérard Moore, whenever she met him where they could converse, and Moore would listen very quietly – too quietly to satisfy her. She would then by her impatient glance demand something more from him – some explanation, or at least some additional remark. Smiling in his way, with that expression which gave a remarkable cast of sweetness to his mouth, while his brow remained grave, he would answer to the effect, that himself, too, trusted in the finite nature of the war; that it was indeed on that ground the anchor of his hopes was fixed: thereon his speculations depended. 'For you are aware,' he would continue, 'that I now work Hollow's mill entirely on speculation: I sell nothing; there is no market for my goods. I manufacture for a future day: I make myself ready to take advantage of the first opening that shall occur. Three months ago this was impossible to me; I had exhausted both credit and capital: you well know who came to my rescue; from what hand I received the loan which saved me. It is on the strength of that loan I am enabled to continue the bold game which, a while since, I feared I should never play more. Total ruin I know will follow loss, and I am aware that gain is doubtful; but I am quite cheerful: so long as I can be active, so long as I can strive, so long, in short, as my hands are not tied, it is impossible for me to be depressed. One year, nay, but six months of the reign of the olive, and I am safe; for, as you say, peace will give an impulse to commerce. In this you are right; but as to the restored tranquillity of the neighbourhood – as to the permanent good effect of your charitable fund – I doubt. Eleemosynary relief never yet tranquillized the working-classes – it never made them grateful; it is not in human nature that it should. I suppose, were all things ordered aright, they ought not to be in a position to need that humiliating relief; and this they feel:

# Shirley

we should feel it were we so placed. Besides, to whom should they be grateful? To you – to the clergy perhaps, but not to us mill-owners. They hate us worse than ever. Then, the disaffected here are in correspondence with the disaffected elsewhere: Nottingham is one of their head-quarters, Manchester another, Birmingham a third. The subalterns receive orders from their chiefs; they are in a good state of discipline: no blow is struck without mature deliberation. In sultry weather, you have seen the sky threaten thunder day by day, and yet night after night the clouds have cleared, and the sun has set quietly; but the danger was not gone, it was only delayed: the long-threatening storm is sure to break at last. There is analogy between the moral and physical atmosphere.'

'Well, Mr Moore' (so these conferences always ended), 'take care of yourself. If you think that I have ever done you any good, reward me by promising to take care of yourself.'

'I do: I will take close and watchful care. I wish to live, not to die: the future opens like Eden before me; and still, when I look deep into the shades of my paradise, I see a vision, that I like better than seraph or cherub, glide across remote vistas.'

'Do you? Pray, what vision?'

'I see –'

The maid came bustling in with the tea-things.

The early part of that May, as we have seen, was fine, the middle was wet; but in the last week, at change of moon, it cleared again. A fresh wind swept off the silver-white, deep-piled rain-clouds, bearing them, mass on mass, to the eastern horizon; on whose verge they dwindled, and behind whose rim they disappeared; leaving the vault behind all pure blue space, ready for the reign of the summer sun. That sun rose broad on Whitsuntide: the gathering of the schools was signalized by splendid weather.

Whit-Tuesday was the great day, in preparation for which the two large schoolrooms of Briarfield, built by the present rector, chiefly at his own expense, were cleaned out, white-washed, re-painted, and decorated with flowers and evergreens – some from the Rectory-garden, two cart-loads from Fieldhead, and a wheelbarrowful from the more stingy domain of De Walden, the residence of Mr Wynne. In these schoolrooms twenty tables, each calculated to accommodate twenty guests, were laid out, surrounded with benches, and covered with white cloths: above them were suspended at least some twenty cages, containing as many canaries, according to a fancy of the district, specially cherished by Mr Helstone's clerk, who delighted in the piercing song of these birds, and knew that amidst confusion of tongues they always caroled loudest. These tables, be it understood, were not spread for the twelve hundred scholars to be assembled from the three parishes, but only for the patrons and teachers of the schools: the children's feast was to be spread in the open air. At one o'clock the troops were to come in; at two they were to be marshalled; till four they were to parade the parish; then came the feast, and afterwards the meeting, with music and speechifying in the church.

Why Briarfield was chosen for the point of rendezvous – the scene of the fête – should be explained. It was not because it was the largest or most populous parish – Whinbury far outdid it in that respect; nor because it was the oldest – antique as were the hoary Church and Rectory, Nunnely's low-roofed Temple and mossy Parsonage, buried both in coëval oaks, outstanding sentinels of

# Shirley

Nunnwood, were older still: it was simply because Mr Helstone willed it so, and Mr Helstone's will was stronger than that of Boultby or Hall; the former *could* not, the latter *would* not, dispute a point of precedence with their resolute and imperious brother: they let him lead and rule.

This notable anniversary had always hitherto been a trying day to Caroline Helstone, because it dragged her perforce into public, compelling her to face all that was wealthy, respectable, influential in the neighbourhood; in whose presence, but for the kind countenance of Mr Hall, she would have appeared unsupported. Obliged to be conspicuous: obliged to walk at the head of her regiment, as the Rector's niece, and first teacher of the first class; obliged to make tea at the first table for a mixed multitude of ladies and gentlemen; and to do all this without the countenance of mother, aunt, or other chaperon – she, meantime, being a nervous person, who mortally feared publicity – it will be comprehended that, under these circumstances, she trembled at the approach of Whitsuntide.

But this year Shirley was to be with her, and that changed the aspect of the trial singularly – it changed it utterly: it was a trial no longer – it was almost an enjoyment. Miss Keeldar was better in her single self than a host of ordinary friends. Quite self-possessed, and always spirited and easy; conscious of her social importance, yet never presuming upon it, it would be enough to give one courage only to look at her. The only fear was, lest the heiress should not be punctual to tryst: she often had a careless way of lingering behind time, and Caroline knew her uncle would not wait a second for any one: at the moment of the church-clock tolling two, the bells would clash out and the march begin. She must look after Shirley, then, in this matter, or her expected companion would fail her.

Whit-Tuesday saw her rise almost with the sun. She, Fanny, and Eliza were busy the whole morning arranging the Rectory-parlours in first-rate company order, and setting out a collation of cooling refreshments – wine, fruit, cakes – on the dining-room sideboard. Then she had to dress in her freshest and fairest attire of white muslin; the perfect fineness of the day and the solemnity of the occasion warranted, and even exacted, such costume. Her new sash – a birthday-present from Margaret Hall, which she had reason to believe Cyril himself had bought, and in return for which she had indeed given him a set of cambric-bands in a handsome case – was tied by the dexterous fingers of Fanny, who took no little pleasure in arraying her fair young mistress for the occasion; her simple bonnet had been trimmed to correspond with her sash; her pretty but inexpensive scarf of white crape suited her dress. When ready, she formed a picture, not bright enough to dazzle, but fair enough to interest; not brilliantly striking, but very delicately pleasing; a picture in which sweetness of tint, purity of air, and grace of mien, atoned for the absence of rich colouring and magnificent contour. What her brown eye and clear forehead showed of her mind, was in keeping with her dress and face – modest, gentle, and, though pensive, harmonious. It appeared that neither lamb nor dove need fear her, but would welcome rather, in her look of simplicity and softness, a sympathy with their own natures, or with the natures we ascribe to them.

After all, she was an imperfect, faulty human being: fair enough of form, hue, and array; but, as Cyril Hall said, neither so good nor so great as the withered

# Shirley

Miss Ainley, now putting on her best black gown and Quaker-drab shawl and bonnet in her own narrow cottage-chamber.

Away Caroline went, across some very sequestered fields and through some quite hidden lanes, to Fieldhead. She glided quickly under the green hedges and across the greener leas. There was no dust – no moisture – to soil the hem of her stainless garment, or to damp her slender sandal: after the late rains all was clean, and under the present glowing sun all was dry: she walked fearlessly, then, on daisy and turf, and through thick plantations; she reached Fieldhead, and penetrated to Miss Keeldar's dressing-room.

It was well she had come, or Shirley would have been too late. Instead of making ready with all speed, she lay stretched on a couch, absorbed in reading: Mrs Pryor stood near, vainly urging her to rise and dress. Caroline wasted no words: she immediately took the book from her, and, with her own hands, commenced the business of disrobing and re-robing her. Shirley, indolent with the heat, and gay with her youth and pleasurable nature, wanted to talk, laugh, and linger; but Caroline, intent on being in time, persevered in dressing her as fast as fingers could fasten strings or insert pins. At length, as she united a final row of hooks and eyes, she found leisure to chide her, saying, she was very naughty to be so unpunctual; that she looked even now the picture of incorrigible carelessness: and so Shirley did – but a very lovely picture of that tiresome quality.

She presented quite a contrast to Caroline: there was style in every fold of her dress and every line of her figure: the rich silk suited her better than a simpler costume; the deep-embroidered scarf became her; she wore it negligently, but gracefully; the wreath on her bonnet crowned her well: the attention to fashion, the tasteful appliance of ornament in each portion of her dress, were quite in place with her: all this suited her, like the frank light in her eyes, the rallying smile about her lips, like her shaft-straight carriage and lightsome step. Caroline took her hand when she was dressed, hurried her downstairs, out of doors, and thus they sped through the fields, laughing as they went, and looking very much like a snow-white dove and gem-tinted bird-of-paradise joined in social flight.

Thanks to Miss Helstone's promptitude, they arrived in good time. While yet trees hid the church, they heard the bell tolling a measured but urgent summons for all to assemble; the trooping in of numbers, the trampling of many steps, and murmuring of many voices were likewise audible. From a rising-ground they presently saw, on the Whinbury-road, the Whinbury-school approaching: it numbered five hundred souls. The Rector and Curate, Boultby and Donne, headed it: the former, looming large in full canonicals, walking, as became a beneficed priest, under the canopy of a shovel-hat, with the dignity of an ample corporation, the embellishment of the squarest and vastest of black coats, and the support of the stoutest of gold-headed canes. As the Doctor walked, he now and then slightly flourished his cane, and inclined his shovel-hat with a dogmatical wag towards his aide-de-camp. That aide-de-camp – Donne, to wit – narrow as the line of his shape was compared to the broad bulk of his principal, contrived, notwithstanding, to look every inch a curate: all about him was pragmatical and self-complacent, from his turned-up nose and elevated chin to his clerical black gaiters, his somewhat short, strapless trousers, and his square-toed shoes.

Walk on, Mr Donne! You have undergone scrutiny. You think you look well

# Shirley

– whether the white and purple figures watching you from yonder hill think so, is another question.

These figures come running down when the regiment has marched by: the churchyard is full of children and teachers, all in their very best holiday attire: and – distressed as is the district, bad as are the times – it is wonderful to see how respectably – how handsomely even – they have contrived to clothe themselves. That British love of decency will work miracles: the poverty which reduces an Irish girl to rags is impotent to rob the English girl of the neat wardrobe she knows necessary to her self-respect. Besides, the lady of the manor – that Shirley, now gazing with pleasure on this well-dressed and happy-looking crowd – has really done them good: her seasonable bounty consoled many a poor family against the coming holiday, and supplied many a child with a new frock or bonnet for the occasion; she knows it, and is elate with the consciousness: glad that her money, example, and influence have really – substantially – benefited those around her. She cannot be charitable like Miss Ainley – it is not in her nature: it relieves her to feel that there is another way of being charitable, practicable for other characters, and under other circumstances.

Caroline, too, is pleased; for she also has done good in her small way; robbed herself of more than one dress, ribbon, or collar she could ill spare, to aid in fitting out the scholars of her class; and, as she could not give money, she has followed Miss Ainley's example, in giving her time and her industry to sew for the children.

Not only is the churchyard full, but the Rectory-garden is also thronged: pairs and parties of ladies and gentlemen are seen walking amongst the waving lilacs and laburnums. The house also is occupied: at the wide-open parlour-windows, gay groups are standing. These are the patrons and teachers, who are to swell the procession. In the parson's croft, behind the Rectory, are the musicians of the three parish bands, with their instruments. Fanny and Eliza, in the smartest of caps and gowns, and the whitest of aprons, move amongst them, serving out quarts of ale; whereof a stock was brewed very sound and strong some weeks since, by the Rector's orders, and under his special super-intendence. Whatever he had a hand in, must be managed handsomely: 'shabby doings,' of any description, were not endured under his sanction: from the erection of a public building, a church, school, or courthouse, to the cooking of a dinner, he still advocated the lordly, liberal and effective. Miss Keeldar was like him in this respect, and they mutually approved each other's arrangements.

Caroline and Shirley were soon in the midst of the company; the former met them very easily for her: instead of sitting down in a retired corner, or stealing away to her own room till the procession should be marshalled, according to her wont, she moved through the three parlours, conversed and smiled, absolutely spoke once or twice ere she was spoken to, and, in short, seemed a new creature. It was Shirley's presence which thus transformed her: the view of Miss Keeldar's air and manner did her a world of good. Shirley had no fear of her kind; no tendency to shrink from, to avoid it. All human beings, men, women, or children, whom low breeding or coarse presumption did not render positively offensive, were welcome enough to her: some much more so than others, of course; but, generally speaking, till a man had indisputably proved himself bad and a nuisance, Shirley was willing to think him good and an acquisition, and to treat him accordingly. This disposition made her a general favourite, for it robbed her

# Shirley

very raillery of its sting, and gave her serious or smiling conversation a happy charm: nor did it diminish the value of her intimate friendship, which was a distinct thing from this social benevolence, depending, indeed, on quite a different part of her character. Miss Helstone was the choice of her affection and intellect; the Misses Pearson, Sykes, Wynne, &c., &c., only the profiters by her good-nature and vivacity.

Donne happened to come into the drawing-room while Shirley, sitting on the sofa, formed the centre of a tolerably wide circle. She had already forgotten her exasperation against him, and she bowed and smiled good-humouredly. The disposition of the man was then seen. He knew neither how to decline the advance with dignity, as one whose just pride has been wounded, nor how to meet it with frankness, as one who is glad to forget and forgive; his punishment had impressed him with no sense of shame, and he did not experience that feeling on encountering his chastiser: he was not vigorous enough in evil to be actively malignant, – he merely passed by sheepishly with a rated, scowling look. Nothing could ever again reconcile him to his enemy; while no passion of resentment, for even sharper and more ignominious inflictions, could his lymphatic nature know.

'He was not worth a scene!' said Shirley to Caroline. 'What a fool I was! To revenge on poor Donne his silly spite at Yorkshire, is something like crushing a gnat for attacking the hide of a rhinoceros. Had I been a gentleman, I believe I should have helped him off the premises by dint of physical force: I am glad now I only employed the moral weapon. But he must come near me no more: I don't like him: he irritates me: there is not even amusement to be had out of him: Malone is better sport.'

It seemed as if Malone wished to justify the preference; for the words were scarcely out of the speaker's mouth, when Peter Augustus came up, all in 'grande tenue,' gloved and scented, with his hair oiled and brushed to perfection, and bearing in one hand a huge bunch of cabbage-roses, five or six in full blow: these he presented to the heiress with a grace to which the most cunning pencil could do but defective justice. And who, after this, could dare to say that Peter was not a lady's man? He had gathered and he had given flowers: he had offered a sentimental – a poetic tribute at the shrine of Love or Mammon. Hercules holding the distaff was but a faint type of Peter bearing the roses. He must have thought this himself, for he seemed amazed at what he had done: he backed without a word; he was going away with a husky chuckle of self-felicitation; then he bethought himself to stop and turn, to ascertain by ocular testimony that he really had presented a bouquet: yes – there were the six red cabbages on the purple satin lap, a very white hand, with some gold rings on the fingers, slightly holding them together, and streaming ringlets, half-hiding a laughing face, drooped over them: only *half*-hiding: Peter saw the laugh – it was unmistakable – he was made a joke of – his gallantry, his chivalry were the subject of a jest for a petticoat – for two petticoats – Miss Helstone too was smiling. Moreover, he felt he was seen through, and Peter grew black as a thunder-cloud. When Shirley looked up, a fell eye was fastened on her: Malone, at least, had energy enough to hate: she saw it in his glances.

'Peter *is* worth a scene, and shall have it, if he likes, one day,' she whispered to her friend.

And now – solemn and sombre as to their colour, though bland enough as to

# Shirley

their faces – appeared at the dining-room door the three rectors: they had hitherto been busy in the church, and were now coming to take some little refreshment for the body, ere the march commenced. The large morocco-covered easy chair had been left vacant for Dr Boultby; he was put into it, and Caroline, obeying the instigations of Shirley, who told her now was the time to play the hostess, hastened to hand to her uncle's vast, revered, and, on the whole, worthy friend, a glass of wine and a plate of macaroons. Boultby's churchwardens, patrons of the Sunday-school both, as he insisted on their being, were already beside him; Mrs Sykes and the other ladies of his congregation were on his right hand and on his left, expressing their hopes that he was not fatigued, their fears that the day would be too warm for him. Mrs Boultby, who held an opinion that when her lord dropped asleep after a good dinner his face became as the face of an angel, was bending over him, tenderly wiping some perspiration, real or imaginary, from his brow: Boultby, in short, was in his glory, and in a round sound 'voix de poitrine,' he rumbled out thanks for attentions, and assurances of his tolerable health. Of Caroline he took no manner of notice as she came near, save to accept what she offered: he did not see her, he never did see her: he hardly knew that such a person existed. He saw the macaroons, however, and being fond of sweets, possessed himself of a small handful thereof. The wine, Mrs Boultby insisted on mingling with hot water, and qualifying with sugar and nutmeg.

Mr Hall stood near an open window, breathing the fresh air and scent of flowers, and talking like a brother to Miss Ainley. To him Caroline turned her attention with pleasure. 'What should she bring him? He must not help himself – he must be served by her;' and she provided herself with a little salver, that she might offer him variety. Margaret Hall joined them; so did Miss Keeldar: the four ladies stood round their favourite pastor: they also had an idea that they looked on the face of an earthly angel: Cyril Hall was their pope, infallible to them as Dr Thomas Boultby to his admirers. A throng, too, enclosed the Rector of Briarfield: twenty or more pressed round him; and no parson was ever more potent in a circle than old Helstone. The curates herding together after their manner, made a constellation of three lesser planets: divers young ladies watched them afar off, but ventured not nigh.

Mr Helstone produced his watch. 'Ten minutes to two,' he announced aloud. 'Time for all to fall into line. Come.' He seized his shovel-hat and marched away; all rose and followed en masse.

The twelve hundred children were drawn up in three bodies of four hundred souls each: in the rear of each regiment was stationed a band; between every twenty there was an interval, wherein Helstone posted the teachers in pairs: to the van of the armies he summoned: –

'Grace Boultby and Mary Sykes lead out Whinbury.'
'Margaret Hall and Mary Ann Ainley conduct Nunnely.'
'Caroline Helstone and Shirley Keeldar head Briarfield.'
Then again he gave command: –
'Mr Donne to Whinbury; Mr Sweeting to Nunnely; Mr Malone to Briarfield.'
And these gentlemen stepped up before the lady-generals.

The rectors passed to the full front – the parish clerks fell to the extreme rear; Helstone lifted his shovel-hat; in an instant out clashed the eight bells in the

tower, loud swelled the sounding bands, flute spoke and clarion answered, deep rolled the drums, and away they marched.

The broad white road unrolled before the long procession, the sun and sky surveyed it cloudless, the wind tossed the tree-boughs above it, and the twelve hundred children, and one hundred and forty adults, of which it was composed, trod on in time and tune, with gay faces and glad hearts. It was a joyous scene, and a scene to do good: it was a day of happiness for rich and poor; the work, first of God, and then of the clergy. Let England's priests have their due: they are a faulty set in some respects, being only of common flesh and blood, like us all; but the land would be badly off without them: Britain would miss her church, if that church fell. God save it! God also reform it!

# Chapter 17

## The School-Feast

Not on combat bent, nor of foemen in search, was this priest-led and woman-officered company: yet their music played martial tunes, and – to judge by the eyes and carriage of some, Miss Keeldar, for instance, – these sounds awoke, if not a martial, yet a longing spirit. Old Helstone, turning by chance, looked into her face, and he laughed, and she laughed at him.

'There is no battle in prospect,' he said; 'our country does not want us to fight for it: no foe or tyrant is questioning or threatening our liberty: there is nothing to be done: we are only taking a walk. Keep your hand on the reins, captain, and slack the fire of that spirit: it is not wanted; the more's the pity.'

'Take your own advice, Doctor,' was Shirley's response. To Caroline, she murmured, 'I'll borrow of imagination what reality will not give me. We are not soldiers – bloodshed is not my desire; or if we are, we are soldiers of the Cross. Time has rolled back some hundreds of years, and we are bound on a pilgrimage to Palestine. But no, – that is too visionary. I need a sterner dream: we are Lowlanders of Scotland, following a covenanting captain up into the hills to hold a meeting out of the reach of persecuting troopers. We know that battle may follow prayer; and, as we believe that in the worst issue of battle, heaven must be our reward, we are ready and willing to redden the peat-moss with our blood. That music stirs my soul; it wakens all my life; it makes my heart beat: not with its temperate daily pulse, but with a new, thrilling vigour. I almost long for danger; for a faith – a land – or, at least, a lover to defend.'

'Look, Shirley!' interrupted Caroline. 'What is that red speck above Stilbro' Brow? You have keener sight than I; just turn your eagle eye to it.'

Miss Keeldar looked. 'I see,' she said: then added, presently, 'there is a line of red. They are soldiers - cavalry soldiers,' she subjoined quickly: 'they ride fast; there are six of them: they will pass us: no – they have turned off to the

# Shirley

right: they saw our procession, and avoid it by making a circuit. Where are they going?'

'Perhaps they are only exercising their horses.'

'Perhaps so. We see them no more now.'

Mr Helstone here spoke.

'We shall pass through Royd-lane, to reach Nunnely Common by a short cut,' said he.

And into the straits of Royd-lane they accordingly defiled. It was very narrow, – so narrow that only two could walk abreast without falling into the ditch which ran along each side. They had gained the middle of it, when excitement became obvious in the clerical commanders: Boultby's spectacles and Helstone's Rehoboam were agitated: the curates nudged each other: Mr Hall turned to the ladies and smiled.

'What is the matter?' was the demand.

He pointed with his staff to the end of the lane before them. Lo and behold! another, – an opposition procession was there entering, headed also by men in black, and followed also, as they could now hear, by music.

'Is it our double?' asked Shirley: 'our manifold wraith? Here is a card turned up.'

'If you wanted a battle, you are likely to get one, – at least of looks,' whispered Caroline, laughing.

'They shall not pass us!' cried the curates, unanimously: 'we'll not give way!'

'Give way!' retorted Helstone, sternly, turning round; 'who talks of giving way? You, boys, mind what you are about: the ladies, I know, will be firm; I can trust them. There is not a churchwoman here but will stand her ground against these folks, for the honour of the Establishment. What does Miss Keeldar say?'

'She asks what is it?'

'The Dissenting and Methodist schools, the Baptists, Independents, and Wesleyans, joined in unholy alliance, and turning purposely into this lane with the intention of obstructing our march and driving us back.'

'Bad manners!' said Shirley; 'and I hate bad manners. Of course, they must have a lesson.'

'A lesson in politeness,' suggested Mr Hall, who was ever for peace: 'not an example of rudeness.'

Old Helstone moved on. Quickening his step, he marched some yards in advance of his company. He had nearly reached the other sable leaders, when he who appeared to act as the hostile commander-in-chief – a large, greasy man, with black hair combed flat on his forehead – called a halt. The procession paused: he drew forth a hymn-book, gave out a verse, set a tune, and they all struck up the most dolorous of canticles.

Helstone signed to his bands: they clashed out with all the power of brass. He desired them to play 'Rule, Britannia,' and ordered the children to join in vocally, which they did with enthusiastic spirit. The enemy was sung and stormed down; his psalm quelled: as far as noise went, he was conquered.

'Now, follow me!' exclaimed Helstone; 'not at a run, but at a firm, smart pace. Be steady, every child and woman of you: – keep together: – hold on by each other's skirts, if necessary.'

And he strode on with such a determined and deliberate gait, and was, besides,

so well seconded by his scholars and teachers – who did exactly as he told them, neither running nor faltering, but marching with cool, solid impetus; the curates, too, being compelled to do the same, as they were between two fires, – Helstone and Miss Keeldar, – both of whom watched any deviation with lynx-eyed vigilance, and were ready, the one with his cane, the other with her parasol, to rebuke the slightest breach of orders, the least independent or irregular demonstration, – that the body of Dissenters were first amazed, then alarmed, then borne down and pressed back, and at last forced to turn tail and leave the outlet from Royd-lane free. Boultby suffered in the onslaught, but Helstone and Malone, between them, held him up, and brought him through the business, whole in limb, though sorely tried in wind.

The fat Dissenter who had given out the hymn was left sitting in the ditch. He was a spirit-merchant by trade, a leader of the Nonconformists, and, it was said, drank more water in that one afternoon than he had swallowed for a twelvemonth before. Mr Hall had taken care of Caroline, and Caroline of him: he and Miss Ainley made their own quiet comments to each other afterwards on the incident. Miss Keeldar and Mr Helstone shook hands heartily when they had fairly got the whole party through the lane. The curates began to exult, but Mr Helstone presently put the curb on their innocent spirits: he remarked that they never had sense to know what to say, and had better hold their tongues; and he reminded them that the business was none of their managing.

About half-past three the procession turned back, and at four once more regained the starting-place. Long lines of benches were arranged in the close-shorn fields round the school: there the children were seated, and huge baskets, covered up with white cloths, and great smoking tin vessels were brought out. Ere the distribution of good things commenced, a brief grace was pronounced by Mr Hall, and sung by the children: their young voices sounded melodious, even touching, in the open air. Large currant buns, and hot, well-sweetened tea, were then administered in the proper spirit of liberality: no stinting was permitted on this day, at least; the rule for each child's allowance being that it was to have about twice as much as it could possibly eat, thus leaving a reserve to be carried home for such as age, sickness, or other impediment, prevented from coming to the feast. Buns and beer circulated, meantime, amongst the musicians and church-singers: afterwards the benches were removed, and they were left to unbend their spirits in licensed play.

A bell summoned the teachers, patrons, and patronesses to the schoolroom; Miss Keeldar, Miss Helstone, and many other ladies were already there, glancing over the arrangement of their separate trays and tables. Most of the female servants of the neighbourhood, together with the clerks', the singers', and the musicians' wives, had been pressed into the service of the day as waiters: each vied with the other in smartness and daintiness of dress, and many handsome forms were seen amongst the younger ones. About half a score were cutting bread and butter; another half-score supplying hot water, brought from the coppers of the Rector's kitchen. The profusion of flowers and evergreens decorating the white walls, the show of silver teapots and bright porcelain on the tables, the active figures, blithe faces, gay dresses flitting about everywhere, formed altogether a refreshing and lively spectacle. Everybody talked, not very loudly, but merrily, and the canary birds sang shrill in their high-hung cages.

Caroline, as the Rector's niece, took her place at one of the three first tables;

Mrs Boultby and Margaret Hall officiated at the others. At these tables the élite of the company were to be entertained; strict rules of equality not being more in fashion at Briarfield than elsewhere. Miss Helstone removed her bonnet and scarf, that she might be less oppressed with the heat; her long curls, falling on her neck, served almost in place of a veil, and for the rest, her muslin dress was fashioned modestly as a nun's robe, enabling her thus to dispense with the encumbrance of a shawl.

The room was filling: Mr Hall had taken his post beside Caroline, who now, as she re-arranged the cups and spoons before her, whispered to him in a low voice remarks on the events of the day. He looked a little grave about what had taken place in Royd-lane, and she tried to smile him out of his seriousness. Miss Keeldar sat near; for a wonder, neither laughing nor talking; on the contrary, very still, and gazing round her vigilantly: she seemed afraid lest some intruder should take a seat she apparently wished to reserve next her own; ever and anon she spread her satin dress over an undue portion of the bench, or laid her gloves or her embroidered handkerchief upon it. Caroline noticed this manège at last, and asked her what friend she expected. Shirley bent towards her, almost touched her ear with her rosy lips, and whispered with a musical softness that often characterized her tones, when what she said tended even remotely to stir some sweet secret source of feeling in her heart: –

'I expect Mr Moore: I saw him last night, and I made him promise to come with his sister, and to sit at our table: he won't fail me, I feel certain, but I apprehend his coming too late, and being separated from us. Here is a fresh batch arriving; every place will be taken: provoking!'

In fact Mr Wynne the magistrate, his wife, his son, and his two daughters, now entered in high state. They were Briarfield gentry: of course their place was at the first table, and being conducted thither, they filled up the whole remaining space. For Miss Keeldar's comfort, Mr Sam Wynne inducted himself into the very vacancy she had kept for Moore, planting himself solidly on her gown, her gloves, and her handkerchief. Mr Sam was one of the objects of her aversion; and the more so because he showed serious symptoms of an aim at her hand. The old gentleman, too, had publicly declared that the Fieldhead estate and the De Walden estate were delightfully *contagious* – a malapropism which rumour had not failed to repeat to Shirley.

Caroline's ears yet rung with that thrilling whisper, 'I expect Mr Moore,' her heart yet beat and her cheek yet glowed with it, when a note from the organ pealed above the confused hum of the place. Dr Boultby, Mr Helstone, and Mr Hall rose, so did all present, and grace was sung to the accompaniment of the music; and then tea began. She was kept too busy with her office for a while to have leisure for looking round, but the last cup being filled, she threw a restless glance over the room. There were some ladies and several gentlemen standing about yet unaccommodated with seats: amidst a group she recognized her spinster friend, Miss Mann, whom the fine weather had tempted, or some urgent friend had persuaded, to leave her drear solitude for one hour of social enjoyment. Miss Mann looked tired of standing: a lady in a yellow bonnet brought her a chair. Caroline knew well that 'chapeau en satin jaune;' she knew the black hair, and the kindly, though rather opinionated and froward-looking face under it; she knew that 'robe de soie noire;' she knew even that 'schal gris de lin;' she knew, in short, Hortense Moore, and she wanted to jump up and run to her and

# Shirley

kiss her – to give her one embrace for her own sake, and two for her brother's. She half rose, indeed, with a smothered exclamation, and perhaps – for the impulse was very strong – she would have run across the room, and actually saluted her, but a hand replaced her in her seat, and a voice behind her whispered: –

'Wait till after tea, Lina, and then I'll bring her to you.'

And when she *could* look up she did, and there was Robert himself close behind, smiling at her eagerness, looking better than she had ever seen him look – looking, indeed, to her partial eyes, so very handsome, that she dared not trust herself to hazard a second glance; for his image struck on her vision with painful brightness, and pictured itself on her memory as vividly as if there daguerreotyped by a pencil of keen lightning.

He moved on, and spoke to Miss Keeldar. Shirley, irritated by some unwelcome attentions from Sam Wynne, and by the fact of that gentleman being still seated on her gloves and handkerchief – and probably, also, by Moore's want of punctuality – was by no means in good humour. She first shrugged her shoulder at him, and then she said a bitter word or two about his 'insupportable tardiness.' Moore neither apologized nor retorted: he stood near her quietly, as if waiting to see whether she would recover her temper; which she did in little more than three minutes, indicating the change by offering him her hand. Moore took it with a smile, half-corrective, half-grateful: the slightest possible shake of the head delicately marked the former quality; it is probable a gentle pressure indicated the latter.

'You may sit where you can now, Mr Moore,' said Shirley, also smiling: 'you see there is not an inch of room for you here; but I discern plenty of space at Mrs Boultby's table, between Miss Armitage and Miss Birtwhistle; go: John Sykes will be your vis-à-vis, and you will sit with your back towards us.'

Moore, however, preferred lingering about where he was: he now and then took a turn down the long room, pausing in his walk to interchange greetings with other gentlemen in his own placeless predicament; but still he came back to the magnet, Shirley, bringing with him, each time he returned, observations it was necessary to whisper in her ear.

Meantime, poor Sam Wynne looked far from comfortable: his fair neighbour, judging from her movements, appeared in a mood the most unquiet and unaccommodating: she would not sit still two seconds: she was hot; she fanned herself; complained of want of air and space. She remarked, that, in her opinion, when people had finished their tea they ought to leave the tables, and announced distinctly that she expected to faint if the present state of things continued. Mr Sam offered to accompany her into the open air; just the way to give her her death of cold, she alleged: in short, his post became untenable; and having swallowed his quantum of tea, he judged it expedient to evacuate.

Moore should have been at hand, whereas he was quite at the other extremity of the room, deep in conference with Christopher Sykes. A large corn-factor, Timothy Ramsden, Esq., happened to be nearer, and feeling himself tired of standing, he advanced to fill the vacant seat. Shirley's expedients did not fail her: a sweep of her scarf upset her teacup, its contents were shared between the bench and her own satin dress. Of course, it became necessary to call a waiter to remedy the mischief: Mr Ramsden, a stout, puffy gentleman, as large in person as he was in property, held aloof from the consequent commotion. Shirley,

usually almost culpably indifferent to slight accidents affecting dress, &c., now made a commotion that might have become the most delicate and nervous of her sex: Mr Ramsden opened his mouth, withdrew slowly, and, as Miss Keeldar again intimated her intention to 'give way' and swoon on the spot, he turned on his heel, and beat a heavy retreat.

Moore at last returned: calmly surveying the bustle, and somewhat quizzically scanning Shirley's enigmatical-looking countenance, he remarked, that in truth this was the hottest end of the room; that he found a climate there calculated to agree with none but cool temperaments like his own; and, putting the waiters, the napkins, the satin robe, the whole turmoil, in short, to one side, he installed himself where destiny evidently decreed he should sit. Shirley subsided; her features altered their lines: the raised knit brow and inexplicable curve of the mouth became straight again: wilfulness and roguery gave place to other expressions; and all the angular movements with which she had vexed the soul of Sam Wynne were conjured to rest as by a charm. Still no gracious glance was cast on Moore: on the contrary, he was accused of giving her a world of trouble, and roundly charged with being the cause of depriving her of the esteem of Mr Ramsden, and the invaluable friendship of Mr Samuel Wynne.

'Wouldn't have offended either gentleman for the world,' she averred: 'I have always been accustomed to treat both with the most respectful consideration, and there, owing to you, how they have been used! I shall not be happy till I have made it up: I never am happy till I am friends with my neighbours; so to-morrow I must make a pilgrimage to Royd corn-mill, soothe the miller, and praise the grain; and next day I must call at De Walden – where I hate to go – and carry in my reticule half an oat-cake to give to Mr Sam's favourite pointers.'

'You know the surest path to the heart of each swain, I doubt not,' said Moore, quietly. He looked very content to have at last secured his present place; but he made no fine speech expressive of gratification, and offered no apology for the trouble he had given. His phlegm became him wonderfully: it made him look handsomer, he was so composed: it made his vicinage pleasant, it was so peace-restoring. You would not have thought, to look at him, that he was a poor, struggling man seated beside a rich woman; the calm of equality stilled his aspect: perhaps that calm, too, reigned in his soul. Now and then, from the way in which he looked down on Miss Keeldar as he addressed her, you would have fancied his station towered above hers as much as his stature did. Almost stern lights sometimes crossed his brow and gleamed in his eyes: their conversation had become animated, though it was confined to a low key; she was urging him with questions – evidently, he refused to her curiosity all the gratification it demanded. She sought his eye once with hers: you read, in its soft yet eager expression, that it solicited clearer replies. Moore smiled pleasantly, but his lips continued sealed. Then she was piqued and turned away, but he recalled her attention in two minutes: he seemed making promises, which he soothed her into accepting, in lieu of information.

It appeared that the heat of the room did not suit Miss Helstone: she grew paler and paler as the process of tea-making was protracted. The moment thanks were returned, she quitted the table, and hastened to follow her cousin Hortense, who, with Miss Mann, had already sought the open air. Robert Moore had risen when she did – perhaps he meant to speak to her; but there was yet a

parting word to exchange with Miss Keeldar, and while it was being uttered, Caroline had vanished.

Hortense received her former pupil with a demeanour of more dignity than warmth: she had been seriously offended by Mr Helstone's proceedings, and had all along considered Caroline to blame, in obeying her uncle too literally.

'You are a very great stranger,' she said, austerely, as her pupil held and pressed her hand. The pupil knew her too well to remonstrate or complain of coldness; she let the punctilious whim pass, sure that her natural *bonté* (I use this French word, because it expresses just what I mean; neither goodness nor good nature, but something between the two) would presently get the upper-hand. It did: Hortense had no sooner examined her face well, and observed the change its somewhat wasted features betrayed, than her mien softened. Kissing her on both cheeks, she asked anxiously after her health: Caroline answered gaily. It would, however, have been her lot to undergo a long cross-examination, followed by an endless lecture on this head, had not Miss Mann called off the attention of the questioner, by requesting to be conducted home. The poor invalid was already fatigued: her weariness made her cross – too cross almost to speak to Caroline; and besides, that young person's white dress and lively look were displeasing in the eyes of Miss Mann: the everyday garb of brown stuff or grey gingham, and the everyday air of melancholy, suited the solitary spinster better: she would hardly know her young friend to-night, and quitted her with a cool nod. Hortense having promised to accompany her home, they departed together.

Caroline now looked round for Shirley. She saw the rainbow scarf and purple dress in the centre of a throng of ladies, all well known to herself, but all of the order whom she systematically avoided whenever avoidance was possible. Shyer at some moments than at others, she felt just now no courage at all to join this company: she could not, however, stand alone where all others went in pairs or parties, so she approached a group of her own scholars, great girls, or rather young women, who were standing watching some hundreds of the younger children playing at blind-man's-buff.

Miss Helstone knew these girls liked her, yet she was shy even with them out of school: they were not more in awe of her than she of them: she drew near them now, rather to find protection in their company than to patronize them with her presence. By some instinct they knew her weakness, and with natural politeness they respected it. Her knowledge commanded their esteem when she taught them; her gentleness attracted their regard; and because she was what they considered wise and good when *on* duty, they kindly overlooked her evident timidity when off: they did not take advantage of it. Peasant girls as they were, they had too much of her own English sensibility to be guilty of the coarse error: they stood round her still, civil, friendly, receiving her slight smiles, and rather hurried efforts to converse, with a good feeling and good breeding: the last quality being the result of the first, which soon set her at her ease.

Mr Sam Wynne coming up with great haste, to insist on the elder girls joining in the game as well as the younger ones, Caroline was again left alone. She was meditating a quiet retreat to the house, when Shirley, perceiving from afar her isolation, hastened to her side.

'Let us go to the top of the fields,' she said: 'I know you don't like crowds, Caroline.'

# Shirley

'But it will be depriving you of a pleasure, Shirley, to take you from all these fine people, who court your society so assiduously, and to whom you can, without art or effort, make yourself so pleasant.'

'Not quite without effort: I am already tired of the exertion: it is but insipid, barren work, talking and laughing with the good gentlefolks of Briarfield. I have been looking out for your white dress for the last ten minutes: I like to watch those I love in a crowd, and to compare them with others: I have thus compared you. You resemble none of the rest, Lina: there are some prettier faces than yours here; you are not a model-beauty like Harriet Sykes, for instance; beside her, your person appears almost insignificant; but you look agreeable – you look reflective – you look what I call interesting.'

'Hush, Shirley! You flatter me.'

'I don't wonder that your scholars like you.'

'Nonsense, Shirley: talk of something else.'

'We will talk of Moore, then, and we will watch him: I see him even now.'

'Where?' And as Caroline asked the question, she looked not over the fields, but into Miss Keeldar's eyes, as was her wont whenever Shirley mentioned any object she descried afar. Her friend had quicker vision than herself; and Caroline seemed to think that the secret of her eagle acuteness might be read in her dark grey irids: or rather, perhaps, she only sought guidance by the direction of those discriminating and brilliant spheres.

'There is Moore,' said Shirley, pointing right across the wide field where a thousand children were playing, and now nearly a thousand adult spectators walking about. 'There – can you miss the tall stature and straight port? He looks amidst the set that surround him like Eliab amongst humbler shepherds – like Saul in a war-council: and a war-council it is, if I am not mistaken.'

'Why so, Shirley?' asked Caroline, whose eye had at last caught the object it sought. 'Robert is just now speaking to my uncle, and they are shaking hands; they are then reconciled.'

'Reconciled not without good reason, depend on it: making common cause against some common foe. And why, think you, are Messrs Wynne and Sykes, and Armitage and Ramsden, gathered in such a close circle round them? And why is Malone beckoned to join them? Where *he* is summoned, be sure a strong arm is needed.'

Shirley, as she watched, grew restless: her eyes flashed.

'They won't trust me,' she said: 'that is always the way when it comes to the point.'

'What about?'

'Cannot you feel? There is some mystery afloat: some event is expected; some preparation is to be made, I am certain: I saw it all in Mr Moore's manner this evening: he was excited, yet hard.'

'Hard to *you*, Shirley!'

'Yes, to *me*. He often is hard to me. We seldom converse tête-à-tête, but I am made to feel that the basis of his character is not of eider down.'

'Yet he seemed to talk to you softly.'

'Did he not? Very gentle tones and quiet manner; yet the man is peremptory and secret: his secrecy vexes me.'

'Yes – Robert is secret.'

'Which he has scarcely a right to be with me; especially as he commenced by

# Shirley

giving me his confidence. Having done nothing to forfeit that confidence, it ought not to be withdrawn: but I suppose I am not considered iron-souled enough to be trusted in a crisis.'

'He fears, probably, to occasion you uneasiness.'

'An unnecessary precaution: I am of elastic materials, not soon crushed; he ought to know that: but the man is proud: he has his faults, say what you will, Lina. Observe how engaged that group appear: they do not know we are watching them.'

'If we keep on the alert, Shirley, we shall perhaps find the clue to their secret.'

'There will be some unusual movements erelong – perhaps to-morrow – possibly to-night. But my eyes and ears are wide open: Mr Moore, you shall be under surveillance. Be you vigilant also, Lina.'

'I will: Robert is going, I saw him turn – I believe he noticed us – they are shaking hands.'

'Shaking hands, with emphasis,' added Shirley; 'as if they were ratifying some solemn league and covenant.'

They saw Robert quit the group, pass through a gate, and disappear.

'And he has not bid us good-bye,' murmured Caroline.

Scarcely had the words escaped her lips, when she tried by a smile to deny the confession of disappointment they seemed to imply. An unbidden suffusion for one moment both softened and brightened her eyes.

'Oh, that is soon remedied!' exclaimed Shirley. 'We'll *make* him bid us good-bye.'

'*Make* him! That is not the same thing,' was the answer.

'It *shall* be the same thing.'

'But he is gone: you can't overtake him.'

'I know a shorter way than that he has taken: we will intercept him.'

'But, Shirley, I would rather not go.'

Caroline said this as Miss Keeldar seized her arm, and hurried her down the fields. It was vain to contend: nothing was so wilful as Shirley, when she took a whim into her head: Caroline found herself out of sight of the crowd almost before she was aware, and ushered into a narrow shady spot, embowered above with hawthorns, and enamelled under foot with daisies. She took no notice of the evening sun chequering the turf, nor was she sensible of the pure incense exhaling at this hour from tree and plant; she only heard the wicket opening at one end, and knew Robert was approaching. The long sprays of the hawthorns, shooting out before them, served as a screen; they saw him before he observed them. At a glance Caroline perceived that his social hilarity was gone: he had left it behind him in the joy-echoing fields round the school; what remained now was his dark, quiet, business countenance. As Shirley had said, a certain hardness characterized his air, while his eye was excited, but austere. So much the worse-timed was the present freak of Shirley's: if he had looked disposed for holiday mirth, it would not have mattered much, but now –

'I told you not to come,' said Caroline, somewhat bitterly, to her friend. She seemed truly perturbed: to be intruded on Robert thus, against her will and his expectation, and when he evidently would rather not be delayed, keenly annoyed her. It did not annoy Miss Keeldar in the least: she stepped forward and faced her tenant, barring his way: –

'You omitted to bid us good-bye,' she said.

# Shirley

'Omitted to bid you good-bye! Where did you come from? Are you fairies? I left two like you, one in purple and one in white, standing at the top of a bank, four fields off, but a minute ago.'

'You left us there and find us here. We have been watching you; and shall watch you still: you must be questioned one day, but not now: at present, all you have to do is to say good-night, and then pass.'

Moore glanced from one to the other, without unbending his aspect. 'Days of fête have their privileges, and so have days of hazard,' observed he, gravely.

'Come – don't moralize: say good-night, and pass,' urged Shirley.

'Must I say good-night to you, Miss Keeldar?'

'Yes, and to Caroline likewise. It is nothing new, I hope: you have bid us both good-night before.'

He took her hand, held it in one of his, and covered it with the other: he looked down at her gravely, kindly, yet commandingly. The heiress could not make this man her subject: in his gaze on her bright face there was no servility, hardly homage; but there was interest and affection, heightened by another feeling: something in his tone when he spoke, as well as in his words, marked that last sentiment to be gratitude.

'Your debtor bids you good-night! – May you rest safely and serenely till morning!'

'And you, Mr Moore, – what are you going to do? What have you been saying to Mr Helstone, with whom I saw you shake hands? Why did all those gentlemen gather round you? Put away reserve for once: be frank with me.'

'Who can resist you? I will be frank: to-morrow, if there is anything to relate, you shall hear it.'

'Just now,' pleaded Shirley: 'don't procrastinate.'

'But I could only tell half a tale; and my time is limited, – I have not a moment to spare: hereafter I will make amends for delay by candour.'

'But are you going home?'

'Yes.'

'Not to leave it any more to-night?'

'Certainly not. At present, farewell to both of you!'

He would have taken Caroline's hand and joined it in the same clasp in which he held Shirley's, but somehow it was not ready for him; she had withdrawn a few steps apart: her answer to Moore's adieu was only a slight bend of the head, and a gentle, serious smile. He sought no more cordial token: again he said 'Farewell!' and quitted them both.

'There! – it is over!' said Shirley, when he was gone. 'We have made him bid us good-night, and yet not lost ground in his esteem, I think, Cary.'

'I hope not,' was the brief reply.

'I consider you very timid and undemonstrative,' remarked Miss Keeldar. 'Why did you not give Moore your hand when he offered you his? He is your cousin: you like him. Are you ashamed to let him perceive your affection?'

'He perceives all of it that interests him: no need to make a display of feeling.'

'You are laconic: you would be stoical if you could. Is love, in your eyes, a crime, Caroline?'

'Love, a crime! No, Shirley: – love is a divine virtue; but why drag that word into the conversation? it is singularly irrelevant!'

'Good!' pronounced Shirley.

The two girls paced the green lane in silence. Caroline first resumed.

'Obtrusiveness is a crime; forwardness is a crime; and both disgust: but love! – no purest angel need blush to love! And when I see or hear either man or woman couple shame with love, I know their minds are coarse, their associations debased. Many who think themselves refined ladies and gentlemen, and on whose lips the word "vulgarity" is for ever hovering, cannot mention "love" without betraying their own innate and imbecile degradation: it is a low feeling in their estimation, connected only with the low ideas for them.'

'You describe three-fourths of the world, Caroline.'

'They are cold – they are cowardly – they are stupid on the subject, Shirley? They never loved – they never were loved!'

'Thou art right, Lina! And in their dense ignorance they blaspheme living fire, seraph-brought from a divine altar.'

'They confound it with sparks mounting from Tophet!'

The sudden and joyous clash of bells here stopped the dialogue by summoning all to the church.

# Chapter 18

## Which the Genteel Reader is Recommended to Skip, Low Persons being Here Introduced

The evening was still and warm; close and sultry it even promised to become. Round the descending sun the clouds glowed purple: summer tints, rather Indian than English, suffused the horizon, and cast rosy reflections on hill-side, house-front, tree-bole; on winding road, and undulating pasture-ground. The two girls came down from the fields slowly: by the time they reached the churchyard the bells were hushed; the multitudes were gathered into the church: the whole scene was solitary.

'How pleasant and calm it is!' said Caroline.

'And how hot it will be in the church!' responded Shirley; 'and what a dreary long speech Dr Boultby will make! and how the curates will hammer over their prepared orations! For my part, I would rather not enter.'

'But my uncle will be angry, if he observes our absence.'

'I will bear the brunt of his wrath: he will not devour me. I shall be sorry to miss his pungent speech. I know it will be all sense for the Church, and all causticity for Schism: he'll not forget the battle of Royd-lane. I shall be sorry also to deprive you of Mr Hall's sincere friendly homily, with all its racy Yorkshireisms; but here I must stay. The grey church and greyer tombs look divine with this crimson gleam on them. Nature is now at her evening prayers: she is kneeling before those red hills. I see her prostrate on the great steps of her altar, praying for a fair night for mariners at sea, for travellers in deserts, for

# Shirley

lambs on moors, and unfledged birds in woods. Caroline, I see her! and I will tell you what she is like: she is like what Eve was when she and Adam stood alone on earth.'

'And that is not Milton's Eve, Shirley.'

'Milton's Eve! Milton's Eve! I repeat. No, by the pure Mother of God, she is not! Cary, we are alone: we may speak what we think. Milton was great; but was he good? His brain was right; how was his heart? He saw heaven: he looked down on hell. He saw Satan, and Sin his daughter, and Death their horrible offspring. Angels serried before him their battalions: the long lines of adamantine shields flashed back on his blind eyeballs the unutterable splendour of heaven. Devils gathered their legions in his sight: their dim, discrowned, and tarnished armies passed rank and file before him. Milton tried to see the first woman; but, Cary, he saw her not.'

'You are bold to say so, Shirley.'

'Not more bold than faithful. It was his cook that he saw; or it was Mrs Gill, as I have seen her, making custards, in the heat of summer, in the cool dairy, with rose-trees and nasturtiums about the latticed window, preparing a cold collation for the rectors, – preserves, and "dulcet creams" – puzzled "what choice to choose for delicacy best; what order so contrived as not to mix tastes, not well-joined, inelegant; but bring taste after taste, upheld with kindliest change." '

'All very well too, Shirley.'

'I would beg to remind him that the first men of the earth were Titans, and that Eve was their mother: from her sprang Saturn, Hyperion, Oceanus; she bore Prometheus –'

'Pagan that you are! what does that signify?'

'I say, there were giants on the earth in those days: giants that strove to scale heaven. The first woman's breast that heaved with life on this world yielded the daring which could contend with Omnipotence: the strength which could bear a thousand years of bondage, – the vitality which could feed that vulture death through uncounted ages, – the unexhausted life and uncorrupted excellence, sisters to immortality, which, after millenniums of crimes, struggles, and woes, could conceive and bring forth a Messiah. The first woman was heaven-born: vast was the heart whence gushed the well-spring of the blood of nations; and grand the undegenerate head where rested the consort-crown of creation.'

'She coveted an apple, and was cheated by a snake: but you have got such a hash of Scripture and mythology into your head that there is no making any sense of you. You have not yet told me what you saw kneeling on those hills.'

'I saw – I now see – a woman-Titan: her robe of blue air spreads to the outskirts of the heath, where yonder flock is grazing; a veil white as an avalanche sweeps from her head to her feet, and arabesques of lightning flame on its borders. Under her breast I see her zone, purple like that horizon: through its blush shines the star of evening. Her steady eyes I cannot picture; they are clear – they are deep as lakes – they are lifted and full of worship – they tremble with the softness of love and the lustre of prayer. Her forehead has the expanse of a cloud, and is paler than the early moon, risen long before dark gathers: she reclines her bosom on the ridge of Stilbro' Moor; her mighty hands are joined beneath it. So kneeling, face to face she speaks with God. That Eve is Jehovah's daughter, as Adam was his son.'

'She is very vague and visionary! Come, Shirley, we ought to go into church.'

# Shirley

'Caroline, I will not: I will stay out here with my mother Eve, in these days called Nature. I love her – undying, mighty being! Heaven may have faded from her brow when she fell in paradise; but all that is glorious on earth shines there still. She is taking me to her bosom, and showing me her heart. Hush, Caroline! you will see her and feel as I do, if we are both silent.'

'I will humour your whim; but you will begin talking again, ere ten minutes are over.'

Miss Keeldar, on whom the soft excitement of the warm summer evening seemed working with unwonted power, leaned against an upright headstone: she fixed her eyes on the deep-burning west, and sank into a pleasurable trance. Caroline, going a little apart, paced to and fro beneath the Rectory garden-wall, dreaming, too, in her way. Shirley had mentioned the word 'mother:' that word suggested to Caroline's imagination not the mighty and mystical parent of Shirley's visions, but a gentle human form – the form she ascribed to her own mother; unknown, unloved, but not unlonged-for.

'Oh, that the day would come when she would remember her child! Oh, that I might know her, and knowing, love her!'

Such was her aspiration.

The longing of her childhood filled her soul again. The desire which many a night had kept her awake in her crib, and which fear of its fallacy had of late years almost extinguished, relit suddenly, and glowed warm in her heart: that her mother might come some happy day, and send for her to her presence – look upon her fondly with loving eyes, and say to her tenderly, in a sweet voice: –

'Caroline, my child. I have a home for you: you shall live with me. All the love you have needed, and not tasted, from infancy, I have saved for you carefully. Come! it shall cherish you now.'

A noise on the road roused Caroline from her filial hopes, and Shirley from her Titan visions. They listened, and heard the tramp of horses: they looked, and saw a glitter through the trees: they caught through the foliage glimpses of martial scarlet; helm shone, plume waved. Silent and orderly, six soldiers rode softly by.

'The same we saw this afternoon,' whispered Shirley: 'they have been halting somewhere till now. They wish to be as little noticed as possible, and are seeking their rendezvous at this quiet hour, while the people are at church. Did I not say we should see unusual things erelong?'

Scarcely were sight and sound of the soldiers lost, when another and somewhat different disturbance broke the night-hush – a child's impatient scream. They looked: a man issued from the church, carrying in his arms an infant – a robust, ruddy little boy, of some two years old – roaring with all the power of his lungs; he had probably just awaked from a church-sleep: two little girls, of nine and ten followed. The influence of the fresh air, and the attraction of some flowers gathered from a grave, soon quieted the child; the man sat down with him, dandling him on his knee as tenderly as any woman; the two little girls took their places one on each side.

'Good-evening, William,' said Shirley, after due scrutiny of the man. He had seen her before, and apparently was waiting to be recognized; he now took off his hat, and grinned a smile of pleasure. He was a rough-headed, hard featured personage, not old, but very weather-beaten; his attire was decent and clean,

# Shirley

that of his children singularly neat; it was our old friend, Farren. The young ladies approached him.

'You are not going into the church?' he inquired, gazing at them complacently, yet with a mixture of bashfulness in his look: a sentiment not by any means the result of awe of their station, but only of appreciation of their elegance and youth. Before gentlemen – such as Moore or Helstone, for instance – William was often a little dogged; with proud or insolent ladies, too, he was quite unmanageable, sometimes very resentful; but he was most sensible of, most tractable to, good-humour and civility. His nature – a stubborn one – was repelled by inflexibility in other natures; for which reason, he had never been able to like his former master, Moore; and, unconscious of that gentleman's good opinion of himself, and of the service he had secretly rendered him in recommending him as gardener to Mr Yorke, and by this means to other families in the neighbourhood, he continued to harbour a grudge against his austerity. Latterly, he had often worked at Fieldhead; Miss Keeldar's frank, hospitable manners were perfectly charming to him. Caroline he had known from her childhood: unconsciously, she was his ideal of a lady. Her gentle mien, step, gestures, her grace of person and attire, moved some artist-fibres about his peasant heart: he had a pleasure in looking at her, as he had in examining rare flowers, or in seeing pleasant landscapes. Both the ladies liked William: it was their delight to lend him books, to give him plants; and they preferred his conversation far before that of many coarse, hard, pretentious people, immeasurably higher in station.

'Who was speaking, William, when you came out?' asked Shirley.

'A gentleman ye set a deal of store on, Miss Shirley – Mr Donne.'

'You look knowing, William. How did you find out my regard for Mr Donne?'

'Ay, Miss Shirley, there's a gleg light i' your een sometimes which betrays you. You look raight down scornful sometimes, when Mr Donne is by.'

'Do you like him yourself, William?'

'Me? I'm stalled o' t' curates, and so is t' wife: they've no manners; they talk to poor folk fair as if they thought they were beneath them. They're allus magnifying their office: it is a pity but their office could magnify them; but it does nought o' t' soart. I fair hate pride.'

'But you are proud in your own way yourself,' interposed Caroline: 'you are what you call house-proud; you like to have everything handsome about you: sometimes you look as if you were almost too proud to take your wages. When you were out of work, you were too proud to get anything on credit; but for your children, I believe you would rather have starved than gone to the shops without money; and when I wanted to give you something, what a difficulty I had in making you take it!'

'It is partly true, Miss Caroline: ony day I'd rather give than take, especially from sich as ye. Look at t' difference between us: ye're a little, young, slender lass, and I'm a great strong man: I'm rather more nor twice your age. It is not *my* part then, I think, to tak' fro' ye – to be under obligations (as they say) to *ye*; and that day ye came to our house, and called me to t' door, and offered me five shillings, which I doubt ye could ill spare, – for ye've no fortin', I know, – that day I war fair a rebel – a radical – an insurrectionist; and *ye* made me so. I thought it shameful that, willing and able as I was to work, I suld be i'

# Shirley

such a condition that a young cratur about the age o' my own eldest lass suld think it needful to come and offer me her bit o' brass.'

'I suppose you were angry with me, William?'

'I almost was, in a way; but I forgave ye varry soon: ye meant well. Ay, *I am* proud, and so are *ye*; but your pride and mine is t' raight mak' – what we call i' Yorkshire "clean pride," – such as Mr Malone and Mr Donne knows nought about: theirs is mucky pride. Now, I shall teach my lasses to be as proud as Miss Shirley there, and my lads to be as proud as myseln; but I dare ony o' 'em to be like t' curates: I'd lick little Michael, if I seed him show any signs o' that feeling.'

'What is the difference, William?'

'Ye know t' difference weel enew, but ye want me to get a gate o' talking. Mr Malone and Mr Donne is almost too proud to do aught for theirsel'n; *we* are almost too proud to let anybody do aught for us. T' curates can hardly bide to speak a civil word to them they think beneath them; *we* can hardly bide to tak' an uncivil word fro' them that thinks themsel'n aboon us.'

'Now, William, be humble enough to tell me truly how you are getting on in the world? Are you well off?'

'Miss Shirley – I am varry well off. Since I got into t' gardening line, wi' Mr Yorke's help, and since Mr Hall (another o' t' raight sort) helped my wife to set up a bit of a shop, I've nought to complain of. My family has plenty to eat and plenty to wear: my pride makes me find means to save an odd pound now and then against rainy days; for I think I'd die afore I'd come to t' parish: and me and mine is content; but th' neighbours is poor yet: I see a great deal of distress.'

'And, consequently, there is still discontent, I suppose?' inquired Miss Keeldar.

'*Consequently* – ye say right – *consequently*. In course, starving folk cannot be satisfied or settled folk. The country's not in a safe condition; – I'll say so mich!'

'But what can be done? What more can I do, for instance?'

'Do? – ye can do naught mich, poor young lass! Ye've gi'en your brass: ye've done well. If ye could transport your tenant, Mr Moore, to Botany Bay, ye'd happen do better. Folks hate him.'

'William, for shame!' exclaimed Caroline, warmly. 'If folks *do* hate him, it is to their disgrace, not his. Mr Moore himself hates nobody; he only wants to do his duty, and maintain his rights: you are wrong to talk so!'

'I talk as I think. He has a cold, unfeeling heart, yond' Moore.'

'But,' interposed Shirley, 'supposing Moore was driven from the country, and his mill razed to the ground, would people have more work?'

'They'd have less. I know that, and they know that; and there is many an honest lad driven desperate by the certainty that whichever way he turns, he cannot better himself, and there is dishonest men plenty to guide them to the devil: scoundrels that reckons to be the "people's friends," and that knows naught about the people, and is as insincere as Lucifer. I've lived aboon forty year in the world, and I believe that "the people" will never have any true friends but theirsel'n, and them two or three good folk i' different stations, that is friends to all the world. Human natur', taking it i' th' lump, is naught but selfishness. It is but excessive few; it is but just an exception here and there, now and then, sich as ye two young 'uns and me, that being in a different sphere,

can understand t' one t' other, and be friends wi'out slavishness o' one hand, or pride o' t' other. Them that reckons to be friends to a lower class than their own fro' political motives is never to be trusted: they always try to make their inferiors tools. For my own part, I will neither be patronized nor misled for no man's pleasure. I've had overtures made to me lately that I saw were treacherous, and I flung 'em back i' the faces o' them that offered 'em.'

'You won't tell us what overtures?'

'I will not: it would do no good; it would mak' no difference: them they concerned can look after theirsel'n.'

'Ay, we'se look after wersel'n,' said another voice. Joe Scott had sauntered forth from the church to get a breath of fresh air, and there he stood.

'I'll warrant *ye*, Joe,' observed William, smiling.

'And I'll warrant my maister,' was the answer. 'Young ladies,' continued Joe, assuming a lordly air, 'ye'd better go into th' house.'

'I wonder what for?' inquired Shirley, to whom the overlooker's somewhat pragmatical manners were familiar, and who was often at war with him; for Joe, holding supercilious theories about women in general, resented greatly, in his secret soul, the fact of his master and his master's mill being, in a manner, under petticoat government, and had felt as wormwood and gall, certain business-visits of the heiress to the Hollow's counting-house.

'Because there is naught agate that fits women to be consarned in.'

'Indeed! There is prayer and preaching agate in that church; are we not concerned in that?'

'Ye have been present neither at the prayer nor preaching, ma'am, if I have observed aright. What I alluded to was politics: William Farren, here, was touching on that subject, if I'm not mista'en.'

'Well, what then? Politics are our habitual study, Joe. Do you know I see a newspaper every day, and two of a Sunday?'

'I should think you'll read the marriages, probably, Miss, and the murders, and the accidents, and sich like?'

'I read the leading articles, Joe, and the foreign intelligence, and I look over the market prices: in short, I read just what gentlemen read.'

Joe looked as if he thought this talk was like the chattering of a pie. He replied to it, by a disdainful silence.

'Joe,' continued Miss Keeldar, 'I never yet could ascertain properly, whether you are a Whig or a Tory: pray which party has the honour of your alliance?'

'It is rayther difficult to explain where you are sure not to be understood,' was Joe's haughty response; 'but, as to being a Tory, I'd as soon be an old woman, or a young one, which is a more flimsier article still. It is the Tories that carries on the war and ruins trade; and, if I be of any party – though political parties is all nonsense – I'm of that which is most favourable to peace, and, by consequence, to the mercantile interests of this here land.'

'So am I, Joe,' replied Shirley, who had rather a pleasure in teazing the overlooker, by persisting in talking on subjects with which he opined she – as a woman – had no right to meddle: 'partly, at least. I have rather a leaning to the agricultural interest, too; as good reason is, seeing that I don't desire England to be under the feet of France, and that if a share of my income comes from Hollow's mill, a larger share comes from the landed estate around it. It would not do to take any measures injurious to the farmers, Joe, I think?'

# Shirley

'The dews at this hour is unwholesome for females,' observed Joe.

'If you make that remark out of interest in me, I have merely to assure you that I am impervious to cold. I should not mind taking my turn to watch the mill one of these summer nights, armed with your musket, Joe.'

Joe Scott's chin was always rather prominent: he poked it out, at this speech, some inches further than usual.

'But – to go back to my sheep,' she proceeded – 'clothier and mill-owner as I am, besides farmer, I cannot get out of my head a certain idea that we manufacturers and persons of business are sometimes a little – a *very little* selfish and short-sighted in our views, and rather *too* regardless of human suffering, rather heartless in our pursuit of gain: don't you agree with me, Joe?'

'I cannot argue, where I cannot be comprehended,' was again the answer.

'Man of mystery! Your master will argue with me sometimes, Joe: he is not so stiff as you are.'

'May be not: we've all our own ways.'

'Joe, do you seriously think all the wisdom in the world is lodged in male skulls?'

'I think that women are a kittle and a froward generation; and I've a great respect for the doctrines delivered in the second chapter of St Paul's first Epistle to Timothy.'

'What doctrines, Joe?'

'Let the woman learn in silence, with all subjection. I suffer not a woman to teach, nor to usurp authority over the man; but to be in silence. For Adam was first formed, then Eve.'

'What has that to do with the business?' interjected Shirley: 'that smacks of rights of primogeniture. I'll bring it up to Mr Yorke the first time he inveighs against those rights.'

'And,' continued Joe Scott, 'Adam was not deceived; but the woman, being deceived, was in the transgression.'

'More shame to Adam to sin with his eyes open!' cried Miss Keeldar. 'To confess the honest truth, Joe, I never was easy in my mind concerning that chapter: it puzzles me.'

'It is very plain, Miss: he that runs may read.'

'He may read it in his own fashion,' remarked Caroline, now joining in the dialogue for the first time. 'You allow the right of private judgment, I suppose, Joe?'

'My certy, that I do! I allow and claim it for every line of the holy Book.'

'Women may exercise it as well as men?'

'Nay: women is to take their husbands' opinion, both in politics and religion: it's wholesomest for them.'

'Oh! oh!' exclaimed both Shirley and Caroline.

'To be sure; no doubt on 't,' persisted the stubborn overlooker.

'Consider yourself groaned down, and cried shame over, for such a stupid observation,' said Miss Keeldar. 'You might as well say, men are to take the opinions of their priests without examination. Of what value would a religion so adopted be? It would be mere blind, besotted superstition.'

'And what is *your* reading, Miss Helstone, o' these words o' St Paul's?'

'Hem! I – I account for them in this way: he wrote that chapter for a particular congregation of Christians, under peculiar circumstances; and besides, I dare

# Shirley

say, if I could read the original Greek, I should find that many of the words have been wrongly translated, perhaps misapprehended altogether. It would be possible, I doubt not, with a little ingenuity, to give the passage quite a contrary turn; to make it say, "Let the woman speak out whenever she sees fit to make an objection;" – "it is permitted to a woman to teach and to exercise authority as much as may be. Man, meantime, cannot do better than hold his peace," and so on.'

'That will n't wash, Miss.'

'I dare say it will. My notions are dyed in faster colours than yours, Joe. Mr Scott, you are a thoroughly dogmatical person, and always were: I like William better than you.'

'Joe is well enough in his own house,' said Shirley: 'I have seen him as quiet as a lamb at home. There is not a better nor a kinder husband in Briarfield. He does not dogmatize to his wife.'

'My wife is a hard-working, plain woman: time and trouble has ta'en all the conceit out of her; but that is not the case with you, young Misses. And then you reckon to have so much knowledge; and i' my thoughts it's only a superficial sort o' vanities you're acquainted with. I can tell – happen a year sin' – one day Miss Caroline coming into our counting-house when I war packing up summut behind t' great desk, and she didn't see me, and she brought a slate wi' a sum on it to t' maister: it were only a bit of a sum in practice, that our Harry would have settled i' two minutes. She couldn't do it; Mr Moore had to show her how; and when he did show her, she couldn't understand him.'

'Nonsense, Joe!'

'Nay, it's no nonsense: and Miss Shirley, there, reckons to hearken to t' maister when he's talking ower trade, so attentive like, as if she followed him word for word, and all war as clear as a lady's looking-glass to her een; and all t' while she's peeping and peeping out o' t' window to see if t' mare stands quiet; and then looking at a bit of a splash on her riding-skirt; and then glancing glegly round at wer counting-house cobwebs and dust, and thinking what mucky folk we are, and what a grand ride she'll have just i' now ower Nunnely-common. She hears no more o' Mr Moore's talk nor if he spake Hebrew.'

'Joe, you are a real slanderer. I would give you your answer, only the people are coming out of church: we must leave you. Man of prejudice, good-bye: William, good-bye. Children, come up to Fieldhead to-morrow, and you shall choose what you like best out of Mrs Gill's store-room.'

# Chapter 19

## A Summer Night

The hour was now that of dusk. A clear air favoured the kindling of the stars.

'There will be just light enough to show me the way home,' said Miss Keeldar, as she prepared to take leave of Caroline at the Rectory garden-door.

'You must not go alone, Shirley. Fanny shall accompany you.'

'That she shall not. Of what need I be afraid in my own parish? I would walk from Fieldhead to the church any fine mid-summer night, three hours later than this, for the mere pleasure of seeing the stars, and the chance of meeting a fairy.'

'But just wait till the crowd is cleared away.'

'Agreed. There are the five Misses Armitage streaming by. Here comes Mrs Sykes's phaeton, Mr Wynne's close carriage, Mrs Birtwhistle's car: I don't wish to go through the ceremony of bidding them all good-bye, so we will step into the garden and take shelter amongst the laburnums for an instant.'

The rectors, their curates and their churchwardens, now issued from the church-porch. There was a great confabulation, shaking of hands, congratulation on speeches, recommendation to be careful of the night air, &c. By degrees the throng dispersed; the carriages drove off. Miss Keeldar was just emerging from her flowery refuge, when Mr Helstone entered the garden and met her.

'Oh! I want you!' he said: 'I was afraid you were already gone. Caroline, come here!'

Caroline came, expecting, as Shirley did, a lecture on not having been visible at church. Other subjects, however, occupied the Rector's mind.

'I shall not sleep at home to-night,' he continued. 'I have just met with an old friend, and promised to accompany him. I shall return probably about noon to-morrow. Thomas, the clerk, is engaged, and I cannot get him to sleep in the house, as I usually do when I am absent for a night; now –'

'Now,' interrupted Shirley, 'you want me as a gentleman – the first gentleman in Briarfield, in short, to supply your place, be master of the Rectory, and guardian of your niece and maids while you are away?'

'Exactly, captain: I thought the post would suit you. Will you favour Caroline so far as to be her guest for one night? Will you stay here instead of going back to Fieldhead?'

'And what will Mrs Pryor do? She expects me home.'

'I will send her word. Come, make up your mind to stay. It grows late; the dew falls heavily: you and Caroline will enjoy each other's society I doubt not.'

'I promise you then to stay with Caroline,' replied Shirley. 'As you say, we

shall enjoy each other's society: we will not be separated to-night. Now, rejoin your old friend, and fear nothing for us.'

'If there should chance to be any disturbance in the night, captain – if you should hear the picking of a lock, the cutting out of a pane of glass, a stealthy tread of steps about the house (and I need not fear to tell *you*, who bear a well-tempered, mettlesome heart under your girl's ribbon-sash, that such little incidents are very possible in the present time), what would you do?'

'Don't know – faint, perhaps – fall down, and have to be picked up again. But, doctor, if you assign me the post of honour, you must give me arms. What weapons are there in your stronghold?'

'You could not wield a sword?'

'No: I could manage the carving-knife better.'

'You will find a good one in the dining-room side-board: a lady's knife, light to handle, and as sharp-pointed as a poniard.'

'It will suit Caroline; but you must give me a brace of pistols: I know you have pistols.'

'I have two pairs; one pair I can place at your disposal. You will find them suspended over the mantelpiece of my study in cloth cases.'

'Loaded?'

'Yes, but not on the cock. Cock them before you go to bed. It is paying you a great compliment, captain, to lend you these: were you one of the awkward squad you should not have them.'

'I will take care. You need delay no longer, Mr Helstone: you may go now. He is gracious to me to lend me his pistols,' she remarked, as the Rector passed out at the garden-gate. 'But come, Lina,' she continued; 'let us go in and have some supper? I was too much vexed at tea with the vicinage of Mr Sam Wynne to be able to eat, and now I am really hungry.'

Entering the house, they repaired to the darkened dining-room, through the open windows of which apartment stole the evening air, bearing the perfume of flowers from the garden, the very distant sound of far-retreating steps from the road, and a soft, vague murmur, whose origin Caroline explained by the remark, uttered as she stood listening at the casement:

'Shirley, I hear the beck in the Hollow.'

Then she rung the bell, asked for a candle and some bread and milk – Miss Keeldar's usual supper and her own. Fanny, when she brought in the tray, would have closed the windows and the shutters, but was requested to desist for the present: the twilight was too calm, its breath too balmy to be yet excluded. They took their meal in silence: Caroline rose once, to remove to the window-sill a glass of flowers which stood on the side-board; the exhalation from the blossoms being somewhat too powerful for the sultry room: in returning, she half opened a drawer, and took from it something that glittered clear and keen in her hand.

'You assigned this to me, then, Shirley – did you? It is bright, keen-edged, finely-tapered: it is dangerous-looking. I never yet felt the impulse which could move me to direct this against a fellow-creature. It is difficult to fancy what circumstances could nerve my arm to strike home with this long knife.'

'I should hate to do it,' replied Shirley; 'but I think I could do it, if goaded by certain exigencies which I can imagine.' And Miss Keeldar quietly sipped

# Shirley

her glass of new milk, looking somewhat thoughtful, and a little pale: though, indeed, when did she not look pale? She was never florid.

The milk sipped and the bread eaten, Fanny was again summoned: she and Eliza were recommended to go to bed, which they were quite willing to do, being weary of the day's exertions, of much cutting of currant-buns, and filling of urns and teapots, and running backwards and forwards with trays. Erelong the maids' chamber-door was heard to close; Caroline took a candle, and went quietly all over the house, seeing that every window was fast and every door barred. She did not even evade the haunted back-kitchen, nor the vault-like cellars. These visited, she returned.

'There is neither spirit nor flesh in the house at present,' she said, 'which should not be there. It is now near eleven o'clock, fully bedtime, yet I would rather sit up a little longer, if you do not object, Shirley. Here,' she continued, 'I have brought the brace of pistols from my uncle's study: you may examine them at your leisure.'

She placed them on the table before her friend.

'Why would you rather sit up longer?' asked Miss Keeldar, taking up the firearms, examining them, and again laying them down.

'Because I have a strange, excited feeling in my heart.'

'So have I.'

'Is this state of sleeplessness and restlessness caused by something electrical in the air, I wonder?'

'No: the sky is clear, the stars numberless; it is a fine night.'

'But very still. I hear the water fret over its stony bed in Hollow's Copse as distinctly as if it ran below the churchyard-wall.'

'I am glad it is so still a night: a moaning wind or rushing rain would vex me to fever just now.'

'Why, Shirley?'

'Because it would baffle my efforts to listen.'

'Do you listen towards the Hollow?'

'Yes, it is the only quarter whence we can hear a sound just now.'

'The only one, Shirley.'

They both sat near the window, and both leaned their arms on the sill, and both inclined their heads towards the open lattice. They saw each other's young faces by the starlight, and that dim, June twilight which does not wholly fade from the west till dawn begins to break in the east.

'Mr Helstone thinks we have no idea which way he is gone,' murmured Miss Keeldar, 'nor on what errand, nor with what expectations, nor how prepared; but I guess much – do not you?'

'I guess something.'

'All those gentlemen – your cousin Moore included – think that you and I are now asleep in our beds, unconscious.'

'Caring nothing about them – hoping and fearing nothing for them,' added Caroline.

Both kept silence for full half an hour. The night was silent, too; only the church-clock measured its course by quarters. Some words were interchanged about the chill of the air: they wrapped their scarves closer round them, resumed their bonnets which they had removed, and again watched.

Towards midnight, the teasing, monotonous bark of the house-dog disturbed

the quietude of their vigil. Caroline rose, and made her way noiselessly through the dark passages to the kitchen, intending to appease him with a piece of bread: she succeeded. On returning to the dining-room, she found it all dark, Miss Keeldar having extinguished the candle: the outline of her shape was visible near the still open window, leaning out. Miss Helstone asked no questions: she stole to her side. The dog recommenced barking furiously; suddenly he stopped, and seemed to listen. The occupants of the dining-room listened too, and not merely now to the flow of the mill-stream: there was a nearer, though a muffled sound on the road below the churchyard; a measured, beating, approaching sound; a dull tramp of marching feet.

It drew near. Those who listened, by degrees comprehended its extent. It was not the tread of two, nor of a dozen, nor of a score of men: it was the tread of hundreds. They could see nothing: the high shrubs of the garden formed a leafy screen between them and the road. To hear, however, was not enough; and this they felt as the troop trod forwards, and seemed actually passing the Rectory. They felt it more when a human voice – though that voice spoke but one word – broke the hush of the night.

'Halt!'

A halt followed! the march was arrested. Then came a low conference, of which no word was distinguishable from the dining-room.

'We *must* hear this,' said Shirley.

She turned, took her pistols from the table, silently passed out through the middle window of the dining-room, which was, in fact, a glass door, stole down the walk to the garden-wall, and stood listening under the lilacs. Caroline would not have quitted the house had she been alone, but where Shirley went she would go. She glanced at the weapon on the side-board, but left it behind her, and presently stood at her friend's side. They dared not look over the wall, for fear of being seen: they were obliged to crouch behind it: they heard these words:–

'It looks a rambling old building. Who lives in it besides the damned parson?'

'Only three women: his niece and two servants.'

'Do you know where they sleep?'

'The lasses behind: the niece in a front room.'

'And Helstone?'

'Yonder is his chamber. He uses burning a light; but I see none now.'

'Where would you get in?'

'If I were ordered to do his job – and he desarves it – I'd try yond' long window: it opens to the dining-room: I could grope my way up-stairs, and I know his chamber.'

'How would you manage about the women folk?'

'Let 'em alone, except they shrieked, and then I'd soon quieten 'em. I could wish to find the old chap asleep: if he waked, he'd be dangerous.'

'Has he arms?'

'Fire-arms, allus, – and allus loadened.'

'Then you're a fool to stop us here; a shot would give the alarm: Moore would be on us before we could turn round. We should miss our main object.'

'You might go on, I tell you. I'd engage Helstone alone.'

A pause. One of the party dropped some weapon which rang on the stone causeway: at this sound the Rectory dog barked again furiously – fiercely.

# Shirley

'That spoils all!' said the voice; 'he'll awake: a noise like that might rouse the dead. You did not say there was a dog. Damn you! Forward!'

Forward they went, – tramp, tramp, – with mustering, manifold, slow-filing tread. They were gone.

Shirley stood erect; looked over the wall, along the road.

'Not a soul remains,' she said.

She stood and mused. 'Thank God!' was the next observation.

Caroline repeated the ejaculation, not in so steady a tone: she was trembling much; her heart was beating fast and thick; her face was cold; her forehead damp.

'Thank God for us!' she reiterated; 'but what will happen elsewhere? They have passed us by that they may make sure of others.'

'They have done well,' returned Shirley, with composure: 'the others will defend themselves, – they can do it, – they are prepared for them: with us it is otherwise. My finger was on the trigger of this pistol. I was quite ready to give that man, if he had entered, such a greeting as he little calculated on; but behind him followed three hundred: I have neither three hundred hands nor three hundred weapons. I could not have effectually protected either you, myself, or the two poor women asleep under that roof; therefore I again earnestly thank God for insult and peril escaped.'

After a second pause, she continued: 'What is it my duty and wisdom to do next? Not to stay here inactive, I am glad to say, but of course to walk over to the Hollow.'

'To the Hollow, Shirley?'

'To the Hollow. Will you go with me?'

'Where those men are gone?'

'They have taken the highway: we should not encounter them: the road over the fields is as safe, silent, and solitary as a path through the air would be. Will you go?'

'Yes,' was the answer, given mechanically, not because the speaker wished, or was prepared to go; or, indeed, was otherwise than scared at the prospect of going, but because she felt she could not abandon Shirley.

'Then we must fasten up these windows, and leave all as secure as we can behind us. Do you know what we are going for, Cary?'

'Yes – no – because you wish it.'

'Is that all? And are you so obedient to a mere caprice of mine? What a docile wife you would make to a stern husband. The moon's face is not whiter than yours at this moment; and the aspen at the gate does not tremble more than your busy fingers; and so tractable and terror-struck, and dismayed and devoted, you would follow me into the thick of real danger! Cary, let me give your fidelity a motive: we are going for Moore's sake; to see if we can be of use to him: to make an effort to warn him of what is coming.'

'To be sure! I am a blind, weak fool, and you are acute and sensible, Shirley! I will go with you! I will gladly go with you!'

'I do not doubt it. You would die blindly and meekly for me, but you would intelligently and gladly die for Moore: but in truth there is no question of death to-night, – we run no risk at all.'

Caroline rapidly closed shutter and lattice. 'Do not fear that I shall not have

# Shirley

breath to run as fast as you can possibly run, Shirley. Take my hand: let us go straight across the fields.'

'But you cannot climb walls?'

'To-night I can.'

'You are afraid of hedges, and the beck which we shall be forced to cross?'

'I can cross it.'

They started: they ran. Many a wall checked but did not baffle them. Shirley was surefooted and agile: she could spring like a deer when she chose. Caroline, more timid, and less dexterous, fell once or twice, and bruised herself; but she rose again directly, saying she was not hurt. A quickset hedge bounded the last field: they lost time in seeking a gap in it: the aperture, when found, was narrow, but they worked their way through: the long hair, the tender skin, the silks and the muslins suffered; but what was chiefly regretted was the impediment this difficulty had caused to speed. On the other side they met the beck, flowing deep in a rough bed: at this point a narrow plank formed the only bridge across it. Shirley had trodden the plank successfully and fearlessly many a time before: Caroline had never yet dared to risk the transit.

'I will carry you across,' said Miss Keeldar: 'you are light, and I am not weak: let me try.'

'If I fall in, you may fish me out,' was the answer, as a grateful squeeze compressed her hand. Caroline, without pausing, trod forward on the trembling plank as if it were a continuation of the firm turf: Shirley, who followed, did not cross it more resolutely or safely. In their present humour, on their present errand, a strong and foaming channel would have been a barrier to neither. At the moment they were above the control either of fire or water: all Stilbro' Moor, alight and aglow with bonfires, would not have stopped them, nor would Calder or Aire thundering in flood. Yet one sound made them pause. Scarce had they set foot on the solid opposite bank, when a shot split the air from the north. One second lapsed. Further off, burst a like note in the south. Within the space of three minutes, similar signals boomed in the east and west.

'I thought we were dead at the first explosion,' observed Shirley, drawing a long breath. 'I felt myself hit in the temples, and I concluded your heart was pierced; but the reiterated voice was an explanation: those are signals – it is their way – the attack must be near. We should have had wings: our feet have not borne us swiftly enough.'

A portion of the copse was now to clear: when they emerged from it, the mill lay just below them: they could look down upon the buildings, the yard; they could see the road beyond. And the first glance in that direction told Shirley she was right in her conjecture: they were already too late to give warning: it had taken more time than they calculated on to overcome the various obstacles which embarrassed the short cut across the fields.

The road, which should have been white, was dark with a moving mass: the rioters were assembled in front of the closed yard gates, and a single figure stood within, apparently addressing them: the mill itself was perfectly black and still; there was neither life, light, nor motion around it.

'Surely he is prepared: surely that is not Moore meeting them alone!' whispered Shirley.

'It is – we must go to him! I *will* go to him.'

'*That* you will not.'

# Shirley

'Why did I come, then? I came only for him. I shall join him.'

'Fortunately, it is out of your power: there is no entrance to the yard.'

'There *is* a small entrance at the back, besides the gates in front: it opens by a secret method which I know – I will try it.'

'Not with my leave.'

Miss Keelder clasped her round the waist with both arms and held her back. 'Not one step shall you stir,' she went on authoritatively. 'At this moment, Moore would be both shocked and embarrassed, if he saw either you or me. Men never want women near them in time of real danger.'

'I would not trouble – I would help him,' was the reply.

'How? By inspiring him with heroism? Pooh! These are not the days of chivalry: it is not a tilt at a tournament we are going to behold, but a struggle about money, and food, and life.'

'It is natural that I should be at his side.'

'As queen of his heart? His mill is his lady-love, Cary! Backed by his factory and his frames, he has all the encouragement he wants or can know. It is not for love or beauty, but for ledger and broadcloth, he is going to break a spear. Don't be sentimental; Robert is not so.'

'I *could* help him – I *will* seek him.'

'Off then – I let you go – seek Moore: you'll not find him.'

She loosened her hold. Caroline sped like levelled shaft from bent bow; after her rang a jesting, gibing laugh. 'Look well there is no mistake!' was the warning given.

But there *was* a mistake. Miss Helstone paused, hesitated, gazed. The figure had suddenly retreated from the gate, and was running back hastily to the mill.

'Make haste, Lina!' cried Shirley: 'meet him before he enters.'

Caroline slowly returned. 'It is not Robert,' she said: 'it has neither his height, form, nor bearing.'

'I saw it was not Robert when I let you go. How could you imagine it? It is a shabby little figure of a private soldier: they had posted him as sentinel. He is safe in the mill now: I saw the door open and admit him. My mind grows easier; Robert is prepared: our warning would have been superfluous, and now I am thankful we came too late to give it: it has saved us the trouble of a scene. How fine to have entered the counting-house "toute éperdue," and to have found oneself in presence of Messrs Armitage and Ramsden smoking, Malone swaggering, your uncle sneering, Mr Sykes sipping a cordial, and Moore himself in his cold man-of-business vein: I am glad we missed it all.'

'I wonder if there are many in the mill, Shirley?'

'Plenty to defend it. The soldiers we have twice seen to-day were going there, no doubt, and the group we noticed surrounding your cousin in the fields will be with him.'

'What are they doing now, Shirley? What is that noise?'

'Hatchets and crow-bars against the yard-gates: they are forcing them. Are you afraid?'

'No; but my heart throbs fast; I have a difficulty in standing: I will sit down. Do you feel unmoved?'

'Hardly that – but I am glad I came: we shall see what transpires with our own eyes: we are here on the spot, and none know it. Instead of amazing the curate, the clothier, and the corn-dealer with a romantic rush on the stage, we

# Shirley

stand alone with the friendly night, its mute stars, and these whispering trees, whose report our friends will not come to gather.'

'Shirley – Shirley, the gates are down! That crash was like the felling of great trees. Now they are pouring through. They will break down the mill-doors as they have broken the gate: what can Robert do against so many? Would to God I were a little nearer him – could hear him speak – could speak to him! With my will – my longing to serve him – I could not be a useless burden in his way: I could be turned to some account.'

'They come on!' cried Shirley. 'How steadily they march in! There is discipline in their ranks – I will not say there is courage: hundreds against tens are no proof of that quality; but' (she dropped her voice) 'there is suffering and desperation enough amongst them – these goads will urge them forwards.'

'Forwards against Robert – and they hate him. Shirley, is there much danger they will win the day?'

'We shall see. Moore and Helstone are of "earth's first blood" – no bunglers – no cravens –'

A crash – smash – shiver – stopped their whispers. A simultaneously-hurled volley of stones had saluted the broad front of the mill, with all its windows; and now every pane of every lattice lay in shattered and pounded fragments. A yell followed this demonstration – a rioters' yell – a North-of-England – a Yorkshire – a West-Riding – a West-Riding-clothing-district-of-Yorkshire rioters' yell. You never heard that sound, perhaps, reader? So much the better for your ears – perhaps for your heart; since, if it rends the air in hate to yourself, or to the men or principles you approve, the interests to which you wish well, Wrath wakens to the cry of Hate: the Lion shakes his mane, and rises to the howl of the Hyena: Caste stands up, ireful, against Caste; and the indignant, wronged spirit of the Middle Rank bears down in zeal and scorn on the famished and furious mass of the Operative Class. It is difficult to be tolerant – difficult to be just – in such moments.

Caroline rose; Shirley put her arm round her: they stood together as still as the straight stems of two trees. That yell was a long one, and when it ceased, the night was yet full of the swaying and murmuring of a crowd.

'What next?' was the question of the listeners. Nothing came yet. The mill remained mute as a mausoleum.

'He *cannot* be alone!' whispered Caroline.

'I would stake all I have, that he is as little alone as he is alarmed,' responded Shirley.

Shots were discharged by the rioters. Had the defenders waited for this signal? It seemed so. The hitherto inert and passive mill woke: fire flashed from its empty window-frames; a volley of musketry pealed sharp through the Hollow.

'Moore speaks at last!' said Shirley, 'and he seems to have the gift of tongues; that was not a single voice.'

'He has been forbearing; no one can accuse him of rashness,' alleged Caroline: 'their discharge preceded his; they broke his gates and his windows; they fired at his garrison before he repelled them.'

What was going on now? It seemed difficult in the darkness, to distinguish, but something terrible, a still-renewing tumult, was obvious; fierce attacks, desperate repulses; the mill-yard, the mill itself, was full of battle-movement: there was scarcely any cessation now of the discharge of firearms; and there was

# Shirley

struggling, rushing, trampling, and shouting between. The aim of the assailants seemed to be to enter the mill, that of the defendants to beat them off. They heard the rebel leader cry, 'To the back, lads!' They heard a voice retort, 'Come round, we will meet you!'

'To the counting-house!' was the order again.

'Welcome! – We shall have you there!' was the response. And accordingly, the fiercest blaze that had yet glowed, the loudest rattle that had yet been heard, burst from the counting-house front, when the mass of rioters rushed up to it.

The voice that had spoken was Moore's own voice. They could tell by its tones that his soul was now warm with the conflict: they could guess that the fighting animal was roused in every one of those men there struggling together, and was for the time quite paramount above the rational human being. Both the girls felt their faces glow and their pulses throb: both knew they would do no good by rushing down into the mêlée: they desired neither to deal nor to receive blows; but they could not have run away – Caroline no more than Shirley; they could not have fainted; they could not have taken their eyes from the dim, terrible scene – from the mass of cloud, of smoke – the musket-lightning – for the world.

'How and when would it end?' was the demand throbbing in their throbbing pulses. 'Would a juncture arise in which they could be useful?' was what they waited to see; for, though Shirley put off their too-late arrival with a jest, and was ever ready to satirize her own or any other person's enthusiasm, she would have given a farm of her best land for a chance of rendering good service.

The chance was not vouchsafed her; the looked-for juncture never came: it was not likely. Moore had expected this attack for days, perhaps weeks: he was prepared for it at every point. He had fortified and garrisoned his mill, which in itself was a strong building: he was a cool, brave man: he stood to the defence with unflinching firmness; those who were with him caught his spirit, and copied his demeanour. The rioters had never been so met before. At other mills they had attacked, they had found no resistance; an organized, resolute defence was what they never dreamed of encountering. When their leaders saw the steady fire kept up from the mill, witnessed the composure and determination of its owner, heard themselves coolly defied and invited on to death, and beheld their men falling wounded round them, they felt that nothing was to be done here. In haste, they mustered their forces, drew them away from the building: a roll was called over, in which the men answered to figures instead of names: they dispersed wide over the fields, leaving silence and ruin behind them. The attack, from its commencement to its termination, had not occupied an hour.

Day was by this time approaching: the west was dim, the east beginning to gleam. It would have seemed that the girls who had watched this conflict would now wish to hasten to the victors, on whose side all their interest had been enlisted; but they only very cautiously approached the now battered mill, and, when suddenly a number of soldiers and gentlemen appeared at the great door opening into the yard, they quickly stepped aside into a shed, the deposit of old iron and timber, whence they could see without being seen.

It was no cheering spectacle: these premises were now a mere blot of desolation on the fresh front of the summer-dawn. All the copse up the Hollow was shady and dewy, the hill at its head was green; but just here in the centre of the sweet glen, Discord, broken loose in the night from control, had beaten the ground with his stamping hoofs, and left it waste and pulverized. The mill yawned all

# Shirley

ruinous with unglazed frames; the yard was thickly bestrewn with stones and brick-bats, and, close under the mill, with the glittering fragments of the shattered windows; muskets and other weapons lay here and there; more than one deep crimson stain was visible on the gravel: a human body lay quiet on its face near the gates; and five or six wounded men writhed and moaned in the bloody dust.

Miss Keeldar's countenance changed at this view: it was the after-taste of the battle, death and pain replacing excitement and exertion: it was the blackness the bright fire leaves when its blaze is sunk, its warmth failed, and its glow faded.

'This is what I wished to prevent,' she said, in a voice whose cadence betrayed the altered impulse of her heart.

'But you could not prevent it; you did your best; it was in vain,' said Caroline, comfortingly. 'Don't grieve, Shirley.'

'I am sorry for those poor fellows,' was the answer, while the spark in her glance dissolved to dew. 'Are any within the mill hurt, I wonder? Is that your uncle?'

'It is, and there is Mr Malone, and, oh Shirley! There is Robert!'

'Well,' (resuming her former tone,) 'don't squeeze your fingers quite into my hand: I see, there is nothing wonderful in that. We knew he, at least, was here, whoever might be absent.'

'He is coming here toward us, Shirley!'

'Towards the pump, that is to say, for the purpose of washing his hands and his forehead, which has got a scratch, I perceive.'

'He bleeds, Shirley: don't hold me; I must go.'

'Not a step.'

'He is hurt, Shirley!'

'Fiddlestick!'

'But I *must* go to him: I wish to go so much: I cannot bear to be restrained.'

'What for?'

'To speak to him, to ask how he is, and what I can do for him?'

'To teaze and annoy him; to make a spectacle of yourself and him before those soldiers, Mr Malone, your uncle, et cetera. Would he like it, think you? Would you like to remember it a week hence?'

'Am I always to be curbed and kept down?' demanded Caroline, a little passionately.

'For his sake, yes. And still more for your own. I tell you, if you showed yourself now, you would repent it an hour hence, and so would Robert.'

'You think he would not like it, Shirley?'

'Far less than he would like our stopping him to say good-night, which you were so sore about.'

'But that was all play; there was no danger.'

'And this is serious work: he must be unmolested.'

'I only wish to go to him because he is my cousin, – you understand?'

'I quite understand. But now, watch him. He has bathed his forehead, and the blood has ceased trickling; his hurt is really a mere graze: I can see it from hence: he is going to look after the wounded men.'

Accordingly Mr Moore and Mr Helstone went round the yard, examining each prostrate form. They then gave directions to have the wounded taken up and carried into the mill. This duty being performed, Joe Scott was ordered to

714

saddle his master's horse, and Mr Helstone's pony, and the two gentlemen rode away full gallop, to seek surgical aid in different directions.

Caroline was not yet pacified.

'Shirley, Shirley, I should have liked to speak one word to him before he went,' she murmured, while the tears gathered glittering in her eyes.

'Why do you cry, Lina?' asked Miss Keeldar a little sternly. 'You ought to be glad instead of sorry. Robert has escaped any serious harm; he is victorious; he has been cool and brave in combat; he is now considerate in triumph: is this a time – are these causes for weeping?'

'You do not know what I have in my heart,' pleaded the other: 'what pain, what distraction; nor whence it arises. I can understand that you should exult in Robert's greatness and goodness; so do I, in one sense, but, in another, I feel *so* miserable. I am too far removed from him: I used to be nearer. Let me alone, Shirley: do let me cry a few minutes; it relieves me.'

Miss Keeldar, feeling her tremble in every limb, ceased to expostulate with her: she went out of the shed, and left her to weep in peace. It was the best plan: in a few minutes Caroline rejoined her, much calmer: she said with her natural, docile, gentle manner –

'Come, Shirley, we will go home now. I promise not to try to see Robert again till he asks for me. I never will try to push myself on him. I thank you for restraining me just now.'

'I did it with a good intention,' returned Miss Keeldar.

'Now, dear Lina,' she continued; 'let us turn our faces to the cool morning breeze, and walk very quietly back to the Rectory. We will steal in as we stole out: none shall know where we have been, or what we have seen to-night: neither taunt nor misconstruction can consequently molest us. To-morrow, we will see Robert, and be of good cheer; but I will say no more, lest I should begin to cry too. I seem hard towards you, but I am not so.'

# Chapter 20

## To-morrow

The two girls met no living soul on their way back to the Rectory: they let themselves in noiselessly; they stole upstairs unheard: the breaking morning gave them what light they needed. Shirley sought her couch immediately; and, though the room was strange – for she had never slept at the Rectory before – and though the recent scene was one unparalleled for excitement and terror by any it had hitherto been her lot to witness, yet, scarce was her head laid on the pillow, ere a deep, refreshing sleep closed her eyes, and calmed her senses.

Perfect health was Shirley's enviable portion; though warm-hearted and

sympathetic, she was not nervous: powerful emotions could rouse and sway, without exhausting, her spirit: the tempest troubled and shook her while it lasted; but it left her elasticity unbent, and her freshness quite unblighted. As every day brought her stimulating emotion, so every night yielded her recreating rest. Caroline now watched her sleeping, and read the serenity of her mind in the beauty of her happy countenance.

For herself, being of a different temperament, she could not sleep. The common-place excitement of the tea-drinking and school-gathering, would alone have sufficed to make her restless all night: the effect of the terrible drama which had just been enacted before her eyes was not likely to quit her for days. It was vain even to try to retain a recumbent posture: she sat up by Shirley's side, counting the slow minutes, and watching the June sun mount the heavens.

Life wastes fast in such vigils as Caroline had of late but too often kept; vigils during which the mind – having no pleasant food to nourish it – no manna of hope – no hived-honey of joyous memories – tries to live on the meagre diet of wishes, and failing to derive thence either delight or support, and feeling itself ready to perish with craving want, turns to philosophy, to resolution, to resignation; calls on all these gods for aid, calls vainly, – is unheard, unhelped, and languishes.

Caroline was a Christian; therefore in trouble she framed many a prayer after the Christian creed; preferred it with deep earnestness; begged for patience, strength, relief. This world, however, we all know, is the scene of trial and probation; and, for any favourable result her petitions had yet wrought, it seemed to her that they were unheard and unaccepted. She believed, sometimes, that God had turned his face from her. At moments she was a Calvinist, and, sinking into the gulf of religious despair, she saw darkening over her the doom of reprobation.

Most people have had a period or periods in their lives when they have felt thus forsaken; when, having long hoped against hope, and still seen the day of fruition deferred, their hearts have truly sickened within them. This is a terrible hour, but it is often the darkest point which precedes the rise of day; that turn of the year when the icy January wind carries over the waste at once the dirge of departing winter, and the prophecy of coming spring. The perishing birds, however, cannot thus understand the blast before which they shiver; and as little can the suffering soul recognize, in the climax of its affliction, the dawn of its deliverance. Yet, let whoever grieves still cling fast to love and faith in God: God will never deceive, never finally desert him. 'Whom He loveth, He chasteneth.' These words are true, and should not be forgotten.

The household was astir at last: the servants were up; the shutters were opened below. Caroline, as she quitted the couch, which had been but a thorny one to her, felt that revival of spirits which the return of day, of action, gives to all but the wholly despairing or actually dying: she dressed herself, as usual, carefully, trying so to arrange her hair and attire that nothing of the forlornness she felt at heart should be visible externally: she looked as fresh as Shirley when both were dressed, only that Miss Keeldar's eyes were lively, and Miss Helstone's languid.

'To-day, I shall have much to say to Moore,' were Shirley's first words; and you could see in her face that life was full of interest, expectation, and occupation for her. 'He will have to undergo cross-examination,' she added: 'I daresay he

thinks he has outwitted me cleverly. And this is the way men deal with women; still concealing danger from them: thinking, I suppose, to spare them pain. They imagined we little knew where they were to-night: we *know* they little conjectured where we were. Men, I believe, fancy women's minds something like those of children. Now, that is a mistake.'

This was said as she stood at the glass, training her naturally waved hair into curls, by twining it round her fingers. She took up the theme again five minutes after, as Caroline fastened her dress and clasped her girdle.

'If men could see us as we really are, they would be a little amazed; but the cleverest, the acutest men are often under an illusion about women: they do not read them in a true light: they misapprehend them, both for good and evil: their good woman is a queer thing, half. doll, half angel; their bad woman almost always a fiend. Then to hear them fall into ecstasies with each other's creations, worshipping the heroine of such a poem – novel – drama, thinking it fine – divine! Fine and divine it may be, but often quite artificial – false as the rose in my best bonnet there. If I spoke all I think on this point; if I gave my real opinion of some first-rate female characters in first-rate works, where should I be? Dead under a cairn of avenging stones in half an hour.'

'Shirley, you chatter so, I can't fasten you: be still. And after all, authors' heroines are almost as good as authoress's heroes.'

'Not at all: women read men more truly than men read women. I'll prove that in a magazine paper some day when I've time; only it will never be inserted: it will be "declined with thanks," and left for me at the publisher's.'

'To be sure: you could not write cleverly enough; you don't know enough; you are not learned, Shirley.'

'God knows, I can't contradict you, Cary: I'm as ignorant as a stone. There's one comfort, however, you are not much better.'

They descended to breakfast.

'I wonder how Mrs Pryor and Hortense Moore have passed the night,' said Caroline, as she made the coffee. 'Selfish being that I am! I never thought of either of them till just now: they will have heard all the tumult, Fieldhead and the Cottage are so near; and Hortense is timid in such matters: so no doubt is Mrs Pryor.'

'Take my word for it, Lina, Moore will have contrived to get his sister out of the way: she went home with Miss Mann; he will have quartered her there for the night. As to Mrs Pryor, I own I am uneasy about her; but in another half-hour we will be with her.'

By this time the news of what had happened at the Hollow was spread all over the neighbourhood. Fanny, who had been to Fieldhead to fetch the milk, returned in panting haste, with tidings that there had been a battle in the night at Mr Moore's mill, and that some said twenty men were killed. Eliza, during Fanny's absence, had been apprized by the butcher's boy that the Mill was burnt to the ground. Both women rushed into the parlour to announce these terrible facts to the ladies, terminating their clear and accurate narrative by the assertion that they were sure master must have been in it all: he and Thomas, the clerk, they were confident, must have gone last night to join Mr Moore and the soldiers: Mr Malone, too, had not been heard of at his lodgings since yesterday afternoon; and Joe Scott's wife and family were in the greatest distress, wondering what had become of their head.

# Shirley

Scarcely was this information imparted when a knock at the kitchen-door announced the Fieldhead errand-boy, arrived in hot haste, bearing a billet from Mrs Pryor. It was hurriedly written, and urged Miss Keeldar to return directly, as the neighbourhood and the house seemed likely to be all in confusion, and orders would have to be given which the mistress of the hall alone could regulate. In a postscript it was entreated that Miss Helstone might not be left alone at the Rectory: she had better, it was suggested, accompany Miss Keeldar.

'There are not two opinions on that head,' said Shirley, as she tied on her own bonnet, and then ran to fetch Caroline's.

'But what will Fanny and Eliza do? And if my uncle returns?'

'Your uncle will not return yet; he has other fish to fry; he will be galloping backwards and forwards from Briarfield to Stilbro' all day, rousing the magistrates in the courthouse, and the officers at the barracks; and Fanny and Eliza can have in Joe Scott's and the clerk's wives to bear them company. Besides, of course, there is no real danger to be apprehended now: weeks will elapse before the rioters can again rally, or plan any other attempt; and I am much mistaken if Moore and Mr Helstone will not take advantage of last night's outbreak to quell them altogether: they will frighten the authorities of Stilbro' into energetic measures. I only hope they will not be too severe – not pursue the discomfited too relentlessly.'

'Robert will not be cruel: we saw that last night,' said Caroline.

'But he will be hard,' retorted Shirley; 'and so will your uncle.'

As they hurried along the meadow and plantation-path to Fieldhead, they saw the distant highway already alive with an unwonted flow of equestrians and pedestrians, tending in the direction of the usually solitary Hollow. On reaching the hall, they found the backyard gates open, and the court and kitchen seemed crowded with excited milk-fetchers – men, women, and children, whom Mrs Gill, the housekeeper, appeared vainly persuading to take their milk-cans and depart. (It *is*, or *was*, by-the-by, the custom in the north of England for the cottagers on a country squire's estate to receive their supplies of milk and butter from the dairy of the Manor-House, on whose pastures a herd of milch kine was usually fed for the convenience of the neighbourhood. Miss Keeldar owned such a herd – all deep-dewlapped, Craven cows, reared on the sweet herbage and clear waters of bonnie Airedale; and very proud she was of their sleek aspect and high condition.) Seeing now the state of matters, and that it was desirable to effect a clearance of the premises, Shirley stepped in amongst the gossiping groups. She bade them good-morning with a certain frank, tranquil ease – the natural characteristic of her manner when she addressed numbers; especially if those numbers belonged to the working-class: she was cooler amongst her equals, and rather proud to those above her. She then asked them if they had all got their milk measured out, and understanding that they had, she further observed that she 'wondered what they were waiting for, then.'

'We're just talking a bit over this battle there has been at your mill, Mistress,' replied a man.

'Talking a bit! Just like you!' said Shirley. 'It is a queer thing all the world is so fond of *talking* over events: you *talk* if anybody dies suddenly; you *talk* if a fire breaks out; you *talk* if a mill-owner fails; you *talk* if he's murdered. What good does your talking do?'

There is nothing the lower orders like better than a little downright good-

# Shirley

humoured rating. Flattery they scorn very much: honest abuse they enjoy. They call it speaking plainly, and take a sincere delight in being the objects thereof. The homely harshness of Miss Keeldar's salutation won her the ear of the whole throng in a second.

'We're no war nor some 'at is aboon us; are we?' asked a man, smiling.

'Nor a whit better: you that should be models of industry are just as gossip-loving as the idle. Fine, rich people that have nothing to do, may be partly excused for trifling their time away: you who have to earn your bread with the sweat of your brow are quite inexcusable.'

'That's queer, Mistress: suld we never have a holiday because we work hard?'

'*Never*,' was the prompt answer; 'unless,' added the 'mistress' with a smile that half-belied the severity of her speech, 'unless you knew how to make a better use of it than to get together over rum and tea, if you are women – or over beer and pipes, if you are men, and *talk* scandal at your neighbour's expense. Come, friends,' she added, changing at once from bluntness to courtesy, 'oblige me by taking your cans and going home. I expect several persons to call to-day, and it will be inconvenient to have the avenues to the house crowded.'

Yorkshire people are as yielding to persuasion as they are stubborn against compulsion: the yard was clear in five minutes.

'Thank you, and good-bye to you, friends,' said Shirley, as she closed the gates on a quiet court.

Now, let me hear the most refined of Cockneys presume to find fault with Yorkshire manners! Taken as they ought to be, the majority of the lads and lasses of the West-Riding are gentlemen and ladies, every inch of them: it is only against the weak affectation and futile pomposity of a would-be aristocrat they turn mutinous.

Entering by the back-way, the young ladies passed through the kitchen (or *house*, as the inner kitchen is called) to the hall. Mrs Pryor came running down the oak staircase to meet them. She was all unnerved: her naturally sanguine complexion was pale: her usually placid, though timid, blue eye was wandering, unsettled, alarmed. She did not, however, break out into any exclamations, or hurried narrative of what had happened. Her predominant feeling had been in the course of the night, and was now this morning, a sense of dissatisfaction with herself that she could not feel firmer, cooler, more equal to the demands of the occasion.

'You are aware,' she began with a trembling voice, and yet the most conscientious anxiety to avoid exaggeration in what she was about to say, – 'that a body of rioters has attacked Mr Moore's mill to-night: we heard the firing and confusion very plainly here: we none of us slept: it was a sad night: the house has been in great bustle all the morning with people coming and going: the servants have applied to me for orders and directions, which I really did not feel warranted in giving. Mr Moore has, I believe, sent up for refreshments for the soldiers and others engaged in the defence; for some conveniences also for the wounded. I could not undertake the responsibility of giving orders or taking measures. I fear delay may have been injurious in some instances; but this is not my house: you were absent, my dear Miss Keeldar – what could I do?'

'Were no refreshments sent?' asked Shirley, while her countenance, hitherto so clear, propitious, and quiet, even while she was rating the milk-fetchers, suddenly turned dark and warm.

# Shirley

'I think not, my dear.'

'And nothing for the wounded? no linen – no wine – no bedding?'

'I think not. I cannot tell what Mrs Gill did; but it seemed impossible to me, at the moment, to venture to dispose of your property by sending supplies to soldiers – provisions for a company of soldiers sounds formidable: how many there are I did not ask; but I could not think of allowing them to pillage the house, as it were. I intended to do what was right; yet I did not see the case quite clearly, I own.'

'It lies in a nutshell, notwithstanding. These soldiers have risked their lives in defence of my property – I suppose they have a right to my gratitude: the wounded are our fellow-creatures – I suppose we should aid them. Mrs Gill!'

She turned and called in a voice more clear than soft. It rung through the thick oak of the hall and kitchen doors more effectually than a bell's summons. Mrs Gill, who was deep in bread-making, came with hands and apron in culinary case, not having dared to stop to rub the dough from the one, or to shake the flour from the other. Her mistress had never called a servant in that voice, save once before, and that was when she had seen from the window Tartar in full tug with two carriers' dogs, each of them a match for him in size, if not in courage, and their masters standing by, encouraging their animals, while hers was unbefriended: then, indeed, she had summoned John as if the Day of Judgment were at hand: nor had she waited for the said John's coming, but had walked out into the lane bonnetless; and after informing the carriers that she held them far less of men than the three brutes whirling and worrying in the dust before them, had put her hands round the thick neck of the largest of the curs and given her whole strength to the essay of choking it from Tartar's torn and bleeding eye, just above and below which organ the vengeful fangs were inserted. Five or six men were presently on the spot to help her, but she never thanked one of them: 'They might have come before, if their will had been good,' she said. She had not a word for anybody during the rest of the day; but sat near the hall fire till evening watching and tending Tartar, who lay all gory, stiff, and swelled, on a mat at her feet. She wept furtively over him sometimes, and murmured the softest words of pity and endearment, in tones whose music the old, scarred, canine warrior acknowledged by licking her hand or her sandal alternately with his own red wounds. As to John, his lady turned a cold shoulder on him for a week afterwards.

Mrs Gill, remembering this little episode, came 'all of a tremble,' as she said herself. In a firm, brief voice, Miss Keeldar proceeded to put questions and give orders. That at such a time Fieldhead should have evinced the inhospitality of a miser's hovel, stung her haughty spirit to the quick; and the revolt of its pride was seen in the heaving of her heart; stirred stormily under the lace and silk which veiled it.

'How long is it since that message came from the mill?'

'Not an hour yet, ma'am,' answered the housekeeper, soothingly.

'Not an hour! You might almost as well have said not a day. They will have applied elsewhere by this time. Send a man instantly down to tell them that everything this house contains is at Mr Moore's, Mr Helstone's, and the soldiers' service. Do that first!'

While the order was being executed, Shirley moved away from her friends, and stood at the hall-window, silent, unapproachable. When Mrs Gill came

back, she turned: the purple flush which painful excitement kindles on a pale cheek, glowed on hers: the spark which displeasure lights in a dark eye fired her glance.

'Let the contents of the larder and the wine-cellar be brought up, put into the hay-carts, and driven down to the Hollow. If there does not happen to be much bread or much meat in the house, go to the butcher and baker, and desire them to send what they have: but I will see for myself.'

She moved off.

'All will be right soon: she will get over it in an hour,' whispered Caroline to Mrs Pryor. 'Go up-stairs, dear madam,' she added, affectionately, 'and try to be as calm and easy as you can. The truth is, Shirley will blame herself more than you before the day is over.'

By dint of a few more gentle assurances and persuasions, Miss Helstone contrived to soothe the agitated lady. Having accompanied her to her apartment, and promised to rejoin her there when things were settled, Caroline left her to see, as she said, 'if she could be useful.' She presently found that she could be very useful; for the retinue of servants at Fieldhead was by no means numerous, and just now their mistress found plenty of occupation for all the hands at her command, and for her own also. The delicate good-nature and dexterous activity which Caroline brought to the aid of the housekeeper and maids, – all somewhat scared by their lady's unwonted mood – did a world of good at once: it helped the assistants and appeased the directress. A chance glance and smile from Caroline moved Shirley to an answering smile directly. The former was carrying a heavy basket up the cellar-stairs.

'This is a shame!' cried Shirley, running to her. 'It will strain your arm.'

She took it from her, and herself bore it out into the yard. The cloud of temper was dispelled when she came back; the flash in her eye was melted; the shade on her forehead vanished: she resumed her usual cheerful and cordial manner to those about her, tempering her revived spirits with a little of the softness of shame at her previous unjust anger.

She was still superintending the lading of the cart, when a gentleman entered the yard and approached her ere she was aware of his presence.

'I hope I see Miss Keeldar well this morning?' he said, examining with rather significant scrutiny her still flushed face.

She gave him a look, and then again bent to her employment, without reply. A pleasant enough smile played on her lips, but she hid it. The gentleman repeated his salutation, stooping, that it might reach her ear with more facility.

'Well enough, if she be good enough,' was the answer; 'and so is Mr Moore too, I dare say. To speak truth, I am not anxious about him; some slight mischance would be only his just due: his conduct has been – we will say *strange*, just now, till we have time to characterize it by a more exact epithet. Meantime, may I ask what brings him here?'

'Mr Helstone and I have just received your message, that everything at Fieldhead was at our service. We judged, by the unlimited wording of the gracious intimation, that you would be giving yourself too much trouble: I perceive, our conjecture was correct. We are not a regiment, remember: only about half a dozen soldiers, and as many civilians. Allow me to retrench something from these too abundant supplies.'

Miss Keeldar blushed, while she laughed at her own over-eager generosity,

and most disproportionate calculations. Moore laughed too – very quietly, though; and as quietly, he ordered basket after basket to be taken from the cart, and remanded vessel after vessel to the cellar.

'The Rector must hear of this,' he said: 'he will make a good story of it. What an excellent army contractor Miss Keeldar would have been!' again he laughed, adding – 'It is precisely as I conjectured.'

'You ought to be thankful,' said Shirley, 'and not mock me. What could I do? How could I gauge your appetites, or number your band? For aught I knew, there might have been fifty of you at least to victual. You told me nothing; and then, an application to provision soldiers naturally suggests large ideas.'

'It appears so,' remarked Moore, levelling another of his keen, quiet glances at the discomfited Shirley. 'Now,' he continued, addressing the carter, 'I think you may take what remains to the Hollow. Your load will be somewhat lighter than the one Miss Keeldar destined you to carry.'

As the vehicle rumbled out of the yard, Shirley, rallying her spirits, demanded what had become of the wounded.

'There was not a single man hurt on our side,' was the answer.

'You were hurt yourself, on the temples,' interposed a quick, low voice – that of Caroline, who, having withdrawn within the shade of the door, and behind the large person of Mrs Gill, had till now escaped Moore's notice: when she spoke, his eye searched the obscurity of the retreat.

'Are you much hurt?' she inquired.

'As you might scratch your finger with a needle in sewing.'

'Lift your hair, and let us see.'

He took his hat off, and did as he was bid, disclosing only a narrow slip of court-plaster. Caroline indicated, by a slight movement of the head, that she was satisfied, and disappeared within the clear obscure of the interior.

'How did she know I was hurt?' asked Moore.

'By rumour, no doubt. But it is too good in her to trouble herself about you. For my part, it was of your victims I was thinking when I inquired after the wounded: what damage have your opponents sustained?'

'One of the rioters, or victims, as you call them, was killed, and six were hurt.'

'What have you done with them?'

'What you will perfectly approve. Medical aid was procured immediately; and as soon as we can get a couple of covered waggons, and some clean straw, they will be removed to Stilbro'.'

'Straw! you must have beds and bedding. I will send my waggon directly, properly furnished; and Mr Yorke, I am sure, will send his.'

'You guess correctly: he has volunteered already; and Mrs Yorke – who, like you, seems disposed to regard rioters as martyrs, and me, and especially Mr Helstone, as murderers – is at this moment, I believe, most assiduously engaged in fitting it up with feather-beds, pillows, bolsters, blankets, &c. The *victims* lack no attentions – I promise you. Mr Hall – your favourite parson – has been with them ever since six o'clock, exhorting them, praying with them, and even waiting on them like any nurse; and Caroline's good friend, Miss Ainley, that *very* plain old maid, sent in a stock of lint and linen, something in the proportion of another lady's allowance of beef and wine.'

'That will do. Where is your sister?'

# Shirley

'Well cared for. I had her securely domiciled with Miss Mann. This very morning, the two set out for Wormwood Wells (a noted watering-place), and will stay there some weeks.'

'So Mr Helstone domiciled me at the Rectory! Mighty clever you gentlemen think you are! I make you heartily welcome to the idea, and hope its savour, as you chew the cud of reflection upon it, gives you pleasure. Acute and astute, why are you not also omniscient? How is it that events transpire, under your very noses, of which you have no suspicion? It should be so, otherwise the exquisite gratification of out-manoeuvring you would be unknown. Ah! friend, you may search my countenance, but you cannot read it.'

Moore, indeed, looked as if he could not.

'You think me a dangerous specimen of my sex. Don't you, now?'

'A peculiar one, at least.'

'But Caroline – is she peculiar?'

'In her way – yes.'

'Her way! What is her way?'

'You know her as well as I do.'

'And knowing her I assert that she is neither eccentric nor difficult of control: is she?'

'That depends –'

'However, there is nothing masculine about *her*.'

'Why lay such emphasis on *her*? Do you consider her a contrast, in that respect, to yourself?'

'You do, no doubt: but that does not signify. Caroline is neither masculine, nor of what they call the spirited order of women.'

'I have seen her flash out.'

'So have I – but not with manly fire: it was a short, vivid, trembling glow, that shot up, shone, vanished –'

'And left her scared at her own daring. You describe others besides Caroline.'

'The point I wish to establish is, that Miss Helstone, though gentle, tractable, and candid enough, is still perfectly capable of defying even Mr Moore's penetration.'

'What have you and she been doing?' asked Moore, suddenly.

'Have you had any breakfast?'

'What is your mutual mystery?'

'If you are hungry, Mrs Gill will give you something to eat here. Step into the oak-parlour, and ring the bell – you will be served as if at an inn; or, if you like better, go back to the Hollow.'

'The alternative is not open to me: I *must* go back. Good-morning: the first leisure I have, I will see you again.'

# Chapter 21

## Mrs Pryor

While Shirley was talking with Moore, Caroline rejoined Mrs Pryor up-stairs. She found that lady deeply depressed. She would not say that Miss Keeldar's hastiness had hurt her feelings; but it was evident an inward wound galled her. To any but a congenial nature, she would have seemed insensible to the quiet, tender attentions by which Miss Helstone sought to impart solace; but Caroline knew that, unmoved or slightly moved as she looked, she felt, valued, and was healed by them.

'I am deficient in self-confidence and decision,' she said at last. 'I always have been deficient in those qualities: yet I think Miss Keeldar should have known my character well enough by this time, to be aware that I always feel an even painful solicitude to do right, to act for the best. The unusual nature of the demand on my judgment puzzled me, especially following the alarms of the night. I could not venture to act promptly for another: but I trust no serious harm will result from my lapse of firmness.'

A gentle knock was here heard at the door: it was half-opened.

'Caroline, come here,' said a low voice.

Miss Helstone went out: there stood Shirley in the gallery, looking contrite, ashamed, sorry as any repentant child.

'How is Mrs Pryor?' she asked.

'Rather out of spirits,' said Caroline.

'I have behaved very shamefully, very ungenerously, very ungratefully to her,' said Shirley. 'How insolent in me to turn on her thus, for what after all was no fault, only an excess of conscientiousness on her part. But I regret my error most sincerely: tell her so, and ask if she will forgive me.'

Caroline discharged the errand with heartfelt pleasure. Mrs Pryor rose, came to the door: she did not like scenes; she dreaded them as all timid people do: she said falteringly –

'Come in, my dear.'

Shirley did come in with some impetuosity: she threw her arms round her governess, and while she kissed her heartily, she said –

'You know you *must* forgive me, Mrs Pryor. I could not get on at all if there was a misunderstanding between you and me.'

'I have nothing to forgive,' was the reply. 'We will pass it over now if you please. The final result of the incident is, that it proves more plainly than ever how unequal I am to certain crises.'

And that was the painful feeling which *would* remain on Mrs Pryor's mind:

no effort of Shirley's or Caroline's could efface it thence: she could forgive her offending pupil, not her innocent self.

Miss Keeldar, doomed to be in constant request during the morning, was presently summoned down-stairs again. The Rector called first: a lively welcome and livelier reprimand were at his service; he expected both, and, being in high spirits, took them in equally good part.

In the course of his brief visit, he quite forgot to ask after his niece: the riot, the rioters, the mill, the magistrates, the heiress, absorbed all his thoughts to the exclusion of family ties. He alluded to the part himself and curate had taken in the defence of the Hollow.

'The vials of pharisaical wrath will be emptied on our heads, for our share in this business,' he said; 'but I defy every calumniator. I was there only to support the law, to play my part as a man and a Briton; which characters I deem quite compatible with those of the priest and Levite, in their highest sense. Your tenant, Moore,' he went on, 'has won my approbation. A cooler commander I would not wish to see, nor a more determined. Besides, the man has shown sound judgment and good sense; first, in being thoroughly prepared for the event which has taken place, and subsequently, when his well-concerted plans had secured him success, in knowing how to use without abusing his victory. Some of the magistrates are now well frightened, and, like all cowards, show a tendency to be cruel; Moore restrains them with admirable prudence. He has hitherto been very unpopular in the neighbourhood; but, mark my words, the tide of opinion will now take a turn in his favour: people will find out that they have not appreciated him, and will hasten to remedy their error; and he, when he perceives the public disposed to acknowledge his merits, will show a more gracious mien than that with which he has hitherto favoured us.'

Mr Helstone was about to add to this speech some half-jesting, half-serious warnings to Miss Keeldar, on the subject of her rumoured partiality for her talented tenant, when a ring at the door, announcing another caller, checked his raillery; and as that other caller appeared in the form of a white-haired, elderly gentleman, with a rather truculent countenance and disdainful eye – in short, our old acquaintance, and the Rector's enemy, Mr Yorke – the priest and Levite seized his hat, and with the briefest of adieux to Miss Keeldar, and the sternest of nods to her guest, took an abrupt leave.

Mr Yorke was in no mild mood, and in no measured terms did he express his opinion on the transaction of the night: Moore, the magistrates, the soldiers, the mob-leaders, each and all came in for a share of his invectives; but he reserved his strongest epithets – and real, racy Yorkshire Doric adjectives they were – for the benefit of the fighting parsons, the 'sanguinary, demoniac' rector and curate. According to him, the cup of ecclesiastical guilt was now full indeed.

'The Church,' he said, 'was in a bonnie pickle now: it was time it came down when parsons took to swaggering amang soldiers, blazing away wi' bullet and gunpowder, taking the lives of far honester men than themselves.'

'What would Moore have done, if nobody had helped him?' asked Shirley.

'Drunk as he'd brewed – eaten as he'd baked.'

'Which means, you would have left him by himself to face that mob. Good. He has plenty of courage; but the greatest amount of gallantry that ever garrisoned one human breast could scarce avail against two hundred.'

# Shirley

'He had the soldiers; those poor slaves who hire out their own blood and spill other folks for money.'

'You abuse soldiers almost as much as you abuse clergymen. All who wear red coats are national refuse in your eyes, and all who wear black are national swindlers. Mr Moore, according to you, did wrong to get military aid, and he did still worse to accept of any other aid. Your way of talking amounts to this: – he should have abandoned his mill and his life to the rage of a set of misguided madmen, and Mr Helstone and every other gentleman in the parish should have looked on, and seen the building razed and its owner slaughtered, and never stirred a finger to save either.'

'If Moore had behaved to his men from the beginning as a master ought to behave, they never would have entertained their present feelings towards him.'

'Easy for you to talk,' exclaimed Miss Keeldar, who was beginning to wax warm in her tenant's cause: 'you, whose family have lived at Briarmains for six generations, to whose person the people have been accustomed for fifty years, who know all their ways, prejudices, and preferences. Easy, indeed, for *you* to act so as to avoid offending them; but Mr Moore came a stranger into the district: he came here poor and friendless, with nothing but his own energies to back him; nothing but his honour, his talent, and his industry to make his way for him. A monstrous crime indeed that, under such circumstances, he could not popularize his naturally grave, quiet manners, all at once: could not be jocular, and free, and cordial with a strange peasantry, as you are with your fellow-townsmen! An unpardonable transgression, that when he introduced improvements he did not go about the business in quite the most politic way; did not graduate his changes as delicately as a rich capitalist might have done! For errors of this sort is he to be the victim of mob-outrage? Is he to be denied even the privilege of defending himself? Are those who have the hearts of men in their breasts (and Mr Helstone – say what you will of him – has such a heart) to be reviled like malefactors because they stand by him – because they venture to espouse the cause of one against two hundred?'

'Come – come now – be cool,' said Mr Yorke, smiling at the earnestness with which Shirley multiplied her rapid questions.

'Cool! Must I listen coolly to downright nonsense – to dangerous nonsense? No. I like you very well, Mr Yorke, as you know; but I thoroughly dislike some of your principles. All that cant – excuse me, but I repeat the word – all that *cant* about soldiers and parsons is most offensive in my ears. All ridiculous, irrational crying up of one class, whether the same be aristocrat or democrat – all howling down of another class, whether clerical or military – all exacting injustice to individuals, whether monarch or mendicant – is really sickening to me: all arraying of ranks against ranks, all party hatreds, all tyrannies disguised as liberties, I reject and wash my hands of. *You* think you are a philanthropist; *you* think you are an advocate of liberty; but I will tell you this – Mr Hall, the parson of Nunnely, is a better friend both of man and freedom, than Hiram Yorke, the Reformer of Briarfield.'

From a man, Mr Yorke would not have borne this language very patiently, nor would he have endured it from some women; but he accounted Shirley both honest and pretty, and her plain-spoken ire amused him: besides he took a secret pleasure in hearing her defend her tenant, for we have already intimated he had Robert Moore's interest very much at heart: moreover, if he wished to avenge

himself for her severity, he knew the means lay in his power: a word, he believed, would suffice to tame and silence her, to cover her frank forehead with the rosy shadow of shame, and veil the glow of her eye under down-drooped lid and lash.

'What more hast thou to say?' he inquired, as she paused, rather it appeared to take breath, than because her subject or her zeal was exhausted.

'Say, Mr Yorke?' was the answer, the speaker meantime walking fast from wall to wall of the oak-parlour. 'Say? I have a great deal to say, if I could get it out in lucid order, which I never *can* do. I have to say that your views, and those of most extreme politicians are such as none but men in an irresponsible position *can* advocate; that they are purely opposition views, meant only to be talked about, and never intended to be acted on. Make you prime minister of England to-morrow, and you would have to abandon them. You abuse Moore for defending his mill: had you been in Moore's place you could not with honour or sense have acted otherwise than he acted. You abuse Mr Helstone for everything he does: Mr Helstone has his faults: he sometimes does wrong, but oftener right. Were you ordained vicar of Briarfield, you would find it no easy task to sustain all the active schemes for the benefit of the parish planned and persevered in by your predecessor. I wonder people cannot judge more fairly of each other and themselves. When I hear Messrs Malone and Donne chatter about the authority of the Church, the dignity and claims of the priesthood, the deference due to them as clergymen; when I hear the outbreaks of their small spite against Dissenters; when I witness their silly narrow jealousies and assumptions; when their palaver about forms, and traditions, and superstitions, is sounding in my ear; when I behold their insolent carriage to the poor, their often base servility to the rich, I think the Establishment is indeed in a poor way, and both she and her sons appear in the utmost need of reformation. Turning away distressed from minster-tower and village-spire – ay, as distressed as a churchwarden who feels the exigence of whitewash, and has not wherewithal to purchase lime – I recall your senseless sarcasms on the "fat bishops," the "pampered parsons," "old mother church," &c. I remember your strictures on all who differ from you, your sweeping condemnation of classes and individuals, without the slightest allowance made for circumstances or temptations; and then Mr Yorke, doubt clutches my inmost heart as to whether men exist clement, reasonable, and just enough to be intrusted with the task of reform. I don't believe *you* are of the number.'

'You have an ill opinion of me, Miss Shirley: you never told me so much of your mind before.'

'I never had an opening; but I have sat on Jessy's stool by your chair in the back-parlour at Briarmains, for evenings together, listening excitedly to your talk, half-admiring what you said, and half-rebelling against it. I think you a fine old Yorkshireman, sir: I am proud to have been born in the same county and parish as yourself – truthful, upright, independent you are, as a rock based below seas; but also you are harsh, rude, narrow, and merciless.'

'Not to the poor, lass – nor to the meek of the earth – only to the proud and high-minded.'

'And what right have you, sir, to make such distinctions? A prouder – a higher-minded man than yourself does not exist. You find it easy to speak comfortably to your inferiors – you are too haughty, too ambitious, too jealous to be civil to those above you. But you are all alike. Helstone also is proud and

prejudiced. Moore, though juster and more considerate than either you or the Rector, is still haughty, stern, and, in a public sense, selfish. It is well there are such men as Mr Hall to be found occasionally: men of large and kind hearts, who can love their whole race, who can forgive others for being richer, more prosperous, or more powerful than they are. Such men may have less originality, less force of character than you, but they are better friends to mankind.'

'And when is it to be?' said Mr Yorke, now rising.

'When is what to be?'

'The wedding.'

'Whose wedding?'

'Only that of Robert Gérard Moore, Esq. of Hollow's Cottage, with Miss Keeldar, daughter and heiress of the late Charles Cave Keeldar of Fieldhead Hall.'

Shirley gazed at the questioner with rising colour; but the light in her eye was not faltering: it shone steadily – yes – it burned deeply.

'That is your revenge,' she said, slowly: then added; 'Would it be a bad match, unworthy of the late Charles Cave Keeldar's representative?'

'My lass, Moore is a gentleman: his blood is pure and ancient as mine or thine.'

'And we two set store by ancient blood? We have family pride, though one of us at least is a Republican?'

Yorke bowed as he stood before her. His lips were mute, but his eye confessed the impeachment. Yes – he had family pride – you saw it in his whole bearing.

'Moore *is* a gentleman,' echoed Shirley, lifting her head with glad grace. She checked herself – words seemed crowding to her tongue, she would not give them utterance; but her look spoke much at the moment: what – Yorke tried to read, but could not – the language was there – visible, but untranslatable – a poem – a fervid lyric in an unknown tongue. It was not a plain story, however – no simple gush of feeling – no ordinary love-confession – that was obvious; it was something other, deeper, more intricate than he guessed at: he felt his revenge had not struck home; he felt that Shirley triumphed – she held him at fault, baffled, puzzled; *she* enjoyed the moment – not *he*.

'And if Moore *is* a gentleman, you *can* be only a lady, therefore –'

'Therefore there would be no inequality in our union?'

'None.'

'Thank you for your approbation. Will you give me away when I relinquish the name of Keeldar for that of Moore?'

Mr Yorke instead of replying, gazed at her much puzzled. He could not divine what her look signified; whether she spoke in earnest or in jest: there was purpose and feeling, banter and scoff playing, mingled, on her mobile lineaments.

'I don't understand thee,' he said, turning away.

She laughed: 'Take courage, sir; you are not singular in your ignorance: but I suppose if Moore understands me that will do – will it not?'

'Moore may settle his own matters henceforward for me; I'll neither meddle nor make with them further.'

A new thought crossed her: her countenance changed magically: with a sudden darkening of the eye, and austere fixing of the features, she demanded,—

'Have you been asked to interfere? Are you questioning me as another's proxy?'

# Shirley

'The Lord save us! Whoever weds thee must look about him! Keep all your questions for Robert; I'll answer no more on 'em. Good-day, lassie!'

The day being fine, or at least fair – for soft clouds curtained the sun, and a dim but not chill or waterish haze slept blue on the hills – Caroline, while Shirley was engaged with her callers, had persuaded Mrs Pryor to assume her bonnet and summer shawl, and to take a walk with her up towards the narrow end of the Hollow.

Here, the opposing sides of the glen approaching each other, and becoming clothed with brushwood and stunted oaks, formed a wooded ravine; at the bottom of which ran the mill-stream, in broken unquiet course, struggling with many stones, chafing against rugged banks, fretting with gnarled tree-roots, foaming, gurgling, battling as it went. Here, when you had wandered half a mile from the mill, you found a sense of deep solitude: found it in the shade of unmolested trees; received it in the singing of many birds, for which that shade made a home. This was no trodden way: the freshness of the woodflowers attested that foot of man seldom pressed them: the abounding wild-roses looked as if they budded, bloomed, and faded under the watch of solitude, as in a sultan's harem. Here you saw the sweet azure of blue-bells, and recognized in pearl-white blossoms, spangling the grass, an humble type of some star-lit spot in space.

Mrs Pryor liked a quiet walk: she ever shunned highroads, and sought byways and lonely lanes: one companion she preferred to total solitude, for in solitude she was nervous: a vague fear of annoying encounters broke the enjoyment of quite lonely rambles; but she feared nothing with Caroline: when once she got away from human habitations, and entered the still demesne of Nature, accompanied by this one youthful friend, a propitious change seemed to steal over her mind and beam in her countenance. When with Caroline – and Caroline only – her heart, you would have said, shook off a burden, her brow put aside a veil, her spirits too escaped from a restraint: with her she was cheerful; with her, at times, she was tender: to her she would impart her knowledge, reveal glimpses of her experience, give her opportunities for guessing what life she had lived, what cultivation her mind had received, of what calibre was her intelligence, how and where her feelings were vulnerable.

To-day, for instance, as they walked along, Mrs Pryor talked to her companion about the various birds singing in the trees, discriminated their species, and said something about their habits and peculiarities. English natural history seemed familiar to her. All the wild flowers round their path were recognized by her: tiny plants springing near stones and peeping out of chinks in old walls – plants such as Caroline had scarcely noticed before – received a name and an intimation of their properties: it appeared that she had minutely studied the botany of English fields and woods. Having reached the head of the ravine, they sat down together on a ledge of grey and mossy rock jutting from the base of a steep green hill, which towered above them: she looked round her, and spoke of the neighbourhood as she had once before seen it long ago. She alluded to its changes, and compared its aspect with that of other parts of England; revealing in quiet, unconscious touches of description, a sense of the picturesque, an appreciation of the beautiful or commonplace, a power of comparing the wild with the

cultured, the grand with the tame, that gave to her discourse a graphic charm as pleasant as it was unpretending.

The sort of reverent pleasure with which Caroline listened – so sincere, so quiet, yet so evident, stirred the elder lady's faculties to gentle animation. Rarely, probably, had she, with her chill, repellent outside – her diffident mien and incommunicative habits, known what it was to excite in one whom she herself could love, feelings of earnest affection and admiring esteem. Delightful, doubtless, was the consciousness that a young girl towards whom it seemed – judging by the moved expression of her eyes and features – her heart turned with almost a fond impulse, looked up to her as an instructor, and clung to her as a friend. With a somewhat more marked accent of interest than she often permitted herself to use, she said, as she bent towards her youthful companion, and put aside from her forehead a pale brown curl which had strayed from the confining comb, –

'I do hope this sweet air blowing from the hill will do you good, my dear Caroline: I wish I could see something more of colour in these cheeks – but perhaps you were never florid?'

'I had red cheeks once,' returned Miss Helstone, smiling. 'I remember a year – two years ago, when I used to look in the glass, I saw a different face there to what I see now – rounder and rosier. But when we are young,' added the girl of eighteen, 'our minds are careless and our lives easy.'

'Do you' – continued Mrs Pryor, mastering by an effort that tyrant timidity which made it difficult for her, even under present circumstances, to attempt the scrutiny of another's heart, – 'Do you, at your age, fret yourself with cares for the future? Believe me, you had better not: let the morrow take thought for the things of itself.'

'True, dear madam: it is not over the future I pine. The evil of the day is sometimes oppressive – *too* oppressive, and I long to escape it.'

'That is – the evil of the day – that is – your uncle perhaps is not – you find it difficult to understand – he does not appreciate –'

Mrs Pryor could not complete her broken sentences: she could not manage to put the question whether Mr Helstone was too harsh with his niece, but Caroline comprehended.

'Oh, that is nothing,' she replied; 'my uncle and I get on very well: we never quarrel – I don't call him harsh – he never scolds me. Sometimes I wish somebody in the world loved me; but I cannot say that I particularly wish him to have more affection for me than he has. As a child, I should perhaps have felt the want of attention, only the servants were very kind to me; but when people are long indifferent to us, we grow indifferent to their indifference. It is my uncle's way not to care for women and girls – unless they be ladies that he meets in company: he could not alter, and I have no wish that he should alter, as far as I am concerned. I believe it would merely annoy and frighten me were he to be affectionate towards me now. But you know, Mrs Pryor, it is scarcely *living* to measure time as I do at the Rectory. The hours pass, and I get them over somehow, but I do not *live*. I endure existence, but I rarely enjoy it. Since Miss Keeldar and you came, I have been – I was going to say – happier, but that would be untrue.' She paused.

'How, untrue? You are fond of Miss Keeldar, are you not, my dear?'

'Very fond of Shirley: I both like and admire her: but I am painfully

circumstanced: for a reason I cannot explain, I want to go away from this place, and to forget it.'

'You told me before you wished to be a governess; but, my dear, if you remember, I did not encourage the idea. I have been a governess myself great part of my life. In Miss Keeldar's acquaintance, I esteem myself most fortunate: her talents and her really sweet disposition have rendered my office easy to me; but when I was young, before I married, my trials were severe, poignant. I should not like a–. I should not like you to endure similar ones. It was my lot to enter a family of considerable pretensions to good birth and mental superiority, and the members of which also believed that "on them was perceptible" an unusual endowment of the "Christian graces:" that all their hearts were regenerate, and their spirits in a peculiar state of discipline. I was early given to understand, that "as I was not their equal," so I could not expect "to have their sympathy." It was in no sort concealed from me that I was held a "burden and a restraint in society." The gentlemen, I found, regarded me as a "tabooed woman," to whom "they were interdicted from granting the usual privileges of the sex," and yet who "annoyed them by frequently crossing their path." The ladies too made it plain that they thought me "a bore." The servants, it was signified, "detested me:" *why*, I could never clearly comprehend. My pupils, I was told, "however much they might love me, and how deep soever the interest I might take in them, could not be my friends." It was intimated, that I must "live alone, and never transgress the invisible but rigid line which established the difference between me and my employers." My life in this house was sedentary, solitary, constrained, joyless, toilsome. The dreadful crushing of the animal spirits, the ever prevailing sense of friendlessness and homelessness consequent on this state of things, began erelong to produce mortal effects on my constitution – I sickened. The lady of the house told me coolly I was the victim of "wounded vanity." She hinted, that if I did not make an effort to quell my "ungodly discontent," to cease "murmuring against God's appointment," and to cultivate the profound humility befitting my station, my mind would very likely "go to pieces" on the rock that wrecked most of my sisterhood – morbid self-esteem; and that I should die an inmate of a lunatic asylum.

'I said nothing to Mrs Hardman; it would have been useless; but to her eldest daughter I one day dropped a few observations, which were answered thus: –

'There were hardships, she allowed, in the position of a governess: "doubtless they had their trials; but," she averred, with a manner it makes me smile now to recall – "but it must be so. *She* (Miss H.) had neither view, hope, nor *wish* to see these things remedied; for, in the inherent constitution of English habits, feelings, and prejudices, there was no possibility that they should be. Governesses," she observed, "must ever be kept in a sort of isolation: it is the only means of maintaining that distance which the reserve of English manners and the decorum of English families exact."

'I remember I sighed as Miss Hardman quitted my bedside: she caught the sound, and turning, said severely, –

' "I fear, Miss Grey, you have inherited in fullest measure the worst sin of our fallen nature – the sin of pride. You are proud, and therefore you are ungrateful too. Mamma pays you a handsome salary; and, if you had average sense, you would thankfully put up with much that is fatiguing to do and irksome to bear, since it is so well made worth your while."

# Shirley

'Miss Hardman, my love, was a very strong-minded young lady, of most distinguished talents: the aristocracy are decidedly a very superior class, you know – both physically and morally and mentally – as a high Tory I acknowledge that – I could not describe the dignity of her voice and mien as she addressed me thus: still, I fear, she was selfish, my dear. I would never wish to speak ill of my superiors in rank; but I think she was a little selfish.

'I remember,' continued Mrs Pryor, after a pause, 'another of Miss H.'s observations, which she would utter with quite a grand air. "WE," she would say, – "WE need the imprudences, extravagances, mistakes, and crimes of a certain number of fathers to sow the seed from which WE reap the harvest of governesses. The daughters of trades-people, however well educated, must necessarily be underbred, and as such unfit to be inmates of OUR dwellings, or guardians of OUR children's minds and persons. WE shall ever prefer to place those about OUR offspring, who have been born and bred with somewhat of the same refinement as OURSELVES."'

'Miss Hardman must have thought herself something better than her fellow-creatures, ma'am, since she held that their calamities, and even crimes, were necessary to minister to her convenience. You say she was religious: her religion must have been that of the Pharisee, who thanked God that he was not as other men are, nor even as that publican.'

'My dear, we will not discuss the point: I should be the last person to wish to instil into your mind any feeling of dissatisfaction with your lot in life, or any sentiment of envy or insubordination towards your superiors. Implicit submission to authorities, scrupulous deference to our betters (under which term I, of course, include the higher classes of society) are, in my opinion, indispensable to the wellbeing of every community. All I mean to say, my dear, is, that you had better not attempt to be a governess, as the duties of the position would be too severe for your constitution. Not one word of disrespect would I breathe towards either Mrs or Miss Hardman; only, recalling my own experience, I cannot but feel that, were you to fall under auspices such as theirs, you would contend a while courageously with your doom; then you would pine and grow too weak for your work: you would come home – if you still had a home – broken down. Those languishing years would follow, of which none but the invalid and her immediate friends feel the heart-sickness and know the burden: consumption or decline would close the chapter. Such is the history of many a life: I would not have it yours. My dear, we will now walk about a little, if you please.'

They both rose and slowly paced a green natural terrace bordering the chasm.

'My dear,' erelong again began Mrs Pryor, a sort of timid, embarrassed abruptness marking her manner as she spoke, 'the young, especially those to whom nature has been favourable – often – frequently – anticipate – look forward to – to marriage as the end, the goal of their hopes.'

And she stopped. Caroline came to her relief with promptitude, showing a great deal more self-possession and courage than herself on the formidable topic now broached:

'They do; and naturally,' she replied, with a calm emphasis that startled Mrs Pryor. 'They look forward to marriage with some one they love as the brightest, – the only bright destiny that can await them. Are they wrong?'

'Oh, my dear!' exclaimed Mrs Pryor, clasping her hands: and again she

paused. Caroline turned a searching, an eager eye on the face of her friend: that face was much agitated. 'My dear,' she murmured, 'life is an illusion.'

'But not love! Love is real: the most real, the most lasting, – the sweetest and yet the bitterest thing we know.'

'My dear – it is very bitter. It is said to be strong – strong as death! Most of the cheats of existence are strong. As to their sweetness – nothing is so transitory: its date is a moment, – the twinkling of an eye: the sting remains for ever: it may perish with the dawn of eternity, but it tortures through time into its deepest night.'

'Yes, it tortures through time,' agreed Caroline, 'except when it is mutual love.'

'Mutual love! My dear, romances are pernicious. You do not read them, I hope?'

'Sometimes – whenever I can get them, indeed; but romance-writers might know nothing of love, judging by the way in which they treat of it.'

'Nothing whatever, my dear!' assented Mrs Pryor, eagerly; 'nor of marriage; and the false pictures they give of those subjects cannot be too strongly condemned. They are not like reality: they show you only the green tempting surface of the marsh, and give not one faithful or truthful hint of the slough underneath.'

'But it is not always slough,' objected Caroline: 'there are happy marriages. Where affection is reciprocal and sincere, and minds are harmonious, marriage *must* be happy.'

'It is never wholly happy. Two people can never literally be as one: there is, perhaps, a possibility of content under peculiar circumstances, such as are seldom combined; but it is as well not to run the risk: you may make fatal mistakes. Be satisfied, my dear: let all the single be satisfied with their freedom.'

'You echo my uncle's words!' exclaimed Caroline, in a tone of dismay: 'you speak like Mrs Yorke, in her most gloomy moments: – like Miss Mann, when she is most sourly and hypochondriacally disposed. This is terrible!'

'No, it is only true. Oh, child! you have only lived the pleasant morning time of life: the hot, weary noon, the sad evening, the sunless night, are yet to come for you! Mr Helstone, you say, talks as I talk; and I wonder how Mrs Matthewson Helstone would have talked had she been living. She died! she died!'

'And, alas! my own mother and father . . .' exclaimed Caroline, struck by a sombre recollection.

'What of them?'

'Did I never tell you that they were separated?'

'I have heard it.'

'They must then have been very miserable.'

'You see all *facts* go to prove what I say.'

'In this case there ought to be no such thing as marriage.'

'There ought, my dear, were it only to prove that this life is a mere state of probation, wherein neither rest nor recompense is to be vouchsafed.'

'But your own marriage, Mrs Pryor?'

Mrs Pryor shrunk and shuddered as if a rude finger had pressed a naked nerve: Caroline felt she had touched what would not bear the slightest contact.

'My marriage was unhappy,' said the lady, summoning courage at last; 'but yet –' she hesitated.

# Shirley

'But yet,' suggested Caroline, 'not immitigably wretched?'

'Not in its results, at least. No,' she added, in a softer tone; 'God mingles something of the balm of mercy even in vials of the most corrosive woe. He can so turn events, that from the very same blind, rash act whence sprang the curse of half our life, may flow the blessing of the remainder. Then, I am of a peculiar disposition, I own that: far from facile, without address, in some points eccentric. I ought never to have married: mine is not the nature easily to find a duplicate, or likely to assimilate with a contrast. I was quite aware of my own ineligibility; and if I had not been so miserable as a governess, I never should have married; and then –'

Caroline's eyes asked her to proceed: they entreated her to break the thick cloud of despair, which her previous words had seemed to spread over life.

'And then, my dear, Mr – , that is, the gentleman I married, was, perhaps, rather an exceptional than an average character. I hope, at least, the experience of few has been such as mine was, or that few have felt their sufferings as I felt mine. They nearly shook my mind: relief was so hopeless, redress so unattainable: but, my dear, I do not wish to dishearten, I only wish to warn you, and to prove that the single should not be too anxious to change their state, as they may change for the worse.'

'Thank you, my dear madam, I quite understand your kind intentions; but there is no fear of my falling into the error to which you allude. I, at least, have no thoughts of marriage, and, for that reason, I want to make myself a position by some other means.'

'My dear, listen to me. On what I am going to say, I have carefully deliberated; having, indeed, revolved the subject in my thoughts ever since you first mentioned your wish to obtain a situation. You know I at present reside with Miss Keeldar in the capacity of companion: should she marry (and that she *will* marry erelong, many circumstances induce me to conclude), I shall cease to be necessary to her in that capacity. I must tell you that I possess a small independency, arising partly from my own savings, and partly from a legacy left me some years since; whenever I leave Fieldhead, I shall take a house of my own: I could not endure to live in solitude: I have no relations whom I care to invite to close intimacy; for, as you must have observed, and as I have already avowed, my habits and tastes have their peculiarities: to you, my dear, I need not say I am attached; with you I am happier than I have ever been with any living thing' (this was said with marked emphasis). 'Your society I should esteem a very dear privilege – an inestimable privilege, a comfort, a blessing. You shall come to me then. Caroline, do you refuse me? I hope you can love me?'

And with these two abrupt questions she stopped.

'Indeed, I *do* love you,' was the reply. 'I should like to live with you: but you are too kind.'

'All I have,' went on Mrs Pryor, 'I would leave to you: you should be provided for, but never again say I am *too kind*. You pierce my heart, child!'

'But, my dear madam – this generosity – I have no claim –'

'Hush! you must not talk about it: there are some things we cannot bear to hear. Oh! it is late to begin, but I may yet live a few years: I can never wipe out the past, but perhaps a brief space in the future may yet be mine!'

Mrs Pryor seemed deeply agitated: large tears trembled in her eyes and rolled down her cheeks. Caroline kissed her, in her gentle caressing way, saying softly –

# Shirley

'I love you dearly. Don't cry.'

But the lady's whole frame seemed shaken: she sat down, bent her head to her knee, and wept aloud. Nothing could console her till the inward storm had had its way. At last the agony subsided of itself.

'Poor thing!' she murmured, returning Caroline's kiss: 'poor lonely lamb! But come,' she added abruptly; 'come, we must go home.'

For a short distance Mrs Pryor walked very fast: by degrees, however, she calmed down to her wonted manner, fell into her usual characteristic pace, – a peculiar one like all her movements, – and by the time they reached Fieldhead, she had re-entered into herself: the outside was, as usual, still and shy.

# Chapter 22

## Two Lives

Only half of Moore's activity and resolution had been seen in his defence of the mill: he showed, the other half (and a terrible half it was) in the indefatigable, the relentless assiduity with which he pursued the leaders of the riot. The mob, the mere followers, he let alone: perhaps an innate sense of justice told him that men misled by false counsel, goaded by privations, are not fit objects of vengeance, and that he who would visit an even violent act on the bent head of suffering, is a tyrant, not a judge. At all events, though he knew many of the number, having recognized them during the latter part of the attack when day began to dawn, he let them daily pass him on street and road without notice or threat.

The leaders he did not know. They were strangers: emissaries from the large towns. Most of these were not members of the operative class: they were chiefly 'downdraughts,' bankrupts, men always in debt and often in drink – men who had nothing to lose, and much – in the way of character, cash, and cleanliness – to gain. These persons Moore hunted like any sleuth-hound; and well he liked the occupation: its excitement was of a kind pleasant to his nature: he liked it better than making cloth.

His horse must have hated these times, for it was ridden both hard and often: he almost lived on the road, and the fresh air was as welcome to his lungs as the policeman's quest to his mood: he preferred it to the steam of dye-houses. The magistrates of the district must have dreaded him: they were slow, timid men; he liked both to frighten and to rouse them. He liked to force them to betray a certain fear, which made them alike falter in resolve and recoil in action – the fear, simply, of assassination. This, indeed, was the dread which had hitherto hampered every manufacturer and almost every public man in the district. Helstone alone had ever repelled it. The old Cossack knew well he

# Shirley

might be shot: he knew there was risk; but such death had for his nerves no terrors: it would have been his chosen – might he have had a choice.

Moore likewise knew his danger: the result was an unquenchable scorn of the quarter whence such danger was to be apprehended. The consciousness that he hunted assassins was the spur in his high-mettled temper's flank. As for fear, he was too proud – too hard-nurtured – (if you will) – too phlegmatic a man to fear. Many a time he rode belated over moors, moonlit or moonless as the case might be, with feelings far more elate, faculties far better refreshed, than when safety and stagnation environed him in the counting-house. Four was the number of the leaders to be accounted for: two, in the course of a fortnight, were brought to bay near Stilbro'; the remaining two it was necessary to seek further off: their haunts were supposed to lie near Birmingham.

Meantime, the clothier did not neglect his battered mill: its reparation was esteemed a light task; carpenters' and glaziers' work alone being needed. The rioters not having succeeded in effecting an entrance, his grim, metal darlings – the machines – had escaped damage.

Whether, during this busy life – whether, while stern justice and exacting business claimed his energies and harassed his thoughts – he now and then gave one moment, dedicated one effort, to keep alive gentler fires than those which smoulder in the fane of Nemesis, it was not easy to discover. He seldom went near Fieldhead; if he did, his visits were brief: if he called at the Rectory, it was only to hold conferences with the Rector in his study. He maintained his rigid course very steadily. Meantime, the history of the year continued troubled: there was no lull in the tempest of war; her long hurricane still swept the Continent. There was not the faintest sign of serene weather: no opening amid 'the clouds of battle-dust and smoke;' no fall of pure dews genial to the olive; no cessation of the red rain which nourishes the baleful and glorious laurel. Meantime, Ruin had her sappers and miners at work under Moore's feet, and whether he rode or walked – whether he only crossed his counting-house hearth, or galloped over sullen Rushedge – he was aware of a hollow echo, and felt the ground shake to his tread.

While the summer thus passed with Moore, how did it lapse with Shirley and Caroline? Let us first visit the heiress. How does she look? Like a love-lorn maiden, pale and pining for a neglectful swain? Does she sit the day long bent over some sedentary task? Has she for ever a book in her hand, or sewing on her knee, and eyes only for that, and words for nothing, and thoughts unspoken?

By no means. Shirley is all right. If her wistful cast of physiognomy is not gone, no more is her careless smile. She keeps her dark old manor-house light and bright with her cheery presence: the gallery, and the low-ceiled chambers that open into it, have learned lively echoes from her voice: the dim entrance-hall, with its one window, has grown pleasantly accustomed to the frequent rustle of a silk dress, as its wearer sweeps across from room to room, now carrying flowers to the barbarous peach-bloom salon, now entering the dining-room to open its casements and let in the scent of mignonette and sweetbriar, anon bringing plants from the staircase-window to place in the sun at the open porch-door.

She takes her sewing occasionally: but, by some fatality, she is doomed never to sit steadily at it for above five minutes at a time: her thimble is scarcely fitted on, her needle scarce threaded, when a sudden thought calls her up-stairs:

736

# Shirley

perhaps she goes to seek some just-then-remembered old ivory-backed needle-book, or older china-topped workbox, quite unneeded, but which seems at the moment indispensable; perhaps to arrange her hair, or a drawer which she recollects to have seen that morning in a state of curious confusion; perhaps only to take a peep from a particular window at a particular view, whence Briarfield Church and Rectory are visible, pleasantly bowered in trees. She has scarcely returned, and again taken up the slip of cambric, or square of half-wrought canvass, when Tartar's bold scrape and strangled whistle are heard at the porch-door, and she must run to open it for him; it is a hot day; he comes in panting; she must convoy him to the kitchen, and see with her own eyes that his water-bowl is replenished. Through the open kitchen-door the court is visible, all sunny and gay, and peopled with turkeys and their poults, peahens and their chicks, pearl-flecked Guinea fowls, and a bright variety of pure white, and purple-necked, and blue and cinnamon-plumed pigeons. Irresistible spectacle to Shirley! She runs to the pantry for a roll, and she stands on the door-step scattering crumbs: around her throng her eager, plump, happy, feathered vassals. John is about the stables, and John must be talked to, and her mare looked at. She is still petting and patting it, when the cows come in to be milked: this is important; Shirley must stay and take a review of them all. There are perhaps some little calves, some little new-yeaned lambs – it may be twins, whose mothers have rejected them: Miss Keeldar must be introduced to them by John – must permit herself the treat of feeding them with her own hand, under the direction of her careful foreman. Meantime, John moots doubtful questions about the farming of certain 'crofts,' and 'ings,' and 'holms,' and his mistress is necessitated to fetch her garden-hat – a gipsy-straw – and accompany him, over stile and along hedgerow, to hear the conclusion of the whole agricultural matter on the spot, and with the said 'crofts,' 'ings,' and 'holms' under her eye. Bright afternoon thus wears into soft evening, and she comes home to a late tea, and after tea she never sews.

After tea Shirley reads, and she is just about as tenacious of her book as she is lax of her needle. Her study is the rug, her seat a foot-stool, or perhaps only the carpet at Mrs Pryor's feet – there she always learned her lessons when a child, and old habits have a strong power over her. The tawny and lion-like bulk of Tartar is ever stretched beside her; his negro muzzle laid on his forepaws, straight, strong, and shapely as the limbs of an Alpine wolf. One hand of the mistress generally reposes on the living serf's rude head, because if she takes it away he groans and is discontented. Shirley's mind is given to her book; she lifts not her eyes; she neither stirs nor speaks: unless, indeed, it be to return a brief respectful answer to Mrs Pryor, who addresses deprecatory phrases to her now and then.

'My dear, you had better not have that great dog so near you: he is crushing the border of your dress.'

'Oh, it is only muslin: I can put a clean one on to-morrow.'

'My dear, I wish you could acquire the habit of sitting to a table when you read.'

'I will try, ma'am, some time; but it is so comfortable to do as one has always been accustomed to do.'

'My dear, let me beg of you to put that book down: you are trying your eyes by the doubtful firelight.'

# Shirley

'No, ma'am, not at all: my eyes are never tired.'

At last, however, a pale light falls on the page from the window: she looks, the moon is up; she closes the volume, rises, and walks through the room. Her book has perhaps been a good one; it has refreshed, refilled, rewarmed her heart; it has set her brain astir, furnished her mind with pictures. The still parlour, the clean hearth, the window opening on the twilight sky, and showing its 'sweet regent,' new throned and glorious, suffice to make earth an Eden, life a poem, for Shirley. A still, deep, inborn delight glows in her young veins; unmingled – untroubled; not to be reached or ravished by human agency, because by no human agency bestowed: the pure gift of God to His creature, the free dower of Nature to her child. This joy gives her experience of a genii-life. Buoyant, by green steps, by glad hills, all verdure and light, she reaches a station scarcely lower than that whence angels looked down on the dreamer of Beth-el, and her eye seeks, and her soul possesses, the vision of life as she wishes it. No – not as she wishes it; she has not time to wish: the swift glory spreads out, sweeping and kindling, and multiplies its splendours faster than Thought can effect his combinations, faster than Aspiration can utter her longings. Shirley says nothing while the trance is upon her – she is quite mute; but if Mrs Pryor speaks to her now, she goes out quietly, and continues her walk up-stairs in the dim gallery.

If Shirley were not an indolent, a reckless, an ignorant being, she would take a pen at such moments; or at least while the recollection of such moments was yet fresh on her spirit: she would seize, she would fix the apparition, tell the vision revealed. Had she a little more of the organ of Acquisitiveness in her head – a little more of the love of property in her nature, she would take a good-sized sheet of paper and write plainly out, in her own queer but clear and legible hand, the story that has been narrated, the song that has been sung to her, and thus possess what she was enabled to create. But indolent she is, reckless she is, and most ignorant, for she does not know her dreams are rare – her feelings peculiar: she does not know, has never known, and will die without knowing, the full value of that spring whose bright fresh bubbling in her heart keeps it green.

Shirley takes life easily: is not that fact written in her eye? In her good-tempered moments, is it not as full of lazy softness as in her brief fits of anger it is fulgent with quick-flashing fire? Her nature is in her eye: so long as she is calm, indolence, indulgence, humour, and tenderness possess that large grey sphere: incense her, – a red ray pierces the dew, – it quickens instantly to flame.

Ere the month of July was passed, Miss Keeldar would probably have started with Caroline on that northern tour they had planned; but just at that epoch an invasion befell Fieldhead: a genteel foraging party besieged Shirley in her castle, and compelled her to surrender at discretion. An uncle, an aunt, and two cousins from the south, a Mr, Mrs, and two Misses Sympson, of Sympson Grove, —shire, came down upon her in state. The laws of hospitality obliged her to give in, which she did with a facility which somewhat surprised Caroline, who knew her to be prompt in action and fertile in expedient, where a victory was to be gained for her will. Miss Helstone even asked her how it was she submitted so readily? – she answered, old feelings had their power: she had passed two years of her early youth at Sympson Grove.

'How did she like her relatives?'

She had nothing in common with them, she replied: little Harry Sympson,

# Shirley

indeed, the sole son of the family, was very unlike his sisters, and of him she had formerly been fond; but he was not coming to Yorkshire: at least, not yet.

The next Sunday the Fieldhead pew in Briarfield church appeared peopled with a prim, trim, fidgety, elderly gentleman, who shifted his spectacles and changed his position every three minutes; a patient, placid-looking elderly lady, in brown satin, and two pattern young ladies, in pattern attire, with pattern deportment. Shirley had the air of a black swan, or a white crow, in the midst of this party; and very forlorn was her aspect. Having brought her into respectable society, we will leave her there a while, and look after Miss Helstone.

Separated from Miss Keeldar for the present, as she could not seek her in the midst of her fine relatives; scared away from Fieldhead by the visiting commotion which the new arrivals occasioned in the neighbourhood, Caroline was limited once more to the grey Rectory; the solitary morning walk in remote bypaths; the long, lonely afternoon sitting in a quiet parlour which the sun forsook at noon, or in the garden alcove where it shone bright, yet sad, on the ripening red currants trained over the trellis, and on the fair monthly roses entwined between, and through them fell chequered on Caroline sitting in her white summer dress, still as a garden statue. There she read old books, taken from her uncle's library: the Greek and Latin were of no use to her; and its collection of light literature was chiefly contained on a shelf which had belonged to her aunt Mary: some venerable Lady's Magazines, that had once performed a sea-voyage with their owner, and undergone a storm, and whose pages were stained with salt water; some mad Methodist Magazines, full of miracles and apparitions, of preternatural warnings, ominous dreams, and frenzied fanaticism; the equally mad Letters of Mrs Elizabeth Rowe from the Dead to the Living, a few old English Classics: – from these faded flowers Caroline had in her childhood extracted the honey, – they were tasteless to her now. By way of change, and also of doing good, she would sew: make garments for the poor, according to good Miss Ainley's direction. Sometimes, as she felt and saw her tears fall slowly on her work, she would wonder how the excellent woman who had cut it out and arranged it for her, managed to be so equally serene in *her* solitude.

'I never find Miss Ainley oppressed with despondency, or lost in grief,' she thought; 'yet her cottage is a still, dim little place, and she is without a bright hope or near friend in the world. I remember, though, she told me once, she had tutored her thoughts to tend upwards to Heaven. She allowed there was, and ever had been, little enjoyment in this world for her; and she looks, I suppose, to the bliss of the world to come. So do nuns – with their close cell, their iron lamp, their robe strait as a shroud, their bed narrow as a coffin. She says, often, she has no fear of death – no dread of the grave: no more, doubtless, had St Simeon Stylites, lifted up terrible on his wild column in the wilderness: no more has the Hindoo votary stretched on his couch of iron spikes. Both these having violated nature, their natural likings and antipathies are reversed: they grow altogether morbid. I do fear death as yet, but I believe it is because I am young: poor Miss Ainley would cling closer to life, if life had more charms for her. God surely did not create us, and cause us to live, with the sole end of wishing always to die. I believe, in my heart, we were intended to prize life and enjoy it, so long as we retain it. Existence never was originally meant to be that useless, blank, pale, slow-trailing thing it often becomes to many, and is becoming to me, among the rest.

# Shirley

'Nobody,' she went on – 'nobody in particular is to blame, that I can see, for the state in which things are; and I cannot tell, however much I puzzle over it, how they are to be altered for the better; but I feel there is something wrong somewhere. I believe single women should have more to do – better chances of interesting and profitable occupation than they possess now. And when I speak thus, I have no impression that I displease God by my words; that I am either impious or impatient, irreligious or sacrilegious. My consolation is, indeed, that God hears many a groan, and compassionates much grief which man stops his ears against, or frowns on with impotent contempt. I say *impotent*, for I observe that to such grievances as society cannot readily cure, it usually forbids utterance, on pain of its scorn: this scorn being only a sort of tinselled cloak to its deformed weakness. People hate to be reminded of ills they are unable or unwilling to remedy: such reminder, in forcing on them a sense of their own incapacity, or a more painful sense of an obligation to make some unpleasant effort, troubles their ease and shakes their self-complacency. Old maids, like the houseless and unemployed poor, should not ask for a place and an occupation in the world: the demand disturbs the happy and rich: it disturbs parents. Look at the numerous families of girls in this neighbourhood: the Armitages, the Birtwhistles, the Sykes. The brothers of these girls are every one in business or in professions; they have something to do: their sisters have no earthly employment, but household work and sewing; no earthly pleasure, but an unprofitable visiting; and no hope, in all their life to come, of anything better. This stagnant state of things makes them decline in health: they are never well; and their minds and views shrink to wondrous narrowness. The great wish – the sole aim of every one of them is to be married, but the majority will never marry: they will die as they now live. They scheme, they plot, they dress to ensnare husbands. The gentlemen turn them into ridicule: they don't want them; they hold them very cheap: they say – I have heard them say it with sneering laughs many a time – the matrimonial market is overstocked. Fathers say so likewise, and are angry with their daughters when they observe their manoeuvres: they order them to stay at home. What do they expect them to do at home? If you ask, – they would answer, sew and cook. They expect them to do this, and this only, contentedly, regularly, uncomplainingly all their lives long, as if they had no germs of faculties for anything else: a doctrine as reasonable to hold, as it would be that the fathers have no faculties but for eating what their daughters cook, or for wearing what they sew. Could men live so themselves? Would they not be very weary? And, when there came no relief to their weariness, but only reproaches at its slightest manifestation, would not their weariness ferment in time to frenzy? Lucretia, spinning at midnight in the midst of her maidens, and Solomon's virtuous woman, are often quoted as patterns of what "the sex" (as they say) ought to be. I don't know: Lucretia, I daresay, was a most worthy sort of person, much like my cousin Hortense Moore; but she kept her servants up very late. I should not have liked to be amongst the number of the maidens. Hortense would just work me and Sarah in that fashion, if she could, and neither of us would bear it. The "virtuous woman," again, had her household up in the very middle of the night; she "got breakfast over" (as Mrs Sykes says) before one o'clock a.m.; but *she* had something more to do than spin and give out portions: she was a manufacturer – she made fine linen and sold it; she was an agriculturist – she bought estates and planted vineyards. *That* woman was a

manager: she was what the matrons hereabouts call "a clever woman." On the whole, I like her a great deal better than Lucretia; but I don't believe either Mr Armitage or Mr Sykes could have got the advantage of her in a bargain: yet, I like her. "Strength and honour were her clothing: the heart of her husband safely trusted in her. She opened her mouth with wisdom; in her tongue was the law of kindness: her children rose up and called her blessed; her husband also praised her." King of Israel! your model of a woman is a worthy model! But are we, in these days, brought up to be like her? Men of Yorkshire! do your daughters reach this royal standard? Can they reach it? Can you help them to reach it? Can you give them a field in which their faculties may be exercised and grow? Men of England! look at your poor girls, many of them fading around you, dropping off in consumption or decline; or, what is worse, degenerating to sour old maids, – envious, backbiting, wretched, because life is a desert to them; or, what is worst of all, reduced to strive, by scarce modest coquetry and debasing artifice, to gain that position and consideration by marriage, which to celibacy is denied. Fathers! cannot you alter these things? Perhaps not all at once; but consider the matter well when it is brought before you, receive it as a theme worthy of thought: do not dismiss it with an idle jest or an unmanly insult. You would wish to be proud of your daughters and not to blush for them – then seek for them an interest and an occupation which shall raise them above the flirt, the manoeuvrer, the mischief-making tale-bearer. Keep your girls' minds narrow and fettered – they will still be a plague and a care, sometimes a disgrace to you: cultivate them – give them scope and work – they will be your gayest companions in health; your tenderest nurses in sickness; your most faithful prop in age.'

# Chapter 23

## An Evening Out

One fine summer day that Caroline had spent entirely alone (her uncle being at Whinbury), and whose long, bright, noiseless, breezeless, cloudless hours (how many they seemed since sunrise!) had been to her as desolate as if they had gone over her head in the shadowless and trackless wastes of Zahara, instead of in the blooming garden of an English home, she was sitting in the alcove, – her task of work on her knee, her fingers assiduously plying the needle, her eyes following and regulating their movements, her brain working restlessly, – when Fanny came to the door, looked round over the lawn and borders, and not seeing her whom she sought, called out – 'Miss Caroline!'

A low voice answered – 'Fanny!' It issued from the alcove, and thither Fanny hastened – a note in her hand, which she delivered to fingers that hardly seemed to have nerve to hold it. Miss Helstone did not ask whence it came, and she did not look at it: she let it drop amongst the folds of her work.

'Joe Scott's son, Harry, brought it,' said Fanny.

The girl was no enchantress, and knew no magic-spell, yet what she said took almost magical effect on her young mistress: she lifted her head with the quick motion of revived sensation; she shot – not a languid, but a life-like, questioning glance at Fanny.

'Harry Scott! Who sent him?'

'He came from the Hollow.'

The dropped note was snatched up eagerly – the seal was broken: it was read in two seconds. An affectionate billet from Hortense, informing her young cousin that she was returned from Wormwood Wells; that she was alone to-day, as Robert was gone to Whinbury market; that nothing would give her greater pleasure than to have Caroline's company to tea; and – the good lady added – she was sure such a change would be most acceptable and beneficial to Caroline, who must be sadly at a loss both for safe guidance and improving society since the misunderstanding between Robert and Mr Helstone had occasioned a separation from her 'meilleure amie, Hortense Gérard Moore.' In a postscript, she was urged to put on her bonnet and run down directly.

Caroline did not need the injunction: glad was she to lay by the child's brown holland slip she was trimming with braid for the Jew's basket, to hasten upstairs, cover her curls with her straw bonnet, and throw round her shoulders the black silk scarf, whose simple drapery suited as well her shape as its dark hue set off the purity of her dress and the fairness of her face; glad was she to escape for a few hours the solitude, the sadness, the nightmare of her life; glad to run down the green lane sloping to the Hollow, to scent the fragrance of hedge-flowers sweeter than the perfume of moss-rose or lily. True, she knew Robert was not at the cottage; but it was delight to go where he had lately been: so long, so totally separated from him, merely to see his home, to enter the room where he had that morning sat, felt like a reunion. As such it revived her; and then Illusion was again following her in Peri-mask: the soft agitation of wings caressed her cheek, and the air, breathing from the blue summer sky, bore a voice which whispered – 'Robert may come home while you are in his house; and then, at least, you may look in his face – at least you may give him your hand: perhaps for a minute, you may sit beside him.'

'Silence!' was her austere response: but she loved the comforter and the consolation.

Miss Moore probably caught from the window the gleam and flutter of Caroline's white attire through the branchy garden-shrubs, for she advanced from the cottage-porch to meet her. Straight, unbending, phlegmatic as usual, she came on: no haste or ecstasy was ever permitted to disorder the dignity of *her* movements; but she smiled, well pleased to mark the delight of her pupil, to feel her kiss, and the gentle, genial strain of her embrace. She led her tenderly in – half-deceived and wholly flattered. Half deceived! had it not been so, she would in all probability have put her to the wicket, and shut her out. Had she known clearly to whose account the chief share of this child-like joy was to be placed, Hortense would most likely have felt both shocked and incensed. Sisters do not like young ladies to fall in love with their brothers: it seems, if not presumptuous, silly, weak, a delusion, an absurd mistake. *They* do not love these gentlemen – whatever sisterly affection they may cherish towards them – and that others should, repels them with a sense of crude romance. The first

# Shirley

movement, in short, excited by such discovery (as with many parents on finding their children to be in love), is one of mixed impatience and contempt. Reason – if they be rational people – corrects the false feeling in time; but if they be irrational, it is never corrected, and the daughter or sister-in-law is disliked to the end.

'You would expect to find me alone, from what I said in my note,' observed Miss Moore, as she conducted Caroline towards the parlour; 'but it was written this morning: since dinner, company has come in.'

And, opening the door, she made visible an ample spread of crimson skirts overflowing the elbow-chair at the fireside, and above them, presiding with dignity, a cap more awful than a crown. That cap had never come to the cottage under a bonnet: no, it had been brought in a vast bag, or rather a middle-sized balloon of black silk, held wide with whalebone. The screed, or frill of the cap, stood a quarter of a yard broad round the face of the wearer: the ribbon, flourishing in puffs and bows about the head, was of the sort called love-ribbon: there was a good deal of it, – I may say, a very great deal. Mrs Yorke wore the cap – it became her: she wore the gown also – it suited her no less.

That great lady was come in a friendly way to take tea with Miss Moore. It was almost as great and as rare a favour as if the Queen were to go uninvited to share pot-luck with one of her subjects: a higher mark of distinction she could not show, – she who, in general, scorned visiting and tea-drinking, and help cheap, and stigmatized as 'gossips,' every maid and matron of the vicinage.

There was no mistake, however; Miss Moore *was* a favourite with her: she had evinced the fact more than once; evinced it by stopping to speak to her in the churchyard on Sundays; by inviting her, almost hospitably, to come to Briarmains; evinced it to-day by the grand condescension of a personal visit. Her reasons for the preference, as assigned by herself, were, that Miss Moore was a woman of steady deportment, without the least levity of conversation or carriage; also, that, being a foreigner, she must feel the want of a friend to countenance her. She might have added, that her plain aspect, homely precise dress, and phlegmatic unattractive manner were, to her, so many additional recommendations. It is certain, at least, that ladies remarkable for the opposite qualities of beauty, lively bearing, and elegant taste in attire, were not often favoured with her approbation. Whatever gentlemen are apt to admire in women, Mrs Yorke condemned; and what they overlook or despise, she patronized.

Caroline advanced to the mighty matron with some sense of diffidence: she knew little of Mrs Yorke; and, as a parson's niece, was doubtful what sort of a reception she might get. She got a very cool one, and was glad to hide her discomfiture by turning away to take off her bonnet. Nor, upon sitting down, was she displeased to be immediately accosted by a little personage in a blue frock and sash, who started up like some fairy from the side of the great dame's chair, where she had been sitting on a foot-stool, screened from view by the folds of the wide red gown, and running to Miss Helstone, unceremoniously threw her arms round her neck and demanded a kiss.

'My mother is not civil to you,' said the petitioner, as she received and repaid a smiling salute; 'and Rose, there, takes no notice of you: it is their way. If, instead of you, a white angel, with a crown of stars, had come into the room, mother would nod stiffly, and Rose never lift her head at all; but I will be your friend: I have always liked you!'

# Shirley

'Jessie, curb that tongue of yours, and repress your forwardness!' said Mrs Yorke.

'But, mother, you are so frozen!' expostulated Jessie. 'Miss Helstone has never done you any harm: why can't you be kind to her? You sit so stiff, and look so cold, and speak so dry: what for? That's just the fashion in which you treat Miss Shirley Keeldar, and every other young lady who comes to our house. And Rose, there, is such an aut – aut – I have forgotten the word, but it means a machine in the shape of a human being. However, between you, you will drive every soul away from Briarmains, – Martin often says so!'

'I am an automaton? Good! Let me alone then,' said Rose, speaking from a corner where she was sitting on the carpet at the foot of a bookcase, with a volume spread open on her knee. 'Miss Helstone – how do you do?' she added, directing a brief glance to the person addressed, and then again casting down her grey, remarkable eyes on the book, and returning to the study of its pages.

Caroline stole a quiet gaze towards her, dwelling on her young, absorbed countenance, and observing a certain unconscious movement of the mouth as she read, – a movement full of character. Caroline had tact, and she had fine instinct: she felt that Rose Yorke was a peculiar child, – one of the unique: she knew how to treat her. Approaching quietly, she knelt on the carpet at her side, and looked over her little shoulder at her book. It was a romance of Mrs Radcliffe's – 'The Italian.'

Caroline read on with her, making no remark: presently Rose showed her the attention of asking, ere she turned a leaf, –

'Are you ready?'

Caroline only nodded.

'Do you like it?' inquired Rose, erelong.

'Long since, when I read it as a child, I was wonderfully taken with it.'

'Why?'

'It seemed to open with such promise, – such foreboding of a most strange tale to be unfolded.'

'And in reading it, you feel as if you were far away from England, – really in Italy – under another sort of sky, – that blue sky of the south which travellers describe.'

'You are sensible of that, Rose?'

'It makes me long to travel, Miss Helstone.'

'When you are a woman, perhaps, you may be able to gratify your wish.'

'I mean to make a way to do so, if one is not made for me. I cannot live always in Briarfield. The whole world is not very large compared with creation: I must see the outside of our own round planet at least.'

'How much of its outside?'

'First this hemisphere where we live; then the other. I am resolved that my life shall be a life: not a black trance like the toad's, buried in marble; nor a long, slow death like yours in Briarfield Rectory.'

'Like mine! What can you mean, child?'

'Might you not as well be tediously dying, as for ever shut up in that glebe-house – a place that, when I pass it, always reminds me of a windowed grave? I never see any movement about the door: I never hear a sound from the wall: I believe smoke never issues from the chimneys. What do you do there?'

'I sew, I read, I learn lessons.'

# Shirley

'Are you happy?'

'Should I be happier wandering alone in strange countries, as you wish to do?'

'Much happier, even if you did nothing but wander. Remember, however, that I shall have an object in view: but if you only went on and on, like some enchanted lady in a fairy tale, you might be happier than now. In a day's wandering, you would pass many a hill, wood, and water-course, each perpetually altering in aspect as the sun shone out or was overcast; as the weather was wet or fair, dark or bright. Nothing changes in Briarfield Rectory: the plaster of the parlour-ceilings, the paper on the walls, the curtains, carpets, chairs, are still the same.'

'Is change necessary to happiness?'

'Yes.'

'It is synonymous with it?'

'I don't know; but I feel monotony and death to be almost the same.'

Here Jessie spoke.

'Isn't she mad?' she asked.

'But, Rose,' pursued Caroline, 'I fear a wanderer's life, for me at least, would end like that tale you are reading, – in disappointment, vanity, and vexation of spirit.'

'Does "the Italian" so end?'

'I thought so when I read it.'

'Better to try all things and find all empty, than to try nothing and leave your life a blank. To do this is to commit the sin of him who buried his talent in a napkin – despicable sluggard!'

'Rose,' observed Mrs Yorke, 'solid satisfaction is only to be realized by doing one's duty.'

'Right, mother! And if my Master has given me ten talents, my duty is to trade with them, and make them ten talents more. Not in the dust of household drawers shall the coin be interred. I will *not* deposit it in a broken-spouted tea-pot, and shut it up in a china-closet among tea-things. I will *not* commit it to your work-table to be smothered in piles of woollen hose. I will *not* prison it in the linen-press to find shrouds among the sheets: and least of all, mother – (she got up from the floor) – least of all will I hide it in a tureen of cold potatoes, to be ranged with bread, butter, pastry, and ham on the shelves of the larder.'

She stopped – then went on: –

'Mother, the Lord who gave each of us our talents will come home some day, and will demand from all an account. The tea-pot, the old stocking-foot, the linen rag, the willow-pattern tureen, will yield up their barren deposit in many a house: suffer your daughters, at least, to put their money to the exchangers, that they may be enabled at the Master's coming to pay him his own with usury.'

'Rose, did you bring your sampler with you, as I told you?'

'Yes, mother.'

'Sit down, and do a line of marking.'

Rose sat down promptly, and wrought according to orders. After a busy pause of ten minutes, her mother asked –

'Do you think yourself oppressed now? A victim?'

'No, mother.'

'Yet, as far as I understood your tirade, it was a protest against all womanly and domestic employment.'

'You misunderstood it, mother. I should be sorry not to learn to sew: you do right to teach me, and to make me work.'

'Even to the mending of your brother's stockings and the making of sheets?'

'Yes.'

'Where is the use of ranting and spouting about it, then?'

'Am I to do nothing but that? I will do that, and then I will do more. Now, mother, I have said my say. I am twelve years old at present, and not till I am sixteen will I speak again about talents: for four years, I bind myself an industrious apprentice to all you can teach me.'

'You see what my daughters are, Miss Helstone,' observed Mrs Yorke: 'how precociously wise in their own conceits! "I would rather this – I prefer that;" such is Jessie's cuckoo-song: while Rose utters the bolder cry, "I *will*, and I will *not!*"'

'I render a reason, mother: besides, if my cry is bold, it is only heard once in a twelvemonth. About each birthday, the spirit moves me to deliver one oracle respecting my own instruction and management: I utter it and leave it; it is for you, mother, to listen or not.'

'I would advise all young ladies,' pursued Mrs Yorke, 'to study the characters of such children as they chance to meet with before they marry, and have any of their own; to consider well how they would like the responsibility of guiding the careless, the labour of persuading the stubborn, the constant burden and task of training the best.'

'But with love it need not be so very difficult,' interposed Caroline. 'Mothers love their children most dearly – almost better than they love themselves.'

'Fine talk! Very sentimental! There is the rough, practical part of life yet to come to you, young Miss!'

'But, Mrs Yorke, if I take a little baby into my arms – any poor woman's infant for instance, – I feel that I love that helpless thing quite peculiarly, though I am not its mother. I could do almost anything for it willingly, if it were delivered over entirely to my care – if it were quite dependent on me.'

'You *feel!* Yes! yes! I daresay, now: you are led a great deal by your *feelings,* and you think yourself a very sensitive, refined personage, no doubt. Are you aware that, with all these romantic ideas, you have managed to train your features into an habitually lackadaisical expression, better suited to a novel-heroine than to a woman who is to make her way in the real world, by dint of common sense?'

'No; I am not at all aware of that, Mrs Yorke.'

'Look in the glass just behind you. Compare the face you see there with that of any early-rising, hard-working milkmaid.'

'My face is a pale one, but it is *not* sentimental, and most milkmaids, however red and robust they may be, are more stupid and less practically fitted to make their way in the world than I am. I think more and more correctly than milkmaids in general do; consequently, where they would often, for want of reflection, act weakly, I, by dint of reflection, should act judiciously.'

'Oh, no! you would be influenced by your feelings. You would be guided by impulse.'

'Of course, I should often be influenced by my feelings: they were given me

# Shirley

to that end. Whom my feelings teach me to love, I *must* and *shall* love; and I hope, if ever I have a husband and children, my feelings will induce me to love them. I hope, in that case, all my impulses will be strong in compelling me to love.'

Caroline had a pleasure in saying this with emphasis: she had a pleasure in daring to say it in Mrs Yorke's presence. She did not care what unjust sarcasm might be hurled at her in reply: she flushed, not with anger, but excitement, when the ungenial matron answered, coolly, –

'Don't waste your dramatic effects. That was well said, – it was quite fine; but it is lost on two women – an old wife and an old maid: there should have been a disengaged gentleman present. Is Mr Robert nowhere hid behind the curtains, do you think, Miss Moore?'

Hortense, who during the chief part of the conversation had been in the kitchen superintending the preparations for tea, did not yet quite comprehend the drift of the discourse. She answered, with a puzzled air, that Robert was at Whinbury. Mrs Yorke laughed her own peculiar short laugh.

'Straightforward Miss Moore!' said she, patronizingly. 'It is like you to understand my question so literally, and answer it so simply. *Your* mind comprehends nothing of intrigue. Strange things might go on around you without your being the wiser: you are not of the class the world calls sharp-witted.'

These equivocal compliments did not seem to please Hortense. She drew herself up, puckered her black eyebrows, but still looked puzzled.

'I have ever been noted for sagacity and discernment from childhood,' she returned: for, indeed, on the possession of these qualities, she peculiarly piqued herself.

'You never plotted to win a husband, I'll be bound,' pursued Mrs Yorke; 'and you have not the benefit of previous experience to aid you in discovering when others plot.'

Caroline felt this kind language where the benevolent speaker intended she should feel it – in her very heart. She could not even parry the shafts: she was defenceless for the present: to answer would have been to avow that the cap fitted. Mrs Yorke, looking at her as she sat with troubled downcast eyes, and cheek burning painfully, and figure expressing in its bent attitude and unconscious tremor all the humiliation and chagrin she experienced, felt the sufferer was fair game. The strange woman had a natural antipathy to a shrinking, sensitive character – a nervous temperament: nor was a pretty, delicate, and youthful face a passport to her affections. It was seldom she met with all these obnoxious qualities combined in one individual: still more seldom she found that individual at her mercy, under circumstances in which she could crush her well. She happened, this afternoon, to be specially bilious and morose: as much disposed to gore as any vicious 'mother of the herd:' lowering her large head, she made a new charge.

'Your cousin Hortense is an excellent sister, Miss Helstone: such ladies as come to try their life's luck here, at Hollow's cottage, may, by a very little clever female artifice, cajole the mistress of the house, and have the game all in their own hands. You are fond of your cousin's society, I dare say, Miss?'

'Of which cousin's?'

'Oh, of the lady's *of course.*'

'Hortense is, and always has been, most kind to me.'

# Shirley

'Every sister, with an eligible single brother, is considered most kind by her spinster friends.'

'Mrs Yorke,' said Caroline, lifting her eyes slowly, their blue orbs at the same time clearing from trouble, and shining steady and full, while the glow of shame left her cheek, and its hue turned pale and settled: 'Mrs Yorke, may I ask what you mean?'

'To give you a lesson on the cultivation of rectitude: to disgust you with craft and false sentiment.'

'Do I need this lesson?'

'Most young ladies of the present day need it. You are quite a modern young lady – morbid, delicate, professing to like retirement; which implies, I suppose, that you find little worthy of your sympathies in the ordinary world. The ordinary world – every-day, honest folks – are better than you think them: much better than any bookish, romancing chit of a girl can be, who hardly ever puts her nose over her uncle, the parson's, garden-wall.'

'Consequently, of whom you know nothing. Excuse me, – indeed, it does not matter whether you excuse me or not – you have attacked me without provocation: I shall defend myself without apology. Of my relations with my two cousins, you are ignorant: in a fit of ill-humour, you have attempted to poison them by gratuitous insinuations, which are far more crafty and false than anything with which you can justly charge me. That I happen to be pale, and sometimes to look diffident, is no business of yours. That I am fond of books, and indisposed for common gossip, is still less your business. That I am a "romancing chit of a girl," is a mere conjecture on your part: I never romanced to you, nor to anybody you know. That I am the parson's niece is not a crime, though you may be narrow-minded enough to think it so. You dislike me: you have no just reason for disliking me; therefore keep the expression of your aversion to yourself. If at any time, in future, you evince it annoyingly, I shall answer even less scrupulously that I have done now.'

She ceased, and sat in white and still excitement. She had spoken in the clearest of tones, neither fast nor loud; but her silver accents thrilled the ear. The speed of the current in her veins was just then as swift as it was viewless.

Mrs Yorke was not irritated at the reproof, worded with a severity so simple, dictated by a pride so quiet. Turning coolly to Miss Moore, she said, nodding her cap approvingly –

'She has spirit in her, after all. Always speak as honestly as you have done just now,' she continued, 'and you'll do.'

'I repel a recommendation so offensive,' was the answer, delivered in the same pure key, with the same clear look. 'I reject counsel poisoned by insinuation. It is my right to speak as I think proper: nothing binds me to converse as you dictate. So far from always speaking as I have done just now, I shall never address any one in a tone so stern, or in language so harsh, unless in answer to unprovoked insult.'

'Mother, you have found your match,' pronounced little Jessie, whom the scene appeared greatly to edify. Rose had heard the whole with an unmoved face. She now said, –

'No: Miss Helstone is not my mother's match – for she allows herself to be vexed: my mother would wear her out in a few weeks. Shirley Keeldar manages

# Shirley

better. Mother, you have never hurt Miss Keeldar's feelings yet. She wears armour under her silk dress that you cannot penetrate.'

Mrs Yorke often complained that her children were mutinous. It was strange, that with all her strictness, with all her 'strong-mindedness,' she could gain no command over them: a look from their father had more influence with them than a lecture from her.

Miss Moore – to whom the position of witness to an altercation in which she took no part was highly displeasing, as being an unimportant secondary post – now, rallying her dignity, prepared to utter a discourse which was to prove both parties in the wrong, and to make it clear to each disputant that she had reason to be ashamed of herself, and ought to submit humbly to the superior sense of the individual then addressing her. Fortunately for her audience, she had not harangued above ten minutes, when Sarah's entrance with the tea-tray called her attention, first, to the fact of that damsel having a gilt comb in her hair, and a red necklace round her throat, and secondly, and subsequently to a pointed remonstrance, to the duty of making tea. After the meal, Rose restored her to good humour by bringing her guitar and asking for a song, and afterwards engaging her in an intelligent and sharp cross-examination about guitar-playing and music in general.

Jessie, meantime, directed her assiduities to Caroline. Sitting on a stool at her feet, she talked to her, first about religion and then about politics. Jessie was accustomed at home to drink in a great deal of what her father said on these subjects, and afterwards in company to retail, with more wit and fluency than consistency or discretion, his opinions, antipathies, and preferences. She rated Caroline soundly for being a member of the Established Church, and for having an uncle a clergyman. She informed her that she lived on the country, and ought to work for her living honestly, instead of passing a useless life, and eating the bread of idleness in the shape of tithes. Thence Jessie passed to a review of the Ministry at that time in office, and a consideration of its deserts. She made familiar mention of the names of Lord Castlereagh and Mr Perceval. Each of these personages she adorned with a character that might have separately suited Moloch and Belial. She denounced the war as wholesale murder, and Lord Wellington as a 'hired butcher.'

Her auditress listened with exceeding edification. Jessie had something of the genius of humour in her nature: it was inexpressibly comic to hear her repeating her sire's denunciations in his nervous northern Doric; as hearty a little Jacobin as ever pent a free mutinous spirit in a muslin frock and sash. Not malignant by nature, her language was not so bitter as it was racy, and the expressive little face gave a piquancy to every phrase which held a beholder's interest captive.

Caroline chid her when she abused Lord Wellington; but she listened delighted to a subsequent tirade against the Prince Regent. Jessie quickly read in the sparkle of her hearer's eye, and the laughter hovering round her lips, that at last she had hit on a topic that pleased. Many a time had she heard the fat 'Adonis of fifty' discussed at her father's breakfast-table, and she now gave Mr Yorke's comments on the theme – genuine as uttered by his Yorkshire lips.

But, Jessie, I will write about you no more. This is an autumn evening, wet and wild. There is only one cloud in the sky; but it curtains it from pole to pole. The wind cannot rest: it hurries sobbing over hills of sullen outline, colourless with twilight and mist. Rain has beat all day on that church-tower: it rises dark

# Shirley

from the stony enclosure of its graveyard: the nettles, the long grass, and the tombs all drip with wet. This evening reminds me too forcibly of another evening some years ago: a howling, rainy autumn evening too – when certain who had that day performed a pilgrimage to a grave new-made in a heretic cemetery, sat near a wood-fire on the hearth of a foreign dwelling. They were merry and social, but they each knew that a gap, never to be filled, had been made in their circle. They knew they had lost something whose absence could never be quite atoned for so long as they lived; and they knew that heavy falling rain was soaking into the wet earth which covered their lost darling; and that the sad, sighing gale was mourning above her buried head. The first warmed them; Life and Friendship yet blessed them; but Jessie lay cold, coffined, solitary, – only the sod screening her from the storm.

Mrs Yorke folded up her knitting, cut short the music-lesson and the lecture on politics, and concluded her visit to the cottage, at an hour early enough to ensure her return to Briarmains before the blush of sunset should quite have faded in heaven, or the path up the fields have become thoroughly moist with evening dew.

The lady and her daughters being gone, Caroline felt that she also ought to resume her scarf, kiss her cousin's cheek, and trip away homeward. If she lingered much later, dusk would draw on, and Fanny would be put to the trouble of coming to fetch her: it was both baking and ironing day at the Rectory, she remembered – Fanny would be busy. Still, she could not quit her seat at the little parlour-window. From no point of view could the West look so lovely as from that lattice with the garland of jessamine round it, whose white stars and green leaves seemed now but grey pencil outlines – graceful in form, but colourless in tint – against the gold incarnadined of a summer evening – against the fire-tinged blue of an August sky, at eight o'clock p.m.

Caroline looked at the wicket-gate, beside which holly-oaks spired up tall; she looked at the close hedge of privet and laurel fencing in the garden; her eyes longed to see something more than the shrubs, before they turned from that limited prospect: they longed to see a human figure, of a certain mould and height, pass the hedge and enter the gate. A human figure she at last saw – nay, two: Frederick Murgatroyd went by, carrying a pail of water; Joe Scott followed, dangling on his forefinger the keys of the mill. They were going to lock up the mill and stables for the night, and then betake themselves home.

'So must I,' thought Caroline, as she half rose and sighed.

'This is all folly – heart-breaking folly,' she added. 'In the first place, though I should stay till dark, there will be no arrival; because I feel in my heart, Fate has written it down in to-day's page of her eternal book, that I am not to have the pleasure I long for. In the second place, if he stepped in this moment, my presence here would be a chagrin to him, and the consciousness that it must be so would turn half my blood to ice. His hand would, perhaps, be loose and chill, if I put mine into it: his eyes would be clouded if I sought its beam. I should look up for that kindling, something I have seen in past days, when my face or my language, or my disposition had at some happy moment pleased him – I should discover only darkness. I had better go home.'

# Shirley

She took her bonnet from the table where it lay, and was just fastening the ribbon, when Hortense, directing her attention to a splendid bouquet of flowers in a glass on the same table, mentioned that Miss Keeldar had sent them that morning from Fieldhead; and went on to comment on the guests that lady was at present entertaining, on the bustling life she had lately been leading; adding divers conjectures that she did not very well like it, and much wonderment that a person who was so fond of her own way as the heiress, did not find some means of sooner getting rid of this cortège of relatives.

'But they say she actually will not let Mr Sympson and his family go,' she added: 'they wanted much to return to the south last week, to be ready for the reception of the only son, who is expected home from a tour. She insists that her cousin Henry shall come and join his friends here in Yorkshire. I daresay she partly does it to oblige Robert and myself.'

'How to oblige Robert and you?' inquired Caroline.

'Why, my child, you are dull. Don't you know – you must often have heard –'

'Please, ma'am,' said Sarah, opening the door, 'the preserves that you told me to boil in treacle – the congfiters, as you call them – is all burnt to the pan.'

'Les confitures! Elles sont brûlées? Ah, quelle négligence coupable! Couqine de cuisinière – fille insupportable!'

And Mademoiselle, hastily taking from a drawer a large linen apron, and tying it over her black apron, rushed 'éperdue' into the kitchen, whence – to speak truth – exhaled an odour of calcined sweets rather strong than savoury.

The mistress and maid had been in full feud the whole day, on the subject of preserving certain black cherries, hard as marbles, sour as sloes. Sarah held that sugar was the only orthodox condiment to be used in that process; Mademoiselle maintained – and proved it by the practice and experience of her mother, grandmother, and great-grandmother – that treacle, 'mélasse,' was infinitely preferable. She had committed an imprudence in leaving Sarah in charge of the preserving-pan, for her want of sympathy in the nature of its contents had induced a degree of carelessness in watching their confection, whereof the result was – dark and cindery ruin. Hubbub followed: high upbraiding, and sobs rather loud than deep or real.

Caroline, once more turning to the little mirror, was shading her ringlets from her cheek to smooth them under her cottage bonnet, certain that it would not only be useless but unpleasant to stay longer; when, on the sudden opening of the back-door, there fell an abrupt calm in the kitchen: the tongues were checked, pulled up as with bit and bridle. 'Was it – was it – Robert?' He often – almost always – entered by the kitchen-way on his return from market. No: it was only Joe Scott, who, having hemmed significantly thrice – every hem being meant as a lofty rebuke to the squabbling womankind – said, –

'Now, I thowt I heerd a crack?'

None answered.

'And,' he continued pragmatically, 'as t' maister's comed, and as he'll enter through this hoyle, I *considered* it desirable to step in and let ye know. A houseful o' women is nivver fit to be comed on wi' out warning. Here he is: walk forrard, sir. They war playing up queerly, but I think I've quietened 'em.'

Another person – it was now audible – entered. Joe Scott proceeded with his rebukes.

'What d'ye mean by being all i' darkness? Sarah, thou quean, canst t' not

751

light a candle? It war sundown an hour syne. He'll brak' his shins agean some o' yer pots, and tables, and stuff. Tak' tent o' this baking-bowl, sir; they've set it i' yer way, fair as if they did it i' malice.'

To Joe's observations succeeded a confused sort of pause, which Caroline, though she was listening with both her ears, could not understand. It was very brief: a cry broke it – a sound of surprise, followed by the sound of a kiss: ejaculations, but half articulate, succeeded.

'Mon Dieu! mon Dieu! Est-ce que je m'y attendais?' were the words chiefly to be distinguished.

'Et tu te portes toujours bien, bonne soeur?' inquired another voice – Robert's, certainly.

Caroline was puzzled. Obeying an impulse, the wisdom of which she had not time to question, she escaped from the little parlour, by way of leaving the coast clear, and running up-stairs took up a position at the head of the banisters, whence she could make further observations ere presenting herself. It was considerably past sunset now; dusk filled the passage, yet not such deep dusk but that she could presently see Robert and Hortense traverse it.

'Caroline! Caroline!' called Hortense, a moment afterwards, 'venez voir mon frère!'

'Strange!' commented Miss Helstone, 'passing strange! What does this unwonted excitement about such an everyday occurrence as a return from market portend? She has not lost her senses, has she? Surely the burnt treacle has not crazed her?'

She descended in a subdued flutter: yet more was she fluttered when Hortense seized her hand at the parlour-door, and leading her to Robert, who stood in bodily presence, tall and dark against the one window, presented her with a mixture of agitation and formality, as though they had been utter strangers, and this was their first mutual introduction.

Increasing puzzle! He bowed rather awkwardly, and turning from her with a stranger's embarrassment, he met the doubtful light from the window: it fell on his face, and the enigma of the dream (a dream it seemed) was at its height: she saw a visage like and unlike, – Robert, and not Robert.

'What is the matter?' said Caroline. 'Is my sight wrong? Is it my cousin?'

'Certainly, it is your cousin,' asserted Hortense.

Then who was this now coming through the passage, – now entering the room? Caroline, looking round, met a new Robert, – the real Robert, as she felt at once.

'Well,' said he, smiling at her questioning, astonished face, 'which is which?'

'Ah! this is *you!* was the answer.

He laughed. 'I believe it is *me:* and do you know who *he* is? You never saw him before; but you have heard of him.'

'It *can* be only one person; your brother, since it is so like you; my other cousin, Louis.'

'Clever little Œdipus! – you would have baffled the Sphynx!' – but now, see us together. Change places. Change again, to confuse her, Louis. – Which is the old love now, Lina?'

'As if it were possible to make a mistake when you speak! You should have told Hortense to ask. But you are not so much alike: it is only your height, your figure, and complexion that are so similar.'

# Shirley

'And I am Robert, am I not?' asked the new comer, making a first effort to overcome what seemed his natural shyness.

Caroline shook her head gently. A soft, expressive ray from her eye beamed on the real Robert: it said much.

She was not permitted to quit her cousins soon: Robert himself was peremptory in obliging her to remain. Glad, simple, and affable in her demeanour (glad for this night, at least), in light, bright spirits for the time, she was too pleasant an addition to the cottage circle to be willingly parted with by any of them. Louis seemed naturally rather a grave, still, retiring man, but the Caroline of this evening, which was not (as you know, reader) the Caroline of every day, thawed his reserve, and cheered his gravity soon. He sat near her, and talked to her. She already knew his vocation was that of tuition; she learned now he had for some years been the tutor of Mrs Sympson's son; that he had been travelling with him, and had accompanied him to the north. She inquired if he liked his post, but got a look in reply which did not invite or license further question. The look woke Caroline's ready sympathy: she thought it a very sad expression to pass over so sensible a face as Louis's: for he *had* a sensible face, – though not handsome, she considered, when seen near Robert's. She turned to make the comparison. Robert was leaning against the wall, a little behind her, turning over the leaves of a book of engravings, and probably listening, at the same time, to the dialogue between her and Louis.

'How could I think them alike?' she asked herself: 'I see now it is Hortense, Louis resembles, not Robert.'

And this was in part true: he had the shorter nose and longer upper-lip of his sister, rather than the fine traits of his brother: he had her mould of mouth and chin – all less decisive, accurate, and clear than those of the young mill-owner. His air, though deliberate and reflective, could scarcely be called prompt and acute. You felt, in sitting near and looking up at him, that a slower and probably a more benignant nature than that of the elder Moore shed calm on your impressions.

Robert – perhaps aware that Caroline's glance had wandered towards and dwelt upon him, though he had neither met nor answered it – put down the book of engravings, and approaching, took a seat at her side. She resumed her conversation with Louis, but, while she talked to him, her thoughts were elsewhere: her heart beat on the side from which her face was half-averted. She acknowledged a steady, manly, kindly air in Louis; but she bent before the secret power of Robert. To be so near him – though he was silent – though he did not touch so much as her scarf-fringe, or the white hem of her dress – affected her like a spell. Had she been obliged to speak to him *only*, it would have quelled – but, at liberty to address another, it excited her. Her discourse flowed freely: it was gay, playful, eloquent. The indulgent look and placid manner of her auditor encouraged her to ease; the sober pleasure expressed by his smile drew out all that was brilliant in her nature. She felt that this evening she appeared to advantage, and, as Robert was a spectator, the consciousness contented her: had he been called away, collapse would at once have succeeded stimulus.

But her enjoyment was not long to shine full-orbed: a cloud soon crossed it.

Hortense, who for some time had been on the move ordering supper, and was now clearing the little table of some books &c., to make room for the tray, called

Robert's attention to the glass of flowers, the carmine and snow and gold of whose petals looked radiant indeed by candlelight.

'They came from Fieldhead,' she said, 'intended as a gift to you, no doubt: we know who is the favourite there – not I, I'm sure.'

It was a wonder to hear Hortense jest; a sign that her spirits were at high-water mark indeed.

'We are to understand, then, that Robert is the favourite?' observed Louis.

'Mon cher,' replied Hortense, 'Robert – c'est tout ce qu'il y a de plus précieux au monde: à côté de lui, le reste du genre humain n'est que du rebut. N'ai-je pas raison, mon enfant?' she added, appealing to Caroline.

Caroline was obliged to reply, 'Yes' – and her beacon was quenched: her star withdrew, as she spoke.

'Et toi, Robert?' inquired Louis.

'When you shall have an opportunity, ask herself,' was the quiet answer. Whether he reddened or paled Caroline did not examine: she discovered it was late, and she must go home. Home she would go: not even Robert could detain her now.

# Chapter 24

## The Valley of the Shadow of Death

The future sometimes seems to sob a low warning of the events it is bringing us, like some gathering though yet remote storm, which, in tones of the wind, in flushings of the firmament, in clouds strangely torn, announces a blast strong to strew the sea with wrecks; or commissioned to bring in fog the yellow taint of pestilence, covering white Western isles with the poisoned exhalations of the East, dimming the lattices of English homes with the breath of Indian plague. At other times this Future bursts suddenly, as if a rock had rent, and in it a grave had opened, whence issues the body of one that slept. Ere you are aware, you stand face to face with a shrouded and unthought-of Calamity – a new Lazarus.

Caroline Helstone went home from Hollow's cottage in good health, as she imagined. On waking the next morning she felt oppressed with unwonted languor: at breakfast, at each meal of the following day, she missed all sense of appetite: palatable food was as ashes and sawdust to her.

'Am I ill?' she asked, and looked at herself in the glass. Her eyes were bright, their pupils dilated, her cheeks seemed rosier and fuller than usual. 'I look well; why can I not eat?'

She felt a pulse beat fast in her temples: she felt, too, her brain in strange activity: her spirits were raised; hundreds of busy and broken, but brilliant thoughts engaged her mind: a glow rested on them, such as tinged her complexion.

# Shirley

Now followed a hot, parched, thirsty, restless night. Towards morning one terrible dream seized her like a tiger: when she woke, she felt and knew she was ill.

How she had caught the fever (fever it was), she could not tell. Probably in her late walk home, some sweet, poisoned breeze, redolent of honey-dew and miasma, had passed into her lungs and veins, and finding there already a fever of mental excitement, and a languor of long conflict and habitual sadness, had fanned the spark to flame, and left a well-lit fire behind it.

It seemed, however, but a gentle fire: after two hot days and worried nights, there was no violence in the symptoms, and neither her uncle, nor Fanny, nor the doctor, nor Miss Keeldar, when she called, had any fear for her: a few days would restore her, every one believed.

The few days passed, and – though it was still thought it could not long delay – the revival had not begun. Mrs Pryor, who had visited her daily, – being present in her chamber one morning when she had been ill a fortnight – watched her very narrowly for some minutes: she took her hand, and placed her finger on her wrist; then, quietly leaving the chamber, she went to Mr Helstone's study. With him she remained closeted a long time – half the morning. On returning to her sick young friend, she laid aside shawl and bonnet: she stood a while at the bedside, one hand placed in the other, gently rocking herself to and fro, in an attitude and with a movement habitual to her. At last she said, –

'I have sent Fanny to Fieldhead to fetch a few things for me, such as I shall want during a short stay here: it is my wish to remain with you till you are better. Your uncle kindly permits my attendance: will it to yourself be acceptable, Caroline?'

'I am sorry you should take such needless trouble. I do not feel very ill, but I cannot refuse resolutely: it will be such comfort to know you are in the house, to see you sometimes in the room; but don't confine yourself on my account, dear Mrs Pryor. – Fanny nurses me very well.'

Mrs Pryor – bending over the pale little sufferer – was now smoothing the hair under her cap, and gently raising her pillow. As she performed these offices, Caroline, smiling, lifted her face to kiss her.

'Are you free from pain? Are you tolerably at ease?' was inquired in a low, earnest voice, as the self-elected nurse yielded to the caress.

'I think I am almost happy.'

'You wish to drink? Your lips are parched.'

She held a glass filled with some cooling beverage to her mouth.

'Have you eaten anything to-day, Caroline?'

'I cannot eat.'

'But soon your appetite will return: it *must* return: that is, I pray God it may!'

In laying her again on the couch, she encircled her in her arms; and while so doing, by a movement which seemed scarcely voluntary, she drew her to her heart, and held her close gathered an instant.

'I shall hardly wish to get well, that I may keep you always,' said Caroline.

Mrs Pryor did not smile at this speech: over her features ran a tremor, which for some minutes she was absorbed in repressing.

# Shirley

'You are more used to Fanny than to me,' she remarked, erelong. 'I should think my attendance must seem strange, officious?'

'No: quite natural, and very soothing. You must have been accustomed to wait on sick people, ma'am. You move about the room so softly, and you speak so quietly, and touch me so gently.'

'I am dexterous in nothing, my dear. You will often find me awkward, but never negligent.'

Negligent, indeed, she was not. From that hour, Fanny and Eliza became ciphers in the sick-room: Mrs Pryor made it her domain: she performed all its duties; she lived in it day and night. The patient remonstrated, – faintly, however, from the first, and not at all erelong: loneliness and gloom were now banished from her bedside; protection and solace sat there instead. She and her nurse coalesced in a wondrous union. Caroline was usually pained to require or receive much attendance: Mrs Pryor, under ordinary circumstances, had neither the habit nor the art of performing little offices of service; but all now passed with such ease – so naturally, that the patient was as willing to be cherished as the nurse was bent on cherishing: no sign of weariness in the latter ever reminded the former that she ought to be anxious. There was, in fact, no very hard duty to perform; but a hireling might have found it hard.

With all this care, it seemed strange the sick girl did not get well; yet such was the case: she wasted like any snow-wreath in thaw; she faded like any flower in drought. Miss Keeldar, on whose thoughts danger or death seldom intruded, had at first entertained no fears at all for her friend; but seeing her change and sink from time to time when she paid her visits, alarm clutched her heart. She went to Mr Helstone and expressed herself with so much energy, that that gentleman was at last obliged, however unwillingly, to admit the idea that his niece was ill of something more than a migraine; and when Mrs Pryor came and quietly demanded a physician, he said she might send for two, if she liked. One came, but that one was an oracle: he delivered a dark saying of which the future was to solve the mystery, wrote some prescriptions, gave some directions – the whole with an air of crushing authority – pocketed his fee, and went. Probably, he knew well enough he could do no good; but didn't like to say so.

Still, no rumour of serious illness got wind in the neighbourhood. At Hollow's-cottage it was thought that Caroline had only a severe cold, she having written a note to Hortense to that effect; and Mademoiselle contented herself with sending two pots of currant jam, a receipt for a tisane, and a note of advice.

Mrs Yorke being told that a physician had been summoned, sneered at the hypochondriac fancies of the rich and idle, who, she said, having nothing but themselves to think about, must needs send for a doctor if only so much as their little finger ached.

The 'rich and idle,' represented in the person of Caroline, were meantime falling fast into a condition of prostration, whose quickly consummated debility puzzled all who witnessed it, except one; for that one alone reflected how liable is the undermined structure to sink in sudden ruin.

Sick people often have fancies inscrutable to ordinary attendants, and Caroline had one which even her tender nurse could not at first explain. On a certain day in the week, at a certain hour, she would – whether worse or better – entreat to be taken up and dressed, and suffered to sit in her chair near the window.

# Shirley

This station she would retain till noon was past: whatever degree of exhaustion or debility her wan aspect betrayed, she still softly put off all persuasion to seek repose until the church-clock had duly tolled mid-day: the twelve strokes sounded, she grew docile, and would meekly lie down. Returned to the couch, she usually buried her face deep in the pillow, and drew the coverlets close round her, as if to shut out the world and sun, of which she was tired: more than once, as she thus lay, a slight convulsion shook the sick-bed, and a faint sob broke the silence round it. These things were not unnoted by Mrs Pryor.

One Tuesday morning, as usual, she had asked leave to rise, and now she sat wrapped in her white dressing-gown, leaning forward in the easy-chair, gazing steadily and patiently from the lattice. Mrs Pryor was seated a little behind, knitting as it seemed, but, in truth, watching her. A change crossed her pale mournful brow, animating its languor; a light shot into her faded eyes, reviving their lustre; she half rose and looked earnestly out. Mrs Pryor, drawing softly near, glanced over her shoulder. From this window was visible the churchyard, beyond it the road, and there, riding sharply by, appeared a horseman. The figure was not yet too remote for recognition: Mrs Pryor had long sight; she knew Mr Moore. Just as an intercepting rising ground concealed him from view, the clock struck twelve.

'May I lie down again?' asked Caroline.

Her nurse assisted her to bed: having laid her down and drawn the curtain, she stood listening near. The little couch trembled, the suppressed sob stirred the air. A contraction as of anguish altered Mrs Pryor's features; she wrung her hands; half a groan escaped her lips. She now remembered that Tuesday was Whinbury market-day: Mr Moore must always pass the Rectory on his way thither, just ere noon of that day.

Caroline wore continually round her neck a slender braid of silk, attached to which was some trinket. Mrs Pryor had seen the bit of gold glisten; but had not yet obtained a fair view of it. Her patient never parted with it: when dressed it was hidden in her bosom; as she lay in bed she always held it in her hand. That Tuesday afternoon the transient doze – more like lethargy than sleep – which sometimes abridged the long days, had stolen over her; the weather was hot: while turning in febrile restlessness, she had pushed the coverlets a little aside; Mrs Pryor bent to replace them; the small, wasted hand lying nerveless on the sick girl's breast, clasped as usual her jealously-guarded treasure: those fingers whose attenuation it gave pain to see, were now relaxed in sleep: Mrs Pryor gently disengaged the braid, drawing out a tiny locket – a slight thing it was, such as it suited her small purse to purchase: under its crystal face appeared a curl of black hair – too short and crisp to have been severed from a female head.

Some agitated movement occasioned a twitch of the silken chain: the sleeper started and woke. Her thoughts were usually now somewhat scattered on waking; her look general wandering. Half-rising, as if in terror, she exclaimed:

'Don't take it from me, Robert! Don't! It is my last comfort – let me keep it. I never tell any one whose hair it is – I never show it.'

Mrs Pryor had already disappeared behind the curtain: reclining far back in a deep arm-chair by the bedside, she was withdrawn from view. Caroline looked abroad into the chamber: she thought it empty. As her stray ideas returned slowly, each folding its weak wings on the mind's sad shore, like birds exhausted,

– beholding void, and perceiving silence round her, she believed herself alone. Collected, she was not yet: perhaps healthy self-possession and self-control were to be hers no more; perhaps that world the strong and prosperous live in had already rolled from beneath her feet for ever: so, at least, it often seemed to herself. In health, she had never been accustomed to think aloud; but now words escaped her lips unawares.

'Oh! I *should* see him once more before all is over: Heaven *might* favour me thus far!' she cried. 'God grant me a little comfort before I die!' was her humble petition.

'But he will not know I am ill, till I am gone; and he will come when they have laid me out, and I am senseless, cold, and stiff.

'What can my departed soul feel then? Can it see or know what happens to the clay? Can spirits, through any medium, communicate with living flesh? Can the dead at all revisit those they leave? Can they come in the elements? Will wind, water, fire, lend me a path to Moore?

'Is it for nothing the wind sounds almost articulately sometimes – sings as I have lately heard it sing at night – or passes the casement sobbing, as if for sorrow to come? Does nothing, then, haunt it – nothing inspire it?

'Why, it suggested to me words one night: it poured a strain which I could have written down, only I was appalled and dared not rise to seek pencil and paper by the dim watchlight.

'What is that electricity they speak of, whose changes make us well or ill; whose lack or excess blasts; whose even balance revives? What are all those influences that are about us in the atmosphere, that keep playing over our nerves like fingers on stringed instruments, and call forth now a sweet note, and now a wail – now an exultant swell, and, anon, the saddest cadence?

'*Where is* the other world? In *what* will another life consist? Why do I ask? Have I not cause to think that the hour is hasting but too fast when the veil must be rent for me? Do I not know the Grand Mystery is likely to burst prematurely on me? Great Spirit! in whose goodness I confide; whom, as my Father, I have petitioned night and morning from early infancy, help the weak creation of thy hands! Sustain me through the ordeal I dread and must undergo! Give me strength! Give me patience! Give me – oh! *give me* FAITH!'

She fell back on her pillow. Mrs Pryor found means to steal quietly from the room: she re-entered it soon after, apparently as composed as if she had really not overheard this strange soliloquy.

The next day several callers came. It had become known that Miss Helstone was worse. Mr Hall and his sister Margaret arrived; both, after they had been in the sick-room, quitted it in tears: they had found the patient more altered than they expected. Hortense Moore came. Caroline seemed stimulated by her presence: she assured her, smiling, she was not dangerously ill; she talked to her in a low voice, but cheerfully: during her stay, excitement kept up the flush of her complexion: she looked better.

'How is Mr Robert?' asked Mrs Pryor, as Hortense was preparing to take leave.

'He was very well when he left.'

'Left! Is he gone from home?'

It was then explained that some police intelligence about the rioters of whom

# Shirley

he was in pursuit, had, that morning, called him away to Birmingham, and probably a fortnight might elapse ere he returned.

'He is not aware that Miss Helstone is very ill?'

'Oh! no. He thought, like me, that she had only a bad cold.'

After this visit, Mrs Pryor took care not to approach Caroline's couch for above an hour: she heard her weep, and dared not look on her tears.

As evening closed in, she brought her some tea. Caroline, opening her eyes from a moment's slumber, viewed her nurse with an unrecognising glance.

'I smelt the honeysuckles in the glen this summer-morning,' she said, 'as I stood at the counting-house window.'

Strange words like these from pallid lips pierce a loving listener's heart more poignantly than steel. They sound romantic, perhaps, in books: in real life, they are harrowing.

'My darling, do you know me?' said Mrs Pryor.

'I went in to call Robert to breakfast: I have been with him in the garden: he asked me to go: a heavy dew has refreshed the flowers: the peaches are ripening.'

'My darling! my darling!' again and again repeated the nurse.

'I thought it was daylight – long after sunrise: it looks dark – is the moon not set?'

That moon, lately risen, was gazing full and mild upon her: floating in deep blue space, it watched her unclouded.

'Then it is not morning? I am not at the cottage? Who is this? – I see a shape at my bedside.'

'It is myself – it is your friend – your nurse – your –. Lean your head on my shoulder: collect yourself.' (In a lower tone.) 'Oh God, take pity! Give *her* life, and *me* strength! Send me courage – teach me words!'

Some minutes passed in silence. The patient lay mute and passive in the trembling arms – on the throbbing bosom of the nurse.

'I am better now,' whispered Caroline, at last, 'much better – I feel where I am: this is Mrs Pryor near me: I was dreaming – I talk when I wake up from dreams: people often do in illness. How fast your heart beats, ma'am! Do not be afraid.'

'It is not fear, child; only a little anxiety, which will pass. I have brought you some tea, Cary; your uncle made it himself. You know he says he can make a better cup of tea than any housewife can. Taste it. He is concerned to hear that you eat so little: he would be glad if you had a better appetite.'

'I am thirsty: let me drink.'

She drank eagerly.

'What o'clock is it, ma'am?' she asked.

'Past nine.'

'Not later? Oh! I have yet a long night before me; but the tea has made me strong: I will sit up.'

Mrs Pryor raised her, and arranged her pillows.

'Thank Heaven! I am not always equally miserable, and ill, and hopeless. The afternoon has been bad since Hortense went: perhaps the evening may be better. It is a fine night, I think? The moon shines clear.'

'Very fine: a perfect summer night. The old church-tower gleams white almost as silver.'

'And does the churchyard look peaceful?'

# Shirley

'Yes, and the garden also: dew glistens on the foliage.'

'Can you see many long weeds and nettles amongst the graves; or do they look turfy and flowery?'

'I see closed daisy-heads, gleaming like pearls on some mounds. Thomas has mown down the dock-leaves and rank grass, and cleared all away.

'I always like that to be done: it soothes one's mind to see the place in order: and, I dare say, within the church just now that moonlight shines as softly as in my room. It will fall through the east window full on the Helstone monument. When I close my eyes I seem to see poor papa's epitaph in black letters on the white marble. There is plenty of room for other inscriptions underneath.'

'William Farren came to look after your flowers this morning: he was afraid, now you cannot tend them yourself, they would be neglected. He has taken two of your favourite plants home to nurse for you.'

'If I were to make a will, I would leave William all my plants; Shirley my trinkets – except one, which must not be taken off my neck; and you, ma'am, my books.' (After a pause.) 'Mrs Pryor, I feel a longing wish for something.'

'For what, Caroline?'

'You know I always delight to hear you sing: sing me a hymn just now: sing that hymn which begins, –

> *"Our God, our help in ages past, –*
> *Our hope for years to come;*
> *Our shelter from the stormy blast;*
> *Our refuge, haven, home!"* '

Mrs Pryor at once complied.

No wonder Caroline liked to hear her sing: her voice, even in speaking, was sweet and silver-clear; in song, it was almost divine: neither flute nor dulcimer has tones so pure. But the tone was secondary compared to the expression which trembled through: a tender vibration from a feeling heart.

The servants in the kitchen, hearing the strain, stole to the stairfoot to listen: even old Helstone, as he walked in the garden, pondering over the unaccountable and feeble nature of women, stood still amongst his borders to catch the mournful melody more distinctly. Why it reminded him of his forgotten dead wife, he could not tell; nor why it made him more concerned than he had hitherto been for Caroline's fading girlhood. He was glad to recollect that he had promised to pay Wynne, the Magistrate, a visit that evening. Low spirits and gloomy thoughts were very much his aversion: when they attacked him he usually found means to make them march in double-quick time. The hymn followed him faintly as he crossed the fields: he hastened his customary sharp pace, that he might get beyond its reach.

> *'Thy word commands our flesh to dust, –*
> *"Return, ye sons of men:"*
> *All nations rose from earth at first,*
> *And turn to earth again.*

# Shirley

*'A thousand ages in thy sight*
*Are like an evening gone;*
*Short as the watch that ends the night*
*Before the rising sun.*

*'Time, like an ever-rolling stream,*
*Bears all its sons away;*
*They fly, forgotten, as a dream*
*Dies at the opening day.*

*'Like flowery fields, the nations stand,*
*Fresh in the morning light;*
*The flowers beneath the mower's hand*
*Lie withering ere 't is night.*

*'Our God, our help in ages past, –*
*Our hope for years to come;*
*Be thou our guard while troubles last, –*
*O Father, be our home!'*

'Now sing a song – a Scottish song,' suggested Caroline, when the hymn was over, – ' "Ye banks and braes o' bonny Doon." '

Again Mrs Pryor obeyed, or essayed to obey. At the close of the first stanza she stopped; she could get no further: her full heart flowed over.

'You are weeping at the pathos of the air: come here, and I will comfort you,' said Caroline, in a pitying accent. Mrs Pryor came: she sat down on the edge of her patient's bed, and allowed the wasted arms to encircle her.

'You often soothe me, let me soothe you,' murmured the young girl, kissing her cheek. 'I hope,' she added, 'it is not for me you weep?'

No answer followed.

'Do you think I shall not get better? I do not feel *very* ill – only weak.'

'But your mind, Caroline: your mind is crushed; your heart is almost broken: you have been so neglected, so repulsed, left so desolate.'

'I believe grief is, and always has been, my worst ailment. I sometimes think, if an abundant gush of happiness came on me, I could revive yet.'

'Do you wish to live?'

'I have no object in life.'

'You love me, Caroline?'

'Very much – very truly, – inexpressibly sometimes: just now, I feel as if I could almost grow to your heart.'

'I will return directly, dear,' remarked Mrs Pryor, as she laid Caroline down.

Quitting her, she glided to the door, softly turned the key in the lock, ascertained that it was fast, and came back. She bent over her. She threw back the curtain to admit the moonlight more freely. She gazed intently on her face.

'Then, if you love me,' said she, speaking quickly, with an altered voice: 'if you feel as if – to use your own words – you could "grow to my heart," it will be neither shock nor pain for you to know that *that* heart is the source whence yours was filled; that from *my* veins issued the tide which flows in *yours*; that you are *mine* – my daughter – my own child.'

# Shirley

'Mrs Pryor – !'

'My own child!'

'That is – that means – you have adopted me?'

'It means that, if I have given you nothing else, I at least gave you life; that I bore you – nursed you; that I am your true mother: no other woman can claim the title – it is *mine*.'

'But Mrs James Helstone – but my father's wife, whom I do not remember ever to have seen, she is my mother?'

'She *is* your mother: James Helstone was *my* husband. I say you are *mine*. I have proved it. I thought perhaps you were all his, which would have been a cruel dispensation for me: I find it is *not* so. God permitted me to be the parent of my child's mind: it belongs to me: it is my property – my *right*. These features are James's own. He had a fine face when he was young, and not altered by error. Papa, my darling, gave you your blue eyes and soft brown hair: he gave you the oval of your face and the regularity of your lineaments: the outside *he* conferred; but the heart and the brain are *mine:* the germs are from *me*, and they are improved, they are developed to excellence. I esteem and approve my child as highly as I do most fondly love her.'

'Is what I hear true? Is it no dream?'

'I wish it were as true that the substance and colour of health were restored to your cheek.'

'My own mother! is she the one I can be so fond of as I can of you? People generally did not like her, so I have been given to understand.'

'They told you that? Well, your mother now tells you, that, not having the gift to please people generally, for their approbation she does not care: her thoughts are centred in her child: does that child welcome or reject her?'

'But if you *are* my mother, the world is all changed to me. Surely I can live – I should like to recover –'

'You *must* recover. You drew life and strength from my breast when you were a tiny, fair infant, over whose blue eyes I used to weep, fearing I beheld in your very beauty the sign of qualities that had entered my heart like iron, and pierced through my soul like a sword. Daughter! we have been long parted: I return now to cherish you again.'

She held her to her bosom: she cradled her in her arms: she rocked her softly, as if lulling a young child to sleep.

'My mother! My own mother!'

The offspring nestled to the parent: that parent, feeling the endearment and hearing the appeal, gathered her closer still. She covered her with noiseless kisses: she murmured love over her, like a cushat fostering its young.

There was silence in the room for a long while.

'Does my uncle know?'

'Your uncle knows: I told him when I first came to stay with you here.'

'Did you recognise me when we first met at Fieldhead?'

'How could it be otherwise? Mr and Miss Helstone being announced, I was prepared to see my child.'

'It was that then which moved you: I saw you disturbed.'

'You saw nothing, Caroline, I can cover my feelings. You can never tell what

762

an age of strange sensation I lived, during the two minutes that elapsed between the report of your name and your entrance. You can never tell how your look, mien, carriage, shook me.'

'Why? Were you disappointed?'

'What will she be like? I had asked myself; and when I saw what you were like, I could have dropped.'

'Mamma, why?'

'I trembled in your presence. I said I will never own her: she shall never know me.'

'But I said and did nothing remarkable. I felt a little diffident at the thought of an introduction to strangers, that was all.'

'I soon saw you were diffident; that was the first thing which reassured me: had you been rustic, clownish, awkward, I should have been content.'

'You puzzle me.'

'I had reason to dread a fair outside, to mistrust a popular bearing, to shudder before distinction, grace and courtesy. Beauty and affability had come in my way when I was recluse, desolate, young, and ignorant: a toil-worn governess perishing of uncheered labour, breaking down before her time. These, Caroline, when they smiled on me, I mistook for angels! I followed them home, and when into their hands I had given without reserve my whole chance of future happiness, it was my lot to witness a transfiguration on the domestic hearth: to see the white mask lifted, the bright disguise put away, and opposite me sat down – oh God! I *have* suffered!'

She sank on the pillow.

'I *have* suffered! None saw – none knew: there was no sympathy – no redemption – no redress!'

'Take comfort, mother: it is over now.'

'It is over, and not fruitlessly. I tried to keep the word of His patience: He kept me in the days of my anguish. I was afraid with terror – I was troubled: through great tribulation He brought me through to a salvation revealed in this last time. My fear had torment – He has cast it out: He has given me in its stead perfect love . . . But, Caroline –'

Thus she invoked her daughter after a pause.

'Mother!'

'I charge you, when you next look on your father's monument, to respect the name chiselled there. To you he did only good. On you he conferred his whole treasure of beauties; nor added to them one dark defect. All *you* derived from him is excellent. You owe him gratitude. Leave, between him and me, the settlement of our mutual account: meddle not: God is the arbiter. This world's laws never came near us – never! They were powerless as a rotten bulrush to protect me! – impotent as idiot babblings to restrain him! As you said, it is all over now: the grave lies between us. There he sleeps – in that church! To his dust I say this night, what I have never said before, "James, slumber peacefully! See! your terrible debt is cancelled! Look! I wipe out the long, black account with my own hand! James, your child atones: this living likeness of you – this thing with your perfect features – this one good gift you gave me has nestled affectionately to my heart, and tenderly called me 'mother.' Husband! rest forgiven!"'

# Shirley

'Dearest mother, that is right! Can papa's spirit hear us? Is he comforted to know that we still love him?'

'I said nothing of love: I spoke of forgiveness. Mind the truth, child – I said nothing of love! On the threshold of eternity, should he be there to see me enter, will I maintain that.'

'Oh, mother! you must have suffered!'

'Oh, child! the human heart *can* suffer. It can hold more tears than the ocean holds waters. We never know how deep – how wide it is, till misery begins to unbind her clouds, and fill it with rushing blackness.'

'Mother, forget.'

'Forget!' she said, with the strangest spectre of a laugh. 'The north pole will rush to the south, and the headlands of Europe be locked into the bays of Australia ere I forget.'

'Hush, mother! rest! – be at peace!'

And the child lulled the parent, as the parent had erst lulled the child. At last, Mrs Pryor wept, she then grew calmer. She resumed those tender cares agitation had for a moment suspended. Replacing her daughter on the couch, she smoothed the pillow and spread the sheet. The soft hair whose locks were loosened, she rearranged, the damp brow she refreshed with a cool fragrant essence.

'Mamma, let them bring a candle, that I may see you; and tell my uncle to come into this room by-and-by: I want to hear him say that I am your daughter: and, mamma, take your supper here; don't leave me for one minute to-night.'

'Oh, Caroline! it is well you are gentle. You will say to me go, and I shall go; come, and I shall come; do this, and I shall do it. You inherit a certain manner as well as certain features. It will be always "mamma" prefacing a mandate: softly spoken though, from you, thank God! Well,' (she added, under her breath), 'he spoke softly too, once, – like a flute breathing tenderness; and then, when the world was not by to listen, discords that split the nerves and curdled the blood – sounds to inspire insanity.'

'It seems so natural, mamma, to ask you for this and that. I shall want nobody but you to be near me, or to do anything for me; but do not let me be troublesome: check me, if I encroach.'

'You must not depend on me to check you: you must keep guard over yourself. I have little moral courage: the want of it is my bane. It is that which has made me an unnatural parent – which has kept me apart from my child during the ten years which have elapsed since my husband's death left me at liberty to claim her: it was that which first unnerved my arms and permitted the infant I might have retained a while longer, to be snatched prematurely from their embrace.'

'How, mamma?'

'I let you go as a babe, because you were pretty, and I feared your loveliness; deeming it the stamp of perversity. They sent me your portrait, taken at eight years old; that portrait confirmed my fears. Had it shown me a sunburnt little rustic – a heavy, blunt-featured, commonplace child – I should have hastened to claim you; but, there, under the silver paper, I saw blooming the delicacy of an aristocratic flower – "little lady" was written on every trait. I had too recently crawled from under the yoke of the fine gentleman – escaped, galled, crushed, paralyzed, dying – to dare to encounter his still finer and most fairy-like representative. My sweet little lady overwhelmed me with dismay: her air of

native elegance froze my very marrow. In my experience I had not met with truth, modesty, good principle as the concomitants of beauty. A form so straight and fine, I argued, must conceal a mind warped and cruel. I had little faith in the power of education to rectify such a mind; or rather, I entirely misdoubted my own ability to influence it. Caroline, I dared not undertake to rear you: I resolved to leave you in your uncle's hands. Matthewson Helstone I knew, if an austere, was an upright man. He and all the world thought hardly of me for my strange, unmotherly resolve, and I deserved to be misjudged.'

'Mamma, why did you call yourself Mrs Pryor?'

'It was a name in my mother's family. I adopted it that I might live unmolested. My married name recalled too vividly my married life: I could not bear it. Besides, threats were uttered of forcing me to return to bondage: it could not be; rather a bier for a bed – the grave for a home. My new name sheltered me: I resumed under its screen my old occupation of teaching. At first, it scarcely procured me the means of sustaining life; but how savoury was hunger when I fasted in peace! How safe seemed the darkness and chill of an unkindled hearth, when no lurid reflection from terror crimsoned its desolation! How serene was solitude, when I feared not the irruption of violence and vice!'

'But, mamma, you have been in this neighbourhood before. How did it happen, that when you reappeared here with Miss Keeldar, you were not recognised?'

'I only paid a short visit, as a bride, twenty years ago; and then I was very different to what I am now – slender, almost as slender as my daughter is at this day: my complexion – my very features are changed; my hair, my style of dress – everything is altered. You cannot fancy me a slim young person, attired in scanty drapery of white muslin, with bare arms, bracelets and necklace of beads, and hair disposed in round Grecian curls above my forehead?'

'You must, indeed, have been different. Mamma, I heard the front door open: if it is my uncle coming in, just ask him to step up-stairs, and let me hear his assurance that I am truly awake and collected, and not dreaming or delirious.'

The Rector, of his own accord, was mounting the stairs; and Mrs Pryor summoned him to his niece's apartment.

'She's not worse, I hope?' he inquired, hastily.

'I think her better: she is disposed to converse – she seems stronger.'

'Good!' said he, brushing quickly into the room. 'Ha, Cary! how do? Did you drink my cup of tea? I made it for you just as I like it myself.'

'I drank it every drop, uncle: it did me good – it has made me quite alive. I have a wish for company, so I begged Mrs Pryor to call you in.'

The respected ecclesiastic looked pleased, and yet embarrassed. He was willing enough to bestow his company on his sick niece for ten minutes, since it was her whim to wish it; but what means to employ for her entertainment, he knew not: he hemmed – he fidgeted.

'You'll be up in a trice,' he observed, by way of saying something. 'The little weakness will soon pass off; and then you must drink port-wine – a pipe, if you can – and eat game and oysters: I'll get them for you, if they are to be had anywhere. Bless me! we'll make you as strong as Samson before we've done with you.'

'Who is that lady, uncle, standing beside you at the bedfoot?'

'Good God!' he ejaculated. 'She's not wandering – is she, ma'am?'

# Shirley

Mrs Pryor smiled.

'I am wandering in a pleasant world,' said Caroline, in a soft, happy voice, 'and I want you to tell me whether it is real or visionary. What lady is that? Give her a name, uncle?'

'We must have Dr Rile again, ma'am, or, better still, MacTurk: he's less of a humbug. Thomas must saddle the pony, and go for him.'

'No: I don't want a doctor; mamma shall be my only physician. Now, do you understand, uncle?'

Mr Helstone pushed up his spectacles from his nose to his forehead, handled his snuff-box, and administered to himself a portion of the contents. Thus fortified, he answered briefly: –

'I see daylight. You've told her then, ma'am?'

'And is it *true*?' demanded Caroline, rising on her pillow. 'Is she *really* my mother?'

'You won't cry, or make any scene, or turn hysterical, if I answer Yes?'

'Cry? I'd cry if you said *No*. It would be terrible to be disappointed now. But give her a name: how do you call her?'

'I call this stout lady in a quaint black dress, who looks young enough to wear much smarter raiment, if she would – I call her Agnes Helstone: she married my brother James, and is his widow.'

'And my mother?'

'What a little sceptic it is! Look at her small face, Mrs Pryor, scarcely larger than the palm of my hand, alive with acuteness and eagerness.' (To Caroline). – 'She had the trouble of bringing you into the world, at any rate: mind you show your duty to her by quickly getting well, and repairing the waste of these cheeks. Heigho! she used to be plump: what she has done with it all, I can't, for the life of me, divine.'

'If *wishing* to get well will help me, I shall not be long sick. This morning, I had no reason and no strength to wish it.'

Fanny here tapped at the door, and said that supper was ready.

'Uncle, if you please, you may send me a little bit of supper – anything you like, from your own plate. That is wiser than going into hysterics, – is it not?'

'It is spoken like a sage, Cary: see if I don't cater for you judiciously. When women are sensible – and, above all, intelligible – I can get on with them. It is only the vague, superfine sensations, and extremely wire-drawn notions, that put me about. Let a woman ask me to give her an edible or a wearable – be the same a roc's egg or the breastplate of Aaron, a share of St John's locusts and honey or the leathern girdle about his loins – I can, at least, understand the demand: but when they pine for they know not what – sympathy – sentiment – some of these indefinite abstractions – I can't do it: I don't know it; I haven't got it. Madam, accept my arm.'

Mrs Pryor signified that she should stay with her daughter that evening. Helstone, accordingly, left them together. He soon returned, bringing a plate in his own consecrated hand.

'This is chicken,' he said; 'but we'll have partridge to-morrow. Lift her up, and put a shawl over her. On my word, I understand nursing. Now, here is the very same little silver fork you used when you first came to the Rectory: that strikes me as being what you may call a happy thought – a delicate attention. Take it, Cary, and munch away cleverly.'

Caroline did her best. Her uncle frowned to see that her powers were so limited: he prophesied, however, great things for the future; and as she praised the morsel he had brought, and smiled gratefully in his face, he stooped over her pillow, kissed her, and said, with a broken, rugged accent, –

'Good-night, bairnie! God bless thee!'

Caroline enjoyed such peaceful rest that night, circled by her mother's arms, and pillowed on her breast, that she forgot to wish for any other stay; and though more than one feverish dream came to her in slumber, yet, when she woke up panting, so happy and contented a feeling returned with returning consciousness, that her agitation was soothed almost as soon as felt.

As to the mother, she spent the night like Jacob at Peniel. Till break of day, she wrestled with God in earnest prayer.

# Chapter 25

## The West Wind Blows

Not always do those who dare such divine conflict prevail. Night after night the sweat of agony may burst dark on the forehead; the supplicant may cry for mercy with that soundless voice the soul utters when its appeal is to the Invisible. 'Spare my beloved,' it may implore. 'Heal my life's life. Rend not from me what long affection entwines with my whole nature. God of heaven – bend – hear – be clement!' And after this cry and strife, the sun may rise and see him worsted. That opening morn, which used to salute him with the whisper of zephyrs, the carol of skylarks, may breathe, as its first accents, from the dear lips which colour and heat have quitted, –

'Oh! I have had a suffering night. This morning I am worse. I have tried to rise. I cannot. Dreams I am unused to have troubled me.'

Then the watcher approaches the patient's pillow, and sees a new and strange moulding of the familiar features, feels at once that the insufferable moment draws nigh, knows that it is God's will his idol shall be broken, and bends his head, and subdues his soul to the sentence he cannot avert, and scarce can bear.

Happy Mrs Pryor! She was still praying, unconscious that the summer sun hung above the hills, when her child softly woke in her arms. No piteous, unconscious moaning – sound which so wastes our strength that, even if we have sworn to be firm, a rush of unconquerable tears sweeps away the oath – preceded her waking. No space of deaf apathy followed. The first words spoken were not those of one becoming estranged from this world, and already permitted to stray at times into realms foreign to the living. Caroline evidently remembered with clearness what had happened.

'Mamma, I have slept *so* well. I only dreamed and woke twice.'

Mrs Pryor rose with a start, that her daughter might not see the joyful tears

called into her eyes by that affectionate word 'mamma,' and the welcome assurance that followed it.

For many days the mother dared rejoice only with trembling. That first revival seemed like the flicker of a dying lamp: if the flame streamed up bright one moment, the next it sank dim in the socket. Exhaustion followed close on excitement.

There was always a touching endeavour to *appear* better, but too often ability refused to second will; too often the attempt to bear up failed: the effort to eat, to talk, to look cheerful, was unsuccessful. Many an hour passed, during which Mrs Pryor feared that the chords of life could never more be strengthened, though the time of their breaking might be deferred.

During this space the mother and daughter seemed left almost alone in the neighbourhood. It was the close of August: the weather was fine – that is to say, it was very dry and very dusty, for an arid wind had been blowing from the east this month past: very cloudless, too, though a pale haze, stationary in the atmosphere, seemed to rob of all depth of tone the blue of heaven, of all freshness the verdure of earth, and of all glow the light of day. Almost every family in Briarfield was absent on an excursion. Miss Keeldar and her friends were at the sea-side; so were Mrs Yorke's household. Mr Hall and Louis Moore, between whom a spontaneous intimacy seemed to have arisen, the result, probably, of harmony of views and temperament, were gone 'up north' on a pedestrian excursion to the Lakes. Even Hortense, who would fain have stayed at home and aided Mrs Pryor in nursing Caroline, had been so earnestly entreated by Miss Mann to accompany her once more to Wormwood Wells, in the hope of alleviating sufferings greatly aggravated by the insalubrious weather, that she felt obliged to comply; indeed, it was not in her nature to refuse a request that at once appealed to her goodness of heart, and – by a confession of dependency – flattered her amour-propre. As for Robert, from Birmingham he had gone on to London, where he still sojourned.

So long as the breath of Asiatic deserts parched Caroline's lips and fevered her veins, her physical convalescence could not keep pace with her returning mental tranquillity: but there came a day when the wind ceased to sob at the eastern gable of the Rectory, and at the oriel window of the church. A little cloud like a man's hand arose in the west: gusts from the same quarter drove it on and spread it wide; wet and tempest prevailed a while. When that was over the sun broke out genially, heaven regained its azure, and earth its green: the livid cholera-tint had vanished from the face of nature: the hills rose clear round the horizon, absolved from that pale malaria-haze.

Caroline's youth could now be of some avail to her, and so could her mother's nurture: both – crowned by God's blessing, sent in the pure west wind blowing soft as fresh through the ever-open chamber lattice – rekindled her long-languishing energies. At last Mrs Pryor saw that it was permitted to hope – a genuine, material convalescence had commenced. It was not merely Caroline's smile which was brighter, or her spirits which were cheered, but a certain look had passed from her face and eye – a look dread and indescribable, but which will easily be recalled by those who have watched the couch of dangerous disease. Long before the emaciated outlines of her aspect began to fill, or its departed colour to return, a more subtle change took place: all grew softer and warmer. Instead of a marble mask and glassy eye, Mrs Pryor saw laid on the pillow a

face pale and wasted enough, perhaps more haggard than the other appearance, but less awful; for it was a sick, living girl – not a mere white mould, or rigid piece of statuary.

Now, too, she was not always petitioning to drink. The words 'I am *so* thirsty,' ceased to be her plaint. Sometimes, when she had swallowed a morsel, she would say it had revived her: all descriptions of food were no longer equally distasteful; she could be induced, sometimes, to indicate a preference. With what trembling pleasure and anxious care did not her nurse prepare what was selected! How she watched her as she partook of it!

Nourishment brought strength. She could sit up. Then she longed to breathe the fresh air, to revisit her flowers, to see how the fruit had ripened. Her uncle, always liberal, had bought a garden-chair for her express use: he carried her down in his own arms and placed her in it himself, and William Farren was there to wheel her round the walks, to show her what he had done amongst her plants, to take her directions for further work.

William and she found plenty to talk about: they had a dozen topics in common; interesting to them, unimportant to the rest of the world. They took a similar interest in animals, birds, insects, and plants: they held similar doctrines about humanity to the lower creation; and had a similar turn for minute observation on points of natural history. The nest and proceedings of some ground-bees, which had burrowed in the turf under an old cherry-tree, was one subject of interest: the haunts of certain hedge-sparrows, and the welfare of certain pearly eggs and callow fledglings, another.

Had 'Chambers' Journal' existed in those days, it would certainly have formed Miss Helstone's and Farren's favourite periodical. She would have subscribed for it; and to him each number would duly have been lent: both would have put implicit faith, and found great savour in its marvellous anecdotes of animal sagacity.

This is a digression; but it suffices to explain why Caroline would have no other hand than William's to guide her chair, and why his society and conversation sufficed to give interest to her garden-airings.

Mrs Pryor, walking near, wondered how her daughter could be so much at ease with a 'man of the people.' *She* found it impossible to speak to him otherwise than stiffly. She felt as if a great gulf lay between her caste and his; and that to cross it, or meet him half-way, would be to degrade herself. She gently asked Caroline, –

'Are you not afraid, my dear, to converse with that person so unreservedly? He may presume, and become troublesomely garrulous.'

'William presume, mamma? You don't know him. He never presumes: he is altogether too proud and sensitive to do so. William has very fine feelings.'

And Mrs Pryor smiled sceptically at the naïve notion of that rough-handed, rough-headed, fustian-clad clown having 'fine feelings.'

Farren, for his part, showed Mrs Pryor only a very sulky brow. He knew when he was misjudged, and was apt to turn unmanageable with such as failed to give him his due.

The evening restored Caroline entirely to her mother, and Mrs Pryor liked the evening; for then, alone with her daughter, no human shadow came between her and what she loved. During the day, she would have her stiff demeanour and cool moments, as was her wont. Between her and Mr Helstone a very

respectful but most rigidly ceremonious intercourse was kept up: anything like familiarity would have bred contempt at once in one or both these personages; but by dint of strict civility and well maintained distance, they got on very smoothly.

Towards the servants, Mrs Pryor's bearing was not uncourteous, but shy, freezing, ungenial. Perhaps it was diffidence rather than pride which made her appear so haughty; but, as was to be expected, Fanny and Eliza failed to make the distinction, and she was unpopular with them accordingly. She felt the effect produced: it rendered her at times dissatisfied with herself for faults she could not help; and with all else, dejected, chill, and taciturn.

This mood changed to Caroline's influence, and to that influence alone. The dependent fondness of her nursling, the natural affection of her child, came over her suavely: her frost fell away; her rigidity unbent: she grew smiling and pliant. Not that Caroline made any wordy profession of love – that would ill have suited Mrs Pryor: she would have read therein the proof of insincerity; but she hung on her with easy dependence; she confided in her with fearless reliance: these things contented the mother's heart.

She liked to hear her daughter say 'Mamma, do this.' 'Please, mamma, fetch me that.' 'Mamma, read to me.' 'Sing a little, mamma.'

Nobody else – not one living thing – had ever so claimed her services, so looked for help at her hand. Other people were always more or less reserved and stiff with her, as she was reserved and stiff with them; other people betrayed consciousness of, and annoyance at her weak points: Caroline no more showed such wounding sagacity or reproachful sensitiveness now, than she had done when a suckling of three months old.

Yet Caroline could find fault. Blind to the constitutional defects that were incurable, she had her eyes wide open to the acquired habits that were susceptible of remedy. On certain points she would quite artlessly lecture her parent; and that parent, instead of being hurt, felt a sensation of pleasure in discovering that the girl *dared* lecture her; that she was so much at home with her.

'Mamma, I am determined you shall not wear that old gown any more; its fashion is not becoming: it is too strait in the skirt. You shall put on your black silk every afternoon; in that you look nice: it suits you; and you shall have a black satin dress for Sundays – a real satin – not a satinet or any of the shams. And, mamma, when you get the new one, mind you must wear it.'

'My dear, I thought of the black silk serving me as a best dress for many years yet, and I wished to buy you several things.'

'Nonsense, mamma: my uncle gives me cash to get what I want: you know he is generous enough; and I have set my heart on seeing you in a black satin. Get it soon, and let it be made by a dressmaker of my recommending; let me choose the pattern. You always want to disguise yourself like a grandmother: you would persuade one that you are old and ugly, – not at all! On the contrary, when well dressed and cheerful, you are very comely indeed. Your smile is so pleasant, your teeth are so white, your hair is still such a pretty light colour. And then you speak like a young lady, with such a clear, fine tone, and you sing better than any young lady I ever heard. Why do you wear such dresses and bonnets, mamma, such as nobody else ever wears?'

'Does it annoy you, Caroline?'

'Very much: it vexes me even. People say you are miserly; and yet you are

# Shirley

not, for you give liberally to the poor and to religious societies: though your gifts are conveyed so secretly and quietly, that you are known to few except the receivers. But I will be your maid myself: when I get a little stronger I will set to work, and you must be good, mamma, and do as I bid you.'

And Caroline, sitting near her mother, rearranged her muslin handkerchief, and resmoothed her hair.

'My own mamma,' then she went on, as if pleasing herself with the thought of their relationship, 'who belongs to me, and to whom I belong! I am a rich girl now: I have something I can love well, and not be afraid of loving. Mamma, who gave you this little brooch? Let me unpin it and look at it.'

Mrs Pryor, who usually shrank from meddling fingers and near approach, allowed the licence complacently.

'Did papa give you this, mamma?'

'My sister gave it me – my only sister, Cary. Would that your aunt Caroline had lived to see her niece!'

'Have you nothing of papa's? – no trinket, no gift of his?'

'I have one thing.'

'That you prize?'

'That I prize.'

'Valuable and pretty?'

'Invaluable and sweet to me.'

'Show it, mamma. Is it here or at Fieldhead?'

'It is talking to me now, leaning on me: its arms are round me.'

'Ah, mamma! you mean your teasing daughter, who will never let you alone; who, when you go into your room, cannot help running to seek for you; who follows you up-stairs and down, like a dog.'

'Whose features still give me such a strange thrill sometimes. I half fear your fair looks yet, child.'

'You don't; you can't. Mamma, I am sorry papa was not good: I do so wish he had been. Wickedness spoils and poisons all pleasant things: it kills love. If you and I thought each other wicked, we could not love each other, could we?'

'And if we could not trust each other, Cary?'

'How miserable we should be! Mother, before I knew you, I had an apprehension that you were not good, that I could not esteem you: that dread damped my wish to see you; and now my heart is elate because I find you perfect, – almost; kind, clever, nice. Your sole fault is that you are old-fashioned, and of that I shall cure you. Mamma, put your work down: read to me. I like your southern accent: it is so pure, so soft. It has no rugged burr, no nasal twang, such as almost everyone's voice here in the north has. My uncle and Mr Hall say that you are a fine reader, mamma. Mr Hall said he never heard any lady read with such propriety of expression, or purity of accent.'

'I wish I could reciprocate the compliment, Cary; but really, the first time I heard your truly excellent friend read and preach, I could not understand his broad, northern tongue.'

'Could you understand me, mamma? Did I seem to speak roughly?'

'No: I almost wished you had, as I wished you had looked unpolished. Your father, Caroline, naturally spoke well; quite otherwise than your worthy uncle: correctly, gently, smoothly. You inherit the gift.'

'Poor papa! When he was so agreeable, why was he not good?'

'Why, he was *as* he was – and, happily, of that you, child, can form no conception – I cannot tell: it is a deep mystery. The key is in the hands of his Maker: there I leave it.'

'Mamma, you will keep stitching, stitching away: put down the sewing; I am an enemy to it. It cumbers your lap, and I want it for my head: it engages your eyes, and I want them for a book. Here is your favourite – Cowper.'

These importunities were the mother's pleasure. If ever she delayed compliance, it was only to hear them repeated, and to enjoy her child's soft, half-playful, half-petulant urgency. And then, when she yielded, Caroline would say, archly, –

'You will spoil me, mamma. I always thought I should like to be spoiled, and I find it very sweet.'

So did Mrs Pryor.

# Chapter 26

## Old Copy-Books

By the time the Fieldhead party returned to Briarfield, Caroline was nearly well. Miss Keeldar, who had received news by post of her friend's convalescence, hardly suffered an hour to elapse between her arrival at home and her first call at the Rectory.

A shower of rain was falling gently, yet fast, on the late flowers and russet autumn shrubs, when the garden-wicket was heard to swing open, and Shirley's well-known form passed the window. On her entrance, her feelings were evinced in her own peculiar fashion. When deeply moved, by serious fears or joys, she was not garrulous. The strong emotion was rarely suffered to influence her tongue; and even her eye refused it more than a furtive and fitful conquest. She took Caroline in her arms, gave her one look, one kiss, then said: –

'You are better.'

And a minute after, – 'I see you are safe now, but take care. God grant your health may be called on to sustain no more shocks!'

She proceeded to talk fluently about the journey. In the midst of vivacious discourse, her eye still wandered to Caroline: there spoke in its light a deep solicitude, some trouble, and some amaze.

'She may be better,' it said; 'but how weak she still is! What peril she has come through!'

Suddenly her glance reverted to Mrs Pryor: it pierced her through.

'When will my governess return to me?' she asked.

'May I tell her all?' demanded Caroline of her mother. Leave being signified by a gesture, Shirley was presently enlightened on what had happened in her absence.

'Very good!' was the cool comment. 'Very good! But it is no news to me.'

'What! Did you know?'

'I guessed long since the whole business. I have heard somewhat of Mrs Pryor's history – not from herself, but from others. With every detail of Mr James Helstone's career and character I was acquainted: an afternoon's sitting and conversation with Miss Mann had rendered me familiar therewith: also he is one of Mrs Yorke's warning-examples – one of the blood-red lights she hangs out to scare young ladies from matrimony. I believe I should have been sceptical about the truth of the portrait traced by such fingers – both these ladies take a dark pleasure in offering to view the dark side of life – but I questioned Mr Yorke on the subject, and he said, – "Shirley, my woman, if you want to know aught about yond' James Helstone, I can only say he was a man-tiger. He was handsome, dissolute, soft, treacherous, courteous, cruel –" Don't cry, Cary; we'll say no more about it.'

'I am not crying, Shirley; or if I am, it is nothing – go on: you are no friend if you withhold from me the truth: I hate that false plan of disguising, mutilating the truth.'

'Fortunately, I have said pretty nearly all that I have to say, except that your uncle himself confirmed Mr Yorke's words: for he too scorns a lie, and deals in none of those conventional subterfuges that are shabbier than lies.'

'But papa is dead: they should let him alone now.'

'They should – and we *will* let him alone. Cry away, Cary, it will do you good: it is wrong to check natural tears; besides, I choose to please myself by sharing an idea that at this moment beams in your mother's eye while she looks at you: every drop blots out a sin. Weep – your tears have the virtue which the rivers of Damascus lacked: like Jordan, they can cleanse a leprous memory.'

'Madam,' she continued, addressing Mrs Pryor, 'did you think I could be daily in the habit of seeing you and your daughter together – marking your marvellous similarity in many points – observing, pardon me – your irrepressible emotions in the presence and still more in the absence of your child, and not form my own conjectures? I formed them, and they are literally correct. I shall begin to think myself shrewd.'

'And you said nothing?' observed Caroline, who soon regained the quiet control of her feelings.

'Nothing. I had no warrant to breathe a word on the subject. *My* business it was not: I abstained from making it such.'

'You guessed so deep a secret, and did not hint that you guessed it?'

'Is that so difficult?'

'It is not like you.'

'How do you know?'

'You are not reserved. You are frankly communicative.'

'I may be communicative, yet know where to stop. In showing my treasure, I may withhold a gem or two – a curious, unbought, graven stone – an amulet, of whose mystic glitter I rarely permit even myself a glimpse. Good-day.'

Caroline thus seemed to get a view of Shirley's character under a novel aspect. Erelong, the prospect was renewed: it opened upon her.

No sooner had she regained sufficient strength to bear a change of scene – the excitement of a little society – than Miss Keeldar sued daily for her presence at Fieldhead. Whether Shirley had become wearied of her honoured relatives

# Shirley

is not known: she did not say she was; but she claimed and retained Caroline with an eagerness which proved that an addition to that worshipful company was not unwelcome.

The Sympsons were Church people: of course, the Rector's niece was received by them with courtesy. Mr Sympson proved to be a man of spotless respectability, worrying temper, pious principles, and worldly views; his lady was a very good woman, patient, kind, well-bred. She had been brought up on a narrow system of views – starved on a few prejudices: a mere handful of bitter herbs; a few preferences, soaked till their natural flavour was extracted, and with no seasoning added in the cooking; some excellent principles, made up in a stiff raised-crust of bigotry, difficult to digest: far too submissive was she to complain of this diet, or to ask for a crumb beyond it.

The daughters were an example to their sex. They were tall, with a Roman nose a-piece. They had been educated faultlessly. All they did was well done. History, and the most solid books, had cultivated their minds. Principles and opinions they possessed which could not be mended. More exactly-regulated lives, feelings, manners, habits, it would have been difficult to find anywhere. They knew by heart a certain young-ladies'-school-room code of laws on language, demeanour, &c.; themselves never deviated from its curious little pragmatical provisions; and they regarded with secret, whispered horror, all deviations in others. The Abomination of Desolation was no mystery to them: they had discovered that unutterable Thing in the characteristic others call Originality. Quick were they to recognize the signs of this evil; and wherever they saw its trace – whether in look, word, or deed; whether they read it in the fresh, vigorous style of a book, or listened to it in interesting, unhackneyed, pure, expressive language – they shuddered – they recoiled: danger was above their heads – peril about their steps. What was this strange Thing? Being unintelligible, it must be bad. Let it be denounced and chained up.

Henry Sympson – the only son, and youngest child of the family – was a boy of fifteen. He generally kept with his tutor; when he left him, he sought his cousin Shirley. This boy differed from his sisters: he was little, lame, and pale; his large eyes shone somewhat languidly in a wan orbit: they were, indeed, usually rather dim – but they were capable of illumination: at times, they could not only shine, but blaze: inward emotion could likewise give colour to his cheek and decision to his crippled movements. Henry's mother loved him; she thought his peculiarities were a mark of election: he was not like other children, she allowed; she believed him regenerate – a new Samuel – called of God from his birth: he was to be a clergyman. Mr and Misses Sympson, not understanding the youth, let him much alone. Shirley made him her pet; and he made Shirley his playmate.

In the midst of this family-circle – or rather outside it – moved the tutor – the satellite.

Yes: Louis Moore was a satellite of the house of Sympson: connected, yet apart; ever attendant – ever distant. Each member of that correct family treated him with proper dignity. The father was austerely civil, sometimes irritable; the mother, being a kind woman, was attentive, but formal; the daughters saw in him an abstraction, not a man. It seemed, by their manner, that their brother's tutor did not live for them. They were learned: so was he – but not for them. They were accomplished: he had talents too, imperceptible to their senses. The

# Shirley

most spirited sketch from his fingers was a blank to their eyes; the most original observation from his lips fell unheard on their ears. Nothing could exceed the propriety of their behaviour.

I should have said, nothing could have equaled it; but I remembered a fact which strangely astonished Caroline Helstone. It was – to discover that her cousin had absolutely *no* sympathizing friend at Fieldhead: that to Miss Keeldar he was as much a mere teacher, as little a gentleman, as little a man, as to the estimable Misses Sympson.

What had befallen the kind-hearted Shirley that she should be so indifferent to the dreary position of a fellow-creature thus isolated under her roof? She was not, perhaps, haughty to him, but she never noticed him: she let him alone. He came and went, spoke or was silent, and she rarely recognized his existence.

As to Louis Moore himself, he had the air of a man used to this life, and who had made up his mind to bear it for a time. His faculties seemed walled up in him, and were unmurmuring in their captivity. He never laughed; he seldom smiled; he was uncomplaining. He fulfilled the round of his duties scrupulously. His pupil loved him; he asked nothing more than civility from the rest of the world. It even appeared that he would accept nothing more: in that abode at least; for when his cousin Caroline made gentle overtures of friendship, he did not encourage them; he rather avoided than sought her. One living thing alone, besides his pale, crippled scholar, he fondled in the house, and that was the ruffianly Tartar; who, sullen and impracticable to others, acquired a singular partiality for him: a partiality so marked that sometimes, when Moore, summoned to a meal, entered the room and sat down unwelcomed, Tartar would rise from his lair at Shirley's feet, and betake himself to the taciturn tutor. Once – but once – she noticed the desertion; and holding out her white hand, and speaking softly, tried to coax him back. Tartar looked, slavered, and sighed, as his manner was, but yet disregarded the invitation, and coolly settled himself on his haunches at Louis Moore's side. That gentleman drew the dog's big, black-muzzled head on to his knee, patted him, and smiled one little smile to himself.

An acute observer might have remarked, in the course of the same evening, that after Tartar had resumed his allegiance to Shirley, and was once more couched near her foot-stool, the audacious tutor by one word and gesture fascinated him again. He pricked up his ears at the word; he started erect at the gesture, and came, with head lovingly depressed, to receive the expected caress: as it was given, the significant smile again rippled across Moore's quiet face.

'Shirley,' said Caroline one day, as they two were sitting alone in the summer-house, 'did you know that my cousin Louis was tutor in your uncle's family before the Sympsons came down here?'

Shirley's reply was not so prompt as her responses usually were, but at last she answered, –

'Yes, – of course: I knew it well.'

'I thought you must have been aware of the circumstance.'

'Well! what then?'

'It puzzles me to guess how it chanced that you never mentioned it to me.'

'Why should it puzzle you?'          •

# Shirley

'It seems odd. I cannot account for it. You talk a great deal, – you talk freely. How was that circumstance never touched on?'

'Because it never was,' and Shirley laughed.

'You are a singular being!' observed her friend: 'I thought I knew you quite well: I begin to find myself mistaken. You were silent as the grave about Mrs Pryor; and now, again, here is another secret. But why you made it a secret is the mystery to me.'

'I never made it a secret: I had no reason for so doing. If you had asked me who Henry's tutor was, I would have told you: besides, I thought you knew.'

'I am puzzled about more things than one in this matter: you don't like poor Louis, – why? Are you impatient at what you perhaps consider his *servile* position? Do you wish that Robert's brother were more highly placed?'

'Robert's brother, indeed!' was the exclamation, uttered in a tone like the accents of scorn; and, with a movement of proud impatience, Shirley snatched a rose from a branch peeping through the open lattice.

'Yes,' repeated Caroline, with mild firmness; 'Robert's brother. He *is* thus closely related to Gérard Moore of the Hollow, though nature has not given him features so handsome, or an air so noble as his kinsman; but his blood is as good, and he is as much a gentleman, were he free.'

'Wise, humble, pious Caroline!' exclaimed Shirley, ironically. 'Men and angels, hear her! We should not despise plain features, nor a laborious yet honest occupation, should we? Look at the subject of your panegyric, – he is there in the garden,' she continued, pointing through an aperture in the clustering creepers; and by that aperture Louis Moore was visible, coming slowly down the walk.

'He is not ugly, Shirley,' pleaded Caroline; 'he is not ignoble; he is sad: silence seals his mind; but I believe him to be intelligent; and be certain, if he had not something very commendable in his disposition, Mr Hall would never seek his society as he does.'

Shirley laughed: she laughed again; each time with a slightly sarcastic sound. 'Well, well,' was her comment. 'On the plea of the man being Cyril Hall's friend and Robert Moore's brother, we'll just tolerate his existence – won't we, Cary? You believe him to be intelligent, do you? Not quite an idiot – eh? Something commendable in his disposition! id est, not an absolute ruffian. Good! Your representations have weight with me; and to prove that they have, should he come this way I will speak to him.'

He approached the summer-house: unconscious that it was tenanted, he sat down on the step. Tartar, now his customary companion, had followed him, and he couched across his feet.

'Old boy!' said Louis, pulling his tawny ear, or rather the mutilated remains of that organ, torn and chewed in a hundred battles, 'the autumn sun shines as pleasantly on us as on the fairest and richest. This garden is none of ours, but we enjoy its greenness and perfume, don't we?'

He sat silent, still caressing Tartar, who slobbered with exceeding affection. A faint twittering commenced among the trees round: something fluttered down as light as leaves: they were little birds, which lighting on the sward at shy distance, hopped as if expectant.

'The small brown elves actually remember that I fed them the other day,'

# Shirley

again soliloquized Louis. 'They want some more biscuit: today, I forgot to save a fragment. Eager little sprites, I have not a crumb for you.'

He put his hand in his pocket and drew it out empty.

'A want easily supplied,' whispered the listening Miss Keeldar.

She took from her reticule a morsel of sweet-cake: for that repository was never destitute of something available to throw to the chickens, young ducks, or sparrows; she crumbled it, and bending over his shoulder, put the crumbs into his hand.

'There,' said she; 'there is a Providence for the improvident.'

'This September afternoon is pleasant,' observed Louis Moore, as – not at all discomposed – he calmly cast the crumbs on to the grass.

'Even for you?'

'As pleasant for me as for any monarch.'

'You take a sort of harsh, solitary triumph in drawing pleasure out of the elements, and the inanimate and lower animate creation.'

'Solitary, but not harsh. With animals I feel I am Adam's son; the heir of him to whom dominion was given over "every living thing that moveth upon the earth." Your dog likes and follows me; when I go into that yard, the pigeons from your dove-cot flutter at my feet; your mare in the stable knows me as well as it knows you, and obeys me better.'

'And my roses smell sweet to you, and my trees give you shade.'

'And,' continued Louis, 'no caprice can withdraw these pleasures from me: they are *mine*.'

He walked off: Tartar followed him, as if in duty and affection bound, and Shirley remained standing on the summer-house step. Caroline saw her face as she looked after the rude tutor: it was pale, as if her pride bled inwardly.

'You see,' remarked Caroline, apologetically, 'his feelings are so often hurt, it makes him morose.'

'You see,' retorted Shirley, with ire, 'he is a topic on which you and I shall quarrel if we discuss it often; so drop it henceforward and for ever.'

'I suppose he has more than once behaved in this way,' thought Caroline to herself; 'and that renders Shirley so distant to him: yet I wonder she cannot make allowance for character and circumstances: I wonder the general modesty, manliness, sincerity of his nature, do not plead with her in his behalf. She is not often so inconsiderate – so irritable.'

The verbal testimony of two friends of Caroline's to her cousin's character augmented her favourable opinion of him. William Farren, whose cottage he had visited in company with Mr Hall, pronounced him a 'real gentleman:' there was not such another in Briarfield: he – William – 'could do aught for that man. And then to see how t' bairns liked him, and how t' wife took to him first minute she saw him: he never went into a house but t' childer wor about him directly: them little things wor like as if they'd a keener sense nor grown-up folks i' finding out folk's natures.'

Mr Hall, in answer to a question of Miss Helstone's, as to what he thought of Louis Moore, replied promptly, that he was the best fellow he had met with since he left Cambridge.

'But he is so grave,' objected Caroline.

# Shirley

'Grave! The finest company in the world! Full of odd, quiet, out-of-the-way humour. Never enjoyed an excursion so much in my life as the one I took with him to the Lakes. His understanding and tastes are so superior, it does a man good to be within their influence; and as to his temper and nature, I call them fine.'

'At Fieldhead he looks gloomy, and, I believe, has the character of being misanthropical.'

'Oh! I fancy he is rather out of place there – in a false position. The Sympsons are most estimable people, but not the folks to comprehend him: they think a great deal about form and ceremony, which are quite out of Louis's way.'

'I don't think Miss Keeldar likes him.'

'She doesn't know him – she doesn't know him; otherwise, she has sense enough to do justice to his merits.'

'Well, I suppose she doesn't know him,' mused Caroline to herself, and by this hypothesis she endeavoured to account for what seemed else unaccountable. But such simple solution of the difficulty was not left her long: she was obliged to refuse Miss Keeldar even this negative excuse for her prejudice.

One day she chanced to be in the school-room with Henry Sympson, whose amiable and affectionate disposition had quickly recommended him to her regard. The boy was busied about some mechanical contrivance: his lameness made him fond of sedentary occupation: he began to ransack his tutor's desk for a piece of wax, or twine, necessary to his work. Moore happened to be absent. Mr Hall, indeed, had called for him to take a long walk. Henry could not immediately find the object of his search: he rummaged compartment after compartment; and, at last opening an inner drawer, he came upon – not a ball of cord, or a lump of bees' wax – but a little bundle of small marble-coloured cahiers, tied with tape. Henry looked at them: –

'What rubbish Mr Moore stores up in his desk!' he said: 'I hope he won't keep my old exercises so carefully.'

'What is it?'

'Old copy-books.'

He threw the bundle to Caroline. The packet looked so neat externally, her curiosity was excited to see its contents.

'If they are only copy-books, I suppose I may open them?'

'Oh! yes; quite freely. Mr Moore's desk is half mine – for he lets me keep all sorts of things in it – and I give you leave.'

On scrutiny they proved to be French compositions, written in a hand peculiar but compact, and exquisitely clean and clear. The writing was recognizable: she scarcely needed the further evidence of the name signed at the close of each theme, to tell her whose they were. Yet that name astonished her: 'Shirley Keeldar, Sympson Grove, —shire' (a southern county), and a date four years back.

She tied up the packet, and held it in her hand, meditating over it. She half felt as if, in opening it, she had violated a confidence.

'They are Shirley's, you see,' said Henry, carelessly.

'Did *you* give them to Mr Moore? She wrote them with Mrs Pryor, I suppose?'

'She wrote them in my school-room at Sympson Grove, when she lived with us there. Mr Moore taught her French: it is his native language.'

778

# Shirley

'I know ... Was she a good pupil, Henry?'

'She was a wild, laughing thing, but pleasant to have in the room: she made lesson-time charming. She learned fast – you could hardly tell when or how. French was nothing to her: she spoke it quick – quick; as quick as Mr Moore himself.'

'Was she obedient? Did she give trouble?'

'She gave plenty of trouble in a way: she was giddy, but I liked her. I'm desperately fond of Shirley.'

'*Desperately* fond – you small simpleton! You don't know what you say.'

'I *am desperately* fond of her: she is the light of my eyes: I said so to Mr Moore last night.'

'He would reprove you for speaking with exaggeration.'

'He didn't. He never reproves and reproves, as girls' governesses do. He was reading, and he only smiled into his book, and said that if Miss Keeldar was no more than that, she was less than he took her to be; for I was but a dim-eyed, short-sighted little chap. I'm afraid I am a poor unfortunate, Miss Caroline Helstone. I am a cripple, you know.'

'Never mind, Henry, you are a very nice little fellow; and if God has not given you health and strength, he has given you a good disposition, and an excellent heart and brain.'

'I shall be despised. I sometimes think both Shirley and you despise me.'

'Listen, Henry. Generally, I don't like school-boys: I have a great horror of them. They seem to me little ruffians, who take an unnatural delight in killing and tormenting birds, and insects, and kittens, and whatever is weaker than themselves; but you are so different, I am quite fond of you. You have almost as much sense as a man (far more, God wot,' she muttered to herself, 'than many men); you are fond of reading, and you can talk sensibly about what you read.'

'I *am* fond of reading. I know I have sense, and I know I have feeling.'

Miss Keeldar here entered.

'Henry,' she said, ' I have brought your lunch here: I shall prepare it for you myself.'

She placed on the table a glass of new milk, a plate of something which looked not unlike leather, and a utensil which resembled a toasting-fork.

'What are you two about,' she continued, 'ransacking Mr Moore's desk?'

'Looking at your old copy-books,' returned Caroline.

'My old copy-books?'

'French exercise-books. Look here! They must be held precious: they are kept carefully.'

She showed the bundle. Shirley snatched it up:

'Did not know one was in existence,' she said. 'I thought the whole lot had long since lit the kitchen-fire, or curled the maid's hair at Sympson Grove. What made you keep them, Henry?'

'It is not my doing: I should not have thought of it: it never entered my head to suppose copy-books of value. Mr Moore put them by in the inner drawer of his desk: perhaps he forgot them.'

'C'est cela: he forgot them, no doubt,' echoed Shirley. 'They are extremely well written,' she observed, complacently.

'What a giddy girl you were, Shirley, in those days! I remember you so well:

# Shirley

a slim, light creature whom, though you were so tall, I could lift off the floor. I see you with your long, countless curls on your shoulders, and your streaming sash. You used to make Mr Moore lively, that is, at first: I believe you grieved him after a while.'

Shirley turned the closely-written pages and said nothing. Presently she observed, 'That was written one winter afternoon. It was a description of a snow-scene.'

'I remember,' said Henry; 'Mr Moore, when he read it, cried "Voilà le Français gagné!" He said it was well done. Afterwards you made him draw, in sepia, the landscape you described.'

'You have not forgotten then, Hal?'

'Not at all. We were all scolded that day for not coming down to tea when called. I can remember my tutor sitting at his easel, and you standing behind him, holding the candle, and watching him draw the snowy cliff, the pine, the deer couched under it, and the half-moon hung above.'

'Where are his drawings, Harry? Caroline should see them.'

'In his portfolio; but it is padlocked: he has the key.'

'Ask him for it when he comes in.'

'You should ask him, Shirley; you are shy of him now: you are grown a proud lady to him, I noticed that.'

'Shirley, you are a real enigma,' whispered Caroline in her ear. 'What queer discoveries I make day by day now! I, who thought I had your confidence. Inexplicable creature! even this boy reproves you.'

'I have forgotten "Auld Langsyne," you see, Harry,' said Miss Keeldar, answering young Sympson, and not heeding Caroline.

'Which you never should have done. You don't deserve to be a man's morning star, if you have so short a memory.'

'A man's morning star indeed! and by "a man" is meant your worshipful self, I suppose? Come, drink your new milk while it is warm.'

The young cripple rose and limped towards the fire: he had left his crutch near the mantel-piece.

'My poor lame darling!' murmured Shirley, in her softest voice, aiding him.

'Whether do you like me or Mr Sam Wynne best, Shirley?' inquired the boy, as she settled him in an arm chair.

'Oh, Harry! Sam Wynne is my aversion: you are my pet.'

'Me or Mr Malone?'

'You again, a thousand times.'

'Yet, they are great whiskered fellows, six feet high each.'

'Whereas, as long as you live, Harry, you will never be anything more than a little pale lameter.'

'Yes, I know.'

'You need not be sorrowful. Have I not often told you who was almost as little, as pale, as suffering as you, and yet potent as a giant, and brave as a lion?'

'Admiral Horatio?'

'Admiral Horatio, Viscount Nelson, and Duke of Bronti; great at heart as a Titan; gallant and heroic as all the world and age of chivalry; leader of the might of England; commander of her strength on the deep; hurler of her thunder over the flood.'

'A great man: but I am not warlike, Shirley: and yet my mind is so restless,

# Shirley

I burn day and night – for what – I can hardly tell – to be – to do – to suffer, I think.'

'Harry, it is your mind, which is stronger and older than your frame, that troubles you. It is a captive. It lies in physical bondage. But it will work its own redemption yet. Study carefully, not only books but the world. You love nature; love her without fear. Be patient – wait the course of time. You will not be a soldier or a sailor, Henry: but, if you live, you will be – listen to my prophecy – you will be an author – perhaps, a poet.'

'An author! It is a flash – a flash of light to me! I will – I *will*! I'll write a book that I may dedicate it to you.'

'You will write it, that you may give your soul its natural release. Bless me! what am I saying? more than I understand, I believe, or can make good. Here, Hal; here is your toasted oat-cake – eat and live!'

'Willingly!' Here cried a voice outside the open window, 'I know that fragrance of meal bread. Miss Keeldar, may I come in and partake?'

'Mr Hall' (it was Mr Hall, and with him was Louis Moore, returned from their walk), 'there is a proper luncheon laid out in the dining-room, and there are proper people seated round it: you may join that society and share that fare if you please; but if your ill-regulated tastes lead you to prefer ill-regulated proceedings, step in here, and do as we do.'

'I approve the perfume, and therefore shall suffer myself to be led by the nose,' returned Mr Hall, who presently entered, accompanied by Louis Moore. That gentleman's eye fell on his desk, pillaged.

'Burglars!' said he. 'Henry, you merit the ferule.'

'Give it to Shirley and Caroline – they did it,' was alleged with more attention to effect than truth.

'Traitor and false witness!' cried both the girls. 'We never laid hands on a thing, except in the spirit of laudable inquiry.'

'Exactly so,' said Moore, with his rare smile. 'And what have you ferreted out, in your "spirit of laudable inquiry?"'

He perceived the inner drawer open.

'This is empty,' said he. 'Who has taken – ?'

'Here! here!' Caroline hastened to say; and she restored the little packet to its place. He shut it up; he locked it in with a small key attached to his watch-guard; he restored the other papers to order, closed the repository, and sat down without further remark.

'I thought you would have scolded much more, sir,' said Henry. 'The girls deserve reprimand.'

'I leave them to their own consciences.'

'It accuses them of crimes intended as well as perpetrated, sir. If I had not been here, they would have treated your portfolio as they have done your desk; but I told them it was padlocked.'

'And will you have lunch with us?' here interposed Shirley, addressing Moore, and desirous, as it seemed, to turn the conversation.

'Certainly, if I may.'

'You will be restricted to new milk and Yorkshire oat-cake.'

'Va – pour le lait frais!' said Louis. 'But for your oat-cake – !' and he made a grimace.

# Shirley

'He cannot eat it,' said Henry: 'he thinks it is like bran, raised with sour yeast.'

'Come, then, by special dispensation, we will allow him a few cracknels; but nothing less homely.'

The hostess rang the bell and gave her frugal orders, which were presently executed. She herself measured out the milk, and distributed the bread round the cozy circle now enclosing the bright little school-room fire. She then took the post of toaster-general; and kneeling on the rug, fork in hand, fulfilled her office with dexterity. Mr Hall, who relished any homely innovation on ordinary usages, and to whom the husky oat-cake was from custom suave as manna – seemed in his best spirits. He talked and laughed gleefully – now with Caroline, whom he had fixed by his side, now with Shirley, and again with Louis Moore. And Louis met him in congenial spirit: he did not laugh much, but he uttered in the quietest tone the wittiest things. Gravely spoken sentences, marked by unexpected turns and a quite fresh flavour and poignancy, fell easily from his lips. He proved himself to be – what Mr Hall had said he was – excellent company. Caroline marvelled at his humour, but still more at his entire self-possession. Nobody there present seemed to impose on him a sensation of unpleasant restraint: nobody seemed a bore – a check – a chill to him; and yet there was the cool and lofty Miss Keeldar kneeling before the fire, almost at his feet.

But Shirley was cool and lofty no longer – at least not as this moment. She appeared unconscious of the humility of her present position – or if conscious, it was only to taste a charm in its lowliness. It did not revolt her pride that the group to whom she voluntarily officiated as handmaid should include her cousin's tutor: it did not scare her that while she handed the bread and milk to the rest, she had to offer it to him also; and Moore took his portion from her hand as calmly as if he had been her equal.

'You are overheated now,' he said, when she had retained the fork for some time: 'let me relieve you.'

And he took it from her with a sort of quiet authority, to which she submitted passively – neither resisting him nor thanking him.

'I should like to see your pictures, Louis,' said Caroline, when the sumptuous luncheon was discussed. 'Would not you, Mr Hall?'

'To please you, I should; but, for my own part, I have cut him as an artist. I had enough of him in that capacity in Cumberland and Westmoreland. Many a wetting we got amongst the mountains because he would persist in sitting on a camp-stool, catching effects of rain-clouds, gathering mists, fitful sunbeams, and what not.'

'Here is the portfolio,' said Henry, bringing it in one hand, and leaning on his crutch with the other.

Louis took it, but he still sat as if he wanted another to speak. It seemed as if he would not open it unless the proud Shirley deigned to show herself interested in the exhibition.

'He makes us wait to whet our curiosity,' she said.

'You understand opening it,' observed Louis, giving her the key. 'You spoiled the lock for me once – try now.'

He held it: she opened it; and, monopolizing the contents, had the first view of every sketch herself. She enjoyed the treat – if treat it were – in silence,

# Shirley

without a single comment. Moore stood behind her chair and looked over her shoulder, and when she had done, and the others were still gazing, he left his post and paced through the room.

A carriage was heard in the lane – the gate-bell rang: Shirley started.

'There are callers,' she said, 'and I shall be summoned to the room. A pretty figure – as they say – I am to receive company: I and Henry have been in the garden gathering fruit half the morning. Oh, for rest under my own vine and my own fig-tree! Happy is the slave-wife of the Indian chief, in that she has no drawing-room duty to perform, but can sit at ease weaving mats, and stringing beads, and peacefully flattening her picaninny's head in an unmolested corner of her wig-wam. I'll emigrate to the western woods.'

Louis Moore laughed.

'To marry a White Cloud or a Big Buffalo; and after wedlock to devote yourself to the tender task of digging your lord's maize-field, while he smokes his pipe or drinks fire-water.'

Shirley seemed about to reply, but here the school-room door unclosed, admitting Mr Sympson. That personage stood aghast when he saw the group around the fire.

'I thought you alone, Miss Keeldar,' he said. 'I find quite a party.'

And evidently from his shocked, scandalized air – had he not recognized in one of the party a clergyman – he would have delivered an extempore philippic on the extraordinary habits of his niece: respect for the cloth arrested him.

'I merely wished to announce,' he proceeded, coldly, 'that the family from De Walden Hall, Mr, Mrs, the Misses, and Mr Sam Wynne, are in the drawing-room.' And he bowed, and withdrew.

'The family from De Walden Hall! Couldn't be a worse set,' murmured Shirley.

She sat still, looking a little contumacious, and very much indisposed to stir. She was flushed with the fire; her dark hair had been more than once dishevelled by the morning wind that day; her attire was a light, neatly fitting, but amply flowing dress of muslin; the shawl she had worn in the garden was still draped in a careless fold round her. Indolent, wilful, picturesque, and singularly pretty was her aspect – prettier than usual, as if some soft inward emotion – stirred who knows how? – had given new bloom and expression to her features.

'Shirley – Shirley, you ought to go,' whispered Caroline.

'I wonder why?'

She lifted her eyes, and saw in the glass over the fireplace both Mr Hall and Louis Moore gazing at her gravely.

'If,' she said, with a yielding smile – 'if a majority of the present company maintain that the De Walden Hall people have claims on my civility, I will subdue my inclinations to my duty. Let those who think I ought to go, hold up their hands.'

Again consulting the mirror, it reflected an unanimous vote against her.

'You must go,' said Mr Hall, 'and behave courteously, too. You owe many duties to society. It is not permitted you to please only yourself.'

Louis Moore assented with a low 'Hear! hear!'

Caroline, approaching her, smoothed her wavy curls, gave to her attire a less artistic and more domestic grace, and Shirley was put out of the room, protesting still, by a pouting lip, against her dismissal.

'There is a curious charm about her,' observed Mr Hall, when she was gone. 'And now,' he added, 'I must away, for Sweeting is off to see his mother, and there are two funerals.'

'Henry, get your books; it is lesson-time,' said Moore, sitting down to his desk.

'A curious charm!' repeated the pupil, when he and his master were left alone. 'True. Is she not a kind of white witch? he asked.

'Of whom are you speaking, sir?'

'Of my cousin Shirley.'

'No irrelevant questions. Study in silence.'

Mr Moore looked and spoke sternly – sourly. Henry knew this mood: it was a rare one with his tutor; but when it came he had an awe of it: he obeyed.

# Chapter 27

## The First Blue-Stocking

iss Keeldar and her uncle had characters that would not harmonize, – that never had harmonized. He was irritable, and she was spirited; he was despotic, and she liked freedom; he was worldly, and she, perhaps, romantic.

Not without purpose had he come down to Yorkshire: his mission was clear, and he intended to discharge it conscientiously: he anxiously desired to have his niece married; to make for her a suitable match; give her in charge to a proper husband, and wash his hands of her for ever.

The misfortune was, from infancy upwards, Shirley and he had disagreed on the meaning of the words 'suitable' and 'proper.' She never yet had accepted his definition; and it was doubtful whether, in the most important step of her life, she would consent to accept it.

The trial soon came.

Mr Wynne proposed in form for his son, Samuel Fawthrop Wynne.

'Decidedly suitable! Most proper!' pronounced Mr Sympson. 'A fine unencumbered estate; real substance; good connexions. *It must be done!*'

He sent for his niece to the oak-parlour; he shut himself up there with her alone; he communicated the offer; he gave his opinion; he claimed her consent.

It was withheld.

'No; I shall not marry Samuel Fawthrop Wynne.'

'I ask why? I must have a reason. In all respects he is more than worthy of you.'

She stood on the hearth; she was pale as the white marble slab and cornice behind her; her eyes flashed large, dilated, unsmiling.

'And *I* ask in what sense that young man is worthy of *me?*'

# Shirley

'He has twice your money, – twice your common sense; – equal connexions, – equal respectability.'

'Had he my money counted five score times, I would take no vow to love him.'

'Please to state your objections.'

'He has run a course of despicable, commonplace profligacy. Accept that as the first reason why I spurn him.'

'Miss Keeldar, you shock me!'

'That conduct alone sinks him in a gulf of immeasurable inferiority. His intellect reaches no standard I can esteem: – there is a second stumbling-block. His views are narrow; his feelings are blunt; his tastes are coarse; his manners vulgar.'

'The man is a respectable, wealthy man. To refuse him is presumption on your part.'

'I refuse, point-blank! Cease to annoy me with the subject: I forbid it!'

'Is it your intention ever to marry, or do you prefer celibacy?'

'I deny your right to claim an answer to that question.'

'May I ask if you expect some man of title – some peer of the realm – to demand your hand?'

'I doubt if the peer breathes on whom I would confer it.'

'Were there insanity in the family, I should believe you mad. Your eccentricity and conceit touch the verge of frenzy.'

'Perhaps, ere I have finished, you will see me overleap it.'

'I anticipate no less. Frantic and impracticable girl! Take warning! – I dare you to sully our name by a mésalliance!'

'*Our* name! Am *I* called Sympson?'

'God be thanked that you are not! But be on your guard! – I will not be trifled with!'

'What, in the name of common law and common sense, would you, or could you do, if my pleasure led me to a choice you disapproved?'

'Take care! take care!' (warning her with voice and hand that trembled alike.)

'Why? What shadow of power have *you* over me? Why should I fear you?'

'Take care, madam!'

'Scrupulous care I will take, Mr Sympson. Before I marry, I am resolved to esteem – and to admire – to *love*.'

'Preposterous stuff! – indecorous! – unwomanly!'

'To love with my whole heart. I know I speak in an unknown tongue; but I feel indifferent whether I am comprehended or not.'

'And if this love of yours should fall on a beggar?'

'On a beggar it will never fall. Mendicancy is not estimable.'

'On a low clerk, a play-actor, a play-writer, or – or –'

'Take courage, Mr Sympson! Or what?'

'Any literary scrub, or shabby, whining artist.'

'For the scrubby, shabby, whining, I have no taste: for literature and the arts, I have. And there I wonder how your Fawthrop Wynne would suit me? He cannot write a note without orthographical errors; he reads only a sporting paper: he was the booby of Stilbro' grammar school!'

'Unladylike language! Great God! – to what will she come?' He lifted hands and eyes.

'Never to the altar of Hymen with Sam Wynne.'

# Shirley

'To what will she come? Why are not the laws more stringent, that I might compel her to hear reason?'

'Console yourself, uncle. Were Britain a serfdom, and you the Czar, you could not *compel* me to this step. *I* will write to Mr Wynne. Give yourself no further trouble on the subject.

Fortune is proverbially called changeful, yet her caprice often takes the form of repeating again and again a similar stroke of luck in the same quarter. It appeared that Miss Keeldar – or her fortune – had by this time made a sensation in the district, and produced an impression in quarters by her unthought of. No less than three offers followed Mr Wynne's – all more or less eligible. All were in succession pressed on her by her uncle, and all in succession she refused. Yet among them was more than one gentleman of unexceptionable character, as well as ample wealth. Many besides her uncle asked what she meant, and whom she expected to entrap, that she was so insolently fastidious.

At last, the gossips thought they had found the key to her conduct, and her uncle was sure of it; and, what is more, the discovery showed his niece to him in quite a new light, and he changed his whole deportment to her accordingly.

Fieldhead had, of late, been fast growing too hot to hold them both: the suave aunt could not reconcile them; the daughters froze at the view of their quarrels: Gertrude and Isabella whispered by the hour together in their dressing-room, and became chilled with decorous dread if they chanced to be left alone with their audacious cousin. But, as I have said, a change supervened: Mr Sympson was appeased and his family tranquillized.

The village of Nunnely has been alluded to: its old church, its forest, its monastic ruins. It had also its Hall, called the Priory – an older, a larger, a more lordly abode than any Briarfield or Whinbury owned; and, what is more, it had its man of title – its baronet, which neither Briarfield nor Whinbury could boast. This possession – its proudest and most prized – had for years been nominal only: the present baronet, a young man hitherto resident in a distant province, was unknown on his Yorkshire estate.

During Miss Keeldar's stay at the fashionable watering-place of Cliffbridge, she and her friends had met with and been introduced to Sir Philip Nunnely. They encountered him again and again on the sands, the cliffs, in the various walks, sometimes at the public balls of the place. He seemed solitary; his manner was very unpretending – too simple to be termed affable; rather timid than proud: he did not *condescend* to their society – he seemed *glad* of it.

With any unaffected individual, Shirley could easily and quickly cement an acquaintance. She walked and talked with Sir Philip; she, her aunt, and cousins, sometimes took a sail in his yacht. She liked him because she found him kind and modest, and was charmed to feel she had the power to amuse him.

One slight drawback there was – where is the friendship without it? – Sir Philip had a literary turn: he wrote poetry, sonnets, stanzas, ballads. Perhaps Miss Keeldar thought him a little too fond of reading and reciting these compositions; perhaps she wished the rhyme had possessed more accuracy – the measure more music – the tropes more freshness – the inspiration more fire; at any rate, she always winced when he recurred to the subject of his poems, and usually did her best to divert the conversation into another channel.

# Shirley

He would beguile her to take moonlight walks with him on the bridge, for the sole purpose, as it seemed, of pouring into her ear the longest of his ballads: he would lead her away to sequestered rustic seats, whence the rush of the surf to the sands was heard soft and soothing; and when he had her all to himself, and the sea lay before them, and the scented shade of gardens spread round, and the tall shelter of cliffs rose behind them, he would pull out his last batch of sonnets, and read them in a voice tremulous with emotion. He did not seem to know, that though they might be rhyme, they were not poetry. It appeared by Shirley's downcast eye and disturbed face that she knew it, and felt heartily mortified by the single foible of this good and amiable gentleman.

Often she tried, as gently as might be, to wean him from this fanatic worship of the Muses: it was his monomania – on all ordinary subjects he was sensible enough; and fain was she to engage him in ordinary topics. He questioned her sometimes about his place at Nunnely; she was but too happy to answer his interrogatories at length: she never wearied of describing the antique Priory, the wild sylvan park, the hoary church and hamlet; nor did she fail to counsel him to come down and gather his tenantry about him in his ancestral halls.

Somewhat to her surprise Sir Philip followed her advice to the letter; and actually, towards the close of September, arrived at the Priory.

He soon made a call at Fieldhead, and his first visit was not his last: he said – when he had achieved the round of the neighbourhood – that under no roof had he found such pleasant shelter as beneath the massive oak-beams of the grey manor-house of Briarfield: a cramped, modest dwelling enough, compared with his own – but he liked it.

Presently, it did not suffice to sit with Shirley in her panelled parlour, where others came and went, and where he could rarely find a quiet moment to show her the latest production of his fertile muse; he must have her out amongst the pleasant pastures, and lead her by the still waters. Tête-à-tête ramblings she shunned; so he made parties for her to his own grounds, his glorious forest; to remoter scenes – woods severed by the Wharfe, vales watered by the Aire.

Such assiduity covered Miss Keeldar with distinction. Her uncle's prophetic soul anticipated a splendid future: he already scented the time afar off when, with nonchalant air, and left foot nursed on his right knee, he should be able to make dashingly-familiar allusion to his 'nephew the baronet.' Now, his niece dawned upon him no longer 'a mad girl,' but a 'most sensible woman.' He termed her, in confidential dialogues with Mrs Sympson, 'a truly superior person: peculiar, but very clever.' He treated her with exceeding deference; rose reverently to open and shut doors for her; reddened his face, and gave himself headaches, with stooping to pick up gloves, handkerchiefs, and other loose property, whereof Shirley usually held but insecure tenure. He would cut mysterious jokes about the superiority of woman's wit over man's wisdom; commence obscure apologies for the blundering mistake he had committed respecting the generalship, the tactics of 'a personage not a hundred miles from Fieldhead:' in short, he seemed elate as any 'midden-cock on pattens.'

His niece viewed his manoeuvres, and received his innuendoes, with phlegm: apparently, she did not above half comprehend to what aim they tended. When plainly charged with being the preferred of the baronet, she said, she believed he did like her, and for her part she liked him: she had never thought a man of

# Shirley

rank – the only son of a proud, fond mother – the only brother of doting sisters – could have so much goodness, and, on the whole, so much sense.

Time proved, indeed, that Sir Philip liked her. Perhaps he had found in her that 'curious charm' noticed by Mr Hall. He sought her presence more and more; and, at last, with a frequency that attested it had become to him an indispensable stimulus. About this time, strange feelings hovered round Field-head; restless hopes and haggard anxieties haunted some of its rooms. There was an unquiet wandering of some of the inmates among the still fields round the mansion; there was a sense of expectancy that kept the nerves strained.

One thing seemed clear. Sir Philip was not a man to be despised: he was amiable; if not highly intellectual, he was intelligent. Miss Keeldar could not affirm of him – what she had so bitterly affirmed of Sam Wynne – that his feelings were blunt, his tastes coarse, and his manners vulgar. There was sensibility in his nature; there was a very real, if not a very discriminating, love of the arts; there was the English gentleman in all his deportment: as to his lineage and wealth, both were, of course, far beyond her claims.

His appearance had at first elicited some laughing, though not ill-natured, remarks from the merry Shirley. It was boyish: his features were plain and slight; his hair sandy; his stature insignificant. But she soon checked her sarcasm on this point; she would even fire up if any one else made uncomplimentary allusion thereto. He had 'a pleasing countenance,' she affirmed; 'and there was that in his heart which was better than three Roman noses, than the locks of Absalom, or the proportions of Saul.' A spare and rare shaft she still reserved for his unfortunate poetic propensity: but, even here, she would tolerate no irony save her own.

In short, matters had reached a point which seemed fully to warrant an observation made about this time by Mr Yorke, to the tutor, Louis.

'Yond' brother Robert of yours seems to me to be either a fool or a madman. Two months ago, I could have sworn he had the game all in his own hands; and there he runs the country, and quarters himself up in London for weeks together, and by the time he comes back, he'll find himself checkmated. Louis, "There is a tide in the affairs of men, which, taken at the flood, leads on to fortune; but, once let slip, never returns again." I'd write to Robert, if I were you, and remind him of that.'

'Robert had views on Miss Keeldar?' inquired Louis, as if the idea were new to him.

'Views I suggested to him myself, and views he might have realized, for she liked him.'

'As a neighbour?'

'As more than that. I have seen her change countenance and colour at the mere mention of his name. Write to the lad, I say, and tell him to come home. He is a finer gentleman than this bit of a baronet, after all.'

'Does it not strike you, Mr Yorke, that for a mere penniless adventurer to aspire to a rich woman's hand is presumptuous – contemptible?'

'Oh! if you are for high notions, and double-refined sentiment, I've naught to say. I'm a plain, practical man myself; and if Robert is willing to give up that royal prize to a lad-rival – a puling slip of aristocracy – I am quite agreeable. At *his* age, in *his* place, with *his* inducements, I would have acted differently. Neither baronet, nor duke, nor prince, should have snatched my sweetheart from

me without a struggle. But you tutors are such solemn chaps: it is almost like speaking to a parson to consult with you.'

Flattered and fawned upon as Shirley was just now, it appeared she was not absolutely spoiled – that her better nature did not quite leave her. Universal report had indeed ceased to couple her name with that of Moore, and this silence seemed sanctioned by her own apparent oblivion of the absentee; but that she had not *quite* forgotten him – that she still regarded him, if not with love yet with interest – seemed proved by the increased attention which at this juncture of affairs a sudden attack of illness induced her to show that tutor-brother of Robert's, to whom she habitually bore herself with strange alternations of cool reserve and docile respect: now sweeping past him in all the dignity of the monied heiress and prospective Lady Nunnely, and anon, accosting him as abashed schoolgirls are wont to accost their stern professors: bridling her neck of ivory, and curling her lip of carmine, if she encountered her glance, one minute; and the next submitting to the grave rebuke of his eye, with as much contrition as if he had the power to inflict penalties in case of contumacy.

Louis Moore had perhaps caught the fever, which for a few days laid him low, in one of the poor cottages of the district, which he, his lame pupil, and Mr Hall, were in the habit of visiting together. At any rate he sickened, and after opposing to the malady a taciturn resistance for a day or two, was obliged to keep his chamber.

He lay tossing on his thorny bed one evening, Henry, who would not quit him, watching faithfully beside him, when a tap – too light to be that of Mrs Gill or the housemaid – summoned young Sympson to the door.

'How is Mr Moore to-night?' asked a low voice from the dark gallery.

'Come in and see him yourself.'

'Is he asleep?'

'I wish he could sleep. Come and speak to him, Shirley.'

'He would not like it.'

But the speaker stepped in, and Henry, seeing her hesitate on the threshold, took her hand and drew her to the couch.

The shaded light showed Miss Keeldar's form but imperfectly, yet it revealed her in elegant attire. There was a party assembled below, including Sir Philip Nunnely; the ladies were now in the drawing-room, and their hostess had stolen from them to visit Henry's tutor. Her pure white dress, her fair arms and neck, the trembling chainlet of gold circling her throat, and quivering on her breast, glistened strangely amid the obscurity of the sick-room. Her mien was chastened and pensive: she spoke gently.

'Mr Moore, how are you to-night?'

'I have not been very ill, and am now better.'

'I heard that you complained of thirst: I have brought you some grapes: can you taste one?'

'No: but I thank you for remembering me.'

'Just one.'

From the rich cluster that filled a small basket held in her hand, she severed a berry and offered it to his lips. He shook his head, and turned aside his flushed face.

'But what then can I bring you instead? You have no wish for fruit; yet I see that your lips are parched. What beverage do you prefer?'

'Mrs Gill supplies me with toast and water: I like it best.'

Silence fell for some minutes.

'Do you suffer? Have you pain?'

'Very little.'

'What made you ill?'

Silence.

'I wonder what caused this fever? To what do you attribute it?'

'Miasma, perhaps – malaria. This is autumn, a season fertile in fevers.'

'I hear you often visit the sick in Briarfield, and Nunnely too, with Mr Hall: you should be on your guard: temerity is not wise.'

'That reminds me, Miss Keeldar, that perhaps you had better not enter this chamber, or come near this couch. I do not believe my illness is infectious: I scarcely fear (with a sort of smile) *you* will take it; but why should you run even the shadow of a risk? Leave me.'

'Patience: I will go soon; but I should like to do something for you before I depart – any little service –'

'They will miss you below.'

'No, the gentlemen are still at table.'

'They will not linger long: Sir Philip Nunnely is no wine-bibber, and I hear him just now pass from the dining-room to the drawing-room.'

'It is a servant.'

'It is Sir Philip, I know his step.'

'Your hearing is acute.'

'It is never dull, and the sense seems sharpened at present. Sir Philip was here to tea last night. I heard you sing to him some song which he had brought you. I heard him, when he took his departure at eleven o'clock, call you out on the pavement, to look at the evening star.'

'You must be nervously sensitive.'

'I heard him kiss your hand.'

'Impossible!'

'No; my chamber is over the hall, the window just above the front door, the sash was a little raised, for I felt feverish: you stood ten minutes with him on the steps: I heard your discourse, every word, and I heard the salute. Henry, give me some water.'

'Let me give it him.'

But he half rose to take the glass from young Sympson, and declined her attendance.

'And can I do nothing?'

'Nothing: for you cannot guarantee me a night's peaceful rest, and it is all I at present want.'

'You do not sleep well?'

'Sleep has left me.'

'Yet you said you were not very ill?'

'I am often sleepless when in high health.'

'If I had power, I would lap you in the most placid slumber; quite deep and hushed, without a dream.'

'Bland annihilation! I do not ask that.'

# Shirley

'With dreams of all you most desire.'

'Monstrous delusions! The sleep would be delirium, the waking death.'

'Your wishes are not so chimerical: you are no visionary?'

'Miss Keeldar, I suppose you think so; but my character is not, perhaps, quite as legible to you as a page of the last new novel might be.'

'That is possible ... But this sleep: I *should* like to woo it to your pillow – to win for you its favour. If I took a book and sat down, and read some pages – ? I can well spare half an hour.'

'Thank you, but I will not detain you.'

'I would read softly.'

'It would not do. I am too feverish and excitable to bear a soft, cooing, vibrating voice close at my ear. You had better leave me.'

'Well, I will go.'

'And no good-night?'

'Yes, sir, yes. Mr Moore, good-night.' (Exit Shirley).

'Henry, my boy, go to bed now: it is time you had some repose.'

'Sir, it would please me to watch at your bed-side all night.'

'Nothing less called for: I am getting better: there, go.'

'Give me your blessing, sir.'

'God bless you, my best pupil!'

'You never call me your dearest pupil!'

'No, nor ever shall.'

Possibly Miss Keeldar resented her former teacher's rejection of her courtesy: it is certain she did not repeat the offer of it. Often as her light step traversed the gallery in the course of a day, it did not again pause at his door; nor did her 'cooing, vibrating voice' disturb a second time the hush of the sick-room. A sick-room, indeed, it soon ceased to be; Mr Moore's good constitution quickly triumphed over his indisposition: in a few days he shook it off, and resumed his duties as tutor.

That 'Auld Langsyne' had still its authority both with preceptor and scholar, was proved by the manner in which he sometimes promptly passed the distance she usually maintained between them, and put down her high reserve with a firm, quiet hand.

One afternoon the Sympson family were gone out to take a carriage airing. Shirley, never sorry to snatch a reprieve from their society, had remained behind, detained by business, as she said. The business – a little letter-writing – was soon despatched after the yard-gates had closed on the carriage: Miss Keeldar betook herself to the garden.

It was a peaceful autumn day. The gilding of the Indian summer mellowed the pastures far and wide. The russet woods stood ripe to be stript, but were yet full of leaf. The purple of heath-bloom, faded but not withered, tinged the hills. The beck wandered down to the Hollow, through a silent district; no wind followed its course, or haunted its woody borders. Fieldhead gardens bore the seal of gentle decay. On the walks, swept that morning, yellow leaves had fluttered down again. Its time of flowers, and even of fruits, was over; but a scantling of apples enriched the trees; only a blossom here and there expanded pale and delicate amidst a knot of faded leaves.

# Shirley

These single flowers – the last of their race – Shirley culled as she wandered thoughtfully amongst the beds. She was fastening into her girdle a hueless and scentless nosegay, when Henry Sympson called to her as he came limping from the house.

'Shirley, Mr Moore would be glad to see you in the school-room and to hear you read a little French, if you have no more urgent occupation.'

The messenger delivered his commission very simply, as if it were a mere matter of course.

'Did Mr Moore tell you to say that?'

'Certainly: why not? And now, do come, and let us once more be as we were at Sympson-grove. We used to have pleasant school-hours in those days.'

Miss Keeldar, perhaps, thought that circumstances were changed since then; however she made no remark, but after a little reflection quietly followed Henry.

Entering the school-room, she inclined her head with a decent obeisance, as had been her wont in former times; she removed her bonnet, and hung it up beside Henry's cap. Louis Moore sat at his desk, turning the leaves of a book, open before him, and marking passages with his pencil; he just moved, in acknowledgment of her curtsey, but did not rise.

'You proposed to read to me a few nights ago,' said he. 'I could not hear you then; my attention is now at your service. A little renewed practice in French may not be unprofitable: your accent, I have observed, begins to rust.'

'What book shall I take?'

'Here are the posthumous works of St Pièrre. Read a few pages of the "Fragments de l'Amazone." '

She accepted the chair which he had placed in readiness near his own – the volume lay on his desk – there was but one between them; her sweeping curls drooped so low as to hide the page from him.

'Put back your hair,' he said.

For one moment, Shirley looked not quite certain whether she would obey the request or disregard it: a flicker of her eye beamed furtive on the professor's face; perhaps if he had been looking at her harshly or timidly, or if one undecided line had marked his countenance, she would have rebelled, and the lesson had ended there and then; but he was only waiting her compliance – as calm as marble, and as cool. She threw the veil of tresses behind her ear. It was well her face owned an agreeable outline, and that her cheek possessed the polish and the roundness of early youth, or, thus robbed of a softening shade, the contours might have lost their grace. But what mattered that in the present society? Neither Calypso nor Eucharis cared to fascinate Mentor.

She began to read. The language had become strange to her tongue; it faltered: the lecture flowed unevenly, impeded by hurried breath, broken by Anglicized tones. She stopped.

'I can't do it. Read me a paragraph, if you please, Mr Moore.'

What *he* read, *she* repeated: she caught his accent in three minutes.

'Très bien,' was the approving comment at the close of the piece.

'C'est presque le Français rattrapé, n'est-ce pas?'

You could not write French as you once could, I daresay – ?'

'Oh! no. I should make strange work of my concords now.'

'You could not compose the devoir of "La Première Femme Savante?" '

'Do you still remember that rubbish?'

# Shirley

'Every line.'

'I doubt you.'

'I will engage to repeat it word for word.'

'You would stop short at the first line.'

'Challenge me to the experiment.'

'I challenge you.'

He proceeded to recite the following: he gave it in French, but we must translate, on pain of being unintelligible to some readers.

'And it came to pass when men began to multiply on the face of the earth, and daughters were born unto them, that the sons of God saw the daughters of men that they were fair; and they took them wives of all which they chose.'

This was in the dawn of time, before the morning stars were set, and while they yet sang together.

The epoch is so remote, the mists and dewy grey of matin twilight veil it with so vague an obscurity, that all distinct feature of custom, all clear line of locality, evade perception and baffle research. It must suffice to know that the world then existed; that men peopled it; that man's nature, with its passions, sympathies, pains, and pleasures, informed the planet and gave it soul.

A certain tribe colonized a certain spot on the globe; of what race this tribe – unknown: in what region that spot – untold. We usually think of the East when we refer to transactions of that date; but who shall declare that there was no life in the West, the South, the North? What is to disprove that this tribe, instead of camping under palm-groves in Asia, wandered beneath island oak-woods rooted in our own seas of Europe?

It is no sandy plain, nor any circumscribed and scant oasis I seem to realize. A forest valley, with rocky sides and brown profundity of shade, formed by tree crowding on tree, descends deep before me. Here, indeed, dwell human beings, but so few, and in alleys so thick branched and over-arched, they are neither heard nor seen. Are they savage? – doubtless. They live by the crook and the bow: half shepherds, half hunters, their flocks wander wild as their prey. Are they happy? – no: not more happy than we are at this day. Are they good? – no: not better than ourselves: their nature is our nature, – human both. There is one in this tribe too often miserable, – a child bereaved of both parents. None cares for this child: she is fed sometimes, but oftener forgotten: a hut rarely receives her: the hollow tree and chill cavern are her home. Forsaken, lost, and wandering, she lives more with the wild beast and bird than with her own kind. Hunger and cold are her comrades: sadness hovers over, and solitude besets her round. Unheeded and unvalued, she should die; but she both lives and grows: the green wilderness nurses her, and becomes to her a mother: feeds her on juicy berry, on saccharine root and nut.

There is something in the air of this clime which fosters life kindly: there must be something, too, in its dews, which heals with sovereign balm. Its gentle seasons exaggerate no passion, no sense; its temperature tends to harmony; its breezes, you would say, bring down from heaven the germ of pure thought, and purer feeling. Not grotesquely fantastic are the forms of cliff and foliage; not

# Shirley

violently vivid the colouring of flower and bird: in all the grandeur of these forests there is repose; in all their freshness there is tenderness.

The gentle charm vouchsafed to flower and tree, – bestowed on deer and dove, – has not been denied to the human nursling. All solitary, she has sprung up straight and graceful. Nature cast her features in a fine mould; they have matured in their pure, accurate first lines, unaltered by the shocks of disease. No fierce dry blast has dealt with the surface of her frame; no burning sun has crisped or withered her tresses: her form gleams ivory-white through the trees; her hair flows plenteous, long, and glossy; her eyes not dazzled by vertical fires, beam in the shade large and open, and full and dewy: above those eyes, when the breeze bares her forehead, shines an expanse fair and ample, – a clear, candid page, whereon knowledge, should knowledge ever come, might write a golden record. You see in the desolate young savage nothing vicious or vacant; she haunts the wood harmless and thoughtful: though of what one so untaught can think, it is not easy to divine.

On the evening of one summer day, before the Flood, being utterly alone – for she had lost all trace of her tribe, who had wandered leagues away, she knew not where, – she went up from the vale, to watch Day take leave and Night arrive. A crag, overspread by a tree, was her station: the oak-roots, turfed and mossed, gave a seat: the oak-boughs, thick-leaved, wove a canopy.

Slow and grand the Day withdrew, passing in purple fire, and parting to the farewell of a wild, low chorus from the woodlands. Then Night entered, quiet as death: the wind fell, the birds ceased singing. Now every nest held happy mates, and hart and hind slumbered blissfully safe in their lair.

The girl sat, her body still, her soul astir; occupied, however, rather in feeling than in thinking, – in wishing, than hoping, – in imagining, than projecting. She felt the world, the sky, the night, boundlessly mighty. Of all things, herself seemed to herself the centre, – a small, forgotten atom of life, a spark of soul, emitted inadvertent from the great creative source, and now burning unmarked to waste in the heart of a black hollow. She asked, was she thus to burn out and perish, her living light doing no good, never seen, never needed, – a star in an else starless firmament, – which nor shepherd, nor wanderer, nor sage, nor priest, tracked as a guide, or read as a prophecy? Could this be, she demanded, when the flame of her intelligence burned so vivid; when her life beat so true, and real, and potent; when something within her stirred disquieted, and restlessly asserted a God-given strength for which it insisted she should find exercise?

She gazed abroad on Heaven and Evening: Heaven and Evening gazed back on her. She bent down, searching bank, hill, river, spread dim below. All she questioned responded by oracles: she heard, – she was impressed; but she could not understand. Above her head she raised her hands joined together.

'Guidance – help – comfort – come!' was her cry.

There was no voice, nor any that answered.

She waited, kneeling, steadfastly looking up. Yonder sky was sealed: the solemn stars shone alien and remote.

At last, one over-stretched chord of her agony slacked: she thought Something above relented: she felt as if Something far round drew nigher: she heard as if Silence spoke. There was no language, no word, only a tone.

Again – a fine, full, lofty tone, a deep, soft sound, like a storm whispering, made twilight undulate.

# Shirley

Once more, profounder, nearer, clearer, it rolled harmonious.

Yet, again – a distinct voice passed between Heaven and Earth.

'Eva!'

If Eva were not this woman's name, she had none. She rose.

'Here am I.'

'Eva!'

'Oh, Night! (it can be but Night that speaks) I am here!'

The voice, descending, reached Earth.

'Eva!'

'Lord!' she cried, 'behold thine handmaid!'

She had her religion: all tribes held some creed.

'I come: a Comforter!'

'Lord, come quickly!'

The Evening flushed full of hope: the Air panted; the Moon – rising before – ascended large, but her light showed no shape.

'Lean towards me, Eva. Enter my arms; repose thus.'

'Thus I lean, O Invisible, but felt! And what art thou?'

'Eva, I have brought a living draught from heaven. Daughter of Man, drink of my cup!'

'I drink – it is as if sweetest dew visited my lips in a full current. My arid heart revives: my affliction is lightened: my strait and struggle are gone. And the night changes! the wood, the hill, the moon, the wide sky – all change!'

'All change, and for ever. I take from thy vision, darkness: I loosen from thy faculties, fetters! I level in thy path, obstacles: I, with my presence, fill vacancy: I claim as mine the lost atom of life: I take to myself the spark of soul – burning, heretofore, forgotten!'

'Oh, take me! Oh, claim me! This is a god.'

'This is a Son of God: one who feels himself in the portion of life that stirs you: he is suffered to reclaim his own, and so to foster and aid that it shall not perish hopeless.'

'A Son of God! Am I indeed chosen?'

'Thou only in this land. I saw thee that thou wert fair: I knew thee that thou were mine. To me it is given to rescue, to sustain, to cherish, mine own. Acknowledge in me that Seraph, on earth, named Genius.'

'My glorious Bridegroom! True Dayspring from on high! All I would have, at last I possess. I receive a revelation. The dark hint, the obscure whisper, which have haunted me from childhood, are interpreted. Thou art He I sought. God-born, take me, thy bride!'

'Unhumbled, I can take what is mine. Did I not give from the altar the very flame which lit Eva's being? Come again into the heaven whence thou wert sent.'

That Presence, invisible, but mighty, gathered her in like a lamb to the fold; that voice, soft, but all pervading, vibrated through her heart like music. Her eye received no image: and yet a sense visited her vision and her brain as of the serenity of stainless air, the power of sovereign seas, the majesty of marching stars, the energy of colliding elements, the rooted endurance of hills wide based, and, above all, as of the lustre of heroic beauty rushing victorious on the Night, vanquishing its shadows like a diviner Sun.

Such was the bridal-hour of Genius and Humanity. Who shall rehearse the

# Shirley

tale of their after-union? Who shall depict its bliss and bale? Who shall tell how He, between whom and the Woman God put enmity, forged deadly plots to break the bond or defile its purity? Who shall record the long strife between Serpent and Seraph? How still the Father of Lies insinuated evil into good – pride into wisdom – grossness into glory – pain into bliss – poison into passion? How the 'dreadless Angel' defied, resisted, and repelled? How, again and again, he refined the polluted cup, exalted the debased emotion, rectified the perverted impulse, detected the lurking venom, baffled the frontless temptation – purified, justified, watched, and withstood? How, by his patience, by his strength, by that unutterable excellence he held from God – his Origin – this faithful Seraph fought for Humanity a good fight through time; and, when Time's course closed, and Death was encountered at the end, barring with fleshless arm the portals of Eternity, how Genius still held close his dying bridge, sustained her through the agony of the passage, bore her triumphant into his own home – Heaven; restored her, redeemed, to Jehovah – her Maker; and at last, before Angel and Archangel, crowned her with the crown of Immortality.

Who shall, of these things, write the chronicle?

'I never could correct that composition,' observed Shirley, as Moore concluded. 'Your censor-pencil scored it with condemnatory lines, whose signification I strove vainly to fathom.'

She had taken a crayon from the tutor's desk, and was drawing little leaves, fragments of pillars, broken crosses, on the margin of the book.

'French may be half-forgotten, but the habits of the French lesson are retained, I see,' said Louis: 'my books would now, as erst, be unsafe with you. My newly bound St Pièrre would soon be like my Racine: Miss Keeldar, her mark – traced on every page.'

Shirley dropped her crayon as if it burned her fingers.

'Tell me what were the faults of that devoir?' she asked. 'Were they grammatical errors, or did you object to the substance?'

'I never said that the lines I drew were indications of fault at all. You would have it that such was the case, and I refrained from contradiction.'

'What else did they denote?'

'No matter now.'

'Mr Moore,' cried Henry, 'make Shirley repeat some of the pieces she used to say so well by heart.'

'If I ask for any, it will be "Le Cheval Dompté,"' said Moore, trimming with his penknife the pencil Miss Keeldar had worn to a stump.

She turned aside her head; the neck, the clear cheek, forsaken by their natural veil, were seen to flush warm.

'Ah! she has not forgotten, you see, sir,' said Henry, exultant. 'She knows how naughty she was.'

A smile, which Shirley would not permit to expand, made her lip tremble; she bent her face, and hid it half with her arms half in her curls, which, as she stooped, fell loose again.

'Certainly, I was a rebel!' she answered.

'A rebel!' repeated Henry. 'Yes: you and papa had quarrelled terribly, and

you set both him and mamma, and Mrs Pryor, and everybody, at defiance: you said he had insulted you –'

'He *had* insulted me,' interposed Shirley.

'And you wanted to leave Sympson Grove directly. You packed your things up, and papa threw them out of your trunk; mamma cried – Mrs Pryor cried; they both stood wringing their hands begging you to be patient, and you knelt on the floor with your things and your upturned box before you, looking, Shirley – looking – why, in one of *your* passions. Your features, in such passions, are not distorted; they are fixed, but quite beautiful: you scarcely look angry, only resolute, and in a certain haste; yet one feels that, at such times, an obstacle cast across your path would be split as with lightning. Papa lost heart, and called Mr Moore.'

'Enough, Henry.'

'No: it is not enough. I hardly know how Mr Moore managed, except that I recollect he suggested to papa that agitation would bring on his gout; and then he spoke quietly to the ladies, and got them away; and afterwards he said to you, Miss Shirley, that it was of no use talking or lecturing now, but that the tea-things were just brought into the school-room, and he was very thirsty, and he would be glad if you would leave your packing for the present and come and make a cup of tea for him and me. You came: you would not talk at first; but soon you softened and grew cheerful. Mr Moore began to tell us about the Continent, the war, and Buonaparte; subjects we were both fond of listening to. After tea he said we should neither of us leave him that evening; he would not let us stray out of his sight, lest we should again get into mischief. We sat one on each side of him: we were so happy. I never passed so pleasant an evening. The next day he gave you, missy, a lecture of an hour, and wound it up by marking you a piece to learn in Bossuet as a punishment-lesson, – "Le Cheval Dompté." You learned it instead of packing up, Shirley. We heard no more of your running away. Mr Moore used to tease you on the subject for a year afterwards.'

'She never said a lesson with greater spirit,' subjoined Moore. 'She then, for the first time, gave me the treat of hearing my native tongue spoken without accent by an English girl.'

'She was as sweet as summer-cherries for a month afterwards,' struck in Henry: 'a good hearty quarrel always left Shirley's temper better than it found it.'

'You talk of me as if I were not present,' observed Miss Keeldar, who had not yet lifted her face.

'Are you sure you *are* present?' asked Moore: 'there have been moments since my arrival here, when I have been tempted to inquire of the lady of Fieldhead if she knew what had become of my former pupil?'

'She is here now.'

'I see her, and humble enough; but I would neither advise Harry, nor others, to believe too implicitly in the humility which one moment can hide its blushing face like a modest little child, and the next lift it pale and lofty as a marble Juno.'

'One man in times of old, it is said, imparted vitality to the statue he had chiselled. Others may have the contrary gift of turning life to stone.'

Moore paused on this observation before he replied to it. His look, at once

struck and meditative, said, 'A strange phrase: what may it mean?' He turned it over in his mind, with thought deep and slow, as some German pondering metaphysics.

'You mean,' he said, at last, 'that some men inspire repugnance, and so chill the kind heart.'

'Ingenious!' responded Shirley. 'If the interpretation pleases you, you are welcome to hold it valid. *I* don't care.'

And with that she raised her head, lofty in look, and statue-like in hue, as Louis had described it.

'Behold the metamorphosis!' he said: 'scarce imagined ere it is realized: a lowly nymph develops to an inaccessible goddess. But Henry must not be disappointed of his recitation, and Olympia will deign to oblige him. Let us begin.'

'I have forgotten the very first line.'

'Which I have not. *My* memory, if a slow, is a retentive one. I acquire deliberately both knowledge and liking: the acquisition grows into my brain, and the sentiment into my breast; and it is not as the rapid springing produce which, having no root in itself, flourishes verdurous enough for a time, but too soon falls withered away. Attention, Henry! Miss Keeldar consents to favour you. "Voyez ce Cheval ardent et impétueux," so it commences.'

Miss Keeldar did consent to make the effort; but she soon stopped.

'Unless I heard the whole repeated, I cannot continue it,' she said.

'Yet it was quickly learned, "soon gained, soon gone," ' moralized the tutor. He recited the passage deliberately, accurately, with slow, impressive emphasis.

Shirley, by degrees, inclined her ear as he went on. Her face, before turned from him, returned towards him. When he ceased, she took the word up as if from his lips: she took his very tone; she seized his very accent; she delivered the periods as he had delivered them: she reproduced his manner, his pronunciation, his expression.

It was now her turn to petition.

'Recall "Le Songe d'Athalie," ' she entreated, 'and say it.'

He said it for her; she took it from him; she found lively excitement in the pleasure of making his language her own: she asked for further indulgence; all the old school-pieces were revived, and with them Shirley's old school-days.

He had gone through some of the best passages of Racine and Corneille, and then had heard the echo of his own deep tones in the girl's voice, that modulated itself faithfully on his:– 'Le Chêne et le Roseau,' that most beautiful of La Fontaine's fables, had been recited, well recited by the tutor, and the pupil had animatedly availed herself of the lesson. Perhaps a simultaneous feeling seized them now, that their enthusiasm had kindled to a glow, which the slight fuel of French poetry no longer sufficed to feed; perhaps they longed for a trunk of English oak to be thrown as a Yule log to the devouring flame. Moore observed,–

'And these are our best pieces! And we have nothing more dramatic, nervous, natural!'

And then he smiled and was silent. His whole nature seemed serenely alight: he stood on the hearth, leaning his elbow on the mantelpiece, musing not unblissfully.

Twilight was closing on the diminished autumn day: the school-room windows – darkened with creeping plants, from which no high October winds had as yet

swept the sere foliage – admitted scarce a gleam of sky; but the fire gave light enough to talk by.

And now Louis Moore addressed his pupil in French; and she answered, at first, with laughing hesitation and in broken phrase: Moore encouraged while he corrected her; Henry joined in the lesson; the two scholars stood opposite the master, their arms round each other's waists: Tartar, who long since had craved and obtained admission, sat sagely in the centre of the rug, staring at the blaze which burst fitful from morsels of coal among the red cinders: the group were happy enough, but –

> *'Pleasures are like poppies spread;*
> *You seize the flower – its bloom is shed.'*

The dull, rumbling sound of wheels was heard on the pavement in the yard.

'It is the carriage returned,' said Shirley; 'and dinner must be just ready, and I am not dressed.'

A servant came in with Mr Moore's candle and tea: for the tutor and his pupil usually dined at luncheon time.

'Mr Sympson and the ladies are returned,' she said, 'and Sir Philip Nunnely is with them.'

'How you did start, and how your hand trembled, Shirley!' said Henry, when the maid had closed the shutter and was gone. 'But I know why – don't you, Mr Moore? I know what papa intends. He is a little ugly man, that Sir Philip: I wish he had not come: I wish sisters and all of them had stayed at De Walden Hall to dine. Shirley should once more have made tea for you and me, Mr Moore, and we would have had a happy evening of it.'

Moore was locking up his desk, and putting away his St Pièrre, – 'That was *your* plan – was it, my boy?'

'Don't you approve it, sir?'

'I approve nothing Utopian. Look Life in its iron face: stare Reality out of its brassy countenance. Make the tea, Henry; I shall be back in a minute.'

He left the room: so did Shirley, by another door.

# Chapter 28

## Phoebe

**S**hirley probably got on pleasantly with Sir Philip that evening, for the next morning she came down in one of her best moods.

'Who will take a walk with me?' she asked, after breakfast, 'Isabella and Gertrude – will you?'

# Shirley

So rare was such an invitation from Miss Keeldar to her female cousins that they hesitated before they accepted it. Their mamma, however, signifying acquiescence in the project, they fetched their bonnets, and the trio set out.

It did not suit these three young persons to be thrown much together: Miss Keeldar liked the society of few ladies: indeed, she had a cordial pleasure in that of none except Mrs Pryor and Caroline Helstone. She was civil, kind, attentive even to her cousins; but still she usually had little to say to them. In the sunny mood of this particular morning, she contrived to entertain even the Misses Sympson. Without deviating from her wonted rule of discussing with them only ordinary themes, she imparted to these themes an extraordinary interest: the sparkle of her spirit glanced along her phrases.

What made her so joyous? All the cause must have been in herself. The day was not bright; it was dim – a pale, waning autumn day: the walks through the dun woods were damp; the atmosphere was heavy, the sky overcast; and yet, it seemed that in Shirley's heart lived all the light and azure of Italy, as all its fervour laughed in her grey English eye.

Some directions necessary to be given to her foreman, John, delayed her behind her cousins as they neared Fieldhead on their return; perhaps an interval of twenty minutes elapsed between her separation from them and her re-entrance into the house: in the mean time she had spoken to John, and then she had lingered in the lane at the gate. A summons to luncheon called her in: she excused herself from the meal, and went up-stairs.

'Is not Shirley coming to luncheon?' asked Isabella: 'she said she was not hungry.'

An hour after, as she did not quit her chamber, one of her cousins went to seek her there. She was found sitting at the foot of the bed, her head resting on her hand: she looked quite pale, very thoughtful, almost sad.

'You are not ill?' was the question put.

'A little sick,' replied Miss Keeldar.

Certainly, she was not a little changed from what she had been two hours before.

This change, accounted for only by those three words, explained no otherwise: this change – whencesoever springing, effected in a brief ten minutes – passed like no light summer cloud. She talked when she joined her friends at dinner, talked as usual; she remained with them during the evening; when again questioned respecting her health, she declared herself perfectly recovered: it had been a mere passing faintness; a momentary sensation, not worth a thought: yet it was felt there was a difference in Shirley.

The next day – the day – the week – the fortnight after – this new and peculiar shadow lingered on the countenance, in the manner of Miss Keeldar. A strange quietude settled over her look, her movements, her very voice. The alteration was not so marked as to court or permit questioning, yet it *was* there, and it would not pass away: it hung over her like a cloud which no breeze could stir or disperse. Soon it became evident that to notice this change was to annoy her. First, she shrunk from remark; and, if persisted in, she, with her own peculiar hauteur, repelled it. 'Was she ill?' The reply came with decision.

'I *am not*.'

'Did anything weigh on her mind? Had anything happened to affect her spirits?'

# Shirley

She scornfully ridiculed the idea. 'What did they mean by spirits? She had no spirits, black or white, blue or grey, to affect.'

'Something must be the matter – she was so altered.'

'She supposed she had a right to alter at her ease. She knew she was plainer: if it suited her to grow ugly, why need others fret themselves on the subject?'

'There must be a cause for the change – what was it?'

She peremptorily requested to be let alone.

Then she would make every effort to appear quite gay, and she seemed indignant at herself that she could not perfectly succeed: brief, self-spurning epithets burst from her lips when alone: 'Fool! Coward!' she would term herself. 'Poltroon!' she would say: 'if you must tremble – tremble in secret! Quail where no eye sees you!'

'How dare you' – she would ask herself – 'how dare you show your weakness and betray your imbecile anxieties? Shake them off: rise above them: if you cannot do this, hide them.'

And to hide them, she did her best. She once more became resolutely lively in company. When weary of effort and forced to relax, she sought solitude: not the solitude of her chamber – she refused to mope, shut up between four walls – but that wilder solitude which lies out of doors, and which she could chase, mounted on Zoë, her mare. She took long rides of half a day. Her uncle disapproved, but he dared not remonstrate: it was never pleasant to face Shirley's anger, even when she was healthy and gay; but now that her face showed thin, and her large eye looked hollow, there was something in the darkening of that face and kindling of that eye which touched as well as alarmed.

To all comparative strangers who, unconscious of the alterations in her spirits, commented on the alteration in her looks, she had one reply:

'I am perfectly well: I have not an ailment.'

And health, indeed, she must have had, to be able to bear the exposure to the weather she now encountered. Wet or fair, calm or storm, she took her daily ride over Stilbro' Moor, Tartar keeping up at her side, with his wolf-like gallop, long and untiring.

Twice – three times, the eyes of gossips – those eyes which are everywhere: in the closet and on the hill-top – noticed that instead of turning on Rushedge, the top-ridge of Stilbro' Moor, she rode forwards all the way to the town. Scouts were not wanting to mark her destination there; it was ascertained that she alighted at the door of one Mr Pearson Hall, a solicitor, related to the Vicar of Nunnely: this gentleman and his ancestors had been the agents of the Keeldar family for generations back: some people affirmed that Miss Keeldar was become involved in business speculations connected with Hollow's Mill; that she had lost money, and was constrained to mortgage her land: others conjectured that she was going to be married, and that the settlements were preparing.

Mr Moore and Henry Sympson were together in the school-room: the tutor was waiting for a lesson which the pupil seemed busied in preparing.

'Henry, make haste! the afternoon is getting on.'

'Is it, sir?'

'Certainly. Are you nearly ready with that lesson?'

'No.'

# Shirley

'Not *nearly* ready?'

'I have not construed a line.'

Mr Moore looked up: the boy's tone was rather peculiar.

'The task presents no difficulties, Henry: or, if it does, bring them to me; we will work together.'

'Mr Moore, I can do no work.'

'My boy, you are ill.'

'Sir, I am not worse in bodily health than usual, but my heart is full.'

'Shut the book. Come hither, Harry. Come to the fireside.'

Harry limped forward; his tutor placed him a chair: his lips were quivering, his eyes brimming. He laid his crutch on the floor, bent down his head, and wept.

'This distress is not occasioned by physical pain, you say, Harry? You have a grief: – tell it me.'

'Sir, I have such a grief as I never had before. I wish it could be relieved in some way: I can hardly bear it.'

'Who knows but, if we talk it over, we may relieve it? What is the cause? Whom does it concern?'

'The cause, sir, is Shirley: it concerns Shirley.'

'Does it?...You think her changed?'

'All who know her think her changed: you too, Mr Moore.'

'Not seriously, – no. I see no alteration but such as a favourable turn might repair in a few weeks: besides, her own word must go for something: she says she is well.'

'There it is, sir: as long as she maintained she was well, I believed her. When I was sad out of her sight, I soon recovered spirits in her presence. Now...'

'Well, Harry, now..? Has she said anything to you? You and she were together in the garden two hours this morning: I saw her talking, and you listening. Now, my dear Harry! if Miss Keeldar has said she is ill, and enjoined you to keep her secret, do not obey her. For her life's sake, avow everything. Speak, my boy!'

'*She* say she is ill! I believe, sir, if she were dying, she would smile, and aver "Nothing ails me." '

'What have you learned, then? What new circumstance..?'

'I have learned that she has just made her will.'

'Made her will!'

The tutor and the pupil were silent.

'She told you that?' asked Moore, when some minutes had elapsed.

'She told me quite cheerfully: not as an ominous circumstance, which I felt it to be. She said I was the only person besides her solicitor, Pearson Hall, and Mr Helstone and Mr Yorke, who knew anything about it; and to me, she intimated, she wished specially to explain its provisions.'

'Go on, Harry.'

' "Because," she said, looking down on me with her beautiful eyes, – oh! they *are* beautiful, Mr Moore! I love them, – I love her! She is my star! Heaven must not claim her! She is lovely in this world, and fitted for this world. Shirley is not an angel; she is a woman, and she shall live with men. Seraphs shall not have her! Mr Moore – if one of the "sons of God," with wings wide and bright as the sky, blue and sounding as the sea, having seen that she was fair, descended

to claim her, his claim should be withstood – withstood by me – boy and cripple as I am!'

'Henry Sympson, go on, when I tell you.'

' "Because," she said, "if I made no will, and died before you Harry, all my property would go to you; and I do not intend that it should be so, though your father would like it. But you," she said, "will have his whole estate, which is large – larger than Fieldhead; your sisters will have nothing, so I have left them some money: though I do not love them, both together, half so much as I love one lock of your fair hair." She said these words, and she called me her "darling," and let me kiss her. She went on to tell me that she had left Caroline Helstone some money too; that this manor-house, with its furniture and books, she had bequeathed to me, as she did not choose to take the old family place from her own blood; and that all the rest of her property, amounting to about twelve thousand pounds, exclusive of the legacies to my sisters and Miss Helstone, she had willed, not to me, seeing I was already rich, but to a good man, who would make the best use of it that any human being could do: a man, she said, that was both gentle and brave, strong and merciful; a man that might not profess to be pious, but she knew he had the secret of religion pure and undefiled before God. The spirit of love and peace was with him: he visited the fatherless and widows in their affliction, and kept himself unspotted from the world. Then she asked, "Do you approve what I have done, Harry?" I could not answer, – my tears choked me, as they do now.'

Mr Moore allowed his pupil a moment to contend with and master his emotion: he then demanded:–

'What else did she say?'

'When I had signified my full consent to the conditions of her will, she told me I was a generous boy, and she was proud of me: "And now," she added, "in case anything should happen, you will know what to say to Malice when she comes whispering hard things in your ear, insinuating that Shirley has wronged you; that she did not love you. You will know that I *did* love you, Harry; that no sister could have loved you better, my own treasure." Mr Moore, sir, when I remember her voice, and recall her look, my heart beats as if it would break its strings. She *may* go to heaven before me – if God commands it, she *must*; but the rest of my life – and my life will not be long – I am glad of that now – shall be a straight, quick, thoughtful, journey in the path her step has pressed. I thought to enter the vault of the Keeldars before her: should it be otherwise, lay my coffin by Shirley's side.'

Moore answered him with a weighty calm, that offered a strange contrast to the boy's perturbed enthusiasm.

'You are wrong, both of you – you harm each other. If youth once falls under the influence of a shadowy terror, it imagines there will never be full sunlight again – its first calamity it fancies will last a lifetime. What more did she say? Anything more?'

'We settled one or two family points between ourselves.'

'I should rather like to know what–'

'But, Mr Moore, you smile – *I* could not smile to see Shirley in such a mood.'

'My boy, I am neither nervous, nor poetic, nor inexperienced. I see things as they are: you don't as yet. Tell me these family points.'

'Only, sir, she asked me whether I considered myself most of a Keeldar or a

# Shirley

Sympson; and I answered I was Keeldar to the core of the heart, and to the marrow of the bones. She said she was glad of it; for, besides her, I was the only Keeldar left in England: and then we agreed on some matters.'

'Well?'

'Well, sir, that if I lived to inherit my father's estate, and her house, I was to take the name of Keeldar, and to make Fieldhead my residence. Henry Shirley Keeldar I said I would be called: and I will. Her name and her manor-house are ages old, and Sympson and Sympson-Grove are of yesterday.'

'Come, you are neither of you going to heaven yet. I have the best hopes of you both, and with your proud distinctions – a pair of half-fledged eaglets. Now, what is your inference from all you have told me? put it into words.'

'That Shirley thinks she is going to die.'

'She referred to her health?'

'Not once; but I assure you she is wasting: her hands are growing quite thin, and so is her cheek.'

'Does she ever complain to your mother or sisters?'

'Never. She laughs at them when they question her. Mr Moore, she is a strange being – so fair and girlish: not a man-like woman at all – not an Amazon, and yet lifting her head above both help and sympathy.'

'Do you know where she is now, Henry? Is she in the house, or riding out?'

'Surely not out, sir – it rains fast.'

'True: which, however, is no guarantee that she is not at this moment cantering over Rushedge. Of late she has never permitted weather to be a hindrance to her rides.'

'You remember, Mr Moore, how wet and stormy it was last Wednesday? so wild, indeed, that she would not permit Zoë to be saddled; yet the blast she thought too tempestuous for her mare, she herself faced on foot; that afternoon she walked nearly as far as Nunnely. I asked her, when she came in, if she was not afraid of taking cold. "Not I," she said, "it would be too much good luck for me. I don't know, Harry; but the best thing that could happen to me would be to take a good cold and fever, and so pass off like other Christians." She is reckless, you see, sir.'

'Reckless indeed! Go and find out where she is; and if you can get an opportunity of speaking to her, without attracting attention, request her to come here a minute.'

'Yes, sir.'

He snatched his crutch, and started up to go.

'Harry!'

He returned.

'Do not deliver the message formally. Word it as, in former days, you would have worded an ordinary summons to the school-room.'

'I see, sir; she will be more likely to obey.'

'And Harry –'

'Sir?'

'I will call you when I want you: till then, you are dispensed from lessons.'

He departed. Mr Moore, left alone, rose from his desk.

'I can be very cool and very supercilious with Henry,' he said. 'I can seem to make light of his apprehensions, and look down "du haut de ma grandeur" on his youthful ardour. To *him* I can speak as if, in my eyes, they were both

children. Let me see if I can keep up the same rôle with her. I have known the moment when I seemed about to forget it; when Confusion and Submission seemed about to crush me with their soft tyranny; when my tongue faltered, and I have almost let the mantle drop, and stood in her presence, not master – no – but something else. I trust I shall never so play the fool: it is well for a Sir Philip Nunnely to redden when he meets her eye: he may permit himself the indulgence of submission – he may even without disgrace suffer his hand to tremble when it touches hers; but if one of her farmers were to show himself susceptible and sentimental, he would merely prove his need of a strait waistcoat. So far I have always done very well. She has sat near me, and I have not shaken – more than my desk. I have encountered her looks and smiles like – why, like a tutor, as I am. Her hand I never yet touched – never underwent that test. Her farmer or her footman I am not – no serf nor servant of hers have I ever been: but I am poor, and it behoves me to look to my self-respect – not to compromise an inch of it. What did she mean by that allusion to the cold people who petrify flesh to marble? It pleased me – I hardly know why – I would not permit myself to inquire – I never do indulge in scrutiny either of her language or countenance; for if I did, I should sometimes forget Common Sense and believe in Romance. A strange, secret ecstasy steals through my veins at moments: I'll not encourage – I'll not remember it. I am resolved, as long as may be, to retain the right to say with Paul – "I am not mad, but speak forth the words of truth and soberness." '

He paused – listening.

'Will she come, or will she not come?' he inquired. 'How will she take the message? naïvely or disdainfully? like a child or like a queen? Both characters are in her nature.

'If she comes, what shall I say to her? How account, firstly, for the freedom of the request? Shall I apologize to her? I could in all humility; but would an apology tend to place us in the positions we ought relatively to occupy in this matter? I *must* keep up the professor, otherwise – I hear a door – .' He waited. Many minutes passed.

'She will refuse me. Henry is entreating her to come: she declines. My petition is presumption in her eyes: let her *only* come, I can teach her to the contrary. I would rather she were a little perverse – it will steel me. I prefer her, cuirassed in pride, armed with a taunt. Her scorn startles me from my dreams – I stand up myself. A sarcasm from her eyes or lips puts strength into every nerve and sinew I have. Some step approaches, and not Henry's. . . .'

The door unclosed; Miss Keeldar came in. The message, it appeared, had found her at her needle: she brought her work in her hand. That day she had not been riding out: she had evidently passed it quietly. She wore her neat indoor dress and silk apron. This was no Thalestris from the fields, but a quiet domestic character from the fireside. Mr Moore had her at advantage: he should have addressed her at once in solemn accents, and with rigid mien; perhaps he would, had she looked saucy; but her air never showed less of crânerie; a soft kind of youthful shyness depressed her eyelid and mantled on her cheek. The tutor stood silent.

She made a full stop between the door and his desk.

'Did you want me, sir?' she asked.

'I ventured, Miss Keeldar, to send for you – that is, to ask an interview of a few minutes.'

She waited: she plyed her needle.

'Well, sir (not lifting her eyes) – what about?'

'Be seated first. The subject I would broach is one of some moment: perhaps I have hardly a right to approach it: it is possible I ought to frame an apology: it is possible no apology can excuse me. The liberty I have taken arises from a conversation with Henry. The boy is unhappy about your health: all your friends are unhappy on that subject. It is of your health I would speak.'

'I am quite well,' she said briefly.

'Yet changed.'

'That matters to none but myself. We all change.'

'Will you sit down? Formerly, Miss Keeldar, I had some influence with you – have I any now? May I feel that what I am saying is not accounted positive presumption?'

'Let me read some French, Mr Moore, or I will even take a spell at the Latin grammar, and let us proclaim a truce to all sanitary discussions.'

'No – no: it is time there were discussions.'

'Discuss away, then, but do not choose me for your text; I am a healthy subject.'

'Do you not think it wrong to affirm, and reaffirm, what is substantially untrue?'

'I say I am well: I have neither cough, pain, nor fever.'

'Is there no equivocation in that assertion? Is it the direct truth?'

'The direct truth.'

Louis Moore looked at her earnestly.

'I can myself,' he said, 'trace no indications of actual disease; but why, then, are you altered?'

'*Am* I altered?'

'We will try: we will seek a proof.'

'How?'

'I ask, in the first place, do you sleep as you used to?'

'I do not: but it is not because I am ill.'

'Have you the appetite you once had?'

'No: but it is not because I am ill.'

'You remember this little ring fastened to my watch-chain? It was my mother's, and is too small to pass the joint of my little finger. You have many a time sportively purloined it: it fitted your forefinger. Try now.'

She permitted the test: the ring dropped from the wasted little hand. Louis picked it up, and re-attached it to the chain. An uneasy flush coloured his brow. Shirley again said:–

'It is not because I am ill.'

'Not only have you lost sleep, appetite, and flesh,' proceeded Moore, 'but your spirits are always at ebb: besides, there is a nervous alarm in your eye – a nervous disquiet in your manner: these peculiarities were not formerly yours.'

'Mr Moore, we will pause here. You have exactly hit it: I am nervous. Now, talk of something else. What wet weather we have! Steady, pouring rain!'

'*You* nervous! Yes: and if Miss Keeldar is nervous, it is not without a cause. Let me reach it. Let me look nearer. The ailment is not physical: I have suspected

# Shirley

that. It came in one moment. I know the day, I noticed the change. Your pain is mental.'

'Not at all: it is nothing so dignified – merely nervous. Oh! dismiss the topic.'

'When it is exhausted: not till then. Nervous alarms should always be communicated, that they may be dissipated. I wish I had the gift of persuasion, and could incline you to speak willingly. I believe confession, in your case, would be half-equivalent to cure.'

'No,' said Shirley, abruptly: 'I wish that were at all probable; but I am afraid it is not.'

She suspended her work a moment. She was now seated. Resting her elbow on the table, she leaned her head on her hand. Mr Moore looked as if he felt he had at last gained some footing in this difficult path. She was serious, and in her wish was implied an important admission; after that, she could no longer affirm that *nothing* ailed her.

The tutor allowed her some minutes for repose and reflection, ere he returned to the charge: once, his lips moved to speak; but he thought better of it, and prolonged the pause. Shirley lifted her eye to his: had he betrayed injudicious emotion, perhaps obstinate persistence in silence would have been the result; but he looked calm, strong, trustworthy.

'I had better tell *you* than my aunt,' she said, 'or than my cousins, or my uncle: they would all make such a bustle – and it is that very bustle I dread; the alarm, the flurry, the éclat: in short, I never liked to be the centre of a small domestic whirlpool. You can bear a little shock – eh?'

'A great one, if necessary.'

Not a muscle of the man's frame moved, and yet his large heart beat fast in his deep chest. What was she going to tell him? Was irremediable mischief done?

'Had I thought it right to go to you, I would never have made a secret of the matter one moment,' she continued: 'I would have told at once, and asked advice.'

'Why was it not right to come to me?'

'It might be *right* – I do not mean that; but I could not do it. I seemed to have no title to trouble you: the mishap concerned me only – I wanted to keep it to myself, and people will not let me. I tell you, I hate to be an object of worrying attention, or a theme for village gossip. Besides, it may pass away without result – God knows!'

Moore, though tortured with suspense, did not demand a quick explanation; he suffered neither gesture, glance, nor word, to betray impatience. His tranquillity tranquillized Shirley; his confidence reassured her.

'Great effects may spring from trivial causes,' she remarked, as she loosened a bracelet from her wrist; then, unfastening her sleeve, and partially turning it up, –

'Look here, Mr Moore.'

She showed a mark in her white arm; rather a deep though healed up indentation: something between a burn and a cut.

'I would not show that to any one in Briarfield but you, because you can take it quietly.'

'Certainly there is nothing in the little mark to shock: its history will explain.'

'Small as it is, it has taken my sleep away, and made me nervous, thin, and

# Shirley

foolish; because, on account of that little mark, I am obliged to look forward to a possibility that has its terrors.'

The sleeve was readjusted; the bracelet replaced.

'Do you know that you try me!' he said smiling. 'I am a patient sort of man, but my pulse is quickening.'

'Whatever happens, you will befriend me, Mr Moore. You will give me the benefit of your self-possession, and not leave me at the mercy of agitated cowards?'

'I make no promise now. Tell me the tale, and then exact what pledge you will.'

'It is a very short tale. I took a walk with Isabella and Gertrude one day, about three weeks ago. They reached home before me: I stayed behind to speak to John. After leaving him, I pleased myself with lingering in the lane, where all was very still and shady: I was tired of chattering to the girls, and in no hurry to rejoin them. As I stood leaning against the gate-pillar, thinking some very happy thoughts about my future life – for that morning I imagined that events were beginning to turn as I had long wished them to turn –'

'Ah! Nunnely had been with her the evening before!' thought Moore, parenthetically.

'I heard a panting sound; a dog came running up the lane. I know most of the dogs in this neighbourhood; it was Phoebe, one of Mr Sam Wynne's pointers. The poor creature ran with her head down, her tongue hanging out; she looked as if bruised and beaten all over. I called her; I meant to coax her into the house, and give her some water and dinner; I felt sure she had been ill-used: Mr Sam often flogs his pointers cruelly. She was too flurried to know me; and when I attempted to pat her head, she turned and snatched at my arm. She bit it so as to draw blood, then ran panting on. Directly after, Mr Wynne's keeper came up, carrying a gun. He asked if I had seen a dog, I told him I had seen Phoebe.

' "You had better chain up Tartar, ma'am," he said, "and tell your people to keep within the house; I am after Phoebe to shoot her, and the groom is gone another way. She is raging mad." '

Mr Moore leaned back in his chair, and folded his arms across his chest; Miss Keeldar resumed her square of silk canvas, and continued the creation of a wreath of Parmese violets.

'And you told no one, sought no help, no cure: you would not come to me?'

'I got as far as the school-room door; there my courage failed: I preferred to cushion the matter.'

'Why? What can I demand better in this world than to be of use to you?'

'I had no claim.'

'Monstrous! And you did nothing?'

'Yes: I walked straight into the laundry, where they are ironing most of the week, now that I have so many guests in the house. While the maid was busy crimping or starching, I took an Italian iron from the fire, and applied the light scarlet glowing tip to my arm: I bored it well in: it cauterized the little wound. Then I went up-stairs.'

'I daresay you never once groaned?'

'I am sure I don't know. I was very miserable. Not firm or tranquil at all, I think: there was no calm in my mind.'

# Shirley

'There was calm in your person. I remember listening the whole time we sat at luncheon, to hear if you moved in the room above: all was quiet.'

'I was sitting at the foot of the bed, wishing Phoebe had not bitten me.'

'And alone! You like solitude.'

'Pardon me.'

'You disdain sympathy.'

'Do I, Mr Moore?'

'With your powerful mind, you must feel independent of help, of advice, of society.'

'So be it – since it pleases you.'

She smiled. She pursued her embroidery carefully and quickly; but her eyelash twinkled, and then it glittered, and then a drop fell.

Mr Moore leaned forward on his desk, moved his chair, altered his attitude.

'If it is not so,' he asked, with a peculiar, mellow change in his voice, 'how is it, then?'

'I don't know.'

'You do know, but you won't speak: all must be locked up in yourself.'

'Because it is not worth sharing.'

'Because nobody can give the high price you require for your confidence. Nobody is rich enough to purchase it. Nobody has the honour, the intellect, the power you demand in your adviser. There is not a shoulder in England on which you would rest your hand for support – far less a bosom which you would permit to pillow your head. Of course you must live alone.'

'I *can* live alone, if need be. But the question is not how to live – but how to die alone. That strikes me in a more grisly light.'

'You apprehend the effects of the virus – ? You anticipate an indefinitely threatening, dreadful doom – ?'

She bowed.

'You are very nervous and womanish.'

'You complimented me two minutes since on my powerful mind.'

'You are very womanish. If the whole affair were coolly examined and discussed, I feel assured it would turn out that there is no danger of your dying at all.'

'Amen! I am very willing to live, if it please God. I have felt life sweet.'

'How can it be otherwise than sweet with your endowments and nature? Do you truly expect that you will be seized with hydrophobia, and die raving mad?'

'I *expect* it, and have *feared* it. Just now, I fear nothing.'

'Nor do I, on your account. I doubt whether the smallest particle of virus mingled with your blood: and if it did, let me assure you that – young, healthy, faultlessly sound as you are – no harm will ensue. For the rest, I shall inquire whether the dog was really mad. I hold she was not mad.'

'Tell nobody that she bit me.'

'Why should I, when I believe the bite innocuous as a cut of this penknife? Make yourself easy: *I* am easy, though I value your life as much as I do my own chance of happiness in eternity. Look up.'

'Why, Mr Moore?'

'I wish to see if you are cheered. Put your work down: raise your head.'

'There –'

'Look at me. Thank you! And is the cloud broken?'

# Shirley

'I fear nothing.'

'Is your mind restored to its own natural sunny clime?'

'I am very content: but I want your promise.'

'Dictate.'

'You know, in case the worst I *have* feared should happen, they will smother me. You need not smile: they will – they always do. My uncle will be full of horror, weakness, precipitation; and that is the only expedient which will suggest itself to him. Nobody in the house will be self-possessed but you: now promise to befriend me – to keep Mr Sympson away from me – not to let Henry come near, lest I should hurt him. Mind – *mind* that you take care of yourself, too: but I shall not injure you, I know I shall not. Lock the chamber-door against the surgeons – turn them out, if they get in. Let neither the young nor the old MacTurk lay a finger on me; nor Mr Graves, their colleague; and, lastly, if I give trouble, with your own hand administer to me a strong narcotic: such a sure dose of laudanum as shall leave no mistake. *Promise to do this.*'

Moore left his desk, and permitted himself the recreation of one or two turns through the room. Stopping behind Shirley's chair, he bent over her, and said, in a low, emphatic voice, –

'I promise all you ask – without comment, without reservation.'

'If female help is needed, call in my housekeeper, Mrs Gill: let her lay me out, if I die. She is attached to me. She wronged me again and again, and again and again I forgave her. She now loves me, and would not defraud me of a pin: confidence has made her honest; forbearance has made her kindhearted. At this day, I can trust both her integrity, her courage, and her affection. Call her; but keep my good aunt and my timid cousins away. Once more, promise.'

'I promise.'

'That is good in you,' she said, looking up at him as he bent above her, and smiling.

'Is it good? Does it comfort?'

'Very much.'

'I will be with you – I and Mrs Gill only – in any, in every extremity where calm and fidelity are needed. No rash or coward hand shall meddle.'

'Yet you think me childish?'

'I do.'

'Ah! you despise me.'

'Do we despise children?'

'In fact, I am neither so strong, nor have I such pride in my strength, as people think, Mr Moore; nor am I so regardless of sympathy; but when I have any grief, I fear to impart it to those I love, lest it should pain them; and to those whom I view with indifference, I cannot condescend to complain. After all, you should not taunt me with being childish; for if you were as unhappy as I have been for the last three weeks, you too would want some friend.'

'We all want a friend, do we not?'

'All of us that have anything good in our natures.'

'Well, you have Caroline Helstone.'

'Yes . . . And you have Mr Hall.'

'Yes . . . Mrs Pryor is a wise, good woman: she can counsel you when you need counsel.'

'For your part, you have your brother Robert.'

# Shirley

'For any right-hand defections, there is the Rev. Matthewson Helstone, M.A., to lean upon; for any left-hand fallings off, there is Hiram Yorke, Esq. Both elders pay you homage.'

'I never saw Mrs Yorke so motherly to any young man as she is to you. I don't know how you have won her heart; but she is more tender to you than she is to her own sons. You have, besides, your sister, Hortense.'

'It appears we are both well provided.'

'It appears so.'

'How thankful we ought to be!'

'Yes.'

'How contented!'

'Yes.'

'For my part, I am almost contented just now, and very thankful. Gratitude is a divine emotion: it fills the heart, but not to bursting: it warms it, but not to fever. I like to taste leisurely of bliss: devoured in haste, I do not know its flavour.'

Still leaning on the back of Miss Keeldar's chair, Moore watched the rapid motion of her fingers, as the green and purple garland grew beneath them. After a prolonged pause, he again asked, –

'Is the shadow *quite* gone?'

'Wholly. As I *was* two hours since, and as I *am* now, are two different states of existence. I believe, Mr Moore, griefs and fears nursed in silence grow like Titan infants.'

'You will cherish such feelings no more in silence?'

'Not if I dare speak.'

'In using the word "*dare*," to whom do you allude?'

'To you.'

'How is it applicable to me?'

'On account of your austerity and shyness.'

'Why am I austere and shy?'

'Because you are proud.'

'Why am I proud?'

'I should like to know: will you be good enough to tell me?'

'Perhaps, because I am poor, for one reason: poverty and pride often go together.'

'That is such a nice reason: I should be charmed to discover another that would pair with it. Mate that turtle, Mr Moore.'

'Immediately. What do you think of marrying to sober Poverty many-tainted Caprice?'

'Are you capricious?'

'*You* are.'

'A libel. I am steady as a rock: fixed as the Polar Star.'

'I look out at some early hour of the day, and see a fine, perfect rainbow, bright with promise, gloriously spanning the beclouded welkin of life. An hour afterwards I look again – half the arch is gone, and the rest is faded. Still later, the stern sky denies that it ever wore so benign a symbol of hope.'

'Well, Mr Moore, you should contend against these changeful humours: they are your besetting sin. One never knows where to have you.'

'Miss Keeldar, I had once – for two years – a pupil who grew very dear to

# Shirley

me. Henry is dear, but she was dearer. Henry never gives me trouble; she – well – she did. I think she vexed me twenty-three hours out of the twenty-four –'

'She was never with you above three hours, or at the most six at a time.'

'She sometimes spilled the draught from my cup, and stole the food from my plate; and when she had kept me unfed for a day (and that did not suit me, for I am a man accustomed to take my meals with reasonable relish, and to ascribe due importance to the rational enjoyment of creature comforts) –'

'I know you do. I can tell what sort of dinners you like best – perfectly well. I know precisely the dishes you prefer –'

'She robbed these dishes of flavour, and made a fool of me besides. I like to sleep well. In my quiet days, when I was my own man, I never quarrelled with the night for being long, nor cursed my bed for its thorns. She changed all this.'

'Mr Moore –'

'And having taken from me peace of mind, and ease of life, she took from me herself; quite coolly, – just as if, when she was gone, the world would be all the same to me. I knew I should see her again at some time. At the end of two years, it fell out that we encountered again under her own roof, where she was mistress. How do you think she bore herself towards me, Miss Keeldar?'

'Like one who had profited well by lessons learned from yourself.'

'She received me haughtily: she meted out a wide space between us, and kept me aloof by the reserved gesture, the rare and alienated glance, the word calmly civil.'

'She was an excellent pupil! Having seen you distant, she at once learned to withdraw. Pray, sir, admire, in her hauteur, a careful improvement on your own coolness.'

'Conscience, and honour, and the most despotic necessity, dragged me apart from her, and kept me sundered with ponderous fetters. She was free: she might have been clement.'

'Never free to compromise her self-respect: to seek where she had been shunned.'

'Then she was inconsistent: she tantalized as before. When I thought I had made up my mind to seeing in her only a lofty stranger, she would suddenly show me such a glimpse of loving simplicity – she would warm me with such a beam of reviving sympathy, she would gladden an hour with converse so gentle, gay, and kindly – that I could no more shut my heart on her image, than I could close that door against her presence. Explain why she distressed me so.'

'She could not bear to be quite outcast; and then she would sometimes get a notion into her head, on a cold, wet day, that the school-room was no cheerful place, and feel it incumbent on her to go and see if you and Henry kept up a good fire; and once there, she liked to stay.'

'But she should not be changeful: if she came at all, she should come oftener.'

'There is such a thing as intrusion.'

'To-morrow, you will not be as you are to-day.'

'I don't know. Will you?'

'I am not mad, most noble Berenice! We may give one day to dreaming, but the next we must awake; and I shall awake to purpose the morning you are married to Sir Philip Nunnely. The fire shines on you and me, and shows us very clearly in the glass, Miss Keeldar; and I have been gazing on the picture

# Shirley

all the time I have been talking. Look up! What a difference between your head and mine! – I look old for thirty!'

'You are so grave; you have such a square brow; and your face is sallow. I never regard you as a young man, nor as Robert's junior.'

'Don't you? I thought not. Imagine Robert's clear-cut, handsome face looking over my shoulder. Does not the apparition make vividly manifest the obtuse mould of my heavy traits? There!' (he started) 'I have been expecting that wire to vibrate this last half-hour.'

The dinner-bell rang, and Shirley rose.

'Mr Moore,' she said, as she gathered up her silks, 'have you heard from your brother lately? Do you know what he means by staying in town so long? Does he talk of returning?'

'He talks of returning; but what has caused his long absence I cannot tell. To speak the truth, I thought none in Yorkshire knew better than yourself why he was reluctant to come home.'

A crimson shadow passed across Miss Keeldar's cheek.

'Write to him, and urge him to come,' she said. 'I know there has been no impolicy in protracting his absence thus far: it is good to let the mill stand, while trade is so bad; but he must not abandon the county.'

'I am aware,' said Louis, 'that he had an interview with you the evening before he left, and I saw him quit Fieldhead afterwards. I read his countenance, or *tried* to read it. He turned from me. I divined that he would be long away. Some fine slight fingers have a wondrous knack at pulverizing a man's brittle pride. I suppose Robert put too much trust in his manly beauty and native gentlemanhood. Those are better off who, being destitute of advantage, cannot cherish delusion. But I will write, and say you advise his return.'

'Do not say *I* advise his return, but that his return is advisable.'

The second bell rang, and Miss Keeldar obeyed its call.

# Chapter 29

## Louis Moore

ouis Moore was used to a quiet life: being a quiet man, he endured it better than most men would: having a large world of his own in his own head and heart, he tolerated confinement to a small, still corner of the real world very patiently.

How hushed is Fieldhead this evening! All but Moore – Miss Keeldar, the whole family of the Sympsons, even Henry – are gone to Nunnely. Sir Philip would have them come: he wished to make them acquainted with his mother and sisters, who are now at the Priory. Kind gentleman as the Baronet is, he asked the Tutor too; but the Tutor would much sooner have made an appointment

813

# Shirley

with the ghost of the Earl of Huntingdon to meet him, and a shadowy ring of his merry men, under the canopy of the thickest, blackest, oldest oak in Nunnely Forest. Yes, he would rather have appointed tryst with a phantom abbess, or mist-pale nun, among the wet and weedy relics of that ruined sanctuary of theirs, mouldering in the core of the wood. Louis Moore longs to have something near him to-night: but not the boy-baronet, nor his benevolent but stern mother, nor his patrician sisters, nor one soul of the Sympsons.

This night is not calm: the equinox still struggles in its storms. The wild rains of the day are abated: the great single cloud disparts and rolls away from heaven, not passing and leaving a sea all sapphire, but tossed buoyant before a continued, long-sounding, high-rushing moonlight tempest. The Moon reigns glorious, glad of the gale; as glad as if she gave herself to his fierce caress with love. No Endymion will watch for his goddess to-night: there are no flocks out on the mountains; and it is well, for to-night she welcomes Aeolus.

Moore – sitting in the school-room – heard the storm roar round the other gable, and along the hall-front: this end was sheltered. He wanted no shelter; he desired no subdued sounds, or screened position.

'All the parlours are empty,' said he: 'I am sick at heart of this cell.'

He left it, and went where the casements, larger and freer than the branch-screened lattice of his own apartment, admitted unimpeded the dark-blue, the silver-fleeced, the stirring and sweeping vision of the autumn night-sky. He carried no candle, unneeded was lamp or fire: the broad and clear, though cloud-crossed and fluctuating, beam of the moon shone on every floor and wall.

Moore wanders through all the rooms: he seems following a phantom from parlour to parlour. In the oak-room he stops; this is not chill, and polished, and fireless like the salon: the hearth is hot and ruddy; and cinders tinkle in the intense heat of their clear glow; near the rug is a little work-table, a desk upon it, a chair near it.

Does the vision Moore has tracked occupy that chair? You would think so, could you see him standing before it. There is as much interest now in his eye, and as much significance in his face, as if in this household solitude he had found a living companion, and was going to speak to it.

He makes discoveries. A bag, a small, satin bag, hangs on the chair-back. The desk is open, the keys are in the lock; a pretty seal, a silver pen, a crimson berry or two of ripe fruit on a green leaf, a small, clean, delicate glove – these trifles at once decorate and disarrange the stand they strew. Order forbids details in a picture: she puts them tidily away; but details give charm.

Moore spoke.

'Her mark,' he said: 'here she has been – careless, attractive thing! – called away in haste, doubtless, and forgetting to return and put all to rights. Why does she leave fascination in her foot-prints? Whence did she acquire the gift to be heedless, and never offend? There is always something to chide in her, and the reprimand never settles in displeasure on the heart; but, for her lover or her husband, when it had trickled a while in words, would naturally melt from his lips in a kiss. Better pass half an hour in remonstrating with her, than a day in admiring or praising any other women alive. Am I muttering – soliloquizing? Stop that!'

He did stop it. He stood thinking; and then he made an arrangement for his evening's comfort.

# Shirley

He dropped the curtains over the broad window and regal moon: he shut out Sovereign and Court and Starry Armies; he added fuel to the hot but fast-wasting fire; he lit a candle, of which there were a pair on the table; he placed another chair opposite that near the work-stand, and then he sat down. His next movement was to take from his pocket a small, thick book of blank paper; to produce a pencil; and to begin to write in a cramp, compact hand. Come near, by all means, reader: do not be shy: stoop over his shoulder fearlessly, and read as he scribbles.

'It is nine o'clock; the carriage will not return before eleven, I am certain. Freedom is mine till then: till then, I may occupy her room; sit opposite her chair; rest my elbow on her table; have her little mementos about me.

'I used rather to like Solitude – to fancy her a somewhat quiet and serious, yet fair nymph; an Oread, descending to me from lone mountain-passes; something of the blue mist of hills in her array, and of their chill breeze in her breath – but much, also, of their solemn beauty in her mien. I once could court her serenely, and imagine my heart easier when I held her to it – all mute, but majestic.

'Since that day I called S. to me in the school-room, and she came and sat so near my side; since she opened the trouble of her mind to me – asked my protection – appealed to my strength: since that hour I abhor Solitude. Cold abstraction – fleshless skeleton – daughter – mother – and mate of Death!

'It is pleasant to write about what is near and dear as the core of my heart: none can deprive me of this little book, and through this pencil, I can say to it what I will – say what I dare utter to nothing living – say what I dare not *think* aloud.

'We have scarcely encountered each other since that evening. Once, when I was alone in the drawing-room, seeing a book of Henry's she entered, dressed for a concert at Stillbro'. Shyness – *her* shyness, not mine – drew a silver veil between us. Much cant have I heard and read about "maiden modesty;" but, properly used, and not hackneyed, the words are good and appropriate words: as she passed to the window, after tacitly but gracefully recognizing me, I could call her nothing in my own mind save "stainless virgin:" to my perception, a delicate splendour robed her, and the modesty of girlhood was her halo. I may be the most fatuitous, as I am one of the plainest, of men; but, in truth, that shyness of hers touched me exquisitely: it flattered my finest sensations. I looked a stupid block, I dare say: I was alive with a life of Paradise, as she turned *her* glance from *my* glance, and softly averted her head to hide the suffusion of her cheek.

'I know this is the talk of a dreamer – of a rapt, romantic lunatic: I *do* dream: I *will* dream now and then; and if she has inspired romance into my prosaic composition, how can I help it?

'What a child she is sometimes! What an unsophisticated, untaught thing! I see her now, looking up into my face, and entreating me to prevent them from smothering her, and to be sure and give her a strong narcotic: I see her confessing that she was not so self-sufficing, so independent of sympathy, as people thought: I see the secret tear drop quietly from her eyelash. She said I thought her childish – and I did. She imagined I despised her. – Despised her! it was unutterably sweet to feel myself at once near her and above her: to be conscious of a natural right and power to sustain her, as a husband should sustain his wife.

# Shirley

'I worship her perfections; but it is her faults, or at least her foibles, that bring her near to me – that nestle her to my heart – that fold her about with my love – and that for a most selfish, but deeply-natural reason: these faults are the steps by which I mount to ascendency over her. If she rose a trimmed, artificial mound, without inequality, what vantage would she offer the foot? It is the natural hill, with its mossy breaks and hollows, whose slope invites ascent – whose summit it is pleasure to gain.

'To leave metaphor. It delights my eye to look on her: she suits me: if I were a king, and she the housemaid that swept my palace-stairs – across all that space between us – my eye would recognize her qualities; a true pulse would beat for her in my heart, though an unspanned gulf made acquaintance impossible. If I were a gentleman, and she waited on me as a servant, I could not help liking that Shirley. Take from her her education – take her ornaments, her sumptuous dress – all extrinsic advantages – take all grace, but such as the symmetry of her form renders inevitable; present her to me at a cottage-door, in a stuff-gown; let her offer me there a draught of water, with that smile – with that warm goodwill with which she now dispenses manorial hospitality – I should like her. I should wish to stay an hour: I should linger to talk with that rustic. I should not feel as I *now* do: I should find in her nothing divine; but whenever I met the young peasant, it would be with pleasure – whenever I left her, it would be with regret.

'How culpably careless in her to leave her desk open, where I know she has money! In the lock hang the keys of all her repositories, of her very jewel-casket. There is a purse in that little satin bag: I see the tassel of silver beads hanging out. That spectacle would provoke my brother Robert: all her little failings would, I know, be a source of irritation to him; if they vex me, it is a most pleasurable vexation: I delight to find her at fault, and were I always resident with her, I am aware she would be no niggard in thus ministering to my enjoyment. She would just give me something to do; to rectify: a theme for my tutor-lectures. I never lecture Henry: never feel disposed to do so: if he does wrong, – and that is very seldom, dear excellent lad! – a word suffices; often I do no more than shake my head; but the moment her "minois mutin" meets my eye, expostulatory words crowd to my lips: from a taciturn man, I believe she would transform me into a talker. Whence comes the delight I take in that talk? It puzzles myself sometimes: the more crâne, malin, taquin is her mood, consequently the clearer occasion she gives me for disapprobation; the more I seek her, the better I like her. She is never wilder than when equipped in her habit and hat; never less manageable than when she and Zoë come in fiery from a race with the wind on the hills; and I confess it – to this mute page I may confess it – I have waited an hour in the court, for the chance of witnessing her return, and for the dearer chance of receiving her in my arms from the saddle. I have noticed (again, it is to this page only I would make the remark) that she will never permit any man but myself to render her that assistance. I have seen her politely decline Sir Philip Nunnely's aid: she is always mighty gentle with her young baronet; mighty tender of his feelings, forsooth, and of his very thin-skinned amour-propre: I have marked her haughtily reject Sam Wynne's. Now I know – my heart knows it, for it has felt it – that she resigns herself to me unreluctantly: is she conscious how my strength rejoices to serve her? I myself am not her slave – I declare it, – but my faculties gather to her beauty, like the

# Shirley

genii to the glisten of the Lamp. All my knowledge, all my prudence, all my
calm, and all my power, stand in her presence humbly waiting a task. How glad
they are when a mandate comes! What joy they take in the toil she assigns! Does
she know it?

'I have called her careless: it is remarkable that her carelessness never
compromises her refinement; indeed, through this very loop-hole of character,
the reality, depth, genuineness of that refinement may be ascertained: a whole
garment sometimes covers meagreness and malformation; through a rent sleeve,
a fair round arm may be revealed. I have seen and handled many of her
possessions, because they are frequently astray. I never saw anything that did
not proclaim the lady: nothing sordid, nothing soiled; in one sense she is as
scrupulous as, in another, she is unthinking: as a peasant girl, she would go ever
trim and cleanly. Look at the pure kid of this little glove, – at the fresh, unsullied
satin of the bag.

'What a difference there is between S. and that pearl C. H.! Caroline, I fancy,
is the soul of conscientious punctuality and nice exactitude; she would precisely
suit the domestic habits of a certain fastidious kinsman of mine: so delicate,
dexterous, quaint, quick, quiet; all done to a minute, all arranged to a straw-
breadth: she would suit Robert; but what could _I_ do with anything so nearly
faultless? _She_ is my equal; poor as myself; she is certainly pretty: a little Raffaelle
head hers; Raffaelle in feature, quite English in expression: all insular grace
and purity; but where is there anything to alter, anything to endure, anything
to reprimand, to be anxious about? There she is, a lily of the valley, untinted,
needing no tint. What change could improve her? What pencil dare to paint?
_My_ sweetheart, if I ever have one, must bear nearer affinity to the rose: a sweet,
lively delight guarded with prickly peril. _My_ wife, if I ever marry, must stir my
great frame with a sting now and then: she must furnish use to her husband's
vast mass of patience. I was not made so enduring to be mated with a lamb: I
should find more congenial responsibility in the charge of a young lioness or
leopardess. I like few things sweet, but what are likewise pungent; few things
bright, but what are likewise hot. I like the summer-day, whose sun makes fruit
blush and corn blanch. Beauty is never so beautiful as when, if I tease it, it
wreathes back on me with spirit. Fascination is never so imperial as when,
roused and half-ireful, she threatens transformation to fierceness. I fear I should
tire of the mute, monotonous innocence of the lamb; I should erelong feel as
burdensome the nestling dove which never stirred in my bosom; but my patience
would exult in stilling the flutterings and training the energies of the restless
merlin. In managing the wild instincts of the scarce manageable "bête fauve,"
my powers would revel.

'Oh, my pupil! Oh, Peri! too mutinous for heaven – too innocent for hell!
never shall I do more than see, and worship, and wish for thee. Alas! knowing
I could make thee happy, will it be my doom to see thee possessed by those who
have not that power?

'However kindly the hand – if it is feeble, it cannot bend Shirley; and she
must be bent: it cannot curb her, and she must be curbed.

'Beware! Sir Philip Nunnely! I never see you walking or sitting at her side,
and observe her lips compressed, or her brow knit, in resolute endurance of
some trait of your character which she neither admires nor likes; in determined
toleration of some weakness she believes atoned for by a virtue, but which annoys

her, despite that belief: I never mark the grave glow of her face, the unsmiling sparkle of her eye, the slight recoil of her whole frame when you draw a little too near, and gaze a little too expressively, and whisper a little too warmly: I never witness these things, but I think of the fable of Semele reversed.

'It is not the daughter of Cadmus I see: nor do I realize her fatal longing to look on Jove in the majesty of his god-head. It is a priest of Juno that stands before me, watching late and lone at a shrine in an Argive temple. For years of solitary ministry, he has lived on dreams: there is divine madness upon him: he loves the idol he serves, and prays day and night that his frenzy may be fed, and that the Ox-eyed may smile on her votary. She has heard; she will be propitious. All Argos slumbers. The doors of the temple are shut: the priest waits at the altar.

'A shock of heaven and earth is felt – not by the slumbering city; only by that lonely watcher, brave and unshaken in his fanaticism. In the midst of silence, with no preluding sound, he is wrapt in sudden light. Through the roof – through the rent, wide-yawning, vast, white-blazing blue of heaven above, pours a wondrous descent – dread as the down-rushing of stars. He has, what he asked: withdraw – forbear to look – I am blinded. I hear in that fane an unspeakable sound – would that I could not hear it! I see an insufferable glory burning terribly between the pillars. Gods be merciful and quench it!

'A pious Argive enters to make an early offering in the cool dawn of morning. There was thunder in the night: the bolt fell here. The shrine is shivered: the marble pavement round, split and blackened. Saturnia's statue rises chaste, grand, untouched: at her feet, piled ashes lie pale. No priest remains: he who watched will be seen no more.

'There is the carriage! Let me lock up the desk and pocket the keys: she will be seeking them to-morrow: she will have to come to me. I hear her –

' "Mr Moore, have you seen my keys?"

'So she will say in her clear voice, speaking with reluctance, looking ashamed, conscious that this is the twentieth time of asking. I will tantalize her: keep her with me, expecting, doubting: and when I *do* restore them, it shall not be without a lecture. Here is the bag, too, and the purse; the glove – pen – seal. She shall wring them all out of me slowly and separately: only by confession, penitence, entreaty. I never can touch her hand, or a ringlet of her head, or a ribbon of her dress, but I will make privileges for myself: every feature of her face, her bright eyes, her lips, shall go through each change they know, for my pleasure: display each exquisite variety of glance and curve, to delight – thrill – perhaps, more hopelessly to enchain me. If I *must* be her slave, I will not lose my freedom for nothing.'

He locked the desk, pocketed all the property, and went.

# Chapter 30

## Rushedge, a Confessional

Everybody said it was high time for Mr Moore to return home: all Briarfield wondered at his strange absence, and Whinbury and Nunnely brought each its separate contribution of amazement.

Was it known why he stayed away? Yes: it was known twenty – forty times over; there being, at least, forty plausible reasons adduced to account for the unaccountable circumstances. Business, it was not – *that* the gossips agreed: he had achieved the business on which he departed long ago: his four ringleaders he had soon scented out and run down; he had attended their trial, heard their conviction and sentence, and seen them safely shipped prior to transportation.

This was known at Briarfield: the newspapers had reported it: the 'Stilbro' Courier' had given every particular, with amplifications. None applauded his perseverance or hailed his success; though the mill-owners were glad of it, trusting that the terrors of Law vindicated would henceforward paralyse the sinister valour of disaffection. Disaffection, however, was still heard muttering to himself. He swore ominous oaths over the drugged beer of alehouses, and drank strange toasts in fiery British gin.

One report affirmed that Moore *dared* not come to Yorkshire: he knew his life was not worth an hour's purchase, if he did.

'I'll tell him that,' said Mr Yorke, when his foreman mentioned the rumour; 'and if *that* does not bring him home full-gallop – nothing will.'

Either that or some other motive prevailed, at last, to recall him. He announced to Joe Scott the day he should arrive at Stilbro', desiring his hackney to be sent to the 'George' for his accommodation; and Joe Scott having informed Mr Yorke, that gentleman made it in his way to meet him.

It was market-day: Moore arrived in time to take his usual place at the market-dinner. As something of a stranger – and as a man of note and action – the assembled manufacturers received him with a certain distinction. Some – who in public would scarcely have dared to acknowledge his acquaintance, lest a little of the hate and vengeance laid up in store for him should perchance have fallen on them – in private hailed him as in some sort their champion. When the wine had circulated, their respect would have kindled to enthusiasm, had not Moore's unshaken nonchalance held it in a damp, low, smouldering state.

Mr Yorke – the permanent president of these dinners – witnessed his young friend's bearing with exceeding complacency. If one thing could stir his temper or excite his contempt more than another, it was to see a man befooled by flattery, or elate with popularity. If one thing smoothed, soothed, and charmed him especially, it was the spectacle of a public character incapable of relishing

his publicity: *incapable*, I say; disdain would but have incensed – it was indifference that appeased his rough spirit.

Robert, leaning back in his chair, quiet and almost surly, while the clothiers and blanket-makers vaunted his prowess and rehearsed his deeds – many of them interspersing their flatteries with coarse invectives against the operative class – was a delectable sight for Mr Yorke. His heart tingled with the pleasing conviction that these gross eulogiums shamed Moore deeply, and made him half scorn himself and his work. On abuse, on reproach, on calumny, it is easy to smile; but painful indeed is the panegyric of those we contemn. Often had Moore gazed with a brilliant countenance over howling crowds from a hostile hustings: he had breasted the storm of unpopularity with gallant bearing and soul elate; but he dropped his head under the half-bred tradesmen's praise, and shrank chagrined before their congratulations.

Yorke could not help asking him how he liked his supporters, and whether he did not think they did honour to his cause. 'But it is a pity, lad,' he added, 'that you did not hang these four samples of the Unwashed. If you had managed *that* feat, the gentry here would have riven the horses out of the coach, yoked to a score of asses, and drawn you into Stilbro' like a conquering general.'

Moore soon forsook the wine, broke from the party, and took the road. In less than five minutes Mr Yorke followed him: they rode out of Stilbro' together.

It was early to go home, but yet it was late in the day: the last ray of the sun had already faded from the cloud-edges, and the October night was casting over the moorlands the shadow of her approach.

Mr Yorke – moderately exhilarated with his moderate libations, and not displeased to see young Moore again in Yorkshire, and to have him for his comrade during the long ride home – took the discourse much to himself. He touched briefly, but scoffingly, on the trials and the conviction; he passed thence to the gossip of the neighbourhood, and, ere-long, he attacked Moore on his own personal concerns.

'Bob, I believe you are worsted; and you deserve it. All was smooth. Fortune had fallen in love with you: she had decreed you the first prize in her wheel – twenty thousand pounds: she only required that you should hold your hand out and take it. And what did you do? You called for a horse and rode a-hunting to Warwickshire. Your sweet-heart – Fortune, I mean – was perfectly indulgent. She said, "I'll excuse him: he's young." She waited like "Patience on a monument," till the chase was over, and the vermin-prey run down. She expected you would come back then, and be a good lad: you might still have had her first prize.

'It capped her beyond expression, and me too, to find that, instead of thundering home in a breakneck gallop, and laying your assize-laurels at her feet, you coolly took coach up to London. What you have done there, Satan knows: nothing in this world, I believe, but sat and sulked: your face was never lily-fair, but it is olive-green now. You're not as bonnie as you were, man.'

'And who is to have this prize you talk so much about?'

'Only a baronet: that is all. I have not a doubt in my own mind you've lost her: she will be Lady Nunnely before Christmas.'

'Hem! Quite probable.'

'But she need not to have been. Fool of a lad! I swear you might have had her!'

# Shirley

'By what token, Mr Yorke?"

'By every token. By the light of her eyes, the red of her cheeks: red they grew when your name was mentioned, though of custom they are pale.'

'My chance is quite over, I suppose?'

'It ought to be; but try: it is worth trying. I call this Sir Philip milk and water. And then he writes verses, they say – tags rhymes. *You* are above that, Bob, at all events.'

'Would you advise me to propose, late as it is, Mr Yorke? at the eleventh hour?'

'You can but make the experiment, Robert. If she has a fancy for you – and, on my conscience, I believe she has, or had – she will forgive much. But, my lad, you are laughing: is it at me? You had better grin at your own perverseness. I see, however, you laugh at the wrong side of your mouth: you have as sour a look at this moment as one need wish to see.'

'I have so quarrelled with myself, Yorke. I have so kicked against the pricks, and struggled in a strait waistcoat, and dislocated my wrists with wrenching them in handcuffs, and battered my hard head, by driving it against a harder wall.'

'Ha! I'm glad to hear that. Sharp exercise yon'! I hope it has done you good; ta'en some of the self-conceit out of you?'

'Self-conceit! What is it? Self-respect, self-tolerance, even, what are they? Do you sell the articles? Do you know anybody who does? Give an indication: they would find in me a liberal chapman. I would part with my last guinea this minute to buy.'

'Is it so with you, Robert? I find that spicy. I like a man to speak his mind. What has gone wrong?'

'The machinery of all my nature; the whole enginery of this human mill: the boiler, which I take to be the heart, is fit to burst.'

'That suld be putten i' print: it's striking. It's almost blank verse. Ye'll be jingling into poetry just e' now. If the afflatus comes, give way, Robert; never heed me: I'll bear it this whet (time).'

'Hideous, abhorrent, base blunder! You may commit in a moment what you will rue for years – what life cannot cancel.'

'Lad, go on. I call it pie, nuts, sugar-candy. I like the taste uncommonly. Go on: it will do you good to talk: the moor is before us now, and there is no life for many a mile round.'

'I *will* talk. I am not ashamed to tell. There is a sort of wild cat in my breast, and I choose that you shall hear how it can yell.'

'To me it is music. What grand voices you and Louis have! When Louis sings – tones off like a soft, deep bell, I've felt myself tremble again. The night is still: it listens: it is just leaning down to you, like a black priest to a blacker penitent. Confess, lad: smooth naught down: be candid as a convicted, justified, sanctified methody at an experience-meeting. Make yourself as wicked as Beelzebub: it will ease your mind.'

'As mean as Mammon, you would say. Yorke, if I got off horse-back and laid myself down across the road, would you have the goodness to gallop over me – backwards and forwards – about twenty times?'

'Wi' all the pleasure in life, if there were no such thing as a coroner's inquest.'

'Hiram Yorke, I certainly believed she loved me. I have seen her eyes sparkle

radiantly when she has found me out in a crowd: she has flushed up crimson when she has offered me her hand, and said, "How do you do, Mr Moore?"

'My name had a magical influence over her: when others uttered it, she changed countenance, – I know she did. She pronounced it herself in the most musical of her many musical tones. She was cordial to me; she took an interest in me; she was anxious about me; she wished me well; she sought, she seized every opportunity to benefit me. I considered, paused, watched, weighed, wondered: I could come to but one conclusion – this is love.

'I looked at her, Yorke: I saw, in her, youth and a species of beauty. I saw power in her. Her wealth offered me the redemption of my honour and my standing. I owed her gratitude. She had aided me substantially and effectually by a loan of five thousand pounds. Could I remember these things? Could I believe she loved me? Could I hear wisdom urge me to marry her, and disregard every dear advantage, disbelieve every flattering suggestion, disdain every well-weighed counsel, turn and leave her? Young, graceful, gracious, – my benefactress, attached to me, enamoured of me, – I used to say so to myself; dwell on the word; mouth it over and over again; swell over it with a pleasant, pompous complacency, – with an admiration dedicated entirely to myself, and unimpaired even by esteem for her; indeed, I smiled in deep secrecy at her naïveté and simplicity, in being the first to love, and to show it. That whip of yours seems to have a good heavy handle, Yorke: you can swing it about your head and knock me out of the saddle, if you choose. I should rather relish a loundering whack.'

'Tak' patience, Robert, till the moon rises, and I can see you. Speak plain out, – did you love her, or not? I could like to know: I feel curious.'

'Sir ... Sir – I say – she is very pretty, in her own style, and very attractive. She has a look, at times, of a thing made out of fire and air, at which I stand and marvel, without a thought of clasping and kissing it. I felt in her a powerful magnet to my interest and vanity: I never felt as if nature meant her to be my other and better self. When a question on that head rushed upon me, I flung it off, saying brutally, I should be rich with her, and ruined without her: vowing I would be practical and not romantic.'

'A very sensible resolve. What mischief came of it, Bob?'

'With this sensible resolve, I walked up to Fieldhead one night last August: it was the very eve of my departure for Birmingham – for – you see – I wanted to secure fortune's splendid prize: I had previously despatched a note, requesting a private interview. I found her at home, and alone.

'She received me without embarrassment, for she thought I came on business: *I* was embarrassed enough, but determined. I hardly know how I got the operation over; but I went to work in a hard, firm fashion, – frightful enough, I daresay. I sternly offered myself – my fine person – with my debts, of course, as a settlement.

'It vexed me; it kindled my ire, to find that she neither blushed, trembled, nor looked down. She responded: –

' "I doubt whether I have understood you, Mr. Moore."

'And I had to go over the whole proposal twice, and word it as plainly as A B C, before she would fully take it in. And then, what did she do? Instead of faltering a sweet Yes, or maintaining a soft, confused silence (which would have

been as good) she started up, walked twice fast through the room, in the way that *she* only does, and no other woman, and ejaculated, –

' "God bless me!"

'Yorke, I stood on the hearth, backed by the mantel-piece; against it I leaned, and prepared for anything – everything. I knew my doom, and I knew myself. There was no misunderstanding her aspect and voice. She stopped and looked at me.

' "God bless me!" she pitilessly repeated, in that shocked, indignant, yet saddened accent. "You have made a strange proposal – strange from *you*; and if you knew how strangely you worded it, and looked it, you would be startled at yourself. You spoke like a brigand who demanded my purse, rather than like a lover who asked my heart."

'A queer sentence, was it not, Yorke? and I knew, as she uttered it, it was true as queer. Her words were a mirror in which I saw myself.

'I looked at her, dumb and wolfish: she at once enraged and shamed me.

' "Gérard Moore, you know you don't love Shirley Keeldar." I might have broken out into false swearing: vowed that I did love her; but I could not lie in her pure face: I could not perjure myself in her truthful presence. Besides, such hollow oaths would have been vain as void: she would no more have believed me than she would have believed the ghost of Judas, had he broken from the night and stood before her. Her female heart had finer perceptions than to be cheated into mistaking my half-coarse, half-cold admiration, for true-throbbing, manly love.

'What next happened? you will say, Mr Yorke.

'Why, she sat down in the window-seat and cried. She cried passionately: her eyes not only rained, but lightened. They flashed, open, large, dark, haughty, upon me: they said – "You have pained me: you have outraged me: you have deceived me."

'She added words soon to looks.

' "I *did* respect – I *did* admire – I *did* like you," she said: "yes – as much as if you were my brother: and *you* – *you* want to make a speculation of me. You would immolate me to that mill – your Moloch!"

'I had the common sense to abstain from any word of excuse – any attempt at palliation: I stood to be scorned.

'Sold to the devil for the time being, I was certainly infatuated: when I did speak, what do you think I said?

' "Whatever my own feelings were, I was persuaded *you* loved *me*, Miss Keeldar."

'Beautiful! – was it not? She sat quite confounded. "Is it Robert Moore that speaks?" I heard her mutter. "Is it a man – or something lower?"

' "Do you mean," she asked aloud – "do you mean you thought I loved you as we love those we wish to marry?"

'It *was* my meaning; and I said so.

' "You conceived an idea obnoxious to a woman's feeling," was her answer: "you have announced it in a fashion revolting to a woman's soul. You insinuate that all the frank kindness I have shown you has been a complicated, a bold, and an immodest manoeuvre to ensnare a husband: you imply that at last you come here out of pity to offer me your hand, because I have courted you. Let me say this: – Your sight is jaundiced: you have been wrong. Your mind is warped: you

# Shirley

have judged wrong. Your tongue betrays you: you now speak wrong. I never loved you. Be at rest there. My heart is as pure of passion for you as yours is barren of affection for me."

'I hope I was answered, Yorke?

' "I seem to be a blind, besotted sort of person," was my remark.

' "*Loved* you!" she cried. "Why, I have been as frank with you as a sister – never shunned you – never feared you. You cannot," she affirmed, triumphantly – "you cannot make me tremble with your coming, nor accelerate my pulse by your influence."

'I alleged that often, when she spoke to me, she blushed, and that the sound of my name moved her.

' "Not for *your* sake!" she declared, briefly: I urged explanation, but could get none.

' "When I sat beside you at the school-feast, did you think I loved you then? When I stopped you in Maythorn-lane, did you think I loved you then? When I called on you in the counting-house – when I walked with you on the pavement – did you think I loved you then?"

'So she questioned me; and I said I did.

'By the Lord! Yorke – she rose – she grew tall – she expanded and refined almost to flame; there was a trembling all through her, as in live coal, when its vivid vermilion is hottest.

' "That is to say, that you have the worst opinion of me: that you deny me the possession of all I value most. That is to say, that I am a traitor to all my sisters: that I have acted as no woman can act, without degrading herself and her sex: that I have sought where the incorrupt of my kind naturally scorn and abhor to seek." She and I were silent, for many a minute. "Lucifer – Star of the Morning!" she went on, "thou art fallen. You – once high in my esteem – are hurled down: you – once intimate in my friendship – are cast out. Go!"

'I went not: I had heard her voice tremble – seen her lip quiver: I knew another storm of tears would fall; and then, I believed, some calm and some sunshine must come, and I would wait for it.

'As fast, but more quietly than before, the warm rain streamed down: there was another sound in her weeping – a softer, more regretful sound. While I watched, her eyes lifted to me a gaze more reproachful than haughty – more mournful than incensed.

' "Oh, Moore!" said she: "it was worse than Et tu, Brute!"

'I relieved myself by what should have been a sigh, but it became a groan. A sense of Cain-like desolation made my breast ache.

' "There has been error in what I have done," I said, "and it has won me bitter wages; which I will go and spend far from her who gave them."

'I took my hat. All the time, I could not have borne to depart so; and I believed she would not let me. Nor would she, but for the mortal pang I had given her pride, that cowed her compassion and kept her silent.

'I was obliged to turn back of my own accord when I reached the door, to approach her and to say, "Forgive me."

' "I could, if there was not myself to forgive, too," was her reply; "but to mislead a sagacious man so far, I must have done wrong."

'I broke out suddenly with some declamation I do not remember: I know that

# Shirley

is was sincere, and that my wish and aim were to absolve her to herself: in fact, in her case, self-accusation was a chimera.

'At last, she extended her hand. For the first time I wished to take her in my arms and kiss her. I *did* kiss her hand many times.

' "Some day we shall be friends again," she said, "when you have had time to read my actions and motives in a true light, and not so horribly to misinterpret them. Time may give you the right key to all: then, perhaps, you will comprehend me; and then we shall be reconciled."

'Farewell drops rolled slow down her cheeks: she wiped them away.

' "I am sorry for what has happened – deeply sorry," she sobbed. So was I, God knows! Thus were we severed.'

'A queer tale!' commented Mr Yorke.

'I'll do it no more,' vowed his companion: 'never more will I mention marriage to a woman, unless I feel love. Henceforth, Credit and Commerce may take care of themselves. Bankruptcy may come when it lists. I have done with slavish fear of disaster. I mean to work diligently, wait patiently, bear steadily. Let the worst come – I will take an axe and an emigrant's berth, and go out with Louis to the West – he and I have settled it. No woman shall ever again look at me as Miss Keeldar looked – ever again feel towards me as Miss Keeldar felt: in no woman's presence will I ever again stand at once such a fool and such a knave – such a brute and such a puppy.'

'Tut!' said the imperturbable Yorke, 'you make too much of it; but still, I say, I am capped: firstly, that she did not love you; and, secondly, that you did not love her. You are both young; you are both handsome; you are both well enough for wit, and even for temper – take you on the right side; what ailed you, that you could not agree?'

'We never *have* been – never *could* be *at home* with each other, Yorke. Admire each other as we might at a distance, still we jarred when we came very near. I have sat at one side of a room and observed her at the other; perhaps in an excited, genial moment, when she had some of her favourites round her – her old beaux, for instance, yourself and Helstone, with whom she is so playful, pleasant, and eloquent. I have watched her when she was most natural, most lively, and most lovely; my judgment has pronounced her beautiful: beautiful she is, at times, when her mood and her array partake of the splendid. I have drawn a little nearer, feeling that our terms of acquaintance gave me the right of approach; I have joined the circle round her seat, caught her eye, and mastered her attention; then we have conversed; and others – thinking me, perhaps, peculiarly privileged – have withdrawn by degrees, and left us alone. Were we happy thus left? For myself, I must say, No. Always a feeling of constraint came over me; always I was disposed to be stern and strange. We talked politics and business: no soft sense of domestic intimacy ever opened our hearts, or thawed our language, and made it flow easy and limpid. If we had confidences, they were confidences of the counting-house, not of the hearth. Nothing in her cherished affection in me – made me better, gentler: she only stirred my brain and whetted my acuteness: she never crept into my heart or influenced its pulse: and for this good reason, no doubt, because I had not the secret of making her love me.'

'Well, lad, it is a queer thing. I might laugh at thee, and reckon to despise thy refinements; but as it is dark night and we are by ourselves, I don't mind

# Shirley

telling thee that thy talk brings back a glimpse of my own past life. Twenty-five years ago, I tried to persuade a beautiful woman to love me, and she would not. I had not the key to her nature: she was a stone wall to me, doorless and windowless.'

'But you loved *her*, Yorke: you worshipped Mary Cave: your conduct, after all, was that of a man – never of a fortune-hunter.'

'Ay! I *did* love her; but then she was beautiful as the moon we do *not* see tonight: there is naught like her in these days: Miss Helstone, maybe, has a look of her, but nobody else.'

'Who has a look of her?'

'That black-coated tyrant's niece; that quiet, delicate Miss Helstone. Many a time I have put on my spectacles to look at the lassie in church, because she has gentle blue een, wi' long lashes; and, when she sits in shadow, and is very still and very pale, and is, happen, about to fall asleep wi' the length of the sermon and the heat of the biggin' – she is as like one of Canova's marbles as aught else.'

'Was Mary Cave in that style?'

'Far grander! Less lass-like and flesh-like. You wondered why she hadn't wings and a crown. She was a stately, peaceful angel – was my Mary.'

'And you could not persuade her to love you?'

'Not with all I could do; though I prayed Heaven many a time, on my bended knees, to help me.'

'Mary Cave was not what you think her, Yorke – I have seen her picture at the Rectory. She is no angel, but a fair, regular-featured, taciturn-looking woman – rather too white and lifeless for my taste. But – supposing she had been something better than she was –'

'Robert,' interrupted Yorke, 'I could fell you off your horse at this moment. However, I'll hold my hand. Reason tells me you are right, and I am wrong. I know well enough that the passion I still have is only the remnant of an illusion. If Miss Cave had possessed either feeling or sense, she could not have been so perfectly impassible to my regard as she showed herself – she must have preferred me to that copper-faced despot.'

'Supposing, Yorke, she had been educated (no women were educated in those days); supposing she had possessed a thoughtful, original mind, a love of knowledge, a wish for information, which she took an artless delight in receiving from your lips, and having measured out to her by your hand; supposing her conversation – when she sat at your side – was fertile, varied, imbued with a picturesque grace and genial interest, quiet-flowing but clear and bounteous; supposing that when you stood near her by chance, or when you sat near her by design, comfort at once became your atmosphere, and content your element; supposing that whenever her face was under your gaze, or her idea filled your thoughts, you gradually ceased to be hard and anxious, and pure affection, love of home, thirst for sweet discourse, unselfish longing to protect and cherish, replaced the sordid, cankering calculations of your trade; supposing – with all this – that many a time, when you had been so happy as to possess your Mary's little hand, you had felt it tremble as you held it – just as a warm little bird trembles when you take it from its nest; supposing you had noticed her shrink into the background on your entrance into a room, yet if you sought her in her retreat she welcomed you with the sweetest smile that ever lit a fair virgin face,

# Shirley

and only turned her eyes from the encounter of your own, lest their clearness should reveal too much; supposing, in short, your Mary had been – not cold, but modest; not vacant, but reflective; not obtuse, but sensitive; not inane, but innocent; not prudish, but pure – would you have left her to court another woman for her wealth?'

Mr Yorke raised his hat, wiped his forehead with his handkerchief.

'The moon is up,' was his first not quite relevant remark, pointing with his whip across the moor. 'There she is, rising into the haze, staring at us wi' a strange red glower. She is no more silver than old Helstone's brow is ivory. What does she mean by leaning her cheek on Rushedge i' that way, and looking at us wi' a scowl and a menace?'

'Yorke, if Mary had loved you silently, yet faithfully – chastely, yet fervently – as you would wish your wife to love, would you have left her?'

'Robert!' he lifted his arm: he held it suspended, and paused. 'Robert! this is a queer world, and men are made of the queerest dregs that Chaos churned up in her ferment. I might swear sounding oaths – oaths that would make the poachers think there was a bittern booming in Bilberry Moss – that, in the case you put, Death only should have parted me from Mary. But I have lived in the world fifty-five years; I have been forced to study human nature; and – to speak a dark truth – the odds are, if Mary had loved and not scorned me; if I had been secure of her affection, certain of her constancy, been irritated by no doubts, stung by no humiliations – the odds are' (he let his hand fall heavy on the saddle) – 'the odds are, I should have left her!'

They rode side by side in silence. Ere either spoke again, they were on the other side of Rushedge: Briarfield lights starred the purple skirt of the moor. Robert, being the youngest, and having less of the part to absorb him than his comrade, recommenced first.

'I believe – I daily find it proved – that we can get nothing in this world worth keeping, not so much as a principle or a conviction, except out of purifying flame, or through strengthening peril. We err; we fall; we are humbled – then we walk more carefully. We greedily eat and drink poison out of the gilded cup of vice, or from the beggar's wallet of avarice; we are sickened, degraded; everything good in us rebels against us; our souls rise bitterly indignant against our bodies; there is a period of civil war; if the soul has strength, it conquers and rules thereafter.'

'What art thou going to do now, Robert? What are thy plans?'

'For my private plans, I'll keep them to myself; which is very easy, as at present I have none: no private life is permitted a man in my position, a man in debt. For my public plans, my views are a little altered. While I was in Birmingham, I looked a little into reality, considered closely, and at their source, the causes of the present troubles of this country; I did the same in London. Unknown, I could go where I pleased, mix with whom I would. I went where there was want of food, of fuel, of clothing; where there was no occupation and no hope. I saw some, with naturally elevated tendencies and good feelings, kept down amongst sordid privations and harassing griefs. I saw many originally low, and to whom lack of education left scarcely anything but animal wants, disappointed in those wants, ahungered, athirst, and desperate as famished animals: I saw what taught my brain a new lesson, and filled my breast with fresh feelings. I have no intention to profess more softness or sentiment than I

have hitherto professed; mutiny and ambition I regard as I have always regarded them: I should resist a riotous mob just as heretofore: I should open on the scent of a runaway ringleader as eagerly as ever, and run him down as relentlessly, and follow him up to condign punishment as rigorously; but I should do it now chiefly for the sake and the security of those he misled. Something there is to look to, Yorke, beyond a man's personal interest: beyond the advancement of well-laid schemes; beyond even the discharge of dishonouring debts. To respect himself, a man must believe he renders justice to his fellow-men. Unless I am more considerate to ignorance, more forbearing to suffering, than I have hitherto been, I shall scorn myself as grossly unjust. What now?' he said, addressing his horse, which, hearing the ripple of water, and feeling thirsty, turned to a wayside trough, where the moonbeam was playing in a crystal eddy.

'Yorke,' pursued Moore, 'ride on: I must let him drink.'

Yorke accordingly rode slowly forwards, occupying himself, as he advanced, in discriminating, amongst the many lights now spangling the distance, those of Briarmains. Stilbro' Moor was left behind; plantations rose dusk on either hand; they were descending the hill; below them lay the valley with its populous parish: they felt already at home.

Surrounded no longer by heath, it was not startling to Mr Yorke to see a hat rise, and to hear a voice speak behind the wall. The words, however, were peculiar.

'When the wicked perisheth, there is shouting,' it said; and added, 'As the whirlwind passeth, so is the wicked no more (with a deeper growl); terrors take hold of him as waters; hell is naked before him. He shall die without knowledge.'

A fierce flash and sharp crack violated the calm of night. Yorke, ere he turned, knew the four convicts of Birmingham were avenged.

# Chapter 31

### Uncle and Niece

The die was cast. Sir Philip Nunnely knew it: Shirley knew it: Mr Sympson knew it. That evening, when all the Fieldhead family dined at Nunnely Priory, decided the business.

Two or three things conduced to bring the baronet to a point. He had observed that Miss Keeldar looked pensive and delicate. This new phase in her demeanour smote him on his weak or poetic side: a spontaneous sonnet brewed in his brain; and while it was still working there, one of his sisters persuaded his ladye-love to sit down to the piano and sing a ballad – one of Sir Philip's own ballads. It was the least elaborate, the least affected – out of all comparison the best of his numerous efforts.

It chanced that Shirley, the moment before, had been gazing from a window

down on the park; she had seen that stormy moonlight which 'le Professeur Louis' was, perhaps, at the same instant contemplating from her own oak-parlour lattice; she had seen the isolated trees of the domain – broad, strong, spreading oaks, and high-towering heroic beeches – wrestling with the gale. Her ear had caught the full roar of the forest lower down; the swift rushing of clouds, the moon, to the eye, hasting swifter still, had crossed her vision: she turned from sight and sound – touched, if not rapt – wakened, if not inspired.

She sang, as requested. There was much about love in the ballad: faithful love that refused to abandon its object; love disaster could not shake; love that, in calamity, waxed fonder, in poverty clung closer. The words were set to a fine old air – in themselves they were simple and sweet: perhaps, when read, they wanted force; when *well* sung, they wanted nothing. Shirley sang them well: she breathed into the feeling, softness; she poured round the passion, force: her voice was fine that evening; its expressions dramatic: she impressed all, and charmed one.

On leaving the instrument, she went to the fire, and sat down on a seat – semi-stool, semi-cushion: the ladies were round her – none of them spoke. The Misses Sympson and the Misses Nunnely looked upon her, as quiet poultry might look on an egret, an ibis, or any other strange fowl. What made her sing so? *They* never sang so. Was it *proper* to sing with such expression, with such originality – so unlike a school-girl? Decidedly not: it was strange; it was unusual. What was *strange* must be *wrong*; what was *unusual* must be *improper*. Shirley was judged.

Moreover, old Lady Nunnely eyed her stonily from her great chair by the fireside: her gaze said, –

'This woman is not of mine or my daughters' kind: I object to her as my son's wife.'

Her son catching the look, read its meaning: he grew alarmed: what he so wished to win, there was danger he might lose. He must make haste.

The room they were in had once been a picture-gallery. Sir Philip's father – Sir Monckton – had converted it into a saloon; but still it had a shadowy, long-withdrawing look. A deep recess with a window – a recess that held one couch, one table, and a fairy cabinet, formed a room within a room. Two persons standing there might interchange a dialogue, and, so it were neither long nor loud, none be the wiser.

Sir Philip induced two of his sisters to perpetrate a duet; he gave occupation to the Misses Sympson: the elder ladies were conversing together. He was pleased to remark that, meantime, Shirely rose to look at the pictures. He had a tale to tell about one ancestress, whose dark beauty seemed as that of a flower of the south: he joined her, and began to tell it.

There were mementos of the same lady in the cabinet adorning the recess; and while Shirley was stooping to examine the missal and the rosary on the inlaid shelf, and while the Misses Nunnely indulged in a prolonged screech, guiltless of expression, pure of originality, perfectly conventional and absolutely unmeaning, Sir Philip stooped too, and whispered a few hurried sentences. At first, Miss Keeldar was struck so still, you might have fancied that whisper a charm which had changed her to a statue; but she presently looked up and answered. They parted. Miss Keeldar returned to the fire, and resumed her

# Shirley

seat: the baronet gazed after her, then went and stood behind his sisters. Mr Sympson – Mr Sympson only – had marked the pantomime.

That gentleman drew his own conclusions. Had he been as acute as he was meddling, as profound as he was prying, he might have found that in Sir Philip's face whereby to correct his inference. Ever shallow, hasty, and positive he went home quite cock-a-hoop.

He was not a man that kept secrets well: when elate on a subject, he could not avoid talking about it. The next morning, having occasion to employ his son's tutor as his secretary, he must needs announce to him, in mouthing accents, and with much flimsy pomp of manner, that he had better hold himself prepared for a return to the south, at an early day, as the important business which had detained him (Mr Sympson) so long in Yorkshire, was now on the eve of fortunate completion: his anxious and laborious efforts were likely, at last, to be crowned with the happiest success: a truly eligible addition was about to be made to the family connexions.

'In Sir Philip Nunnely?' Louis Moore conjectured.

Whereupon Mr Sympson treated himself simultaneously to a pinch of snuff and a chuckling laugh, checked only by a sudden choke of dignity, and an order to the tutor to proceed with business.

For a day or two, Mr Sympson continued as bland as oil; but also he seemed to sit on pins, and his gait, when he walked, emulated that of a hen treading a hot girdle. He was for ever looking out of the window, and listening for chariot-wheels: Bluebeard's wife – Sisera's mother – were nothing to him. He waited when the matter should be opened in form; when himself should be consulted; when lawyers should be summoned; when settlement discussions, and all the delicious worldly fuss, should pompously begin.

At last there came a letter; he himself handed it to Miss Keeldar out of the bag: he knew the handwriting; he knew the crest on the seal. He did not see it opened and read, for Shirley took it to her own room; nor did he see it answered, for she wrote her reply shut up, and was very long about it, – the best part of a day. He questioned her whether it was answered; she responded, 'Yes.'

Again he waited – waited in silence – absolutely not daring to speak: kept mute by something in Shirley's face, – a very awful something – inscrutable to him as the writing on the wall to Belshazzar. He was moved more than once to call Daniel, in the person of Louis Moore, and to ask an interpretation; but his dignity forbade the familiarity. Daniel himself, perhaps, had his own private difficulties connected with that baffling bit of translation: he looked like a student for whom grammars are blank, and dictionaries dumb.

Mr Sympson had been out, to while away an anxious hour in the society of his friends at De Walden Hall. He returned a little sooner than was expected; his family and Miss Keeldar were assembled in the oak-parlour; addressing the latter, he requested her to step with him into another room: he wished to have with her a '*strictly* private interview.'

She rose, asking no questions, and professing no surprise.

'Very well, sir,' she said in the tone of a determined person, who is informed that the dentist is come to extract that large double tooth of his, from which he

has suffered such a purgatory this month past. She left her sewing and her thimble in the window-seat, and followed her uncle where he led.

Shut into the drawing-room, the pair took seats, each in an armchair, placed opposite, a few yards between them.

'I have been to De Walden Hall,' said Mr Sympson. He paused. Miss Keeldar's eyes were on the pretty white and green carpet. *That* information required no response: she gave none.

'I have learned,' he went on, slowly, – 'I have learned a circumstance which surprises me.'

Resting her cheek on her forefinger, she waited to be told *what* circumstance.

'It seems that Nunnely Priory is shut up; that the family are gone back to their place in – shire. It seems that the baronet – that the baronet – that Sir Philip himself has accompanied his mother and sisters.'

'Indeed!' said Shirley.

'May I ask if you share the amazement with which I received this news?'

'No, sir.'

'*Is* it news to you?'

'Yes, sir.'

'I mean – I mean –' pursued Mr Sympson, now fidgeting in his chair, quitting his hitherto brief and tolerably clear phraseology, and returning to his customary wordy, confused, irritable style; 'I mean to have a *thorough* explanation. I will *not* be put off. I – I – shall *insist* on being heard; and on – on having my own way. My questions *must* be answered. I will have clear, satisfactory replies. I am not to be trifled with. Silence!'

'It is a strange and an extraordinary thing – a very singular – a most odd thing! I thought all was right: knew no other: and there – the family are gone!'

'I suppose, sir, they had a right to go.'

'*Sir Philip is gone!*' (with emphasis).

Shirley raised her brows: 'Bon voyage!' said she.

'This will not do: this must be altered, ma'am.'

He drew his chair forward; he pushed it back; he looked perfectly incensed, and perfectly helpless.

'Come, come, now, uncle,' expostulated Shirley, 'do not begin to fret and fume, or we shall make no sense of the business. Ask me what you want to know: I am as willing to come to an explanation as you: I promise you truthful replies.'

'I want – I demand to know, Miss Keeldar, whether Sir Philip has made you an offer?'

'He has.'

'You avow it?'

'I avow it. But now, go on: consider that point settled.'

'He made you an offer that night we dined at the Priory?'

'It is enough to say that he made it. Go on.'

'He proposed in the recess – in the room that used to be a picture-gallery – that Sir Monckton converted into a saloon?'

No answer.

'You were both examining a cabinet: I saw it all: my sagacity was not at fault – it never is. Subsequently, you received a letter from him. On what subject – of what nature were the contents?'

# Shirley

'No matter.'

'Ma'am, is that the way in which you speak to me?'

Shirley's foot tapped quick on the carpet.

'There you sit, silent and sullen – *you* who promised truthful replies!'

'Sir, I have answered you thus far: proceed.'

'I should like to see that letter.'

'You *cannot* see it.'

'I *must* and *shall*, ma'am. I am your guardian.'

'Having ceased to be a ward, I have no guardian.'

'Ungrateful being! Reared by me as my own daughter –'

'Once more, uncle, have the kindness to keep to the point. Let us both remain cool. For my part, I do not wish to get into a passion; but, you know, once drive me beyond certain bounds, I care little what I say: I am not then soon checked. Listen! You have asked me whether Sir Philip made me an offer: that question is answered. What do you wish to know next?'

'I desire to know whether you accepted or refused him? and know it I will.'

'Certainly: you ought to know it. I refused him.'

'Refused him! You – *you*, Shirley Keeldar, *refused* Sir Philip Nunnely?'

'I did.'

The poor gentleman bounced from his chair, and first rushed, and then trotted, through the room.

'There it is! There it is! There it is!'

'Sincerely speaking, I am sorry, uncle, you are so disappointed.'

Concession – contrition – never do any good with some people. Instead of softening and conciliating, they but embolden and harden them: of that number was Mr Sympson.

'*I* disappointed! What is it to me? Have *I* an interest in it? You would insinuate, perhaps, that I have motives?'

'Most people have motives, of some sort, for their actions.'

'She accuses me to my face! I – that have been a parent to her – she charges with bad motives!'

'*Bad* motives, I did not say.'

'And now you prevaricate. You have no principles!'

'Uncle, you tire me: I want to go away.'

'Go you shall not! I will be answered. What are your intentions, Miss Keeldar?'

'In what respect?'

'In respect of matrimony.'

'To be quiet – and to do just as I please.'

'Just as you please! The words are to the last degree indecorous.'

'My Sympson, I advise you not to become insulting: you know I will not bear that.'

'You read French. Your mind is poisoned with French novels. You have imbibed French principles.'

'The ground you are treading now returns a mighty hollow sound under your feet. Beware!'

'It will end in infamy, sooner or later: I have foreseen it all along.'

'Do you assert, sir, that something in which *I* am concerned will end in infamy?'

# Shirley

'That it will – that it will. You said just now you would act as you please. You acknowledge no rules – no limitations.'

'Silly stuff! and vulgar as silly!'

'Regardless of decorum, you are prepared to fly in the face of propriety.'

'You tire me, uncle.'

'What, madam – *what* could be your reasons for refusing Sir Philip?'

'At last, there is another sensible question: I shall be glad to reply to it. Sir Philip is too young for me: I regard him as a boy: all his relations – his mother especially – would be annoyed if he married me: such a step would embroil him with them: I am not his equal in the world's estimation.'

'Is that all?'

'Our dispositions are not compatible.'

'Why, a more amiable gentleman never breathed.'

'He is very amiable – very excellent – truly estimable, but *not my master*: not in one point. I could not trust myself with his happiness: I would not undertake the keeping of it for thousands: I will accept no hand which cannot hold me in check.'

'I thought you liked to do as you please: you are vastly inconsistent.'

'When I promise to obey, it shall be under the conviction that I can keep that promise: I could not obey a youth like Sir Philip. Besides, he would never command me: he would expect me always to rule – to guide, and I have no taste whatever for the office.'

'*You* no taste for swaggering, and subduing, and ordering, and ruling?'

'Not my husband: only my uncle.'

'Where is the difference?'

'There *is* a slight difference: that is certain. And I know full well, any man who wishes to live in decent comfort with me as a husband must be able to control me.'

'I wish you had a real tyrant.'

'A tyrant would not hold me for a day – not for an hour. I would rebel – break from him – defy him.'

'Are you not enough to bewilder one's brain with your self-contradiction?'

'It is evident I bewilder your brain.'

'You talk of Sir Philip being young: he is two-and-twenty.'

'My husband must be thirty, with the sense of forty.'

'You had better pick out some old man – some white-headed or bald-headed swain.'

'No, thank you.'

'You could lead some doting fool: you might pin him to your apron.'

'I might do that with a boy: but it is not my vocation. Did I not say I prefer a *master*? One in whose presence I shall feel obliged and disposed to be good. One whose control my impatient temper must acknowledge. A man whose approbation can reward – whose displeasure punish me. A man I shall feel it impossible not to love, and very possible to fear.'

'What is there to hinder you from doing all this with Sir Philip? He is a baronet; a man of rank, property, connexions, far above yours. If you talk of intellect, he is a poet: he writes verses: which you, I take it, cannot do, with all your cleverness.'

'Neither his title, wealth, pedigree, nor poetry, avail to invest him with the

power I describe. These are feather-weights: they want ballast: a measure of sound, solid practical sense would have stood him in better stead with me.'

'You and Henry rave about poetry: you used to catch fire like tinder on the subject when you were a girl.'

'Oh! uncle, there is nothing really valuable in this world, there is nothing glorious in the world to come, that is not poetry!'

'Marry a poet, then, in God's name!'

'Show him me, and I will.'

'Sir Philip.'

'Not at all. You are almost as good a poet as he.'

'Madam, you are wandering from the point.'

'Indeed, uncle, I wanted to do so; and I shall be glad to lead you away with me. Do not let us get out of temper with each other: it is not worth while.'

'Out of temper, Miss Keeldar! I should be glad to know who is out of temper?'

'*I* am not, yet.'

'If you mean to insinuate that *I* am, I consider that you are guilty of impertinence.'

'You will be soon, if you go on at that rate.'

'There it is! With your pert tongue, you would try the patience of a Job.'

'I know I should.'

'No levity, Miss! This is not a laughing matter. It is an affair I am resolved to probe thoroughly, convinced that there is mischief at the bottom. You described just now, with far too much freedom for your years and sex, the sort of individual you would prefer as a husband. – Pray, did you paint from the life?'

Shirley opened her lips; but instead of speaking she only glowed rose-red.

'I shall have an answer to that question,' affirmed Mr Sympson, assuming vast courage and consequence on the strength of this symptom of confusion.

'It was an historical picture, uncle, from several originals.'

'Several originals! Bless my heart!'

'I have been in love several times.'

'This is cynical.'

'With heroes of many nations.'

'What next – ?'

'And philosophers.'

'She is mad – '

'Don't ring the bell, uncle; you will alarm my aunt.'

'Your poor dear aunt, what a niece has she!'

'Once I loved Socrates.'

'Pooh! No trifling, ma'am.'

'I admired Themistocles, Leonidas, Epaminondas.'

'Miss Keeldar – '

'To pass over a few centuries, Washington was a plain man, but I liked him: but, to speak of the actual present – '

'Ah! the actual present.'

'To quit crude school-girl fancies, and come to realities.'

'Realities! That is the test to which you shall be brought, ma'am.'

'To avow before what altar I now kneel – to reveal the present idol of my soul –'

'You will make haste about it, if you please; it is near luncheon time, and confess *you shall.*'

'Confess, I must: my heart is full of the secret; it must be spoken: I only wish you were Mr Helstone instead of Mr Sympson, you would sympathize with me better.'

'Madam – it is a question of common sense and common prudence, not of sympathy and sentiment, and so on. Did you say it was Mr Helstone?'

'Not precisely, but as near as may be: they are rather alike.'

'I will know the name – I will have particulars.'

'They positively *are* rather alike; their very faces are not dissimilar – a pair of human falcons – and dry, direct, decided both. But my hero is the mightier of the two: his mind has the clearness of the deep sea, the patience of its rocks, the force of its billows.'

'Rant and fustian!'

'I daresay he can be harsh as a saw-edge, and gruff as a hungry raven.'

'Miss Keeldar, does the person reside in Briarfield? answer me that.'

'Uncle – I am going to tell you – his name is trembling on my tongue.'

'Speak, girl!'

'That was well said, uncle. "Speak, girl!" it is quite tragic. England has howled savagely against this man, uncle; and she will one day roar exultingly over him. He has been unscared by the howl, and he will be unelated by the shout.'

'I said she was mad – she is.'

'This country will change and change again in her demeanour to him: he will never change in his duty to her. Come, cease to chafe, uncle, I'll tell you his name.'

'You shall tell me, or –'

'Listen! Arthur Wellesley, Lord Wellington.'

Mr Sympson rose up furious: he bounced out of the room, but immediately bounced back again, shut the door, and resumed his seat.

'Ma'am you *shall* tell me *this:* will your principles permit you to marry a man without money – a man below you?'

'Never a man below me.'

(In a high voice.) 'Will you, Miss Keeldar, marry a poor man?'

'What right have you, Mr Sympson, to ask me?'

'I insist upon knowing.'

'You don't go the way to know.'

'My family respectability shall not be compromised.'

'A good resolution: keep it.'

'Madam, it is you who shall keep it.'

'Impossible, sir, since I form no part of your family.'

'Do you disown us?'

'I disdain your dictatorship.'

'Whom *will* you marry, Miss Keeldar?'

'Not Mr Sam Wynne, because I scorn him: not Sir Philip Nunnely, because I *only* esteem him.'

'Whom have you in your eye?'

'Four rejected candidates.'

'Such obstinacy could not be, unless you were under improper influence.'

# Shirley

'What do you mean? There are certain phrases potent to make my blood boil, – improper influence! What old woman's cackle is that?'

'Are you a young lady?'

'I am a thousand times better: I am an honest woman, and as such I will be treated.'

'Do you know (leaning mysteriously forward, and speaking with ghastly solemnity), do you know the whole neighbourhood teems with rumours respecting you and a bankrupt tenant of yours – the foreigner Moore?'

'Does it?'

'It does. Your name is in every mouth.'

'It honours the lips it crosses, and I wish to the gods it may purify them.'

'Is it *that* person who has power to influence you?'

'Beyond any whose cause you have advocated.'

'It is he you will marry?'

'He is handsome, and manly, and commanding.'

'You declare it to my face! The Flemish knave! The low trader!'

'He is talented, and venturous, and resolute. Prince is on his brow, and ruler in his bearing.'

'She glories in it! She conceals nothing! No shame, no fear!'

'When we speak the name of Moore, shame should be forgotten and fear discarded: the Moores know only honour and courage.'

'I say she is mad.'

'You have taunted me till my blood is up. You have worried me till I turn again.'

'That Moore is the brother of my son's tutor. Would you let the Usher call you Sister?'

Bright and broad shone Shirley's eye, as she fixed it on her questioner now.

'No: no. Not for a province of possession, – not for a century of life.'

'You cannot separate the husband from his family.'

'What then?'

'Mr Louis Moore's sister you will be.'

'Mr Sympson... I am sick at heart with all this weak trash: I will bear no more. Your thoughts are not my thoughts, your aims are not my aims, your gods are not my gods. We do not view things in the same light; we do not measure them by the same standard; we hardly speak in the same tongue. Let us part.

'It is not,' she resumed, much excited, – 'It is not that I hate you; you are a good sort of man: perhaps you mean well in your way; but we cannot suit: we are ever at variance. You annoy me with small meddling, with petty tyranny; you exasperate my temper, and make and keep me passionate. As to your small maxims, your narrow rules, your little prejudices, aversions, dogmas, bundle them off: Mr Sympson – go, offer them a sacrifice to the deity you worship; I'll none of them: I wash my hands of the lot. I walk by another creed, light, faith, and hope, than you.'

'Another creed! I believe she is an infidel.'

'An infidel to *your* religion; an atheist to *your* god.'

'*An – atheist!!!*'

'Your god, sir, is the World. In my eyes, you too, if not an infidel, are an idolater. I conceive that you ignorantly worship: in all things you appear to me too superstitious. Sir, your god, your great Bel, your fish-tailed Dagon, rises

before me as a demon. You, and such as you, have raised him to a throne, put on him a crown, given him a sceptre. Behold how hideously he governs! See him busied at the work he likes best – making marriages. He binds the young to the old, the strong to the imbecile. He stretches out the arm of Mezentius, and fetters the dead to the living. In his realm there is hatred – secret hatred: there is disgust – unspoken disgust: there is treachery – family treachery: there is vice – deep, deadly, domestic vice. In his dominions, children grow unloving between parents who have never loved: infants are nursed on deception from their very birth; they are reared in an atmosphere corrupt with lies. Your god rules at the bridal of kings – look at your royal dynasties! your deity is the deity of foreign aristocracies – analyse the blue blood of Spain! Your god is the Hymen of France – what is French domestic life? All that surrounds him hastens to decay: all declines and degenerates under his sceptre. *Your* god is a masked Death.'

'This language is terrible! My daughters and you must associate no longer, Miss Keeldar: there is danger in such companionship. Had I known you a little earlier – but, extraordinary as I thought you, I could not have believed –'

'Now, sir, do you begin to be aware that it is useless to scheme for me? That, in doing so, you but sow the wind to reap the whirlwind? I sweep your cobweb-projects from my path, that I may pass on unsullied. I am anchored on a resolve you cannot shake. My heart, my conscience shall dispose of my hand – *they only*. Know this at last.'

Mr Sympson was becoming a little bewildered.

'Never heard such language!' he muttered again and again. 'Never was so addressed in my life – never was so used.'

'You are quite confused, sir. You had better withdraw, or I will.'

He rose hastily.

'We must leave this place: they must pack up at once.'

'Do not hurry my aunt and cousins: give them time.'

'No more intercourse: she's not proper.'

He made his way to the door; he came back for his handkerchief; he dropped his snuff-box: leaving the contents scattered on the carpet, he stumbled out: Tartar lay outside across the mat – Mr Sympson almost fell over him: in the climax of his exasperation he hurled an oath at the dog, and a coarse epithet at his mistress.

'Poor Mr Sympson! He is both feeble and vulgar,' said Shirley to herself. 'My head aches, and I am tired,' she added; and leaning her head upon a cushion, she softly subsided from excitement to repose. One, entering the room a quarter of an hour afterwards, found her asleep. When Shirley had been agitated, she generally took this natural refreshment: it would come at her call.

The intruder paused in her unconscious presence, and said – 'Miss Keeldar.'

Perhaps his voice harmonized with some dream into which she was passing – it did not startle, it hardly roused her: without opening her eyes, she but turned her head a little, so that her cheek and profile, before hidden by her arm, became visible: she looked rosy, happy, half-smiling, but her eyelashes were wet; she had wept in slumber; or perhaps, before dropping asleep, a few natural tears had fallen after she had heard that epithet: no man – no woman is always strong, always able to bear up against the unjust opinion – the vilifying word: calumny, even from the mouth of a fool, will sometimes cut into unguarded

# Shirley

feelings. Shirley looked like a child that had been naughty and punished, but was now forgiven and at rest.

'Miss Keeldar,' again said the voice: this time it woke her; she looked up and saw at her side Louis Moore – not close at her side, but standing, with arrested step, two or three yards from her.

'Oh, Mr Moore!' she said; 'I was afraid it was my uncle again: he and I have quarrelled.'

'Mr Sympson should let you alone,' was the reply: 'can he not see that you are as yet far from strong?'

'I assure you he did not find me weak: I did not cry when he was here.'

'He is about to evacuate Fieldhead – so he says. He is now giving orders to his family: he has been in the school-room issuing commands in a manner which, I suppose, was a continuation of that with which he has harassed you.'

'Are you and Henry to go?'

'I believe, as far as Henry is concerned, that was the tenor of his scarcely-intelligible directions; but he may change all to-morrow: he is just in that mood when you cannot depend on his consistency for two consecutive hours: I doubt whether he will leave you for weeks yet. To myself he addressed some words which will require a little attention and comment by-and-by, when I have time to bestow on them. At the moment he came in, I was busied with a note I had got from Mr Yorke – so fully busied that I cut short the interview with him somewhat abruptly: I left him raving: here is the note – I wish you to see it – it refers to my brother Robert.' And he looked at Shirley.

'I shall be glad to hear news of him: is he coming home?'

'He is come: he is in Yorkshire: Mr Yorke went yesterday to Stilbro' to meet him.'

'Mr Moore – something is wrong – ?'

'Did my voice tremble? He is now at Briarmains – and I am going to see him.'

'What has occurred?'

'If you turn so pale I shall be sorry I have spoken. It might have been worse: Robert is not dead, but much hurt.'

'Oh! sir; it is you who are pale. Sit down near me.'

'Read the note – let me open it.'

Miss Keeldar read the note: it briefly signified that last night Robert Moore had been shot at from behind the wall of Milldean plantation, at the foot of the Brow; that he was wounded severely, but it was hoped not fatally: of the assassin, or assassins, nothing was known – they had escaped. 'No doubt,' Mr Yorke observed, 'it was done in revenge: it was a pity ill-will had ever been raised; but that could not be helped now.'

'He is my only brother,' said Louis, as Shirley returned the note. 'I cannot hear unmoved that ruffians have laid in wait for him, and shot him down like some wild beast from behind a wall.'

'Be comforted: be hopeful. He will get better – I know he will.'

Shirley, solicitous to soothe, held her hand over Mr Moore's, as it lay on the arm of the chair: she just touched it lightly, scarce palpably.

'Well, give me your hand,' he said; 'it will be for the first time: it is in a moment of calamity – give it me.'

Awaiting neither consent nor refusal, he took what he asked.

'I am going to Briarmains now,' he went on. 'I want you to step over to the Rectory, and tell Caroline Helstone what has happened: will you do this? she will hear it best from you.'

'Immediately,' said Shirley, with docile promptitude. 'Ought I to say that there is no danger?'

'Say so.'

'You will come back soon, and let me know more?'

'I will either come or write.'

'Trust me for watching over Caroline. I will communicate with your sister, too; but, doubtless, she is already with Robert?'

'Doubtless; or will be soon. Good-morning, now.'

'You will bear up, come what may?'

'We shall see that.'

Shirley's fingers were obliged to withdraw from the Tutor's: Louis was obliged to relinquish that hand folded, clasped, hidden in his own.

'I thought I should have had to support her,' he said, as he walked towards Briarmains, 'and it is she who has made me strong. That look of pity – that gentle touch! No down was ever softer – no elixir more potent! It lay like a snow-flake: it thrilled like lightning. A thousand times I have longed to possess that hand – to have it in mine. I *have* possessed it – for five minutes I held it. Her fingers and mine can never be strangers more – having met once, they must meet again.'

# Chapter 32

## The Schoolboy and the Wood-Nymph

Briarmains being nearer than the Hollow, Mr Yorke had conveyed his young comrade there. He had seen him laid in the best bed of the house, as carefully as if he had been one of his own sons. The sight of his blood, welling from the treacherously-inflicted wound, made him indeed the son of the Yorkshire gentleman's heart. The spectacle of the sudden event; of the tall, straight shape prostrated in its pride across the road; of the fine southern head laid low in the dust; of that youth in prime flung at once before him pallid, lifeless, helpless – this was the very combination of circumstances to win for the victim Mr Yorke's liveliest interest.

No other hand was there to raise – to aid; no other voice to question kindly; no other brain to concert measures: he had to do it all himself. This utter dependence of the speechless, bleeding youth (as a youth he regarded him) on his benevolence, secured that benevolence most effectually. Well did Mr Yorke like to have power, and to use it: he had now between his hands power over a fellow-creature's life: it suited him.

# Shirley

No less perfectly did it suit his saturnine better-half: the incident was quite in her way, and to her taste. Some women would have been terror-struck to see a gory man brought in over their threshold, and laid down in their hall in the 'howe of the night.' There, you would suppose, was subject-matter for hysterics. No: Mrs Yorke went into hysterics when Jessie would not leave the garden to come to her knitting, or when Martin proposed starting for Australia, with a view to realize freedom, and escape the tyranny of Matthew; but an attempted murder near her door – a half-murdered man in her best bed – set her straight, cheered her spirits, gave her cap the dash of a turban.

Mrs Yorke was just the woman who, while rendering miserable the drudging life of a simple maid-servant, would nurse like a heroine an hospital full of plague patients. She almost loved Moore: her tough heart almost yearned towards him, when she found him committed to her charge, – left in her arms, as dependent on her as her youngest-born in the cradle. Had she seen a domestic, or one of her daughters, give him a draught of water, or smooth his pillow, she would have boxed the intruder's ears. She chased Jessie and Rose from the upper realm of the house: she forbade the housemaids to set their foot in it.

Now, if the accident had happened at the Rectory gates, and old Helstone had taken in the martyr, neither Yorke nor his wife would have pitied him: they would have adjudged him right served for his tyranny and meddling: as it was, he became, for the present, the apple of their eye.

Strange! Louis Moore was permitted to come, – to sit down on the edge of the bed, and lean over the pillow, – to hold his brother's hand, and press his pale forehead with his fraternal lips: and Mrs Yorke bore it well. She suffered him to stay half the day there; she once suffered him to sit up all night in the chamber; she rose herself at five o'clock of a wet November morning, and with her own hands lit the kitchen fire, and made the brothers a breakfast, and served it to them herself. Majestically arrayed in a boundless flannel wrapper, a shawl, and her nightcap, she sat and watched them eat, as complacently as a hen beholds her chickens feed. Yet she gave the cook warning that day for venturing to make and carry up to Mr Moore a basin of sago-gruel; and the housemaid lost her favour because, when Mr Louis was departing, she brought him his surtout aired from the kitchen, and like a 'forward piece,' as she was, helped him on with it, and accepted, in return, a smile, a 'thank you, my girl,' and a shilling. Two ladies called one day, pale and anxious, and begged earnestly, humbly, to be allowed to see Mr Moore one instant: Mrs Yorke hardened her heart, and sent them packing, – not without opprobrium.

But how was it when Hortense Moore came? – Not so bad as might have been expected: the whole family of the Moores really seemed to suit Mrs Yorke so as no other family had ever suited her. Hortense and she possessed an exhaustless mutual theme of conversation in the corrupt propensities of servants. Their views of this class were similar: they watched them with the same suspicion, and judged them with the same severity. Hortense, too, from the very first, showed no manner of jealousy of Mrs Yorke's attentions to Robert: she let her keep the post of nurse with little interference; and, for herself, found ceaseless occupation in fidgeting about the house, holding the kitchen under surveillance, reporting what passed there, and, in short, making herself generally useful. Visitors, they both of them agreed in excluding sedulously from the sick-room.

840

# Shirley

They held the young millowner captive, and hardly let the air breathe or the sun shine on him.

Mr MacTurk, the surgeon to whom Moore's case had been committed, pronounced his wound of a dangerous, but, he trusted, not of a hopeless character. At first, he wished to place with him a nurse of his own selection; but this neither Mrs Yorke nor Hortense would hear of: they promised faithful observance of directions. He was left, therefore, for the present, in their hands.

Doubtless, they executed the trust to the best of their ability; but something got wrong: the bandages were displaced, or tampered with; great loss of blood followed. MacTurk, being summoned, came with steed afoam. He was one of those surgeons whom it is dangerous to vex: abrupt in his best moods; in his worst, savage. On seeing Moore's state, he relieved his feelings by a little flowery language, with which it is not necessary to strew the present page. A bouquet or two of the choicest blossoms fell on the unperturbed head of one Mr Graves, a stony young assistant, he usually carried about with him; with a second nosegay he gifted another young gentleman in his train – an interesting facsimile of himself, being, indeed, his own son; but the full corbeille of blushing bloom fell to the lot of meddling womankind, en masse.

For the best part of one winter night, himself and satellites were busied about Moore. There, at his bedside, shut up alone with him in his chamber, they wrought and wrangled over his exhausted frame. They three were on one side of the bed, and Death on the other. The conflict was sharp: it lasted till day broke, when the balance between the belligerents seemed so equal that both parties might have claimed the victory.

At dawn, Graves and young MacTurk were left in charge of the patient, while the senior went himself in search of additional strength, and secured it in the person of Mrs Horsfall, the best nurse on his staff. To this woman he gave Moore in charge, with the sternest injunctions respecting the responsibility laid on her shoulders. She took this responsibility stolidly, as she did also the easy chair at the bed-head. That moment she began her reign.

Mrs Horsfall had one virtue, – orders received from MacTurk she obeyed to the letter: the Ten Commandments were less binding in her eyes than her surgeon's dictum. In other respects, she was no woman, but a dragon. Hortense Moore fell effaced before her; Mrs Yorke withdrew – crushed: yet both these women were personages of some dignity in their own estimation, and of some bulk in the estimation of others. Perfectly cowed by the breadth, the height, the bone, and the brawn of Mrs Horsfall, they retreated to the back-parlour. She, for her part, sat up-stairs when she liked, and down-stairs when she preferred it; she took her dram three times a-day, and her pipe of tobacco four times.

As to Moore, no one now ventured to inquire about him: Mrs Horsfall had him at dry-nurse: it was she who was to do for him; and the general conjecture now ran that she did for him accordingly.

Morning and evening MacTurk came to see him: his case, thus complicated by a new mischance, was become one of interest in the surgeon's eyes: he regarded him as a damaged piece of clock-work, which it would be creditable to his skill to set a-going again. Graves and young MacTurk – Moore's sole other visitors – contemplated him in the light in which they were wont to contemplate the occupant for the time being of the dissecting-room at Stilbro' Infirmary.

# Shirley

Robert Moore had a pleasant time of it: in pain; in danger; too weak to move; almost too weak to speak; a sort of giantess his keeper; the three surgeons his sole society. Thus he lay through the diminishing days and lengthening nights of the whole drear month of November.

In the commencement of his captivity, Moore used feebly to resist Mrs Horsfall: he hated the sight of her rough bulk, and dreaded the contact of her hard hands; but she taught him docility in a trice. She made no account whatever of his six feet – his manly thews and sinews: she turned him in his bed as another woman would have turned a babe in its cradle. When he was good, she addressed him as 'my dear,' and 'honey;' and when he was bad, she sometimes shook him. Did he attempt to speak when MacTurk was there, she lifted her hand and bade him 'hush!' like a nurse checking a forward child. If she had not smoked – if she had not taken gin, it would have been better, he thought; but she did both. Once – in her absence – he intimated to MacTurk, that 'that woman was a dram-drinker.'

'Pooh! my dear sir; they are all so,' was the reply he got for his pains. 'But Horsfall has this virtue,' added the surgeon, – 'drunk or sober, she always remembers to obey *me*.'

At length the latter autumn passed: its fogs, its rains withdrew from England their mourning and their tears; its winds swept on to sigh over lands far away. Behind November came deep winter; clearness, stillness, frost accompanying.

A calm day had settled into a crystalline evening; the world wore a North Pole colouring: all its lights and tints looked like the 'reflets'* of white, or violet, or pale green gems. The hills wore a lilac-blue; the setting sun had purple in its red; the sky was ice, all silvered azure; when the stars rose, they were of white crystal – not gold; gray, or cerulean, or faint emerald hues – cool, pure, and transparent – tinged the mass of the landscape.

What is this by itself in a wood no longer green, no longer even russet; a wood, neutral tint – this dark blue moving object? Why, it is a schoolboy – a Briarfield grammar-schoolboy – who has left his companions, now trudging home by the high road, and is seeking a certain tree, with a certain mossy mound at its root – convenient as a seat. Why is he lingering here? – the air is cold, and the time wears late. He sits down: what is he thinking about? Does he feel the chaste charm nature wears to-night? A pearl-white moon smiles through the grey trees: Does he care for her smile?

Impossible to say; for he is silent, and his countenance does not speak: as yet, it is no mirror to reflect sensation, but rather a mask to conceal it. This boy is a stripling of fifteen – slight, and tall of his years; in his face there is as little of amenity as of servility: his eye seems prepared to note any incipient attempt to control or overreach him, and the rest of his features indicate faculties alert for resistance. Wise ushers avoid unnecessary interference with that lad. To break him in by severity would be a useless attempt; to win him by flattery would be an effort worse than useless. He is best let alone. Time will educate, and experience train him.

Professedly, Martin Yorke (it is a young Yorke, of course) tramples on the

* Find me an English word as good, reader, and I will gladly dispense with the French word. Reflections won't do.

# Shirley

name of poetry: talk sentiment to him, and you would be answered by sarcasm. Here he is, wandering alone, waiting duteously on Nature, while she unfolds a page of stern, of silent, and of solemn poetry, beneath his attentive gaze.

Being seated, he takes from his satchel a book – not the Latin grammar, but a contraband volume of Fairy tales; there will be light enough yet for an hour to serve his keen young vision: besides, the moon waits on him – her beam, dim and vague as yet, fills the glade where he sits.

He reads: he is led into a solitary mountain region; all round him is rude and desolate, shapeless, and almost colourless. He hears bells tinkle on the wind; forth-riding from the formless folds of the mist, dawns on him the brightest vision – a green-robed lady, on a snow-white palfrey; he sees her dress, her gems, and her steed; she arrests him with some mysterious question: he is spellbound, and must follow her into Fairy-land.

A second legend bears him to the seashore: there tumbles in a strong tide, boiling at the base of dizzy cliffs: it rains and blows. A reef of rocks, black and rough, stretches far into the sea; all along, and among, and above these crags, dash and flash, sweep and leap, swells, wreaths, drifts of snowy spray. Some lone wanderer is out on these rocks, treading, with cautious step, the wet, wild sea-weed; glancing down into hollows where the brine lies fathoms deep and emerald-clear, and seeing there wilder, and stranger, and huger vegetation, than is found on land, with treasure of shells – some green, some purple, some pearly – clustered in the curls of the snaky plants. He hears a cry. Looking up, and forward, he sees, at the bleak point of the reef a tall, pale thing – shaped like man, but made of spray – transparent, tremulous, awful: it stands not alone: they are all human figures that wanton in the rocks – a crowd of foam-women – a band of white, evanescent Nereides.

Hush! – shut the book: hide it in the satchel. – Martin hears a tread. He listens: No – Yes: Once more, the dead leaves, lightly crushed, rustle on the wood-path. Martin watches: the trees part, and a woman issues forth.

She is a lady dressed in dark silk, a veil covering her face. Martin never met a lady in this wood before – nor any female, save, now and then, a village-girl come to gather nuts. To-night, the apparition does not displease him. He observes, as she approaches, that she is neither old nor plain, but, on the contrary, very youthful; and, but that he now recognizes her for one whom he has often wilfully pronounced ugly, he would deem that he discovered traits of beauty behind the thin gauze of that veil.

She passes him, and says nothing. He knew she would: all women are proud monkeys – and he knows no more conceited doll than that Caroline Helstone. The thought is hardly hatched in his mind, when the lady retraces those two steps she had got beyond him, and, raising her veil, reposes her glance on his face, while she softly asks: –

'Are you one of Mr Yorke's sons?'

No human evidence would ever have been able to persuade Martin Yorke that he blushed when thus addressed; yet blush he did, to the ears.

'I am,' he said, bluntly; and encouraged himself to wonder, superciliously, what would come next.

'You are Martin, I think?' was the observation that followed.

It could not have been more felicitous: it was a simple sentence – very artlessly,

843

# Shirley

a little timidly, pronounced; but it chimed in harmony to the youth's nature: it stilled him like a note of music.

Martin had a keen sense of his personality: he felt it right and sensible that the girl should discriminate him from his brothers. Like his father, he hated ceremony: it was acceptable to hear a lady address him as 'Martin,' and not Mr Martin, or Master Martin, which form would have lost her his good graces for ever. Worse, if possible, than ceremony, was the other extreme of slipshod familiarity: the slight tone of bashfulness – the scarcely-perceptible hesitation – was considered perfectly in place.

'I am Martin,' he said.

'Are your father and mother well?' – (it was lucky she did not say *papa* and *mamma*: that would have undone all,) – 'and Rose and Jessie?'

'I suppose so.'

'My cousin Hortense is still at Briarmains?'

'Oh, yes!'

Martin gave a comic half-smile and demi-groan: the half-smile was responded to by the lady, who could guess in what sort of odour Hortense was likely to be held by the young Yorkes.

'Does your mother like her?'

'They suit so well about the servants, they can't help liking each other.'

'It is cold to-night.'

'Why are you out so late?'

'I lost my way in this wood.'

Now, indeed, Martin allowed himself a refreshing laugh of scorn.

'Lost your way in the mighty forest of Briarmains! You deserve never more to find it.'

'I never was here before, and I believe I am trespassing now: you might inform against me if you chose, Martin, and have me fined: it is your father's wood.'

'I should think I knew that; but since you are so simple as to lose your way, I will guide you out.'

'You need not: I have got into the track now: I shall be right. Martin,' (a little quickly), 'how is Mr Moore?'

Martin had heard certain rumours: it struck him that it might be amusing to make an experiment.

'Going to die. Nothing can save him. All hope flung overboard!'

She put her veil aside. She looked into his eyes, and said, –

'To die!'

'To die. All along of the women, my mother and the rest: they did something about his bandages that finished everything: he would have got better but for them. I am sure they should be arrested, cribbed, tried, and brought in for Botany Bay, at the very least.'

The questioner, perhaps, did not hear this judgment: she stood motionless. In two minutes, without another word, she moved forwards: no goodnight, no further inquiry. This was not amusing, nor what Martin had calculated on: he expected something dramatic and demonstrative: it was hardly worth while to frighten the girl, if she would not entertain him in return. He called, –

'Miss Helstone!'

She did not hear or turn. He hastened after and overtook her.

'Come. Are you uneasy about what I said?'

# Shirley

'You know nothing about death, Martin: you are too young for me to talk to concerning such a thing.'

'Did you believe me? It's all flummery! Moore eats like three men: they are always making sago or tapioca, or something good for him: I never go into the kitchen but there is a saucepan on the fire, cooking him some dainty. I think I will play the old soldier, and be fed on the fat of the land like him.'

'Martin! Martin!' here her voice trembled, and she stopped.

'It is exceedingly wrong of you, Martin: you have almost killed me.'

Again she stopped: she leaned against a tree, trembling, shuddering, and as pale as death.

Martin contemplated her with inexpressible curiosity. In one sense it was, as he would have expressed it, 'nuts' to him to see this: it told him so much, and he was beginning to have a great relish for discovering secrets; in another sense, it reminded him of what he had once felt when he had heard a blackbird lamenting for her nestlings, which Matthew had crushed with a stone, and that was not a pleasant feeling. Unable to find anything very appropriate to *say*, in order to comfort her, he began to cast about in his mind what he could *do*: he smiled: the lad's smile gave wondrous transparency to his physiognomy.

'Eureka!' he cried. 'I'll set all straight by-and-by. You are better now, Miss Caroline: walk forward,' he urged.

Not reflecting that it would be more difficult for Miss Helstone than for himself to climb a wall or penetrate a hedge, he piloted her by a short cut which led to no gate. The consequence was he had to help her over some formidable obstacles, and, while he railed at her for helplessness, he perfectly liked to feel himself of use.

'Martin, before we separate, assure me seriously, and on your word of honour, that Mr Moore is better.'

'How very much you think of that Moore!'

'No – but – many of his friends may ask me, and I wish to be able to give an authentic answer.'

'You may tell them he is well enough, only idle: you may tell them that he takes mutton-chops for dinner, and the best of arrowroot for supper. I intercepted a basin myself one night on its way up-stairs, and ate half of it.'

'And who waits on him, Martin? Who nurses him?'

'Nurses him? – the great baby! Why, a woman as round and big as our largest water-butt – a rough, hard-favoured old girl. I make no doubt she leads him a rich life: nobody else is let near him: he is chiefly in the dark. It is my belief she knocks him about terribly in that chamber. I listen at the wall sometimes when I am in bed, and I think I hear her thumping him. You should see her fist: she could hold half a dozen hands like yours in her one palm. After all, notwithstanding the chops and jellies he gets, I would not be in his shoes. In fact, it is my private opinion that she eats most of what goes up on the tray to Mr Moore. I wish she may not be starving him.'

Profound silence and meditation on Caroline's part, and a sly watchfulness on Martin's.

'You never see him, I suppose, Martin?'

'I? No: I don't care to see him, for my own part.'

Silence again.

# Shirley

'Did not you come to our house once with Mrs Pryor, about five weeks since, to ask after him?' again inquired Martin.

'Yes.'

'I dare say you wished to be shown up-stairs?'

'We *did* wish it: we entreated it; but your mother declined.'

'Aye! she declined. I heard it all: she treated you as it is her pleasure to treat visitors now and then: she behaved to you rudely and harshly.'

'She was not kind; for, you know Martin, we are relations, and it is natural we should take an interest in Mr Moore. But here we must part: we are at your father's gate.'

'Very well – what of that? I shall walk home with you.'

'They will miss you, and wonder where you are.'

'Let them . . . I can take care of myself, I suppose.'

Martin knew that he had already incurred the penalty of a lecture, and dry bread for tea. No matter, the evening had furnished him with an adventure: it was better than muffins and toast.

He walked home with Caroline. On the way he promised to see Mr Moore, in spite of the dragon who guarded his chamber, and appointed an hour on the next day, when Caroline was to come to Briarmains Wood and get tidings of him: he would meet her at a certain tree. The scheme led to nothing: still he liked it.

Having reached home, the dry bread and the lecture were duly administered to him, and he was dismissed to bed at an early hour. He accepted his punishment with the toughest stoicism.

Ere ascending to his chamber he paid a secret visit to the dining-room, a still, cold, stately apartment, seldom used; for the family customarily dined in the back parlour. He stood before the mantel-piece, and lifted his candle to two pictures hung above – female heads: one, a type of serene beauty – happy and innocent; the other, more lovely – but forlorn and desperate.

'She looked like *that*,' he said, gazing on the latter sketch, 'when she sobbed, turned white, and leaned against the tree.'

'I suppose,' he pursued, when he was in his room, and seated on the edge of his pallet-bed, – 'I suppose she is, what they call, "*in love*;" yes, *in love* with that long thing in the next chamber. Whisht! is that Horsfall clattering him? I wonder he does not yell out. It really sounds as if she had fallen on him tooth and nail; but I suppose she is making the bed. I saw her at it once – she hit into the mattresses as if she was boxing. It is queer, Zillah (they call her Zillah) – Zillah Horsfall is a woman, and Caroline Helstone is a woman: they are two individuals of the same species – not much alike though. Is she a pretty girl, that Caroline? I suspect she is – very nice to look at – something so clear in her face – so soft in her eyes. I approve of her looking at me; it does me good. She has long eyelashes: their shadow seems to rest where she gazes, and to instil peace and thought. If she behaves well, and continues to suit me, as she has suited me to-day, I may do her a good turn. I rather relish the notion of circumventing my mother and that ogress, old Horsfall. Not that I like humouring Moore; but whatever I do I'll be paid for, and in coin of my own choosing: I know what reward I will claim – one displeasing to Moore, and agreeable to myself.'

He turned into bed.

# Chapter 33

## Martin's Tactics

t was necessary to the arrangement of Martin's plan, that he should stay at home that day. Accordingly, he found no appetite for breakfast; and, just about school-time, took a severe pain about his heart, which rendered it advisable that, instead of setting out to the grammar-school with Mark, he should succeed to his father's armchair by the fireside, and also to his morning-paper. This point being satisfactorily settled, and Mark being gone to Mr Sumner's class, and Matthew and Mr Yorke withdrawn to the counting-house, three other exploits, nay four, remained to be achieved.

The first of these was to realize the breakfast he had not yet tasted, and with which his appetite of fifteen could ill afford to dispense; the second, third, fourth, to get his mother, Miss Moore, and Mrs Horsfall successively, out of the way before four o'clock that afternoon.

The first was, for the present, the most pressing, since the work before him demanded an amount of energy which the present empty condition of his youthful stomach did not seem likely to supply.

Martin knew the way to the larder; and knowing this way, he took it. The servants were in the kitchen, breakfasting solemnly with closed doors; his mother and Miss Moore were airing themselves on the lawn, and discussing the closed doors aforesaid: Martin, safe in the larder, made fastidious selection from its stores. His breakfast had been delayed – he was determined it should be recherché: it appeared to him that a variety on his usual somewhat insipid fare of bread and milk was both desirable and advisable: the savoury and the salutary he thought might be combined. There was store of rosy apples laid in straw upon a shelf; he picked out three. There was pastry upon a dish; he selected an apricot-puff and a damson tart. On the plain household bread his eye did not dwell; but he surveyed with favour some currant tea-cakes, and condescended to make choice of one. Thanks to his clasp-knife, he was able to appropriate a wing of fowl and a slice of ham; a cantlet of cold custard-pudding he thought would harmonize with these articles; and having made this final addition to his booty, he at length sallied forth into the hall.

He was already half-way across – three steps more would have anchored him in the harbour of the back-parlour – when the front door opened, and there stood Matthew. Better far had it been the Old Gentleman, in full equipage of horns, hoofs, and tail.

Matthew, sceptic and scoffer, had already failed to subscribe a prompt belief in that pain about the heart: he had muttered some words, amongst which the phrase 'shamming Abraham' had been very distinctly audible; and the succession

# Shirley

to the arm-chair and newspaper had appeared to affect him with mental spasms: the spectacle now before him, the apples, the tarts, the tea-cake, the fowl, ham and pudding, offered evidence but too well calculated to inflate his opinion of his own sagacity.

Martin paused 'interdit' one minute, one instant; the next he knew his ground, and pronounced all well. With the true perspicacity 'des âmes élites,' he at once saw how this – at first sight untoward event – might be turned to excellent account: he saw how it might be so handled as to secure the accomplishment of his second task, viz. the disposal of his mother. He knew that a collision between him and Matthew always suggested to Mrs Yorke the propriety of a fit of hysterics; he further knew that, on the principle of calm succeeding to storm, after a morning of hysterics, his mother was sure to indulge in an afternoon of bed. This would accommodate him perfectly.

The collison duly took place in the hall. A dry laugh, an insulting sneer, a contemptuous taunt, met by a nonchalant but most cutting reply, were the signals. They rushed at it. Martin, who usually made little noise on these occasions, made a great deal now. In flew the servants, Mrs Yorke, Miss Moore: ιо female hand could separate them: Mr Yorke was summoned.

'Sons,' said he, 'one of you must leave my roof if this occurs again: I will have no Cain and Abel strife here.'

Martin now allowed himself to be taken off: he had been hurt; he was the youngest and slightest: he was quite cool, in no passion: he even smiled, content that the most difficult part of the labour he had set himself was over.

Once he seemed to flag in the course of the morning.

'It is not worth while to bother myself for that Caroline,' he remarked. But, a quarter of an hour afterwards, he was again in the dining-room, looking at the head with dishevelled tresses and eyes turbid with despair.

'Yes,' he said, 'I made her sob, shudder, almost faint: I'll see her smile before I've done with her: besides, I want to outwit all these womenites.'

Directly after dinner, Mrs Yorke fulfilled her son's calculation, by withdrawing to her chamber. Now for Hortense.

That lady was just comfortably settled to stocking-mending in the back-parlour, when Martin – laying down a book which, stretched on the sofa (he was still indisposed, according to his own account), he had been perusing in all the voluptuous ease of a yet callow pacha – lazily introduced some discourse about Sarah, the maid at the Hollow. In the course of much verbal meandering, he insinuated information that this damsel was said to have three suitors, Frederic Murgatroyd, Jeremiah Pighills, and John-of-Mally's-of-Hannah's-of-Deb's; and that Miss Mann had affirmed she knew for a fact, that, now the girl was left in sole charge of the cottage, she often had her swains to meals, and entertained them with the best the house afforded.

It needed no more. Hortense could not have lived another hour without betaking herself to the scene of these nefarious transactions, and inspecting the state of matters in person. Mrs Horsfall remained.

Martin, master of the field now, extracted from his mother's work-basket a bunch of keys; with these he opened the sideboard cupboard, produced thence a black bottle and a small glass, placed them on the table, nimbly mounted the stairs, made for Mr Moore's door, tapped, the nurse opened.

# Shirley

'If you please, ma'am, you are invited to step into the back-parlour and take some refreshment: you will not be disturbed: the family are out.'

He watched her down; he watched her in; himself shut the door: he knew she was safe.

The hard work was done; now for the pleasure. He snatched his cap, and away for the wood.

It was yet but half-past three; it had been a fine morning, but the sky looked dark now: it was beginning to snow; the wind blew cold; the wood looked dismal, the old tree grim. Yet Martin approved the shadow on his path: he found a charm in the spectral aspect of the doddered oak.

He had to wait: to and fro he walked, while the flakes fell faster; and the wind, which at first had but moaned, pitifully howled.

'She is long in coming,' he muttered, as he glanced along the narrow track. 'I wonder,' he subjoined, 'what I wish to see her so much for? She is not coming for me. But I have power over her, and I want her to come that I may use that power.'

He continued his walk.

'Now,' he resumed, when a further period had elapsed, 'if she fails to come, I shall hate and scorn her.'

It struck four: he heard the church-clock far away. A step so quick, so light, that, but for the rustling of leaves, it would scarcely have sounded on the wood-walk, checked his impatience. The wind blew fiercely now, and the thickened white storm waxed bewildering; but on she came, and not dismayed.

'Well, Martin,' she said eagerly, 'how is he?'

'It is queer how she thinks of *him*,' reflected Martin: 'the blinding snow and bitter cold are nothing to her, I believe: yet she is but a "chitty-faced creature," as my mother would say. I could find in my heart to wish I had a cloak to wrap her in.'

Thus meditating to himself, he neglected to answer Miss Helstone.

'You have seen him?'

'No.'

'Oh! You promised you would.'

'I mean to do better by you than that. Didn't I say, *I* don't care to see him?'

'But now it will be so long before I get to know anything certain about him, and I am sick of waiting. Martin, *do* see him, and give him Caroline Helstone's regards, and say she wished to know how he was, and if anything could be done for his comfort.'

'I won't.'

'You are changed: you were so friendly last night.'

'Come: we must not stand in this wood; it is too cold.'

'But, before I go, promise me to come again to-morrow with news.'

'No such thing; I am much too delicate to make and keep such appointments in the winter season: if you knew what a pain I had in my chest this morning, and how I went without breakfast, and was knocked down besides, you'd feel the impropriety of bringing me here in the snow. Come, I say.'

'Are you really delicate, Martin?'

'Don't I look so?'

'You have rosy cheeks.'

'That's hectic. Will you come – or you won't?'

# Shirley

'Where?'

'With me. I was a fool not to bring a cloak: I would have made you cozy.'

'You are going home: my nearest road lies in the opposite direction.'

'Put your arm through mine. I'll take care of you.'

'But, the wall – the hedge – it is such hard work climbing, and you are too slender and young to help me without hurting yourself.'

'You shall go through the gate.'

'But –'

'But! – but! Will you trust me or not?'

She looked into his face.

'I think I will. Anything rather than return as anxious as I came.'

'I can't answer for that. This, however, I promise you; be ruled by me, and you shall see Moore yourself.'

'See him myself?'

'Yourself.'

'But, dear Martin, does he know?'

'Ah! I'm dear now. No: he doesn't know.'

'And your mother and the others?'

'All is right.'

Caroline fell into a long silent fit of musing, but still she walked on with her guide: they came in sight of Briarmains.

'Have you made up your mind?' he asked.

She was silent.

'Decide. We are just on the spot. *I won't* see him – that I tell you – except to announce your arrival.'

'Martin, you are a strange boy, and this is a strange step; but all I feel *is* and *has* been, for a long time, strange. I will see him.'

'Having said that, you will neither hesitate nor retract?'

'No.'

'Here we are, then. Do not be afraid of passing the parlour-window: no one will see you. My father and Matthew are at the mill; Mark is at school; the servants are in the back-kitchen; Miss Moore is at the cottage; my mother in her bed; and Mrs Horsfall in Paradise. Observe – I need not ring: I open the door; the hall is empty; the staircase quiet; so is the gallery: the whole house and all its inhabitants are under a spell, which I will not break till you are gone.'

'Martin, I trust you.'

'You never said a better word. Let me take your shawl: I will shake off the snow and dry it for you. You are cold and wet: never mind; there is a fire upstairs. Are you ready?'

'Yes.'

'Follow me.'

He left his shoes on the mat; mounted the stair unshod; Caroline stole after, with noiseless step: there was a gallery, and there was a passage; at the end of that passage Martin paused before a door and tapped: he had to tap twice – thrice: a voice, known to one listener, at last said, –

'Come in.'

The boy entered briskly.

'Mr Moore, a lady called to inquire after you: none of the women were about:

it is washing-day, and the maids are over the crown of the head in soap-suds in the back-kitchen; so I asked her to step up.'

'Up here, sir?'

'Up here, sir; but if you object, she shall go down again.'

'Is this a place, or am I a person to bring a lady to, you absurd lad?'

'No: so I'll take her off.'

'Martin, you will stay here. Who is she?'

'Your grandmother from that château on the Scheldt Miss Moore talks about.'

'Martin,' said the softest whisper at the door, 'don't be foolish.'

'Is she there?' inquired Moore, hastily. He had caught an imperfect sound.

'She is there, fit to faint: she is standing on the mat, shocked at your want of filial affection.'

'Martin, you are an evil cross between an imp and a page. What is she like?'

'More like me than you; for she is young and beautiful.'

'You are to show her forward. Do you hear?'

'Come, Miss Caroline.'

'Miss Caroline!' repeated Moore.

And when Miss Caroline entered, she was encountered in the middle of the chamber by a tall, thin, wasted figure, who took both her hands.

'I give you a quarter of an hour,' said Martin, as he withdrew: 'no more. Say what you have to say in that time: till it is past, I will wait in the gallery: nothing shall approach: I'll see you safe away. Should you persist in staying longer, I leave you to your fate.'

He shut the door. In the gallery he was as elate as a king: he had never been engaged in an adventure he liked so well; for no adventure had ever invested him with so much importance, or inspired him with so much interest.

'You are come at last,' said the meagre man, gazing on his visitress with hollow eyes.

'Did you expect me before?'

'For a month – near two months, we have been very near; and I have been in sad pain, and danger, and misery, Cary.'

'I could not come.'

'Couldn't you? But the Rectory and Briarmains are very near: not two miles apart.'

There was pain – there was pleasure in the girl's face as she listened to these implied reproaches: it was sweet – it was bitter to defend herself.

'When I say I could not come, I mean I could not see you; for I came with mamma the very day we heard what had happened. Mr MacTurk then told us it was impossible to admit any stranger.'

'But afterwards – every fine afternoon these many weeks past I have waited and listened. Something here, Cary, (laying his hand on his breast), told me it was impossible but that you should think of me. Not that I merit thought; but we are old acquaintance; we are cousins.'

'I came again, Robert: mamma and I came again.'

'Did you? Come, that is worth hearing: since you came again, we will sit down and talk about it.'

They sat down. Caroline drew her chair up to his. The air was now dark with snow: an Iceland blast was driving it wildly. This pair neither heard the

long 'wuthering' rush, nor saw the white burden it drifted: each seemed conscious but of one thing – the presence of the other.

'So mamma and you came again?'

'And Mrs Yorke did treat us strangely. We asked to see you. "No," said she; "not in my house. I am at present responsible for his life: it shall not be forfeited for half an hour's idle gossip." But I must not tell you all she said: it was very disagreeable. However, we came yet again – mamma, Miss Keeldar, and I. This time we thought we should conquer, as we were three against one, and Shirley was on our side. But Mrs Yorke opened such a battery.'

Moore smiled. 'What did she say?'

'Things that astonished us. Shirley laughed at last; I cried; mamma was seriously annoyed: we were all three driven from the field. Since that time I have only walked once a-day past the house, just for the satisfaction of looking up at your window, which I could distinguish by the drawn curtains. I really dared not come in.'

'I *have* wished for you, Caroline.'

'I did not know that. I never dreamt one instant that you thought of me. If I had but most distantly imagined such a possibility —'

'Mrs Yorke would still have beaten you.'

'She would not. Stratagem should have been tried, if persuasion failed. I would have come to the kitchen door; the servant should have let me in; and I would have walked straight up-stairs. In fact, it was far more the fear of intrusion – the fear of yourself, that baffled me, than the fear of Mrs Yorke.'

'Only last night, I despaired of ever seeing you again. Weakness has wrought terrible depression in me – terrible depressions.'

'And you sit alone?'

'Worse than alone.'

'But you must be getting better, since you can leave your bed?'

'I doubt whether I shall live: I see nothing for it, after such exhaustion, but decline.'

'You – you shall go home to the Hollow.'

'Dreariness would accompany – nothing cheerful come near me.'

'I *will* alter this: this *shall* be altered, were there ten Mrs Yorkes to do battle with.'

'Cary, you make me smile.'

'Do smile: smile again. Shall I tell you what I should like?'

'Tell me anything – only keep talking. I am Saul: but for music I should perish.'

'I should like you to be brought to the Rectory, and given to me and mamma.'

'A precious gift! I have not laughed since they shot me till now.'

'Do you suffer pain, Robert?'

'Not so much pain now; but I am hopelessly weak, and the state of my mind is inexpressible – dark, barren, impotent. Do you not read it all in my face? I look a mere ghost.'

'Altered, yet I should have known you anywhere: but I understand your feelings: I experienced something like it. Since we met, I too have been very ill.'

'*Very* ill?'

'I thought I should die. The tale of my life seemed told. Every night, just at

midnight, I used to wake from awful dreams – and the book lay open before me at the last page, where was written "Finis." I had strange feelings.'

'You speak my experience.'

'I believed I should never see you again; and I grew so thin – as thin as you are now: I could do nothing for myself – neither rise nor lie down; and I could not eat – yet, you see I am better.'

'Comforter! sad as sweet: I am too feeble to say what I feel; but, while you speak, I *do* feel.'

'Here I am at your side, where I thought never more to be: here I speak to you – I see you listen to me willingly – look at me kindly. Did I count on that? I despaired.'

Moore sighed – a sigh so deep, it was nearly a groan: he covered his eyes with his hand.

'May I be spared to make some atonement!'

Such was his prayer.

'And for what?'

'We will not touch on it now, Cary: unmanned as I am, I have not the power to cope with such a topic. Was Mrs Pryor with you during your illness?'

'Yes,' (Caroline smiled brightly) – 'you know she is mamma?'

'I have heard: Hortense told me; but that tale too I will receive from yourself. Does she add to your happiness?'

'What! mamma? She is *dear* to me; *how* dear I cannot say. I was altogether weary, and she held me up.'

'I deserve to hear that in a moment when I can scarce lift my hand to my head. I deserve it.'

'It is no reproach against you.'

'It is a coal of fire heaped on my head: and so is every word you address to me, and every look that lights your sweet face. Come still nearer, Lina, and give me your hand – if my thin fingers do not scare you.'

She took those thin fingers between her two little hands – she bent her head 'et les effleura de ses lèvres' (I put that in French, because the word 'effleurer' is an exquisite word). Moore was much moved: a large tear or two coursed down his hollow cheek.

'I'll keep these things in my heart, Cary: that kiss I will put by, and you shall hear of it again one day.'

'Come out!' cried Martin, opening the door, 'Come away – you have had twenty minutes instead of a quarter of an hour.'

'She will not stir yet – you hempseed.'

'I dare not stay longer, Robert.'

'Can you promise to return?'

'No, she can't,' responded Martin. 'The thing musn't become customary: I can't be troubled. It's very well for once: I'll not have it repeated.'

'*You*'ll not have it repeated!'

'Hush! don't vex him – we could not have met to-day but for him: but I will come again, if it is your wish that I should come.'

'It *is* my wish – my *one* wish – almost the only wish I can feel.'

'Come this minute: my mother has coughed, got up, set her feet on the floor. Let her only catch you on the stairs, Miss Caroline: you're not to bid him good-bye' (stepping between her and Moore), – 'you are to march.'

'My shawl, Martin.'

'I have it. I'll put it on for you when you are in the hall.'

He made them part: he would suffer no farewell but what could be expressed in looks: he half carried Caroline down the stairs. In the hall he wrapped her shawl round her, and – but that his mother's tread then creaked in the gallery, and but that a sentiment of diffidence – the proper, natural, therefore the noble impulse of his boy's heart, held him back, he would have claimed his reward – he would have said, 'Now, Miss Caroline, for all this give me one kiss.' But ere the words had passed his lips, she was across the snowy road, rather skimming than wading the drifts.

'She is my debtor, and I *will* be paid.'

He flattered himself that it was opportunity, not audacity, which had failed him: he misjudged the quality of his own nature, and held it for something lower than it was.

# Chapter 34

## Case of Domestic Persecution – Remarkable Instance of Pious Perseverance in the Discharge of Religious Duties

artin, having known the taste of excitement, wanted a second draught; having felt the dignity of power, he loathed to relinquish it. Miss Helstone – that girl he had always called ugly, and whose face was now perpetually before his eyes, by day and by night, in dark and in sunshine – had once come within his sphere: it fretted him to think the visit might never be repeated.

Though a schoolboy, he was no ordinary schoolboy: he was destined to grow up an original. At a few years later date, he took great pains to pare and polish himself down to the pattern of the rest of the world, but he never succeeded: an unique stamp marked him always. He now sat idle at his desk in the grammar-school, casting about in his mind for the means of adding another chapter to his commenced romance: he did not yet know how many commenced life-romances are doomed never to get beyond the first – or, at most, the second chapter. His Saturday half-holiday he spent in the wood with his book of fairy legends, and that other unwritten book of his imagination.

Martin harboured an irreligious reluctance to see the approach of Sunday. His father and mother – while disclaiming community with the Establishment – failed not duly, once on the sacred day, to fill their large pew in Briarfield church with the whole of their blooming family. Theoretically, Mr Yorke placed all sects and churches on a level: Mrs Yorke awarded the palm to Moravians and Quakers, on account of that crown of humility by these worthies worn: neither of them were ever known, however, to set foot in a conventicle.

# Shirley

Martin, I say, disliked Sunday, because the morning service was long, and the sermon usually little to his taste: this Saturday afternoon, however, his woodland musings disclosed to him a new-found charm in the coming day.

It proved a day of deep snow: so deep, that Mrs Yorke, during breakfast, announced her conviction that the children, both boys and girls, would be better at home: and her decision that, instead of going to church, they should sit silent for two hours in the back-parlour, while Rose and Martin alternately read a succession of sermons – John Wesley's Sermons: John Wesley, being a Reformer and an Agitator, had a place both in her own and her husband's favour.

'Rose will do as she pleases,' said Martin, not looking up from the book which, according to his custom then and in after-life, he was studying over his bread and milk.

'Rose will do as she is told, and Martin too,' observed the mother.

'I am going to church.'

So her son replied, with the ineffable quietude of a true Yorke, who knows his will and means to have it, and who, if pushed to the wall, will let himself be crushed to death, provided no way of escape can be found – but will never capitulate.

'It is not fit weather,' said the father.

No answer: the youth read studiously; he slowly broke his bread and sipped his milk.

'Martin hates to go to church, but he hates still more to obey,' said Mrs Yorke.

'I suppose I am influenced by pure perverseness?'

'Yes – you are.'

'Mother – I *am not.*'

'By what, then, are you influenced?'

'By a complication of motives; the intricacies of which I should as soon think of explaining to you as I should of turning myself inside out to exhibit the internal machinery of my frame.'

'Hear Martin! Hear him!' cried Mr Yorke. 'I must see and have this lad of mine brought up to the Bar: Nature meant him to live by his tongue. Hesther, your third son must certainly be a lawyer: he has the stock in trade – brass, self-conceit, and words – words – words.'

'Some bread, Rose, if you please,' requested Martin, with intense gravity, serenity, phlegm: the boy had naturally a low, plaintive voice, which, in his 'dour' moods, rose scarcely above a lady's whisper: the more inflexibly stubborn the humour, the softer, the sadder the tone. He rang the bell, and gently asked for his walking-shoes.

'But, Martin,' urged his sire, 'there is drift all the way – a man could hardly wade through it. However, lad,' he continued, seeing that the boy rose as the church-bell began to toll, 'this is a case wherein I would by no means balk the obdurate chap of his will. Go to church by all means. There is a pitiless wind, and a sharp, frozen sleet, besides the depth underfoot. Go out into it, since thou prefers it to a warm fireside.'

Martin quietly assumed his cloak, comforter, and cap, and deliberately went out.

'My father has more sense than my mother,' he pronounced. 'How women

miss it! They drive the nail into the flesh, thinking they are hammering away at insensate stone.'

He reached church early.

'Now, if the weather frightens her (and it is a real December tempest), or if that Mrs Pryor objects to her going out, and I should miss her after all, it will vex me: but, tempest or tornado, hail or ice, she *ought* to come; and, if she has a mind worthy of her eyes and features, she *will* come: she will be here for the chance of seeing me, as I am here for the chance of seeing her: she will want to get a word respecting her confounded sweetheart, as I want to get another flavour of what I think the essence of life: a taste of existence, with the spirit preserved in it, and not evaporated. Adventure is to stagnation what champagne is to flat porter.'

He looked round. The church was cold, silent, empty, but for one old woman. As the chimes subsided, and the single bell tolled slowly, another and another elderly parishioner came dropping in, and took a humble station in the free sittings. It is always the frailest, the oldest, and the poorest that brave the worst weather, to prove and maintain their constancy to dear old mother Church: this wild morning, not one affluent family attended, not one carriage party appeared – all the lined and cushioned pews were empty; only on the bare oaken seats sat ranged the grey-haired elders and feeble paupers.

'I'll scorn her, if she doesn't come,' muttered Martin shortly and savagely to himself. The Rector's shovel-hat had passed the porch: Mr Helstone and his clerk were in the vestry.

The bells ceased – the reading-desk was filled – the doors were closed – the service commenced: void stood the Rectory-pew – she was not there: Martin scorned her.

'Worthless thing! Vapid thing! Commonplace humbug! Like all other girls – weakly, selfish, shallow!'

Such was Martin's liturgy.

'She is not like our picture: her eyes are not large and expressive: her nose is not straight, delicate, Hellenic: her mouth has not that charm I thought it had – which, I imagined, could beguile me of sullenness in my worst moods. What is she? A thread-paper, a doll, a toy – a *girl*, in short.'

So absorbed was the young cynic, he forgot to rise from his knees at the proper place, and was still in an exemplary attitude of devotion when – the litany over – the first hymn was given out. To be so caught did not contribute to soothe him: he started up red (for he was so sensitive to ridicule as any girl). To make the matter worse, the church-door had re-opened, and the aisles were filling: patter, patter, patter, a hundred little feet trotted in. It was the Sunday-scholars. According to Briarfield winter custom, these children had till now been kept where there was a warm stove, and only led into church just before the Communion and Sermon.

The little ones were settled first, and at last, when the boys and the younger girls were all arranged – when the organ was swelling high, and the choir and congregation were rising to uplift a spiritual song – a tall class of young women came quietly in, closing the procession. Their teacher, having seen them seated, passed into the Rectory-pew. The French-grey cloak and small beaver bonnet were known to Martin: it was the very costume his eyes had ached to catch. Miss Helstone had not suffered the storm to prove an impediment: after all, she

was come to church. Martin probably whispered his satisfaction to his hymn-book; at any rate, he therewith hid his face two minutes.

Satisfied or not, he had time to get very angry with her again before the sermon was over; she had never once looked his way: at least, he had not been so lucky as to encounter a glance.

'If,' he said – 'if she takes no notice of me; if she shows I am not in her thoughts, I shall have a worse, a meaner opinion of her than ever. Most despicable would it be to come for the sake of those sheep-faced Sunday-scholars, and not for my sake, or that long skeleton Moore's.'

The sermon found an end; the benediction was pronounced; the congregation dispersed: she had not been near him.

Now, indeed, as Martin set his face homeward, he felt that the sleet was sharp, and the east wind cold.

His nearest way lay through some fields: it was a dangerous, because an untrodden way: he did not care; he would take it. Near the second stile rose a clump of trees: was that an umbrella waiting there? Yes: an umbrella held with evident difficulty against the blast: behind it fluttered a French-grey cloak. Martin grinned as he toiled up the steep encumbered field, difficult to the foot as a slope in the upper realms of Etna. There was an inimitable look in his face when, having gained the stile, he seated himself coolly thereupon, and thus opened a conference which, for his own part, he was willing to prolong indefinitely.

'I think you had better strike a bargain: exchange me for Mrs Pryor.'

'I was not sure whether you would come this way, Martin; but I thought I would run the chance: there is no such thing as getting a quiet word spoken in the church or churchyard.'

'Will you agree? Make over Mrs Pryor to my mother, and put me in her skirts?'

'As if I could understand you! What puts Mrs Pryor into your head?'

'You call her "mamma," don't you?'

'She *is* my mamma.'

'Not possible – or so inefficient, so careless a mamma – I should make a five times better one. You *may* laugh: I have no objection to see you laugh: your teeth – I hate ugly teeth; but yours are as pretty as a pearl necklace, and a necklace, of which the pearls are very fair, even, and well matched too.'

'Martin, what now? I thought the Yorkes never paid compliments?'

'They have not done till this generation; but I feel as if it were my vocation to turn out a new variety of the Yorke species. I am rather tired of my own ancestors: we have traditions going back for four ages – tales of Hiram, which was the son of Hiram, which was the son of Samuel, which was the son of John, which was the son of Zerubbabel Yorke. All, from Zerubbabel down to the last Hiram, were such as you see my father. Before that, there was a Godfrey: we have his picture; it hangs in Moore's bed-room: it is like me. Of his character we know nothing; but I am sure it was different to his descendants: he has long curling dark hair; he is carefully and cavalierly dressed. Having said that he is like me, I need not add that he is handsome.'

'You are not handsome, Martin.'

'No; but wait a while: just let me take my time: I mean to begin from this day to cultivate, to polish – and we shall see.'

# Shirley

'You are a very strange – a very unaccountable boy, Martin; but don't imagine you ever will be handsome: you cannot.'

'I mean to try. But we were talking about Mrs Pryor: she must be the most unnatural mamma in existence, coolly to let her daughter come out in this weather. Mine was in such a rage, because I would go to church: she was fit to fling the kitchen-brush after me.'

'Mamma was very much concerned about me; but I am afraid I was obstinate: I *would* go.'

'To see me?'

'Exactly: I thought of nothing else. I greatly feared the snow would hinder you from coming: you don't know how pleased I was to see you all by yourself in the pew.'

'*I* came to fulfil my duty, and set the parish a good example. And so you were obstinate, were you? I should like to see you obstinate, I should. Wouldn't I have you in good discipline if I owned you? Let me take the umbrella.'

'I can't stay two minutes: our dinner will be ready.'

'And so will ours; and we have always a hot dinner on Sundays. Roast goose today, with apple-pie and rice-pudding. I always contrive to know the bill of fare: well, I like these things uncommonly; but I'll make the sacrifice, if you will.'

'We have a cold dinner: my uncle will allow no unnecessary cooking on the Sabbath. But I must return: the house would be in commotion, if I failed to appear.'

'So will Briarmains, bless you! I think I hear my father sending out the overlooker and five of the dyers, to look in six directions for the body of his prodigal son in the snow; and my mother repenting her of her many misdeeds towards me, now I am gone.'

'Martin, how is Mr Moore?'

'*That* is what you came for – just to say that word.'

'Come, tell me quickly.'

'Hang him! he is no worse; but as ill-used as ever – mewed up, kept in solitary confinement. They mean to make either an idiot or a maniac of him, and take out a commission of lunacy. Horsfall starves him: you saw how thin he was.'

'You were very good the other day, Martin.'

'What day? I am always good – a model.'

'When will you be so good again?'

'I see what you are after; but you'll not wheedle me: I am no cat's paw.'

'But it must be done: it is quite a right thing, and a necessary thing.'

'How you encroach! Remember, I managed the matter of my own free will before.'

'And you will again.'

'I won't: the business gave me far too much trouble: I like my ease.'

'Mr Moore wishes to see me, Martin; and I wish to see him.'

'I daresay' (coolly).

'It is too bad of your mother to exclude his friends.'

'Tell her so.'

'His own relations.'

'Come and blow her up.'

'You know that would advance nothing. Well, I shall stick to my point. See him I will. If you won't help me, I'll manage without help.'

'Do: there is nothing like self-reliance – self-dependence.'

'I have no time to reason with you now; but I consider you provoking. Good-morning.'

Away she went – the umbrella shut; for she could not carry it against the wind.

'She is not vapid; she is not shallow,' said Martin. 'I shall like to watch, and mark how she will work her way without help. If the storm were not of snow, but of fire – such as came refreshingly down on the cities of the plain – she would go through it to procure five minutes' speech of that Moore. Now, I consider I have had a pleasant morning: the disappointments got time on: the fears and fits of anger only made that short discourse pleasanter, when it came at last. She expected to coax me at once: she'll not manage that in one effort: she shall come again, again, and yet again. It would please me to put her in a passion – to make her cry: I want to discover how far she will go – what she will do and dare – to get her will. It seems strange and new to find one human being thinking so much about another as she thinks about Moore. – But it is time to go home: my appetite tells me the hour: won't I walk into that goose? – and we'll try whether Matthew or I shall get the largest cut of the apple-pie to-day.'

# Chapter 35

## Wherein Matters Make Some Progress, But Not Much

Martin had planned well: he had laid out a dexterously concerted scheme for his private amusement; but older and wiser schemers than he are often doomed to see their finest-spun projects swept to annihilation by the sudden broom of Fate – that fell housewife, whose red arm none can control. In the present instance, this broom was manufactured out of the tough fibres of Moore's own stubborn purpose, bound tight with his will. He was now resuming his strength, and making strange head against Mrs Horsfall. Each morning he amazed that matron with a fresh astonishment. First, he discharged her from her valet-duties: he would dress himself. Then, he refused the coffee she brought him: he would breakfast with the family. Lastly, he forbade her his chamber. On the same day, amidst the outcries of all the women in the place, he put his head out of doors. The morning after, he followed Mr Yorke to his counting-house, and requested an envoy to fetch a chaise from the Red-House Inn. He was resolved, he said, to return home to the Hollow that very afternoon. Mr Yorke, instead of opposing, aided and abetted him: the chaise was sent for, though Mrs Yorke declared the step would be his death. It came. Moore, little

disposed to speak, made his purse do duty for his tongue: he expressed his gratitude to the servants and to Mrs Horsfall, by the chink of his coin. The latter personage approved and understood this language perfectly; it made amends for all previous contumacy: she and her patient parted the best friends in the world.

The kitchen visited and soothed, Moore betook himself to the parlour: he had Mrs Yorke to appease: not quite so easy a task as the pacification of her housemaids. There she sat plunged in sullen dudgeon; the gloomiest speculations on the depths of man's ingratitude absorbing her thoughts. He drew near and bent over her; she was obliged to look up, if it were only to bid him 'avaunt.' There was beauty still in his pale, wasted features; there was earnestness, and a sort of sweetness – for he was smiling – in his hollow eyes.

'Good-bye!' he said; and as he spoke the smile glittered and melted. He had no iron mastery of his sensations now: a trifling emotion made itself apparent in his present weak state.

'And what are you going to leave us for?' she asked: 'we will keep you, and do anything in the world for you, if you will only stay till you are stronger.'

'Good-bye!' he again said: and added, 'you have been a mother to me: give your wilful son one embrace.'

Like a foreigner, as he was, he offered her first one cheek, then the other: she kissed him.

'What a trouble – what a burden I have been to you!' he muttered.

'You are the worst trouble now, headstrong youth!' was the answer. 'I wonder who is to nurse you at Hollow's cottage: your sister Hortense knows no more about such matters than a child.'

'Thank God! for I have had nursing enough to last me my life.'

Here the little girls came in; Jessie crying, Rose quiet, but grave. Moore took them out into the hall to soothe, pet, and kiss them. He knew it was not in their mother's nature to bear to see any living thing caressed but herself: she would have felt annoyed had he fondled a kitten in her presence.

The boys were standing about the chaise as Moore entered it; but for them he had no farewell. To Mr Yorke he only said, –

'You have a good riddance of me: that was an unlucky shot for you, Yorke; it turned Briarmains into an hospital. Come and see me at the cottage soon.'

He drew up the glass; the chaise rolled away. In half an hour he alighted at his own garden-wicket. Having paid the driver and dismissed the vehicle, he leaned on that wicket an instant, at once to rest and to muse.

'Six months ago I passed out at this gate,' said he, 'a proud, angry, disappointed man; I come back sadder and wiser: weakly enough, but not worried. A cold, grey, yet quiet world lies round – a world where, if I hope little, I fear nothing. All slavish terrors of embarrassment have left me: let the worst come, I can work, as Joe Scott does, for an honourable living: in such doom, I yet see some hardship, but no degradation. Formerly, pecuniary ruin was equivalent in my eyes to personal dishonour. It is not so now: I know the difference. Ruin *is* an evil; but one for which I am prepared; the day of whose coming I know, for I have calculated. I can yet put it off six months – not an hour longer: if things by that time alter – which is not probable; if fetters, which now seem indissoluble, should be loosened from our trade (of all things the most unlikely to happen) – I might conquer in this long struggle yet – I might – Good God! what might

# Shirley

I not do? But the thought is a brief madness: let me see things with sane eyes. Ruin will come, lay her axe to my fortune's roots, and hew them down. I shall snatch a sapling, I shall cross the sea, and plant it in American woods. Louis will go with me. Will none but Louis go? I cannot tell – I have no right to ask.'

He entered the house.

It was afternoon, twilight yet out of doors: starless and moonless twilight; for, though keenly freezing with a dry black frost, heaven wore a mask of clouds congealed and fast-locked. The mill-dam too was frozen: the Hollow was very still: indoors it was already dark. Sarah had lit a good fire in the parlour; she was preparing tea in the kitchen.

'Hortense,' said Moore, as his sister bustled up to help him off with his cloak, 'I am pleased to come home.'

Hortense did not feel the peculiar novelty of this expression coming from her brother, who had never before called the cottage his home; and to whom its narrow limits had always heretofore seemed rather restrictive than protective: still, whatever contributed to his happiness pleased her; and she expressed herself to that effect.

He sat down, but soon rose again: he went to the window; he came back to the fire.

'Hortense!'

'Mon frère?'

'This little parlour looks very clean and pleasant: unusually bright, somehow.'

'It is true, brother: I have had the whole house thoroughly and scrupulously cleaned in your absence.'

'Sister, I think on this first day of your return home, you ought to have a friend or so to tea; if it were only to see how fresh and spruce you have made the little place.'

'True, brother: if it were not late, I might send for Miss Mann.'

'So you might; but it really is too late to disturb that good lady; and the evening is much too cold for her to come out.'

'How thoughtful in you, dear Gérard! We must put it off till another day.'

'I want some one to-day, dear sister: some quiet guest, who would tire neither of us.'

'Miss Ainley?'

'An excellent person, they say; but she lives too far off. Tell Harry Scott to step up to the Rectory with a request from you, that Caroline Helstone should come and spend the evening with you.'

'Would it not be better to-morrow, dear brother?'

'I should like her to see the place as it is just now: its brilliant cleanliness and perfect neatness are so much to your credit.'

'It might benefit her in the way of example.'

'It might and must: she ought to come.'

He went into the kitchen.

'Sarah, delay tea half an hour.' He then commissioned her to despatch Harry Scott to the Rectory, giving her a twisted note hastily scribbled in pencil by himself, and addressed 'Miss Helstone.'

Scarcely had Sarah time to get impatient under the fear of damage to her toast already prepared, when the messenger returned; and with him the invited guest.

# Shirley

She entered through the kitchen, quietly tripped up Sarah's stairs to take off her bonnet and furs, and came down as quietly, with her beautiful curls nicely smoothed; her graceful merino dress and delicate collar all trim and spotless; her gay little work-bag in her hand. She lingered to exchange a few kindly words with Sarah; and to look at the new tortoise-shell kitten basking on the kitchen hearth; and to speak to the canary-bird, which a sudden blaze from the fire had startled on its perch; and then she betook herself to the parlour.

The gentle salutation, the friendly welcome, were interchanged in such tranquil sort as befitted cousins meeting; a sense of pleasure, subtle and quiet as a perfume, diffused itself through the room; the newly kindled lamp burned up bright; the tray and the singing urn were brought in.

'I am pleased to come home,' repeated Mr Moore.

They assembled round the table. Hortense chiefly talked. She congratulated Caroline on the evident improvement in her health: her colour and her plump cheeks were returning, she remarked. It was true: there was an obvious change in Miss Helstone: all about her seemed elastic; depression, fear, forlornness, were withdrawn: no longer crushed, and saddened, and slow, and drooping, she looked like one who had tasted the cordial of heart's-ease, and been lifted on the wing of hope.

After tea, Hortense went up-stairs: she had not rummaged her drawers for a month past, and the impulse to perform that operation was now become resistless. During her absence, the talk passed into Caroline's hands: she took it up with ease; she fell into her best tone of conversation. A pleasing facility and elegance of language gave fresh charm to familiar topics: a new music in the always soft voice gently surprised and pleasingly captivated the listener; unwonted shades and lights of expression elevated the young countenance with character, and kindled it with animation.

'Caroline, you look as if you had heard good tidings,' said Moore, after earnestly gazing at her for some minutes.

'Do I?'

'I sent for you this evening that I might be cheered; but you cheer me more than I had calculated.'

'I am glad of that. And I *really* cheer you?'

'You look brightly; move buoyantly; speak musically.'

'It is pleasant to be here again.'

'Truly it is pleasant: I feel it so. And to see health on your cheek, and hope in your eye, is pleasant, Cary: but what is this hope, and what is the source of this sunshine I perceive about you?'

'For one thing, I am happy in mamma: I love her so much, and she loves me. Long and tenderly she nursed me; now, when her care has made me well, I can occupy myself for and with her all the day. I say it is my turn to attend to her; and I *do* attend to her: I am her waiting-woman, as well as her child: I like – you would laugh if you knew what pleasure I have in making dresses and sewing for her. She looks so nice now, Robert: I will not let her be old-fashioned. And then, she is charming to talk to: full of wisdom; ripe in judgment; rich in information; exhaustless in stores her observant faculties have quietly amassed. Every day that I live with her, I like her better; I esteem her more highly; I love her more tenderly.'

'*That* for one thing, then, Cary: you talk in such a way about "mamma", it is enough to make one jealous of the old lady.'

'She is not old, Robert.'

'Of the young lady, then.'

'She does not pretend to be young.'

'Well – of the matron. But you said, "mamma's" affection was *one* thing that made you happy: now for the other thing.'

'I am glad you are better.'

'What besides?'

'I am glad we are friends.'

'You and I?'

'Yes; I once thought we never should be.'

'Cary, some day I mean to tell you a thing about myself that is not to my credit, and, consequently, will not please you.'

'Ah! – don't! I cannot bear to think ill of you.'

'And I cannot bear that you should think better of me than I deserve.'

'Well, but I half know your "thing:" indeed, I believe I know all about it.'

'You do not.'

'I believe I do.'

'Whom does it concern besides me?'

She coloured; she hesitated; she was silent.

'Speak, Cary! – whom does it concern?'

She tried to utter a name, and could not.

'Tell me: there is none present but ourselves: be frank.'

'But if I guess wrong?'

'I will forgive. Whisper, Cary.'

He bent his ear to her lips: still she would not, or could not, speak clearly to the point. Seeing that Moore waited, and was resolved to hear something, she at last said, –

'Miss Keeldar spent a day at the Rectory about a week since. The evening came on very wintry, and we persuaded her to stay all night.'

'And you and she curled your hair together?'

'How do you know that?'

'And then you chatted; and she told you –'

'It was not at curling-hair time; so you are not as wise as you think: and besides, she didn't tell me.'

'You slept together afterwards?'

'We occupied the same room and bed. We did not sleep much: we talked the whole night through.'

'I'll be sworn you did! and then it all came out – tant pis. I would rather you had heard it from myself.'

'You are quite wrong: she did not tell me what you suspect: she is not the person to proclaim such things; but yet I inferred something from parts of her discourse: I gathered more from rumour, and I made out the rest by instinct.'

'But if she did not tell you that I wanted to marry her for the sake of her money, and that she refused me indignantly and scornfully (you need neither start nor blush; nor yet need you prick your trembling fingers with your needle: that is the plain truth, whether you like it or not) – if such was not the subject

# Shirley

of her august confidences, on what point did they turn? You say you talked the whole night through: what about?'

'About things we never thoroughly discussed before, intimate friends as we have been: but you hardly expect I should tell you?'

'Yes, yes, Cary – you will tell me: you said we were friends; and friends should always confide in each other.'

'But you are sure you won't repeat it?'

'Quite sure.'

'Not to Louis?'

'Not even to Louis? What does Louis care for young ladies' secrets?'

'Robert – Shirley is a curious, magnanimous being.'

'I daresay: I can imagine there are both odd points and grand points about her.'

'I have found her chary in showing her feelings; but when they rush out, river-like, and pass full and powerful before you, – almost without leave from her – you gaze, wonder, you admire, and – I think – love her.'

'You saw this spectacle?'

'Yes: at dead of night; when all the house was silent, and starlight, and the cold reflection from the snow glimmered in our chamber, – then I saw Shirley's heart.'

'Her heart's core? Do you think she showed you that?'

'Her heart's core.'

'And how was it?'

'Like a shrine, – for it was holy; like snow, – for it was pure; like flame, – for it was warm; like death, – for it was strong.'

'Can she love? Tell me that.'

'What think you?'

'She has loved none that have loved her yet.'

'Who are those that have loved her?'

He named a list of gentlemen, closing with Sir Philip Nunnely.

'She has loved none of these.'

'Yet some of them were worthy of a woman's affection.'

'Of some women's; but not of Shirley's.'

'Is she better than others of her sex?'

'She is peculiar, and more dangerous to take as a wife – rashly.'

'I can imagine that.'

'She spoke of you –'

'Oh! she did! I thought you denied it.'

'She did not speak in the way you fancy; but I asked her, and I would make her tell me what she thought of you, or rather, how she felt towards you. I wanted to know: I had long wanted to know.'

'So had I; but let us hear: she thinks meanly – she feels contemptuously, doubtless?'

'She thinks of you almost as highly as a woman can think of a man. You know she can be eloquent: I yet feel in fancy the glow of the language in which her opinion was conveyed.'

'But how does she feel?'

'Till you shocked her (she said you had shocked her, but she would not tell

me how), she felt as a sister feels towards a brother of whom she is at once fond and proud.'

'I'll shock her no more, Cary, for the shock rebounded on myself till I staggered again: but that comparison about sister and brother is all nonsense: she is too rich and proud to entertain fraternal sentiments for me.'

'You don't know her, Robert; and somehow, I fancy *now* (I had other ideas formerly), that you cannot know her: you and she are not so constructed as to be able thoroughly to understand each other.'

'It may be so. I esteem her; I admire her; and yet my impressions concerning her are harsh – perhaps uncharitable. I believe, for instance, that she is incapable of love –'

'Shirley incapable of love!'

'That she will never marry: Imagine her jealous of compromising her pride, of relinquishing her power, of sharing her property.'

'Shirley has hurt your amour-propre.'

'She did hurt it – though I had not an emotion of tenderness, not a spark of passion for her.'

'Then, Robert, it was very wicked in you to want to marry her.'

'And very mean, my little pastor, my pretty priestess. I never wanted to kiss Miss Keeldar in my life, though she has fine lips, scarlet and round, as ripe cherries; or, if I did wish it, it was the mere desire of the eye.'

'I doubt, now, whether you are speaking the truth: the grapes or the cherries are sour – "hung too high." '

'She has a pretty figure, a pretty face, beautiful hair: I acknowledge all her charms and feel none of them; or only feel them in a way she would disdain. I suppose I was truly tempted, by the mere gilding of the bait. Caroline, what a noble fellow your Robert is – great, good, disinterested, and then so pure!'

'But not perfect: he made a great blunder once, and we will hear no more about it.'

'And shall we think no more about it, Cary? Shall we not despise him in our heart, gentle but just, compassionate but upright?'

'Never! We will remember that with what measure we mete it shall be measured unto us, and so we will give no scorn – only affection.'

'Which won't satisfy, I warn you of that. Something besides affection – something far stronger, sweeter, warmer – will be demanded one day: is it there to give?'

Caroline was moved – much moved.

'Be calm, Lina,' said Moore, soothingly; 'I have no intention, because I have no right, to perturb your mind now, nor for months to come: don't look as if you would leave me: we will make no more agitating allusions: we will resume our gossip. Do not tremble: look me in the face: see what a poor, pale, grim phantom I am – more pitiable than formidable.'

She looked shyly. 'There is something formidable still, pale as you are,' she said, as her eye fell under his.

'To return to Shirley,' pursued Moore; 'is it your opinion that she is ever likely to marry?'

'She loves.'

'Platonically – theoretically – all humbug!'

'She loves, what I call, sincerely.'

'Did she say so?'

'I cannot affirm that she said so: no such confession as, I love this man or that, passed her lips.'

'I thought not.'

'But the feeling made its way in spite of her, and I saw it. She spoke of one man in a strain not to be misunderstood: her voice alone was sufficient testimony. Having wrung from her an opinion on your character, I demanded a second opinion of – another person about whom I had my conjectures; though they were the most tangled and puzzled conjectures in the world. I would *make* her speak: I shook her, I chid her, I pinched her fingers when she tried to put me off with gibes and jests in her queer, provoking way, and at last, out it came: the voice, I say, was enough; hardly raised above a whisper, and yet such a soft vehemence in its tones. There was no confession – no confidence in the matter: to these things she cannot condescend; but I am sure that man's happiness is dear to her as her own life.'

'Who is it?'

'I charged her with the fact; she did not deny; she did not avow, but looked at me: I saw her eyes by the snow-gleam. It was quite enough: I triumphed over her mercilessly.'

'What right had *you* to triumph? Do you mean to say *you* are fancy-free?'

'Whatever *I* am, Shirley is a bondswoman. Lioness! She has found her captor. Mistress she may be of all round her – but her own mistress she is not.'

'So you exulted at recognizing a fellow-slave in one so fair and imperial?'

'I did; Robert, you say right, in one so fair and imperial.'

'You confess it – a *fellow*-slave?'

'I confess nothing; but I say that haughty Shirley is no more free than was Hagar.'

'And who, pray, is the Abraham; the hero of a patriarch who has achieved such a conquest?'

'You still speak scornfully, and cynically, and sorely; but I will make you change your note before I have done with you.'

'We will see that: can she marry this Cupidon?'

'Cupidon! he is just about as much a Cupidon as you are a Cyclops.'

'Can she marry him?'

'You will see.'

'I want to know his name, Cary.'

'Guess it.'

'Is it any one in this neighbourhood?'

'Yes, in Briarfield parish.'

'Then it is some person unworthy of her. I don't know a soul in Briarfield parish her equal.'

'Guess.'

'Impossible. I suppose she is under a delusion, and will plunge into some absurdity after all.'

Caroline smiled.

'Do *you* approve the choice?' asked Moore.

'Quite, *quite*.'

'Then I *am* puzzled; for the head which owns this bounteous fall of hazel

# Shirley

curls is an excellent little thinking machine, most accurate in its working: it boasts a correct, steady judgment, inherited from "mamma," I suppose.'

'And I *quite* approve, and mamma was charmed.'

' "Mamma" charmed! Mrs Pryor. It can't be romantic then?'

'It *is* romantic, but it is also right.'

'Tell me, Cary. Tell me out of pity: I am too weak to be tantalized.'

'You shall be tantalized: it will do you no harm: you are not so weak as you pretend.'

'I have twice this evening had some thoughts of falling on the floor at your feet.'

'You had better not: I shall decline to help you up.'

'And worshipping you downright. My mother was a Roman Catholic; you look like the loveliest of her pictures of the Virgin: I think I will embrace her faith, and kneel and adore.'

'Robert, Robert, sit still; don't be absurd: I will go to Hortense, if you commit extravagances.'

'You have stolen my senses: just now nothing will come into my mind but "les litanies de la sainte Vièrge. Rose céleste, reine des Anges!" '

' "Tour d'ivoire, maison d'or": is not that the jargon? Well, sit down quietly, and guess your riddle.'

'But, "mamma" charmed! There's the puzzle.'

'I'll tell you what mamma said when I told her: "Depend upon it, my dear, such a choice will make the happiness of Miss Keeldar's life." '

'I'll guess once, and no more. It is old Helstone. She is going to be your aunt.'

'I'll tell my uncle; I'll tell Shirley!' cried Caroline, laughing gleefully. 'Guess again, Robert; your blunders are charming.'

'It is the parson, Hall.'

'Indeed, no: he is mine, if you please.'

'Yours! Ay! the whole generation of women in Briarfield seem to have made an idol of that priest: I wonder why: he is bald, sand-blind, grey-haired.'

'Fanny will be here to fetch me, before you have solved the riddle, if you don't make haste.'

'I'll guess no more, I am tired: and then I don't care. Miss Keeldar may marry "le grand Turc" for me.'

'Must I whisper?'

'That you must, and quickly: here comes Hortense: come near, a little nearer, my own Lina: I care for the whisper more than the words.'

She whispered: Robert gave a start, a flash of the eye, a brief laugh: Miss Moore entered, and Sarah followed behind, with information that Fanny was come. The hour of converse was over.

Robert found a moment to exchange a few more whispered sentences: he was waiting at the foot of the staircase, as Caroline descended after putting on her shawl.

'Must I call Shirley a noble creature now?' he asked.

'If you wish to speak the truth, certainly.'

'Must I forgive her?'

'Forgive her? Naughty Robert! Was she in the wrong, or were you?'

'Must I at length love her downright, Cary?'

Caroline looked keenly up, and made a movement towards him, something between the loving and the petulant.

'Only give the word, and I'll try to obey you.'

'Indeed, you must not love her: the bare idea is perverse.'

'But then she is handsome, peculiarly handsome: hers is a beauty that grows on you: you think her but graceful, when you first see her; you discover her to be beautiful, when you have known her for a year.'

'It is not you who are to say these things. Now, Robert, be good.'

'Oh! Cary, I have no love to give. Were the goddess of beauty to woo me, I could not meet her advances: there is no heart which I can call mine in this breast.'

'So much the better: you are a great deal safer without: good-night.'

'Why must you always go, Lina, at the very instant when I most want you to stay?'

'Because you most wish to retain when you are most certain to lose.'

'Listen; one other word. Take care of your own heart: do you hear me?'

'There is no danger.'

'I am not convinced of that: the Platonic parson, for instance.'

'Who? Malone?'

'Cyril Hall: I owe more than one twinge of jealousy to that quarter.'

'As to you, you have been flirting with Miss Mann: she showed me the other day a plant you had given her. – Fanny, I am ready.'

# Chapter 36

## Written in the Schoolroom

ouis Moore's doubts, respecting the immediate evacuation of Fieldhead by Mr Sympson, turned out to be perfectly wellfounded. The very next day after the grand quarrel about Sir Philip Nunnely, a sort of reconciliation was patched up between uncle and niece: Shirley, who could never find in her heart to be or to seem inhospitable (except in the single instance of Mr Donne), begged the whole party to stay a little longer: she begged in such earnest, it was evident she wished it, for some reason. They took her at her word: indeed, the uncle could not bring himself to leave her quite unwatched – at full liberty to marry Robert Moore, as soon as that gentleman should be able (Mr Sympson piously prayed this might never be the case) to reassert his supposed pretensions to her hand. They all stayed.

In his first rage against all the house of Moore, Mr Sympson had so conducted himself towards Mr Louis, that that gentleman – patient of labour or suffering, but intolerant of coarse insolence – had promptly resigned his post, and could now be induced to resume and retain it only till such time as the family should

# Shirley

quit Yorkshire: Mrs Sympson's entreaties prevailed with him thus far; his own attachment to his pupil constituted an additional motive for concession; and probably he had a third motive, stronger than either of the other two: probably he would have found it very hard indeed to leave Fieldhead just now.

Things went on, for some time, pretty smoothly; Miss Keeldar's health was re-established; her spirits resumed their flow: Moore had found means to relieve her from every nervous apprehension; and, indeed, from the moment of giving him her confidence, every fear seemed to have taken wing: her heart became as lightsome, her manner as careless, as those of a little child, that, thoughtless of its own life or death, trusts all responsibility to its parents. He and William Farren – through whose medium he made inquiries concerning the state of Phoebe – agreed in asserting that the dog was not mad: that it was only ill-usage which had driven her from home: for it was proved that her master was in the frequent habit of chastising her violently. Their assertion might, or might not, be true: the groom and gamekeeper affirmed to the contrary; both asserting that, if hers was not a clear case of hydrophobia, there was no such disease. But to this evidence Louis Moore turned an incredulous ear: he reported to Shirley only what was encouraging: she believed him; and, right or wrong, it is certain that in her case the bite proved innocuous.

November passed; December came: the Sympsons were now really departing; it was incumbent on them to be at home by Christmas; their packages were preparing; they were to leave in a few days. One winter evening, during the last week of their stay, Louis Moore again took out his little blank book, and discoursed with it as follows: –

'She is lovelier than ever. Since that little cloud was dispelled, all the temporary waste and wanness have vanished. It was marvellous to see how soon the magical energy of youth raised her elastic, and revived her blooming.

'After breakfast this morning, when I had seen her, and listened to her, and – so to speak – felt her, in every sentient atom of my frame, I passed from her sunny presence into the chill drawing-room. Taking up a little gilt volume, I found it to contain a selection of lyrics. I read a poem or two: whether the spell was in me or in the verse, I know not, but my heart filled genially – my pulse rose: I glowed, notwithstanding the frost-air. I too, am young as yet; though she said she never considered me young, I am barely thirty: there are moments when life – for no other reason than my own youth – beams with sweet hues upon me.

'It was time to go to the school-room: I went. That same school-room is rather pleasant in a morning; the sun then shines through the low lattice; the books are in order; there are no papers strewn about; the fire is clear and clean; no cinders have fallen, no ashes accumulated. I found Henry there, and he had brought with him Miss Keeldar: they were together.

'I said she was lovelier than ever: she is. A fine rose, not deep, but delicate, opens on her cheek; her eye, always dark, clear, and speaking, utters now a language I cannot render – it is the utterance, seen not heard, through which angels must have communed when there was "silence in heaven." Her hair was always dusk as night, and fine as silk; her neck was always fair, flexible, polished – but both have now a new charm: the tresses are soft as shadow, the shoulders they fall on wear a goddess-grace. Once I only *saw* her beauty, now I *feel* it.

# Shirley

'Henry was repeating his lesson to her before bringing it to me – one of her hands was occupied with the book, he held the other: that boy gets more than his share of privileges; he dares caress and is caressed. What indulgence and compassion she shows him! Too much: if this went on, Henry, in a few years, when his soul was formed, would offer it on her altar as I have offered mine.

'I saw her eyelid flitter when I came in, but she did not look up: *now* she hardly ever gives me a glance. She seems to grow silent too – to *me* she rarely speaks, and, when I am present, she says little to others. In my gloomy moments, I attribute this change to indifference, – aversion, – what not? In my sunny intervals I give it another meaning: I say, were I her equal, I could find in this shyness – coyness, and in that coyness – love. As it is, dare I look for it? What could I do with it, if found?

'This morning I dared, at least, contrive an hour's communion for her and me; I dared not only *wish* – but *will* an interview with her: I dared summon solitude to guard us. Very decidedly I called Henry to the door: without hesitation, I said, "Go where you will, my boy; but, till I call you, return not here."

'Henry, I could see, did not like his dismissal: that boy is young, but a thinker: his meditative eye shines on me strangely sometimes: he half feels what links me to Shirley; he half guesses that there is a dearer delight in the reserve with which I am treated, than in all the endearments he is allowed. The young, lame, half-grown lion would growl at me now and then, because I have tamed his lioness and am her keeper, did not the habit of discipline and the instinct of affection hold him subdued. Go, Henry; you must learn to take your share of the bitter of life with all of Adam's race that have gone before, or will come after you: your destiny can be no exception to the common lot: be grateful that your love is overlooked thus early, before it can claim any affinity to passion: an hour's fret, a pang of envy, suffice to express what you feel: Jealousy hot as the sun above the line, Rage destructive as the tropic storm, the clime of your sensations ignores – as yet.

'I took my usual seat at the desk, quite in my usual way: I am blessed in that power to cover all inward ebullition with outward calm. No one who looks at my slow face can guess the vortex sometimes whirling in my heart, and engulfing thought, and wrecking prudence. Pleasant is it to have the gift to proceed peacefully and powerfully in your course without alarming by one eccentric movement. It was not my present intention to utter one word of love to her, or to reveal one glimpse of the fire in which I wasted. Presumptuous, I never have been; presumptuous, I never will be: rather than even *seem* selfish and interested, I would resolutely rise, gird my loins, part and leave her, and seek, on the other side of the globe, a new life, cold and barren as the rock the salt tide daily washes. My design this morning was to take of her a near scrutiny – to read a line in the page of her heart: before I left, I determined to know *what* I was leaving.

'I had some quills to make into pens: most men's hands would have trembled when their hearts were so stirred; mine went to work steadily, and my voice, when I called it into exercise, was firm.

' "This day-week you will be alone at Fieldhead, Miss Keeldar."

' "Yes: I rather think my uncle's intention to go is a settled one now."

' "He leaves you dissatisfied."

# Shirley

' "He is not pleased with me."

' "He departs as he came – no better for his journey: this is mortifying."

' "I trust the failure of his plans will take from him all inclination to lay new ones."

' "In his way, Mr Sympson honestly wished you well. All he has done, or intended to do, he believed to be for the best."

' "You are kind to undertake the defence of a man who has permitted himself to treat you with so much insolence."

' "I never feel shocked at, or bear malice for, what is spoken in character; and most perfectly in character was that vulgar and violent onset against me, when he had quitted you worsted."

' "You cease now to be Henry's tutor?"

' "I shall be parted from Henry for a while – (if he and I live we shall meet again somehow, for we love each other) – and be ousted from the bosom of the Sympson family for ever. Happily this change does not leave me stranded: it hurries into premature execution designs long formed."

' "No change finds you off your guard: I was sure, in your calm way, you would be prepared for sudden mutation. I always think you stand in the world like a solitary but watchful, thoughtful archer in a wood; and the quiver on your shoulder holds more arrows than one; your bow is provided with a second string. Such too is your brother's wont. You two might go forth homeless hunters to the loneliest western wilds; all would be well with you. The hewn tree would make you a hut, the cleared forest yield you fields from its stripped bosom, the buffalo would feel your rifle-shot, and with lowered horns and hump pay homage at your feet."

' "And any Indian tribe of Black-feet, or Flat-heads, would afford us a bride, perhaps?"

' "No (hestitating), I think not. The savage is sordid: I think, – that is, I *hope*, – you would neither of you share your hearth with that to which you could not give your heart."

' "What suggested the wild West to your mind, Miss Keeldar? Have you been with me in spirit when I did not see you? Have you entered into my day-dreams, and beheld my brain labouring at its scheme of a future?"

'She had separated a slip of paper for lighting tapers – a spill, as it is called – into fragments: she threw morsel by morsel into the fire, and stood pensively watching them consume. She did not speak.

' "How did you learn what you seem to know about my intentions?"

' "I know nothing: I am only discovering them now: I spoke at hazard."

' "Your hazard sounds like divination. A tutor I will never be again: never take a pupil after Henry and yourself: not again will I sit habitually at another man's table – no more be the appendage of a family. I am now a man of thirty: I have never been free since I was a boy of ten. I have such a thirst for freedom – such a deep passion to know her and call her mine – such a day-desire and night-longing to win her and possess her, I will not refuse to cross the Atlantic for her sake: her I will follow deep into virgin woods. Mine it shall not be to accept a savage girl as a slave – she could not be a wife. I know no white woman whom I love that would accompany me; but I am certain Liberty will await me, sitting under a pine: when I call her she will come to my log-house, and she shall fill my arms."

# Shirley

'She could not hear me speak so unmoved, and she *was* moved. It was right – I meant to move her. She could not answer me, nor could she look at me: I should have been sorry if she could have done either. Her cheek glowed as if a crimson flower, through whose petals the sun shone, had cast its light upon it. On the white lid and dark lashes of her downcast eye, trembled all that is graceful in the sense of half-painful, half-pleasing shame.

'Soon she controlled her emotion, and took all her feelings under command. I saw she had felt insurrection, and was waking to empire – she sat down. There was that in her face which I could read: it said, I see the line which is my limit – nothing shall make me pass it. I feel – I know how far I may reveal my feelings, and when I must clasp the volume. I have advanced to a certain distance, as far as the true and sovereign and undegraded nature of my kind permits – now here I stand rooted. My heart may break if it is baffled: let it break – it shall never dishonour me – it shall never dishonour my sisterhood in me. Suffering before degradation! death before treachery!

'I, for my part, said, "If she were poor, I would be at her feet. If she were lowly, I would take her in my arms. Her Gold and her Station are two griffins, that guard her on each side. Love looks and longs, and dares not: Passion hovers round, and is kept at bay: Truth and Devotion are scared. There is nothing to lose in winning her – no sacrifice to make – it is all clear gain, and therefore unimaginably difficult."

'Difficult or not, something must be done; something must be said. I could not, and would not, sit silent with all that beauty modestly mute in my presence. I spoke thus; and still I spoke with calm: quiet as my words were, I could hear they fell in a tone distinct, round, and deep.

' "Still, I know I shall be strangely placed with that mountain nymph, Liberty. She is, I suspect, akin to that Solitude which I once wooed, and from which I now seek a divorce. These Oreads are peculiar: they come upon you with an unearthly charm, like some starlight evening; they inspire a wild but not warm delight; their beauty is the beauty of spirits: their grace is not the grace of life, but of seasons or scenes in Nature: theirs is the dewy bloom of morning – the languid flush of evening – the peace of the moon – the changefulness of clouds. I want and will have something different. This elfish splendour looks chill to my vision, and feels frozen to my touch. I am not a poet: I cannot live with abstractions. You, Miss Keeldar, have sometimes, in your laughing satire, called me a material philosopher, and implied that I live sufficiently for the substantial. Certainly I feel material from head to foot; and glorious as Nature is, and deeply as I worship her with the solid powers of a solid heart, I would rather behold her through the soft human eyes of a loved and lovely wife, than through the wild orbs of the highest goddess of Olympus."

' "Juno could not cook a buffalo steak as you like it," said she.

' "She could not: but I will tell you who could – some young, penniless, friendless orphan girl. I wish I could find such a one: pretty enough for me to love, with something of the mind and heart suited to my taste: not uneducated – honest and modest. I care nothing for attainments; but I would fain have the germ of those sweet natural powers which nothing acquired can rival: any temper Fate wills, – I can manage the hottest. To such a creature as this, I should like to be first tutor and then husband. I would teach her my language, my habits, and my principles, and then I would reward her with my love."

# Shirley

' "*Reward* her! lord of the creation! *Reward* her!" ejaculated she, with a curled lip.

' "And be repaid a thousandfold."

' "If she willed it, Monseigneur."

' "And she *should* will it."

' "You have stipulated for any temper Fate wills. Compulsion is flint and a blow to the metal of some souls."

' "And love the spark it elicits."

' "Who cares for the love that is but a spark – seen, flown upward, and gone?"

' "I must find my orphan girl. Tell me how, Miss Keeldar."

' "Advertise; and be sure you add, when you describe the qualifications, she must be a good plain cook."

' "I must find her; and when I do find her, I shall marry her."

' "Not you!" and her voice took a sudden accent of peculiar scorn.

'I liked this: I had roused her from the pensive mood in which I had first found her: I would stir her further.

' "Why doubt it?"

' "*You* marry!"

' "Yes, – of course; nothing more evident than that I can, and shall."

' "The contrary is evident, Mr Moore."

'She charmed me in this mood: waxing disdainful, half insulting, pride, temper, derision, blent in her large fine eye, that had, just now, the look of a merlin's.

' "Favour me with your reasons for such an opinion, Miss Keeldar."

' "How will *you* manage to marry, I wonder?"

' "I shall manage it with ease and speed when I find the proper person."

' "Accept celibacy!" (and she made a gesture with her hand as if she gave me something) "take it as your doom!"

' "No: you cannot give what I already have. Celibacy has been mine for thirty years. If you wish to offer me a gift, a parting present, a keepsake, you must change the boon."

' "Take worse, then!"

' "How? What?"

'I now felt, and looked, and spoke eagerly. I was unwise to quit my sheet-anchor of calm even for an instant: it deprived me of an advantage and transferred it to her. The little spark of temper dissolved in sarcasm, and eddied over her countenance in the ripples of a mocking smile.

' "Take a wife that has paid you court to save your modesty, and thrust herself upon you to spare your scruples."

' "Only show me where."

' "Any stout widow that has had a few husbands already, and can manage these things."

' "She must not be rich then. Oh these riches!"

' "Never would you have gathered the produce of the gold-bearing garden. You have not courage to confront the sleepless dragon: you have not craft to borrow the aid of Atlas!"

' "You look hot and haughty."

' "And you far haughtier. Yours is the monstrous pride which counterfeits humility."

# Shirley

' "I am a dependant: I know my place."

' "I am a woman: I know mine."

' "I am poor: I must be proud."

' "I have received ordinances, and own obligations stringent as yours."

'We had reached a critical point now, and we halted and looked at each other. *She* would not give in, I felt. Beyond this, I neither felt nor saw. A few moments yet were mine: the end was coming – I heard its rush – but not come; I would dally, wait, talk, and when impulse urged, I would act. I am never in a hurry: I never was in a hurry in my whole life. Hasty people drink the nectar of existence scalding hot: I taste it cool as dew. I proceeded: –

' "Apparently, Miss Keeldar, you are as little likely to marry as myself. I know you have refused three, nay, four advantageous offers, and, I believe, a fifth. Have you rejected Sir Philip Nunnely?"

'I put this question suddenly and promptly.

' "Did you think I should take him?"

' "I thought you might."

' "On what grounds, may I ask?"

' "Conformity of rank; age; pleasing contrast of temper, for *he* is mild and amiable; harmony of intellectual tastes."

' "A beautiful sentence! Let us take it to pieces. 'Conformity of rank.' – He is quite above me: compare my grange with his palace, if you please: I am disdained by his kith and kin. 'Suitability of age.' – We were born in the same year; consequently, he is still a boy, while I am a woman: ten years his senior to all intents and purposes. 'Contrast of temper.' – Mild and amiable, is he: I – what? Tell me."

' "Sister of the spotted, bright, quick fiery leopard."

' "And you would mate me with a kid – the Millennium being yet millions of centuries from mankind; being yet, indeed, an archangel high in the seventh heaven, uncommissioned to descend –? Unjust barbarian! 'Harmony of intellectual tastes.' – He is fond of poetry, and I hate it –"

' "Do you? That is news."

' "I absolutely shudder at the sight of metre or at the sound of rhyme, whenever I am at the Priory or Sir Philip at Fieldhead. Harmony, indeed! When did I whip up syllabub sonnets, or string stanzas fragile as fragments of glass? and when did I betray a belief that those penny-beads were genuine brilliants?"

' "You might have the satisfaction of leading him to a higher standard – of improving his tastes."

' "Leading and improving! teaching and tutoring! bearing and forbearing! Pah! My husband is not to be my baby. I am not to set him his daily lesson and see that he learns it, and give him a sugar-plum if he is good, and a patient, pensive, pathetic lecture if he is bad. But it is like a tutor to talk of the 'satisfaction of teaching' – I suppose *you* think it the finest employment in the world. I don't – I reject it. Improving a husband! No. I shall insist upon my husband improving me, or else we part."

' "God knows it is needed!"

' "What do you mean by that, Mr Moore?"

' "What I say. Improvement is imperatively needed."

' "If you were a woman you would school Monsieur, votre mari, charmingly: it would just suit you; schooling is your vocation."

874

# Shirley

' "May I ask whether, in your present just and gentle mood, you mean to taunt me with being a tutor?"

' "Yes – bitterly; and with anything else you please: any defect of which you are painfully conscious."

' "With being poor, for instance?"

' "Of course; that will sting you; you are sore about your poverty: you brood over that."

' "With having nothing but a very plain person to offer the woman who may master my heart?"

' "Exactly. You have a habit of calling yourself plain. You are sensitive about the cut of your features, because they are not quite on an Apollo-pattern. You abuse them more than is needful, in the faint hope that others may say a word in their behalf – which won't happen. Your face is nothing to boast of, certainly: not a pretty line, nor a pretty tint, to be found therein."

' "Compare it with your own."

' "It looks like a god of Egypt: a great sand-buried stone head; or rather I will compare it to nothing so lofty: it looks like Tartar: you are my mastiff's cousin: I think you as much like him as a man can be like a dog."

' "Tartar is your dear companion. In summer, when you rise early, and run out into the fields to wet your feet with the dew, and freshen your cheek and uncurl your hair with the breeze, you always call him to follow you: you call him sometimes with a whistle that you learned from me. In the solitude of your wood, when you think nobody but Tartar is listening, you whistle the very tunes you imitated from my lips, or sing the very songs you have caught up by ear from my voice: I do not ask whence flows the feeling which you pour into these songs, for I know it flows out of your heart, Miss Keeldar. In the winter evenings, Tartar lies at your feet: you suffer him to rest his head on your perfumed lap; you let him couch on the borders of your satin raiment: his rough hide is familiar with the contact of your hand: I once saw you kiss him on that snow-white beauty-spot which stars his broad forehead. It is dangerous to say I am like Tartar: it suggests to me a claim to be treated like Tartar."

' "Perhaps, sir, you can extort as much from your penniless and friendless young orphan-girl, when you find her."

' "Oh! could I find her such as I imagine her. Something to tame first, and teach afterwards: to break in, and then to fondle. To lift the destitute proud thing out of poverty; to establish power over, and then to be indulgent to the capricious moods that never were influenced and never indulged before; to see her alternately irritated and subdued about twelve times in the twenty-four hours; and perhaps, eventually, when her training was accomplished, to behold her the exemplary and patient mother of about a dozen children, only now and then lending little Louis a cordial cuff by way of paying the interest of the vast debt she owes his father. Oh!" (I went on) "my orphan-girl would give me many a kiss; she would watch on the threshold for my coming home of an evening; she would run into my arms; should keep my hearth as bright as she would make it warm. God bless the sweet idea! Find her I must."

'Her eyes emitted an eager flash, her lips opened; but she reclosed them, and impetuously turned away.

' "Tell me, tell me where she is, Miss Keeldar!"

'Another movement: all haughtiness, and fire, and impulse.

# Shirley

' "I must know. You *can* tell me. You *shall* tell me."

' "I *never will.*"

'She turned to leave me. Could I now let her part as she had always parted from me? No: I had gone too far not to finish. I had come too near the end not to drive home to it. All the encumbrance of doubt, all the rubbish of indecision must be removed at once, and the plain truth must be ascertained. She must take her part, and tell me what it was. I must take mine, and adhere to it.

' "A minute, madam," I said, keeping my hand on the doorhandle before I opened it. "We have had a long conversation this morning, but the last word has not been spoken yet: it is yours to speak it."

' "May I pass?"

' "No. I guard the door. I would almost rather die than let you leave me just now, without speaking the word I demand."

' "What dare you expect me to say?"

' "What I am dying and perishing to hear; what I *must* and *will* hear; what you dare not now suppress."

' "Mr Moore, I hardly know what you mean: you are not like yourself."

'I suppose I hardly was like my usual self, for I scared her; that I could see: it was right; she must be scared to be won.

' "You *do* know what I mean, and for the first time I stand before you *myself.* I have flung off the tutor, and beg to introduce you to the man: and, remember, he is a gentleman."

'She trembled. She put her hand to mine as if to remove it from the lock; she might as well have tried to loosen, by her soft touch, metal welded to metal. She felt she was powerless, and receded; and again she trembled.

'What change I underwent, I cannot explain; but out of her emotion passed into me a new spirit. I neither was crushed nor elated by her hands and gold; I thought not of them, cared not for them: they were nothing: dross that could not dismay me. I saw only herself; her young beautiful form; the grace, the majesty, the modesty of her girlhood.

' "My pupil," I said.

' "My master," was the low answer.

' "I have a thing to tell you."

'She waited with declined brow, and ringlets drooped.

' "I have to tell you, that four years you have been growing into your tutor's heart, and that you are rooted there now. I have to declare that you have bewitched me, in spite of sense and experience, and difference of station and estate: you have so looked, and spoken, and moved; so shown me your faults and your virtues – beauties rather; they are hardly so stern as virtues, – that I love you – love you with my life and strength. It is out now."

'She sought what to say, but could not find a word: she tried to rally; but vainly. I passionately repeated that I loved her.

' "Well, Mr Moore, what then?" was the answer I got uttered in a tone that would have been petulant, if it had not faltered.

' "Have you nothing to say to me? Have you no love for me?"

' "A little bit."

' "I am not to be tortured: I will not even play at present."

' "I don't want to play; I want to go."

' "I wonder you dare speak of going at this moment. *You* go! What! with my

876

# Shirley

heart in your hand, to lay it on your toilet and pierce it with your pins? From my presence you do not stir; out of my reach you do not stray, till I receive a hostage – pledge for pledge – your heart for mine."

' "The thing you want is mislaid – lost some time since: let me go and seek it."

' "Declare that it is where your keys often are – in my possession."

' "You ought to know. And where are my keys, Mr Moore? indeed and truly, I have lost them again; and Mrs Gill wants some money, and I have none, except this sixpence."

'She took the coin out of her apron-pocket, and showed it in her palm. I could have trifled with her; but it would not do: life and death were at stake. Mastering at once the sixpence and the hand that held it, I demanded, –

' "Am I to die without you, or am I to live for you?"

' "Do as you please: far be it from me to dictate your choice."

' "You shall tell me with your own lips, whether you doom me to exile, or call me to hope."

' "Go. I can bear to be left."

' "Perhaps, I too *can* bear to leave you: but reply, Shirley, my pupil, my sovereign – reply."

' "Die without me, if you will. Live for me if you dare."

' "I am not afraid of you, my leopardess: I *dare* live for and with you, from this hour till my death. Now, then, I have you: you are mine: I will never let you go. Wherever my home be, I have chosen my wife. If I stay in England, in England you will stay; if I cross the Atlantic, you will cross it also: our lives are riveted; our lots intertwined."

' "And are we equal then, sir? Are we equal at last."

' "You are younger, frailer, feebler, more ignorant than I."

' "Will you be good to me, and never tryrannize?"

' "Will you let me breathe, and not bewilder me? You must not smile at present. The world swims and changes round me. The sun is a dizzying scarlet blaze; the sky a violet vortex whirling over me."

'I am a strong man, but I staggered as I spoke. All creation was exaggerated: colour grew more vivid; motion more rapid; life itself more vital. I hardly saw her for a moment; but I heard her voice – pitilessly sweet. She would not subdue one of her charms in compassion: perhaps she did not know what I felt.

' "You name me leopardess: remember, the leopardess is tameless," said she.

' "Tame or fierce, wild or subdued, you are *mine*."

' "I am glad I know my keeper, and am used to him. Only his voice will I follow; only his hand shall manage me; only at his feet will I repose."

'I took her back to her seat, and sat down by her side: I wanted to hear her speak again: I could never have enough of her voice and her words.

' "How much do you love me?" I asked.

' "Ah! you know: I will not gratify you: I will not flatter."

' "I don't know half enough: my heart craves to be fed. If you knew how hungry and ferocious it is, you would hasten to stay it with a kind word or two."

' "Poor Tartar!" said she, touching and patting my hand: "poor fellow; stalwart friend; Shirley's pet and favourite, lie down!"

' "But I will not lie down till I am fed with one sweet word."

'And at last she gave it.

# Shirley

' "Dear Louis, be faithful to me: never leave me. I don't care for life, unless I may pass it at your side."

' "Something more."

'She gave me a change: it was not her way to offer the same dish twice.

' "Sir!" she said, starting up, "at your peril, you ever again name such sordid things as money, or poverty, or inequality. It will be absolutely dangerous to torment me with these maddening scruples. I defy you to do it."

'My face grew hot. I did once more wish I were not so poor, or she were not so rich. She saw the transient misery; and then, indeed, she caressed me. Blent with torment, I experienced rapture.

' "Mr Moore,' said she, looking up with a sweet, open, earnest countenance, "teach me and help me to be good. I do not ask you to take off my shoulders all the cares and duties of property; but I ask you to share the burden, and to show me how to sustain my part well. Your judgment is well-balanced; your heart is kind; your principles are sound. I know you are wise; I feel you are benevolent; I believe you are conscientious. Be my companion through life; be my guide where I am ignorant: be my master where I am faulty; be my friend always!"

' "So help me God, I will" '

Yet again, a passage from the blank book, if you like, reader; if you don't like it, pass it over: –

'The Sympsons are gone; but not before discovery and explanation. My manner must have betrayed something, or my looks: I was quiet, but I forgot to be guarded sometimes. I stayed longer in the room than usual; I could not bear to be out of her presence; I returned to it; and basked in it, like Tartar in the sun. If she left the oak-parlour, instinctively I rose, and left it too. She chid me for this procedure more than once: I did it with a vague, blundering idea of getting a word with her in the hall, or elsewhere. Yesterday, towards dusk, I had her to myself for five minutes, by the hall-fire: we stood side by side; she was railing at me, and I was enjoying the sound of her voice: the young ladies passed, and looked at us; we did not separate: erelong, they repassed, and again looked. Mrs Sympson came; we did not move: Mr Sympson opened the dining-room door; Shirley flashed him back full payment for his spying gaze: she curled her lip, and tossed her tresses. The glance she gave was at once explanatory and defiant; it said – "I like Mr Moore's society, and I dare you to find fault with my taste."

'I asked, "Do you mean him to understand how matters are?"

' "I do," said she; "but I leave the development to chance. There will be a scene. I neither invite it nor fear it – only, you must be present; for I am inexpressibly tired of facing him solus. I don't like to see him in a rage; he then puts off all his fine proprieties and conventional disguises, and the real human being below is what you would call 'commun, plat, bas – vilain et un peu méchant.' His ideas are not clean, Mr Moore; they want scouring with soft soap and fuller's earth. I think, if he could add his imagination to the contents of Mrs Gill's bucking-basket, and let her boil it in her copper, with rain-water and bleaching-powder (I hope you think me a tolerable laundress), it would do him incalculable good."

'This morning, fancying I heard her descend somewhat early, I was down

instantly. I had not been deceived: there she was, busy at work, in the breakfast-parlour, of which the housemaid was completing the arrangement and dusting. She had risen betimes to finish some little keepsake she intended for Henry. I got only a cool reception; which I accepted till the girl was gone, taking my book to the window-seat very quietly. Even when we were alone, I was slow to disturb her: to sit with her in sight was happiness, and the proper happiness, for early morning – serene, incomplete, but progressive. Had I been obtrusive, I knew I should have encountered rebuff. "Not at home to suitors," was written on her brow; therefore, I read on – stole, now and then, a look; watched her countenance soften and open, as she felt I respected her mood, and enjoyed the gentle content of the moment.

'The distance between us shrank, and the light hoar-frost thawed insensibly: ere an hour elapsed, I was at her side, watching her sew, gathering her sweet smiles and her merry words, which fell for me abundantly. We sat, as we had a right to sit, side by side: my arm rested on her chair; I was near enough to count the stitches of her work, and to discern the eye of her needle. The door suddenly opened.

'I believe, if I had just then started from her, she would have despised me: thanks to the phlegm of my nature, I rarely start. When I am well-off, bien, comfortable, I am not soon stirred: bien I was – très bien – consequently, immutable: no muscle moved. I hardly looked to the door.

' "Good-morning, uncle," said she, addressing that personage; who paused on the threshold in a state of petrifaction.

' "Have you been long down-stairs, Miss Keeldar, and alone with Mr Moore?"

' "Yes, a very long time: we both came down early; it was scarcely light."

' "The proceeding is improper –"

' "It was at first: I was rather cross, and not civil; but you will perceive that we are now friends."

' "I perceive more than you would wish me to perceive."

' "Hardly, sir," said I: "we have no disguises. Will you permit me to intimate, that any further observations you have to make may as well be addressed to me. Henceforward, I stand between Miss Keeldar and all annoyan e."

' "*You!* What have *you* to do with Miss Keeldar?"

' "To protect, watch over, serve her."

' "You, sir? – you, the tutor?"

' "Not one word of insult, sir," interposed she: "not one syllable of disrespect to Mr Moore, in this house."

' "Do you take his part?"

' "*His* part! Oh, yes!"

'She turned to me with a sudden, fond movement, which I met by circling her with my arm. She and I both rose.

' "Good Ged!" was the cry from the morning-gown standing quivering at the door. *Ged*, I think, must be the cognomen of Mr Sympson's Lares: when hard-pressed, he always invokes his idol.

' "Come forward, uncle: you shall hear all. Tell him all, Louis."

' "I dare him to speak! The beggar! the knave! the specious hypocrite! the vile, insinuating, infamous menial! Stand apart from my niece, sir: let her go!"

# Shirley

'She clung to me with energy. "I am near my future husband," she said: "who dares touch him or me?"

' "Her husband!" he raised and spread his hands: he dropped into a seat.

' "A while ago, you wanted much to know whom I meant to marry: my intention was then formed, but not mature for communication; now it is ripe, sun-mellowed, perfect: take the crimson-peach – take Louis Moore!"

' "But" (savagely) "you *shall not* have him – he *shall not* have you."

' "I would die before I would have another. I would die if I might not have him."

'He uttered words with which this page shall never be polluted.

'She turned white as death: she shook all over: she lost her strength. I laid her down on the sofa: just looked to ascertain that she had not fainted – of which, with a divine smile, she assured me; I kissed her, and then, if I were to perish, I cannot give a clear account of what happened in the course of the next five minutes: she has since – through tears, laughter, and trembling – told me that I turned terrible, and gave myself to the demon; she says I left her, made one bound across the room – that Mr Sympson vanished through the door as if shot from a cannon – I also vanished, and she heard Mrs Gill scream.

'Mrs Gill was still screaming when I came to my senses: I was then in another apartment – the oak-parlour, I think: I held Sympson before me crushed into a chair, and my hand was on his cravat: his eyes rolled in his head – I was strangling him, I think: the housekeeper stood wringing her hands, entreating me to desist; I desisted that moment, and felt at once as cool as stone. But I told Mrs Gill to fetch the Red-House Inn chaise instantly, and informed Mr Sympson he must depart from Fieldhead the instant it came: though half-frightened out of his wits, he declared he would not. Repeating the former order, I added a commission to fetch a constable. I said: –

' "You *shall* go – by fair means or foul."

'He threatened prosecution – I cared for nothing: I had stood over him once before, not quite so fiercely as now, but full as austerely. It was one night when burglars attempted the house at Sympson-Grove; and in his wretched cowardice he would have given a vain alarm, without daring to offer defence: I had then been obliged to protect his family and his abode by mastering himself – and I had succeeded. I now remained with him till the chaise came: I marshalled him to it, he scolding all the way. He was terribly bewildered, as well as enraged: he would have resisted me, but knew not how: he called for his wife and daughters to come. I said they should follow him as soon as they could prepare: the smoke, the fume, the fret of his demeanour was inexpressible, but it was a fury incapable of producing a deed: that man, properly handled, must ever remain impotent. I know he will never touch me with the law: I know his wife, over whom he tyrannizes in trifles, guides him in matters of importance. I have long since earned her undying mother's gratitude by my devotion to her boy: in some of Henry's ailments I have nursed him – better, she said, than any woman could nurse: she will never forget that. She and her daughters quitted me to-day, in mute wrath and consternation – but she respects me. When Henry clung to my neck, as I lifted him into the carriage and placed him by her side – when I arranged her own wrapping to make her warm, though she turned her head from me, I saw the tears start to her eyes. She will but the more zealously

advocate my cause, because she has left me in anger. I am glad of this: not for my own sake, but for that of my life and idol - my Shirley.'

Once again he writes - a week after: -

'I am now at Stilbro': I have taken up my temporary abode with a friend - a professional man - in whose business I can be useful. Every day I ride over to Fieldhead. How long will it be before I can call that place my home, and its mistress mine? I am not easy - not tranquil: I am tantalized - sometimes tortured. To see her now, one would think she had never pressed her cheek to my shoulder, or clung to me with tenderness or trust. I feel unsafe: she renders me miserable: I am shunned when I visit her: she withdraws from my reach. Once, this day, I lifted her face, resolved to get a full look down her deep, dark eyes: difficult to describe what I read there! Pantheress! - beautiful forest-born! - wily, tameless, peerless nature! She gnaws her chain: I see the white teeth working at the steel! She has dreams of her wild woods, and pinings after virgin freedom. I wish Sympson would come again, and oblige her again to entwine her arms about me. I wish there was danger she should lose me, as there is risk I shall lose her. No: final loss, I do not fear; but long delay —

'It is now night - midnight. I have spent the afternoon and evening at Fieldhead. Some hours ago she passed me, coming down the oak-staircase to the hall: she did not know I was standing in the twilight, near the staircase-window, looking at the frost-bright constellations. How closely she glided against the banisters! How shyly shone her large eyes upon me! How evanescent, fugitive, fitful, she looked, - slim and swift as a Northern Streamer!

'I followed her into the drawing-room: Mrs Pryor and Caroline Helstone were both there: she has summoned them to bear her company awhile. In her white evening dress; with her long hair flowing full and wavy; with her noiseless step, her pale cheek, her eye full of night and lightning, she looked, I thought, spirit-like, - a thing made of an element, - the child of a breeze and a flame, - the daughter of ray and rain-drop, - a thing never to be overtaken, arrested, fixed. I wished I could avoid following her with my gaze, as she moved here and there, but it was impossible. I talked with the other ladies as well as I could, but still I looked at her. She was very silent: I think she never spoke to me, - not even when she offered me tea. It happened that she was called out a minute by Mrs Gill. I passed into the moon-lit hall, with the design of getting a word as she returned; nor in this did I fail.

' "Miss Keeldar, stay one instant!" said I, meeting her.

' "Why? - the hall is too cold.'

' "It is not cold for me: at my side, it should not be cold for you."

' "But I shiver."

' "With fear, I believe. What makes you fear me? You are quiet and distant: why?"

' "I may well fear what looks like a great dark goblin meeting me in the moonlight."

' "*Do not - do not* pass! - stay with me awhile: let us exchange a few quiet words. It is three days since I spoke to you alone: such changes are cruel.'

' "I have no wish to be cruel," she responded, softly enough: indeed, there was softness in her whole deportment, - in her face, in her voice; but there was also reserve, and an air fleeting, evanishing, intangible.

' "You certainly give me pain," said I. "It is hardly a week since you called

me your future husband, and treated me as such; now I am once more the tutor for you: I am addressed as Mr Moore, and Sir; your lips have forgotten Louis."

' "No, Louis, no: it is an easy, liquid name; not soon forgotten."

' "Be cordial to Louis, then: approach him, – let him approach."

' "I *am* cordial," said she, hovering aloof like a white shadow.

' "Your voice is very sweet, and very low," I answered, quietly advancing: "you seem subdued, but still startled."

' "No, – quite calm, and afraid of nothing," she assured me.

' "Of nothing but your votary."

'I bent a knee to the flags at her feet.

' "You see I am in a new world, Mr Moore. I don't know myself, – I don't know you: but rise; when you do so, I feel troubled and disturbed."

'I obeyed: it would not have suited me to retain that attitude long. I courted serenity and confidence for her, and not vainly: she trusted, and clung to me again.

' "Now, Shirley," I said, "you can conceive I am far from happy in my present uncertain unsettled state."

' "Oh, yes; you *are* happy!" she cried, hastily: "you don't know how happy you are! – any change will be for the worse!"

' "Happy or not, I cannot bear to go on so much longer: you are too generous to require it."

' "Be reasonable, Louis, – be patient! I like you because you are patient."

' "Like me no longer, then, – love me instead: fix our marriage-day. Think of it to-night, and decide."

'She breathed a murmur, inarticulate yet expressive; darted, or melted, from my arms – and I lost her.'

# Chapter 37

## The Winding-Up

Yes, reader, we must settle accounts now. I have only briefly to narrate the final fates of some of the personages whose acquaintance we have made in this narrative, and then you and I must shake hands, and for the present separate.

Let us turn to the Curates, – to the much-loved, though long-neglected. Come forward, modest merit! Malone, I see, promptly answers the invocation: he knows his own description when he hears it.

No, Peter Augustus, we can have nothing to say to you: it won't do. Impossible to trust ourselves with the touching tale of your deeds and destinies. Are you not aware, Peter, that a discriminating public has its crotchets: that the unvarnished truth does not answer; that plain facts will not digest? Do you not know that

# Shirley

the squeak of the real pig is no more relished now than it was in days of yore?
Were I to give the catastrophe of your life and conversation, the public would
sweep off in shrieking hysterics, and there would be a wild cry for sal-volatile
and burnt feathers. 'Impossible!' would be pronounced here: 'untrue!' would be
responded there. 'Inartistic!' would be solemnly decided. Note well! Whenever
you present the actual, simple truth, it is, somehow, always denounced as a lie:
they disown it, cast it off, throw it on the parish; whereas the product of your
own imagination, the mere figment, the sheer fiction, is adopted, petted, termed
pretty, proper, sweetly natural: the little, spurious wretch gets all the comfits,
– the honest, lawful bantling, all the cuffs. Such is the way of the world, Peter;
and, as you are the legitimate urchin, rude, unwashed, and naughty, you must
stand down.

Make way for Mr Sweeting.

Here he comes, with his lady on his arm; the most splendid and the weightiest
woman in Yorkshire: Mrs Sweeting, formerly Miss Dora Sykes. They were
married under the happiest auspices. Mr Sweeting having been just inducted
to a comfortable living, and Mr Sykes being in circumstances to give Dora a
handsome portion. They lived long and happily together, beloved by their
parishioners, and by a numerous circle of friends.

There! I think the varnish has been put on very nicely.

Advance, Mr Donne.

This gentleman turned out admirably: far better than either you or I could
possibly have expected, reader. He, too, married a most sensible, quiet, lady-like
little woman: the match was the making of him: he became an exemplary
domestic character, and a truly active parish-priest (as a pastor, he, to his dying
day, conscientiously refused to act). The outside of the cup and platter he
burnished up with the best polishing-powder; the furniture of the altar and
temple he looked after with the zeal of an upholsterer, – the care of a cabinet-
maker. His little school, his little church, his little parsonage, all owed their
erection to him; and they did him credit: each was a model in its way: if
uniformity and taste in architecture had been the same thing as consistency and
earnestness in religion, what a shepherd of a Christian flock Mr Donne would
have made! There was one art in the mastery of which nothing mortal ever
surpassed Mr Donne – it was that of begging. By his own unassisted efforts, he
begged all the money for all his erections. In this matter he had a grasp of plan,
a scope of action quite unique: he begged of high and low, – of the shoeless
cottage brat and the coronetted duke: he sent out begging-letters far and wide
– to old Queen Charlotte, to the princesses her daughters, to her sons the royal
dukes, to the Prince Regent, to Lord Castlereagh, to every member of the
ministry then in office; and, what is more remarkable, he screwed something out
of every one of these personages. It is on record that he got five pounds from the
close-fisted old lady, Queen Charlotte, and two guineas from the royal profligate,
her eldest son. When Mr Donne set out on begging expeditions, he armed
himself in a complete suit of brazen mail: that you had given a hundred pounds
yesterday, was, with him, no reason why you should not give two hundred to-
day: he would tell you so to your face, and, ten to one, get the money out of you:
people gave to get rid of him. After all, he did some good with the cash; he was
useful in his day and generation.

Perhaps I ought to remark, that on the premature and sudden vanishing of

# Shirley

Mr Malone from the stage of Briarfield parish (you cannot know how it happened, reader; your curiosity must be robbed to pay your elegant love of the pretty and pleasing), there came as his successor another Irish curate, Mr Macarthey. I am happy to be able to inform you, *with truth*, that this gentleman did as much credit to his country as Malone had done it discredit: he proved himself as decent, decorous, and conscientious, as Peter was rampant, boisterous, and – (this last epithet I choose to suppress, because it would let the cat out of the bag). He laboured faithfully in the parish: the schools, both Sunday and day schools, flourished under his sway like green bay-trees. Being human, of course he had his faults; these, however, were proper, steady-going, clerical faults: what many would call virtues: the circumstance of finding himself invited to tea with a Dissenter would unhinge him for a week: the spectacle of a Quaker wearing his hat in the church, the thought of an unbaptized fellow-creature being interred with Christian rites – these things could make strange havoc in Mr Macarthey's physical and mental economy; otherwise, he was sane and rational, diligent and charitable.

I doubt not a justice-loving public will have remarked, ere this, that I have thus far shown a criminal remissness in pursuing, catching, and bringing to condign punishment the would-be assassin of Mr Robert Moore: here was a fine opening to lead my willing readers a dance, at once decorous and exciting: a dance of law and gospel, of the dungeon, the dock, and the 'dead-thraw.' You might have liked it, reader, but *I* should not: I and my subject would presently have quarrelled, and then I should have broken down: I was happy to find that facts perfectly exonerated me from the attempt. The murderer was never punished; for the good reason, that he was never caught; the result of the further circumstance, that he was never pursued. The magistrates made a shuffling, as if they were going to rise and do valiant things: but, since Moore himself, instead of urging and leading them as heretofore, lay still on his little cottage-couch, laughing in his sleeve and sneering with every feature of his pale, foreign face, they considered better of it; and, after fulfilling certain indispensable forms, prudently resolved to let the matter quietly drop: which they did.

Mr Moore knew who had shot him, and all Briarfield knew: it was no other than Michael Hartley, the half-crazed weaver once before alluded to, a frantic Antinomian in religion, and a mad leveller in politics; the poor soul died of delirium tremens a year after the attempt on Moore, and Robert gave his wretched widow a guinea to bury him.

The winter is over and gone: spring has followed with beamy and shadowy, with flowery and showery flight: we are now in the heart of summer – in mid-June, – the June of 1812.

It is burning weather: the air is deep azure and red gold: it fits the time; it fits the age; it fits the present spirit of the nations. The nineteenth century wantons in its giant adolescence: the Titan-boy uproots mountains in his game, and hurls rocks in his wild sport. This summer, Bonaparte is in the saddle: he and his host scour Russian deserts: he has with him Frenchmen and Poles, Italians and children of the Rhine, six hundred thousand strong. He marches on old Moscow: under old Moscow's walls the rude Cossack waits him. Barbarian stoic! he waits without fear of the boundless ruin rolling on. He puts his trust

# Shirley

in a snow-cloud: the Wilderness, the Wind, and the Hail-Storm are his refuge: his allies are the elements – Air, Fire, Water. And what are these? Three terrible archangels ever stationed before the throne of Jehovah. They stand clothed in white, girdled with golden girdles: they uplift vials, brimming with the wrath of God. Their time is the day of vengeance; their signal, the word of the Lord of Hosts, 'thundering with the voice of His excellency.'

'Hast thou entered into the treasures of the snow? or hast thou seen the treasures of the hail, which I have reserved against the time of trouble, against the day of battle and war?

'Go your ways: pour out the vials of the wrath of God upon the earth.'

It is done: the earth is scorched with fire: the sea becomes 'as the blood of a dead man:' the islands flee away; the mountains are not found.

In this year, Lord Wellington assumed the reins in Spain: they made him Generalissimo, for their own salvation's sake. In this year, he took Badajos, he fought the field of Vittoria, he captured Pampeluna, he stormed St Sebastian; in this year, he won Salamanca.

Men of Manchester! I beg your pardon for this slight résumé of warlike facts: but it is of no consequence. Lord Wellington is, for you, only a decayed old gentleman now: I rather think some of you have called him a 'dotard' – you have taunted him with his age, and the loss of his physical vigour. What fine heroes you are yourselves! Men like you have a right to trample on what is mortal in a demigod. Scoff at your ease – your scorn can never break his grand, old heart.

But come, friends, whether Quakers or Cotton-printers, let us hold a Peace-Congress, and let out our venom quietly. We have been talking with unseemly zeal about bloody battles and butchering generals; we arrive now at a triumph in your line. On the 18th of June 1812, the Orders in Council were repealed, and the blockaded ports thrown open. You know very well – such of you as are old enough to remember – you made Yorkshire and Lancashire shake with your shout on that occasion: the ringers cracked a bell in Briarfield belfry; it is dissonant to this day. The Association of Merchants and Manufacturers dined together at Stilbro', and one and all went home in such a plight as their wives would never wish to witness more. Liverpool started and snorted like a river-horse roused amongst his reeds by thunder. Some of the American merchants felt threatenings of apoplexy, and had themselves bled: all, like wise men, at this first moment of prosperity, prepared to rush into the bowels of speculation, and to delve new difficulties, in whose depths they might lose themselves at some future day. Stocks, which had been accumulating for years, now went off in a moment, in the twinkling of an eye; warehouses were lightened, ships were laden; work abounded, wages rose: the good time seemed come. These prospects might be delusive, but they were brilliant – to some they were even true. At that epoch, in that single month of June, many a solid fortune was realized.

When a whole province rejoices, the humblest of its inhabitants tastes a festal feeling: the sound of public bells rouses the most secluded abode, as if with a call to be gay. And so Caroline Helstone thought, when she dressed herself more carefully than usual on the day of this trading triumph, and went, attired in her neatest muslin, to spend the afternoon at Fieldhead, there to superintend certain

885

# Shirley

millinery preparations for a great event: the last appeal in these matters being reserved for her unimpeachable taste. She decided on the wreath, the veil, the dress to be worn at the altar: she chose various robes and fashions for more ordinary occasions, without much reference to the bride's opinion; that lady, indeed, being in a somewhat impracticable mood.

Louis had presaged difficulties, and he had found them: in fact, his mistress had shown herself exquisitely provoking; putting off her marriage day by day, week by week, month by month. At first coaxing him with soft pretences of procrastination, and in the end rousing his whole deliberate but determined nature to revolt against her tyranny, at once so sweet and so intolerable.

It had needed a sort of tempest-shock to bring her to the point; but there she was at last, fettered to a fixed day: there she lay, conquered by love, and bound with a vow.

Thus vanquished and restricted, she pined, like any other chained denizen of deserts. Her captor alone could cheer her; his society only could make amends for the lost privilege of liberty: in his absence, she sat or wandered alone; spoke little, and ate less.

She furthered no preparations for her nuptials; Louis was himself obliged to direct all arrangements: he was virtually master of Fieldhead, weeks before he became so nominally: the least presumptuous, the kindest master that ever was; but with his lady absolute. She abdicated without a word or a struggle. 'Go to Mr Moore; ask Mr Moore,' was her answer when applied to for orders. Never was wooer of wealthy bride so thoroughly absolved from the subaltern part; so inevitably compelled to assume a paramount character.

In all this, Miss Keeldar partly yielded to her disposition; but a remark she made a year afterwards proved that she partly also acted on system. 'Louis,' she said, 'would never have learned to rule, if she had not ceased to govern: the incapacity of the sovereign had developed the powers of the premier.'

It had been intended that Miss Helstone should act as bridesmaid at the approaching nuptials; but Fortune had destined her another part.

She came home in time to water her plants. She had performed this little task. The last flower attended to was a rose-tree, which bloomed in a quiet green nook at the back of the house. This plant had received the refreshing shower: she was now resting a minute. Near the wall stood a fragment of sculptured stone – a monkish relic; once, perhaps, the base of a cross: she mounted it, that she might better command the view. She had still the watering-pot in one hand; with the other, her pretty dress was held lightly aside, to avoid trickling drops: she gazed over the wall, along some lonely fields; beyond three dusk trees, rising side by side against the sky; beyond a solitary thorn, at the head of a solitary lane far off: she surveyed the dusk moors, where bonfires were kindling: the summer evening was warm; the bell-music was joyous; the blue smoke of the fires looked soft; their red flame bright: above them, in the sky whence the sun had vanished, twinkled a silver point – the Star of Love.

Caroline was not unhappy that evening; far otherwise: but as she gazed she sighed, and as she sighed a hand circled her, and rested quietly on her waist. Caroline thought she knew who had drawn near: she received the touch unstartled.

'I am looking at Venus, mamma: see, she is beautiful. How white her lustre is, compared with the deep red of the bonfires!'

# Shirley

The answer was a closer caress; and Caroline turned, and looked, not into Mrs Pryor's matron face, but up at a dark manly visage. She dropped her watering-pot, and stepped down from the pedestal.

'I have been sitting with "mamma" an hour,' said the intruder. 'I have had a long conversation with her. Where, meantime, have you been?'

'To Fieldhead. Shirley is as naughty as ever, Robert: she will neither say Yes nor No to any question put. She sits alone: I cannot tell whether she is melancholy or nonchalant: if you rouse her, or scold her, she gives you a look half wistful, half reckless, which sends you away as queer and crazed as herself. What Louis will make of her, I cannot tell: for my part, if I were a gentleman, I think I would not dare undertake her.'

'Never mind them: they were cut out for each other. Louis, strange to say, likes her all the better for these freaks: he will manage her, if any one can. She tires him, however: he has had a stormy courtship for such a calm character; but you see it all ends in victory for him. Caroline, I have sought you to ask an audience. Why are those bells ringing?'

'For the repeal of your terrible law; the Orders you hate so much. You are pleased, are you not?'

'Yesterday evening at this time, I was packing some books for a sea-voyage: they were the only possessions, except some clothes, seeds, roots, and tools, which I felt free to take with me to Canada. I was going to leave you.'

'To leave me? To leave *me?*'

Her little fingers fastened on his arm: she spoke and looked affrighted.

'Not now – not now. Examine my face; yes, look at me well: is the despair of parting legible thereon?'

She looked into an illuminated countenance, whose characters were all beaming, though the page itself was dusk: this face, potent in the majesty of its traits, shed down on her hope, fondness, delight.

'Will the repeal do you good; *much* good – *immediate* good?' she inquired.

'The repeal of the Orders in Council saves me. Now I shall not turn bankrupt; now I shall not give up business; now I shall not leave England; now I shall be no longer poor; now I can pay my debts; now all the cloth I have in my warehouses will be taken off my hands, and commissions given me for much more: this day lays for my fortunes abroad, firm foundation; on which, for the first time in my life, I can securely build.'

Caroline devoured his words: she held his hand in hers; she drew a long breath.

'You are saved? Your heavy difficulties are lifted?'

'They are lifted: I breathe: I can act.'

'At last! Oh! Providence is kind. Thank Him, Robert.'

'I do thank Providence.'

'And I also, for your sake!' She looked up devoutly.

'Now, I can take more workmen; give better wages; lay wiser and more liberal plans; do some good; be less selfish: *now*, Caroline, I can have a house – a home which I can truly call mine – and *now –*'

He paused; for his deep voice was checked.

'And *now*,' he resumed – 'now I can think of marriage; *now* I can seek a wife.'

This was no moment for her to speak: she did not speak.

# Shirley

'Will Caroline, who meekly hopes to be forgiven as she forgives – will she pardon all I have made her suffer – all that long pain I have wickedly caused her – all that sickness of body and mind she owed to me? Will she forget what she knows of my poor ambition – my sordid schemes? Will she let me expiate these things? Will she suffer me to prove that, as I once deserted cruelly, trifled wantonly, injured basely, I can now love faithfully, cherish fondly, treasure tenderly?'

His hand was in Caroline's still: a gentle pressure answered him.

'Is Caroline mine?'

'Caroline is yours.'

'I will prize her: the sense of her value is here, in my heart; the necessity for her society is blended with my life: not more jealous shall I be of the blood whose flow moves my pulses, than of her happiness and well-being.'

'I love you, too, Robert, and will take faithful care of you.'

'Will you take faithful care of me? – faithful care! as if that rose should promise to shelter from tempest this hard, grey stone? But she *will* care for me, in her way: these hands will be the gentle ministrants of every comfort I can taste. I know the being I seek to entwine with my own will bring me a solace – a charity – a purity – to which, of myself, I am a stranger.'

Suddenly, Caroline was troubled; her lip quivered.

'What flutters my dove?' asked Moore, as she nestled to, and then uneasily shrank from him.

'Poor mamma! I am all mamma has: must I leave her?'

'Do you know, I thought of that difficulty: I and "mamma" have discussed it.'

'Tell me what you wish – what you would like – and I will consider if it is possible to consent; but I cannot desert her, even for you: I cannot break her heart, even for your sake.'

'She was faithful when I was false – was she not? I never came near your sick-bed, and she watched it ceaselessly.'

'What must I do? Anything but leave her.'

'At my wish, you never shall leave her.'

'She may live very near us?'

'With us – only she will have her own rooms and servant: for this she stipulates herself.'

'You know she has an income, that, with her habits, makes her quite independent?'

'She told me that, with a gentle pride that reminded me of somebody else.'

'She is not at all interfering, and incapable of gossip.'

'I know her, Cary: but if – instead of being the personification of reserve and discretion – she were something quite opposite, I should not fear her.'

'Yet she will be your mother-in-law?' The speaker gave an arch little nod: Moore smiled.

'Louis and I are not of the order of men who fear their mothers-in-law, Cary: our foes never have been, nor will be, those of our own household. I doubt not, my mother-in-law will make much of me.'

'That she will – in her quiet way, you know. She is not demonstrative; and when you see her silent, or even cool, you must not fancy her displeased – it is

# Shirley

only a manner she has. Be sure to let me interpret for her, whenever she puzzles you: always believe my account of the matter, Robert.'

'Oh, implicitly! Jesting apart, I feel that she and I will suit – on ne peut mieux. Hortense, you know, is exquisitely susceptible – in our French sense of the word – and not, perhaps, always reasonable in her requirements; yet – dear, honest girl – I never painfully wounded her feelings, or had a serious quarrel with her, in my life.'

'No: you are most generously considerate – indeed, most tenderly indulgent to her; and you will be considerate with mamma. You are a gentleman all through, Robert, to the bone, and nowhere so perfect a gentleman as at your own fireside.'

'An eulogium I like: it is very sweet. I am well pleased my Caroline should view me in this light.'

'Mamma just thinks of you as I do.'

'Not quite, I hope?'

'She does not want to marry you – don't be vain; but she said to me the other day, "My dear, Mr Moore has pleasing manners; he is one of the few gentlemen I have seen who combine politeness with an air of sincerity."'

' "Mamma" is rather a misanthropist, is she not? Not the best opinion of the sterner sex?'

'She forbears to judge them as a whole, but she has her exceptions whom she admires. Louis and Mr Hall, and, of late – yourself. She did not like you once: I knew that, because she would never speak of you. But, Robert –'

'Well, what now? What is the new thought?'

'You have not seen my uncle yet?'

'I have: "mamma" called him into the room. He consents conditionally: if I prove that I can keep a wife, I may have her: and I *can* keep her better than he thinks – better than I choose to boast.'

'If you get rich, you will do good with your money, Robert?'

'I *will* do good; you shall tell me how: indeed, I have some schemes of my own, which you and I will talk about on our own hearth one day. I have seen the necessity of doing good: I have learned the downright folly of being selfish. Caroline, I foresee what I will now foretell. This war *must* erelong draw to a close: Trade is likely to prosper for some years to come: there may be a brief misunderstanding between England and America, but that will not last. What would you think if, one day – perhaps ere another ten years elapse – Louis and I divide Briarfield parish betwixt us? Louis, at any rate, is certain of power and property: he will not bury his talents: he is a benevolent fellow, and has besides an intellect of his own of no trifling calibre. His mind is slow but strong: it must work: it may work deliberately, but it will work well. He will be made magistrate of the district – Shirley says he shall: she would proceed impetuously and prematurely to obtain for him this dignity, if he would let her, but he will not; as usual, he will be in no haste: ere he has been master of Fieldhead a year, all the district will feel his quiet influence, and acknowledge his unassuming superiority: a magistrate is wanted – they will, in time, invest him with the office voluntarily and unreluctantly. Everybody admires his future wife: and everybody will, in time, like him: he is of the "pâte" generally approved, "bon comme le pain" – daily bread for the most fastidious: good for the infant and the aged, nourishing for the poor, wholesome for the rich. Shirley, in spite of

# Shirley

her whims and oddities, her dodges and delays, has an infatuated fondness for him: she will one day see him as universally beloved as even *she* could wish: he will also be universally esteemed, considered, consulted, depended on – too much so: his advice will be always judicious, his help always good-natured – erelong, both will be in inconvenient request: he will have to impose restrictions. As for me, if I succeed as I intend to do, my success will add to his and Shirley's income: I can double the value of their mill-property: I can line yonder barren Hollow with lines of cottages, and rows of cottage-gardens —'

'Robert! And root up the copse?'

'The copse shall be firewood ere five years elapse: the beautiful wild ravine shall be a smooth descent; the green natural terrace shall be a paved street: there shall be cottages in the dark ravine, and cottages on the lonely slopes: the rough pebbled track shall be an even, firm, broad, black, sooty road, bedded with the cinders from my mill: and my mill, Caroline – my mill shall fill its present yard.'

'Horrible! You will change our blue hill-country air into the Stilbro' smoke atmosphere.'

'I will pour the waters of Pactolus through the valley of Briarfield.'

'I like the beck a thousand times better.'

'I will get an act for enclosing Nunnely Common, and parcelling it out into farms.'

'Stilbro' Moor, however, defies you, thank Heaven! What can you grow in Bilberry Moss! What will flourish on Rushedge?'

'Caroline, the houseless, the starving, the unemployed, shall come to Hollow's mill from far and near; and Joe Scott shall give them work, and Louis Moore, Esq., shall let them a tenement, and Mrs Gill shall mete them a portion till the first pay-day.'

She smiled up in his face.

'Such a Sunday-school as you will have, Cary! such collections as you will get! such a day-school as you and Shirley, and Miss Ainley, will have to manage between you! The mill shall find salaries for a master and mistress, and the Squire or the Clothier shall give a treat once a-quarter.'

She mutely offered a kiss, an offer taken unfair advantage of, to the extortion of about a hundred kisses.

'Extravagant day-dreams!' said Moore, with a sigh and smile, 'yet perhaps we may realize some of them. Meantime, the dew is falling: Mrs Moore, I shall take you in.'

It is August: the bells clash out again, not only through Yorkshire but through England: from Spain, the voice of a trumpet has sounded long: it now waxes louder and louder; it proclaims Salamanca won. This night is Briarfield to be illuminated. On this day the Fieldhead tenantry dine together; the Hollow's mill work-people will be assembled for a like festal purpose; the schools have a grand treat. This morning there were two marriages solemnized in Briarfield church, – Louis Gérard Moore, Esq., late of Antwerp, to Shirley, daughter of the late Charles Cave Keeldar, Esq. of Fieldhead: Robert Gérard Moore, Esq., of Hollow's mill, to Caroline, niece of the Rev. Matthewson Helstone, M.A., Rector of Briarfield.

# Shirley

The ceremony, in the first instance, was performed by Mr Helstone; Hiram Yorke, Esq. of Briarmains, giving the bride away. In the second instance, Mr Hall, Vicar of Nunnely, officiated. Amongst the bridal train, the two most noticeable personages were the youthful bridesmen, Henry Sympson and Martin Yorke.

I suppose Robert Moore's prophecies were, partially, at least, fulfilled. The other day I passed up the Hollow, which tradition says was once green, and lone, and wild; and there I saw the manufacturer's day-dreams embodied in substantial stone and brick and ashes – the cinder-black highway, the cottages, and the cottage-gardens; there I saw a mighty mill, and a chimney, ambitious as the tower of Babel. I told my old housekeeper when I came home where I had been.

'Ay!' said she; 'this world has queer changes. I can remember the old mill being built – the very first it was in all the district; and then, I can remember it being pulled down, and going with my lake-lasses (companions) to see the foundation-stone of the new one laid: the two Mr Moores made a great stir about it; they were there, and a deal of fine folk beside, and both their ladies; very bonnie and grand they looked; but Mrs Louis was the grandest, she always wore such handsome dresses: Mrs Robert was quieter-like. Mrs Louis smiled when she talked: she had a real happy, glad, good-natured look; but she had een that pierced a body through: there is no such ladies now-a-days.'

'What was the Hollow like then, Martha?'

'Different to what it is now; but I can tell of it clean different again: when there was neither mill, nor cot, nor hall, except Fieldhead, within two miles of it. I can tell, one summer-evening, fifty years syne, my mother coming running in just at the edge of dark, almost fleyed out of her wits, saying, she had seen a fairish (fairy) in Fieldhead Hollow; and that was the last fairish that ever was seen on this country side (though they've been heard within these forty years). A lonesome spot it was – and a bonnie spot – full of oak trees and nut trees. It is altered now.'

The story is told. I think I now see the judicious reader putting on his spectacles to look for the moral. It would be an insult to his sagacity to offer directions. I only say, God speed him in the quest!

# Jane
# Eyre

# Chapter 1

There was no possibility of taking a walk that day. We had been wandering, indeed, in the leafless shrubbery an hour in the morning; but since dinner (Mrs Reed, when there was no company, dined early) the cold winter wind had brought with it clouds so sombre, and a rain so penetrating, that further outdoor exercise was now out of the question.

I was glad of it; I never liked long walks, especially on chilly afternoons: dreadful to me was the coming home in the raw twilight, with nipped fingers and toes, and a heart saddened by the chidings of Bessie, the nurse, and humbled by the consciousness of my physical inferiority to Eliza, John, and Georgiana Reed.

The said Eliza, John, and Georgiana were now clustered round their mamma in the drawing-room: she lay reclined on a sofa by the fireside, and with her darlings about her (for the time neither quarrelling nor crying) looked perfectly happy. Me, she had dispensed from joining the group, saying, 'She regretted to be under the necessity of keeping me at a distance; but that until she heard from Bessie, and could discover by her own observation that I was endeavouring in good earnest to acquire a more sociable and childlike disposition, a more attractive and sprightly manner – something lighter, franker, more natural, as it were – she really must exclude me from privileges intended only for contented, happy little children.'

'What does Bessie say I have done?' I asked.

'Jane, I don't like cavillers or questioners; besides, there is something truly forbidding in a child taking up her elders in that manner. Be seated somewhere; and until you can speak pleasantly, remain silent.'

A small breakfast-room adjoined the drawing-room, I slipped in there. It contained a bookcase; I soon possessed myself of a volume, taking care that it should be one stored with pictures. I mounted into the window-seat: gathering up my feet, I sat cross-legged, like a Turk; and, having drawn the red moreen curtain nearly close, I was shrined in double retirement.

Folds of scarlet drapery shut in my view to the right hand; to the left were the clear panes of glass, protecting, but not separating me from the drear November day. At intervals, while turning over the leaves in my book, I studied the aspect of that winter afternoon. Afar, it offered a pale blank of mist and cloud; near, a scene of wet lawn and storm-beat shrub, with ceaseless rain sweeping away wildly before a long and lamentable blast.

I returned to my book – Bewick's *History of British Birds*: the letterpress thereof I cared little for, generally speaking; and yet there were certain intro-ductory pages that, child as I was, I could not pass quite as a blank. They were

those which treat of the haunts of sea-fowl; of 'the solitary rocks and promontories' by them only inhabited; of the coast of Norway, studded with isles from its southern extremity, the Lindeness, or Naze, to the North Cape –

> *Where the Northern Ocean, in vast whirls,*
> *Boils round the naked, melancholy isles*
> *Of farthest Thule; and the Atlantic surge*
> *Pours in among the stormy Hebrides.*

Nor could I pass unnoticed the suggestion of the bleak shores of Lapland, Siberia, Spitzbergen, Nova Zembla, Iceland, Greenland, with 'the vast sweep of the Arctic Zone, and those forlorn regions of dreary space – that reservoir of frost and snow, where firm fields of ice, the accumulation of centuries of winters, glazed in Alpine heights above heights, surround the pole, and concentre the multiplied rigours of extreme cold'. Of these death-white realms I formed an idea of my own: shadowy, like all the half-comprehended notions that float dim through children's brains, but strangely impressive. The words in these introductory pages connected themselves with the succeeding vignettes, and gave significance to the rock standing up alone in a sea of billow and spray; to the broken boat stranded on a desolate coast; to the cold and ghastly moon glancing through bars of cloud at a wreck just sinking.

I cannot tell what sentiment haunted the quite solitary churchyard, with its inscribed headstone; its gate, its two trees, its low horizon, girdled by a broken wall, and its newly risen crescent, attesting the hour of eventide.

The two ships becalmed on a torpid sea, I believed to be marine phantoms.

The fiend pinning down the thief's pack behind him, I passed over quickly: it was an object of terror.

So was the black, horned thing seated aloof on a rock, surveying a distant crowd surrounding a gallows.

Each picture told a story; mysterious often to my undeveloped understanding and imperfect feelings, yet ever profoundly interesting: as interesting as the tales Bessie sometimes narrated on winter evenings, when she chanced to be in good humour; and when, having brought her ironing-table to the nursery-hearth, she allowed us to sit about it, and while she got up Mrs Reed's lace frills, and crimped her nightcap borders, fed our eager attention with passages of love and adventure taken from old fairy tales and older ballads; or (as at a later period I discovered) from the pages of *Pamela*, and *Henry, Earl of Moreland*.

With Bewick on my knee, I was then happy: happy at least in my way. I feared nothing but interruption, and that came too soon. The breakfast-room door was opened.

'Boh! Madam Mope!' cried the voice of John Reed; then he paused: he found the room apparently empty.

'Where the dickens is she?' he continued. 'Lizzy! Georgy! (calling to his sisters) Jane is not here: tell mamma she is run out into the rain – bad animal!'

'It is well I drew the curtain,' thought I, and I wished fervently he might not discover my hiding-place: nor would John Reed have found it out himself; he was not quick either of vision or conception; but Eliza just put her head in at the door, and said at once: 'She is in the window-seat, to be sure, Jack.'

# Jane Eyre

And I came out immediately, for I trembled at the idea of being dragged forth by the said Jack.

'What do you want?' I asked with awkward diffidence.

'Say, "what do you want, Master Reed,"' was the answer. 'I want you to come here'; and seating himself in an arm-chair, he intimated by a gesture that I was to approach and stand before him.

John Reed was a schoolboy of fourteen years old; four years older than I, for I was but ten; large and stout for his age, with a dingy and unwholesome skin; thick lineaments in a spacious visage, heavy limbs and large extremities. He gorged himself habitually at table, which made him bilious, and gave him a dim and bleared eye with flabby cheeks. He ought now to have been at school; but his mamma had taken him home for a month or two, 'on account of his delicate health'. Mr Miles, the master, affirmed that he would do very well if he had fewer cakes and sweetmeats sent him from home; but the mother's heart turned from an opinion so harsh, and inclined rather to the more refined idea that John's sallowness was owing to over-application, and, perhaps, to pining after home.

John had not much affection for his mother and sisters, and an antipathy to me. He bullied and punished me; not two or three times in the week, nor once or twice in a day, but continually: every nerve I had feared him, and every morsel of flesh on my bones shrank when he came near. There were moments when I was bewildered by the terror he inspired, because I had no appeal whatever against either his menaces or his inflictions; the servants did not like to offend their young master by taking my part against him, and Mrs Reed was blind and deaf on the subject: she never saw him strike or heard him abuse me, though he did both now and then in her very presence; more frequently, however, behind her back.

Habitually obedient to John, I came up to his chair: he spent some three minutes in thrusting out his tongue at me as far as he could without damaging the roots: I knew he would soon strike, and while dreading the blow, I mused on the disgusting and ugly appearance of him who would presently deal it. I wonder if he read that notion in my face; for, all at once, without speaking, he struck suddenly and strongly. I tottered, and on regaining my equilibrium retired back a step or two from his chair.

'That is for your impudence in answering mamma a while since,' said he, 'and for your sneaking way of getting behind curtains, and for the look you had in your eyes two minutes since, you rat!'

Accustomed to John Reed's abuse, I never had an idea of replying to it: my care was how to endure the blow which would certainly follow the insult.

'What were you doing behind the curtain?' he asked.

'I was reading.'

'Show the book.'

I returned to the window and fetched it thence.

'You have no business to take our books; you are a dependant, mamma says; you have no money; your father left you none; you ought to beg, and not to live here with gentlemen's children like us, and eat the same meals we do, and wear clothes at our mamma's expense. Now, I'll teach you to rummage my book-shelves: for they *are* mine; all the house belongs to me, or will do in a few years. Go and stand by the door, out of the way of the mirror and the windows.'

I did so, not at first aware what was his intention; but when I saw him lift and poise the book and stand in act to hurl it, I instinctively started aside with a cry of alarm: not soon enough, however; the volume was flung, it hit me, and I fell, striking my head against the door and cutting it. The cut bled, the pain was sharp: my terror had passed its climax; other feeling succeeded.

'Wicked and cruel boy!' I said. 'You are like a murderer – you are like a slave-driver – you are like the Roman emperors!'

I had read Goldsmith's *History of Rome*, and had formed my opinion of Nero, Caligula, &c. Also I had drawn parallels in silence, which I never thought thus to have declared aloud.

'What! what!' he cried. 'Did she say that to me? Did you hear her, Eliza and Georgiana? Won't I tell mamma? but first—'

He ran headlong at me: I felt him grasp my hair and my shoulder: he had closed with a desperate thing. I really saw in him a tyrant: a murderer. I felt a drop or two of blood from my head trickle down my neck, and was sensible of somewhat pungent suffering: these sensations for the time predominated over fear, and I received him in frantic sort. I don't very well know what I did with my hands, but he called me 'Rat! rat!' and bellowed out aloud. Aid was near him: Eliza and Georgiana had run for Mrs Reed, who was gone upstairs; she now came upon the scene, followed by Bessie and her maid Abbot. We were parted: I heard the words –

'Dear! dear! What a fury to fly at Master John!'

'Did ever anybody see such a picture of passion!'

Then Mrs Reed subjoined: 'Take her away to the red-room, and lock her in there.' Four hands were immediately laid upon me, and I was borne upstairs.

# Chapter 2

I resisted all the way: a new thing for me, and a circumstance which greatly strengthened the bad opinion Bessie and Miss Abbot were disposed to entertain of me. The fact is, I was a trifle beside myself; or rather *out* of myself, as the French would say. I was conscious that a moment's mutiny had already rendered me liable to strange penalties, and, like any other rebel slave, I felt resolved, in my desperation, to go all lengths.

'Hold her arms, Miss Abbot: she's like a mad cat.'

'For shame, for shame!' cried the lady's-maid. 'What shocking conduct, Miss Eyre, to strike a young gentleman, your benefactress's son! Your young master.'

'Master! How is he my master? Am I a servant?'

'No; you are less than a servant, for you do nothing for your keep. There, sit down, and think over your wickedness.'

They had got me by this time into the apartment indicated by Mrs Reed, and

# Jane Eyre

had thrust me upon a stool: my impulse was to rise from it like a spring; their two pair of hands arrested me instantly.

'If you don't sit still, you must be tied down,' said Bessie. 'Miss Abbot, lend me your garters; she would break mine directly.'

Miss Abbot turned to divest a stout leg of the necessary ligature. This preparation for bonds, and the additional ignominy it inferred, took a little of the excitement out of me.

'Don't take them off,' I cried; 'I will not stir.'

In guarantee whereof, I attached myself to my seat by my hands.

'Mind you don't,' said Bessie; and when she had ascertained that I was really subsiding, she loosened her hold of me; then she and Miss Abbot stood with folded arms, looking darkly and doubtfully on my face, as incredulous of my sanity.

'She never did so before,' at last said Bessie, turning to the Abigail.

'But it was always in her,' was the reply. 'I've told missis often my opinion about the child, and missis agreed with me. She's an underhand little thing: I never saw a girl of her age with so much cover.'

Bessie answered not; but ere long, addressing me, she said:

'You ought to be aware, miss, that you are under obligations to Mrs Reed: she keeps you: if she were to turn you off you would have to go to the poorhouse.'

I had nothing to say to these words: they were not new to me: my very first recollections of existence included hints of the same kind. This reproach of my dependence had become a vague sing-song in my ear; very painful and crushing, but only half intelligible. Miss Abbot joined in:

'And you ought not to think yourself on an equality with the Misses Reed and Master Reed, because missis kindly allows you to be brought up with them. They will have a great deal of money and you will have none: it is your place to be humble, and to try to make yourself agreeable to them.'

'What we tell you is for your good,' added Bessie, in no harsh voice: 'you should try to be useful and pleasant, then, perhaps, you would have a home here; but if you become passionate and rude, missis will send you away, I am sure.'

'Besides,' said Miss Abbot, 'God will punish her: He might strike her dead in the midst of her tantrums, and then where would she go? Come, Bessie, we will leave her: I wouldn't have her heart for anything. Say your prayers, Miss Eyre, when you are by yourself; for if you don't repent, something bad might be permitted to come down the chimney and fetch you away.'

They went, shutting the door, and locking it behind them.

The red-room was a spare chamber, very seldom slept in: I might say never, indeed, unless when a chance influx of visitors at Gateshead Hall rendered it necessary to turn to account all the accommodation it contained: yet it was one of the largest and stateliest chambers in the mansion. A bed supported on massive pillars of mahogany, hung with curtains of deep red damask, stood out like a tabernacle in the centre, the two large windows, with their blinds always drawn down, were half shrouded in festoons and falls of similar drapery; the carpet was red; the table at the foot of the bed was covered with a crimson cloth; the walls were a soft fawn colour, with a blush of pink in it; the wardrobe, the toilet-table, the chairs, were of darkly-polished old mahogany. Out of these deep surrounding shades rose high, and glared white, the piled-up mattresses and

pillows of the bed, spread with a snowy Marseilles counterpane. Scarcely less prominent was an ample cushioned easy-chair near the head of the bed, also white, with a footstool before it, and looking, as I thought, like a pale throne.

This room was chill, because it seldom had a fire; it was silent, because remote from the nursery and kitchens; solemn, because it was known to be so seldom entered. The housemaid alone came here on Saturdays, to wipe from the mirrors and the furniture a week's quiet dust; and Mrs Reed herself, at far intervals, visited it to review the contents of a certain secret drawer in the wardrobe, where were stored divers parchments, her jewel-casket, and a miniature of her deceased husband; and in those last words lies the secret of the red-room – the spell which kept it so lonely in spite of its grandeur.

Mr Reed had been dead nine years: it was in this chamber he breathed his last; here he lay in state; hence his coffin was borne by the undertaker's men; and, since that day, a sense of dreary consecration had guarded it from frequent intrusion.

My seat, to which Bessie and the bitter Miss Abbot had left me riveted, was a low ottoman near the marble chimney-piece; the bed rose before me; to my right hand there was the high, dark wardrobe, with subdued, broken reflections varying the gloss of its panels; to my left were the muffled windows; a great looking-glass between them repeated the vacant majesty of the bed and room. I was not quite sure whether they had locked the door; and, when I dared move, I got up and went to see. Alas, yes! no jail was ever more secure. Returning, I had to cross before the looking-glass; my fascinated glance involuntarily explored the depth it revealed. All looked colder and darker in that visionary hollow than in reality: and the strange little figure there gazing at me with a white face and arms specking the gloom, and glittering eyes of fear moving where all else was still, had the effect of a real spirit: I thought it like one of the tiny phantoms, half fairy, half imp, Bessie's evening stories represented as coming out of lone, ferny dells in moors, and appearing before the eyes of belated travellers. I returned to my stool.

Superstition was with me at that moment: but it was not yet her hour for complete victory: my blood was still warm; the mood of the revolted slave was still bracing me with its bitter vigour; I had to stem a rapid rush of retrospective thought before I quailed to the dismal present.

All John Reed's violent tyrannies, all his sisters' proud indifference, all his mother's aversion, all the servant's partiality, turned up in my disturbed mind like a dark deposit in a turbid well. Why was I always suffering, always browbeaten, always accused, forever condemned?

Why could I never please? Why was it useless to try to win anyone's favour? Eliza, who was headstrong and selfish, was respected. Georgiana, who had a spoiled temper, a very acrid spite, a captious and insolent carriage, was universally indulged. Her beauty, her pink cheeks, and golden curls, seemed to give delight to all who looked at her, and to purchase indemnity for every fault. John no one thwarted, much less punished, though he twisted the necks of the pigeons, killed the little pea-chicks, set the dogs at the sheep, stripped the hothouse vines of their fruit, and broke the buds off the choicest plants in the conservatory; he called his mother 'old girl', too; sometimes reviled her for her dark skin, similar to his own; bluntly disregarded her wishes; not infrequently tore and spoiled her silk attire; and he was still 'her own darling'. I dared commit

# Jane Eyre

no fault; I strove to fulfil every duty; and I was termed naughty and tiresome, sullen and sneaking, from morning to noon, and from noon to night.

My head still ached and bled with the blow and fall I had received; no one had reproved John for wantonly striking me; and because I had turned against him to avert further irrational violence, I was loaded with general opprobrium.

'Unjust! – unjust!' said my reason, forced by the agonizing stimulus into precocious though transitory power; and Resolve, equally wrought up, instigated some strange expedient to achieve escape from insupportable oppression – as running away, or, if that could not be effected, never eating or drinking more, and letting myself die.

What a consternation of soul was mine that dreary afternoon! How all my brain was in tumult, and all my heart in insurrection! Yet in what darkness, what dense ignorance, was the mental battle fought! I could not answer the ceaseless inward question – *why* I thus suffered; now, at the distance of – I will not say how many years – I see it clearly.

I was a discord in Gateshead Hall; I was like nobody there; I had nothing in harmony with Mrs Reed or her children, or her chosen vassalage. If they did not love me, in fact, as little did I love them. They were not bound to regard with affection a thing that could not sympathize with one amongst them; a heterogeneous thing, opposed to them in temperament, in capacity, in propensities; a useless thing, incapable of serving their interest, or adding to their pleasure; a noxious thing, cherishing the germs of indignation at their treatment, of contempt of their judgement. I know that had I been a sanguine, brilliant, careless, exacting, handsome, romping child – though equally dependent and friendless – Mrs Reed would have endured my presence more complacently; her children would have entertained for me more of the cordiality of fellow-feeling; the servants would have been less prone to make me the scapegoat of the nursery.

Daylight began to forsake the red-room; it was past four o'clock, and the beclouded afternoon was tending to drear twilight. I heard the rain still beating continuously on the staircase window, and the wind howling in the grove behind the hall; I grew by degrees cold as a stone, and then my courage sank. My habitual mood of humiliation, self-doubt, forlorn depression, fell damp on the embers of my decaying ire. All said I was wicked, and perhaps I might be so: what thought had I been but just conceiving of starving myself to death? That certainly was a crime: and was I fit to die? Or was the vault under the chancel of Gateshead Church an inviting bourne? In such vault I had been told did Mr Reed lie buried; and led by this thought to recall his idea, I dwelt on it with gathering dread. I could not remember him, but I knew that he was my own uncle – my mother's brother – that he had taken me when a parentless infant to his house; and that in his last moments he had required a promise of Mrs Reed that she would rear and maintain me as one of her own children. Mrs Reed probably considered she had kept this promise; and so she had, I dare say, as well as her nature would permit her: but how could she really like an interloper, not of her race, and unconnected with her, after her husband's death, by any tie? It must have been most irksome to find herself bound by a hard-wrung pledge to stand in the stead of a parent to a strange child she could not love, and to see an uncongenial alien permanently intruded on her own family group.

A singular notion dawned upon me. I doubted not – never doubted – that if

# Jane Eyre

Mr Reed had been alive he would have treated me kindly; and now, as I sat looking at the white bed and overshadowed walls – occasionally also turning a fascinated eye towards the dimly gleaming mirror – I began to recall what I had heard of dead men, troubled in their graves by the violation of their last wishes, revisiting the earth to punish the perjured and avenge the oppressed; and I thought Mr Reed's spirit, harassed by the wrongs of his sister's child, might quit its abode – whether in the church vault or in the unknown world of the departed – and rise before me in this chamber. I wiped my tears and hushed my sobs, fearful lest any sign of violent grief might waken a preternatural voice to comfort me, or elicit from the gloom some haloed face, bending over me with strange pity. This idea, consolatory in theory, I felt would be terrible if realized: with all my might I endeavoured to stifle it – I endeavoured to be firm. Shaking my hair from my eyes, I lifted my head and tried to look boldly round the dark room; at this moment a light gleamed on the wall. Was it, I asked myself, a ray from the moon penetrating some aperture in the blind? No; moonlight was still, and this stirred; while I gazed, it glided up to the ceiling and quivered over my head. I can now conjecture readily that this streak of light was, in all likelihood, a gleam from a lantern carried by some one across the lawn; but then, prepared as my mind was for horror, shaken as my nerves were by agitation, I thought the swift-darting beam was a herald of some coming vision from another world. My heart beat thick, my head grew hot; a sound filled my ears, which I deemed the rushing of wings; something seemed near me; I was oppressed, suffocated: endurance broke down; I rushed to the door and shook the lock in desperate effort. Steps came running along the outer passage; the key turned, Bessie and Abbot entered.

'Miss Eyre, are you ill?' said Bessie.

'What a dreadful noise! It went quite through me!' exclaimed Abbot.

'Take me out! Let me go into the nursery!' was my cry.

'What for? Are you hurt? Have you seen something?' again demanded Bessie.

'Oh! I saw a light, and I thought a ghost would come.' I had now got hold of Bessie's hand, and she did not snatch it from me.

'She has screamed out on purpose,' declared Abbot, in some disgust. 'And what a scream! If she had been in great pain one would have excused it, but she only wanted to bring us all here; I know her naughty tricks.'

'What is all this?' demanded another voice peremptorily; and Mrs Reed came along the corridor, her cap flying wide, her gown rustling stormily. 'Abbot and Bessie, I believe I gave orders that Jane Eyre should be left in the red-room till I came to her myself.'

'Miss Jane screamed so loud, ma'am,' pleaded Bessie.

'Let her go,' was the only answer. 'Loose Bessie's hands, child: you cannot succeed in getting out by these means, be assured. I abhor artifice, particularly in children; it is my duty to show you that tricks will not answer; you will now stay here an hour longer, and it is only on condition of perfect submission and stillness that I shall liberate you then.'

'Oh, aunt! have pity! Forgive me! I cannot endure it – let me be punished some other way! I shall be killed if—'

'Silence! This violence is almost repulsive'; and so, no doubt, she felt it. I was a precocious actress in her eyes: she sincerely looked on me as a compound of virulent passions, mean spirit, and dangerous duplicity.

# Jane Eyre

Bessie and Abbot having retreated, Mrs Reed, impatient of my now frantic anguish and wild sobs, abruptly thrust me back and locked me in, without further parley. I heard her sweeping away; and soon after she was gone, I suppose I had a species of fit: unconsciousness closed the scene.

# Chapter 3

The next thing I remember is waking up with a feeling as if I had had a frightful nightmare, and seeing before me a terrible red glare, crossed with thick black bars. I heard voices, too, speaking with a hollow sound, and as if muffled by a rush of wind or water: agitation, uncertainty, and an all-predominating sense of terror confused my faculties. Ere long, I became aware that some one was handling me; lifting me up and supporting me in a sitting posture, and that more tenderly than I had ever been raised or upheld before. I rested my head against a pillow or an arm, and felt easy.

In five minutes more the cloud of bewilderment dissolved: I knew quite well that I was in my own bed, and that the red glare was the nursery fire. It was night: a candle burnt on the table: Bessie stood at the bed-foot with a basin in her hand, and a gentleman sat in a chair near my pillow, leaning over me.

I felt an inexpressible relief, a soothing conviction of protection and security, when I knew that there was a stranger in the room, an individual not belonging to Gateshead, and not related to Mrs Reed. Turning from Bessie (though her presence was far less obnoxious to me than that of Abbot, for instance, would have been), I scrutinized the face of the gentleman: I knew him; it was Mr Lloyd, an apothecary, sometimes called in by Mrs Reed when the servants were ailing: for herself and the children she employed a physician.

'Well, who am I?' he asked.

I pronounced his name, offering him at the same time my hand: he took it, smiling and saying, 'We shall do very well by and by.' Then he laid me down, and addressing Bessie, charged her to be very careful that I was not disturbed during the night. Having given some further directions, and intimated that he should call again the next day, he departed, to my grief: I felt so sheltered and befriended while he sat in the chair near my pillow; and as he closed the door after him, all the room darkened and my heart again sank: inexpressible sadness weighed it down.

'Do you feel as if you should sleep, miss?' asked Bessie, rather softly.

Scarcely dared I answer her; for I feared the next sentence might be rough. 'I will try.'

'Would you like to drink, or could you eat anything?'

'No, thank you, Bessie.'

# Jane Eyre

'Then I think I shall go to bed, for it is past twelve o'clock; but you may call me if you want anything in the night.'

Wonderful civility this! It emboldened me to ask a question.

'Bessie, what is the matter with me? Am I ill?'

'You felt sick, I suppose, in the red-room with crying; you'll be better soon, no doubt.'

Bessie went into the housemaid's apartment which was near. I heard her say, –

'Sarah, come and sleep with me in the nursery; I daren't for my life be alone with that poor child to-night; she might die; it's such a strange thing she should have that fit: I wonder if she saw anything. Missis was rather too hard.'

Sarah came back with her; they both went to bed; they were whispering together for half an hour before they fell asleep. I caught scraps of their conversation, from which I was able only too distinctly to infer the main subject discussed.

'Something passed her, all dressed in white, and vanished' – 'A great black dog behind him' – 'Three loud raps on the chamber door' – 'A light in the churchyard just over his grave' – &c., &c.

At last both slept; the fire and the candle went out. For me, the watches of that long night passed in ghastly wakefulness; ear, eye, and mind were alike strained by dread, such dread as children only can feel.

No severe or prolonged bodily illness followed this incident of the red-room: it only gave my nerves a shock, on which I feel the reverberation to this day. Yes, Mrs Reed, to you I owe some fearful pangs of mental suffering. But I ought to forgive you, for you knew not what you did: while rending my heartstrings, you thought you were only uprooting my bad propensities.

Next day, by noon, I was up and dressed, and sat wrapped in a shawl by the nursery hearth. I felt physically weak and broken down: but my worst ailment was an unutterable wretchedness of mind: a wretchedness which kept drawing from me silent tears. No sooner had I wiped one salt drop from my cheek than another followed. Yet I thought I ought to have been happy, for none of the Reeds were there – they were all gone out in the carriage with their mamma. Abbot, too, was sewing in another room, and Bessie, as she moved hither and thither, putting away toys and arranging drawers, addressed to me every now and then a word of unwonted kindness. This state of things should have been to me a paradise of peace, accustomed as I was to a life of ceaseless reprimand and thankless fagging; but, in fact, my racked nerves were now in such a state that no calm could soothe, and no pleasure excite them agreeably.

Bessie had been down into the kitchen, and she brought up with her a tart on a certain brightly painted china plate, whose bird of paradise, nestling in a wreath of convolvuli and rosebuds, had been wont to stir in me a most enthusiastic sense of admiration; and which plate I had often petitioned to be allowed to take in my hand in order to examine it more closely, but had always hitherto been deemed unworthy of such a privilege. This precious vessel was now placed on my knee, and I was cordially invited to eat the circlet of delicate pastry upon it. Vain favour! coming, like most other favours long deferred and often wished for, too late! I could not eat the tart: and the plumage of the bird, the tints of the flowers, seemed strangely faded! I put both plate and tart away. Bessie asked if I would have a book: the word *book* acted as a transient stimulus, and I

# Jane Eyre

begged her to fetch *Gulliver's Travels* from the library. This book I had again and again perused with delight. I considered it a narrative of facts, and discovered in it a vein of interest deeper than what I found in fairy tales: for as to the elves, having sought them in vain among foxglove leaves and bells, under mushrooms and beneath the ground-ivy mantling old wall-nooks, I had at length made up my mind to the sad truth, that they were all gone out of England to some savage country where the woods were wilder and thicker, and the population more scant; whereas Lilliput and Brobdingnag being, in my creed, solid parts of the earth's surface, I doubted not that I might one day, by taking a long voyage, see with my own eyes the little fields, houses, and trees, the diminutive people, the tiny cows, sheep, and birds of the one realm; and the cornfields forest-high, the mighty mastiffs, the monster cats, the tower-like men and women of the other. Yet, when this cherished volume was now placed in my hands – when I turned over its leaves, and sought in its marvellous pictures the charm I had, till now, never failed to find – all was eerie and dreary; the giants were gaunt goblins, the pigmies malevolent and fearful imps, Gulliver a most desolate wanderer in most dread and dangerous regions. I closed the book, which I dared no longer peruse, and put it on the table beside the untasted tart.

Bessie had now finished dusting and tidying the room, and, having washed her hands, she opened a certain little drawer, full of splendid shreds of silk and satin, and began making a new bonnet for Georgiana's doll. Meantime she sang: her song was, –

> *'In the days when we went gipsying,*
> *A long time ago.'*

I had often heard the song before, and always with lively delight; for Bessie had a sweet voice – at least, I thought so. But now, though her voice was still sweet, I found in its melody an indescribable sadness. Sometimes, preoccupied with her work, she sang the refrain very low, very lingerly: '*A long time ago*' came out like the saddest cadence of a funeral hymn. She passed into another ballad, this time a really doleful one.

> *'My feet they are sore, and my limbs they are weary;*
> *Long is the way, and the mountains are wild;*
> *Soon will the twilight close moonless and dreary*
> *Over the path of the poor orphan child.*
>
> *Why did they send me so far and so lonely,*
> *Up where the moors spread and gray rocks are piled?*
> *Men are hard-hearted, and kind angels only*
> *Watch o'er the steps of a poor orphan child.*
>
> *Yet, distant and soft, the night-breeze is blowing,*
> *Clouds there are none, and clear stars beam mild;*
> *God, in His mercy, protection is showing,*
> *Comfort and hope to the poor orphan child.*

# Jane Eyre

*Ev'n should I fall o'er the broken bridge passing,*
*Or stray in the marshes, by false lights beguiled,*
*Still will my Father, with promise and blessing,*
*Take to His bosom the poor orphan child.*

*There is a thought that for strength should avail me;*
*Though both of shelter and kindred despoiled;*
*Heaven is a home, and a rest will not fail me;*
*God is a friend to the poor orphan child.'*

'Come, Miss Jane, don't cry,' said Bessie, as she finished. She might as well have said to the fire, 'Don't burn!' but how could she divine the morbid suffering to which I was a prey? In the course of the morning Mr Lloyd came again.

'What, already up!' said he, as he entered the nursery. 'Well, nurse, how is she?'

Bessie answered that I was doing very well.

'Then she ought to look more cheerful. Come here, Miss Jane: your name is Jane, is it not?'

'Yes, sir; Jane Eyre.'

'Well, you have been crying, Miss Jane Eyre: can you tell me what about? Have you any pain?'

'No, sir.'

'Oh! I dare say she is crying because she could not go out with missis in the carriage,' interposed Bessie.

'Surely not! why, she is too old for such pettishness.'

I thought so too; and my self-esteem being wounded by a false charge, I answered promptly, 'I never cried for such a thing in my life: I hate going out in the carriage. I cry because I am miserable.'

'Oh, fie, Miss!' said Bessie.

The good apothecary appeared a little puzzled I was standing before him: he fixed his eyes on me very steadily: his eyes were small and gray, not very bright; but I dare say I should think them shrewd now: he had a hard-featured yet good-natured looking face. Having considered me at leisure, he said, 'What made you ill yesterday?'

'She had a fall,' said Bessie, again putting in her word.

'Fall! why, that is like a baby again! Can't she manage to walk at her age? She must be eight or nine years old.'

'I was knocked down,' was the blunt explanation, jerked out of me by another pang of mortified pride; 'but that did not make me ill,' I added; while Mr Lloyd helped himself to a pinch of snuff.

As he was returning the box to his waistcoat pocket, a loud bell rang for the servants' dinner; he knew what it was. 'That's for you, nurse,' said he; 'you can go down; I'll give Miss Jane a lecture till you come back.'

Bessie would rather have stayed, but she was obliged to go, because punctuality at meals was rigidly enforced at Gateshead Hall.

'The fall did not make you ill; what did, then?' pursued Mr Lloyd, when Bessie was gone.

'I was shut up in a room where there is a ghost, till after dark.'

# Jane Eyre

I saw Mr Lloyd smile and frown at the same time: 'Ghost! What, you are a baby after all! You are afraid of ghosts?'

'Of Mr Reed's ghost I am; he died in that room, and was laid out there. Neither Bessie nor anyone else will go into it at night, if they can help it; and it was cruel to shut me up alone without a candle – so cruel that I think I shall never forget it.'

'Nonsense! And is it that makes you so miserable? Are you afraid now in daylight?'

'No: but night will come again before long; and besides, I am unhappy – very unhappy, for other things.'

'What other things? Can you tell me some of them?'

How much I wished to reply fully to this question! How difficult it was to frame any answer! Children can feel, but they cannot analyse their feelings; and if the analysis is partially effected in thought, they know not how to express the result of the process in words. Fearful, however, of losing this first and only opportunity of relieving my grief by imparting it, I, after a disturbed pause, contrived to frame a meagre, though, as far as it went, true response.

'For one thing, I have no father or mother, brothers or sisters.'

'You have a kind aunt and cousins.'

Again I paused; then bunglingly enounced,

'But John Reed knocked me down, and my aunt shut me up in the red-room.'

Mr Lloyd a second time produced his snuff-box.

'Don't you think Gateshead Hall a very beautiful house?' asked he. 'Are you not very thankful to have such a fine place to live at?'

'It is not my house, sir; and Abbot says I have less right to be here than a servant.'

'Pooh! you can't be silly enough to wish to leave such a splendid place?'

'If I had anywhere else to go, I should be glad to leave it; but I can never get away from Gateshead till I am a woman.'

'Perhaps you may – who knows? Have you any relations besides Mrs Reed?'

'I think not, sir.'

'None belonging to your father?'

'I don't know: I asked Aunt Reed once, and she said possibly I might have some poor, low relations called Eyre, but she knew nothing about them.'

'If you had such, would you like to go to them?'

I reflected. Poverty looks grim to grown people; still more so to children: they have not much idea of industrious, working, respectable poverty; they think of the word only as connected with ragged clothes, scanty food, fireless grates, rude manners, and debasing vices: poverty for me was synonymous with degradation.

'No; I should not like to belong to poor people,' was my reply.

'Not even if they were kind to you?'

I shook my head; I could not see how poor people had the means of being kind, and then to learn to speak like them, to adopt their manners, to be uneducated, to grow up like one of the poor women I saw sometimes nursing their children or washing their clothes at the cottage doors of the village of Gateshead: no, I was not heroic enough to purchase liberty at the price of caste.

'But are your relatives so very poor? Are they working people?'

'I cannot tell; Aunt Reed says if I have any they must be a beggarly set; I should not like to go a-begging.'

# Jane Eyre

'Would you like to go to school?'

Again I reflected: I scarcely knew what school was; Bessie sometimes spoke of it as a place where young ladies sat in the stocks, wore backboards, and were expected to be exceedingly genteel and precise; John Reed hated his school and abused his master; but John Reed's tastes were no rule for mine, and if Bessie's accounts of school discipline (gathered from the young ladies of a family where she had lived before coming to Gateshead) were somewhat appalling, her details of certain accomplishments attained by these same young ladies were, I thought, equally attractive. She boasted of beautiful paintings of landscapes and flowers by them executed; of songs they could sing and pieces they could play, of purses they could net, of French books they could translate; till my spirit was moved to emulation, as I listened. Besides, school would be a complete change; it implied a long journey, an entire separation from Gateshead, an entrance into a new life.

'I should indeed like to go to school,' was the audible conclusion of my musings.

'Well, well; who knows what may happen?' said Mr Lloyd, as he got up. 'The child ought to have change of air and scene,' he added, speaking to himself; 'nerves not in a good state.'

Bessie now returned; at the same moment the carriage was heard rolling up the gravel-walk.

'Is that your mistress, nurse?' asked Mr Lloyd. 'I should like to speak to her before I go.'

Bessie invited him to walk into the breakfast-room and led the way out. In the interview which followed between him and Mrs Reed, I presume, from after-occurrences, that the apothecary ventured to recommend my being sent to school; and the recommendation was no doubt readily enough adopted; for as Abbot said, in discussing the subject with Bessie, when both sat sewing in the nursery one night after I was in bed, and, as they thought, asleep, 'Missis was, she dared say, glad enough to get rid of such a tiresome ill-conditioned child, who always looked as if she were watching everybody, and scheming plots underhand.' Abbot, I think, gave me credit for being a sort of infantine Guy Fawkes.

On that same occasion I learned, for the first time, from Miss Abbot's communications to Bessie, that my father had been a poor clergyman; that my mother had married him against the wishes of her friends, who considered the match beneath her; that my grandfather Reed was so irritated at her disobedience, he cut her off without a shilling; that after my mother and father had been married a year, the latter caught the typhus fever while visiting among the poor of a large manufacturing town where his curacy was situated, and where that disease was then prevalent; that my mother took the infection from him, and both died within a month of each other.

Bessie, when she heard this narrative, sighed and said, 'Poor Miss Jane is to be pitied too, Abbot.'

'Yes,' responded Abbot; 'if she were a nice, pretty child, one might compassionate her forlornness; but one really cannot care for such a little toad as that.'

'Not a great deal, to be sure,' agreed Bessie: 'at any rate, a beauty like Miss Georgiana would be more moving in the same condition.'

'Yes, I dote on Miss Georgiana!' cried the fervent Abbot. 'Little darling! –

with her long curls and her blue eyes, and such a sweet colour as she has; just as if she were painted! – Bessie, I could fancy a Welsh rabbit for supper.'

'So could I – with a roast onion. Come, we'll go down.' They went.

# Chapter 4

From my discourse with Mr Lloyd, and from the above reported conference between Bessie and Abbot, I gathered enough of hope to suffice as a motive for wishing to get well: a change seemed near – I desired and waited it in silence. It tarried, however; days and weeks passed; I had regained my normal state of health, but no new allusion was made to the subject over which I brooded. Mrs Reed surveyed me at times with a severe eye, but seldom addressed me; since my illness she had drawn a more marked line of separation than ever between me and her own children, appointing me a small closet to sleep in by myself, condemning me to take my meals alone, and pass all my time in the nursery, while my cousins were constantly in the drawing-room. Not a hint, however, did she drop about sending me to school; still I felt an instinctive certainty that she would not long endure me under the same roof with her; for her glance, now more than ever, when turned on me, expressed an insuperable and rooted aversion.

Eliza and Georgiana, evidently acting according to orders, spoke to me as little as possible; John thrust his tongue in his cheek whenever he saw me, and once attempted chastisement; but as I instantly turned against him, roused by the same sentiment of deep ire and desperate revolt which had stirred my corruption before, he thought it better to desist, and ran from me, uttering execrations, and vowing I had burst his nose. I had, indeed, levelled at that prominent feature as hard a blow as my knuckles could inflict; and when I saw that either that or my look daunted him I had the greatest inclination to follow up my advantage to purpose, but he was already with his mamma. I heard him in a blubbering tone commence the tale of how 'that nasty Jane Eyre' had flown at him like a wild cat; he was stopped rather harshly –

'Don't talk to me about her, John: I told you not to go near her: she is not worthy of notice. I do not choose that either you or your sisters should associate with her.'

Here, leaning over the banister, I cried out suddenly, and without at all deliberating on my words –

'They are not fit to associate with me.'

Mrs Reed was rather a stout woman; but, on hearing this strange and audacious declaration, she ran nimbly up the stair, swept me like a whirlwind into the nursery, and crushing me down on the edge of my crib, dared me in an

emphatic voice to rise from that place, or utter one syllable, during the remainder of the day.

'What would Uncle Reed say to you, if he were alive?' was my scarcely voluntary demand. I say scarcely voluntary, for it seemed as if my tongue pronounced words without my will consenting to their utterance: something spoke out of me over which I had no control.

'What?' said Mrs Reed under her breath: her usually cold, composed gray eye became troubled with a look of fear; she took her hand from my arm, and gazed at me as if she really did not know whether I were child or fiend. I was now in for it.

'My Uncle Reed is in heaven, and can see all you do and think; and so can papa and mamma; they know how you shut me up all day long, and how you wish me dead.'

Mrs Reed soon rallied her spirits: she shook me most soundly, she boxed both my ears, and then left me without a word. Bessie supplied the hiatus by a homily of an hour's length, in which she proved beyond a doubt that I was the most wicked and abandoned child ever reared under a roof. I half believed her, for I felt, indeed, only bad feelings surging in my breast.

November, December, and half of January passed away. Christmas and the New Year had been celebrated at Gateshead with the usual festive cheer; presents had been interchanged, dinners and evening parties given. From every enjoyment I was, of course, excluded: my share of the gaiety consisted in witnessing the daily apparelling of Eliza and Georgiana, and seeing them descend to the drawing-room, dressed out in thin muslin frocks and scarlet sashes, with hair elaborately ringleted; and afterwards, in listening to the sound of the piano or the harp played below, to the passing to and fro of the butler and footman, to the jingling of glass and china as refreshments were handed, to the broken hum of conversation as the drawing-room doors opened and closed. When tired of this occupation, I would retire from the stairhead to the solitary and silent nursery: there, though somewhat sad, I was not miserable. To speak truth, I had not the least wish to go into company, for in company I was very rarely noticed: and if Bessie had but been kind and companionable, I should have deemed it a treat to spend the evenings quietly with her, instead of passing them under the formidable eye of Mrs Reed, in a room full of ladies and gentlemen. But Bessie, as soon as she had dressed her young ladies, used to take herself off to the lively regions of the kitchen and housekeeper's room, generally bearing the candle along with her. I then sat with my doll on my knee, till the fire got low, glancing round occasionally to make sure that nothing worse than myself haunted the shadowy room; and when the embers sank to a dull red, I undressed hastily, tugging at knots and strings as I best might, and sought shelter from cold and darkness in my crib. To this crib I always took my doll; human beings must love something, and, in the dearth of worthier objects of affection, I contrived to find a pleasure in loving and cherishing a faded graven image, shabby as a miniature scarecrow. It puzzles me now to remember with what absurd sincerity I doted on this little toy, half fancying it alive and capable of sensation. I could not sleep unless it was folded in my nightgown; and when it lay there safe and warm, I was comparatively happy, believing it to be happy likewise.

Long did the hours seem while I waited the departure of the company, and

listened for the sound of Bessie's step on the stairs. Sometimes she would come up in the interval to seek her thimble or her scissors, or perhaps to bring me something by way of supper—a bun or a cheese-cake – then she would sit on the bed while I ate it, and when I had finished, she would tuck the clothes round me, and twice she kissed me, and said, 'Good-night, Miss Jane.' When thus gentle, Bessie seemed to me the best, prettiest, kindest being in the world; and I wished most intensely that she would always be so pleasant and amiable, and never push me about, or scold, or task me unreasonably, as she was too often wont to do. Bessie Lee must, I think, have been a girl of good natural capacity, for she was smart in all she did, and had a remarkable knack of narrative; so, at least, I judged from the impression made on me by her nursery tales. She was pretty, too, if my recollections of her face and person are correct. I remember her as a slim young woman, with black hair, dark eyes, very nice features, and good, clear complexion; but she had a capricious and hasty temper, and indifferent ideas of principle or justice; still, such as she was, I preferred her to any one else at Gateshead Hall.

It was the fifteenth of January, about nine o'clock in the morning. Bessie was gone down to breakfast; my cousins had not yet been summoned to their mamma; Eliza was putting on her bonnet and warm garden-coat to go and feed her poultry – an occupation of which she was fond, and not less so of selling the eggs to the housekeeper and hoarding up the money she thus obtained. She had a turn for traffic, and a marked propensity for saving – shown not only in the vending of eggs and chickens, but also in driving hard bargains with the gardener about flower-roots, seeds, and slips of plants – that functionary having orders from Mrs Reed to buy of his young lady all the products of her parterre she wished to sell: and Eliza would have sold the hair off her head if she could have made a handsome profit thereby. As to her money, she first secreted it in odd corners, wrapped in a rag or an old curl-paper; but some of these hoards having been discovered by the housemaid, Eliza, fearful of one day losing her valued treasure, consented to entrust it to her mother, at a usurious rate of interest – fifty or sixty per cent – which interest she exacted every quarter, keeping her accounts in a little book with anxious accuracy.

Georgiana sat on a high stool, dressing her hair at the glass, and interweaving her curls with artificial flowers and faded feathers, of which she had found a store in a drawer in the attic. I was making my bed, having received strict orders from Bessie to get it arranged before she returned (for Bessie now frequently employed me as a sort of under nursery-maid, to tidy the room, dust the chairs, &c). Having spread the quilt and folded my nightdress, I went to the window-seat to put in order some picture-books and doll's-house furniture scattered there; an abrupt command from Georgiana to let her playthings alone (for the tiny chairs and mirrors, the fairy plates and cups, were her property) stopped my proceedings; and then, for lack of other occupation, I fell to breathing on the frost-flowers with which the window was fretted, and thus clearing a space in the glass through which I might look out on the grounds, where all was still and petrified under the influence of a hard frost.

From this window were visible the porter's lodge and the carriage-road, and just as I had dissolved so much of the silver-white foliage veiling the panes as left room to look out, I saw the gates thrown open and a carriage roll through. I watched it ascending the drive with indifference: carriages often came to

# Jane Eyre

Gateshead, but none ever brought visitors in whom I was interested; it stopped in front of the house, the door-bell rang loudly, the new-comer was admitted. All this being nothing to me, my vacant attention soon found livelier attraction in the spectacle of a little hungry robin, which came and chirruped on the twigs of the leafless cherry-tree nailed against the wall near the casement. The remains of my breakfast of bread and milk stood on the table, and, having crumbled a morsel of roll, I was tugging at the sash to put out the crumbs on the window-sill, when Bessie came running upstairs into the nursery.

'Miss Jane, take off your pinafore. What are you doing there? Have you washed your hands and face this morning?'

I gave another tug before I answered, for I wanted the bird to be secure of its bread: the sash yielded, I scattered the crumbs – some on the stone sill, some on the cherry-tree bough; then, closing the window, I replied –

'No, Bessie; I have only just finished dusting.'

'Troublesome, careless child! – and what are you doing now? You look quite red, as if you had been about some mischief: what were you opening the window for?'

I was spared the trouble of answering, for Bessie seemed to be in too great a hurry to listen to explanations; she hauled me to the washstand, inflicted a merciless, but happily brief scrub on my face and hands with soap, water, and a coarse towel; disciplined my head with a bristly brush, denuded me of my pinafore, and then hurrying me to the top of the stairs, bid me go down directly, as I was wanted in the breakfast-room.

I would have asked who wanted me – I would have demanded if Mrs Reed was there; but Bessie was already gone, and had closed the nursery door upon me. I slowly descended. For nearly three months I had never been called to Mrs Reed's presence; restricted so long to the nursery, the breakfast-, dining-, and drawing-rooms were become to me awful regions, on which it dismayed me to intrude.

I now stood in the empty hall; before me was the breakfast-room door, and I stopped, intimidated and trembling. What a miserable little poltroon had fear, engendered of unjust punishment, made of me in those days! I feared to return to the nursery, and feared to go forward to the parlour; ten minutes I stood in agitated hesitation; the vehement ringing of the breakfast-room bell decided me; I *must* enter.

'Who could want me?' I asked inwardly, as with both hands I turned the stiff door-handle which, for a second or two, resisted my efforts. 'What should I see besides Aunt Reed in the apartment? – a man or a woman?' The handle turned, the door unclosed, and passing through and curtseying low, I looked up at – a black pillar! – such, at least, appeared to me, at first sight, the straight, narrow, sable-clad shape standing erect on the rug; the grim face at the top was like a carved mask, placed above the shaft by way of capital.

Mrs Reed occupied her usual seat by the fireside; she made a signal to me to approach; I did so, and she introduced me to the stony stranger with the words –

'This is the little girl respecting whom I applied to you.'

*He* – for it was a man – turned his head slowly towards where I stood, and having examined me with the two inquisitive looking gray eyes which twinkled under a pair of bushy brows, said solemnly, and in a bass voice –

'Her size is small; what is her age?'

# Jane Eyre

'Ten years.'

'So much?' was the doubtful answer; and he prolonged his scrutiny for some minutes. Presently he addressed me –

'Your name, little girl?'

'Jane Eyre, sir.'

In uttering these words I looked up: he seemed to me a tall gentleman, but then I was very little; his features were large, and they and all the lines of his frame were equally harsh and prim.

'Well, Jane Eyre, and are you a good child?'

Impossible to reply to this in the affirmative: my little world held a contrary opinion: I was silent. Mrs Reed answered for me by an expressive shake of the head, adding soon, 'Perhaps the less said on that subject the better, Mr Brocklehurst.'

'Sorry indeed to hear it! She and I must have some talk'; and bending from the perpendicular, he installed his person in the arm-chair, opposite Mrs Reed's. 'Come here,' he said.

I stepped across the rug: he placed me square and straight before him. What a face he had, now that it was almost on a level with mine! what a great nose! and what a mouth! and what large, prominent teeth!

'No sight so sad as that of a naughty child,' he began, 'especially a naughty little girl. Do you know where the wicked go after death?'

'They go to hell,' was my ready and orthodox answer.

'And what is hell? Can you tell me that?'

'A pit full of fire.'

'And should you like to fall into that pit, and to be burning there for ever?'

'No, sir.'

'What must you do to avoid it?'

I deliberated a moment: my answer, when it did come, was objectionable: 'I must keep in good health, and not die.'

'How can you keep in good health? Children younger than you die daily. I buried a little child of five years old only a day or two since – a good little child, whose soul is now in heaven. It is to be feared the same could not be said of you, were you to be called thence.'

Not being in a condition to remove his doubt, I only cast my eyes down on the two large feet planted on the rug, and sighed, wishing myself far enough away.

'I hope that sigh is from the heart, and that you repent of ever having been the occasion of discomfort to your excellent benefactress.'

'Benefactress! benefactress!' said I inwardly: 'they all call Mrs Reed my benefactress; if so, a benefactress is a disagreeable thing.'

'Do you say your prayers night and morning?' continued my interrogator.

'Yes, sir.'

'Do you read your Bible?'

'Sometimes.'

'With pleasure? Are you fond of it?'

'I like Revelations, and the Book of Daniel, and Genesis, and Samuel, and a little bit of Exodus, and some parts of Kings and Chronicles, and Job and Jonah.'

'And the Psalms? I hope you like them?'

# Jane Eyre

'No, sir.'

'No? Oh, shocking! I have a little boy, younger than you, who knows six Psalms by heart: and when you ask him which he would rather have, a ginger-bread-nut to eat, or a verse of a Psalm to learn, he says: "Oh! the verse of a Psalm! angels sing Psalms," says he; "I wish to be a little angel here below." He then gets two nuts in recompense for his infant piety.'

'Psalms are not interesting,' I remarked.

'That proves you to have a wicked heart; and you must pray to God to change it: to give you a new and clean one: to take away your heart of stone and give you a heart of flesh.'

I was about to propound a question, touching the manner in which that operation of changing my heart was to be performed, when Mrs Reed interposed, telling me to sit down; she then proceeded to carry on the conversation herself.

'Mr Brocklehurst, I believe I intimated in the letter which I wrote to you three weeks ago, that this little girl has not quite the character and disposition I could wish: should you admit her into Lowood school, I should be glad if the superintendent and teachers were requested to keep a strict eye on her, and, above all, to guard against her worst fault, a tendency to deceit. I mention this in your hearing, Jane, that you may not attempt to impose on Mr Brocklehurst.'

Well might I dread, well might I dislike Mrs Reed; for it was her nature to wound me cruelly: never was I happy in her presence. However carefully I obeyed, however strenuously I strove to please her, my efforts were still repulsed, and repaid by such sentences as the above. Now, uttered before a stranger, the accusation cut me to the heart: I dimly perceived that she was already obliterating hope from the new phase of existence which she destined me to enter. I felt, though I could not have expressed the feeling, that she was sowing aversion and unkindness along my future path: I saw myself transformed, under Mr Brock-lehurst's eye, into an artful, noxious child, and what could I do to remedy the injury?

'Nothing, indeed,' thought I, as I struggled to repress a sob, and hastily wiped away some tears, the impotent evidences of my anguish.

'Deceit is, indeed, a sad fault in a child,' said Mr Brocklehurst; 'it is akin to falsehood, and all liars will have their portion in the lake burning with fire and brimstone; she shall, however, be watched, Mrs Reed. I will speak to Miss Temple and the teachers.'

'I should wish her to be brought up in a manner suiting her prospects,' continued my benefactress; 'to be made useful, to be kept humble. As for the vacations she will, with your permission, spend them always at Lowood.'

'Your decisions are perfectly judicious, madam,' returned Mr Brocklehurst. 'Humility is a Christian grace, and one peculiarly appropriate to the pupils of Lowood; I, therefore, direct that special care shall be bestowed on its cultivation amongst them. I have studied how best to mortify in them the worldly sentiment of pride, and, only the other day, I had a pleasing proof of my success. My second daughter, Augusta, went with her mamma to visit the school, and on her return she exclaimed, "Oh, dear papa, how quiet and plain all the girls at Lowood look; with their hair combed behind their ears, and their long pinafores, and those little holland pockets outside their frocks, they are almost like poor people's children! and," said she, "they looked at my dress and mamma's, as if they had never seen a silk gown before".'

# Jane Eyre

'This is the state of things I quite approve,' returned Mrs Reed. 'Had I sought all England over, I could scarcely have found a system more exactly fitting a child like Jane Eyre. Consistency, my dear Mr Brocklehurst – I advocate consistency in all things.'

'Consistency, madam, is the first of Christian duties, and it has been observed in every arrangement connected with the establishment of Lowood: plain fare, simple attire, unsophisticated accommodations, hardy and active habits: such is the order of the day in the house and its inhabitants.'

'Quite right, sir. I may then depend upon this child being received as a pupil at Lowood, and there being trained in conformity to her position and prospects?'

'Madam, you may: she shall be placed in that nursery of chosen plants, and I trust she will show herself grateful for the inestimable privilege of her election.'

'I will send her, then, as soon as possible, Mr Brocklehurst; for, I assure you, I feel anxious to be relieved of a responsibility that was becoming too irksome.'

'No doubt, no doubt, madam. And now I wish you good-morning. I shall return to Brocklehurst Hall in the course of a week or two; my good friend, the Archdeacon, will not permit me to leave him sooner. I shall send Miss Temple notice that she is to expect a new girl, so that there will be no difficulty about receiving her. Good-bye.'

'Good-bye, Mr Brocklehurst; remember me to Mrs and Miss Brocklehurst, and to Augusta and Theodore, and Master Broughton Brocklehurst.'

'I will, madam. – Little girl, here is a book entitled the *Child's Guide*; read it with prayer, especially that part containing "an account of the awfully sudden death of Martha G—, a naughty child addicted to falsehood and deceit".'

With these words Mr Brocklehurst put into my hand a thin pamphlet, sewn in a cover, and, having rung for his carriage, he departed.

Mrs Reed and I were left alone. Some minutes passed in silence; she was sewing, I was watching her. Mrs Reed might be at that time some six or seven-and-thirty; she was a woman of robust frame, square-shouldered and strong limbed, not tall, and, though stout, not obese; she had a somewhat large face, the under-jaw being much developed and very solid; her brow was low, her chin large and prominent, mouth and nose sufficiently regular; under her light eyebrows glimmered an eye devoid of truth; her skin was dark and opaque, her hair nearly flaxen; her constitution was sound as a bell – illness never came near her; she was an exact, clever manager, her household and tenantry were thoroughly under her control; her children only, at times, defied her authority, and laughed it to scorn; she dressed well, and had a presence and port calculated to set off handsome attire.

Sitting on a low stool, a few yards from her arm-chair, I examined her figure, I perused her features. In my hand I held the tract containing the sudden death of the Liar: to which narrative my attention had been pointed as to an appropriate warning. What had just passed; what Mrs Reed had said concerning me to Mr Brocklehurst; the whole tenor of their conversation, was recent, raw, and stinging in my mind; I had felt every word as acutely as I had heard it plainly, and a passion of resentment fomented now within me.

Mrs Reed looked up from her work: her eyes settled on mine, her fingers at the same time suspended their nimble movements.

'Go out of the room; return to the nursery,' was her mandate. My look or something else must have struck her as offensive, for she spoke with extreme

# Jane Eyre

though suppressed irritation. I got up; I went to the door; I came back again; I walked to the window across the room, then close up to her.

*Speak* I must: I had been trodden on severely, and *must* turn: but how? What strength had I to dart retaliation at my antagonist? I gathered my energies and launched them in this blunt sentence –

'I am not deceitful: if I were, I should say I loved *you*; but I declare I do not love you: I dislike you the worst of anybody in the world except John Reed: and this book about the Liar, you may give to your girl, Georgiana, for it is she who tells lies, and not I.'

Mrs Reed's hands lay still on her work inactive: her eye of ice continued to dwell freezingly on mine.

'What more have you to say?' she asked, rather in the tone in which a person might address an opponent of adult age than such as is ordinarily used to a child.

That eye of hers, that voice, stirred every antipathy I had. Shaking from head to foot, thrilled with ungovernable excitement, I continued –

'I am glad you are no relation of mine. I will never call you aunt again as long as I live. I will never come to see you when I am grown up; and if any one asks me how I liked you, and how you treated me, I will say the very thought of you makes me sick, and that you treated me with miserable cruelty.'

'How dare you affirm that, Jane Eyre?'

'How dare I, Mrs Reed? How dare I? Because it is the *truth*. You think I have no feelings, and that I can do without one bit of love or kindness; but I cannot live so: and you have no pity. I shall remember how you thrust me back – roughly and violently thrust me back – into the red-room, and locked me up there, to my dying day, though I was in agony, though I cried out, while suffocating with distress, "Have mercy! Have mercy, Aunt Reed!" And that punishment you made me suffer because your wicked boy struck me – knocked me down for nothing. I will tell anybody who asks me questions this exact tale. People think you a good woman, but you are bad, hard-hearted. *You* are deceitful!'

Ere I had finished this reply, my soul began to expand, to exult, with the strangest sense of freedom, of triumph, I ever felt. It seemed as if an invisible bond had burst, and that I had struggled out into unhoped-for liberty. Not without cause was this sentiment: Mrs Reed looked frightened: her work had slipped from her knee; she was lifting up her hands, rocking herself to and fro, and even twisting her face as if she would cry.

'Jane, you are under a mistake: what is the matter with you? Why do you tremble so violently? Would you like to drink some water?'

'No, Mrs Reed.'

'Is there anything else you wish for, Jane? I assure you, I desire to be your friend.'

'Not you. You told Mr Brocklehurst I had a bad character, a deceitful disposition; and I'll let everybody at Lowood know what you are, and what you have done.'

'Jane, you don't understand these things: children must be corrected for their faults.'

'Deceit is not my fault!' I cried out in a savage, high voice.

# Jane Eyre

'But you are passionate, Jane, that you must allow; and now return to the nursery – there's a dear – and lie down a little.'

'I am not your dear; I cannot lie down. Send me to school soon, Mrs Reed, for I hate to live here.'

'I will indeed send her to school soon,' murmured Mrs Reed, *sotto voce*; and gathering up her work, she abruptly quitted the apartment.

I was left there alone – winner of the field. It was the hardest battle I had fought, and the first victory I had gained. I stood awhile on the rug, where Mr Brocklehurst had stood, and I enjoyed my conqueror's solitude. First, I smiled to myself and felt elate; but this fierce pleasure subsided in me as fast as did the accelerated throb of my pulses. A child cannot quarrel with its elders, as I had done – cannot give its furious feelings uncontrolled play, as I had given mine – without experiencing afterwards the pang of remorse and the chill of reaction. A ridge of lighted heath, alive, glancing, devouring, would have been a great emblem of my mind when I accused and menaced Mrs Reed; the same ridge, black and blasted after the flames are dead, would have represented as meetly my subsequent condition, when half an hour's silence and reflection had shown me the madness of my conduct, and the dreariness of my hates and hating position.

Something of vengeance I had tasted for the first time. An aromatic wine it seemed, on swallowing, warm and racy; its after-flavour, metallic and corroding, gave me a sensation as if I had been poisoned. Willingly would I now have gone and asked Mrs Reed's pardon; but I knew, partly from experience and partly from instinct, that was the way to make her repulse me with double scorn, thereby re-exciting every turbulent impulse of my nature.

I would fain exercise some better faculty than that of fierce speaking – fain find nourishment for some less fiendish feeling than that of sombre indignation. I took a book – some Arabian tales; I sat down and endeavoured to read. I could make no sense of the subject; my own thoughts swam always between me and the page I had usually found fascinating. I opened the glass-door in the breakfast-room: the shrubbery was quite still: the black frost reigned, unbroken by sun or breeze, through the grounds. I covered my head and arms with the skirt of my frock, and went out to walk in a part of the plantation which was quite sequestered; but I found no pleasure in the silent trees, the falling fir-cones, the congealed relics of autumn, russet leaves, swept by past winds in heaps, and now stiffened together. I leaned against a gate, and looked into an empty field where no sheep were feeding, where the short grass was nipped and blanched. It was a very gray day; a most opaque sky, 'onding on snaw', canopied all; then flakes fell at intervals, which settled on the hard path and on the hoary lea without melting. I stood, a wretched child enough, whispering to myself over and over again, 'What shall I do? – what shall I do?'

All at once I heard a clear voice call, 'Miss Jane, where are you? Come to lunch!'

It was Bessie, I knew well enough; but I did not stir. Her light step came tripping down the path.

'You naughty little thing!' she said. 'Why don't you come when you are called?'

Bessie's presence, compared with the thoughts over which I had been brooding, seemed cheerful, even though, as usual, she was somewhat cross. The fact is,

# Jane Eyre

after my conflict with and victory over Mrs Reed, I was not disposed to care much for the nursemaid's transitory anger; and I *was* disposed to bask in her youthful lightness of heart. I just put my two arms round her, and said, 'Come, Bessie! don't scold!'

The action was more frank and fearless than any I was habituated to indulge in. Somehow, it pleased her.

'You are a strange child, Miss Jane,' she said, as she looked down at me; 'a little roving, solitary thing. And you are going to school, I suppose?'

I nodded.

'And won't you be sorry to leave poor Bessie?'

'What does Bessie care for me? She is always scolding me.'

'Because you're such a queer, frightened, shy little thing. You should be bolder.'

'What! To get more knocks!'

'Nonsense! But you are rather put upon, that's certain. My mother said, when she came to see me last week, that she would not like a little one of her own to be in your place. Now, come in, and I've some good news for you.'

'I don't think you have, Bessie.'

'Child! What do you mean? What sorrowful eyes you fix on me! Well! but missis and the young ladies and Master John are going out to tea this afternoon, and you shall have tea with me. I'll ask cook to bake you a little cake, and then you shall help me to look over your drawers, for I am soon to pack your trunks. Missis intends you to leave Gateshead in a day or two, and you shall choose what toys you like to take with you.'

'Bessie, you must promise not to scold me any more till I go.'

'Well, I will: but mind you are a very good girl, and don't be afraid of me. Don't start when I chance to speak rather sharply: it's so provoking.'

'I don't think I shall ever be afraid of you again, Bessie, because I have got used to you; and I shall soon have another set of people to dread.'

'If you dread them, they'll dislike you.'

'As you do, Bessie?'

'I don't dislike you, miss; I believe I am fonder of you than of all the others.'

'You don't show it.'

'You little sharp thing! you've got quite a new way of talking. What makes you so venturesome and hardy?'

'Why, I shall soon be away from you, and besides –' I was going to say something about what had passed between me and Mrs Reed; but on second thoughts I considered it better to remain silent on that head.

'And so you're glad to leave me?'

'Not at all, Bessie; indeed, just now I am rather sorry.'

'Just now! and rather! How coolly my little lady says it! I dare say now if I were to ask you for a kiss you wouldn't give it me: you'd say you'd *rather* not.'

'I'll kiss you and welcome: bend your head down.' Bessie stooped; we mutually embraced, and I followed her into the house quite comforted. That afternoon lapsed in peace and harmony; and in the evening Bessie told me some of her most enchanting stories, and sang me some of her sweetest songs. Even for me life had its gleams of sunshine.

918

# Chapter 5

Five o'clock had hardly struck on the morning of the nineteenth of January, when Bessie brought a candle into my closet and found me already up and nearly dressed. I had risen half an hour before her entrance, and had washed my face, and put on my clothes by the light of a half-moon just setting, whose rays streamed through the narrow window near my crib. I was to leave Gateshead that day by a coach which passed the lodge gates at six a.m. Bessie was the only person yet risen; she had lit a fire in the nursery, where she now proceeded to make my breakfast. Few children can eat when excited with the thoughts of a journey; nor could I. Bessie, having pressed me in vain to take a few spoonfuls of the boiled milk and bread she had prepared for me, wrapped some biscuits in a paper and put them into my bag; then she helped me on with my pelisse and bonnet, and wrapping herself in a shawl she and I left the nursery. As we passed Mrs Reed's bedroom she said, 'Will you go in and bid missis good-bye?'

'No, Bessie: she came to my crib last night when you were gone down to supper, and said I need not disturb her in the morning, or my cousins either; and she told me to remember that she had always been my best friend, and to speak of her and be grateful to her accordingly.'

'What did you say, miss?'

'Nothing: I covered my face with the bedclothes, and turned from her to the wall.'

'That was wrong, Miss Jane.'

'It was quite right, Bessie: your missis has not been my friend: she has been my foe.'

'Oh, Miss Jane! don't say so!'

'Good-bye to Gateshead!' cried I, as we passed through the hall and went out at the front door.

The moon was set, and it was very dark; Bessie carried a lantern, whose light glanced on wet steps and gravel road sodden by a recent thaw. Raw and chill was the winter morning: my teeth chattered as I hastened down the drive. There was a light in the porter's lodge: when we reached it, we found the porter's wife just kindling her fire: my trunk, which had been carried down the evening before, stood corded at the door. It wanted but a few minutes of six, and shortly after that hour had struck, the distant roll of wheels announced the coming coach; I went to the door and watched its lamps approach rapidly through the gloom.

'Is she going by herself?' asked the porter's wife.

'Yes.'

# Jane Eyre

'And how far is it?'

'Fifty miles.'

'What a long way! I wonder Mrs Reed is not afraid to trust her so far alone.'

The coach drew up; there it was at the gates with its four horses and its top laden with passengers: the guard and coachman loudly urged haste; my trunk was hoisted up; I was taken from Bessie's neck, to which I clung with kisses.

'Be sure and take good care of her,' cried she to the guard, as he lifted me into the inside.

'Ay, ay!' was the answer: the door was slapped to, a voice exclaimed 'All right,' and on we drove. Thus was I severed from Bessie and Gateshead: thus whirled away to unknown, and, as I then deemed, remote and mysterious regions.

I remember but little of the journey; I only know that the day seemed to me of a preternatural length, and that we appeared to travel over hundreds of miles of road. We passed through several towns, and in one, a very large one, the coach stopped; the horses were taken out, and the passengers alighted to dine. I was carried into an inn, where the guard wanted me to have some dinner; but, as I had no appetite, he left me in an immense room with a fireplace at each end, a chandelier pendant from the ceiling, and a little red gallery high up against the wall filled with musical instruments. Here I walked about for a long time, feeling very strange, and mortally apprehensive of someone coming in and kidnapping me; for I believed in kidnappers, their exploits having frequently figured in Bessie's fireside chronicles. At last the guard returned: once more I was stowed away in the coach, my protector mounted his own seat, sounded his hollow horn, and away we rattled over the 'stony street' of L—

The afternoon came on wet and somewhat misty: as it waned into dusk, I began to feel that we were getting very far indeed from Gateshead: we ceased to pass through towns; the country changed; great gray hills heaved up round the horizon: as twilight deepened, we descended a valley, dark with wood, and long after night had overclouded the prospect, I heard a wild wind rushing amongst trees.

Lulled by the sound, I at last dropped asleep: I had not long slumbered when the sudden cessation of motion awoke me; the coach-door was open, and a person like a servant was standing at it: I saw her face and dress by the light of the lamps.

'Is there a little girl called Jane Eyre here?' she asked. I answered 'Yes,' and was then lifted out; my trunk was handed down, and the coach instantly drove away.

I was stiff with long sitting, and bewildered with the noise and motion of the coach: gathering my faculties, I looked about me. Rain, wind, and darkness filled the air; nevertheless, I dimly discerned a wall before me and a door open in it; through this door I passed with my new guide: she shut and locked it behind her. There was now visible a house or houses – for the building spread far – with many windows, and lights burning in some; we went up a broad pebbly path, splashing wet, and were admitted at a door; then the servant led me through a passage into a room with a fire, where she left me alone.

I stood and warmed my numbed fingers over the blaze, then I looked round; there was no candle, but the uncertain light from the hearth showed, by intervals, papered walls, carpets, curtains, shining mahogany furniture: it was a parlour,

# Jane Eyre

not so spacious or splendid as the drawing-room at Gateshead, but comfortable enough. I was puzzling to make out the subject of a picture on the wall, when the door opened, and an individual carrying a light entered; another followed close behind.

The first was a tall lady with dark hair, dark eyes, and a pale and large forehead; her figure was partly enveloped in a shawl, her countenance was grave, her bearing erect.

'The child is very young to be sent alone,' said she, putting her candle down on the table. She considered me attentively for a minute or two, then further added –

'She had better be put to bed soon; she looks tired. Are you tired?' she asked, placing her hand on my shoulder.

'A little, ma'am.'

'And hungry too, no doubt: let her have some supper before she goes to bed, Miss Miller. Is this the first time you have left your parents to come to school, my little girl?'

I explained to her that I had no parents. She inquired how long they had been dead; then how old I was, what was my name, whether I could read, write, and sew a little: then she touched my cheek gently with her forefinger, and saying, 'She hoped I should be a good child,' dismissed me along with Miss Miller.

The lady I had left might be about twenty-nine; the one who went with me appeared some years younger: the first impressed me by her voice, look, and air. Miss Miller was more ordinary; ruddy in complexion, though of a careworn countenance: hurried in gait and action, like one who had always a multiplicity of tasks on hand; she looked, indeed, what I afterwards found she really was, an under-teacher. Led by her, I passed from compartment to compartment, from passage to passage, of a large and irregular building; till, emerging from the total and somewhat dreary silence pervading that portion of the house we had traversed, we came upon the hum of many voices, and presently entered a wide, long room, with great deal tables, two at each end, on each of which burnt a pair of candles, and seated all round on benches, a congregation of girls of every age, from nine or ten to twenty. Seen by the dim light of the dips, their number to me appeared countless, though not in reality exceeding eighty; they were uniformly dressed in brown stuff frocks of quaint fashion, and long holland pinafores. It was the hour of study; they were engaged in conning over their to-morrow's tasks, and the hum I had heard was the combined result of their whispered repetitions.

Miss Miller signed to me to sit on a bench near the door, then walking up to the top of the long room, she cried out, –

'Monitors, collect the lesson-books and put them away!'

Four tall girls arose from different tables, and going round, gathered the books and removed them. Miss Miller again gave the word of command –

'Monitors, fetch the supper-trays!'

The tall girls went out and returned presently, each bearing a tray, with portions of something, I knew not what, arranged thereon, and a pitcher of water and mug in the middle of each tray. The portions were handed round; those who liked took a draught of the water, the mug being common to all. When it came to my turn, I drank, for I was thirsty, but did not touch the food,

# Jane Eyre

excitement and fatigue rendering me incapable of eating: I now saw, however, that it was a thin oaten cake, shared into fragments.

The meal over, prayers were read by Miss Miller, and the classes filed off, two and two, upstairs. Overpowered by this time with weariness, I scarcely noticed what sort of a place the bedroom was; except that, like the schoolroom, I saw it was very long. To-night I was to be Miss Miller's bed-fellow; she helped me to undress: when laid down I glanced at the long row of beds, each of which was quickly filled with two occupants; in ten minutes the single light was extinguished; amidst silence and complete darkness, I fell asleep.

The night passed rapidly: I was too tired even to dream; I only once awoke to hear the wind rave in furious gusts, and the rain fall in torrents, and to be sensible that Miss Miller had taken her place by my side. When I again unclosed my eyes, a loud bell was ringing; the girls were up and dressing; day had not yet begun to dawn, and a rushlight or two burnt in the room. I too rose reluctantly; it was bitter cold, and I dressed as well as I could for shivering, and washed when there was a basin at liberty, which did not occur soon, as there was but one basin to six girls, on the stands down the middle of the room. Again the bell rang: all formed in file, two and two, and in that order descended the stairs and entered the cold and dimly-lit schoolroom: here prayers were read by Miss Miller; afterwards she called out –

'Form classes!'

A great tumult succeeded for some minutes, during which Miss Miller repeatedly exclaimed, 'Silence!' and 'Order!' When it subsided, I saw them all drawn up in four semicircles, before four chairs, placed at the four tables: all held books in their hands, and a great book, like a Bible, lay on each table, before the vacant seat. A pause of some seconds succeeded, filled up by the low, vague hum of numbers; Miss Miller walked from class to class, hushing this indefinite sound.

A distant bell tinkled: immediately three ladies entered the room, each walked to a table and took her seat; Miss Miller assumed the fourth vacant chair, which was that nearest the door, and around which the smallest of the children were assembled: to this inferior class I was called, and placed at the bottom of it.

Business now began: the day's Collect was repeated, then certain texts of Scripture were said, and to these succeeded a protracted reading of chapters in the Bible, which lasted an hour. By the time that exercise was terminated, day had fully dawned. The indefatigable bell now sounded for the fourth time: the classes were marshalled and marched into another room to breakfast. How glad I was to behold a prospect of getting something to eat! I was now nearly sick from inanition, having taken so little the day before.

The refectory was a great, low-ceiled, gloomy room; on two long tables smoked basins of something hot, which, however, to my dismay, sent forth an odour far from inviting. I saw a universal manifestation of discontent when the fumes of the repast met the nostrils of those destined to swallow it; from the van of the procession, the tall girls of the first class, rose the whispered words –

'Disgusting! The porridge is burnt again!'

'Silence!' ejaculated a voice; not that of Miss Miller, but one of the upper teachers, a little dark personage, smartly dressed, but of somewhat morose aspect, who installed herself at the top of one table, while a more buxom lady presided at the other. I looked in vain for her I had first seen the night before; she was

# Jane Eyre

not visible. Miss Miller occupied the foot of the table where I sat; and a strange foreign-looking, elderly lady, the French teacher, as I afterwards found, took the corresponding seat at the other board. A long grace was said, and a hymn sung; then a servant brought in some tea for the teachers, and the meal began.

Ravenous, and now very faint, I devoured a spoonful or two of my portion without thinking of its taste, but the first edge of hunger blunted, I perceived I had got in hand a nauseous mess – burnt porridge is almost as bad as rotten potatoes; famine itself soon sickens over it. The spoons were moved slowly: I saw each girl taste her food and try to swallow it; but in most cases the effort was soon relinquished. Breakfast was over, and none had breakfasted. Thanks having been returned for what we had not got, and a second hymn chanted, the refectory was evacuated for the schoolroom. I was one of the last to go out, and in passing the tables, I saw one teacher take a basin of the porridge and taste it; she looked at the others; all their countenances expressed displeasure, and one of them, the stout one, whispered –

'Abominable stuff! How shameful!'

A quarter of an hour passed before lessons again began, during which the schoolroom was in a glorious tumult; for that space of time, it seemed to be permitted to talk loud and more freely, and they used their privilege. The whole conversation ran on the breakfast, which one and all abused roundly. Poor things! it was the sole consolation they had. Miss Miller was now the only teacher in the room: a group of great girls standing about her, spoke with serious and sullen gestures. I heard the name of Mr Brocklehurst pronounced by some lips, at which Miss Miller shook her head disapprovingly; but she made no great effort to check the general wrath: doubtless she shared in it.

A clock in the schoolroom struck nine: Miss Miller left her circle, and standing in the middle of the room, cried –

'Silence! To your seats!'

Discipline prevailed: in five minutes the confused throng was resolved into order, and comparative silence quelled the Babel clamour of tongues. The upper teachers now punctually resumed their posts: but still, all seemed to wait. Ranged on benches down the sides of the room, the eighty girls sat motionless and erect: a quaint assemblage they appeared, all with plain locks combed from their faces, not a curl visible; in brown dresses, made high, and surrounded by a narrow tucker about the throat, with little pockets of holland (shaped something like a Highlander's purse) tied in front of their frocks, and destined to serve the purpose of a workbag: all, too, wearing woollen stockings and country-made shoes, fastened with brass buckles. Above twenty of those clad in this costume were full-grown girls, or rather young women; it suited them ill, and gave an air of oddity even to the prettiest.

I was still looking at them, and also at intervals examining the teachers – none of whom precisely pleased me; for the stout one was a little coarse, the dark one not a little fierce, the foreigner harsh and grotesque, and Miss Miller, poor thing! looked purple, weather-beaten, and overworked – when, as my eye wandered from face to face, the whole school rose simultaneously, as if moved by a common spring.

What was the matter? I had heard no order given; I was puzzled. Ere I had gathered my wits the classes were again seated, but, as all eyes were now turned to one point, mine followed the general direction, and encountered the personage

# Jane Eyre

who had received me last night. She stood at the bottom of the long room, on the hearth, for there was a fire at each end; she surveyed the two rows of girls silently and gravely. Miss Miller, approaching, seemed to ask her a question, and having received her answer, went back to her place, and said aloud, –

'Monitor of the first class, fetch the globes!'

While the direction was being executed, the lady consulted moved slowly up the room. I suppose I have a considerable organ of veneration, for I retain yet the sense of admiring awe with which my eyes traced her steps. Seen now, in broad daylight, she looked tall, fair, and shapely; brown eyes with a benignant light in their irises, and a fine pencilling of long lashes round, relieved the whiteness of her large front; on each of her temples her hair, of a very dark brown, was clustered in round curls, according to the fashion of those times, when neither smooth bands nor long ringlets were in vogue; her dress, also in the mode of the day, was of purple cloth, relieved by a sort of Spanish trimming of black velvet; a gold watch (watches were not so common then as now) shone at her girdle. Let the reader add, to complete the picture, refined features; a complexion, if pale, clear; and a stately air and carriage, and he will have at least as clearly as words can give it, a correct idea of the exterior of Miss Temple – Maria Temple, as I afterwards saw the name written in a Prayer Book entrusted to me to carry to church.

The superintendent of Lowood (for such was this lady) having taken her seat before a pair of globes placed on one of the tables, summoned the first class round her, and commenced giving a lesson in geography; the lower classes were called by the teachers. Repetitions in history, grammar, &c., went on for an hour; more writing and arithmetic succeeded, and music lessons were given by Miss Temple to some of the elder girls. The duration of each lesson was measured by the clock, which at last struck twelve. The superintendent rose.

'I have a word to address to the pupils,' said she.

The tumult of cessation from lessons was already breaking forth, but it sank at her voice. She went on –

'You had this morning a breakfast which you could not eat; you must be hungry. I have ordered that a lunch of bread and cheese shall be served to all.'

The teachers looked at her with a sort of surprise.

'It is to be done on my responsibility,' she added, in an explanatory tone to them, and immediately afterwards left the room.

The bread and cheese was presently brought in and distributed to the high delight and refreshment of the whole school. The order was now given, 'To the garden!' Each put on a coarse straw bonnet, with strings of coloured calico, and a cloak of gray frieze. I was similarly equipped, and, following the stream, I made my way into the open air.

The garden was a wide enclosure, surrounded with walls so high as to exclude every glimpse of prospect; a covered veranda ran down one side, and broad walks bordered a middle space divided into scores of little beds; these beds were assigned as gardens for the pupils to cultivate, and each bed had an owner. When full of flowers they would doubtless look pretty, but now, at the latter end of January, all was wintry blight and brown decay. I shuddered as I stood and looked round me: it was an inclement day for outdoor exercise – not positively rainy, but darkened by a drizzling yellow fog; all under foot was still soaking wet with the floods of yesterday. The stronger among the girls ran about and

# Jane Eyre

engaged in active games, but sundry pale and thin ones herded together for shelter and warmth in the veranda; and amongst these, as the dense mist penetrated to their shivering frames, I heard frequently the sound of a hollow cough.

As yet I had spoken to no one, nor did anybody seem to take notice of me; I stood lonely enough, but to that feeling of isolation I was accustomed: it did not oppress me much. I leant against a pillar of the veranda, drew my gray mantle close about me, and, trying to forget the cold which nipped me without, and the unsatisfied hunger which gnawed me within, delivered myself up to the employment of watching and thinking. My reflections were too undefined and fragmentary to merit record. I hardly yet knew where I was. Gateshead and my past life seemed floated away to an immeasurable distance. The present was vague and strange, and of the future I could form no conjecture. I looked round the convent-like garden, and then up at the house – a large building, half of which seemed gray and old, the other half quite new. The new part, containing the schoolroom and dormitory, was lit by mullioned and latticed windows, which gave it a church-like aspect. A stone tablet over the door bore this inscription:

'Lowood Institution. – This portion was rebuilt A.D. —, by Naomi Brocklehurst, of Brocklehurst Hall, in this county.' 'Let your light so shine before men that they may see your good works, and glorify your Father which is in Heaven.' – St Matt. v. 16.

I read these words over and over again. I felt that an explanation belonged to them, and was unable fully to penetrate their import. I was still pondering the significance of 'Institution', and endeavouring to make out a connexion between the first words and the verse of Scripture, when the sound of a cough close behind me made me turn my head. I saw a girl sitting on a stone bench near. She was bent over a book, on the perusal of which she seemed intent. From where I stood I could see the title – it was *Rasselas* – a name that struck me as strange, and consequently attractive. In turning a leaf she happened to look up, and I said to her directly –

'Is your book interesting?' I had already formed the intention of asking her to lend it to me some day.

'I like it,' she answered, after a pause of a second or two, during which she examined me.

'What is it about?' I continued. I hardly know where I found the hardihood thus to open a conversation with a stranger. The step was contrary to my nature and habits; but I think her occupation touched a chord of sympathy somewhere, for I, too, liked reading, though of a frivolous and childish kind. I could not digest or comprehend the serious or substantial.

'You may look at it,' replied the girl, offering me the book.

I did so. A brief examination convinced me that the contents were less taking than the title. *Rasselas* looked dull to my trifling taste. I saw nothing about fairies, nothing about genii; no bright variety seemed spread over the closely-printed pages. I returned it to her. She received it quietly, and, without saying anything, she was about to relapse into her former studious mood. Again I ventured to disturb her –

'Can you tell me what the writing on that stone over the door means? What is Lowood Institution?'

'This house where you are come to live.'

# Jane Eyre

'And why do they call it Institution? Is it in any way different from other schools?'

'It is partly a charity-school. You and I, and all the rest of us, are charity-children. I suppose you are an orphan. Are not either your father or your mother dead?'

'Both died before I can remember.'

'Well, all the girls here have lost either one or both parents, and this is called an Institution for educating orphans.'

'Do we pay no money? Do they keep us for nothing?'

'We pay, or our friends pay, fifteen pounds a year for each.'

'Then why do they call us charity-children?'

'Because fifteen pounds is not enough for board and teaching, and the deficiency is supplied by subscription.'

'Who subscribes?'

'Different benevolent-minded ladies and gentlemen in this neighbourhood and in London.'

'Who was Naomi Brocklehurst?'

'The lady who built the new part of this house, as that tablet records, and whose son overlooks and directs everything here.'

'Why?'

'Because he is treasurer and manager of the establishment.'

'Then this house does not belong to that tall lady who wears a watch, and who said we were to have some bread and cheese?'

'To Miss Temple? Oh, no! I wish it did. She has to answer to Mr Brocklehurst for all she does. Mr Brocklehurst buys all our food and all our clothes.'

'Does he live here?'

'No – two miles off, at a large hall.'

'Is he a good man?'

'He is a clergyman, and is said to do a great deal of good.'

'Did you say that tall lady was called Miss Temple?'

'Yes.'

'And what are the other teachers called?'

'The one with red cheeks is called Miss Smith; she attends to the work, and cuts out – for we make our own clothes, our frocks, and pelisses, and everything; the little one with black hair is Miss Scatcherd; she teaches history and grammar, and hears the second class repetitions; and the one who wears a shawl, and has a pocket-handkerchief tied to her side with a yellow riband, is Madame Pierrot; she comes from Lisle, in France, and teaches French.'

'Do you like the teachers?'

'Well enough.'

'Do you like the little black one, and the Madame —? – I cannot pronounce her name as you do.'

'Miss Scatcherd is hasty – you must take care not to offend her; Madame Pierrot is not a bad sort of person.'

'But Miss Temple is the best – isn't she?'

'Miss Temple is very good, and very clever; she is above the rest, because she knows far more than they do.'

'Have you been long here?'

'Two years.'

# Jane Eyre

'Are you an orphan?'

'My mother is dead.'

'Are you happy here?'

'You ask rather too many questions. I have given you answers enough for the present. Now I want to read.'

But at the moment the summons sounded for dinner. All re-entered the house. The odour which now filled the refectory was scarcely more appetizing than that which had regaled our nostrils at breakfast. The dinner was served in two huge tin-plated vessels, whence rose a strong steam redolent of rancid fat. I found the mess to consist of indifferent potatoes and strange shreds of rusty meat, mixed and cooked together. Of this preparation a tolerably abundant plateful was apportioned to each pupil. I ate what I could, and wondered within myself whether every day's fare would be like this.

After dinner, we immediately adjourned to the schoolroom. Lessons recommenced, and were continued till five o'clock.

The only marked event of the afternoon was, that I saw the girl with whom I had conversed in the veranda, dismissed in disgrace, by Miss Scatcherd, from a history class, and sent to stand in the middle of the large schoolroom. The punishment seemed to me in a high degree ignominious, especially for so great a girl – she looked thirteen or upwards. I expected she would show signs of great distress and shame; but to my surprise she neither wept nor blushed. Composed, though grave, she stood, the central mark of all eyes. 'How can she bear it so quietly – so firmly?' I asked of myself. 'Were I in her place, it seems to me I should wish the earth to open and swallow me up. She looks as if she were thinking of something beyond her punishment – beyond her situation: of something not round her nor before her. I have heard of day-dreams – is she in a day-dream now? Her eyes are fixed on the floor, but I am sure they do not see it – her sight seems turned in, gone down into her heart: she is looking at what she can remember, I believe; not at what is really present. I wonder what sort of a girl she is – whether good or naughty.'

Soon after five p.m. we had another meal, consisting of a small mug of coffee, and half a slice of brown bread. I devoured my bread and drank my coffee with relish: but I should have been glad of as much more – I was still hungry. Half an hour's recreation succeeded, then study; then the glass of water and the piece of oatcake, prayers, and bed. Such was my first day at Lowood.

# Chapter 6

he next day commenced as before, getting up and dressing by rush-light; but this morning we were obliged to dispense with the ceremony of washing: the water in the pitchers was frozen. A change had taken place in the weather the preceding evening, and a keen north-east wind, whistling through the crevices of our bedroom windows all night long, had made us shiver in our beds, and turned the contents of the ewers to ice.

Before the long hour and a half of prayers and Bible-reading was over, I felt ready to perish with cold. Breakfast-time came at last, and this morning the porridge was not burnt; the quality was eatable, the quantity small; how small my portion seemed! I wished it had been doubled.

In the course of the day I was enrolled a member of the fourth class, and regular tasks and occupations were assigned me; hitherto, I had only been a spectator of the proceedings at Lowood, I was now to become an actor therein. At first, being little accustomed to learn by heart, the lessons appeared to me both long and difficult: the frequent change from task to task, too, bewildered me; and I was glad, when, about three o'clock in the afternoon, Miss Smith put into my hands a border of muslin two yards long, together with needle, thimble, &c., and sent me to sit in a quiet corner of the schoolroom, with directions to hem the same. At that hour most of the others were sewing likewise; but one class still stood round Miss Scatcherd's chair reading, and as all was quiet, the subject of their lessons could be heard, together with the manner in which each girl acquitted herself, and the animadversions or commendations of Miss Scatcherd on the performance. It was English history: among the readers, I observed my acquaintance of the veranda: at the commencement of the lesson, her place had been at the top of the class, but for some error of pronunciation or some inattention to stops, she was suddenly sent to the very bottom. Even in that obscure position, Miss Scatcherd continued to make her an object of constant notice; she was continually addressing to her such phrases as the following:

'Burns (such it seems was her name: the girls here were all called by their surnames, as boys are elsewhere), Burns, you are standing on the side of your shoe, turn your toes out immediately.' 'Burns, you poke your chin most unpleasantly; draw it in.' 'Burns, I insist on your holding your head up; I will not have you before me in that attitude,' &c., &c.

A chapter having been read through twice, the books were closed and the girls examined. The lesson had comprised part of the reign of Charles I, and there were sundry questions about tonnage, and poundage, and ship-money, which most of them appeared unable to answer; still every little difficulty was solved instantly when it reached Burns: her memory seemed to have retained the

# Jane Eyre

substance of the whole lesson, and she was ready with answers on every point. I kept expecting that Miss Scatcherd would praise her attention; but, instead of that, she suddenly cried out –

'You dirty, disagreeable girl! you have never cleaned your nails this morning!'

Burns made no answer: I wondered at her silence.

'Why,' thought I, 'does she not explain that she could neither clean her nails nor wash her face, as the water was frozen?'

My attention was now called off by Miss Smith desiring me to hold a skein of thread: while she was winding it, she talked to me from time to time, asking whether I had ever been at school before, whether I could mark, stitch, knit, &c.; till she dismissed me, I could not pursue my observations on Miss Scatcherd's movements. When I returned to my seat, that lady was just delivering an order, of which I did not catch the import; but Burns immediately left the class, and going into the small inner room where the books were kept, returned in half a minute, carrying in her hand a bundle of twigs tied together at one end. This ominous tool she presented to Miss Scatcherd with a respectful curtsey; then she quietly and without being told, unloosed her pinafore, and the teacher instantly and sharply inflicted on her neck a dozen strokes with the bunch of twigs. Not a tear rose to Burns's eye; and, while I paused from my sewing, because my fingers quivered at this spectacle with a sentiment of unavailing and impotent anger, not a feature of her pensive face altered its ordinary expression.

'Hardened girl!' exclaimed Miss Scatcherd; 'nothing can correct you of your slatternly habits: carry the rod away.'

Burns obeyed: I looked at her narrowly as she emerged from the book-closet; she was just putting back her handkerchief into her pocket, and the trace of a tear glistened on her thin cheek.

The play-hour in the evening I thought the pleasantest fraction of the day at Lowood: the bit of bread, the draught of coffee swallowed at five o'clock had revived vitality, if it had not satisfied hunger; the long restraint of the day was slackened; the schoolroom felt warmer than in the morning – its fires being allowed to burn a little more brightly to supply, in some measure, the place of candles, not yet introduced: the ruddy gloaming, the licensed uproar, the confusion of many voices gave one a welcome sense of liberty.

On the evening of the day on which I had seen Miss Scatcherd flog her pupil, Burns, I wandered as usual among the forms and tables and laughing groups without a companion, yet not feeling lonely: when I passed the windows I now and then lifted a blind and looked out; it snowed fast, a drift was already forming against the lower panes; putting my ear close to the window, I could distinguish from the gleeful tumult within, the disconsolate moan of the wind outside.

Probably, if I had lately left a good home and kind parents, this would have been the hour when I should most keenly have regretted the separation: that wind would then have saddened my heart: this obscure chaos would have disturbed my peace: as it was, I derived from both a strange excitement, and, reckless and feverish, I wished the wind to howl more wildly, the gloom to deepen to darkness, and the confusion to rise to clamour.

Jumping over forms, and creeping under tables, I made my way to one of the fireplaces; there, kneeling by the high wire fender, I found Burns, absorbed, silent, abstracted from all round her by the companionship of a book, which she read by the dim glare of the embers.

# Jane Eyre

'Is it still *Rasselas?*' I asked, coming behind her.

'Yes,' she said, 'and I have just finished it.'

And in five minutes more she shut it up. I was glad of this.

'Now,' thought I, 'I can perhaps get her to talk.' I sat down by her on the floor.

'What is your name beside Burns?'

'Helen.'

'Do you come a long way from here?'

'I come from a place farther north; quite on the borders of Scotland.'

'Will you ever go back?'

'I hope so; but nobody can be sure of the future.'

'You must wish to leave Lowood?'

'No: why should I? I was sent to Lowood to get an education; and it would be of no use going away until I have attained that object.'

'But that teacher, Miss Scatcherd, is so cruel to you?'

'Cruel? Not at all! She is severe; she dislikes my faults.'

'And if I were in your place I should dislike her; I should resist her; if she struck me with that rod, I should get it from her hand; I should break it under her nose.'

'Probably you would do nothing of the sort: but if you did, Mr Brocklehurst would expel you from the school: that would be a great grief to your relations. It is far better to endure patiently a smart which nobody feels but yourself, than to commit a hasty action whose evil consequences will extend to all connected with you; and, besides, the Bible bids us return good for evil.'

'But then it seems disgraceful to be flogged, and to be sent to stand in the middle of a room full of people; and you are such a great girl: I am far younger than you, and I could not bear it.'

'Yet it would be your duty to bear it, if you could not avoid it: it is weak and silly to say you *cannot bear* what it is your fate to be required to bear.'

I heard her with wonder: I could not comprehend this doctrine of endurance; and still less could I understand or sympathize with the forbearance she expressed for her chastiser. Still I felt that Helen Burns considered things by a light invisible to my eyes. I suspected she might be right and I wrong; but I would not ponder the matter deeply: like Felix, I put it off to a more convenient season.

'You say you have faults, Helen: what are they? To me you seem very good.'

'Then learn from me, not to judge by appearances. I am, as Miss Scatcherd said, slatternly; I seldom put, and never keep, things in order; I am careless; I forget rules; I read when I should learn my lessons; I have no method; and sometimes I say, like you, I cannot *bear* to be subjected to systematic arrangements. This is all very provoking to Miss Scatcherd, who is naturally neat, punctual, and particular.'

'And cross and cruel,' I added; but Helen Burns would not admit my addition: she kept silence.

'Is Miss Temple as severe to you as Miss Scatcherd?'

At the utterance of Miss Temple's name, a soft smile flitted over her grave face.

'Miss Temple is full of goodness: it pains her to be severe to any one, even the worst in the school: she sees my errors, and tells me of them gently; and, if I do anything worthy of praise, she gives me my meed liberally. One strong

# Jane Eyre

proof of my wretchedly defective nature is that even her expostulations, so mild, so rational, have not influence to cure me of my faults; and even her praise, though I value it most highly, cannot stimulate me to continued care and foresight.'

'That is curious,' said I; 'it is so easy to be careful.'

'For *you* I have no doubt it is. I observed you in your class this morning, and saw you were closely attentive: your thoughts never seemed to wander while Miss Miller explained the lesson and questioned you. Now, mine continually rove away: when I should be listening to Miss Scatcherd, and collecting all she says with assiduity, often I lose the very sound of her voice; I fall into a sort of dream. Sometimes I think I am in Northumberland, and that the noises I hear round me are the bubbling of a little brook which runs through Deepden, near our house; – then, when it comes to my turn to reply, I have to be wakened; and, having heard nothing of what was read for listening to the visionary brook, I have no answer ready.'

'Yet how well you replied this afternoon.'

'It was mere chance: the subject on which we had been reading had interested me. This afternoon, instead of dreaming of Deepden, I was wondering how a man who wished to do right could act so unjustly and unwisely as Charles the First sometimes did; and I thought what a pity it was that, with his integrity and conscientiousness, he could see no farther than the prerogatives of the Crown. If he had but been able to look to a distance, and see how what they call the spirit of the age was tending! Still, I like Charles – I respect him – I pity him, poor murdered king! Yes, his enemies were the worst: they shed blood they had no right to shed. How dared they kill him!'

Helen was talking to herself now: she had forgotten I could not very well understand her – that I was ignorant, or nearly so, of the subject she discussed. I recalled her to my level.

'And when Miss Temple teaches you, do your thoughts wander then?'

'No, certainly, not often; because Miss Temple has generally something to say which is newer than my own reflections; her language is singularly agreeable to me, and the information she communicates is often just what I wished to gain.'

'Well, then, with Miss Temple you are good?'

'Yes, in a passive way; I made no effort; I follow as inclination guides me. There is no merit in such goodness.'

'A great deal; you are good to those who are good to you. It is all I ever desire to be. If people were always kind and obedient to those who are cruel and unjust, the wicked people would have it all their own way; they would never feel afraid, and so they would never alter, but would grow worse and worse. When we are struck at without a reason, we should strike back again very hard; I am sure we should – so hard as to teach the person who struck us never to do it again.'

'You will change your mind, I hope, when you grow older; as yet you are but a little untaught girl.'

'But I feel this, Helen: I must dislike those who, whatever I do to please them, persist in disliking me; I must resist those who punish me unjustly. It is as natural as that I should love those who show me affection, or submit to punishment when I feel it is deserved.'

# Jane Eyre

'Heathens and savage tribes hold that doctrine; but Christians and civilized nations disown it.'

'How? I don't understand.'

'It is not violence that best overcomes hate – nor vengeance that most certainly heals injury.'

'What then?'

'Read the New Testament, and observe what Christ says, and how He acts; make His word your rule, and His conduct your example.'

'What does He say?'

'Love your enemies; bless them that curse you; do good to them that hate you and despitefully use you.'

'Then I should love Mrs Reed, which I cannot do: I should bless her son John, which is impossible.'

In her turn, Helen Burns asked me to explain; and I proceeded forthwith to pour out, in my own way, the tale of my sufferings and resentments. Bitter and truculent when excited, I spoke as I felt, without reoerve or softening.

Helen heard me patiently to the end; I expected she would then make a remark, but she said nothing.

'Well,' I asked impatiently, 'is not Mrs Reed a hard-hearted, bad woman?'

'She has been unkind to you, no doubt, because, you see, she dislikes your cast of character, as Miss Scatcherd does mine; but how minutely you remember all she has done and said to you! What a singularly deep impression her injustice seems to have made on your heart! No ill-usage so brands its record on my feelings. Would you not be happier if you tried to forget her severity, together with the passionate emotions it excited? Life appears to me too short to be spent in nursing animosity, or registering wrongs. We are, and must be, one and all, burdened with faults in this world: but the time will soon come when, I trust, we shall put them off in putting off our corruptible bodies; when debasement and sin will fall from us with this cumbrous frame of flesh, and only the spark of the spirit will remain – the impalpable principle of life and thought, pure as when it left the Creator to inspire the creature; whence it came it will return, perhaps again to be communicated to some being higher than man – perhaps to pass through gradations of glory, from the pale human soul to brighten to the seraph! Surely it will never, on the contrary, be suffered to degenerate from man to fiend? No, I cannot believe that: I hold another creed, which no one ever taught me, and which I seldom mention, but in which I delight, and to which I cling, for it extends hope to all; it makes eternity a rest – a mighty home – not a terror and an abyss. Besides, with this creed, I can so clearly distinguish between the criminal and his crime, I can so sincerely forgive the first while I abhor the last; with this creed, revenge never worries my heart, degradation never too deeply disgusts me, injustice never crushes me too low; I live in calm, looking to the end.'

Helen's head, always drooping, sank a little lower as she finished this sentence. I saw by her look she wished no longer to talk to me, but rather to converse with her own thoughts. She was not allowed much time for meditation. A monitor, a great rough girl, presently came up, exclaiming in a strong Cumberland accent –

'Helen Burns, if you don't go and put your drawer in order, and fold up your work this minute, I'll tell Miss Scatcherd to come and look at it!'

Helen sighed as her reverie fled, and getting up, obeyed the monitor without reply as without delay.

# Chapter 7

y first quarter at Lowood seemed an age, and not the golden age either; it comprised an irksome struggle with difficulties in habituating myself to new rules and unwonted tasks. The fear of failure in these points harassed me worse than the physical hardships of my lot, though these were no trifles.

During January, February, and part of March, the deep snows, and after their melting, the almost impassable roads, prevented our stirring beyond the garden walls, except to go to church, but within these limits we had to pass an hour every day in the open air. Our clothing was insufficient to protect us from the severe cold; we had no boots, the snow got into our shoes, and melted there; our ungloved hands became numbed and covered with chilblains, as were our feet. I remember well the distracting irritation I endured from this cause every evening, when my feet inflamed, and the torture of thrusting the swelled, raw, and stiff toes into my shoes in the morning. Then the scanty supply of food was distressing: with the keen appetites of growing children, we had scarcely sufficient to keep alive a delicate invalid. From this deficiency of nourishment resulted an abuse which pressed hardly on the younger pupils: whenever the famished great girls had an opportunity they would coax or menace the little ones out of their portion. Many a time I have shared between two claimants the precious morsel of brown bread distributed at teatime, and after relinquishing to a third half the contents of my mug of coffee, I have swallowed the remainder with an accompaniment of secret tears, forced from me by the exigency of hunger.

Sundays were dreary days in that wintry season. We had to walk two miles to Brocklebridge Church, where our patron officiated. We set out cold, we arrived at church colder: during the morning service we became almost paralysed. It was too far to return to dinner, and an allowance of cold meat and bread, in the same penurious proportion observed in our ordinary meals, was served round between the services.

At the close of the afternoon service we returned by an exposed and hilly road, where the bitter winter wind, blowing over a range of snowy summits to the north, almost flayed the skin from our faces.

I can remember Miss Temple walking lightly and rapidly along our drooping line, her plaid cloak, which the frosty wind fluttered, gathered close about her, and encouraging us, by precept and example, to keep up our spirits, and march forward, as she said, 'like stalwart soldiers'. The other teachers, poor things,

# Jane Eyre

were generally themselves too much dejected to attempt the task of cheering others.

How we longed for the light and heat of a blazing fire when we got back! But, to the little ones at least, this was denied; each hearth in the schoolroom was immediately surrounded by a double row of great girls, and behind them the younger children crouched in groups, wrapping their starved arms in their pinafores.

A little solace came at tea-time, in the shape of a double ration of bread – a whole, instead of a half, slice – with the delicious addition of a thin scrape of butter; it was the hebdomadal treat to which we all looked forward from Sabbath to Sabbath. I generally contrived to reserve a moiety of this bounteous repast for myself: but the remainder I was invariably obliged to part with.

The Sunday evening was spent in repeating, by heart, the Church Catechism, and the fifth, sixth, and seventh chapters of St Matthew; and in listening to a long sermon read by Miss Miller, whose irrepressible yawns attested her weariness. A frequent interlude of these performances was the enactment of the part of Eutychus by some half-dozen of little girls: who, overpowered with sleep, would fall down, if not out of the third loft, yet off the fourth form, and be taken up half dead. The remedy was, to thrust them forward into the centre of the schoolroom, and oblige them to stand there till the sermon was finished. Sometimes their feet failed them, and they sank together in a heap; they were then propped up with the monitor's high stools.

I have not yet alluded to the visits of Mr Brocklehurst; and indeed that gentleman was from home during the greater part of the first month after my arrival, perhaps prolonging his stay with his friend the archdeacon: his absence was a relief to me. I need not say that I had my own reasons for dreading his coming: but come he did at last.

One afternoon (I had then been three weeks at Lowood), as I was sitting with a slate in my hand, puzzling over a sum in long division, my eyes, raised in abstraction to the window, caught sight of a figure just passing. I recognized almost instinctively that gaunt outline; and when, two minutes after, all the school, teachers included, rose *en masse*, it was not necessary for me to look up in order to ascertain whose entrance they thus greeted. A long stride measured the schoolroom, and presently beside Miss Temple, who herself had risen, stood the same black column which had frowned on me so ominously from the hearthrug of Gateshead. I now glanced sideways at this piece of architecture. Yes, I was right: it was Mr Brocklehurst, buttoned up in a surtout, and looking longer, narrower, and more rigid than ever.

I had my own reasons for being dismayed at this apparition: too well I remembered the perfidious hints given by Mrs Reed, about my disposition, &c.; the promise pledged by Mr Brocklehurst to apprise Miss Temple and the teachers of my vicious nature. All along I had been dreading the fulfilment of this promise – I had been looking out daily for the 'Coming Man', whose information respecting my past life and conversation was to brand me as a bad child for ever: now there he was. He stood at Miss Temple's side; he was speaking low in her ear: I did not doubt he was making disclosures of my villainy; and I watched her eye with painful anxiety, expecting every moment to see its dark orb turn on me a glance of repugnance and contempt. I listened

# Jane Eyre

too; and as I happened to be seated quite at the top of the room, I caught most what he said: its import relieved me from immediate apprehension.

'I suppose, Miss Temple, the thread I bought at Lowton will do: it struck me that it would be just of the quality for the calico chemises, and I sorted the needles to match. You may tell Miss Smith that I forgot to make a memorandum of the darning needles, but she shall have some papers sent in next week; and she is not, on any account, to give out more than one at a time to each pupil – if they have more, they are apt to be careless and lose them. And oh, ma'am! I wish the woollen stockings were better looked to! When I was here last, I went into the kitchen-garden and examined the clothes drying on the line; there was a quantity of black hose in a very bad state of repair; from the size of the holes in them I was sure they had not been well mended from time to time.'

He paused.

'Your directions shall be attended to, sir,' said Miss Temple.

'And, ma'am,' he continued, 'the laundress tells me some of the girls have two clean tuckers in a week: it is too much; the rules limit them to one.'

'I think I can explain that circumstance, sir. Agnes and Catherine Johnstone were invited to tea with some friends at Lowton last Thursday, and I gave them leave to put on clean tuckers for the occasion.'

Mr Brocklehurst nodded.

'Well, for once it may pass; but please not to let the circumstance occur too often. And there is another thing which surprised me: I find in settling accounts with the housekeeper, that a lunch, consisting of bread and cheese, has twice been served out to the girls during the past fortnight. How is this? I look over the regulations, and I find no such meal as lunch mentioned. Who introduced this innovation? and by what authority?'

'I must be responsible for the circumstance, sir,' replied Miss Temple: 'the breakfast was so ill-prepared that the pupils could not possibly eat it; and I dared not allow them to remain fasting till dinner-time.'

'Madam, allow me an instant. You are aware that my plan in bringing up these girls is, not to accustom them to habits of luxury and indulgence, but to render them hardy, patient, self-denying. Should any little accidental disappointment of the appetite occur, such as the spoiling of a meal, the under or the over-dressing of a dish, the incident ought not to be neutralized by replacing with something more delicate the comfort lost, thus pampering the body and obviating the aim of this institution; it ought to be improved to the spiritual edification of the pupils, by encouraging them to evince fortitude under the temporary privation. A brief address on those occasions would not be mistimed, wherein a judicious instructor would take the opportunity of referring to the sufferings of the primitive Christians; to the torments of martyrs; to the exhortations of Our Blessed Lord Himself, calling upon His disciples to take up their cross and follow Him; to His warnings that man shall not live by bread alone, but by every word that proceedeth out of the mouth of God; to His divine consolations, "If ye suffer hunger or thirst for My sake, happy are ye." Oh, madam, when you put bread and cheese, instead of burnt porridge, into these children's mouths, you may indeed feed their vile bodies, but you little think how you starve their immortal souls!'

Mr Brocklehurst again paused – perhaps overcome by his feelings. Miss Temple had looked down when he first began to speak to her; but she now

# Jane Eyre

gazed straight before her, and her face, naturally pale as marble, appeared to be assuming also the coldness and fixity of that material; especially her mouth, closed as if it would have required a sculptor's chisel to open it, and her brow settled gradually into petrified severity.

Meantime, Mr Brocklehurst, standing on the hearth with his hands behind his back, majestically surveyed the whole school. Suddenly his eye gave a blink, as if it had met something that either dazzled or shocked its pupil; turning, he said in more rapid accents than he had hitherto used –

'Miss Temple, Miss Temple, what – *what* is that girl with curled hair? Red hair, ma'am, curled – curled all over?' And extending his cane he pointed to the awful object, his hand shaking as he did so.

'It is Julia Severn,' replied Miss Temple very quietly.

'Julia Severn, ma'am! And why has she, or any other, curled hair? Why, in defiance of every precept and principle of this house, does she conform to the world so openly – here in an evangelical, charitable establishment – as to wear her hair one mass of curls?'

'Julia's hair curls naturally,' returned Miss Temple still more quietly.

'Naturally! Yes, but we are not to conform to nature. I wish these girls to be the children of Grace: and why that abundance? I have again and again intimated that I desire the hair to be arranged closely, modestly, plainly. Miss Temple, that girl's hair must be cut off entirely; I will send a barber to-morrow: and I see others who have far too much of the excrescence – that tall girl, tell her to turn round. Tell all the first form to rise up and direct their faces to the wall.'

Miss Temple passed her handkerchief over her lips, as if to smooth away the involuntary smile that curled them; she gave the order, however, and when the first class could take in what was required of them, they obeyed. Leaning a little back on my bench, I could see the looks and grimaces with which they commented on this manoeuvre: it was a pity Mr Brocklehurst could not see them too; he would perhaps have felt that, whatever he might do with the outside of the cup and platter, the inside was farther beyond his interference than he imagined.

He scrutinized the reverse of these living medals some five minutes, then pronounced sentence. These words fell like the knell of doom –

'All these top-knots must be cut off.'

Miss Temple seemed to remonstrate.

'Madam,' he pursued, 'I have a Master to serve whose kingdom is not of this world: my mission is to mortify in these girls the lusts of the flesh, to teach them to clothe themselves with shamefacedness and sobriety, not with braided hair and costly apparel; and each of the young persons before us has a string of hair twisted in plaits which vanity itself might have woven: these, I repeat, must be cut off; think of the time wasted, of —'

Mr Brocklehurst was here interrupted; three other visitors, ladies, now entered the room. They ought to have come a little sooner to have heard his lecture on dress, for they were splendidly attired in velvet, silk, and furs. The two younger of the trio (fine girls of sixteen and seventeen) had gray beaver hats, then in fashion, shaded with ostrich plumes, and from under the brim of this graceful headdress fell a profusion of light tresses, elaborately curled; the elder lady was enveloped in a costly velvet shawl, trimmed with ermine, and she wore a false front of French curls.

These ladies were deferentially received by Miss Temple, as Mrs and the

# Jane Eyre

Misses Brocklehurst, and conducted to seats of honour at the top of the room. It seems they had come in the carriage with their reverend relative, and had been conducting a rummaging scrutiny of the rooms upstairs, while he transacted business with the housekeeper, questioned the laundress, and lectured the superintendent. They now proceeded to address divers remarks and reproofs to Miss Smith, who was charged with the care of the linen and the inspection of the dormitories: but I had no time to listen to what they said, other matters called off and enchained my attention.

Hitherto, while gathering up the discourse of Mr Brocklehurst and Miss Temple, I had not, at the same time, neglected precautions to procure my personal safety, which I thought would be effected, if I only could elude observation. To this end, I had sat well back on the form, and while seeming to be busy with my sum, had held my slate in such a manner as to conceal my face. I might have escaped notice, had not my treacherous slate somehow happened to slip from my hand, and falling with an obtrusive crash, directly drawn every eye upon me; I knew it was all over now, and, as I stooped to pick up the two fragments of slate, I rallied my forces for the worst. It came.

'A careless girl!' said Mr Brocklehurst, and immediately after – 'it is the new pupil, I perceive.' And before I could draw breath, 'I must not forget I have a word to say respecting her.' Then aloud – how loud it seemed to me! 'Let the child who broke her slate come forward!'

Of my own accord, I could not have stirred: I was paralysed; but the two great girls who sat on each side of me set me on my legs and pushed me towards the dread judge, and then Miss Temple gently assisted me to his very feet, and I caught her whispered counsel –

'Don't be afraid, Jane, I saw it was an accident; you shall not be punished.'

The kind whisper went to my heart like a dagger.

'Another minute and she will despise me for a hypocrite,' thought I; and an impulse of fury against Reed, Brocklehurst, and Co. bounded in my pulses at the conviction. I was no Helen Burns.

'Fetch that stool,' said Mr Brocklehurst, pointing to a very high one from which a monitor had just risen: it was brought.

'Place the child upon it.'

And I was placed there, by whom I don't know. I was in no condition to note particulars. I was only aware that they had hoisted me up to the height of Mr Brocklehurst's nose, and that he was within a yard of me, and that a spread of shot orange and purple silk pelisses, and a cloud of silvery plumage extended and waved below me.

Mr Brocklehurst hemmed.

'Ladies,' said he, turning to his family; 'Miss Temple, teachers, and children, you all see this girl?'

Of course they did; for I felt their eyes directed like burning-glasses against my scorched skin.

'You see she is yet young; you observe she possesses the ordinary form of childhood; God has graciously given her the shape that He has given to all of us; no single deformity points her out as a marked character. Who would think that the Evil One had already found a servant and agent in her? Yet such, I grieve to say, is the case.'

A pause – in which I began to study the palsy of my nerves, and to feel that

the Rubicon was passed, and that the trial, no longer to be shirked, must be firmly sustained.

'My dear children,' pursued the black marble clergyman with pathos, 'this is a sad, a melancholy occasion; for it becomes my duty to warn you that this girl, who might be one of God's own lambs, is a little castaway – not a member of the true flock, but evidently an interloper and an alien. You must be on your guard against her; you must shun her example – if necessary, avoid her company, exclude her from your sports, and shut her out from your converse. Teachers, you must watch her; keep your eyes on her movements, weigh well her words, scrutinize her actions, punish her body to save her soul – if, indeed, such salvation be possible, for (my tongue falters while I tell it) this girl, this child, the native of a Christian land, worse than many a little heathen who says its prayers to Brahma and kneels before Juggernaut – this girl is – a liar!'

Now came a pause of ten minutes, during which I – by this time in perfect possession of my wits – observed all the female Brocklehursts produce their pocket-handerkerchiefs and apply them to their optics, while the elderly lady swayed herself to and fro, and the two younger ones whispered, 'How shocking!'

Mr Brocklehurst resumed.

'This I learned from her benefactress – from the pious and charitable lady who adopted her in her orphan state, reared her as her own daughter, and whose kindness, whose generosity the unhappy girl repaid by an ingratitude so bad, so dreadful, that at last her excellent patroness was obliged to separate her from her own young ones, fearful lest her vicious example should contaminate their purity. She has sent her here to be healed, even as the Jews of old sent their diseased to the troubled pool of Bethesda; and, teachers, superintendent, I beg of you not to allow the waters to stagnate round her.'

With this sublime conclusion, Mr Brocklehurst adjusted the top button of his surtout, muttered something to his family, who rose, bowed to Miss Temple, and then all the great people sailed in state from the room. Turning at the door, my judge said –

'Let her stand half an hour longer on that stool, and let no one speak to her during the remainder of the day.'

There was I, then, mounted aloft: I, who had said I could not bear the shame of standing on my natural feet in the middle of the room, was now exposed to general view on a pedestal of infamy. What my sensations were, no language can describe; but, just as they all rose, stifling my breath and constricting my throat, a girl came up and passed me: in passing, she lifted her eyes. What a strange light inspired them! What an extraordinary sensation that ray sent through me! How the new feeling bore me up! It was as if a martyr, a hero, had passed a slave or victim, and imparted strength in the transit. I mastered the rising hysteria, lifted up my head, and took a firm stand on the stool. Helen Burns asked some slight question about her work of Miss Smith, was chidden for the triviality of the inquiry, returned to her place, and smiled at me as she again went by. What a smile! I remember it now, and I know that it was the effluence of fine intellect, of true courage; it lit up her marked lineaments, her thin face, her sunken gray eye, like a reflection from the aspect of an angel. Yet at that moment Helen Burns wore on her arm 'the untidy badge'; scarcely an hour ago I had heard her condemned by Miss Scatcherd to a dinner of bread and water on the morrow, because she had blotted an exercise in copying it out.

Jane Eyre

Such is the imperfect nature of man! Such spots are there on the disc of the clearest planet; and eyes like Miss Scatcherd's can only see these minute defects, and are blind to the full brightness of the orb.

# Chapter 8

Ere the half-hour ended, five o'clock struck; school was dismissed, and all were gone into the refectory to tea. I now ventured to descend: it was deep dusk; I retired into a corner and sat down on the floor. The spell by which I had been so far supported began to dissolve; reaction took place, and soon, so overwhelming was the grief that seized me, I sank prostrate with my face to the ground. Now I wept: Helen Burns was not there; nothing sustained me; left to myself I abandoned myself, and my tears watered the boards. I had meant to be so good, and to do so much at Lowood: to make so many friends, to earn respect, and win affection. Already I had made visible progress: that very morning I had reached the head of my class; Miss Miller had praised me warmly; Miss Temple had smiled approbation; she had promised to teach me drawing, and to let me learn French, if I continued to make similar improvement two months longer: and then I was well received by my fellow-pupils; treated as an equal by those of my own age, and not molested by any; now, here I lay again crushed and trodden on; and could I ever rise more?

'Never,' I thought; and ardently I wished to die. While sobbing out this wish in broken accents, some one approached: I started up – again Helen Burns was near me; the fading fires just showed her coming up the long, vacant room; she brought my coffee and bread.

'Come, eat something,' she said; but I put both away from me, feeling as if a drop or a crumb would have choked me in my present condition. Helen regarded me, probably, with surprise: I could not now abate my agitation, though I tried hard; I continued to weep aloud. She sat down on the ground near me, embraced her knees with her arms, and rested her head upon them; in that attitude she remained silent as an Indian. I was the first who spoke –

'Helen, why do you stay with a girl whom everybody believes to be a liar?'

'Everybody, Jane? Why, there are only eighty people who have heard you called so, and the world contains hundreds of millions.'

'But what have I to do with millions! The eighty I know despise me.'

'Jane, you are mistaken: probably not one in the school either despises or dislikes you; many, I am sure, pity you much.'

'How can they pity me after what Mr Brocklehurst said?'

'Mr Brocklehurst is not a god: nor is he even a great and admired man: he is little liked here; he never took steps to make himself liked. Had he treated you as an especial favourite, you would have found enemies, declared or covert, all

# Jane Eyre

around you; as it is, the greater number would offer you sympathy if they dared. Teachers and pupils may look coldly on you for a day or two, but friendly feelings are concealed in their hearts; and if you persevere in doing well, these feelings will ere long appear so much the more evidently for the temporary suppression. Besides, Jane—' She paused.

'Well, Helen?' said I, putting my hand into hers. She chafed my fingers gently to warm them, and went on –

'If all the world hated you, and believed you wicked, while your own conscience approved you, and absolved you from guilt, you would not be without friends.'

'No; I know I should think well of myself; but that is not enough; if others don't love me, I would rather die than live – I cannot bear to be solitary and hated, Helen. Look here; to gain some real affection from you, or Miss Temple, or any other whom I truly love, I would willingly submit to have the bone of my arm broken, or to let a bull toss me, or to stand behind a kicking horse, and let it dash its hoof at my chest—'

'Hush, Jane! you think too much of the love of human beings; you are too impulsive, too vehement: the sovereign Hand that created your frame, and put life into it, has provided you with other resources than your feeble self, or than creatures feeble as you. Besides this earth, and besides the race of men, there is an invisible world and a kingdom of spirits: that world is round us, for it is everywhere; and those spirits watch us, for they are commissioned to guard us; and if we were dying in pain and shame, if scorn smote us on all sides, and hatred crushed us, angels see our tortures, recognize our innocence (if innocent we be: as I know you are of this charge which Mr Brocklehurst has weakly and pompously repeated at secondhand from Mrs Reed; for I read a sincere nature in your ardent eyes and on your clear front), and God waits only a separation of spirit from flesh to crown us with a full reward. Why, then, should we ever sink overwhelmed with distress, when life is so soon over, and death is so certain an entrance to happiness – to glory?'

I was silent: Helen had calmed me; but in the tranquillity she imparted there was an alloy of inexpressible sadness. I felt the impression of woe as she spoke, but I could not tell whence it came; and when, having done speaking, she breathed a little fast, and coughed a short cough, I momentarily forgot my own sorrows to yield to a vague concern for her.

Resting my head on Helen's shoulder, I put my arms round her waist; she drew me to her, and we reposed in silence. We had not sat long thus, when another person came in. Some heavy clouds, swept from the sky by a rising wind, had left the moon bare; and her light, streaming in through a window near, shone full both on us and on the approaching figure, which we at once recognized as Miss Temple.

'I came on purpose to find you, Jane Eyre,' said she; 'I want you in my room; and as Helen Burns is with you, she may come too.'

We went: following the superintendent's guidance, we had to thread some intricate passages, and mount a staircase before we reached her apartment; it contained a good fire, and looked cheerful. Miss Temple told Helen Burns to be seated in a low arm-chair on one side of the hearth, and herself taking another, she called me to her side.

'Is it all over?' she asked, looking down at my face. 'Have you cried your grief away?'

# Jane Eyre

'I am afraid I never shall do that.'

'Why?'

'Because I have been wrongly accused; and you, ma'am, and everybody else will now think me wicked.'

'We shall think you what you prove yourself to be, my child. Continue to act as a good girl, and you will satisfy us.'

'Shall I, Miss Temple?'

'You will,' said she, passing her arm round me. 'And now tell me who is the lady whom Mr Brocklehurst called your benefactress?'

'Mrs Reed, my uncle's wife. My uncle is dead, and he left me to her care.'

'Did she not, then, adopt you of her own accord?'

'No, ma'am; she was sorry to have to do it: but my uncle, as I have often heard the servants say, got her to promise before he died, that she would always keep me.'

'Well, now, Jane, you know, or at least I will tell you, that when a criminal is accused, he is always allowed to speak in his own defence. You have been charged with falsehood; defend yourself to me as well as you can. Say whatever your memory suggests as true; but add nothing and exaggerate nothing.'

I resolved in the depth of my heart, that I would be most moderate – most correct; and, having reflected a few minutes in order to arrange coherently what I had to say, I told her all the story of my sad childhood. Exhausted by emotion, my language was more subdued than it generally was when it developed that sad theme; and mindful of Helen's warnings against the indulgence of resentment. I infused into the narrative far less of gall and wormwood than ordinary. Thus restrained and simplified, it sounded more credible: I felt as I went on that Miss Temple fully believed me.

In the course of the tale I had mentioned Mr Lloyd as having come to see me after the fit: for I never forgot the, to me, frightful episode of the red-room; in detailing which, my excitement was sure, in some degree, to break bounds; for nothing could soften in my recollection the spasm of agony which clutched my heart when Mrs Reed spurned my wild supplication for pardon, and locked me a second time in the dark and haunted chamber.

I had finished: Miss Temple regarded me a few minutes in silence; she then said –

'I know something of Mr Lloyd; I shall write to him; if his reply agrees with your statement, you shall be publicly cleared from every imputation: to me, Jane, you are clear now.'

She kissed me, and still keeping me at her side (where I was well contented to stand, for I derived a child's pleasure from the contemplation of her face, her dress, her one or two ornaments, her white forehead, her clustered and shining curls, and beaming dark eyes), she proceeded to address Helen Burns.

'How are you to-night, Helen? Have you coughed much to-day?'

'Not quite so much, I think, ma'am.'

'And the pain in your chest?'

'It is a little better.'

Miss Temple got up, took her hand and examined her pulse; then she returned to her own seat; as she resumed it, I heard her sigh low. She was pensive a few minutes, then rousing herself, she said cheerfully –

# Jane Eyre

'But you two are my visitors to-night; I must treat you as such.' She rang her bell.

'Barbara,' she said to the servant who answered it, 'I have not yet had tea; bring the tray, and place cups for these two young ladies.'

And a tray was soon brought. How pretty, to my eyes, did the china cups and bright teapot look, placed on the little round table near the fire! How fragrant was the steam of the beverage, and the scent of the toast! of which, however, I, to my dismay (for I was beginning to be hungry), discerned only a very small portion: Miss Temple discerned it too.

'Barbara,' said she, 'can you not bring a little more bread and butter? There is not enough for three.'

Barbara went out. She returned soon.

'Madam, Mrs Harden says she has sent up the usual quantity.'

Mrs Harden, be it observed, was the housekeeper, a woman after Mr Brocklehurst's own heart, made up of equal parts of whalebone and iron.

'Oh, very well!' returned Miss Temple; 'we must make it do, Barbara, I suppose.' And as the girl withdrew, she added, smiling, 'Fortunately, I have it in my power to supply deficiencies for this once.'

Having invited Helen and me to approach the table, and placed before each of us a cup of tea with one delicious but thin morsel of toast, she got up, unlocked a drawer, and taking from it a parcel wrapped in paper, disclosed presently to our eyes a good-sized seed-cake.

'I meant to give each of you some of this to take with you,' said she; 'but as there is so little toast, you must have it now,' and she proceeded to cut slices with a generous hand.

We feasted that evening as on nectar and ambrosia; and not the least delight of the entertainment was the smile of gratification with which our hostess regarded us, as we satisfied our famished appetites on the delicate fare she liberally supplied. Tea over and the tray removed, she again summoned us to the fire; we sat one on each side of her, and now a conversation followed between her and Helen, which it was indeed a privilege to be admitted to hear.

Miss Temple had always something of serenity in her air, of state in her mien, of refined propriety in her language, which precluded deviation into the ardent, the excited, the eager: something which chastened the pleasure of those who looked on her, and listened to her, by a controlling sense of awe; and such was my feeling now: but as to Helen Burns, I was struck with wonder.

The refreshing meal, the brilliant fire, the presence and kindness of her beloved instructress, or, perhaps, more than all these, something in her own unique mind, had roused her powers within her. They woke, they kindled: first, they glowed in the bright tint of her cheek, which till this hour I had never seen but pale and bloodless; then they shone in the liquid lustre of her eyes, which suddenly acquired a beauty more singular than that of Miss Temple's – a beauty neither of fine colour nor long eyelash, nor pencilled brow, but of meaning, of movement, of radiance. Then her soul sat on her lips, and language flowed, from what source I cannot tell; has a girl of fourteen a heart large enough, vigorous enough to hold the swelling spring of pure, full, fervid eloquence? Such was the characteristic of Helen's discourse on that, to me, memorable evening; her spirit seemed hastening to live within a very brief span as much as many live during a protracted existence.

# Jane Eyre

They conversed of things I had never heard of; of nations and times past; of countries far away; of secrets of nature discovered or guessed at: they spoke of books: how many they had read! What stores of knowledge they possessed! Then they seemed so familiar with French names and French authors: but my amazement reached its climax when Miss Temple asked Helen if she sometimes snatched a moment to recall the Latin her father had taught her, and, taking a book from a shelf, bade her read and construe a page of Virgil; and Helen obeyed, my organ of veneration expanding at every sounding line. She had scarcely finished ere the bell announced bedtime; no delay could be admitted; Miss Temple embraced us both, saying, as she drew us to her heart –

'God bless you, my children!'

Helen she held a little longer than me; she let her go more reluctantly. It was Helen her eye followed to the door; it was for her she a second time breathed a sad sigh; for her she wiped a tear from her cheek.

On reaching the bedroom we heard the voice of Miss Scatcherd: she was examining drawers, she had just pulled out Helen Burns's, and when we entered Helen was greeted with a sharp reprimand, and told that to-morrow she should have half a dozen of untidily folded articles pinned to her shoulder.

'My things were indeed in shameful disorder,' murmured Helen to me, in a low voice. 'I intended to have arranged them, but I forgot.'

Next morning Miss Scatcherd wrote in conspicuous characters on a piece of pasteboard the word 'Slattern', and bound it like a phylactery round Helen's large, mild, intelligent, and benign-looking forehead. She wore it till evening, patient, unresentful, regarding it as a deserved punishment. The moment Miss Scatcherd withdrew, after afternoon school, I ran to Helen, tore it off, and thrust it into the fire. The fury of which she was incapable had been burning in my soul all day, and tears, hot and large, had continually been scalding my cheek; for the spectacle of her sad resignation gave me an intolerable pain at the heart.

About a week subsequently to the incidents above narrated, Miss Temple, who had written to Mr Lloyd, received his answer: it appeared that what he said went to corroborate my account. Miss Temple, having assembled the whole school, announced that inquiry had been made into the charges alleged against Jane Eyre, and that she was most happy to be able to pronounce her completely cleared from every imputation. The teachers then shook hands with me and kissed me, and a murmur of pleasure ran through the ranks of my companions.

Thus relieved of a grievous load, I from that hour set to work afresh, resolved to pioneer my way through every difficulty. I toiled hard, and my success was proportionate to my efforts; my memory, not naturally tenacious, improved with practice; exercise sharpened my wits. In a few weeks I was promoted to a higher class; in less than two months I was allowed to commence French and drawing. I learned the first two tenses of the verb *Etre*, and sketched my first cottage (whose walls, by the way, outrivalled in slope those of the leaning tower of Pisa) on the same day. That night, on going to bed, I forgot to prepare in imagination the Barmecide supper, of hot roast potatoes, or white bread and new milk, with which I was wont to amuse my inward cravings. I feasted instead on the spectacle of ideal drawings, which I saw in the dark – all the work of my own hands; freely pencilled houses and trees, picturesque rocks and ruins, Cuyp-like groups of cattle, sweet paintings of butterflies hovering over unblown roses, of birds picking at ripe cherries, of wrens' nests enclosing pearl-like eggs, wreathed about

with young ivy sprays. I examined, too, in thought, the possibility of my ever being able to translate currently a certain little French story-book which Madame Pierrot had that day shown me; nor was that problem solved to my satisfaction ere I fell sweetly asleep.

Well had Solomon said, 'Better is a dinner of herbs where love is, than a stalled ox and hatred therewith.'

I would not now have exchanged Lowood with all its privations for Gateshead and its daily luxuries.

# Chapter 9

But the privations, or rather the hardships, of Lowood lessened. Spring drew on` - she was indeed already come; the frosts of winter had ceased; its snows were melted, its cutting winds ameliorated. My wretched feet, flayed and swollen to lameness by the sharp air of January, began to heal and subside under the gentler breathings of April; the nights and mornings no longer by their Canadian temperature froze the very blood in our veins; we could now endure the playhour passed in the garden; sometimes on a sunny day it began even to be pleasant and genial, and a greenness grew over those brown beds, which, freshening daily, suggested the thought that Hope traversed them at night, and left each morning brighter traces of her steps. Flowers peeped out among the leaves: snowdrops, crocuses, purple auriculas, and golden-eyed pansies. On Thursday afternoons (half-holidays) we now took walks, and found still sweeter flowers opening by the wayside under the hedges.

I discovered, too, that a great pleasure, an enjoyment which the horizon only bounded, lay all outside the high and spike-guarded walls of our garden: this pleasure consisted in prospect of noble summits girdling a great hill-hollow, rich in verdure and shadow; in a bright beck, full of dark stones and sparkling eddies. How different had this scene looked when I viewed it laid out beneath the iron sky of winter, stiffened in frost, shrouded with snow! - when mists as chill as death wandered to the impulse of east winds along those purple peaks, and rolled down 'ing' and holm till they blended with the frozen fog of the beck! That beck itself was then a torrent, turbid and curbless; it tore asunder the wood, and sent a raving sound through the air, often thickened with wild rain or whirling sleet; and for the forest on its banks, *that* showed only ranks of skeletons.

April advanced to May - a bright serene May it was; days of blue sky, placid sunshine, and soft western or southern gales filled up its duration. And now vegetation matured with vigour; Lowood shook loose its tresses; it became all green, all flowers; its great elm, ash, and oak skeletons were restored to majestic life; woodland plants sprang up profusely in its recesses; unnumbered varieties

# Jane Eyre

of moss filled its hollows, and it made a strange ground-sunshine out of the wealth of its wild primrose plants: I have seen their pale gold gleam in overshadowed spots like scatterings of the sweetest lustre. All this I enjoyed often and fully, free, unwatched, and almost alone: for this unwonted liberty and pleasure there was a cause, to which it now becomes my task to advert.

Have I not described a pleasant site for a dwelling, when I speak of it as bosomed in hill and wood, and rising from the verge of a stream? Assuredly, pleasant enough, but whether healthy or not is another question.

That forest dell, where Lowood lay, was the cradle of fog and fog-bred pestilence; which, quickening with the quickening spring, crept into the Orphan Asylum, breathed typhus through its crowded schoolroom and dormitory, and, ere May arrived, transformed the seminary into a hospital.

Semi-starvation and neglected colds had predisposed most of the pupils to receive infection: forty-five out of the eighty girls lay ill at one time. Classes were broken up, rules relaxed. The few who continued well were allowed almost unlimited licence; because the medical attendant insisted on the necessity of frequent exercise to keep them in health: and had it been otherwise, no one had leisure to watch or restrain them. Miss Temple's whole attention was absorbed by the patients: she lived in the sick-room, never quitting it except to snatch a few hours' rest at night. The teachers were fully occupied with packing up and making other necessary preparations for the departure of those girls who were fortunate enough to have friends and relations able and willing to remove them from the seat of contagion. Many, already smitten, went home only to die: some died at the school, and were buried quietly and quickly, the nature of the malady forbidding delay.

While disease had thus become an inhabitant of Lowood, and death its frequent visitor; while there was gloom and fear within its walls; while its rooms and passages steamed with hospital smells, the drug and the pastille striving vainly to overcome the effluvia of mortality, that bright May shone unclouded over the bold hills and beautiful woodland out of doors. Its garden, too, glowed with flowers: hollyhocks had sprung up tall as trees, lilies had opened, tulips and roses were in bloom; the borders of the little beds were gay with pink thrift and crimson double daisies; the sweetbriars gave out, morning and evening, their scent of spice and apples; and these fragrant treasures were all useless for most of the inmates of Lowood, except to furnish now and then a handful of herbs and blossoms to put on a coffin.

But I, and the rest who continued well, enjoyed fully the beauties of the scene and season: they let us ramble in the wood like gipsies, from morning till night; we did what we liked, went where we liked: we lived better too. Mr Brocklehurst and his family never came near Lowood now: household matters were not scrutinized into; the cross housekeeper was gone, driven away by the fear of infection; her successor, who had been matron at the Lowton Dispensary, unused to the ways of her new abode, provided with comparative liberality. Besides, there were fewer to feed: the sick could eat little; our breakfast basins were better filled: when there was no time to prepare a regular dinner, which often happened, she would give us a large piece of cold pie, or a thick slice of bread and cheese, and this we carried away with us to the wood, where we each chose the spot we liked best, and dined sumptuously.

My favourite seat was a smooth and broad stone, rising white and dry from

# Jane Eyre

the very middle of the beck, and only to be got at by wading through the water; a feat I accomplished barefoot. The stone was just broad enough to accommodate, comfortably, another girl and me, at that time my chosen comrade – one Mary Ann Wilson, a shrewd, observant personage, whose society I took pleasure in, partly because she was witty and original, and partly because she had a manner which set me at my ease. Some years older than I, she knew more of the world, and could tell me many things I liked to hear: with her my curiosity found gratification: to my faults also she gave ample indulgence, never imposing curb or rein on anything I said. She had a turn for narrative, I for analysis; she liked to inform, I to question; so we got on swimmingly together, deriving much entertainment, if not much improvement, from our mutual intercourse.

And where, meantime, was Helen Burns? Why did I not spend these sweet days of liberty with her? Had I forgotten her? or was I so worthless as to have grown tired of her pure society? Surely the Mary Ann Wilson I have mentioned was inferior to my first acquaintance: she could only tell me amusing stories, and reciprocate any racy and pungent gossip I chose to indulge in; while, if I have spoken truth of Helen, she was qualified to give those who enjoyed the privilege of her converse, a taste of far higher things.

True, reader, and I knew and felt this; and though I am a defective being, with many faults and few redeeming points, yet I never tired of Helen Burns, nor ever ceased to cherish for her a sentiment of attachment, as strong, tender, and respectful as any that ever animated my heart. How could it be otherwise, when Helen, at all times and under all circumstances, evinced for me a quiet and faithful friendship, which ill-humour never soured, nor irritation ever troubled? But Helen was ill at present: for some weeks she had been removed from my sight to I knew not what room upstairs. She was not, I was told, in the hospital portion of the house with the fever patients, for her complaint was consumption, not typhus; and by consumption I, in my ignorance, understood something mild, which time and care would be sure to alleviate.

I was confirmed in this idea by the fact of her once or twice coming downstairs on very warm sunny afternoons, and being taken by Miss Temple into the garden: but, on these occasions, I was not allowed to go and speak to her; I only saw her from the schoolroom window, and then not distinctly, for she was much wrapped up, and sat at a distance under the veranda.

One evening, in the beginning of June, I had stayed out very late with Mary Ann in the wood; we had, as usual, separated ourselves from the others, and had wandered far: so far that we lost our way, and had to ask it at a lonely cottage, where a man and woman lived, who looked after a herd of half-wild swine that fed on the mast in the wood. When we got back, it was after moonrise: a pony, which we knew to be the surgeon's, was standing at the garden door. Mary Ann remarked that she supposed some one must be very ill, as Mr Bates had been sent for at that time of the evening. She went into the house; I stayed behind a few minutes to plant in my garden a handful of roots I had dug up in the forest, and which I feared would wither if I left them till the morning. This done I lingered yet a little longer; the flowers smelt so sweet as the dew fell; it was such a pleasant evening, so serene, so warm; the still glowing west promised so fairly another fine day on the morrow; the moon rose with such majesty in the grave east. I was noting these things and enjoying them as a child might, when it entered my mind as it had never done before –

# Jane Eyre

'How sad to be lying now on a sick-bed, and to be in danger of dying! This world is pleasant – it would be dreary to be called from it, and to have to go, who knows where?'

And then my mind made its first earnest effort to comprehend what had been infused into it concerning heaven and hell: and for the first time it recoiled baffled; and for the first time glancing behind, on each side, and before it, it saw all round an unfathomed gulf: it felt the one point where it stood – the present; all the rest was formless cloud and vacant depth; and it shuddered at the thought of tottering, and plunging amid that chaos. While pondering this new idea, I heard the front door open; Mr Bates came out, and with him was a nurse. After she had seen him mount his horse and depart, she was about to close the door, but I ran up to her.

'How is Helen Burns?'

'Very poorly,' was the answer.

'Is it her Mr Bates has been to see?'

'Yes.'

'And what does he say about her?'

'He says she'll not be here long.'

This phrase, uttered in my hearing yesterday, would have only conveyed the notion that she was about to be removed to Northumberland, to her own home. I should not have suspected that it meant she was dying; but I knew instantly now; it opened clear on my comprehension that Helen Burns was numbering her last days in this world, and that she was going to be taken to the region of spirits, if such region there were. I experienced a shock of horror, then a strong thrill of grief, then a desire – a necessity to see her; and I asked in what room she lay.

'She is in Miss Temple's room,' said the nurse.

'May I go up and speak to her?'

'Oh, no, child! It is not likely; and now it is time for you to come in; you'll catch the fever if you stop out when the dew is falling.'

The nurse closed the front door; I went in by the side entrance which led to the schoolroom: I was just in time; it was nine o'clock, and Miss Miller was calling the pupils to go to bed.

It might be two hours later, probably near eleven, when I – not having been able to fall asleep, and deeming, from the perfect silence of the dormitory, that my companions were all wrapt in profound repose – rose softly, put on my frock over my nightdress, and, without shoes, crept from the apartment, and set off in quest of Miss Temple's room. It was quite at the other end of the house; but I knew my way, and the light of the unclouded summer moon, entering here and there at passage windows, enabled me to find it without difficulty. An odour of camphor and burnt vinegar warned me when I came near the fever-room: and I passed its door quickly, fearful lest the nurse who sat up all night should hear me. I dreaded being discovered and sent back; for I *must* see Helen – I must embrace her before she died – I must give her one last kiss, exchange with her one last word.

Having descended a staircase, traversed a portion of the house below, and succeeded in opening and shutting, without noise, two doors, I reached another flight of steps; these I mounted, and then just opposite to me was Miss Temple's room. A light shone through the keyhole, and from under the door; a profound

# Jane Eyre

stillness pervaded the vicinity. Coming near, I found the door slightly ajar; probably to admit some fresh air into the close abode of sickness. Indisposed to hesitate, and full of impatient impulses – soul and senses quivering with keen throes – I put it back and looked in. My eye sought Helen, and feared to find death.

Close by Miss Temple's bed, and half covered with its white curtains, there stood a little crib. I saw the outline of a form under the clothes, but the face was hid by the hangings; the nurse I had spoken to in the garden sat in an easy-chair, asleep; an unsnuffed candle burnt dimly on the table. Miss Temple was not to be seen: I knew afterwards that she had been called to a delirious patient in the fever-room. I advanced: then paused by the crib side: my hand was on the curtain, but I preferred speaking before I withdrew it. I still recoiled at the dread of seeing a corpse.

'Helen!' I whispered softly; 'are you awake?'

She stirred herself, put back the curtain, and I saw her face, pale, wasted, but quite composed; she looked so little changed, that my fear was instantly dissipated.

'Can it be you, Jane?' she asked, in her own gentle voice.

'Oh!' I thought, 'she is not going to die; they are mistaken; she could not speak and look so calmly if she were.'

I got on to her crib and kissed her: her forehead was cold, and her cheek both cold and thin, and so were her hand and wrist: but she smiled as of old.

'Why are you come here, Jane? It is past eleven o'clock: I heard it strike some minutes since.'

'I came to see you, Helen: I heard you were very ill, and I could not sleep till I had spoken to you.'

'You came to bid me good-bye, then: you are just in time probably.'

'Are you going somewhere, Helen? Are you going home?'

'Yes; to my long home – my last home.'

'No, no, Helen!' I stopped distressed. While I tried to devour my tears, a fit of coughing seized Helen; it did not, however, wake the nurse. When it was over, she lay some minutes exhausted; then she whispered –

'Jane, your little feet are bare; lie down and cover yourself with my quilt.'

I did so: she put her arm over me, and I nestled close to her. After a long silence, she resumed, still whispering –

'I am very happy, Jane; and when you hear that I am dead, you must be sure and not grieve: there is nothing to grieve about. We all must die one day, and the illness which is removing me is not painful; it is gentle and gradual; my mind is at rest. I leave no one to regret me much: I have only a father, and he is lately married, and will not miss me. By dying young, I shall escape great sufferings. I had not qualities or talents to make my way very well in the world: I should have been continually at fault.'

'But where are you going to, Helen? Can you see? Do you know?'

'I believe; I have faith: I am going to God.'

'Where is God? What is God?'

'My Maker and yours, who will never destroy what He created. I rely implicitly on His power, and confide wholly in His goodness: I count the hours till that eventful one arrives which shall restore me to Him, reveal Him to me.'

'You are sure, then, Helen, that there is such a place as heaven; and that our souls can get to it when we die?'

948

# Jane Eyre

'I am sure there is a future state; I believe God is good; I can resign my immortal part to Him without any misgiving. God is my father; God is my friend; I love Him; I believe He loves me.'

'And shall I see you again, Helen, when I die?'

'You will come to the same region of happiness: be received by the same mighty universal Parent, no doubt, dear Jane.'

Again I questioned; but this time only in thought. 'Where is that region? Does it exist?' And I clasped my arms closer round Helen; she seemed dearer to me than ever; I felt as if I could not let her go; I lay with my face hidden on her neck. Presently she said in the sweetest tone –

'How comfortable I am! The last fit of coughing has tired me a little; I feel as if I could sleep; but don't leave me, Jane; I like to have you near me.'

'I'll stay with you, *dear* Helen: no one shall take me away.'

'Are you warm, darling?'

'Yes.'

'Good-night, Jane.'

'Good-night, Helen.'

She kissed me, and I her, and we both soon slumbered.

When I awoke it was day: an unusual movement roused me; I looked up; I was in somebody's arms; the nurse held me; she was carrying me through the passage back to the dormitory. I was not reprimanded for leaving my bed; people had something else to think about; no explanation was afforded then to my many questions; but a day or two afterwards I learned that Miss Temple, on returning to her own room at dawn, had found me laid in a little crib; my face against Helen Burns's shoulder, my arms round her neck. I was asleep, and Helen was – dead.

Her grave is in Brocklebridge Churchyard: for fifteen years after her death it was only covered by a grassy mound; but now a gray marble tablet marks the spot, inscribed with her name, and the word '*Resurgam*'.

# Chapter 10

itherto I have recorded in detail the events of my insignificant existence: to the first ten years of my life I have given almost as many chapters. But this is not to be a regular autobiography: I am only bound to invoke memory where I know her reponses will possess some degree of interest; therefore I now pass a space of eight years almost in silence: a few lines only are necessary to keep up the links of connection.

When the typhus fever had fulfilled its mission of devastation at Lowood, it gradually disappeared from thence; but not till its virulence and the number of its victims had drawn public attention on the school. Inquiry was made into the

# Jane Eyre

origin of the scourge, and by degrees various facts came out which excited public indignation in a high degree. The unhealthy nature of the site; the quantity and quality of the children's food; the brackish, fetid water used in its preparation; the pupil's wretched clothing and accommodations – all these things were discovered; and the discovery produced a result mortifying to Mr Brocklehurst, but beneficial to the institution.

Several wealthy and benevolent individuals in the county subscribed largely for the erection of a more convenient building in a better situation; new regulations were made; improvements in diet and clothing introduced; the funds of the school were entrusted to the management of a committee. Mr Brocklehurst, who, from his wealth and family connections, could not be overlooked, still retained the post of treasurer; but he was aided in the discharge of his duties by gentlemen of rather more enlarged and sympathizing minds: his office of inspector, too, was shared by those who knew how to combine reason with strictness, comfort with economy, compassion with uprightness. The school, thus improved, became in time a truly useful and noble institution. I remained an inmate of its walls, after its regeneration, for eight years – six as pupil, and two as teacher; and in both capacities I bear my testimony to its value and importance.

During these eight years my life was uniform, but not unhappy, because it was not inactive. I had the means of an excellent education placed within my reach; a fondness for some of my studies, and a desire to excel in all, together with a great delight in pleasing my teachers, especially such as I loved, urged me on. I availed myself fully of the advantages offered me. In time I rose to be the first girl of the first class; then I was invested with the office of teacher; which I discharged with zeal for two years; but at the end of that time I altered.

Miss Temple, through all changes, had thus far continued superintendent to the seminary; to her instruction I owed the best part of my acquirements; her friendship and society had been my continual solace; she had stood me in the stead of mother, governess, and, latterly, companion. At this period she married, removed with her husband (a clergyman, an excellent man, almost worthy of such a wife), to a distant county, and consequently was lost to me.

From the day she left I was no longer the same: with her was gone every settled feeling, every association that had made Lowood in some degree a home to me. I had imbibed from her something of her nature and much of her habits; more harmonious thoughts; what seemed better regulated feelings had become the inmates of my mind. I had given in allegiance to duty and order; I was quiet; I believed I was content; to the eyes of others, usually even to my own, I appeared a disciplined and subdued character.

But destiny, in the shape of the Rev. Mr Nasmyth, came between me and Miss Temple: I saw her in her travelling dress step into a post-chaise, shortly after the marriage ceremony. I watched the chaise mount the hill and disappear beyond its brow; and then retired to my own room, and there spent in solitude the greatest part of the half-holiday granted in honour of the occasion.

I walked about the chamber most of the time. I imagined myself only to be regretting my loss, and thinking how to repair it; but when my reflections were concluded, and I looked up and found that the afternoon was gone, and evening far advanced, another discovery dawned on me – namely, that in the interval I had undergone a transforming process; that my mind had put off all it had borrowed of Miss Temple – or rather, that she had taken with her the serene

# Jane Eyre

atmosphere I had been breathing in her vicinity – and that now I was left in my natural element, and beginning to feel the stirring of old emotions. It did not seem as if a prop were withdrawn, but rather as if a motive had gone: it was not the power to be tranquil which had failed me, but the reason for tranquillity was no more. My world had for some years been in Lowood: my experience had been of its rules and systems; now I remembered that the real world was wide, and that a varied field of hopes and fears, of sensations and excitements, awaited those who had courage to go forth into its expanse, to seek real knowledge of life amidst its perils.

I went to my window, opened it, and looked out. There were the two wings of the building; there was the garden; there were the skirts of Lowood; there was the hilly horizon. My eye passed all other objects to rest on those most remote, the blue peaks. It was those I longed to surmount; all within their boundary of rock and heath seemed prison-ground, exile limits. I traced the white road winding round the base of one mountain, and vanishing in a gorge between two. How I longed to follow it farther! I recalled the time when I had travelled that very road in a coach: I remembered descending that hill at twilight. An age seemed to have elapsed since the day which brought me first to Lowood, and I have never quitted it since. My vacations had all been spent at school. Mrs Reed had never sent for me to Gateshead; neither she nor any of her family had ever been to visit me. I had had no communication by letter, or message with the outer world. School rules, school duties, school habits and notions, and voices, and faces, and phrases, and costumes, and preferences, and antipathies: such was what I knew of existence. And now I felt that it was not enough. I tired of the routine of eight years in one afternoon. I desired liberty; for liberty I gasped; for liberty I uttered a prayer; it seemed scattered on the wind then faintly blowing. I abandoned it and framed a humbler supplication. For change, stimulus. That petition, too, seemed swept off into vague space. 'Then,' I cried, half desperate, 'grant me at least a new servitude!'

Here a bell, ringing the hour of supper, called me downstairs.

I was not free to resume the interrupted chain of my reflections till bedtime; even then a teacher who occupied the same room with me kept me from the subject to which I longed to recur, by a prolonged effusion of small talk. How I wished sleep would silence her! It seemed as if, could I but go back to the idea which had last entered my mind as I stood at the window, some inventive suggestion would rise for my relief.

Miss Gryce snored at last. She was a heavy Welsh woman, and till now her habitual nasal strains had never been regarded by me in any other light than as a nuisance. To-night I hailed the first deep notes with satisfaction. I was debarrassed of interruption; my half-effaced thought instantly revived.

A new servitude! There is something in that,' I soliloquized (mentally, be it understood; I did not talk aloud). 'I know there is, because it does not sound too sweet. It is not like such words as Liberty, Excitement, Enjoyment: delightful sounds truly, but no more than sounds for me, and so hollow and fleeting that it is mere waste of time to listen to them. But Servitude! That must be a matter of fact. Any one may serve. I have served here eight years; now all I want is to serve elsewhere. Can I not get so much of my own will! Is not the thing feasible! Yes – yes – the end is not so difficult, if I had only a brain active enough to ferret out the means of attaining it.'

# Jane Eyre

I sat up in bed by way of arousing this said brain. It was a chilly night; I covered my shoulders with a shawl, and then I proceeded to *think* again with all my might.

'What do I want? A new place, in a new house, amongst new faces, under new circumstances. I want this because it is of no use wanting anything better. How do people do to get a new place? They apply to friends, I suppose. I have no friends. There are many others who have no friends, who must look about for themselves and be their own helpers; and what is their resource?'

I could not tell: nothing answered me. I then ordered my brain to find a response, and quickly. It worked and worked faster. I felt the pulses throb in my head and temples; but for nearly an hour it worked in chaos, and no result came of its efforts. Feverish, with vain labour, I got up and took a turn in the room, undrew the curtain, noted a star or two, shivered with cold, and again crept to bed.

A kind fairy in my absence had surely dropped the required suggestion on my pillow, for as I lay down it came quietly and naturally to my mind: 'Those who want situations advertise: you must advertise in the —*shire Herald.*'

'How? I know nothing about advertising.'

Replies rose smooth and prompt now –

'You must enclose the advertisement and the money to pay for it under a cover directed to the editor of the *Herald*. You must put it, the first opportunity you have, into the post at Lowton. Answers must be addressed to J.E. at the post office there. You can go and inquire, in about a week after you send the letter, if any are come, and act accordingly.'

This scheme I went over twice, thrice; it was then digested in my mind: I had it in a clear, practical form: I felt satisfied, and fell asleep.

With earliest day, I was up; I had my advertisement written, enclosed, and directed before the bell rang to rouse the school; it ran thus –

'A young lady accustomed to tuition' (had I not been a teacher two years?) 'is desirous of meeting with a situation in a private family where the children are under fourteen.' (I thought that as I was barely eighteen, it would not do to undertake the guidance of pupils nearer my own age.) 'She is qualified to teach the usual branches of a good English education, together with French, Drawing, and Music' (in those days, reader, this now narrow catalogue of accomplishments would have been held tolerably comprehensive). 'Address J.E., Post Office, Lowton, —shire.'

This document remained locked in my drawer all day. After tea, I asked leave of the new superintendent to go to Lowton, in order to perform some small commissions for myself and one or two of my fellow-teachers; permission was readily granted; I went. It was a walk of two miles, and the evening was wet, but the days were still long; I visited a shop or two, slipped the letter into the post office, and came back through heavy rain, with streaming garments, but with a relieved heart.

The succeeding week seemed long: it came to an end at last, however, like all sublunary things, and once more, towards the close of a pleasant autumn day, I found myself afoot on the road to Lowton. A picturesque track it was, by the way; lying along the side of the beck and through the sweetest curves of the dale; but that day I thought more of the letters, that might or might not be awaiting me at the little burgh whither I was bound, than of the charms of lea and water.

# Jane Eyre

My ostensible errand on this occasion was to get measured for a pair of shoes; so I discharged that business first, and when it was done I stepped across the clean and quiet little street from the shoemaker's to the post office: it was kept by an old dame, who wore horn spectacles on her nose, and black mittens on her hands.

'Are there any letters for J.E.?' I asked.

She peered at me over her spectacles, and then she opened a drawer and fumbled among its contents for a long time, so long that my hopes began to falter. At last, having held a document before her glasses for nearly five minutes, she presented it across the counter, accompanying the act by another inquisitive and mistrustful glance – it was for J.E.

'Is there only one?' I demanded.

'There are no more,' said she; and I put it in my pocket and turned my face homeward: I could not open it then; rules obliged me to be back by eight, and it was already half-past seven.

Various duties awaited me on my arrival. I had to sit with the girls during their hour of study; then it was my turn to read prayers; to see them to bed; afterwards I supped with the other teachers. Even when we finally retired for the night, the inevitable Miss Gryce was still my companion: we had only a short end of candle in our candlestick, and I dreaded lest she should talk till it was all burnt out; fortunately, however, the heavy supper she had eaten produced a soporific effect: she was already snoring, before I had finished undressing. There still remained an inch of candle: I now took out my letter; the seal was an initial F.; I broke it; the contents were brief.

'If J.E. who advertised in the —*shire Herald* of last Thursday, possess the acquirements mentioned; and if she is in a position to give satisfactory references as to character and competency; a situation can be offered her where there is but one pupil, a little girl, under ten years of age; and where the salary is thirty pounds per annum. J.E. is requested to send references, name, and address, and all particulars to the direction: "Mrs Fairfax, Thornfield, near Millcote, —shire."'

I examined the document long: the writing was old-fashioned and rather uncertain, like that of an elderly lady. This circumstance was satisfactory: a private fear had haunted me, that in thus acting for myself, and by my own guidance, I ran the risk of getting into some scrape; and above all things, I wished the result of my endeavours to be respectable, proper, *en règle*. I now felt that an elderly lady was no bad ingredient in the business I had on hand. Mrs Fairfax! I saw her in a black gown and widow's cap; frigid perhaps, but not uncivil: a model of elderly English respectability. Thornfield! that, doubtless, was the name of her house: a neat orderly spot, I was sure; though I failed in my efforts to conceive a correct plan of the premises. Millcote, —shire; I brushed up my recollections of the map of England; yes, I saw it; both the shire and the town. —shire was seventy miles nearer London than the remote county where I now resided: that was a recommendation to me. I longed to go where there was life and movement. Millcote was a large manufacturing town on the banks of the A—; a busy place enough, doubtless; so much the better; it would be a complete change at least. Not that my fancy was much captivated by the idea of the long chimneys and clouds of smoke – 'but,' I argued, 'Thornfield will, probably, be a good way from the town.'

# Jane Eyre

Here the socket of the candle dropped, and the wick went out.

Next day new steps were to be taken: my plans could no longer be confined to my own breast; I must impart them in order to achieve their success. Having sought and obtained an audience of the superintendent, during the noontide recreation, I told her I had a prospect of getting a new situation where the salary would be double what I now received (for at Lowood I only got fifteen pounds per annum); and requested she would break the matter for me to Mr Brocklehurst, or some of the committee, and ascertain whether they would permit me to mention them as references. She obligingly consented to act as mediatrix in the matter. The next day she laid the affair before Mr Brocklehurst, who said that Mrs Reed must be written to, as she was my natural guardian. A note was accordingly addressed to that lady, who returned for answer, that 'I might do as I pleased: she had long relinquished all interference in my affairs.' This note went the round of the committee, and at last, after what appeared to me most tedious delay, formal leave was given me to better my condition if I could; and an assurance added, that as I had always conducted myself well, both as teacher and pupil, at Lowood, a testimonial of character and capacity, signed by the inspectors of that institution, should forthwith be furnished me.

This testimonial I accordingly received in about a month, forwarded a copy of it to Mrs Fairfax, and got that lady's reply, stating that she was satisfied, and fixing that day fortnight as the period for my assuming the post of governess in her house.

I now busied myself in preparations: the fortnight passed rapidly. I had not a very large wardrobe, though it was adequate to my wants; and the last day sufficed to pack my trunk – the same I had brought with me eight years ago from Gateshead.

The box was corded, the card nailed on. In half an hour the carrier was to call for it to take it to Lowton, whither I myself was to repair at an early hour the next morning to meet the coach. I had brushed my black stuff travelling-dress, prepared my bonnet, gloves, and muff; sought in all my drawers to see that no article was left behind; and now, having nothing more to do, I sat down and tried to rest. I could not; though I had been on foot all day, I could not now repose an instant; I was too much excited. A phase of my life was closing to-night, a new one opening to-morrow: impossible to slumber in the interval; I must watch feverishly while the change was being accomplished.

'Miss,' said the servant who met me in the lobby, where I was wandering like a troubled spirit, 'a person below wishes to see you.'

'The carrier, no doubt,' I thought, and ran downstairs without inquiry. I was passing the back-parlour, or teacher's sitting-room, the door of which was half open, to go to the kitchen, when some one ran out –

'It's her, I am sure! – I could have told her anywhere!' cried the individual, who stopped my progress and took my hand.

I looked: I saw a woman attired like a well-dressed servant, matronly yet still young; very good-looking, with black hair and eyes, and lively complexion.

'Well, who is it?' she asked, in a voice and with a smile I half recognized; 'you've not forgotten me, I think, Miss Jane?'

In another second I was embracing and kissing her rapturously: 'Bessie! Bessie! Bessie!' that was all I said; whereat she half laughed, half cried, and we

# Jane Eyre

both went into the parlour. By the fire stood a little fellow of three years old, in plaid frock and trousers.

'That is my little boy,' said Bessie directly.

'Then you are married, Bessie?'

'Yes: nearly five years since, to Robert Leaven, the coachman; and I've a little girl besides Bobby there, that I've christened Jane.'

'And you don't live at Gateshead?'

'I live at the lodge: the old porter has left.'

'Well, and how do they all get on? Tell me everything about them, Bessie: but sit down first, and, Bobby, come and sit on my knee, will you?' but Bobby preferred sidling over to his mother.

'You're not grown so very tall, Miss Jane, nor so very stout,' continued Mrs Leaven. 'I dare say they've not kept you too well at school; Miss Reed is the head and shoulders taller than you are; and Miss Georgiana would make two of you in breadth.'

'Georgiana is handsome, I suppose, Bessie?'

'Very. She went up to London last winter with her mamma, and there everybody admired her, and a young lord fell in love with her: but his relations were against the match; and – what do you think? – he and Miss Georgiana made it up to run away: but they were found out and stopped. It was Miss Reed that found them out; I believe she was envious; and now she and her sister lead a cat-and-dog life together; they are always quarrelling.'

'Well, and what of John Reed?'

'Oh, he is not doing so well as his mamma could wish. He went to college, and he got – plucked, I think they call it. And then his uncles wanted him to be a barrister, and study the law: but he is such a dissipated young man, they will never make much of him, I think.'

'What does he look like?'

'He is very tall. Some people call him a fine-looking young man; but he has such thick lips.'

'And Mrs Reed?'

'Missis looks stout and well enough in the face, but I think she's not quite easy in her mind. Mr John's conduct does not please her – he spends a deal of money.'

'Did she send you here, Bessie?'

'No, indeed: but I have long wanted to see you, and when I heard that there had been a letter from you and that you were going to another part of the country, I thought I'd just set off, and get a look at you before you were quite out of my reach.'

'I am afraid you are disappointed in me, Bessie?' I said this, laughing. I perceived that Bessie's glance, though it expressed regard, did in no shape denote admiration.

'No, Miss Jane, not exactly. You are genteel enough; you look like a lady, and it is as much as I ever expected of you: you were no beauty as a child.'

I smiled at Bessie's frank answer; I felt that it was correct, but I confess I was not quite indifferent to its import. At eighteen most people wish to please, and the conviction that they have not an exterior likely to second that desire brings anything but gratification.

# Jane Eyre

'I dare say you are clever, though,' continued Bessie, by way of solace. 'What can you do? Can you play on the piano?'

'A little.'

There was one in the room; Bessie went and opened it and then asked me to sit down and give her a tune. I played a waltz or two, and she was charmed.

'The Miss Reeds could not play as well!' said she exultingly. 'I always said you could surpass them in learning: and can you draw?'

'That is one of my paintings over the chimney-piece.' It was a landscape in water colours, of which I had made a present to the superintendent, in acknowledgement of her obliging mediation with the committee on my behalf, and which she had framed and glazed.

'Well, that is beautiful, Miss Jane! It is as fine a picture as any Miss Reed's drawing-master could paint, let alone the young ladies themselves, who could not come near it: and have you learnt French?'

'Yes, Bessie, I can both read it and speak it.'

'And you can work on muslin and canvas?'

'I can.'

'Oh, you are quite a lady, Miss Jane! I knew you would be; you will get on whether your relations notice you or not. There was something I wanted to ask you. Have you ever heard anything from your father's kinsfolk, the Eyres?'

'Never in my life.'

'Well, you know missis always said they were poor and quite despicable: and they may be poor; but I believe they are as much gentry as the Reeds are; for one day, nearly seven years ago, a Mr Eyre came to Gateshead and wanted to see you. Missis said you was at school fifty miles off: he seemed so much disappointed, for he could not stay; he was going on a voyage to a foreign country, and the ship was to sail from London in a day or two. He looked quite a gentleman, and I believe he was your father's brother.'

'What foreign country was he going to, Bessie?'

'An island thousands of miles off, where they make wine – the butler did tell me –'

'Madeira?' I suggested.

'Yes; that is it – that is the very word.'

'So he went?'

'Yes; he did not stay many minutes in the house: Missis was very high with him; she called him afterwards a "sneaking tradesman". My Robert believes he was a wine merchant.'

'Very likely,' I returned; 'or perhaps clerk or agent to a wine merchant.'

Bessie and I conversed about old times an hour longer, and then she was obliged to leave me: I saw her again for a few minutes the next morning at Lowton, while I was waiting for the coach. We parted finally at the door of the Brocklehurst Arms there: each went her separate way: she set off for the brow of Lowood Fell to meet the conveyance which was to take her back to Gateshead; I mounted the vehicle which was to bear me to new duties and a new life in the unknown environs of Millcote.

# Chapter 11

A new chapter in a novel is something like a new scene in a play; and when I draw up the curtain this time, reader – you must fancy you see a room in the George Inn at Millcote, with such large-figured papering on the walls as inn rooms have; such a carpet, such furniture, such ornaments on the mantelpiece, such prints – including a portrait of George the Third and another of the Prince of Wales, and a representation of the death of Wolfe. All this is visible to you by the light of an oil lamp hanging from the ceiling, and by that of an excellent fire, near which I sit in my cloak and bonnet; my muff and umbrella lie on the table, and I am warming away the numbness and chill contracted by sixteen hours' exposure to the rawness of an October day: I left Lowton at four o'clock a.m. and the Millcote town clock is now just striking eight.

Reader, though I look comfortably accommodated, I am not very tranquil in my mind. I thought when the coach stopped here there would be some one to meet me; I looked anxiously round as I descended the wooden steps the 'boots' placed for my convenience, expecting to hear my name pronounced and to see some description of carriage waiting to convey me to Thornfield. Nothing of the sort was visible; and when I asked a waiter if anyone had been to inquire after a Miss Eyre, I was answered in the negative; so I had no resource but to request to be shown into a private room: and here I am waiting, while all sorts of doubts and fears are troubling my thoughts.

It is a very strange sensation to inexperienced youth to feel itself quite alone in the world, cut adrift from every connexion, uncertain whether the port to which it is bound can be reached, and prevented by many impediments from returning to that it has quitted. The charm of adventure sweetens that sensation, the glow of pride warms it: but then the throb of fear disturbs it, and fear with me became predominant when half an hour elapsed and still I was alone. I bethought myself to ring the bell.

'Is there a place in this neighbourhood called Thornfield?' I asked of the waiter who answered the summons.

'Thornfield? I don't know, ma'am: I'll inquire at the bar.' He vanished, but reappeared instantly.

'Is your name Eyre, miss?'

'Yes'

'Person here waiting for you.'

I jumped up, took my muff and umbrella, and hastened into the inn passage: a man was standing by the open door, and in the lamp-lit street I dimly saw a one-horse conveyance.

# Jane Eyre

'This will be your luggage, I suppose?' said the man rather abruptly when he saw me, pointing to my trunk in the passage.

'Yes.' He hoisted it on to the vehicle, which was a sort of car, and then I got in: before he shut me up, I asked him how far it was to Thornfield.

'A matter of six miles.'

'How long shall we be before we get there?'

'Happen an hour and a half.'

He fastened the car door, and climbed to his own seat outside, and we set off. Our progress was leisurely, and gave me ample time to reflect: I was content to be at length so near the end of my journey; and as I leaned back in the comfortable though not elegant conveyance, I meditated much at my ease.

'I suppose,' thought I, 'judging from the plainness of the servant and the carriage, Mrs Fairfax is not a very dashing person: so much the better; I have never lived amongst fine people but once, and I was very miserable with them. I wonder if she lives alone except this little girl; if so, and she is in any degree amiable, I shall surely be able to get on with her; I will do my best: it is a pity that doing one's best does not always answer. At Lowood, indeed, I took that resolution, kept it, and succeeded in pleasing; but with Mrs Reed, I remember my best was always spurned with scorn. I pray God Mrs Fairfax may not turn out a second Mrs Reed: but if she does, I am not bound to stay with her: let the worst come to the worst I can advertise again. How far are we on our road now, I wonder?'

I let down the window and looked out; Millcote was behind us; judging by the number of its lights, it seemed a place of considerable magnitude, much larger than Lowton. We were now, as far as I could see, on a sort of common; but there were houses scattered all over the district; I felt we were in a different region to Lowood, more populous, less picturesque: more stirring, less romantic.

The roads were heavy, the night misty: my conductor let his horse walk all the way, and the hour and a half extended, I verily believe, to two hours; at last he turned in his seat and said –

'You're noan so far fro' Thornfield now.'

Again I looked out: we were passing a church: I saw its low, broad tower against the sky, and its bell was tolling a quarter; I saw a narrow galaxy of lights too, on a hillside, marking a village or hamlet. About ten minutes after, the driver got down and opened a pair of gates; we passed through, and they clashed to behind us. We now slowly ascended a drive, and came upon the long front of a house; candlelight gleamed from one curtained bow-window; all the rest were dark. The cab stopped at the front door; it was opened by a maidservant; I alighted and went in.

'Will you walk this way, ma'am?' said the girl, and I followed her across a square hall with high doors all round: she ushered me into a room whose double illumination of fire and candle at first dazzled me, contrasting as it did with the darkness to which my eyes had been for two hours inured; when I could see, however, a cosy and agreeable picture presented itself to my view.

A snug, small room; a round table by a cheerful fire; an arm-chair, high-backed and old-fashioned, wherein sat the neatest imaginable little elderly lady, in widow's cap, black silk gown, and snowy muslin apron; exactly like what I had fancied Mrs Fairfax, only less stately and milder looking. She was occupied in knitting; a large cat sat demurely at her feet; nothing, in short, was wanting

# Jane Eyre

to complete the beau-ideal of domestic comfort. A more reassuring introduction for a new governess could scarcely be conceived: there was no grandeur to overwhelm, no stateliness to embarrass; and then, as I entered, the old lady got up and promptly and kindly came forward to meet me.

'How do you do, my dear? I am afraid you have had a tedious ride; John drives so slowly; you must be cold; come to the fire.'

'Mrs Fairfax, I suppose?' said I.

'Yes, you are right: sit down.'

'She conducted me to her own chair, and then began to remove my shawl and untie my bonnet strings: I begged she would not give herself so much trouble.

'Oh, it is no trouble: I dare say your own hands are almost numbed with cold. Leah, make a little hot negus and cut a sandwich or two: here are the keys of the storeroom.'

And she produced from her pocket a most housewifely bunch of keys, and delivered them to the servant.

'Now, then, draw nearer to the fire,' she continued. 'You've brought your luggage with you, haven't you, my dear?'

'Yes, ma'am.'

'I'll see it carried into your room,' she said, and bustled out.

'She treats me like a visitor,' thought I. 'I little expected such a reception; I anticipated only coldness and stiffness: this is not like what I have heard of the treatment of governesses; but I must not exult too soon.'

She returned; with her own hands cleared her knitting apparatus and a book or two from the table, to make room for the tray which Leah now brought, and then herself handed me the refreshments. I felt rather confused at being the object of more attention than I had ever before received, and that, too, shown by my employer and superior; but as she did not herself seem to consider she was doing anything out of her place, I thought it better to take her civilities quietly.

'Shall I have the pleasure of seeing Miss Fairfax to-night?' I asked when I had partaken of what she offered me.

'What did you say, my dear? I am a little deaf,' returned the good lady, approaching her ear to my mouth.

I repeated the question more distinctly.

'Miss Fairfax? Oh, you mean Miss Varens! Varens is the name of your future pupil.'

'Indeed! Then she is not your daughter?'

'No – I have no family.'

I should have followed up my first inquiry, by asking in what way Miss Varens was connected with her; but I recollected it was not polite to ask too many questions: besides, I was sure to hear in time.

'I am so glad,' she continued, as she sat down opposite to me, and took the cat on her knee; 'I am so glad you are come; it will be quite pleasant living here now with a companion. To be sure it is pleasant at any time; for Thornfield is a fine old hall, rather neglected of late years, perhaps, but still it is a respectable place; yet you know in winter time one feels dreary quite alone, in the best quarters. I say alone – Leah is a nice girl to be sure, and John and his wife are very decent people; but then you see they are only servants, and one can't converse with them on terms of equality; one must keep them at due distance

# Jane Eyre

for fear of losing one's authority. I'm sure last winter (it was a very severe one if you recollect, and when it did not snow, it rained and blew), not a creature but the butcher and postman came to the house, from November till February; and I really got quite melancholy with sitting night after night alone; I had Leah in to read to me sometimes, but I don't think the poor girl liked the task much: she felt it confining. In spring and summer one got on better; sunshine and long days make such a difference; and then, just at the commencement of this autumn, little Adela Varens came and her nurse; a child makes a house alive all at once; and, now you are here, I shall be quite gay.'

My heart really warmed to the worthy lady, as I heard her talk; and I drew my chair a little nearer to her, and expressed my sincere wish that she might find my company as agreeable as she anticipated.

'But I'll not keep you sitting up late to-night,' said she; 'it is on the stroke of twelve now, and you have been travelling all day; you must feel tired. If you have got your feet well warmed, I'll show you your bedroom. I've had the room next to mine prepared for you; it is only a small apartment, but I thought you would like it better than one of the large front chambers: to be sure they have finer furniture, but they are so dreary and solitary, I never sleep in them myself.'

I thanked her for her considerate choice, and as I really felt fatigued with my long journey, expressed my readiness to retire. She took her candle, and I followed her from the room. First she went to see if the hall-door was fastened; having taken the key from the lock, she led the way upstairs. The steps and banisters were of oak; the staircase window was high and latticed; both it and the long gallery into which the bedroom doors opened looked as if they belonged to a church rather than a house. A very chill and vault-like air pervaded the stairs and the gallery, suggesting cheerless ideas of space and solitude; and I was glad when finally ushered into my chamber, to find it of small dimensions, and furnished in ordinary modern style.

When Mrs Fairfax had bidden me a kind good-night, and I had fastened my door, gazed leisurely round, and in some measure effaced the eerie impression made by that wide hall, that dark and spacious staircase, and that long, cold gallery, by the livelier aspect of my little room, I remembered that after a day of bodily fatigue and mental anxiety, I was now at last in safe haven. The impulse of gratitude swelled my heart, and I knelt down at the bedside, and offered up thanks where thanks were due; not forgetting, ere I rose, to implore aid on my farther path, and the power of meriting the kindness which seemed so frankly offered me before it was earned. My couch had no thorns in it that night; my solitary room no fears. At once weary and content, I slept soon and soundly: when I awoke it was broad day.

The chamber looked such a bright little place to me as the sun shone in between the gay blue chintz window curtains, showing papered walls and a carpeted floor, so unlike the bare planks and stained plaster of Lowood, that my spirits rose at the view. Externals have a great effect on the young. I thought that a fairer era of life was beginning for me, one that was to have its flowers and pleasures, as well as its thorns and toils. My faculties, roused by the change of scene, the new field offered to hope, seemed all astir. I cannot precisely define what they expected, but it was something pleasant: not perhaps that day or that day month, but at an indefinite future period.

I rose; I dressed myself with care: obliged to be plain – for I had no article

of attire that was not made with extreme simplicity – I was still by nature solicitous to be neat. It was not my habit to be disregardful of appearance, or careless of the impression I made; on the contrary, I ever wished to look as well as I could, and to please as much as my want of beauty would permit. I sometimes regretted that I was not handsomer: I sometimes wished to have rosy cheeks, a straight nose, and small cherry mouth: I desired to be tall, stately, and finely developed in figure; I felt it a misfortune that I was so little, so pale, and had features so irregular and so marked. And why had I these aspirations and these regrets? It would be difficult to say: I could not then distinctly say it to myself; yet I had a reason, and a logical, natural reason too. However, when I had brushed my hair very smooth, and put on my black frock – which, Quaker-like as it was, at least had the merit of fitting to a nicety – and adjusted my clean white tucker, I thought I should do respectably enough to appear before Mrs Fairfax; and that my new pupil would not at least recoil from me with antipathy. Having opened my chamber window, and seen that I had left all things straight and neat on the toilet-table, I ventured forth.

Traversing the long and matted gallery, I descended the slippery steps of oak; then I gained the hall: I halted there a minute; I looked at some pictures on the walls (one, I remember, represented a grim man in a cuirass, and one a lady with powdered hair and a pearl necklace), at a bronze lamp pendant from the ceiling, at a great clock whose case was of oak curiously carved, and ebon black with time and rubbing. Everything appeared very stately and imposing to me: but then I was so little accustomed to grandeur. The hall-door, which was half of glass, stood open; I stepped over the threshold. It was a fine autumn morning; the early sun shone serenely on embrowned groves and still green fields; advancing on to the lawn, I looked up and surveyed the front of the mansion. It was three stories high, of proportions not vast, though considerable; a gentleman's manor-house, not a nobleman's seat: battlements round the top gave it a picturesque look. Its gray front stood out well from the background of a rookery, whose cawing tenants were now on the wing. They flew over the lawn and grounds to alight in a great meadow, from which these were separated by a sunk fence, and where an array of mighty old thorn trees, strong, knotty, and broad as oaks, at once explained the etymology of the mansion's designation. Farther off were hills: not so lofty as those round Lowood, nor so craggy, nor so like barriers of separation from the living world; but yet quiet and lonely hills enough, and seeming to embrace Thornfield with a seclusion I had not expected to find existent so near the stirring locality of Millcote. A little hamlet, whose roofs were blent with trees, straggled up the side of one of these hills: the church of the district stood nearer Thornfield; its old tower-top looked over a knoll between the house and gates.

I was yet enjoying the calm prospect and pleasant fresh air, yet listening with delight to the cawing of the rooks, yet surveying the wide, hoary front of the hall, and thinking what a great place it was for one lonely little dame like Mrs Fairfax to inhabit, when that lady appeared at the door.

'What! out already?' said she. 'I see you are an early riser.' I went up to her, and was received with an affable kiss and shake of the hand.

'How do you like Thornfield?' she asked. I told her I liked it very much.

'Yes,' she said, 'it is a pretty place; but I fear it will be getting out of order, unless Mr Rochester should take it into his head to come and reside here

# Jane Eyre

permanently – or, at least, visit it rather oftener. Great houses and fine grounds require the presence of the proprietor.'

'Mr Rochester!' I exclaimed. 'Who is he?'

'The owner of Thornfield,' she responded quietly. 'Did you not know he was called Rochester?'

Of course I did not: I had never heard of him before; but the old lady seemed to regard his existence as a universally understood fact, with which everybody must be acquainted by instinct.

'I thought,' I continued, 'Thornfield belonged to you.'

'To me? Bless you, child; what an idea! To me? I am only the housekeeper – the manager. To be sure, I am distantly related to the Rochesters by the mother's side – or, at least, my husband was. He was a clergyman, incumbent of Hay – that little village yonder on the hill – and that church near the gate was his. The present Mr Rochester's mother was a Fairfax, and second cousin to my husband; but I never presume on the connexion – in fact, it is nothing to me. I consider myself quite in the light of an ordinary housekeeper. My employer is always civil, and I expect nothing more.'

'And the little girl – my pupil?'

'She is Mr Rochester's ward. He commissioned me to find a governess for her. He intends to have her brought up in – shire, I believe. Here she comes, with her "bonne", as she calls her nurse.' The enigma then explained: this affable and kind little widow was no great dame, but a dependant like myself. I did not like her the worse for that; on the contrary. I felt better pleased than ever. The equality between her and me was real: not the mere result of condescension on her part. So much the better; my position was all the freer.

As I was meditating on this discovery, a little girl, followed by her attendant, came running up the lawn. I looked at my pupil, who did not at first appear to notice me. She was quite a child – perhaps seven or eight years old – slightly built, with a pale, small-featured face, and a redundancy of hair falling in curls to her waist.

'Good morning, Miss Adela,' said Mrs Fairfax. 'Come and speak to the lady who is to teach you, and to make you a clever woman some day.' She approached.

'C'est la gouvernante?' said she, pointing to me, and addressing her nurse, who answered –

'Mais oui, certainement.'

'Are they foreigners?' I inquired, amazed at hearing the French language.

'The nurse is a foreigner, and Adela was born on the Continent; and, I believe, never left it till within six months ago. When she first came here she could speak no English; now she can make shift to talk it a little. I don't understand her, she mixes it so with French; but you will make out her meaning very well, I dare say.'

Fortunately I had had the advantage of being taught French by a French lady; and as I had always made a point of conversing with Madame Pierrot as often as I could, and had, besides, during the last seven years, learnt a portion of French by heart daily – applying myself to take pains with my accent, and imitating as closely as possible the pronunciation of my teacher – I had acquired a certain degree of readiness and correctness in the language, and was not likely to be much at a loss with Mademoiselle Adela. She came and shook hands with me when she heard that I was her governess; and, as I led her into breakfast,

# Jane Eyre

I addressed some phrases to her in her own tongue. She replied briefly at first; but after we were seated at the table, and she had examined me some ten minutes with her large hazel eyes, she suddenly commenced chattering fluently.

'Ah!' cried she in French, 'you speak my language as well as Mr Rochester does. I can talk to you as I can to him, and so can Sophie. She will be glad; nobody here understands her; Madame Fairfax is all English. Sophie is my nurse; she came with me over the sea in a great ship with a chimney that smoked – how it did smoke! – and I was sick, and so was Sophie, and so was Mr Rochester. Mr Rochester lay down on a sofa in a pretty room called the salon, and Sophie and I had little beds in another place. I nearly fell out of mine; it was like a shelf. And, Mademoiselle – What is your name?'

'Eyre – Jane Eyre.'

'Aire? Bah! I cannot say it. Well, our ship stopped in the morning, before it was quite daylight, at a great city – a huge city, with very dark houses and all smoky; not at all like the pretty clean town I came from; and Mr Rochester carried me in his arms over a plank to the land, and Sophie came after, and we all got into a coach, which took us to a beautiful large house, larger than this and finer, called a hotel. We stayed there nearly a week: I and Sophie used to walk every day in a great green place full of trees, called the Park; and there were many children there besides me, and a pond with beautiful birds in it, that I fed with crumbs.'

'Can you understand her when she runs on so fast?' asked Mrs Fairfax.

I undestood her very well, for I had been accustomed to the fluent tongue of Madame Pierrot.

'I wish,' continued the good lady, 'you would ask her a question or two about her parents. I wonder if she remembers them?'

'Adèle,' I inquired, 'with whom did you live when you were in that pretty clean town you spoke of?'

'I lived long ago with mamma; but she is gone to the Holy Virgin. Mamma used to teach me to dance and sing, and to say verses. A great many gentlemen and ladies came to see mamma, and I used to dance before them, or sit on their knees and sing to them: I liked it. Shall I let you hear me sing now?'

She had finished her breakfast, so I permitted her to give a specimen of her accomplishments. Descending from her chair, she came and placed herself on my knee; then, folding her little hands demurely before her, shaking back her curls, and lifting her eyes to the ceiling, she commenced singing a song from some opera. It was the strain of a forsaken lady, who, after bewailing the perfidy of her lover, calls pride to her aid; desires her attendant to deck her in her brightest jewels and richest robes, and resolves to meet the false one that night at the ball, and prove to him, by the gaiety of her demeanour, how little his desertion has affected her.

The subject seemed strangely chosen for an infant singer; but I suppose the point of the exhibition lay in hearing the notes of love and jealousy warbled with the lisp of childhood, and in very bad taste that point was – at least I thought so.

Adèle sang the conzonette tunefully enough, and with the *naïveté* of her age. This achieved, she jumped from my knee and said, 'Now mademoiselle, I will repeat you some poetry.'

Assuming an attitude, she began *La Ligue des Rats; fable de La Fontaine*. She

# Jane Eyre

then declaimed the little piece with an attention to punctuation and emphasis, a flexibility of voice, and an appropriateness of gesture, very unusual indeed at her age, and which proved she had been carefully trained.

'Was it your mamma who taught you that piece?' I asked.

'Yes; and she just used to say it in this way: "Qu'avez-vous donc? lui dit un de ces rats; parlez!" She made me lift my hand – so – to remind me to raise my voice at the question. Now shall I dance for you?'

'No, that will do. But after your mamma went to the Holy Virgin, as you say, with whom did you live then?'

'With Madame Frédéric and her husband: she took care of me, but she is nothing related to me. I think she is poor, for she had not so fine a house as mamma. I was not long there. Mr Rochester asked me if I would like to go and live with him in England, and I said yes: for I knew Mr Rochester before I knew Madame Frédéric, and he was always kind to me, and gave me pretty dresses and toys; but you see he has not kept his word, for he has brought me to England, and now he has gone back again himself, and I never see him.'

After breakfast, Adèle and I withdrew to the library, which room, it appears, Mr Rochester had directed should be used as the schoolroom. Most of the books were locked up behind glass doors; but there was one bookcase left open containing everything that could be needed in the way of elementary works, and several volumes of light literature, poetry, biography, travels, a few romances, &c. I suppose he had considered that these were all the governess would require for her private perusal; and, indeed, they contented me amply for the present; compared with the scanty pickings I had now and then been able to glean at Lowood, they seemed to offer an abundant harvest of entertainment and information. In this room, too, there was a cabinet piano, quite new and of superior tone; also an easel for painting, and a pair of globes.

I found my pupil sufficiently docile, though disinclined to apply: she had not been used to regular occupation of any kind. I felt it would be injudicious to confine her too much at first; so, when I had talked to her a great deal, and got her to learn a little, and when the morning had advanced to noon, I allowed her to return to her nurse. I then proposed to occupy myself till dinner-time in drawing some little sketches for her use.

As I was going upstairs to fetch my portfolio and pencils, Mrs Fairfax called to me: 'Your morning school-hours are over now, I suppose,' said she. She was in a room the folding doors of which stood open. I went in when she addressed me. It was a large, stately apartment, with purple chairs and curtains, a Turkey carpet, walnut-panelled walls, one vast window rich in stained glass, and a lofty ceiling, nobly moulded. Mrs Fairfax was dusting some vases of fine purple spar, which stood on a sideboard.

'What a beautiful room!' I exclaimed, as I looked round; for I had never before seen any half so imposing.

'Yes; this is the dining-room. I have just opened the window, to let in a little air and sunshine; for everything gets so damp in apartments that are seldom inhabited: the drawing-room yonder feels like a vault.'

She pointed to a wide arch corresponding to the window, and hung like it with a Tyrian-dyed curtain, now looped up. Mounting to it by two broad steps, and looking through, I thought I caught a glimpse of a fairy place, so bright to my novice eyes appeared the view beyond. Yet it was merely a very pretty

# Jane Eyre

drawing-room, and within it a boudoir, both spread with white carpets, on which seemed laid brilliant garlands of flowers; both ceiled with snowy mouldings of white grapes and vine leaves, beneath which glowed in rich contrast crimson couches and ottomans: while the ornaments on the pale Parian mantelpiece were of sparkling Bohemian glass, ruby red; and between the windows large mirrors repeated the general blending of snow and fire.

'In what order you keep these rooms, Mrs Fairfax!' said I. 'No dust, no canvas coverings: except that the air feels chilly, one would think they were inhabited daily.'

'Why, Miss Eyre, though Mr Rochester's visits here are rare, they are always sudden and unexpected; and as I observed that it put him out to find everything swathed up, and to have a bustle of arrangement on his arrival, I thought it best to keep the rooms in readiness.'

'Is Mr Rochester an exacting, fastidious sort of man?'

'Not particularly so; but he has a gentleman's tastes and habits, and he expects to have things managed in conformity to them.'

'Do you like him? Is he generally liked?'

'Oh, yes; the family have always been respected here. Almost all the land in this neighbourhood, as far as you can see, has belonged to the Rochesters time out of mind.'

'Well, but leaving his land out of the question, do you like him? Is he liked for himself?'

'*I* have no cause to do otherwise than like him; and I believe he is considered a just and liberal landlord by his tenants: but he has never lived much amongst them.'

'But he has no peculiarities? What, in short, is his character?'

'Oh! his character is unimpeachable, I suppose. He is rather peculiar, perhaps: he has travelled a great deal, and seen a great deal of the world, I should think. I dare say he is clever: but I never had much conversation with him.'

'In what way is he peculiar?'

'I don't know – it is not easy to describe – nothing striking, but you feel it when he speaks to you: you cannot be always sure whether he is in jest or earnest, whether he is pleased or the contrary: you don't thoroughly understand him, in short – at least, I don't: but that is of no consequence, he is a very good master.'

This was all the account I got from Mrs Fairfax of her employer and mine. There are people who seem to have no notion of sketching a character, or observing and describing salient points, either in persons or things: the good lady evidently belonged to this class; my queries puzzled, but did not draw her out. Mr Rochester was Mr Rochester in her eyes; a gentleman, a landed proprietor – nothing more: she inquired and searched no further, and evidently wondered at my wish to gain a more definite notion of his identity.

When we left the dining-room, she proposed to show me over the rest of the house: and I followed her upstairs and downstairs, admiring as I went; for all was well arranged and handsome. The large front chambers I thought especially grand; and some of the third-story rooms, though dark and low, were interesting from their air of antiquity. The furniture once appropriate to the lower apartments had from time to time been removed here, as fashions changed: and the imperfect light entering by their narrow casements showed bedsteads of a

hundred years old; chests in oak or walnut, looking, with their strange carving of palm branches and cherubs' heads, like types of the Hebrew ark; rows of venerable chairs, high-backed and narrow; stools still more antiquated, on whose cushioned tops were yet apparent traces of half-effaced embroideries, wrought by fingers that for two generations had been coffin-dust. All these relics gave to the third story of Thornfield Hall the aspect of a home of the past – a shrine of memory. I liked the hush, the gloom, the quaintness of these retreats in the day; but I by no means coveted a night's repose on one of those wide and heavy beds; shut in, some of them, with doors of oak; shaded others, with wrought English old hangings crusted with thick work, portraying effigies of strange flowers, and stranger birds, and strangest human beings – all which would have looked strange, indeed, by the pallid gleam of moonlight.

'Do the servants sleep in these rooms?' I asked.

'No: they occupy a range of smaller apartments to the back; no one ever sleeps here. One would almost say that, if there were a ghost at Thornfield Hall, this would be its haunt.'

'So I think. You have no ghost then?'

'None that I ever heard of,' returned Mrs Fairfax, smiling.

'Nor any traditions of one? No legends or ghost stories?'

'I believe not. And yet it is said the Rochesters have been rather a violent than a quiet race in their time. Perhaps, though, that is the reason they rest tranquilly in their graves now.'

'Yes – "after life's fitful fever they sleep well",' I muttered. 'Where are you going now, Mrs Fairfax?' for she was moving away.

'On to the leads; will you come and see the view from thence?' I followed still, up a very narrow staircase to the attics, and thence by a ladder and through a trapdoor to the roof of the hall. I was now on a level with the crow colony, and could see into their nests. Leaning over the battlements and looking far down, I surveyed the grounds laid out like a map; the bright and velvet lawn closely girdling the gray base of the mansion; the field, wide as a park, dotted with its ancient timber; the wood, dun and sere, divided by a path visibly overgrown, greener with moss than the trees with foliage; the church at the gates, the road, the tranquil hills, all reposing in the autumn day's sun; the horizon bounded by a propitious sky, azure, marbled with pearly white. No feature in the scene was extraordinary, but all was pleasing. When I turned from it and repassed the trapdoor, I could scarcely see my way down the ladder; the attic seemed black as a vault compared with that arch of blue air to which I had been looking up, and to that sunlit scene of grove, pasture, and green hill of which the hall was the centre, and over which I had been gazing with delight.

Mrs Fairfax stayed behind a moment to fasten the trapdoor. I, by dint of groping, found the outlet from the attic, and proceeded to descend the narrow garret staircase. I lingered in the long passage to which this led, separating the front and back rooms of the third story – narrow, low, and dim, with only one little window at the far end, and looking, with its two rows of small black doors all shut, like a corridor in some Bluebeard's castle.

While I paced softly on, the last sound I expected to hear in so still a region, a laugh, struck my ears. It was a curious laugh – distinct, formal, mirthless, I stopped. The sound ceased, only for an instant. It began again, louder – for at first, though very distinct, it was very low. It passed off in a clamourous peal

that seemed to echo in every lonely chamber, though it originated but in one, and I could have pointed out the door whence the accents issued.

'Mrs Fairfax!' I called out – for I now heard her descending the great stairs. 'Did you hear that loud laugh? Who is it?'

'Some of the servants, very likely,' she answered; 'perhaps Grace Poole.'

'Did you hear it?' I again inquired.

'Yes, plainly; I often hear her. She sews in one of these rooms. Sometimes Leah is with her; they are frequently noisy together.'

The laugh was repeated in its low, syllabic tone, and terminated in an odd murmur.

'Grace!' exclaimed Mrs Fairfax.

I really did not expect any Grace to answer, for the laugh was as tragic, as preternatural a laugh as any I ever heard; and, but that it was high noon, and that no circumstance of ghostliness accompanied the curious cachinnation; but that neither scene nor season favoured fear, I should have been superstitiously afraid. However, the event showed me I was a fool for entertaining a sense even of surprise.

The door nearest me opened, and a servant came out – a woman of between thirty and forty; a set, square-made figure, red-haired, and with a hard, plain face: any apparition less romantic or less ghostly could scarcely be conceived.

'Too much noise, Grace,' said Mrs Fairfax. 'Remember directions!' Grace curtseyed silently and went in.

'She is a person we have to sew and assist Leah in her housemaid's work,' continued the widow; 'not altogether unobjectionable in some points, but she does well enough. By the by, how have you got on with your new pupil this morning?'

The conversation, thus turned on Adèle, continued till we reached the light and cheerful region below. Adèle came running to meet us in the hall, exclaiming–

'Mesdames, vous êtes servies!' adding, 'J'ai bien faim, moi!'

We found dinner ready, and waiting for us in Mrs Fairfax's room.

# Chapter 12

The promise of a smooth career, which my first calm introduction to Thornfield Hall seemed to pledge, was not belied on a longer acquaintance with the place and its inmates. Mrs Fairfax turned out to be what she appeared, a placid-tempered, kind-natured woman, of competent education and average intelligence. My pupil was a lively child, who had been spoilt and indulged, and therefore was sometimes wayward; but as she was committed entirely to my care, and no injudicious interference from any quarter ever thwarted my plans for her improvement, she soon forgot her little freaks, and

# Jane Eyre

became obedient and teachable. She had no great talents, no marked traits of character, no peculiar development of feeling or taste, which raised her one inch above the ordinary level of childhood; but neither had she any deficiency or vice which sunk her below it. She made reasonable progress, entertained for me a vivacious, though perhaps not very profound affection; and by her simplicity, gay prattle, and efforts to please, inspired me, in return, with a degree of attachment sufficient to make us both content in each other's society.

This, *par parenthèse*, will be thought cool language by persons who entertain solemn doctrines about the angelic nature of children, and the duty of those charged with their education to conceive for them an idolatrous devotion. But I am not writing to flatter parental egotism, to echo cant, or prop up humbug; I am merely telling the truth. I felt a conscientious solicitude for Adèle's welfare and progress, and a quiet liking to her little self; just as I cherished towards Mrs Fairfax a thankfulness for her kindness, and a pleasure in her society proportionate to the tranquil regard she had for me, and the moderation of her mind and character.

Anybody may blame me who likes, when I add further, that, now and then, when I took a walk by myself in the grounds; when I went down to the gates and looked through them along the road; or when, while Adèle played with her nurse, and Mrs Fairfax made jellies in the storeroom, I climbed the three staircases, raised the trapdoor of the attic, and having reached the leads, looked out afar over sequestered field and hill, and along dim skyline – that then I longed for a power of vision which might overpass that limit; which might reach the busy world, towns, regions full of life I had heard of but never seen; that then I desired more of practical experience than I possessed; more of intercourse with my kind, of acquaintance with variety of character, than was here within my reach. I valued what was good in Mrs Fairfax, and what was good in Adèle; but I believed in the existence of other and more vivid kinds of goodness, and what I believed in I wished to behold.

Who blames me? Many, no doubt; and I shall be called discontented. I could not help it; the restlessness was in my nature; it agitated me to pain sometimes. Then my sole relief was to walk along the corridor of the third story, backwards and forwards, safe in the silence and solitude of the spot, and allow my mind's eye to dwell on whatever bright visions rose before it – and, certainly, they were many and glowing; to let my heart be heaved by the exultant movement, which, while it swelled it in trouble, expanded it with life; and, best of all, to open my inward ear to a tale that was never ended – a tale my imagination created, and narrated continuously; quickened with all of incident, life, fire, feeling, that I desired and had not in my actual existence.

It is in vain to say human beings ought to be satisfied with tranquillity: they must have action; and they will make it if they cannot find it. Millions are condemned to a stiller doom than mine, and millions are in silent revolt against their lot. Nobody knows how many rebellions besides political rebellions ferment in the masses of life which people earth. Women are supposed to be very calm generally: but women feel just as men feel; they need exercise for their faculties, and a field for their efforts as much as their brothers do; they suffer from too rigid a restraint, too absolute a stagnation, precisely as men would suffer; and it is narrow-minded in their more privileged fellow-creatures to say that they ought to confine themselves to making puddings and knitting stockings, to

# Jane Eyre

playing on the piano and embroidering bags. It is thoughtless to condemn them, or laugh at them, if they seek to do more or learn more than custom has pronounced necessary for their sex.

When thus alone, I not unfrequently heard Grace Poole's laugh: the same peal, the same low, slow ha! ha! which, when first heard, had thrilled me: I heard, too, her eccentric murmurs; stranger than her laugh. There were days when she was quite silent; but there were others when I could not account for the sounds she made. Sometimes I saw her: she would come out of her room with a basin, or a plate, or a tray in her hand, go down to the kitchen, and shortly return, generally (oh, romantic reader, forgive me for telling the plain truth!) bearing a pot of porter. Her appearance always acted as a damper to the curiosity raised by her oral oddities: hard-featured and staid, she had no point to which interest could attach. I made some attempts to draw her into conversation, but she seemed a person of few words: a monosyllabic reply usually cut short every effort of that sort.

The other members of the household, viz., John and his wife, Leah the housemaid, and Sophie the French nurse, were decent people; but in no respect remarkable; with Sophie I used to talk French, and sometimes I asked her questions about her native country; but she was not of a descriptive or narrative turn, and generally gave such vapid and confused answers as were calculated rather to check than encourage inquiry.

October, November, December passed away. One afternoon in January, Mrs Fairfax had begged a holiday for Adèle, because she had a cold; and, as Adèle seconded the request with an ardour that reminded me how precious occasional holidays had been to me in my own childhood, I accorded it, deeming that I did well in showing pliability on the point. It was a fine, calm day, though very cold; I was tired of sitting still in the library through a whole long morning: Mrs Fairfax had just written a letter which was waiting to be posted, so I put on my bonnet and cloak and volunteered to carry it to Hay; the distance, two miles, would be a pleasant winter afternoon walk. Having seen Adèle comfortably seated in her little chair by Mrs Fairfax's parlour fireside, and given her her best wax doll (which I usually kept enveloped in silver paper in a drawer) to play with, and a story-book for change of amusement; and having replied to her 'Revenez bientôt, ma bonne amie, ma chère Mdlle Jeannette,' with a kiss, I set out.

The ground was hard, the air was still, my road was lonely: I walked fast till I got warm, and then I walked slowly to enjoy and to analyse the species of pleasure brooding for me in the hour and situation. It was three o'clock; the church bell tolled as I passed under the belfry: the charm of the hour lay in its approaching dimness, in the low-gliding and pale-beaming sun. I was a mile from Thornfield, in a lane noted for wild roses in summer, for nuts and blackberries in autumn, and even now possessing a few coral treasures in hips and haws, but whose best winter delight lay in its utter solitude and leafless repose. If a breath of air stirred, it made no sound here; for there was not a holly, not an evergreen to rustle, and the stripped hawthorn and hazel bushes were as still as the white worn stones which causewayed the middle of the path. Far and wide, on each side, there were only fields, where no cattle now browsed; and the little brown birds, which stirred occasionally in the hedge, looked like single russet leaves that had forgotten to drop.

# Jane Eyre

This lane inclined uphill all the way to Hay; having reached the middle, I sat down on a stile which led thence into a field. Gathering my mantle about me, and sheltering my hands in my muff, I did not feel the cold, though it froze keenly; as was attested by a sheet of ice covering the causeway, where a little brooklet, now congealed, had overflowed after a rapid thaw some days since. From my seat I could look down on Thornfield: the gray and battlemented hall was the principal object in the vale below me; its woods and dark rookery arose against the west. I lingered till the sun went down amongst the trees, and sank crimson and clear behind them. I then turned eastward.

On the hilltop above me sat the rising moon; pale yet as a cloud, but brightening momently; she looked over Hay, which, half lost in trees, sent up a blue smoke from its few chimneys; it was yet a mile distant, but in the absolute hush I could hear plainly its thin murmurs of life. My ear, too, felt the flow of currents; in what dales and depths I could not tell: but there were many hills beyond Hay, and doubtless many becks threading their passes. That evening calm betrayed alike the tinkle of the nearest streams, the sough of the most remote.

A rude noise broke out on these fine ripplings and whisperings, at once so far away and so clear: a positive tramp, tramp, a metallic clatter, which effaced the soft wave-wanderings; as, in a picture, the solid mass of a crag, or the rough boles of a great oak, drawn in dark and strong in the foreground, efface the aerial distance of azure hill, sunny horizon, and blended clouds, where tint melts into tint.

The din was on the causeway: a horse was coming; the windings of the lane yet hid it, but it approached. I was just leaving the stile; yet as the path was narrow, I sat still to let it go by. In those days I was young, and all sorts of fancies bright and dark tenanted my mind: the memories of nursery stories were there amongst other rubbish; and when they recurred, maturing youth added to them a vigour and vividness beyond what childhood could give. As this horse approached, and as I watched for it to appear through the dusk, I remembered certain of Bessie's tales, wherein figured a North-of-England spirit, called a 'Gytrash'; which, in the form of horse, mule, or large dog, haunted solitary ways, and sometimes came upon belated travellers, as this horse was now coming upon me.

It was very near, but not yet in sight; when, in addition to the tramp, tramp, I heard a rush under the hedge, and close down by the hazel stems glided a great dog, whose black and white colour made him a distinct object against the trees. It was exactly one mask of Bessie's Gytrash – a lion-like creature with long hair and a huge head: it passed me, however, quietly enough; not staying to look up, with strange pretercanine eyes, in my face, as I half expected it would. The horse followed – a tall steed, and on its back a rider. The man, the human being, broke the spell at once. Nothing ever rode the Gytrash: it was always alone; and goblins, to my notions, though they might tenant the dumb carcasses of beasts, could scarce covet shelter in the commonplace human form. No Gytrash was this – only a traveller taking a short cut to Millcote. He passed, and went on; a few steps, and I turned; a sliding sound and an exclamation of 'What the deuce is to do now?' and a clattering tumble, arrested my attention. Man and horse were down; they had slipped on the sheet of ice which glazed the causeway. The dog came bounding back, and seeing his master in a predicament, and

# Jane Eyre

hearing the horse groan, barked till the evening hills echoed the sound, which was deep in proportion to his magnitude. He sniffed round the prostrate group, and then he ran up to me; it was all he could do – there was no other help at hand to summon. I obeyed him, and walked down to the traveller, by this time struggling himself free of his steed. His efforts were so vigorous, I thought he could not be much hurt; but I asked him the question –

'Are you injured, sir?'

I think he was swearing, but I am not certain; however, he was pronouncing some formula which prevented him from replying to me directly.

'Can I do anything?' I asked again.

'You must just stand on one side,' he answered as he rose, first to his knees, and then to his feet. I did; whereupon began a heaving, stamping, clattering process, accompanied by a barking and baying which removed me effectually some yards distance; but I would not be driven quite away till I saw the event. This was finally fortunate; the horse was re-established, and the dog was silenced with a 'Down Pilot!' The traveller now; stooping, felt his foot and leg, as if trying whether they were sound; apparently something ailed them, for he halted to the stile whence I had just risen, and sat down.

I was in the mood for being useful, or at least officious, I think, for I now drew near him again.

'If you are hurt, and want help, sir, I can fetch some one either from Thornfield Hall or from Hay.'

'Thank you; I shall do: I have no broken bones – only a sprain'; and again he stood up and tried his foot, but the result extorted an involuntary 'Ugh!'

Something of daylight still lingered, and the moon was waxing bright; I could see him plainly. His figure was enveloped in a riding cloak, fur collared and steel clasped; its details were not apparent, but I traced the general points of middle height, and considerable breadth of chest. He had a dark face, with stern features and a heavy brow; his eyes and gathered eyebrows looked ireful and thwarted just now; he was past youth, but had not reached middle age; perhaps he might be thirty-five. I felt no fear of him, and but little shyness. Had he been a handsome, heroic-looking young gentleman, I should not have dared to stand thus questioning him against his will, and offering my services unasked. I had hardly ever seen a handsome youth; never in my life spoken to one. I had a theoretical reverence and homage for beauty, elegance, gallantry, fascination; but had I met those qualities incarnate in masculine shape, I should have known instinctively that they neither had nor could have sympathy with anything in me, and should have shunned them as one would fire, lightning, or anything else that is bright but antipathetic.

If even this stranger had smiled and been good-humoured to me when I addressed him; if he had put off my offer of assistance gaily and with thanks, I should have gone on my way and not felt any vocation to renew inquiries: but the frown, the roughness of the traveller set me at my ease: I retained my station when he waved to me to go, and announced –

'I cannot think of leaving you, sir, at so late an hour, in this solitary lane, till I see you are fit to mount your horse.'

He looked at me when I said this: he had hardly turned his eyes in my direction before.

# Jane Eyre

'I should think you ought to be at home yourself,' said he, 'if you have a home in this neighbourhood. Where do you come from?'

'From just below; and I am not at all afraid of being out late when it is moonlight. I will run over to Hay for you with pleasure, if you wish it; indeed, I am going there to post a letter.'

'You live just below – do you mean at that house with the battlements?' pointing to Thornfield Hall, on which the moon cast a hoary gleam, bringing it out distinct and pale from the woods, that, by contrast with the western sky, now seemed one mass of shadow.

'Yes, sir.'

'Whose house is it?'

'Mr Rochester's.'

'Do you know Mr Rochester?'

'No, I have never seen him.'

'He is not resident, then?'

'No.'

'Can you tell me where he is?'

'I cannot.'

'You are not a servant at the Hall, of course. You are—' He stopped, ran his eye over my dress, which as usual, was quite simple – a black merino cloak, a black beaver bonnet; neither of them half fine enough for a lady's-maid. He seemed puzzled to decide what I was – I helped him.

'I am the governess.'

'Ah, the governess!' he repeated; 'deuce take me if I had not forgotten! The governess!' and again my raiment underwent scrutiny. In two minutes he rose from the stile; his face expressed pain when he tried to move.

'I cannot commission you to fetch help,' he said; 'but you may help me a little yourself, if you will be so kind.'

'Yes, sir.'

'You have not an umbrella that I can use as a stick?'

'No.'

'Try to get hold of my horse's bridle and lead him to me. You are not afraid?'

I should have been afraid to touch a horse when alone, but when told to do it I was disposed to obey. I put down my muff on the stile, and went up to the tall steed; I endeavoured to catch the bridle, but it was a spirited thing, and would not let me come near its head; I made effort on effort, though in vain: meantime I was mortally afraid of its trampling forefeet. The traveller waited and watched for some time, and at last he laughed.

'I see,' he said; 'the mountain will never be brought to Mahomet, so all you can do is to aid Mahomet to go to the mountain; I must beg of you to come here.'

I came. 'Excuse me,' he continued; 'necessity compels me to make you useful.' He laid a heavy hand on my shoulder, and, leaning on me with some stress, limped to his horse. Having once caught the bridle he mastered it directly, and sprang to his saddle, grimacing grimly as he made the effort, for it wrenched his sprain.

'Now,' said he, releasing his under lip from a hard bite, 'just hand me my whip; it lies there under the hedge.'

I sought it and found it.

# Jane Eyre

'Thank you; now make haste with the letter to Hay, and return as fast as you can.'

A touch of a spurred heel made his horse first start and rear, and then bound away; the dog rushed in his traces: all three vanished –

> 'Like heath that, in the wilderness,
> The wild wind whirls away.'

I took up my muff and walked on. The incident had occurred and was gone for me: it *was* an incident of no moment, no romance, no interest in a sense; yet it marked with change one single hour of a monotonous life. My help had been needed and claimed: I had given it: I was pleased to have done something; trivial, transitory though the deed was, it was yet an active thing, and I was weary of an existence all passive. The new face, too, was like a new picture introduced to the gallery of memory, and it was dissimilar to all the others hanging there: firstly, because it was masculine; and, secondly, because it was dark, strong, and stern. I had it still before me when I entered Hay, and slipped the letter into the post office; I saw it as I walked fast downhill all the way home. When I came to the stile, I stopped a minute, looked round and listened, with an idea that a horse's hoofs might ring on the causeway again, and that a rider in a cloak, and a Gytrash-like Newfoundland dog, might be again apparent: I saw only the hedge and a pollard willow before me, rising up still and straight to meet the moonbeams; I heard only the faintest waft of wind roaming fitful among the trees round Thornfield, a mile distant; and when I glanced down in the direction of the murmur, my eye, traversing the hall front, caught a light kindling in a window: it reminded me that I was late, and I hurried on.

I did not like re-entering Thornfield. To pass its threshold was to return to stagnation; to cross the silent hall, to ascend the darksome staircase, to seek my own lonely little room, and then to meet tranquil Mrs Fairfax, and spend the long winter evening with her, and her only, was to quell wholly the faint excitement wakened by my walk – to slip again over my faculties the viewless fetters of a uniform and too still existence; of an existence whose very privileges of security and ease I was becoming incapable of appreciating. What good it would have done me at that time to have been tossed in the storms of an uncertain, struggling life, and to have been taught by rough and bitter experience to long for the calm amidst which I now repined! Yes; just as much good as it would do a man tired of sitting still in a 'too easy chair' to take a long walk: and just as natural was the wish to stir, under my circumstances, as it would be under his.

I lingered at the gates; I lingered on the lawn; I paced backwards and forwards on the pavement: the shutters of the glass door were closed; I could not see into the interior; and both my eyes and spirit seemed drawn from the gloomy house – from the gray hollow filled with rayless cells, as it appeared to me – to that sky expanded before me – a blue sea absolved from taint of cloud; the moon ascending it in solemn march, her orb seeming to look up as she left the hilltops, from behind which she had come, far and farther below her, and aspired to the zenith, midnight dark in its fathomless depth and measureless distance; and for those trembling stars that followed her course, they made my heart tremble, my veins glow when I viewed them. Little things recall us to earth: the clock struck

973

# Jane Eyre

in the hall; that sufficed. I turned from moon and stars, opened a side-door, and went in.

The hall was dark, nor yet was it lit, only by the high-hung bronze lamp. A warm glow suffused both it and the lower steps of the oak staircase. This ruddy shine issued from the great dining-room, whose two-leaved door stood open, and showed a genial fire in the grate, glancing on marble hearth and brass fireirons, and revealing the purple draperies and polished furniture in the most pleasant radiance. It revealed, too, a group near the mantelpiece. I had scarcely caught it, and scarcely become aware of a cheerful mingling of voices, amongst which I seemed to distinguish the tones of Adèle, when the door closed.

I hastened to Mrs Fairfax's room. There was a fire there too, but no candle, and no Mrs Fairfax. Instead, all alone, sitting upright on the rug, and gazing with gravity at the blaze, I beheld a great black and white long-haired dog, just like the Gytrash of the lane. It was so like it that I went forward and said 'Pilot', and the thing got up and came to me and snuffed me. I caressed him, and he wagged his great tail; but he looked an eerie creature to be alone with, and I could not tell whence he had come. I rang the bell, for I wanted a candle; and I wanted, too, to get an account of this visitant. Leah entered.

'What dog is this?'

'He came with master.'

'With whom?'

'With master – Mr Rochester – he is just arrived.'

'Indeed! and is Mrs Fairfax with him?'

'Yes, and Miss Adela; they are in the dining-room, and John is gone for a surgeon, for the master has had an accident. His horse fell, and his ankle is sprained.'

'Did the horse fall in Hay Lane?'

'Yes, coming downhill; it slipped on some ice.'

'Ah! Bring me a candle, will you, Leah?'

Leah brought it. She entered, followed by Mrs Fairfax, who repeated the news, adding that Mr Carter, the surgeon, was come, and was now with Mr Rochester. Then she hurried out to give orders about tea, and I went upstairs to take off my things.

# Chapter 13

Mr Rochester, it seems, by the surgeon's orders, went to bed early that night; nor did he rise soon next morning. When he did come down, it was to attend to business. His agent and some of his tenants were arrived, and waiting to speak with him.

Adèle and I had now to vacate the library: it would be in daily requisition

# Jane Eyre

as a reception-room for callers. A fire was lit in an apartment upstairs, and there I carried our books, and arranged it for the future schoolroom. I discerned in the course of the morning that Thornfield Hall was a changed place. No longer silent as a church, it echoed every hour or two to a knock at the door or a clang of the bell. Steps, too, often traversed the hall, and new voices spoke in different keys below. A rill from the outer world was flowing through it. It had a master; for my part, I liked it better.

Adèle was not easy to teach that day; she could not apply. She kept running to the door and looking over the banisters to see if she could get a glimpse of Mr Rochester. Then she coined pretexts to go downstairs, in order, as I shrewdly suspected, to visit the library, where I knew she was not wanted. Then, when I got a little angry, and made her sit still, she continued to talk incessantly of her 'ami Monsieur Edouard Fairfax *de* Rochester', as she dubbed him (I had not before heard his prenomens), and to conjecture what presents he had brought her; for it appears that he had intimated the night before that, when his luggage came from Millcote, there would be found amongst it a little box in whose contents she had an interest.

'Et cela doit signifier,' said she, 'qu'il y aura là-dedans un cadeau pour moi, et peut-être pour vous aussi, mademoiselle. Monsieur a parlé de vous: il m'a demandé le nom de ma gouvernante, et si elle n'était pas une petite personne, assez mince et un peu pâle. J'ai dit qu'oui: car c'est vrai, n'est-ce pas, mademoiselle?'

I and my pupil dined as usual in Mrs Fairfax's parlour. The afternoon was wild and snowy, and we passed it in the schoolroom. At dark, I allowed Adèle to put away books and work, and to run downstairs: for, from the comparative silence below, and from the cessation of appeals to the doorbell, I conjectured that Mr Rochester was now at liberty. Left alone, I walked to the window; but nothing was to be seen thence. Twilight and snowflakes together thickened the air, and hid the very shrubs on the lawn. I let down the curtain and went back to the fireside.

In the clear embers I was tracing a view, not unlike a picture I remembered to have seen of the castle of Heidelberg on the Rhine, when Mrs Fairfax came in, breaking up by her entrance the fiery mosaic I had been piecing together, and scattering, too, some heavy unwelcome thoughts that were beginning to throng on my solitude.

'Mr Rochester would be glad if you and your pupil would take tea with him in the drawing-room this evening,' said she. 'He has been so much engaged all day that he could not ask to see you before.'

'When is his tea-time?' I inquired.

'Oh, at six o'clock. He keeps early hours in the country. You had better change your frock now: I will go with you and fasten it. Here is a candle.'

'Is it necessary to change my frock?'

'Yes, you had better. I always dress for the evening when Mr Rochester is here.'

This additional ceremony seemed somewhat stately. However, I repaired to my room, and, with Mrs Fairfax's aid, replaced my black stuff dress by one of black silk; the best and the only additional one I had, except one of light gray, which, in my Lowood notions of the toilette, I thought too fine to be worn, except on first-rate occasions.

# Jane Eyre

'You want a brooch,' said Mrs Fairfax. I had a single little pearl ornament which Miss Temple gave me as a parting keepsake. I put it on, and then we went downstairs. Unused as I was to strangers, it was rather a trial to appear thus formally summoned in Mr Rochester's presence. I let Mrs Fairfax precede me into the dining-room, and kept in her shade as we crossed that apartment; and, passing the arch, whose curtain was now dropped, entered the elegant recess beyond.

Two wax candles stood lighted on the table, and two on the mantelpiece; basking in the light and heat of a superb fire, lay Pilot – Adèle knelt near him. Half reclined on a couch appeared Mr Rochester, his foot supported by a cushion; he was looking at Adèle and the dog. The fire shone full on his face. I knew my traveller, with his broad and jetty eyebrows, his square forehead, made squarer by the horizontal sweep of his black hair. I recognized his decisive nose, more remarkable for character than beauty; his full nostrils, denoting, I thought, choler; his grim mouth, chin, and jaw – yes, all three were very grim, and no mistake. His shape, now divested of cloak, I perceived harmonized in squareness with his physiognomy. I suppose it was a good figure in the athletic sense of the term – broad-chested and thin-flanked, though neither tall nor graceful.

Mr Rochester must have been aware of the entrance of Mrs Fairfax and myself; but it appeared he was not in the mood to notice us, for he never lifted his head as we approached.

'Here is Miss Eyre, sir,' said Mrs Fairfax, in her quiet way. He bowed, still not taking his eyes from the group of the dog and child.

'Let Miss Eyre be seated,' said he; and there was something in the forced stiff bow, in the impatient yet formal tone, which seemed further to express, 'What the deuce is it to me whether Miss Eyre be there or not? At this moment I am not disposed to accost her.'

I sat down quite disembarrassed. A reception of finished politeness would probably have confused me: I could not have returned or repaid it by answering grace and elegance on my part; but harsh caprice laid me under no obligation; on the contrary, a decent quiescence, under the freak of manner, gave me the advantage. Besides, the eccentricity of the proceedings was piquant: I felt interested to see how he would go on.

He went on as a statue would, that is, he neither spoke nor moved. Mrs Fairfax seemed to think it necessary that some one should be amiable, and she began to talk. Kindly, as usual – and, as usual, rather trite – she condoled with him on the pressure of business he had had all day; on the annoyance it must have been to him with that painful sprain: then she commended his patience and perseverance in going through with it.

'Madam, I should like some tea,' was the sole rejoinder she got. She hastened to ring the bell; and when the tray came, she proceeded to arrange the cups, spoons, &c., with assiduous celerity. I and Adèle went to the table; but the master did not leave his couch.

'Will you hand Mr Rochester's cup?' said Mrs Fairfax to me; 'Adèle might perhaps spill it.'

I did as requested. As he took the cup from my hand, Adèle thinking the moment propitious for making a request in my favour, cried out –

# Jane Eyre

'N'est-ce pas, monsieur, qu'il y a un cadeau pour Mademoiselle Eyre dans votre petite coffre?'

'Who talks of cadeaux?' said he gruffly. 'Did you expect a present, Miss Eyre? Are you fond of presents?' and he searched my face with eyes that I saw were dark, irate, and piercing.

'I hardly know, sir; I have little experience of them; they are generally thought pleasant things.'

'Generally thought? But what do *you* think?'

'I should be obliged to take time, sir, before I could give you an answer worthy of your acceptance: a present has many faces to it, has it not? and one should consider all, before pronouncing an opinion as to its nature.'

'Miss Eyre, you are not so unsophisticated as Adèle: she demands a "cadeau" clamorously, the moment she sees me: you beat about the bush.'

'Because I have less confidence in my deserts than Adèle has: she can prefer the claim of old acquaintance, and the right, too, of custom; for she says you have always been in the habit of giving her playthings; but if I had to make out a case I should be puzzled, since I am a stranger, and have done nothing to entitle me to an acknowledgement.'

'Oh, don't fall back on over-modesty! I have examined Adèle, and find you have taken great pains with her: she is not bright, she has no talents; yet in a short time she has made much improvement.'

'Sir, you have now given me my "cadeau"; I am obliged to you: it is the meed teachers most covet – praise of their pupil's progress.'

'Humph!' said Mr Rochester, and he took his tea in silence.

'Come to the fire,' said the master, when the tray was taken away, and Mrs Fairfax had settled into a corner with her knitting; while Adèle was leading me by the hand round the room, showing me the beautiful books and ornaments on the consoles and chiffonnières. We obeyed, as in duty bound; Adèle wanted to take a seat on my knee, but she was ordered to amuse herself with Pilot.

'You have been resident in my house three months?'

'Yes, sir.'

'And you come from —?'

'From Lowood school, in —shire.'

'Ah! a charitable concern. How long were you there?'

'Eight years.'

'Eight years! you must be tenacious of life. I thought half the time in such a place would have done up any constitution! No wonder you have rather the look of another world. I marvelled where you had got that sort of face. When you came on me in Hay Lane last night, I thought unaccountably of fairy tales, and had half a mind to demand whether you had bewitched my horse: I am not sure yet. Who are your parents?'

'I have none.'

'Nor ever had, I suppose; do you remember them?'

'No.'

'I thought not. And so you were waiting for your people when you sat on that stile?'

'For whom, sir?'

'For the men in green: it was a proper moonlight evening for them. Did I

break through one of your rings, that you spread that damned ice on the causeway?'

I shook my head. 'The men in green all forsook England a hundred years ago,' said I, speaking as seriously as he had done. 'And not even in Hay Lane, or the fields about it, could you find a trace of them. I don't think either summer or harvest, or winter moon, will ever shine on their revels more.'

Mrs Fairfax had dropped her knitting, and, with raised eyebrows, seemed wondering what sort of talk this was.

'Well,' resumed Mr Rochester, 'if you disown parents, you must have some sort of kinsfolk: uncles and aunts?'

'No; none that I ever saw.'

'And your home?'

'I have none.'

'Where do your brothers and sisters live?'

'I have no brothers or sisters.'

'Who recommended you to come here?'

'I advertised, and Mrs Fairfax answered my advertisement.'

'Yes,' said the good lady, who knew now what ground we were upon, 'and I am daily thankful for the choice Providence led me to make. Miss Eyre has been an invaluable companion to me, and a kind and careful teacher to Adèle.'

'Don't trouble yourself to give her a character,' returned Mr Rochester: 'eulogiums will not bias me; I shall judge for myself. She began by felling my horse.'

'Sir?' said Mrs Fairfax.

'I have to thank her for this sprain.'

The widow looked bewildered.

'Miss Eyre, have you ever lived in a town?'

'No, sir.'

'Have you seen much society?'

'None but the pupils and teachers of Lowood, and now the inmates of Thornfield.'

'Have you read much?'

'Only such books as came in my way; and they have not been numerous, or very learned.'

'You have lived the life of a nun: no doubt you are well drilled in religious forms; Brocklehurst, who I understand directs Lowood, is a parson, is he not?'

'Yes, sir.'

'And you girls probably worshipped him, as a convent full of religieuses would worship their director.'

'Oh, no.'

'You are very cool! No! What! a novice not worship her priest! That sounds blasphemous.'

'I disliked Mr Brocklehurst; and I was not alone in the feeling. He is a harsh man; at once pompous and meddling: he cut off our hair; and for economy's sake bought us bad needles and thread, with which we could hardly sew.'

'That was very false economy,' remarked Mrs Fairfax, who now again caught the drift of the dialogue.

'And was that the head and front of his offending?' demanded Mr Rochester.

'He starved us when he had sole superintendence of the provision department,

# Jane Eyre

before the committee was appointed; and he bored us with long lectures once a week, and with evening readings from books of his own inditing, about sudden deaths and judgements, which made us afraid to go to bed.'

'What age were you when you went to Lowood?'

'About ten.'

'And you stayed there eight years: you are now, then, eighteen?'

I assented.

'Arithmetic, you see, is useful; without its aid, I should hardly have been able to guess your age. It is a point difficult to fix where the features and countenance are so much at variance as in your case. And now what did you learn at Lowood? Can you play?'

'A little.'

'Of course: that is the established answer. Go into the library – I mean if you please. (Excuse my tone of command; I am used to say, "Do this," and it is done: I cannot alter my customary habits for one new inmate.) Go, then, into the library; take a candle with you; leave the door open; sit down at the piano, and play a tune.'

I departed, obeying his directions.

'Enough!' he called out in a few minutes. 'You play a *little*, I see; like any other English schoolgirl; perhaps rather better than some, but not well.'

I closed the piano, and returned. Mr Rochester continued –

'Adèle showed me some sketches this morning, which she said were yours. I don't know whether they were entirely of your doing; probably a master aided you.'

'No, indeed!' I interjected.

'Ah! that pricks pride. Well, fetch me your portfolio, if you can vouch for its contents being original; but don't pass your word unless you are certain: I can recognize patchwork.'

'Then I will say nothing, and you shall judge for yourself, sir.'

I brought the portfolio from the library.

'Approach the table,' said he; and I wheeled it to his couch. Adèle and Mrs Fairfax drew near to see the pictures.

'No crowding,' said Mr Rochester: 'take the drawings from my hand as I finish with them; but don't push your faces up to mine.'

He deliberately scrutinized each sketch and painting. Three he laid aside; the others, when he had examined them, he swept from him.

'Take them off to the other table, Mrs Fairfax,' said he, 'and look at them with Adèle; – you' (glancing at me) 'resume your seat, and answer my questions. I perceive those pictures were done by one hand; was that hand yours?'

'Yes.'

'And when did you find time to do them? They have taken much time, and some thought.'

'I did them in the last two vacations I spent at Lowood, when I had no other occupation.'

'Where did you get your copies?'

'Out of my head.'

'That head I see now on your shoulders?'

'Yes, sir.'

'Has it other furniture of the same kind within?'

# Jane Eyre

'I should think it may have: I should hope – better.'

He spread the pictures before him, and again surveyed them alternately.

While he is so occupied, I will tell you, reader, what they are: and first, I must premise that they are nothing wonderful. The subjects had, indeed, risen vividly on my mind. As I saw them with the spiritual eye, before I attempted to embody them, they were striking; but my hand would not second my fancy, and in each case it had wrought out but a pale portrait of the thing I had conceived.

These pictures were in water-colours. The first represented clouds low and livid, rolling over a swollen sea: all the distance was in eclipse; so, too, was the foreground; or, rather, the nearest billows, for there was no land. One gleam of light lifted into relief a half-submerged mast, on which sat a cormorant, dark and large, with wings flecked with foam; its beak held a gold bracelet, set with gems, that I had touched with as brilliant tints as my palette could yield, and as glittering distinctness as my pencil could impart. Sinking below the bird and mast, a drowned corpse glanced through the green water; a fair arm was the only limb clearly visible, whence the bracelet had been washed or torn.

The second picture contained for foreground only the dim peak of a hill, with grass and some leaves slanting as if by a breeze. Beyond and above spread an expanse of sky, dark-blue as at twilight: rising into the sky was a woman's shape to the bust, portrayed in tints as dusk and soft as I could combine. The dim forehead was crowned with a star; the lineaments below were seen as through the suffusion of vapour; the eyes shone dark and wild; the hair streamed shadowy, like a beamless cloud torn by storm, or by electric travail. On the neck lay a pale reflection like moonlight; the same faint lustre touched the train of thin clouds from which rose and bowed this vision of the Evening Star.

The third showed the pinnacle of an iceberg piercing a polar winter sky: a muster of northern lights reared their dim lances, close serried, along the horizon. Throwing these into distance, rose, in the foreground, a head – a colossal head, inclined towards the iceberg, and resting against it. Two thin hands, joined under the forehead, and supporting it, drew up before the lower features a sable veil; a brow quite bloodless, white as bone, and an eye hollow and fixed, blank of meaning, but for the glassiness of despair, alone were visible. Above the temples, amidst wreathed turban folds of black drapery, vague in its character and consistency as cloud, gleamed a ring of white flame, gemmed with sparkles of a more lurid tinge. This pale crescent was 'the likeness of a kingly crown'; what it diademed was 'the shape which shape had none'.

'Were you happy when you painted these pictures?' asked Mr Rochester presently.

'I was absorbed, sir: yes, and I was happy. To paint them, in short, was to enjoy one of the keenest pleasures I have ever known.'

'That is not saying much. Your pleasures, by your own account, have been few; but I dare say you did exist in a kind of artist's dreamland while you blent and arranged these strange tints. Did you sit at them long each day?'

'I had nothing else to do, because it was the vacation, and I sat at them from morning till noon, and from noon till night: the length of the mid-summer days favoured my inclination to apply.'

'And you felt self-satisfied with the result of your ardent labours?'

'Far from it. I was tormented by the contrast between my idea and my

# Jane Eyre

handiwork: in each case I had imagined something which I was quite powerless to realize.'

'Not quite: you have secured the shadow of your thought; but no more, probably. You had not enough of the artist's skill and science to give it full being: yet the drawings are, for a schoolgirl, peculiar. As to the thoughts, they are elfish. These eyes in the Evening Star you must have seen in a dream. How could you make them look so clear, and yet not at all brilliant? for the planet above quells their rays. And what meaning is that in their solemn depth? And who taught you to paint wind? There is a high gale in that sky, and on this hilltop. Where did you see Latmos? For that is Latmos. There – put the drawings away!'

I had scarce tied the strings of the portfolio, when, looking at his watch, he said abruptly –

'It is nine o'clock: what are you about, Miss Eyre, to let Adèle sit up so long? take her to bed.'

Adèle went to kiss him before quitting the room: he endured the caress, but scarcely seemed to relish it more than Pilot would have done, nor so much.

'I wish you all good-night, now,' said he, making a movement of the hand towards the door, in token that he was tired of our company, and wished to dismiss us. Mrs Fairfax folded up her knitting: I took my portfolio: we curtseyed to him, and received a frigid bow in return, and so withdrew.

'You said Mr Rochester was not strikingly peculiar, Mrs Fairfax,' I observed, when I rejoined her in her room after putting Adèle to bed.

'Well, is he?'

'I think so: he is very changeful and abrupt.'

'True: no doubt he may appear so to a stranger, but I am so accustomed to his manner, I never think of it; and then, if he has peculiarities of temper, allowance should be made.

'Why?'

'Partly because it is his nature – and we can none of us help our nature; and partly because he has painful thoughts, no doubt, to harass him, and make his spirits unequal.'

'What about?'

'Family troubles, for one thing.'

'But he has no family.'

'Not now, but he has had – or, at least, relatives. He lost his elder brother a few years since.'

'His *elder* brother?'

'Yes. The present Mr Rochester has not been very long in possession of the property; only about nine years.'

'Nine years is a tolerable time. Was he so very fond of his brother as to be still inconsolable for his loss?'

'Why, no – perhaps not. I believe there were some misunderstandings between them. Mr Rowland Rochester was not quite just to Mr Edward; and perhaps he prejudiced his father against him. The old gentleman was fond of money, and anxious to keep the family estate together. He did not like to diminish the property by division, and yet he was anxious that Mr Edward should have wealth, too, to keep up the consequence of the name; and, soon after he was of age, some steps were taken that were not quite fair, and made a great deal of

# Jane Eyre

mischief. Old Mr Rochester and Mr Rowland combined to bring Mr Edward into what he considered a painful position, for the sake of making his fortune; what the precise nature of that position was I never clearly knew, but his spirit could not brook what he had to suffer in it. He is not very forgiving: he broke with his family, and now for many years he has led an unsettled kind of life. I don't think he has ever been resident at Thornfield for a fortnight together, since the death of his brother without a will left him master of the estate; and, indeed, no wonder he shuns the old place.'

'Why should he shun it?'

'Perhaps he thinks it gloomy.'

The answer was evasive. I should have liked something clearer: but Mrs Fairfax either could not, or would not, give me more explicit information of the origin and nature of Mr Rochester's trials. She averred they were a mystery to herself, and that what she knew was chiefly from conjecture. It was evident, indeed, that she wished me to drop the subject, which I did accordingly.

# Chapter 14

For several subsequent days I saw little of Mr Rochester. In the mornings he seemed much engaged with business, and, in the afternoon, gentlemen from Millcote or the neighbourhood called, and sometimes stayed to dine with him. When his sprain was well enough to admit of horse exercise, he rode out a good deal; probably to return these visits, as he generally did not come back till late at night.

During this interval, even Adèle was seldom sent for to his presence; and all my acquaintance with him was confined to an occasional rencontre in the hall, on the stairs, or in the gallery, when he would sometimes pass me haughtily and coldly, just acknowledging my presence by a distant nod or a cool glance, and sometimes bow and smile with gentleman-like affability. His changes of mood did not offend me, because I saw that I had nothing to do with their alteration; the ebb and flow depended on causes quite disconnected with me.

One day he had had company to dinner, and had sent for my portfolio; in order, doubtless, to exhibit its contents: the gentlemen went away early to attend a public meeting at Millcote, as Mrs Fairfax informed me; but the night being wet and inclement, Mr Rochester did not accompany them. Soon after they were gone, he rang the bell; a message came that I and Adèle were to go downstairs. I brushed Adèle's hair and made her neat, and having ascertained that I was myself in my usual Quaker trim, where there was nothing to retouch – all being too close and plain, braided locks included, to admit of disarrangement – we descended, Adèle wondering whether the *petit coffre* was at length come; for, owing to some mistake, its arrival had hitherto been delayed. She was

# Jane Eyre

gratified: there it stood, a little carton, on the table when we entered the dining-room. She appeared to know by instinct.

'Ma boîte! ma boîte!' exclaimed she, running towards the table.

'Yes, there is your "boîte" at last: take it into a corner, you genuine daughter of Paris, and amuse youself with disembowelling it,' said the deep and rather sarcastic voice of Mr Rochester, proceeding from the depths of an immense easy-chair at the fireside. 'And mind,' he continued, 'don't bother me with any details of the anatomical process, or any notice of the condition of the entrails: let your operations be conducted in silence: tiens-toi tranquille, enfant; comprends-tu?'

Adèle seemed scarcely to need the warning: she had already retired to a sofa with her treasure, and was busy untying the cord which secured the lid. Having removed this impediment, and lifted certain silvery envelopes of tissue paper, she merely exclaimed –

'Oh, ciel! Que c'est beau!' and then remained absorbed in ecstatic contemplation.

'Is Miss Eyre there?' now demanded the master, half rising from his seat to look round to the door, near which I still stood.

'Ah! well, come forward; be seated here.' He drew a chair near his own. 'I am not fond of the prattle of children,' he continued; 'for, old bachelor as I am, I have no pleasant associations connected with their lisp. It would be intolerable to me to pass a whole evening *tête-à-tête* with a brat. Don't draw that chair farther off, Miss Eyre; sit down exactly where I placed it – if you please, that is. Confound these civilities! I continually forget them. Nor do I particularly affect simple-minded old ladies. By the by, I must have mine in mind; it won't do to neglect her; she is a Fairfax, or wed to one; and blood is said to be thicker than water.'

He rang, and despatched an invitation to Mrs Fairfax, who soon arrived, knitting-basket in hand.

'Good-evening, madam; I sent to you for a charitable purpose. I have forbidden Adèle to talk to me about her presents, and she is bursting with repletion; have the goodness to serve her as auditress and interlocutrice; it will be one of the most benevolent acts you have ever performed.'

Adèle, indeed, no sooner saw Mrs Fairfax, than she summoned her to the sofa, and there quickly filled her lap with the porcelain, the ivory, the waxen contents of her 'boîte'; pouring out, meantime, explanations and raptures in such broken English as she was mistress of.

'Now I have performed the part of a good host,' pursued Mr Rochester; 'put my guests into the way of amusing each other, I ought to be at liberty to attend to my own pleasure. Miss Eyre, draw your chair still a little farther forward: you are yet too far back: I cannot see you without disturbing my position in this comfortable chair, which I have no mind to do.'

I did as I was bid, though I would have much rather have remained somewhat in the shade; but Mr Rochester had such a direct way of giving orders, it seemed a matter of course to obey him promptly.

We were, as I have said, in the dining-room: the lustre which had been lit for dinner filled the room with a festal breadth of light; the large fire was all red and clear; the purple curtains hung rich and ample before the lofty window and loftier arch; everything was still save the subdued chat of Adèle (she dared not

speak loud), and, filling up each pause, the beating of winter rain against the panes.

Mr Rochester, as he sat in the damask-covered chair, looked different to what I had seen him look before; not quite so stern – much less gloomy. There was a smile on his lips, and his eyes sparkled, whether with wine or not, I am not sure, but I think it very probable. He was, in short, in his after-dinner mood; more expanded and genial, and also more self-indulgent than the frigid and rigid temper of the morning: still, he looked preciously grim, cushioning his massive head against the swelling back of his chair, and receiving the light of the fire on his granite-hewn features, and in his great dark eyes; for he had great dark eyes, and very fine eyes, too – not without a certain change in their depths sometimes, which, if it was not softness, reminded you, at least, of that feeling.

He had been looking two minutes at the fire, and I had been looking the same length of time at him, when, turning suddenly, he caught my gaze fastened on his physiognomy.

'You examine me, Miss Eyre,' said he: 'do you think me handsome?'

I should, if I had deliberated, have replied to this question by something conventionally vague and polite; but the answer somehow slipped from my tongue before I was aware, 'No, sir.'

'Ah! By my word! there is something singular about you, he said: 'you have the air of a little *nonnette*; quaint, quiet, grave, and simple, as you sit with your hands before you, and your eyes generally bent on the carpet (except, by the by, when they are directed piercingly to my face; as just now, for instance); and when one asks you a question, or makes a remark to which you are obliged to reply, you rap out a round rejoinder, which, if not blunt, is at least brusque. What do you mean by it?'

'Sir, I was too plain: I beg your pardon. I ought to have replied that it was not easy to give an impromptu answer to a question about appearances; that tastes mostly differ; and that beauty is of little consequence, or something of that sort.'

'You ought to have replied no such thing. Beauty of little consequence, indeed! And so, under pretence of softening the previous outrage, of stroking and soothing me into placidity, you stick a sly pen-knife under my ear! Go on: what faults do you find with me, pray? I suppose I have all my limbs and all my features like any other man?'

'Mr Rochester, allow me to disown my first answer: I intended no pointed repartee: it was only a blunder.'

'Just so: I think so: and you shall be answerable for it. Criticize me: does my forehead not please you?'

He lifted up the sable waves of hair which lay horizontally over his brow, and showed a solid enough mass of intellectual organs, but an abrupt deficiency where the suave sign of benevolence should have risen.

'Now, ma'am, am I a fool?'

'Far from it, sir. You would, perhaps, think me rude if I inquired in return whether you are a philanthropist?'

'There again! Another stick of the penknife, when she pretended to pat my head: and that is because I said I did not like the society of children and old women (low be it spoken!). No, young lady, I am not a general philanthropist; but I bear a conscience': and he pointed to the prominences which are said to

# Jane Eyre

indicate that faculty and which, fortunately for him, were sufficiently conspicuous; giving, indeed, a marked breadth to the upper part of his head: 'and, besides, I once had a kind of rude tenderness of heart. When I was as old as you, I was a feeling fellow enough; partial to the unfledged, unfostered, and unlucky; but fortune has knocked me about since: she has even kneaded me with her knuckles, and now I flatter myself I am hard and tough as an indiarubber ball; pervious, though, through a chink or two still, and with one sentient point in the middle of the lump. Yes: does that leave hope for me?'

'Hope of what, sir?'

'Of my final retransformation from india-rubber back to flesh?'

'Decidedly he has had too much wine,' I thought; and I did not know what answer to make to his queer question: how could I tell whether he was capable of being retransformed?

'You look very much puzzled, Miss Eyre: and though you are not pretty any more than I am handsome, yet a puzzled air becomes you; besides it is convenient, for it keeps those searching eyes of yours away from my physiognomy, and busies them with the worsted flowers of the rug; so puzzle on. Young lady, I am disposed to be gregarious and communicative to-night.'

With this announcement he rose from his chair, and stood, leaning his arm on the marble mantelpiece: in that attitude his shape was seen plainly as well as his face; his unusual breadth of chest, disproportionate almost to his length of limb. I am sure most people would have thought him an ugly man; yet there was so much unconscious pride in his port; so much ease in his demeanour; such a look of complete indifference to his own external appearance; so haughty a reliance, on the power of other qualities, intrinsic or adventitious, to atone for the lack of mere personal attractiveness, that, in looking at him, one inevitably shared the indifference, and, even in a blind, imperfect sense, put faith in the confidence.

'I am disposed to be gregarious and communicative to-night,' he repeated, 'and that is why I sent for you: the fire and the chandelier were not sufficient company for me; nor would Pilot have been, for none of these can talk. Adèle is a degree better, but still far below the mark; Mrs Fairfax ditto; you, I am persuaded, can suit me if you will: you puzzled me the first evening I invited you down here. I have almost forgotten you since: other ideas have driven yours from my head; but to-night I am resolved to be at ease; to dismiss what importunes, and recall what pleases. It would please me now to draw you out – to learn more of you – therefore speak.'

Instead of speaking, I smiled; and not a very complacent or submissive smile either.

'Speak,' he urged.

'What about, sir?'

'Whatever you like. I leave both the choice of subject and the manner of treating it entirely to yourself.'

Accordingly I sat and said nothing: 'If he expects me to talk for the mere sake of talking and showing off, he will find he has addressed himself to the wrong person,' I thought.

'You are dumb, Miss Eyre.'

I was dumb still. He bent his head a little towards me, and with a single hasty glance seemed to dive into my eyes.

# Jane Eyre

'Stubborn?' he said, 'and annoyed. Ah! it is consistent. I put my request in an absurd, almost insolent form. Miss Eyre, I beg your pardon. The fact is, once for all, I don't wish to treat you like an inferior: that is (correcting himself), I claim only such superiority as must result from twenty years' difference in age and a century's advance in experience. This is legitimate, *et j'y tiens*, as Adèle would say: and it is by virtue of this superiority, and this alone, that I desire you to have the goodness to talk to me a little now, and divert my thoughts, which are galled with dwelling on one point – cankering as a rusty nail.'

He had designed an explanation; almost an apology; and I did not feel insensible to his condescension, and would not seem so.

'I am willing to amuse you, if I can, sir – quite willing; but I cannot introduce a topic, because how do I know what will interest you? Ask me questions, and I will do my best to answer them.'

'Then, in the first place, do you agree with me that I have a right to be a little masterful, abrupt, perhaps exacting, sometimes, on the grounds I stated, namely, that I am old enough to be your father, and that I have battled through a varied experience with many men of many nations, and roamed over half the globe, while you have lived quietly with one set of people in one house.'

'Do as you please, sir.'

'That is no answer; or rather, it is very irritating because a very evasive one. Reply clearly.'

'I don't think, sir, you have the right to command me, merely because you are older than I, or because you have seen more of the world than I have; your claim to superiority depends on the use you have made of your time and experience.'

'Humph! Promptly spoken. But I won't allow that, seeing that it would never suit my case, as I have made an indifferent, not to say bad, use of both advantages. Leaving superiority out of the question, then, you must still agree to receive my orders now and then, without being piqued or hurt by the tone of command. Will you?'

I smiled: I thought to myself Mr Rochester *is* peculiar – he seems to forget that he pays me thirty pounds per annum for receiving his orders.

'The smile is very well,' said he, catching instantly the passing expression; 'but speak too.'

'I was thinking, sir, that very few masters would trouble themselves to inquire whether or not their paid subordinates were piqued and hurt by their orders.'

'Paid subordinates! What! you are my paid subordinate, are you? Oh, yes, I had forgotten the salary! Well, then, on that mercenary ground, will you agree to let me hector a little?'

'No, sir, not on that ground; but on the ground that you did forget it, and that you care whether or not a dependent is comfortable in his dependency, I agree heartily.'

'And will you consent to dispense with a great many conventional forms and phrases, without thinking that the omission arises from insolence?'

'I am sure, sir, I should never mistake informality for insolence: one I rather like, the other nothing free-born would submit to, even for a salary.'

'Humbug! Most things free-born will submit to anything for a salary; therefore, keep to yourself, and don't venture on generalities of which you are intensely ignorant. However, I mentally shake hands with you for your answer, despite its inaccuracy; and as much for the manner in which it was said, as for

# Jane Eyre

the substance of the speech; the manner was frank and sincere; one does not often see such a manner: no, on the contrary, affectation, or coldness, or stupid, coarse-minded misapprehension of one's meaning are the usual rewards of candour. Not three in three thousand raw schoolgirl-governesses would have answered me as you have just done. But I don't mean to flatter you: if you are cast in a different mould to the majority, it is no merit of yours: Nature did it. And then, after all, I go too fast in my conclusions: for what I yet know, you may be no better than the rest; you may have intolerable defects to counterbalance your few good points.'

'And so may you,' I thought. My eye met his as the idea crossed my mind: he seemed to read the glance, answering as if its import had been spoken as well as imagined –

'Yes, yes, you are right,' said he; 'I have plenty of faults of my own: I know it, and I don't wish to palliate them, I assure you. God wot I need not be too severe about others; I have a past experience, a series of deeds, a colour of life to contemplate within my own breast, which might well call many sneers and censures from my neighbours to myself. I started, or rather (for, like other defaulters, I like to lay half the blame on ill-fortune and adverse circumstances) was thrust on to a wrong tack, at the age of one and twenty, and have never recovered the right course since; but I might have been very different; I might have been as good as you – wiser – almost as stainless. I envy you your peace of mind, your clean conscience, your unpolluted memory. Little girl, a memory without blot or contamination must be an exquisite treasure – an inexhaustible source of pure refreshment: is it not?'

'How was your memory when you were eighteen, sir?'

'All right then; limpid, salubrious: no gush of bilge water had turned it to fetid puddle. I was your equal at eighteen – quite your equal. Nature meant me to be, on the whole, a good man, Miss Eyre; one of the better kind, and you see I am not so. You would say you don't see it: at least I flatter myself I read as much in your eye (beware, by the by, what you express with that organ; I am quick at interpreting its language). Then take my word for it – I am not a villain: you are not to suppose that – not to attribute to me any such bad eminence; but owing, I verily believe, rather to circumstances than to my natural bent, I am a trite, commonplace sinner, hackneyed in all the poor petty dissipations with which the rich and worthless try to put on life. Do you wonder that I avow this to you? Know that in the course of your future life you will often find yourself elected the involuntary confidante of your acquaintances' secrets: people will instinctively find out, as I have done, that it is not your forte to tell of yourself, but to listen while others talk of themselves; they will feel, too, that you listen with no malevolent scorn of their indiscretion, but with a kind of innate sympathy, not the less comforting and encouraging because it is very unobtrusive in its manifestations.'

'How do you know? – how can you guess all this, sir?'

'I know it well; therefore I proceed almost as freely as if I were writing my thoughts in a diary. You would say, I should have been superior to circumstances; so I should – so I should; but you see I was not. When fate wronged me, I had not the wisdom to remain cool; I turned desperate; then I degenerated. Now, when any vicious simpleton excites my disgust by his paltry ribaldry, I cannot flatter myself that I am better than he: I am forced to confess that he and I are

987

# Jane Eyre

on a level. I wish I had stood firm – God knows I do! Dread remorse when you are tempted to err, Miss Eyre: remorse is the poison of life.'

'Repentance is said to be its cure, sir.'

'It is not its cure. Reformation may be its cure; and I could reform – I have strength yet for that – if – but where is the use of thinking of it, hampered, burdened, cursed as I am? Besides, since happiness is irrevocably denied me, I have a right to get pleasure out of life: and I *will* get it, cost what it may.'

'Then you will degenerate still more, sir.'

'Possibly: yet why should I, if I can get sweet, fresh pleasure? And I may get it as sweet and fresh as the wild honey the bee gathers on the moor.'

'It will sting – it will taste bitter, sir.'

'How do you know? – you never tried it. How very serious – how very solemn you look; and you are as ignorant of the matter as this cameo head' (taking one from the mantelpiece). 'You have no right to preach to me, you neophyte, that have not passed the porch of life, and are absolutely unacquainted with its mysteries.'

'I only remind you of your own words, sir: you said error brought remorse, and you pronounced remorse the poison of existence.'

'And who talks of error now? I scarcely think the notion that flitted across my brain was an error. I believe it was an inspiration rather than a temptation: it was very genial, very soothing – I know that. Here it comes again! It is no devil, I assure you; or if it be, it has put on the robes of an angel of light. I think I must admit so fair a guest when it asks entrance to my heart.'

'Distrust it, sir; it is not a true angel.'

'Once more, how do you know? By what instinct do you pretend to distinguish between a fallen seraph of the abyss and a messenger from the eternal throne – between a guide and a seducer?'

'I judged by your countenance, sir; which was troubled when you said the suggestion had returned upon you. I feel sure it will work you more misery if you listen to it.'

'Not at all – it bears the most gracious message in the world: for the rest, you are not my conscience-keeper, so don't make yourself uneasy. Here, come in, bonny wanderer!'

He said this as if he spoke to a vision, viewless to any eye but his own; then, folding his arms, which he had half extended on his chest, he seemed to enclose in their embrace the invisible being.

'Now,' he continued, again addressing me, 'I have received the pilgrim – a disguised deity, as I verily believe. Already it has done me good: my heart was a sort of charnel; it will now be a shrine.'

'To speak truth, sir, I don't understand you at all; I cannot keep up the conversation, because it has got out of my depth. Only one thing I know: you said you were not as good as you would like to be, and that you regretted your own imperfection; one thing I can comprehend: you intimated that to have a sullied memory was a perpetual bane. It seems to me, that if you tried hard, you would in time find it possible to become what you yourself would approve; and that if from this day you began with resolution to correct your thoughts and actions, you would in a few years have laid up a new and stainless store of recollections, to which you might revert with pleasure.'

# Jane Eyre

'Justly thought; rightly said, Miss Eyre; and at this moment, I am paving hell with energy.'

'Sir?'

'I am laying down good intentions, which I believe durable as flint. Certainly, my associates and pursuits shall be other than they have been.'

'And better?'

'And better – so much better as pure ore is than foul dross. You seem to doubt me; I don't doubt myself: I know what my aim is, what my motives are; and at this moment I pass a law, unalterable as that of the Medes and Persians, that both are right.'

'They cannot be, sir, if they require a new statute to legalize them.'

'They are, Miss Eyre, though they absolutely require a new statute: unheard-of combinations of circumstances demand unheard-of rules.'

'That sounds a dangerous maxim, sir; because one can see at once that it is liable to abuse.'

'Sententious sage! so it is: but I swear by my household gods not to abuse it.'

'You are human and fallible.'

'I am: so are you – what then?'

'The human and fallible should not arrogate a power with which the divine and perfect alone can be safely entrusted.'

'What power?'

'That of saying of any strange, unsanctioned line of action, "Let it be right".'

'"Let it be right" – the very words: you have pronounced them.'

'*May* it be right then,' I said, as I rose, deeming it useless to continue a discourse which was all darkness to me; and, besides, sensible that the character of my interlocutor was beyond my penetration, at least, beyond its present reach; and feeling the uncertainty, the vague sense of insecurity, which accompanies a conviction of ignorance.

'Where are you going?'

'To put Adèle to bed: it is past her bedtime.'

'You are afraid of me, because I talk like a sphinx.'

'Your language is enigmatical, sir: but though I am bewildered, I am certainly not afraid.'

'You *are* afraid – your self-love dreads a blunder.'

'In that sense I do feel apprehensive – I have no wish to talk nonsense.'

'If you did, it would be in such a grave, quiet manner, I should mistake it for sense. Do you never laugh, Miss Eyre? Don't trouble yourself to answer – I see you laugh rarely; but you can laugh very merrily; believe me, you are not naturally austere, any more than I am naturally vicious. The Lowood constraint still clings to you somewhat; controlling your features, muffling your voice, and restricting your limbs; and you fear in the presence of a man and a brother – or father, or master, or what you will – to smile too gaily, speak too freely, or move too quickly: but in time, I think you will be natural with me, as I find it impossible to be conventional with you; and then your looks and movements will have more vivacity and variety than they dare offer now. I see at intervals the glance of a curious sort of bird through the close-set bars of a cage: a vivid, restless, resolute captive is there; were it but free, it would soar cloud-high. You are still bent on going?'

'It has struck nine, sir.'

# Jane Eyre

'Never mind – wait a minute: Adèle is not ready to go to bed yet. My position, Miss Eyre, with my back to the fire, and my face to the room, favours observation. While talking to you, I have also occasionally watched Adèle (I have my own reasons for thinking her a curious study – reasons that I may, nay, that I shall, impart to you some day). She pulled out of her box, about ten minutes ago, a little pink frock; rapture lit her face as she unfolded it; coquetry runs in her blood, blends with her brains, and seasons the marrow of her bones. "Il faut que je l'essaie!" cried she, "et à l'instant même!" and she rushed out of the room. She is now with Sophie, undergoing a robing process: in a few minutes she will re-enter; and I know what I shall see – a miniature of Céline Varens, as she used to appear on the boards at the rising of—but never mind that. However, my tenderest feelings are about to receive a shock: such is my presentiment; stay now, to see whether it will be realized.'

Ere long, Adèle's little foot was heard tripping across the hall. She entered, transformed as her guardian had predicted. A dress of rose-coloured satin, very short, and as full in the skirt as it could be gathered, replaced the brown frock she had previously worn; a wreath of rosebuds circled her forehead; her feet were dressed in silk stockings and small white satin sandals.

'Est-ce que ma robe va bien?' cried she, bounding forward; 'et mes souliers? et mes bas? Tenez, je crois que je vais danser!'

And spreading out her dress, she chasséed across the room; till, having reached Mr Rochester, she wheeled lightly round before him on tiptoe, then dropped on one knee at his feet, exclaiming –

'Monsieur, je vous remercie mille fois de votre bonté'; then rising, she added, 'C'est comme cela que maman faisait, n'est-ce pas, monsieur?'

'Pre-cise-ly!' was the answer; 'and, "comme cela", she charmed my English gold out of my British breeches pocket. I have been green, too, Miss Eyre – ay, grass green: not a more vernal tint freshens you now that once freshened me. My Spring is gone, however, but it has left me that French floweret on my hands, which, in some moods, I would fain be rid of. Not valuing now the root whence it sprang; having found that it was of a sort which nothing but gold dust could manure, I have but half a liking to the blossom, especially when it looks so artificial as just now. I keep it and rear it on the Roman Catholic principle of expiating numerous sins, great or small, by one good work. I'll explain all this some day. Good-night.'

# Chapter 15

r Rochester did, on a future occasion, explain it. It was one afternoon, when he chanced to meet me and Adèle in the grounds: and while she played with Pilot and her shuttlecock, he asked me to walk up and down a long beech avenue within sight of her.

He then said that she was the daughter of a French opera-dancer, Céline Varens, towards whom he had once cherished, what he called a '*grande passion*'. This passion Céline had professed to return with even superior ardour. He thought himself her idol, ugly as he was: he believed, as he said, that she preferred his '*taille d'athlète*' to the elegance of the Apollo Belvedere.

'And, Miss Eyre, so much was I flattered by this preference of the Gallic sylph for her British gnome, that I installed her in an hotel, gave her a complete establishment of servants, a carriage, cashmeres, diamonds, dentelles, &c. In short, I began the process of ruining myself in the received style, like any other spoony. I had not, it seems, the originality to chalk out a new road to shame and destruction, but trod the old track with stupid exactness not to deviate an inch from the beaten centre. I had – as I deserved to have – the fate of all other spoonies. Happening to call one evening when Céline did not expect me, I found her out; but it was a warm night, and I was tired with strolling through Paris, so I sat down in her boudoir, happy to breathe the air consecrated so lately by her presence. No – I exaggerate; I never thought there was any consecrating virtue about her: it was rather a sort of pastille perfume she had left, a scent of musk and amber, than an odour of sanctity. I was just beginning to stifle with the fumes of conservatory flowers and sprinkled essences, when I bethought myself to open the window and step out on to the balcony. It was moonlight and gaslight besides, and very still and serene. The balcony was furnished with a chair or two. I sat down, and took out a cigar – I will take one now, if you will excuse me.'

Here ensued a pause, filled up by the producing and lighting of a cigar; having placed it to his lips and breathed a trail of Havannah incense on the freezing and sunless air, he went on –

'I liked bonbons too in those days, Miss Eyre, and I was *croquant* – (overlook the barbarism) – *croquant* chocolate comfits, and smoking alternately, watching meantime the equipages that rolled along the fashionable streets towards the neighbouring opera-house, when in an elegant close carriage drawn by a beautiful pair of English horses, and distinctly seen in the brilliant city-night, I recognized the "voiture" I had given Céline. She was returning: of course my heart thumped with impatience against the iron rails I leant upon. The carriage stopped, as I had expected, at the hotel door; my flame (that is the very word

# Jane Eyre

for an opera inamorata) alighted: though muffled in a cloak – an unnecessary encumbrance, by the by, on so warm a June evening – I knew her instantly by her little foot, seen peeping from the skirt of her dress, as she skipped from the carriage step. Bending over the balcony, I was about to murmur "Mon ange" – in a tone, of course, which should be audible to the ear of love alone – when a figure jumped from the carriage after her; cloaked also; but that was a spurred heel which had rung on the pavement, and that was a hatted head which now passed under the arched *porte cochère* of the hotel.

'You never felt jealousy, did you, Miss Eyre? Of course not: I need not ask you; because you never felt love. You have both sentiments yet to experience: your soul sleeps: the shock is yet to be given which shall waken it. You think all existence lapses in as quiet a flow as that in which your youth has hitherto slid away. Floating on with closed eyes and muffled ears, you neither see the rocks bristling not far off in the bed of the flood, nor hear the breakers boil at their base. But I tell you – and you may mark my words – you will come some day to a craggy pass in the channel, where the whole of life's stream will be broken up into whirl and tumult, foam and noise: either you will be dashed to atoms on crag points, or lifted up and borne on by some master-wave into a calmer current – as I am now.

'I like this day; I like that sky of steel; I like the sternness and stillness of the world under this frost. I like Thornfield, its antiquity, its retirement, its old crow-trees and thorn-trees, its gray façade, and lines of dark windows reflecting that metal welkin: and yet how long have I abhorred the very thought of it, shunned it like a great plague-house? How do I still abhor—'

He ground his teeth and was silent: he arrested his step and struck his boot against the hard ground. Some hated thought seemed to have him in its grip, and to hold him so tightly that he could not advance –

We were ascending the avenue when he thus paused; the hall was before us. Lifting his eyes to its battlements, he cast over them a glare, such as I never saw before or since. Pain, shame, ire – impatience, disgust, detestation – seemed momentarily to hold a quivering conflict in the large pupil dilating under his ebon eyebrow. Wild was the wrestle which should be paramount; but another feeling rose and triumphed: something hard and cynical; self-willed and resolute: it settled his passion and petrified his countenance: he went on –

'During the moment I was silent, Miss Eyre, I was arranging a point with my destiny. She stood there by that beech trunk – a hag like one of those who appeared to Macbeth on the heath at Forres. "You like Thornfield?" she said, lifting her finger; and then she wrote in the air a memento, which ran in lurid hieroglyphics all along the house front, between the upper and lower row of windows, "Like it if you can! Like it if you dare!"

'"I will like it," said I; "I dare like it"; and' (he subjoined moodily) 'I will keep my word: I will break obstacles to happiness, to goodness – yes, goodness. I wish to be a better man than I have been, than I am; as Job's leviathan broke the spear, the dart, and the habergeon, hindrances which others count as iron and brass I will esteem but straw and rotten wood.'

Adèle here ran before him with her shuttlecock.

'Away!' he cried harshly; 'keep at a distance, child; or go in to Sophie!' Continuing then to pursue his walk in silence, I ventured to recall him to the point whence he had abruptly diverged –

# Jane Eyre

'Did you leave the balcony, sir,' I asked, 'when Mdlle Varens entered?'
I almost expected a rebuff for this hardly well-timed question: but, on the contrary, waking out of his scowling abstraction, he turned his eyes towards me, and the shade seemed to clear off his brow. 'Oh, I had forgotten Céline! Well, to resume. When I saw my charmer thus come in accompanied by a cavalier, I seemed to hear a hiss, and the green snake of jealousy, rising on undulating coils from the moonlit balcony, glided within my waistcoat, and ate its way in two minutes to my heart's core. Strange!' he exclaimed, suddenly starting again from the point. 'Strange that I should choose you for the confidante of all this, young lady; passing strange that you should listen to me quietly, as if it were the most usual thing in the world for a man like me to tell stories of his opera-mistresses to a quaint, inexperienced girl like you! But the last singularity explains the first, as I intimated once before you, with your gravity, consider-ateness, and caution, were made to be the recipient of secrets. Besides, I know what sort of a mind I have placed in communication with my own: I know it is one not liable to take infection: it is a peculiar mind: it is a unique one. Happily, I do not mean to harm it: but if I did, it would not take harm from me. The more you and I converse the better; for while I cannot blight you, you may refresh me.' After this digression he proceeded –
'I remained in the balcony. "They will come to her boudoir, no doubt", thought I: "let me prepare an ambush." So, putting my hand in through the open window, I drew the curtain over it, leaving only an opening through which I could take observations; then I closed the casement, all but a chink just wide enough to furnish an outlet to lovers' whispered vows: then I stole back to my chair, and as I resumed it the pair came in. My eyes were quickly at the aperture. Céline's chambermaid entered, lit a lamp, left it on the table and withdrew. The couple were thus revealed to me clearly: both removed their cloaks, and there was "the Varens", shining in satin and jewels – my gifts of course – and there was her companion in an officer's uniform; and I knew him for a young roué of a vicomte – a brainless and vicious youth whom I had sometimes met in society, and had never thought of hating because I despised him so absolutely. On recognizing him, the fang of the snake jealousy was instantly broken; because at that same moment my love for Céline sank under an extinguisher. A woman who could betray me for such a rival was not worth contending for; she deserved only scorn; less, however, than I, who had been her dupe.
'They began to talk; their conversation eased me completely: frivolous, mercenary, heartless, and senseless, it was rather calculated to weary than enrage a listener. A card of mine lay on the table; this being perceived, brought my name under discussion. Neither of them possessed energy or wit to belabour me soundly, but they insulted me as coarsely as they could in their little way: especially Céline, who even waxed rather brilliant on my personal defects – deformities, she termed them. Now it had been her custom to launch out into fervent admiration of what she called my *"beauté mâle"*; wherein she differed diametrically from you, who told me point-blank, at the second interview, that you did not think me handsome. The contrast struck me at the time and—'
Adèle here came running up again.
'Monsieur, John has just been to say that your agent has called and wishes to see you.'

'Ah! in that case I must abridge. Opening the window, I walked in upon them; liberated Céline from my protection; gave her notice to vacate her hotel; offered her a purse for immediate exigencies; disregarded screams, hysterics, prayers, protestations, convulsions; made an appointment with the vicomte for a meeting at the Bois de Boulogne. Next morning I had the pleasure of encountering him; left a bullet in one of his poor etiolated arms, feeble as the wing of a chicken in the pip, and then thought I had done with the whole crew. But unluckily the Varens, six months before, had given me this fillette Adèle, who, she affirmed, was my daughter; and perhaps she may be, though I see no proofs of such grim paternity written in her countenance: Pilot is more like me than she. Some years after I had broken with the mother, she abandoned her child, and ran away to Italy with a musician or singer. I acknowledged no natural claim on Adèle's part to be supported by me, nor do I now acknowledge any, for I am not her father; but hearing that she was quite destitute, I e'en took the poor thing out of the slime and mud of Paris, and transplanted it here, to grow up clean in the wholesome soil of an English country garden. Mrs Fairfax found you to train it; but now you know that it is the illegitimate offspring of a French opera-girl, you will perhaps think differently of your post and protégée: you will be coming to me some day with notice that you have found another place – that you beg me to look out for a new governess, &c. – eh?'

'No: Adèle is not answerable for either her mother's faults or yours: I have a regard for her; and now that I know she is, in a sense, parentless – forsaken by her mother and disowned by you, sir – I shall cling closer to her than before. How could I possibly prefer the spoilt pet of a wealthy family, who would hate her governess as a nuisance, to a lonely little orphan who leans towards her as a friend?'

'Oh, that is the light in which you view it! Well, I must go in now; and you too; it darkens.'

But I stayed out a few minutes longer with Adèle and Pilot – ran a race with her, and played a game of battledore and shuttlecock. When we went in, and I had removed her bonnet and coat, I took her on my knee; kept her there an hour, allowing her to prattle as she liked: not rebuking even some little freedoms and trivialities into which she was apt to stray when much noticed, and which betrayed in her a superficiality of character, inherited probably from her mother, hardly congenial to an English mind. Still, she had her merits; and I was disposed to appreciate all that was good in her to the utmost. I sought in her countenance and features a likeness to Mr Rochester, but found none; no trait, no turn of expression announced relationship. It was pity: if she could have been proved to resemble him, he would have thought more of her.

It was not until after I had withdrawn to my own chamber for the night, that I steadily reviewed the tale Mr Rochester had told me. As he had said, there was probably nothing at all extraordinary in the substance of the narrative itself: a wealthy Englishman's passion for a French dancer, and her treachery to him, were everyday matters enough, no doubt, in society; but there was something decidedly strange in the paroxysm of emotion which had suddenly seized him when he was in the act of expressing the present contentment of his mood, and his newly revived pleasure in the old hall and its environs. I meditated wonderingly on this incident; but gradually quitting it, as I found it for the present inexplicable, I turned to the consideration of my master's manner to

# Jane Eyre

myself. The confidence he had thought fit to repose in me seemed a tribute to my discretion: I regarded and accepted it as such. His deportment had now for some weeks been more uniform towards me than at the first. I never seemed in his way; he did not take fits of chilling hauteur: when he met me unexpectedly, the encounter seemed welcome; he always had a word and sometimes a smile for me: when summoned by formal invitation to his presence, I was honoured by a cordiality of reception that made me feel I really possessed the power to amuse him, and that these evening conferences were sought as much for his pleasure as for my benefit.

I, indeed, talked comparatively little, but I heard him talk with relish. It was his nature to be communicative; he liked to open to a mind unacquainted with the world, glimpses of its scenes and ways (I do not mean its corrupt scenes and wicked ways, but such as derived their interest from the great scale on which they were acted, the strange novelty by which they were characterized); and I had a keen delight in receiving the new ideas he offered, imagining the new pictures he portrayed, and following him in thought through the new regions he disclosed, never startled or troubled by one noxious allusion.

The ease of his manner freed me from painful restraint; the friendly frankness, as correct as cordial, with which he treated me, drew me to him. I felt at times as if he were my relation rather than my master: yet he was imperious sometimes still; but I did not mind that; I saw it was his way. So happy, so gratified did I become with this new interest added to life, that I ceased to pine after kindred: my thin-crescent destiny seemed to enlarge; the blanks of existence were filled up; my bodily health improved; I gathered flesh and strength.

And was Mr Rochester now ugly in my eyes: No, reader: gratitude and many associations, all pleasurable and genial, made his face the object I best liked to see; his presence in a room was more cheering than the brightest fire. Yet I had not forgotten his faults; indeed, I could not, for he brought them frequently before me. He was proud, sardonic, harsh to inferiority of every description: in my secret soul I knew that his great kindness to me was balanced by unjust severity to many others. He was moody, too, unaccountably so; I more than once, when sent for to read to him, found him sitting in his library alone, with his head bent on his folded arms; and, when he looked up, a morose, almost a malignant scowl blackened his features. But I believed that his moodiness, his harshness, and his former faults of morality (I say *former*, for now he seemed corrected of them) had their source in some cruel cross of fate. I believed he was naturally a man of better tendencies, higher principles, and purer tastes than such as circumstances had developed, education instilled, or destiny encouraged. I thought there were excellent materials in him; though for the present they hung together somewhat spoiled and tangled. I cannot deny that I grieved for his grief, whatever that was, and would have given much to assuage it.

Though I had now extinguished my candle and was laid down in bed, I could not sleep for thinking of his look when he paused in the avenue, and told how his destiny had risen up before him, and dared him to be happy at Thornfield.

'Why not?' I asked myself. 'What alienates him from the house? Will he leave it again soon? Mrs Fairfax said he seldom stayed here longer than a fortnight at a time; and he has now been resident eight weeks. If he does go, the change will be doleful. Suppose he should be absent spring, summer, and autumn: how joyless sunshine and fine days will seem!'

# Jane Eyre

I hardly know whether I had slept or not after this musing; at any rate, I started wide awake on hearing a vague murmur, peculiar and lugubrious, which sounded, I thought, just above me. I wished I had kept my candle burning: the night was drearily dark; my spirits were depressed. I rose and sat up in bed, listening. The sound was hushed.

I tried again to sleep; but my heart beat anxiously: my inward tranquillity was broken. The clock, far down in the hall, struck two. Just then it seemed my chamber door was touched; as if fingers had swept the panels in groping a way along the dark gallery outside. I said, 'Who is there?' Nothing answered. I was chilled with fear.

All at once I remembered that it might be Pilot, who, when the kitchen door chanced to be left open, not infrequently found his way up to the threshold of Mr Rochester's chamber: I had seen him lying there myself in the mornings. The idea calmed me somewhat: I lay down. Silence composes the nerves; and as an unbroken hush now reigned again through the whole house, I began to feel the return of slumber. But it was not fated that I should sleep that night. A dream had scarcely approached my ear, when it fled affrighted, scared by a marrow-freezing incident enough.

This was a demoniac laugh – low, suppressed, and deep – uttered, as it seemed, at the very keyhole of my chamber door. The head of my bed was near the door, and I thought at first the goblin-laughter stood at my bedside – or rather crouched by my pillow: but I rose, looked round, and could see nothing; while, as I still gazed, the unnatural sound was reiterated: and I knew it came from behind the panels. My first impulse was to rise and fasten the bolt; my next again to cry out, 'Who is there?'

Something gurgled and moaned. Ere long, steps retreated up the gallery towards the third-story staircase: a door had lately been made to shut in that staircase; I heard it open and close, and all was still.

'Was that Grace Poole? and is she possessed with a devil?' thought I. Impossible now to remain longer by myself; I must go to Mrs Fairfax. I hurried on my frock and a shawl; I withdrew the bolt and opened the door with a trembling hand. There was a candle burning just outside, and on the matting in the gallery. I was surprised at this circumstance: but still more was I amazed to perceive the air quite dim, as if filled with smoke: and, while looking to the right hand and left, to find whence these blue wreaths issued, I became further aware of a strong smell of burning.

Something creaked: it was a door ajar; and that door was Mr Rochester's, and the smoke rushed in a cloud from thence. I thought no more of Mrs Fairfax; I thought no more of Grace Poole, or the laugh: in an instant, I was within the chamber. Tongues of flame darted round the bed: the curtains were on fire. In the midst of blaze and vapour, Mr Rochester lay stretched motionless, in deep sleep.

'Wake! wake!' I cried. I shook him, but he only murmured and turned: the smoke had stupefied him. Not a moment could be lost: the very sheets were kindling. I rushed to his basin and ewer; fortunately, one was wide and the other deep, and both were filled with water. I heaved them up, deluged the bed and its occupant, flew back to my own room, brought my own water-jug, baptized the couch afresh, and, by God's aid, succeeded in extinguishing the flames which were devouring it.

# Jane Eyre

The hiss of the quenched element, the breakage of the pitcher which I had flung from my hand when I had emptied it, and, above all, the splash of the shower-bath I had liberally bestowed, roused Mr Rochester at last. Though it was now dark, I knew he was awake; because I heard him fulminating strange anathemas at finding himself lying in a pool of water.

'Is there a flood?' he cried.

'No, sir,' I answered; 'but there has been a fire: get up, do; you are quenched now; I will fetch you a candle.'

'In the name of all the elves in Christendom, is that Jane Eyre?' he demanded. 'What have you done with me, witch, sorceress? Who is in the room besides you? Have you plotted to drown me?'

'I will fetch you a candle, sir; and, in Heaven's name, get up. Somebody has plotted something: you cannot too soon find out who and what it is.'

'There! I am up now; but at your peril you fetch a candle yet: wait two minutes till I get into some dry garments, if any dry there be – yes, here is my dressing-gown. Now run!'

I did run; I brought the candle which still remained in the gallery. He took it from my hand, held it up, and surveyed the bed, all blackened and scorched, the sheets drenched, the carpet round swimming in water.

'What is it? and who did it?' he asked.

I briefly related to him what had transpired: the strange laugh I had heard in the gallery: the step ascending to the third story; the smoke – the smell of fire which had conducted me to his room; in what state I had found matters there, and how I had deluged him with all the water I could lay hands on.

He listened very gravely; his face, as I went on, expressed more concern than astonishment; he did not immediately speak when I had concluded.

'Shall I call Mrs Fairfax?' I asked.

'Mrs Fairfax? No: what the deuce would you call her for? What can she do? Let her sleep unmolested.'

'Then I will fetch Leah, and wake John and his wife.'

'Not at all: just be still. You have a shawl on. If you are not warm enough, you may take my cloak yonder; wrap it about you: and sit down on the arm-chair: there – I will put it on. Now place your feet on the stool, to keep them out of the wet. I am going to leave you a few minutes. I shall take the candle. Remain where you are till I return; be as still as a mouse. I must pay a visit to the third story. Don't move, remember, or call any one.'

He went: I watched the light withdraw. He passed up the gallery very softly, unclosed the staircase door with as little noise as possible, shut it after him, and the last ray vanished. I was left in total darkness. I listened for some noise, but heard nothing. A very long time elapsed. I grew weary: it was cold, in spite of the cloak; and then I did not see the use of staying, as I was not to rouse the house. I was on the point of risking Mr Rochester's displeasure by disobeying his orders, when the light once more gleamed dimly on the gallery wall, and I heard his unshod feet tread the matting. 'I hope it is he,' thought I, 'and not something worse.'

He re-entered, pale and very gloomy. 'I have found it all out,' said he, setting the candle down on the washstand; 'it is as I thought.'

'How, sir?'

# Jane Eyre

He made no reply, but stood with his arms folded, looking on the ground. At the end of a few minutes he inquired in rather a peculiar tone –

'I forget whether you said you saw anything when you opened your chamber-door.'

'No, sir, only the candlestick on the ground.'

'But you heard an odd laugh? You have heard that laugh before, I should think, or something like it?'

'Yes, sir: there is a woman who sews here, called Grace Poole – she laughs in that way. She is a singular person.'

'Just so. Grace Poole – you have guessed it. She is as you say, singular – very. Well, I shall reflect on the subject. Meantime, I am glad that you are the only person, besides myself, acquainted with the precise details of to-night's incident. You are no talking fool: say nothing about it. I will account for this state of affairs' (pointing to the bed) 'and now return to your own room. I shall do very well on the sofa in the library for the rest of the night. It is near four: in two hours the servants will be up.'

'Good-night, then, sir,' said I, departing.

He seemed surprised – very inconsistently so, as he had just told me to go.

'What!' he exclaimed, 'are you quitting me already, and in that way?'

'You said I might go, sir.'

'But not without taking leave; not without a word or two of acknowledgement and goodwill: not, in short, in that brief dry fashion. Why, you have saved my life – snatched me from a horrible and excruciating death! and you walk past me as if we were mutual strangers! At least shake hands.'

He held out his hand: I gave him mine: he took it first in one, then in both of his own.

'You have saved my life: I have a pleasure in owing you so immense a debt. I cannot say more. Nothing else that has being would have been tolerable to me in the character of creditor for such an obligation: but you: it is different – I feel your benefit no burden Jane.'

He paused; gazed at me: words almost visible trembled on his lips – but his voice was checked.

'Good-night again, sir. There is no debt, benefit, burden, obligation, in the case.'

'I knew,' he continued, 'you would do me good in some way, at some time: I saw it in your eyes when I first beheld you: their expression and smile did not' – (again he stopped) – 'did not' (he proceeded hastily) 'strike delight to my very inmost heart so for nothing. People talk of natural sympathies: I have heard of good genii: there are grains of truth in the wildest fable. My cherished preserver, good-night!'

Strange energy was in his voice, strange fire in his look.

'I am glad I happened to be awake,' I said: and then I was was going.

'What! you *will* go?'

'I am cold, sir.'

'Cold? Yes – and standing in a pool! Go, then, Jane; go! But he still retained my hand, and I could not free it. I bethought myself of an expedient.

'I think I hear Mrs Fairfax move, sir,' said I.

'Well, leave me': he relaxed his fingers, and I was gone.

I regained my couch, but never thought of sleep. Till morning dawned I was

tossed on a buoyant but unquiet sea, where billows of trouble rolled under surges of joy. I thought sometimes I saw beyond its wild waters a shore, sweet as the hills of Beulah; and now and then a freshening gale, wakened by hope, bore my spirit triumphantly towards the bourne: but I could not reach it, even in fancy – a counteracting breeze blew off the land, and continually drove me back. Sense would resist delirium: judgement would warn passion. Too feverish to rest, I rose as soon as day dawned.

# Chapter 16

I both wished and feared to see Mr Rochester on the day which followed this sleepless night: I wanted to hear his voice again, yet feared to meet his eye. During the early part of the morning I momentarily expected his coming; he was not in the frequent habit of entering the schoolroom, but he did step in for a few minutes sometimes, and I had the impression that he was sure to visit it that day.

But the morning passed just as usual: nothing happened to interrupt the quiet course of Adèle's studies; only, soon after breakfast, I heard some bustle in the neighbourhood of Mr Rochester's chamber, Mrs Fairfax's voice, and Leah's and the cook's – that is, John's wife – and even John's own gruff tones. There were exclamations of 'What a mercy master was not burnt in bed!' 'It is always dangerous to keep a candle lit at night.' 'How providential that he had the presence of mind to think of the water-jug!' 'I wonder he waked nobody!' 'It is to be hoped he will not take cold with sleeping on the library sofa,' &c.

To much confabulation succeeded a sound of scrubbing and setting to rights; and when I passed the room in going downstairs to dinner, I saw through the open door that all was again restored to complete order; only the bed was stripped of its hangings. Leah stood up in the window seat, rubbing the panes of glass dimmed with smoke. I was about to address her, for I wished to know what account had been given of the affair; but, on advancing, I saw a second person in the chamber – a woman sitting on a chair by the bedside, and sewing rings to new curtains. That woman was no other than Grace Poole.

There she sat, staid and taciturn-looking, as usual, in her brown stuff gown, her check apron, white handkerchief, and cap. She was intent on her work, in which her whole thoughts seemed absorbed: on her hard forehead, and in her commonplace features, was nothing either of the paleness or desperation one would have expected to see marking the countenance of a woman who had attempted murder, and whose intended victim had followed her last night to her lair, and (as I believed) charged her with the crime she wished to perpetrate. I was amazed – confounded. She looked up while I still gazed at her: no start, no increase or failure of colour betrayed emotion, consciousness of guilt, or fear

of detection. She said 'Good-morning, miss,' in her usual phlegmatic and brief manner; and taking up another ring and more tape, went on with her sewing.

'I will put her to some test,' thought I: 'such absolute impenetrability is past comprehension.'

'Good-morning, Grace,' I said, 'Has anything happened here? I thought I heard the servants all talking together a while ago.'

'Only master had been reading in his bed last night; he fell asleep with his candle lit, and the curtains got on fire; but, fortunately, he awoke before the bedclothes or the woodwork caught, and contrived to quench the flames with the water in the ewer.'

'A strange affair!' I said, in a low voice: then, looking at her fixedly, 'Did Mr Rochester wake nobody? Did no one hear him move?'

She again raised her eyes to me; and this time there was something of consciousness in their expression. She seemed to examine me warily; then she answered –

'The servants sleep so far off, you know, miss, they would not be likely to hear. Mrs Fairfax's room and yours are the nearest to master's; but Mrs Fairfax said she heard nothing: when people get elderly, they often sleep heavy.' She paused, and then added with a sort of assumed indifference, but still in a marked and significant tone, 'But you are young, miss; and I should say a light sleeper: perhaps you may have heard a noise?'

'I did,' said I, dropping my voice, so that Leah, who was still polishing the panes, could not hear me, 'and at first I thought it was Pilot: but Pilot cannot laugh; and I am certain I heard a laugh, and a strange one.'

She took a needleful of thread, waxed it carefully, threaded her needle with a steady hand, and then observed with perfect composure –

'It is hardly likely master would laugh, I should think, miss, when he was in such danger: you must have been dreaming.'

'I was not dreaming,' I said, with some warmth, for her brazen coolness provoked me. Again she looked at me: and with the same scrutinizing and conscious eye.

'Have you told master that you heard a laugh?' she inquired.

'I have not had the opportunity of speaking to him this morning.'

'You did not think of opening your door and looking out into the gallery?' she further asked.

She appeared to be cross-questioning me, attempting to draw from me information unawares. The idea struck me that if she discovered I knew or suspected her guilt, she would be playing off some of her malignant pranks on me; I thought it advisable to be on my guard.

'On the contrary,' said I, 'I bolted my door.'

'Then you are not in the habit of bolting your door every night before you get into bed?'

'Fiend! she wants to know my habits, that she may lay her plans accordingly!' Indignation again prevailed over prudence: I replied sharply, 'Hitherto I have often omitted to fasten the bolt: I did not think it necessary. I was not aware any danger or annoyance was to be dreaded at Thornfield Hall: but in future' (and I laid marked stress on the words) 'I shall take good care to make all secure before I venture to lie down.'

'It will be a wise thing to do,' was her answer; 'this neighbourhood is as quiet

# Jane Eyre

as any I know, and I never heard of the Hall being attempted by robbers since it was a house; though there are hundreds of pounds' worth of plate in the plate-closet, as is well known. And you see, for such a large house, there are very few servants, because master has never lived here much; and when he does come, being a bachelor, he needs little waiting on: but I always think it best to err on the safe side; a door is soon fastened, and it is as well to have a drawn bolt between one and any mischief that may be about. A deal of people, miss, are for trusting all to Providence; but I say Providence will not dispense with the means, though He often blesses them when they are used discreetly.' And here she closed her harangue: a long one for her, and uttered with the demureness of a Quakeress.

I still stood absolutely dumbfounded at what appeared to me her miraculous self-possession and most inscrutable hypocrisy, when the cook entered.

'Mrs Poole,' said she, addressing Grace, 'the servants' dinner will soon be ready: will you come down?'

'No; just put my pint of porter and a bit of pudding on a tray, and I'll carry it upstairs.'

'You'll have some meat?'

'Just a morsel, and a taste of cheese, that's all.'

'And the sago?'

'Never mind it at present; I shall be coming down before tea-time; I'll make it myself.'

The cook here turned to me, saying that Mrs Fairfax was waiting for me: so I departed.

I hardly heard Mrs Fairfax's account of the curtain conflagration during dinner, so much was I occupied in puzzling my brains over the enigmatical character of Grace Poole, and still more in pondering the problem of her position at Thornfield, and questioning why she had not been given into custody that morning, or, at the very least, dismissed from her master's service. He had almost as much as declared his conviction of her criminality last night: what mysterious cause withheld him from accusing her? Why had he enjoined me, too, to secrecy? It was strange: a bold, vindictive, and haughty gentleman seemed somehow in the power of one of the meanest of his dependants; so much in her power, that even when she lifted her hand against his life, he dared not openly charge her with the attempt, much less punish her for it.

Had Grace been young and handsome, I should have been tempted to think that tenderer feelings than prudence or fear influenced Mr Rochester in her behalf; but, hard-favoured and matronly as she was, the idea could not be admitted. 'Yet,' I reflected, 'she has been young once; her youth would be contemporary with her master's: Mrs Fairfax told me once, she had lived here many years. I don't think she can ever have been pretty; but, for aught I know, she may possess originality and strength of character to compensate for the want of personal advantages. Mr Rochester is an amateur of the decided and eccentric: Grace is eccentric at least. What if a former caprice (a freak very possible to a nature so sudden and headstrong as his) has delivered him into her power, and she now exercises over his actions a secret influence, the result of his own indiscretion, which he cannot shake off, and dare not disregard?' But, having reached this point of conjecture, Mrs Poole's square, flat figure, and uncomely, dry, even coarse face, recurred so distinctly to my mind's eye, that I though. 'No;

impossible! my supposition cannot be correct. Yet,' suggested the secret voice which talks to us in our own hearts, '*you* are not beautiful either, and perhaps Mr Rochester approves you: at any rate, you have often felt as if he did; and last night – remember his words: remember his look: remember his voice!'

I well remembered all – language, glance, and tone seemed at the moment vividly renewed. I was now in the schoolroom; Adèle was drawing; I bent over her and directed her pencil. She looked up with a sort of start.

'Qu'avez-vous, mademoiselle?' said she; 'vos doigts tremblent comme la feuille, et vos joues sont rouges: mais, rouges comme des cerises!'

'I am hot, Adèle, with stooping!' She went on sketching; I went on thinking.

I hastened to drive from my mind the hateful notion I had been conceiving respecting Grace Poole: it disgusted me. I compared myself with her, and found we were different. Bessie Leaven had said I was quite a lady: and she spoke the truth – I was a lady. And now I looked much better than I did when Bessie saw me; I had more colour and more flesh, more life, more vivacity, because I had brighter hopes and keener enjoyments.

'Evening approaches,' said I, as I looked towards the window. 'I have never heard Mr Rochester's voice or step in the house to-day; but surely I shall see him before night: I feared the meeting in the morning; now I desire it, because expectation has been so long baffled that it is grown impatient.'

When dusk actually closed, and when Adèle left me to go and play in the nursery with Sophie, I did most keenly desire it. I listened for the bell to ring below; I listened for Leah coming up with a message; I fancied sometimes I heard Mr Rochester's own tread, and I turned to the door, expecting it to open and admit him. The door remained shut; darkness only came in through the window. Still it was not too late; he often sent for me at seven and eight o'clock and it was not yet six. Surely I would not be wholly disappointed to-night when I had so many things to say to him! I wanted again to introduce the subject of Grace Poole, and to hear what he would answer; I wanted to ask him plainly if he really believed it was she who had made last night's hideous attempt; and if so, why he kept her wickedness a secret. It little mattered whether my curiosity irritated him; I knew the pleasure of vexing and soothing him by turns; it was one I chiefly delighted in, and a sure instinct always prevented me from going too far; beyond the verge of provocation I never ventured; on the extreme brink I liked well to try my skill. Retaining every minute form of respect, every propriety of my station, I could still meet him in argument without fear or uneasy restraint; this suited both him and me.

A tread creaked on the stairs at last; Leah made her appearance; but it was only to intimate that tea was ready in Mrs Fairfax's room. Thither I repaired, glad at least to go downstairs; for that brought me, I imagined, nearer to Mr Rochester's presence.

'You must want your tea,' said the good lady, as I joined her; 'you ate so little at dinner. I am afraid,' she continued, 'you are not well to-day: you look flushed and feverish.'

'Oh, quite well! I never felt better.'

'Then you must prove it by evincing a good appetite; will you fill the teapot while I knit off this needle?' Having completed her task, she rose to draw down the blind, which she had hitherto kept up, by way I suppose, of making the most of daylight, though dusk was now fast deepening into total obscurity.

# Jane Eyre

'It is fair to-night,' said she, as she looked through the panes, 'though not starlight; Mr Rochester has, on the whole, had a favourable day for his journey.'

'Journey! – Is Mr Rochester gone anywhere? I did not know he was out.'

'Oh, he set off the moment he had breakfasted! He is gone to the Leas, Mr Eshton's place, ten miles on the other side Millcote. I believe there is quite a party assembled there; Lord Ingram, Sir George Lynne, Colonel Dent, and others.'

'Do you expect him back to-night?'

'No – nor to-morrow either; I should think he is very likely to stay a week or more: when these fine, fashionable people get together, they are so surrounded by elegance and gaiety, so well provided with all that can please and entertain, they are in no hurry to separate. Gentlemen, especially, are often in request on such occasions; and Mr Rochester is so talented and so lively in society, that I believe he is a general favourite: the ladies are very fond of him: though you would not think his appearance calculated to recommend him particularly in their eyes: but I suppose his acquirements and abilities, perhaps his wealth and good blood, make amends for any little fault of look.'

'Are there ladies at the Leas?'

'There are Mrs Eshton and her three daughters – very elegant young ladies indeed: and there are the Hon. Blanche and Mary Ingram, most beautiful women, I suppose: indeed I have seen Blanche, six or seven years since, when she was a girl of eighteen. She came here to a Christmas ball and party Mr Rochester gave. You should have seen the dining-room that day – how richly it was decorated, how brilliantly lit up! I should think there were fifty ladies and gentlemen present – all of the first county families: and Miss Ingram was considered the belle of the evening.'

'You saw her, you say, Mrs Fairfax: what was she like?'

'Yes, I saw her. The dining-room doors were thrown open; and, as it was Christmas-time, the servants were allowed to assemble in the hall, to hear some of the ladies sing and play. Mr Rochester would have me to come in, and I sat down in a quiet corner and watched them. I never saw a more splendid scene; the ladies were magnificently dressed; most of them – at least most of the younger ones – looked handsome; but Miss Ingram was certainly the queen.'

'And what was she like?'

'Tall, fine bust, sloping shoulders; long, graceful neck; olive complexion, dark and clear; noble features; eyes rather like Mr Rochester's, large and black, and as brilliant as her jewels. And then she had such a fine head of hair, raven-black, and so becomingly arranged; a crown of thick plaits behind, and in front the longest, the glossiest curls I ever saw. She was dressed in pure white; an amber-coloured scarf was passed over her shoulder and across her breast, tied at the side, and descending in long, fringed ends below her knee. She wore an amber-coloured flower, too, in her hair: it contrasted well with the jetty mass of her curls.'

'She was greatly admired, of course?'

'Yes, indeed: and not only for her beauty, but for her accomplishments. She was one of the ladies who sang: a gentleman accompanied her on the piano. She and Mr Rochester sang a duet.'

'Mr Rochester? I was not aware he could sing.'

'Oh! he has a fine bass voice, and an excellent taste for music.'

# Jane Eyre

'And Miss Ingram: what sort of a voice had she?'

'A very rich and powerful one: she sang delightfully; it was a treat to listen to her; and she played afterwards. I am no judge of music, but Mr Rochester is; and I heard him say her execution was remarkably good.'

'And this beautiful and accomplished lady, she is not yet married?'

'It appears not: I fancy neither she nor her sister have very large fortunes. Old Lord Ingram's estates were chiefly entailed, and the eldest son came in for everything almost.'

'But I wonder no wealthy nobleman or gentleman has taken a fancy to her: Mr Rochester, for instance. He is rich, is he not?'

'Oh, yes. But you see there is a considerable different in age. Mr Rochester is nearly forty; she is but twenty-five.'

'What of that? More unequal matches are made every day.'

'True: yet I should scarcely fancy Mr Rochester would entertain an idea of the sort. But you eat nothing; you have scarcely tasted since you began tea.'

'No: I am too thirsty to eat. Will you let me have another cup?'

I was about again to revert to the probability of a union between Mr Rochester and the beautiful Blanche; but Adèle came in, and the conversation was turned into another channel.

When once more alone, I reviewed the information I had got; looked into my heart, examined its thoughts and feelings, and endeavoured to bring back with a strict hand such as had been straying through imagination's boundless and trackless waste, into the safe fold of common sense.

Arraigned at my own bar, Memory having given her evidence of the hopes, wishes, sentiments I had been cherishing since last night – of the general state of mind in which I had indulged for nearly a fortnight past; Reason having come forward, and told, in her own quiet way, a plain, unvarnished tale, showing how I had rejected the real, and rapidly devoured the ideal; – I pronounced judgement to this effect:

That a greater fool than Jane Eyre had never breathed the breath of life: that a more fantastic idiot had never surfeited herself on sweet lies, and swallowed poison as if it were nectar.

'*You*,' I said, 'a favourite with Mr Rochester? *You* gifted with the power of pleasing him? *You* of importance to him in any way? Go! your folly sickens me. And you have derived pleasure from occasional tokens of preference – equivocal tokens shown by a gentleman of family and a man of the world to a dependant and a novice. How dared you? Poor stupid dupe! – Could not even self-interest make you wiser? You repeated to yourself this morning the brief scene of last night? – Cover your face and be ashamed! He said something in praise of your eyes, did he? Blind puppy! Open their bleared lids and look on your own accursed senselessness! It does good to no woman to be flattered by her superior, who cannot possibly intend to marry her; and it is madness in all women to let a secret love kindle within them, which, if unreturned and unknown, must devour the life that feeds it; and, if discovered and responded to, must lead *ignis-fatuus*-like, into miry wilds whence there is no extrication.

'Listen, then, Jane Eyre, to your sentence: to-morrow, place the glass before you, and draw in chalk you own picture, faithfully, without softening one defect; omit no harsh line, smooth away no displeasing irregularity, write under it, "Portrait of a Governess, disconnected, poor, and plain".

'Afterwards take a piece of smooth ivory – you have one prepared in your drawing box: take your palette; mix your freshest, finest, clearest tints; choose your most delicate camel-hair pencils; delineate carefully the loveliest face you can imagine; paint it in your softest shades and sweetest hues, according to the description given by Mrs Fairfax of Blanche Ingram: remember the raven ringlets, the oriental eye; – What! you revert to Mr Rochester as a model! Order! No snivel! – no sentiment! – no regret! I will endure only sense and resolution. Recall the august yet harmonious lineaments, the Grecian neck and bust; let the round and dazzling arm be visible, and the delicate hand; omit neither diamond ring nor gold bracelet; portray faithfully the attire, aerial lace and glistening satin, graceful scarf and golden rose: call it, "Blanche, an accomplished lady of rank."

'Whenever in future you should chance to fancy Mr Rochester thinks well of you, take out these two pictures and compare them: say, "Mr Rochester might probably win that noble lady's love, if he chose to strive for it; is it likely he would waste a serious thought on this indigent and insignificant plebeian?"'

'I'll do it,' I resolved: and having framed this determination, I grew calmer, and fell asleep.

I kept my word. An hour or two sufficed to sketch my own portrait in crayons; and in less than a fortnight I had completed an ivory miniature of an imaginary Blanche Ingram. It looked a lovely face enough, and when compared with the real head in chalk, the contrast was as great as self-control could desire. I derived benefit from the task: it had kept my head and hands employed, and had given force and fixedness to the new impressions I wished to stamp indelibly on my heart.

Ere long, I had reason to congratulate myself on the course of wholesome discipline to which I had thus forced my feelings to submit: thanks to it, I was able to meet subsequent occurrences with a decent calm; which, had they found me unprepared, I should probably have been unequal to maintain, even externally.

# Chapter 17

 week passed, and no news arrived of Mr Rochester: ten days, and still he did not come. Mrs Fairfax said she should not be surprised if he were to go straight from the Leas to London, and thence to the Continent, and not show his face again at Thornfield for a year to come; he had not infrequently quitted it in a manner quite as abrupt and unexpected. When I heard this, I was beginning to feel a strange chill and failing at the heart. I was actually permitting myself to experience a sickening sense of disappointment; but rallying my wits, and recollecting my principles, I at once called my

# Jane Eyre

sensations to order; and it was wonderful how I got over the temporary blunder – how I cleared up the mistake of supposing Mr Rochester's movements a matter in which I had any cause to take a vital interest. Not that I humbled myself by a slavish notion of inferiority: on the contrary, I just said –

'You have nothing to do with the master of Thornfield, further than to receive the salary he gives you for teaching his protégée, and to be grateful for such respectful and kind treatment as, if you do your duty, you have a right to expect at his hands. Be sure that this is the only tie he seriously acknowledges between you and him; so don't make him the object of your fine feelings, your raptures, agonies, and so forth. He is not of your order: keep to your caste, and be too self-respecting to lavish the love of the whole heart, soul and strength, where such a gift is not wanted and would be despised.'

I went on with my day's business tranquilly; but ever and anon vague suggestions kept wandering across my brain, of reasons why I should quit Thornfield; and I kept involuntarily framing advertisements and pondering conjectures about new situations: these thoughts I did not think it necessary to check; they might germinate and bear fruit if they could.

Mr Rochester had been absent upwards of a fortnight when the post brought Mrs Fairfax a letter.

'It is from the master,' said she, as she looked at the direction. 'Now I suppose we shall know whether we are to expect his return or not.'

And while she broke the seal and perused the document, I went on taking my coffee (we were at breakfast): it was hot, and I attributed to that circumstance a fiery glow which suddenly rose to my face. Why my hand shook, and why I voluntarily spilt half the contents of my cup into my saucer, I did not choose to consider.

'Well, I sometimes think we are too quiet; but we run a chance of being busy enough now, for a little while at least,' said Mrs Fairfax, still holding the note before her spectacles.

Ere I permitted myself to request an explanation, I tied the string of Adèle's pinafore, which happened to be loose: having helped her also to another bun and refilled her mug with milk, I said nonchalantly –

'Mr Rochester is not likely to return soon, I suppose?'

'Indeed he is – in three days, he says: that will be next Thursday; and not alone either. I don't know how many of the fine people at the Leas are coming with him: he sends directions for all the best bedrooms to be prepared; and the library and the drawing-rooms are to be cleaned out; and I am to get more kitchen hands from the George Inn, at Millcote, and from wherever else I can; and the ladies will bring their maids and the gentlemen their valets: so we shall have a full house of it.' And Mrs Fairfax swallowed her breakfast and hastened away to commence operations.

The three days were, as she had foretold, busy enough. I had thought all the rooms at Thornfield beautifully clean and well arranged; but it appears I was mistaken. Three women were got to help; and such scrubbing, such brushing, such washing of paint and beating of carpets, such taking down and putting up of pictures, such polishing of mirrors and lustres, such lighting of fires in bedrooms, such airing of sheets and feather-beds on hearths, I never beheld, either before or since. Adèle ran quite wild in the midst of it: the preparations for the company and the prospect of their arrival, seemed to throw her into

ecstasies. She would have Sophie to look over her 'toilettes,' as she called frocks; to furbish up any that were *'passées'*, and to air and arrange the new. For herself, she did nothing but caper about in the front chambers, jump on and off the bedsteads, and lie on the mattresses and piled-up bolsters and pillows before the enormous fires roaring in the chimneys. From school duties she was exonerated: Mrs Fairfax has pressed me into her service, and I was all day in the store-room, helping (or hindering) her and the cook; learning to make custards and cheese-cakes and French pastry, to truss game and garnish dessert-dishes.

The party were expected to arrive on Thursday afternoon, in time for dinner at six. During the intervening period I had no time to nurse chimeras; and I believe I was as active and gay as anybody – Adèle excepted. Still, now and then, I received a damping check to my cheerfulness; and was, in spite of myself, thrown back on the region of doubts and portents and dark conjectures. This was when I chanced to see the third-story staircase door (which of late had always been kept locked) open slowly, and give passage to the form of Grace Poole, in prim cap, white apron, and handkerchief; when I watched her glide along the gallery, her quiet tread muffled in a list slipper; when I saw her look into the bustling, topsy-turvey bedrooms – just say a word, perhaps, to the charwoman about the proper way to polish a grate, or clean a marble mantelpiece, or take stains from papered walls, and then pass on. She would thus descend to the kitchen once a day, eat her dinner, smoke a moderate pipe on the hearth, and go back, carrying her pot of porter with her, for her private solace, in her own gloomy upper haunt. Only one hour in the twenty-four did she pass with her fellow-servants below; all the rest of her time was spent in some low-ceiled, oaken chamber of the third story; there she sat and sewed – as companionless as a prisoner in his dungeon.

The strangest thing of all, was, that not a soul in the house, except me, noticed her habits, or seemed to marvel at them: no one discussed her position or employment; no one pitied her solitude or isolation. I once, indeed, overheard part of a dialogue between Leah and one of the charwomen, of which Grace had formed the subject. Leah had been saying something I had not caught, and the charwoman remarked –

'She gets good wages, I guess?'

'Yes,' said Leah; 'I wish I had as good; not that mine are to complain of – there's no stinginess at Thornfield; but they're not one-fifth of the sum Mrs Poole receives. And she is laying by: she goes every quarter to the bank at Millcote. I should not wonder but she has saved enough to keep her independent if she liked to leave; but I suppose she's got used to the place; and then she's not forty yet, and strong and able for anything. It is too soon for her to give up business.'

'She is a good hand, I dare say,' said the charwoman.

'Ah! – she understands what she has to do – nobody better,' rejoined Leah significantly; 'and it is not every one who could fill her shoes – not for all the money she gets.'

'That it is not!' was the reply. 'I wonder whether the master –'

The charwoman was going on; but here Leah turned and perceived me, and she instantly gave her companion a nudge.

'Doesn't she know?' I heard the woman whisper.

Leah shook her head, and the conversation was of course dropped. All I had gathered from it amounted to this – that there was a mystery at Thornfield; and that from participation in that mystery I was purposely excluded.

Thursday came: all work had been completed the previous evening; carpets were laid down, bed-hangings festooned, radiant white counterpanes spread, toilet tables arranged, furniture rubbed, flowers piled in vases: both chambers and saloons looked as fresh and bright as hands could make them. The hall, too, was scoured; and the great carved clock, as well as the steps and banisters of the staircase, were polished to the brightness of glass; in the dining-room the sideboard flashed resplendent with plate; in the drawing-room and boudoir, vases of exotics bloomed on all sides.

Afternoon arrived: Mrs Fairfax assumed her best black satin gown, her gloves, and her gold watch; for it was her part to receive the company – to conduct the ladies to their rooms, etc. Adèle, too, would be dressed: though I thought she had little chance of being introduced to the party that day at least. However, to please her, I allowed Sophie to apparel her in one of her short, full muslin frocks. For myself, I had no need to make any change; I should not be called upon to quit my sanctum of the schoolroom; for a sanctum it was now become to me – 'a very pleasant refuge in time of trouble'.

It had been a mild, serene spring day – one of those days, which towards the end of March or the beginning of April, rise shining over the earth as heralds of summer. It was drawing to an end now; but the evening was even warm, and I sat at work in the schoolroom with the window open.

'It gets late,' said Mrs Fairfax, entering in rustling state. 'I am glad I ordered dinner an hour after the time Mr Rochester mentioned; for it is past six now. I have sent John down to the gates to see if there is anything on the road: one can see a long way from thence in the direction of Millcote.' She went to the window. 'Here he is!' said she. 'Well, John' (leaning out), 'any news?'

'They're coming, ma'am,' was the answer. 'They'll be here in ten minutes.'

Adèle flew to the window. I followed, taking care to stand on one side, so that, screened by the curtain, I could see without being seen.

The ten minutes John had given seemed very long, but at last wheels were heard; four equestrians galloped up the drive, and after them came two open carriages. Fluttering veils and waving plumes filled the vehicles; two of the cavaliers were young, dashing-looking gentlemen; the third was Mr Rochester, on his black horse, Mesrour, Pilot bounding before him; at his side rode a lady, and he and she were the first of the party. Her purple riding-habit almost swept the ground, her veil streamed long on the breeze; mingling with its transparent folds, and gleaming through them, shone rich raven ringlets.

'Miss Ingram!' exclaimed Mrs Fairfax, and away she hurried to her post below.

The calvacade, following the sweep of the drive, quickly turned the angle of the house, and I lost sight of it. Adèle now petitioned to go down: but I took her on my knee, and gave her to understand that she must not on any account think of venturing in sight of the ladies, either now or at any other time, unless expressly sent for: that Mr Rochester would be very angry, etc. 'Some natural tears she shed' on being told this; but as I began to look very grave, she consented at last to wipe them.

A joyous stir was now audible in the hall: gentlemen's deep tones and ladies

# Jane Eyre

silvery accents blent harmoniously together, and distinguishable above all, though not loud, was the sonorous voice of the master of Thornfield Hall, welcoming his fair and gallant guests under its roof. Then light steps ascended the stairs; and there was a tripping through the gallery, and soft cheerful laughs, and opening and closing doors, and, for a time, a hush.

'Elles changent de toilettes,' said Adèle; who, listening attentively, had followed every movement; and she sighed.

'Chez maman,' said she, 'quand il y avait du monde, je le suivais partout au salon et à leurs chambres; souvent je regardais les femmes de chambre coiffer et habiller les dames, et c'était si amusant: comme cela on apprend.'

'Don't you feel hungry, Adèle?'

'Mais oui, mademoiselle: voilà cinq ou six heures que nous n'avons pas mangé.'

'Well, now, while the ladies are in their rooms, I will venture down and get you something to eat.'

And issuing from my asylum with precaution, I sought a backstairs which conducted directly to the kitchen. All in that region was fire and commotion; the soup and fish were in the last stage of projection, and the cook hung over her crucibles in a frame of mind and body threatening spontaneous combustion. In the servants' hall two coachmen and three gentlemen's gentlemen stood or sat round the fire; the abigails, I suppose, were upstairs with their mistresses; the new servants, that had been hired from Millcote, were bustling about everywhere. Threading this chaos, I at last reached the larder; there I took possession of a cold chicken, a roll of bread, some tarts, a plate or two, and a knife and fork: with this booty I made a hasty retreat. I had regained the gallery and was just shutting the back-door behind me, when an accelerated hum warned me that the ladies were about to issue from their chambers. I could not proceed to the schoolroom without passing some of their doors, and running the risk of being surprised with my cargo of victualage; so I stood still at this end, which, being windowless, was dark: quite dark now, for the sun was set and twilight gathering.

Presently the chambers gave up their fair tenants one after another: each came out gaily and airily, with dresses that gleamed lustrous through the dusk. For a moment they stood grouped together at the other extremity of the gallery, conversing in a key of sweet subdued vivacity: they then descended the staircase almost as noiselessly as a bright mist rolls down a hill. Their collective appearance had left on me an impression of high-born elegance, such as I had never before received.

I found Adèle peeping through the schoolroom door, which she held ajar. 'What beautiful ladies!' cried she in English. 'Oh, I wish I might go to them! Do you think Mr Rochester will send for us by and by, after dinner?'

'No, indeed I don't; Mr Rochester has something else to think about. Never mind the ladies to-night; perhaps you will see them to-morrow: here is your dinner.'

She was really hungry, so the chicken and tarts served to divert her attention for a time. It was well I secured this forage, or both she, I and Sophie, to whom I conveyed a share of our repast, would have run a chance of getting no dinner at all: every one downstairs was too much engaged to think of us. The dessert was not carried out till after nine; and at ten footmen were still running to and fro with trays and coffee-cups. I allowed Adèle to sit up much later than usual;

# Jane Eyre

for she declared she could not possibly go to sleep while the doors kept opening and shutting below, and people bustling about. Besides, she added, a message might possibly come from Mr Rochester when she was undressed; 'et alors quel dommage!'

I told her stories as long as she would listen to them; and then for a change I took her out into the gallery. The hall lamp was now lit, and it amused her to look over the balustrade and watch the servants passing backwards and forwards. When the evening was far advanced a sound of music issued from the drawing-room, whither the piano had been removed; Adèle and I sat down on the top step of the stairs to listen. Presently a voice blent with the rich tones of the instrument; it was a lady who sang, and very sweet her notes were. The solo over, a duet followed, and then a glee: a joyous conversational murmur filled up the intervals. I listened long: suddenly discovered that my ears were wholly intent on analysing the mingled sounds, and trying to discriminate amidst the confusion of accents those of Mr Rochester; and when it caught them, which it soon did, it found a further task in framing the tones, rendered by distance inarticulate, into words.

The clock struck eleven. I looked at Adèle, whose head leant against my shoulder; her eyes were waxing heavy, so I took her up in my arms and carried her off to bed. It was near one before the gentlemen and ladies sought their chambers.

The next day was as fine as its predecessor: it was devoted by the party to an excursion to some site in the neighbourhood. They set out early in the forenoon, some on horseback, the rest in carriages; I witnessed both the departure and the return. Miss Ingram, as before, was the only lady equestrian; and, as before, Mr Rochester galloped at her side; the two rode a little apart from the rest. I pointed out this circumstance to Mrs Fairfax, who was standing at the window with me –

'You said it was not likely they should think of being married,' said I, 'but you see Mr Rochester evidently prefers her to any of the other ladies.'

'Yes, I dare say: no doubt he admires her.'

'And she him,' I added; 'look how she leans her head towards him as if she were conversing confidentially: I wish I could see her face; I have never had a glimpse of it yet.'

'You will see her this evening,' answered Mrs Fairfax. 'I happened to remark to Mr Rochester how much Adèle wished to be introduced to the ladies, and he said: "Oh! let her come into the drawing-room after dinner; and request Miss Eyre to accompany her."'

'Yes; he said that from mere politeness: I need not go, I am sure,' I answered.

'Well, I observed to him that as you were unused to company, I did not think you would like appearing before so gay a party – all strangers; and he replied in his quick way, "Nonsense! If she objects, tell her it is my particular wish; and if she resists, say I shall come and fetch her in case of contumacy."'

'I will not give him that trouble,' I answered. 'I will go, if no better may be; but I don't like it. Shall you be there, Mrs Fairfax?'

'No; I pleaded off, and he admitted my plea. I'll tell you how to manage so as to avoid the embarrassment of making a formal entrance, which is the most disagreeable part of the business. You must go into the drawing-room while it is empty, before the ladies leave the dinner-table; choose your seat in any quiet

nook you like; you need not stay long after the gentlemen come in, unless you please: just let Mr Rochester see you are there and then slip away – nobody will notice you.'

'Will these people remain long, do you think?'

'Perhaps two or three weeks, certainly not more. After the Easter recess, Sir George Lynn, who was lately elected member for Millcote, will have to go up to town and take his seat; I dare say Mr Rochester will accompany him: it surprises me that he has already made so protracted a stay at Thornfield.'

It was with some trepidation that I perceived the hour approach when I was to repair with my charge to the drawing-room. Adèle had been in a state of ecstasy all day, after hearing she was to be presented to the ladies in the evening; and it was not till Sophie commenced the operation of dressing her that she sobered down. Then the importance of the process quickly steadied her, and by the time she had her curls arranged in well-smoothed, drooping clusters, her pink satin frock on, her long sash tied, and her lace mittens adjusted, she looked as grave as any judge. No need to warn her not to disarrange her attire: when she was dressed, she sat demurely down in her little chair, taking care previously to lift up the satin skirt for fear she should crease it, and assured me she would not stir thence till I was ready. This I quickly was: my best dress (the silver-gray one, purchased for Miss Temple's wedding, and never worn since) was soon put on; my hair was soon smoothed; my sole ornament, the pearl brooch, soon assumed. We descended.

Fortunately, there was another entrance to the drawing-room than that through the saloon where they were all seated at dinner. We found the apartment vacant; a large fire burning silently on the marble hearth, and wax candles shining in bright solitude amid the exquisite flowers with which the tables were adorned. The crimson curtain hung before the arch: slight as was the separation this drapery formed from the party in the adjoining saloon, they spoke in so low a key that nothing of their conversation could be distinguished beyond a soothing murmur.

Adèle who appeared to be still under the influence of a most solemnizing impression, sat down, without a word, on the footstool I pointed out to her. I retired to a window-seat, and, taking a book from a table near, endeavoured to read. Adèle brought her stool to my feet; ere long she touched my knee.

'What is it, Adèle?'

'Est-ce que je ne puis pas prendre une seule de ces fleurs magnifiques, mademoiselle? Seulement pour completer ma toilette.'

'You think too much of your "toilette", Adèle: but you may have a flower.' And I took a rose from a vase and fastened it on her sash. She sighed a sigh of ineffable satisfaction, as if her cup of happiness were now full. I turned my face away to conceal a smile I could not suppress: there was something ludicrous as well as painful in the little Parisienne's earnest and innate devotion to matters of dress.

A soft sound of rising now became audible; the curtain was swept back from the arch; through it appeared the dining-room, with its lit lustre pouring down light on the silver and glass of a magnificent dessert-service covering a long table; a band of ladies stood in the opening; they entered, and the curtain fell behind them.

There were but eight; yet, somehow, as they flocked in, they gave the

impression of a much larger number. Some of them were very tall; many were dressed in white; and all had a sweeping amplitude of array that seemed to magnify their persons as a mist magnifies the moon. I rose and curtseyed to them: one or two bent their heads in return; the others only stared at me.

They dispersed about the room, reminding me, by the lightness and buoyancy of their movements, of a flock of white plumy birds. Some of them threw themselves in half-reclining positions on the sofas and ottomans: some bent over the tables and examined the flowers and books: the rest gathered in a group round the fire: all talked in a low but clear tone which seemed habitual to them. I knew their names afterwards, and may as well mention them now.

First, there was Mrs Eshton and two of her daughters. She had evidently been a handsome woman, and was well preserved still. Of her daughters, the eldest, Amy, was rather little: naïve, and child-like, in face and manner, and piquant in form; her white muslin dress and blue sash became her well. The second, Louisa, was taller and more elegant in figure; with a very pretty face, of that order the French term *minois chiffonné*: both sisters were fair as lilies.

Lady Lynn was a large and stout personage of about forty, very erect, very haughty-looking, richly dressed in a satin robe of changeful sheen: her dark hair shone glossily under the shade of an azure plume, and within the circlet of a band of gems.

Mrs Colonel Dent was less showy; but, I thought, more ladylike. She had a slight figure, a pale, gentle face, and fair hair. Her black satin dress, her scarf of rich foreign lace, and her pearl ornaments, pleased me better than the rainbow radiance of the titled dame.

But the three most distinguished – partly, perhaps, because the tallest figures of the band – were the Dowager Lady Ingram and her daughters, Blanche and Mary. They were all three of the loftiest stature of woman. The dowager might be between forty and fifty: her shape was still fine; her hair (by candlelight at least) still black; her teeth, too, were still apparently perfect. Most people would have termed her a splendid woman of her age: and so she was, no doubt, physically speaking; but then there was an expression of almost insupportable haughtiness in her bearing and countenance. She had Roman features and a double chin, disappearing into a throat like a pillar: these features appeared to me not only inflated and darkened, but even furrowed with pride; and the chin was sustained by the same principle, in a position of almost preternatural erectness. She had, likewise, a fierce and hard eye: it reminded me of Mrs Reed's; she mouthed her words in speaking; her voice was deep, its inflections very pompous, very dogmatical – very intolerable, in short. A crimson velvet robe, and a shawl turban of some gold-wrought Indian fabric, invested her (I suppose she thought) with a truly imperial dignity.

Blanche and Mary were of equal stature – straight and tall as poplars. Mary was too slim for her height, but Blanche was moulded like a Diana. I regarded her, of course, with special interest. First, I wished to see whether her appearance accorded with Mrs Fairfax's description; secondly, whether it at all resembled the fancy miniature I had painted of her; and thirdly – it will out! – whether it were such as I should fancy likely to suit Mr Rochester's taste.

As far as person went, she answered point for point, both to my picture and Mrs Fairfax's description. The noble bust, the sloping shoulders, the graceful neck, the dark eyes and black ringlets were all there: but her face? Her face was

like her mother's; a youthful unfurrowed likeness: the same low brow, the same high features, the same pride: it was not, however, so saturnine a pride. She laughed continually: her laugh was satirical, and so was the habitual expression of her arched and haughty lip.

Genius is said to be self-conscious: I cannot tell whether Miss Ingram was a genius, but she was self-conscious – remarkably self-conscious indeed. She entered into a discourse on botany with the gentle Mrs Dent. It seemed Mrs Dent had not studied the science: though, as she said, she liked flowers, 'especially wild ones'; Miss Ingram had, and she ran over its vocabulary with an air. I presently perceived she was (what is vernacularly termed) *trailing* Mrs Dent; that is, playing on her ignorance: her *trail* might be clever, but it was decidedly not good-natured. She played: her execution was brilliant; she sang: her voice was fine; she talked French apart to her mamma: and she talked it well, with fluency and with a good accent.

Mary had a milder and more open countenance than Blanche; softer features too, and a skin some shades fairer (Miss Ingram was dark as a Spaniard) – but Mary was deficient in life: her face lacked expression, her eye lustre; she had nothing to say, and having once taken her seat, remained fixed like a statue in its niche. The sisters were both attired in spotless white.

And did I now think Miss Ingram such a choice as Mr Rochester would be likely to make? I could not tell – I did not know his taste in female beauty. If he liked the majestic, she was the very type of majesty; then she was accomplished, sprightly. Most gentlemen would admire her, I thought; and that he *did* admire her, I already seemed to have obtained proof: to remove the last shade of doubt, it remained but to see them together.

You are not to suppose, reader, that Adèle has all this time been sitting motionless on the stool at my feet: no; when the ladies entered, she rose, advanced to meet them, made a stately reverence, and said with gravity–

'Bon jour, mesdames.'

And Miss Ingram had looked down at her with a mocking air, and exclaimed, 'Oh, what a little puppet!'

Lady Lynn had remarked, 'It is Mrs Rochester's ward, I suppose – the little French girl he was speaking of.'

Mrs Dent had kindly taken her hand, and given her a kiss. Amy and Louisa Eshton had cried out simultaneously –

'What a love of a child!'

And then they had called her to a sofa, where she now sat, ensconced between them, chattering alternately in French and broken English; absorbing not only the young ladies' attention, but that of Mrs Eshton and Lady Lynn, and getting spoilt to her heart's content.

At last coffee is brought in, and the gentlemen are summoned. I sit in the shade – if any shade there be in this brilliantly lit apartment; the window-curtain half hides me. Again the arch yawns; they come. The collective appearance of the gentlemen, like that of the ladies, is very imposing: they are all costumed in black; most of them are tall, some young. Henry and Frederick Lynn are very dashing sparks indeed; and Colonel Dent is a fine soldierly man. Mr Eshton, the magistrate of the district, is gentleman-like: his hair is quite white, his eyebrows and whiskers still dark, which gives him something of the appearance of a 'père noble de théâtre'. Lord Ingram, like his sisters, is very

# Jane Eyre

tall; like them, also, he is handsome; but he shares Mary's apathetic and listless look: he seems to have more length of limb than vivacity of blood or vigour of brain.

And where is Mr Rochester?

He comes in last: I am not looking at the arch, yet I see him enter. I try to concentrate my attention on those netting-needles, on the meshes of the purse I am forming – I wish to think only of the work I have in my hands, to see only the silver beads and silk threads that lie in my lap; whereas, I distinctly behold his figure, and I inevitably recall the moment when I last saw it; just after I had rendered him what he deemed an essential service, and he, holding my hand, and looking down on my face, surveyed me with eyes that revealed a heart full and eager to overflow; in whose emotions I had a part. How near had I approached him at that moment! What had occurred since, calculated to change his and my relative positions? Yet now, how distant, how far estranged we were! So far estranged, that I did not expect him to come and speak to me. I did not wonder, when without looking at me, he took a seat at the other side of the room, and began conversing with some of the ladies.

No sooner did I see that his attention was riveted on them, and that I might gaze without being observed, than my eyes were drawn involuntarily to his face; I could not keep their lids under control: they would rise, and the irids would fix on him. I looked, and had an acute pleasure in looking – a precious yet poignant pleasure; pure gold, with a steely point of agony: a pleasure like what the thirst-perishing man might feel who knows the well to which he has crept is poisoned, yet stoops and drinks divine draughts nevertheless.

Most true is it that 'beauty is in the eye of the gazer'. My master's colourless, olive face, square, massive brow, broad and jetty eyebrows, deep eyes, strong features, firm, grim mouth – all energy, decision, will – were not beautiful, according to rule; but they were more than beautiful to me: they were full of an interest, an influence that quite mastered me – that took my feelings from my own power and fettered them in his. I had not intended to love him; the reader knows I had wrought hard to extirpate from my soul the germs of love there detected; and now, at the first renewed view of him they spontaneously revived, green and strong! He made me love him without looking at me.

I compared him with his guests. What was the gallant grace of the Lynns, the languid elegance of Lord Ingram – even the military distinction of Colonel Dent, contrasted with his look of native pith and genuine power? I had no sympathy in their appearance, their expression: yet I could imagine that most observers would call them attractive, handsome, imposing; while they would pronounce Mr Rochester at once harsh featured and melancholy looking. I saw them smile, laugh – it was nothing; the light of the candles had as much soul in it as their smile; the tinkle of the bell as much significance as their laugh. I saw Mr Rochester smile – his stern features softened; his eye grew both brilliant and gentle, its ray both searching and sweet. He was talking, at the moment, to Louisa and Amy Eshton. I wondered to see them receive with calm that look which seemed to me so penetrating: I expected their eyes to fall, their colour to rise under it; yet I was glad when I found they were in no sense moved. 'He is not to them what he is to me,' I thought: 'he is not of their kind. I believe he is of mine – I am sure he is – I feel akin to him – I understand the language of his countenance and movements: though rank and wealth sever us widely, I

# Jane Eyre

have something in my brain and heart, in my blood and nerves, that assimilates me mentally to him. Did I say, a few days since, that I had nothing to do with him but to receive my salary at his hands? Did I forbid myself to think of him in any other light than as a paymaster? Blasphemy against nature! Every good, true, vigorous feeling I have gathers impulsively round him. I know I must conceal my sentiments: I must smother hope; I must remember that he cannot care much for me. For when I say that I am of his kind, I do not mean that I have his force to influence, and his spell to attract; I mean only that I have certain tastes and feelings in common with him. I must, then, repeat continually that we are for ever sundered – and yet, while I breathe and I think, I must love him.'

Coffee is handed. The ladies, since the gentlemen entered, have become lively as larks; conversation waxes brisk and merry. Colonel Dent and Mr Eshton argue on politics; their wives listen. The two proud dowagers, Lady Lynn and Lady Ingram, confabulate together. Sir George – whom, by the by, I have forgotten to describe – a very big, and very fresh-looking country gentleman, stands before their sofa, coffee-cup in hand, and occasionally puts in a word. Mr Frederick Lynn has taken a seat beside Mary Ingram and is showing her the engravings of a splendid volume: she looks, smiles now and then, but apparently says little. The tall and phlegmatic Lord Ingram leans with folded arms on the chair-back of the little and lively Amy Eshton; she glances up at him, and chatters like a wren; she likes him better than she does Mr Rochester. Henry Lynn has taken possession of an ottoman at the feet of Louisa: Adèle shares it with him: he is trying to talk French with her, and Louisa laughs at his blunders. With whom will Blanche Ingram pair? She is standing alone at the table, bending gracefully over an album. She seems waiting to be sought; but she will not wait too long: she herself selects a mate.

Mr Rochester having quitted the Eshtons, stands on the hearth as solitary as she stands by the table: she confronts him, taking her station on the opposite side of the mantelpiece.

'Mr Rochester, I thought you were not fond of children?'

'Nor am I.'

'Then what induced you to take charge of such a little doll as that?' (pointing to Adèle). 'Where did you pick her up?'

'I did not pick her up; she was left on my hands.'

'You should have sent her to school.'

'I could not afford it: schools are so dear.'

'Why, I suppose you have a governess for her: I saw a person with her just now – is she gone? Oh, no! there she is still, behind the window-curtain. You pay her, of course; I should think it quite as expensive – more so; for you have them both to keep in addition.'

I feared – or should I say, hoped – the allusion to me would make Mr Rochester glance my way; and I involuntarily shrank further into the shade: but he never turned his eyes.

'I have not considered the subject,' said he indifferently, looking straight before him.

'No, you men never do consider economy and common sense. You should hear mamma on the chapter of governesses. Mary and I have had, I should think,

# Jane Eyre

a dozen at least in our day; half of them detestable and the rest ridiculous, and all incubi – were they not, mamma?'

'Did you speak, my own?'

The young lady thus claimed as the dowager's special property, reiterated her question with an explanation.

'My dearest, don't mention governesses; the word makes me nervous. I have suffered a martyrdom from their incompetency and caprice. I thank Heaven I have now done with them!'

Mrs Dent here bent over to the pious lady, and whispered something in her ear; I suppose, from the answer elicited, it was a reminder that one of the anathematized race was present.

'Tant pis!' said her ladyship. 'I hope it may do her good!' Then, in a lower tone, but still loud enough for me to hear, 'I noticed her; I am a judge of physiognomy, and in hers I see all the faults of her class.'

'What are they, madam?' inquired Mr Rochester aloud.

'I will tell you in your private ear,' replied she, wagging her turban three times with portentous significance.

'But my curiosity will be past its appetite; it craves food now.'

'Ask Blanche; she is nearer you than I.'

'Oh, don't refer him to me, mamma! I have just one word to say of the whole tribe; they are a nuisance. Not that I ever suffered much from them; I took care to turn the tables. What tricks Theodore and I used to play on our Miss Wilsons, and Mrs Greys, and Madame Jouberts! Mary was always too sleepy to join in a plot with spirit. The best fun was with Madame Joubert: Miss Wilson was a poor, sickly thing, lachrymose and low-spirited, not worth the trouble of vanquishing, in short; and Mrs Grey was coarse and insensible; no blow took effect on her. But poor Madame Joubert! I see her yet in her raging passions, when we had driven her to extremities – spilt our tea, crumbled our bread and butter, tossed our books up to the ceiling, and played a charivari with the ruler and desk, the fender and fire-irons. Theodore, do you remember those merry days?'

'Yaas, to be sure I do,' drawled Lord Ingram; 'and the poor old stick used to cry out, "Oh you villains childs!" and then we sermonized her on the presumption of attempting to teach such clever blades as we were, when she was herself so ignorant.'

'We did; and, Tedo, you know, I helped you in prosecuting (or persecuting) your tutor, whey-faced Mr Vining – the parson in the pip, as we used to call him. He and Miss Wilson took the liberty of falling in love with each other – at least Tedo and I thought so; we surprised sundry tender glances and sighs which we interpreted as tokens of "la belle passion", and I promise you the public soon had the benefit of our discovery; we employed it as a sort of lever to hoist our deadweights from the house. Dear mamma there, as soon as she got an inkling of the business, found out that it was of an immoral tendency. Did you not, my lady-mother?'

'Certainly, my best. And I was quite right: depend on that: there are a thousand reasons why liaisons between governesses and tutors should never be tolerated a moment in any well-regulated house; firstly –'

'Oh, gracious, mamma! Spare us the enumeration! *Au reste*, we all know them: danger of bad example to innocence of childhood; distractions and

consequent neglect of duty on the part of the attached – mutual alliance and reliance; confidence thence resulting – insolence accompanying – mutiny and general blow-up. Am I right, Baroness Ingram, of Ingram Park?'

'My lily-flower, you are right now, as always.'

'Then no more need be said: change the subject.'

Amy Eshton, not hearing or not heeding this dictum, joined in with her soft, infantine tone: 'Louisa and I used to quiz our governess too; but she was such a good creature, she would bear anything: nothing put her out. She was never cross with us; was she, Louisa?'

'No, never; we might do what we pleased – ransack her desk and her workbox, and turn her drawers inside out; and she was so good-natured, she would give us anything we asked for.'

'I suppose, now,' said Miss Ingram, curling her lips sarcastically, 'we shall have an abstract of the memoirs of all the governesses extant. In order to avert such a visitation, I again move the introduction of a new topic. Mr Rochester, do you second my motion?'

'Madam, I support you on this point, as on every other.'

'Then on me be the onus of bringing it forward. Signior Eduardo, are you in voice to-night?'

'Donna Bianca, if you command it, I will be.'

'Then, signior, I lay on you my sovereign behest to furbish up your lungs and other vocal organs, as they will be wanted on my royal service.'

'Who would not be the Rizzio of so divine a Mary?'

'A fig for Rizzio!' cried she, tossing her head with all its curls, as she moved to the piano. 'It is my opinion, the fiddler David must have been an insipid sort of a fellow; I like black Bothwell better: to my mind a man is nothing without a spice of the devil in him; and history may say what it will of James Hepburn, but I have a notion he was just the sort of wild, fierce, bandit hero whom I could have consented to gift with my hand.'

'Gentlemen, you hear! Now, which of you most resembles Bothwell?' cried Rochester.

'I should say the preference lies with you,' responded Colonel Dent.

'On my honour, I am much obliged to you,' was the reply.

Miss Ingram, who had now seated herself with proud grace at the piano, spreading out her snowy robes in queenly amplitude, commenced a brilliant prelude; talking meantime. She appeared to be on her high-horse to-night; both her words and her air seemed intended to excite not only the admiration, but the amazement of her auditors: she was evidently bent on striking them as something very dashing and daring indeed.

'Oh, I am so sick of the young men of the present day!' exclaimed she, rattling away at the instrument. 'Poor, puny things, not fit to stir a step beyond papa's park gates: nor to go even so far without mamma's permission and guardianship! Creatures so absorbed in care about their pretty faces, and their white hands, and their small feet; as if a man had anything to do with beauty! As if loveliness were not the special prerogative of woman – her legitimate appanage and heritage! I grant an ugly *woman* is a blot on the fair face of creation; but as to the *gentlemen*, let them be solicitous to possess only strength and valour: let their motto be – hunt, shoot, and fight: the rest is not worth a fillip. Such should be my device, were I a man.

# Jane Eyre

'Whenever I marry,' she continued after a pause which none interrupted, 'I am resolved my husband shall not be a rival, but a foil to me. I will suffer no competitor near the throne; I shall exact an undivided homage; his devotion shall not be shared between me and the shape he sees in his mirror. Mr Rochester, now sing, and I will play for you.'

'I am all obedience,' was the response.

'Here then is a Corsair-song. Know that I dote on Corsairs; and for that reason, sing it *con spirito.*'

'Commands from Miss Ingram's lips would put spirit into a mug of milk and water.'

'Take care, then: if you don't please me, I will shame you by showing how such things *should* be done.'

'That is offering a premium on incapacity: I shall now endeavour to fail.'

'Gardez-vous-en bien! If you err wilfully, I shall devise a proportionate punishment.'

'Miss Ingram ought to be clement, for she has it in her power to inflict a chastisement beyond mortal endurance.'

'Ha! explain!' commanded the lady.

'Pardon me, madam: no need of explanation; your own fine sense must inform you that one of your frowns would be a sufficient substitute for capital punishment.'

'Sing!' said she, and again touching the piano, she commenced an accompaniment in spirited style.

'Now is my time to slip away,' thought I: but the tones that then severed the air arrested me. Mrs Fairfax had said Mr Rochester possessed a fine voice: he did – a mellow, powerful bass, into which he threw his own feeling, his own force; finding a way through the ear to the heart, and there waking sensation strangely. I waited till the last deep and full vibration had expired – till the tide of talk, checked an instant, had resumed its flow; I then quitted my sheltered corner and made my exit by the side-door, which was fortunately near. Thence a narrow passage led into the hall: in crossing it, I perceived my sandal was loose; I stopped to tie it, kneeling down for that purpose on the mat at the foot of the staircase. I heard the dining-room door unclose; a gentleman came out; rising hastily, I stood face to face with him: it was Mr Rochester.

'How do you do?' he asked.

'I am very well, sir.'

'Why did you not come and speak to me in the room?'

I thought I might have retorted the question on him who put it: but I would not take that freedom. I answered –

'I did not wish to disturb you, as you seemed engaged, sir.'

'What have you been doing during my absence?'

'Nothing particular; teaching Adèle as usual.'

'And getting a good deal paler than you were – as I saw at first sight. What is the matter?'

'Nothing at all, sir.'

'Did you take any cold that night you half drowned me?'

'Not the least.'

'Return to the drawing-room: you are deserting too early.'

'I am tired, sir.'

He looked at me for a minute.

'And a little depressed,' he said 'What about? Tell me.'

'Nothing – nothing sir. I am not depressed.'

'But I affirm that you are: so much depressed that a few more words would bring tears to your eyes – indeed, they are there now, shining and swimming; and a bead has slipped from the lash and fallen on the flag. If I had time, and was not in mortal dread of some prating prig of a servant passing, I would know what all this means. Well, to-night I excuse you; but understand that so long as my visitors stay, I expect you to appear in the drawing-room, every evening; it is my wish; don't neglect it. Now go, and send Sophie for Adèle. Goodnight, my –' He stopped, bit his lip, and abruptly left me.

# Chapter 18

Merry days were these at Thornfield Hall; and busy days too: how different from the first three months of stillness, monotony, and solitude I had passed beneath its roof! All sad feelings seemed now driven from the house, all gloomy associations forgotten: there was life everywhere, movement all day long. You could not now traverse the gallery, once so hushed, nor enter the front chambers, once so tenantless, without encountering a smart lady's maid or a dandy valet.

The kitchen, the butler's pantry, the servants' hall, the entrance hall, were equally alive; and the saloons were only left void and still when the blue sky and halcyon sunshine of the genial spring weather called their occupants out into the grounds. Even when that weather was broken, and continuous rain set in for some days, no damp seemed cast over enjoyment: indoor amusements only became more lively and varied, in consequence of the stop put to outdoor gaiety.

I wondered what they were going to do the first evening a change of entertainment was proposed: they spoke of 'playing charades', but in my ignorance I did not understand the term. The servants were called in, the dining-room tables wheeled away, the lights otherwise disposed, the chairs placed in a semicircle opposite the arch. While Mr Rochester and the other gentlemen directed these alterations, the ladies were running up and down stairs ringing for their maids. Mrs Fairfax was summoned to give information respecting the resources of the house in shawls, dresses, draperies of any kind; and certain wardrobes of the third story were ransacked, and their contents, in the shape of brocaded and hooped petticoats, satin sacques, black modes, lace lappets, &c., were brought down in armfuls by the abigails; then a selection was made, and such things as were chosen were carried to the boudoir within the drawing-room.

Meantime, Mr Rochester had again summoned the ladies round him, and

# Jane Eyre

was selecting certain of their number to be of his party. 'Miss Ingram is mine, of course,' said he: afterwards he named the two Misses Eshton, and Mrs Dent. He looked at me: I happened to be near him, as I had been fastening the clasp of Mrs Dent's bracelet, which had got loose.

'Will you play?' he asked. I shook my head. He did not insist, which I rather feared he would have done; he allowed me to return quietly to my usual seat.

He and his aids now withdrew behind the curtain: the other party, which was headed by Colonel Dent, sat down on the crescent of chairs. One of the gentlemen, Mr Eshton, observing me, seemed to propose that I should be asked to join them; but Lady Ingram instantly negatived the notion.

'No,' I heard her say: 'she looks too stupid for any game of the sort.'

Ere long, a bell tinkled, and the curtain drew up. Within the arch, the bulky figure of Sir George Lynn, whom Mr Rochester had likewise chosen, was seen enveloped in a white sheet: before him, on a table, lay open a large book; and at his side stood Amy Eshton, draped in Mr Rochester's cloak, and holding a book in her hand. Somebody unseen, rang the bell merrily; then Adèle (who had insisted on being one of her guardian's party), bounded forward, scattering round her the contents of a basket of flowers she carried on her arm. Then appeared the magnificent figure of Miss Ingram, clad in white, a long veil on her head, and a wreath of roses round her brow; by her side walked Mr Rochester, and together they drew near the table. They knelt; while Mrs Dent and Louisa Eshton, dressed also in white, took up their stations behind them. A ceremony followed, in dumb show, in which it was easy to recognize the pantomime of marriage. At its termination, Colonel Dent and his party consulted in whispers for two minutes, then the Colonel called out –

'Bride!' Mr Rochester bowed, and the curtain fell.

A considerable interval elapsed before it again rose. Its second rising displayed a more elaborately prepared scene than the last. The drawing-room, as I have before observed, was raised two steps above the dining-room, and on the top of the upper step, placed a yard or two back within the room, appeared a large marble basin, which I recognized as an ornament of the conservatory – where it usually stood, surrounded by exotics, and tenanted by gold fish – and whence it must have been transported with some trouble, on account of its size and weight.

Seated on the carpet, by the side of this basin, was seen Mr Rochester, costumed in shawls, with a turban on his head. His dark eyes and swarthy skin and Paynim features suited the costume exactly: he looked the very model of an Eastern emir, an agent or a victim of the bowstring. Presently advanced into view Miss Ingram. She, too, was attired in oriental fashion: a crimson scarf tied sash-like round the waist: an embroidered handkerchief knotted about her temples: her beautifully-moulded arms bare, one of them upraised in the act of supporting a pitcher, poised gracefully on her head. Both her cast of form and feature, her complexion and her general air, suggested the idea of some Israelitish princess of the patriarchal days; and such was doubtless the character she intended to represent.

She approached the basin, and bent over it as if to fill her pitcher; she again lifted it to her head. The personage on the well-brink now seemed to accost her; to make some request: 'She hasted, let down her pitcher on her hand, and gave him to drink.' From the bosom of his robe he then produced a casket, opened

it, and showed magnificent bracelets and ear-rings; she acted astonishment and admiration; kneeling, he laid the treasure at her feet; incredulity and delight were expressed by her looks and gestures; the stranger fastened the bracelets on her arms and the rings in her ears. It was Eleizer and Rebecca: the camels only were wanting.

The divining party again laid their heads together: apparently they could not agree about the word or syllable the scene illustrated. Colonel Dent, their spokesman, demanded 'the tableau of the whole'; whereupon the curtain again descended.

On its third rising, only a portion of the drawing-room was disclosed, the rest being concealed by a screen, hung with some sort of dark and coarse drapery. The marble basin was removed; in its place stood a deal table and a kitchen chair: these objects were visible by a very dim light proceeding from a horn lantern, the wax candles being all extinguished.

Amidst this sordid scene, sat a man with his clenched hands resting on his knees, and his eyes bent on the ground. I knew Mr Rochester; though the begrimed face, the disordered dress (his coat hanging loose from one arm, as if it had been almost torn from his back in a scuffle), the desperate and scowling countenance, the rough, bristling hair might well have disguised him. As he moved, a chain clanked; to his wrists were attached fetters.

'Bridewell!' exclaimed Colonel Dent, and the charade was solved.

A sufficient interval having elapsed for the performers to resume their ordinary costume, they re-entered the dining-room. Mr Rochester led in Miss Ingram; she was complimenting him on his acting.

'Do you know,' said she, 'that, of the three characters, I liked you in the last best? Oh, had you but lived a few years earlier, what a gallant gentleman-highwayman you would have made!'

'Is all the soot washed from my face?' he asked, turning it towards her.

'Alas! yes: the more's the pity! Nothing could be more becoming to your complexion than that ruffian's rouge.'

'You would like a hero of the road then?'

'An English hero of the road would be the next best thing to an Italian bandit; and that could only be surpassed by a Levantine pirate.'

'Well, whatever I am, remember you are my wife; we were married an hour since, in the presence of all these witnesses.' She giggled, and her colour rose.

'Now, Dent,' continued Mr Rochester, 'it is your turn.' And as the other party withdrew, he and his band took the vacated seats. Miss Ingram placed herself at her leader's right hand; the other diviners filled the chairs on each side of him and her. I did not now watch the actors; I no longer waited with interest for the curtain to rise; my attention was absorbed by the spectators; my eyes, erewhile fixed on the arch, were now irresistibly attracted to the semicircle of chairs. What charade Colonel Dent and his party played, what word they chose, how they acquitted themselves, I no longer remember; but I still see the consultation which followed each scene: I see Mr Rochester turn to Miss Ingram, and Miss Ingram to him; I see her incline her head towards him, till the jetty curls almost touch his shoulder and wave against his cheek; I hear their mutual whisperings; I recall their interchanged glances; and something even of the feeling roused by the spectacle returns in memory at this moment.

I have told you, reader, that I had learnt to love Mr Rochester: I could not

# Jane Eyre

unlove him now, merely because I found that he had ceased to notice me – because I might pass hours in his presence and he would never once turn his eyes in my direction – because I saw all his attentions appropriated by a great lady, who scorned to touch me with the hem of her robes as she passed; who, if ever her dark and imperious eye fell on me by chance, would withdraw it instantly as from an object too mean to merit observation. I could not unlove him, because I felt sure he would soon marry this very lady – because I read daily in her a proud security in his intentions respecting her – because I witnessed hourly in him a style of courtship which, if careless and choosing rather to be sought than to seek, was yet, in its very carelessness, captivating, and in its very pride, irresistible.

There was nothing to cool or banish love in these circumstances, though much to create despair. Much too, you will think, reader, to engender jealousy: if a woman in my position could presume to be jealous of a woman in Miss Ingram's. But I was not jealous, or very rarely; the nature of the pain I suffered could not be explained by that word. Miss Ingram was a mark beneath jealousy: she was too inferior to excite the feeling. Pardon the seeming paradox; I mean what I say. She was very showy, but she was not genuine; she had a fine person, many brilliant attainments, but her mind was poor, her heart barren by nature; nothing bloomed spontaneously on that soil; no unforced natural fruit delighted by its freshness. She was not good; she was not original: she used to repeat sounding phrases from books: she never offered, nor had, an opinion of her own. She advocated a high tone of sentiment, but she did not know the sensations of sympathy and pity; tenderness and truth were not in her. Too often she betrayed this, by the undue vent she gave to a spiteful antipathy she had conceived against little Adèle, pushing her away with some contumelious epithet if she happened to approach her; sometimes ordering her from the room, and always treating her with coldness and acrimony. Other eyes besides mine watched these manifestations of character – watched them closely, keenly, shrewdly. Yes; the future bridegroom, Mr Rochester himself, exercised over his intended a ceaseless surveillance: and it was from this sagacity – this guardedness of his – this perfect, clear consciousness of his fair one's defects – this obvious absence of passion in his sentiments towards her, that my ever-torturing pain arose.

I saw he was going to marry her, for family, perhaps political reasons; because her rank and connections suited him; I felt he had not given her his love, and that her qualifications were ill-adapted to win from him that treasure. This was the point – this was where the nerve was touched and teased – this was where the fever was sustained and fed: *she could not charm him.*

If she had managed the victory at once, and he had yielded and sincerely laid his heart at her feet, I should have covered my face, turned to the wall, and (figuratively) have died to them. If Miss Ingram had been a good and noble woman, endowed with force, fervour, kindness, sense, I should have had one vital struggle with two tigers – jealousy and despair: then, my heart torn out and devoured, I should have admired her – acknowledged her excellence, and been quiet for the rest of my days: and the more absolute her superiority, the deeper would have been my admiration – the more truly tranquil my quiescence. But, as matters really stood, to watch Miss Ingram's efforts at fascinating Mr Rochester, to witness their repeated failure – herself unconscious that they did fail; vainly fancying that each shaft launched hit the mark, and infatuatedly

# Jane Eyre

pluming herself on success, when her pride and self-complacency repelled further and further what she wished to allure – to witness *this*, was to be at once under ceaseless excitation and ruthless restraint.

Because, when she failed, I saw how she might have succeeded. Arrows that continually glanced off from Mr Rochester's breast and fell harmless at his feet, might, I knew, if shot by a surer hand, have quivered keen in his proud heart – have called love into his stern eye, and softness into his sardonic face; or, better still, without weapons a silent conquest might have been won.

'Why can she not influence him more, when she is privileged to draw so near to him?' I asked myself, 'Surely she cannot truly like him, or not like him with true affection! If she did, she need not coin her smiles so lavishly, flash her glances so unremittingly, manufacture airs so elaborate, graces to multitudinous. It seems to me that she might, by merely sitting quietly at his side saying little and looking less, get nigher his heart. I have seen in his face a far different expression from that which hardens it now while she is so vivaciously accosting him; but then it came of itself: it was not elicited by meretricious arts and calculated manoeuvres; and one had but to accept it – to answer what he asked without pretension, to address him when needful without grimace – and it increased and grew kinder and more genial, and warmed one like a fostering sunbeam. How will she manage to please him when they are married? I do not think they will manage it; and yet it might be managed; and his wife might, I verily believe, be the very happiest woman the sun shines on.'

I have not yet said anything condemnatory of Mr Rochester's project of marrying for interest and connexions. It surprised me when I first discovered that such was his intention: I had thought him a man unlikely to be influenced by motives so commonplace in his choice of a wife; but the longer I considered the position, education, &c., of the parties, the less I felt justified in judging and blaming either him or Miss Ingram for acting in conformity to ideas and principles instilled into them, doubtless, from their childhood. All their class held these principles: I supposed, then, they had reasons for holding them, such as I could not fathom. It seemed to me that, were I a gentleman like him, I would take to my bosom only such a wife as I could love; but the very obviousness of the advantages to the husband's own happiness offered by this plan convinced me that there must be arguments against its general adoption of which I was quite ignorant: otherwise I felt sure all the world would act as I wished to act.

But in other points, as well as this, I was growing very lenient to my master: I was forgetting all his faults, for which I had once kept a sharp lookout. It had formerly been my endeavour to study all sides of his character: to take the bad with the good; and from the just weighing of both, to form an equitable judgement. Now I saw no bad. The sarcasm that had repelled, the harshness that had startled me once, were only like keen condiments in a choice dish: their presence was pungent, but their absence would be felt as comparatively insipid. And as for the vague something – was it a sinister or a sorrowful, a designing or a desponding expression? – that opened upon a careful observer, now and then, in his eye, and closed again before one could fathom the strange depth partially disclosed; that something which used to make me fear and shrink, as if I had been wandering amongst volcanic-looking hills, and had suddenly felt the ground quiver, and seen it gape; that something, I, at intervals beheld still, and with throbbing heart, but not with palsied nerves. Instead of wishing to

shun, I longed only to dare – to divine it; and I thought Miss Ingram happy, because one day she might look into the abyss at her leisure, explore its secrets and analyze their nature.

Meantime, while I thought only of my master and his future bride – saw only them, heard only their discourse, and considered only their movements of importance – the rest of the party were occupied with their own separate interests and pleasures. The Ladies Lynn and Ingram continued to consort in solemn conferences, where they nodded their two turbans at each other, and held up their four hands in confronting gestures of surprise, or mystery, or horror, according to the theme on which their gossip ran, like a pair of magnified puppets. Mild Mrs Dent talked with good-natured Mrs Eshton; and the two sometimes bestowed a courteous word or smile on me. Sir George Lynn, Colonel Dent, and Mr Eshton discussed politics, or county affairs, or justice business. Lord Ingram flirted with Amy Eshton; Louisa played and sang to and with one of the Messrs Lynn; and Mary Ingram listened languidly to the gallant speeches of the other. Sometimes all, as with one consent, suspended their byplay to observe and listen to the principal actors; for, after all, Mr Rochester and – because closely connected with him – Miss Ingram were the life and soul of the party. If he was absent from the room an hour, a perceptible dullness seemed to steal over the spirits of his guests; his re-entrance was sure to give a fresh impulse to the vivacity of conversation.

The want of his animating influence appeared to be peculiarly felt one day that he had been summoned to Millcote on business, and was not likely to return till late. The afternoon was wet: a walk the party had proposed to take to see a gipsy camp, lately pitched on a common beyond Hay, was consequently deferred. Some of the gentlemen were gone to the stables: the younger ones, together with the younger ladies, were playing billiards in the billiard-room. The Dowagers Ingram and Lynn sought solace in a quiet game at cards. Blanche Ingram, after having repelled, by supercilious taciturnity, some efforts of Mrs Dent and Mrs Eshton to draw her into conversation, had first murmured over some sentimental tunes and airs on the piano, and then, having fetched a novel from the library, had flung herself in haughty listlessness on a sofa, and prepared to beguile, by the spell of fiction, the tedious hours of absence. The room and the house were silent: only now and then the merriment of the billiard-players was heard from above.

It was verging on dusk, and the clock had already given warning of the hour to dress for dinner, when little Adèle, who knelt by me in the drawing-room window-seat, suddenly exclaimed –

'Voilà Monsieur Rochester, qui revient!'

I turned, and Miss Ingram darted forward from her sofa: the others, too, looked up from their several occupations; for at the same time a crunching of wheels, and a splashing tramp of horse-hoofs became audible on the wet gravel. A post-chaise was approaching.

'What can possess him to come home in that style?' said Miss Ingram. 'He rode Mesrour (the black horse), did he not, when he went out? and Pilot was with him – what has he done with the animals?'

As she said this, she approached her tall person and ample garments so near the window, that I was obliged to bend back almost to the breaking of my spine: in her eagerness she did not observe me at first, but when she did, she curled

# Jane Eyre

her lip and moved to another casement. The post-chaise stopped; the driver rang the door-bell, and a gentleman alighted, attired in travelling garb; but it was not Mr Rochester; it was a tall, fashionable-looking man, a stranger.

'How provoking!' exclaimed Miss Ingram: 'you tiresome monkey!' (apostrophizing Adèle) 'who perched you up in the window to give false intelligence?' and she cast on me an angry glance, as if I were in fault.

Some parleying was audible in the hall, and soon the new-comer entered. He bowed to Lady Ingram, as deeming her the eldest lady present.

'It appears I come at an inopportune time, madam,' said he, 'when my friend, Mr Rochester, is from home; but I arrive from a very long journey, and I think I may presume so far on old and intimate acquaintance as to instal myself here till he returns.'

His manner was polite; his accent, in speaking, struck me as being somewhat unusual – not precisely foreign, but still not altogether English: his age might be about Mr Rochester's – between thirty and forty; his complexion was singularly sallow: otherwise he was a fine-looking man, at first sight especially. On closer examination, you detected something in his face that displeased; or rather, that failed to please. His features were regular, but too relaxed: his eye was large and well cut, but the life looking out of it was a tame, vacant life – at least so I thought.

The sound of the dressing-bell dispersed the party. It was not till after dinner that I saw him again: he then seemed quite at his ease. But I liked his physiognomy even less than before: it struck me as being at the same time unsettled and inanimate. His eye wandered, and had no meaning in its wandering: this gave him an odd look, such as I never remembered to have seen. For a handsome and not an unamiable-looking man, he repelled me exceedingly: there was no power in that smooth-skinned face of a full oval shape; no firmness in that aquiline nose and small cherry mouth; there was no thought on the low, even forehead; no command in that blank, brown eye.

As I sat in my usual nook, and looked at him with the light of the girandoles on the mantelpiece beaming full over him – for he occupied an arm-chair drawn close to the fire, and kept shrinking still nearer, as if he were cold – I compared him with Mr Rochester. I think (with deference be it spoken) the contrast could not be much greater between a sleek gander and a fierce falcon: between a meek sheep and the rough-coated, keen-eyed dog, its guardian.

He had spoken of Mr Rochester as an old friend. A curious friendship theirs must have been: a pointed illustration, indeed, of the old adage that 'extremes meet'.

Two or three of the gentlemen sat near him, and I caught at times scraps of their conversation across the room. At first I could not make much sense of what I heard; for the discourse of Louisa Eshton and Mary Ingram, who sat nearer to me, confused the fragmentary sentences that reached me at intervals. These last were discussing the stranger; they both called him 'a beautiful man'. Louisa said he was 'a love of a creature', and she 'adored him'; and Mary instanced his 'pretty little mouth, and nice nose', as her ideal of the charming.

'And what a sweet-tempered forehead he has!' cried Louisa, 'so smooth – none of those frowning irregularities I dislike so much; and such a placid eye and smile!'

And then, to my great relief, Mr Henry Lynn summoned them to the other

# Jane Eyre

side of the room, to settle some point about the deferred excursion to Hay Common.

I was now able to concentrate my attention on the group by the fire, and I presently gathered that the new-comer was called Mr Mason; then I learned that he was but just arrived in England, and that he came from some hot country: which was the reason, doubtless, his face was so sallow, and that he sat so near the hearth, and wore a surtout in the house. Presently the words Jamaica, Kingston, Spanish Town, indicated the West Indies as his residence; and it was with no little surprise I gathered, ere long, that he had there first seen and become acquainted with Mr Rochester. He spoke of his friend's dislike of the burning heats, the hurricanes, and rainy seasons of that region. I knew Mr Rochester had been a traveller: Mrs Fairfax had said so; but I thought the continent of Europe had bounded his wanderings; till now I had never heard a hint given of visits to more distant shores.

I was pondering these things, when an incident, and a somewhat unexpected one, broke the thread of my musings. Mr Mason, shivering as some one chanced to open the door, asked for more coal to be put on the fire, which had burnt out its flame, though its mass of cinder still shone hot and red. The footman who brought the coal, in going out, stopped near Mr Eshton's chair, and said something to him in a low voice, of which I heard only the words 'old woman' – 'quite troublesome'.

'Tell her she shall be put in the stocks if she does not take herself off,' replied the magistrate.

'No – stop!' interrupted Colonel Dent. 'Don't send her away, Eshton; we might turn the thing to account; better consult the ladies.' And, speaking aloud, he continued – 'Ladies, you talked of going to Hay Common to visit the gipsy camp; Sam, here, says that one of the old Mother Bunches is in the servants' hall at this moment, and insists upon being brought in before "the quality", to tell them their fortunes. Would you like to see her?'

'Surely, colonel,' cried Lady Ingram, 'you would not encourage such a low impostor? Dismiss her, by all means, at once!'

'But I cannot persuade her to go away, my lady,' said the footman; 'nor can any of the servants: Mrs Fairfax is with her just now, entreating her to be gone; but she has taken a chair in the chimney corner, and says nothing shall stir her from it till she gets leave to come in here.'

'What does she want?' asked Mrs Eshton.

'"To tell the gentry their fortunes," she says, ma'am; and she swears she must and will do it.'

'What is she like?' inquired the Misses Eshton, in a breath.

'A shockingly ugly old creature, miss; almost as black as a crock.'

'Why, she's a real sorceress!' cried Frederick Lynn. 'Let us have her in, of course.'

'To be sure,' rejoined his brother; 'it would be a thousand pities to throw away such a chance of fun.'

'My dear boys, what are you thinking about?' exclaimed Mrs Lynn.

'I cannot possibly countenance any such inconsistent proceeding,' chimed in the Dowager Ingram.

'Indeed, mamma, but you can – and will,' pronounced the haughty voice of Blanche, as she turned round on the piano-stool; where till now she had sat

# Jane Eyre

silent, apparently examining sundry sheets of music. 'I have a curiosity to hear my fortune told: therefore, Sam, order the beldame forward.'

'My darling Blanche! recollect —'

'I do – I recollect all you can suggest: and I must have my will – quick, Sam!'

'Yes – yes – yes!' cried all the juveniles, both ladies and gentlemen. 'Let her come – it will be excellent sport!'

The footman still lingered. 'She looks such a rough one,' said he.

'Go!' ejaculated Miss Ingram, and the man went.

Excitement instantly seized the whole party: a running fire of raillery and jests was proceeding when Sam returned.

'She won't come now,' said he. 'She says it's not her mission to appear before the "vulgar herd" (them's her words). I must show her into a room by herself, and then those who wish to consult her must go to her one by one.'

'You see now, my queenly Blanche,' began Lady Ingram, 'she encroaches. Be advised, my angel girl – and —'

'Show her into the library, of course,' cut in the 'angel girl'. 'It is not my mission to listen to her before the vulgar herd either: I mean to have her all to myself. Is there a fire in the library?'

'Yes, ma'am – but she looks such a tinkler.'

'Cease that chatter, blockhead! and do my bidding.'

Again Sam vanished; and mystery, animation, expectation rose to full flow once more.

'She's ready now,' said the footman, as he reappeared.

'She wishes to know who will be her first visitor.'

'I think I had better just look in upon her before any of the ladies go,' said Colonel Dent.

'Tell her, Sam, a gentleman is coming.'

Sam went and returned.

'She says, sir, that she'll have no gentlemen; they need not trouble themselves to come near her; nor,' he added, with difficulty suppressing a titter, 'any ladies either, except the young and single.'

'By jove, she has taste!' exlaimed Henry Lynn.

Miss Ingram rose solemnly: 'I go first,' she said, in a tone which might have befitted the leader of a forlorn hope, mounting a breach in the van of his men.

'Oh, my best! oh, my dearest! pause – reflect!' was her mamma's cry: but she swept past her in stately silence, passed through the door which Colonel Dent held open, and we heard her enter the library.

A comparative silence ensued. Lady Ingram thought it 'le cas' to wring her hands: which she did accordingly. Miss Mary declared she felt, for her part, she never dared venture. Amy and Louisa Eshton tittered under their breath, and looked a little frightened.

The minutes passed very slowly: fifteen were counted before the library door again opened. Miss Ingram returned to us through the arch.

Would she laugh? Would she take it as a joke? All eyes met her with a glance of eager curiosity, and she met all eyes with one of rebuff and coldness: she looked neither flurried nor merry; she walked stiffly to her seat, and took it in silence.

'Well, Blanche?' said Lord Ingram.

'What did she say, sister?' asked Mary.

'What did you think? How do you feel? Is she a real fortune-teller?' demanded the Misses Eshton.

'Now, now, good people,' returned Miss Ingram, 'don't press upon me. Really your organs of wonder and credulity are easily excited: you seem, by the importance you all – my good mamma included – ascribe to this matter, absolutely to believe we have a genuine witch in the house, who is in close alliance with the old gentleman. I have seen a gipsy vagabond; she has practised in hackneyed fashion the science of palmistry and told me what such people usually tell. My whim is gratified; and now I think Mr Eshton will do well to put the hag in the stocks to-morrow morning, as he threatened.'

Miss Ingram took a book, leant back in her chair, and so declined further conversation. I watched her for nearly half an hour: during all that time she never turned a page, and her face grew momently darker, more dissatisfied, and more sourly expressive of disappointment. She had obviously not heard anything to her advantage: and it seemed to me, from her prolonged fit of gloom and taciturnity, that she herself, notwithstanding her professed indifference, attached undue importance to whatever revelations had been made her.

Meantime, Mary Ingram, Amy and Louisa Eshton, declared they dared not go alone; and yet they all wished to go. A negotiation was opened through the medium of the ambassador, Sam; and after much pacing to and fro, till, I think, she said Sam's calves must have ached with the exercise, permission was at last, with great difficulty, extorted from the rigorous sibyl, for the three to wait upon her in a body.

Their visit was not so still as Miss Ingram's had been: we heard hysterical giggling and little shrieks proceeding from the library; and at the end of about twenty minutes they burst the door open, and came running across the hall, as if they were half-scared out of their wits.

'I am sure she is something not right!' they cried, one and all. 'She told us such things! She knows all about us!' and they sank breathless into the various seats the gentlemen hastened to bring them.

Pressed for further explanations, they declared she had told them of things they had said and done when they were mere children; described books and ornaments they had in their boudoirs at home: keepsakes that different relations had presented to them. They affirmed that she had even divined their thoughts, and had whispered in the ear of each the name of the person she liked best in the world, and informed them of what they most wished for.

Here the gentlemen interposed with earnest petitions to be further enlightened on these two last-named points, but they got only blushes, ejaculations, tremors, and titters, in return for the importunity. The matrons, meantime, offered vinaigrettes and wielded fans; and again reiterated the expression of their concern that their warning had not been taken in time; and the elder gentlemen laughed, and the younger urged their services on the agitated fair ones.

In the midst of the tumult, and while my eyes and ears were fully engaged in the scene before me, I heard a 'hem' close at my elbow; I turned, and saw Sam.

'If you please, miss, the gipsy declares that there is another young single lady in the room who has not been to her yet, and she swears she will not go till she has seen all. I thought it must be you: there is no one else for it. What shall I tell her?'

'Oh, I will go by all means,' I answered; and I was glad of the unexpected opportunity to gratify my much-excited curiosity. I slipped out of the room, unobserved by an eye – for the company were gathered in one mass about the trembling trio just returned – and I closed the door quietly behind me.

'If you like, miss,' said Sam, 'I'll wait in the hall for you; if she frightens you, just call and I'll come in.'

'No, Sam, return to the kitchen: I am not in the least afraid.' Nor was I; but I was a good deal interested and excited.

# Chapter 19

The library looked tranquil enough as I entered it, and the sibyl – if sibyl she were – was seated snugly enough in an easy-chair at the chimney corner. She had on a red cloak and a black bonnet: or rather, a broad-brimmed gipsy hat, tied down with a striped handkerchief under the chin. An extinguished candle stood on the table; she was bending over the fire, and seemed reading in a little black book, like a Prayer Book, by the light of the blaze: she muttered the words to herself, as most old women do, while she read; she did not desist immediately on my entrance: it appeared she wished to finish a paragraph.

I stood on the rug and warmed my hands, which were rather cold with sitting at a distance from the drawing-room fire. I felt now as composed as ever I did in my life: there was nothing indeed in the gipsy's appearance to trouble one's calm. She shut her book and slowly looked up; her hat-brim partially shaded her face, yet I could see, as she raised it, that it was a strange one. It looked all brown and black: elf-locks bristled out from beneath a white band which passed under her chin, and came half over her cheeks, or rather jaws: her eye confronted me at once, with a bold and direct gaze.

'Well, and you want your fortune told?' she said, in a voice as decided as her glance, as harsh as her features.

'I don't care about it, mother; you may please yourself: but I ought to warn you, I have no faith.'

'It's like your impudence to say so: I expected it of you: I heard it in your step as you crossed the threshold.'

'Did you? You've a quick ear.'

'I have; and a quick eye, and a quick brain.'

'You need them all in your trade.'

'I do: especially when I've customers like you to deal with. Why don't you tremble?'

'I'm not cold.'

'Why don't you turn pale?'

# Jane Eyre

'I am not sick.'

'Why don't you consult my art?'

'I'm not silly.'

The old crone 'nichered' a laugh under her bonnet and bandage; she then drew out a short black pipe, and lighting it, began to smoke. Having indulged a while in this sedative, she raised her bent body, took the pipe from her lips, and while gazing steadily at the fire, said very deliberately –

'You are cold; you are sick; you are silly.'

'Prove it,' I rejoined.

'I will in a few words. You are cold, because you are alone: no contact strikes the fire from you that is in you. You are sick, because the best of feelings, the highest and the sweetest given to man, keeps far away from you. You are silly, because, suffer as you may, you will not beckon it to approach, nor will you stir one step to meet it where it waits for you.'

She again put her short black pipe to her lips, and renewed her smoking with vigour.

'You might say all that to almost any one who, you knew, lived as a solitary dependant in a great house.'

'I might say it to almost any one: but would it be true of almost any one?'

'In my circumstances.'

'Yes; just so, in *your* circumstances: but find me another precisely placed as you are.'

'It would be easy to find you thousands.'

'You could scarcely find me one. If you knew it, you are peculiarly situated: very near happiness; yes, within reach of it. The materials are all prepared; there only wants a movement to combine them. Chance laid them somewhat apart; let them be once approached and bliss results.'

'I don't understand enigmas. I never could guess a riddle in my life.'

'If you wish me to speak more plainly, show me your palm.'

'And I must cross it with silver, I suppose?'

'To be sure.'

I gave her a shilling: she put it into an old stocking-foot which she took out of her pocket, and having tied it round and returned it, she told me to hold out my hand. I did. She approached her face to the palm, and pored over it without touching it.

'It is too fine,' said she. 'I can make nothing of such a hand as that; almost without lines; besides, what is in a palm? Destiny is not written there.'

'I believe you,' said I.

'No,' she continued, 'it is in the face: on the forehead, about the eyes, and in the eyes themselves, in the lines of the mouth. Kneel, and lift up your head.'

'Ah! now you are coming to reality,' I said, as I obeyed her. 'I shall begin to put some faith in you presently.'

I knelt within half a yard of her. She stirred the fire, so that a ripple of light broke from the disturbed coal: the glare, however, as she sat, only threw her face into deeper shadow: mine, it illumined.

'I wonder with what feelings you came to me to-night,' she said, when she had examined me a while. 'I wonder what thoughts were busy in your heart during all the hours you sit in yonder room with the fine people flitting before you like shapes in a magic-lantern: just as little sympathetic communion passing

between you and them as if they were really mere shadows of human forms, and not the actual substance.'

'I feel tired often, sleepy sometimes, but seldom sad.'

'Then you have some secret hope to buoy you up and please you with the whispers of the future?'

'Not I. The utmost I hope is, to save enough money out of my earnings to set up a school some day in a little house rented by myself.'

'A mean nutriment for the spirit to exist on: and sitting in that window-seat (you see I know your habits) —'

'You have learned them from the servants.'

'Ah! you think yourself sharp. Well, perhaps I have: to speak truth, I have an acquaintance with one of them, Mrs Poole —'

I started to my feet when I heard the name.

'You have - have you?' thought I; 'there is diablerie in the business after all, then!'

'Don't be alarmed,' continued the strange being; 'she's a safe hand is Mrs Poole: close and quiet; any one might repose confidence in her. But, as I was saying: sitting in that window-seat, do you think of nothing but your future school? Have you no present interest in any of the company who occupy the sofas and chairs before you? Is there not one face you study? one figure whose movements you follow with at least curiosity?'

'I like to observe all the faces, and all the figures.'

'But do you never single one from the rest - or it may be two?'

'I do frequently; when the gestures or looks of a pair seem telling a tale: it amuses me to watch them.'

'What tale do you like best to hear?'

'Oh, I have not much choice! They generally run on the same theme – courtship; and promise to end in the same catastrophe - marriage.'

'And do you like that monotonous theme?'

'Positively, I don't care about it: it is nothing to me.'

'Nothing to you? When a lady, young and full of life and health, charming, with beauty, and endowed with the gifts of rank and fortune, sits and smiles in the eyes of a gentleman you —'

'I what?'

'You know - and perhaps think well of.'

'I don't know the gentlemen here. I have scarcely interchanged a syllable with one of them; and as to thinking well of them, I consider some respectable, and stately, and middle-aged; and others young, dashing, handsome, and lively: but certainly they are all at liberty to be the recipients of whose smiles they please, without my feeling disposed to consider the transaction of any moment to me.'

'You don't know the gentlemen here? You have not exchanged a syllable with one of them? Will you say that of the master of the house?'

'He is not at home.'

'A profound remark! A most ingenious quibble! He went to Millcote this morning, and will be back here to-night or to-morrow: does that circumstance exclude him from the list of your acquaintance - blot him, as it were, out of existence?'

'No; but I can scarcely see what Mr Rochester has to do with the theme you had introduced.'

# Jane Eyre

'I was talking of ladies smiling in the eyes of gentlemen; and of late so many smiles have been shed into Mr Rochester's eyes that they overflow like two cups filled above the brim: have you never remarked that?'

'Mr Rochester has a right to enjoy the society of his guests.'

'No question about his right: but have you never observed that, of all the tales told here about matrimony, Mr Rochester has been favoured with the most lively and the most continuous?'

'The eagerness of a listener quickens the tongue of a narrator.' I said this rather to myself than to the gipsy, whose strange talk, voice, manner, had by this time wrapped me in a kind of dream. One unexpected sentence came from her lips after another, till I got involved in a web of mystification; and wondered what unseen spirit had been sitting for weeks by my heart watching its workings and taking record of every pulse.

'Eagerness of a listener!' repeated she: 'yes; Mr Rochester has sat by the hour, his ear inclined to the fascinating lips that took such delight in their task of communicating; and Mr Rochester was so willing to receive and looked so grateful for the pastime given him: you have noticed this?'

'Grateful! I cannot remember detecting gratitude in his face.'

'Detecting! You have analysed, then. And what did you detect, if not gratitude?' I said nothing.

'You have seen love: have you not? – and, looking forward, you have seen him married, and beheld his bride happy?'

'Humph! Not exactly. Your witch's skill is rather at fault sometimes.'

'What the devil have you seen then?'

'Never mind: I came here to inquire, not to confess. Is it known that Mr Rochester is to be married?'

'Yes; and to the beautiful Miss Ingram.'

'Shortly?'

'Appearances would warrant that conclusion; and, no doubt (though, with an audacity that wants chastising out of you, you seem to question it), they will be a superlatively happy pair. He must love such a handsome, noble, witty, accomplished lady; and probably she loves him, or, if not his person, at least his purse. I know she considers the Rochester estate eligible to the last degree; though (God pardon me!) I told her something on that point about an hour ago which made her look wondrous grave: the corners of her mouth fell half an inch. I would advise her blackavised suitor to look out: if another comes, with a longer or clearer rent-roll – he's dished —'

'But, Mother, I did not come to hear Mr Rochester's fortune: I came to hear my own; and you have told me nothing of it.'

'Your fortune is yet doubtful: when I examined your face, one trait contradicted another. Chance has meted you a measure of happiness: that I know. I knew it before I came here this evening. She has laid it carefully on one side for you. I saw her do it. It depends on yourself to stretch out your hand, and take it up: but whether you will do so is the problem I study. Kneel again on the rug.'

'Don't keep me long; the fire scorches me.'

I knelt. She did not stoop towards me, but only gazed, leaning back in her chair. She began muttering:

'The flame flickers in the eye; the eye shines like dew; it looks soft and full of feeling; it smiles at my jargon: it is susceptible; impression follows impression

# Jane Eyre

through its clear sphere; where it ceases to smile, it is sad; an unconscious lassitude weighs on the lid: that signifies melancholy resulting from loneliness. It turns from me; it will not suffer further scrutiny: it seems to deny, by a mocking glance, the truth of the discoveries I have already made – to disown the charge both of sensibility and chagrin: its pride and reserve only confirm me in my opinion. The eye is favourable.

'As to the mouth, it delights at times in laughter; it is disposed to impart all that the brain conceives; though I dare say it would be silent on much the heart experiences. Mobile and flexible, it was never intended to be compressed in the eternal silence of solitude: it is a mouth which should speak much and smile often, and have human affection for its interlocutor. That feature too is propitious.

'I see no enemy to a fortunate issue but in the brow; and that brow professes to say – "I can live alone, if self-respect and circumstances require me so to do. I need not sell my soul to buy bliss. I have an inward treasure born with me, which can keep me alive if all extraneous delights should be withheld, or offered only at a price I cannot afford to give." The forehead declares, "Reason sits firm and holds the reins, and she will not let the feelings burst away and hurry her to wild chasms. The passions may rage furiously, like true heathens, as they are; and the desires may imagine all sorts of vain things: but judgement shall still have the last word in every argument, and the casting vote in every decision. Strong wind, earthquake-shock, and fire may pass by: but I shall follow the guiding of that still small voice which interprets the dictates of conscience."

'Well said, forehead; your declaration shall be respected. I have formed my plans – right plans I deem them – and in them I have attended to the claims of conscience, the counsels of reason. I know how soon youth would fade and bloom perish, if, in the cup of bliss offered, but one dreg of shame, or one flavour of remorse were detected; and I do not want sacrifice, sorrow, dissolution – such is not my taste. I wish to foster, not to blight – to earn gratitude, not to wring tears of blood – no, nor of brine: my harvest must be in smiles, in endearments, in sweet – That will do. I think I rave in a kind of exquisite delirium. I should wish now to protract this moment *ad infinitum*; but I dare not. So far I have governed myself thoroughly. I have acted as I inwardly swore I would act; but further might try me beyond my strength. Rise, Miss Eyre: leave me; "the play is played out".'

Where was I? Did I wake or sleep? Had I been dreaming? Did I dream still? The old woman's voice had changed: her accent, her gesture, and all, were familiar to me as my own face in a glass – as the speech of my own tongue. I got up, but did not go. I looked; I stirred the fire, and looked again: but she drew her bonnet and her bandage closer about her face, and again beckoned me to depart. The flame illuminated her hand stretched out: roused now, and on the alert for discoveries, I at once noticed that hand. It was no more the withered limb of eld than my own; it was a rounded, supple member, with smooth fingers, symmetrically turned; a broad ring flashed on the little finger, and stooping forward, I looked at it, and saw a gem I had seen a hundred times before. Again I looked at the face; which was no longer turned from me – on the contrary, the bonnet was doffed, the bandage displaced, the head advanced.

'Well, Jane, do you know me?' asked the familiar voice.

'Only take off the red cloak, sir, and then—'

'But the string is in a knot – help me.'

# Jane Eyre

'Break it, sir.'

'There, then – "Off, ye lendings!" ' And Mr Rochester stepped out of his disguise.

'Now, sir, what a strange idea!'

'But well carried out, eh? Don't you think so?'

'With the ladies you must have managed well.'

'But not with you?'

'You did not act the character of a gipsy with me.'

'What character did I act? My own?'

'No; some unaccountable one. In short I believe you have been trying to draw me out – or in; you have been talking nonsense to make me talk nonsense. It is scarcely fair, sir.'

'Do you forgive me, Jane?'

'I cannot tell till I have thought it all over. If, on reflection, I find I have fallen into no great absurdity, I shall try to forgive you; but it was not right.'

'Oh, you have been very correct – very careful, very sensible.'

I reflected, and thought, on the whole, I had. It was a comfort; but, indeed, I had been on my guard almost from the beginning of the interview. Something of masquerade I suspected. I knew gipsies and fortune-tellers did not express themselves as this seeming old woman had expressed herself; besides, I had noted her feigned voice, her anxiety to conceal her features. But my mind had been running on Grace Poole – that living enigma, that mystery of mysteries, as I considered her. I had never thought of Mr Rochester.

'Well,' said he, 'what are you musing about? What does that grave smile signify?'

'Wonder and self-congratulation, sir. I have your permission to retire now, I suppose?'

'No; stay a moment; and tell me what the people in the drawing-room yonder are doing.'

'Discussing the gipsy, I dare say.'

'Sit down! – Let me hear what they said about me.'

'I had better not stay long, sir; it must be near eleven o'clock. – Oh! are you aware, Mr Rochester, that a stranger has arrived here since you left this morning?'

'A stranger! – no; who can it be? I expected no one; is he gone?'

'No; he said he had known you long, and that he could take the liberty of installing himself here till you returned.'

'The devil he did! Did he give his name?'

'His name is Mason, sir; and he comes from the West Indies; from Spanish Town, in Jamaica, I think.'

Mr Rochester was standing near me; he had taken my hand, as if to lead me to a chair. As I spoke he gave my wrist a convulsive grip; the smile on his lips froze: apparently a spasm caught his breath.

'Mason! – the West Indies!' he said, in a tone one might fancy a speaking automaton to enounce its single words; 'Mason! – the West Indies!' he reiterated; and he went over the syllables three times, growing, in the intervals of speaking, whiter than ashes: he hardly seemed to know what he was doing.

'Do you feel ill, sir?' I inquired.

'Jane, I've got a blow – I've got a blow, Jane!' He staggered.

# Jane Eyre

'Oh, lean on me, sir.'

'Jane, you offered me your shoulder once before; let me have it now.'

'Yes, sir, yes; and my arm.'

He sat down and made me sit beside him. Holding my hand in both his own, he chafed it; gazing on me, at the same time, with the most troubled, and dreary look.

'My little friend!' said he, 'I wish I were in a quiet island with only you; and trouble, and danger, and hideous recollections removed from me.'

'Can I help you, sir? – I'd give my life to serve you.'

'Jane, if aid is wanted, I'll seek it at your hands; I promise you that.'

'Thank you, sir. Tell me what to do – I'll try, at least, to do it.'

'Fetch me now, Jane, a glass of wine from the dining-room; they will be at supper there; and tell me if Mason is with them, and what he is doing.'

I went. I found all the party in the dining-room at supper, as Mr Rochester had said; they were not seated at table – the supper was arranged on the sideboard; each had taken what he chose, and they stood about here and there in groups, their plates and glasses in their hands. Every one seemed in high glee; laughter and conversation were general and animated. Mr Mason stood near the fire, talking to Colonel and Mrs Dent, and appeared as merry as any of them. I filled a wine-glass (I saw Miss Ingram watch me frowningly as I did so: she thought I was taking a liberty, I dare say), and I returned to the library.

Mr Rochester's extreme pallor had disappeared, and he looked once more firm and stern. He took the glass from my hand.

'Here is to your health, ministrant spirit!' he said. He swallowed the contents and returned it to me. 'What are they doing, Jane?'

'Laughing and talking, sir.'

'They don't look grave and mysterious, as if they had heard something strange?'

'Not at all: they are full of jests and gaiety.'

'And Mason?'

'He was laughing too.'

'If all those people came in a body and spat at me, what would you do, Jane?'

'Turn them out of the room, sir, if I could.'

He half-smiled. 'But if I were to go to them, and they only looked at me coldly, and whispered sneeringly amongst each other, and then dropped off and left me one by one, what then? Would you go with them?'

'I rather think not, sir: I should have more pleasure in staying with you.'

'To comfort me?'

'Yes, sir, to comfort you, as well as I could.'

'And if they laid you under a ban for adhering to me?'

'I probably should know nothing about their ban; and if I did, I should care nothing about it.'

'Then you could dare censure for my sake?'

'I could dare it for the sake of any friend who deserved my adherence; as you, I am sure, do.'

'Go back now into the room; step quietly up to Mason, and whisper in his ear that Mr Rochester is come and wishes to see him: show him in here, and then leave me.'

'Yes, sir.'

I did his behest. The company all stared at me as I passed straight among them. I sought Mr Mason, delivered the message, and preceded him from the room: I ushered him into the library, and then I went upstairs.

At a late hour, after I had been in bed some time, I heard the visitors repair to their chambers; I distinguished Mr Rochester's voice, and heard him say, 'This way, Mason; this is your room.'

He spoke cheerfully: the gay tones set my heart at ease. I was soon asleep.

# Chapter 20

I had forgotten to draw my curtain, which I usually did, and also to let down my window-blind. The consequence was, that when the moon, which was full and bright (for the night was fine), came in her course to that space in the sky opposite my casement, and looked in at me through the unveiled panes, her glorious gaze roused me. Awakening in the dead of night, I opened my eyes on her disc – silver-white and crystal clear. It was beautiful, but too solemn: I half rose, and stretched my arm to draw the curtain.

Good God! What a cry!

The night – its silence – its rest, was rent in twain by a savage, a sharp, a shrilly sound that ran from end to end of Thornfield Hall.

My pulse stopped: my heart stood still; my stretched arm was paralysed. The cry died, and was not renewed. Indeed, whatever being uttered that fearful shriek could not soon repeat it: not the wildest-winged condor on the Andes could, twice in succession, send out such a yell from the cloud shrouding his eyrie. The thing delivering such utterance must rest ere it could repeat the effort.

It came out of the third story; for it passed overhead. And overhead – yes, in the room just above my chamber-ceiling – I now heard a struggle: a deadly one it seemed from the noise; and a half-smothered voice shouted –

'Help! help! help!' three times rapidly.

'Will no one come?' it cried; and then, while the staggering and stamping went on wildly, I distinguished through plank and plaster:

'Rochester! Rochester! for God's sake, come!'

A chamber-door opened: some one ran, or rushed, along the gallery. Another step stamped on the flooring above and something fell: and there was silence.

I had put on some clothes, though horror shook all my limbs; I issued from my apartment. The sleepers were all aroused: ejaculations, terrified murmurs sounded in every room; door after door unclosed; one looked out and another looked out; the gallery filled. Gentlemen and ladies alike had quitted their beds; and 'Oh! what is it?' – 'Who is hurt?' – 'What has happed?' – 'Fetch a light!' – 'Is it fire?' – 'Are there robbers?' – 'Where shall we run?' was demanded confusedly on all hands. But for the moonlight they would have been in complete

# Jane Eyre

darkness. They ran to and fro; they crowded together: some sobbed, some stumbled: the confusion was inextricable.

'Where the devil is Rochester?' cried Colonel Dent. 'I cannot find him in his bed.'

'Here! here!' was shouted in return. 'Be composed all of you: I'm coming.'

And the door at the end of the gallery opened, and Mr Rochester advanced with a candle: he had just descended from the upper story. One of the ladies ran to him directly; she seized his arm: it was Miss Ingram.

'What awful event has taken place?' said she. 'Speak! let us know the worst at once!'

'But don't pull me down or strangle me,' he replied; for the Misses Eshton were clinging about him now: and the two dowagers, in vast white wrappers, were bearing down on him like ships in full sail.

'All's right! – all's right!' he cried. 'It's a mere rehearsal of "Much Ado about Nothing". Ladies, keep off, or I shall wax dangerous.'

And dangerous he looked: his black eyes darted sparks. Calming himself by an effort, he added –

'A servant has had the nightmare; that is all. She's an excitable, nervous person: she construed her dream into an apparition, or something of that sort, no doubt; and has taken a fit with fright. Now, then, I must see you all back into your rooms; for, till the house is settled, she cannot be looked after. Gentlemen, have the goodness to set the ladies the example. Miss Ingram, I am sure you will not fail in evincing superiority to idle terrors. Amy and Louisa, return to your nests like a pair of doves, as you are. Mesdames' (to the dowagers) 'you will take cold to a dead certainty, if you stay in this chill gallery any longer.'

And so, by dint of alternate coaxing and commanding, he contrived to get them all once more enclosed in their separate dormitories. I did not wait to be ordered back to mine, but retreated unnoticed, as unnoticed I had left it.

Not, however, to go to bed: on the contrary, I began and dressed myself carefully. The sound I had heard after the scream, and the words that had been uttered, had probably been heard only by me; for they had proceeded from the room above mine: but they assured me that it was not a servant's dream which had thus struck horror through the house; and that the explanation Mr Rochester had given was merely an invention framed to pacify the guests. I dressed, then, to be ready for emergencies. When dressed, I sat a long time by the window, looking out over the silent grounds and silvered fields, and waiting for I knew not what. It seemed to me that some event must follow the strange cry, struggle, and call.

No: stillness returned: each murmur and movement ceased gradually, and in about an hour Thornfield Hall was again as hushed as a desert. It seemed that sleep and night had resumed their empire. Meantime the moon declined: she was about to set. Not liking to sit in the cold and darkness, I thought I would lie down on my bed, dressed as I was. I left the window, and moved with little noise across the carpet; as I stooped to take off my shoes, a cautious hand tapped low at the door.

'Am I wanted?' I asked.

'Are you up?' asked the voice I expected to hear, namely, my master's.

'Yes, sir.'

'And dressed?'

'Yes.'

'Come out, then, quietly.'

I obeyed. Mr Rochester stood in the gallery, holding a light.

'I want you,' he said: 'come this way: take your time, and make no noise.'

My slippers were thin: I could walk the matted floor as softly as a cat. He glided up the gallery and up the stairs, and stopped in the dark, low corridor of the fateful third story: I had followed and stood at his side.

'Have you a sponge in your room?' he asked in a whisper.

'Yes, sir.'

'Have you any salts – volatile salts?'

'Yes.'

'Go back and fetch both.'

I returned, sought the sponge on the washstand, the salts in my drawer, and once more retraced my steps. He still waited; he held a key in his hand: approaching one of the small, black doors, he put it in the lock; he paused, and addressed me again.

'You don't turn sick at the sight of blood?'

'I think I shall not: I have never been tried yet.'

I felt a thrill while I answered him; but no coldness, and no faintness.

'Just give me your hand,' he said: 'it will not do to risk a fainting fit.'

I put my fingers into his. 'Warm and steady,' was his remark: he turned the key and opened the door.

I saw a room I remembered to have seen before, the day Mrs Fairfax showed me over the house: it was hung with tapestry; but the tapestry was now looped up in one part, and there was a door apparent, which had then been concealed. This door was open; a light shone out of the room within: I heard thence a snarling, snatching sound, almost like a dog quarrelling. Mr Rochester, putting down his candle, said to me, 'Wait a minute,' and he went forward to the inner apartment. A shout of laughter greeted his entrance; noisy at first, and terminating in Grace Poole's own goblin ha! ha! *She* then was there. He made some sort of arrangement without speaking, though I heard a low voice address him: he came out and closed the door behind him.

'Here, Jane!' he said; and I walked round to the other side of the large bed, which with its drawn curtains concealed a considerable portion of the chamber. An easy-chair was near the bed-head: a man sat in it, dressed with the exception of his coat; he was still; his head leant back; his eyes were closed. Mr Rochester held the candle over him; I recognized in his pale and seemingly lifeless face – the stranger, Mason: I saw, too, that his linen on one side, and one arm, was almost soaked in blood.

'Hold the candle,' said Mr Rochester, and I took it; he fetched a basin of water from the washstand: 'Hold that,' said he. I obeyed. He took the sponge, dipped it in, and moistened the corpse-like face; he asked for my smelling bottle, and applied it to the nostrils. Mr Mason shortly unclosed his eyes; he groaned. Mr Rochester opened the shirt of the wounded man, whose arm and shoulder were bandaged: he sponged away blood, trickling fast down.

'Is there immediate danger?' murmured Mr Mason.

'Pooh! No – a mere scratch. Don't be so overcome, man: bear up! I'll fetch a surgeon for you now, myself: you'll be able to be removed by morning, I hope. Jane,' he continued.

# Jane Eyre

'Sir?'

'I shall have to leave you in this room with this gentleman, for an hour, or perhaps two hours: you will sponge the blood as I do when it returns: if he feels faint, you will put the glass of water on that stand to his lips, and your salts to his nose. You will not speak to him on any pretext – and – Richard, it will be at the peril of your life if you speak to her: open your lips – agitate yourself – and I'll not answer for the consequences.'

Again the poor man groaned; he looked as if he dared not move; fear, either of death or something else, appeared almost to paralyse him. Mr Rochester put the now bloody sponge into my hand, and I proceeded to use it as he had done. He watched me a second, then saying, 'Remember! – no conversation,' he left the room. I experienced a strange feeling as the key grated in the lock, and the sound of his retreating step ceased to be heard.

Here, then, was I in the third story, fastened into one of its mystic cells; night around me; a pale and bloody spectacle under my eyes and hands; a murderess hardly separated from me by a single door: yes – that was appalling – the rest I could bear; but I shuddered at the thought of Grace Poole bursting out upon me.

I must keep to my post, however. I must watch this ghastly countenance – these blue, still lips forbidden to unclose – these eyes now shut, now opening, now wandering through the room, now fixing on me, and ever glazed with the dullness of horror. I must dip my hand again and again in the basin of blood and water, and wipe away the trickling gore. I must see the light of the unsnuffed candle wane on my employment; the shadows darken on the wrought, antique tapestry round me, and grow black under the hangings of the vast old bed, and quiver strangely over the doors of a great cabinet opposite – whose front, divided into twelve panels, bore, in grim design, the heads of the twelve apostles, each enclosed in its separate panel as in a frame; while above them at the top rose an ebon crucifix and a dying Christ.

According as the shifting obscurity and flickering gleam hovered here or glanced there, it was now the bearded physician, Luke, that bent his brow; now St John's long hair that waved; and anon the devilish face of Judas, that grew out of the panel, and seemed gathering life and threatening a revelation of the arch-traitor – of Satan himself – in his subordinate's form.

Amidst all this, I had to listen as well as watch: to listen for the movements of the wild beast or fiend in yonder side-den. But since Mr Rochester's visit it seemed spellbound: all the night I heard but three sounds at three long intervals – a sharp creak, a momentary renewal of the snarling, canine noise, and a deep human groan.

Then my own thoughts worried me. What crime was this, that lived incarnate in this sequestered mansion, and could neither be expelled nor subdued by the owned? – what mystery, that broke out, now in fire and now in blood, at the deadest hours of night? What creature was it, that, masked in an ordinary woman's face and shape, uttered the voice, now of a mocking demon, and anon of a carrion-seeking bird of prey?

And this man I bent over – this commonplace, quiet stranger – how had he become involved in the web of horror? and why had the fury flown at him? What made him seek this quarter of the house at an untimely season, when he should have been asleep in bed? I had heard Mr Rochester assign him an

apartment below – what brought him here? And why, now, was he so tame under the violence of treachery done him? Why did he so quietly submit to the concealment Mr Rochester enforced? Why *did* Mr Rochester enforce this concealment? His guest had been outraged, his own life on a former occasion had been hideously plotted against; and both attempts he smothered in secrecy and sank in oblivion! Lastly, I saw Mr Mason was submissive to Mr Rochester; that the impetuous will of the latter held complete sway over the inertness of the former: the few words which has passed between them assured me of this. It was evident that in their former intercourse, the passive disposition of the one had been habitually influenced by the active energy of the other; whence then had arisen Mr Rochester's dismay when he heard of Mr Mason's arrival? Why had the mere name of this unresisting individual – whom his word now sufficed to control like a child – fallen on him, a few hours since, as a thunderbolt might fall on an oak?

Oh! I could not forget his look and his paleness when he whispered: 'Jane, I have got a blow – I have got a blow, Jane.' I could not forget how the arm had trembled which he rested on my shoulder: and it was no light matter which could thus bow the resolute spirit and thrill the vigorous frame of Fairfax Rochester.

'When will he come? When will he come?' I cried inwardly as the night lingered and lingered – as my bleeding patient drooped, moaned, sickened: and neither day nor aid arrived. I had, again and again, held the water to Mason's white lips; again and again offered him the stimulating salts: my efforts seemed ineffectual: either bodily or mental suffering, or loss of blood, or all three combined, were fast prostrating his strength. He moaned so, and looked so weak, wild, and lost, I feared he was dying; and I might not even speak to him.

The candle, wasted at last, went out; as it expired, I perceived streaks of gray light edging the window curtains: dawn was then approaching. Presently I heard Pilot bark far below, out of his distant kennel in the courtyard: hope revived. Nor was it unwarranted: in five minutes more the grating key, the yielding lock, warned me my watch was relieved. It could not have lasted more than two hours: many a week has seemed shorter.

Mr Rochester entered, and with him the surgeon he had been to fetch.

'Now, Carter, be on the alert,' he said to this last: 'I give you but half an hour for dressing the wound, fastening the bandages, getting the patient downstairs and all.'

'But is he fit to move, sir?'

'No doubt of it; it is nothing serious; he is nervous, his spirits must be kept up. Come, set to work.'

Mr Rochester drew back the thick curtain, drew up the holland blind, let in all the daylight he could; and I was surprised and cheered to see how far dawn was advanced: what rosy streaks were beginning to brighten the east. Then he approached Mason, whom the surgeon was already handling.

'Now, my good fellow, how are you?' he asked.

'She's done for me, I fear,' was the faint reply.

'Not a whit! – courage! This day fortnight you'll hardly be a pin the worse of it: you've lost a little blood; that's all – Carter, assure him there's no danger.'

'I can do that conscientiously,' said Carter, who had now undone the bandages; 'only I wish I could have got here sooner: he would not have bled so much – but

how is this? The flesh on the shoulder is torn as well as cut. This wound was not done with a knife: there have been teeth here!'

'She bit me,' he murmured. 'She worried me like a tigress, when Rochester got the knife from her.'

'You should not have yielded: you should have grappled with her at once,' said Mr Rochester.

'But under such circumstances, what could one do?' returned Mason. 'Oh, it was frightful!' he added shuddering. 'And I did not expect it: she looked so quiet at first.'

'I warned you,' was his friend's answer; 'I said – be on your guard when you go near her. Besides, you might have waited till to-morrow, and had me with you: It was mere folly to attempt the interview to-night, and alone.'

'I thought I could have done some good.'

'You thought! you thought! Yes, it makes me impatient to hear you: but, however, you have suffered, and are likely to suffer enough for not taking my advice; so I'll say no more. Carter – hurry! – hurry! The sun will soon rise, and I must have him off.'

'Directly, sir; the shoulder is just bandaged. I must look to this other wound in the arm: she has had her teeth here too, I think.'

'She sucked the blood: she said she'd drain my heart,' said Mason.

I saw Mr Rochester shudder: a singularly marked expression of disgust, horror, hatred, warped his countenance almost to distortion; but he only said –

'Come, be silent, Richard, and never mind her gibberish; don't repeat it.'

'I wish I could forget it,' was the answer.

'You will when you are out of the country: when you get back to Spanish Town, you may think of her as dead and buried – or rather, you need not think of her at all.'

'Impossible to forget this night!'

'It is not impossible: have some energy, man. You thought you were as dead as a herring two hours since, and you are all alive and talking now. There! – Carter has done with you, or nearly so; I'll make you decent in a trice. Jane' (he turned to me for the first time since his re-entrance), 'take this key: go down into my bedroom, and walk straight forward into my dressing-room; open the top drawer of the wardrobe and take out a clean shirt and neck-handkerchief: bring them here; and be nimble.'

I went; sought the repository he had mentioned, found the articles named, and returned with them.

'Now,' said he, 'go to the other side of the bed while I order his toilet; but don't leave the room: you may be wanted again.'

I retired as directed.

'Was anybody stirring below when you went down Jane?' inquired Mr Rochester presently.

'No, sir: all was very still.'

'We shall get you off cannily, Dick: and it will be better, both for your sake, and for that of the poor creature in yonder. I have striven long to avoid exposure, and I should not like it to come at last. Here, Carter, help him on with his waistcoat. Where did you leave your furred cloak? You can't travel a mile without that, I know, in this damned cold climate. In your room? – Jane, run

down to Mr Mason's room – the one next mine – and fetch a cloak you will see there.'

Again I ran, and again returned, bearing an immense mantle, lined and edged with fur.

'Now, I've another errand for you,' said my untiring master; 'you must away to my room again. What a mercy you are shod with velvet, Jane! – a clodhopping messenger would never do at this juncture. You must open the middle drawer of my toilet-table and take out a little phial and a little glass you will find there – quick!'

I flew thither and back, bringing the desired vessels.

'That's well! Now, doctor, I shall take the liberty of administering a dose myself, on my own responsibility. I got this cordial at Rome, of an Italian charlatan – a fellow you would have kicked, Carter. It is not a thing to be used indiscriminately, but it is good upon occasion: as now, for instance. Jane, a little water.'

He held out the tiny glass, and I half-filled it from the water-bottle on the washstand.

'That will do: now wet the lip of the phial.'

I did so; he measured twelve drops of a crimson liquid and presented it to Mason.

'Drink, Richard: it will give you the heart you lack, for an hour or so.'

'But will it hurt me – is it inflammatory?'

'Drink! drink! drink!'

Mr Mason obeyed, because it was evidently useless to resist. He was dressed now: he still looked pale, but he was no longer gory and sullied. Mr Rochester let him sit three minutes after he had swallowed the liquid; he then took his arm –

'Now I am sure you can get on your feet,' he said; 'try.'

The patient rose.

'Carter, take him under the other shoulder. Be of good cheer, Richard; step out – that's it!'

'I do feel better,' remarked Mr Mason.

'I am sure you do. Now, Jane, trip on before us away to the back-stairs; unbolt the side-passage door, and tell the driver of the post-chaise you will see in the yard – or just outside, for I told him not to drive his rattling wheels over the pavement – to be ready; we are coming: and, Jane, if anyone is about, come to the foot of the stairs and hem.'

It was by this time half-past five, and the sun was on the point of rising; but I found the kitchen still dark and silent. The side-passage door was fastened; I opened it with as little noise as possible: all the yard was quiet; but the gates stood wide open, and there was a post-chaise, with horses ready harnessed, and driver seated on the box, stationed outside. I approached him, and said the gentlemen were coming; he nodded: then I looked carefully round and listened. The stillness of the early morning slumbered everywhere; the curtains were yet drawn over the servants' chamber windows; little birds were just twittering in the blossom-blanched orchard-trees, whose boughs drooped like white garlands over the wall enclosing one side of the yard; the carriage horses stamped from time to time in their closed stables: all else was still.

The gentlemen now appeared. Mason, supported by Mr Rochester and the

surgeon, seemed to walk with tolerable ease: they assisted him into the chaise; Carter followed.

'Take care of him,' said Mr Rochester to the latter, 'and keep him at your house till he is quite well: I shall ride over in a day or two to see how he gets on. Richard, how is it with you?'

'The fresh air revives me, Fairfax.'

'Leave the window open on this side, Carter; there is no wind – good-bye, Dick.'

'Fairfax —'

'Well, what is it?'

'Let her be taken care of: let her be treated as tenderly as may be; let her —' He stopped and burst into tears.

'I do my best; and have done it, and will do it,' was the answer: he shut up the chaise door, and the vehicle drove away.

'Yet would to God there was an end of all this!' added Mr Rochester, as he closed and barred the heavy yard-gates.

This done, he moved with slow step and abstracted air towards a door in the wall bordering the orchard. I, supposing he had done with me, prepared to return to the house; again, however, I heard him call 'Jane!' He had opened the portal and stood at it, waiting for me.

'Come where there is some freshness, for a few moments,' he said; 'that house is a mere dungeon; don't you feel it so?'

'It seems to me a splendid mansion, sir.'

'The glamour of inexperience is over your eyes,' he answered; 'and you see it through a charmed medium; you cannot discern that the gilding is slime and the silk draperies cobwebs; that the marble is sordid slate, and the polished woods mere refuse chips and scaly bark. Now *here*' (he pointed to the leafy enclosure we had entered) 'all is real, sweet and pure.'

He strayed down a walk edged with box, with apple-trees, pear-trees, and cherry-trees on one side, and a border on the other full of all sorts of old-fashioned flowers, stocks, sweet-williams, primroses, pansies, mingled with southernwood, sweet-briar, and various fragrant herbs. They were fresh now as a succession of April showers and gleams, followed by a lovely spring morning, could make them: the sun was just entering the dappled east, and his light illumined the wreathed and dewy orchard-trees and shone down the quiet walks under them.

'Jane, will you have a flower?'

He gathered a half-blown rose, the first on the bush, and offered it to me.

'Thank you, sir.'

'Do you like this sunrise, Jane? That sky, with its high and light clouds, which are sure to melt away as the day waxes warm, this placid and balmy atmosphere?'

'I do, very much.'

'You have passed a strange night, Jane.'

'Yes, sir.'

'And it has made you look pale – were you afraid when I left you alone with Mason?'

'I was afraid of some one coming out of the inner room.'

'But I had fastened the door – I had the key in my pocket: I should have been

# Jane Eyre

a careless shepherd if I had left a lamb – my pet lamb – so near a wolf's den, unguarded: you were safe.'

'Will Grace Poole live here still, sir?'

'Oh, yes! don't trouble your head about her – put the thing out of your thoughts.'

'Yet it seems to me your life is hardly secure while she stays.'

'Never fear – I will take care of myself.'

'Is the danger you apprehended last night gone by now, sir?'

'I cannot vouch for that till Mason is out of England: nor even then. To live, for me, Jane, is to stand on a crater-crust which may crack and spew fire any day.'

'But Mr Mason seems a man easily led. Your influence, sir, is evidently potent with him: he will never set you at defiance or wilfully injure you.'

'Oh, no! Mason will not defy me; nor, knowing it, will he hurt me – but, unintentionally, he might in a moment, by one careless word, deprive me, if not of life, yet for ever of happiness.'

'Tell him to be cautious, sir: let him know what you fear, and show him how to avert the danger.'

He laughed sardonically, hastily took my hand, and as hastily threw it from him.

'If I could do that, simpleton, where would the danger be? Annihilated in a moment. Ever since I have known Mason, I have only had to say to him "Do that," and the thing has been done. But I cannot give him orders in this case: I cannot say "Beware of harming me, Richard"; for it is imperative that I should keep him ignorant that harm to me is possible. Now you look puzzled; and I will puzzle you further. You are my little friend, are you not?'

'I like to serve you, sir, and to obey you in all that is right.'

'Precisely: I see you do. I see genuine contentment in your gait and mien, your eye and face, when you are helping me and pleasing me – working for me, and with me, in, as you characteristically say, "*all that is right*": for if I bid you to do what you thought wrong, there would be no light-footed running, no neat-handed alacrity, no lively glance and animated complexion. My friend would then turn to me, quiet and pale, and would say, "No, sir; that is impossible: I cannot do it, because it is wrong"; and would become immutable as a fixed star. Well, you too have power over me, and may injure me: yet I dare not show you where I am vulnerable, lest, faithful and friendly as you are, you should transfix me at once.'

'If you have no more to fear from Mr Mason than you have from me, sir, you are very safe.'

'God grant it may be so! Here, Jane, is an arbour; sit down.'

The arbour was an arch in the wall, lined with ivy; it contained a rustic seat. Mr Rochester took it, leaving room, however, for me: but I stood before him.

'Sit,' he said; 'the bench is long enough for two. You don't hesitate to take a place at my side, do you? Is that wrong, Jane?'

I answered him by assuming it: to refuse would, I felt, have been unwise.

'Now, my little friend, while the sun drinks the dew – while all the flowers in this old garden awake and expand, and the birds fetch their young ones' breakfast out of the cornfield, and the early bees do their first spell of work – I'll put a case to you, which you must endeavour to suppose your own: but first,

# Jane Eyre

look at me, and tell me you are at ease, and not fearing that I err in detaining you, or that you err in staying.'

'No, sir: I am content.'

'Well, then Jane, call to aid your fancy: suppose you were no longer a girl well reared and disciplined, but a wild boy indulged from childhood upwards; imagine yourself in a remote foreign land; conceive that you there commit a capital error, no matter of what nature or from what motives, but one whose consequences must follow you through life and taint all your existence. Mind, I don't say a *crime*; I am not speaking of shedding of blood or any other guilty act, which might make the perpetrator amenable to the law: my word is *error*. The results of what you have done become in time to you utterly insupportable; you take measures to obtain relief: unusual measures, but neither unlawful nor culpable. Still you are miserable; for the hope has quitted you on the very confines of life: your sun at noon darkens in an eclipse, which you feel will not leave it till the time of setting. Bitter and base associations have become the sole food of your memory: you wander here and there, seeking rest in exile: happiness in pleasure – I mean in heartless, sensual pleasure – such as dulls intellect and blights feeling. Heart-weary and soul-withered, you come home after years of voluntary banishment: you make a new acquaintance – how or where no matter: you find in this stranger much of the good and bright qualities which you have sought for twenty years, and never before encountered; and they are all fresh, healthy, without soil and without taint. Such society revives, regenerates; you feel better days come back – higher wishes, purer feelings; you desire to recommence your life, and to spend what remains to you of days in a way more worthy of an immortal being. To attain this end, are you justified in overleaping an obstacle of custom – a mere conventional impediment which neither your conscience sanctifies nor your judgement approves?'

He paused for an answer: and what was I to say? Oh, for some good spirit to suggest a judicious and satisfactory response! Vain aspiration! The west wind whispered in the ivy round me; but no gentle Ariel borrowed its breath as a medium of speech: the birds sang in the tree-tops; but their song, however sweet, was inarticulate.

Again Mr Rochester propounded his query –

'Is the wandering and sinful, but now rest-seeking and repentant, man justified in daring the world's opinion, in order, to attach to him for ever this gentle, gracious, genial stranger, thereby securing his own peace of mind and regeneration of life?'

'Sir,' I answered, 'a wanderer's repose or a sinner's reformation should never depend on a fellow-creature. Men and women die; philosophers falter in wisdom, and Christians in goodness; if any one you know has suffered and erred, let him look higher than his equals for strength to amend and solace to heal.'

'But the instrument – the instrument! God, who does the work, ordains the instrument. I have myself – I tell it you without parable – been a worldly, dissipated, restless man; and I believe I have found the instrument for my cure in —'

He paused: the birds went on carolling, the leaves lightly rustling. I almost wondered they did not check their songs and whispers to catch the suspended revelation; but they would have had to wait many minutes – so long was the

silence protracted. At last I looked up at the tardy speaker: he was looking eagerly at me.

'Little friend,' said he, in quite a changed tone – while his face changed too, losing all its softness and gravity, and becoming harsh and sarcastic – 'you have noticed my tender penchant for Miss Ingram: don't you think if I married her she would regenerate me with a vengeance?'

He got up instantly, went quite to the other end of the walk, and when he came back he was humming a tune.

'Jane, Jane,' said he, stopping before me, 'you are quite pale with your vigils: don't you curse me for disturbing your rest?'

'Curse you? No, sir.'

'Shake hands in confirmation of the word. What cold fingers! They were warmer last night when I touched them at the door of the mysterious chamber. Jane, when will you watch with me again?'

'Whenever I can be useful, sir.'

'For instance, the night before I am married I am sure I shall not be able to sleep. Will you promise to sit up with me to bear me company? To you I can talk of my lovely one: for now you have seen her and know her.'

'Yes, sir.'

'She's a rare one, is she not, Jane?'

'Yes, sir.'

' A strapper – a real strapper, Jane: big, brown, and buxom; with hair just such as the ladies of Carthage must have had. Bless me! there's Dent and Lynn in the stables! Go in by the shrubbery, through that wicket.'

As I went in one way, he went another, and I heard him in the yard, saying cheerfully –

'Mason got the start of you all this morning; he was gone before sunrise: I rose at four to see him off.'

# Chapter 21

Presentiments are strange things! and so are sympathies; and so are signs; and the three combined make one mystery to which humanity had not yet found the key. I never laughed at presentiments in my life, because I have had strange ones of my own. Sympathies, I believe, exist (for instance, between far-distant, long-absent, wholly estranged relatives asserting, notwithstanding their alienation, the unity of the source to which each traces his origin) whose workings baffle mortal comprehension. And signs, for aught we know, may be but the sympathies of Nature with man.

When I was a little girl, only six years old, I one night heard Bessie Leaven say to Martha Abbot that she had been dreaming about a little child: and that

to dream of children was a sure sign of trouble, either to oneself or one's kin. The saying might have worn out of my memory had not a circumstance immediately followed which served indelibly to fix it there. The next day Bessie was sent for, home to the deathbed of her little sister.

Of late I had often recalled this saying and this incident; for during the past week scarcely a night had gone over my couch that had not brought with it a dream of an infant, which I sometimes hushed in my arms, sometimes dandled on my knee, sometimes watched playing with daisies on a lawn, or again, dabbling its hands in running water. It was a wailing child this night, and a laughing one the next: now it nestled close to me, and now it ran from me; but whatever mood the apparition evinced, whatever aspect it wore, it failed not for seven successive nights to meet me the moment I entered the land of slumber.

I did not like this iteration of one idea – this strange recurrence of one image: and I grew nervous as bedtime approached, and the hour of the vision drew near. It was from companionship with this baby-phantom I had been roused on that moonlight night when I heard the cry; and it was on the afternoon of the day following I was summoned downstairs by a message that some one wanted me in Mrs Fairfax's room. On repairing thither, I found a man waiting for me, having the appearance of a gentleman's servant: he was dressed in deep mourning, and the hat he held in his hand was surrounded with a crape band.

'I dare say you hardly remember me, miss,' he said, rising as I entered; 'but my name is Leaven: I lived coachman with Mrs Reed when you were at Gateshead, eight or nine years since, and I live there still.'

'Oh, Robert! how do you do? I remember you very well: you used to give me a ride sometimes on Miss Georgiana's bay pony. And how is Bessie? You are married to Bessie?'

'Yes, miss: my wife is very hearty, thank you; she brought me another little one about two months since – we have three now – and both mother and child are thriving.'

'And are the family well at the house, Robert?'

'I am sorry I can't give you better news of them, miss: they are very badly at present – in great trouble.'

'I hope no one is dead,' I said, glancing at his black dress. He too looked down at the crape round his hat and replied –

'Mr John died yesterday was a week, at his chambers in London.'

'Mr John?'

'Yes.'

'And how does his mother bear it?'

'Why, you see, Miss Eyre, it is not a common mishap: his life has been very wild: these last three years he gave himself up to strange ways, and his death was shocking.'

'I heard from Bessie he was not doing well.'

'Doing well! He could not do worse: he ruined his health and his estate amongst the worst men and the worst women. He got into debt and into jail: his mother helped him out twice, but as soon as he was free he returned to his old companions and habits. His head was not strong: the knaves he lived amongst fooled him beyond anything I ever heard. He came down to Gateshead about three weeks ago and wanted missis to give up all to him. Missis refused: her means have long been much reduced by his extravagance; so he went back again,

and the next news was that he was dead. How he died, God knows! – they say he killed himself.'

I was silent: the tidings were frightful. Robert Leaven resumed –

'Missis had been out of health herself for some time; she had got very stout, but was not strong with it; and the loss of money and fear of poverty were quite breaking her down. The information about Mr John's death and the manner of it came too suddenly: it brought on a stroke. She was three days without speaking: but last Tuesday she seemed rather better: she appeared as if she wanted to say something, and kept making signs to my wife and mumbling. It was only yesterday morning however, that Bessie understood she was pronouncing your name; and at last she made out of the words, "Bring Jane – fetch Jane Eyre: I want to speak to her." Bessie is not sure whether she is in her right mind, or means anything by the words; but she told Miss Reed and Miss Georgiana, and advised them to send for you. The young ladies put it off at first; but their mother grew so restless, and said, "Jane, Jane," so many times, that at last they consented. I left Gateshead yesterday; and if you can get ready, miss, I should like to take you back with me early to-morrow morning.'

'Yes, Robert, I shall be ready: it seems to me that I ought to go.'

'I think so too, miss. Bessie said she was sure you would not refuse: but I suppose you will have to ask leave before you can get off?'

'Yes; and I will do it now'; and having directed him to the servants' hall, and recommended him to the care of John's wife, and the attentions of John himself, I went in search of Mr Rochester.

He was not in any of the lower rooms; he was not in the yard, the stables, or the grounds. I asked Mrs Fairfax if she had seen him – yes; she believed he was playing billiards with Miss Ingram. To the billiard room I hastened: the click of balls and the hum of voices resounded thence; Mr Rochester, Miss Ingram, the two Misses Eshton, and their admirers, were all busied in the game. It required some courage to disturb so interesting a party; my errand, however, was one I could not defer, so I approached the master where he stood at Miss Ingram's side. She turned as I drew near, and looked at me haughtily: her eyes seemed to demand, 'What can the creeping creature want now?' and when I said in a low voice, 'Mr Rochester', she made a movement as if tempted to order me away. I remember her appearance at the moment – it was very graceful and very striking: she wore a morning robe of sky-blue crape; a gauzy azure scarf was twisted in her hair. She had been all animation with the game, and irritated pride did not lower the expression of her haughty lineaments.

'Does that person want you?' she inquired of Mr Rochester; and Mr Rochester turned to see who 'the person' was. He made a curious grimace – one of his strange and equivocal demonstrations – threw down his cue, and followed me from the room.

'Well, Jane?' he said, as he rested his back against the schoolroom door, which he had shut.

'If you please, sir, I want leave of absence for a week or two.'

'What to do – where to go?'

'To see a sick lady who has sent for me.'

'What sick lady? where does she live?'

'At Gateshead, in —shire.'

# Jane Eyre

'—shire? That is a hundred miles off! Who may she be that sends for people to see her that distance?'

'Her name is Reed, sir – Mrs Reed.'

'Reed of Gateshead? There was a Reed of Gateshead, a magistrate.'

'It is his widow, sir.'

'And what have you to do with her? How do you know her?'

'Mr Reed was my uncle – my mother's brother.'

'The deuce he was! You never told me that before: you always said you had no relations.'

'None that would own me, sir. Mr Reed is dead, and his wife cast me off.'

'Why?'

'Because I was poor and burdensome, and she disliked me.'

'But Reed left children? – you must have cousins? Sir George Lynn was talking of a Reed of Gateshead yesterday, who, he said, was one of the veriest rascals in town; and Ingram was mentioning a Georgiana Reed of the same place, who was much admired for her beauty a season or two ago in London.'

'John Reed is dead, too, sir: he ruined himself and half-ruined his family, and is supposed to have committed suicide. The news so shocked his mother that it brought on an apoplectic attack.'

'And what good can you do her? Nonsense, Jane! I would never think of running a hundred miles to see an old lady who will, perhaps, be dead before you reach her: besides you say she cast you off.'

'Yes, sir, but that is long ago; and when her circumstances were very different: I could not be easy to neglect her wishes now.'

'How long will you stay?'

'As short a time as possible, sir.'

'Promise me only to stay a week—'

'I had better not pass my word: I might be obliged to break it.'

'At all events you will come back: you will not be induced under any pretext to take up a permanent residence with her?'

'Oh, no! I shall certainly return if all be well.'

'And who goes with you? You don't travel a hundred miles alone.'

'No, sir, she has sent her coachman.'

'A person to be trusted?'

'Yes, sir, he has lived ten years in the family.'

Mr Rochester meditated. 'When do you wish to go?'

'Early to-morrow morning, sir.'

'Well, you must have some money; you can't travel without money, and I dare say you have not much: I have given you no salary yet. How much have you in the world, Jane?' he asked, smiling.

I drew out my purse; a meagre thing it was. 'Five shillings, sir.' He took the purse, poured the hoard into his palm, and chuckled over it as if its scantiness amused him. Soon he produced his pocket-book: 'Here,' said he, offering me a note; it was fifty pounds, and he owed me but fifteen. I told him I had no change.

'I don't want change; you know that. Take your wages.'

I declined accepting more than was my due. He scowled at first; then as if recollecting something, he said—

# Jane Eyre

'Right, right! Better not give you all now: you would, perhaps, stay away three months if you had fifty pounds. There is ten; is it not plenty?'

'Yes, sir, but now you owe me five.'

'Come back for it, then; I am your banker for forty pounds.'

'Mr Rochester, I may as well mention another matter of business to you while I have the opportunity.'

'Matter of business? I'm curious to hear it.'

'You have as good as informed me, sir, that you are going shortly to be married?'

'Yes; what then?'

'In that case, sir, Adèle ought to go to school: I am sure you will perceive the necessity of it.'

'To get her out of my bride's way, who might otherwise walk over her rather too emphatically? There's sense in the suggestion; not a doubt of it, Adèle, as you say, must go to school; and you, of course, must march straight to – the devil?'

'I hope not, sir; but I must seek another situation somewhere.'

'In course!' he exclaimed, with a twang of voice and a distortion of features equally fantastic and ludicrous. He looked at me some minutes.

'And old Madam Reed, or the Misses, her daughters, will be solicited by you to seek a place, I suppose?'

'No, sir; I am not on such terms with my relatives as would justify me in asking favours of them – but I shall advertise.'

'You shall walk up the pyramids of Egypt!' he growled. 'At your peril you advertise! I wish I had only offered you a sovereign instead of ten pounds. Give me back nine pounds, Jane; I've a use for it.'

'And so have I, sir,' I returned, putting my hands and my purse behind me. 'I could not spare the money on any account.'

'Little niggard!' said he, 'refusing me a pecuniary request! Give me five pounds, Jane.'

'Not five shillings, sir; nor five pence.'

'Just let me look at the cash.'

'No, sir; you are not to be trusted.'

'Jane!'

'Sir?'

'Promise me one thing.'

'I'll promise you anything, sir, that I think I am likely to perform.'

'Not to advertise: and to trust this quest of a situation to me. I'll find you one in time.'

'I shall be glad so to do, sir, if you, in your turn, will promise that I and Adèle shall be both safe out of the house before your bride enters it.'

'Very well! very well! I'll pledge my word on it. You go to-morrow, then?'

'Yes, sir; early.'

'Shall you come down to the drawing-room after dinner?'

'No, sir, I must prepare for the journey.'

'Then you and I must bid good-bye for a little while?'

'I suppose so, sir.'

'And how do people perform that ceremony of parting, Jane? Teach me; I'm not quite up to it.'

1050

'They say, Farewell, or any other form they prefer.'

'Then, say it.'

'Farewell, Mr Rochester, for the present.'

'What must I say?'

'The same if you like, sir.'

'Farewell, Miss Eyre, for the present; is that all?'

'Yes.'

'It seems stingy to my notions, and dry, and unfriendly. I should like something else: a little addition to the rite. If one shook hands for instance; but no – that would not content me either. So you'll do no more than say Farewell, Jane?'

'It is enough, sir: as much goodwill may be conveyed in one hearty word as in many.'

'Very likely; but it is blank and cool – "Farewell".'

'How long is he going to stand with his back against that door?' I asked myself; 'I want to commence my packing.' The dinner-bell rang, and suddenly away he bolted, without another syllable: I saw him no more during the day, and was off before he had risen in the morning.

I reached the lodge at Gateshead about five o'clock in the afternoon of the first of May: I stepped in there before going up to the hall. It was very clean and neat: the ornamental windows were hung with little white curtains; the floor was spotless; the grate and fire-irons were burnished bright, and the fire burnt clear. Bessie sat on the hearth nursing her last-born, and Robert and his sister played quietly in a corner.

'Bless you! – I knew you would come!' exclaimed Mrs Leaven as I entered.

'Yes, Bessie,' said I, after I had kissed her; 'and I trust I am not too late. How is Mrs Reed? – Alive still, I hope.'

'Yes, she is alive; and more sensible and collected than she was. The doctor says she may linger a week or two yet; but he hardly thinks she will finally recover.'

'Has she mentioned me lately?'

'She was talking of you only this morning, and wishing you would come: but she is sleeping now, or was ten minutes ago, when I was up at the house. She generally lies in a kind of lethargy all the afternoon and wakes up about six or seven. Will you rest yourself here an hour, miss, and then I will go up with you?'

Robert here entered, and Bessie laid her sleeping child in the cradle and went to welcome him: afterwards she insisted on my taking off my bonnet and having some tea; for she said I looked pale and tired. I was glad to accept her hospitality; and I submitted to be relieved of my travelling garb just as passively as I used to let her undress me when a child.

Old times crowded back on me as I watched her bustling about – setting out the tea-tray with her best china, cutting bread and butter, toasting a tea-cake, and, between whiles, giving little Robert or Jane an occasional tap or push, just as she used to give me in former days. Bessie had retained her quick temper as well as her light foot and good looks.

Tea ready, I was going to approach the table; but she desired me to sit still, quite in her old peremptory tones. I must be served at the fireside, she said: and she placed before me a little round stand with my cup and a plate of toast,

# Jane Eyre

absolutely as she used to accommodate me with some privately purloined dainty on a nursery chair: and I smiled and obeyed her as in bygone days.

She wanted to know if I was happy at Thornfield Hall, and what sort of a person the mistress was; and when I told her there was only a master, whether he was a nice gentleman, and if I liked him. I told her he was rather an ugly man, but quite a gentleman; and that he treated me kindly, and I was content. Then I went on to describe to her the gay company that had lately been staying at the house; and to these details Bessie listened with interest: they were precisely of the kind she relished.

In such conversation an hour was soon gone: Bessie restored to me my bonnet, &c., and, accompanied by her, I quitted the lodge for the hall. It was also accompanied by her that I had, nearly nine years ago, walked down the path I was now ascending. On a dark, misty, raw morning in January, I had left a hostile roof with a desperate and embittered heart – a sense of outlawry and almost of reprobation – to seek the chilly harbourage of Lowood: that bourne so far away and unexplored. The same hostile roof now again rose before me: my prospects were doubtful yet; and I had an aching heart. I still felt as a wanderer on the face of the earth; but I experienced firmer trust in myself and my own powers, and less withering dread of oppression. The gaping wound of my wrongs, too, was now quite healed; and the flame of resentment extinguished.

'You shall go into the breakfast-room first,' said Bessie, as she preceded me through the hall; 'the young ladies will be there.'

In another moment I was within that apartment. There was every article of furniture looking just as it did on the very morning I was first introduced to Mr Brocklehurst: the rug he had stood upon still covered the hearth. Glancing at the bookcases, I thought I could distinguish the two volumes of Bewick's *British Birds* occupying their old place on the third shelf, and *Gulliver's Travels* and the *Arabian Nights* ranged just above. The inanimate objects were not changed; but the living things had altered past recognition.

Two young ladies appeared before me; one very tall, almost as tall as Miss Ingram – very thin, too, with a sallow face and severe mien. There was something ascetic in her look which was augmented by the extreme plainness of a straight-skirted, black stuff dress, a starched linen collar, hair combed away from the temples, and the nun-like ornament of a string of ebony beads and a crucifix. This I felt sure was Eliza, though I could trace little resemblance to her former self in that elongated and colourless visage.

The other was certainly Georgiana: but not the Georgiana I remembered – the slim and fairy-like girl of eleven. This was a full-blown, very plump damsel, fair as waxwork, with handsome and regular features, languishing blue eyes, and ringleted yellow hair. The hue of her dress was black too; but its fashion was so different from her sister's – so much more flowing and becoming – it looked as stylish as the other's looked puritanical.

In each of the sisters there was one trait of the mother – and only one; the thin and pallid elder daughter had her parent's Cairngorm eye: the blooming and luxuriant younger girl had her contour of jaw and chin – perhaps a little softened, but still imparting an indescribable hardness to the countenance, otherwise so voluptuous and buxom.

Both ladies, as I advanced, rose to welcome me, and both addressed me by the name of 'Miss Eyre'. Eliza's greeting was delivered in a short, abrupt voice,

without a smile; and then she sat down again, fixed her eyes on the fire, and seemed to forget me. Georgiana added to her 'How d'ye do?' several common-places about my journey, the weather, and so on, uttered in rather a drawling tone: and accompanied by sundry side-glances that measured me from head to foot – now traversing the folds of my drab merino pelisse, and now lingering on the plain trimming of my cottage bonnet. Young ladies have a remarkable way of letting you know that they think you a 'quiz' without actually saying the words. A certain superciliousness of look, coolness of manner, nonchalance of tone, express fully their sentiments on the point, without committing them by any positive rudeness in word or deed.

A sneer, however, whether covert or open, had now no longer that power over me it once possessed: as I sat between my cousins, I was surprised to find how easy I felt under the total neglect of the one and the semi-sarcastic attentions of the other – Eliza did not mortify, nor Georgiana ruffle me. The fact was, I had other things to think about; within the last few months feelings had been stirred in me so much more potent than any they could raise – pains and pleasures so much more acute and exquisite had been excited than any it was in their power to inflict or bestow – that their airs gave me no concern either for good or bad.

'How is Mrs Reed?' I asked soon, looking calmly at Georgiana, who thought fit to bridle at the direct address, as if it were an unexpected liberty.

'Mrs Reed? Ah! mama, you mean; she is extremely poorly: I doubt if you can see her to-night.'

'If,' said I, 'you would just step upstairs and tell her I am come, I should be much obliged to you.'

Georgiana almost started, and she opened her blue eyes wild and wide. 'I know she had a particular wish to see me,' I added, 'and I would not defer attending to her desire longer than is absolutely necessary.'

'Mama dislikes being disturbed in an evening,' remarked Eliza. I soon rose, quietly took off my bonnet and gloves, uninvited, and said I would just step out to Bessie – who was, I dared say, in the kitchen – and ask her to ascertain whether Mrs Reed was disposed to receive me or not to-night. I went, and having found Bessie and despatched her on my errand, I proceeded to take further measures. It had heretofore been my habit always to shrink from arrogance: received as I had been today, I should, a year ago, have resolved to quit Gateshead the very next morning; now, it was disclosed to me all at once that that would be a foolish plan. I had taken a journey of a hundred miles to see my aunt, and I must stay with her till she was better – or dead: as to her daughter's pride or folly, I must put it on one side, make myself independent of it. So I addressed the housekeeper; asked her to show me a room, told her I should probably be a visitor here for a week or two, had my trunk conveyed to my chamber, and followed it thither myself: I met Bessie on the landing.

'Missis is awake,' said she; 'I have told her you are here: come and let us see if she will know you.'

I did not need to be guided to the well-known room, to which I had so often been summoned for chastisement or reprimand in former days. I hastened before Bessie; I softly opened the door: a shaded light stood on the table, for it was now getting dark. There was the great four-post bed with amber hangings as of old; there the toilet table, the arm-chair, and the footstool, at which I had a hundred times been sentenced to kneel, to ask pardon for offences by me uncommitted.

# Jane Eyre

I looked into a certain corner near, half-expecting to see the slim outline of a once dreaded switch which used to lurk there, waiting to leap out imp-like and lace my quivering palm or shrinking neck. I approached the bed; I opened the curtains and leant over the high-piled pillows.

Well did I remember Mrs Reed's face, and I eagerly sought the familiar image. It is a happy thing that time quells the longings of vengeance and hushes the promptings of rage and aversion. I had left this woman in bitterness and hate, and I came back to her now with no other emotion than a sort of ruth for her great sufferings, and a strong yearning to forget and forgive all injuries – to be reconciled and clasp hands in amity.

The well-known face was there: stern, relentless as ever – there was that peculiar eye which nothing could melt, and the somewhat raised, imperious, despotic eyebrow. How often had it lowered on me menace and hate! and how the recollection of childhood's terrors and sorrows revived as I traced its harsh line now! And yet I stooped down and kissed her: she looked at me.

'Is this Jane Eyre?' she said.

'Yes, Aunt Reed. How are you, dear aunt?'

I had once vowed that I would never call her aunt again: I thought it no sin to forget and break that vow now. My fingers had fastened on her hand, which lay outside the sheet: had she pressed mine kindly, I should at that moment have experienced true pleasure. But unimpressionable natures are not so soon softened, nor are natural antipathies so readily eradicated. Mrs Reed took her hand away, and, turning her face rather from me, she remarked that the night was warm. Again she regarded me so icily, I felt at once that her opinion of me – her feeling towards me – was unchanged and unchangeable. I knew by her stony eye – opaque to tenderness, indissoluble to tears – that she was resolved to consider me bad to the last; because to believe me good would give her no generous pleasure: only a sense of mortification.

I felt pain, and then I felt ire; and then I felt a determination to subdue her – to be her mistress in spite both of her nature and her will. My tears had risen, just as in childhood: I ordered them back to their source. I brought a chair to the bed-head: I sat down and leaned over the pillow.

'You sent for me,' I said, 'and I am here; and it is my intention to stay till I see how you get on.'

'Oh, of course! You have seen my daughters?'

'Yes.'

'Well, you may tell them I wish you to stay till I can talk some things over with you I have on my mind: to-night it is too late and I have a difficulty in recalling them. But there was something I wished to say – let me see—'

The wandering look and changed utterance told what wreck had taken place in her once vigorous frame. Turning restlessly, she drew the bedclothes round her; my elbow, resting on a corner of the quilt, fixed it down: she was at once irritated.

'Sit up!' said she; 'don't annoy me with holding the clothes fast. Are you Jane Eyre?'

'I am Jane Eyre.'

'I have had more trouble with that child than any one would believe. Such a burden to be left on my hands – and so much annoyance as she caused me daily and hourly, with her incomprehensible disposition and her sudden fits of

# Jane Eyre

temper, and her continual, unnatural watchings of one's movements! I declare she talked to me once like something mad, or like a fiend – no child ever spoke or looked as she did; I was glad to get her away from the house. What did they do with her at Lowood? The fever broke out there, and many of the pupils died. She, however, did not die: but I said she did – I wish she had died!'

'A strange wish, Mrs Reed; why do you hate her so?'

'I had a dislike to her mother always; for she was my husband's only sister, and a great favourite with him: he opposed the family disowning her when she made her low marriage; and when news came of her death, he wept like a simpleton. He would send for the baby; though I entreated him rather to put it out to nurse and pay for its maintenance. I hated it the first time I set my eyes on it – a sickly, whining, pining thing! It would wail in its cradle all night long – not screaming heartily like any other child, but whimpering and moaning. Reed pitied it; and he used to nurse it and notice it as if it had been his own: more indeed, than he ever noticed his own at that age. He would try to make my children friendly to the little beggar: the darlings could not bear it, and he was angry with them when they showed their dislike. In his last illness, he had it brought continually to his bedside; and but an hour before he died, he bound me by vow to keep the creature. I would as soon have been charged with a pauper brat out of the workhouse: but he was weak, naturally weak. John does not at all resemble his father, and I am glad of it: John is like me and like my brothers – he is quite a Gibson. Oh, I wish he would cease tormenting me with letters for money! I have no more money to give him: we are getting poor. I must send away half the servants and shut up part of the house; or let it off. I can never submit to do that – yet how are we to get on? Two-thirds of my income goes in paying the interest of mortgages. John gambles dreadfully, and always loses – poor boy! He is beset with sharpers: John is sunk and degraded – his look is frightful – I feel ashamed for him when I see him.'

She was getting much excited. 'I think I had better leave her now,' said I to Bessie, who stood on the other side of the bed.

'Perhaps you had, miss: but she often talks in this way towards night – in the morning she is calmer.'

I rose. 'Stop!' exclaimed Mrs Reed, 'there is another thing I wished to say. He threatens me – he continually threatens me with his own death, or mine: and I dream sometimes that I see him laid out with a great wound in his throat, or with a swollen and blackened face. I am come to a strange pass: I have heavy troubles. What is to be done? How is the money to be had?'

Bessie now endeavoured to persuade her to take a sedative draught: she succeeded with difficulty. Soon after, Mrs Reed grew more composed, and sank into a dozing state. I then left her.

More than ten days elapsed before I had again any conversation with her. She continued either delirious or lethargic; and the doctor forbade everything which could painfully excite her. Meantime, I got on as well as I could with Georgiana and Eliza. They were very cold, indeed, at first. Eliza would sit half the day sewing, reading, or writing, and scarcely utter a word either to me or her sister. Georgiana would chatter nonsense to her canary bird by the hour, and take no notice of me. But I was determined not to seem at a loss for occupation or amusement: I had brought my drawing materials with me, and they served me for both.

# Jane Eyre

Provided with a case of pencils, and some sheets of paper, I used to take a seat apart from them, near the window, and busy myself in sketching fancy vignettes representing any scene that happened momentarily to shape itself in the ever-shifting kaleidoscope of imagination; a glimpse of sea between two rocks; the rising moon, and a ship crossing its disc; a group of reeds and water-flags, and a naiad's head, crowned with lotus-flowers, rising out of them; an elf sitting in a hedge-sparrow's nest, under a wreath of hawthorn bloom.

One morning I fell to sketching a face: what sort of a face it was to be, I did not care or know. I took a soft black pencil, gave it a broad point, and worked away. Soon I had traced on the paper a broad and prominent forehead and a square lower outline of visage: that contour gave me pleasure; my fingers proceeded actively to fill it with features. Strongly-marked horizontal eyebrows must be traced under that brow; then followed, naturally, a well-defined nose, with a straight ridge and full nostrils; then a flexible looking mouth, by no means narrow; then a firm chin, with a decided cleft down the middle of it: of course, some black whiskers were wanted, and some jetty hair, tufted on the temples, and waved above the forehead. Now for the eyes: I had left them to the last, because they required the most careful working. I drew them large; I shaped them well: the eyelashes I traced long and sombre; the irids lustrous and large. 'Good! but not quite the thing,' I thought as I surveyed the effect: 'they want more force and spirit'; and I wrought the shades blacker, that the lights might flash more brilliantly – a happy touch or two secured success. There, I had a friend's face under my gaze: and what did it signify that those young ladies turned their backs on me? I looked at it; I smiled at the speaking likeness: I was absorbed and content.

'Is that a portrait of some one you know?' asked Eliza, who had approached me unnoticed. I responded that it was merely a fancy head, and hurried it beneath the other sheets. Of course, I lied: it was, in fact, a very faithful representation of Mr Rochester. But what was that to her, or to any one but myself? Georgiana also advanced to look. The other drawings pleased her much, but she called that 'an ugly man'. They both seemed surprised at my skill. I offered to sketch their portraits; and each, in turn, sat for a pencil outline. Then Georgiana produced her album. I promised to contribute a water-colour drawing: this put her at once into good humour. She proposed a walk in the grounds. Before we had been out two hours, we were deep in a confidential conversation: she had favoured me with a description of the brilliant winter she had spent in London two seasons ago – of the admiration she had there excited – the attention she had received; and I even got hints of the titled conquest she had made. In the course of the afternoon and evening these hints were enlarged on; various soft conversations were reported, and sentimental scenes represented; and, in short, a volume of a novel of fashionable life was that day improvised by her for my benefit. The communications were renewed from day to day: they always ran on the same theme – herself, her loves, and woes. It was strange she never once adverted either to her mother's illness, or her brother's death, or the present gloomy state of the family prospects. Her mind seemed wholly taken up with reminiscences of past gaiety, and aspirations after dissipations to come. She passed about five minutes each day in her mother's sick-room, and no more.

Eliza still spoke little: she had evidently no time to talk. I never saw a busier person than she seemed to be: yet it was difficult to say what she did: or rather,

to discover any result of her diligence. She had an alarm to call her up early.
I know not how she occupied herself before breakfast, but after that meal she
divided her time into regular portions, and each hour had its allotted task. Three
times a day she studied a little book, which I found, on inspection, was a
Common Prayer Book. I asked her once what was the great attraction of that
volume, and she said, 'the Rubric'. Three hours she gave to stitching with gold
thread, the border of a square crimson cloth, almost large enough for a carpet.
In answer to my inquiries after the use of this article, she informed me it was
a covering for the altar of a new church lately erected near Gateshead. Two
hours she devoted to her diary; two to working by herself in the kitchen garden;
and one to the regulation of her accounts. She seemed to want no company: no
conversation. I believe she was happy in her way: this routine sufficed for her;
and nothing annoyed her so much as the occurrence of any incident which forced
her to vary its clockwork regularity.

She told me one evening, when more disposed to be communicative than usual,
that John's conduct, and the threatened ruin of the family, had been a source
of profound affliction to her: but she had now, she said, settled her mind, and
formed her resolution. Her own fortune she had taken care to secure: and when
her mother died – and it was wholly improbable, she tranquilly remarked, that
she should either recover or linger long – she would execute a long-cherished
project: seek a retirement where punctual habits would be permanently secured
from disturbance, and place safe barriers between herself and a frivolous world.
I asked if Georgiana would accompany her.

Of course not. Georgiana and she had nothing in common: they never had
had. She would not be burdened with her society for any consideration. Georgiana
should take her own course; and she, Eliza, would take hers.

Georgiana, when not unburdening her heart to me, spent most of her time
in lying on the sofa, fretting about the dullness of the house, and wishing over
and over again that her Aunt Gibson would send her an invitation up to town.
'It would be so much better,' she said, 'if she could only get out of the way for
a month or two, till all was over.' I did not ask what she meant by 'all being
over', but I suppose she referred to the expected decease of her mother and the
gloomy sequel of funeral rites. Eliza generally took no more notice of her sister's
indolence and complaints than if no such murmuring, lounging object had been
before her. One day, however, as she put away her account-book and unfolded
her embroidery, she suddenly took her up thus—

'Georgiana, a more vain and absurd animal than you was certainly never
allowed to cumber the earth. You had no right to be born; for you make no use
of life. Instead of living for, in, and with yourself, as a reasonable being ought,
you seek only to fasten your feebleness on some other person's strength: if no
one can be found willing to burden her or himself with such a fat, weak, puffy,
useless thing, you cry out that you are ill-treated, neglected, miserable. Then,
too, existence for you must be a scene of continual change and excitement, or
else the world is a dungeon: you must be admired, you must be courted, you
must be flattered – you must have music, dancing, and society – or you languish,
you die away. Have you no sense to devise a system which will make you
independent of all efforts, and all wills, but your own? Take one day; share it
into sections; to each section apportion its task: leave no stray unemployed
quarters of an hour, ten minutes, five minutes – include all; do each piece of

# Jane Eyre

business in its turn with method, with rigid regularity. The day will close almost before you are aware it has begun; and you are indebted to no one for helping you to get rid of one vacant moment: you have had to seek no one's company, conversation, sympathy, forbearance; you have lived, in short, as an independent being ought to do. Take this advice: the first and last I shall offer you; that you will not want me or any one else, happen what may. Neglect it – go on as heretofore, craving, whining, and idling – and suffer the results of your idiocy, however bad and insufferable they may be. I tell you this plainly: and listen: for though I shall no more repeat what I am about to say, I shall steadily act on it. After my mother's death, I wash my hands of you: from the day her coffin is carried to the vault in Gateshead Church, you and I will be as separate as if we had never known each other. You need not think that because we chanced to be born of the same parents, I shall suffer you to fasten me down by even the feeblest claim: I can tell you this – if the whole human race, ourselves excepted, were swept away, and we two stood alone on the earth, I would leave you in the old world, and betake myself to the new.'

She closed her lips.

'You might have saved yourself the trouble of delivering that tirade,' answered Georgiana. 'Everybody knows you are the most selfish, heartless creature in existence: and *I* know your spiteful hatred towards me: I have had a specimen of it before in the trick you played me about Lord Edwin Vere: you could not bear me to be raised above you, to have a title, to be received into circles where you dare not show your face, and so you acted the spy and informer, and ruined my prospects for ever.' Georgiana took out her handkerchief and blew her nose for an hour afterwards; Eliza sat cold, impassible, and assiduously industrious.

True, generous feeling is made small account of by some; but here were two natures rendered, the one intolerably acrid, the other despicably savourless, for the want of it. Feeling without judgement is a washy draught indeed; but judgement untempered by feeling is too bitter and husky a morsel for human deglutition.

It was a wet and windy afternoon: Georgiana had fallen asleep on the sofa over the perusal of a novel; Eliza was gone to attend a saint's day service at the new church – for in matters of religion she was a rigid formalist; no weather ever prevented the punctual discharge of what she considered her devotional duties; fair or foul, she went to church thrice every Sunday, and as often on week-days as there were prayers.

I bethought myself to go upstairs and see how the dying woman sped, who lay there almost unheeded: the very servants paid her but a remittent attention: the hired nurse, being little looked after, would slip out of the room whenever she could. Bessie was faithful; but she had her own family to mind, and could only come occasionally to the hall. I found the sick-room unwatched, as I had expected: no nurse was there; the patient lay still and seemingly lethargic: her livid face sunk in the pillows: the fire was dying in the grate. I renewed the fuel, re-arranged the bedclothes, gazed awhile on her who could not now gaze on me, and then I moved away to the window.

The rain beat strongly against the panes, the wind blew tempestuously: 'One lies there,' I thought, 'who will soon be beyond the war of earthly elements. Whither will that spirit – now struggling to quit its material tenement – flit when at length released?'

# Jane Eyre

In pondering the great mystery, I thought of Helen Burns, recalled her dying words – her faith – her doctrine of the equality of disembodied souls. I was still listening in thought to her well-remembered tones – still picturing her pale and spiritual aspect, her wasted face and sublime gaze, as she lay on her placid deathbed, and whispered her longing to be restored to her divine Father's bosom – when a feeble voice murmured from the couch behind, 'Who is that?'

I knew Mrs Reed had not spoken for days: was she reviving? I went up to her. 'It is I, Aunt Reed.'

'Who – I?' was her answer. 'Who are you?' looking at me with surprise and a sort of alarm, but still not wildly. 'You are quite a stranger to me – where is Bessie?'

'She is at the lodge, aunt.'

'Aunt!' she repeated. 'Who calls me aunt? You are not one of the Gibsons; and yet I know you – that face, and the eyes and forehead, are quite familiar to me: you are like – why, you are like Jane Eyre!'

I said nothing: I was afraid of occasioning some shock by declaring my identity.

'Yet,' said she, 'I am afraid it is a mistake: my thoughts deceive me. I wished to see Jane Eyre, and I fancy a likeness where none exists: besides, in eight years she must be changed.' I now gently assured her that I was the person she supposed and desired me to be: and seeing that I was understood, and that her senses were quite collected, I explained how Bessie had sent her husband to fetch me from Thornfield.

'I am very ill, I know,' she said ere long. 'I was trying to turn myself a few minutes since, and find I cannot move a limb. It is as well I should ease my mind before I die: what we think little of in health, burdens us at such an hour as the present is to me. Is the nurse here? or is there no one in the room but you?'

I assured her we were alone.

'Well, I have twice done you a wrong which I regret now. One was in breaking the promise which I gave my husband to bring you up as my own child; the other –' she stopped. 'After all, it is of no great importance, perhaps,' she murmured to herself: 'and then I may get better; and to humble myself so to her is painful.'

She made an effort to alter her position, but failed: her face changed; she seemed to experience some inward sensation – the precursor, perhaps, of the last pang.

'Well, I must get it over. Eternity is before me: I had better tell her. Go to my dressing-case, open it, and take out a letter you will see there.'

I obeyed her directions. 'Read the letter,' she said.

It was short, and thus conceived —

*Madam,*
*Will you have the goodness to send me the address of my niece, Jane Eyre, and to tell me how she is. It is my intention to write shortly and desire her to come to me at Madeira. Providence has blessed my endeavours to secure a competency: and as I am unmarried and childless, I wish to adopt her during my life, and bequeath her at my death whatever I may have to leave.*
*I am, Madam, &c., &c.,*
*John Eyre, Madeira.*

# Jane Eyre

It was dated three years back.

'Why did I never hear of this?' I asked.

'Because I disliked you too fixedly and thoroughly ever to lend a hand in lifting you to prosperity. I could not forget your conduct to me, Jane – the fury with which you once turned on me; the tone in which you declared you abhorred me the worst of anybody in the world; the unchildlike look and voice with which you affirmed that the very thought of me made you sick, and asserted that I had treated you with miserable cruelty. I could not forget my own sensations when you thus started up and poured out the venom of your mind: I felt fear as if an animal that I had struck or pushed had looked up at me with human eyes and cursed me in a man's voice – Bring me some water! Oh, make haste!'

'Dear Mrs Reed,' said I, as I offered her the draught she required, 'think no more of all this, let it pass away from your mind. Forgive me for my passionate language; I was a child then; eight, nine years have passed since that day.'

She heeded nothing of what I said; but when she had tasted the water and drawn breath, she went on thus—

'I tell you I could not forget it; and I took my revenge: for you to be adopted by your uncle, and placed in a state of ease and comfort, was what I could not endure. I wrote to him; I said I was sorry for his disappointment, but Jane Eyre was dead: she had died of typhus fever at Lowood. Now act as you please: write and contradict my assertion – expose my falsehood as soon as you like. You were born, I think, to be my torment: my last hour is racked by the recollection of a deed which, but for you, I should never have been tempted to commit.'

'If you could be persuaded to think no more of it, aunt, and to regard me with kindness and forgiveness—'

'You have a very bad disposition,' said she, 'and one to this day I feel it impossible to understand: how for nine years you could be patient and quiescent under any treatment, and in the tenth break out all fire and violence, I can never comprehend.'

'My disposition is not so bad as you think. I am passionate, but not vindictive. Many a time, as a little child, I should have been glad to love you if you would have let me: and I long earnestly to be reconciled to you now: kiss me, aunt.'

I approached my cheek to her lips: she would not touch it. She said I oppressed her by leaning over the bed, and again demanded water. As I laid her down – for I raised her and supported her on my arm while she drank – I covered her ice-cold and clammy hand with mine: the feeble fingers shrank from my touch – the glazing eyes shunned my gaze.

'Love me, then, or hate me, as you will,' I said at last, 'you have my full and free forgiveness: ask now for God's and be at peace.'

Poor suffering woman! it was too late for her to make now the effort to change her habitual frame of mind: living, she had ever hated me – dying, she must hate me still.

The nurse now entered, and Bessie followed. I yet lingered half an hour longer, hoping to see some sign of amity: but she gave none. She was fast relapsing into stupor; nor did her mind again rally: at twelve o'clock that night she died. I was not present to close her eyes: nor were either of her daughters. They came to tell us the next morning that all was over. She was by that time laid out. Eliza and I went to look at her: Georgiana, who had burst out into loud weeping, said she dared not go. There was stretched Sarah Reed's once robust

and active frame, rigid and still: her eye of flint was covered with its cold lid; her brow and strong traits wore yet the impress of her inexorable soul. A strange and solemn object was that corpse to me. I gazed on it with gloom and pain; nothing soft, nothing sweet, nothing pitying, or hopeful, or subduing did it inspire; only a grating anguish for *her* woes – not *my* loss – and a sombre, tearless dismay at the fearfulness of death in such a form.

Eliza surveyed her parent calmly. After a silence of some minutes she observed—

'With her constitution she should have lived to a good old age: her life was shortened by trouble.' And then a spasm constricted her mouth for an instant: as it passed away she turned and left the room, and so did I. Neither of us had dropped a tear.

# Chapter 22

Mr Rochester had given me but one week's leave of absence: yet a month elapsed before I quitted Gateshead. I wished to leave immediately after the funeral, but Georgiana entreated me to stay till she could get off to London, whither she was now at last invited by her uncle, Mr Gibson, who had come down to direct his sister's interment and settle the family affairs. Georgiana said she dreaded being left alone with Eliza; from her she got neither sympathy in her dejection, support in her fears, nor aid in her preparations; so I bore with her feeble-minded wailings and selfish lamentations as well as I could, and did my best in sewing for her and packing her dresses. It is true, that while I worked, she would idle; and I thought to myself, 'If you and I were destined to live always together, cousin, we would commence matters on a different footing. I should not settle tamely down into being the forbearing party; I should assign you your share of labour, and compel you to accomplish it, or else it should be left undone: I should insist, also, on your keeping some of those drawling, half-insincere complaints hushed in your own breast. It is only because our connexion happens to be very transitory, and comes at a peculiarly mournful season, that I consent thus to render it so patient and compliant on my part.'

At last I saw Georgiana off; but now it was Eliza's turn to request me to stay another week. Her plans required all her time and attention, she said; she was about to depart for some unknown bourne; and all day long she stayed in her own room, her door bolted within, filling trunks, emptying drawers, burning papers, and holding no communication with anyone. She wished me to look after the house, to see callers, and answer notes of condolence.

One morning, she told me I was at liberty. 'And,' she added, 'I am obliged

to you for your valuable services and discreet conduct! There is some difference between living with such a one as you and with Georgiana: you perform your own part in life, and burden no one. To-morrow,' she continued, 'I set out for the Continent. I shall take up my abode in a religious house near Lisle – a nunnery, you would call it; there I shall be quiet and unmolested. I shall devote myself for a time to the examination of the Roman Catholic dogmas, and to a careful study of the workings of their system; if I find it to be, as I half suspect it is, the one best calculated to ensure the doing of all things decently and in order, I shall embrace the tenets of Rome and probably take the veil.'

I neither expressed surprise at this resolution nor attempted to dissuade her from it. 'The vocation will fit you to a hair,' I thought: 'much good may it do you!'

When we parted she said: 'Good-bye, cousin Jane Eyre; I wish you well: you have some sense.'

I then returned: 'You are not without sense, cousin Eliza; but what you have, I suppose, in another year will be walled up alive in a French convent. However, it is not my business, and so it suits you – I don't much care.'

'You are in the right,' said she; and with these words we each went our separate way. As I shall not have occasion to refer either to her or her sister again, I may as well mention here, that Georgiana made an advantageous match with a wealthy, worn-out man of fashion; and that Eliza actually took the veil, and is at this day Superior of the convent where she passed the period of her novitiate, and which she endowed with her fortune.

How people feel when they are returning home from an absence, long or short, I did not know: I had never experienced the sensation. I had known what it was to come back to Gateshead, when a child, after a long walk – to be scolded for looking cold or gloomy; and later, what it was to come back from church to Lowood – to long for a plenteous meal and a good fire, and to be unable to get either. Neither of these returnings was very pleasant or desirable: no magnet drew me to a given point, increasing in its strength of attraction the nearer I came. The return to Thornfield was yet to be tried.

My journey seemed tedious – very tedious: fifty miles one day, a night spent at an inn; fifty miles the next day. During the first twelve hours I thought of Mrs Reed in her last moments; I saw her disfigured and discoloured face, and heard her strangely altered voice. I mused on the funeral day, the coffin, the hearse, the black train of tenants and servants – few was the number of relatives – the gaping vault, the silent church, the solemn service. Then I thought of Eliza and Georgiana; I beheld one the cynosure of a ballroom, the other the inmate of a convent cell; and I dwelt on and analysed their separate peculiarities of person and character. The evening arrival at the great town of — scattered these thoughts; night gave them quite another turn: laid down on my traveller's bed I left reminiscence for anticipation.

I was going back to Thornfield: but how long was I to stay there? Not long; of that I was sure. I had heard from Mrs Fairfax in the interim of my absence: the party at the hall was dispersed; Mr Rochester had left for London three weeks ago, but he was then expected to return in a fortnight. Mrs Fairfax surmised that he was gone to make arrangements for his wedding as he had talked of purchasing a new carriage: she said the idea of his marrying Miss Ingram still seemed strange to her; but from what everybody said, and from

what she had herself seen, she could no longer doubt that the event would shortly take place. 'You would be strangely incredulous if you did doubt it,' was my mental comment. 'I don't doubt it.'

The question followed, 'Where was I to go?' I dreamt of Miss Ingram all the night: in a vivid morning dream I saw her closing the gates of Thornfield against me and pointing me out another road; and Mr Rochester looked on with his arms folded – smiling sardonically, as it seemed, at both her and me.

I had not notified to Mrs Fairfax the exact day of my return; for I did not wish either car or carriage to meet me at Millcote. I proposed to walk the distance quietly by myself; and very quietly, after leaving my box in the ostler's care, did I slip away from the George Inn, about six o'clock of a June evening, and take the old road to Thornfield: a road which lay chiefly through fields, and was now little frequented.

It was not a bright or splendid summer evening, though fair and soft: the haymakers were at work all along the road; and the sky, though far from cloudless, was such as promised well for the future: its blue – where blue was visible – was mild and settled, and its cloud strata high and thin. The west, too, was warm: no watery gleam chilled it – it seemed as if there was a fire lit, an altar burning behind its screen of marbled vapour, and out of apertures shone a golden redness.

I felt glad as the road shortened before me: so glad that I stopped once to ask myself what the joy meant: and to remind reason that it was not to my home I was going, or to a permanent resting-place, or to a place where fond friends looked out for me and waited my arrival. 'Mrs Fairfax will smile you a calm welcome, to be sure,' said I; 'and little Adèle will clap her hands and jump to see you: but you know very well you are thinking of another than they, and that he is not thinking of you.'

But what is so headstrong as youth? What so blind as inexperience? These affirmed that it was pleasure enough to have the privilege of again looking at Mr Rochester, whether he looked on me or not; and they added – 'Hasten! hasten! be with him while you may: but a few more days or weeks, at most, and you are parted from him for ever!' And I then strangled a newborn agony – a deformed thing which I could not persuade myself to own and rear – and ran on.

They are making hay, too, in Thornfield meadows: or rather, the labourers are just quitting their work, and returning home with their rakes on their shoulders, now, at the hour I arrive. I have but a field or two to traverse, and then I shall cross the road and reach the gates. How full the hedges are of roses! But I have no time to gather any; I want to be at the house. I passed a tall brier, shooting leafy and flowery branches across the path; I see the narrow stile with stone steps; and I see – Mr Rochester sitting there, a book and a pencil in his hand; he is writing.

Well, he is not a ghost; yet every nerve I have is unstrung: for a moment I am beyond my own mastery. What does it mean? I did not think I should tremble in this way when I saw him, or lose my voice or the power of motion in his presence. I will go back as soon as I can stir: I need not make an absolute fool of myself. I know another way to the house. It does not signify if I knew twenty ways; for he has seen me.

# Jane Eyre

'Hallo!' he cries; and he puts up his book and his pencil. 'There you are! Come on, if you please.'

I suppose I do come on; though in what fashion I know not; being scarcely cognizant of my movements, and solicitous only to appear calm; and, above all, to control the working muscles of my face – which I feel rebel insolently against my will, and struggle to express what I had resolved to conceal. But I have a veil – it is down: I may make shift yet to behave with decent composure.

'And this is Jane Eyre? Are you coming from Millcote, and on foot? Yes – just one of your tricks: not to send for a carriage, and come clattering over street and road like a common mortal, but to steal into the vicinage of your home along with twilight, just as if you were a dream or a shade. What the deuce have you done with yourself this last month?'

'I have been with my aunt, sir, who is dead.'

'A true Janian reply! Good angels be my guard! She comes from the other world – from the abode of people who are dead; and tells me so when she meets me alone here in the gloaming! If I dared, I'd touch you, to see if you are substance or shadow, you elf! but I'd as soon offer to take hold of a blue *ignis fatuus* light in a marsh. Truant! truant!' he added, when he had paused an instant. 'Absent from me a whole month, and forgetting me quite, I'll be sworn.'

I knew there would be pleasure in meeting my master again; even though broken by the fear that he was so soon to cease to be my master, and by the knowledge that I was nothing to him: but there was ever in Mr Rochester (so at least I thought) such a wealth of the power of communicating happiness, that to taste but of the crumbs he scattered to stray and stranger birds like me was to feast genially. His last words were balm: they seemed to imply that it imported something to him whether I forgot him or not. And he had spoken of Thornfield as my home – would that it were my home!

He did not leave the stile, and I hardly liked to ask to go by. I inquired soon if he had not been to London.

'Yes; I suppose you found that out by second sight.'

'Mrs Fairfax told me in a letter.'

'And did she inform you what I went to do?'

'Oh, yes, sir! Everybody knew your errand.'

'You must see the carriage, Jane, and tell me if you don't think it will suit Mrs Rochester exactly; and whether she won't look like Queen Boadicea, leaning back against those purple cushions. I wish, Jane, I were a trifle better adapted to match with her externally. Tell me now, fairy as you are – can't you give me a charm, or a philter, or something of that sort, to make me a handsome man?'

'It would be past the power of magic, sir'; and, in thought, I added, 'A loving eye is all the charm needed: to such you are handsome enough; or rather your sternness has a power beyond beauty.'

Mr Rochester had sometimes read my unspoken thoughts with an acumen to me incomprehensible: in the present instance he took no notice of my abrupt vocal response; but he smiled at me with a certain smile he had of his own, and which he used but on rare occasions. He seemed to think it too good for common purposes: it was the real sunshine of feeling – he shed it over me now.

'Pass, Janet,' said he, making room for me to cross the stile: 'go up home, and stay your weary little wandering feet at a friend's threshold.'

All I had now to do was to obey him in silence: no need for me to colloquize

further. I got over the stile without a word, and meant to leave him calmly. An impulse held me fast – a force turned me round. I said – or something in me said for me, and in spite of me—

'Thank you, Mr Rochester, for your great kindness. I am strangely glad to get back again to you; and wherever you are is my home – my only home.'

I walked on so fast that even he could hardly have overtaken me had he tried. Little Adèle was half wild with delight when she saw me. Mrs Fairfax received me with her usual plain friendliness. Leah smiled, and even Sophie bid me 'bon soir' with glee. This was very pleasant; there is no happiness like that of being loved by your fellow-creatures, and feeling that your presence is an addition to their comfort.

I, that evening, shut my eyes resolutely against the future: I stopped my ears against the voice that kept warning me of near separation and coming grief. When tea was over, and Mrs Fairfax had taken her knitting, and I had assumed a low seat near her, and Adèle, kneeling on the carpet, had nestled close up to me, and a sense of mutual affection seemed to surround us with a ring of golden peace, I uttered a silent prayer that we might not be parted far or soon; but when, as we thus sat, Mr Rochester entered unannounced, and, looking at us, seemed to take pleasure in the spectacle of a group so amicable – when he said he supposed the old lady was all right now that she had got her adopted daughter back again, and added that he saw Adèle was 'prête à croquer sa petite maman Anglaise' – I had ventured to hope that he would, even after his marriage, keep us together somewhere under the shelter of his protection, and not quite exiled from the sunshine of his presence.

A fortnight of dubious calm succeeded my return to Thornfield Hall. Nothing was said of the master's marriage, and I saw no preparation going on for such an event. Almost every day I asked Mrs Fairfax if she had yet heard anything decided: her answer was always in the negative. Once, she said, she had actually put the question to Mr Rochester as to when he was going to bring his bride home; but he answered her only by a joke and one of his queer looks, and she could not tell what to make of him.

One thing specially surprised me, and that was, there was no journeying backward and forward, no visits to Ingram Park: to be sure it was twenty miles off, on the borders of another county; but what was that distance to an ardent lover? To so practised and indefatigable a horseman as Mr Rochester, it would be but a morning's ride. I began to cherish hopes I had no right to conceive: that the match was broken off; that rumour had been mistaken; that one or both parties had changed their minds. I used to look at my master's face to see if it were sad or fierce; but I could not remember the time when it had been so uniformly clear of clouds or evil feelings. If, in the moments I and my pupil spent with him, I lacked spirits and sank into inevitable dejection, he became even gay. Never had he called me more frequently to his presence; never been kinder to me when there – and, alas! never had I loved him so well.

# Chapter 23

A splendid Midsummer shone over England: skies so pure, suns so radiant as were then seen in long succession, seldom favour, even singly, our wave-girt land. It was as if a band of Italian days had come from the South, like a flock of glorious passenger birds, and lighted to rest them on the cliffs of Albion. The hay was all got in; the fields round Thornfield were green and shorn; the roads white and baked; the trees were in their dark prime; hedge and wood, full-leaved and deeply tinted, contrasted well with the sunny hue of the cleared meadows between.

On Midsummer-eve, Adèle, weary with gathering wild strawberries in Hay Lane half the day, had gone to bed with the sun. I watched her drop asleep, and when I left her, I sought the garden.

It was now the sweetest hour of the twenty-four: 'day its fervid fires had wasted', and dew fell cool on panting plain and scorched summit. Where the sun had gone down in simple state – pure of the pomp of clouds – spread a solemn purple, burning with the light of red jewel and furnace flame at one point, on one hill-peak, and extending high and wide, soft and still softer, over half heaven. The east had its own charm of fine, deep blue, and its own modest gem, a rising and solitary star: soon it would boast the moon; but she was yet beneath the horizon.

I walked a while on the pavement; but a subtle, well-known scent – that of a cigar – stole from some window; I saw the library casement open a hand-breadth; I knew I might be watched thence; so I went apart into the orchard. No nook in the grounds more sheltered and more Eden-like; a very high wall shut it out from the court on one side; on the other a beech avenue screened it from the lawn. At the bottom was a sunk fence, its sole separation from lonely fields: a winding walk, bordered with laurels and terminating in a giant horse-chestnut, circled at the base by a seat, led down to the fence. Here one could wander unseen. While such honeydew fell, such silence reigned, such gloaming gathered, I felt as if I could haunt such shade for ever; but in treading the flower and fruit parterres at the upper part of the enclosure, enticed there by the light the now rising moon cast on this more open quarter, my step is stayed – not by sound, not by sight, but once more by a warning fragrance.

Sweet-brier and southernwood, jasmine, pink, and rose have long been yielding their evening sacrifice of incense: this new scent is neither of shrub nor flower; it is – I know it well – it is Mr Rochester's cigar. I look round and listen. I see trees laden with ripening fruit. I hear a nightingale warbling in a wood half a mile off: no moving form is visible, no coming step audible; but that perfume increases: I must flee. I make for the wicket leading to the shrubbery, and I see

# Jane Eyre

Mr Rochester entering. I step aside into the ivy recess; he will not stay long: he will soon return whence he came, and if I sit still he will never see me.

But no – eventide is as pleasant to him as to me, and this antique garden as attractive; and he strolls on, now lifting the gooseberry-tree branches to look at the fruit, large as plums, with which they are laden; now taking a ripe cherry from the wall; now stooping towards a knot of flowers, either to inhale their fragrance or to admire the dew-beads on their petals. A great moth goes humming by me; it alights on a plant at Mr Rochester's foot: he sees it, and bends to examine it.

'Now he has his back towards me,' thought I, 'and he is occupied too; perhaps if I walk softly, I can slip away unnoticed.'

I trod on an edging of turf that the crackle of the pebbly gravel might not betray me: he was standing among the beds at a yard or two distant from where I had to pass; the moth apparently engaged him. 'I shall get by very well,' I meditated. As I crossed his shadow, thrown long over the garden by the moon, not yet risen high, he said quietly, without turning –

'Jane, come and look at this fellow.'

I had made no noise: he had not eyes behind – could his shadow feel? I started at first, and then I approached him.

'Look at his wings,' said he; 'he reminds me rather of a West Indian insect; one does not often see so large and gay a night-rover in England; there! he is flown.'

The moth roamed away. I was sheepishly retreating also; but Mr Rochester followed me, and when we reached the wicket he said –

'Turn back: on so lovely a night it is a shame to sit in the house; and surely no one can wish to go to bed while sunset is thus at meeting with moonrise.'

It is one of my faults, that though my tongue is sometimes prompt enough at answer, there are times when it sadly fails me in framing an excuse; and always the lapse occurs at some crisis, when a facile word or plausible pretext is specially wanted to get me out of a painful embarrassment. I did not like to walk at this hour alone with Mr Rochester in the shadowy orchard; but I could not find a reason to allege for leaving him. I followed with lagging step, and thoughts busily bent on discovering a means of extrication; but he himself looked so composed and so grave also, I became ashamed of feeling any confusion: the evil – if evil existent or prospective there was – seemed to lie with me only; his mind was unconscious and quiet.

'Jane,' he recommenced, as we entered the laurel walk and slowly strayed down in the direction of the sunk fence and the horse-chestnut, 'Thornfield is a pleasant place in summer, is it not?'

'Yes, sir.'

'You must have become in some degree attached to the house – you who have an eye for natural beauties, and a good deal of the organ of Adhesiveness?'

'I am attached to it, indeed.'

'And though I don't comprehend how it is, I perceive you have acquired a degree of regard for that foolish little child Adèle, too; and even for simple Dame Fairfax?'

'Yes, sir; in different ways, I have an affection for both.'

'And would be sorry to part with them?'

'Yes.'

# Jane Eyre

'Pity!' he said, and sighed and paused.

'It is always the way of events in this life,' he continued presently: 'no sooner have you got settled in a pleasant resting-place, than a voice calls out to you to rise and move on, for the hour of repose is expired.'

'Must I move on, sir?' I asked. 'Must I leave Thornfield?'

'I believe you must, Jane. I am sorry, Janet, but I believe indeed you must.'

This was a blow: but I did not let it prostrate me.

'Well, sir, I shall be ready when the order to march comes.'

'It is come now – I must give it to-night.'

'Then you *are* going to be married, sir?'

'Ex-act-ly – pre-cise-ly: with your usual acuteness, you have hit the nail straight on the head.'

'Soon, sir?'

'Very soon, my — that is, Miss Eyre: and you'll remember, Jane, the first time I, or Rumour, plainly intimated to you that it was my intention to put my old bachelor's neck into the sacred noose, to enter into the holy state of matrimony – to take Miss Ingram to my bosom, in short (she's an extensive armful: but that's not to the point – one can't have too much of such a very excellent thing as my beautiful Blanche): well, as I was saying – listen to me, Jane! You're not turning your head to look after more moths, are you? That was only a ladyclock, child, "flying away home". I wish to remind you that it was you who first said to me, with that discretion I respect in you – with that foresight, prudence, and humility which befit your responsible and dependent position – that in case I married Miss Ingram, both you and little Adèle had better trot forthwith. I pass over the sort of slur conveyed in this suggestion on the character of my beloved; indeed, when you are far away, Janet, I'll try to forget it: I shall notice only its wisdom; which is such that I have made it my law of action. Adèle must go to school; and you, Miss Eyre, must get a new situation.'

'Yes, sir, I will advertise immediately: and meantime, I suppose —' I was going to say, 'I suppose I must stay here, till I find another shelter to betake myself to': but I stopped, feeling it would not do to risk a long sentence, for my voice was not quite under command.

'In about a month I hope to be a bridegroom,' continued Mr Rochester; 'and in the interim, I shall myself look out for employment and an asylum for you.'

'Thank you, sir; I am sorry to give —'

'Oh, no need to apologize! I consider that when a dependent does her duty as well as you have done yours, she has a sort of claim upon her employer for any little assistance he can conveniently render her; indeed, I have already, through my future mother-in-law, heard of a place that I think will suit: it is to undertake the education of the five daughters of Mrs Dionysius O'Gall of Bitternutt Lodge, Connaught, Ireland. You'll like Ireland, I think: they're such warm-hearted people there, they say.'

'It is a long way off, sir.'

'No matter – a girl of your sense will not object to the voyage or the distance.'

'Not the voyage but the distance: and then the sea is a barrier —'

'From what, Jane?'

'From England and from Thornfield: and —'

'Well?'

'From *you*, sir.'

# Jane Eyre

I said this almost involuntarily, and with as little sanction of free will, my tears gushed out. I did not cry so as to be heard, however; I avoided sobbing. The thought of Mrs O'Gall and Bitternutt Lodge struck cold to my heart; and colder the thought of all the brine and foam destined, as it seemed, to rush between me and the master at whose side I now walked; and coldest the remembrance of the wider ocean – wealth, caste, custom – intervened between me and what I naturally and inevitably loved.

'It is a long way,' I said again.

'It is, to be sure; and when you get to Bitternutt Lodge, Connaught, Ireland, I shall never see you again, Jane: that's morally certain. I never go over to Ireland, not having myself much of a fancy for the country. We have been good friends, Jane; have we not?'

'Yes, sir.'

'And when friends are on the eve of separation, they like to spend the little time that remains to them close to each other. Come! we'll talk over the voyage and the parting quietly, half an hour or so, while the stars enter into their shining life up in heaven yonder: here is the chestnut-tree: here is the bench at its old roots. Come, we will sit there in peace to-night, though we should never more be destined to sit there together.'

He seated me and himself.

'It is a long way to Ireland, Janet, and I am sorry to send my little friend on such weary travels: but if I can't do better, how is it to be helped? Are you anything akin to me, do you think, Jane?'

I could risk no sort of answer by this time: my heart was still.

'Because,' he said, 'I sometimes have a queer feeling with regard to you – especially when you are near to me, as now: it is as if I had a string somewhere under my left ribs, tightly and inextricably knotted to a similar string situated in the corresponding quarter of your little frame. And if that boisterous Channel, and two hundred miles or so of land, come broad between us, I am afraid that cord of communion will be snapped; and then I've a nervous notion I should take to bleeding inwardly. As for you – you'd forget me.'

'That I *never* should, sir: you know —' Impossible to proceed.

'Jane, do you hear that nightingale singing in the wood? Listen!'

In listening, I sobbed convulsively; for I could repress what I endured no longer; I was obliged to yield, and I was shaken from head to foot with acute distress. When I did speak, it was only to express an impetuous wish that I had never been born, or never come to Thornfield.

'Because you are sorry to leave it?'

The vehemence of emotion, stirred by grief and love within me, was claiming mastery, and struggling for full sway, and asserting a right to predominate, to overcome, to live, rise, and reign at last: yes – and to speak.

'I grieve to leave Thornfield: I love Thornfield: I love it, because I have lived in it a full and delightful life – momentarily at least. I have not been trampled on. I have not been petrified. I have not been buried with inferior minds, and excluded from every glimpse of communion with what is bright and energetic and high. I have talked, face to face, with what I reverence, with what I delight in – with an original, a vigorous, an expanded mind. I have known you, Mr Rochester; and it strikes me with terror and anguish to feel I absolutely must

# Jane Eyre

be torn from you for ever. I see the necessity of departure; and it is like looking on the necessity of death.'

'Where do you see the necessity?' he asked suddenly.

'Where? You, sir, have placed it before me.'

'In what shape?'

'In the shape of Miss Ingram; a noble and beautiful woman – your bride.'

'My bride! What bride? I have no bride!'

'But you will have.'

'Yes – I will! – I will!' he set his teeth.

'Then I must go – you have said it yourself.'

'No: you must stay! I swear it – and the oath shall be kept.'

'I tell you I must go!' I retorted, roused to something like passion. 'Do you think I can stay to become nothing to you? Do you think I am an automaton? – a machine without feelings? and can bear to have my morsel of bread snatched from my lips, and my drop of living water dashed from my cup? Do you think, because I am poor, obscure, plain, and little, I am soulless and heartless? You think wrong! – I have as much soul as you – and full as much heart! And if God had gifted me with some beauty and much wealth, I should have made it as hard for you to leave me, as it is now for me to leave you. I am not talking to you now through the medium of custom, conventionalities, nor even of mortal flesh: it is my spirit that addresses your spirit; just as if both had passed through the grave, and we stood at God's feet, equal – as we are!'

'As we are!' repeated Mr Rochester – 'so,' he added, enclosing me in his arms, gathering me to his breast, pressing his lips to my lips: 'so, Jane!'

'Yes, so, sir,' I rejoined: 'and yet not so: for you are a married man – or as good as a married man, and wed to one inferior to you – to one with whom you have no sympathy – whom I do not believe you truly love; for I have seen and heard you sneer at her. I would scorn such a union: therefore I am better than you – let me go!'

'Where, Jane? To Ireland?'

'Yes – to Ireland. I have spoken my mind, and can go anywhere now.'

'Jane, be still; don't struggle so, like a wild frantic bird that is rendering its own plumage in its desperation.'

'I am no bird; and no net ensnares me; I am a free human being with an independent will, which I now exert to leave you.'

Another effort set me at liberty, and I stood erect before him.

'And your will shall decide your destiny,' he said. 'I offer you my heart, my hand, and a share of all my possessions.'

'You play a farce, which I merely laugh at.'

'I ask you to pass through life at my side – to be my second self, and best earthly companion.'

'For that fate you have already made your choice, and must abide by it.'

'Jane, be still a few moments: you are over-excited: I will be still too.'

A waft of wind came sweeping down the laurel-walk, and trembled through the boughs of the chestnut: it wandered away – away – to an indefinite distance – it died. The nightingale's song was then the only voice of the hour: in listening to it I again wept. Mr Rochester sat quiet, looking at me gently and seriously. Some time passed before he spoke; he at last said —

'Come to my side, Jane, and let us explain and understand one another.'

# Jane Eyre

'I will never again come to your side: I am torn away now, and cannot return.'

'But, Jane, I summon you as my wife: it is you only I intend to marry.'

I was silent: I thought he mocked me.

'Come, Jane – come hither.'

'Your bride stands between us.'

He rose, and with a stride reached me.

'My bride is here,' he said, again drawing me to him, 'because my equal is here, and my likeness. Jane, will you marry me?'

Still I did not answer, and still I writhed myself from his grasp: for I was still incredulous.

'Do you doubt me, Jane?'

'Entirely.'

'You have no faith in me?'

'Not a whit.'

'Am I a liar in your eyes?' he asked passionately. 'Little sceptic, you *shall* be convinced. What love have I for Miss Ingram? None: and that you know. What love has she for me? None: as I have taken pains to prove: I caused a rumour to reach her that my fortune was not a third of what was supposed, and after that I presented myself to see the result; it was coldness both from her and her mother. I would not – I could not – marry Miss Ingram. You – you strange, you almost unearthly thing! – I love you as my own flesh. You – poor and obscure, and small and plain as you are – I entreat to accept me as a husband.'

'What, me!' I ejaculated, beginning in his earnestness – and especially in his incivility – to credit his sincerity: 'me who have not a friend in the world but you – if you are my friend: not a shilling but what you have given me?'

'You, Jane, I must have you for my own – entirely my own. Will you be mine? Say yes, quickly.'

'Mr Rochester, let me look at your face: turn to the moonlight.'

'Why?'

'Because I want to read your countenance – turn!'

'There! you will find it scarcely more legible than a crumpled, scratched page. Read on: only make haste, for I suffer.'

His face was very much agitated and very much flushed, and there were strong workings in the features, and strange gleams in the eyes.

'Oh, Jane, you torture me!' he exclaimed. 'With that searching and yet faithful and generous look, you torture me!'

'How can I do that? If you are true, and your offer real, my only feelings to you must be gratitude and devotion – they cannot torture.'

'Gratitude!' he ejaculated; and added wildly – 'Jane, accept me quickly. Say, Edward – give me my name – Edward – I will marry you.'

'Are you in earnest? Do you truly love me? Do you sincerely wish me to be your wife?'

'I do; and if an oath is necessary to satisfy, I swear it.'

'Then, sir, I will marry you.'

'Edward – my little wife!'

'Dear Edward!'

'Come to me – come to me entirely now,' said he; and added in his deepest tone, speaking in my ear as his cheek was laid on mine, 'Make my happiness – I will make yours.'

# Jane Eyre

'God pardon me!' he subjoined ere long; 'and man meddle not with me: I have her, and will hold her.'

'There is no one to meddle, sir. I have no kindred to interfere.'

'No – that is the best of it,' he said. And if I had loved him less I should have thought his accent and look of exultation savage; but, sitting by him, roused from the nightmare of parting – called to the paradise of union – I thought only of the bliss given me to drink in so abundant a flow. Again and again he said, 'Are you happy, Jane?' And again and again I answered, 'Yes.' After which he murmured, 'It will atone – it will atone. Have I not found her friendless, and cold, and comfortless? Will I not guard, and cherish, and solace her? Is there not love in my heart, and constancy in my resolves? It will expiate at God's tribunal. I know my Maker sanctions what I do. For the world's judgement – I wash my hands thereof. For man's opinion – I defy it.'

But what had befallen the night? The moon was not yet set, and we were all in shadow: I could scarcely see my master's face, near as I was. And what ailed the chestnut tree? it writhed and groaned; while wind roared in the laurel walk, and came sweeping over us.

'We must go in,' said Mr Rochester: 'the weather changes. I could have sat with thee till morning, Jane.'

'And so,' thought I, 'could I with you.' I should have said so, perhaps, but a livid, vivid spark leapt out of a cloud at which I was looking, and there was a crack, a crash, and a close rattling peal; and I thought only of hiding my dazzled eyes against Mr Rochester's shoulder.

The rain rushed down. He hurried me up the walk, through the grounds, and into the house; but we were quite wet before we could pass the threshold. He was taking off my shawl in the hall, and shaking the water out of my loosened hair, when Mrs Fairfax emerged from her room. I did not observe her at first, nor did Mr Rochester. The lamp was lit. The clock was on the stroke of twelve.

'Hasten to take off your wet things,' said he; 'and before you go, good-night – good-night, my darling.'

He kissed me repeatedly. When I looked up, on leaving his arms, there stood the widow, pale, grave, and amazed. I only smiled at her, and ran upstairs. 'Explanation will do for another time,' thought I. Still, when I reached my chamber, I felt a pang at the idea she should even temporarily misconstrue what she had seen. But joy soon effaced every other feeling; and loud as the wind blew, near and deep as the thunder crashed, fierce and frequent as the lightning gleamed, cataract-like as the rain fell during a storm of two hours' duration, I experienced no fear and little awe. Mr Rochester came thrice to my door in the course of it, to ask if I was safe and tranquil: and that was comfort, that was strength for anything.

Before I left my bed in the morning, little Adèle came running in to tell me that the great horse-chestnut at the bottom of the orchard had been struck by lightning in the night, and half of it split away.

# Chapter 24

As I rose and dressed, I thought over what had happened, and wondered if it were a dream. I could not be certain of the reality till I had seen Mr Rochester again, and heard him renew his words of love and promise.

While arranging my hair, I looked at my face in the glass, and felt it was no longer plain: there was hope in its aspect and life in its colour; and my eyes seemed as if they had beheld the fount of fruition, and borrowed beams from the lustrous ripple. I had often been unwilling to look at my master, because I feared he could not be pleased at my look: but I was sure I might lift my face to his now, and not cool his affection by its expression. I took a plain but clean and light summer dress from my drawer and put it on: it seemed no attire had ever so well become me, because none had I ever worn in so blissful a mood.

I was not surprised, when I ran down into the hall, to see that a brilliant June morning had succeeded to the tempest of the night; and to feel, through the open glass door, the breathing of a fresh and fragrant breeze. Nature must be gladsome when I was so happy. A beggar-woman and her little boy – pale, ragged objects both – were coming up the walk, and I ran down and gave them all the money I happened to have in my purse – some three or four shillings: good or bad, they must partake of my jubilee. The rooks cawed, and blither birds sang; but nothing was so merry or so musical as my own rejoicing heart.

Mrs Fairfax surprised me by looking out of the window with a sad countenance, and saying gravely, 'Miss Eyre, will you come to breakfast?' During the meal she was quiet and cool: but I could not undeceive her then. I must wait for my master to give explanations; and so must she. I ate what I could, and then I hastened upstairs. I met Adèle leaving the schoolroom.

'Where are you going? It is time for lessons.'

'Mr Rochester has sent me away to the nursery.'

'Where is he?'

'In there,' pointing to the apartment she had left; and I went in, and there he stood.

'Come and bid me good-morning,' said he. I gladly advanced; and it was not merely a cold word now, or even a shake of the hand that I received, but an embrace and a kiss. It seemed natural: it seemed genial to be so well loved, so caressed by him.

'Jane, you look blooming, and smiling, and pretty,' said he: 'truly pretty this morning. Is this my pale little elf? Is this my mustard-seed? This little sunny-faced girl with the dimpled cheek and rosy lips; the satin-smooth hazel hair, and the radiant hazel eyes? (I had green eyes, reader; but you must excuse the mistake; for him they were new-dyed, I suppose.)

# Jane Eyre

'It is Jane Eyre, sir.'

'Soon to be Jane Rochester,' he added: 'in four weeks, Janet; not a day more. Do you hear that?'

I did, and I could not quite comprehend it: it made me giddy. The feeling the announcement sent through me was something stronger than was consistent with joy – something that smote and stunned: it was, I think, almost fear.

'You blushed, and now you are white, Jane: what is that for?'

'Because you gave me a new name – Jane Rochester; and it seems so strange.'

'Yes, Mrs Rochester,' said he; 'young Mrs Rochester – Fairfax Rochester's girl-bride.'

'It can never be, sir; it does not sound likely. Human beings never enjoy complete happiness in this world. I was not born for a different destiny to the rest of my species: to imagine such a lot befalling me is a fairy-tale – a daydream.'

'Which I can and will realize. I shall begin to-day. This morning I wrote to my banker in London to send me certain jewels he has in his keeping – heirlooms for the ladies of Thornfield. In a day or two I hope to pour them into your lap: for every privilege, every attention shall be yours that I would accord a peer's daughter, if about to marry her.'

'Oh, sir! – never mind jewels! I don't like to hear them spoken of. Jewels for Jane Eyre sounds unnatural and strange: I would rather not have them.'

'I will myself put the diamond chain around your neck, and the circlet on your forehead – which it will become: for nature, at least, has stamped her patent of nobility on this brow, Jane; and I will clasp the bracelets on these fine wrists, and load these fairy-like fingers with rings.'

'No, no, sir! Think of other subjects, and speak of other things, and in another strain. Don't address me as if I were a beauty; I am your plain, Quakerish governess.'

'You are a beauty in my eyes, and a beauty just the desire of my heart – delicate and aerial.'

'Puny and insignificant, you mean. You are dreaming, sir – or are you sneering? For God's sake, don't be ironical!'

'I will make the world acknowledge you a beauty, too,' he went on, while I really became uneasy at the strain he had adopted, because I felt he was either deluding himself or trying to delude me. 'I will attire my Jane in satin and lace, and she shall have roses in her hair; and I will cover the head I love best with a priceless veil.'

'And then you won't know me, sir; and I shall not be your Jane Eyre any longer, but an ape in a harlequin's jacket – a jay in borrowed plumes. I would as soon see you, Mr Rochester, tricked out in stage-trappings, as myself clad in a court-lady's robe; and I don't call you handsome, sir, though I love you most dearly; far too dearly to flatter you. Don't flatter me.'

He pursued his theme, however, without noticing my deprecation. 'This very day I shall take you in the carriage to Millcote, and you must choose some dresses for yourself. I told you we shall be married in four weeks. The wedding is to take place quietly, in the church down below yonder; and then I shall waft you away at once to town. After a brief stay there I shall bear my treasure to regions nearer the sun: to French vineyards and Italian plains; and she shall see whatever is famous in old story and in modern record: she shall taste, too, of the life of cities; and she shall learn to value herself by just comparison with others.'

# Jane Eyre

'Shall I travel? – and with you, sir?'

'You shall sojourn at Paris, Rome, and Naples: at Florence, Venice, and Vienna: all the ground I have wandered over shall be re-trodden by you: wherever I stamped my hoof, your sylph's foot shall step also. Ten years since, I flew through Europe half mad: with disgust, hate, and rage as my companions: now I shall revisit it healed and cleansed, with a very angel as my comforter.'

I laughed at him as he said this. 'I am not an angel,' I asserted; 'and I will not be one till I die: I will be myself. Mr Rochester, you must neither expect nor exact anything celestial of me – for you will not get it, any more than I shall get it of you: which I do not at all anticipate.'

'What do you anticipate of me?'

'For a little while you will perhaps be as you are now – a very little while; and then you will turn cool; and then you will be capricious; and then you will be stern, and I shall have much ado to please you; but when you get used to me, you will perhaps like me again – *like* me, I say, not *love* me. I suppose your love will effervesce in six months or less. I have observed in books written by men, that period assigned as the furthest to which a husband's ardour extends. Yet, after all, as a friend and companion, I hope never to become quite distasteful to my dear master.'

'Distasteful! and like you again! I think I shall like you again, and yet again: and I will make you confess I do not only *like*, but *love* you – with truth, fervour, constancy.'

'Yet are you not capricious, sir?'

'To women who please me only by their faces, I am the very devil when I find out they have neither souls or hearts – when they open to me a perspective of flatness, triviality, and perhaps imbecility, coarseness, and ill-temper; but to the clear eye and eloquent tongue, to the soul made of fire, and the character that bends but does not break – at once supple and stable, tractable and consistent – I am ever tender and true.'

'Had you ever experience of such a character, sir? Did you ever love such a one?'

'I love it now.'

'But before me: if I, indeed, in any respect come up to your difficult standard?'

'I never met your likeness. Jane, you please me, and you master me – you seem to submit, and I like the sense of pliancy you impart; and while I am twining the soft, silken hair round my finger, it sends a thrill up my arm to my heart. I am influenced – conquered; and the influence is sweeter than I can express; and the conquest I undergo has a witchery beyond any triumph I can win. Why do you smile, Jane? What does that inexplicable, that uncanny turn of countenance, mean?'

'I was thinking, sir (you will excuse the idea; it was involuntary), I was thinking of Hercules and Samson with their charmers —'

'You were, my little elfish —'

'Hush, sir! You don't talk very wisely just now; any more than those gentlemen acted very wisely. However, had they been married, they would no doubt by their severity as husbands have made up for their softness as suitors; and so will you, I fear. I wonder how you will answer me a year hence, should I ask a favour it does not suit your convenience or pleasure to grant.'

'Ask me something now, Janet – the least thing: I desire to be entreated —'

# Jane Eyre

'Indeed I will, sir; I have my petition all ready.'

'Speak! But if you look up and smile with that countenance, I shall swear concession before I know to what, and that will make a fool of me.'

'Not at all, sir; I ask only this: don't send for the jewels, and don't crown me with roses: you might as well put a border of gold lace round that plain pocket-handkerchief you have there.'

'I might as well "gild refined gold". I know it: your request is granted then – for the time. I will remand the order I despatched to my banker. But you have not yet asked for anything; you have prayed a gift to be withdrawn; try again.'

'Well then, sir, have the goodness to gratify my curiosity, which is much piqued on one point.'

He looked disturbed. 'What? What?' he said hastily. 'Curiosity is a dangerous petition: it is well I have not taken a vow to accord every request —'

'But there can be no danger in complying with this, sir.'

'Utter it, Jane; but I wish that instead of a mere inquiry into, perhaps, a secret, it was a wish for half my estate.'

'Now, King Ahasuerus! What do I want with half your estate? Do you think I am a Jew usurer, seeking good investment in land? I would much rather have all your confidence. You will not exclude me from your confidence if you admit me to your heart?'

'You are welcome to all my confidence that is worth having, Jane; but for God's sake, don't desire a useless burden! Don't long for poison – don't turn out a downright Eve on my hands!'

'Why not, sir? You have just been telling me how much you liked to be conquered, and how pleasant overpersuasion is to you. Don't you think I had better take advantage of the confession, and begin and coax and entreat – even cry and be sulky if necessary – for the sake of a mere essay of my power?'

'I dare you to any such experiment. Encroach, presume, and the game is up.'

'Is it, sir? You soon give in. How stern you look now! Your eyebrows have become as thick as my finger, and your forehead resembles what, in some very astonishing poetry, I once saw styled, "a blue-piled thunderloft". That will be your married look, sir, I suppose?'

'If that will be *your* married look, I, as a Christian, will soon give up the notion of consorting with a mere sprite or salamander. But what had you to ask, thing – out with it?'

'There, you are less than civil now; and I like rudeness a great deal better than flattery. I had rather be a *thing* than an angel. This is what I have to ask. Why did you take such pains to make me believe you wished to marry Miss Ingram?'

'Is that all? Thank God it is no worse!' And now he unknit his black brows; looked down, smiling at me, and stroked my hair, as if well pleased at seeing a danger averted. 'I think I may confess,' he continued, 'even although I should make you a little indignant, Jane – and I have seen what a fire-spirit you can be when you are indignant. You glowed in the cool moonlight last night, when you mutinied against fate, and claimed your rank as my equal. Janet, by the by, it was you who made me the offer.'

'Of course I did. But to the point, if you please, sir – Miss Ingram?'

'Well, I feigned courtship of Miss Ingram, because I wished to render you

as madly in love with me as I was with you; and I knew jealousy would be the best ally I could call in for the furtherance of that end.'

'Excellent! Now you are small – not one whit bigger than the end of my little finger. It was a burning shame and a scandalous disgrace to act in that way. Did you think nothing of Miss Ingram's feelings, sir?'

'Her feelings are concentrated in one – pride; and that needs humbling. Were you jealous, Jane?'

'Never mind, Mr Rochester; it is in no way interesting to you to know that. Answer me truly once more. Do you think Miss Ingram will not suffer from your dishonest coquetry? Won't she feel forsaken and deserted?'

'Impossible! – when I told you how she, on the contrary, deserted me: the idea of my insolvency cooled, or rather extinguished, her flame in a moment.'

'You have a curious, designing mind, Mr Rochester. I am afraid your principles on some points are eccentric.'

'My principles were never trained, Jane: they may have grown a little awry for want of attention.'

'Once again, seriously: may I enjoy the great good that has been vouchsafed to me, without fearing that anyone else is suffering the bitter pain I myself felt a while ago?'

'That you may, my good little girl; there is not another being in the world has the same pure love for me as yourself – for I lay that pleasant unction to my soul, Jane, a belief in your affection.'

I turned my lips to the hand that lay on my shoulder. I loved him very much – more than I could trust myself to say – more than words had power to express.

'Ask something more,' he said presently; 'it is my delight to be entreated, and to yield.'

I was again ready with my request. 'Communicate your intentions to Mrs Fairfax, sir: she saw me with you last night in the hall, and she was shocked. Give her some explanation before I see her again. It pains me to be misjudged by so good a woman.'

'Go to your room, and put on your bonnet,' he replied. 'I mean you to accompany me to Millcote this morning; and while you prepare for the drive, I will enlighten the old lady's understanding. Did she think, Janet, you had given the world for love, and considered it well lost?'

'I believe she thought I had forgotten my station, and yours, sir.'

'Station! station – your station is in my heart, and on the necks of those who would insult you, now or hereafter. – Go.'

I was soon dressed; and when I heard Mr Rochester quit Mrs Fairfax's parlour, I hurried down to it. The old lady had been reading her morning portion of Scripture – the Lesson for the day; her Bible lay open before her, and her spectacles were upon it. Her occupation, suspended by Mr Rochester's announcement, seemed now forgotten; her eyes, fixed on the blank wall opposite, expressed the surprise of a quiet mind stirred by unwonted tidings. Seeing me, she roused herself: she made a sort of effort to smile, and framed a few words of congratulation; but the smile expired, and the sentence was abandoned unfinished. She put up her spectacles, shut the Bible, and pushed her chair back from the table.

'I feel so astonished,' she began, 'I hardly know what to say to you, Miss Eyre. I have surely not been dreaming, have I? Sometimes I half fall asleep

# Jane Eyre

when I am sitting alone and fancy things that have never happened. It has seemed to me more than once when I have been in a doze, that my dear husband, who died fifteen years since, has come in and sat down beside me; and that I have even heard him call me by my name, Alice, as he used to do. Now, can you tell me whether it is actually true that Mr Rochester has asked you to marry him? Don't laugh at me. But I really thought he came in here five minutes ago, and said that in a month you would be his wife.'

'He has said the same thing to me,' I replied.

'He has! Do you believe him? Have you accepted him?'

'Yes.'

She looked at me bewildered.

'I could never have thought it. He is a proud man; all the Rochesters were proud: and his father at least, liked money. He, too, has always been called careful. He means to marry you?'

'He tells me so.'

She surveyed my whole person: in her eyes I read that they had there found no charm powerful enough to solve the enigma.

'It passes me!' she continued; 'but no doubt it is true since you say so. How it will answer I cannot tell: I really don't know. Equality of position and fortune is often advisable in such cases; and there are twenty years of difference in your ages. He might almost be your father.'

'No, indeed, Mrs Fairfax!' I exclaimed, nettled; 'he is nothing like my father! No one, who saw us together, would suppose it for an instant. Mr Rochester looks as young, and is as young, as some men at five-and-twenty.'

'Is it really for love he is going to marry you?' she asked.

I was so hurt by her coldness and scepticism, that the tears rose to my eyes.

'I am sorry to grieve you,' pursued the widow; 'but you are so young, and so little acquainted with men, I wished to put you on your guard. It is an old saying that "all is not gold that glitters"; and in this case I do fear there will be something found to be different to what either you or I expect.'

'Why? – am I a monster?' I said: 'Is it impossible that Mr Rochester should have a sincere affection for me?'

'No: you are very well; and much improved of late; and Mr Rochester, I dare say, is fond of you. I have always noticed that you were a sort of pet of his. There are times when, for your sake, I have been a little uneasy at his marked preference, and have wished to put you on your guard; but I did not like to suggest even the possibility of wrong. I knew such an idea would shock, perhaps offend you; and you were so discreet, and so thoroughly modest and sensible, I hoped you might be trusted to protect yourself. Last night I cannot tell you what I suffered when I sought all over the house, and could find you nowhere, nor the master either; and then, at twelve o'clock, saw you come in with him.'

'Well, never mind that now,' I interrupted impatiently; 'it is enough that all was right.'

'I hope all will be right in the end,' she said: 'but, believe me, you cannot be too careful. Try and keep Mr Rochester at a distance: distrust yourself as well as him. Gentlemen in his station are not accustomed to marry their governesses.'

I was growing truly irritated: happily, Adèle ran in.

'Let me go – let me go to Millcote too!' she cried. 'Mr Rochester won't: though there is so much room in the new carriage. Beg him to let me go, mademoiselle.'

# Jane Eyre

'That I will, Adèle;' and I hastened away with her, glad to quit my gloomy monitress. The carriage was ready: they were bringing it round to the front, and my master was pacing the pavement, Pilot following him backwards and forwards.

'Adèle may accompany us, may she not, sir?'

'I told her no. I'll have no brats! – I'll have only you.'

'Do let her go, Mr Rochester, if you please: it would be better.'

'Not it: she will be a restraint.'

He was quite peremptory, both in look and voice. The chill of Mrs Fairfax's warnings, and the damp of her doubts were upon me: something of unsubstantiality and uncertainty had beset my hopes. I half lost the sense of power over him. I was about mechanically to obey him, without further remonstrance; but as he helped me into the carriage, he looked at my face.

'What is the matter?' he asked; 'all the sunshine is gone. Do you really wish the bairn to go? Will it annoy you if she is left behind?'

'I would far rather she went, sir.'

'Then off for your bonnet, and back like a flash of lightning!' cried he to Adèle.

She obeyed him with what speed she might.

'After all, a single morning's interruption will not matter much,' said he, 'when I mean shortly to claim you – your thoughts, conversation, and company – for life.'

Adèle, when lifted in, commenced kissing me, by way of expressing her gratitude for my intercession: she was instantly stowed away into a corner on the other side of him. She then peeped round to where I sat; so stern a neighbour was too restrictive: to him, in his present fractious mood, she dared whisper no observations, nor ask of him any information.

'Let her come to me,' I entreated: 'she will, perhaps, trouble you, sir: there is plenty of room on this side.'

He handed her over as if she had been a lap-dog. 'I'll send her to school yet,' he said, but now he was smiling.

Adèle heard him, and asked if she was to go to school 'sans mademoiselle?'

'Yes,' he replied, 'absolutely sans mademoiselle; for I am to take mademoiselle to the moon, and there I shall seek a cave in one of the white valleys among the volcano-tops, and mademoiselle shall live with me there, and only me.'

'She will have nothing to eat: you will starve her,' observed Adèle.

'I shall gather manna for her morning and night: the plains and hillsides in the moon are bleached with manna, Adèle.'

'She will want to warm herself: what will she do for a fire?'

'Fire rises out of the lunar mountains: when she is cold, I'll carry her up to a peak, and lay her down on the edge of a crater.'

'Oh, qu'elle y sera mal – peu confortable! and her clothes, they will wear out: how can she get new ones?'

Mr Rochester professed to be puzzled. 'Hem!' said he. 'What would you do, Adèle? Cudgel your brains for an expedient. How would a white or a pink cloud answer for a gown, do you think? And one could cut a pretty enough scarf out of a rainbow.'

'She is far better as she is,' concluded Adèle, after musing some time: 'besides,

# Jane Eyre

she would get tired of living with only you in the moon. If I were mademoiselle, I would never consent to go with you.'

'She has consented: she has pledged her word.'

'But you can't get her there; there is no road to the moon; it is all air; and neither you nor she can fly.'

'Adèle, look at that field.' We were now outside Thornfield gates, and bowling lightly along the smooth road to Millcote, where the dust was well laid by the thunderstorm, and where the low hedges and lofty timber trees on each side glistened green and rain-refreshed.

'In that field, Adèle, I was walking late one evening about a fortnight since – the evening of the day you helped me to make hay in the orchard meadows; and as I was tired with raking swaths, I sat down to rest me on a stile; and there I took out a little book and a pencil, and began to write about a misfortune that befell me long ago, and a wish I had for happy days to come. I was writing away very fast, though daylight was fading from the leaf, when something came up the path and stopped two yards off me. I looked at it. It was a little thing with a veil of gossamer on its head. I beckoned it to come near me; it stood soon at my knee. I never spoke to it, and it never spoke to me, in words; but I read its eyes, and it read mine; and our speechless colloquy was to this effect –

'It was a fairy, and come from Elf-land, it said; and its errand was to make me happy: I must go with it out of the common world to a lonely place – such as the moon, for instance – and it nodded its head towards her horn, rising over Hayhill: it told me of the alabaster cave and silver vale where we might live. I said I should like to go; but reminded it, as you did me, that I had no wings to fly.

' "Oh," returned the fairy, "that does not signify! Here is a talisman will remove all difficulties"; and she held out a pretty gold ring. "Put it," she said, "on the fourth finger of my left hand, and I am yours, and you are mine; and we shall leave earth, and make our own heaven yonder." She nodded again at the moon. The ring, Adèle, is in my breeches pocket, under the disguise of a sovereign; but I mean soon to change it to a ring again.'

'But what has mademoiselle to do with it? I don't care for the fairy: you said it was mademoiselle you would take to the moon?'

'Mademoiselle is a fairy,' he said, whispering mysteriously. Whereupon I told her not to mind his badinage; and she, on her part, evinced a fund of genuine French scepticism; denominating Mr Rochester, 'un vrai menteur', and assuring him that she made no account whatever of his 'contes de fée', and that 'du reste, il n'y avait pas de fées, et quand même il y en avait', she was sure they would never appear to him, nor ever give him rings, or offer to live with him in the moon.

The hour spent at Millcote was a somewhat harassing one to me. Mr Rochester obliged me to go to a certain silk warehouse: there I was ordered to choose half a dozen dresses. I hated the business, I begged leave to defer it: no – it should be gone through with now. By dint of entreaties expressed in energetic whispers, I reduced the half-dozen to two: these, however, he vowed he would select himself. With anxiety I watched his eye rove over the gay stores: he fixed on a rich silk of the most brilliant amethyst dye, and a superb pink satin. I told him in a new series of whispers, that he might as well buy me a gold gown and a silver bonnet at once: I should certainly never venture to wear his choice. With

infinite difficulty, for he was stubborn as a stone, I persuaded him to make an exchange in favour of a sober black satin and pearl-gray silk. 'It might pass for the present,' he said; but he would yet see me glittering like a parterre.'

Glad was I to get him out of the silk warehouse, and then out of a jeweller's shop: the more he bought me, the more my cheek burned with a sense of annoyance and degradation. As we re-entered the carriage, and I sat back, feverish and fagged, I remembered what, in the hurry of events, dark and bright, I had wholly forgotten – the letter of my uncle, John Eyre, to Mrs Reed: his intention to adopt me and make me his legatee. 'It would, indeed, be a relief', I thought, 'if I had ever so small an independency; I never can bear being dressed like a doll by Mr Rochester, or sitting like a second Danae with the golden shower falling daily round me. I will write to Madeira the moment I get home, and tell my Uncle John I am going to be married, and to whom: if I had but a prospect of one day bringing Mr Rochester an accession of fortune, I could better endure to be kept by him now.' And somewhat relieved by this idea (which I failed not to execute that day), I ventured once more to meet my master's and lover's eye, which most pertinaciously sought mine, though I averted both face and gaze. He smiled; and I thought his smile was such as a sultan might, in a blissful and fond moment, bestow on a slave his gold and gems had enriched: I crushed his hand, which was ever hunting mine, vigorously, and thrust it back to him red with the passionate pressure.

'You need not look in that way,' I said: 'if you do, I'll wear nothing but my old Lowood frocks to the end of the chapter. I'll be married in this lilac gingham: you may make a dressing-gown for yourself out of the pearl-gray silk, and an infinite series of waistcoats out of the black satin.'

He chuckled; he rubbed his hands, 'Oh, it is rich to see and hear her!' he exclaimed. 'Is she original? Is she piquant? I would not exchange this one little English girl for the Grand Turk's whole seraglio – gazelle-eyes, houri forms, and all!'

The Eastern allusion bit me again. 'I'll not stand you an inch in the stead of a seraglio,' I said; 'so don't consider me an equivalent for one. If you have a fancy for anything in that line, away with you, sir, to the bazaars of Stamboul, without delay, and lay out in extensive slave-purchases some of that spare cash you seem at a loss to spend satisfactorily here.'

'And what will you do, Janet, while I am bargaining for so many tons of flesh and such an assortment of black eyes?'

'I'll be preparing myself to go out as a missionary to preach liberty to them that are enslaved – your harem inmates amongst the rest. I'll get admitted there, and I'll stir up mutiny; and you, three-tailed bashaw as you are, sir, shall in a trice find yourself fettered amongst our hands: nor will I, for one, consent to cut your bonds till you have signed a charter, the most liberal that despot ever yet conferred.'

'I would consent to be at your mercy, Jane.'

'I would have no mercy, Mr Rochester, if you supplicated for it with an eye like that. While you look so, I should be certain that whatever charter you might grant under coercion, your first act, when released, would be to violate its conditions.'

'Why, Jane, what would you have? I fear you will compel me to go through

a private marriage ceremony, besides that performed at the altar. You will stipulate, I see, for peculiar terms – what will they be?'

'I only want an easy mind, sir; not crushed by crowded obligations. Do you remember what you said of Céline Varens? – of the diamonds, the cashmeres you gave her? I will not be your English Céline Varens. I shall continue to act as Adèle's governess; by that I shall earn my board and lodging, and thirty pounds a year besides. I shall furnish my own wardrobe out of that money, and you shall give me nothing but —'

'Well, but what?'

'Your regard; and if I give you mine in return, that debt will be quit.'

'Well, for cool native impudence and pure innate pride, you haven't your equal,' said he. We were now approaching Thornfield. 'Will it please you to dine with me to-day?' he asked, as we re-entered the gates.

'No, thank you, sir.'

'And what for "no, thank you", if one may inquire?'

'I never have dined with you, sir; and I see no reason why I should now: till —'

'Till what? You delight in half-phrases.'

'Till I can't help it.'

'Do you suppose I eat like an ogre or a ghoul, that you dread being the companion of my repast?'

'I have formed no supposition on the subject, sir; but I want to go on as usual for another month.'

'You will give up your governessing slavery at once.'

'Indeed, begging your pardon, sir, I shall not. I shall just go on with it as usual. I shall keep out of your way all day as I have been accustomed to do: you may send for me in the evening, when you feel disposed to see me, and I'll come then; but at no other time.'

'I want a smoke, Jane, or a pinch of snuff, to comfort me under all this, "pour me donner une contenance", as Adèle would say; and unfortunately I have neither my cigar-case, nor my snuff-box. But listen – whisper. It is your time now, little tyrant, but it will be mine presently; and when once I have fairly seized you, to have and to hold, I'll just – figuratively speaking – attach you to a chain like this' (touching his watch-guard). 'Yes, bonny wee thing, I'll wear you in my bosom, lest my jewel I should tyne.'

He said this as he helped me to alight from the carriage; and while he afterwards lifted out Adèle, I entered the house, and made good my retreat upstairs.

He duly summoned me to his presence in the evening. I had prepared an occupation for him; for I was determined not to spend the whole time in a tête-à-tête conversation. I remembered his fine voice; I knew he liked to sing – good singers generally do. I was no vocalist myself, and, in his fastidious judgement, no musician either; but I delighted in listening when the performance was good. No sooner had twilight, that hour of romance, began to lower her blue and starry banner over the lattice, than I rose, opened the piano, and entreated him, for the love of Heaven, to give me a song. He said I was a capricious witch, and that he would rather sing another time; but I averred that no time was like the present.

'Did I like his voice?' he asked.

# Jane Eyre

'Very much.' I was not fond of pampering that susceptible vanity of his; but for once, and from motives of expediency, I would e'en soothe and stimulate it.

'Then, Jane, you must play the accompaniment.'

'Very well, sir, I'll try.'

I did try, but was presently swept off the stool and denominated 'a little bungler'. Being pushed unceremoniously to one side – which was precisely what I wished – he usurped my place, and proceeded to accompany himself: for he could play as well as sing. I hied me to the window-recess; and while I sat there and looked out on the still trees and dim lawn, to a sweet air was sung in mellow tones the following strain:

> 'The truest love that ever heart
>     Felt at its kindled core,
> Did through each vein, in quickened start,
>     The tide of being pour.
>
> 'Her coming was my hope each day,
>     Her parting was my pain;
> The chance that did her steps delay
>     Was ice in every vein.
>
> 'I dreamed it would be nameless bliss,
>     As I loved, loved to be;
> And to this object did I press
>     As blind as eagerly.
>
> 'But wide as pathless was the space
>     That lay our lives between,
> And dangerous as the foamy race
>     Of ocean-surges green.
>
> 'And haunted as a robber-path
>     Through wilderness or wood;
> For Might and Right and Woe and Wrath,
>     Between our spirits stood.
>
> 'I dangers dared; I hindrance scorned;
>     I omens did defy;
> Whatever menaced, harassed, warned,
>     I passed impetuous by.
>
> 'On sped my rainbow, fast as light;
>     I flew as in a dream;
> For glorious rose upon my sight
>     That child of Shower and Gleam.
>
> 'Still bright on clouds of suffering dim
>     Shines that soft, solemn joy;
> Nor care I now, how dense and grim
>     Disasters gather nigh.

# Jane Eyre

*'I care not in this moment sweet,*
*Though all I have rushed o'er*
*Should come on pinion, strong and fleet,*
*Proclaiming vengeance sore:*

*'Though Haughty hate should strike me down,*
*Right, bar approach to me,*
*And grinding Might, with furious frown,*
*Swear endless enmity.*

*'My love has placed her little hand*
*With noble faith in mine,*
*And vowed that wedlock's sacred band*
*Our nature shall entwine.*

*'My love has sworn, with sealing kiss,*
*With me to live – to die;*
*I have at last my nameless bliss:*
*As I love – loved am I!'*

He rose and came towards me, and I saw his face all kindled, and his full falcon-eye flashing, and tenderness and passion in every lineament. I quailed momentarily – then I rallied. Soft scene, daring demonstration, I would not have; and I stood in peril of both; a weapon of defence must be prepared – I whetted my tongue; as he reached me, I asked with asperity, 'whom he was going to marry now?'

'That was a strange question to be put by his darling Jane.'

'Indeed! I considered it a very natural and necessary one: he had talked of his future wife dying with him. What did he mean by such a pagan idea? *I* had no intention of dying with him – he might depend on that.'

'Oh, all he longed, all he prayed for, was that I might live with him! Death was not for such as I.'

'Indeed it was: I had as good a right to die when my time came as he had: but I should bide that time, and not be hurried away in a suttee.'

'Would I forgive him for the selfish idea, and prove my pardon by a reconciling kiss?'

'No: I would rather be excused.'

Here I heard myself apostrophized as a 'hard little thing'; and it was added, 'any other woman would have been melted to marrow at hearing such stanzas crooned in her praise'.

I assured him I was naturally hard – very flinty, and that he would often find me so; and that, moreoever, I was determined to show him divers rugged points in my character before the ensuing four weeks elapsed: he should know fully what sort of a bargain he had made, while there was yet time to rescind it.

'Would I be quiet and talk rationally?'

'I would be quiet if he liked; and as to talking rationally, I flattered myself I was doing that now.'

He fretted, pished, and pshawed. 'Very good,' I thought; 'you may fume and fidget as you please: but this is the best plan to pursue with you, I am certain. I like you more than I can say; but I'll not sink into a bathos of sentiment: and

with this needle of repartee I'll keep you from the edge of the gulf, too; and, moreoever, maintain by its pungent aid that distance between you and myself most conducive to our real mutual advantage.'

From less to more, I worked him up to considerable irritation; then, after he had retired in dudgeon, quite to the other end of the room, I got up, and saying, 'I wish you good-night, sir,' in my natural and wonted respectful manner, I slipped out by the side-door and got away.

The system thus entered on, I pursued during the whole season of probation; and with the best success. He was kept, to be sure, rather cross and crusty; but on the whole I could see he was excellently entertained, and that a lamb-like submission and turtle-dove sensibility, while fostering his despotism more, would have pleased his judgement, satisfied his common sense, and even suited his taste less.

In other people's presence I was, as formerly, deferential and quiet; any other line of conduct being uncalled for: it was only in the evening conferences I thus thwarted and afflicted him. He continued to send for me punctually the moment the clock struck seven; though when I appeared before him now, he had no such honeyed terms as 'love' and 'darling' on his lips: the best words at my service were 'provoking puppet', 'malicious elf', 'sprite', 'changeling', &c. For caresses, too, I now got grimaces; for a pressure of the hand, a pinch on the arm; for a kiss on the cheek, a severe tweak of the ear. It was all right: at present I decidedly preferred these fierce favours to anything more tender. Mrs Fairfax, I saw, approved me: her anxiety on my account vanished; therefore I was certain I did well. Meantime, Mr Rochester affirmed I was wearing him to skin and bone, and threatened awful vengeance for my present conduct at some period fast coming. I laughed in my sleeve at his menaces. 'I can keep you in reasonable check now', I reflected; 'and I don't doubt to be able to do it hereafter: if one expedient loses its virtue, another must be devised'.

Yet after all my task was not an easy one; often I would rather have pleased than teased him. My future husband was becoming to me my whole world; and more than the world; almost my hope of heaven. He stood between me and every thought of religion, as an eclipse intervenes between man and the broad sun. I could not, in those days, see God for His creature: of whom I had made an idol.

# Chapter 25

The month of courtship had wasted: its very last hours were being numbered. There was no putting off the day that advanced – the bridal day; and all preparations for its arrival were complete. *I*, at least, had nothing more to do: there were my trunks, packed, locked, corded, ranged in a row along

the wall of my little chamber; to-morrow, at this time, they would be far on their road to London: and so should I (*D.V.*) – or rather, not I, but one Jane Rochester, a person whom as yet I knew not. The cards of address alone remained to nail on: they lay, four little squares, in the drawer. Mr Rochester had himself written the direction, 'Mrs Rochester, – Hotel, London', on each: I could not persuade myself to affix them, or to have them affixed. Mrs Rochester! She did not exist: she would not be born till to-morrow, some time after eight o'clock a.m.; and I would wait to be assured she had come into the world alive before I assigned to her all that property. It was enough that in yonder closet, opposite my dressing-table, garments said to be hers had already displaced my black stuff Lowood frock and straw bonnet: for not to me appertained that suit of wedding raiment; the pearl-coloured robe, the vapoury veil pendent from the usurped portmanteau. I shut the closet to conceal the strange, wraith-like apparel it contained; which, at this evening hour – nine o'clock – gave out certainly a most ghostly shimmer through the shadow of my apartment. 'I will leave you by yourself, white dream,' I said, 'I am feverish: I hear the wind blowing: I will go out of doors and feel it.'

It was not only the hurry of preparation that made me feverish: not only the anticipation of the great change – the new life which was to commence to-morrow: both these circumstances had their share, doubtless, in producing that restless, excited mood which hurried me forth at this late hour into the darkening grounds; but a third cause influenced my mind more than they.

I had at heart a strange and anxious thought. Something had happened which I could not comprehend; no one knew of or had seen the event but myself: it had taken place the preceding night. Mr Rochester that night was absent from home; nor was he yet returned; business had called him to a small estate of two or three farms he possessed thirty miles off – business it was requisite he should settle in person, previous to this meditated departure from England. I waited now his return; eager to disburthen my mind, and to seek of him the solution of the enigma that perplexed me. Stay till he comes, reader; and, when I disclose my secret to him, you shall share the confidence.

I sought the orchard, driven to its shelter by the wind, which all day had blown strong and full from the south, without, however, bringing a speck of rain. Instead of subsiding as night drew on, it seemed to augment its rush and deepen its roar: the trees blew steadfastly one way, never writhing round, and scarcely tossing back their boughs once in an hour; so continuous was the strain bending their branchy heads northward – the clouds drifted from pole to pole, fast following, mass on mass: no glimpse of blue sky had been visible that July day.

It was not without a certain wild pleasure I ran before the wind, delivering my trouble of mind to the measureless air-torrent thundering through space. Descending the laurel walk, I faced the wreck of the chestnut-tree; it stood up, black and riven: the trunk, split down the centre, gasped ghastly. The cloven halves were not broken from each other, for the firm base and strong roots kept them unsundered below; though community of vitality was destroyed – the sap could flow no more: their great boughs on each side were dead, and next winter's tempests would be sure to fell one or both to earth: as yet, however, they might be said to form one tree – a ruin, but an entire ruin.

'You did right to hold fast to each other,' I said: as if the monster splinters

# Jane Eyre

were living things, and could hear me. 'I think, scathed as you look, and charred and scorched, there must be a little sense of life in you yet, rising out of that adhesion at the faithful, honest roots: you will never have green leaves more – never more see birds making nests and singing idylls in your boughs; the time of pleasure and love is over with you; but you are not desolate: each of you has a comrade to sympathize with him in his decay.' As I looked up at them, the moon appeared momentarily in that part of the sky which filled their fissure; her disc was blood-red and half overcast; she seemed to throw on me one bewildered, dreary glance, and buried herself again instantly in the deep drift of cloud. The wind fell, for a second, round Thornfield; but far away over wood and water poured a wild, melancholy wail: it was sad to listen to, and I ran off again.

Here and there I strayed through the orchard, gathered up the apples with which the grass round the tree roots was thickly strewn; then I employed myself in dividing the ripe from the unripe; I carried them into the house and put them away in the storeroom. Then I repaired to the library to ascertain whether the fire was lit, for, though summer, I knew on such a gloomy evening Mr Rochester would like to see a cheerful hearth when he came in: yes, the fire had been kindled some time, and burnt well. I placed his arm-chair by the chimney-corner; I wheeled the table near it; I let down the curtain, and had the candles brought in ready for lighting.

More restless than ever, when I had completed these arrangements, I could not sit still, nor even remain in the house: a little timepiece in the room and the old clock in the hall simultaneously struck ten.

'How late it grows!' I said. 'I will run down to the gates: it is moonlight at intervals: I can see a good way on the road. He may be coming now, and to meet him will save some minutes of suspense.'

The wind roared high in the great trees which embowered the gates; but the road as far as I could see, to the right hand and the left, was all still and solitary: save for the shadows of clouds crossing it at intervals as the moon looked out, it was but a long, pale line, unvaried by one moving speck.

A puerile tear dimmed my eye while I looked – a tear of disappointment and impatience; ashamed of it, I wiped it away. I lingered; the moon shut herself wholly within her chamber, and drew close her curtain of dense cloud; the night grew dark; rain came driving fast on the gale.

'I wish he would come! I wish he would come!' I exclaimed, seized with hypochondriac foreboding. I had expected his arrival before tea; now it was dark: what could keep him? Had an accident happened? The event of last night again recurred to me. I interpreted it as a warning of disaster. I feared my hopes were too bright to be realized; and I had enjoyed so much bliss lately that I imagined my fortune had passed its meridian, and must now decline.

'Well, I cannot return to the house,' I thought; 'I cannot sit by the fireside, while he is abroad in inclement weather: better tire my limbs than strain my heart; I will go forward and meet him.'

I set out; I walked fast, but not far: ere I had measured a quarter of a mile, I heard the tramp of hoofs; a horseman came on, full gallop; a dog ran by his side. Away with evil presentiment! It was he: here he was, mounted on Mesrour, followed by Pilot. He saw me; for the moon had opened a blue field in the sky,

# Jane Eyre

and rode in it watery bright: he took his hat off, and waved it round his head. I now ran to meet him.

'There!' he exclaimed, as he stretched out his hand and bent from the saddle: 'you can't do without me, that is evident. Step on my boot-toe; give me both hands: mount!'

I obeyed: joy made me agile: I sprang up before him. A hearty kissing I got for a welcome, and some boastful triumph, which I swallowed as well as I could. He checked himself in his exultation to demand, 'But is there anything the matter, Janet, that you come to meet me at such an hour? Is there anything wrong?'

'No, but I thought you would never come. I could not bear to wait in the house for you, especially with this rain and wind.'

'Rain and wind, indeed! Yes, you are dripping like a mermaid; pull my cloak round you: but I think you are feverish, Jane: both your cheek and hand are burning hot. I ask again, is there anything the matter?'

'Nothing now; I am neither afraid nor unhappy.'

'Then you have been both?'

'Rather; but I'll tell you all about it by and by, sir; and I dare say you will only laugh at me for my pains.'

'I'll laugh at you heartily when to-morrow is past; till then I dare not: my prize is not certain. This is you, who have been as slippery as an eel this last month, and as thorny as a brier-rose? I could not lay a finger anywhere but I was pricked; and now I seem to have gathered up a stray lamb in my arms. You wandered out of the fold to seek your shepherd, did you Jane?'

'I wanted you: but don't boast. Here we are at Thornfield: now let me get down.'

He landed me on the pavement. As John took his horse, and he followed me into the hall, he told me to make haste and put something dry on, and then return to him in the library; and he stopped me, as I made for the staircase, to extort a promise that I would not be long: nor was I long; in five minutes I rejoined him. I found him at supper.

'Take a seat and bear me company, Jane: please God, it is the last meal but one you will eat at Thornfield Hall for a long time.'

I sat down near him, but told him I could not eat.

'Is it because you have the prospect of a journey before you, Jane? Is it the thoughts of going to London that takes away your appetite?'

'I cannot see my prospects clearly to-night, sir; and I hardly know what thoughts I have in my head. Everything in life seems unreal.'

'Except me: I am substantial enough – touch me.'

'You sir, are the most phantom-like of all: you are a mere dream.'

He held out his hand, laughing. 'Is that a dream?' said he, placing it close to my eyes. He had a rounded, muscular, and vigorous hand, as well as a long, strong arm.

'Yes: though I touch it, it is a dream,' said I, as I put it down from before my face. 'Sir, have you finished supper?'

'Yes, Jane.'

I rang the bell, and ordered away the tray. When we were again alone, I stirred the fire, and then took a low seat at my master's knee.

'It is near midnight,' I said.

# Jane Eyre

'Yes: but remember, Jane, you promised to wake with me the night before my wedding.'

'I did; and I will keep my promise, for an hour or two at least: I have no wish to go to bed.'

'Are all your arrangements complete?'

'All, sir.'

'And on my part likewise,' he returned, 'I have settled everything; and we shall leave Thornfield to-morrow, within half an hour after our return from church.'

'Very well, sir.'

'With an extraordinary smile you uttered that word – "very well", Jane! What a bright spot of colour you have on each cheek! and how strangely your eyes glitter! Are you well?'

'I believe I am.'

'Believe! What is the matter? Tell me what you feel.'

'I could not, sir: no words could tell you what I feel. I wish this present hour would never end: who knows with what fate the next may come charged?'

'This is hypochondria, Jane. You have been over-excited, or over-fatigued.'

'Do you, sir, feel calm and happy?'

'Calm? – no: but happy – to the heart's core.'

I looked up at him to read the signs of bliss in his face: it was ardent and flushed.

'Give me your confidence, Jane,' he said: 'relieve your mind of any weight that oppresses it, by imparting it to me. What do you fear? – that I shall not prove a good husband?'

'It is the idea farthest from my thoughts.'

'Are you apprehensive of the new sphere you are about to enter? – of the new life into which you are passing?'

'No.'

'You puzzle me, Jane: your look and tone of sorrowful audacity perplex and pain me. I want an explanation.'

'Then, sir, listen. You were from home last night?'

'I was: I know that; and you hinted a while ago at something which had happened in my absence: nothing, probably, of consequence; but, in short, it has disturbed you. Let me hear it. Mrs Fairfax has said something, perhaps? or you have overheard the servants talk? – your sensitive self-respect has been wounded?'

'No, sir.' It struck twelve – I waited till the timepiece had concluded its silver chime, and the clock its hoarse, vibrating stroke, and then I proceeded –

'All day yesterday I was very busy, and very happy in my ceaseless bustle; for I am not, as you seem to think, troubled by any haunting fears about the new sphere, et cetera: I think it a glorious thing to have the hope of living with you, because I love you. No, sir, don't caress me now – let me talk undisturbed. Yesterday I trusted well in Providence, and believed that events were working together for your good and mine: it was a fine day, if you recollect – the calmness of the air and sky forbade apprehensions respecting your safety or comfort on your journey. I walked a little while on the pavement after tea, thinking of you; and I beheld you in imagination so near me, I scarcely missed your actual presence. I thought of the life that lay before me – *your* life, sir – an existence more expansive and stirring than my own: as much more so as the depths of the

sea to which the brook runs are than the shallows of its own strait channel. I wondered why moralists call this world a dreary wilderness: for me it blossomed like a rose. Just at sunset, the air turned cold and the sky cloudy: I went in. Sophie called me upstairs to look at my wedding-dress, which they had just brought; and under it in the box I found your present – the veil which, in your princely extravagance, you sent for from London: resolved, I suppose, since I would not have jewels, to cheat me into accepting something as costly. I smiled as I unfolded it, and devised how I would tease you about your aristocratic tastes, and your efforts to mask your plebeian bride in the attributes of a peeress. I thought how I would carry down to you the square of unembroidered blond I had myself prepared as a covering for my low-born head, and ask if that was not good enough for a woman who could bring her husband neither fortune, beauty, nor connexions. I saw plainly how you would look; and heard your impetuous republican answers, and your haughty disavowal of any necessity on your part to augment your wealth, or elevate your standing by marrying either a purse or a coronet.'

'How well you read me, you witch!' interposed Mr Rochester: 'but what did you find in the veil besides its embroidery? Did you find poison, or a dagger, that you look so mournful now?'

'No, no, sir; besides the delicacy and richness of the fabric, I found nothing save Fairfax Rochester's pride; and that did not scare me, because I am used to the sight of the demon. But, sir, as it grew dark, the wind rose: it blew yesterday evening, not as it blows now – wild and high – but "with a sullen, moaning sound" far more eerie. I wished you were at home. I came into this room, and the sight of the empty chair and fireless hearth chilled me. For some time after I went to bed, I could not sleep – a sense of anxious excitement distressed me. The gale, still rising, seemed to my ear to muffle a mournful under-sound; whether in the house or abroad I could not at first tell, but it recurred, doubtful yet doleful at every lull; at last I made out it must be some dog howling at a distance. I was glad when it ceased. On sleeping, I continued in dreams the idea of a dark and gusty night. I continued also the wish to be with you, and experienced a strange, regretful consciousness of some barrier dividing us. During all my first sleep, I was following the windings of an unknown road; total obscurity environed me; rain pelted me; I was burdened with the charge of a little child: a very small creature, too young and feeble to walk, and which shivered in my cold arms, and wailed piteously in my ear. I thought, sir, that you were on the road a long way before me; and I strained every nerve to overtake you, and made effort on effort to utter your name and entreat you to stop – but my movements were fettered, and my voice still died away inarticulate; while you, I felt, withdrew farther and farther every moment.'

'And these dreams weigh on your spirits now, Jane, when I am close to you? Little nervous subject! Forget visionary woe, and think only of real happiness! You say you love me Janet: yes – I will not forget that; and you cannot deny it. *Those words* did not die inarticulate on your lips. I heard them clear and soft; a thought too solemn, perhaps, but sweet as music – "I think it is a glorious thing to have the hope of living with you, Edward, because I love you." Do you love me, Jane? – repeat it.'

'I do, sir – I do, with my whole heart.'

'Well,' he said, after some minutes' silence, 'it is strange; but that sentence

# Jane Eyre

has penetrated my breast painfully. Why? I think because you said it with such an earnest, religious energy, and because your upward gaze at me now is the very sublime of faith, truth, and devotion: it is too much as if some spirit were near me. Look wicked, Jane: as you know well how to look: coin one of your wild, shy, provoking smiles; tell me you hate me – tease me, vex me; do anything but move me: I would rather be incensed than saddened.'

'I will tease you and vex you to your heart's content, when I have finished my tale: but hear me to the end.'

'I thought, Jane, you had told me all. I thought I had found the source of your melancholy in a dream.'

I shook my head. 'What! is there more? But I will not believe it to be anything important. I warn you of incredulity beforehand. Go on.'

The disquietude of his air, the somewhat apprehensive impatience of his manner, surprised me: but I proceeded.

'I dreamt another dream, sir: that Thornfield Hall was a dreary ruin, the retreat of bats and owls. I thought that of all the stately front nothing remained but a shell-like wall, very high and very fragile-looking. I wandered, on a moonlight night, through the grass-grown enclosure within: here I stumbled over a marble hearth, and there over a fallen fragment of cornice. Wrapped up in a shawl, I still carried the unknown little child: I might not lay it down anywhere, however tired were my arms – however much its weight impeded my progress, I must retain it. I heard the gallop of a horse at a distance on the road; I was sure it was you; and you were departing for many years, and for a distant country. I climbed the thin wall with frantic, perilous haste, eager to catch one glimpse of you from the top: the stones rolled from under my feet, the ivy branches I grasped gave way, the child clung round my neck in terror, and almost strangled me; at last I gained the summit. I saw you like a speck on a white track, lessening every moment. The blast blew so strong I could not stand. I sat down on the narrow ledge; I hushed the scared infant in my lap: you turned an angle of the road: I bent forward to take a last look; the wall crumbled; I was shaken; the child rolled from my knee, I lost my balance, fell, and woke.'

'Now, Jane, that is all.'

'All the preface, sir; the tale is yet to come. On waking, a gleam dazzled my eyes; I thought – oh, it is daylight! But I was mistaken; it was only candlelight. Sophie, I supposed, had come in. There was a light on the dressing-table, and the door of the closet, where, before going to bed, I had hung my wedding-dress and veil, stood open; I heard a rustling there. I asked, "Sophie, what are you doing?" No one answered; but a form emerged from the closet; it took the light, held it aloft, and surveyed the garments pendent from the portmanteau. "Sophie! Sophie!" I again cried: and still it was silent. I had risen up in bed, I bent forward: first surprise, then bewilderment, came over me; and and then my blood crept cold through my veins. Mr Rochester, this was not Sophie, it was not Leah, it was not Mrs Fairfax; it was not – no, I was sure of it, and am still – it was not even that strange woman, Grace Poole.'

'It must have been one of them,' interrupted my master.

'No, sir, I solemnly assure you to the contrary. The shape standing before me had never crossed my eyes within the precincts of Thornfield Hall before; the height, the contour were new to me.'

'Describe it, Jane.'

# Jane Eyre

'It seemed, sir, a woman, tall and large, with thick and dark hair hanging long down her back. I know not what dress she had on: it was white and straight; but whether gown, sheet, or shroud, I cannot tell.'

'Did you see her face?'

'Not at first. But presently she took my veil from its place: she held it up, gazed at it long, and then, she threw it over her own head, and turned to the mirror. At that moment I saw the reflection of the visage and features quite distinctly in the dark oblong glass.'

'And how were they?'

'Fearful and ghastly to me – oh, sir, I never saw a face like it! It was a discoloured face – it was a savage face. I wish I could forget the roll of the red eyes and the fearful blackened inflation of the lineaments!'

'Ghosts are usually pale, Jane.'

'This, sir, was purple: the lips were swelled and dark; the brow furrowed: the black eyebrows widely raised over the bloodshot eyes. Shall I tell you of what it reminded me?'

'You may.'

'Of the foul German spectre – the vampire.'

'Ah! – what did it do?'

'Sir, it removed my veil from its gaunt head, rent it in two parts, and flinging both on the floor, trampled on them.'

'Afterwards?'

'It drew aside the window-curtain and looked out; perhaps it saw dawn approaching, for, taking the candle, it retreated to the door. Just at my bedside the figure stopped: the fiery eyes glared upon me – she thrust up her candle close to my face, and extinguished it under my eyes. I was aware her lurid visage flamed over mine, and I lost consciousness: for the second time in my life – only the second time – I became insensible from terror.'

'Who was with you when you revived?'

'No one, sir, but the broad day. I rose, bathed my head and face in water, drank a long draught; felt that though enfeebled I was not ill, and determined that to none but you would I impart this vision. Now, sir, tell me who and what that woman was?'

'The creature of an over-stimulated brain; that is certain, I must be careful of you, my treasure: nerves like yours were not made for rough handling.'

'Sir, depend on it, my nerves were not in fault; the thing was real: the transaction actually took place.'

'And your previous dreams, were they real too? Is Thornfield Hall a ruin? Am I severed from you by insuperable obstacles? Am I leaving you without a tear – without a kiss – without a word?'

'Not yet.'

'Am I about to do it? Why, the day is already commenced which is to bind us indissolubly; and whence we are once united, there shall be no recurrence of these mental terrors: I guarantee that.'

'Mental terrors, sir! I wish I could believe them to be only such: I wish it more now than ever; since even you cannot explain to me the mystery of that awful visitant.'

'And since I cannot do it, Jane, it must have been unreal.'

'But, sir, when I said to myself on rising this morning, and when I looked

# Jane Eyre

round the room to gather courage and comfort from the cheerful aspect of each familiar object in full daylight, there – on the carpet – I saw what gave the distinct lie to my hypothesis – the veil, torn from top to bottom in two halves!'

I felt Mr Rochester start and shudder; he hastily flung his arms round me. 'Thank God!' he exclaimed, 'that if anything malignant did come near you last night, it was only the veil that was harmed. Oh, to think what might have happened!'

He drew his breath short, and strained me so close to him, I could scarcely pant. After some minutes silence, he continued cheerily –

'Now, Janet, I'll explain to you all about it. It was half-dream, half-reality. A woman did, I doubt not, enter your room: and that woman was – must have been – Grace Poole. You call her a strange being yourself: from all you know, you have reason so to call her – what did she do to me? what to Mason? In a state between sleeping and waking, you noticed her entrance and her actions; but feverish, almost delirious as you were, you ascribed to her a goblin appearance different from her own: the long dishevelled hair, the swelled black face, the exaggerated stature, were figments of imagination; results of nightmare: the spiteful tearing of the veil was real: and it is like her. I see you would ask why I keep such a woman in my house: when we have been married a year and a day, I will tell you; but not now. Are you satisfied, Jane? Do you accept my solution of the mystery?'

I reflected, and in truth it appeared to me the only possible one: satisfied I was not, but to please him I endeavoured to appear so – relieved, I certainly did feel: so I answered him with a contented smile. And now, as it was long past one, I prepared to leave him.

'Does not Sophie sleep with Adèle in the nursery?' he asked as I lit my candle. 'Yes, sir.'

'And there is room enough in Adèle's little bed for you. You must share it with her to-night, Jane: it is no wonder that the incident you have related should make you nervous, and I would rather you did not sleep alone: promise me to go to the nursery.'

'I shall be very glad to do so, sir.'

'And fasten the door securely on the inside. Wake Sophie when you go upstairs, under pretence of requesting her to rouse you in good time to-morrow; for you must be dressed and finished breakfast before eight. And now, no more sombre thoughts: chase dull care away, Janet. Don't you hear to what soft whispers the wind has fallen? and there is no more beating of rain against the window-panes: look here' (he lifted up the curtain) – 'it is a lovely night!'

It was. Half heaven was pure and stainless: the clouds, now trooping before the wind, which had shifted to the west, were filing off eastward in long, silvered columns. The moon shone peacefully.

'Well,' said Mr Rochester, gazing inquiringly into my eyes, 'how is my Janet, now?'

'The night is serene, sir; and so am I.'

'And you will not dream of separation and sorrow to-night; but of happy love and blissful union.'

This prediction was but half fulfilled: I did not indeed dream of sorrow, but as little did I dream of joy; for I never slept at all. With little Adèle in my arms, I watched the slumber of childhood – so tranquil, so passionless, so innocent –

and waited for the coming day: all my life was awake and astir in my frame: and as soon as the sun rose I rose too. I remember Adèle clung to me as I left her: I remember I kissed her as I loosened her little hands from my neck; and I cried over her with strange emotion, and quitted her because I feared my sobs would break her still sound repose. She seemed the emblem of my past life; and he I was now to array myself to meet, the dread, but adored, type of my unknown future day.

# Chapter 26

Sophie came at seven to dress me: she was very long indeed in accomplishing her task; so long that Mr Rochester, grown, I suppose, impatient of my delay, sent up to ask why I did not come. She was just fastening my veil (the plain square of blond after all) to my hair with a brooch; I hurried from under her hands as soon as I could.

'Stop!' she cried in French. 'Look at yourself in the mirror: you have not taken one peep.'

So I turned at the door: I saw a robed and veiled figure, so unlike my usual self that it seemed almost the image of a stranger. 'Jane!' called a voice, and I hastened down. I was received at the foot of the stairs by Mr Rochester.

'Lingerer!' he said, 'my brain is on fire with impatience, and you tarry so long!'

He took me into the dining-room, surveyed me keenly all over, pronounced me 'fair as a lily, and not only the pride of his life, but the desire of his eyes', and then telling me he would give me about ten minutes to eat some breakfast, he rang the bell. One of his lately hired servants, a footman, answered it.

'Is John getting the carriage ready?'

'Yes, sir.'

'Is the luggage brought down?'

'They are bringing it down, sir.'

'Go you to the church: see if Mr Wood (the clergyman) and the clerk are there: return and tell me.'

The church, as the reader knows, was but just beyond the gates; the footman soon returned.

'Mr Wood is in the vestry sir, putting on his surplice.'

'And the carriage?'

'The horses are harnessing.'

'We shall not want it to go to church; but it must be ready the moment we return: all the boxes and luggage arranged and strapped on, and the coachman in his seat.'

'Yes, sir.'

# Jane Eyre

'Jane, are you ready?'

I rose. There was no groomsmen, no bridesmaids, no relatives to wait for or marshal: none but Mr Rochester and I. Mrs Fairfax stood in the hall as we passed. I would fain have spoken to her, but my hand was held by a grasp of iron: I was hurried along by a stride I could hardly follow; and to look at Mr Rochester's face was to feel that not a second of delay would be tolerated for any purpose. I wonder what other bridegroom ever looked as he did – so bent up to a purpose, so grimly resolute: or who, under such steadfast brows ever revealed such flaming and flashing eyes.

I know not whether the day was fair or foul; in descending the drive, I gazed neither on sky nor earth: my heart was with my eyes; and both seemed migrated into Mr Rochester's frame. I wanted to see the invisible thing on which, as we went along, he appeared to fasten a glance fierce and fell. I wanted to feel the thoughts whose force he seemed breasting and resisting.

At the churchyard wicket he stopped: he discovered I was quite out of breath. 'Am I cruel in my love?' he said. 'Delay an instant: lean on me, Jane.'

And now I can recall the picture of the gray old house of God rising calm before me, of a rook wheeling round the steeple, of a ruddy morning sky beyond. I remember something, too, of the green grave-mounds; and I have not forgotten, either, two figures of strangers straying among the low hillocks and reading the mementoes graven on the few mossy headstones. I noticed them, because, as they saw us, they passed round to the back of the church; and I doubted not they were going to enter by the side-aisle door and witness the ceremony. By Mr Rochester they were not observed; he was earnestly looking at my face, from which the blood had, I dare say, momentarily fled: for I felt my forehead dewy, and my cheeks and lips cold. When I rallied, which I soon did, he walked gently with me up the path to the porch.

We entered the quiet and humble temple; the priest waited in his white surplice at the lowly altar, the clerk beside him. All was still: two shadows only moved in a remote corner. My conjecture had been correct: the strangers had slipped in before us, and they now stood by the vault of the Rochesters, their backs towards us, viewing through the rails the old-time stained marble tomb, where a kneeling angel guarded the remains of Damer de Rochester, slain at Marston Moor, in the time of the civil wars, and of Elizabeth, his wife.

Our place was taken at the communion rails. Hearing a cautious step behind me, I glanced over my shoulder: one of the strangers – a gentleman, evidently – was advancing up the chapel. The service began. The explanation of the intent of matrimony was gone through; and then the clergyman came a step farther forward, and, bending slightly towards Mr Rochester, went on:

'I require and charge you both (as ye will answer at the dreadful Day of Judgement when the secrets of all hearts shall be disclosed), that if either of you know any impediment why ye may not lawfully be joined together in matrimony, ye do now confess it; for be ye well assured that so many as are coupled together otherwise than God's Word doth allow, are not joined together by God, neither is their matrimony lawful.'

He paused, as the custom is. When is the pause after that sentence ever broken by reply? Not perhaps, once in a hundred years. And the clergyman, who had not lifted his eyes from his book, and had held his breath but for a moment, was proceeding: his hand was already stretched towards Mr Rochester, as his lips

unclosed to ask, 'Wilt thou have this woman for thy wedded wife?' – when a distinct and near voice said –

'The marriage cannot go on: I declare the existence of an impediment.'

The clergyman looked up at the speaker and stood mute; the clerk did the same; Mr Rochester moved slightly, as if an earthquake had rolled under his feet: taking a firmer footing, and not turning his head or eyes, he said, 'Proceed.'

Profound silence fell when he uttered that word, with deep but low intonation. Presently Mr Wood said –

'I cannot proceed without some investigation into what has been asserted, and evidence of its truth or falsehood.'

'The ceremony is quite broken off,' subjoined the voice behind us. 'I am in a condition to prove my allegation: an insuperable impediment to this marriage exists.'

Mr Rochester heard, but heeded not: he stood stubborn and rigid, making no movement but to possess himself of my hand. What a hot and strong grasp he had! and how like quarried marble was his pale, firm, massive front at this moment! How his eyes shone, still watchful, and yet wild beneath!

Mr Wood seemed at a loss. 'What is the nature of the impediment?' he asked. 'Perhaps it may be got over – explained away?'

'Hardly,' was the answer. 'I have called it insuperable, and I speak advisedly.'

The speaker came forward and leaned on the rails. He continued, uttering each word distinctly, calmly, steadily, but not loudly –

'It simply consists in the existence of a previous marriage. Mr Rochester has a wife now living.'

My nerves vibrated to those low-spoken words as they had never vibrated to thunder – my blood felt their subtle violence as it had never felt frost or fire; but I was collected, and in no danger of swooning. I looked at Mr Rochester; I made him look at me. His whole face was colourless rock; his eye was both spark and flint. He disavowed nothing: he seemed as if he would defy all things. Without speaking, without smiling, without seeming to recognize in me a human being, he only twined my waist with his arm and riveted me to his side.

'Who are you?' he asked of the intruder.

'My name is Briggs, a solicitor of — Street, London.'

'And you would thrust on me a wife?'

'I would remind you of your lady's existence, sir, which the law recognizes, if you do not.'

'Favour me with an account of her – with her name, her parentage, her place of abode.'

'Certainly.' Mr Briggs calmly took a paper from his pocket, and read out in a sort of official, nasal voice:

'"I affirm and can prove that on the 20th October, A.D. — (a date of fifteen years back), Edward Fairfax Rochester, of Thornfield Hall, in the county of —, and of Ferndean Manor, in —shire, England, was married to my sister, Bertha Antoinetta Mason, daughter of Jonas Mason, merchant, and of Antoinetta Mason, his wife, a Creole, at — Church, Spanish Town, Jamaica. The record of the marriage will be found in the register of that church – a copy of it is now in my possession. Signed, Richard Mason."'

'That – if a genuine document – may prove I have been married, but it does not prove that the woman mentioned therein as my wife is still living.'

# Jane Eyre

'She was living three months ago,' returned the lawyer.

'How do you know?'

'I have a witness to the fact, whose testimony even you, sir, will scarcely controvert.'

'Produce him – or go to hell.'

'I will produce him first – he is on the spot. Mr Mason, have the goodness to step forward.'

Mr Rochester, on hearing the name, set his teeth; he experienced, too, a sort of strong convulsive quiver; near to him as I was, I felt the spasmodic movement of fury or despair run through his frame. The second stranger, who had hitherto lingered in the background, now drew near; a pale face looked over the solicitor's shoulder – yes, it was Mason himself. Mr Rochester turned and glared at him. His eye, as I have often said, was a black eye: it had now a tawny, nay, a bloody light in its gloom; and his face flushed – olive cheeks and hueless forehead received a glow as from spreading ascending heart-fire: and he stirred, lifted his strong arm – he could have struck Mason, dashed him on the church floor, shocked by ruthless blow the breath from his body – but Mason shrank away, and cried faintly, 'Good God?' Contempt fell cool on Mr Rochester – his passion died as if a blight had shrivelled it up: he only asked, 'What have *you* to say?'

An inaudible reply escaped Mason's white lips.

'The devil is in it if you cannot answer distinctly. I again demand what have *you* to say?'

'Sir – sir,' interrupted the clergyman, 'do not forget you are in a sacred place.' Then addressing Mason, he inquired gently. 'Are you aware, sir, whether or not this gentleman's wife is still living?'

'Courage,' urged the lawyer; 'speak out.'

'She is now at Thornfield Hall,' said Mason, in more articulate tones: 'I saw her there last April. I am her brother.'

'At Thornfield Hall!' ejaculated the clergyman. 'Impossible! I am an old resident in this neighbourhood, sir, and I never heard of a Mrs Rochester at Thornfield Hall.'

I saw a grim smile contort Mr Rochester's lips, and he muttered –

'No, by God! I took care that none should hear of it – or of her under that name.' He mused – for ten minutes he held counsel with himself: he formed his resolve and announced it.

'Enough! all shall bolt out at once, like the bullet from the barrel. Wood, close your book, and take off your surplice; John Green (to the clerk), leave the church: there will be no wedding today.' The man obeyed.

Mr Rochester continued, hardily and recklessly, 'Bigamy is an ugly word! – I meant, however, to be a bigamist; but fate has out-manoeuvred me, or Providence has checked me – perhaps the last. I am little better than a devil at this moment; and, as my pastor there would tell me, deserve no doubt the sternest judgements of God, even to the quenchless fire and deathless worm. Gentlemen, my plan is broken up! – what this lawyer and his client say is true: I have been married, and the woman to whom I was married lives! You say you have never heard of a Mrs Rochester at the house up yonder, Wood; but I daresay you have many a time inclined your ear to gossip about the mysterious lunatic kept there under watch and ward. Some have whispered to you that she is my bastard half-sister: some, my cast-off mistress. I now inform you that she is my wife, whom

# Jane Eyre

I married fifteen years ago – Bertha Mason by name; sister of this resolute personage, who is now, with his quivering limbs and white cheeks, showing you what a stout heart men may bear. Cheer up, Dick – never fear me! – I'd almost as soon strike a woman as you. Bertha Mason is mad; and she came of a mad family; idiots and maniacs through three generations! Her mother, the Creole, was both a madwoman and a drunkard! – as I found out after I had wed the daughter: for they were silent on family secrets before. Bertha, like a dutiful child, copied her parent in both points. I had a charming partner – pure, wise, modest: you can fancy I was a happy man. I went through rich scenes! Oh! my experience has been heavenly, if you only knew it! But I owe you no further explanation. Briggs, Wood, Mason, I invite you all to come up to the house and visit Mrs Poole's patient, and *my wife*! You shall see what sort of a being I was cheated into espousing, and judge whether or not I had a right to break the compact, and seek sympathy with something at least human. This girl,' he continued, looking at me, 'knew no more than you, Wood, of the disgusting secret: she thought all was fair and legal, and never dreamt she was going to be entrapped into a feigned union with a defrauded wretch, already bound to a bad, mad, and embruted partner! Come all of you – follow!'

Still holding me fast, he left the church: the three gentlemen came after. At the front door of the hall we found the carriage.

'Take it back to the coach-house, John,' said Mr Rochester coolly; 'it will not be wanted today.'

At our entrance Mrs Fairfax, Adèle, Sophie, Leah, advanced to meet and greet us.

'To the right about – every soul!' cried the master; 'away with your congratulations! Who wants them? Not I! – they are fifteen years too late!'

He passed on and ascended the stairs, still holding my hand, and still beckoning the gentlemen to follow him, which they did. We mounted the first staircase, passed up the gallery, proceeded to the third story: the low, black door, opened by Mr Rochester's master-key, admitted us to the tapestried room, with its great bed and its pictorial cabinet.

'You know this place, Mason,' said our guide; 'she bit and stabbed you here.'

He lifted the hangings from the wall, uncovering the second door: this, too, he opened. In a room without a window, there burnt a fire, guarded by a high and strong fender, and a lamp suspended from the ceiling by a chain. Grace Poole bent over the fire, apparently cooking something in a saucepan. In the deep shade, at the farther end of the room, a figure ran backwards and forwards. What it was, whether beast or human being, one could not, at first sight tell: it grovelled, seemingly, on all fours; it snatched and growled like some strange wild animal: but it was covered with clothing, and a quantity of dark, grizzled hair, wild as a mane, hid its head and face.

'Good-morrow, Mrs Poole!' said Mr Rochester. 'How are you? and how is your charge today?'

'We're tolerable, sir, I thank you,' replied Grace, lifting the boiling mess carefully on to the hob: 'rather snappish, but not 'rageous.'

A fierce cry seemed to give the lie to her favourable report: the clothed hyena rose up, and stood tall on its hind-feet.

'Ah! sir, she sees you!' exclaimed Grace: 'you'd better not stay.'

'Only a few moments, Grace: you must allow me a few moments.'

# Jane Eyre

'Take care, then, sir! – for God's sake, take care!'

The maniac bellowed: she parted her shaggy locks from her visage, and gazed wildly at her visitors. I recognized well that purple face – those bloated features. Mrs Poole advanced.

'Keep out of the way,' said Mr Rochester, thrusting her aside: 'she has no knife now, I suppose? and I'm on my guard.'

'One never knows what she has, sir: she is so cunning: it is not in mortal discretion to fathom her craft.'

'We had better leave her,' whispered Mason.

'Go to the devil!' was his brother-in-law's recommendation.

''Ware!' cried Grace. The three gentlemen retreated simultaneously. Mr Rochester flung me behind him: the lunatic sprang and grappled his throat viciously, and laid her teeth to his cheek: they struggled. She was a big woman, in stature almost equalling her husband, and corpulent besides: she showed virile force in the contest – more than once she almost throttled him, athletic as he was. He could have settled her with a well-planted blow; but he would not strike: he would only wrestle. At last he mastered her arms; Grace Poole gave him a cord, and he pinioned them behind her: with more rope, which was at hand, he bound her to a chair. The operation was performed amidst the fiercest yells and the most convulsive plunges. Mr Rochester then turned to the spectators: he looked at them with a smile both acrid and desolate.

'That is *my wife*,' said he. 'Such is the sole conjugal embrace I am ever to know – such are the endearments which are to solace my leisure hours! And *this* is what I wished to have' (laying his hand on my shoulder) 'this young girl, who stands so grave and quiet at the mouth of hell, looking collectedly at the gambols of a demon. I wanted her just as a change after that fierce ragout. Wood and Briggs, look at the difference! Compare these clear eyes with the red balls yonder – this face with that mask – this form with that bulk; then judge me, priest of the gospel and man of the law, and remember with what judgement ye judge ye shall be judged! Off with you now. I must shut up my prize.'

We all withdrew. Mr Rochester stayed a moment behind us, to give some further order to Grace Poole. The solicitor addressed me as he descended the stair.

'You, madam,' said he, 'are cleared from all blame: your uncle will be glad to hear it – if, indeed, he should be still living – when Mr Mason returns to Madeira.'

'My uncle! What of him? Do you know him?'

'Mr Mason does. Mr Eyre has been the Funchal correspondent of his house for some years. When your uncle received your letter intimating the contemplated union between yourself and Mr Rochester, Mr Mason, who was staying at Madeira to recruit his health, on his way back to Jamaica, happened to be with him. Mr Eyre mentioned the intelligence; for he knew that my client here was acquainted with a gentleman of the name of Rochester. Mr Mason, astonished and distressed as you may suppose, revealed the real state of matters. Your uncle, I am sorry to say, is now on a sick-bed; from which, considering the nature of his disease – decline – and the stage it has reached, it is unlikely he will ever rise. He could not then hasten to England himself, to extricate you from the snare into which you had fallen, but he implored Mr Mason to lose no time in taking steps to prevent the false marriage. He referred him to me for

assistance. I used all despatch, and am thankful I was not too late: as you, doubtless, must be also. Were I not morally certain that your uncle will be dead ere you reach Madeira, I would advise you to accompany Mr Mason back; but as it is, I think you had better remain in England, till you can hear further, either from or of Mr Eyre. Have we anything else to stay for?' he inquired of Mr Mason.

'No, no – let us begone,' was the anxious reply; and without waiting to take leave of Mr Rochester, they made their exit at the hall door. The clergyman stayed to exchange a few sentences, either of admonition or reproof, with his haughty parishioner; this duty done, he too departed.

I heard him go as I stood at the half-open door of my own room, to which I had now withdrawn. The house cleared, I shut myself in, fastened the bolt that none might intrude, and proceeded – not to weep, not to mourn, I was yet too calm for that, but – mechanically to take off the wedding-dress, and replace it by the stuff gown I had worn yesterday, as I thought, for the last time. I then sat down: I felt weak and tired. I leaned my arms on a table, and my head dropped on them. And now I thought: till now I had only heard, seen, moved – followed up and down where I was led or dragged – watched event rushed on event, disclosure open beyond disclosure: but *now, I thought.*

The morning had been a quiet morning enough – all except the brief scene with the lunatic: the transaction in the church had not been noisy; there was no explosion of passion, no loud altercation, no dispute, no defiance or challenge, no tears, no sobs: a few words had been spoken, a calmly pronounced objection to the marriage made; some stern, short questions put by Mr Rochester; answers, explanations given, evidence adduced; an open admission of the truth had been uttered by my master; then the living proof had been seen; the intruders were gone, and all was over.

I was in my own room as usual – just myself, without obvious change: nothing had smitten me, or scathed me, or maimed me. And yet where was the Jane Eyre of yesterday? – where was her life? – where were her prospects?

Jane Eyre, who had been an ardent expectant woman – almost a bride – was a cold, solitary girl again: her life was pale; her prospects were desolate. A Christmas frost had come at midsummer; a white December storm had whirled over June; ice glazed the ripe apples, drifts crushed the blowing roses; on hayfield and cornfield lay a frozen shroud: lanes which last night blushed full of flowers, to-day were pathless with untrodden snow; and the woods, which twelve hours since waved leafy and fragrant as groves between the tropics, now spread, waste, wild, and white as pine-forests in wintry Norway. My hopes were all dead – struck with a subtle doom, such as, in one night, fell on all the first born in the land of Egypt. I looked on my cherished wishes, yesterday so blooming and glowing; they lay stark, chill, livid corpses that could never revive. I looked at my love: that feeling which was my master's – which he had created; it shivered in my heart, like a suffering child in a cold cradle: sickness and anguish had seized it; it could not seek Mr Rochester's arms – it could not derive warmth from his breast. Oh, never more could it turn to him; for faith was blighted – confidence destroyed! Mr Rochester was not to me what he had been; for he was not what I had thought him. I would not ascribe vice to him; I would not say he had betrayed me; but the attribute of stainless truth was gone from his idea, and from his presence I must go: *that* I perceived well. When – how – whither,

I could not yet discern; but he himself, I doubted not, would hurry me from Thornfield. Real affection, it seemed, he could not have for me; it had only been fitful passion: that was balked; he would want me no more. I should fear even to cross his path now: my view must be hateful to him. Oh, how blind had been my eyes! How weak my conduct!

My eyes were covered and closed: eddying darkness seemed to swim round me, and reflection came in as black and confused a flow. Self-abandoned, relaxed, and effortless, I seemed to have laid me down in the dried-up bed of a great river; I heard a flood loosened in remote mountains, and I felt the torrent come: to rise I had no will, to flee I had no strength. I lay faint, longing to be dead. One idea only still throbbed lifelike within me – a remembrance of God: it begot an unuttered prayer: these words went wandering up and down in my rayless mind, as something that should be whispered, but no energy was found to express them.

'Be not far from me, for trouble is near: there is none to help.'

It was near; and as I had lifted no petition to Heaven to avert it – as I had neither joined my hands, nor bent my knees, nor moved my lips – it came: in full heavy swing the torrent poured over me. The whole consciousness of my life lorn, my love lost, my hope quenched, my faith death-struck, swayed full and mighty above me in one sullen mass. That bitter hour cannot be described: in truth, 'the waters came into my soul; I sank in deep mire: I felt no standing; I came into deep waters; the floods overflowed me.'

# Chapter 27

Some time in the afternoon I raised my head, and looking round and seeing the western sun gilding the sign of its decline on the wall, I asked, 'What am I to do?'

But the answer my mind gave – 'Leave Thornfield at once' – was so prompt, so dread, that I stopped my ears. I said I could not bear such words now. 'That I am not Edward Rochester's wife is the least part of my woe,' I alleged: 'that I have awakened out of most glorious dreams, and found them all void and vain, is a horror I could bear and master; but that I must leave him decidedly, instantly, entirely, is intolerable. I cannot do it.'

But, then a voice within me averred that I could do it, and foretold that I should do it. I wrestled with my own resolution: I wanted to be weak that I might avoid the awful passage of further suffering I saw laid out for me; and Conscience, turned tyrant, held Passion by the throat, told her tauntingly, she had yet but dipped her dainty feet in the slough, and swore that with that arm of iron he would thrust her down to unsounded depths of agony.

'Let me be torn away, then!' I cried. 'Let another help me!'

# Jane Eyre

'No; you shall tear yourself away, none shall help you: you shall yourself pluck out your right eye; yourself cut off your right hand: your heart shall be the victim, and you the priest to transfix it.'

I rose up suddenly, terror-struck at the solitude which so ruthless a judge haunted – at the silence which so awful a voice filled. My head swam as I stood erect. I perceived that I was sickening from excitement and inanition; neither meat nor drink had passed my lips that day, for I had taken no breakfast. And, with a strange pang, I now reflected that, long as I had been shut up here, no message had been sent to ask how I was, or to invite me to come down: not even little Adèle had tapped at the door; not even Mrs Fairfax had sought me. 'Friends always forget those whom fortune forsakes,' I murmured, as I undrew the bolt and passed out. I stumbled over an obstacle: my head was still dizzy, my sight was dim, and my limbs were feeble. I could not soon recover myself. I fell, but not on the ground: an outstretched arm caught me, I looked up – I was supported by Mr Rochester, who sat in a chair across my chamber threshold.

'You come out at last,' he said. 'Well, I have been waiting for you long, and listening: yet not one movement have I heard, nor one sob: five minutes more of that deathlike hush, and I should have forced the lock like a burglar. So you shun me? – you shut yourself up and grieve alone! I would rather you had come and upbraided me with vehemence. You are passionate: I expected a scene of some kind. I was prepared for the hot rain of tears; only I wanted them to be shed on my breast: now a senseless floor has received them, or your drenched handkerchief. But I err: you have not wept at all! I see a white cheek and a faded eye, but no trace of tears. I suppose, then, your heart has been weeping blood?

'Well, Jane! not a word of reproach? Nothing bitter – nothing poignant? Nothing to cut a feeling or sting a passion? You sit quietly where I have placed you, and regard me with a weary, passive look.

'Jane, I never meant to wound you thus. If the man who had but one little ewe lamb that was dear to him as a daughter, that ate of his bread and drank of his cup, and lay in his bosom, had by some mistake slaughtered it at the shambles, he would not have rued his bloody blunder more than I now rue mine. Will you ever forgive me?'

Reader, I forgave him at the moment and on the spot. There was such deep remorse in his eye, such true pity in his tone, such manly energy in his manner: and besides, there was such unchanged love in his whole look and mien – I forgave him all: yet not in words, not outwardly; only at my heart's core.

'You know I am a scoundrel, Jane?' ere long he inquired wistfully – wondering, I suppose, at my continued silence and tameness, the result rather of weakness than of will.

'Yes, sir.'

'Then tell me so roundly and sharply – don't spare me.'

'I cannot: I am tired and sick. I want some water.'

He heaved a sort of shuddering sigh, and taking me in his arms, carried me downstairs. At first I did not know to what room he had borne me: all was cloudy to my glazed sight: presently I felt the reviving warmth of a fire; for summer as it was, I had become icy cold in my chamber. He put wine to my lips; I tasted it and revived; then I ate something he offered me, and was soon myself. I was in the library – sitting in his chair – he was quite near. 'If I could

go out of life now, without too sharp a pang, it would be well for me,' I thought: 'then I should not have to make the effort of cracking my heart-strings in rending them from among Mr Rochester's. I must leave him, it appears. I do not want to leave him – I cannot leave him.'

'How are you now, Jane?'

'Much better, sir; I shall be well soon.'

'Taste the wine again, Jane.'

I obeyed him; then he put the glass on the table, stood before me, and looked at me attentively. Suddenly he turned away, with an inarticulate exclamation, full of passionate emotion of some kind; he walked fast through the room and came back: he stooped towards me as if to kiss me; but I remembered caresses were now forbidden. I turned my face away, and put his aside.

'What! – How is this?' he exclaimed hastily. 'Oh, I know! you won't kiss the husband of Bertha Mason? You consider my arms filled and my embraces appropriated?'

'At any rate there is neither room nor claim for me, sir.'

'Why, Jane? I will spare you the trouble of much talking; I will answer for you – because I have a wife already, you would reply – I guess rightly?'

'Yes.'

'If you think so, you must have a strange opinion of me; you must regard me as a plotting profligate – a base and low rake who has been simulating disinterested love in order to draw you into a snare deliberately laid, and strip you of honour and rob you of self-respect. What do you say to that? I see you can say nothing: in the first place, you are faint still, and have enough to do to draw your breath; in the second place, you cannot yet accustom yourself to accuse and revile me, and besides, the floodgates of tears are opened, and they would rush out if you spoke much; and you have no desire to expostulate, to upbraid, to make a scene: you are thinking how *to act* – *talking* you consider is of no use. I know you – I am on my guard.'

'Sir, I do not wish to act against you,' I said; and my unsteady voice warned me to curtail my sentence.

'Not in *your* sense of the word, but in *mine* you are scheming to destroy me. You have as good as said that I am a married man – as a married man you will shun me, keep out of my way: just now you have refused to kiss me. You intend to make yourself a complete stranger to me: to live under this roof only as Adèle's governess; if ever I say a friendly word to you, if ever a friendly feeling inclines you again to me, you will say, "That man had nearly made me his mistress: I must be ice and rock to him"; and ice and rock you will accordingly become.'

I cleared and steadied my voice to reply: 'All is changed about me, sir; I must change, too – there is no doubt of that; and to avoid fluctuations of feeling, and continual combats with recollections and associations, there is only one way – Adèle must have a new governess, sir.'

'Oh, Adèle will go to school – I have settled that already; nor do I mean to torment you with the hideous associations and recollections of Thornfield Hall – this accursed place – this tent of Achan – this insolent vault, offering the ghastliness of living death to the light of the open sky – this narrow stone hell, with its one real fiend, worse than a legion of such as we imagine. Jane, you shall not stay here, nor will I. I was wrong ever to bring you to Thornfield Hall, knowing as I did how it was haunted. I charged them to conceal from you,

# Jane Eyre

before I ever saw you, all knowledge of the curse of the place; merely because I feared Adèle never would have a governess to stay if she knew with what inmate she was housed, and my plans would not permit me to remove the maniac elsewhere – though I possess an old house, Ferndean Manor, even more retired and hidden than this, where I could have lodged her safely enough, had not a scruple about the unhealthiness of the situation, in the heart of a wood, made my conscience recoil from the arrangement. Probably those damp walls would soon have eased me of her charge; but to each villain his own vice; and mine is not a tendency to indirect assassination, even of what I most hate.

'Concealing the madwoman's neighbourhood from you, however, was something like covering a child with a cloak, and laying it down near a upas-tree: that demon's vicinage is poisoned, and always was. But I'll shut up Thornfield Hall: I'll nail up the front door, and board the lower windows: I'll give Mrs Poole two hundred a year to live here with *my wife*, as you term that fearful hag: Grace will do much for money, and she shall have her son, the keeper at Grimsby Retreat, to bear her company and be at hand to give her aid in the paroxysms, when *my wife* is prompted by her familiar to burn people in their beds at night, to stab them, to bite their flesh from their bones, and so on—'

'Sir,' I interrupted him, 'you are inexorable for that unfortunate lady: you speak of her with hate – with vindictive antipathy. It is cruel – she cannot help being mad.'

'Jane, my little darling (so I will call you, for so you are), you don't know what you are talking about; you misjudge me again: it is not because she is mad I hate her. If you were mad, do you think I should hate you?'

'I do indeed, sir.'

'Then you are mistaken, and you know nothing about me, and nothing about the sort of love of which I am capable. Every atom of your flesh is as dear to me as my own: in pain and sickness it would still be dear. Your mind is my treasure, and if it were broken, it would be my treasure still: if you raved, my arms should confine you, and not a strait waistcoat – your grasp, even in fury, would have a charm for me: if you flew at me as wildly as that woman did this morning, I should receive you in an embrace, at least as fond as it would be restrictive. I should not shrink from you with disgust as I did from her: in your quiet moments you should have no watcher and no nurse but me; and I could hang over you with untiring tenderness, though you gave me no smile in return; and never weary of gazing into your eyes, though they had no longer a ray of recognition for me. – But why do I follow that train of ideas? I was talking of removing you from Thornfield. All, you know, is prepared for prompt departure: to-morrow you shall go. I only ask you to endure one more night under this roof, Jane; and then, farewell to its miseries and terrors for ever! I have a place to repair to, which will be a secure sanctuary from hateful reminiscences, from unwelcome intrusion – even from falsehood and slander.'

'And take Adèle with you, sir,' I interrupted; 'she will be a companion for you.'

'What do you mean, Jane? I told you I would send Adèle to school; and what do I want with a child for a companion, and not my own child – a French dancer's bastard? Why do you importune me about her! I say, why do you assign Adèle to me for a companion?'

# Jane Eyre

'You spoke of a retirement, sir; and retirement and solitude are dull: too dull for you.'

'Solitude! solitude! he reiterated with irritation. 'I see I must come to an explanation. I don't know what sphinx-like expression is forming in your countenance. *You* are to share my solitude. Do you understand?'

I shook my head: it required a degree of courage, excited as he was becoming, even to risk that mute sign of dissent. He had been walking fast about the room, and he stopped, as if suddenly rooted to one spot. He looked at me long and hard: I turned my eyes from him, fixed them on the fire, and tried to assume and maintain a quiet, collected aspect.

'Now for the hitch in Jane's character,' he said at last, speaking more calmly than from his look I had expected him to speak. 'The reel of silk has run smoothly enough so far; but I always knew there would come a knot and a puzzle: here it is. Now for vexation, and exasperation, and endless trouble! By God! I long to exert a fraction of Samson's strength, and break the entanglement like tow!'

He recommenced his walk, but soon again stopped and this time just before me.

'Jane! will you hear reason?' (he stooped and approached his lips to my ear); 'because, if you won't, I'll try violence.' His voice was hoarse; his look that of a man who is just about to burst an insufferable bond and plunge headlong into wild licence. I saw that in another moment, and with one impetus of frenzy more, I should be able to do nothing with him. The present – the passing second of time – was all I had in which to control and restrain him: a movement of repulsion, flight, fear would have sealed my doom – and his. But I was not afraid: not in the least. I felt an inward power; a sense of influence, which supported me. The crisis was perilous; but not without its charm: such as the Indian, perhaps, feels when he slips over the rapid in his canoe. I took hold of his clenched hand, loosened the contorted fingers, and said to him, soothingly –

'Sit down; I'll talk to you as long as you like, and hear all you have to say, whether reasonable or unreasonable.'

He sat down: but he did not get leave to speak directly. I had been struggling with tears for some time: I had taken great pains to repress them, because I knew he would not like to see me weep. Now, however, I considered it well to let them flow as freely and as long as they liked. If the flood annoyed him, so much the better. So I gave way and cried heartily.

Soon I heard him earnestly entreating me to be composed. I said I could not while he was in such a passion.

'But I am not angry, Jane: I only love you too well; and you had steeled you little pale face with such a resolute, frozen look, I could not endure it. Hush, now, and wipe your eyes.'

His softened voice announced that he was subdued; so I, in my turn, became calm. Now he made an effort to rest his head on my shoulder, but I would not permit it. Then he would draw me to him: no.

'Jane! Jane!' he said, in such an accent of bitter sadness, it thrilled along every nerve I had; 'you don't love me, then? It was only my station, and the rank of my wife, that you valued? Now that you think me disqualified to become your husband, you recoil from my touch as if I were some toad or ape.'

These words cut me: yet what could I do or say? I ought probably to have

# Jane Eyre

done or said nothing; but I was so tortured by a sense of remorse at thus hurting his feelings, I could not control the wish to drop balm where I had wounded.

'I *do* love you,' I said, 'more than ever: but I must not show or indulge the feeling: and this is the last time I must express it.'

'The last time, Jane! What! do you think you can live with me, and see me daily, and yet, if you still love me, be always cold and distant?'

'No, sir; that I am certain I could not; and therefore I see there is but one way: but you will be furious if I mention it.'

'Oh, mention it! If I storm, you have the art of weeping.'

'Mr Rochester, I must leave you.'

'For how long, Jane? For a few minutes, while you smooth your hair – which is somewhat dishevelled; and bathe your face – which looks feverish?'

'I must leave Adèle and Thornfield. I must part with you for my whole life: I must begin a new existence among strange faces and strange scenes.'

'Of course: I told you you should. I pass over the madness about parting from me. You mean you must become a part of me. As to the new existence, it is all right: you shall yet be my wife: I am not married. You shall be Mrs Rochester – both virtually and nominally I shall keep only to you so long as you and I live. You shall go to a place I have in the south of France: a whitewashed villa on the shores of the Mediterranean. There you shall live a happy, and guarded, and most innocent life. Never fear that I wish to lure you into error – to make you my mistress. Why did you shake your head? Jane, you must be reasonable, or in truth I shall again become frantic.'

His voice and hand quivered: his large nostrils dilated: his eye blazed: still I dared to speak.

'Sir, your wife is living: that is a fact acknowledged this morning by yourself. If I lived with you as you desire – I should then be your mistress: to say otherwise is sophistical – is false.'

'Jane, I am not a gentle-tempered man – you forget that: I am not long-enduring; I am not cool and dispassionate. Out of pity to me and yourself, put your finger on my pulse, feel how it throbs, and – beware!'

He bared his wrist, and offered it to me: the blood was forsaking his cheek and lips, they were growing livid; I was distressed on all hands. To agitate him thus deeply, by a resistance he so abhorred, was cruel: to yield was out of the question. I did what human beings do instinctively when they are driven to utter extremity – looked for aid to one higher than man: the words 'God help me!' burst involuntarily from my lips.

'I am a fool!' cried Mr Rochester suddenly. 'I keep telling her I am not married, and do not explain to her why. I forget she knows nothing of the character of that woman, or of the circumstances attending my infernal union with her. Oh, I am certain Jane will agree with me in opinion, when she knows all that I know! Just put your hand in mine, Janet – that I may have the evidence of touch as well as sight, to prove you are near me – and I will in a few words show you the real state of the case. Can you listen to me?'

'Yes, sir; for hours, if you will.'

'I only ask minutes. Jane, did you ever hear or know that I was not the eldest son of my house; that I had once a brother older than I?'

'I remember Mrs Fairfax told me so once.'

'And did you ever hear that my father was an avaricious, grasping man?'

# Jane Eyre

'I have understood something to that effect.'

'Well, Jane, being so, it was his resolution to keep the property together; he could not bear the idea of dividing his estate and leaving me a fair portion: all, he resolved, should go to my brother, Rowland. Yet as little could he endure that a son of his should be a poor man. I must be provided for by a wealthy marriage. He sought me a partner betimes. Mr Mason, a West India planter and merchant, was his old acquaintance. He was certain his possessions were real and vast: he made inquiries. Mr Mason, he found, had a son and daughter; and he learned from him that he could and would give the latter a fortune of thirty thousand pounds: that sufficed. When I left college, I was sent out to Jamaica, to espouse a bride already courted for me. My father said nothing about her money; but he told me Miss Mason was the boast of Spanish Town for her beauty: and this was no lie. I found her a fine woman, in the style of Blanche Ingram: tall, dark, and majestic. Her family wished to secure me, because I was of a good race; and so did she. They showed her to me in parties splendidly dressed. I seldom saw her alone, and had very little private conversation with her. She flattered me, and lavishly displayed for my pleasure her charms and accomplishments. All the men in her circle seemed to admire her and envy me. I was dazzled, stimulated: my senses were excited; and being ignorant, raw, and inexperienced, I thought I loved her. There is no folly so besotted that the idiotic rivalries of society, the prurience, the rashness, the blindness of youth, will not hurry a man to its commission. Her relatives encouraged me: competitors piqued me: she allured me: a marriage was achieved almost before I knew where I was. Oh, I have no respect for myself when I think of that act! – an agony of inward contempt masters me. I never loved, I never esteemed, I did not even know her. I was not sure of the existence of one virtue in her nature: I have marked neither modesty nor benevolence, nor candour, nor refinement in her mind or manners – and, I married her: gross, grovelling, mole-eyed blockhead that I was! With less sin I might have – but let me remember to whom I am speaking.

'My bride's mother I had never seen: I understood she was dead. The honeymoon over, I learned my mistake; she was only mad, and shut up in a lunatic asylum. There was a younger brother, too – a complete dumb idiot. The elder one, whom you have seen (and whom I cannot hate, whilst I abhor all his kindred, because he has some gains of affection in his feeble mind, shown in the continued interest he takes in his wretched sister, and also in a dog-like attachment he once bore me), will probably be in the same state one day. My father and my brother Rowland knew all this; but they thought only of the thirty thousand pounds, and joined in the plot against me.

'These were vile discoveries; but except for the treachery of concealment, I should have made them no subject of reproach to my wife, even when I found her nature wholly alien to mine, her tastes obnoxious to me, her cast of mind common, low, narrow, and singularly incapable of being led to anything higher, expanded to anything larger – when I found that I could not pass a single evening, nor even a single hour of the day with her in comfort; that kindly conversation could not be sustained between us, because whatever topic I started, immediately received from her a turn at once coarse and trite, perverse and imbecile – when I perceived that I should never have a quiet or settled household, because no servant would bear the continued outbreaks of her violent and

# Jane Eyre

unreasonable temper, or the vexations of her absurd, contradictory, exacting orders – even when I restrained myself: I eschewed upbraiding, I curtailed remonstrance; I tried to devour my repentance and disgust in secret; I repressed the deep antipathy I felt.

'Jane, I will not trouble you with abominable details; some strong words shall express what I have to say. I lived with that woman upstairs four years, and before that time she had tried me indeed: her character ripened and developed with frightful rapidity; her vices sprang up fast and rank: they were so strong, only cruelty could check them, and I would not use cruelty. What a pigmy intellect she had, and what giant propensities! How fearful were the curses those propensities entailed on me! Bertha Mason, the true daughter of an infamous mother, dragged me through all the hideous and degrading agonies which must attend a man bound to a wife at once intemperate and unchaste.

'My brother in the interval was dead, and at the end of the four years my father died, too. I was rich enough now – yet poor to hideous indigence: a nature the most gross, impure, depraved I ever saw, was associated with mine, and called by the law and by society a part of me. And I could not rid myself of it by any legal proceedings: for the doctors now discovered that *my wife* was mad – her excesses had prematurely developed the germs of insanity. Jane, you don't like my narrative; you look almost sick – shall I defer the rest to another day?'

'No, sir, finish it now; I pity you – I do pity you.'

'Pity, Jane, from some people is a noxious and insulting sort of tribute, which one is justified in hurling back in the teeth of those who offer it; but that is a sort of pity native to callous, selfish hearts; it is a hybrid, egotistical pain at hearing of woes, crossed with ignorant contempt for those who have endured them. But that is not your pity, Jane; it is not the feeling of which your whole face is full at this moment – with which your eyes are now almost overflowing – with which your heart is heaving – with which your hand is trembling in mine. Your pity, my darling, is the suffering mother of love: its anguish is the very natal pang of the divine passion. I accept it, Jane; let the daughter have free advent – my arms wait to receive her.'

'Now, sir, proceed; what did you do when you found she was mad?'

'Jane, I approached the verge of despair; a remnant of self-respect was all that intervened between me and the gulf. In the eyes of the world, I was doubtless covered with grimy dishonour; but I resolved to be clean in my own sight – and to the last I repudiated the contamination of her crimes, and wrenched myself from connexion with her mental defects. Still, society associated my name and person with hers; I yet saw her and heard her daily: something of her breath (faugh!) mixed with the air I breathed; and besides, I remembered I had once been her husband – that recollection was then, and is now, inexpressibly odious to me; moreover, I knew that while she lived I could never be the husband of another and better wife; and, though five years my senior (her family and her father had lied to me even in the particular of her age), she was likely to live as long as I, being as robust in frame as she was infirm in mind. Thus, at the age of twenty-six, I was hopeless.

'One night I had been awakened by her yells – (since the medical men had pronounced her mad, she had, of course, been shut up) – it was a fiery West Indian night; one of the description that frequently precede the hurricanes of those climates. Being unable to sleep in bed, I got up and opened the window.

# Jane Eyre

The air was like sulphur-streams – I could find no refreshment anywhere. Mosquitoes came buzzing in and hummed sullenly round the room; the sea, which I could hear from thence, rumbled dull like an earthquake – black clouds were casting up over it; the moon was setting in the waves, broad and red, like a hot cannon-ball – she threw her last bloody glance over a world quivering with the ferment of tempest. I was physically influenced by the atmosphere and scene, and my ears were filled with the curses the maniac still shrieked out: wherein she momentarily mingled my name with such a tone of demon-hate, with such language! – no professed harlot ever had a fouler vocabulary than she: though two rooms off, I heard every word – the thin partitions of the West Indian house opposing but slight obstruction to her wolfish cries.

'"This life", said I at last, "is hell: this is the air – those are the sounds of the bottomless pit! I have a right to deliver myself from it if I can. The sufferings of this mortal state will leave me with the heavy flesh that now cumbers my soul. Of the fanatic's burning eternity I have no fear: there is not a future state worse than this present one – let me break away, and go home to God!"

'I said this whilst I knelt down at and unlocked a trunk which contained a brace of loaded pistols: I meant to shoot myself. I only entertained the intention for a moment; for, not being insane, the crisis of exquisite and unalloyed despair, which had originated the wish and design of self-destruction, was past in a second.

'A wind fresh from Europe blew over the ocean and rushed through the open casement: the storm broke, streamed, thundered, blazed, and the air grew pure. I then framed and fixed a resolution. While I walked under the dripping orange-trees of my wet garden, and amongst its drenched pomegranates and pineapples, and while the refulgent dawn of the tropics kindled round me – I reasoned thus, Jane – and now listen; for it was true Wisdom that consoled me in that hour, and showed me the right path to follow.

'The sweet wind from Europe was still whispering in the refreshed leaves, and the Atlantic was thundering in glorious liberty; my heart, dried up and scorched for a long time, swelled to the tone, and filled with living blood – my being longed for renewal – my soul thirsted for a pure draught. I saw hope revive – and felt regeneration possible. From a flowery arch at the bottom of my garden I gazed over the sea – bluer than the sky: the old world was beyond; clear prospects opened thus:

'"Go", said Hope, "and live again in Europe: there it is not known what a sullied name you bear, nor what a filthy burden is bound to you. You may take the maniac with you to England; confine her with due attendance and precautions at Thornfield: then travel yourself to what clime you will, and form what new tie you like. That woman, who has so abused your long-suffering, so sullied your name, so outraged your honour, so blighted your youth, is not your wife, nor are you her husband. See that she is cared for as her condition demands, and you have done all that God and humanity require of you. Let her identity, her connexion with yourself, be buried in oblivion: you are bound to impart them to no living being. Place her in safety and comfort: shelter her degradation with secrecy, and leave her."

'I acted precisely on this suggestion. My father and brother had not made my marriage known to their acquaintance; because, in the very first letter I wrote to apprise them of the union – having already begun to experience extreme

disgust of its consequences, and, from the family character and constitution, seeing a hideous future opening to me – I added an urgent charge to keep it secret: and very soon the infamous conduct of the wife my father had selected for me was such as to make him blush to own her as his daughter-in-law. Far from desiring to publish the connexion, he became as anxious to conceal it as myself.

'To England, then, I conveyed her; a fearful voyage I had with such a monster in the vessel. Glad was I when I at last got her to Thornfield, and saw her safely lodged in that third-story room, of whose secret inner cabinet she has now for ten years made a wild beast's den – a goblin's cell. I had some trouble in finding an attendant for her, as it was necessary to select one on whose fidelity dependence could be placed; for her ravings would inevitably betray my secret: besides, she had lucid intervals of days – sometimes weeks – which she filled up with abuse of me. At last I hired Grace Poole from the Grimsby Retreat. She and the surgeon, Carter (who dressed Mason's wounds that night he was stabbed and worried) are the only two I have ever admitted to my confidence. Mrs Fairfax may indeed have suspected something, but she could have gained no precise knowledge as to facts. Grace has, on the whole, proved a good keeper; though, owing partly to a fault of her own, of which it appears nothing can cure her, and which is incident to her harassing profession, her vigilance has been more than once lulled and baffled. The lunatic is both cunning and malignant; she has never failed to take advantage of her guardian's temporary lapses; once to secrete the knife with which she stabbed her brother, and twice to possess herself of the key of her cell, and issue therefrom in the night-time. On the first of these occasions, she perpetrated the attempt to burn me in my bed; on the second, she paid that ghastly visit to you. I thank Providence, who watched over you, that she then spent her fury on your wedding apparel, which perhaps brought back vague reminiscences of her own bridal days: but on what might have happened, I cannot endure to reflect. When I think of the thing which flew at my throat this morning, hanging its black and scarlet visage over the nest of my dove, my blood curdles —'

'And what, sir,' I asked, while he paused, 'did you do when you had settled her here? Where did you go?'

'What did I do, Jane? I transformed myself into a will-o'-the-wisp. Where did I go? I pursued wanderings as wild as those of the March spirit. I sought the Continent, and went devious through all its lands. My fixed desire was to seek and find a good and intelligent woman, whom I could love: a contrast to the fury I left at Thornfield —'

'But you could not marry, sir.'

'I had determined and was convinced that I could and ought. It was not my original intention to deceive, as I have deceived you. I meant to tell my tale plainly, and make my proposals openly: and it appeared to me so absolutely rational that I should be considered free to love and be loved, I never doubted some woman might be found willing and able to understand my case and accept me, in spite of the curse with which I was burdened.'

'Well, sir?'

'When you are inquisitive, Jane, you always make me smile. You open your eyes like an eager bird, and make every now and then a restless movement, as if answers in speech did not flow fast enough for you, and you wanted to read

# Jane Eyre

the tablet of one's heart. But before I go on, tell me what you mean by your "Well, sir?" It is a small phrase very frequent with you; and which many a time has drawn me on and on through interminable talk: I don't very well know why.'

'I mean – What next? How did you proceed? What came of such an event?'

'Precisely! and what do you wish to know now?'

'Whether you found any one you liked: whether you asked her to marry you; and what she said.'

'I can tell you whether I found anyone I liked, and whether I asked her to marry me: but what she said is yet to be recorded in the book of Fate. For ten long years I roved about, living first in one capital, then another: sometimes in St Petersburg, oftener in Paris, occasionally in Rome, Naples, and Florence. Provided with plenty of money and the passport of an old name, I could choose my own society: no circles were closed against me. I sought my ideal of a woman amongst English ladies, French countesses, Italian signoras, and German gräfinnen. I could not find her. Sometimes, for a fleeting moment, I thought I caught a glance, heard a tone, beheld a form, which announced the realization of my dream: but I was presently undeceived. You are not to suppose that I desired perfection, either of mind or person. I longed only for what suited me – for the antipodes of the Creole: and I longed vainly. Amongst them all I found not one whom, had I been ever so free, I – warned as I was of the risks, the horrors, the loathings of incongruous unions – would have asked to marry me. Disappointment made me reckless. I tried dissipation – never debauchery: that I hated, and hate. That was my Indian Messalina's attribute: rooted disgust at it and her restrained me much, even in pleasure. Any enjoyment that bordered on riot seemed to approach me to her and her vices, and I eschewed it.

'Yet I could not live alone; so I tried the companionship of mistresses. The first I chose was Céline Varens – another of those steps which make a man spurn himself when he recalls them. You already know what she was, and how my liaison with her terminated. She had two successors: an Italian, Giacinta, and a German, Clara; both considered singularly handsome. What was their beauty to me in a few weeks? Giacinta was unprincipled and violent: I tired of her in three months. Clara was honest and quiet; but heavy, mindless, and unimpressible: not one whit to my taste. I was glad to give her a sufficient sum to set her up in a good line of business, and so get decently rid of her. But, Jane, I see by your face you are not forming a very favourable opinion of me just now. You think me an unfeeling, loose-principled rake: don't you?'

'I don't like you so well as I have done sometimes, indeed, sir. Did it not seem to you in the least wrong to live in that way, first with one mistress and then another? You talk of it as a mere matter of course.'

'It was with me; and I did not like it. It was a grovelling fashion of existence: I should never like to return to it. Hiring a mistress is the next worse thing to buying a slave: both are often by nature, and always by position, inferior: and to live familiarly with inferiors is degrading. I now hate the recollection of the time I passed with Céline, Giacinta, and Clara.'

I felt the truth of these words; and I drew from them the certain inference, that if I were so far to forget myself and all the teaching that had ever been instilled into me, as – under any pretext – with any justification – through any temptation – to become the successor of these poor girls, he would one day regard

me with the same feeling which now in his mind desecrated their memory. I did not give utterance to this conviction: it was enough to feel it. I impressed it on my heart, that it might remain there to serve me as aid in the time of trial.

'Now, Jane, why don't you say, "Well, sir?" I have not done. You are looking grave. You disapprove of me still, I see. But let me come to the point. Last January, rid of all mistresses – in a harsh, bitter frame of mind, the result of a useless, roving, lonely life – corroded with disappointment, sourly disposed against all men, and especially against all *woman*kind (for I began to regard the notion of an intellectual, faithful, loving woman as a mere dream), recalled by business, I came back to England.

'On a frosty winter afternoon, I rode in sight of Thornfield Hall. Abhorred spot! I expected no peace, no pleasure there. On a stile in Hay Lane I saw a quiet little figure sitting by itself. I passed it as negligently as I did the pollard willow opposite to it: I had no presentiment of what it would be to me; no inward warning that the arbitress of my life – my genius for good or evil – waited there in humble guise. I did not know it, even when, on the occasion of Mesrour's accident, it came up and gravely offered me help. Childish and slender creature! It seemed as if a linnet had hopped to my foot and proposed to bear me on its tiny wing. I was surly; but the thing would not go: it stood by me with strange perseverance, and looked and spoke with a sort of authority. I must be aided, and by that hand: and aided I was.

'When once I had pressed the frail shoulder, something new – a fresh sap and sense – stole into my frame. It was well I had learnt that this elf must return to me – that it belonged to my house down below – or I could not have felt it pass away from under my hand, and seen it vanish behind the dim hedge, without singular regret. I heard you come home that night, Jane: though probably you were not aware that I thought of you, or watched for you. The next day I observed you – myself unseen – for half an hour, while you played with Adèle in the gallery. It was a snowy day, I recollect, and you could not go out of doors. I was in my room; the door was ajar: I could both listen and watch. Adèle claimed your outward attention for a while; yet I fancied your thoughts were elsewhere: but you were very patient with her, my little Jane; you talked to her and amused her a long time. When at last she left you, you lapsed at once into deep reverie: you betook yourself slowly to pace the gallery. Now and then, in passing a casement, you glanced out at the thick falling snow; you listened to the sobbing wind, and again you paced gently on and dreamed. I think those day visions were not dark: there was a pleasurable illumination in your eye occasionally, a soft excitement in your aspect, which told of no bitter, bilious, hypochondriac brooding: your look revealed rather the sweet musings of youth when its spirit follows on willing wings the flight of Hope up and on to an ideal Heaven. The voice of Mrs Fairfax, speaking to a servant in the hall, wakened you: and how curiously you smiled to and at yourself, Janet! There was much sense in your smile: it was very shrewd, and seemed to make light of your own abstraction. It seemed to say, "My fine visions are all very well, but I must not forget they are absolutely unreal. I have a rosy sky and a green flowery Eden in my brain; but without, I am perfectly aware, lies at my feet a rough tract to travel, and around me gather black tempests to encounter." You ran downstairs and demanded of Mrs Fairfax some occupation: the weekly house accounts to

make up, or something of that sort, I think it was. I was vexed with you for getting out of my sight.

'Impatiently I waited for evening, when I might summon you to my presence. An unusual – to me – a perfectly new character, I suspected, was yours: I desired to search it deeper and know it better. You entered the room with a look and air at once shy and independent: you were quaintly dressed – much as you are now. I made you talk: ere long I found you full of strange contrasts. Your garb and manner were restricted by rule; your air was often diffident, and altogether that of one refined by nature, but absolutely unused to society, and a good deal afraid of making herself disadvantageously conspicuous by some solecism or blunder; yet when addressed, you lifted a keen, a daring, and a glowing eye to your interlocutor's face: there was penetration and power in each glance you gave; when plied by close questions, you found ready and round answers. Very soon you seemed to get used to me: I believe you felt the existence of sympathy between you and your grim and cross master, Jane; for it was astonishing to see how quickly a certain pleasant ease tranquillized your manner: snarl as I would, you showed no surprise, fear, annoyance, or displeasure at my moroseness; you watched me, and now and then smiled at me with a simple yet sagacious grace I cannot describe. I was at once content and stimulated with what I saw: I liked what I had seen, and wished to see more. Yet, for a long time, I treated you distantly, and sought your company rarely. I was an intellectual epicure, and wished to prolong the gratification of making this novel and piquant acquaintance: besides, I was for a while troubled with a haunting fear that if I handled the flower freely its bloom would fade – the sweet charm of freshness would leave it. I did not then know that it was no transitory blossom, but rather the radiant resemblance of one, cut in an indestructible gem. Moreover, I wished to see whether you would seek me if I shunned you – but you did not; you kept in the schoolroom as still as your own desk and easel; if by chance I met you, you passed me as soon, and with as little token of recognition, as was consistent with respect. Your habitual expression in those days, Jane, was a thoughtful look; not despondent, for you were not sickly; but not buoyant, for you had little hope, and no actual pleasure. I wondered what you thought of me – or if you ever thought of me; to find this out, I resumed my notice of you. There was something glad in your glance, and genial in your manner, when you conversed: I saw you had a social heart; it was the silent schoolroom – it was the tedium of your life – that made you mournful. I permitted myself the delight of being kind to you; kindness stirred emotion soon: your face became soft in expression, your tones gentle; I liked my name pronounced by your lips in a grateful, happy accent. I used to enjoy a chance meeting with you, Jane, at this time: there was a curious hesitation in your manner: you glanced at me with a slight trouble – a hovering doubt: you did not know what my caprice might be – whether I was going to play the master and be stern, or the friend and be benignant. I was now too fond of you often to simulate the first whim; and, when I stretched my hand out cordially, such bloom and light and bliss rose to your young, wistful features, I had much ado often to avoid straining you then and there to my heart.'

'Don't talk any more of those days, sir,' I interrupted, furtively dashing away some tears from my eyes; his language was torture to me; for I knew what I must do – and do soon – and all these reminiscences, and these revelations of his feelings only made my work more difficult.

# Jane Eyre

'No, Jane,' he returned: 'what necessity is there to dwell on the past, when the Present is so much surer – the Future so much brighter?'

I shuddered to hear the infatuated assertion.

'You see now how the case stands – do you not?' he continued. 'After a youth and manhood passed half in unutterable misery and half in dreary solitude, I have for the first time found what I can truly love – I have found *you*. You are my sympathy – my better self – my good angel. I am bound to you with a strong attachment. I think you good, gifted, lovely: a fervent, a solemn passion is conceived in my heart; it leans to you, draws you to my centre and spring of life, wraps my existence about you, and, kindling in pure, powerful flame, fuses you and me in one.

'It was because I felt and knew this, that I resolved to marry you. To tell me that I had already a wife is empty mockery: you know now that I had but a hideous demon. I was wrong to attempt to deceive you; but I feared a stubbornness that exists in your character. I feared early instilled prejudice: I wanted to have you safe before hazarding conferences. This was cowardly: I should have appealed to your nobleness and magnanimity at first, as I do now – opened to you plainly my life of agony – described to you my hunger and thirst after a higher and worthier existence – shown to you, not my *resolution* (that word is weak), but my resistless *bent* to love faithfully and well, where I am faithfully and well loved in return. Then I should have asked you to accept my pledge of fidelity and to give me yours. Jane – give it me now.'

A pause.

'Why are you silent, Jane?'

I was experiencing an ordeal: a hand of fiery iron grasped my vitals. Terrible moment: full of struggle, blackness, burning! Not a human being that ever lived could wish to be loved better than I was loved; and him who thus loved me I absolutely worshipped: and I must renounce love and idol. One drear word comprised my intolerable duty – 'Depart!'

'Jane, you understand what I want of you? Just this promise – "I will be yours, Mr Rochester."'

'Mr Rochester, I will *not* be yours.'

Another long silence.

'Jane!' recommenced he, with a gentleness that broke me down with grief, and turned me stone-cold with ominous terror – for this still voice was the pant of a lion rising – 'Jane, do you mean to go one way in the world, and to let me go another?'

'I do.'

'Jane' (bending towards and embracing me), 'do you mean it now?'

'I do.'

'And now?' softly kissing my forehead and cheek.

'I do,' extricating myself from restraint rapidly and completely.

'Oh, Jane, this is bitter! This – this is wicked. It would not be wicked to love me.'

'It would to obey you.'

A wild look raised his brows – crossed his features: he rose; but he forebore yet. I laid my hand on the back of a chair for support: I shook, I feared – but I resolved.

'One instant, Jane. Give one glance to my horrible life when you are gone.

# Jane Eyre

All happiness will be torn away with you. What then is left? For a wife I have but the maniac upstairs: as well might you refer me to some corpse in yonder churchyard. What shall I do, Jane? Where turn for a companion, and for some hope?'

'Do as I do: trust in God and yourself. Believe in heaven. Hope to meet again there.'

'Then you will not yield?'

'No.'

'Then you condemn me to live wretched, and to die accursed?' His voice rose.

'I advise you to live sinless, and I wish you to die tranquil.'

'Then you snatch love and innocence from me? You fling me back on lust for a passion – vice for an occupation?'

'Mr Rochester, I no more assign this fate to you than I grasp at it for myself. We were born to strive and endure – you as well as I: do so. You will forget me before I forget you.'

'You make me a liar by such language: you sully my honour. I declared I could not change: you tell me to my face I shall change soon. And what a distortion in your judgement, what a perversity in your ideas, is proved by your conduct! Is it better to drive a fellow-creature to despair than to transgress a mere human law, no man being injured by the breach? – for you have neither relatives nor acquaintances whom you need fear to offend by living with me.'

This was true: and while he spoke my very conscience and reason turned traitors against me, and charged me with crime in resisting him. They spoke almost as loud as Feeling: and that clamoured wildly. 'Oh, comply!' it said. 'Think of his misery; think of his danger; look at his state when left alone; remember his headlong nature: consider the recklessness following on despair – soothe him; save him; love him; tell him you love him and will be his. Who in the world cares for *you*? or who will be injured by what you do?'

Still indomitable was the reply: '*I* care for myself. The more solitary, the more friendless, the more unsustained I am, the more I will respect myself. I will keep the law given by God; sanctioned by man. I will hold to the principles received by me when I was sane, and not mad – as I am now. Laws and principles are not for times when there is no temptation: they are for such moments as this, when body and soul rise in mutiny against their rigour; stringent are they; inviolate they shall be. If at my individual convenience I might break them, what would be their worth? They have a worth – so I have always believed; and if I cannot believe it now, it is because I am insane – quite insane, with my veins running fire, and my heart beating faster than I can count its throbs. Preconceived opinions, foregone determinations are all I have at this hour to stand by; there I plant my foot.'

I did. Mr Rochester, reading my countenance, saw I had done so. His fury was wrought to the highest: he must yield to it for a moment, whatever followed; he crossed the floor and seized my arm and grasped my waist. He seemed to devour me with his flaming glance: physically, I felt, at the moment, powerless as stubble exposed to the draught and glow of a furnace: mentally, I still possessed my soul, and with it the certainty of ultimate safety. The soul, fortunately, has an interpreter – often an unconscious but still a faithful interpreter – in the eye. My eye rose to his; and while I looked in his fierce face

# Jane Eyre

I gave an involuntary sigh; his grip was painful, and my overtaxed strength almost exhausted.

'Never,' said he, as he ground his teeth, 'never was anything at once so frail and so indomitable. A mere reed she feels in my hand!' (And he shook me with the force of his hold.) 'I could bend her with my finger and thumb: and what good would it do if I bent, if I uptore, if I crushed her? Consider that eye: consider the resolute, wild, free thing looking out of it, defying me, with more than courage - with a stern triumph. Whatever I do with its cage, I cannot get at it - the savage, beautiful creature! If I tear, if I rend the slight prison, my outrage will only let the captive loose. Conqueror I might be of the house; but the inmate would escape to heaven before I could call myself possessor of its clay dwelling-place. And it is you, spirit - with will and energy, and virtue and purity - that I want: not alone your brittle frame. Of yourself you could come with a soft flight and nestle against my heart, if you would: seized against your will, you will elude the grasp like an essence - you will vanish ere I inhale your fragrance. Oh! come, Jane, come!'

As he said this, he released me from his clutch, and only looked at me. The look was far worse to resist than the frantic strain: only an idiot, however, would have succumbed now. I had dared and baffled his fury; I must elude his sorrow: I retired to the door.

'You are going, Jane?'

'I am going, sir.'

'You are leaving me?'

'Yes.'

'You will not come? You will not be my comforter, my rescuer? My deep love, my wild woe, my frantic prayer, are all nothing to you?'

What unutterable pathos was in his voice! How hard it was to reiterate firmly. 'I am going.'

'Jane!'

'Mr Rochester!'

'Withdraw, then - I consent; but remember, you leave me here in anguish. Go up to your own room; think over all I have said, and, Jane, cast a glance on my sufferings - think of me.'

He turned away; he threw himself on his face on the sofa. 'Oh, Jane! my hope - my love - my life!' broke in anguish from his lips. Then came a deep, strong sob.

I had already gained the door; but, reader, I walked back - walked back as determinedly as I had retreated. I knelt down by him; I turned his face from the cushion to me; I kissed his cheek; I smoothed his hair with my hand.

'God bless you, my dear master!' I said. 'God keep you from harm and wrong - direct you, solace you - reward you well for your past kindness to me.'

'Little Jane's love would have been my best reward,' he answered; 'without it, my heart is broken. But Jane will give me her love: yes - nobly, generously.'

Up the blood rushed to his face; forth flashed the fire from his eyes; erect he sprang; he held his arms out; but I evaded the embrace, and at once quitted the room.

'Farewell!' was the cry of my heart as I left him. Despair added, 'Farewell for ever!'

# Jane Eyre

That night I never thought to sleep; but a slumber fell on me as soon as I lay down in bed. I was transported in thought to the scenes of childhood: I dreamt I lay in the red-room at Gateshead; that the night was dark, and my mind impressed with strange fears. The light that long ago had struck me into syncope, recalled in this vision, seemed glidingly to mount the wall, and tremblingly to pause in the centre of the obscured ceiling. I lifted up my head to look: the roof resolved to clouds, high and dim; the gleam was such as the moon imparts to vapours she is about to sever. I watched her come – watched with the strangest anticipation; as though some words of doom were to be written on her disc. She broke forth as never moon yet burst from cloud: a hand first penetrated the sable folds and waved them away; then, not a moon, but a white human form shone in the azure, inclining a glorious brow earthward. It gazed and gazed on me. It spoke to my spirit: immeasurably distant was the tone, yet so near, it whispered in my heart –

'My daughter, flee temptation.'

'Mother, I will.'

So I answered after I had waked from the trance-like dream. It was yet night, but July nights are short: soon after midnight, dawn comes. 'It cannot be too early to commence the task I have to fulfil,' thought I. I rose: I was dressed; for I had taken off nothing but my shoes. I knew where to find in my drawers some linen, a locket, a ring. In seeking these articles, I encountered the beads of a pearl necklace Mr Rochester had forced me to accept a few days ago. I left that; it was not mine: it was the visionary bride's who had melted in air. The other articles I made up in a parcel; my purse, containing twenty shillings (it was all I had), I put in my pocket: I tied on my straw bonnet, pinned my shawl, took the parcel and my slippers, which I would not put on yet, and stole from my room.

'Farewell, kind Mrs Fairfax!' I whispered, as I glided past her door. 'Farewell, my darling Adèle!' I said, as I glanced towards the nursery. No thought could be admitted of entering to embrace her. I had to deceive a fine ear: for aught I knew, it might now be listening.

I would have got past Mr Rochester's chamber without a pause; but my heart momentarily stopping its beat at that threshold, my foot was forced to stop also. No sleep was there: the inmate was walking restlessly from wall to wall; and again and again he sighed while I listened. There was a heaven – a temporary heaven – in this room for me, if I chose: I had but to go in and to say –

'Mr Rochester, I will love you and live with you through life till death,' and a fount of rapture would spring to my lips. I thought of this.

That kind master, who could not sleep now, was waiting with impatience for day. He would send for me in the morning; I should be gone. He would have me sought for: vainly. He would feel himself forsaken; his love rejected: he would suffer; perhaps grow desperate. I thought of this, too. My hand moved towards the lock: I caught it back, and glided on.

Drearily I wound my way downstairs: I knew what I had to do, and I did it mechanically. I sought the key of the side-door in the kitchen; I sought, too, a phial of oil and a feather; I oiled the key and the lock. I got some water, I got some bread: for perhaps I should have to walk far; and my strength, sorely shaken of late, must not break down. All this I did without one sound. I opened the door, passed out, shut it softly. Dim dawn glimmered in the yard. The great

# Jane Eyre

gates were closed and locked; but a wicket in one of them was only latched. Through that I departed: it, too, I shut; and now I was out of Thornfield.

A mile off, beyond the fields, lay a road which stretched in the contrary direction to Millcote; a road I had never travelled, but often noticed, and wondered where it led: thither I bent my steps. No reflection was to be allowed now: not one glance was to be cast back; not even one forward. Not one thought was to be given either to the past or the future. The first was a page so heavenly sweet – so deadly sad – that to read one line of it would dissolve my courage and break down my energy. The last was an awful blank: something like the world when the deluge was gone by.

I skirted fields and hedges and lanes till after sunrise. I believe it was a lovely summer morning: I know my shoes, which I had put on when I left the house, were soon wet with dew. But I looked neither to rising sun, nor smiling sky, nor wakening nature. He who is taken out to pass through a fair scene to the scaffold, thinks not of the flowers that smile on his road, but of the block and axe-edge; of the disseverment of bone and vein; of the grave gaping at the end: and I thought of drear flight and homeless wandering – and oh! with agony I thought of what I left. I could not help it. I thought of him now – in his room – watching the sunrise; hoping I should soon come to say I would stay with him and be his. I longed to be his; I panted to return: it was not too late. I could yet spare him the bitter pang of bereavement. As yet my flight, I was sure, was undiscovered. I could go back and be his comforter – his pride; his redeemer from misery, perhaps from ruin. Oh, that fear of his self-abandonment – far worse than my abandonment – how it goaded me! It was a barbed arrowhead in my breast; it tore me when I tried to extract it; it sickened me when remembrance thrust it farther in. Birds began singing in brake and copse: birds were faithful to their mates; birds were emblems of love. What was I? In the midst of my pain of heart and frantic effort of principle, I abhorred myself. I had no solace from self-approbation: none even from self-respect. I had injured – wounded – left my master. I was hateful in my own eyes. Still I could not turn, nor retrace one step. God must have led me on. As to my own will or conscience, impassioned grief had trampled one and stifled the other. I was weeping wildly as I walked along my solitary way; fast, fast I went like one delirious. A weakness, beginning inwardly, extending to the limbs, seized me, and I fell; I lay on the ground some minutes, pressing my face to the wet turf. I had some fear – or hope – that here I should die; but I was soon up, crawling forward on my hands and knees, and then again raised my feet – as eager and as determined as ever to reach the road.

When I got there, I was forced to sit to rest me under the hedge; and while I sat I heard wheels, and saw a coach come on. I stood up and lifted my hand; it stopped. I asked where it was going: the driver named a place a long way off, and where I was sure Mr Rochester had no connections. I asked for what sum he would take me there; he said thirty shillings; I answered I had but twenty; well, he would try to make it do. He further gave me leave to get into the inside, as the vehicle was empty: I entered, was shut in, and it rolled on its way.

Gentle reader, may you never feel what I then felt! May your eyes never shed such stormy, scalding, heart-wrung tears as poured from mine. May you never appeal to Heaven in prayers so hopeless and so agonized as in that hour left my

lips; for never may you, like me, dread to be the instrument of evil to what you wholly love.

# Chapter 28

wo days are passed. It is a summer evening; the coachman has set me down at a place called Whitcross: he could take me no farther for the sum I had given and I was not possessed of another shilling in the world. The coach is a mile off by this time; I am alone. At this moment I discover that I forgot to take my parcel out of the pocket of the coach, where I had placed it for safety; there it remains, there it must remain; and now, I am absolutely destitute.

Whitcross is no town, nor even a hamlet; it is but a stone pillar set up where four roads meet: whitewashed, I suppose, to be more obvious at a distance and in darkness. Four arms spring from its summit: the nearest town to which these point is, according to the inscription, distant ten miles; the farthest, above twenty. From the well-known names of these towns I learn in what county I have lighted; a north-midland shire, dusk with moorland, ridged with mountain: this I see. There are great moors behind and on each hand of me; there are waves of mountains far beyond that deep valley at my feet. The population here must be thin, and I see no passengers on these roads; they stretch out east, west, north, and south – white, broad, lonely; they are all cut in the moor, and the heather grows deep and wild to their very verge. Yet a chance traveller might pass by; and I wish no eye to see me now: strangers would wonder what I am doing, lingering here at the signpost, evidently objectless and lost. I might be questioned: I could give no answer but what would sound incredible and excite suspicion. Not a tie holds me to human society at this moment – not a charm or hope calls me where my fellow-creatures are – none that saw me would have a kind thought or a good wish for me. I have no relative but the universal mother, Nature: I will seek her breast and ask repose.

I struck straight into the heath; I held on to a hollow I saw deeply furrowing the brown moorside; I waded kneedeep in its dark growth; I turned with its turnings, and finding a moss-blackened granite crag in a hidden angle, I sat down under it. High banks of moor were about me; the crag protected my head: the sky was over that. Some time passed before I felt tranquil even here: I had a vague dread that wild cattle might be near, or that some sportsman or poacher might discover me. If a gust of wind swept the waste, I looked up, fearing it was the rush of a bull; if a plover whistled, I imagined it a man. Finding my apprehensions unfounded, however, and calmed by the deep silence that reigned as evening declined at nightfall, I took confidence. As yet I had not thought: I had only listened, watched, dreaded; now I regained the faculty of reflection.

# Jane Eyre

What was I to do? Where to go? Oh, intolerable questions, when I could do nothing and go nowhere! – when a long way must yet be measured by my weary, trembling limbs before I could reach human habitation – when cold charity must be entreated before I could get a lodging: reluctant sympathy importuned, almost certain repulse incurred, before my tale could be listened to, or one of my wants relieved!

I touched the heath: it was dry, and yet warm with the heat of the summer day. I looked at the sky; it was pure: a kindly star twinkled just above the chasm ridge. The dew fell, but with propitious softness; No breeze whispered. Nature seemed to me benign and good; I thought she loved me, outcast as I was; and I, who from man could anticipate only mistrust, rejection, insult, clung to her with filial fondness. To-night, at least, I would be her guest, as I was her child: my mother would lodge me without money and without price. I had one morsel of bread yet: the remnant of a roll I had bought in a town we had passed through at noon with a stray penny – my last coin. I saw ripe bilberries gleaming here and there, like jet beads in the heath: I gathered a handful, and ate them with the bread. My hunger, sharp before, was, if not satisfied, appeased by this hermit's meal. I said my evening prayers at its conclusion, and then chose my couch.

Beside the crag the heath was very deep: when I lay down my feet were buried in it; rising high on each side, it left only a narrow space for the night-air to invade. I folded my shawl double, and spread it over me for a coverlet; a low, mossy swell was my pillow. Thus lodged, I was not, at least at the commencement of the night, cold.

My rest might have been blissful enough, only a sad heart broke it. It plained of its gaping wounds, its inward bleeding, its riven chords. It trembled for Mr Rochester and his doom; it bemoaned him with bitter pity; it demanded him with ceaseless longing; and, impotent as a bird with both wings broken, it still quivered its shattered pinions in vain attempts to seek him.

Worn out with this torture of thought, I rose to my knees. Night was come, and her planets were risen: a safe, still night: too serene for the companionship of fear. We know that God is everywhere; but certainly we feel His presence most when His works are on the grandest scale spread before us; and it is in the unclouded night-sky, where His worlds wheel their silent course, that we read clearest His infinitude, His omnipotence, His omnipresence. I had risen to my knees to pray for Mr Rochester. Looking up, I, with tear-dimmed eyes, saw the mighty Milky Way. Remembering what it was – what countless systems there swept space like a soft trace of light – I felt the might and strength of God. Sure was I of His efficiency to save what He had made: convinced I grew that neither earth should perish, nor one of the souls it treasured. I turned my prayer to thanksgiving: the Source of Life was also the Saviour of spirits. Mr Rochester was safe: he was God's, and by God would he be guarded. I again nestled to the breast of the hill; and ere long in sleep forgot sorrow.

But next day, Want came to me, pale and bare. Long after the little birds had left their nests; long after bees had come in the sweet prime of day to gather the heath honey before the dew was dried – when the long morning shadows were curtailed, and the sun filled earth and sky – I got up, and I looked round me.

What a still, hot, perfect day! What a golden desert this spreading moor! Everywhere sunshine. I wished I could live in it and on it. I saw a lizard run

over the crag; I saw a bee busy among the sweet bilberries. I would fain at the moment have become bee or lizard, that I might have found fitting nutriment, permanent shelter here. But I was a human being, and had a human being's wants: I must not linger where there was nothing to supply them. I rose; I looked back at the bed I had left. Hopeless of the future, I wished but this – that my Maker had that night thought good to require my soul of me while I slept; and that this weary frame, absolved by death from further conflict with fate, had now but to decay quietly, and mingle in peace with the soil of this wilderness. Life, however, was yet in my possession, with all its requirements, and pains, and responsibilities. The burden must be carried; the want provided for; the suffering endured; the responsibility fulfilled. I set out.

Whitcross regained, I followed a road which led from the sun, now fervent and high. But no other circumstance had I will to decide my choice. I walked a long time, and when I thought I had nearly done enough, and might conscientiously yield to the fatigue that almost overpowered me – might relax this forced action, and sitting down on a stone I saw near, submit resistlessly to the apathy that clogged heart and limb – I heard a bell chime – a church bell.

I turned in the direction of the sound, and there, amongst the romantic hills, whose changes and aspect I had ceased to note an hour ago, I saw a hamlet and a spire. All the valley at my right hand was full of pasture fields, and cornfields, and wood; and a glittering stream ran zigzag through the varied shades of green, the mellowing grain, the sombre woodland, the clear and sunny lea. Recalled by the rumbling of wheels to the road before me, I saw a heavily-laden wagon labouring up the hill, and not far beyond were two cows and their drover. Human life and human labour were near. I must struggle on: strive to live and bend to toil like the rest.

About two o'clock p.m. I entered the village. At the bottom of its one street there was a little shop with some cakes of bread in the window. I coveted a cake of bread. With that refreshment I could perhaps regain a degree of energy; without it, it would be difficult to proceed. The wish to have some strength and some vigour returned to me as soon as I was amongst my fellow-beings. I felt it would be degrading to faint with hunger on the causeway of a hamlet. Had I nothing about me I could offer in exchange for one of these rolls? I considered. I had a small silk handkerchief tied round my throat; I had my gloves. I could hardly tell how men and women in extremities of destitution proceeded. I did not know whether either of these articles would be accepted: probably they would not; but I must try.

I entered the shop: a woman was there. Seeing a respectably dressed person, a lady as she supposed, she came forward with civility. How could she serve me? I was seized with shame: my tongue would not utter the request I had prepared. I dared not offer her the half-worn gloves, the creased handkerchief: besides, I felt it would be absurd. I only begged permission to sit down a moment, as I was tired. Disappointed in the expectation of a customer, she coolly acceded to my request. She pointed to a seat; I sank into it. I felt sorely urged to weep; but conscious how unseasonable such a manifestation would be, I restrained it. Soon I asked her 'if there were any dressmaker or plainwork-woman in the village?'

'Yes; two or three. Quite as many as there was employment for.'

I reflected. I was driven to the point now. I was brought face to face with

Necessity. I stood in the position of one without a resource, without a friend, without a coin. I must do something. What? I must apply somewhere. Where?

'Did she know of any place in the neighbourhood where a servant was wanted?'

'Nay; she couldn't say.'

'What was the chief trade in this place? What did most of the people do?'

'Some were farm labourers; a good deal worked at Mr Oliver's needle-factory, and at the foundry.'

'Did Mr Oliver employ women?'

'Nay; it was men's work.'

'And what do the women do?'

'I knawn't,' was the answer. 'Some does one thing, and some another. Poor folk mun get on as they can.'

She seemed to be tired of my questions: and, indeed, what claim had I to importune her? A neighbour or two came in; my chair was evidently wanted. I took leave.

I passed up the street, looking as I went at all the houses to the right hand and to the left; but I could discover no pretext, nor see an inducement, to enter any. I rambled round the hamlet, going sometimes to a little distance and returning again, for an hour or more. Much exhausted, and suffering greatly now for want of food, I turned aside into a lane and sat down under the hedge. Ere many minutes had elapsed, I was again on my feet, however, and again searching something – a resource, or at least an informant. A pretty little house stood at the top of the lane, with a garden before it, exquisitely neat and brilliantly blooming. I stopped at it. What business had I to approach the white door or touch the glittering knocker? In what way could it possibly be the interest of the inhabitants of that dwelling to serve me? Yet I drew near and knocked. A mild-looking, cleanly-attired young woman opened the door. In such a voice as might be expected from a hopeless heart and fainting frame – a voice wretchedly low and faltering – I asked if a servant was wanted here?

'No,' said she; 'we do not keep a servant.'

'Can you tell me where I could get employment of any kind?' I continued. 'I am a stranger, without acquaintance in this place. I want some work: no matter what.'

But it was not her business to think for me, or to seek a place for me: besides, in her eyes, how doubtful must have appeared my character, position, tale. She shook her head, she 'was sorry she could give me no information', and the white door closed, quite gently and civilly: but it shut me out. If she had held it open a little longer, I believe I should have begged a piece of bread; for I was now brought low.

I could not bear to return to the sordid village, where, besides, no prospect of aid was visible. I should have longed rather to deviate to a wood I saw not far off, which appeared in its thick shade to offer inviting shelter; but I was so sick, so weak, so gnawed with nature's cravings, instinct kept me roaming round abodes where there was a chance of food. Solitude would be no solitude – rest no rest – while the vulture, hunger, thus sank beak and talons in my side.

I drew near the houses; I left them, and came back again, and again I wandered away: always repelled by the consciousness of having no claim to ask – no right to expect interest in my isolated lot. Meantime, the afternoon advanced,

# Jane Eyre

while I thus wandered about like a lost and starving dog. In crossing a field, I saw the church spire before me: I hastened towards it. Near the churchyard, and in the middle of a garden, stood a well-built though small house, which I had no doubt was the parsonage. I remembered that strangers who arrive at a place where they have no friends, and who want employment, sometimes apply to the clergyman for introduction and aid. It is the clergyman's function to help – at least with advice – those who wished to help themselves. I seemed to have something like a right to seek counsel here. Renewing, then, my courage, and gathering my feeble remains of strength, I pushed on. I reached the house, and knocked at the kitchen-door. An old woman opened: I asked was this the parsonage?

'Yes.'

'Was the clergyman in?'

'No.'

'Would he be in soon?'

'No, he was gone from home.'

'To a distance?'

'Not so far – happen three miles. He had been called away by the sudden death of his father: he was at Marsh End now, and would very likely stay there for a fortnight longer.'

'Was there any lady of the house?'

'Nay, there was naught but her, and she was housekeeper'; and of her, reader, I could not bear to ask relief for want of which I was sinking; I could not yet beg, and again I crawled away.

Once more I took off my handkerchief – once more I thought of the cakes of bread in the little shop. Oh, for but a crust! for but one mouthful to allay the pang of famine! Instinctively I turned my face again to the village; I found the shop again, and I went in; and though others were there besides the woman I ventured the request, 'Would she give me a roll for this handkerchief?'

She looked at me with evident suspicion: 'Nay, she never sold stuff i' that way.'

Almost desperate, I asked for half a cake; she again refused. 'How could she tell where I had got the handkerchief?' she said.

'Would she take my gloves?'

'No! what could she do with them?'

Reader, it is not pleasant to dwell on these details. Some say there is enjoyment in looking back to painful experience past; but at this day I can scarcely bear to review the times to which I allude; the moral degradation, blent with the physical suffering, form too distressing a recollection ever to be willingly dwelt on. I blamed none of those who repulsed me. I felt it was what was to be expected, and what could not be helped: an ordinary beggar is frequently an object of suspicion; a well-dressed beggar inevitably so. To be sure, what I begged was employment; but whose business was it to provide me with employment? Not, certainly, that of persons who saw me then for the first time, and who knew nothing about my character. And as to the woman who would not take my handkerchief in exchange for her bread, why, she was right, if the offer appeared to her sinister or the exchange unprofitable. Let me condense now. I am sick of the subject.

# Jane Eyre

A little before dark I passed a farm-house, at the open door of which the farmer was sitting, eating his supper of bread and cheese. I stopped and said –
'Will you give me a piece of bread? for I am very hungry.' He cast on me a glance of surprise; but without answering, he cut a thick slice from his loaf, and gave it to me. I imagine he did not think I was a beggar, but only an eccentric sort of lady, who had taken a fancy to his brown loaf. As soon as I was out of sight of his house, I sat down and ate it.

I could not hope to get a lodging under a roof, and sought it in the wood I have before alluded to. But my night was wretched, my rest broken: the ground was damp, the air cold: besides, intruders passed near me more than once, and I had again and again to change my quarters: no sense of safety or tranquillity befriended me. Towards morning it rained; the whole of the following day was wet. Do not ask me, reader, to give a minute account of that day; as before, I sought work; as before, I was repulsed; as before, I starved; but once did food pass my lips. At the door of a cottage was a little girl about to throw a mess of cold porridge into a pig trough.

'Will you give me that?' I asked.

She stared at me. 'Mother!' she exclaimed, 'there is a women wants me to give her these porridge.'

'Well lass,' replied a voice within, 'give it her if she's a begger. T' pig doesn't want it.'

The girl emptied the stiffened mould into my hand, and I devoured it ravenously.

As the wet twilight deepened, I stopped in a solitary bridle-path, which I had been pursuing an hour or more.

'My strength is quite failing me,' I said in a soliloquy. 'I feel I cannot go much farther. Shall I be an outcast again this night? While the rain descends so, must I lay my head on the cold, drenched ground? I fear I cannot do otherwise: for who will receive me? But it will be very dreadful, with this feeling of hunger, faintness, chill, and the sense of desolation – this total prostration of hope. In all likelihood, though, I should die before morning. And why cannot I reconcile myself to the prospect of death? Why do I struggle to retain a valueless life? Because I know, or believe, Mr Rochester is living: and then, to die of want and cold is a fate to which nature cannot submit passively. Oh, Providence! sustain me a little longer! Aid! – direct me!'

My glazed eye wandered over the dim and misty landscape. I saw I had strayed far from the village: it was quite out of sight. The very cultivation surrounding it had disappeared. I had, by cross-ways and bypaths, once more drawn near the tract of moorland; and now, only a few fields, almost as wild and unproductive as the heath from which they were scarcely reclaimed, lay between me and the dusky hill.

'Well, I would rather die yonder than in a street or on a frequented road,' I reflected. 'And far better that crows and ravens – if any ravens there be in these regions – should pick my flesh from my bones, than that they should be prisoned in a workhouse coffin and moulder in a pauper's grave.'

To the hill, then, I turned. I reached it. It remained now only to find a hollow where I could lie down, and feel at least hidden, if not secure. But all the surface of the waste looked level. It showed no variation but of tint: green, where rush and moss overgrew the marshes; black, where the dry soil bore only death. Dark

# Jane Eyre

as it was getting, I could still see these changes, though but as mere alternations of light and shade; for colour had faded with the daylight.

My eyes still roved over the sullen swell and along the moor edge, vanishing amidst the wildest scenery, when at one dim point, far in among the marshes and the ridges, a light sprang up. 'That is an *ignis fatuus*', was my first thought; and I expected it would soon vanish. It burnt on, however, quite steadily, neither receding nor advancing. 'Is it, then, a bonfire just kindled?' I questioned. I watched to see whether it would spread: but no; as it did not diminish, so it did not enlarge. 'It may be a candle in a house,' I then conjectured; 'but if so, I can never reach it. It is much too far away: and were it within a yard of me, what would it avail? I should but knock at the door to have it shut in my face.'

And I sank down where I stood, and hid my face against the ground. I lay still a while: the night-wind swept over the hill and over me, and died moaning in the distance; the rain fell fast, wetting me afresh to the skin. Could I but have stiffened to the still frost – the friendly numbness of death – it might have pelted on; I should not have felt it; but my yet living flesh shuddered at its chilling influence. I rose ere long.

The light was yet there, shining dim but constant through the rain. I tried to walk again: I dragged my exhausted limbs slowly towards it. It led me aslant over the hill, through a wide bog, which would have been impassable in winter, and was splashy and shaking even now, in the height of summer. Here I fell twice; but as often I rose and rallied my faculties. This light was my forlorn hope: I must gain it.

Having crossed the marsh, I saw a trace of white over the moor. I approached it; it was a road or a track: it led straight up to the light, which now beamed from a sort of knoll, amidst a clump of trees – firs, apparently, from what I could distinguish of the character of their forms and foliage through the gloom. My star vanished as I drew near; some obstacle had intervened between me and it. I put out my hand to feel the dark mass before me: I discriminated the rough stones of a low wall – above it, something like palisades, and within, a high and prickly hedge. I groped on. Again a whitish object gleamed before me: it was a gate – a wicket; it moved on its hinges as I touched it. On each side stood a sable bush – holly or yew.

Entering the gate and passing the shrubs, the silhouette of a house rose to view, black, low, and rather long; but the guiding light shone nowhere. All was obscurity. Were the inmates retired to rest? I feared it must be so. In seeking the door, I turned an angle; there shot out the friendly gleam again, from the lozenged panes of a very small latticed window, within a foot of the ground, made still smaller by the growth of ivy or some other creeping plant, whose leaves clustered thick over the portion of the house wall in which it was set. The aperture was so screened and narrow, that curtain or shutter had been deemed unnecessary; and when I stooped down and put aside the spray of foliage shooting over it, I could see all within. I could see clearly a room with a sanded floor, clean scoured; a dresser of walnut, with pewter plates ranged in rows, reflecting the redness and radiance of a glowing peat fire. I could see a clock, a white deal table, some chairs. The candle, whose rays had been my beacon, burnt on the table; and by its light an elderly woman, somewhat rough-looking, but scrupulously clean, like all about her, was knitting a stocking.

I noticed these objects cursorily only – in them there was nothing extraordinary.

# Jane Eyre

A group of more interest appeared near the hearth, sitting still amidst the rosy peace and warmth suffusing it. Two young, graceful women – ladies in every point – sat, one in a low rocking-chair, the other on a lower stool; both wore deep mourning of crape and bombazeen, which sombre garb singularly set off very fair necks and faces: a large old pointer dog rested its massive head on the knee of one girl – in the lap of the other was cushioned a black cat.

A strange place was this humble kitchen for such occupants! Who were they? They could not be the daughters of the elderly person at the table; for she looked like a rustic, and they were all delicacy and cultivation. I had nowhere seen such faces as theirs: and yet, as I gazed on them, I seemed intimate with every lineament. I cannot call them handsome – they were too pale and grave for the word; as they each bent over a book, they looked thoughtful almost to severity. A stand between them supported a second candle and two great volumes, to which they frequently referred, comparing them, seemingly, with the smaller books they held in their hands, like people consulting a dictionary to aid them in the task of translation. This scene was as silent as if all the figures had been shadows and the firelit apartment a picture: so hushed was it, I could hear the cinders fall from the grate, the clock tick in its obscure corner; and I even fancied I could distinguish the click-click of the woman's knitting-needles. When, therefore, a voice broke the strange stillness at last, it was audible enough to me.

'Listen, Diana,' said one of the absorbed students, 'Franz and old Daniel are together in the night-time, and Franz is telling a dream from which he has awakened in terror – listen!' And in a low voice she read something, of which not one word was intelligible to me; for it was in an unknown tongue – neither French nor Latin. Whether it were Greek or German I could not tell.

'That is strong,' she said, when she had finished: 'I relish it.' The other girl, who had lifted her head to listen to her sister, repeated, while she gazed at the fire, a line of what had been read. At a later day, I knew the language and the book; therefore, I will here quote the line: though, when I first heard it, it was only like a stroke on sounding brass to me – conveying no meaning –

'"Da trat hervor Einer, anzusehen wie die Sternen Nacht." Good! good!' she exclaimed, while her dark and deep eye sparkled. 'There you have a dim and mighty archangel fitly set before you! The line is worth a hundred pages of fustian. "Ich wäge die Gedanken in der Schale meines Zornes und die Werke mit dem Gewichte meines Grimms." I like it!'

Both were again silent.

'Is there ony country where they talk i' that way?' asked the old woman, looking up from her knitting.

'Yes, Hannah – a far larger country than England, where they talk in no other way.'

'Well, for sure case, I knawn't how they can understand t' one t'other: and if either o' ye went there, ye could tell what they said, I guess?'

'We could probably tell something of what they said, but not all – for we are not as clever as you think us, Hannah. We don't speak German, and we cannot read it without a dictionary to help us.'

'And what good does it do you?'

'We mean to teach it sometime – or at least, elements, as they say; and then we shall get more money than we do now.'

'Varry like: but give ower studying; ye've done enough for to-night.'

# Jane Eyre

'I think we have: at least I am tired. Mary, are you?'

'Mortally: after all, it's tough work fagging away at a language with no master but a lexicon.'

'It is: especially with such a language as this crabbed but glorious Deutsch. I wonder when St John will come home.'

'Surely he will not be long now; it is just ten (looking at a little gold watch she drew from her girdle). It rains fast. Hannah, will you have the goodness to look at the fire in the parlour?'

The woman rose: she opened a door, through which I dimly saw a passage: soon I heard her stir a fire in an inner room: she presently came back.

'Ah, childer!' said she, 'it fair troubles me to go into yond' room now: it looks so lonesome wi' the chair empty and set back in the corner.'

She wiped her eyes with her apron: the two girls, grave before, looked sad now.

'But he is in a better place,' continued Hannah: 'we shouldn't wish him here again. And then, nobody need have a quieter death nor he had.'

'You say he never mentioned us?' inquired one of the ladies.

'He hadn't time, bairn: he was gone in a minute, was your father. He had been a bit ailing like the day before, but naught to signify; and when Mr St John asked if he would like either of you to be sent for, he fair laughed at him. He began again with a bit of a heaviness in his head the next day – that is, a fortnight sin' – and he went to sleep and niver wakened: he wor a'most stark when your brother went into t' chamber and fand him. Ah, childer! that's t' last o' t' old stock, for ye and Mr St John is like of different soart to them 'at's gone: for all your mother wor mich i' your way, and a'most as book-learned. She wor the pictur' o' ye, Mary: Diana is more like your father.'

I thought them so similar I could not tell where the old servant (for such I now concluded her to be) saw the difference. Both were fair complexioned and slenderly made; both possessed faces full of distinction and intelligence. One, to be sure, had hair a shade darker than the other, and there was a difference in their style of wearing it: Mary's pale brown locks were parted and braided smooth; Diana's duskier tresses covered her neck with thick curls. The clock struck ten.

'Ye'll want your supper, I am sure,' observed Hannah; 'and so will Mr St John when he comes in.'

And she proceeded to prepare the meal. The ladies rose; they seemed about to withdraw to the parlour. Till this moment, I had been so intent on watching them, their appearance and conversation had excited in me so keen an interest, I had half-forgotten my own wretched position: now it recurred to me. More desolate, more desperate than ever, it seemed from contrast. And how impossible did it appear to touch the inmates of this house with concern on my behalf; to make them believe in the truth of my wants and woes; to induce them to vouchsafe a rest for my wanderings! As I groped out the door, and knocked at it hesitatingly, I felt that last idea to be a mere chimera. Hannah opened.

'What do you want?' she inquired in a voice of surprise, as she surveyed me by the light of the candle she held.

'May I speak to your mistresses?' I said.

'You had better tell me what you have to say to them. Where do you come from?'

'I am a stranger.'

'What is your business here at this hour?'

'I want a night's shelter in an outhouse or anywhere, and a morsel of bread to eat.'

Distrust, the very feeling I dreaded, appeared in Hannah's face. 'I'll give you a piece of bread,' she said, after a pause: 'but we can't take in a vagrant to lodge. It isn't likely.'

'Do let me speak to your mistresses.'

'No, not I. What can they do for you? You should not be roving about now; it looks very ill.'

'But where shall I go if you drive me away? What shall I do?'

'Oh, I'll warrant you know where to go and what to do. Mind you don't do wrong, that's all. Here is a penny; now go –'

'A penny cannot feed me, and I have no strength to go farther. Don't shut the door: oh, don't, for God's sake!'

'I must; the rain is driving in –'

'Tell the young ladies. Let me see them –'

'Indeed I will not. You are not what you ought to be, or you wouldn't make such a noise. Move off.'

'But I must die if I am turned away.'

'Not you. I'm feared you have some ill plans agate, that bring you about folks' houses at this time o' night. If you've any followers – housebreakers or such like – anywhere near, you may tell them we are not by ourselves in the house; we have a gentleman, and dogs, and guns.' Here the honest but inflexible servant clapped the door to and bolted it within.

This was the climax. A pang of exquisite suffering – a throe of true despair – rent and heaved my heart. Worn out, indeed, I was; not another step could I stir. I sank on the wet doorstep; I groaned – I wrung my hands – I wept in utter anguish. Oh, this spectre of death! Oh, this last hour, approaching in such horror! Alas, this isolation – this banishment from my kind! Not only the anchor of hope, but the footing of fortitude was gone – at least for a moment; but the last I soon endeavoured to regain.

'I can but die,' I said, 'and I believe in God. Let me try to wait His will in silence.'

These words I not only thought, but uttered; and thrusting back all my misery into my heart, I made an effort to compel it to remain there – dumb and still.

'All men must die,' said a voice quite close at hand; 'but all are not condemned to meet a lingering and premature doom, such as yours would be if you perished here of want.'

'Who or what speaks?' I asked, terrified at the unexpected sound, and incapable now of deriving from any occurrence a hope of aid. A form was near – what form, the pitch-dark night and my enfeebled vision prevented me from distinguishing. With a loud, long knock, the new-comer appealed to the door.

'Is that you, Mr St John?' cried Hannah.

'Yes – yes; open quickly.'

'Well, how wet and cold you must be, such a wild night as it is! Come in – your sisters are quite uneasy about you, and I believe there are bad folks about. There has been a beggar-woman – I declare she is not gone yet! – laid down there. Get up! for shame! Move off, I say!'

# Jane Eyre

'Hush, Hannah! I have a word to say to the woman. You have done your duty in excluding, now let me do mine in admitting her. I was near, and listened to both you and her. I think this is a peculiar case – I must at least examine into it. Young woman, rise, and pass before me into the house.'

With difficulty I obeyed him. Presently I stood within that clean, bright kitchen – on the very hearth – trembling, sickening; conscious of an aspect in the last degree ghastly, wild, and weather-beaten. The two ladies, their brother, Mr St John, the old servant, were all gazing at me.

'St John, who is it?' I heard one ask.

'I cannot tell: I found her at the door,' was the reply.

'She does look white,' said Hannah.

'As white as clay or death,' was responded. 'She will fall: let her sit.'

And indeed my head swam: I dropped; but a chair received me. I still possessed my senses, though just now I could not speak.

'Perhaps a little water would restore her, Hannah, fetch some. But she is worn to nothing. How very thin, and how very bloodless!'

'A mere spectre!'

'Is she ill, or only famished?'

'Famished I think. Hannah, is that milk? Give it me, and a piece of bread.'

Diana (I knew her by the long curls which I saw drooping between me and the fire as she bent over me) broke some bread, dipped it in milk, and put it to my lips. Her face was near mine: I saw there was pity in it, and I felt sympathy in her hurried breathing. In her simple words, too, the same balm-like emotion spoke: 'Try to eat.'

'Yes – try,' repeated Mary gently; and Mary's hand removed my sodden bonnet and lifted my head. I tasted what they offered me: feebly at first, eagerly soon.

'Not too much at first – restrain her,' said the brother; 'she has had enough.' And he withdrew the cup of milk and the plate of bread.

'A little more, St John – look at the avidity in her eyes.'

'No more at present, sister. Try if she can speak now – ask her her name.'

I felt I could speak, and I answered, 'My name is Jane Elliott.' Anxious as ever to avoid discovery I had before resolved to assume an *alias*.

'And where do you live? Where are your friends?'

I was silent.

'Can we send for any one you know?'

I shook my head.

'What account can you give of yourself?'

Somehow, now that I had once crossed the threshold of this house, and once was brought face to face with its owners, I felt no longer outcast, vagrant, and disowned by the wide world. I dared to put off the mendicant – to resume my natural manner and character. I began once more to know myself; and when Mr St John demanded an account – which at present I was far too weak to render – I said after a brief pause –

'Sir, I can give you no details to-night.'

'But what then,' said he, 'do you expect me to do for you?'

'Nothing,' I replied. My strength sufficed but for short answers. Diana took the word –

'Do you mean,' she asked, 'that we have now given you what aid you require? and that we may dismiss you to the moor and the rainy night?'

I looked at her. She had, I thought, a remarkable countenance, instinct both with power and goodness. I took sudden courage. Answering her compassionate gaze with a smile, I said, 'I will trust you. If I were a masterless and stray dog, I know that you would not turn me from your hearth to-night: as it is, I really have no fear. Do with me and for me as you like; but excuse me from much discourse – my breath is short – I feel a spasm when I speak.' All three surveyed me, and all three were silent.

'Hannah,' said Mr St John at last, 'let her sit there at present, and ask her no questions; in ten minutes more, give her the remainder of that bread and milk. Mary and Diana, let us go into the parlour and talk the matter over.'

They withdrew. Very soon one of the ladies returned – I could not tell which. A kind of pleasant stupor was stealing over me as I sat by the genial fire. In an undertone she gave some directions to Hannah. Ere long, with the servant's aid, I contrived to mount a staircase; my dripping clothes were removed; soon a warm, dry bed received me. I thanked God – experienced amidst unutterable exhaustion a glow of grateful joy – and slept.

# Chapter 29

The recollection of about three days and nights succeeding this is very dim in my mind. I can recall some sensations felt in that interval; but few thoughts framed, and no actions performed. I knew I was in a small room and in a narrow bed. To that bed I seemed to have grown; I lay on it motionless as a stone; and to have torn me from it would have been almost to kill me. I took no note of the lapse of time – of the change from morning to noon, from noon to evening. I observed when any one entered or left the apartment: I could even tell who they were; I could understand what was said when the speaker stood near me; but I could not answer; to open my lips or move my limbs was equally impossible. Hannah, the servant, was my most frequent visitor. Her coming disturbed me. I had a feeling that she wished me away; that she did not understand me or my circumstances; that she was prejudiced against me. Diana and Mary appeared in the chamber once or twice a day. They would whisper sentences of this sort at my bedside –

'It is very well we took her in.'

'Yes; she would certainly have been found dead at the door in the morning, had she been left out all night. I wonder what she has gone through?'

'Strange hardships, I imagine – poor, emaciated, pallid wanderer!'

'She is not an uneducated person, I should think, by her manner of speaking;

her accent was quite pure; and the clothes she took off, though splashed and wet, were little worn and fine.'

'She has a peculiar face; fleshless and haggard as it is, I rather like it; and when in good health and animated I can fancy her physiognomy would be agreeable.'

Never once in their dialogues did I hear a syllable of regret at the hospitality they had extended to me, or of suspicion of, or aversion to, myself. I was comforted.

Mr St John came but once: he looked at me, and said my state of lethargy was the result of reaction from excessive and protracted fatigue. He pronounced it needless to send for a doctor: nature, he was sure, would manage best, left to herself. He said every nerve had been overstrained in some way, and the whole system must sleep torpid a while. There was no disease. He imagined my recovery would be rapid enough when once commenced. These opinions he delivered in a few words, in a quiet, low voice; and added, after a pause, in the tone of a man little accustomed to expansive comment, 'Rather an unusual physiognomy; certainly, not indicative of vulgarity or degradation.'

'Far otherwise,' responded Diana. 'To speak truth, St John, my heart rather warms to the poor little soul. I wish we may be able to benefit her permanently.'

'That is hardly likely,' was the reply. 'You will find she is some young lady who has had a misunderstanding with her friends, and has probably injudiciously left them. We may, perhaps, succeed in restoring her to them, if she is not obstinate: but I trace lines of force in her face which make me sceptical of her tractability.' He stood considering me some minutes; then added, 'She looks sensible, but not at all handsome.'

'She is so ill, St John.'

'Ill or well, she would always be plain. The grace and harmony of beauty are quite wanting in those features.'

On the third day I was better; on the fourth, I could speak, move, rise in bed, and turn. Hannah had brought me some gruel and dry toast, about, as I supposed, the dinner-hour. I had eaten with relish: the food was good – void of the feverish flavour which had hitherto poisoned what I had swallowed. When she left me. I felt comparatively strong and revived: ere long, satiety of repose and desire for action stirred me. I wished to rise; but what could I put on? Only my damp and bemired apparel, in which I had slept on the ground and fallen in the marsh. I felt ashamed to appear before my benefactors so clad. I was spared the humiliation.

On a chair by the bedside were all my own things, clean and dry. My black silk frock hung against the wall. The traces of the bog were removed from it; the creases left by the wet smoothed out: it was quite decent. My very shoes and stockings were purified and rendered presentable. There were the means of washing in the room, and a comb and brush to smooth my hair. After a weary process, and resting every five minutes, I succeeded in dressing myself. My clothes hung loose on me, for I was much wasted; but I covered deficiencies with a shawl, and once more, clean and respectable-looking – no speck of the dirt, no trace of the disorder I so hated, and which seemed so to degrade me, left – I crept down a stone staircase with the aid of the banisters, to a narrow, low passage, and found my way presently to the kitchen.

It was full of the fragrance of new bread and the warmth of a generous fire.

# Jane Eyre

Hannah was baking. Prejudices, it is well known, are most difficult to eradicate from the heart whose soil has never been loosened or fertilized by education; they grow there, firm as weeds among stones. Hannah had been cold and stiff, indeed, at the first: latterly she had begun to relent a little; and when she saw me come in tidy and well-dressed, she even smiled.

'What, you have got up!' she said. 'You are better, then. You may sit you down in my chair on the hearthstone, if you will.'

She pointed to the rocking-chair: I took it. She bustled about, examining me every now and then with the corner of her eye. Turning to me, as she took some loaves from the oven, she asked bluntly –

'Did you ever go a-begging afore you came here?'

I was indignant for a moment; but remembering that anger was out of the question, and that I had indeed appeared as a beggar to her, I answered quietly, but still not without a certain marked firmness –

'You are mistaken in supposing me a beggar. I am no beggar; any more than yourself or your young ladies.'

After a pause she said, 'I dunnut understand that: you've like no house, nor no brass, I guess?'

'The want of house or brass (by which I suppose you mean money) does not make a beggar in your sense of the word.'

'Are you book-learned?' she inquired presently.

'Yes, very.'

'But you've never been to a boarding-school?'

'I was at a boarding-school eight years.'

She opened her eyes wide. 'Whatever cannot ye keep yourself for, then?'

'I have kept myself; and, I trust, shall keep myself again. What are you going to do with these gooseberries?' I inquired, as she brought out a basket of the fruit.

'Mak' 'em into pies.'

'Give them to me and I'll pick them.'

'Nay; I dunnut want ye to do nought.'

'But I must do something. Let me have them.'

She consented; and she even brought me a clean towel to spread over my dress, 'lest,' as she said, 'I should mucky it.'

'Ye've not been used to sarvant's wark, I see by your hands,' she remarked. 'Happen ye've been a dressmaker?'

'No, you are wrong. And now, never mind what I have been: don't trouble your head further about me; but tell me the name of the house where we are.'

'Some calls it Marsh End, and some calls it Moor House.'

'And the gentleman who lives here is called Mr St John?'

'Nay; he doesn't live here: he is only staying a while. When he is at home, he is in his own parish at Morton.'

'That village a few miles off?'

'Ay.'

'And what is he?'

'He is a parson.'

I remembered the answer of the old housekeeper at the parsonage, when I had asked to see the clergyman. 'This, then, was his father's residence?'

# Jane Eyre

'Ay; old Mr Rivers lived here, and his father, and grandfather, and gurt (great) grandfather afore him.'

'The name, then, of that gentleman is Mr St John Rivers?'

'Ay; St John is like his kirstened name.'

'And his sisters are called Diana and Mary Rivers?'

'Yes.'

'Their father is dead?'

'Dead three weeks sin' of a stroke.'

'They have no mother?'

'The mistress has been dead this mony a year.'

'Have you lived with the family long?'

'I've lived here thirty year. I nursed them all three.'

'That proves you must have been an honest and faithful servant. I will say so much for you, though you have had the incivility to call me a beggar.'

She again regarded me with a surprised stare. 'I believe,' she said, 'I was quite mista'en in my thoughts of you: but there is so mony cheats goes about, you mun forgie me.'

'And though,' I continued, rather severely, 'you wished to turn me from the door, on a night when you should not have shut out a dog.'

'Well, it was hard: but what can a body do? I thought more o' th' childer nor of mysel': poor things! They've like nobody to tak' care on 'em but me. I'm like to look sharpish.'

I maintained a grave silence for some minutes.

'You munnit think too hardly of me,' she again remarked.

'But I do think hardly of you,' I said; 'and I'll tell you why – not so much because you refused to give me shelter, or regarded me as an impostor, as because you just now made it a species of reproach that I had no "brass" and no house. Some of the best people that ever lived here have been as destitute as I am; and if you are a Christian, you ought not to consider poverty a crime.'

'No more I ought,' said she: 'Mr St John tells me so, too; and I see I wor wrang – but I've clear a different notion on you now to what I had. You look a raight down dacent little crater.'

'That will do – I forgive you now. Shake hands.'

She put her floury and horny hand into mine; another and heartier smile illumined her rough face, and from that moment we were friends.

Hannah was evidently fond of talking. While I picked the fruit, and she made the paste for the pies, she proceeded to give me sundry details about her deceased master and mistress, and 'the childer', as she called the young people.

Old Mr Rivers, she said, was a plain man enough, but a gentleman, and of as ancient a family as could be found. Marsh End had belonged to the Rivers ever since it was a house: and it was, she affirmed, 'aboon two hundred years old – for all it looked but a small, humble place, naught to compare wi' Mr Oliver's grand hall down i' Morton Vale. But she could remember Bill Oliver's father, a journeyman needlemaker; and th' Rivers wor gentry i' th' owd days o' th' Henrys, as onybody might see by looking into th' registers i' Morton Church vestry.' Still, she allowed, 'the owd maister was like other folk – naught mich out o' t' common way: stark mad o' shooting, and farming, and sich-like.' The mistress was different. She was a great reader, and studied a deal; and the 'bairns' had taken after her. There was nothing like them in these parts, nor

ever had been; they had liked learning, all three, almost from the time they could speak; and they had always been 'of a mak' of their own'. Mr St John, when he grew up, would go to a college and be a parson; and the girls, as soon as they left school, would seek places as governesses: for they had told her their father had some years ago lost a great deal of money by a man he had trusted turning bankrupt; and as he was now not rich enough to give them fortunes, they must provide for themselves. They had lived very little at home for a long while, and were only come now to stay a few weeks on account of their father's death; but they did so like Marsh End and Morton, and all these moors and hills about. They had been in London, and many other grand towns: but they always said there was no place like home; and then they were so agreeable with each other – never fell out nor 'threaped'. She did not know where there was such a family for being united.

Having finished my task of gooseberry picking, I asked where the two ladies and their brother were now.

'Gone over to Morton for a walk; but they would be back in half an hour to tea.'

They returned within the time Hannah had allotted them; they entered by the kitchen door. Mr St John, when he saw me, merely bowed and passed through; the two ladies stopped: Mary, in a few words, kindly and calmly expressed the pleasure she felt in seeing me well enough to be able to come down; Diana took my hand: she shook her head at me.

'You should have waited for my leave to descend,' she said. 'You still look very pale – and so thin! Poor child! – poor girl!'

Diana had a voice toned, to my ear, like the cooing of a dove. She possessed eyes whose gaze I delighted to encounter. Her whole face seemed to me full of charm. Mary's countenance was equally intelligent – her features equally pretty; but her expression was more reserved, and her manners, though gentle, more distant. Diana looked and spoke with a certain authority: she had a will, evidently. It was my nature to feel pleasure in yielding to an authority supported like hers, and to bend, where my conscience and self-respect permitted, to an active will.

'And what business have you here?' she continued. 'It is not your place. Mary and I sit in the kitchen sometimes, because at home we like to be free, even to licence – but you are a visitor, and must go into the parlour.'

'I am very well here.'

'Not at all, with Hannah bustling about and covering you with flour.'

'Besides, the fire is too hot for you.' interposed Mary.

'To be sure,' added her sister. 'Come, you must be obedient.' And still holding my hand she made me rise, and led me into the inner room.

'Sit there,' she said, placing me on the sofa, 'while we take our things off and get the tea ready; it is another privilege we exercise in our little moorland home – to prepare our own meals when we are so inclined, or when Hannah is baking, brewing, washing, or ironing.'

She closed the door, leaving me solus with Mr St John, who sat opposite, a book or newspaper in his hand. I examined first the parlour, and then its occupant.

The parlour was rather a small one, very plainly furnished, yet comfortable, because clean and neat. The old-fashioned chairs were very bright, and the

# Jane Eyre

walnut-wood table was like a looking-glass. A few strange, antique portraits of the men and women of other days decorated the stained walls; a cupboard with glass doors contained some books and an ancient set of china. There was no superfluous ornament in the room – not one modern piece of furniture, save a brace of work-boxes and a lady's desk in rosewood, which stood on a side-table: everything – including the carpet and curtains – looked at once well worn and well saved.

Mr St John – sitting as still as one of the study pictures on the walls, keeping his eyes fixed on the page he perused, and his lips mutely sealed – was easy enough to examine. Had he been a statue instead of a man, he could not have been easier. He was young – perhaps from twenty-eight to thirty – tall, slender; his face riveted the eye; it was like a Greek face, very pure in outline: quite a straight, classic nose; quite an Athenian mouth and chin. It is seldom, indeed, an English face comes so near the antique models as did his. He might well be a little shocked at the irregularity of my lineaments, his own being so harmonious. His eyes were large and blue, with brown lashes; his high forehead, colourless as ivory, was partially streaked over by careless locks of fair hair.

This is a gentle delineation, is it not, reader? Yet he whom it describes scarcely impressed one with the idea of a gentle, a yielding, an impressible, or even of a placid nature. Quiescent as he now sat, there was something about his nostril, his mouth, his brow, which, to my perceptions, indicated elements within either restless, or hard, or eager. He did not speak to me one word, nor even direct to me one glance, till his sisters returned. Diana, as she passed in and out, in the course of preparing tea, brought me a little cake, baked on the top of the oven.

'Eat that now,' she said: 'you must be hungry. Hannah says you have had nothing but some gruel since breakfast.'

I did not refuse it, for my appetite was awakened and keen. Mr Rivers now closed his book, approached the table, and, as he took a seat, fixed his blue pictorial-looking eyes full on me. There was an unceremonious directness, a searching, decided steadfastness in his gaze now, which told that intention, and not diffidence, had hitherto kept it averted from the stranger.

'You are very hungry,' he said.

'I am sir.' It is my way – it always was my way, by instinct – ever to meet the brief with brevity, the direct with plainness.

'It is well for you that a low fever has forced you to abstain for the last three days: there would have been danger in yielding to the cravings of your appetite at first. Now you may eat, though still not immoderately.'

'I trust I shall not eat long at your expense, sir,' was my very clumsily-contrived, unpolished answer.

'No,' he said coolly: 'when you have indicated to us the residence of your friends, we can write to them, and you may be restored to home.'

'That, I must plainly tell you, is out of my power to do; being absolutely without home and friends.'

The three looked at me, but not distrustfully; I felt there was no suspicion in their glances, there was more of curiosity. I speak particularly of the young ladies. St John's eyes, though clear enough in a literal sense, in a figurative one were difficult to fathom. He seemed to use them rather as instruments to search other people's thoughts, than as agents to reveal his own: the which combination

of keenness and reserve was considerably more calculated to embarrass than to encourage.

'Do you mean to say,' he asked, 'that you are completely isolated from every connexion?'

'I do. Not a tie links me to any living thing: not a claim do I possess to admittance under any roof in England.'

'A most singular position at your age!'

Here I saw his glance directed to my hands, which were folded on the table before me. I wondered what he sought there: his words soon explained the quest.

'You have never been married? You are a spinster?'

Diana laughed. 'Why, she can't be above seventeen or eighteen years old, St John,' said she.

'I am near nineteen: but I am not married. No.'

I felt a burning glow mount to my face; for bitter and agitating recollections were awakened by the allusion to marriage. They all saw the embarrassment and the emotion. Diana and Mary relieved me by turning their eyes elsewhere than to my crimsoned visage: but the colder and sterner brother continued to gaze, till the trouble he had excited forced out tears as well as colour.

'Where did you last reside?' he now asked.

'You are too inquisitive, St John,' murmured Mary in a low voice; but he leaned over the table and required answer by a second firm and piercing look.

'The name of the place where, and of the person with whom I lived, is my secret,' I replied concisely.

'Which, if you like, you have, in my opinion, a right to keep, both from St John and every other questioner,' remarked Diana.

'Yet if I know nothing about you or your history, I cannot help you,' he said. 'And you need help, do you not?'

'I need it, and I seek it so far, sir, that some true philanthropist will put me in the way of getting work which I can do, and the remuneration for which will keep me, if but in the barest necessaries of life.'

'I know not whether I am a true philanthropist; yet I am willing to aid you to the utmost of my power in a purpose so honest. First, then, tell me what you have been accustomed to do, and what you *can* do.'

I had now swallowed my tea. I was mightily refreshed by the beverage; as much so as a giant with wine: it gave new tone to my unstrung nerves, and enabled me to address this penetrating young judge steadily.

'Mr Rivers,' I said, turning to him, and looking at him, as he looked at me, openly and without diffidence, 'you and your sisters have done me a great service – the greatest man can do his fellow-being; you have rescued me, by your noble hospitality, from death. This benefit conferred gives you an unlimited claim on my gratitude, and a claim, to a certain extent, on my confidence. I will tell you as much of the history of the wanderer you have harboured, as I can tell without compromising my own peace of mind – my own security, moral and physical, and that of others.

'I am an orphan, the daughter of a clergyman. My parents died before I could know them. I was brought up a dependant; educated in a charitable institution. I will even tell you the name of the establishment, where I passed six years as a pupil, and two as a teacher – Lowood Orphan Asylum, —shire: you will have heard of it, Mr Rivers? – the Rev. Robert Brocklehurst is the treasurer.'

# Jane Eyre

'I have heard of Mr Brocklehurst, and I have seen the school.'

'I left Lowood nearly a year since to become a private governess. I obtained a good situation, and was happy. This place I was obliged to leave four days before I came here. The reason of my departure I cannot and ought not to explain: it would be useless, dangerous, and would sound incredible. No blame attached to me: I am as free from culpability as any one of you three. Miserable I am, and must be for a time; for the catastrophe which drove me from a house I had found a paradise was of a strange and direful nature. I observed but two points in planning my departure – speed, secrecy: to secure these, I had to leave behind me everything I possessed except a small parcel; which, in my hurry, and trouble of mind, I forgot to take out of the coach that brought me to Whitcross. To this neighbourhood, then, I came, quite destitute. I slept two nights in the open air, and wandered about two days without crossing a threshold: but twice in that space of time did I taste food; and it was when brought by hunger, exhaustion, and despair almost to the last gasp, that you, Mr Rivers, forbade me to perish of want at your door, and took me under the shelter of your roof. I know all your sisters have done for me since – for I have not been insensible during my seeming torpor – and I owe to their spontaneous, genuine, genial compassion as large a debt as to your evangelical charity.'

'Don't make her talk any more now, St John,' said Diana, as I paused; 'she is evidently not yet for excitement. Come to the sofa and sit down now, Miss Elliott.'

I gave an involuntary half-start at hearing the *alias*: I had forgotten my new name. Mr Rivers, whom nothing seemed to escape, noticed it at once.

'You said your name was Jane Elliot?' he observed.

'I did say so; and it is the name by which I think it expedient to be called at present; but it is not my real name, and when I hear it, it sounds strange to me.'

'Your real name you will not give?'

'No: I fear discovery above all things; and whatever disclosure would lead to it, I avoid.'

'You are quite right, I am sure,' said Diana. 'Now do, brother, let her be at peace a while.'

But when St John had mused a few movements he recommenced as imperturbably and with as much acumen as ever.

'You would not like to be long dependent on our hospitality – you would wish, I see, to dispense as soon as may be with my sisters' compassion, and, above all, with my *charity* (I am quite sensible of the distinction drawn, nor do I resent it – it is just): you desire to be independent of us?'

'I do: I have already said so. Show me how to work, or how to seek work; that is all I now ask; then let me go, if it be but to the meanest cottage; but *till then,* allow me to stay here: I dread another essay of the horrors of homeless destitution.'

'Indeed you *shall* stay here,' said Diana, putting her white hand on my head, 'You *shall,*' repeated Mary, in the tone of undemonstrative sincerity which seemed natural to her.

'My sisters, you see, have a pleasure in keeping you,' said Mr St John, 'as they would have a pleasure in keeping and cherishing a half-frozen bird some wintry wind might have driven through their casement. *I* feel more inclination to put you in the way of keeping yourself, and shall endeavour to do so; but

observe, my sphere is narrow. I am but the incumbent of a poor country parish: my aid must be of the humblest sort. And if you are inclined to despise the day of small things, seek some more efficient succour than such as I can offer.'

'She has already said that she is willing to do anything honest she *can* do,' answered Diana for me; 'and you know, St John, she has no choice of helpers: she is forced to put up with such crusty people as you.'

'I will be a dressmaker; I will be a plain-workwoman; I will be a servant, a nurse-girl, if I can be no better,' I answered.

'Right,' said Mr St John, quite coolly. 'If such is your spirit, I promise to aid you, in my own time and way.'

He now resumed the book with which he had been occupied before tea. I soon withdrew, for I had talked as much, and sat up as long, as my present strength would permit.

# Chapter 30

The more I knew of the inmates of Moor House, the better I liked them. In a few days I had so far recovered my health that I could sit up all day, and walk out sometimes. I could join with Diana and Mary in all their occupations, converse with them as much as they wished, and aid them when and where they would allow me. There was a reviving pleasure in this intercourse, of a kind now tasted by me for the first time – the pleasure arising from perfect congeniality of tastes, sentiments, and principles.

I liked to read what they liked to read: what they enjoyed, delighted me; what they approved I reverenced. They loved their sequestered home. I, too, in the gray, small, antique structure – with its low roof, its latticed casements, its mouldering walls, its avenue of aged firs, all grown aslant under the stress of mountain winds; its garden, dark with yew and holly, and where no flowers but of the hardiest species would bloom – found a charm both potent and permanent. They clung to the purple moors behind and around their dwelling – to the hollow vale into which the pebbly bridle-path leading from their gate descended, and which wound between fern-banks first, and then among a few of the wildest little pasture-fields that ever bordered, a wilderness of heath, or gave sustenance to a flock of gray moorland sheep, with their little mossy-faced lambs – they clung to this scene, I say, with a perfect enthusiasm of attachment. I could comprehend the feeling, and share both its strength and truth. I saw the fascination of the locality. I felt the consecration of its loneliness: my eye feasted on the outline of swell and sweep – on the wild colouring communicated to ridge and dell by moss, by heathbell, by flower-sprinkled turf, by brilliant bracken, and mellow granite crag. These details were just to me what they were to them – so many pure and sweet sources of pleasure. The strong blast and the soft

# Jane Eyre

breeze, the rough and the halcyon day, the hours of sunrise and sunset, the moonlight and the clouded night, developed for me, in these regions, the same attraction as for them – wound round my faculties the same spell that entranced theirs.

Indoors we agreed equally well. They were both more accomplished and better read than I was; but with eagerness I followed in the path of knowledge they had trodden before me. I devoured the books they lent me: then it was full satisfaction to discuss with them in the evening what I had perused during the day. Thought fitted thought: opinion met opinion: we coincided, in short, perfectly.

If in our trio there was a superior and a leader it was Diana. Physically, she far excelled me: she was handsome: she was vigorous. In her animal spirits there was an affluence of life and certainty of flow, such as excited my wonder, while it baffled my comprehension. I could talk a while when the evening commenced, but the first gush of vivacity and fluency gone, I was fain to sit on a stool at Diana's feet, to rest my head on her knee, and listen alternately to her and Mary, while they sounded thoroughly the topic on which I had but touched. Diana offered to teach me German. I liked to learn of her; I saw the part of instructress pleased and suited her; that of scholar pleased and suited me no less. Our natures dovetailed: mutual affection – of the strongest kind – was the result. They discovered I could draw: their pencils and colour-boxes were immediately at my service. My skill, greater in this one point than theirs, surprised and charmed them. Mary would sit and watch me by the hour together: then she would take lessons: and a docile, intelligent, assiduous pupil she made. Thus occupied, and mutually entertained, days passed like hours, and weeks like days.

As to Mr St John, the intimacy which had arisen so naturally and rapidly between me and his sisters did not extend to him. One reason of the distance yet observed between us was, that he was comparatively seldom at home: a large proportion of his time appeared devoted to visiting the sick and poor among the scattered population of his parish.

No weather seemed to hinder him in these pastoral excursions: rain or fair, he would, when his hours of morning study were over, take his hat, and, followed by his father's old pointer, Carlo, go out on his mission of love or duty – I scarcely know in which light he regarded it. Sometimes, when the day was very unfavourable, his sisters would expostulate. He would then say, with a peculiar smile, more solemn than cheerful –

'And if I let a gust of wind or a sprinkling of rain turn me aside from these easy tasks, what preparation would such sloth be for the future I propose to myself?'

Diana and Mary's general answer to this question was a sigh, and some minutes of apparently mournful meditation.

But besides his frequent absences, there was another barrier to friendship with him: he seemed of a reserved, an abstracted, and even of a brooding nature. Zealous in his ministerial labours, blameless in his life and habits, he yet did not appear to enjoy that mental serenity, that inward content, which should be the reward of every sincere Christian and practical philanthropist. Often, of an evening, when he sat at the window, his desk and papers before him, he would cease reading or writing, rest his chin on his hand, and deliver himself up to I

know not what course of thought; but that it was perturbed and exciting might be seen in the frequent flash and changeful dilation of his eye.

I think, moreover, that nature was not to him that treasury of delight it was to his sisters. He expressed once, and but once in my hearing, a strong sense of the rugged charm of the hills, and an inborn affection for the dark and hoary walls he called his home; but there was more of a gloom than pleasure in the tone and words in which the sentiment was manifested; and never did he seem to roam the moors for the sake of their soothing silence – never seek out or dwell upon the thousand peaceful delights they could yield.

Incommunicative as he was, some time elaspsed before I had an opportunity of gauging his mind. I first got an idea of its calibre when I heard him preach in his own church at Morton. I wish I could describe that sermon: but it is past my power. I cannot even render faithfully the effect it produced on me.

It began calm – and indeed, as far as delivery and pitch of voice went, it was calm to the end: an earnestly felt, yet strictly restrained zeal breathed soon in the distinct accents, and prompted the nervous language. This grew to force – compressed, condensed, controlled. The heart was thrilled, the mind astonished, by the power of the preacher: neither were softened. Throughout there was a strange bitterness; an absence of consolatory gentleness; stern allusions to Calvinistic doctrines – election, predestination, reprobation – were frequent; and each reference to these points sounded like a sentence pronounced for doom. When he had done, instead of feeling better, calmer, more enlightened by his discourse, I experienced an inexpressible sadness: for it seemed to me – I know not whether equally so to others – that the eloquence to which I had been listening had sprung from a depth where lay turbid dregs of disappointment, where moved troubling impulses of insatiate yearnings and disquieting aspirations. I was sure St John Rivers – pure-lived, conscientious, zealous as he was – had not yet found that peace of God which passeth all understanding: he had no more found it, I thought, than had I, with my concealed and racking regrets for my broken idol and lost elysium – regrets to which I have latterly avoided referring, but which possessed me and tyrannized over me ruthlessly.

Meantime a month was gone. Diana and Mary were soon to leave Moor House, and return to the far different life and scene which awaited them, as governesses in a large, fashionable south-of-England city, where each held a situation in families by whose wealthy and haughty members they were regarded only as humble dependants, and who neither knew nor sought one of their innate excellences, and appreciated only their acquired accomplishments as they appreciated the skill of their cook or the taste of their waiting-woman. Mr St John had said nothing to me yet about the employment he had promised to obtain for me: yet it became urgent that I should have a vocation of some kind. One morning, being left alone with him a few minutes in the parlour, I ventured to approach the window-recess which his table, chair, and desk consecrated as a kind of study; and I was going to speak, though not very well knowing in what words to frame my inquiry – for it is at all times difficult to break the ice of reserve glassing over such natures as his – when he saved me the trouble by being the first to commence a dialogue.

Looking up as I drew near – 'You have a question to ask of me?' he said.

'Yes, I wish to know whether you have heard of any service I can offer myself to undertake?'

# Jane Eyre

'I found or devised something for you three weeks ago; but as you seemed both useful and happy here – as my sisters had evidently become attached to you, and your society gave them unusual pleasure – I deemed it inexpedient to break in on your mutual comfort till their approaching departure from Marsh End should render yours necessary.'

'And they will go in three days now?' I said.

'Yes; and when they go, I shall return to the parsonage at Morton; Hannah will accompany me; and this old house will be shut up.'

I waited a few moments, expecting he would go on with the subject first broached: but he seemed to have entered another train of reflection: his look denoted abstraction from me and my business. I was obliged to recall him to a theme which was of necessity one of close and anxious interest to me.

'What is the employment you had in view, Mr Rivers? I hope this delay will not have increased the difficulty of securing it.'

'Oh, no; since it is an employment which depends only on me to give, and you to accept.'

He again paused: there seemed a reluctance to continue, I grew impatient: a restless movement or two, and an eager and exacting glance fastened on his face, conveyed the feeling to him as effectually as words could have done, and with less trouble.

'You need be in no hurry to hear,' he said; 'let me frankly tell you, I have nothing eligible or profitable to suggest. Before I explain, recall, if you please, my notice, early given, that if I helped you, it must be as the blind man would help the lame. I am poor; for I find that, when I have paid my father's debts, all the patrimony remaining to me will be this crumbling grange, the row of scathed firs behind, and the patch of moorish soil, with the yew-trees and holly-bushes in front. I am obscure: Rivers is an old name; but of the three sole descendants of the race, two earn the dependant's crust among strangers, and the third considers himself an alien from his native country – not only for life, but in death. Yes, and deems, and is bound to deem, himself honoured by the lot, and aspires but after the day when the cross of separation from fleshly ties shall be laid on his shoulders, and when the Head of that Church militant, of whose humblest members he is one, shall give the word, "Rise, follow Me!"'

St John said these words as he pronounced his sermons, with a quiet, deep voice; with an unflushed cheek, and a coruscating radiance of glance. He resumed –

'And since I am myself poor and obscure, I can offer you but a service of poverty and obscurity. *You* may even think it degrading – for I see now your habits have been what the world calls refined: your tastes lean to the ideal, and your society has at least been among the educated; but I consider that no service degrades which can better our race. I hold that the more arid and unreclaimed the soil where the Christian labourer's task of tillage is appointed him – the scantier the meed his toil brings – the higher the honour. His, under such circumstances, is the destiny of the pioneer; and the first pioneers of the Gospel were the Apostles – their captain was Jesus, the Redeemer, Himself.'

'Well?' I said, as he again paused, 'proceed.'

He looked at me before he proceeded: indeed, he seemed leisurely to read my face, as if its features and lines were characters on a page. The conclusions drawn from this scrutiny he partially expressed in his succeeding observations.

# Jane Eyre

'I believe you will accept the post I offer you,' said he, 'and hold it for a while: not permanently, though: any more than I could permanently keep the narrow and narrowing – the tranquil, hidden office of English country incumbent; for in your nature is an alloy as detrimental to repose as that in mine, though of a different kind.'

'Do explain,' I urged, when he halted once more.

'I will; and you shall hear how poor the proposal is – how trivial, how cramping. I shall not stay long at Morton, now that my father is dead, and that I am my own master. I shall leave the place probably in the course of a twelvemonth; but while I do stay, I will exert myself to the utmost for its improvement. Morton, when I came to it two years ago, had no school: the children of the poor were excluded from every hope of progress. I established one for boys: I mean now to open a second school for girls. I have hired a building for the purpose, with a cottage of two rooms attached to it for the mistress's house. Her salary will be thirty pounds a year: her house is already furnished, very simply, but sufficiently, by the kindness of a lady, Miss Oliver, the only daughter of the sole rich man in my parish – Mr Oliver, the proprietor of a needle-factory and iron-foundry in the valley. The same lady pays for the education and clothing of an orphan from the workhouse, on condition that she shall aid the mistress in such menial offices connected with her own house and the school as her occupation of teaching will prevent her having time to discharge in person. Will you be this mistress?'

He put the question rather hurriedly; he seemed half to expect an indignant or at least a disdainful rejection of the offer: not knowing all my thoughts and feelings, though guessing some, he could not tell in what light the lot would appear to me. In truth it was humble – but then it was sheltered, and I wanted a safe asylum; it was plodding – but then, compared with that of a governess in a rich house, it was independent, and the fear of servitude with strangers entered my soul like iron; it was not ignoble – not unworthy – not mentally degrading. I made my decision.

'I thank you for the proposal, Mr Rivers, and I accept it with all my heart.'

'But you comprehend me?' he said. 'It is a village school: your scholars will be only poor girls – cottagers' children – at the best, farmers' daughters. Knitting, sewing, reading, writing, ciphering, will be all you will have to teach. What will you do with your accomplishments? What, with the largest portion of your mind – sentiments – tastes?'

'Save them till they are wanted. They will keep.'

'You know what you undertake, then?'

'I do.'

He now smiled: and not a bitter or a sad smile, but one well pleased and deeply gratified.

'And when will you commence the exercise of your function?'

'I will go to my house to-morrow, and open the school, if you like, next week.'

'Very well: so be it.'

He rose and walked through the room. Standing still, he again looked at me. He shook his head.

'What do you disapprove of Mr Rivers?' I asked.

'You will not stay at Morton long: no, no!'

'Why? What is your reason for saying so?'

# Jane Eyre

'I read it in your eyes; it is not of that description which promises the maintenance of an even tenor in life.'

'I am not ambitious.'

He started at the word 'ambitious'. He repeated, 'No. What made you think of ambition? Who is ambitious? I know I am: but how did you find it out?'

'I was speaking of myself.'

'Well, if you are not ambitious, you are—' He paused.

'What?'

'I was going to say, impassioned: but perhaps you would have misunderstood the word, and been displeased. I mean that human affections and sympathies have a most powerful hold on you. I am sure you cannot long be content to pass your leisure in solitude, and to devote your working hours to a monotonous labour wholly void of stimulus: any more than I can be content,' he added, with emphasis, 'to live here buried in morass, pent in with mountain – my nature, that God gave me, contravened; my faculties, Heaven-bestowed, paralysed – made useless. You hear now how I contradict myself, I, who preached contentment with a humble lot, and justified the vocation even of hewers of wood and drawers of water in God's service – I, His ordained minister, almost rave in my restlessness. Well, propensities and principles must be reconciled by some means.'

He left the room. In this brief hour I had learnt more of him than in the whole previous month: yet still he puzzled me.

Diana and Mary Rivers became more sad and silent as the day approached for leaving their brother and their home. They both tried to appear as usual; but the sorrow they had to struggle against was one that could not be entirely conquered or concealed. Diana intimated that this would be a different parting from any they had ever yet known. It would probably, as far as St John was concerned, be a parting for years: it might be a parting for life.

'He will sacrifice all to his long-framed resolves,' she said: 'natural affection and feelings more potent still. St John looks quiet, Jane; but he hides a fever in his vitals. You would think him gentle, yet in some things he is inexorable as death; and the worst of it is, my conscience will hardly permit me to dissuade him from his severe decision: certainly, I cannot for a moment blame him for it. It is right, noble, Christian: yet it breaks my heart!' And the tears gushed to her fine eyes. Mary bent her head low over her work.

'We are now without father: we shall soon be without home and brother,' she murmured.

At that moment a little accident supervened, which seemed decreed by fate purposely to prove the truth of the adage, that 'misfortunes never come singly', and to add to their distresses the vexing one of the slip between the cup and the lip. St John passed the window reading a letter. He entered.

'Our Uncle John is dead,' said he.

Both the sisters seemed struck: not shocked or appalled; the tidings appeared in their eyes rather momentous than afflicting.

'Dead?' repeated Diana.

'Yes.'

She riveted a searching gaze on her brother's face. 'And what then?' she demanded, in a low voice.

'What then, Di?' he replied, maintaining a marble immobility of feature. 'What then? Why – nothing. Read.'

He threw the letter into her lap. She glanced over it, and handed it to Mary. Mary perused it in silence and returned it to her brother. All three looked at each other, and all three smiled – a dreary, pensive smile enough.

'Amen! We can yet live,' said Diana at last.

'At any rate, it makes us no worse off than we were before,' remarked Mary.

'Only it forces rather strongly on the mind the picture of what *might have been*,' said Mr Rivers, 'and contrasts it somewhat too vividly with what *is*.'

He folded the letter, locked it in his desk, and again went out.

For some minutes no one spoke. Diana then turned to me.

'Jane, you will wonder at us and our mysteries,' she said, 'and think us hard-hearted beings not to be more moved at the death of so near a relation as an uncle; but we have never seen him or known him. He was my mother's brother. My father and he quarrelled long ago. It was by his advice that my father risked most of his property in the speculation that ruined him. Mutual recrimination passed between them: they parted in anger, and were never reconciled. My uncle engaged afterwards in more prosperous undertakings: it appears he realized a fortune of twenty thousand pounds. He was never married, and had no near kindred but ourselves and one other person, not more closely related than we. My father always cherished the idea that he would atone for his error by leaving his possessions to us; that letter informs us that he has bequeathed every penny to the other relation, with the exception of thirty guineas, to be divided between St John, Diana, and Mary Rivers, for the purchase of three mourning rings. He had a right, of course, to do as he pleased; and yet a momentary damp is cast on the spirits by the receipt of such news. Mary and I would have esteemed ourselves rich with a thousand pounds each; and to St John such a sum would have been valuable, for the good it would have enabled him to do.'

This explanation given, the subject was dropped, and no further reference made to it by either Mr Rivers or his sisters. The next day I left Marsh End for Morton. The day after, Diana and Mary quitted it for distant B—. In a week Mr Rivers and Hannah repaired to the parsonage: and so the old grange was abandoned.

# Chapter 31

My home, then – when I at last find a home – is a cottage; a little room with whitewashed walls and a sanded floor, containing four painted chairs and a table, a clock, cupboard, with two or three plates and dishes, and a set of tea-things in delf. Above, a chamber of the same dimensions as the kitchen, with a deal bedstead and chest of drawers – small, yet too large to be filled with my scanty wardrobe, though the kindness of my gentle and generous friends has increased that by a modest stock of such things as are necessary.

# Jane Eyre

It is evening. I have dismissed, with the fee of an orange, the little orphan who serves me as a handmaid. I am sitting alone on the hearth. This morning the village school opened. I had twenty scholars. But three of the number can read: none write or cipher. Several knit, and a few sew a little. They speak with the broadest accent of the district. At present, they and I have a difficulty in understanding each other's language. Some of them are unmannered, rough, intractable, as well as ignorant; but others are docile, have a wish to learn, and evince a disposition that pleases me. I must not forget that these coarsely-clad little peasants are of flesh and blood as good as the scions of gentlest genealogy; and that the germs of native excellence, refinement, intelligence, kind feeling, are as likely to exist in their hearts as in those of the best-born. My duty will be to develop these germs: surely I shall find some happiness in discharging that office. Much enjoyment I do not expect in the life opening before me: yet it will, doubtless, if I regulate my mind, and exert my powers as I ought, yield me enough to live on from day to day.

Was I very gleeful, settled, content, during the hours I passed in yonder bare, humble schoolroom this morning and afternoon? Not to deceive myself, I must reply – no: I felt desolate to a degree. I felt – yes, idiot that I am – I felt degraded. I doubted I had taken a step which sank instead of raising me in the scale of social existence. I was weakly dismayed at the ignorance, the poverty, the coarseness of all I heard and saw round me. But let me not hate and despise myself too much for these feelings; I know them to be wrong – that is a great step gained; I shall strive to overcome them. To-morrow, I trust, I shall get the better of them partially; and in a few weeks, perhaps, they will be quite subdued. In a few months, it is possible, the happiness of seeing progress and a change for the better in my scholars may substitute gratification for disgust.

Meantime, let me ask myself one question: Which is better? – To have surrendered to temptation; listened to passion; made no painful effort – no struggle – but to have sunk down in the silken snare; fallen asleep on the flowers covering it; wakened in a southern clime, amongst the luxuries of a pleasure villa; to have been now living in France, Mr Rochester's mistress; delirious with his love half my time – for he would – oh, yes, he would have loved me well for a while. He *did* love me– no one will ever love me so again. I shall never more know the sweet homage given to beauty, youth, and grace – for never to any one else shall I seem to possess these charms. He was fond and proud of me – it is what no man besides will ever be. But where am I wandering, and what am I saying, and above all, feeling? Whether is it better, I ask, to be a slave in a fool's paradise at Marseilles – fevered with delusive bliss one hour – suffocating with the bitterest tears of remorse and shame the next – or to be a village schoolmistress, free and honest, in a breezy mountain nook in the healthy heart of England?

Yes; I feel now that I was right when I adhered to principle and law, and scorned and crushed the insane promptings of a frenzied moment. God directed me to a correct choice: I thank His Providence for the guidance!

Having brought my eventide musings to this point, I rose, went to my door, and looked at the sunset of the harvest-day, and at the quiet fields before my cottage, which, with the school, was distant half a mile from the village. The birds were singing their last strains –

*'The air was mild, the dew was balm.'*

# Jane Eyre

While I looked, I thought myself happy, and was surprised to find myself ere long weeping – and why? For the doom which had left me from adhesion to my master; for him I was no more to see; for the desperate grief and fatal fury – consequences of my departure – which might now, perhaps, be dragging him from the path of right, too far to leave hope of ultimate restoration thither. At this thought, I turned my face aside from the lovely sky of eve and lonely vale of Morton – I say *lonely*, for in that bend of it visible to me there was no building apparent save the church and the parsonage, half-hid in trees, and, quite at the extremity, the roof of Vale Hall, where the rich Mr Oliver and his daughter lived. I hid my eyes, and leant my head against the stone frame of my door; but soon a slight noise near the wicket which shut in my tiny garden from the meadow beyond it made me look up. A dog – old Carlo, Mr Rivers' pointer, as I saw in a moment – was pushing the gate with his nose, and St John himself leant upon it with folded arms; his brow knit, his gaze, grave almost to displeasure, fixed on me. I asked him to come in.

'No, I cannot stay; I have only brought you a little parcel my sisters left for you. I think it contains a colour-box, pencils, and paper.'

I approached to take it: a welcome gift it was, He examined my face, I thought, with austerity, as I came near: the traces of tears were doubtless very visible upon it.

'Have you found your first day's work harder than you expected?' he asked.

'Oh, no! On the contrary, I think in time I shall get on with my scholars very well.'

'But perhaps your accommodations – your cottage – your furniture – have disappointed your expectations? They are, in truth scanty enough; but —' I interrupted –

'My cottage is clean and weather-proof; my furniture sufficient and commodious. All I see has made me thankful, not despondent. I am not absolutely such a fool and sensualist as to regret the absence of a carpet, a sofa, and silver-plate; besides, five weeks ago I had nothing – I was an outcast, a beggar, a vagrant; now I have acquaintance, a home, a business. I wonder at the goodness of God, the generosity of my friends, the bounty of my lot. I do not repine.'

'But you feel solitude an oppression? The little house there behind you is dark and empty.'

'I have hardly had time yet to enjoy a sense of tranquillity, much less to grow impatient under one of loneliness.'

'Very well; I hope you feel the content you express: at any rate, your good sense will tell you that it is too soon yet to yield to the vacillating fears of Lot's wife. What you had left before I saw you, of coarse, I do not know; but I counsel you to resist firmly every temptation which would incline you to look back; pursue your present career steadily, for some months at least.'

'It is what I mean to do,' I answered. St John continued –

'It is hard work to control the workings of inclination and turn the bent of nature; but that it may be done, I know from experience. God has given us, in a measure, the power to make our own fate; and when our energies seem to demand a sustenance they cannot get – when our will strains after a path we may not follow – we need neither starve from inanition, nor stand still in despair: we have but to seek another nourishment for the mind, as strong as the forbidden fruit it longed to taste – and perhaps purer; and to hew out for the adventurous

foot a road as direct and broad as the one Fortune has blocked up against us, if rougher than it.

'A year ago I was myself intensely miserable, because I thought I had made a mistake in entering the ministry: its uniform duties wearied me to death. I burned for the more active life of the world – for the more exciting toils of a literary career – for the destiny of an artist, author, orator, anything rather than that of a priest: yes, the heart of a politician, of a soldier, of a votary of glory, a lover of renown, a luster after power, beat under my curate's surplice. I considered; my life was so wretched it must be changed, or I must die. After a season of darkness and struggling, light broke and relief fell: my cramped existence all at once spread out to a plain without bounds; my powers heard a call from Heaven to rise, gather their full strength, spread their wings, and mount beyond ken. God had an errand for me; to bear which afar, to deliver it well, skill and strength, courage and eloquence, the best qualifications of soldier, statesman, and orator, were all needed: for these all centre in the good missionary.

'A missionary I resolved to be. From that moment my state of mind changed: the fetters dissolved and dropped from every faculty, leaving nothing of bondage but its galling soreness – which time only can heal. My father, indeed, opposed the determination; but since his death I have not a legitimate obstacle to contend with; some affairs settled, a successor for Morton provided, an entanglement or two of the feelings broken through or cut asunder – a last conflict with human weakness, in which I know I shall overcome, because I have vowed that I *will* overcome – and I leave Europe for the East.'

He said this, in his peculiar subdued, yet emphatic voice; looking, when he had ceased speaking, not at me, but at the setting sun, at which I looked too. Both he and I had our backs toward the path leading up the field to the wicket. We had heard no step on the grass-grown track; the water running in the vale was the one lulling sound of the hour and scene; we might well then start when a gay voice, sweet as a silver bell, exclaimed –

'Good-evening, Mr Rivers. And good-evening, old Carlo. Your dog is quicker to recognize his friends than you are, sir; he pricked his ears and wagged his tail when I was at the bottom of the field, and you have your back towards me now.'

It was true. Though Mr Rivers had started at the first of those musical accents, as if a thunderbolt had split a cloud over his head, he stood yet, at the close of the sentence, in the same attitude in which the speaker had surprised him – his arms resting on a gate, his face directed towards the west. He turned at last, with measured deliberation. A vision, as it seemed to me, had risen at his side. There appeared within three feet of him, a form clad in pure white – a youthful, graceful form: full, yet fine in contour; and when, after bending to caress Carlo, it lifted up its head, and threw back a long veil, there bloomed under his glance a face of perfect beauty. Perfect beauty is a strong expression; but I do not retract or qualify it; as sweet features as ever the temperate clime of Albion moulded, as pure hues of rose and lily as ever her humid gales and vapoury skies generated and screened, justified, in this instance, the term. No charm was wanting, no defect was perceptible; the young girl had regular and delicate lineaments; eyes shaped and coloured as we see them in lovely pictures, large, and dark, and full; the long and shadowy eyelash which encircles a fine eye with so soft a fascination; the pencilled brow which gives such clearness; the white, smooth forehead, which adds such repose to the livelier beauties of tint

and ray; the cheek oval, fresh, and smooth; the lips, too, ruddy, healthy, sweetly formed; the even and gleaming teeth without flaw; the small dimpled chin; the ornament of rich, plenteous tresses – all advantages, in short, which, combined, realized the ideal of beauty, were fully hers. I wondered, as I looked at this fair creature: I admired her with my whole heart. Nature had surely formed her in a partial mood; and, forgetting her usual stinted stepmother dole of gifts, had endowed this her darling with a grand-dame's bounty.

What did St John Rivers think of this earthly angel? I naturally asked myself that question as I saw him turn to her and look at her; and, as naturally, I sought the answer to the inquiry in his countenance. He had already withdrawn his eyes from the Peri, and was looking at a humble tuft of daisies which grew by the wicket.

'A lovely evening, but late for you to be out alone,' he said, as he crushed the snowy heads of the closed flowers with his foot.

'Oh, I only came home from S—' (she mentioned the name of a large town some twenty miles distant) 'this afternoon. Papa told me you had opened your school, and that the new mistress was come; and so I put on my bonnet after tea, and ran up the valley to see her: this is she?' pointing to me.

'It is,' said St John.

'Do you think you shall like Morton?' she asked of me, with a direct and naïve simplicity of tone and manner, pleasing, if childlike.

'I hope I shall. I have many inducements to do so.'

'Did you find your scholars as attentive as you expected?'

'Quite.'

'Do you like your house?'

'Very much.'

'Have I furnished it nicely?'

'Very nicely, indeed.'

'And made a good choice of an attendant for you in Alice Wood?'

'You have indeed. She is teachable and handy.' (This, then, I thought, is Miss Oliver, the heiress; favoured, it seems, in the gifts of fortune, as well as in those of nature! What happy combination of the planets presided over her birth, I wonder?)

'I shall come up and help you to teach sometimes,' she added. 'It will be a change for me to visit you now and then; and I like a change. Mr Rivers, I have been *so* gay during my stay at S—. Last night, or rather this morning, I was dancing till two o'clock. The —th regiment are stationed there since the riots; and the officers are the most agreeable men in the world: they put all our young knife-grinders and scissor-merchants to shame.'

It seemed to me that Mr St John's under lip protruded, and his upper lip curled a moment. His mouth certainly looked a good deal compressed, and the lower part of his face unusually stern and square, as the laughing girl gave him this information. He lifted his gaze, too, from the daisies, and turned it to her. An unsmiling, a searching, a meaning gaze it was. She answered it with a second laugh; and laughter well became her youth, her roses, her dimples, her bright eyes.

As he stood mute and grave, she again fell to caressing Carlo. 'Poor Carlo loves me,' she said. '*He* is not stern and distant to his friends; and if he could speak, he would not be silent.'

# Jane Eyre

As she patted the dog's head, bending with native grace before his young and austere master, I saw a glow rise to that master's face. I saw his solemn eye melt with sudden fire, and flicker with resistless emotion. Flushed and kindled thus, he looked nearly as beautiful for a man as she for a woman. His chest heaved once, as if his large heart, weary of despotic constriction, had expanded, despite the will, and made a vigorous bound for the attainment of liberty. But he curbed it, I think, as a resolute rider would curb a rearing steed. He responded neither by word nor movement to the gentle advances made him.

'Papa says you never come to see us now,' continued Miss Oliver, looking up. 'You are quite a stranger at Vale Hall. He is alone this evening, and not very well: will you return with me and visit him?'

'It is not a seasonable hour to intrude on Mr Oliver,' answered St John.

'Not a seasonable hour! But I declare it is. It is just the hour when papa most wants company: when the works are closed, and he has no business to occupy him. Now, Mr Rivers, *do* come. Why are you so very shy, and so very sombre?' She filled up the hiatus his silence left by a reply of her own.

'I forgot!' she exclaimed, shaking her beautiful curled head, as if shocked at herself. 'I am so giddy and thoughtless! *Do* excuse me. It had slipped my memory that you have good reason to be indisposed for joining in my chatter. Diana and Mary have left you, and Moor House is shut up, and you are so lonely. I am sure I pity you. Do come and see papa.'

'Not to-night, Miss Rosamond, not to-night.'

Mr St John spoke almost like an automaton: himself only knew the effort it cost him thus to refuse.

'Well, if you are so obstinate, I will leave you; for I dare not stay any longer: the dew begins to fall. Good-evening!'

She held out her hand. He just touched it. 'Good-evening!' he repeated, in a voice low and hollow as an echo. She turned, but in a moment returned.

'Are you well?' she asked. Well might she put the question: his face was blanched as her gown.

'Quite well,' he enunciated; and, with a bow, he left the gate. She went one way; he another. She turned twice to gaze after him as she tripped fairy-like down the field; he, as he strode firmly across, never turned at all.

This spectacle of another's suffering and sacrifice rapt my thoughts from exclusive meditation on my own. Diana Rivers had designated her brother 'inexorable as death'. She had not exaggerated.

# Chapter 32

continued the labours of the village school as actively and faithfully as I could. It was truly hard work at first. Some time elapsed before, with all my efforts, I could comprehend my scholars and their nature. Wholly untaught, with faculties quite torpid, they seemed to me hopelessly dull; and, at first sight, all dull alike: but I soon found I was mistaken. There was a difference amongst them as amongst the educated; and when I got to know them, and they me, this difference rapidly developed itself. Their amazement at me, my language, my rules, and ways, once subsided, I found some of these heavy-looking, gaping rustics wake up into sharp-witted girls enough. Many showed themselves obliging, and amiable too; and I discovered amongst them not a few examples of natural politeness, and innate self-respect, as well as of excellent capacity, that won both my goodwill and my admiration. These soon took a pleasure in doing their work well, in keeping their persons neat, in learning their tasks regularly, in acquiring quiet and orderly manners. The rapidity of their progress, in some instances, was even surprising; and an honest and happy pride I took in it: besides, I began personally to like some of the best girls; and they liked me. I had amongst my scholars several farmers' daughters – young women grown, almost. These could already read, write, and sew; and to them I taught the elements of grammar, geography, history, and the finer kinds of needlework. I found estimable characters amongst them – characters desirous of information and disposed for improvement – with whom I passed many a pleasant evening hour in their own homes. Their parents then (the farmer and his wife) loaded me with attentions. There was an enjoyment in accepting their simple kindness, and in repaying it by a consideration – a scrupulous regard to their feelings – to which they were not, perhaps, at all times accustomed, and which both charmed and benefited them; because, while it elevated them in their own eyes, it made them emulous to merit the deferential treatment they received.

I felt I became a favourite in the neighbourhood. Whenever I went out, I heard on all sides cordial salutations, and was welcomed with friendly smiles. To live amidst general regard, though it be but the regard of working people, is like 'sitting in sunshine, calm and sweet': serene inward feelings bud and bloom under the ray. At this period of my life, my heart far oftener swelled with thankfulness than sank with dejection: and yet, reader, to tell you all, in the midst of this calm, this useful existence – after a day passed in honourable exertion amongst my scholars, an evening spent in drawing or reading contentedly alone – I used to rush into strange dreams at night: dreams many-coloured, agitated, full of the ideal, the stirring, the stormy – dreams where, amidst unusual scenes, charged with adventure, with agitating risk and romantic chance,

# Jane Eyre

I still again and again met Mr Rochester, always at some exciting crisis; and then the sense of being in his arms, hearing his voice, meeting his eye, touching his hand and cheek, loving him, being loved by him – the hope of passing a lifetime at his side, would be renewed, with all its first force and fire. Then I awoke. Then I recalled where I was, and how situated. Then I rose up on my curtainless bed, trembling and quivering; and then the still, dark night witnessed the convulsion of despair, and heard the burst of passion. By nine o'clock the next morning I was punctually opening the school; tranquil, settled, prepared for the steady duties of the day.

Rosamond Oliver kept her word in coming to visit me. Her call at the school was generally made in the course of her morning ride. She would canter up to the door on her pony, followed by a mounted livery servant. Anything more exquisite than her appearance, in her purple habit with her Amazon's cap of black velvet placed gracefully above the long curls that kissed her cheek and floated to her shoulders, can scarcely be imagined: and it was thus she would enter the rustic building, and glide through the dazzled ranks of the village children. She generally came at the hour when Mr Rivers was engaged in giving his daily catechizing lesson. Keenly, I fear, did the eye of the visitress pierce the young pastor's heart. A sort of instinct seemed to warn him of her entrance, even when he did not see it; and when he was looking quite away from the door, if she appeared at it, his cheek would glow, and his marble-seeming features, though they refused to relax, changed indescribably, and in their very quiescence became expressive of a repressed fervour, stronger than working muscle or darting glance could indicate.

Of course, she knew her power: indeed, he did not, because he could not, conceal it from her. In spite of his Christian stoicism, when she went up and addressed him, and smiled gaily, encouragingly, even fondly in his face, his hands would tremble and his eye burn. He seemed to say, with his sad and resolute look, if he did not say it with his lips, 'I love you, and I know you prefer me. It is not despair of success that keeps me dumb. If I offered my heart, I believe you would accept it. But that heart is already laid on a sacred altar: the fire is arranged around it. It will soon be no more than a sacrifice consumed.'

And then she would pout like a disappointed child; a pensive cloud would soften her radiant vivacity; she would withdraw her hand hastily from his, and turn in transient petulance from his aspect, at once so heroic and so martyr-like. St John, no doubt, would have given the world to follow, recall, retain her, when she thus left him; but he would not give one chance of heaven, nor relinquish, for the elysium of her love, one hope of the true, eternal Paradise. Besides, he could not bind all that he had in his nature – the rover, the aspirant, the poet, the priest – in the limits of a single passion. He could not – he would not – renounce his wide field of mission warfare for the parlours and the peace of Vale Hall. I learnt so much from himself in an inroad I once, despite his reserve, had the daring to make on his confidence.

Miss Oliver already honoured me with frequent visits to my cottage. I had learnt her whole character, which was without mystery or disguise. She was coquettish, but not heartless; exacting, but not worthlessly selfish. She had been indulged from her birth, but was not absolutely spoilt. She was hasty, but good humoured; vain (she could not help it, when every glance in the glass showed her such a flush of loveliness), but not affected; liberal-handed; innocent of the

1151

pride of wealth; ingenuous; sufficiently intelligent; gay, lively, and unthinking. She was very charming, in short, even to a cool observer of her own sex like me; but she was not profoundly interesting or thoroughly impressive. A very different sort of mind was hers from that, for instance, of the sisters of St John. Still, I liked her almost as I liked my pupil Adèle; except that, for a child whom we have watched over and taught, a closer affection is engendered than we can give an equally attractive adult acquaintance.

She had taken an amiable caprice to me. She said I was like Mr Rivers, only, certainly, she allowed, 'not one-tenth so handsome, though I was a nice, neat little soul enough, but he was an angel'. I was, however, good, clever, composed, and firm, like him. I was a *lusus naturae*, she affirmed, as a village schoolmistress: she was sure my previous history, if known, would make a delightful romance.

One evening, while, with her usual childlike activity, and thoughtless yet not offensive inquisitiveness, she was rummaging the cupboard and the table-drawer of my little kitchen, she discovered first two French books, a volume of Schiller, a German grammar and dictionary, and then my drawing materials and some sketches, including a pencil-head of a pretty little cherub-like girl, one of my scholars, and sundry views from nature, taken in the Vale of Morton and on the surrounding moors. She was first transfixed with surprise, and then electrified with delight.

'Had I done these pictures? Did I know French and German? What a love – what a miracle I was! I drew better than her master in the first school in S— Would I sketch a portrait of her, to show to papa?'

'With pleasure,' I replied; and I felt a thrill of artist-delight at the idea of copying from so perfect and radiant a model. She had then on a dark-blue silk dress; her arms and her neck were bare; her only ornament was her chestnut tresses, which waved over her shoulders with all the wild grace of natural curls. I took a sheet of fine cardboard, and drew a careful outline. I promised myself the pleasure of colouring it; and, as it was getting late then, I told her she must come and sit another day.

She made such a report of me to her father, that Mr Oliver himself accompanied her next evening – a tall, massive-featured, middle-aged, and gray-headed man, at whose side his lovely daughter looked like a bright flower near a hoary turret. He appeared a taciturn, and perhaps a proud personage; but he was very kind to me. The sketch of Rosamond's portrait pleased him highly: he said I must make a finished picture of it. He insisted, too, on my coming the next day to spend the evening at Vale Hall.

I went. I found it a large, handsome residence, showing abundant evidences of wealth in the proprietor. Rosamond was full of glee and pleasure all the time I stayed. Her father was affable; and when he entered into conversation with me after tea, he expressed in strong terms his approbation of what I had done in Morton School, and said he only feared, from what he saw and heard, I was too good for the place, and would soon quit it for one more suitable.

'Indeed,' cried Rosamond, 'she is clever enough to be a governess in a high family, papa.'

I thought I would far rather be where I am than in any high family in the land. Mr Oliver spoke of Mr Rivers – of the Rivers family – with great respect. He said it was a very old name in that neighbourhood; that the ancestors of the house were wealthy; that all Morton had once belonged to them; that even now

# Jane Eyre

he considered the representative of that house might, if he liked, make an alliance with the best. He accounted it a pity that so fine and talented a young man should have formed the design of going out as a missionary; it was quite throwing a valuable life away. It appeared, then, that her father would throw no obstacle in the way of Rosamond's union with St John. Mr Oliver evidently regarded the young clergyman's good birth, old name, and sacred profession as sufficient compensation for the want of fortune.

It was the fifth of November, and a holiday. My little servant, after helping me to clean my house, was gone, well satisfied with the fee of a penny for her aid. All about me was spotless and bright – scoured floor, polished grate, and well-rubbed chairs. I had also made myself neat, and now the afternoon before me to spend as I would.

The translation of a few pages of German occupied an hour; then I got my palette and pencils, and fell to the more soothing, because easier, occupation of completing Rosamond Oliver's miniature. The head was finished already: there was but the background to tint and the drapery to shade off; a touch of carmine, too, to add to the ripe lips; a soft curl here and there to the tresses, a deeper tinge to the shadow of the lash under the azured eyelid. I was absorbed in the execution of these nice details, when, after one rapid tap, my door unclosed, admitting St John Rivers.

'I am come to see how you are spending your holiday,' he said. 'Not, I hope, in thought? No, that is well: while you draw you will not feel lonely. You see, I mistrust you still, though you have borne up wonderfully so far. I have brought you a book for evening solace,' and he laid on the table a new publication – a poem: one of those genuine productions so often vouchsafed to the fortunate public of those days – the golden age of modern literature. Alas! the readers of our era are less favoured. But courage! I will not pause either to accuse or repine. I know poetry is not dead, nor genius lost; nor has Mammon gained power over either, to bind or slay; they will both assert their existence, their presence, their liberty and strength again one day. Powerful angels, safe in heaven! they smile when sordid souls triumph, and feeble ones weep over their destruction. Poetry destroyed. Genius banished? No! Mediocrity, no: do not let envy prompt you to the thought. No; they not only live, but reign and redeem: and without their divine influence spread everywhere, you would be in hell – the hell of your own meanness.

While I was eagerly glancing at the bright pages of *Marmion* (for *Marmion* it was), St John stooped to examine my drawing. His tall figure sprang erect again with a start: he said nothing. I looked up at him: he shunned my eye. I knew his thoughts well, and could read his heart plainly; at the moment I felt calmer and cooler than he: I had then temporarily the advantage of him, and I conceived an inclination to do him some good, if I could.

'With all his firmness and self-control,' thought I, 'he tasks himself too far: locks every feeling and pang within – expresses, confesses, imparts nothing. I am sure it would benefit him to talk a little about this sweet Rosamond, whom he thinks he ought not to marry: I will make him talk.'

I said first, 'Take a chair, Mr Rivers.' But he answered, as he always did, that he could not stay. 'Very well,' I responded mentally, 'stand if you like; but you shall not go just yet, I am determined: solitude is at least as bad for you as it is for me. I'll try if I cannot discover the secret spring of your confidence, and

# Jane Eyre

find an aperture in that marble breast through which I can shed one drop of the balm of sympathy.'

'Is this portrait like?' I asked bluntly.

'Like! Like whom? I did not observe it closely.'

'You did, Mr Rivers.'

He also started at my sudden and strange abruptness: he looked at me astonished. 'Oh, that is nothing yet,' I muttered within. 'I don't mean to be baffled by a little stiffness on your part; I'm prepared to go to considerable lengths.' I continued, 'You observed it closely and distinctly; but I have no objection to your looking at it again,' and I rose and placed it in his hand.

'A well-executed picture,' he said; 'very soft, clear colouring; very graceful and correct drawing.'

'Yes, yes; I know all that. But what of the resemblance? Who is it like?'

Mastering some hesitation, he answered, 'Miss Oliver, I presume.'

'Of course. And now, sir, to reward you for the accurate guess, I will promise to paint you a careful and faithful duplicate of this very picture, provided you admit that the gift would be acceptable to you. I don't wish to throw away my time and trouble on an offering you would deem worthless.'

He continued to gaze at the picture: the longer he looked, the firmer he held it, the more he seemed to covet it. 'It is like!' he murmured; 'the eye is well managed: the colour, light, expression, are perfect. It smiles!'

'Would it comfort, or would it wound you to have a similar painting? Tell me that! When you are at Madagascar, or at the Cape, or in India, would it be a consolation to have that memento in your possession? or would the sight of it bring recollections calculated to enervate and distress?'

He now furtively raised his eyes: he glanced at me, irresolute, disturbed: he again surveyed the picture.

'That I should like to have it is certain: whether it would be judicious or wise is another question.'

Since I had ascertained that Rosamond really preferred him, and that her father was not likely to oppose the match, I – less exalted in my views than St John – had been strongly disposed in my own heart to advocate their union. It seemed to me that, should he become the possessor of Mr Oliver's large fortune, he might do as much good with it as if he went and laid his genius out to wither, and his strength to waste, under a tropical sun. With this persuasion I now answered –

'As far as I can see, it would be wiser and more judicious if you were to take to yourself the original at once.'

By this time he had sat down: he had laid the picture on the table before him, and with his brow supported on both hands, hung fondly over it. I discerned he was now neither angry nor shocked at my audacity. I saw even that to be thus frankly addressed on a subject he had deemed unapproachable – to hear it thus freely handled – was beginning to be felt by him as a new pleasure – an unhoped-for relief. Reserved people often really need the frank discussion of their sentiments and griefs more than the expansive. The sternest-seeming stoic is human after all; and to 'burst' with boldness and good will into 'the silent sea' of their souls is often to confer on them the first of obligations.

'She likes you, I am sure,' said I, as I stood behind his chair, 'and her father

respects you. Moreover, she is a sweet girl – rather thoughtless; but you would have sufficient thought for both yourself and her. You ought to marry her.'

'*Does* she like me?' he asked.

'Certainly; better than she likes any one else. She talks of you continually: there is no subject she enjoys so much or touches upon so often.'

'It is very pleasant to hear this,' he said, 'very: go on for another quarter of an hour.' And he actually took out his watch and laid it upon the table to measure the time.

'But where is the use of going on,' I asked, 'when you are probably preparing some iron blow of contradiction, or forging a fresh chain to fetter your heart?'

'Don't imagine such hard things. Fancy me yielding and melting, as I am doing: human love rising like a freshly opened fountain in my mind and overflowing with sweet inundation all the field I have so carefully and with such labour prepared – so assiduously sown with the seeds of good intentions, of self-denying plans. And now it is deluged with a nectarous flood – the young germs swamped – delicious poison cankering them: now I see myself stretched on an ottoman in the drawing-room at Vale Hall at my bride Rosamond Oliver's feet: she is talking to me with her sweet voice – gazing down on me with those eyes your skilful hand has copied so well – smiling at me with these coral lips. She is mine – I am hers – this present life and passing world suffice to me. Hush! say nothing – my heart is full of delight – my senses are entranced – let the time I marked pass in peace.'

I humoured him: the watch ticked on: he breathed fast and low: I stood silent. Amidst this hush the quarter sped; he replaced the watch, laid the picture down, rose, and stood on the hearth.

'Now,' said he, 'that little space was given to delirium and delusion. I rested my temples on the breast of temptation, and put my neck voluntarily under her yoke of flowers; I tasted her cup. The pillow was burning: there is an asp in the garland: the wine has a bitter taste: her promises are hollow – her offers false: I see and know all this.'

I gazed at him in wonder.

'It is strange,' pursued he, 'that while I love Rosamond Oliver so wildly – with all the intensity, indeed, of a first passion, the object of which is exquisitely beautiful, graceful, and fascinating – I experience at the same time a calm, unwarped consciousness that she would not make me a good wife; that she is not the partner suited to me; that I should discover this within a year after marriage; and that to twelve months' rapture would succeed a lifetime of regret. This I know.'

'Strange, indeed!' I could not help ejaculating.

'While something in me,' he went on, 'is acutely sensible to her charms, something else is as deeply impressed with her defects: they are such that they could sympathize in nothing I aspired to – co-operate in nothing I undertook. Rosamond a sufferer, a labourer, a female apostle? Rosamond a missionary's wife? No!'

'But you need not be a missionary. You might relinquish that scheme.'

'Relinquish! What! my vocation? My great work? My foundation laid on earth for a mansion in heaven? My hopes of being numbered in the band who have merged all ambitions in the glorious one of bettering their race – of carrying knowledge into the realms of ignorance – of substituting peace for war, freedom

for bondage, religion for superstition, the hope of heaven for the fear of hell? Must I relinquish that? It is dearer than the blood in my veins. It is what I have to look forward to, and to live for.'

After a considerable pause, I said, 'And Miss Oliver? Are her disappointment and sorrow of no interest to you?'

'Miss Oliver is ever surrounded by suitors and flatterers: in less than a month, my image will be effaced from her heart. She will forget me; and will marry, probably, some one who will make her far happier than I should do.'

'You speak coolly enough; but you suffer in the conflict. You are wasting away.'

'No. If I get a little thin, it is with anxiety about my prospects, yet unsettled – my departure, continually procrastinated. Only this morning I received intelligence that the successor, whose arrival I have been so long expecting, cannot be ready to replace me for three months to come yet; and perhaps the three months may extend to six.'

'You tremble and become flushed whenever Miss Oliver enters the schoolroom.'

Again the surprised expression crossed his face. He had not imagined that a woman would dare to speak so to a man. For me, I felt at home in this sort of discourse. I could never rest in communication with strong, discreet, and refined minds, whether male or female, till I had passed the outworks of conventional reserve, and crossed the threshold of confidence, and won a place by their heart's very hearthstone.

'You *are* original,' said he, 'and not timid. There is something brave in your spirit, as well as penetrating in your eye; but allow me to assure you that you partially misinterpret my emotions. You think them more profound and potent than they are. You give me a larger allowance of sympathy than I have a just claim to. When I colour, and when I shake before Miss Oliver, I do not pity myself, I scorn the weakness. I know it is ignoble: a mere fever of the flesh: not, I declare, the convulsion of the soul. *That* is just as fixed as a rock, firm set in the depths of a restless sea. Know me to be what I am – a cold, hard man.'

I smiled incredulously.

'You have taken my confidence by storm,' he continued, 'and now it is much at your service. I am simply, in my original state – stripped of that blood-bleached robe with which Christianity covers human deformity – a cold, hard, ambitious man. Natural affection only, of all the sentiments, has permanent power over me. Reason, and not feeling, is my guide: my ambition is unlimited; my desire to rise higher, to do more than others, insatiable. I honour endurance, perseverance, industry, talent; because these are the means by which men achieve great ends and mount to lofty eminence. I watch your career with interest, because I consider you a specimen of a diligent, orderly, energetic woman: not because I deeply compassionate what you have gone through, or what you still suffer.'

'You would describe yourself as a mere pagan philosopher,' I said.

'No. There is this difference between me and deistic philosophers: I believe; and I believe the Gospel. You missed your epithet. I am not a pagan, but a Christian philosopher – a follower of the sect of Jesus. As His disciple I adopt His pure, His merciful, His benignant doctrines. I advocate them: I am sworn to spread them. Won in youth to religion, she has cultivated my original qualities thus: From the minute germ, natural affection, she has developed the oversha-

dowing tree, philanthropy. From the wild stringy root of human uprightness she has reared a due sense of the divine justice. Of the ambition to win power and renown for my wretched self she has formed the ambition to spread my Master's Kingdom, to achieve victories for the standard of the Cross. So much has religion done for me: turning the original materials to the best account; pruning and training nature. But she could not eradicate nature; nor will it be eradicated "till this mortal shall put on immortality".'

Having said this, he took his hat, which lay on the table beside my palette. Once more he looked at the portrait.

'She *is* lovely,' he murmured. 'She is well named the Rose of the World, indeed!'

'And may I not paint one like it for you?'

'*Cui bono?* No.'

He drew over the picture the sheet of thin paper on which I was accustomed to rest my hand in painting, to prevent the cardboard from being sullied. What he suddenly saw on this blank paper, it was impossible for me to tell; but something had caught his eye. He took it up with a snatch; he looked at the edge; then shot a glance at me, inexpressibly peculiar and quite incomprehensible: a glance that seemed to take and make a note of every point in my shape, face, and dress; for it traversed all, quick, keen as lightning. His lips parted, as if to speak: but he checked the coming sentence, whatever it was.

'What is the matter?' I asked.

'Nothing in the world,' was the reply; and replacing the paper, I saw him dexterously tear a narrow slip from the margin. It disappeared in his glove; and, with one hasty nod and 'good-afternoon', he vanished.

'Well!' I exclaimed, using an expression of the district, 'that caps the globe, however!'

I, in my turn, scrutinized the paper; but saw nothing on it save a few dingy stains of paint where I had tried the tint in my pencil. I pondered the mystery a minute or two; but finding it insolvable, and being certain it could not be of much moment, I dismissed, and soon forgot it.

# Chapter 33

When Mr St John went, it was beginning to snow; the whirling storm continued all night. The next day a keen wind brought fresh and blinding falls; by twilight the valley was drifted up and almost impassable. I had closed my shutter, laid a mat to the door to prevent the snow from blowing in under it, trimmed my fire, and after sitting nearly an hour on the hearth listening to the muffled fury of the tempest, I lit a candle, took down *Marmion*, and beginning—

# Jane Eyre

*'Day set on Norham's castled steep,*
*And Tweed's fair river broad and deep,*
*And Cheviot's mountains lone;*
*The massive towers, the donjon keep,*
*The flanking walls that round them sweep,*
*In yellow lustre shone'*—

I soon forgot storm in music.

I heard a noise: the wind, I thought, shook the door. No; it was St John Rivers, who, lifting the latch, came in out of the frozen hurricane, the howling darkness, and stood before me: the cloak that covered his tall figure all white as a glacier. I was almost in consternation, so little had I expected any guests from the blocked-up vale that night.

'Any ill news?' I demanded. 'Has anything happened?'

'No. How very easily alarmed you are!' he answered, removing his cloak and hanging it up against the door, towards which he again coolly pushed the mat which his entrance had deranged. He stamped the snow from his boots.

'I shall sully the purity of your floor,' said he, 'but you must excuse me for once.' Then he approached the fire. 'I have had hard work to get here, I assure you,' he observed, as he warmed his hands over the flame. 'One drift took me up to the waist; happily the snow is quite soft yet.'

'But why are you come?' I could not forbear saying.

'Rather an inhospitable question to put to a visitor: but since you ask it, I answer simply to have a little talk with you; I got tired of my mute books and empty rooms. Besides, since yesterday I have experienced the excitement of a person to whom a tale has been half-told, and who is impatient to hear the sequel.'

He sat down. I recalled his singular conduct of yesterday, and really I began to fear his wits were touched. If he were insane, however, his was a very cool and collected insanity: I had never seen that handsome featured face of his look more like chiselled marble than it did just now, as he put aside his snow-wet hair from his forehead and let the firelight shine free on his pale brow and cheek as pale, where it grieved me to discover the hollow trace of care or sorrow now so plainly graved. I waited, expecting he would say something I could at least comprehend; but his hand was now at his chin, his finger on his lip: he was thinking. It struck me that his hand looked wasted like his face. A perhaps uncalled-for gush of pity came over my heart: I was moved to say—

'I wish Diana or Mary would come and live with you: it is too bad that you should be quite alone; and you are recklessly rash about your own health.'

'Not at all,' said he: 'I care for myself when necessary. I am well now. What do you see amiss in me?'

This was said with a careless, abstracted indifference, which showed that my solicitude was, at least in his opinion, wholly superfluous. I was silenced.

He still slowly moved his finger over his upper lip, and still his eye dwelt dreamily on the glowing grate. Thinking it urgent to say something, I asked him presently if he felt any cold draught from the door, which was behind him.

'No, no!' he responded shortly and somewhat testily.

'Well,' I reflected, 'if you won't talk, you may be still; I'll let you alone now, and return to my book.'

# Jane Eyre

So I snuffed the candle and resumed the perusal of *Marmion*. He soon stirred; my eye was instantly drawn to his movements; he only took out a morocco pocket-book, thence produced a letter, which he read in silence, folded it, put it back, relapsed into meditation. It was vain to try to read with such an inscrutable fixture before me; nor could I, in my impatience, consent to be dumb; he might rebuff me if he liked, but talk I would.

'Have you heard from Diana and Mary lately?'

'Not since the letter I showed you a week ago.'

'There has not been any change made about your own arrangements? You will not be summoned to leave England sooner than you expected?'

'I fear not, indeed: such chance is too good to befall me.' Baffled so far, I changed my ground. I bethought myself to talk about the school and my scholars.

'Mary Garrett's mother is better, and Mary came back to the school this morning, and I shall have four new girls next week from the Foundry Close; they would have come to-day but for the snow.'

'Indeed!'

'Mr Oliver pays for two.'

'Does he?'

'He means to give the whole school a treat at Christmas.'

'I know.'

'Was it your suggestion?'

'No.'

'Whose then?'

'His daughter's, I think.'

'It is like her: she is so good-natured.'

'Yes.'

Again came the blank of a pause: the clock struck eight strokes. It aroused him; he uncrossed his legs, sat erect, turned to me.

'Leave your book a moment, and come a little nearer the fire,' he said.

Wondering, and of my wonder finding no end, I complied.

'Half an hour ago,' he pursued, 'I spoke of my impatience to hear the sequel of a tale: on reflection, I find the matter will be better managed by my assuming the narrator's part, and converting you into a listener. Before commencing, it is but fair to warn you that the story will sound somewhat hackneyed in your ears; but stale details often regain a degree of freshness when they pass through new lips. For the rest, whether trite or novel, it is short.

'Twenty years ago, a poor curate – never mind his name at this moment – fell in love with a rich man's daughter; she fell in love with him, and married him, against the advice of all her friends, who consequently disowned her immediately after the wedding. Before two years passed, the rash pair were both dead, and laid quietly side by side under one slab. (I have seen their grave: it formed part of the pavement of a huge churchyard surrounding the grim, soot-black old cathedral of an overgrown manufacturing town in —shire.) They left a daughter, which, at its very birth, Charity received in her lap – cold as that of the snowdrift I almost stuck fast in to-night. Charity carried the friendless thing to the house of its rich, maternal relations; it was reared by an aunt-in-law, called (I come to names now) Mrs Reed of Gateshead. You start – did you hear a noise? I dare say it is only a cat scrambling along the rafters of the adjoining schoolroom: it was a barn before I had it repaired and altered, and

barns are generally haunted by rats. – To proceed. Mrs Reed kept the orphan ten years: whether it was happy or not with her, I cannot say, never having been told: but at the end of that time she transferred it to a place you know – being no other than Lowood School, where you so long resided yourself. It seems her career there was very honourable: from a pupil, she became a teacher, like yourself – really it strikes me there are parallel points in her history and yours. She left it to be a governess: there, again, your fates were analogous; she undertook the education of the ward of a certain Mr Rochester.'

'Mr Rivers!' I interrupted.

'I can guess your feelings,' he said, 'but restrain them for a while; I have nearly finished; hear me to the end. Of Mr Rochester's character I know nothing, but the one fact that he professed to offer honourable marriage to this young girl, and that at the very altar she discovered he had a wife yet alive, though a lunatic. What his subsequent conduct and proposals were is a matter of pure conjecture; but when an event transpired which rendered inquiry after the governess necessary, it was discovered she was gone – no one could tell when, where, or how. She had left Thornfield Hall in the night; every research after her course had been vain: the country had been scoured far and wide; no vestige of information could be gathered respecting her. Yet that she should be found is become a matter of serious urgency; advertisements have been put in all the papers; I myself have received a letter from one Mr Briggs, a solicitor, communicating the details I have just imparted. Is it not an odd tale?'

'Just tell me this,' said I, 'and since you know so much, you surely *can* tell it me – what of Mr Rochester? How and where is he? What is he doing? Is he well?'

'I am ignorant of all concerning Mr Rochester: the letter never mentions him but to narrate the fraudulent and illegal attempt I have adverted to. You should rather ask the name of the governess – the nature of the event which requires her appearance.'

'Did no one go to Thornfield Hall, then? Did no one see Mr Rochester?'

'I suppose not.'

'But they wrote to him?'

'Of course.'

'And what did he say? Who has his letters?'

'Mr Briggs intimates that the answer to his application was not from Mr Rochester, but from a lady: it is signed "Alice Fairfax".'

I felt cold and dismayed: my worst fears then were probably true: he had in all probability left England and rushed in reckless desperation to some former haunt on the Continent. And what opiate for his severe sufferings – what object for his strong passions – had he sought there? I dared not answer the question. Oh, my poor master – once almost my husband – whom I had often called 'my dear Edward!'

'He must have been a bad man,' observed Mr Rivers.

'You don't know him – don't pronounce an opinion upon him,' I said with warmth.

'Very well,' he answered quietly: 'and indeed my head is otherwise occupied than with him: I have my tale to finish. Since you won't ask the governess's name, I must tell it of my own accord. Stay! I have it here – it is always more

# Jane Eyre

satisfactory to see important points written down, fairly committed to black and white.'

And the pocket-book was again deliberately produced, opened, sought through; from one of its compartments was extracted a shabby slip of paper, hastily torn off: I recognized in its texture and its stains of ultramarine, and lake, and vermilion, the ravished margin of the portrait-cover. He got up, held it close to my eyes: and I read, traced in Indian ink, in my own handwriting, the words 'JANE EYRE' – the work doubtless of some moment of abstraction.

'Briggs wrote to me of a Jane Eyre,' he said; 'the advertisements demanded a Jane Eyre: I knew a Jane Elliott. I confess I had my suspicions, but it was only yesterday afternoon they were at once resolved into certainty. You own the name and renounce the *alias*?'

'Yes – yes; but where is Mr Briggs? He perhaps knows more of Mr Rochester than you do.'

'Briggs is in London. I should doubt his knowing anything at all about Mr Rochester; it is not in Mr Rochester he is interested. Meantime, you forget essential points in pursuing trifles: you do not inquire why Mr Briggs sought after you – what he wanted with you.'

'Well, what did he want?'

'Merely to tell you that your uncle, Mr Eyre of Madeira, is dead; that he has left you all his property, and that you are now rich – merely that – nothing more.'

'I! – rich?'

'Yes, you rich – quite an heiress.'

Silence succeeded.

'You must prove your identity, of course,' resumed St John presently: 'a step which will offer no difficulties; you can then enter on immediate possession. Your fortune is vested in the English funds; Briggs has the will and the necessary documents.'

Here was a new card turned up! It is a fine thing, reader, to be lifted in a moment from indigence to wealth – a very fine thing; but not a matter one can comprehend, or consequently enjoy, all at once. And then there are other chances in life far more thrilling and rapture-giving: *this* is solid, an affair of the actual world, nothing ideal about it: all its associations are solid and sober, and its manifestations are the same. One does not jump, and spring, and shout hurrah! at hearing one has got a fortune; one begins to consider responsibilities, and to ponder business; on a base of steady satisfaction rise certain grave cares, and we contain ourselves, and brood over our bliss with a solemn brow.

Besides, the words Legacy, Bequest, go side by side with the words Death, Funeral. My uncle I had heard was dead – my only relative; ever since being made aware of his existence, I had cherished the hope of one day seeing him: now, I never should. And then this money came only to me: not to me and a rejoicing family, but to my isolated self. It was a grand boon doubtless; and independence would be glorious – yes, I felt that – *that* thought swelled my heart.

'You unbend your forehead at last,' said Mr Rivers. 'I thought Medusa had looked at you, and that you were turning to stone. Perhaps now you will ask how much you are worth?'

'How much am I worth?'

I apologize—let me provide the clean output.

'Oh, a trifle! Nothing of course to speak of – twenty thousand pounds, I think they say; but what is that?'

'Twenty thousand pounds?'

Here was a new stunner – I had been calculating on four or five thousand. This news actually took my breath for a moment: Mr St John, whom I had never heard laugh before, laughed now.

'Well,' said he, 'if you had committed a murder, and I had told you your crime was discovered, you could scarcely look more aghast.'

'It is a large sum – don't you think there is a mistake?'

'No mistake at all.'

'Perhaps you have read the figures wrong – it may be two thousand!'

'It is written in letters, not figures – twenty thousand.'

I again felt rather like an individual of but average gastronomical powers sitting down to feast alone at a table spread with provisions for a hundred. Mr Rivers rose now and put his cloak on.

'If it were not such a very wild night,' he said, 'I would send Hannah down to keep you company: you look too desperately miserable to be left alone. But Hannah, poor woman! could not stride the drifts so well as I: her legs are not quite so long: so I must e'en leave you to your sorrows. Good-night.'

He was lifting the latch: a sudden thought occurred to me.

'Stop one minute!' I cried.

'Well?'

'It puzzles me to know why Mr Briggs wrote to you about me; or how he knew you, or could fancy that you, living in such an out-of-the-way place, had the power to aid in my discovery.'

'Oh! I am a clergyman,' he said; 'and the clergy are often appealed to about odd matters.' Again the latch rattled.

'No; that does not satisfy me!' I exclaimed: and indeed there was something in the hasty and unexplanatory reply which, instead of allaying, piqued my curiosity more than ever.

'It is a very strange piece of business,' I added; 'I must know more about it.'

'Another time.'

'No; to-night! to-night!' and as he turned from the door, I placed myself between it and him. He looked rather embarrassed.

'You certainly shall not go till you have told me all,' I said.

'I would rather not just now.'

'You shall! – you must!'

'I would rather Diana or Mary informed you.'

Of course these objections wrought my eagerness to a climx: gratified it must be, and that without delay; and I told him so.

'But I apprised you that I was a hard man,' said he, 'difficult to persuade.'

'And I am a hard woman – impossible to put off.'

'And then,' he pursued, 'I am cold: no fervour infects me.'

'Whereas I am hot, and fire dissolves ice. The blaze there has thawed all the snow from your cloak; by the same token, it has streamed on to my floor, and made it like a trampled street. As you hope ever to be forgiven, Mr Rivers, the high crime and misdemeanour of spoiling a sanded kitchen, tell me what I wish to know.'

'Well, then,' he said, 'I yield; if not to your earnestness, to your perseverance:

as stone is worn by continual dropping. Besides, you must know some day – as well now as later. Your name is Jane Eyre?'

'Of course: that was all settled before.'

'You are not, perhaps, aware that I am your namesake? – that I was christened St John Eyre Rivers?'

'No, indeed! I remember now seeing the letter E comprised in your initials written in books you have at different times lent me; but I never asked for what name it stood. But what then? Surely —'

I stopped: I could not trust myself to entertain, much less to express, the thought that rushed upon me – that embodied itself – that, in a second, stood out a strong, solid probability. Circumstances knit themselves, fitted themselves, shot into order: the chain that had been lying hitherto a formless lump of links was drawn out straight – every ring was perfect, the connexion complete. I knew, by instinct, how the matter stood, before St John had said another word; but I cannot expect the reader to have the same intuitive perception, so I must repeat his explanation.

'My mother's name was Eyre; she had two brothers; one a clergyman, who married Miss Jane Reed of Gateshead; the other, John Eyre, Esq., Merchant, late of Funchal, Madeira. Mr Briggs, being Mr Eyre's solicitor, wrote to us last August to inform us of our uncle's death, and to say that he had left his property to his brother the clergyman's orphan daughter, overlooking us, in consequence of a quarrel, never forgiven, between him and my father. He wrote again a few weeks since, to intimate that the heiress was lost, and asking if we knew anything of her. A name casually written on a slip of paper has enabled me to find her out. You know the rest.' Again he was going, but I set my back against the door.

'Do let me speak,' I said; 'let me have one moment to draw breath and reflect.' I paused – he stood before me, hat in hand, looking composed enough. I resumed—

'Your mother was my father's sister?'

'Yes.'

'My aunt, consequently?'

He bowed.

'My uncle John was your uncle John? You, Diana, and Mary are his sister's children, as I am his brother's child?'

'Undeniably.'

'You three, then, are my cousins; half our blood on each side flows from the same source?'

'We are cousins; yes.'

I surveyed him. It seemed I had found a brother: one I could be proud of – one I could love; and two sisters, whose qualities were such, that when I knew them but as mere strangers, they had inspired me with genuine affection and admiration. The two girls, on whom, kneeling down on the wet ground, and looking through the low, latticed window of Moor House kitchen, I had gazed with so bitter a mixture of interest and despair, were my near kinswomen; and the young and stately gentleman who had found me almost dying at his threshold was my blood relation. Glorious discovery to a lonely wretch! This was wealth indeed! – wealth to the heart! – a mine of pure, genial affections. This was a blessing, bright, vivid, and exhilarating – not like the ponderous gift of gold:

# Jane Eyre

rich and welcome enough in its way, but sobering from its weight. I now clapped my hands in sudden joy – my pulse bounded, my veins thrilled.

'Oh, I am glad! – I am glad!' I exclaimed.

St John smiled. 'Did I not say you neglected essential points to pursue trifles?' he asked. 'You were serious when I told you you had got a fortune; and now, for a matter of no moment, you are excited.'

'What *can* you mean? It may be of no moment to you; you have sisters and don't care for a cousin; but I had nobody; and now three relations – or two, if you don't choose to be counted – are born into my world full-grown. I say again, I am glad!'

I walked fast through the room: I stopped, half suffocated with the thoughts that rose faster than I could receive, comprehend, settle them: thoughts of what might, could, would, and should be, and that ere long. I looked at the blank wall: it seemed a sky thick with ascending stars – every one lit me to a purpose or delight. Those who had saved my life, whom, till this hour, I had loved barrenly, I could now benefit. They were under a yoke – I could free them: they were scattered – I could reunite them: the independence, the affluence which was mine, might be theirs too. Were we not four? Twenty thousand pounds shared equally, would be five thousand each – enough and to spare: justice would be done – mutual happiness secured. Now the wealth did not weigh on me: now it was not a mere bequest of coin – it was a legacy of life, hope, enjoyment.

How I looked while these ideas were taking my spirit by storm, I cannot tell; but I perceived soon that Mr Rivers had placed a chair behind me, and was gently attempting to make me sit down on it. He also advised me to be composed; I scorned the insinuation of helplessness and distraction, shook off his hand and began to walk about again.

'Write to Diana and Mary to-morrow,' I said, 'and tell them to come home directly. Diana said they would both consider themselves rich with a thousand pounds, so with five thousand they will do very well.'

'Tell me where I can get you a glass of water,' said St John; 'you must really make an effort to tranquillize your feelings.'

'Nonsense! and what sort of an effect will the bequest have on you? Will it keep you in England, induce you to marry Miss Oliver, and settle down like an ordinary mortal?'

'You wander: your head becomes confused. I have been too abrupt in communicating the news; it has excited you beyond your strength.'

'Mr Rivers! you quite put me out of patience: I am rational enough; it is you who misunderstand, or rather who affect to misunderstand.'

'Perhaps, if you explained yourself a little more fully, I should comprehend better.'

'Explain! What is there to explain? You cannot fail to see that twenty thousand pounds, the sum in question, divided equally between the nephew and three nieces of our uncle, will give five thousand to each? What I want is, that you should write to your sisters and tell them of the fortune that has accrued to them.'

'To you, you mean.'

'I have intimated my view of the case: I am incapable of taking any other. I am not brutally selfish, blindly unjust, or fiendishly ungrateful. Besides, I am resolved I will have a home and connexions. I like Moor House, and I will live

# Jane Eyre

at Moor House; I like Diana and Mary, and I will attach myself for life to Diana and Mary. It would please and benefit me to have five thousand pounds; it would torment and oppress me to have twenty thousand; which, moreover, could never be mine in justice, though it might in law. I abandon to you, then, what is absolutely superfluous to me. Let there be no opposition, and no discussion about it; let us agree amongst each other, and decide the point at once.'

'This is acting on first impulses; you must take days to consider such a matter, ere your word can be regarded as valid.'

'Oh! if all you doubt is my sincerity, I am easy: you see the justice of the case?'

'I *do* see a certain justice; but it is contrary to all custom. Besides, the entire fortune is your right: my uncle gained it by his own efforts; he was free to leave it to whom he would: he left it to you. After all, justice permits you to keep it: you may, with a clear conscience, consider it absolutely your own.'

'With me,' said I, 'it is fully as much a matter of feeling as of conscience: I must indulge my feelings; I so seldom have had an opportunity of doing so. Were you to argue, object, and annoy me for a year, I could not forgo the delicious pleasure of which I have caught a glimpse – that of repaying, in part, a mighty obligation, and winning to myself lifelong friends.'

'You think so now,' rejoined St John, 'because you do not know what it is to possess, nor consequently to enjoy wealth: you cannot form a notion of the importance twenty thousand pounds would give you; of the place it would enable you to take in society; of the prospects it would open to you: you cannot—'

'And you,' I interrupted, 'cannot at all imagine the craving I have for fraternal and sisterly love. I never had a home, I never had brothers or sisters; I must and will have them now: you are not reluctant to admit me, and own me, are you?'

'Jane, I will be your brother – my sisters will be your sisters – without stipulating for this sacrifice of your just rights.'

'Brother? Yes; at the distance of a thousand leagues! Sisters? Yes; slaving amongst strangers! I, wealthy – gorged with gold I never earned and do not merit! You, penniless! Famous equality and fraternization! Close union! Intimate attachment!'

'But, Jane, your aspirations after family ties and domestic happiness may be realized otherwise than by the means you contemplate: you may marry.'

'Nonsense, again! Marry! I don't want to marry, and never shall marry.'

'That is saying too much: such hazardous affirmations are a proof of the excitement under which you labour.'

'It is not saying too much: I know what I feel, and how averse are my inclinations to the bare thought of marriage. No one would take me for love; and I will not be regarded in the light of a mere money speculation. And I do not want a stranger – unsympathizing, alien, different from me; I want my kindred: those with whom I have full fellow-feeling. Say again you will be my brother: when you uttered the words I was satisfied, happy; repeat them, if you can repeat them sincerely.'

'I think I can. I know I have always loved my own sisters; and I know on what my affection for them is grounded – respect for their worth, and admiration of their talents. You too have principle and mind: your tastes and habits resemble Diana's and Mary's; your presence is always agreeable to me; in your conver-

# Jane Eyre

sation I have already for some time found a salutary solace. I feel I can easily and naturally make room in my heart for you, as my third and youngest sister.'

'Thank you: that contents me for to-night. Now you had better go; for if you stay longer, you will perhaps irritate me afresh by some mistrustful scruple.'

'And the school, Miss Eyre? It must now be shut up, I suppose?'

'No. I will retain my post of mistress till you get a substitute.'

He smiled approbation: we shook hands, and he took leave.

I need not narrate in detail the further struggles I had, and arguments I used, to get matters regarding the legacy settled as I wished. My task was a very hard one; but, as I was absolutely resolved – as my cousins saw at length that my mind was really and immutably fixed on making a just division of the property; as they must in their own hearts have felt the equity of the intention; and must, besides, have been innately conscious that in my place they would have done precisely what I wished to do – they yielded at length so far as to consent to put the affair to arbitration. The judges chosen were Mr Oliver and an able lawyer: both coincided in my opinion: I carried my point. The instruments of transfer were drawn out: St John, Diana, Mary, and I, each became possessed of a competency.

# Chapter 34

It was near Christmas by the time all was settled: the season of general holiday approached. I now closed Morton school, taking care that the parting should not be barren on my side. Good fortune opens the hand as well as the heart wonderfully; and to give somewhat when we have largely received, is but to afford a vent to the unusual ebullition of the sensations. I had long felt with pleasure that many of my rustic scholars liked me, and when we parted, that consciousness was confirmed: they manifested their affection plainly and strongly. Deep was my gratification to find I had really a place in their unsophisticated hearts: I promised them that never a week should pass in future that I did not visit them, and give them an hour's teaching in their school.

Mr Rivers came up as, having seen the classes, now numbering sixty girls, file out before me, and locked the door, I stood with the key in my hand, exchanging a few words of special farewell with some half-dozen of my best scholars: as decent, respectable, modest, and well-informed young women as could be found in the ranks of the British peasantry. And that is saying a great deal; for, after all, the British peasantry are the best taught, best mannered, most self-respecting of any in Europe: since those days I have seen paysannes and Bäuerinnen; and the best of them seemed to me ignorant, coarse, and besotted, compared with my Morton girls.

# Jane Eyre

'Do you consider you have got your reward for a season of exertion?' asked Mr Rivers, when they were gone. 'Does not the consciousness of having done some real good in your day and generation give pleasure?'

'Doubtless.'

'And you have only toiled a few months! Would not a life devoted to the task of regenerating your race be well spent?'

'Yes,' I said; ' but I could not go on for ever so: I want to enjoy my own faculties as well as to cultivate those of other people. I must enjoy them now; don't recall either my mind or body to the school; I am out of it and disposed for full holiday.'

He looked grave. 'What now? What sudden eagerness is this you evince? What are you going to do?'

'To be active: as active as I can. And first I must beg you to set Hannah at liberty, and get somebody else to wait on you.'

'Do you want her?'

'Yes; to go with me to Moor House. Diana and Mary will be at home in a week, and I want to have everything in order against their arrival.'

'I understand. I thought you were for flying off on some excursion. It is better so: Hannah shall go with you.'

'Tell her to be ready by to-morrow then; and here is the school-room key: I will give you the key of my cottage in the morning.'

He took it. 'You give it up very gleefully,' said he; 'I don't quite understand your light-heartedness, because I cannot tell what employment you propose to yourself as a substitute for the one you are relinquishing. What aim, what purpose, what ambition in life have you now?'

'My first aim will be to *clean down* (do you comprehend the full force of the expression?) - to *clean down* Moor House from chamber to cellar; my next to rub it up with beeswax, oil, and an indefinite number of cloths, till it glitters again; my third, to arrange every chair, table, bed, carpet, with mathematical precision, afterwards I shall go near to ruin you in coals and peat to keep up good fires in every room; and lastly, the two days preceding that on which your sisters are expected will be devoted by Hannah and me to such a beating of eggs, sorting of currants, grating of spices, compounding of Christmas cakes, chopping up of materials for mince pies, and solemnizing of other culinary rites, as words can convey but an inadequate notion of to the uninitiated like you. My purpose, in short, is to have all things in an absolutely perfect state of readiness for Diana and Mary before next Thursday; and my ambition is to give them a beau ideal of a welcome when they come.'

St John smiled slightly: still he was dissatisfied.

'It is all very well for the present,' said he; 'but seriously, I trust when the first flush of vivacity is over, you will look a little higher than domestic endearments and household joys.'

'The best thing the world has!' I interrupted.

'No, Jane, no; this world is not the scene of fruition; do not attempt to make it so: nor of rest; do not turn slothful.'

'I mean, on the contrary, to be busy.'

'Jane, I excuse you for the present: two months' grace I allow you for the full enjoyment of your new position, and for pleasing yourself with this late-found charm of relationship; but *then*, I hope you will begin to look beyond Moor

House and Morton, and sisterly society and the selfish calm and sensual comfort of civilized affluence. I hope your energies will then once more trouble you with their strength.'

I looked at him with surprise. 'St John,' I said, 'I think you are almost wicked to talk so. I am disposed to be as content as a queen, and you try to stir me up to restlessness! To what end?'

'To the end of turning to profit the talents which God has committed to your keeping; and of which He will surely one day demand a strict account. Jane, I shall watch you closely and anxiously – I warn you of that. And try to restrain the disproportionate fervour with which you throw yourself into commonplace home pleasures. Don't cling so tenaciously to ties of the flesh; save your constancy and ardour for an adequate cause; forbear to waste them on trite transient objects. Do you hear, Jane?'

'Yes; just as if you were speaking Greek. I feel I have adequate cause to be happy, and I *will* be happy. Good-bye!'

Happy at Moor House I was, and hard I worked; and so did Hannah: she was charmed to see how jovial I could be amidst the bustle of a house turned topsy-turvey – how I could brush, and dust, and clean, and cook. And really, after a day or two of confusion worse confounded, it was delightful by degrees to invoke order from the chaos ourselves had made. I had previously taken a journey to S— to purchase some new furniture: my cousins having given me *carte blanche* to effect what alterations I pleased, and a sum having been set aside for that purpose. The ordinary sitting-room and bedrooms I left much as they were: for I knew Diana and Mary would derive more pleasure from seeing again the old homely tables, and chairs, and beds, than from the spectacle of the smartest innovations. Still some novelty was necessary, to give to their return the piquancy with which I wished it to be invested. Dark handsome new carpets and curtains, an arrangement of some carefully selected antique ornaments in porcelain and bronze, new coverings, and mirrors, and dressing-cases, for the toilet-tables, answered the end: they looked fresh without being glaring. A spare parlour and bedroom I refurnished entirely, with old mahogany and crimson upholstery: I laid canvas on the passage, and carpets on the stairs. When all was finished, I thought Moor House as complete a model of bright modest snugness within, as it was, at this season, a specimen of wintry waste and desert dreariness without.

The eventful Thursday at length came. They were expected about dark, and ere dusk fires were lit upstairs and below; the kitchen was in perfect trim; Hannah and I were dressed, and all was in readiness.

St John arrived first. I had entreated him to keep quite clear of the house till everything was arranged: and, indeed, the bare idea of the commotion, at once sordid and trivial, going on within its walls, sufficed to scare him to estrangement. He found me in the kitchen, watching the progress of certain cakes for tea, then baking. Approaching the hearth, he asked, 'If I was at last satisfied with housemaid's work?' I answered by inviting him to accompany me on a general inspection of the result of my labours. With some difficulty, I got him to make the tour of the house. He just looked in at the doors I opened; and when he had wandered upstairs and downstairs, he said I must have gone through a great deal of fatigue and trouble to have effected such considerable changes in so short

a time: but not a syllable did he utter indicating pleasure in the improved aspect of his abode.

This silence damped me. I thought perhaps the alterations had disturbed some old associations he valued. I inquired whether this was the case, no doubt in a somewhat crestfallen tone.

'Not at all; he had, on the contrary, remarked that I had scrupulously respected every association: he feared, indeed, I must have bestowed more thought on the matter than it was worth. How many minutes, for instance, had I devoted to studying the arrangement of this very room? By the by, could I tell him where such a book was?'

I showed him the volume on the shelf: he took it down, and withdrawing to his accustomed window recess, he began to read it.

Now, I did not like this, reader. St John was a good man; but I began to feel he had spoken truth of himself when he said he was hard and cold. The humanities and amenities of life had no attraction for him – its peaceful enjoyments no charm. Literally, he lived only to aspire – after what was good and great, certainly; but still he would never rest, nor approve of others resting round him. As I looked at his lofty forehead, still and pale as a white stone – at his fine lineaments fixed in study – I comprehended all at once that he would hardly make a good husband: that it would be a trying thing to be his wife. I understood, as by inspiration, the nature of his love for Miss Oliver; I agreed with him that it was but a love of the senses. I comprehended how he should despise himself for the feverish influence it exercised over him; how he should wish to stifle and destroy it; how he should mistrust its ever conducing permanently to his happiness or hers. I saw he was of the material from which nature hews her heroes – Christian and Pagan – her lawgivers, her statesmen, her conquerors: a steadfast bulwark for great interests to rest upon; but, at the fireside, too often a cold cumbrous column, gloomy and out of place.

'This parlour is not his sphere,' I reflected: 'The Himalayan ridge, or Caffre bush, even the plague-cursed Guinea Coast swamp, would suit him better. Well may he eschew the calm of domestic life; it is not his element: there his faculties stagnate – they cannot develop or appear to advantage. It is in scenes of strife and danger – where courage is proved, and energy exercised, and fortitude tasked – that he will speak and move, the leader and superior. A merry child would have the advantage of him on this hearth. He is right to choose a missionary career – I see it now.'

'They are coming! They are coming!' cried Hannah, throwing open the parlour door. At the same moment old Carlo barked joyfully. Out I ran. It was now dark; but a rumbling of wheels was audible. Hannah soon had a lantern lit. The vehicle had stopped at the wicket; the driver opened the door: first one well-known form, then another, stepped out. In a minute I had my face under their bonnets, in contact with Mary's soft cheek, then with Diana's flowing curls. They laughed – kissed me – then Hannah: patted Carlo, who was half wild with delight; asked eagerly if all was well; and being assured in the affirmative, hastened into the house.

They were stiff with their long and jolting drive from Whitcross, and chilled with the frosty night air; but their pleasant countenances expanded to the cheerful firelight. While the driver and Hannah brought in the boxes, they demanded St John. At this moment he advanced from the parlour. They both

threw their arms round his neck at once. He gave each one a quiet kiss, said in a low tone a few words of welcome, stood a while to be talked to, and then, intimating that he supposed they would soon rejoin him in the parlour, withdrew there as to a place of refuge.

I had lit their candles to go upstairs, but Diana had first to give hospitable orders respecting the driver; this done, both followed me. They were delighted with the renovation and decorations of their rooms; with the new drapery, and fresh carpets, and rich-tinted china vases: they expressed their gratification ungrudgingly. I had the pleasure of feeling that my arrangements met their wishes exactly, and that what I had done added a vivid charm to their joyous return home.

Sweet was that evening. My cousins, full of exhilaration, were so eloquent in narrative and comment, that their fluency covered St John's taciturnity: he was sincerely glad to see his sisters; but in their glow of fervour and flow of joy he could not sympathize. The event of the day – that is, the return of Diana and Mary – pleased him; but the accompaniments of that event, the glad tumult, the garrulous glee of reception, irked him: I saw he wished the calmer morrow was come. In the very meridian of the night's enjoyment, about an hour after tea, a rap was heard at the door. Hannah entered with the intimation that 'a poor lad was come, at that unlikely time, to fetch Mr Rivers to see his mother, who was drawing away.'

'Where does she live, Hannah?'

'Clear up at Whitcross Brow, almost four miles off, and moor and moss all the way.'

'Tell him I will go.'

'I'm sure, sir, you had better not. It's the worst road to travel after dark that can be: there's no track at all over the bog. And then it is such a bitter night – the keenest wind you ever felt. You had better send word, sir, that you will be there in the morning.'

But he was already in the passage, putting on his cloak; and without one objection, one murmur, he departed. It was then nine o'clock: he did not return till midnight. Starved and tired enough he was: but he looked happier than when he set out. He had performed an act of duty; made an exertion; felt his own strength to do and deny, and was on better terms with himself.

I am afraid the whole of the ensuing week tried his patience. It was Christmas week: we took to no settled employment, but spent it in a sort of merry domestic dissipation. The air of the moors, the freedom of home, the dawn of prosperity, acted on Diana and Mary's spirits like some life-giving elixir: they were gay from morning till noon, and from noon till night. They could always talk; and their discourse, witty, pithy, original, had such charms for me, that I preferred listening to, and sharing in it, to doing anything else. St John did not rebuke our vivacity; but he escaped from it: he was seldom in the house; his parish was large, the population scattered, and he found daily business in visiting the sick and poor in its different districts.

One morning at breakfast, Diana, after looking a little pensive for some minutes, asked him, 'If his plans were yet unchanged?'

'Unchanged and unchangeable,' was the reply. And he proceeded to inform us that his departure from England was now definitely fixed for the ensuing year.

# Jane Eyre

'And Rosamond Oliver?' suggested Mary, the words seeming to escape her lips involuntarily: for no sooner had she uttered them, than she made a gesture as if wishing to recall them. St John had a book in his hand – it was his unsocial custom to read at meals – he closed it, and looked up.

'Rosamond Oliver,' said he, 'is about to be married to Mr Granby, one of the best connected and most estimable residents in S—, grandson and heir to Sir Frederic Granby: I had the intelligence from her father yesterday.'

His sisters looked at each other and at me; we all three looked at him: he was serene as glass.

'The match must have been got up hastily,' said Diana: 'they cannot have known each other long.'

'But two months: they met in October at the county ball at S—. But where there are no obstacles to a union, as in the present case, where the connexion is in every point desirable, delays are unnecessary; they will be married as soon as S— Place, which Sir Frederic gives up to them, can be refitted for their reception.'

The first time I found St John alone after this communication, I felt tempted to inquire if the event distressed him; but he sensed so little to need sympathy, that, so far from venturing to offer him more, I experienced some shame at the recollection of what I had already hazarded. Besides, I was out of practice in talking to him: his reserve was again frozen over, and my frankness was congealed beneath it. He had not kept his promise of treating me like his sisters; he continually made little chilling differences between us, which did not at all tend to the development of cordiality: in short, now that I was acknowledged his kinswoman and lived under the same roof with him, I felt the distance between us to be far greater than when he had known me only as the village schoolmistress. When I remembered how far I had once been admitted to his confidence, I could hardly comprehend his present frigidity.

Such being the case, I felt not a little surprised when he raised his head suddenly from the desk over which he was stooping, and said –

'You see, Jane, the battle is fought and the victory won.'

Startled at being thus addressed, I did not immediately reply: after a moment's hesitation, I answered—

'But are you sure you are not in the position of those conquerors whose triumphs have cost them too dear? Would not such another ruin you?'

'I think not; and if I were, it does not much signify; I shall never be called upon to contend for such another. The event of the conflict is decisive: my way is now clear; I thank God for it!' So saying he returned to his papers and his silence.

As our mutual happiness (i.e. Diana's, Mary's, and mine) settled into a quieter character, and we resumed our usual habits and regular studies, St John stayed more at home: he sat with us in the same room, sometimes for hours together. While Mary drew, Diana pursued a course of encyclopaedic reading she had (to my awe and amazement) undertaken, and I fagged away at German, he pondered a mystic lore of his own – that of some eastern tongue, the acquisition of which he thought necessary to his plans.

Thus engaged, he appeared, sitting in his own recess, quiet, and absorbed enough: but that blue eye of his had a habit of leaving the outlandish-looking grammar, and wandering over, and sometimes fixing upon us, his fellow-

# Jane Eyre

students, with a curious intensity of observation: if caught, it would be instantly withdrawn; yet ever and anon, it returned searchingly to our table. I wondered what it meant: I wondered too, at the punctual satisfaction he never failed to exhibit on an occasion that seemed to me of small moment, namely, my weekly visit to Morton school; and still more was I puzzled when, if the day was unfavourable, if there was snow, or rain, or high wind, and his sisters urged me not to go, he would invariably make light of their solicitude, and encourage me to accomplish the task without regard to the elements.

'Jane is not such a weakling as you would make her,' he would say: 'she can bear a mountain blast, or a shower, or a few flakes of snow, as well as any of us. Her constitution is both sound and elastic; better calculated to endure variations of climate than many more robust.'

And when I returned, sometimes a good deal tired, and not a little weather-beaten, I never dared complain, because I saw that to murmur would be to vex him: on all occasions fortitude pleased him; the reverse was a special annoyance.

One afternoon, however, I got leave to stay at home, because I really had a cold. His sisters were gone to Morton in my stead: I sat reading Schiller; he, deciphering his crabbed Oriental scrolls. As I exchanged a translation for an exercise, I happened to look his way: there I found myself under the influence of the ever-watchful blue eye. How long it had been searching me through and through, and over and over, I cannot tell: so keen was it, and yet so cold, I felt for the moment superstitious – as if I were sitting in the room with something uncanny.

'Jane, what are you doing?'

'Learning German.'

'I want you to give up German and learn Hindustani.'

'You are not in earnest?'

'In such earnest that I must have it so: and I will tell you why.'

He then went on to explain that Hindustani was the language he was himself at present studying; that, as he advanced, he was apt to forget the commencement; that it would assist him greatly to have a pupil with whom he might again and again go over the elements, and so fix them thoroughly in his mind; that his choice had hovered for some time between me and his sisters; but that he had fixed on me because he saw I could sit at a task the longest of the three. Would I do him this favour? I should not, perhaps, have to make the sacrifice long, as it wanted now barely three months to his departure.

St John was not a man to be lightly refused: you felt that every impression made on him, either for pain or pleasure, was deep-graved and permanent. I consented. When Diana and Mary returned, the former found her scholar transferred from her to her brother: she laughed, and both she and Mary agreed that St John should never have persuaded them to such a step. He answered quietly –

'I know it.'

I found him a very patient, very forbearing, and yet an exacting master: he expected me to do a great deal; and when I fulfilled his expectations, he, in his own way, fully testified his approbation. By degrees, he acquired a certain influence over me that took away my liberty of mind: his praise and notice were more restraining than his indifference. I could no longer talk or laugh freely when he was by, because a tiresomely importunate instinct reminded me that

vivacity (at least in me) was distasteful to him. I was so fully aware that only serious moods and occupations were acceptable, that in his presence every effort to sustain or follow any other became vain: I fell under a freezing spell. When he said 'go', I went; 'come', I came; 'do this', I did it. But I did not love my servitude: I wished, many a time, he had continued to neglect me.

One evening, when, at bedtime, his sisters and I stood round him, bidding him good-night, he kissed each of them, as was his custom; and, as equally his custom, he gave me his hand. Diana, who chanced to be in a frolicsome humour (*she* was not painfully controlled by his will; for hers, in another way, was as strong), exclaimed –

'St John! you used to call Jane your third sister, but you don't treat her as such: you should kiss her too.'

She pushed me towards him. I thought Diana very provoking, and felt uncomfortably confused; and while I was thus thinking and feeling, St John bent his head; his Greek face was brought to a level with mine, his eyes questioned my eyes piercingly – he kissed me. There are no such things as marble kisses or ice kisses, or I should say my ecclesiastical cousin's salute belonged to one of these classes; but there may be experiment kisses, and his was an experiment kiss. When given, he viewed me to learn the result; it was not striking: I am sure I did not blush; perhaps I might have turned a little pale, for I felt as if this kiss were a seal affixed to my fetters. He never omitted the ceremony afterwards, and the gravity and quiescence with which I underwent it, seemed to invest it for him with a certain charm.

As for me, I daily wished more to please him; but to do so, I felt daily more and more that I must disown half my nature, stifle half my faculties, wrest my tastes from their original bent, force myself to the adoption of pursuits for which I had no natural vocation. He wanted to train me to an elevation I could never reach; it racked me hourly to aspire to the standard he uplifted. The thing was as impossible as to mould my irregular features to his correct and classic pattern, to give to my changeable green eyes the sea-blue tint and solemn lustre of his own.

Not his ascendancy alone, however, held me in thrall at present. Of late it had been easy enough for me to look sad: a cankering evil sat at my heart and drained my happiness at its source – the evil of suspense.

Perhaps you think I had forgotten Mr Rochester, reader, amidst these changes of place and fortune. Not for a moment. His idea was still with me, because it was not a vapour sunshine could disperse, not a sand-traced effigy storms could wash away; it was a name graven on a tablet, fated to last as long as the marble it inscribed. The craving to know what had become of him followed me everywhere; when I was at Morton, I re-entered my cottage every evening to think of that; and now at Moor House, I sought my bedroom each night to brood over it.

In the course of my necessary correspondence with Mr Briggs about the will, I had inquired if he knew anything of Mr Rochester's present residence and state of health; but as St John had conjectured, he was quite ignorant of all concerning him. I then wrote to Mrs Fairfax, entreating information on the subject. I had calculated with certainty on this step answering my end: I felt sure it would elicit an early answer. I was astonished when a fortnight passed

# Jane Eyre

without reply; but when two months wore away, and day after day the post arrived and brought nothing for me, I fell a prey to the keenest anxiety.

I wrote again: there was a chance of my first letter having missed. Renewed hope followed renewed effort: it shone like the former for some weeks, then, like it, it faded, flickered: not a line, not a word reached me. When half a year wasted in vain expectancy, my hope died out, and then I felt dark indeed.

A fine spring shone round me, which I could not enjoy. Summer approached; Diana tried to cheer me: she said I looked ill, and wished to accompany me to the seaside. This St John opposed; he said I did not want dissipation, I wanted employment; my present life was too purposeless, I required an aim; and, I suppose, by way of supplying deficiencies, he prolonged still further my lessons in Hindustani, and grew more urgent in requiring their accomplishment: and I, like a fool, never thought of resisting him – I could not resist him.

One day I had come to my studies in lower spirits than usual; the ebb was occasioned by a poignantly felt disappointment. Hannah had told me in the morning there was a letter for me, and when I went down to take it, almost certain that the long-looked-for tidings were vouchsafed me at last, I found only an unimportant note from Mr Briggs on business. The bitter check had wrung from me some tears; and now, as I sat poring over the crabbed characters and flourishing tropes of an Indian scribe, my eyes filled again.

St John called me to his side to read; in attempting to do this my voice failed me: words were lost in sobs. He and I were the only occupants of the parlour: Diana was practising her music in the drawing-room, Mary was gardening – it was a very fine May day, clear, sunny, and breezy. My companion expressed no surprise at this emotion, nor did he question me as to its cause; he only said –

'We will wait a few minutes, Jane, till you are more composed.' And while I smothered the paroxysm with all haste, he sat calm and patient, leaning on his desk, and looking like a physician watching with the eye of science an expected and fully understood crisis in a patient's malady. Having stifled my sobs, wiped my eyes, and muttered something about not being very well that morning, I resumed my task, and succeeded in completing it. St John put away my books and his, locked his desk, and said –

'Now, Jane, you shall take a walk; and with me.'

'I will call Diana and Mary.'

'No; I want only one companion this morning, and that must be you. Put on your things; go out by the kitchen door: take the road towards the head of Marsh Glen: I will join you in a moment.'

I know no medium: I never in my life have known any medium in my dealings with positive, hard characters, antagonistic of my own, between absolute submission and determined revolt. I have always faithfully observed the one, up to the very moment of bursting, sometimes with volcanic vehemence, into the other; and as neither present circumstances warranted, nor my present mood inclined me to mutiny, I observed careful obedience to St John's directions, and in ten minutes I was treading the wild track of the glen, side by side with him.

The breeze was from the west: it came over the hills, sweet with scents of heath and rush; the sky was of stainless blue; the stream descending the ravine, swelled with past spring rains, poured along plentiful and clear, catching golden gleams from the sun, and sapphire tints from the firmament. As we advanced and left the track, we trod a soft turf, mossy fine and emerald green, minutely

# Jane Eyre

enamelled with a tiny white flower, and spangled with a star-like yellow blossom: the hills, meantime, shut us quite in; for the glen, towards its head, wound to their very core.

'Let us rest here,' said St John, as we reached the first stragglers of the battalion of rocks, guarding a sort of pass, beyond which the beck rushed down a waterfall; and where, still a little further, the mountain shook off turf and flower, had only heath for raiment and crag for gem – where it exaggerated the wild to the savage, and exchanged the fresh for the frowning – where it guarded the forlorn hope of solitude, and a last refuge for silence.

I took a seat: St John stood near me. He looked up the pass and down the hollow; his glance wandered away with the stream, and returned to traverse the unclouded heaven which coloured it: he removed his hat, let the breeze stir his hair and kiss his brow. He seemed in communion with the genius of the haunt: with his eye he bade farewell to something.

'And I shall see it again,' he said aloud, 'in dreams, when I sleep by the Ganges; and again, in a more remote hour – when another slumber overcomes me, on the shore of a darker stream!'

Strange words of a strange love! An austere patriot's passion for his fatherland! He sat down; for half an hour we never spoke; neither he to me nor I to him: that interval past, he recommenced –

'Jane, I go in six weeks; I have taken my berth in an East Indiaman which sails on the twentieth of June.'

'God will protect you; for you have undertaken His work,' I answered.

'Yes,' said he, 'there is my glory and joy. I am the servant of an infallible Master. I am not going out under human guidance, subject to the defective laws and erring control of my feeble fellow-worms: my king, my lawgiver, my captain, is the all-perfect. It seems strange to me that all round me do not burn to enlist under the same banner – to join in the same enterprise.'

'All have not your powers; and it would be folly for the feeble to wish to march with the strong.'

'I do not speak to the feeble, or think of them: I address only such as are worthy of the work, and competent to accomplish it.'

'Those are few in number, and difficult to discover.'

'You say truly: but when found, it is right to stir them up – to urge and exhort them to the effort – to show them what their gifts are, and why they were given – to speak Heaven's message in their ear – to offer them, direct from God, a place in the ranks of His chosen.'

'If they are really qualified for the task, will not their own hearts be the first to inform them of it?'

I felt as if an awful charm was framing round and gathering over me: I trembled to hear some fatal word spoken which would at once declare and rivet the spell.

'And what does *your* heart say?' demanded St John.

'My heart is mute – my heart is mute,' I answered, struck and thrilled.

'Then I must speak of it,' continued the deep, relentless voice. 'Jane, come with me to India: come as my helpmeet and fellow-labourer.'

The glen and sky spun round: the hills heaved! It was as if I had heard a summons from Heaven – as if a visionary messenger, like him of Macedonia,

had enounced, 'Come over and help us!' But I was no apostle – I could not behold the herald – I could not receive his call.

'Oh, St John!' I cried, 'have some mercy!'

I appealed to one who, in the discharge of what he believed his duty, knew neither mercy nor remorse. He continued –

'God and nature intended you for a missionary's wife. It is not personal, but mental endowments they have given you: you are formed for labour, not for love. A missionary's wife you must – shall be. You shall be mine: I claim you – not for my pleasure, but for my Sovereign's service.'

'I am not fit for it: I have no vocation,' I said.

He had calculated on these first objections: he was not irritated by them. Indeed, as he leaned back against the crag behind him, folded his arms on his chest, and fixed his countenance, I saw he was prepared for a long and trying opposition, and had taken in a stock of patience to last him to its close – resolved, however, that that close should be conquest for him.

'Humility, Jane,' said he, 'is the groundwork of Christian virtues: you say right that you are not fit for the work. Who is fit for it? Or who, that ever was truly called, believed himself worthy of the summons? I, for instance, am but dust and ashes. With St Paul, I acknowledge myself the chiefest of sinners; but I do not suffer this sense of my personal vileness to daunt me. I know my Leader: that He is just as well as mighty; and while He has chosen a feeble instrument to perform a great task, He will, from the boundless stores of His providence, supply the inadequacy of the means to the end. Think like me, Jane – trust like me. It is the Rock of Ages I ask you to lean on: do not doubt but it will bear the weight of your human weakness.'

'I do not understand a missionary life: I have never studied missionary labours.'

'There I, humble as I am, can give you the aid you want; I can set your task from hour to hour; stand by you always; help you from moment to moment. This I could do in the beginning: soon (for I know your powers) you would be as strong and apt as myself, and would not require my help.'

'But my powers – where are they for this undertaking? I do not feel them. Nothing speaks or stirs in me while you talk. I am sensible of no light kindling – no life quickening – no voice counselling or cheering. Oh, I wish I could make you see how much my mind is at this moment like a rayless dungeon, with one shrinking fear fettered in its depths – the fear of being persuaded by you to attempt what I cannot accomplish!'

'I have an answer for you – hear it. I have watched you ever since we first met: I have made you my study for ten months. I have proved you in that time by sundry tests: and what have I seen and elicited? In the village school I found you could perform well, punctually, uprightly, labour uncongenial to your habits and inclinations; I saw you could perform it with capacity and tact: you could win while you controlled. In the calm with which you learnt you had become suddenly rich, I read a mind clear of the vice of Demas – lucre had no undue power over you. In the resolute readiness with which you cut your wealth into four shares, keeping but one to yourself, and relinquishing the three others to the claim of abstract justice, I recognized a soul that revelled in the flame and excitement of sacrifice. In the tractability with which, at my wish, you forsook a study in which you were interested, and adopted another because it interested

# Jane Eyre

me; in the untiring assiduity with which you have since persevered in it – in the unflagging energy and unshaken temper with which you have met its difficulties – I acknowledge the complement of the qualities I seek. Jane, you are docile, diligent, disinterested, faithful, constant, and courageous; very gentle, and very heroic: cease to mistrust yourself – I can trust you unreservedly. As a conductress of Indian schools, and a helper amongst Indian women, your assistance will be to me invaluable.'

My iron shroud contracted round me; persuasion advanced with slow, sure step. Shut my eyes as I would, these last words of his succeeded in making the way, which had seemed blocked up, comparatively clear. My work, which had appeared so vague, so hopelessly diffuse, condensed itself as he proceeded, and assumed a definite form under his shaping hand. He wanted for an answer. I demanded a quarter of an hour to think, before I again hazarded a reply.

'Very willingly,' he rejoined; and rising, he strode a little distance up the pass, threw himself down on a swell of heath, and there lay still.

'I *can* do what he wants me to do: I am forced to see and acknowledge that,' I meditated – 'that is, if life be spared me. But I feel mine is not the existence to be long protracted under an Indian sun. What then? He does not care for that: when my time came to die, he would resign me, in all serenity and sanctity, to the God who gave me. The case is very plain before me. In leaving England, I should leave a loved but empty land – Mr Rochester is not there; and if he were, what is, what can that ever be to me? My business is to live without him now: nothing so absurd, so weak as to drag on from day to day, as if I were waiting some impossible change in circumstances, which might re-unite me to him. Of course (as St John once said) I must seek another interest in life to replace the one lost: is not the occupation he now offers me truly the most glorious man can adopt or God assign. Is it not, by its noble cares and sublime results, the one best calculated to fill the void left by uptorn affections and demolished hopes? I believe I must say yes – and yet I shudder. Alas! If I join St John, I abandon half myself; if I go to India, I go to premature death. And how will the interval between leaving England for India, and India for the grave, be filled? Oh, I know well! That, too, is very clear to my vision. By straining to satisfy St John till my sinews ache. I *shall* satisfy him – to the finest central point and farthest outward circle of his expectations. If I *do* go with him – if I *do* make the sacrifice he urges, I will make it absolutely: I will throw all on the altar – heart, vitals, the entire victim. He will never love me; but he shall approve me; I will show him energies he has not yet seen, resources he has never suspected. Yes, I can work as hard as he can, and with as little grudging.

'Consent, then, to his demand is possible: but for one item – one dreadful item. It is – that he asks me to be his wife, and has no more of a husband's heart for me than that frowning giant of a rock, down which the stream is foaming in yonder gorge. He prizes me as a soldier would a good weapon, and that is all. Unmarried to him, this would never grieve me; but can I let him complete his calculations – coolly put into practice his plans – go through the wedding ceremony? Can I receive from him the bridal ring, endure all the forms of love (which I doubt not he would scrupulously observe) and know that the spirit was quite absent? Can I bear the consciousness that every endearment he bestows is a sacrifice made on principle? No: such a martyrdom would be montrous. I

# Jane Eyre

will never undergo it. As his sister, I might accompany him – not as his wife: I will tell him so.'

I looked towards the knoll: there he lay, still as a prostrate column; his face turned to me: his eye beaming, watchful, and keen. He started to his feet and approached me.

'I am ready to go to India, if I may go free.'

'Your answer requires a commentary,' he said; 'it is not clear.'

'You have hitherto been my adopted brother – I, your adopted sister: let us continue as such: you and I had better not marry.'

He shook his head. 'Adopted fraternity will not do in this case. If you were my real sister it would be different: I should take you, and seek no wife. But as it is, either our union must be consecrated and sealed by marriage, or it cannot exist: practical obstacles oppose themselves to any other plan. Do you not see it, Jane? Consider a moment – your strong sense will guide you.'

I did consider; and still my sense, such as it was, directed me only to the fact that we did not love each other as man and wife should: and therefore it inferred we ought not to marry. I said so. 'St John,' I returned, 'I regard you as a brother – you, me as a sister: so let us continue.'

'We cannot – we cannot,' he answered, with short sharp determination: 'it would not do. You have said you will go with me to India: remember – you have said that.'

'Conditionally.'

'Well – well. To the main point – the departure with me from England, the co-operation with me in my future labours – you do not object. You have already as good as put your hand to the plough: you are too consistent to withdraw it. You have but one end to keep in view – how the work you have undertaken can best be done. Simplify your complicated interests, feeling, thoughts, wishes, aims; merge all considerations in one purpose: that of fulfilling with effect – with power – the mission of your great Master. To do so, you must have a coadjutor: not a brother – that is a loose tie – but a husband. I, too, do not want a sister: a sister might any day be taken from me. I want a wife: the sole helpmeet I can influence efficiently in life, and retain absolutely till death.'

I shuddered as he spoke: I felt his influence in my marrow – his hold on my limbs.

'Seek one elsewhere than in me, St John: seek one fitted to you.'

'One fitted to my purpose, you mean – fitted to my vocation. Again I tell you it is not the significant private individual – the mere man, with the man's selfish senses – I wish to mate: it is the missionary.'

'And I will give the missionary my energies – it is all he wants – but not myself: that would be only adding the husk and shell to the kernel. For them he has no use: I retain them.'

'You cannot – you ought not. Do you think God will be satisfied with half an oblation? Will He accept a mutilated sacrifice? It is the cause of God I advocate: it is under His standard I enlist you. I cannot accept on His behalf a divided allegiance: it must be entire.'

'Oh! I will give my heart to God,' I said, '*You* do not want it.'

I will not swear, reader, that there was not something of repressed sarcasm both in the tone in which I uttered this sentence, and in the feeling that accompanied it. I had silently feared St John till now, because I had not

# Jane Eyre

understood him. He had held me in awe, because he had held me in doubt. How much of him was saint, how much mortal, I could not heretofore tell: but revelations were being made in this conference: the analysis of his nature was proceeding before my eyes. I saw his fallibilities: I comprehended them. I understood that, sitting there where I did, on the bank of heath, and with that handsome form before me, I sat at the feet of a man, erring as I. The veil fell from his hardness and despotism. Having felt in him the presence of these qualities, I felt his imperfection, and took courage. I was with an equal – one with whom I might argue – one whom, if I saw good, I might resist.

He was silent after I had uttered the last sentence, and I presently risked an upward glance at his countenance. His eye, bent on me, expressed at once stern surprise and keen inquiry. 'Is she sarcastic, and sarcastic to *me!*' it seemed to say. 'What does this signify?'

'Do not let us forget that this is a solemn matter,' he said ere long; 'one of which we may neither think nor talk lightly without sin. I trust, Jane, you are in earnest when you say you will give your heart to God: it is all I want. Once wrench your heart from man, and fix it on your Maker, the advancement of that Maker's spiritual kingdom on earth will be your chief delight and endeavour; you will be ready to do at once whatever furthers that end. You will see what impetus would be given to your efforts and mine by your physical and mental union in marriage – the only union that gives a character of permanent conformity to the destinies and designs of human beings – and, passing over all minor caprices – all trivial difficulties and delicacies of feeling, all scruple about the degree, kind, strength, or tenderness of mere personal inclination – you will hasten to enter into that union at once.'

'Shall I?' I said briefly; and I looked at his features, beautiful in their harmony, but strangely formidable in their still severity; at his brow, commanding, but not open; at his eyes, bright and deep and searching, but never soft; at his tall imposing figure; and fancied myself in idea *his wife*. Oh! it would never do! As his curate, his comrade, all would be right: I would cross oceans with him in that capacity; toil under Eastern suns, in Asian deserts with him in that office; admire and emulate his courage and devotion and vigour: accommodate quietly to his masterhood; smile undisturbed at his ineradicable ambition; discriminate the Christian from the man: profoundly esteem the one, and freely forgive the other. I should suffer often, no doubt, attached to him only in this capacity: my body would be under rather a stringent yoke, but my heart and mind would be free. I should still have my unblighted self to turn to: my natural unenslaved feelings with which to communicate in moments of loneliness. There would be recesses in my mind which would be only mine, to which he never came; and sentiments growing there, fresh and sheltered, which his austerity could never blight, nor his measured warrior-march trample down. But as his wife – at his side always, and always restrained, and always checked – forced to keep the fire of my nature continually low, to compel it to burn inwardly and never utter a cry, though the imprisoned flame consumed vital after vital – *this* would be unendurable.

'St John!' I exclaimed, when I had got so far in my meditation.

'Well?' he answered icily.

'I repeat I freely consent to go with you as your fellow-missionary, but not as your wife; I cannot marry you, and become part of you.'

# Jane Eyre

'A part of me you must become,' he answered steadily; 'otherwise the whole bargain is void. How can I, a man, not yet thirty, take out with me to India a girl of nineteen, unless she be married to me? How can we be for ever together – sometimes in solitudes, sometimes amidst savage tribes – and unwed?'

'Very well,' I said shortly; 'under the circumstances, quite as well as if I were either your real sister, or a man and a clergyman like yourself.'

'It is known that you are not my sister; I cannot introduce you as such: to attempt it would be to fasten injurious suspicions on us both. And for the rest, though you have a man's vigorous brain, you have a woman's heart and – it would not do.'

'It would do,' I affirmed with some disdain, 'perfectly well. I have a woman's heart, but not where you are concerned; for you I have only a comrade's constancy; a fellow-soldier's frankness, fidelity, fraternity, if you like; a neophyte's respect and submission to his hierophant: nothing more – don't fear.'

'It is what I want,' he said, speaking to himself; 'it is just what I want. And there are obstacles in the way: they must be hewn down. Jane, you would not repent marrying me; be certain of that. We *must* be married – I repeat it: there is no other way; and undoubtedly enough of love would follow upon marriage to render the union right even in your eyes.'

'I scorn your idea of love,' I could not help saying, as I rose up and stood before him, leaning my back against the rock. 'I scorn the counterfeit sentiment you offer: yes, St John, and I scorn you when you offer it.'

He looked at me fixedly, compressing his well-cut lips while he did so. Whether he was incensed or surprised, or what, it was not easy to tell: he could command his countenance thoroughly.

'I scarcely expected to hear that expression from you,' he said; 'I think I have done and uttered nothing to deserve scorn.'

I was touched by his gentle tone, and overawed by his high, calm mien.

'Forgive me the words, St John; but it is your own fault that I have been roused to speak so unguardedly. You have introduced a topic on which our natures are at variance – a topic we should never discuss: the very name of love is an apple of discord between us. If the reality were required, what should we do? How should we feel? My dear cousin, abandon your scheme of marriage – forget it.'

'No,' said he; 'it is a long-cherished scheme, and the only one which can secure my great end: but I shall urge you no further at present. To-morrow, I leave home for Cambridge: I have many friends there to whom I should wish to say farewell. I shall be absent a fortnight – take that space of time to consider my offer; and do not forget that if you reject it, it is not me you deny, but God. Through my means, He opens to you a noble career, as my wife only can you enter upon it. Refuse to be my wife, and you limit yourself for ever to a track of selfish ease and barren obscurity. Tremble lest in that case you should be numbered with those who have denied the faith, and are worse than infidels!'

He had done. Turning from me he once more

*Looked to river, looked to hill.*

But this time his feelings were all pent in his heart: I was not worthy to hear them uttered. As I walked by his side homeward, I read well in his iron silence all he felt towards me: the disappointment of an austere and despotic nature,

which has met resistance where it expected submission – the disapprobation of a cool, inflexible judgement, which has detected in another feelings and views in which it has no power to sympathize: in short, as a man, he would have wished to coerce me into obedience: it was only as a sincere Christian he bore so patiently with my perversity, and allowed so long a space for reflection and repentance.

That night, after he had kissed his sisters, he thought proper to forget even to shake hands with me, but left the room in silence. I – who though I had no love, had much friendship for him – was hurt by the marked omission: so much hurt that tears started to my eyes.

'I see you and St John have been quarrelling, Jane,' said Diana, 'during your walk on the moor. But go after him; he is now lingering in the passage expecting you – he will make it up.'

I have not much pride under such circumstances: I would always rather be happy than dignified; and I ran after him: he stood at the foot of the stairs.

'Good-night, St John,' said I.

'Good-night, Jane,' he replied calmly.

'Then shake hands,' I added.

What a cold, loose touch he impressed on my fingers! He was deeply displeased by what had occurred that day; cordiality would not warm, nor tears move him. No happy reconciliation was to be had with him – no cheering smile or generous word: but still the Christian was patient and placid; and when I asked him if he forgave me, he answered that he was not in the habit of cherishing the remembrance of vexation; that he had nothing to forgive, not having been offended.

And with that answer he left me. I would much rather he had knocked me down.

# Chapter 35

He did not leave for Cambridge the next day, as he had said he would. He deferred his departure a whole week, and during that time he made me feel what severe punishment a good yet stern, a conscientious yet implacable man can inflict on one who has offended him. Without one overt act of hostility, one upbraiding word, he contrived to impress me momently with the conviction that I was put beyond the pale of his favour.

Not that St John harboured a spirit of unchristian vindictiveness – not that he would have injured a hair of my head, if it had been fully in his power to do so. Both by nature and principle he was superior to the mean gratification of vengeance: he had forgiven me for saying I scorned him and his love, but he had not forgotten the words; and as long as he and I lived he never would forget

# Jane Eyre

them. I saw by his look, when he turned to me, that they were always written on the air between me and him; whenever I spoke, they sounded in my voice to his ear, and their echo toned every answer he gave me.

He did not abstain from conversing with me: he even called me as usual each morning to join him at his desk: and I fear the corrupt man within him had a pleasure unimparted to, and unshared by, the pure Christian, in evincing with what skill he could, while acting and speaking apparently just as usual, extract from every deed and every phrase the spirit of interest and approval which had formerly communicated a certain austere charm to his language and manner. To me, he was in reality become no longer flesh, but marble; his eye was a cold, bright, blue gem; his tongue a speaking instrument – nothing more.

All this was torture to me – refined, lingering torture. It kept up a slow fire of indignation and a trembling trouble of grief, which harassed and crushed me altogether. I felt how, if I were his wife, this good man, pure as the deep sunless source, could soon kill me, without drawing from my veins a single drop of blood, or receiving on his own crystal conscience the faintest stain of crime. Especially I felt this when I made any attempt to propitiate him. No ruth met my ruth. *He* experienced no suffering from estrangement – no yearning after reconciliation; and though, more than once, my fast-falling tears blistered the page over which we both bent, they produced no more effect on him than if his heart had been really a matter of stone or metal. To his sisters, meantime, he was somewhat kinder than usual: as if afraid that mere coldness would not sufficiently convince me how completely I was banished and banned, he added the force of contrast; and this I am sure he did not by malice, but on principle.

The night before he left home, happening to see him walking in the garden about sunset, and remembering, as I looked at him, that this man, alienated as he now was, had once saved my life, and that we were near relations, I was moved to make a last attempt to regain his friendship. I went out and approached him as he stood leaning over the little gate; I spoke to the point at once.

'St John, I am unhappy because you are still angry with me. Let us be friends.'

'I hope we are friends,' was the unmoved reply; while he still watched the rising of the moon, which he had been contemplating as I approached.

'No, St John, we are not friends as we were. You know that.'

'Are we not? That is wrong. For my part I wish you no ill, and all good.'

'I believe you, St John; for I am sure you are incapable of wishing any one ill; but, as I am your kinswoman, I should desire somewhat more affection than that sort of general philanthropy you extend to mere strangers.'

'Of course,' he said. 'Your wish is reasonable, and I am far from regarding you as a stranger.'

This, spoken in a cool, tranquil tone, was mortifying, and baffling enough. Had I attended to the suggestions of pride and ire, I should immediately have left him; but something worked within me more strongly than those feelings could. I deeply venerated my cousin's talent and principle. His friendship was of value to me: to lose it tried me severely. I would not so soon relinquish the attempt to reconquer it.

'Must we part in this way, St John? And when you go to India, will you leave me so, without a kinder word than you have yet spoken?'

He now turned quite from the moon and faced me.

# Jane Eyre

'When I go to India, Jane, will I leave you! What! do you not go to India?'

'You said I could not unless I married you.'

'And you will not marry me! You adhere to that resolution?'

Reader, do you know, as I do, what terror those cold people can put into the ice of their questions? How much of the fall of the avalanche is in their anger? of the breaking up of the frozen sea in their displeasure?

'No, St John, I will not marry you. I adhere to my resolution.'

The avalanche had shaken and slid a little forward, but it did not yet crash down.

'Once more, why this refusal?' he asked.

'Formerly,' I answered, 'because you did not love me; now, I reply, because you almost hate me. If I were to marry you, you would kill me. You are killing me now.'

His lips and cheeks turned white – quite white.

'*I should kill you – I am killing you?* Your words are such as ought not to be used: violent, unfeminine, and untrue. They betray an unfortunate state of mind: they merit severe reproof: they would seem inexcusable, but that it is the duty of man to forgive his fellow even until seventy-and-seven times.'

I had finished the business now. While earnestly wishing to erase from his mind the trace of my former offence, I had stamped on that tenacious surface another and far deeper impression: I had burnt it in.

'Now you will indeed hate me,' I said. 'It is useless to attempt to conciliate you: I see I have made an eternal enemy of you.'

A fresh wrong did these words inflict: the worse, because they touched on the truth. That bloodless lip quivered to a temporary spasm. I knew the steely ire I had whetted. I was heart-wrung.

'You utterly misinterpret my words,' I said, at once seizing his hand: 'I have no intention to grieve or pain you – indeed, I have not.'

Most bitterly he smiled – most decidedly he withdrew his hand from mine. 'And now you recall your promise, and will not go to India at all, I presume?' said he, after a considerable pause.

'Yes, I will, as your assistant,' I answered.

A very long silence succeeded. What struggle there was in him between Nature and Grace in this interval, I cannot tell: only singular gleams scintillated in his eyes, and strange shadows passed over his face. He spoke at last.

'I before proved to you the absurdity of a single woman of your age proposing to accompany abroad a single man of mine. I proved it to you in such terms as, I should have thought, would have prevented your ever again alluding to the plan. That you have done so, I regret – for your sake.'

I interrupted him. Anything like a tangible reproach gave me courage at once. 'Keep to common sense, St John: you are verging on nonsense. You pretend to be shocked by what I have said. You are not really shocked; for, with your superior mind, you cannot be either so dull or so conceited as to misunderstand my meaning. I say again, I will be your curate, if you like, but never your wife.'

Again he turned lividly pale; but, as before, controlled his passion perfectly. He answered emphatically but calmly –

'A female curate, who is not my wife, would never suit me. With me, then it seems, you cannot go: but if you are sincere in your offer, I will, while in town, speak to a married missionary, whose wife needs a coadjutor. Your own

fortune will make you independent of the Society's aid; and thus you may still be spared the dishonour of breaking your promise and deserting the band you engaged to join.'

Now I never had, as the reader knows, either given any formal promise or entered into any engagement; and this language was all much too hard and much too despotic for the occasion. I replied –

'There is no dishonour, no breach of promise, no desertion in the case. I am not under the slightest obligation to go to India, especially with strangers. With you I would have ventured much, because I admire, confide in, and, as a sister, I love you; but I am convinced that, go when and with whom I would, I should not live long in that climate.'

'Ah! you are afraid of yourself,' he said, curling his lip.

'I am. God did not give me my life to throw away; and to do as you wish me would, I begin to think, be almost equivalent to committing suicide. Moreover, before I definitively resolve on quitting England, I will know for certain whether I cannot be of greater use by remaining in it than by leaving it.'

'What do you mean?'

'It would be fruitless to attempt to explain; but there is a point on which I have long endured painful doubt, and I can go nowhere till by some means that doubt is removed.'

'I know where your heart turns and to what it clings. The interest you cherish is lawless and unconsecrated. Long since you ought to have crushed it: now you should blush to allude to it. You think of Mr Rochester?'

It was true. I confessed it by silence.

'Are you going to seek Mr Rochester?'

'I must find out what is become of him.'

'It remains for me, then,' he said, 'to remember you in my prayers, and to entreat God for you, in all earnestness, that you may not indeed become a castaway. I had thought I recognized in you one of the chosen. But God sees not as man sees: *His* will be done.'

He opened the gate, passed through it, and strayed away down the glen. He was soon out of sight.

On re-entering the parlour, I found Diana standing at the window, looking very thoughtful. Diana was a great deal taller than I: she put her hand on my shoulder, and, stooping, examined my face.

'Jane,' she said, 'you are always agitated and pale now, I am sure there is something the matter. Tell me what business St John and you have on hand. I have watched you this half-hour from the window; you must forgive my being such a spy, but for a long time I have fancied I hardly know what. St John is a strange being —'

She paused – I did not speak: soon she resumed –

'That brother of mine cherishes peculiar views of some sort respecting you, I am sure: he has long distinguished you by a notice and interest he never showed to anyone else – to what end? I wish he loved you – does he, Jane?'

I put her cool hand to my hot forehead; 'No, Di, not one whit.'

'Then why does he follow you so with his eyes, and get you so frequently alone with him, and keep you so continually at his side? Mary and I had both concluded he wished you to marry him.'

'He does – he has asked me to be his wife.'

# Jane Eyre

Diana clapped her hands. 'That is just what we hoped and thought!
And you will marry him, Jane, won't you? And then he will stay in England.'

'Far from that, Diana; his sole idea in proposing to me is to procure a fitting
fellow-labourer in his Indian toils.'

'What! He wishes you to go to India?'

'Yes.'

'Madness!' she exclaimed. 'You would not live three months there, I am
certain. You never shall go: you have not consented, have you, Jane?'

'I have refused to marry him –'

'And have consequently displeased him?' she suggested.

'Deeply: he will never forgive me, I fear: yet I offered to accompany him as
his sister.'

'It was frantic folly to do so, Jane. Think of the task you undertook – one of
incessant fatigue, where fatigue kills even the strong, and you are weak. St John
– you know him – would urge you to impossibilities: with him there would be
no permission to rest during the hot hours; and unfortunately, I have noticed,
whatever he exacts, you force yourself to perform. I am astonished you found
courage to refuse his hand. You do not love him then, Jane?'

'Not as a husband.'

'Yet he is a handsome fellow.'

'And I am so plain, you see, Di. We should never suit.'

'Plain! You? Not at all. You are much too pretty, as well as too good, to be
grilled alive in Calcutta.' And again she earnestly conjured me to give up all
thoughts of going out with her brother.

'I must indeed,' I said; 'for when just now I repeated the offer of serving him
for a deacon, he expressed himself shocked at my want of decency. He seemed
to think I had committed an impropriety in proposing to accompany him
unmarried: as if I had not from the first hoped to find in him a brother, and
habitually regarded him as such.'

'What make you say he does not love you, Jane?'

'You should hear himself on the subject. He has again and again explained
that it is not himself, but his office, he wishes to mate. He has told me I am
formed for labour – not for love: which is true, no doubt. But, in my opinion,
if I am not formed for love, it follows that I am not formed for marriage. Would
it not be strange, Di, to be chained for life to a man who regarded one but as
a useful tool?'

'Insupportable – unnatural – out of the question!'

'And then,' I continued, 'though I have only sisterly affection for him now,
yet, if forced to be his wife, I can imagine the possibility of conceiving an
inevitable, strange, torturing kind of love for him, because he is so talented, and
there is often a certain heroic grandeur in his look, manner, and conversation.
In that case, my lot would become unspeakably wretched. He would not want
me to love him; and if I showed the feeling, he would make me sensible that it
was a superfluity, unrequired by him, unbecoming in me. I know he would.'

'And yet St John is a good man,' said Diana.

'He is a good and a great man; but he forgets, pitilessly, the feelings and
claims of little people, in pursuing his own large views. It is better, therefore,
for the insignificant to keep out of his way lest, in his progress, he should trample

them down. Here he comes! I will leave you, Diana.' And I hastened upstairs as I saw him entering the garden.

But I was forced to meet him again at supper. During that meal he appeared just as composed as usual. I had thought he would hardly speak to me, and I was certain he had given up his pursuit of his matrimonial scheme: the sequel showed I was mistaken on both points. He addressed me precisely in his ordinary manner, or what had, of late, been his ordinary manner – one scrupulously polite. No doubt he had invoked the help of the Holy Spirit to subdue the anger I had roused in him, and now believed he had forgiven me once more.

For the evening reading before prayers, he selected the twenty-first chapter of Revelation. It was at all times pleasant to listen while from his lips fell the words of the Bible: never did his fine voice sound at once so sweet and full – never did his manner become so impressive in its noble simplicity, as when he delivered the oracles of God: and to-night that voice took a more solemn tone – that manner a more thrilling meaning – as he sat in the midst of his household circle (the May moon shining in through the uncurtained window, and rendering almost unnecessary the light of the candle on the table): as he sat there, bending over the great old Bible, and described from its page the vision of the new heaven and the new earth – told how God would come to dwell with men, how He would wipe away all the tears from their eyes, and promised that there should be no more death, neither sorrow nor crying, nor any more pain, because the former things were passed away.

The succeeding words thrilled me strangely as he spoke them: especially as I felt, by the slight, indescribable alteration in sound, that in uttering them his eye had turned on me.

'He that overcometh shall inherit all things; and I will be his God, and he shall be My son. But,' was slowly, distinctly read, 'the fearful, the unbelieving . . . shall have their part in the lake which burneth with fire and brimstone, which is the second death.'

Henceforward, I knew what fate St John feared for me.

A calm, subdued triumph, blent with a longing earnestness, marked his enunciation of the last glorious verses of that chapter. The reader believed his name was already written in the Lamb's Book of Life, and yearned after the hour which should admit him to the city to which the kings of the earth bring their glory and honour; which has no need of sun or moon to shine in it, because the glory of God lighten it, and the Lamb is the light thereof.

In the prayer following the chapter, all his energy gathered – all his stern zeal woke: he was in deep earnest, wrestling with God, and resolved on a conquest. He supplicated strength for the weak-hearted; guidance for wanderers from the fold: a return, even at the eleventh hour, for those whom the temptations of the world and the flesh were luring from the narrow path. He asked, he urged, he claimed the boon of a brand snatched from the burning. Earnestness is ever deeply solemn: first, as I listened to that prayer, I wondered at his; then, when it continued and rose, I was touched by it, and at last awed. He felt the greatness and goodness of his purpose so sincerely; others who heard him plead for it, could not but feel it too.

The prayer over, we took leave of him: he was to go at a very early hour in the morning. Diana and Mary, having kissed him, left the room – in compliance,

# Jane Eyre

I think with a whispered hint from him: I tendered my hand, and wished him a pleasant journey.

'Thank you, Jane. As I said, I shall return from Cambridge in a fortnight: that space, then, is yet left you for reflection. If I listened to human pride, I should say no more to you of marriage with me; but I listen to my duty, and keep steadily in view my first aim – to do all things to the glory of God. My Master was long-suffering: so will I be. I cannot give you up to perdition as a vessel of wrath: repent – resolve, while there is yet time. Remember, we are bid to work while it is day – warned that "the night cometh when no man shall work". Remember the fate of Dives, who had his good things in this life. God give you strength to choose that better part which shall not be taken from you!'

He laid his hand on my head as he uttered the last words. He had spoken earnestly, mildly: his look was not, indeed, that of a lover beholding his mistress, but it was that of a pastor recalling his wandering sheep – or better, of a guardian angel watching the soul for which he is responsible. All men of talent, whether they be men of feeling or not, whether they be zealots, or aspirants, or despots – provided only they be sincere – have their sublime moments, when they subdue and rule. I felt veneration for St John – veneration so strong that its impetus thrust me at once to the point I had so long shunned. I was tempted to cease struggling with him – to rush down the torrent of his will into the gulf of his existence, and there lose my own. I was almost as hard beset by him now as I had been once before, in a different way, by another. I was a fool both times. To have yielded then would have been an error of principle; to have yielded now would have been an error of judgement. So I think at this hour, when I look back to the crisis through the quiet medium of time: I was unconscious of folly at the instant.

I stood motionless under my hierophant's touch. My refusals were forgotten – my fears overcome – my wrestlings paralysed. The Impossible – that is, my marriage with St John – was fast becoming the Possible. All was changing utterly with a sudden sweep. Religion called – Angels beckoned – God commanded – life rolled together like a scroll – death's gates opening showed eternity beyond: it seemed, that for safety and bliss there, all here might be sacrificed in a second. The dim room was full of visions.

'Could you decide now?' asked the missionary. The inquiry was put in gentle tones: he drew me to him as gently. Oh, that gentleness! how far more potent is it than force! I could resist St John's wrath: I grew pliant as a reed under his kindness. Yet I knew all the time, if I yielded now, I should not the less be made to repent, some day, of my former rebellion. His nature was not changed by one hour of solemn prayer: it was only elevated.

'I could decide if I were but certain,' I answered: 'were I but convinced that it is God's will I should marry you, I could vow to marry you here and now – come afterwards what would!'

'My prayers are heard!' ejaculated St John. He pressed his hand firmer on my head, as if he claimed me: he surrounded me with his arm, *almost* as if he loved me (I say *almost* – I knew the difference – for I had felt what it was to be loved; but, like him, I had now put love out of the question, and thought only of duty). I contended with my inward dimness of vision, before which clouds yet rolled. I sincerely, deeply, fervently longed to do what was right; and only that. 'Show me, show me the path!' I entreated of Heaven. I was excited more than

# Jane Eyre

I had ever been; and whether what followed was the effect of excitement the reader shall judge.

All the house was still; for I believe all, except St John and myself, were now retired to rest. The one candle was dying out: the room was full of moonlight. My heart beat fast and thick: I heard its throb. Suddenly it stood still to an inexpressible feeling that thrilled it through, and passed at once to my head and extremities. The feeling was not like an electric shock, but it was quite as sharp, as strange, as startling: it acted on my senses as if their utmost activity hitherto had been but torpor, from which they were now summoned and forced to wake. They rose expectant: eye and ear waited while the flesh quivered on my bones.

'What have you heard? What do you see?' asked St John. I saw nothing, but I heard a voice somewhere cry –

'Jane! Jane! Jane!' – nothing more.

'O God! what is it?' I gasped.

I might have said, 'Where is it?' for it did not seem in the room, nor in the house, nor in the garden; it did not come out of the air, nor from under the earth, nor from overhead. I had heard it – where, or whence, for ever impossible to know! And it was the voice of a human being – a known, loved, well-remembered voice – that of Edward Fairfax Rochester; and it spoke in pain and woe, wildly, eerily, urgently.

'I am coming!' I cried. 'Wait for me! Oh, I will come!' I flew to the door and looked into the passage: it was dark. I ran out into the garden: it was void.

'Where are you?' I exclaimed.

The hills beyond March Glen sent the answer faintly back, 'Where are you!' I listened. The wind sighed low in the firs: all was moorland loneliness and midnight hush.

'Down superstition!' I commented, as that spectre rose up black by the black yew at the gate. 'This is not thy deception, nor thy witchcraft: it is the work of nature. She was roused, and did – no miracle – but her best.'

I broke from St John, who had followed, and would have detained me. It was *my* time to assume ascendancy. *My* powers were in play and in force. I told him to forbear question or remark; I desired him to leave me: I must and would be alone. He obeyed at once. Where there is energy to command well enough, obedience never fails. I mounted to my chamber; locked myself in; fell on my knees; and prayed in my way – a different way to St John's, but effective in its own fashion. I seemed to penetrate very near a Mighty Spirit; and my soul rushed out in gratitude at His feet. I rose from the thanksgiving – took a resolve – and lay down, unscared, enlightened – eager but for the daylight.

# Chapter 36

The daylight came. I rose at dawn. I busied myself for an hour or two with arranging my things in my chamber, drawers, and wardrobe, in order wherein I should wish to leave them during a brief absence. Meantime, I heard St John quit his room. He stopped at my door. I feared he would knock – no, but a slip of paper was passed under the door. I took it up. It bore these words:

'You left me too suddenly last night. Had you stayed but a little longer, you would have laid your hand on the Christian's cross and the angel's crown. I shall expect your clear decision when I return this day fortnight. Meantime, watch and pray that you enter not into temptation: the spirit, I trust, is willing, but the flesh, I see, is weak. I shall pray for you hourly. – Yours, St John.'

'My spirit,' I answered mentally, 'is willing to do what is right; and my flesh, I hope, is strong enough to accomplish the will of Heaven, when once that will is distinctly known to me. At any rate, it shall be strong enough to search – inquire – to grope an outlet from this cloud of doubt, and find the open day of certainty.'

It was the first of June; yet the morning was overcast and chilly: rain beat fast on my casement. I heard the front door open, and St John pass out. Looking through the window, I saw him traverse the garden. He took the way over the misty moors in the direction of Whitcross; there he would meet the coach.

'In a few more hours I shall succeed you in that track, cousin, thought I: 'I too have a coach to meet at Whitcross. I too have some to see and ask after in England, before I depart for ever.'

It wanted yet two hours of breakfast-time. I filled the interval in walking softly about my room, and pondering the visitation which had given my plans their present bent. I recalled the inward sensation I had experienced: for I could recall it, with all its unspeakable strangeness. I recalled the voice I had heard; again I questioned whence it came, as vainly as before: it seemed in *me* – not in the external world. I asked was it a mere nervous impression – a delusion? I could not conceive or believe: it was more like an inspiration. The wonderous shock of feeling had come like the earthquake which shook the foundations of Paul and Silas's prison; it had opened the doors of the soul's cell and loosed its bands – it had wakened it out of its sleep, whence it sprang trembling, listening, aghast; then vibrated thrice a cry on my startled ear, and in my quaking heart and through my spirit, which neither feared nor shook, but exulted as if in joy over the success of one effort it had been privileged to make, independent of the cumbrous body.

'Ere many days,' I said, as I terminated my musings, 'I will know something

# Jane Eyre

of him whose voice seemed last night to summon me. Letters have proved of no avail – personal inquiry shall replace them.'

At breakfast I announced to Diana and Mary that I was going a journey, and should be absent at least four days.

'Alone, Jane?' they asked.

'Yes; it was to see or hear news of a friend about whom I had for some time been uneasy.'

They might have said, as I have no doubt they thought, that they had believed me to be without any friends save them, for indeed I had often said so; but, with their true natural delicacy, they abstained from comment, except that Diana asked me if I was sure I was well enough to travel. I looked very pale, she observed. I replied, that nothing ailed me save anxiety of mind, which I hoped soon to alleviate.

It was easy to make my further arrangements; for I was troubled with no inquiries – no surmises. Having once explained to them that I could not now be explicit about my plans, they kindly and wisely acquiesced in the silence with which I pursued them, according to me the privilege of free action I should under similar circumstances have accorded them.

I left Moor House at three o'clock p.m., and soon after four I stood at the foot of the signpost of Whitcross, waiting the arrival of the coach which was to take me to distant Thornfield. Amidst the silence of those solitary roads and desert hills, I heard it approach from a great distance. It was the same vehicle whence, a year ago, I had alighted one summer evening on this very spot, how desolate, and hopeless, and objectless! It stopped as I beckoned. I entered – not now obliged to part with my whole fortune as the price of its accommodation. Once more on the road to Thornfield, I felt like the messenger-pigeon flying home.

It was a journey of six-and-thirty hours. I had set out from Whitcross on a Tuesday afternoon, and early on the succeeding Thursday morning the coach stopped to water the horses at a wayside inn, situated in the midst of scenery whose green hedges and large fields and low pastoral hills (how mild of feature and verdant of hue compared with the stern North-Midland moors of Morton!) met my eye like the lineaments of a once familiar face. Yes, I knew the character of this landscape: I was sure we were near my bourne.

'How far is Thornfield Hall from here?' I asked the ostler.

'Just two miles, ma'am, across the fields.'

'My journey is closed,' I thought to myself. I got out of the coach, gave a box I had into the ostler's charge, to be kept till I called for it; paid my fare; satisfied the coachman, and was going: the brightening day gleamed on the sign of the inn, and I read in gilt letters, 'The Rochester Arms'. My heart leapt up: I was already on my master's very lands. It fell again: the thought struck it –

'Your master himself may be beyond the British Channel, for aught you know: and then, if he is at Thornfield Hall, towards which you hasten, who besides him is there? His lunatic wife: and you have nothing to do with him: you dare not speak to him or seek his presence. You have lost your labour – you had better go no farther,' urged the monitor. 'Ask information of the people at the inn; they can give you all you seek: they can solve your doubts at once. Go up to that man, and inquire if Mr Rochester be at home.'

The suggestion was sensible, and yet I could not force myself to act on it. I so dreaded a reply that would crush me with despair. To prolong doubt was to

# Jane Eyre

prolong hope. I might yet once more see the Hall under the ray of her star. There was the stile before me – the very fields through which I had hurried, blind, deaf, distracted with a revengeful fury tracking and scourging me, on the morning I fled from Thornfield: ere I well knew what course I had resolved to take, I was in the midst of them. How fast I walked! How I ran sometimes! How I looked forward to catch the first view of the well-known woods! With what feelings I welcomed single trees I knew and familiar glimpses of meadow and hill between them!

At last the woods rose; the rookery clustered dark; a loud cawing broke the morning stillness. Strange delight inspired me: on I hastened. Another field crossed, a lane threaded, and there was the courtyard walls, the back offices; the house itself, the rookery still hid. 'My first view of it shall be in front,' I determined, 'where its bold battlements will strike the eye nobly at once, and where I can single out my master's very window: perhaps he will be standing at it – he rises early: perhaps he is now walking in the orchard, or on the pavement in front. Could I but see him! Surely, in that case, I should not be so mad as to run to him? I cannot tell – I am not certain. And if I did – what then? God bless him! What then! Who would be hurt by my once more tasting the life his glance can give me? I rave: perhaps at this moment he is watching the sun rise over the Pyrenees, or on the tideless sea of the south.'

I had coasted along the lower wall of the orchard – turned its angle: there was a gate just there, opening into the meadow, between two stone pillars crowned by stone balls. From behind one pillar I could peep round quietly at the full front of the mansion. I advanced my head with precaution, desirous to ascertain if any bedroom window-blinds were yet drawn up: battlements, windows, long front – all from this sheltered station were at my command.

The crows sailing overhead perhaps watched me while I took this survey. I wonder what they thought. They must have considered I was very careful and timid at first, and that gradually I grew very bold and reckless. A peep, and then a long stare; and then a departure from my niche and a straying out into the meadow; a sudden stop full in front of the great mansion, and a protracted, hardy gaze towards it. 'What affectation of diffidence was this at first?' they might have demanded; 'what stupid regardlessness now?'

Hear an illustration, reader.

A lover finds his mistress asleep on a mossy bank; he wishes to catch a glimpse of her fair face without waking her. He steals softly over the grass, careful to make no sound; he pauses – fancying she has stirred: he withdraws: not for worlds would he be seen. All is still: he again advances: he bends above her; a light veil rests on her features: he lifts it, bends lower; now his eyes anticipate the vision of beauty – warm, and blooming, and lovely, in rest. How hurried was their first glance! But how they fix! How he starts! How he suddenly and vehemently clasps in both arms the form he dared not, a moment since, touch with his finger! How he calls aloud a name, and drops his burden, and gazes on it wildly! He thus grasps, and cries, and gazes, because he no longer fears to waken by any sound he can utter – by any movement he can make. He thought his love slept sweetly: he finds she is stone dead.

I looked with timorous joy towards a stately house; I saw a blackened ruin.

No need to cower behind a gatepost, indeed! – to peep up at chamber lattices, fearing life was astir behind them! No need to listen for doors opening – to fancy

steps on the pavements or the gravel walk! The lawn, the grounds were trodden and waste: the portal yawned void. The front was, as I had once seen it in a dream, but a shell-like wall, very high and very fragile-looking, perforated with paneless windows: no roof, no battlements, no chimneys – all had crashed in.

And there was the silence of death about it, the solitude of a lonesome wild. No wonder that letters addressed to people here had never received an answer: as well despatch epistles to a vault in a church aisle. The grim blackness of the stones told by what fate the Hall had fallen – by conflagration. But how kindled? What story belonged to this disaster? What loss, besides mortar and marble and woodwork had followed upon it? Had life been wrecked as well as property? If so, whose? Dreadful question: there was no one here to answer it – not even dumb sign, mute token.

In wandering round the shattered walls and through the devastated interior, I gathered evidence that the calamity was not of late occurrence. Winter snows, I thought, had drifted through that void arch, winter rains beaten in at those hollow casements; for, amidst the drenched piles of rubbish, spring had cherished vegetation: grass and weed grew here and there between the stones and fallen rafters. And oh! where meantime was the hapless owner of this wreck? In what land? Under what auspices? My eye involuntarily wandered to the gray church tower near the gates, and I asked, 'Is he with Damer de Rochester, sharing the shelter of his narrow Marble house?'

Some answer must be had to these questions. I could find it nowhere but at the inn, and thither, ere long, I returned. The host himself brought my breakfast into the parlour. I requested him to shut the door and sit down: I had some questions to ask him. But when he complied, I scarcely knew how to begin; such horror had I of the possible answers. And yet the spectacle of desolation I had just left prepared me in a measure for a tale of misery. The host was a respectable-looking, middle-aged man.

'You know Thornfield Hall, of course?' I managed to say at last.

'Yes, ma'am; I lived there once.'

'Did you?' Not in my time, I thought: you are a stranger to me.

'I was the late Mr Rochester's butler,' he added.

The late! I seem to have received, with full force, the blow I had been trying to evade.

'The late!' I gasped. 'Is he dead?'

'I mean the present gentleman Mr Edward's father,' he explained. I breathed again: my blood resumed its flow. Fully assured by these words that Mr Edward – *my* Mr Rochester (God bless him, wherever he was!) – was at least alive: was, in short, 'the present gentleman'. Gladdening words! It seemed I could hear all that was to come – whatever the disclosures might be – with comparative tranquillity. Since he was not in the grave, I could bear, I thought, to learn that he was at the Antipodes.

'Is Mr Rochester living at Thornfield Hall now?' I asked, knowing, of course, what the answer would be but yet desirous of deferring the direct question as to where he really was.

'No, ma'am – oh, no! No one is living there. I suppose you are a stranger in these parts, or you would have heard what happened last autumn – Thornfield Hall is quite a ruin: it was burnt down just about harvest-time. A dreadful calamity! such an immense quantity of valuable property destroyed: hardly any

of the furniture could be saved. The fire broke out at dead of night, and before the engines arrived from Millcote, the building was one mass of flames. It was a terrible spectacle: I witnessed it myself.'

'At dead of night!' I muttered. Yes, that was ever the hour of fatality at Thornfield. 'Was it known how it originated?' I demanded.

'They guessed, ma'am: they guessed. Indeed, I should say it was ascertained beyond a doubt. You are not perhaps aware,' he continued, edging his chair a little nearer the table, and speaking low, 'that there was a lady – a – a lunatic, kept in the house?'

'I have heard something of it.'

'She was kept in very close confinement, ma'am; people even for some years were not absolutely certain of her existence. No one saw her: they only knew by rumour that such a person was at the hall; and who or what she was it was difficult to conjecture. They said Mr Edward had brought her from abroad, and some believed she had been his mistress. But a queer thing happened a year since – a very queer thing.'

I feared now to hear my own story. I endeavoured to recall him to the main fact.

'And this lady?'

'This lady, ma'am,' he answered, 'turned out to be Mr Rochester's wife! The discovery was brought about in the strangest way. There was a young lady, a governess at the Hall, that Mr Rochester fell in—'

'But the fire,' I suggested.

'I am coming to that, ma'am – that Mr Edward fell in love with. The servants say they never saw anybody so much in love as he was: he was after her continually. They used to watch him – servants will, you know, ma'am – and he set store on her past everything: for all, nobody but him thought her so very handsome. She was a little, small thing, they say, almost like a child. I never saw her myself; but I've heard Leah, the housemaid, tell of her. Leah liked her well enough. Mr Rochester was about forty, and this governess not twenty; and you see, when gentlemen of his age fall in love with girls, they are often like as if they were bewitched. Well, he would marry her.'

'You shall tell me this part of the story another time,' I said; 'but now I have a particular reason for wishing to hear all about the fire. Was it suspected that this lunatic, Mrs Rochester, had any hand in it?'

'You've hit it, ma'am: it's quite certain that it was her, and nobody but her, that set it going. She had a woman to take care of her called Mrs Poole – an able woman in her line, and very trustworthy, but for one fault – a fault common to a deal of them nurses and matrons – *she kept a private bottle of gin by her*, and now and then took a drop over-much. It is excusable, for she had a hard life of it: but it still was dangerous; for when Mrs Poole was fast asleep after the gin and water, the mad lady, who was as cunning as a witch, would take the keys out of her pocket, let herself out of her chamber, and go roaming about the house, doing any wild mischief that came into her head. They say she had nearly burnt her husband in his bed once: but I don't know about that. However, on this night, she set fire first to the hangings of the room next her own, and then she got down to a lower story, and made her way to the chamber that had been the governess's – (she was like as if she knew somehow how matters had gone on, and had a spite at her) – and she kindled the bed there; but there was

nobody sleeping in it, fortunately. The governess had run away two months before; and for all Mr Rochester sought her as if she had been the most precious thing he had in the world, he never could hear a word of her; and he grew savage – quite savage on his disappointment: he never was a mild man, but he got dangerous after he lost her. He would be alone, too. He sent Mrs Fairfax, the housekeeper, away to her friends at a distance; but he did it handsomely, for he settled an annuity on her for life: and she deserved it – she was a very good woman. Miss Adèle, a ward he had, was put to school. He broke off acquaintance with all the gentry, and shut himself up like a hermit at the Hall.'

'What! did he not leave England?'

'Leave England? Bless you, no! He would not cross the doorstones of the house, except at night, when he walked just like a ghost about the grounds and in the orchard, as if he had lost his senses – which it is my opinion he had; for a more spirited, bolder, keener gentleman that he was before that midge of a governess crossed him, you never saw, ma'am. He was not a man given to wine, or cards, or racing, as some are, and he was not so very handsome; but he had a courage and a will of his own, if ever man had. I knew him from a boy, you see: and for my part, I have often wished that Miss Eyre had been sunk in the sea before she came to Thornfield Hall.'

'Then Mr Rochester was at home when the fire broke out?'

'Yes, indeed was he; and he went up to the attics when all was burning above and below, and got the servants out of their beds and helped them down himself, and went back to get his mad wife out of her cell. And then they called out to him that she was on the roof, where she was standing, waving her arms above the battlements, and shouting out till they could hear her a mile off: I saw her and heard her with my own eyes. She was a big woman, and had long black hair: we could see it streaming against the flames as she stood. I witnessed, and several more witnessed, Mr Rochester ascend through the skylight on to the roof; we heard him call "Bertha!" We saw him approach her; and then, ma'am, she yelled and gave a spring, and the next minute she lay smashed on the pavement.'

'Dead?'

'Dead! Ay, dead as the stones on which her brains and blood were scattered.'

'Good God!'

'You may well say so, ma'am: it was frightful!'

He shuddered.

'And afterwards?' I urged.

'Well, ma'am, afterwards the house was burnt to the ground: there are only some bits of walls standing now.'

'Were any other lives lost?'

'No – perhaps it would have been better if there had.'

'What do you mean?'

'Poor Mr Edward!' he ejaculated, 'I little thought ever to have seen it! Some say it was a just judgement on him for keeping his first marriage secret, and wanting to take another wife while he had one living: but I pity him, for my part.'

'You said he was alive?' I exclaimed.

'Yes, yes: he is alive; but many think he had better be dead.'

'Why? How?' My blood was again running cold. 'Where is he?' I demanded. 'Is he in England?'

'Ay – ay – he's in England; he can't get out of England, I fancy – he's a fixture now.'

What agony was this! And the man seemed resolved to protract it.

'He is stone-blind,' he said at last. 'Yes, he is stone-blind, is Mr Edward.'

I had dreaded worse. I had dreaded he was mad. I summond strength to ask what had caused this calamity.

'It was all his own courage, and a body may say, his kindness, in a way, ma'am: he wouldn't leave the house till every one else was out before him. As he came down the great staircase at last, after Mrs Rochester had flung herself from the battlements, there was a great crash – all fell. He was taken out from under the ruins, alive, but sadly hurt: a beam had fallen in such a way as to protect him partly; but one eye was knocked out, and one hand so crushed that Mr Carter, the surgeon, had to amputate it directly. The other eye inflamed: he lost the sight of that also. He is now helpless, indeed – blind, and a cripple.'

'Where is he? Where does he now live?'

'At Ferndean, a manor-house on a farm he has, about thirty miles off: quite a desolate spot.'

'Who is with him?'

'Old John and his wife: he would have none else. He is quite broken down, they say.'

'Have you any sort of conveyance?'

'We have a chaise, ma'am, a very handsome chaise.'

'Let it be got ready instantly; and if your postboy can drive me to Ferndean before dark this day, I'll pay both you and him twice the hire you usually demand.'

# Chapter 37

The manor-house of Ferndean was a building of considerable antiquity, moderate size, and no architectural pretensions, deep buried in a wood. I had heard of it before. Mr Rochester often spoke of it, and sometimes went there. His father had purchased the estate for the sake of the game coverts. He would have let the house, but could find no tenant, in consequence of its ineligible and insalubrious site. Ferndean then remained uninhabited and unfurnished with the exception of some two or three rooms fitted up for the accommodation of the squire when he went there in the season to shoot.

To this house I came just ere dark, on an evening marked by the characteristics of sad sky, cold gale, and continued, small, penetrating rain. The last mile I performed on foot, having dismissed the chaise and driver with the double

remuneration I had promised. Even when within a very short distance of the manor-house, you could see nothing of it, so thick and dark grew the timber of the gloomy wood about it. Iron gates between granite pillars showed me where to enter, and passing through them, I found myself at once in the twilight of close ranked trees. There was a grass-grown track descending the forest aisle between hoar and knotty shafts and under branched arches. I followed it, expecting soon to reach the dwelling, but it stretched on and on, it wound far and farther: no sign of habitation or grounds was visible.

I thought I had taken a wrong direction and lost my way. The darkness of natural as well as of sylvan dusk gathered over me. I looked round in search of another road. There was none: all was interwoven stem, columnar trunk, dense summer foliage – no opening anywhere.

I proceeded: at last my way opened, the trees thinned a little; presently I beheld a railing, then the house – scarce, by this dim light, distinguishable from the trees; so dank and green were its decaying walls. Entering a portal, fastened only by a latch, I stood amidst a space of enclosed ground, from which the wood swept away in a semicircle. There were no flowers, no garden-beds; only a broad gravel walk girdling a grass plot, and this set in the heavy frame of the forest. The house presented two pointed gables in its front; the windows were latticed and narrow, the front door was narrow too, one step led up to it. The whole looked, as the host of the Rochester Arms had said, 'quite a desolate spot'. It was as still as a church on a week-day: the pattering rain on the forest leaves was the only sound audible in its vicinage.

'Can there be life here?' I asked.

Yes, life of some kind there was; for I heard a movement – that narrow front door was unclosing, and some shape was about to issue from the grange.

It opened slowly: a figure came out into the twilight and stood on the step – a man without a hat. He stretched forth his hand as if to feel whether it rained. Dusk as it was, I had recognized him; it was my master, Edward Fairfax Rochester, and no other.

I stayed my step, almost my breath, and stood to watch him – to examine him, myself unseen, and alas! to him invisible. It was a sudden meeting, and one in which rapture was kept well in check by pain. I had no difficulty in restraining my voice from exclamation, my step from hasty advance.

His form was of the same strong and stalwart contour as ever: his port was still erect, his hair was still raven black: nor were his features altered or sunk: not in one year's space, by any sorrow, could his athletic strength be quelled or his vigorous prime blighted. But in his countenance I saw a change; that looked desperate and brooding – that reminded me of some wronged and fettered wild beast or bird, dangerous to approach in his sullen woe. The caged eagle, whose gold-ringed eyes cruelty has extinguished, might look as looked that sightless Samson.

And reader, do you think I feared him in his blind ferocity? – if you do, you little know me. A soft hope blent with my sorrow that soon I should dare to drop a kiss on that brow of rock, and on those lips so sternly sealed beneath it; but not yet. I would not accost him yet.

He descended the one step, and advanced slowly and gropingly towards the grass plot. Where was his daring stride now? Then he paused, as if he knew not which way to turn. He lifted his hand and opened his eyelids; gazed blank,

and with a straining effort, on the sky, and toward the amphitheatre of trees: one saw that all to him was void darkness. He stretched his right hand (the left arm, the multilated one, he kept hidden in his bosom); he seemed to wish by touch to gain an idea of what lay around him: he met but vacancy still; for the trees were some yards off where he stood. He relinquished the endeavour, folded his arms, and stood quiet and mute in the rain, now falling fast on his uncovered head. At this moment John approached him from some quarter.

'Will you take my arm, sir?' he said; 'there is a heavy shower coming on: had you not better go in?'

'Let me alone,' was the answer.

John withdrew, without having observed me. Mr Rochester now tried to walk about: vainly – all was too uncertain. He groped his way back to the house, and re-entering it, closed the door.

I now drew near and knocked: John's wife opened for me. 'Mary,' I said, 'how are you?'

She started as if she had seen a ghost: I calmed her. To her hurried, 'Is it really you, miss, come at this late hour to this lonely place?' I answered by taking her hand; and then I followed her into the kitchen, where John now sat by a good fire. I explained to them, in few words, that I had heard all which had happened since I left Thornfield, and that I was come to see Mr Rochester. I asked John to go down to the turnpike-house, where I had dismissed the chaise, and bring my trunk, which I had left there: and then, while I removed my bonnet and shawl, I questioned Mary as to whether I could be accommodated at the Manor House for the night; and finding that arrangements to that effect, though difficult, would not be impossible, I informed her I should stay. Just at this moment the parlour-bell rang.

'When you go in,' said I, 'tell your master that a person wishes to speak to him, but do not give my name.'

'I don't think he will see you,' she answered; 'he refuses everybody.'

When she returned, I inquired what he had said.

'You are to send in your name and your business,' she replied. She then proceeded to fill a glass with water, and place it on a tray, together with candles.

'Is that what he rang for?' I asked.

'Yes: he always has candles brought in at dark, though he is blind.'

'Give the tray to me; I will carry it in.'

I took it from her hand: she pointed me out the parlour door. The tray shook as I held it; the water spilt from the glass; my heart struck my ribs loud and fast. Mary opened the door for me, and shut it behind me.

This parlour looked gloomy: a neglected handful of fire burnt low in the grate; and, leaning over it, with his head supported against the high, old-fashioned mantelpiece, appeared the blind tenant of the room. His old dog, Pilot, lay on one side, removed out of the way, and coiled up as if afraid of being inadvertently trodden upon. Pilot pricked up his ears when I came in: then he jumped up with a yelp and a whine, and bounded towards me: he almost knocked the tray from my hands. I set it on the table; then patted him, and said softly, 'Lie down!' Mr Rochester turned mechanically to *see* what the commotion was: but as he *saw* nothing, he returned and sighed.

'Give me the water, Mary,' he said.

# Jane Eyre

I approached him with the now only half-filled glass; Pilot followed me, still excited.

'What is the matter?' he inquired.

'Down, Pilot!' I again said. He checked the water on its way to his lips, and seemed to listen: he drank, and put the glass down. 'This is you, Mary, is it not?'

'Mary is in the kitchen,' I answered.

He put out his hand with a quick gesture, but not seeing where I stood, he did not touch me. 'Who is this? Who is this?' he demanded, trying, as it seemed, to *see* with those sightless eyes – unavailing and distressing attempt! 'Answer me – speak again!' he ordered, imperiously and aloud.

'Will you have a little more water, sir? I spilt half of what was in the glass,' I said.

'*Who* is it? *What* is it? Who speaks?'

'Pilot knows me, and John and Mary know I am here. I came only this evening,' I answered.

'Great God! – what delusion has come over me? What sweet madness has seized me?'

'No delusion – no madness: your mind, sir, is too strong for delusion, your health too sound for frenzy.'

'And where is the speaker? Is it only a voice? Oh! I *cannot* see, but I must feel, or my heart will stop and my brain burst. Whatever, whoever you are, be perceptible to the touch, or I cannot live!'

He groped; I arrested his wandering hand, and prisoned it in both mine.

'Her very fingers!' he cried; 'her small, slight fingers! If so, there must be more of her.'

The muscular hand broke from my custody; my arm was seized, my shoulder, neck, waist – I was entwined and gathered to him.

'Is it Jane? *What* is it? This is her shape – this is her size —'

'And this her voice,' I added. 'She is all here: her heart, too. God bless you, sir! I am glad to be so near you again.'

'Jane Eyre! – Jane Eyre!' was all he said.

'My dear master,' I answered, 'I am Jane Eyre: I have found you out – I am come back to you.'

'In truth? – in the flesh? My living Jane?'

'You touch me, sir – you hold me, and fast enough: I am not cold like a corpse, nor vacant like air, am I?'

'My living darling! These are certainly her limbs, and these her features; but I cannot be so blest, after all my misery. It is a dream; such dreams as I have had at night when I have clasped her once more to my heart, as I do now; and kissed her, as thus – and felt that she loved me, and trusted that she would not leave me.'

'Which I never will, sir, from this day.'

'Never will, says the vision? But I always woke and found it an empty mockery; and I was desolate and abandoned – my life dark, lonely, hopeless – my soul athirst and forbidden to drink – my heart famished and never to be fed. Gentle, soft dream, nestling in my arms now, you will fly, too, as your sisters have fled before you: but kiss me before you go – embrace me, Jane.'

'There, sir – and there!'

# Jane Eyre

I pressed my lips to his once brilliant and now rayless eyes – I swept his hair from his brow, and kissed that too. He suddenly seemed to arouse himself: the conviction of the reality of all this seized him.

'It is you – is it, Jane? you are come back to me, then?'

'I am.'

'And you do not lie dead in some ditch, under some stream? And you are not a pining outcast amongst strangers?'

'No, sir! I am an independent woman now.'

'Independent! What do you mean, Jane?'

'My uncle in Madeira is dead, and he left me five thousand pounds.'

'Ah! this is practical – this is real!' he cried: 'I should never dream that. Besides, there is that peculiar voice of hers, so animating and piquant, as well as soft: it cheers my withered heart; it puts life into it. What, Janet! Are you an independent woman? A rich woman?'

'Quite rich, sir. If you won't let me live with you, I can build a house of my own close up to your door, and you may come and sit in my parlour when you want company of an evening.'

'But as you are rich, Jane, you have now, no doubt, friends who will look after you, and not suffer you to devote yourself to a blind lamenter like me?'

'I told you I am independent, sir, as well as rich: I am my own mistress.'

'And you will stay with me?'

'Certainly – unless you object. I will be your neighbour, your nurse, your housekeeper. I find you lonely: I will be your companion – to read to you, to walk with you, to sit with you, to wait on you, to be eyes and hands to you. Cease to look so melancholy, my dear master; you shall not be left desolate, so long as I live.'

He replied not: he seemed serious – abstracted; he sighed; he half-opened his lips as if to speak: he closed them again. I felt a little embarrassed. Perhaps I had too rashly overleaped conventionalities; and he, like St John, saw impropriety in my inconsiderateness. I had indeed made my proposal from the idea that he wished and would ask me to be his wife: an expectation, not the less certain because unexpressed, had buoyed me up, that he could claim me at once as his own. But no hint to that effect escaping him, and his countenance becoming more overcast, I suddenly remembered that I might have been all wrong, and was perhaps playing the fool unwittingly; and I began to gently withdraw myself from his arms – but he eagerly snatched me closer.

'No – no – Jane; you must not go. No – I have touched you, heard you, felt the comfort of your presence – the sweetness of your consolation: I cannot give up these joys. I have little left in myself – I must have you. The world may laugh – may call me absurd, selfish – but it does not signify. My very soul demands you; it will be satisfied, or it will take deadly vengeance on its frame.'

'Well, sir, I will stay with you: I have said so.'

'Yes; but you understand one thing by staying with me; and I understand another. You, perhaps, could make up your mind to be about my hand and chair – to wait on me as a kind little nurse (for you have an affectionate heart and a generous spirit, which prompt you to make sacrifices for those you pity), and that ought to suffice for me, no doubt. I suppose I should now entertain none but fatherly feelings for you: do you think so? Come, tell me.'

# Jane Eyre

'I will think what you like, sir: I am content to be only your nurse, if you think it better.'

'But you cannot always be my nurse, Janet: you are young – you must marry some day.'

'I don't care about being married.'

'You should care, Janet: if I were what I once was, I would try to make you care – but – a sightless block!'

He relapsed again into gloom. I, on the contrary, became more cheerful, and took fresh courage: these last words gave me an insight as to where the difficulty lay; and as it was no difficulty with me, I felt quite relieved from my previous embarrassment. I resumed a livelier vein of conversation.

'It is time some one undertook to rehumanize you,' said I, parting his thick and long uncut locks; 'for I see you are being metamorphosed into a lion, or something of that sort. You have a *faux air* of Nebuchadnezzar in the fields about you, that is certain: your hair reminds me of eagles' feathers; whether your nails are grown like bird's claws or not, I have not yet noticed.'

'On this arm I have neither hand nor nails,' he said, drawing the mutilated limb from his breast, and showing it to me. 'It is a mere stump – a ghastly sight! Don't you think so, Jane?'

'It is a pity to see it; and a pity to see your eyes – and the scar of fire on your forehead: and the worst of it is, one is in danger of loving you too well for all this; and making too much of you.'

'I thought you would be revolted, Jane, when you saw my arm, and my cicatrized visage.'

'Did you? Don't tell me so – lest I should say something disparaging to your judgement. Now, let me leave you an instant to make a better fire, and have the hearth swept up. Can you tell when there is a good fire?'

'Yes; with the right eye I see a glow – a ruddy haze.'

'And you see the candles?'

'Very dimly – each is a luminous cloud.'

'Can you see me?'

'No, my fairy: but I am only too thankful to hear and feel you.'

'When do you take supper?'

'I never take supper.'

'But you shall have some tonight. I am hungry: so are you, I dare say, only you forget.'

Summoning Mary, I soon had the room in more cheerful order: I prepared him, likewise, a comfortable repast. My spirits were excited, and with pleasure and ease I talked to him during supper, and for a long time after. There was no harassing restraint, no repressing of glee and vivacity with him; for with him I was at perfect ease, because I knew I suited him; all I said or did seemed either to console or revive him. Delightful consciousness! It brought to life and light my whole nature: in his presence I thoroughly lived; and he lived in mine. Blind as he was, smiles played over his face, joy dawned on his forehead; his lineaments softened and warmed.

After supper, he began to ask me many questions, of where I had been, what I had been doing, how I had found him out; but I gave him only very partial replies: it was too late to enter into particulars that night. Besides, I wished to touch no deep-thrilling chord – to open no fresh well of emotion in his heart,

# Jane Eyre

my sole present aim was to cheer him. Cheered, as I have said, he was: and yet
but by fits. If a moment's silence broke the conversation he would turn restless,
touch me, then say, 'Jane.'

'You are altogether a human being, Jane? You are certain of that?'

'I conscientiously believe so, Mr Rochester.'

'Yet, how, on this dark and doleful evening could you so suddenly rise on my
lone hearth? I stretched my hand to take a glass of water from a hireling, and
it was given me by you: I asked a question, expecting John's wife to answer me,
and your voice spoke at my ear.'

'Because I had come in, in Mary's stead, with the tray.'

'And the enchantment there is in the very hour I am now spending with you.
Who can tell what a dark, dreary, hopeless life I have dragged on for months
past? Doing nothing, expecting nothing; merging night in day; feeling but the
sensation of cold when I let the fire go out, of hunger when I forgot to eat; and
then a ceaseless sorrow, and, at times, a very delirium of desire to behold my
Jane again. Yes: for her restoration I longed, far more than for that of my lost
sight. How can it be that Jane is with me, and says she loves me? Will she not
depart as suddenly as she came? To-morrow, I fear I shall find her no more.'

A commonplace, practical reply, out of the train of his own disturbed ideas,
was, I was sure, the best and most reassuring for him in this frame of mind. I
passed my finger over his eyebrows, and remarked that they were scorched, and
that I should apply something which would make them grow as broad and black
as ever.

'Where is the use of doing me good in any way, beneficent spirit, when, at
some fatal moment, you will again desert me – passing like a shadow, whither
and how to me unknown, and for me remaining afterwards undiscoverable?'

'Have you a pocket-comb about you, sir?'

'What for, Jane?'

'Just to comb out this shaggy black mane. I find you rather alarming, when
I examine you close at hand: you talk of my being a fairy, but I am sure you
are more like a brownie.'

'Am I hideous, Jane?'

'Very, sir; you always were, you know.'

'Humph! The wickedness has not been taken out of you, wherever you have
sojourned.'

'Yet I have been with good people; for better than you: a hundred times better
people; possessed of ideas and views you never entertained in your life: quite
more refined and exalted.'

'Who the deuce have you been with?'

'If you twist in that way you will make me pull the hair out of your head;
and then I think you will cease to entertain doubts of my substantiality.'

'Who have you been with, Jane?'

'You shall not get it out of me to-night, sir; you must wait till tomorrow; to
leave my tale half told, will, you know, be a sort of security that I shall appear
at your breakfast-table to finish it. By the by, I must mind not to rise on your
hearth with only a glass of water then: I must bring you an egg at least, to say
nothing of fried ham.'

'You mocking changeling – fairy-born and human-bred! You make me feel

as I have not felt these twelve months. If Saul could have had you for his David, the evil spirit would have been exorcised without the aid of the harp.'

'There, sir, you are redd up and made decent. Now I'll leave you: I have been travelling these last three days, and I believe I am tired. Good-night.'

'Just one word, Jane: were there only ladies in the house where you have been?'

I laughed and made my escape, still laughing as I ran upstairs. 'A good idea!' I thought with glee. 'I see I have the means of fretting him out of his melancholy for some time to come.'

Very early the next morning I heard him up and astir, wandering from one room to another. As soon as Mary came down I heard the question: 'Is Miss Eyre here?' Then: 'Which room did you put her into? Was it dry? Is she up? Go and ask if she wants anything; and when she will come down.'

I came down as soon as I thought there was a prospect of breakfast. Entering the room very softly, I had a view of him before he discovered my presence. It was mournful indeed, to witness the subjugation of that vigorous spirit to a corporeal infirmity. He sat in his chair – still, but not at rest: expectant evidently; the lines of now habitual sadness marking his strong features. His countenance reminded one of the lamp quenched, waiting to be re-lit; and alas! it was not himself that could now kindle the lustre of animated expression: he was dependent on another for that office! I had meant to be gay and careless, but the powerlessness of the strong man touched my heart to the quick: still I accosted him with what vivacity I could.

'It is a bright sunny morning, sir,' I said. 'The rain is over and gone, and there is a tender shining after it: you shall have a walk soon.'

I had wakened the glow: his features beamed.

'Oh, you are indeed there, my skylark! Come to me. You are not gone, not vanished? I heard one of your kind an hour ago, singing high over the wood; but its song had no music for me, any more than the rising sun had rays. All the melody on earth is concentrated in my Jane's tongue to my ear (I am glad it is not naturally a silent one); all the sunshine I can feel is in her presence.'

The water stood in my eyes to hear this avowal of his dependence; just as if a royal eagle, chained to a perch, should be forced to entreat a sparrow to become its purveyor. But I would not be lachrymose: I dashed off the salt drops, and busied myself with preparing breakfast.

Most of the morning was spent in the open air. I led him out of the wet and wild wood into some cheerful fields: I described to him how brilliantly green they were; how the flowers and hedges looked refreshed; how sparklingly blue was the sky. I sought a seat for him in a hidden and lovely spot, a dry stump of a tree; nor did I refuse to let him, when seated, place me on his knee. Why should I, when both he and I were happier near than apart? Pilot lay beside us: all was quiet. He broke out suddenly while clasping me in his arms –

'Cruel, cruel deserter! Oh, Jane, what did I feel when I discovered you had fled from Thornfield, and when I could nowhere find you: and, after examining your apartment, ascertained that you had taken no money, nor anything which could serve as an equivalent! A pearl necklace I had given you lay untouched in its little casket; your trunks were left corded and locked as they had been prepared for the bridal tour. What could my darling do, I asked, left destitute and penniless? And what did she do? Let me hear now.'

# Jane Eyre

Thus urged, I began the narrative of my experience for the last year. I softened considerably what related to the three days of wandering and starvation, because to have told him all would have been to inflict unnecessary pain: the little I did say lacerated his faithful heart deeper than I wished.

I should not have left him thus, he said, without any means of making my way: I should have told him my intention. I should have confided in him: he would never have forced me to be his mistress. Violent as he had seemed in his despair, he, in truth, loved me far too well and too tenderly to constitute himself my tyrant: he would have given me half his fortune, without demanding so much as a kiss in return, rather than I should have flung myself friendless on the wide world. I had endured, he was certain, more than I had confessed to him.

'Well, whatever my sufferings had been, they were very short,' I answered: and then I proceeded to tell him how I had been received at Moor House; how I had obtained the office of schoolmistress, etc. The accession of fortune, the discovery of my relations, followed in due order. Of course St John Rivers' name came in frequently in the progress of the tale. When I had done, that name was immediately taken up.

'This St John, then is your cousin?'

'Yes.'

'You have spoken of him often: do you like him?'

'He was a very good man, sir; I could not help liking him.'

'A good man. Does that mean a respectable, well-conducted man of fifty? Or what does it mean?'

'St John was only twenty-nine, sir.'

' "Jeune encore", as the French say. Is he a person of low stature, phlegmatic, and plain? A person whose goodness consists rather in his guiltlessness of vice, than in his prowess in virtue?'

'He is untiringly active. Great and exalted deeds are what he lives to perform.'

'But his brain? That is probably rather soft? He means well: but you shrug your shoulders to hear him talk?'

'He talks little, sir: what he does say is ever to the point. His brain is first-rate, I should think not impressible, but vigorous.'

'Is he an able man, then?'

'Truly able,'

'A thoroughly educated man?'

'St John is an accomplished and profound scholar.'

'His manners, I think you said, are not to your taste? – priggish and parsonic?'

'I never mentioned his manners; but, unless I had a very bad taste, they must suit it; they are polished, calm, and gentleman-like.'

'His appearance – I forgot what description you gave of his appearance; – a sort of raw curate, half strangled with his white neckcloth, and stilted up on his thick-soled high-lows, eh?'

'St John dresses well. He is a handsome man: tall, fair, with blue eyes, and a Grecian profile.'

(Aside) 'Damn him!' – (To me) 'Did you like him, Jane?'

'Yes, Mr Rochester, I liked him: but you asked me that before.'

I perceived, of course, the drift of my interlocutor. Jealousy had got hold of him: she stung him; but the sting was salutary: it gave him respite from the

gnawing fang of melancholy. I would not, therefore, immediately charm the snake.

'Perhaps you would rather not sit any longer on my knee, Miss Eyre?' was the next somewhat unexpected observation.

'Why not, Mr Rochester?'

'The picture you have just drawn is suggestive of a rather too overwhelming contrast. Your words have delineated very prettily a graceful Apollo: he is present to your imagination – tall, fair, blue-eyed, and with a Grecian profile. Your eyes dwell on a Vulcan – a real blacksmith, brown, broad-shouldered; and blind and lame into the bargain.'

'I never thought of it before; but you certainly are rather like Vulcan, sir.'

'Well, you can leave me, ma'am: but before you go' (and he retained me by a firmer grasp than ever), 'you will be pleased just to answer me a question or two.' He paused.

'What questions, Mr Rochester?'

Then followed this cross-examination.

'St John made you schoolmistress of Morton before he knew you were his cousin?'

'Yes.'

'You would often see him? He would visit the school sometimes?'

'Daily.'

'He would approve of your plans, Jane? I know they would be clever, for you are a talented creature!'

'He approved of them – yes.'

'He would discover many things in you he could not have expected to find? Some of your accomplishments are not ordinary.'

'I don't know about that.'

'You had a little cottage near the school, you say: did he ever come there to see you?'

'Now and then.'

'Of an evening?'

'Once or twice.'

A pause.

'How long did you reside with him and his sisters after the cousinship was discovered?'

'Five months.'

'Did Rivers spend much time with the ladies of his family?'

'Yes; the back parlour was both his study and ours: he sat near the window, and we by the table.'

'Did he study much?'

'A good deal.'

'What?'

'Hindustani.'

'And what did you do meantime?'

'I learnt German at first.'

'Did he teach you?'

'He did not understand German.'

'Did he teach you nothing?'

'A little Hindustani.'

# Jane Eyre

'Rivers taught you Hindustani?'

'Yes, sir.'

'And his sisters also?'

'No.'

'Only you?'

'Only me.'

'Did you ask to learn?'

'No.'

'He wished to teach you?'

'Yes.'

A second pause.

'Why did he wish it? Of what use could Hindustani be to you?'

'He intended me to go with him to India.'

'Ah! here I reach the root of the matter. He wanted you to marry him?'

'He asked me to marry him.'

'That is a fiction – an impudent invention to vex me.'

'I beg your pardon, it is the literal truth: he asked me more than once, and was as stiff about urging his point as ever you could be.'

'Miss Eyre, I repeat it, you can leave me. How often am I to say the same thing? Why do you remain pertinaciously perched on my knee, when I have given you notice to quit?'

'Because I am comfortable there.'

'No, Jane, you are not comfortable there, because your heart is not with me: it is with this cousin – this St John. Oh, till this moment, I thought my little Jane was all mine! I had a belief she loved me even when she left me: that was an atom of sweet in much bitter. Long as we have been parted, hot tears as I have wept over our separation, I never thought that while I was mourning her, she was loving another! But it is useless grieving. Jane, leave me: go and marry Rivers.'

'Shake me off, then, sir – push me away, for I'll not leave you of my own accord.'

'Jane, I ever like your tone of voice: it still renews hope, it sounds so truthful. When I hear it, it carries me back a year. I forget that you have formed a new tie. But I am not a fool – go —'

'Where must I go, sir?'

'Your own way – with the husband you have chosen.'

'Who is that?'

'You know – this St John Rivers.'

'He is not my husband, nor ever will be. He does not love me: I do not love him. He loves (as he *can* love, and that is not as you love) a beautiful young lady called Rosamond. He wanted to marry me only because he thought I should make a suitable missionary's wife, which she would not have done. He is good and great, but severe; and, for me, cold as an iceberg. He is not like you, sir. I am not happy at his side, nor near him, nor with him. He has no indulgence for me – no fondness. He sees nothing attractive in me; not even youth – only a few useful mental points – Then I must leave you, sir, to go to him?'

I shuddered involuntarily, and clung instinctively closer to my blind but beloved master. He smiled.

'What, Jane! Is this true? Is such really the state of matters between you and Rivers?'

'Absolutely, sir! Oh, you need not be jealous! I wanted to tease you a little to make you less sad: I thought anger would be better than grief. But if you wish me to love you, could you but see how much I *do* love you, you would be proud and content. All my heart is yours, sir: it belongs to you; and with you it would remain, were fate to exile the rest of me from your presence for ever.'

Again, as he kissed me, painful thoughts darkened his aspect.

'My seared vision! My crippled strength!' he murmured regretfully.

I caressed, in order to soothe him. I knew of what he was thinking, and wanted to speak for him, but dared not. As he turned aside his face a minute, I saw a tear slide from under the sealed eyelid, and trickle down the manly cheek. My heart swelled.

'I am no better than the old lightning-struck chestnut-tree in Thornfield orchard,' he remarked ere long. 'And what right would that ruin have to bid a budding woodbine cover its decay with freshness?'

'You are no ruin, sir - no lightning-struck tree: you are green and vigorous. Plants will grow about your roots, whether you ask them or not, because they take delight in your bountiful shadow; and as they grow they will lean towards you, and wind round you, because your strength offers them so safe a prop.'

Again he smiled: I gave him comfort.

'You speak of friends, Jane?' he asked.

'Yes, of friends,' I answered rather hesitatingly: for I knew I meant more than friends, but could not tell what other word to employ. He helped me.

'Ah! Jane. But I want a wife.'

'Do you, sir?'

'Yes: it is news to you?'

'Of course: you said nothing about it before.'

'Is it unwelcome news?'

'That depends on circumstances, sir - on your choice.'

'Which you shall make for me, Jane. I will abide by your decision.'

'Choose then, sir - *her who loves you best.*'

'I will at least choose - *her I love best.* Jane, will you marry me?'

'Yes, sir.'

'A poor blind man, whom you will have to lead about by the hand?'

'Yes, sir.'

'A crippled man, twenty years older than you, whom you will have to wait on?'

'Yes, sir.'

'Truly, Jane?'

'Most truly, sir.'

'Oh! my darling! God bless you and reward you!'

'Mr Rochester, if ever I did a good deed in my life - if ever I thought a good thought - if ever I prayed a sincere and blameless prayer - if ever I wished a righteous wish - I am rewarded now. To be your wife is, for me, to be as happy as I can be on earth.'

'Because you delight in sacrifice.'

'Sacrifice! What do I sacrifice? Famine for food, expectation for content. To be privileged to put my arms round what I value - to press my lips to what I

love – to repose on what I trust; is that to make a sacrifice? If so, then certainly I delight in sacrifice.'

'And to bear with my infirmities, Jane: to overlook my deficiencies.'

'Which are none, sir, to me. I love you better now, when I can really be useful to you, than I did in your state of proud independence, when you disdained every part but that of the giver and protector.'

'Hitherto I have hated to be helped – to be led: henceforth, I feel I shall hate it no more. I did not like to put my hand into a hireling's, but it is pleasant to feel it circled by Jane's little fingers. I preferred utter loneliness to the constant attendance of servants; but Jane's soft ministry will be a perpetual joy. Jane suits me: do I suit her?'

'To the finest fibre of my nature, sir.'

'The case being so, we have nothing in the world to wait for: we must be married instantly.'

He looked and spoke with eagerness: his old impetuosity was rising.

'We must become one flesh without any delay, Jane: there is but the licence to get – then we marry.'

'Mr Rochester, I have just discovered the sun is far declined from its meridian, and Pilot is actually gone home to his dinner. Let me look at your watch.'

'Fasten it into your girdle, Janet, and keep it henceforward: I have no use for it.'

'It is nearly four o'clock in the afternoon, sir. Don't you feel hungry?'

'The third day from this must be our wedding day, Jane. Never mind fine clothes and jewels, now: all that is not worth a fillip.'

'The sun has dried up all the raindrops, sir. The breeze is still: it is quite hot.'

'Do you know, Jane, I have your little pearl necklace at this moment fastened round my bronze scrag under my cravat? I have worn it since the day I lost my only treasure, as a memento of her.'

'We will go home through the wood: that will be the shadiest way.'

He pursued his own thoughts without heeding me.

'Jane! you think me, I dare say, an irreligious dog: but my heart swells with gratitude to the beneficent God of this earth just now. He sees not as man sees, but far clearer: judges not as man judges, but far more wisely. I did wrong: I would have sullied my innocent flower – breathed guilt on its purity: the Omnipotent snatched it from me. I, in my stiff-necked rebellion, almost cursed the dispensation: instead of bending to the decree, I defied it. Divine justice pursued its course; disasters came thick on me: I was forced to pass through the valley of the shadow of death. *His* chastisements are mighty; and one smote me which has humbled me for ever. You know I was proud of my strength: but what is it now, when I must give it over to foreign guidance, as a child does its weakness? Of late, Jane – only – only of late – I began to see and acknowledge the hand of God in my doom. I began to experience remorse, repentance, the wish for reconcilement to my Maker. I began sometimes to pray: very brief prayers they were, but very sincere.

'Some days since: nay, I can number them – four; it was last Monday night, a singular mood came over me; one in which grief replaced frenzy – sorrow, sullenness. I had long had the impression that since I could nowhere find you, you must be dead. Late that night – perhaps it might be between eleven and twelve o'clock – ere I retired to my dreary rest, I supplicated God, that, if it

seemed good to Him, I might soon be taken from this life, and admitted to that world to come, where there was still hope of joining Jane.

'I was in my own room and sitting by the window, which was open: it soothed me to feel the balmy night-air; though I could see no stars, and only by a vague luminous haze knew the presence of the moon. I longed for thee, Janet! Oh, how I longed for thee both with soul and flesh! I asked of God, at once in anguish and humility, if I had not been long enough desolate, afflicted, tormented; and might not soon taste bliss and peace once more. That I merited all I endured, I acknowledged – that I could scarcely endure more, I pleaded; and the alpha and omega of my heart's wishes broke involuntarily from my lips in the words, – "Jane! Jane! Jane!" '

'Did you speak these words aloud?'

'I did, Jane. If any listener had heard me, he would have thought me mad, I pronounced them with such frantic energy.'

'And it was last Monday night, somewhere near midnight?'

'Yes; but the time is of no consequence: what followed is the strangest point. You will think me superstitious – some superstition I have in my blood, and always had: nevertheless, this is true – true at least it is that I heard what I now relate.

'As I exclaimed, "Jane! Jane! Jane!" a voice – I cannot tell whence the voice came, but I know whose voice it was – replied, "I am coming; wait for me"; and a moment after, went whispering on the wind the words, "Where are you?"

'I tell you, if I can, the idea, the picture these words opened to my mind: yet it is difficult to express what I want to express. Ferndean is buried, as you see, in a heavy wood, where sound falls dull, and dies unreverberating. "Where are you?" seemed spoken amongst mountains; for I heard a hill-sent echo repeat the words. Cooler and fresher at the moment the gale seemed to visit my brow: I could have deemed that in some wild, lone scene, I and Jane were meeting. In spirit, I believe, we must have met. You no doubt were, at the hour, in unconscious sleep, Jane: perhaps your soul wandered from its cell to comfort mine; for those were your accents – as certain as I live – they were yours!'

Reader, it was on Monday night – near midnight – that I too had received the mysterious summons: those were the very words by which I replied to it. I listened to Mr Rochester's narrative, but made no disclosure in return. The coincidence struck me as too awful and inexplicable to be communicated or discussed. If I told anything, my tale would be such as must necessarily make a profound impression on the mind of my hearer: and that mind, yet from its sufferings too prone to gloom, needed not the deeper shade of the supernatural. I kept these things then, and pondered them in my heart.

'You cannot now wonder,' continued my master, 'that when you rose upon me so unexpectedly last night, I had difficulty in believing you any other than a mere voice and vision, something that would melt to silence and annihilation, as the midnight whisper and mountain echo had melted before. Now, I thank God! I know it to be otherwise. Yes, I thank God!'

He put me off his knee, rose, and reverently lifting his hat from his brow, and bending his sightless eyes to the earth, he stood in mute devotion. Only the last words of the worship were audible –

'I thank my Maker, that, in the midst of judgement, He has remembered

mercy. I humbly entreat my Redeemer to give me strength to lead henceforth a purer life than I have done hitherto!'

Then he stretched his hand out to be led. I took that dear hand, held it a moment to my lips, and then let it pass round my shoulder: being so much lower of stature than he, I served both for his prop and guide. We entered the wood, and wended homeward.

# Chapter 38

Reader, I married him. A quiet wedding we had: he and I, the parson and clerk, were alone present. When we got back from church, I went into the kitchen of the manor-house, where Mary was cooking the dinner, and John cleaning the knives, and I said –

'Mary, I have been married to Mr Rochester this morning.' The housekeeper and her husband were both of that decent, phlegmatic order of people, to whom one may at any time safely communicate a remarkable piece of news without incurring the danger of having one's ears pierced by some shrill ejaculation, and subsequently stunned by a torrent of wordy wonderment. Mary did look up, and she did stare at me; the ladle with which she was basting a pair of chickens roasting at the fire, did for some three minutes hang suspended in air, and for the same space of time John's knives also had rest from the polishing process; but Mary, bending again over the roast, said only –

'Have you, miss? Well, for sure!'

A short time after she pursued, 'I seed you go out with the master, but I didn't know you were gone to church to be wed'; and she basted away. John, when I turned to him, was grinning from ear to ear.

'I told Mary how it would be,' he said: 'I knew what Mr Edward' (John was an old servant, and had known his master when he was the cadet of the house, therefore he often gave him his Christian name) – 'I knew what Mr Edward would do; and I was certain he would not wait long either: and he's done right, for aught I know. I wish you joy, miss!' and he politely pulled his forelock.

'Thank you, John. Mr Rochester told me to give you and Mary this.'

I put into his hand a five-pound note. Without waiting to hear more, I left the kitchen. In passing the door of that sanctum some time after, I caught the words –

'She'll happen do better for him nor ony o' t' grand ladies.' And again, 'if she ben't one o' th' handsomest, she's noan faàl, and varry good-natured; and i' his een she's fair beautiful, onybody may see that.'

I wrote to Moor House and to Cambridge immediately, to say what I had done: fully explaining also why I had thus acted. Diana and Mary approved the

step unreservedly. Diana announced that she would just give me time to get over the honeymoon, and then she would come and see me.

'She had better not wait till then, Jane,' said Mr Rochester, when I read her letter to him; 'if she does, she will be too late, for our honeymoon will shine our life long: its beams will only fade over your grave or mine.'

How St John received the news I don't know: he never answered the letter in which I communicated it: yet six months after he wrote to me, without, however, mentioning Mr Rochester's name or alluding to my marriage. His letter was then calm, and though very serious, kind. He has maintained a regular, though not frequent correspondence ever since: he hopes I am happy, and trusts I am not of those who live without God in the world, and only mind earthly things.

You have not quite forgotten little Adèle, have you, reader? I had not; I soon asked and obtained leave of Mr Rochester, to go and see her at the school where he had placed her. Her frantic joy at beholding me again moved me much. She looked pale and thin: she said she was not happy. I found the rules of the establishment were too strict, its course of study too severe, for a child of her age: I took her home with me. I meant to become her governess once more, but I soon found this impracticable; my time and cares were now required by another – my husband needed them all. So I sought out a school conducted on a more indulgent system, and near enough to permit of my visiting her often, and bringing her home sometimes. I took care she should never want for anything that could contribute to her comfort: she soon settled in her new abode, became very happy there, and made fair progress in her studies. As she grew up, a sound English education corrected in a great measure her French defects; and when she left school, I found in her a pleasing and obliging companion – docile, good-tempered, and well-principled. By her grateful attention to me and mine, she has long since well repaid any little kindness I ever had it in my power to offer her.

My tale draws to its close: one word respecting my experience of married life, and one brief glance at the fortunes of those whose names have most frequently recurred in this narrative, and I have done.

I have now been married ten years. I know what it is to live entirely for and with what I love best on earth. I hold myself supremely blest – blest beyond what language can express; because I am my husband's life as fully as he is mine. No woman was ever nearer to her mate than I am: ever more absolutely bone of his bone and flesh of his flesh. I know no weariness of my Edward's society: he knows none of mine, any more than we each do of the pulsation of the heart that beats in our separate bosoms; consequently, we are ever together. To be together is for us to be at once as free as in solitude, as gay as in company. We talk, I believe, all day long: to talk to each other is but a more animated and an audible thinking. All my confidence is bestowed on him, all his confidence is devoted to me; we are precisely suited in character – perfect concord is the result.

Mr Rochester continued blind the first two years of our union: perhaps it was that circumstance that drew us so very near – that knit us so very close: for I was then his vision, as I am still his right hand. Literally, I was (what he often called me) the apple of his eye. He saw nature – he saw books through me; and never did I weary of gazing for his behalf, and of putting into words the effect

of field, tree, town, river, cloud, sunbeam – of the landscape before us; of the weather round us – and impressing by sound on his ear what light could no longer stamp on his eye. Never did I weary of reading to him; never did I weary of conducting him where he wished to go: of doing for him what he wished to be done. And there was a pleasure in my services, most full, most exquisite, even though sad – because he claimed these services without painful shame or damping humiliation. He loved me so truly that he knew no reluctance in profiting by my attendance; he felt I loved him so fondly, that to yield that attendance was to indulge my sweetest wishes.

One morning at the end of the two years, as I was writing a letter to his dictation, he came and bent over me and said –

'Jane, have you a glittering ornament round your neck?'

I have a gold watch-chain: I answered 'Yes.'

'And have you a pale blue dress on?'

I had. He informed me then, that for some time he had fancied the obscurity clouding one eye was becoming less dense; and that now he was sure of it.

He and I went up to London. He had the advice of an eminent oculist; and he eventually recovered the sight of that one eye. He cannot now see very distinctly; he cannot read or write much; but he can find his way without being led by the hand: the sky is no longer a blank to him – the earth no longer a void. When his first-born was put into his arms, he could see that the boy had inherited his own eyes, as they once were – large, brilliant, and black. On that occasion, he again, with a full heart, acknowledged that God had tempered judgement with mercy.

My Edward and I, then, are happy: and the more so, because those we love most are happy likewise. Diana and Mary Rivers are both married: alternately, once every year, they come to see us, and we go to see them. Diana's husband is a captain in the navy, a gallant officer, and a good man. Mary's is a clergyman, a college friend of her brother's, and, from his attainments and principles, worthy of the connexion. Both Captain Fitzjames and Mr Wharton love their wives, and are loved by them.

As to St John Rivers, he left England: he went to India. He entered on the path he had marked for himself; he pursues it still. A more resolute, indefatigable pioneer never wrought amidst rocks and dangers. Firm, faithful, and devoted, full of energy and zeal, and truth, he labours for his race; he clears their painful way to improvement; he hews down like a giant the prejudices of creed and caste that encumber it. He may be stern; he may be exacting; he may be ambitious yet; but his is the sternness of the warrior Greatheart, who guards his pilgrim convoy from the onslaught of Apollyon. His is the exaction of the apostle, who speaks but for Christ, when he says, 'Whosoever will come after Me, let him deny himself, and take up his cross and follow Me.' His is the ambition of the high master-spirit, which aims to fill a place in the first rank of those who are redeemed from the earth – who stand without fault before the throne of God, who share the last mighty victories of the Lamb, who are called, and chosen, and faithful.

St John is unmarried: he never will marry now. Himself has hither-to sufficed to the toil, and the toil draws near its close: his glorious sun hastens to its setting. The last letter I received from him drew from my eyes human tears and yet filled my heart with divine joy: he anticipated his sure reward, his incorruptible

crown. I know that a stranger's hand will write to me next, to say that the good and faithful servant has been called at length into the joy of his Lord. And why weep for this? No fear of death will darken St John's last hour: his mind will be unclouded, his heart will be undaunted, his hope will be sure, his faith steadfast. His own words are a pledge of this –

'My Master,' he says, 'has forewarned me. Daily he announces more distinctly, "Surely I come quickly!" and hourly I more eagerly respond, "Amen; even so, come Lord Jesus!"'